The University of Chicago Spanish Dictionary

Universidad de Chicago Diccionario Español–Inglés, Inglés–Español

Universidad de Chicago Diccionario Español–Inglés, Inglés–Español

Compilación original de Carlos Castillo y Otto F. Bond

QUINTA EDICIÓN

David Pharies
Director

María Irene Moyna
Redactora Adjunta

Gary K. Baker
Asistente de Dirección

Erica Fischer Dorantes
Ayudante de Dirección

The University of Chicago Press
Chicago & London

The University of Chicago Spanish Dictionary

Spanish–English · English–Spanish

Originally Compiled by Carlos Castillo and Otto F. Bond

FIFTH EDITION

David Pharies
Editor in Chief

María Irene Moyna
Associate Editor

Gary K. Baker
Assistant Editor

Erica Fischer Dorantes
Editorial Assistant

The University of Chicago Press
Chicago & London

DAVID PHARIES, Professor of Spanish at the University of Florida, enjoys an
international reputation as an expert on the history and development of
the Spanish language. His publications deal chiefly with Spanish
morphology, lexicology, and etymology.

The University of Chicago Press, Chicago 60637
The University of Chicago Press, Ltd., London
© 2002 by The University of Chicago
All rights reserved. Published 2002
First Edition published 1948
Printed in the United States of America

11 10 09 08 07 06 05 04   3 4 5

ISBN: 0-226-66688-3 (cloth)
ISBN: 0-226-66689-1 (paper)

Library of Congress Cataloging-in-Publication Data

The University of Chicago Spanish dictionary : Spanish–English,
English–Spanish / originally compiled by Carlos Castillo and Otto F.
Bond.—5th ed. / David Pharies, editor in chief ; María Irene Moyna,
associate editor ; Gary K. Baker, assistant editor.
        p.   cm.
        Added t.p. in Spanish: Universidad de Chicago diccionario
español–inglés, inglés–español.
        ISBN 0-226-66688-3 (cloth : alk. paper)—ISBN 0-226-66689-1 (paper
: alk. paper)
        1. Spanish language—Dictionaries—English. 2. English
language—Dictionaries—Spanish. I. Castillo, Carlos, 1890– . II. Bond,
Otto Ferdinand, 1885– . III. Pharies, David A. IV. Moyna, María Irene. V.
Baker, Gary K. VI. University of Chicago. VII. Title: Spanish dictionary.
VIII. Title: Universidad de Chicago diccionario español–inglés,
inglés–español.
PC4640 .U5 2002
463'.21—dc21
                                                2002017358

⊚ The paper used in this publication meets the minimum requirements of
the American National Standard for Information Sciences—Permanence of
Paper for Printed Library Materials, ANSI Z39.48-1992.

Contents

Preface to the Fifth Edition

The University of Chicago Spanish Dictionary has been compiled for the general use of the American English-speaking learner of Spanish and the Spanish-speaking learner of American English. With this purpose in mind, the editors of the fifth edition have introduced a number of significant improvements. One of the most important changes is the addition of many new words and meanings in order to bring the dictionary up to date with the latest technical advancements and cultural changes. Especially significant are additions in the fields of medicine (*anorexia, antioxidant, clone, defibrillate, gene splicing, HIV, hypoglycemia, liposuction, mammography, melanoma, metastasis, progesterone, scoliosis*), electronics (*CD, fax, magnetic resonance imaging, microwave, satellite dish*), computers (*browser, cache, chat room, megabyte, on-line, scanner, search engine, URL, website*), and science and technology (*entropy, genome, nanosecond, polyurethane, pulsar, smart bomb*). Recent cultural phenomena are captured in items such as *bungee jumping, e-commerce, mountain bike, politically correct, pro-life, sexual harassment*, and *surrogate mother*, as well as in slang terms such as *bigtime, bimbo, ditsy, douchebag, hype*, and *no-brainer*. In order to provide the most up-to-date picture of the language, many obsolescent or obsolete terms have been eliminated, such as *aught, ere, forenoon, fortnight, kerchief, knave, morrow*, and *o'er*.

Another significant improvement in the fifth edition is the consistent use of parenthetical words meant to guide the choice of equivalents from a series. For example, among the various equivalents of *soft*, the user is advised to choose *blando* to apply to butter, *suave* to apply to skin, and *tenue* to apply to light. Similarly, users are enabled by these parenthetical words to choose appropriate equivalents for *sheet* according to whether reference is being made to a sheet of paper (*hoja*), of ice (*capa*), of glass (*lámina*), or to a bed covering (*sábana*).

A change that will enhance the usability of the dictionary is the integration into the entries themselves of material that was formerly presented in charts and lists, such as idioms, proverbs, names of nations, and cardinal and ordinal numbers.

The amount and quality of grammatical information has been expanded. For the first time, gender markings for Spanish noun equivalents are provided on the English–Spanish side, thus freeing users from having to seek this information on the Spanish–English side. Additionally, transitive and intransitive verbal meanings are distinguished.

The frequent references to regional usage characteristic of the fourth edition have been de-emphasized here, partly for reasons of space, partly because of the notorious unreliability of the available information on regional dialects. In the present edition, such information is provided only where a word of more general currency might not be understood (see the various equivalents of Eng. *bean*), where the use of a particular word might cause embarrassment (see Sp. *coger*), or where the word is universally recognized as being characteristic of a given dialect (see Sp. *che, cuate*).

Acknowledgments

The Editor in Chief and the University of Chicago Press wish to acknowledge with thanks the contributions to early project planning made by the following Advisory Board, all from the University of Chicago: Paolo Cherchi, Gene B. Gragg, Eric P. Hamp, Salikoko Mufwene, and Michael Silverstein.

Preámbulo a la quinta edición

Este libro se ha compilado para el uso general del anglohablante estadounidense que estudia español y para el hispanohablante que estudia el inglés americano. Con este propósito, los editores de la presente edición han incorporado una cantidad sustancial de mejoras. Uno de los cambios más importantes es la adición de muchos términos y significados nuevos que han puesto el diccionario al día con los avances tecnológicos y las transformaciones culturales. De especial importancia son las incorporaciones en los campos de la medicina (*anorexia, antioxidante, clon, desfibrilar, empalme genético, escoliosis, hipoglucemia, VIH, liposucción, mamografía, melanoma, metástasis, progesterona*), la electrónica (*CD, fax, imagen por resonancia magnética, microondas, parabólica, píxel*), la informática (*bit, caché, en línea, escáner, megabyte, motor de búsqueda, navegador, protector de tensión, sitio web, URL*) y la ciencia y la tecnología (*bomba inteligente, entropía, genoma, nanosegundo, púlsar, poliuretano*). Los recientes fenómenos culturales se ven reflejados en términos tales como *antiaborto, bicicleta de montaña, lifting, limpieza étnica, madre de alquiler, políticamente correcto*, y *puénting* además de palabras familiares, tales como *chute, coca, curro, gachí, mala leche, mamado, truja*. Al mismo tiempo, para captar la lengua en su forma más actualizada se han eliminado muchas palabras arcaicas o caídas en desuso como *acullá, albéitar, asaz, luengo* y *postrer*.

Otra mejora considerable de la quinta edición es el uso sistemático de indicadores semánticos, que van entre paréntesis y cuyo objetivo es guiar en la elección del equivalente apropiado a partir de una serie de posibilidades. Por ejemplo, entre los diferentes equivalentes de *destino*, se advierte al usuario que opte por *fate* cuando significa 'hado', por *destination* cuando significa 'lugar adonde se viaja' y por *use* cuando significa 'uso'. Del mismo modo, la presencia de estos indicadores semánticos posibilita al usuario elegir con certeza entre los equivalentes de *calmar* según se hable de los nervios (*to calm*), dolor (*to soothe*), miedo (*to allay, to quell*) o sed (*to quench*).

Otro cambio que sin duda facilitará el empleo del diccionario es la integración, en el cuerpo del mismo, de material que en ediciones anteriores se presentaba en forma de cuadros y listas, tal como expresiones idiomáticas, refranes, nombres de países y números cardinales y ordinales.

También se ha incrementado la cantidad y calidad de la información gramatical. Por primera vez se proporcionan las marcas de género gramatical para los sustantivos en la sección inglés–español, lo cual elimina la necesidad de consultar la sección español–inglés para obtener esta información. Además, se distinguen los significados verbales transitivos e intransitivos.

En comparación con la edición anterior, la nueva insiste mucho menos en las diferencias dialectales en el vocabulario del español, en parte por razones de espacio y en parte porque la información disponible sobre ese aspecto del vocabulario es incompleta y poco fidedigna. En la presente edición las referencias al léxico regional se limitan a unos cuantos tipos de términos, concretamente, aquellos que pueden resultar desconocidos en una determinada comunidad lingüística (como los muchos equivalentes españoles del ingl. *bean*), aquellos que pueden resultar ofensivos (ver *coger*) y aquellos que son universalmente reconocidos como típicos de un dialecto dado (ver *che*, *cuate*).

Agradecimiento

El Director y la Editorial de la Universidad de Chicago desean expresar su gratitud por las contribuciones a la planificación de la obra hechas por los miembros del Consejo Editorial, concretamente por Paolo Cherchi, Gene B. Gragg, Eric P. Hamp, Salikoko Mufwene y Michael Silverstein.

How to Use *The University of Chicago Spanish Dictionary*

Order of Entries

Alphabetical order is observed irrespective of hyphens or spaces, such that *air conditioner* precedes *aircraft* and *middle school* precedes *middle-sized*. Homographs are placed under a single entry (*lie* 'to prevaricate', *lie* 'to recline', both pronounced [laɪ]), with different pronunciations if applicable (e.g., *bow* [baʊ] 'forward end of a vessel', *bow* [bo] 'bend, curve'). Regarding Spanish, according to the current policy of the Spanish Royal Academy,[1] *ch* and *ll* are no longer recognized as separate letters, such that *ch* now follows *ce* and precedes *ci*, and *ll* follows *li* and precedes *lo* in alphabetization.

Compounds listed within entries are also alphabetized. However, the need to list compounds under their first element sometimes interferes with alphabetization, as when *slumlord*, a compound listed under *slum*, comes before the next headword, *slumber*, even though strict alphabetization would require the reverse.

Spelling

Spelling of English words reflects common American usage, variants being noted where applicable (*ax, axe; sulphur, sulfur; stymie, stymy*). The spelling of Spanish words, where possible, follows the conventions of the Spanish Royal Academy. For the orthography of problematic Spanish words such as recent borrowings (*escáner, scooter*), country names (*Malí, Irak*) and adjectives of nationality (*zimbabuo*), a variety of authorities were consulted, including the *Diccionario del español actual*, the *Diccionario de dudas*, the *Libro de estilo* published by the Madrid newspaper *El País*, and various Internet sources.[2] It should be noted that there is vacillation in some cases, cf. *Bahrain*, which is listed as *Bahrein* in the *Libro de estilo* and as *Bahráin* or *Bahréin* in the *Diccionario de dudas*. In these cases, we either opt for the form that appears to be most generally accepted or provide multiple equivalents.

---

1. Real Academia Española, *Ortografía de la lengua española* (Madrid: Espasa-Calpe, 1999), p. 2.
2. Manuel Seco, Olimpia Andrés, and Gabino Ramos, *Diccionario del español actual* (Madrid: Aguilar, 1999); Manuel Seco, *Diccionario de dudas y dificultades de la lengua española*, 10th ed. (Madrid: Espasa-Calpe, 1998), *El País: Libro de estilo*, 9th ed. (Madrid: Ediciones El País, 1990).

Omissions

Some categories of words are systematically omitted from the vocabulary entries. First, irregular English past tense and participial forms (e.g., *drunk, smitten*), formerly included among the entries, have been removed and are presented instead in a verb table (p. 282). Second, adverbial forms in *-ly* (English) and *-mente* (Spanish) are included only when their usage and meaning are not transparently derivable from their adjectival bases. Thus, *clearly* is omitted, as its usage is predictable from its adjectival base ('in a clear way'), while *surely* is included, since it means, in addition to 'in a sure way', also 'undoubtedly' or 'without fail'. Similarly, *claramente* 'clearly' is omitted, while *atentamente* is retained, since the latter, in addition to meaning 'in an attentive manner', is also used as a farewell, equivalent to 'yours truly'. Third, English nouns in *-ing* and adjectives in *-ed*, which may appear as glosses of Spanish words, are not always accorded separate entries on the English–Spanish side, due to their derivational regularity and to considerations of space.

Structure of Entries

1. HEADWORD. Spelling variants, if any, follow the most frequent form, which appears first. In Spanish, occupational designations, titles, and kinship terms are shown in both masculine and feminine forms, as in *abogado -da*.

2. PRONUNCIATION. Pronunciation of English words is indicated through a modified version of the International Phonetic Alphabet, whose conventions are explained on p. 276. No individual transcription of Spanish words is required, given the simplicity and consistency of the Spanish orthographic system. See "The Spanish Spelling System and the Sounds Represented" (p. 2) for an explanation.

3. GRAMMATICAL CATEGORY. Meanings are marked according to whether they reflect usage as a noun (*n*), adjective (*adj*), adverb (*adv*), conjunction (*conj*), preposition (*prep*), pronoun (*pron*), interjection (*interj*), transitive verb (*vt*), or intransitive verb (*vi*). The exception to this rule is that nouns on the Spanish–English side are marked only by gender, i.e., *m* (masculine noun) or *f* (feminine noun).

   Order of meanings within an entry reflects frequency of usage. Where more than one grammatical category can be rendered by the same gloss, the two are listed together, cf. Eng. *red*, which can be glossed as Sp. *rojo* in both its adjective and noun meanings.

   Traditionally, Spanish adjectives are listed in their masculine form only. However, where the adjective normally functions as a noun as well, it is shown with both masculine and feminine forms if both are possible, cf. the case of *africano -na*, which can mean *African* in the adjectival sense as well as *African* (*man*) and *African* (*woman*).

   Special mention must be made of the combination "vi/vt." Occasionally, a single verb form may function both transitively and intransitively, e.g., both *to eat* and its Spanish equivalent *comer*. Not infrequently, however, Spanish glosses of English intransitives require the addition of the pronominal particle *-se*. Thus, in cases such as *to bathe*, marked "vi/vt" and glossed *bañar(se)*, it should be understood that the bare form is transitive, and the *-se* form intransitive. Finally, where transitivity differs between a headword and its equivalent in the second language, particles must be added to reflect this, as in the case of the transitive English verb *to regret*, which is glossed in Spanish as *arrepentirse de*, since *arrepentirse* alone is intransitive. Where an English verb can be used both transitively and intransitively and its Spanish equivalent is only intransitive, the latter may sometimes be made transitive through the addition of a preposition, which appears in parentheses. Thus, English *fight* is glossed as *pelear* (*con*) to show that its intransitive equivalent is *pelear*, whereas its transitive equivalent is *pelear con*.

Again for reasons of economy, pronominal forms of Spanish verbs are omitted in two cases: First, when the particle *-se* functions as a direct object, either reflexive or reciprocal, cf. *mirarse*, which can mean both *to look at oneself*, and *to look at each other*, and second, when the addition of *-se* does not affect the English translation, cf. *bañar(se)*, glossed in both meanings as *to bathe*. In contrast, pronominal forms of verbs are included when they differ substantially in meaning from the bare forms, cf. *ir*, glossed as *to go*, vs. *irse*, which means *to leave*.

4. DELIMITERS. Whenever a word, within a grammatical category, is considered to have two or more meanings, these are differentiated by means of delimiters, that is, explanatory markers. Most commonly, synonyms are used, cf. *retort*, which in the meaning 'reply' is glossed as *réplica* and in the meaning 'vessel' as *retorta*, though on occasion other strategies may be adopted. Thus, transitive verbs are sometimes best differentiated according to the objects they take, cf. *to negotiate* (a contract), which is glossed *negociar*, while *to negotiate* (an obstacle) is glossed *salvar*. Similarly, adjectives may be most easily distinguished by showing the referents to which they regularly apply, cf. *refreshing*, which applied to drink is *refrescante*, to sleep is *reparador*, and to honesty is *amable*. Not infrequently, a single equivalent covers almost all meanings of a headword in a single grammatical category. In such cases, only the "exceptional" meaning, placed second, is delimited. For example, the equivalent of Eng. *net* in almost all its meanings is Sp. *red*, though when it refers specifically to a hairnet it is *redecilla*. Although delimiters typically precede the gloss they are meant to distinguish, occasionally they are placed afterward. In these cases they are meant to erase doubts about the applicability of a given gloss in a specific secondary context, cf. *site*, whose gloss *sitio* is followed by the delimiter "also Internet."

5. GLOSSES. Insofar as is possible, glosses are intended to match the headword in terms of meaning, register, and frequency. Thus, *cop* is glossed as *poli* rather than the more formal *policía*. Similarly, *orinar* is glossed as *to urinate* rather than the informal and vulgar *to piss*. Glosses separated by a comma are to be considered interchangeable, if not perfectly synonymous. Semicolons, on the other hand, indicate separate meanings.

6. REGIONAL USAGE. No systematic attempt has been made to reflect regional usage in either English or Spanish, since in the great majority of cases a word of more general currency is available as a gloss. Thus, among the many Spanish equivalents of Eng. *peasant*, Sp. *campesino* is understood everywhere, even where a local term also exists, such as Puerto Rican *jíbaro*, Cuban *guajiro*, and Chilean *guaso*. However, Spanish regional usage is marked where any of the following conditions are met: (1) there is no term of international currency, or it might not be understood in a given location (cf. the various regional Spanish equivalents of Eng. *bean*), (2) the use of a given term in a given region could cause embar-

rassment or misunderstanding, as in the case of *coger*, which means 'to catch' or 'to get' in Spain and Cuba, but is a vulgar term meaning 'to have sexual relations with' in large parts of Spanish America, or (3) a specific regionalism is known throughout the Spanish-speaking world to be typical of a given dialect, cf. River Plate *che*, Mexican *ándale*, *cuate*.

7.   STYLISTIC MARKERS. Because, as mentioned earlier, equivalents are chosen in order to match headwords in all aspects of their meaning, including register and frequency, stylistic markers are only infrequently employed. They are included, redundantly, in the case of taboo or offensive words, in order to provide a second level of warning to potential users. Thus, whereas there is no need to mark the Spanish gloss *tonto* as familiar, since it is meant to be equivalent to the equally familiar Eng. *fool*, the gloss of Eng. *whore*, viz., *puta*, is marked "offensive," on the chance that a given user might not realize that this is also true of *whore*. Only five register markers are employed: literary (*lit*), which also includes poetic and formal language, familiar (*fam*), which designates words used among family and friends, vulgar (*vulg*), for words whose use is socially censured, pejorative (*pej*), which implies a negative evaluation, and *offensive* (not abbreviated), for words meant to insult people.

   Taboo and offensive words are included in this dictionary because of its purely descriptive rather than prescriptive nature; that is, this dictionary is intended to reflect how the vocabularies of English and Spanish are actually used by their speakers, rather than how we or other people may feel that they should be used. The inclusion of vulgar and offensive words here should not be construed as an indication that we condone or encourage their use.

8.   COMPOUNDS. Ease of usage would dictate that each lexical item receive its own entry, but for reasons of economy this is not possible in a concise dictionary. This explains why compound words, which are composed of two or more preexisting words, are listed in almost all cases under the entry of their initial constituent, at the end of the corresponding grammatical category. Thus, *doghouse* is listed as —*house*, under *dog*. There are certain exceptions to this convention, however. First, compounds are listed under the headword of their second constituent when the first is extremely frequent, as are the so-called empty verbs such as Eng. *keep*, *take*, *turn*, Sp. *hacer*, *tener*, *tomar*. Thus, *to have a good time*, glossed *divertirse*, is listed under *time* rather than *have*, and *tener paciencia*, glossed *to be patient*, is under *paciencia* rather than *tener*. Second, English compounds whose first element is a preposition (*offsides*, *outcast*, *overcome*) are listed as separate headwords, chiefly because of their frequent grammatical complexity, cf. *overhead*, which can be an adverb (*it flew overhead*), an adjective (*overhead projector*), or a noun (*overhead from grant money*). Conversely, derived words, that is, words that contain one or more affixes (e.g., *antiabortion*, composed of the prefix *anti-* plus *abortion*, and *kingdom*, composed of *king* plus the suffix *-dom*), are listed as separate headwords.

9.   ILLUSTRATIVE PHRASES. Appearing together with the compound words pertinent to any given grammatical category are illustrative phrases, a category defined so as to include idioms, collocations, proverbs, and, especially, sentences required to clarify usage in some way, as when the usage of *gustarle a uno* as a gloss of *to like* is illustrated by the phrase *he likes dogs*, with the translation *le gustan los perros*.

Cómo usar el *Universidad de Chicago Diccionario Español–Inglés, Inglés–Español*

Orden de las entradas

Se respeta el orden alfabético, independientemente de la presencia de guiones o espacios, de tal manera que *air conditioning* precede a *aircraft* y *middle school* precede a *middle-sized*. Los homógrafos se ubican en una sola entrada (*lie* 'mentir' y *lie* 'yacer', ambos con la pronunciación [laɪ]), y se indican sus distintas pronunciaciones si corresponde (e.g., *bow* [baʊ] 'proa' y *bow* [bo] 'curva'). En cuanto al español y siguiendo la política oficial de la Real Academia Española,[1] *ch* y *ll* ya no se reconocen como letras independientes, de tal manera que *ch* ahora sigue a *ce* y precede a *ci*, y *ll* sigue a *li* y precede a *lo* en el orden alfabético.

Asimismo, los compuestos incluidos dentro de una entrada determinada aparecen en orden alfabético a continuación de su primer elemento, lo cual a veces interfiere con el orden alfabético general. Así, por ejemplo, *rompeolas* aparece a continuación de *romper*, porque se trata de un compuesto de dicho verbo, si bien el orden alfabético requeriría lo contrario.

Ortografía

La ortografía de los vocablos ingleses refleja el uso general en inglés americano, y las variantes se incluyen en los casos pertinentes (*ax, axe; sulphur, sulfur; stymie, stymy*). La ortografía española sigue las convenciones de la Real Academia Española. Para la grafía española de palabras problemáticas, tales como préstamos recientes (*escáner, scooter*), nombres de países (*Malí, Irak*) y gentilicios (*zimbabuo*), se consultaron fuentes tales como el *Diccionario del español actual*, el *Diccionario de dudas*, el *Libro de estilo* de *El País* de Madrid y varios sitios en el Internet.[2] Corresponde hacer notar que la grafía de algunos términos vacila entre varias posibles, cf. la versión española de *Bahrain*, que aparece como *Bahrein* en el *Libro de estilo* y como *Bahráin* o *Bahréin* en el *Diccionario de dudas*, en cuyo caso damos la forma que parece más generalmente aceptada u ofrecemos varias.

---

1. Real Academia Española, *Ortografía de la lengua española* (Madrid: Espasa-Calpe, 1999), p. 2.

2. Manuel Seco, Olimpia Andrés y Gabino Ramos, *Diccionario del español actual* (Madrid: Aguilar, 1999); Manuel Seco, *Diccionario de dudas y dificultades de la lengua española,*10ª ed. (Madrid: Espasa-Calpe, 1998), *El País: Libro de estilo,* 9ª ed. (Madrid: Ediciones El País, 1990).

Omisiones

Algunas categorías de palabras se omiten sistemáticamente de las entradas del diccionario. En primer lugar, las formas irregulares de los pretéritos y participios pasados del inglés (e.g., *drunk, smitten*), que en ediciones anteriores aparecían incluidas en el cuerpo del diccionario, se han eliminado y se presentan ahora tabuladas (p. 282). En segundo lugar, las formas adverbiales en *-mente* (español) y en *-ly* (inglés), se incluyen solamente cuando su uso y significado no pueden deducirse claramente de sus bases adjetivas. De esta forma, *claramente* se omite, ya que su significado es predecible a partir de su base adjetiva ('de manera clara'), mientras que *atentamente* se incluye, ya que además de significar 'de manera atenta', también se usa como fórmula de despedida epistolar. Del mismo modo, se omite *clearly*, porque su equivalente, *de manera clara*, se deduce de su base adjetiva, mientras que se incluye *surely* porque además de significar *de forma segura* también quiere decir *sin duda*. Finalmente, debe notarse que los sustantivos ingleses terminados en *-ing* y los adjetivos en *-ed*, que pueden aparecer como traducción de palabras españolas en la parte español–inglés, no figuran siempre como cabezas de artículo en la parte inglés–español debido a la total regularidad de su formación y a consideraciones de espacio.

Estructura de las entradas

1. PALABRAS CABEZA DE ARTÍCULO. Las variantes ortográficas, si las hay, siguen a la forma más frecuente, que aparece en primer término. En español, las designaciones de profesiones y oficios, los títulos y las relaciones de parentesco aparecen tanto en la forma masculina como en la femenina, como por ejemplo, *abogado -da*.

2. PRONUNCIACIÓN. La pronunciación de las palabras inglesas se indica mediante una versión modificada del Alfabético Fonético Internacional, cuyas convenciones se explican en la p. 276. No se requiere transcripción individual de las palabras españolas, gracias a la simplicidad y sistematicidad de la ortografía española. Para detalles, ver la sección titulada "The Spanish Spelling System" en la p. 2.

3. CATEGORÍA GRAMATICAL. Los significados se marcan según reflejen el uso de la palabra como sustantivo masculino (*m*), sustantivo femenino (*f*), adjetivo (*adj*), adverbio (*adv*), conjunción (*conj*), preposición (*prep*), pronombre (*pron*), interjección (*interj*), verbo transitivo (*vt*) o verbo intransitivo (*vi*). En inglés, en cambio, los sustantivos se marcan con *n*, abreviación de *noun*.

    Los significados dentro de una entrada aparecen ordenados de manera que el más frecuente figure primero. Cuando la misma traducción cubre el significado de dos categorías gramaticales, ambas aparecen juntas, cf. el inglés *red*, que puede traducirse como *rojo* tanto en su significado sustantivo como en el adjetivo.

    Siguiendo la tradición, los adjetivos españoles aparecen exclusivamente en su forma masculina. Sin embargo, cuando el adjetivo frecuentemente funciona además como sustantivo, se muestra tanto en la forma masculina como en la femenina si ambas son posibles, cf. el caso de *africano -na*, traducido al inglés como *African*, forma adecuada para todos sus usos.

    La combinación "vi/vt" merece mención especial. En ocasiones, una única forma verbal funciona tanto transitiva como intransitivamente, v.g., tanto *comer* como su equivalente inglés *to eat*. Sin embargo, es también frecuente que las traducciones españolas de verbos intransitivos ingleses requieran el agregado de una partícula pronominal *-se*. Así, en casos tales como *to bathe* que se marca "vi/ vt," y se traduce como *bañar(se)*, debe entenderse que la forma no pronominalizada es transitiva y la forma con *-se* es intransitiva. En aquellos casos en los que la palabra cabeza de artículo y su equivalente en la otra lengua difieren en transitividad, se deben agregar partículas para reflejar esta diferencia. Tal es el caso del verbo *aprobar*, que se traduce al inglés como *to approve of* en algunos de sus significados, ya que *to approve* es intransitivo si no va acompañado de preposición. Finalmente, en los casos en los que un verbo español puede usarse tanto intransitiva como transitivamente y su equivalente inglés es exclusivamente intransitivo, este último puede a veces volverse transitivo mediante el agregado de una preposición entre paréntesis. Así, el esp. *chivar* se traduce como *to snitch (on)* para mostrar que su forma intransitiva en inglés es *to snitch* mientras que el equivalente transitivo es *to snitch on*.

Por razones de espacio se omiten las formas pronominales de los verbos españoles en dos casos. En primer lugar, se omiten si la partícula pronominal hace las veces de complemento directo reflexivo o recíproco, cf. *mirarse* (a sí mismo o el uno al otro). En segundo lugar no se incluyen tampoco si la partícula pronominal no afecta la traducción al inglés, como en el caso de *bañar* y *bañarse*, ambos *to bathe*. Sí se incluyen aquellas formas pronominales que difieren semánticamente de sus verbos de base, cf. *ir* vs. *irse*.

4. INDICADORES SEMÁNTICOS. En aquellos casos en los que una palabra, dentro de una misma categoría gramatical, tiene dos o más acepciones, estas se distinguen por medio de indicadores semánticos, o sea, explicaciones parentéticas. Lo más frecuente es que se empleen sinónimos, cf. *arco*, que se traduce *arc* cuando se trata de una curva, como *arch* cuando se refiere a una estructura arquitectónica, y como *bow* cuando se trata de un arma, aunque en otras ocasiones se adoptan otras estrategias. Así, los verbos transitivos a veces se distinguen con mayor facilidad mediante los tipos de complementos directos que los acompañan, cf. *acordonar* (un zapato) *to lace*, (un lugar) *to rope off*, (una moneda) *to mill*, mientras que la forma más sencilla de distinguir adjetivos es mostrar los tipos de referentes a los cuales se aplican con mayor frecuencia, cf. *inseguro*, que aplicado a una personalidad se traduce por *insecure*, a un vehículo por *unsafe*, y al andar por *unsteady*. Es frecuente que un único equivalente abarque casi todas las acepciones de una palabra cabeza de artículo dentro de una categoría gramatical determinada. En esos casos, solamente el significado "excepcional," que aparece en segundo lugar, se acompaña de un indicador semántico. Por ejemplo, el equivalente de *acceso* en casi todas sus acepciones es *access*, excepto cuando se refiere a un ataque de tos o rabia, en cuyo caso se traduce como *fit*. Aunque los indicadores semánticos normalmente preceden a la traducción que les corresponde, en ocasiones se ubican después. En estos casos tienen como objetivo eliminar dudas acerca del empleo de una traducción determinada en un contexto secundario específico, cf. *acompañar*, cuya traducción *to accompany* va seguida de un indicador semántico "también en música" para confirmar al lector su aplicación a ese contexto.

5. TRADUCCIONES. En la medida de lo posible, se ha tratado de que las traducciones sean equivalentes a la palabra cabeza de artículo en cuanto a su significado,

registro y frecuencia. Así, *poli* se traduce como *cop* y no como *policeman*, palabra más formal. De la misma forma, *to urinate* se traduce como *orinar* y no como *mear*, palabra más familiar. Las traducciones separadas por una coma deben considerarse equivalentes, aunque no sean exactamente sinónimas. El uso del punto y coma indica acepciones distintas.

6. USO REGIONAL. No se ha hecho ningún esfuerzo sistemático por reflejar usos regionales, ni en inglés ni en español, ya que en la gran mayoría de los casos existe una palabra de uso general. Así, entre los muchos equivalentes españoles de la palabra inglesa *peasant*, su equivalente español *campesino* se entiende en todo el mundo de habla hispana, aun cuando existan términos locales, tales como *jíbaro* en Puerto Rico, *guajiro* en Cuba y *guaso* en Chile. Sin embargo, el uso regional se indica para el español en tres casos específicos. En primer lugar se encuentran los casos en los que una palabra determinada podría resultar desconocida en una región dada, como los varios equivalentes españoles del ingl. *bean*. En segundo lugar, hay casos en que el empleo de una palabra podría dar lugar a situaciones bochornosas o equívocas. Tal es el caso de *coger*, que significa 'tomar' u 'obtener' en España y Cuba, pero es un vulgarismo para 'tener relaciones sexuales con' en gran parte de Hispanoamérica. En tercer término, se han incluido regionalismos que se reconocen en todo el mundo de habla hispana como típicos de un dialecto determinado, cf. español rioplatense *che*, mexicano *ándale, cuate*.

7. INDICADORES DE ESTILO. Ya que, como se mencionó anteriormente, los equivalentes se eligen para que correspondan a las palabras cabeza de artículo en todos los aspectos de su significado, incluyendo nivel de lengua y frecuencia, los indicadores de estilo se usan poco. Aunque son redundantes, se incluyen en los casos de palabras tabú o términos ofensivos para reforzar la advertencia a los usuarios potenciales del término. Así, aunque no hay necesidad de indicar que la palabra inglesa *fool* es familiar, ya que figura como equivalente del español *tonto*, la traducción de *puta* como *whore* va acompañada del indicador *ofensivo* por si el usuario ignora las connotaciones de la palabra española. Se han empleado cinco indicadores de estilo: literario (*lit*), que incluye lenguaje poético y formal, familiar (*fam*), que designa palabras que se usan en situaciones de intimidad, vulgar (*vulg*), que designa términos cuyo uso está censurado socialmente, peyorativo (*pey*), que designa palabras que tienen una carga connotativa negativa hacia el referente y *ofensivo* (sin abreviar), que designa insultos. Las palabras tabú y los términos ofensivos se incluyen en el diccionario debido a la naturaleza descriptiva y no prescriptiva del mismo. Es decir, el diccionario tiene como objetivo reflejar el uso que los hablantes nativos dan a los términos y no las opiniones nuestras o ajenas de cómo deberían usarse, de manera que la inclusión de estas palabras no debe interpretarse como una indicación de que preconizamos su empleo.

8. COMPUESTOS. El criterio de facilidad de uso requeriría que cada palabra recibiera su propia entrada, pero por razones de economía de espacio esto no es posible en un diccionario conciso. Por lo tanto, las palabras compuestas, que están formadas por dos o más vocablos preexistentes, aparecen en casi todos los casos en la entrada de su primer constituyente, al final de la categoría gramatical correspondiente. De tal forma, *hombre rana* aparece como — *rana*, en la entrada de *hombre*. Hay ciertas excepciones a esta regla, sin embargo. En primer lugar, los compuestos aparecen bajo la cabeza de artículo de su segundo constituyente cuando el primero es extremadamente frecuente, tal como lo son los verbos se-

mánticamente "vacíos" como el español *hacer, tener, tomar* y el inglés *keep, take, turn.* De este modo, *tener paciencia* aparece en la entrada de *paciencia* y no en la de *tener*, y *to have a good time* figura bajo *time* y no bajo *to have*. En segundo lugar, los compuestos ingleses cuyo primer elemento es una preposición (*offsides, overcome, outcast*), aparecen como cabezas de artículo independientes, sobre todo debido a su complejidad gramatical, cf. *overhead*, que puede ser adverbio (*it flew overhead*, que equivale a *voló en lo alto*), adjetivo (*overhead projector*, es decir, *retroproyector*) y sustantivo (*overhead from grant money*, o sea, *gastos generales de una subvención*). No obstante, las palabras derivadas, i.e., aquellas que contienen uno o más afijos (e.g., *anticuerpo*, compuesta del prefijo *anti-* y *cuerpo*, y *cabezón*, compuesta por *cabeza* y el sufijo *-ón*), figuran como cabezas de artículo independientes.

9. FRASES ILUSTRATIVAS. Junto con las palabras compuestas de una determinada categoría gramatical figuran las frases ilustrativas, una categoría que incluye expresiones idiomáticas, colocaciones típicas, refranes y especialmente, oraciones necesarias para aclarar el uso de alguna palabra, como cuando el uso de *like* como traducción de *gustar* se ilustra con la frase *he likes dogs*, que se traduce *le gustan los perros*.

Spanish–English · Español–Inglés

List of Abbreviations / Lista de abreviaturas

adj	adjetivo	adjective
adv	adverbio, adverbial	adverb, adverbial
Am	América	America
art	artículo	article
conj	conjunción	conjunction
def	definido	definite
dem	demostrativo	demonstrative
Esp	España	Spain, Spanish
f	femenino	feminine
fam	familiar	familiar
indef	indefinido	indefinite
interj	interjección	interjection
interr	interrogativo	interrogative
inv	invariable	invariable
lit	literario	literary
loc	locución	locution
m	masculino	masculine
Méx	México	Mexico
num	numeral	numeral
pej	peyorativo	pejorative
pers	personal	personal
pl	plural	plural
pos	posesivo	possessive
prep	preposición, preposicional	preposition, prepositional
pron	pronombre	pronoun
rel	relativo	relative
RP	Río de la Plata	River Plate
sg	singular	singular
v aux	verbo auxiliar	auxiliary verb
vi	verbo intransitivo	intransitive verb
vt	verbo transitivo	transitive verb
vulg	vulgar	vulgar

Spanish Pronunciation

Spanish orthography very closely mirrors Spanish pronunciation, much more so than is the case in English. This explains why, in bilingual dictionaries such as this, each English entry must be accompanied by a phonetic representation, while Spanish pronunciation may be presented in synoptic form.

This synopsis is only meant as an introduction, however. In spite of the clarity of the orthographical system of Spanish, the individual sounds of the language are difficult for adult native speakers of English to pronounce, and this difficulty is compounded by the syllabic structure of the language. For these reasons, readers who wish to perfect their pronunciation of Spanish are strongly advised to seek the help of a competent teacher.

To say that orthography mirrors pronunciation means that there is a close correlation between letters and sounds. Thus, most Spanish letters correspond to a single sound, or to a single family of closely related sounds, as is the case for all vowels, and the consonants *f, l, m, n, p, t,* and *s.* In a few cases a single letter represents two very different sounds, as *c,* which is pronounced as *k* before *a, o,* and *u,* but *th* (as in *thin,* or as *s* in America) before *e* or *i.* Rarely, two letters represent a single sound, as in the case of *ch.*

The overarching differences between Spanish and English pronunciation are tenseness of articulation and syllabification within the breath group. Due to the tenseness of their articulation, for example, all Spanish vowels have a clear nondiphthongal character, unlike English long vowels, which tend to be bipartite (e.g., *late,* pronounced [leⁱt]). Syllabification is a problem for English speakers because in Spanish, syllables are formed without respect to word boundaries, such that *el hado* 'fate' and *helado* 'ice cream' are both pronounced as e-la-do, and the phrase *tus otras hermanas* 'your other sisters' is syllabified as tu-so-tra-ser-ma-nas. In fast speech, vowels may combine, as in *lo ofendiste* 'you offended him', pronounced lo-fen-dis-te. Finally, when Spanish consonants occur in clusters, very often the articulation of the second influences that of the first, as when *un peso* 'one peso' is pronounced um-pe-so, and *en que* 'in which' is pronounced eŋ ke, where ŋ represents the sound of the letters *ng* in English.

The Spanish Spelling System and the Sounds Represented

I. VOWELS

i as a single vowel always represents a sound similar to the second vowel of *police.* Examples: **hilo, camino, piso.** As a part of a diphthong, it sounds like the *y* of English *yes, year.* Examples: **bien, baile, reina.**

e is similar to the vowel of *late* ([leⁱt]), but without the diphthong. Examples: **mesa, hablé, tres.**

a is similar to the vowel of *pod.* Examples: **casa, mala, América.** Notably, **a** is always pronounced this way, even when not stressed. This contrasts with the English tendency to reduce unstressed vowels to schwa ([ə]), as in *America,* pronounced in English as [ə-mé-rɪ-kə].

o has a value similar to that of the vowel in Eng. *coat* [ko^wt], but without the diphthong. Examples: **no, modo, amó.**

u has a value similar to that of English *oo*, as in *boot* [bu^wt], but without the diphthong. Examples: **cura, agudo, uno.** Note that the letter **u** is not pronounced in the syllables **qui, que, gui,** and **gue** (unless spelled with dieresis, as in *bilingüe*). When **u** occurs in diphthongs such as those of **cuida, cuento, deuda,** it has the sound of *w* (as in *way*).

II. CONSONANTS

b and **v** represent the same sounds in Spanish. At the beginning of a breath group or when preceded by the *m* sound (which may be spelled *n*), they are both pronounced like English *b*. Examples: **bomba, en vez de, vine, invierno.** In other environments, especially between vowels, both letters are pronounced as a very relaxed *b*, in which the lips do not completely touch and the air is not completely stopped. This sound has no equivalent in English. Examples: **haba, uva, la vaca, la banda.**

c represents a *k* sound before **a, o, u, l,** and **r.** However, this sound is not accompanied by a puff of air as it is in Eng. *can* and *coat* (compare the *c* in *scan*, which is more similar to the Spanish sound). Examples: **casa, cosa, cuna, quinto, queso, crudo, aclamar.** (Note that, as mentioned above, the vowel **u** is not pronounced in **quinto** and **queso.**) In contrast, when appearing before the vowels **e** and **i, c** is pronounced as *s* in Spanish America and the southwest of Spain, and as *th* (as in *thin*) in other parts of Spain (see **s** for more information).

ch is no longer considered to be a separate letter in the Spanish alphabet. However, it represents a single sound, which is similar to the English *ch* in *church* and *cheek*. Examples: **chato, chaleco, mucho.**

d is phonetically complex in Spanish. In terms of articulation, it is pronounced by the tongue striking the teeth rather than the alveolar ridge as in English. Second, it is represented by two variants. The first of these, which is similar to that of English *dame* and *did*, occurs at the beginning of breath groups or after **n** and **l.** Examples: **donde, falda, conde.** In all other situations the letter represents a sound similar to the *th* of English *then*. Examples: **hado, cuerda, cuadro, usted.** This sound tends to be very relaxed, to the point of disappearing in certain environments, such as word-final and intervocalic.

f is very similar to the English *f* sound. Examples: **faro, elefante, alfalfa.**

g is phonetically complex. Before the vowels **e** and **i,** it is pronounced as *h* in most American dialects, while in northern Spain it is realized like the *ch* in the German word *Bach*. Examples: **gente, giro.** At the beginning of breath groups before the vowels **a, o, u,** and before the consonants **l** and **r,** it is pronounced like the **g** of English *go*. Examples: **ganga, globo, grada.** In all other environments it is pronounced as a very relaxed *g*. Examples: **lago, la goma, agrado.**

h is silent. Examples: **hoja, humo, harto.**

j is realized in most American dialects as *h*, while in northern Spain it is pronounced like the *ch* in the German word *Bach*. Examples: **jamás, jugo, jota.**

k sounds like Eng. *k*, but without the accompanying puff of air. Examples: **kilo, keroseno.**

l is pronounced forward in the mouth, as the *l* in *leaf, leak*, never in the back, as in *bell, full*. Examples: **lado, ala, sol.**

ll is no longer considered to be a separate letter in the Spanish alphabet. However, it does represent a single sound, which differs widely in pronunciation throughout the Spanish-speaking world. In most areas, it is pronounced like the *y* of Eng. *yes*, though with greater tension. In extreme northern Spain and in parts of the Andes, it sounds like the *lli* in Eng. *million*. In the River Plate area it is pronounced like the *g* in *beige* or the *sh* in *ship*. Examples: **calle, llano, olla.**

m is essentially the same as in English. Examples: **madre, mano, cama.** However, in final position, as in **álbum** 'album', it is pronounced *n*.

n is normally pronounced like Eng. *n*. Examples: **no, mano, hablan.** There are exceptions, however. For example, before **b, v, p,** and **m**, it is pronounced *m*, as in **en Barcelona, en vez de, un peso,** while before **k, g, j, ge-,** and **gi-,** it is realized as [ŋ], the final sound of Eng. *sing*, as in **anca, tengo, naranja, engendrar.**

ñ is similar to but more tense than the *ny* of Eng. *canyon*. Examples: **cañón, año, ñato.**

p is like English *p* except that it is not accompanied by a puff of air, as it is in Eng. *pill* and *papa* (compare the *p* in *spot*, which is more similar to the Spanish sound). Examples: **padre, capa, apuro.**

q combined with **u** has the sound of *k*. Examples: **queso, aquí, quien.**

r usually represents a sound similar to that of the *tt* in Eng. *kitty*, and the *dd* in *ladder*. Examples: **caro, tren, comer.** In contrast, at the beginning of words, and after **n, l, s,** the letter **r** is realized as a trill, as in **rosa, Enrique, alrededor, Israel.** The double letter **rr** always represents a trill, as in **carro, correr, guerrero.**

s is pronounced the same as in standard American English in most parts of Spanish America and in parts of southern Spain. In most of Spain, in contrast, it is realized with the tip of the tongue against the alveolar ridge, producing a whistling sound that is also common in southern dialects of American English. Examples: **solo, casa, es.** In the Caribbean and in coastal Spanish generally, there is a strong tendency to pronounce **s** in certain environments (usually preconsonantal) as *h*, or to eliminate it entirely. In these dialects, *esta* may be pronounced as *ehta* or *eta*.

t differs from English *t* in two respects: first, it is articulated by the tongue touching the teeth rather than the alveolar ridge, and second, it is not accompanied by a puff of air, as it is in English *too* and *titillate* (compare the *t* in *stop*, which is more similar to the Spanish sound). Examples: **tela, tino, tinta.**

x has a wide range of phonetic realizations. Between vowels, it is usually pronounced *ks* or *gs* (but never *gz*), as in **examen, próximo,** though in a few words it is pronounced as *s*, e.g., *exacto, auxilio*. Before a consonant, **x** is almost always pronounced *s*, as in **extranjero, experiencia.** In many Mexican and Central American words of indigenous origin, **x** represents *h*, as in **México.**

y varies regionally in its pronunciation. In most areas it is pronounced like the *y* of Eng. *yes*, though with greater tension. In the River Plate area it is pronounced like the *g* in *beige* or the *sh* in *ship*. Examples: **yo, ayer.**

z is subject to dialectal variation as well. In most parts of Spain, except the southwest, it is pronounced as the *th* in Eng. *thin, cloth*. In southwestern Spain and all of Spanish America, in contrast, it is pronounced *s*. Examples: **zagal, hallazgo, luz.**

Stress Assignment in Spanish and the Use of the Written Accent

Spanish words are normally stressed on the next-to-last syllable when they end in a vowel or the consonants **n** or **s**. Examples: **mesa, zapato, acontecimiento, hablan, mujeres.** Words whose pronunciation does not conform to this rule are considered exceptions, and their stressed syllable is indicated with an accent mark. Examples: **lámpara, estómago, género, acá, varón, además.**

Conversely, Spanish words are normally stressed on the final syllable when they end in a consonant other than **n** or **s**. Examples: **mujer, actualidad, pedal, voraz.** Words whose pronunciation does not conform to this rule are considered exceptions, and their stressed syllable is indicated with an accent mark. Examples: **nácar, volátil, lápiz.**

For the purposes of stress assignment, diphthongs are considered the same as simple vowels. Thus, **arduo** and **industria** are considered to have two and three syllables respectively, with regular stress on the penultimate syllable. However, some sequences of vowels are not considered diphthongs. For example, **alegría** and **continúo** are both considered to have four syllables, with the stress mark indicating the absence of a diphthong.

Until recently certain words received written accents in order to differentiate functions, even though they are pronounced identically (this is still true in certain cases, such as **de** 'of', **dé** 'give'). Thus, the orthography **esta** was assigned to the demonstrative adjective ('this', fem.), while the demonstrative pronoun ('this one', fem.) was written **ésta.** This convention is no longer observed by most writers.

Notes on Spanish Grammar

The Noun

Gender. All Spanish nouns, not just those that denote male or female beings, are assigned either masculine or feminine gender. As a general rule, male beings (**muchacho** 'boy', **toro** 'bull') and all nouns ending in **-o** (**lodo** 'mud') are assigned masculine gender (exceptions: **mano** 'hand', **radio** 'radio', **foto** 'photo', all feminine). Similarly, female beings (**mujer** 'woman', **vaca** 'cow') and nouns ending in **-a** (**envidia** 'envy') tend to be assigned feminine gender (exceptions: **mapa** 'map', **drama** 'drama', **día** 'day', all masculine). In addition, nouns ending in **-ción, -tad, -dad, -tud,** and **-umbre** are always feminine: **canción** 'song', **facultad** 'college', **ciudad** 'city', **virtud** 'virtue', and **muchedumbre** 'crowd'. Otherwise, nouns ending in consonants and vowels other than **-o** and **-a** are of unpredictable gender. Some are feminine (**barbarie** 'savagery', **clase** 'class', **nariz** 'nose', **tribu** 'tribe'), while others are masculine (**antílope** 'antelope', **corte** 'cut', **mesón** 'lodge', **nácar** 'mother of pearl').

Nouns in **-o** that denote human beings (and to some extent, animals) form the feminine by replacing **-o** with **-a**, as in **tío** 'uncle' / **tía** 'aunt', **niño** 'boy' / **niña** 'girl', **oso** 'bear' / **osa** 'she-bear'. Where the masculine noun does not end in **-o**, the rules of formation are more complex. For example, nouns ending in **-ón, -or,** and **-án** require the addition of **-a**, as in the pairs **patrón** / **patrona** 'patron', **pastor** / **pastora** 'shepherd', **holgazán** / **holgazana** 'lazy person'. In other cases the difference is more unpredictable: **poeta** / **poetisa** 'poet', **emperador** 'emperor' / **emperatriz** 'empress', **abad** 'abbot' / **abadesa** 'abbess'.

Some nouns have different genders according to their meanings: **corte** (m) 'cut', (f) 'court', **capital** (m) 'money capital', (f) 'capital city', while others have invariable endings which are used for both the masculine and the feminine: **artista** 'artist' (and all nouns ending in **-ista**), **amante** 'lover', **aristócrata** 'aristocrat', **homicida** 'murderer', **cliente** 'customer'. Finally, some words vacillate as to gender, e.g., **mar** 'sea', which is normally masculine but is feminine in certain expressions (**en alta mar** 'on the high seas') and in poetic contexts, and **arte,** which is masculine in the singular but feminine in the plural. Some words, such as **armazón** and **esperma,** can be both masculine and feminine.

Pluralization. Nouns ending in an unaccented vowel and **-é** add **-s** to form the plural: **libro / libros, casa / casas, café / cafés,** while nouns ending in a consonant, in **-y,** or in an accented vowel other than **-é** add **-es: papel / papeles, canción / canciones, ley / leyes, rubí / rubíes.** Exceptions to this rule include the words **papá / papás, mamá / mamás,** and the small group of nouns ending in unaccented **-es** and **-is,** which do not change in the plural: **lunes** 'Monday', 'Mondays', **tesis** 'thesis', 'theses'.

Articles

Definite Article. The equivalent of English **the** is as follows: masculine singular, **el;** feminine singular, **la;** masculine plural, **los;** feminine plural, **las.** Feminine words beginning with stressed **a** or **ha** take **el** in the singular and **las** in the plural: **el alma** 'the soul' / **las almas** 'the souls', **el hacha** 'the hatchet' / **las hachas** 'the hatchets'. In spite of this, these nouns remain feminine in the singular, as shown by adjective agreement: **el alma bendita** 'the blessed soul'. When preceded by the prepositions **a** and **de,** the masculine singular article **el** forms the contractions **al** and **del.**

Indefinite Article. The equivalent of English **a, an** is as follows: masculine singular, **un;** feminine singular, **una.** In the plural, masculine **unos** and feminine **unas** are equivalent to English **some.** Feminine words beginning with stressed **a** or **ha** take **un** in the singular and **unas** in the plural: **un alma** 'a soul' / **unas almas** 'some souls', **un hacha** 'a hatchet' / **unas hachas** 'some hatchets'.

Adjectives

Agreement. The adjective in Spanish agrees in gender and number with the noun it modifies: **el lápiz rojo** 'the red pencil', **la casa blanca** 'the white house', **los libros interesantes** 'the interesting books', **las flores hermosas** 'the beautiful flowers'.

Formation of the Plural. Adjectives follow the same rules as nouns for the formation of the plural: **pálido, pálidos** 'pale', **fácil, fáciles** 'easy', **cortés, corteses** 'courteous', **capaz, capaces** 'capable'.

Formation of the Feminine. Adjectives ending in **-o** change to **-a: blanco, blanca** 'white'. Adjectives ending in other vowels are invariable: **verde** 'green', **fuerte** 'strong', **indígena** 'indigenous, native', **pesimista** 'pessimistic', **baladí** 'trivial', as are adjectives ending in a consonant: **fácil** 'easy', **cortés** 'courteous', **mayor** 'older', 'larger'. Some cases are more complex: (a) adjectives ending in **-ón, -án, -or** (except comparatives like **mayor**) add **-a** to form the feminine: **holgazán, holgazana** 'lazy', **preguntón, preguntona** 'inquisitive', **hablador, habladora** 'talkative', (b) adjectives of nationality ending in a consonant add **-a** to form the feminine: **francés, francesa** 'French', **español, española** 'Spanish', **alemán, alemana** 'German'.

Adverbs

Most adverbs are formed by adding **-mente** to the feminine form of the adjective: **clara** 'clear' / **claramente** 'clearly', **fácil** 'easy' / **fácilmente** 'easily'.

Comparison of Inequality in Adjectives and Adverbs

The comparative of inequality is formed by placing **más** or **menos** before the positive form of the adjective or adverb: **más rico que** 'richer than', **menos rico que** 'less rich than', **más tarde** 'later', **menos tarde** 'less late'. The superlative is formed by placing the definite article **el** before the comparative: **el más rico** 'the richest', **el menos rico** 'the least rich'.

The following adjectives and adverbs have irregular forms of comparison:

Positive	Comparative	Superlative
bueno	**mejor**	**el (la) mejor**
malo	**peor**	**el (la) peor**
grande	**mayor**	**el (la) mayor**
pequeño	**menor**	**el (la) menor**

Common Spanish Suffixes

-aco   is a pejorative suffix: **pajarraco** 'ugly bird' (from **pájaro** 'bird'), **libraco** 'large, bulky book' (**libro** 'book')

-ada *a.* attaches to verbal stems to indicate an action: **mirada** 'look' (**mirar** 'to look'), **empujada** 'push' (**empujar** 'to push')

b. attaches to noun stems to indicate a blow: **cachetada** 'blow on the cheek' (**cachete** 'cheek'), **puñalada** 'stab with a dagger' (**puñal** 'dagger')

c. attaches to nominal stems to indicate an action characteristic of a person or group: **bobada** 'foolish act' (**bobo** 'fool'), **niñada** 'childish act' (**niño** 'child')

-al, -ar   attach to nouns indicating trees to form nouns that denote a grove: **naranjal** 'orange grove' (from **naranjo** 'orange tree'), **pinar** 'pine grove' (**pino** 'pine tree')

-azo   attaches to noun stems, forming nouns that indicate

a. augmentation: **hombrazo** 'big man' (**hombre** 'man'), **marranazo** 'large hog' (**marrano** 'hog')

b. a blow or explosion: **porrazo** 'blow with a club' (**porra** 'club'), **cañonazo** 'cannon shot' (**cañón** 'cannon')

-cito   is a diminutive suffix: **cochecito** 'a little car' (**coche** 'car'), **mujercita** 'little woman' (**mujer** 'woman')

-dor   forms agent nouns from verbs: **hablador** 'talker' (**hablar** 'to talk'), **regulador** 'regulator' (**regular** 'to regulate'), which are sometimes used as adjectives: **hablador** 'talkative', **regulador** 'regulating'

-ejo   is a pejorative suffix: **librejo** 'worthless book' (**libro** 'book'), **lugarejo** 'Podunk' (**lugar** 'place')

-ería   attaches to noun stems to denote

a. a place where something is made or sold: **zapatería** 'shoestore' (**zapato** 'shoe'), **pastelería** 'pastry shop' (**pastel** 'pastry')

b. a profession, business, or occupation: **carpintería** 'carpentry' (**carpintero** 'carpenter'), **ingeniería** 'engineering' (**ingeniero** 'engineer')

c. a group: **chiquillería** 'bunch of children' (**chiquillo** 'little kid')

-ero *a.* attaches to nouns to indicate a person who makes, sells, or is in charge of something: **librero** 'bookseller' (**libro** 'book'), **zapatero** 'shoemaker' (**zapato** 'shoe'), **carcelero** 'jailer' (**cárcel** 'jail')

b. attaches to nominal stems to form adjectives: **guerrero** 'warlike' (**guerra** 'war'), **conejero** 'for hunting rabbits' (**conejo** 'rabbit')

-ez, -eza	are used to make abstract nouns from adjectival bases: **vejez** 'old age' (**viejo** 'old'), **niñez** 'childhood' (**niño** 'child'), **grandeza** 'greatness' (**grande** 'large, great'), **rareza** 'rarity' (**raro** 'rare')
-ía	forms adjective abstracts: **valentía** 'courage' (**valiente** 'brave'), **cobardía** 'cowardice' (**cobarde** 'coward')
-ico	is a diminutive suffix: **ratico** 'little while' (**rato** 'while'), **momentico** 'brief moment' (**momento** 'moment')
-(i)ento	attaches to adjectives to indicate attenuation, as in **amarillento** 'yellowish' (**amarillo** 'yellow'), or an undesirable quality, as in **hambriento** 'hungry' (**hambre** 'hunger')
-illo	is sometimes a diminutive suffix: **politiquillo** 'insignificant politician' (**político** 'politician'), **chiquillo** 'little kid' (**chico** 'child')
-ísimo	attaches to adjectives to indicate an extreme degree of a quality: **hermosísimo** 'very beautiful' (**hermoso** 'beautiful')
-ito	is a diminutive suffix: **librito** 'small book' (**libro** 'book'), **casita** 'little house' (**casa** 'house')
-izo	forms adjectives from nominal stems, indicating a tendency or attenuation: **rojizo** 'reddish' (**rojo** 'red'), **olvidadizo** 'forgetful' (**olvidar** 'to forget')
-mente	is the adverbial ending attached to the feminine form of the adjective: **generosamente** 'generously' (**generoso** 'generous'), **claramente** 'clearly' (**claro** 'clear')
-ón	*a.* is an augmentative adjectival suffix: **barrigón** 'pot-bellied' (**barriga** 'belly'), **cabezón** 'large-headed' (**cabeza** 'head')
	b. attaches to verb stems to denote sudden actions: **tirón** 'pull, jerk' (**tirar** 'to pull'), **apretón** 'push' (**apretar** 'to push')
-oso	forms adjectives from nouns, indicating abundance or character: **rocoso** 'rocky' (**roca** 'rock'), **tormentoso** 'stormy' (**tormenta** 'storm')
-ote, -ota	is an augmentative and pejorative suffix attached to nouns: **discursote** 'long, boring speech' (**discurso** 'speech'), **narizota** 'big ugly nose' (**nariz** 'nose')
-udo	forms adjectives from nouns, indicating an excess: **peludo** 'hairy' (**pelo** 'hair'), **panzudo** 'big-bellied' (**panza** 'belly')

-ura	forms abstract nouns from adjectives: **negrura** 'blackness' (**negro** 'black'), **altura** 'height' (**alto** 'high')
-uzco	forms adjectives from other adjectives, indicating attenuation: **blancuzco** 'whitish' (**blanco** 'white'), **negruzco** 'blackish' (**negro** 'black')

Spanish Regular Verbs

First Conjugation

Infinitive	**hablar**
Pres. Indic.	hablo, hablas, habla, hablamos, habláis, hablan
Pres. Subj.	hable, hables, hable, hablemos, habléis, hablen
Pret. Indic.	hablé, hablaste, habló, hablamos, hablasteis, hablaron
Imp. Indic.	hablaba, hablabas, hablaba, hablábamos, hablabais, hablaban
Imp. Subj.	hablara, hablaras, hablara, habláramos, hablarais, hablaran, *or*
	hablase, hablases, hablase, hablásemos, hablaseis, hablasen
Fut. Indic.	hablaré, hablarás, hablará, hablaremos, hablaréis, hablarán
Cond.	hablaría, hablarías, hablaría, hablaríamos, hablaríais, hablarían
Imperatives	habla (tú), hable (usted), hablad (vosotros), hablen (ustedes)
Pres. Part.	hablando
Past Part.	hablado

Second Conjugation

Infinitive	**comer**
Pres. Indic.	como, comes, come, comemos, coméis, comen
Pres. Subj.	coma, comas, coma, comamos, comáis, coman
Pret. Indic.	comí, comiste, comió, comimos, comisteis, comieron
Imp. Indic.	comía, comías, comía, comíamos, comíais, comían
Imp. Subj.	comiera, comieras, comiera, comiéramos, comierais, comieran, *or*
	comiese, comieses, comiese, comiésemos, comieseis, comiesen
Fut. Indic.	comeré, comerás, comerá, comeremos, comeréis, comerán
Cond.	comería, comerías, comería, comeríamos, comeríais, comerían
Imperatives	come (tú), coma (usted), comed (vosotros), coman (ustedes)
Pres. Part.	comiendo
Past Part.	comido

Third Conjugation

Infinitive	**vivir**
Pres. Indic.	vivo, vives, vive, vivimos, vivís, viven
Pres. Subj.	viva, vivas, viva, vivamos, viváis, vivan
Pret. Indic.	viví, viviste, vivió, vivimos, vivisteis, vivieron
Imp. Indic.	vivía, vivías, vivía, vivíamos, vivíais, vivían

Imp. Subj.	viviera, vivieras, viviera, viviéramos, vivierais, vivieran, *or*
	viviese, vivieses, viviese, viviésemos, vivieseis, viviesen
Fut. Indic.	viviré, vivirás, vivirá, viviremos, viviréis, vivirán
Cond.	viviría, vivirías, viviría, viviríamos, viviríais, vivirían
Imperative	vive (tú), viva (usted), vivid (vosotros), vivan (ustedes)
Pres. Part.	viviendo
Past Part.	vivido

Spanish Irregular and Orthographic Changing Verbs

The superscript number or numbers listed as part of a verb entry indicate that the verb is to be conjugated like the model verb in this section that has the corresponding number. Only the tenses that have irregular forms or spelling changes are given, wherein irregular forms and spelling changes are shown in boldface type.

1. **pensar**
   Pres. Indic. **pienso, piensas, piensa,** pensamos, pensáis, **piensan**
   Pres. Subj. **piense, pienses, piense,** pensemos, penséis, **piensen**
   Imper. **piensa** (tú), **piense** (usted), pensad (vosotros), **piensen** (ustedes)

2. **contar**
   Pres. Indic. **cuento, cuentas, cuenta,** contamos, contáis, **cuentan**
   Pres. Subj. **cuente, cuentes, cuente,** contemos, contéis, **cuenten**
   Imper. **cuenta** (tú), **cuente** (usted), contad (vosotros), **cuenten** (ustedes)

3. *a.* **sentir**
   Pres. Indic. **siento, sientes, siente,** sentimos, sentís, **sienten**
   Pres. Subj. **sienta, sientas, sienta, sintamos, sintáis,** sientan
   Pret. Indic. sentí, sentiste, **sintió,** sentimos, sentisteis, **sintieron**
   Imp. Subj. **sintiera, sintieras, sintiera, sintiéramos, sintierais, sintieran,** or **sintiese, sintieses, sintiese, sintiésemos, sintieseis, sintiesen**
   Imperative **siente** (tú), **sienta** (usted), sentid (vosotros), **sientan** (ustedes)
   Pres. Part. **sintiendo**

   b. **erguir**
   Pres. Indic. **yergo, yergues, yergue,** erguimos, erguís, **yerguen**
   Pres. Subj. **yerga, yergas, yerga, irgamos, irgáis, yergan**
   Pret. Indic. erguí, erguiste, **irguió,** erguimos, erguisteis, **irguieron**
   Imp. Subj. **irguiera, irguieras, irguiera, irguiéramos, irguierais, irguieran,** or **irguiese,** irguieses, **irguieses, irguiésemos, irguieseis, irguiesen**
   Imperative **yergue** (tú), **yerga** (usted), erguid (vosotros), **yergan** (ustedes)
   Pres. Part. **irguiendo**

4. **dormir**

Pres. Indic.	**duermo, duermes, duerme,** dormimos, dormís, **duermen**
Pres. Subj.	**duerma, duermas, duerma, durmamos, durmáis, duerman**
Pret. Indic.	dormí, dormiste, **durmió,** dormimos, dormisteis, **durmieron**
Imp. Subj.	**durmiera, durmieras, durmiera, durmiéramos, durmierais, durmieran,** or **durmiese, durmieses, durmiese, durmiésemos, durmieseis, durmiesen**
Imperative	**duerme** (tú), **duerma** (usted), dormid (vosotros), **duerman** (ustedes)
Pres. Part.	**durmiendo**

5. **pedir**

Pres. Indic.	**pido, pides, pide,** pedimos, pedís, **piden**
Pres. Subj.	**pida, pidas, pida, pidamos, pidáis, pidan**
Pret. Indic.	**pedí,** pediste, **pidió,** pedimos, pedisteis, **pidieron**
Imp. Subj.	**pidiera, pidieras, pidiera, pidiéramos, pidierais, pidieran,** or **pidiese, pidieses, pidiese, pidiésemos, pidieseis, pidiesen**
Imperative	**pide** (tú), **pida** (usted), pedid (vosotros), **pidan** (ustedes)
Pres. Part.	**pidiendo**

6. **buscar**

Pres. Subj.	**busque, busques, busque, busquemos, busquéis, busquen**
Pret. Indic.	**busqué,** buscaste, buscó, buscamos, buscasteis, buscaron
Imperative	busca (tú), **busque** (usted), buscad (vosotros), **busquen** (ustedes)

7. **llegar**

Pres. Subj.	**llegue, llegues, llegue, lleguemos, lleguéis, lleguen**
Pret. Indic.	**llegué,** llegaste, llegó, llegamos, llegasteis, llegaron
Imperative	llega (tú), **llegue** (usted), llegad (vosotros), **lleguen** (ustedes)

8. **averiguar**

Pres. Subj.	**averigüe, averigües, averigüe, averigüemos, averigüéis, averigüen**
Pret. Indic.	**averigüé,** averiguaste, averiguó, averiguamos, averiguasteis, averiguaron
Imperative	averigua (tú), **averigüe** (usted), averiguad (vosotros), **averigüen** (ustedes)

9. **abrazar**

Pres. Subj.	**abrace, abraces, abrace, abracemos, abracéis, abracen**

Pret. Indic.	**abracé,** abrazaste, abrazó, abrazamos, abrazasteis, abrazaron
Imperative	abraza (tú), **abrace** (usted), abrazad (vosotros), **abracen** (ustedes)

10. *a.* **convencer**

Pres. Indic.	**convenzo,** convences, convence, convencemos, convencéis, convencen
Pres. Subj.	**convenza, convenzas, convenza, convenzamos, convenzáis, convenzan**
Imperative	convence (tú), **convenza** (usted), convenced (vosotros), **convenzan** (ustedes)

b. **esparcir**

Pres. Indic.	**esparzo,** esparces, esparce, esparcimos, esparcís, esparcen
Pres. Subj.	**esparza, esparzas, esparza, esparzamos, esparzáis, esparzan**
Imperative	esparce (tú), **esparza** (usted), esparcid (vosotros), **esparzan** (ustedes)

c. **cocer**

Pres. Indic.	**cuezo,** cueces, cuece, cocemos, cocéis, cuecen
Pres. Subj.	**cueza, cuezas, cueza, cozamos, cozáis, cuezan**
Imperative	cuece (tú), **cueza** (usted), coced (vosotros), **cuezan** (ustedes)

11. *a.* **dirigir**

Pres. Indic.	**dirijo,** diriges, dirige, dirigimos, dirigís, dirigen
Pres. Subj.	**dirija, dirijas, dirija, dirijamos, dirijáis, dirijan**
Imper.	dirige (tú), **dirija** (usted), dirigid (vosotros), **dirijan** (ustedes)

b. **coger**

Pres. Indic.	**cojo,** coges, coge, cogemos, cogéis, cogen
Pres. Subj.	**coja, cojas, coja, cojamos, cojáis, cojan**
Imperative	coge (tú), **coja** (usted), coged (vosotros), **cojan** (ustedes)

12. **distinguir**

Pres. Indic.	**distingo,** distingues, distingue, distinguimos, distinguís, distinguen
Pres. Subj.	**distinga, distingas, distinga, distingamos, distingáis, distingan**
Imperative	distingue (tú), **distinga** (usted), distinguid (vosotros), **distingan** (ustedes)

13. *a.* **conocer**

Pres. Indic.	**conozco,** conoces, conoce, conocemos, conocéis, conocen
Pres. Subj.	**conozca, conozcas, conozca, conozcamos, conozcáis, conozcan**
Imperative	conoce (tú), **conozca** (usted), conoced (vosotros), **conozcan** (ustedes)

13

b. **lucir**
    Pres. Indic.   **luzco,** luces, luce, lucimos, lucís, lucen
    Pres. Subj.   **luzca, luzcas, luzca, luzcamos, luzcáis, luzcan**
    Imperative   luce (tú), **luzca** (usted), lucid (vosotros), **luzcan** (ustedes)

14. **creer**
    Pret. Indic.   creí, creíste, **creyó,** creímos, creísteis, **creyeron**
    Imp. Subj.   **creyera, creyeras, creyera, creyéramos, creyerais, creyeran,** or **creyese, creyeses, creyese, creyésemos, creyeseis, creyesen**
    Pret. Part.   **creyendo**

15. **reír**
    Pres. Indic.   **río, ríes, ríe,** reímos, reís, **ríen**
    Pres. Subj.   **ría, rías, ría, riamos, riáis, rían**
    Pret. Indic.   reí, reíste, **rió,** reímos, reísteis, **rieron**
    Imp. Subj.   **riera, rieras, riera, riéramos, rierais, rieran,** or **riese, rieses, riese, riésemos, rieseis, riesen**
    Imperative   **ríe** (tú), **ría** (usted), reíd (vosotros), **rían** (ustedes)
    Pres. Part.   **riendo**

16. **enviar**
    Pres. Indic.   envío, envías, envía, enviamos, enviáis, envían
    Pres. Subj.   envíe, envíes, enviemos, enviéis, envíen
    Imperative   envía (tú), envíe (usted), enviad (vosotros), envíen (ustedes)

17. **continuar**
    Pres. Indic.   continúo, continúas, continúa, continuamos, continuáis, continúan
    Pres. Subj.   continúe, continúes, continúe, continuemos, continuéis, continúen
    Imperative   continúa (tú), continúe (usted), continuad (vosotros), continúen (ustedes)

18. **gruñir**
    Pret. Indic.   gruñí, gruñiste, **gruñó,** gruñisteis, **gruñeron**
    Imp. Subj.   **gruñera, gruñeras, gruñera, gruñéramos, gruñerais, gruñeran,** or **gruñese, gruñeses, gruñese, gruñésemos, gruñeseis, gruñesen**
    Pres. Part.   **gruñendo**

19. **bullir**
    Pret. Indic.   bullí, bulliste, **bulló,** bullimos, bullisteis, **bulleron**
    Imp. Subj.   **bullera, bulleras, bullera, bulléramos, bullerais, bulleran,** or **bullese, bulleses, bullese, bullésemos, bulleseis, bullesen**
    Pres. Part.   **bullendo**

20. **andar**
    Pret. Indic. **anduve, anduviste, anduvo, anduvimos, anduvisteis, anduvieron**
    Imp. Subj. **anduviera, anduvieras, anduviera, anduviéramos, anduvierais, anduvieran,** or **anduviese, anduvieses, anduviese, anduviésemos, anduvieseis, anduviesen**

21. **asir**
    Pres. Indic. **asgo,** ases, ase, asimos, asís, asen
    Pres. Subj. **asga, asgas, asga, asgamos, asgáis, asgan**
    Imperative ase (tú), **asga** (usted), asid (vosotros), **asgan** (ustedes)

22. **caber**
    Pres. Indic. **quepo,** cabes, cabe, cabemos, cabéis, caben
    Pres. Subj. **quepa, quepas, quepa, quepamos, quepáis, quepan**
    Pret. Indic. **cupe, cupiste, cupo, cupimos, cupisteis, cupieron**
    Imp. Subj. **cupiera, cupieras, cupiera, cupiéramos, cupierais, cupieran,** or **cupiese, cupieses, cupiese, cupiésemos, cupieseis, cupiesen**
    Fut. Indic. **cabré, cabrás, cabrá, cabremos, cabréis, cabrán**
    Cond. **cabría, cabrías, cabría, cabríamos, cabríais, cabrían**
    Imperative cabe (tú), **quepa** (usted), cabed (vosotros), **quepan** (ustedes)

23. **caer**
    Pres. Indic. **caigo,** caes, cae, caemos, caéis, caen
    Pres. Subj. **caiga, caigas, caiga, caigamos, caigáis, caigan**
    Pret. Indic. caí, caiste, **cayó,** caímos, caísteis, **cayeron**
    Imp. Subj. **cayera, cayeras, cayera, cayéramos, cayerais, cayeran,** or **cayese, cayeses, cayese, cayésemos, cayeseis, cayesen**
    Imperative cae (tú), **caiga** (usted), caed (vosotros), **caigan** (ustedes)
    Pres. Part. **cayendo**

24. **conducir**
    Pres. Indic. **conduzco,** conduces, conduce, conducimos, conducís, conducen
    Pres. Subj. **conduzca, conduzcas, conduzca, conduzcamos, conduzcáis, conduzcan**
    Pret. Indic. **conduje, condujiste, condujo, condujimos, condujisteis, condujeron**
    Imp. Subj. **condujera, condujeras, condujera, condujéramos, condujerais, condujeran,** or **condujese, condujeses, condujese, condujésemos, condujeseis, condujesen**
    Imperative conduce (tú), **conduzca** (usted), conducid (vosotros), **conduzcan** (ustedes)

25. **dar**
    Pres. Indic. **doy,** das, da, damos, dais, dan
    Pres. Subj. **dé,** des, **dé,** demos, deis, den
    Pret. Indic. **di, diste, dio, dimos, disteis, dieron**
    Imp. Subj. **diera, dieras, diera, diéramos, dierais, dieran,** or
    diese, dieses, diese, diésemos, dieseis, diesen

26. **decir**[1]
    Pres. Indic. **digo, dices, dice,** decimos, decís, **dicen**
    Pres. Subj. **diga, digas, diga, digamos, digáis, digan**
    Pret. Indic. **dije, dijiste, dijo, dijimos, dijisteis, dijeron**
    Imp. Subj. **dijera, dijeras, dijera, dijéramos, dijerais, dijeran,** or
    dijese, dijeses, dijese, dijésemos, dijeseis, dijesen
    Fut. Indic. **diré, dirás, dirá, diremos, diréis, dirán**
    Cond. **diría, dirías, diría, diríamos, diríais, dirían**
    Imperative **di** (tú), **diga** (usted), decid (vosotros), **digan** (ustedes)
    Pres. Part. **diciendo**
    Past Part. **dicho**

27. **errar**
    Pres. Indic. **yerro, yerras, yerra,** erramos, erráis, **yerran**
    Pres. Subj. **yerre, yerres, yerre,** erremos, erréis, **yerren**
    Imperative **yerra** (tú), **yerre** (usted), errad (vosotros), **yerren** (ustedes)

28. **estar**
    Pres. Indic. **estoy, estás, está,** estamos, estáis, **están**
    Pres. Subj. **esté, estés, esté,** estemos, estéis, **estén**
    Pret. Indic. **estuve, estuviste, estuvo, estuvimos, estuvisteis,
    estuvieron**
    Imp. Subj. **estuviera, estuvieras, estuviera, estuviéramos,
    estuvierais, estuvieran,** or **estuviese, estuvieses,
    estuviese, estuviésemos, estuvieseis, estuviesen**
    Imperative **está** (tú), **esté** (usted), estad (vosotros), **estén** (ustedes)

29. **haber**
    Pres. Indic. **he, has, ha, hemos,** habéis, **han**
    Pres. Subj. **haya, hayas, haya, hayamos, hayáis, hayan**
    Pret. Indic. **hube, hubiste, hubo, hubimos, hubisteis, hubieron**
    Imp. Subj. **hubiera, hubieras, hubiera, hubiéramos, hubierais,
    hubieran,** or **hubiese, hubieses, hubiese, hubiésemos,
    hubieseis, hubiesen**
    Fut. Indic. **habré, habrás, habrá, habremos, habréis, habrán**

---

1. The compound verbs of *decir* have the same irregularities with the exception of the following: The future and conditional of the compound verbs *bendecir* and *maldecir* are regular: *bendeciré, maldeciré,* etc.; *bendeciría, maldeciría,* etc. The familiar imperative is regular: *bendice tu, maldice tu, contradice tu,* etc. The past participles of *bendecir* and *maldecir* are regular when used with haber or in the passive with ser: *bendecido, maldecido.*

Cond.	**habría, habrías, habría, habríamos, habríais, habrían**

30. **hacer**

Pres. Indic.	**hago,** haces, hace, hacemos, hacéis, hacen
Pres. Subj.	**haga, hagas, haga, hagamos, hagáis, hagan**
Pret. Indic.	**hice, hiciste, hizo, hicimos, hicisteis, hicieron**
Imp. Subj.	**hiciera, hicieras, hiciera, hiciéramos, hicierais, hicieran,** or **hiciese, hicieses, hiciese, hiciésemos, hicieseis, hiciesen**
Fut. Indic.	**haré, harás, hará, haremos, haréis, harán**
Cond.	**haría, harías, haría, haríamos, haríais, harían**
Imperative	**haz** (tú), **haga** (usted), haced (vosotros), **hagan** (ustedes)
Past Part.	**hecho**

31. *a.* **huir**

Pres. Indic.	**huyo, huyes, huye,** huimos, huís, **huyen**
Pres. Subj.	**huya, huyas, huya, huyamos, huyáis, huyan**
Pret. Indic.	huí, huiste, **huyó,** huimos, huisteis, **huyeron**
Imp. Subj.	**huyera, huyeras, huyera, huyéramos, huyerais, huyeran,** or **huyese, huyeses, huyese, huyésemos, huyeseis, huyesen**
Imperative	**huye** (tú), **huya** (usted), huid (vosotros), **huyan** (ustedes)
Pres. Part.	**huyendo**

    b. **argüir**

Pres. Indic.	**arguyo, arguyes, arguye,** argüimos, argüís, **arguyen**
Pres. Subj.	**arguya, arguyas, arguya, arguyamos, arguyáis, arguyan**
Pret. Indic.	argüí, argüiste, **arguyó,** argüimos, argüisteis, **arguyeron**
Imp. Subj.	**arguyera, arguyeras, arguyera, arguyéramos, arguyerais, arguyeran,** or **arguyese, arguyeses, arguyese, arguyésemos, arguyeseis, arguyesen**
Imperative	**arguye** (tú), **arguya** (usted), argüid (vosotros), **arguyan** (ustedes)
Pres. Part.	**arguyendo**

32. **ir**

Pres. Indic.	**voy, vas, va, vamos, vais, van**
Pres. Subj.	**vaya, vayas, vaya, vayamos, vayáis, vayan**
Imp. Indic.	**iba, ibas, iba, íbamos, ibais, iban**
Pret. Indic.	**fui, fuiste, fue, fuimos, fuisteis, fueron**
Imp. Subj.	**fuera, fueras, fuera, fuéramos, fuerais, fueran,** or **fuese, fueses, fuese, fuésemos, fueseis, fuesen**
Imperative	**ve** (tú), **vaya** (usted), id (vosotros), **vayan** (ustedes)
Pres. Part.	**yendo**

33. **jugar**
Pres. Indic. **juego, juegas, juega,** jugamos, jugáis, **juegan**
Pres. Subj. **juegue, juegues, juegue,** juguemos, juguéis, **jueguen**
Pret. Indic. **jugué,** jugaste, jugó, jugamos, jugasteis, jugaron
Imperative **juega** (tú), **juegue** (usted), jugad (vosotros), **jueguen** (ustedes)

34. **adquirir**
Pres. Indic. **adquiero, adquieres, adquiere,** adquirimos, adquirís, **adquieren**
Pres. Subj. **adquiera, adquieras, adquiera,** adquiramos, adquiráis, **adquieran**
Imperative **adquiere** (tú), **adquiera** (usted), adquirid (vosotros), **adquieran** (ustedes)

35. **oír**
Pres. Indic. **oigo, oyes, oye,** oímos, oís, **oyen**
Pres. Subj. **oiga, oigas, oiga, oigamos, oigáis, oigan**
Pret. Indic. oí, oíste, **oyó,** oímos, oísteis, **oyeron**
Imp. Subj. **oyera, oyeras, oyera, oyéramos, oyerais, oyeran,** or **oyese, oyeses, oyese, oyésemos, oyeseis, oyesen**
Imperative **oye** (tú), **oiga** (usted), oíd (vosotros), **oigan** (ustedes)
Pres. Part. **oyendo**

36. **oler**
Pres. Indic. **huelo, hueles, huele,** olemos, oléis, **huelen**
Pres. Subj. **huela, huelas, huela,** olamos, oláis, **huelan**
Imperative **huele** (tú), **huela** (usted), oled (vosotros), **huelan** (ustedes)

37. **placer**
Pres. Indic. **plazco,** places, place, placemos, placéis, placen
Pres. Subj. **plazca, plazcas, plazca, plazcamos, plazcáis, plazcan**

38. **poder**
Pres. Indic. **puedo, puedes, puede,** podemos, podéis, **pueden**
Pres. Subj. **pueda, puedas, pueda,** podamos, podáis, **puedan**
Pret. Indic. **pude, pudiste, pudo, pudimos, pudisteis, pudieron**
Imp. Subj. **pudiera, pudieras, pudiera, pudiéramos, pudierais, pudieran,** or **pudiese, pudieses, pudiese, pudiésemos, pudieseis, pudiesen**
Fut. Indic. **podré, podrás, podrá, podremos, podréis, podrán**
Cond. **podría, podrías, podría, podríamos, podríais, podrían**
Pres. Part. **pudiendo**

39. **poner**
Pres. Indic. **pongo,** pones, pone, ponemos, ponéis, ponen

Pres. Subj.	**ponga, pongas, ponga, pongamos, pongáis, pongan**
Pret. Indic.	**puse, pusiste, puso, pusimos, pusisteis, pusieron**
Imp. Subj.	**pusiera, pusieras, pusiera, pusiéramos, pusierais, pusieran,** or **pusiese, pusieses, pusiese, pusiésemos, pusieseis, pusiesen**
Fut. Indic.	**pondré, pondrás, pondrá, pondremos, pondréis, pondrán**
Cond.	**pondría, pondrías, pondría, pondríamos, pondríais, pondrían**
Imperative	**pon** (tú), **ponga** (usted), poned (vosotros), **pongan** (ustedes)
Past Part.	**puesto**

40. **querer**

Pres. Indic.	**quiero, quieres, quiere,** queremos, queréis, **quieren**
Pres. Subj.	**quiera, quieras, quiera,** queramos, queráis, **quieran**
Pret. Indic.	**quise, quisiste, quiso, quisimos, quisisteis, quisieron**
Imp. Subj.	**quisiera, quisieras, quisiera, quisiéramos, quisierais, quisieran,** or **quisiese, quisieses, quisiese, quisiémos, quisieseis, quisiesen**
Fut. Indic.	**querré, querrás, querrá, querremos, querréis, querrán**
Cond.	**querría, querrías, querría, querríamos, querríais, querrían**
Imperative	**quiere** (tú), **quiera** (usted), quered (vosotros), **quieran** (ustedes)

41. **saber**

Pres. Indic.	**sé,** sabes, sabe, sabemos, sabéis, saben
Pres. Subj.	**sepa, sepas, sepa, sepamos, sepáis, sepan**
Pret. Indic.	**supe, supiste, supo, supimos, supisteis, supieron**
Imp. Subj.	**supiera, supieras, supiera, supiéramos, supierais, supieran,** or **supiese, supieses, supiese, supiésemos, supieseis, supiesen**
Fut. Indic.	**sabré, sabrás, sabrá, sabremos, sabréis, sabrán**
Cond.	**sabría, sabrías, sabría, sabríamos, sabríais, sabrían**
Imperative	sabe (tú), **sepa** (usted), sabed (vosotros), **sepan** (ustedes)

42. **salir**

Pres. Indic.	**salgo,** sales, sale, salimos, salís, salen
Pres. Subj.	**salga, salgas, salga, salgamos, salgáis, salgan**
Fut. Indic.	**saldré, saldrás, saldrá, saldremos, saldréis, saldrán**
Cond.	**saldría, saldrías, saldría, saldríamos, saldríais, saldrían**
Imperative	**sal** (tú),[2] **salga** (usted), salid (vosotros), **salgan** (ustedes)

2. The compound *sobresalir* is regular in the familiar imperative: **sobresale tú.**

43. **ser**

Pres. Indic.	**soy, eres, es, somos, sois, son**
Pres. Subj.	**sea, seas, sea, seamos, seáis, sean**
Imp. Indic.	**era, eras, era, éramos, erais, eran**
Pret. Indic.	**fui, fuiste, fue, fuimos, fuisteis, fueron**
Imp. Subj.	**fuera, fueras, fuera, fuéramos, fuerais, fueran**, or **fuese, fueses, fuese, fuésemos, fueseis, fuesen**
Imperative	**sé** (tú), **sea** (usted), sed (vosotros), **sean** (ustedes)

44. **tener**

Pres. Indic.	**tengo, tienes, tiene,** tenemos, tenéis, **tienen**
Pres. Subj.	**tenga, tengas, tenga, tengamos, tengáis, tengan**
Pret. Indic.	**tuve, tuviste, tuvo, tuvimos, tuvisteis, tuvieron**
Imp. Subj.	**tuviera, tuvieras, tuviera, tuviéramos, tuvierais, tuvieran,** or **tuviese, tuvieses, tuviese, tuviésemos, tuvieseis, tuviesen**
Fut. Indic.	**tendré, tendrás, tendrá, tendremos, tendréis, tendrán**
Cond.	**tendría, tendrías, tendría, tendríamos, tendríais, tendrían**
Imperative	**ten** (tú), **tenga** (usted), tened (vosotros), **tengan** (ustedes)

45. **traer**

Pres. Indic.	**traigo,** traes, trae, traemos, traéis, traen
Pres. Subj.	**traiga, traigas, traiga, traigamos, traigáis, traigan**
Pret. Indic.	**traje, trajiste, trajo, trajimos, trajisteis, trajeron**
Imp. Subj.	**trajera, trajeras, trajera, trajéramos, trajerais, trajeran,** or **trajese, trajeses, trajese, trajésemos, trajeseis, trajesen**
Imperative	trae (tú), **traiga** (usted), traed (vosotros), **traigan** (ustedes)
Pres. Part.	**trayendo**

46. **valer**

Pres. Indic.	**valgo,** vales, vale, valemos, valéis, valen
Pres. Subj.	**valga, valgas, valga, valgamos, valgáis, valgan**
Fut. Indic.	**valdré, valdrás, valdrá, valdremos, valdréis, valdrán**
Cond.	**valdría, valdrías, valdría, valdríamos, valdríais, valdrían**
Imperative	**val** *or* vale (tú), **valga** (usted), valed (vosotros), **valgan** (ustedes)

47. **venir**

Pres. Indic.	**vengo, vienes, viene,** venimos, venís, **vienen**
Pres. Subj.	**venga, vengas, venga, vengamos, vangáis, vengan**
Pret. Indic.	**vine, viniste, vino, vinimos, vinisteis, vinieron**
Imp. Subj.	**viniera, vinieras, viniera, viniéramos, vinierais, vinieran,** or **viniese, vinieses, viniese, viniésemos, vinieseis, viniesen**

Fut. Indic.	**vendré, vendrás, vendrá, vendremos, vendréis, vendrán**
Cond.	**vendría, vendrías, vendría, vendríamos, vendríais, vendrían**
Imperative	**ven** (tú), **venga** (usted), venid (vosotros), **vengan** (ustedes)
Pres. Part.	**viniendo**

48. **ver**

Pres. Indic.	**veo,** ves, ve, vemos, veis, ven
Pres. Subj.	**vea, veas, vea, veamos, veáis, vean**
Imp. Indic.	**veía, veías, veía, veíamos, veíais, veían**
Imperative	ve (tú), **vea** (usted), ved (vosotros), **vean** (ustedes)
Past Part.	**visto**

49. **yacer**

Pres. Indic.	**yazco** or **yazgo,** yaces, yace, yacemos, yacéis, yacen
Pres. Subj.	**yazca, yazcas, yazca, yazcamos, yazcáis, yazcan,** or **yazga, yazgas, yazga, yazgamos, yazgáis, yazgan**
Imperative	yace (tú), **yazca** or **yazga** (usted), yaced (vosotros), **yazcan** or **yazgan** (ustedes)

50. Defective Verbs

The following verbs are used only in the forms that have an **i** in the ending: **abolir, agredir, aterirse, empedernirse, transgredir.**

The verb **atañer** is used only in the third person, most frequently in the present indicative: atañe, atañen.

The verb **concernir** is used only in the third person of the following tenses:

Pres. Indic.	**concierne, conciernen**
Pres. Subj.	**concierna, conciernan**
Imp. Indic.	concernía, concernían
Imp. Subj.	concerniera *or* concerniese, concernieran *or* concerniesen
Pres. Part.	concerniendo

The verb **roer** (also **corroer**) has three forms in the first person of the present indicative: **roo, royo, roigo,** all of which are infrequently used. In the present subjunctive the preferable form is **roa, roas, roa,** etc., although the forms **roya** and **roiga** are found.

The verb **soler** is used most frequently in the present and imperfect indicative. It is less frequently used in the present subjunctive.

Pres. Indic.	**suelo, sueles, suele,** solemos, soléis, **suelen**
Pres. Subj.	**suela, suelas, suela,** solamos, soláis, **suelan**
Imp. Indic.	solía, solías, solía, solíamos, solíais, solían

51.   Additional Irregular Past Participles
        absolver—**absuelto**
        abrir—**abierto**
        circunscribir—**circunscrito**
        componer—**compuesto**
        cubrir—**cubierto**
        decir—**dicho**
        deponer—**depuesto**
        descomponer—**descompuesto**
        describir—**descrito**
        descubrir—**descubierto**
        desenvolver—**desenvuelto**
        deshacer—**deshecho**
        devolver—**devuelto**
        disolver—**disuelto**
        encubrir—**encubierto**
        entreabrir—**entreabierto**
        entrever—**entrevisto**
        envolver—**envuelto**
        escribir—**escrito**
        hacer—**hecho**
        imprimir—**impreso** (often regular, **imprimido**)
        inscribir—**inscrito**
        morir—**muerto**
        poner—**puesto**
        prescribir—**prescrito**
        proscribir—**proscrito**
        proveer—**provisto** (often regular, **proveído**)
        pudrir—**podrido**
        reabrir—**reabierto**
        reescribir—**reescrito**
        resolver—**resuelto**
        revolver—**revuelto**
        romper—**roto**
        satisfacer—**satisfecho**
        subscribir—**subscrito**
        transcribir—**transcrito**
        ver—**visto**
        volver—**vuelto**

Aa

a PREP **voy — Londres** I'm going to London; **te lo doy — ti** I'm giving it to you; **se sentó — la sombra** she sat down in the shade; **tumbarse —l sol** to lie down in the sun; **una soga —l cuello** a rope around his neck; **lo miraba — la luz de una vela** she looked at him by the light of a candle; **— dos pesetas cada uno** at two pesetas each; **— las tres y media** at three-thirty; **sentarse — la mesa** to sit down at the table; **prestar dinero —l 15%** to lend money at 15%; **en grupos de — cinco** in groups of five; **cocina — gas** gas cooker; **fotos — todo color** full-color photos; **nadie le gana — testaruda** no one touches her for stubbornness; **terminaron — puñetazos** they ended up fighting; **¡— jugar!** let's play! **¿— qué vienen?** what are they coming for? **veo — mi mamá** I see my mother

abacá M manila

abad -esa M abbot; F abbess

abadejo M cod

abadía F abbey

abajo ADV (dirección) down; (posición relativa) below; **mirar para —** to look down; **el piso de —** the apartment below; **véase —** see below; **— de** under, underneath; **Stefan está — del coche** Stefan is under / underneath the car; **¡— el rey!** down with the king! **—firmante** undersigned; **echar —** to knock down; **río —** downstream; **venirse —** to go to ruin

abalanzarse⁹ VI to lunge at, to swoop down upon

abanderado -da MF standard-bearer

abandonado ADJ abandoned; **es una persona muy abandonada** she's very unkempt

abandonar VT (a una persona, a una familia) to leave, to desert; (el hogar, un partido) to abandon; (una carrera, el poder) to give up; (una carrera, a un enamorado, el hábito de fumar) to quit; (en los naipes) to fold; (un curso) to drop out of

abandono M (acción de descuidar) neglect; (acción de abandonar, condición de abandonado) abandonment; **por —** by default

abanicar⁶ VT to fan

abanico M (utensilio) fan; (de posibilidades) array; **abrirse en —** to fan out

abaratar VT (bajar el precio) to lower the price of; (desprestigiar) to cheapen

abarcar⁶ VT (categorías) to embrace, to encompass; (un período de tiempo) to span

abarrotería F Méx grocery store

abarrotero -ra MF Méx grocer

abarrotes M PL Méx groceries; **tienda de —** Méx grocery store

abastecer¹³ VT (un ejército, una ciudad) to supply; (una tienda) to stock

abastecimiento M supply

abasto M supply; **mercado de —s** farmers' market; **yo sola no doy —** I can't cope alone

abatido ADJ dejected, despondent, downcast

abatimiento M dejection, despondency

abatir VT (bajar) to lower; (derribar) to knock down; (desanimar) to depress; (matar a tiros) to shoot; **—se** to swoop down

abdicar⁶ VI/VT to abdicate

abdomen M abdomen

abdominal ADJ abdominal; M sit-up

abecedario M alphabet

abedul M birch

abeja F bee; **— asesina** killer bee

abejón M bumblebee

abejorro M bumblebee

aberración F aberration

abertura F (acción) opening; (de una cueva) mouth

abeto M fir

abierto ADJ (no cerrado, no determinado, sin cubierta) open; (franco) frank; **— de par en par** wide open

abigarrado ADJ motley

abigeato M cattle rustling

abismal ADJ abysmal

abismo M abyss, chasm; **— generacional** generation gap

ablandar VT to soften

abnegación F self-denial

abobado ADJ silly

abocar⁶ VI to turn onto; **—se a** to devote oneself to

abochornar VT (calentar) to make too hot; (avergonzar) to embarrass; **—se** to get embarrassed

abocinar VT to flare

abofetear VT to slap

abogacía F legal profession; **ejercer la —** to practice law

abogado -da MF lawyer, attorney

abogar⁷ VI **— por** to advocate, to plead for

abolengo M ancestry
abolición F abolition
abolir[50] VT to abolish
abollado ADJ dented
abolladura F dent
abollar VT to dent; —**se** to get dented
abolsarse VI to sag
abombar VT to make bulge
abominable ADJ abominable, loathsome
abominación F abomination
abominar VI to detest
abonado -da MF subscriber
abonar VT (suscribir) to subscribe; (pagar) to make a payment; (poner abono) to fertilize; —**se** to subscribe
abono M (a una revista) subscription; (para una temporada deportiva) season ticket; (para el autobús) pass; (para la tierra) fertilizer
abordar VT (un avión, un buque) to board; (un problema) to tackle, to approach; (a una persona en la calle) to accost
aborigen ADJ aboriginal; M primitive inhabitant; — **australiano** Australian aborigine
aborrascarse[6] VI to become stormy
aborrecer[13] VT to abhor, to loathe
aborrecible ADJ hateful, abhorrent
aborrecimiento M abhorrence
abortador -ora MF abortionist
abortar VI to miscarry, to have a miscarriage; VI/VT to abort
abortero -ra MF abortionist
aborto M (espontáneo) miscarriage; (provocado) abortion
abotargarse[7] VI to bloat
abotonar VT to button; —**se** to button up
abovedar VT (una iglesia) to vault, to cover with a vault; (una calle) to arch, to cover as a vault
abozalar VT to muzzle
abracadabra M abracadabra
abrasador ADJ burning
abrasar VT to burn; —**se** to be consumed
abrasión F abrasion
abrasivo ADJ abrasive
abrazadera F clamp
abrazar[9] VT (rodear con los brazos) to hug, to embrace; (rodear una cosa sujetando) to clasp; (una opinión) to espouse
abrazo M hug, embrace
abrevadero M trough
abrevar VT (dar de beber) to water; (beber) to drink
abreviación F abbreviation
abreviar VT to abbreviate, to abridge
abreviatura F abbreviation

abridor M opener
abrigado ADJ (ropa) warm; (lugar) sheltered
abrigar[7] VT to shelter; (emociones) to harbor; —**se** to bundle up
abrigo M (refugio) shelter; (prenda de vestir) coat, wrap
abril M April
abrillantar VT to make shiny
abrir[51] VI/VT to open; VT (con llave) to unlock; (un grifo) to turn on; — **el apetito** to whet one's appetite; — **paso** to make way; M SG **abrebotellas** bottle opener; **abrelatas** can opener; VI (el cielo) to clear up; —**se** to open up; —**se paso** to press through; **en un — y cerrar de ojos** in the twinkle of an eye
abrochar VT to fasten; —**se** to buckle (up)
abrogación F repeal
abrogar[7] VT to repeal
abrojo M bur, sticker
abrumador ADJ overwhelming
abrumar VT to overwhelm, to weigh down; —**se** to become foggy
abrupto ADJ abrupt
absceso M abscess
absolución F acquittal
absoluto ADJ absolute; **en —** absolutely not
absolver[2,51] VT to absolve, to acquit
absorbente ADJ absorbent
absorber VT to absorb
absorción F absorption
absorto ADJ absorbed, engrossed
abstemio -mia ADJ abstemious; MF teetotaler
abstenerse[44] VI to abstain; — **de** to abstain from, to refrain from
abstinencia F abstinence
abstracción F abstraction
abstracto ADJ abstract
abstraer[45] VT to abstract; —**se de** to shut out
abstraído ADJ lost in thought
absurdo ADJ absurd, preposterous; M absurdity
abuchear VI/VT to boo, to jeer
abucheo M boo, jeer
abuelo -la M grandfather; F grandmother; —**s** grandparents
abulia F apathy
abultado ADJ bulgy
abultar VI to bulge
abundancia F abundance, plenty
abundante ADJ abundant, plentiful
abundar VI to abound; — **en** to abound in
aburrido ADJ (sin entretenimiento) bored; (pesado) boring, tiresome
aburrimiento M boredom
aburrir VT to bore; —**se** to become bored

abusar VT — **de** to abuse; (sexualmente) to molest

abuso M abuse; — **de confianza** breach of trust; — **de sustancias** substance abuse

abyecto ADJ abject

acá ADV (en este lugar) here; (a este lugar) over here, *lit* hither; — **y allá** here and there

acabado ADJ finished; M finish

acabar VT to finish; VI to end; (llegar al orgasmo) *vulg* to come; — **de** to have just; — **por** to end up by; — **con** (la corrupción) to put an end to; (las cucarachas) to get rid of; **él y yo hemos acabado** he and I are through; **se acabaron los dulces** the candy is all gone; **se nos acabaron las ideas** we ran out of ideas; **y se acabó** and that's that

academia F (corporación, escuela militar) academy; (centro privado de enseñanza) private school

académico ADJ academic

acallar VT to silence, to quiet

acalorado ADJ heated

acaloramiento M **sufrió un** — he got too hot

acalorarse VI/VT (sofocarse) to overheat; (emocionarse) to get excited

acampada F camping

acampante MF camper

acampar VT to camp

acanalar VT to groove

acantilado ADJ sheer, steep; M bluff, cliff

acantonar VT to quarter

acaparar VT (productos) to hoard; (atención) to capture; (monopolizar) *fam* to hog

acaramelar VT to candy

acariciar VT to caress; — **una esperanza** to harbor a hope

ácaro M mite

acarrear VT (transportar) to cart, to transport; (ocasionar) to bring about

acarreo M cartage, carriage, transport

acaso ADV perhaps; **por si** — just in case

acatamiento M compliance

acatar VT to abide by, to comply with

acatarrar VI to chill; —**se** to catch cold

acaudalado ADJ wealthy

acceder VI — **a** to accede to

accesible ADJ accessible, convenient

acceso M access; (de ira) fit

accesorio ADJ & M accessory

accidentado -da ADJ (viaje) eventful; (terreno) uneven; MF accident victim

accidental ADJ accidental

accidentarse VI to have an accident

accidente M (suceso imprevisto) accident; (del terreno) feature; (automovilístico) wreck; **por** — by accident

acción F (acto) action; (valor de bolsa) share of stock; — **de gracias** thanksgiving; **las buenas acciones** good deeds; **acciones preferenciales** preferred stock; **acciones ordinarias** common stock

accionar VT to operate

accionista MF shareholder, stockholder

acebo M holly

acechar VT (emboscar) to lie in ambush; (amenazar) to stalk

acecho M **rondar en** — to prowl; **estar al** — to lie in wait

aceitar VT to oil

aceite M oil; — **de linaza** linseed oil; — **de oliva** olive oil; — **de ricino** castor oil; — **vegetal** vegetable oil

aceitera F oilcan

aceitoso ADJ oily

aceituna F olive

aceleración F acceleration

acelerador M accelerator

acelerar VT to accelerate, to speed up; VI to accelerate, to step on the gas; — **en vacío** to rev, to race; —**se** to get nervous

acémila F pack animal

acento M (rasgos fonéticos, signo) accent; (especial intensidad) stress

acentuar[17] VT (la hermosura) to accentuate; (ortográficamente) to accent; (oralmente) to stress; —**se** to accentuate

acepción F gloss, meaning

aceptable ADJ acceptable

aceptación F acceptance

aceptar VT to accept

acequia F irrigation ditch

acera F sidewalk

acerado ADJ made of steel

acerar VT to steel

acerca PREP — **de** about, concerning

acercamiento M approach

acercar[6] VT to bring near; **os acerco a la estación** I'll give you a ride to the station; —**se** to come near, to approach

acería F steel mill

acero M steel; — **inoxidable** stainless steel

acérrimo ADJ bitter

acertado ADJ right

acertar[1] VT to hit; VI to be right; — **con** to hit upon; — **a** to happen to; **no** — to miss the mark

acertijo M riddle, conundrum

acervo M heritage

acetona F acetone

achacar[6] VI to blame

achacoso ADJ infirm

achaparrado ADJ (planta) stunted; (persona) squat

achaque M affliction, ailment; **—s** aches and pains

achicado ADJ weak-kneed

achicar[6] VT (empequeñecer) to make small; (un vestido) to take in; (agua) to bail; **—se** (acobardarse) to feel intimidated; (empequeñecerse) to get smaller

achicoria F chicory

aciago ADJ unlucky

acicalado ADJ clean-cut

acicalarse VI to dress up

acicate M incentive

acidez F (de un ácido) acidity; (del vinagre) sourness; **— de estómago** heartburn

ácido M acid; ADJ (como el ácido) acidic; (fruta) sour, tart

acierto M (contestación correcta) right answer; (buena elección) felicitous choice

aclamación F acclamation, acclaim; **por —** by acclamation

aclamar VT to acclaim, to hail

aclaración F clarification

aclarar VT (con explicaciones) to clarify; (con agua) to rinse; (la voz) to clear; VI to dawn; **aclaró despúes de la tormenta** it cleared up after the storm; **—se** to lighten

aclimatar VT to acclimate

acné M acne

acobardar VT to intimidate

acogedor ADJ (persona) hospitable; (cuarto) cozy

acoger[11b] VT (una sugerencia) to receive; (a un refugiado) to shelter; **—se** to take refuge; **—se a la ley** to have recourse to the law

acogida F reception

acogimiento M reception

acolchar VT (pespuntear) to quilt; (rellenar) to pad

acollarar VT to collar

acometer VT (atacar) to attack; (emprender) to undertake

acometida F attack

acomodado ADJ well-off

acomodador -ora MF usher

acomodar VT (arreglar) to arrange; (ajustar) to adjust; (adaptar) to adapt; **—se** (ponerse cómodo) to make oneself comfortable; (adaptarse) to adapt oneself

acomodo M position

acompañamiento M (acción, música) accompaniment; (grupo de personas que acompaña) retinue; (comida) side dish

acompañante ADJ accompanying; MF (compañero) companion; (en música) accompanist

acompañar VI/VT to accompany (también en música); (escoltar) to escort; (en una carta) to enclose; **—se de** to be accompanied by; **esperemos que el tiempo acompañe** we hope the weather cooperates; **te acompaño en el sentimiento** my thoughts are with you

acompasado ADJ rhythmical, measured

acomplejado ADJ self-conscious

acondicionar VT to prepare

acongojar VT to distress; **—se** to become distressed

aconsejable ADJ advisable

aconsejar VT to advise, to counsel

acontecer[13] VI to take place

acontecimiento M event; **todo un —** quite a happening; **a esta altura de los —s** at this point in the proceedings

acopiar VT to stockpile

acopio M (acción de guardar) storing; (cosas guardadas) stockpile

acoplamiento M coupling; **— universal de cardán** universal joint

acoplar VT to couple; **—se** (juntarse) to couple, to join; (parlantes) to have feedback

acople M coupling, connection

acorazado ADJ armored; M battleship, warship

acorazar[9] VT to armor

acordar[2] VI **— en** to arrange to; **—se (de)** to remember

acorde ADJ in agreement; **— con** in agreement with; M chord

acordeón M accordion

acordonar VT (un zapato) to tie with a lace; (un lugar) to rope off, to seal off; (una moneda) to mill

acorralar VT (meter en un corral) to corral; (impedir la salida) to corner

acortamiento M shortening

acortar VT to shorten

acosar VT (perseguir) to harry; (atacar) to beset; (atormentar) to badger; (solicitar sexualmente) to harass

acostar[2] VT to put to bed; **—se** to go to bed; **—se con** to sleep with

acostumbrado ADJ accustomed; (habitual) customary; **estar — a** to be used / accustomed to

acostumbrar VT to accustom; (soler) to be accustomed to; **—se (a)** to get accustomed (to)

acotación F (anotación) marginal note; (en una obra de teatro) stage directions

acotar VT (un terreno) to mark off; (un texto) to make marginal notes on

acre ADJ acrid, pungent, sharp; M acre

acrecentamiento M growth, increase

acrecentar[1] VI to grow

acreditar VT (una cuenta) to credit; (a un profesional) to accredit; **a quien pueda — ser el dueño de** to whoever can prove he is the owner of

acreedor -ora ADJ deserving; **saldo —** positive balance; MF creditor

acribillar VI (a balazos) to riddle; (a pedradas) to pelt

acrílico ADJ & M acrylic

acritud F acrimony

acrobacia F (arte) acrobatics; (ejercicio de acróbata) stunt

acróbata MF INV acrobat

acrobático ADJ acrobatic

acrofobia F acrophobia

acrónimo M acronym

acta F (de nacimiento) certificate; (de una reunión) minutes; (de un congreso) proceedings

actitud F attitude

activar VT to activate

actividad F activity

activismo M activism

activista MF activist

activo ADJ active; **en —** working; M assets; **— líquido** liquid assets

acto M (solemne, sexual, de una obra de teatro) act; (acción) action; **— seguido** immediately after; **— fallido** Freudian slip; **en el —** on the spot; **hacer — de presencia** to show up

actor -triz M actor; F actress; **— de carácter** character actor

actuación F (acción de actuar) acting; (modo de actuar) performance

actual ADJ current, present

actualidad F present time; **—es** latest news; **de —** up-to-date

actualización F (de información) update; (de ordenador) upgrade

actualizado ADJ up-to-date

actualizar[9] VT to update; (ordenador) to upgrade

actualmente ADV presently

actuar[17] VI to act; (ante el público) to perform

actuario -ria MF (judicial) clerk; (de seguros) actuary

acuarela F watercolor

acuario M aquarium

acuartelar VT to quarter

acuático ADJ aquatic

acuchillar VT to stab, to slash

acuclillado ADJ squatting

acuclillarse VI to squat

acudir VI (ir) to go; (asistir) to attend; **— a** to turn to; **— al llamado** to respond to the call; **— al socorro de** to go to the rescue of; **— en masa** to flock

acueducto M aqueduct

acuerdo M agreement; **estar de —** to be in agreement; **ponerse de —** to come to an agreement; **de — con** in accordance with

acumulación F accumulation, build-up

acumulador M storage battery

acumular VT to accumulate; (una fortuna) to amass; **—se** to collect

acumulativo ADJ cumulative

acuñación F coinage, minting

acuñar VT (hacer monedas, una expresión) to coin; (meter cuñas) to wedge

acuoso ADJ watery

acupuntor -ora MF acupuncturist

acupuntura F acupuncture

acurrucarse[6] VI to nestle, to huddle

acusación F accusation, charge

acusado -da MF accused; (en un juicio) defendant

acusador -ora MF accuser

acusar VT (señalar como culpable) to accuse; (detectar) to detect; (revelar) to betray; (entre niños) to tattle, to tell; **— el golpe** to feel the blow; **— recibo** to acknowledge receipt

acuse M acknowledgment

acusetas MF SG tattletale

acusica MF INV tattletale

acústica F acoustics

acústico ADJ acoustic

adagio M adage

adaptabilidad F resilience

adaptación F adaptation

adaptar VT to adapt

adecuado ADJ appropriate

adecuar VT to adapt; **—se a** to be suitable for

adefesio M sight, hideous thing

adelantado ADJ (economía, alumno) advanced; (reloj) fast; (tren) ahead of time, ahead of schedule; **por —** in advance

adelantamiento M (de una fecha) bringing forward; (de un coche) overtaking

adelantar VT (una fecha, dinero) to advance; (la mano) to move forward; (un coche) to pass; (una noticia) to tell before; VI (un reloj) to gain; **— en** to make progress in; **—se** (sacar ventaja) to get ahead; (actuar antes) to go ahead; (innovar) to be ahead; (hablar antes) to get ahead of oneself

adelante ADV forward; **— con los faroles** let's get started; **— de mí** in front of me; **de aquí en —** from now on; **hacia —** forward; **ir —** to go ahead; **más —** later; **sacar —** to make prosper; **seguir —** to go on

adelanto M (de la ciencia) advance, breakthrough; (de un coche) passing; (pago) advance; **el — de los relojes** setting the clocks forward

adelfa F oleander

adelgazar[9] VI to lose weight; VT to lose; (hacer perder peso) to make one lose weight; (hacer menos espeso) to thin; (hacer parecer delgado) to make one look thinner; **—se** to get thinner

ademán M gesture; **hacer un — a alguien** to motion to someone

además ADV moreover, besides, in addition; **— de deberme dinero** besides / in addition to owing me money

adentro ADV inside; **ir para / hacia —** to go inside; **hablar para sus —s** to talk to oneself; **con lo de — para afuera** inside out

aderezar[9] VT (embellecer) to adorn; (condimentar) to season, to garnish

aderezo M (adorno) adornment; (de un alimento) seasoning; (de una ensalada) salad dressing

adeudar VT (deber) to owe; (cargar en cuenta) to debit

adeudo M (endeudamiento) indebtedness; (a una cuenta) debit

adherencia F adhesion

adherir[3] VI to adhere; **—se a** (una cosa) to stick to; (una huelga) to join; (una idea) to subscribe to

adhesión F (a una cosa) adhesion; (a una doctrina) adherence

adhesivo ADJ adhesive; M (pegamento) cement, adhesive; (calcomanía) sticker

adicción F addiction

adición F addition

adicional ADJ additional

adictivo ADJ addictive

adicto -ta ADJ addicted; MF addict

adiestramiento M training

adiestrar VT to train

adinerado ADJ wealthy, well-to-do

adiós INTERJ goodbye; **hacer — con la mano** to wave goodbye

adiposo ADJ fatty

aditivo M additive

adivinanza F riddle

adivinar VT to guess

adivino -na MF fortune teller

adjetivo ADJ & M adjective

adjudicación F award

adjudicar[6] VT to award; **—se** to be awarded

adjuntar VT (incluir en una carta) to enclose; (añadir) to add

adjunto ADJ (unido) attached; (en un mismo envío) enclosed; (asistente) adjunct; ADV herewith

adminículo M gadget

administración F administration; **— pública** civil service

administrador -ora MF administrator

administrar VT (una empresa, un medicamento) to administer; (justicia) to dispense; **—se** to budget

administrativo ADJ administrative

admirable ADJ admirable

admiración F admiration

admirador -ora MF admirer; (de una estrella de cine) fan

admirar VT to admire; **—se** to be amazed; **—se de** to wonder at

admisible ADJ admissible, allowable

admisión F (aceptación) admission; (reconocimiento) acknowledgment

admitir VT (dejar entrar, reconocer) to admit; (aceptar) to accept; (permitir) to allow

ADN (ácido desoxirribonucleico) M DNA

adobar VT (aderezar una comida) to fix; (curtir una piel) to tan; (encurtir) to pickle

adobe M adobe

adobo M sauce for seasoning

adoctrinar VT to indoctrinate

adolecer[13] VI **— de** to suffer from

adolescencia F adolescence

adolescente ADJ adolescent; MF adolescent, teenager

adonde ADV REL **esa es la casa — vamos** that's the house (where) we're going to

adónde ADV INTERR & PRON where

adopción F adoption

adoptar VT to adopt

adoptivo ADJ adoptive

adoquín M cobblestone

adorable ADJ adorable

adoración F (a un ser amado) adoration; (a un dios) worship

adorador -ora MF worshiper

adorar VT (a una persona) to adore; (a un dios) to worship

adormecer[13] VT (dar sueño) to make drowsy; (entumecer) to numb; **—se** (de sueño) to become drowsy; (de frío) to go numb

adormilado ADJ sleepy

adornar VT to adorn, to embellish

adorno M adornment, ornament, decoration

adquirir[34] VT to acquire; (una característica)

to take on

adquisición F acquisition; (a una colección, al personal) addition; (de una compañía) takeover

adrede ADV on purpose

adrenalina F adrenaline

aduana F customs; (edificio) customshouse

aduanero -ra MF customs officer

aducir[24] VT to offer as proof

adueñarse VI to take possession

adulación F flattery

adulador -ora ADJ flattering; MF flatterer

adular VI/VT to flatter

adulón -ona ADJ flattering; MF *fam* brownnoser

adulterar VT to adulterate

adulterio M adultery

adúltero -ra MF adulterer

adulto -ta ADJ & MF adult

adusto ADJ stern

advenedizo ADJ upstart

advenimiento M advent

adverbio MF adverb

adversario -ria MF adversary, opponent

adversidad F adversity

adverso ADJ adverse

advertencia F (aviso) notice; (amonestación) warning, admonition

advertir[3] VT (avisar) to warn; (notar) to notice; (notificar) to advise, to tip off

Adviento M Advent

adyacente ADJ adjacent

aéreo ADJ aerial; **correo —** air mail

aeróbic M aerobics

aeróbico ADJ aerobic

aerobio ADJ aerobic

aerodeslizador M hovercraft

aerodinámica F aerodynamics

aerodinámico ADJ aerodynamic, streamlined

aeródromo M airport

aeroespacial ADJ aerospace

aeronáutica F aeronautics

aeronave F aircraft

aeropuerto M airport

aerosol M (suspensión) aerosol; (aparato) spray can

aerotransportado ADJ airborne

aerotransportar VT to airlift

afabilidad F affability, friendliness

afable ADJ affable, friendly

afamado ADJ famed

afán M eagerness

afanar VT *fam* to swipe; **—se** to work hard

afanoso ADJ hardworking

afasia F aphasia

afear VT to make ugly; **—se** to become ugly

afección F condition

afectación F affectation

afectado ADJ (por un desastre) affected, stricken; (modales) affected, unnatural

afectar VT to affect

afecto M affection, fondness; **— a** fond of

afectuoso ADJ affectionate, loving

afeitado ADJ clean-shaven; M shave

afeitadora F shaver

afeitar VT to shave

afelpado ADJ & M plush

afeminado ADJ effeminate, sissy

aferrado ADJ stubborn, obstinate

aferrar VT (agarrar) to grasp; (atar) to grapple; **—se** to cling

affaire M affair

Afganistán M Afghanistan

afgano -na ADJ & MF Afghan, Afghani

afianzar[9] VT to secure; (un préstamo) to guarantee

afiche M poster

afición F (inclinación) inclination; (afecto) fondness; (conjunto de aficionados) fans

aficionado -da ADJ **— a** fond of; MF (no profesional) amateur; (hincha) fan

aficionarse VI **— a** to become fond of

afilado ADJ sharp; M sharpening

afilador -ora MF grinder, sharpener

afilar VT to sharpen, to grind

afiliarse VI **— con** to affiliate oneself with

afín ADJ kindred, related

afinación F tune-up

afinado ADJ in tune

afinador -ora MF tuner

afinar VT (una destreza) to perfect; (un plan) to fine-tune; (un piano) to tune; **—se** to become thinner

afinidad F (afecto) affinity; (parentesco) kinship

afirmación F (aseveración) assertion; (aseveración positiva) affirmation

afirmar VT (decir) to assert, to declare; (decir que algo es cierto) to affirm; (sujetar) to secure; **—se** to steady oneself

afirmativa F affirmative answer

afirmativo ADJ affirmative

aflicción F affliction, woe

afligir[11] VT (dar dolor) to afflict; (entristecer) to distress

aflojar VT (una soga) to slacken, to loosen; (la vigilancia) to relax; **— el dinero** to hand over the money; VI to ease up, to slack off; **—se** to work loose

afluencia F influx

afluente M tributary

afluir[31] VI (ríos) to flow (into); (turistas) to flock

afortunado ADJ fortunate, lucky

afrecho M bran
afrenta F affront
afrentar VT to offend
África F Africa
africano -na ADJ & MF African
afroamericano -na ADJ & MF African-American
afrodisíaco M aphrodisiac
afrontar VT to face
afuera ADV outdoors, outside; F PL. **—s** outskirts
agachar VT to lower; **—se** to crouch, to stoop
agalla F (de pez) gill; (de roble) gallnut; **tener —s** to have guts / spunk
agarrado ADJ tight-fisted
agarrar VT (sujetar) to seize, to grasp, to grab; (capturar) to catch; (adherirse) to grip; **— por sorpresa** to catch by surprise; **—le la onda a algo** to get the swing of something; **—se una sífilis** to catch a case of syphilis; **—se** to hold on; **—se de** to latch onto; **agarré por la calle ocho** I took eighth street; **agarró y se fue** he up and went
agarre M grip
agarrón M grab
agarrotarse VI (el cuerpo) to stiffen up; (un motor) to seize (up)
agasajar VT to entertain
agasajo M entertainment
agazaparse VI to crouch
agencia F agency, bureau; **— de viajes** travel agency
agenciar VT to wrangle
agente MF agent; (espía) operative; **— de policía** police officer
ágil ADJ agile, nimble
agilidad F agility
agitación F (acción de agitar, nerviosismo) agitation; (protesta) turmoil, unrest
agitado ADJ (estado) agitated; (vida) eventful, hectic; (mar) choppy; (sueño) uneasy
agitador -ora M (aparato) agitator; MF agitator, troublemaker
agitar VT (sacudir) to agitate, to shake up; (incitar a la protesta) to agitate; **—se** (ponerse nervioso) to get worked up; (moverse) to thrash around
aglomeración F crowd
aglomerado M particle board
aglomerarse VI to crowd together
agnóstico -ca ADJ & MF agnostic
agobiado ADJ (por los enemigos) embattled; (por el trabajo) overwhelmed
agobiante ADJ overwhelming
agobiar VT (con una carga excesiva) to weigh down; (con el trabajo) to overwhelm; (con impuestos) to burden
agolparse VI to crowd together
agonía F throes of death; **ser un —s** to be a whiner
agonizante ADJ dying
agonizar[9] VI to be in the throes of death
agorafobia F agoraphobia
agorero -ra ADJ ominous; MF soothsayer
agosto M August; **hacer su —** to make hay while the sun shines
agotado ADJ (una persona) worn-out; (un libro) out-of-print; (una mercancía) out-of-stock
agotamiento M (de una persona) exhaustion; (de un recurso) depletion
agotar VT (un recurso) to exhaust, to use up, to deplete; (la energía) to sap; (un libro) to go out of print; (a una persona) to wear down; **—se** (acabarse) to be all gone; (venderse) to sell out; (secarse) to dry up
agraciado ADJ attractive
agraciar VT to grace
agradable ADJ (persona) agreeable, pleasant, congenial; (situación) pleasant, enjoyable
agradar VT to please
agradecer[13] VT (dar las gracias) to thank; (sentir gratitud) to be grateful for; **se agradece** thank you
agradecido ADJ thankful, grateful
agradecimiento M thankfulness, appreciation; (en un libro) acknowledgment
agrado M pleasure; **de su —** to his liking
agrandamiento M enlargement
agrandar VT to enlarge
agrario ADJ agrarian
agravar VT to aggravate, to make worse; **—se** to get worse
agraviar VT to outrage
agravio M outrage
agredir[50] VT to assault
agregado -da MF (funcionario de embajada) attaché; (profesor asociado) adjunct; M (mezcla) aggregate
agregar[7] VT to add
agresión F (violencia) aggression; (ataque) assault; **— con lesiones** assault and battery
agresivo ADJ aggressive
agresor -ora MF aggressor, assailant
agreste ADJ rough
agriar[16] VT to make sour; **—se** to go sour
agrícola ADJ INV agricultural
agricultor -ora MF agriculturist, farmer
agricultura F agriculture, farming
agridulce ADJ (sabor) sweet-and-sour;

(memoria) bittersweet
agrietarse VI to crack; (los labios) to chap
agrimensor -ora MF surveyor
agrimensura F surveying
agrio ADJ sour
agrisarse VI to gray
agropecuario ADJ agricultural
agrumarse VI to lump
agrupación F group
agrupar VT to group
agua F water; — **con gas** sparkling water; —
    corriente running water; — **de colonia**
    cologne; — **de grifo** tap water; — **de**
    manantial spring water; — **dulce** fresh
    water; —**marina** aquamarine; —
    mineral mineral water; — **oxigenada**
    hydrogen peroxide; — **salada** salt water;
    —**s abajo** downstream; —**s arriba**
    upstream; —**s negras** sewer water; **hacer**
    — *fam* to take a leak; **se me hace — la**
    boca my mouth is watering
aguacate M avocado
aguacero M shower, cloudburst, downpour
aguada F watering hole
aguadero M watering hole
aguado ADJ (fruta) watery; (vino, sopa)
    watered-down
aguantar VT (miserias) to endure; (a una
    persona molesta) to bear, to stand; (un
    peso) to bear; (la respiración) to hold; VI
    (mantenerse) to stand; (durar) to last;
    (esperar) to wait; (no pudrirse) to keep;
    aguántate grin and bear it
aguante M (para el trabajo) endurance,
    stamina; (para el vino) tolerance
aguar[8] VT (añadir agua, despojar de fuerza)
    to water down; (estropear) to spoil; —**se**
    to become diluted; MF SG **aguafiestas**
    killjoy, wet blanket
aguardar VI to wait; VT to wait for, to await
aguardentoso ADJ hoarse
aguardiente M brandy
aguarrás M turpentine
agudeza F (visual) sharpness, keenness; (del
    ingenio) quickness; (para los negocios)
    acumen; (dicho agudo) witticism
agudo ADJ (dolor, enfermedad, ángulo) acute;
    (vista, mente) sharp, keen; (mentón)
    pointed; (voz) high-pitched; (chiste) witty
agüero M portent, omen; **de mal —**
    portentous
aguijada F goad
aguijar VT to goad
aguijón M (de planta) spur; (de insecto)
    sting, stinger
aguijonear VT (a un animal) to goad, to
    prod; (insecto) to sting

águila F eagle; **es un —** he is sharp
aguilucho M eaglet
aguinaldo M Christmas bonus
aguja F (para coser, tejer, de tocadiscos, de
    pino, de velocímetro) needle; (de reloj)
    hand; (riel móvil) railroad switch;
    (chapitel) steeple, spire; — **de croché**
    crochet hook; — **de punto** knitting
    needle; — **de zurcir** darning needle;
    como una — en un pajar like a needle
    in a haystack
agujerear VT to pierce
agujero M hole; (de una ley) loophole;
    (déficit) shortfall; — **negro** black hole;
    tapar —s to pay debts
aguzar[9] VT to sharpen; — **el oído** to prick
    up one's ears
ahechaduras F PL chaff
ahí ADV there; **por —** over there,
    thereabouts; **de —** hence; — **te quiero**
    ver I want to see you in that situation
ahijado -a M godson; F goddaughter
ahínco M **trabajar con —** to work hard
ahogar[7] VT (asfixiar en agua) to drown;
    (inundar un motor con combustible) to
    flood; (asfixiar por falta de aire) to
    smother; (reprimir un grito) to stifle;
    (asfixiar por presión al cuello) to throttle,
    to strangle, to choke; — **las penas**
    bebiendo to drown one's sorrows in
    drink; —**se** (en agua) to drown
ahogo M (por calor, falta de aire) suffocation;
    (por un esfuerzo) breathlessness; **vivir sin**
    —**s** to live a comfortable life
ahondar VT (un hoyo) to deepen; (un
    asunto) to dig deeper into; —**se** to become
    deeper
ahora ADV now; — **bien** now then; —
    mismo right now; **por —** for the present,
    for now; **hasta —** to date, up to now, so
    far
ahorcar[6] VT to hang, *fam* to string up
ahorrar VT to save; (librar de una molestia)
    to spare
ahorrativo ADJ frugal, thrifty
ahorro M thriftiness; —**s** savings
ahuecar[6] VT to hollow out; — **la voz** to
    speak in a hollow voice
ahumado ADJ smoked; M smoking
ahumar VT to smoke
ahuyentar VT to drive away, to scare away;
    —**se** to get scared
airado ADJ irate
airarse VI to get angry
airbag M airbag
aire M air; (melodía) tune; (manera de ser)
    manner; — **acondicionado** air

conditioning; — **libre** outdoors; **al —
libre** outdoors; **andar con el culo al —**
to walk around buck naked; **cambiar de
—s** to change surroundings; **darse —s** to
posture; **en el —** up in the air; **estar en
el —** to be on the air; **tener — de** to look
like; **tomar —** to breathe in; **tomar el —**
to get some air
airear VT to air out
airoso ADJ graceful
aislacionismo M isolationism
aislado ADJ (persona) isolated; (lugar)
secluded
aislador M insulator; ADJ insulating
aislamiento M (acción de aislarse) isolation;
(cosa que aísla) insulation; (soledad)
seclusion
aislante M insulator
aislar VT (dejar separado, separar) to isolate;
(poner fuera de contacto) to insulate;
(rechazar socialmente) to ostracize
ajar VT (una planta) to wither; (las manos) to
make rough; (la piel) to age
ajedrez M chess
ajeno ADJ (de otro) belonging to someone
else; (extraño) alien; **— a un peligro**
oblivious to a danger; **— a mi voluntad**
beyond my control; **— a mi experiencia**
foreign to my experience
ajetrearse VI to bustle about
ajetreo M bustle, hustle and bustle
ají M chili
ajo M garlic
ajuar M (de novia) trousseau; (mobiliario)
furnishings
ajustado ADJ tight, snug; **— a la ley** in
accordance with the law
ajustar VT (hacer corresponder, retocar una
prenda) to adjust; (retocar un contrato) to
tweak; (apretar) to tighten; VI to fit tight;
— cuentas to settle accounts; **—se a
derecho** to be in accordance with the law
ajuste M (acción de ajustar) adjustment; (del
cinturón) tightening; (de una máquina)
fine-tuning; (de cuentas) settlement; (de
una prenda) alteration; **hacer —s** to
tinker with
ala F (de ave) wing; (de sombrero) brim;
cortarle las —s a alguien to clip
someone's wings
alabanza F praise
alabar VT to praise
alabeo M warp
alacena F pantry
alacrán M scorpion
alamar M (adorno con flecos) frog; (presilla)
clasp

alambique M still
alambrada F wire fence
alambrado M (barrera) wire fence; (acción
de alambrar) wiring
alambrar VT to wire
alambre M wire; **— de púas** barbed wire
alameda F poplar grove
álamo M poplar (tree)
alancear VT to wound with a lance, to spear
alano M mastiff
alarde M show; **hacer — de** to boast of, to
show off
alardear VI **— de** to boast about
alargar[7] VT (hacer más largo) to lengthen;
(un brazo, un guiso) to stretch (out); **— la
vista** to peer into the distance; **—se** to go
on (longer than expected)
alarido M scream, howl
alarma F alarm; **— antirrobo** burglar alarm;
— contra incendios fire alarm
alarmar VT to alarm
alba F dawn
albacea MF INV executor
albanés -esa ADJ & MF Albanian
Albania F Albania
albañal M sewer
albañil M mason, bricklayer
albañilería F masonry
albaricoque M apricot
albatros M albatross
alberca F (depósito) reservoir; (piscina) *Méx*
swimming pool
albergar[7] VT (dar refugio) to shelter;
(hospedar) to lodge; (ser sede de) to
house; (guardar rencor, un secreto) to
harbor; **—se** to take shelter
albino -na MF albino
albóndiga F meatball
albor M dawn
alborada F dawn; reveille
albornoz M bathrobe
alborotador -ora ADJ rowdy; MF
troublemaker
alborotar VT (el pelo) to muss; (la casa) to
mess up; (la calle) to cause trouble in; (a
los niños) to excite; **—se** to get excited
alboroto M hubbub, fuss
alborozado ADJ joyful
alborozar[9] VT to gladden; **—se** to rejoice
alborozo M joy
albricias F PL & INTERJ congratulations
álbum M album
alcachofa F artichoke
alcahuete -ta MF (soplón) tattletale;
(mediador, encubridor) procurer
alcaide M warden
alcalde -esa MF mayor

álcali M alkali

alcalino ADJ alkaline

alcance M (de una persona) reach; (de los deseos) attainment; (de un misil) range; (de una ley) scope; **de corto(s) —(s)** meager intellect; **al —** at hand, within reach; **a su —** within his reach; **al — del oído** within hearing; **dar — a** to catch up with; **de gran —** far-reaching; **de largo —** long-range

alcancía F piggybank

alcanfor M camphor

alcantarilla F (para agua sucia) sewer; (para lluvias) gully, gutter

alcantarillado M sewage system

alcanzar[9] VT (llegar a un punto, cumplir un deseo) to reach; (igualar) to catch up with; (pasar, poner en la mano) to pass; (herir a balazos) to get; **no alcanzo a verlo** I can't quite see it; **no me alcanza el dinero** I don't have enough money; **alcancé a conocer a mi abuela** I was born soon enough to meet my grandmother

alcaparra F caper

alcaucil M artichoke

alcázar M fortress

alce M elk; (norteamericano) moose

alcoba F bedroom

alcohol M alcohol; **— etílico** ethyl alcohol

alcohólico -ca ADJ & MF alcoholic

alcoholismo M alcoholism

alcornoque M (árbol) cork tree; (persona) blockhead

alcuza F oilcan

aldaba F (para llamar) knocker; (para cerrar) bolt

aldabón M large knocker

aldea F village, hamlet

aldeano -na MF villager; **joven aldeana** village girl

aleación F alloy

alear VT (metales) to alloy; (alas) to flap

aleatorio ADJ random

aleccionar VT to teach a lesson

aledaños M PL vicinity

alegar[7] VT (aducir) to adduce; (pretender) to claim

alegato M (a favor de) plea; (en contra de) allegation

alegoría F allegory

alegrar VT (a una persona) to gladden; (una fiesta) to brighten up; **—se** to be glad; (por efecto del alcohol) to get tipsy

alegre ADJ joyful, cheerful, lighthearted; (ebrio) tipsy, lit

alegría F joy, merriment, cheer

alejamiento M withdrawal

alejar VT (distanciar) to move away; (ahuyentar) to scare off; **—se** (físicamente) to move away; (emocionalmente) to withdraw

alelar VT to stupefy

alemán -ana ADJ & MF German; M (lengua) German

Alemania F Germany

alentar[1] VT (animar) to encourage, to cheer up; VI to breathe

alergia F allergy

alérgico ADJ allergic

alergólogo -ga MF allergist

alero M eaves

alerón M (de avión) aileron, flap; (de coche) spoiler

alerta ADJ INV, ADV & F alert

alertar VT to alert

aleta F (de pez) fin; (de ballena) fluke; (de buceador) flipper

aletargado ADJ sluggish

aletargarse[7] VI to fall into a lethargy

aletazo M flap of a wing

aletear VI to flap, to flutter

aleteo M flapping, flutter

alevín M small fry

alevosía F treachery

alevoso ADJ treacherous

alfabetismo M literacy

alfabetización F literacy

alfabetizar[9] VI (enseñar a leer y a escribir) to teach to read and write; VT (disponer en orden alfabético) to alphabetize

alfabeto M alphabet

alfalfa F alfalfa

alfanumérico ADJ alphanumeric

alfarería F pottery

alfarero -ra MF potter

alféizar M windowsill

alfeñique M (golosina) sugar paste; (persona) weakling

alférez MF second lieutenant; **— de fragata** ensign

alfil M bishop

alfiler M pin; **— de corbata** tiepin; **no cabe un —** it's totally full

alfiletero M pincushion

alfombra F carpet; (suelta) rug

alfombrar VT to carpet

alfombrilla F mat

alforja F saddlebag

alga F seaweed; **—s** algae

algarabía F uproar

algarrobo M locust tree

algazara F merriment

álgebra F algebra

algo PRON something, anything; ADV somewhat; **— es —** something is better than nothing; **por — será** there must be reason

algodón M cotton; **— de azúcar** cotton candy; **se crió entre algodones** he had a protected childhood

algoritmo M algorithm

alguacil M sheriff, marshal; (en un tribunal) bailiff

alguien PRON INDEF somebody, someone; **vino — a hablarte** someone came to talk to you; (en preguntas) anybody, anyone; **¿— lo vio?** did anyone see him?

alguno ADJ some; **—s** some, a few; **sin ruido —** without a sound; **en alguna parte** somewhere; **de alguna manera** somehow; **en algún momento** sometime; **¿lo has visto alguna vez?** have you ever seen him? **¿hay alguna forma de hacer esto?** is there any way to do this?

alhaja F jewel (también persona); **—s** jewelry

alhajero M jewelry box

alharaca F fuss

alhelí M wallflower

aliado -da ADJ allied; MF ally

alianza F alliance; (de Dios) covenant

aliar[16] VT to ally

alias M alias

alicaído ADJ crestfallen

alicates M PL pliers

aliciente M inducement

aliento M (aire respirado) breath; (ánimo) encouragement; **cobrar —** to catch one's breath; **contener el —** to hold one's breath; **sin —** out of breath, breathless

aligerar VT to lighten; **— el paso** to quicken one's pace

alijo M cache, stash

alimentación F (de una persona) nourishment, food; (de una máquina) feeding

alimentar VT (a una persona) to feed, to nourish; (un fuego) to stoke

alimenticio ADJ nutritious, nourishing; **industria alimenticia** food industry; **pensión alimenticia** alimony

alimento M food, nourishment

alineación F (de un equipo deportivo) lineup; (de un coche) alignment

alinear VT (un grupo de cosas) to line up; (a un deportista) to put in the lineup; **—se con** to align oneself with

aliño M condiment, seasoning

alisar VT to smooth; (pelo) to straighten

alistamiento M enlistment

alistar VT to enlist

aliviar VT (hacer menos pesado) to lighten; (mitigar) to alleviate, to relieve; (tranquilizar) to relieve; **—se** (mejorarse) to get better; (hacer sus necesidades) to relieve oneself

alivio M relief

aljaba F quiver

aljibe M cistern

allá ADV there, over there; **más —** farther, beyond; **el más —** the hereafter; **— tú** that's your problem

allanamiento M raid; **— de morada** forcible entry

allanar VT (la tierra) to level, to smooth; (una dificultad) to iron out; (una casa) to raid; **— el camino** to smooth the way

allegado -da ADJ close to; MF relative

allegar[7] VT to gather; **—se** to arrive

allí ADV (punto en el espacio) there; (punto en el tiempo) then; **por —** through there

alma F soul; **con toda el —** from the bottom of one's heart; **hasta el —** to the bone; **ni un —** not a soul; **no me cabía el — en el cuerpo** I was overjoyed; **se me fue el — al piso** my heart sank

almacén M (depósito) warehouse, storehouse, depot; (tienda) department store; **almacenes** department store

almacenaje M storage

almacenamiento M storage

almacenar VT to store, to stock up on

almacenista MF wholesaler

almáciga F nursery

almádena F sledgehammer

almanaque M (publicación anual) almanac; (calendario) calendar

almeja F clam

almendra F almond

almendro M almond tree

almiar M haystack

almíbar M syrup

almidón M starch

almidonado ADJ stiff

almidonar VT to starch

almirante M admiral

almohada F pillow; **consultarlo con la —** to sleep on it

almohadilla F (para sentarse) cushion; (en las patas de los perros) pad

almohadón M cushion

almohaza F currycomb

almohazar[9] VT to groom

almorranas F PL piles, hemorrhoids

almorzar[2,9] VT to lunch, to eat lunch

almuerzo M lunch

alocado ADJ wild

áloe M aloe vera
alojamiento M lodging, accommodations; (militar) quarters
alojar VT (a un invitado) to lodge, to accommodate; (a unos huérfanos) to house; (a las tropas) to quarter; **—se** (una bala) to lodge; (una persona) to board, to room
alondra F lark
alpaca F alpaca
alpinismo M mountain climbing
alpinista MF mountain climber, mountaineer
alpino ADJ alpine
alpiste M birdseed
alquería F farmhouse
alquilar VT to rent; **se alquila** for rent
alquiler M (pago mensual) rent; (acción de alquilar) renting; **coche de —** rental car; **dar en —** to hire out
alquitrán M tar
alquitranar VT to tar
alrededor ADV around; **— de la casa** around the house; M **—es** (de un área) surroundings; (de una ciudad) outskirts
alta F discharge; **dar de —** to discharge
altanería F haughtiness
altanero ADJ haughty
altar M altar
alteración F alteration; **alteraciones al orden público** public disturbances
alterar VT to alter; **— el ánimo** to upset; **—se** to get upset
altercado M altercation
altercar[6] VT **— con** to quarrel with
alternador M alternator
alternar VT to alternate; **— con** to rub elbows with
alternativa F alternative
alternativo ADJ (cambiante) alternating; (optativo) alternative
alterno ADJ alternate; **alterna y continua** AC/DC
alteza F highness
altibajos M PL ups and downs
altillo M attic
altímetro M altimeter
altiplano M high plateau
altisonante ADJ high-sounding
altitud F altitude
altivez F haughtiness
altivo ADJ haughty
alto ADJ (que está arriba) high; (que tiene mayor altura vertical) tall; **de alta fidelidad** high fidelity; **de alta potencia** high-powered; **de alta velocidad** high-speed; **en — grado** to a great extent; **en alta mar** on the high

seas; M **altavoz** loudspeaker; **altoparlante** loudspeaker; M (altura) height; (piso) upper story; **— el fuego** cease-fire; ADV loud; **hablar —** to talk loud; **cotizarse —** to be set high; INTERJ halt!
altruismo M altruism
altura F (de persona, edificio, ola, epidemia) height; (de avión) altitude; (del suelo sobre el mar, lugar alto) elevation; **a estas —s** at this stage; **a la — de la calle ocho** at eighth street; **a la — de las circunstancias** equal to the circumstances
alubia F bean
alucinar VT (causar alucinaciones) to hallucinate; (fascinar) to fascinate; (deslumbrar) to bowl over; VI (sufrir alucinaciones) to hallucinate
alud M avalanche
aludir VI **— a** to allude to, to refer to
alumbrado M lighting; ADJ lit
alumbramiento M childbirth
alumbrar VT to light up; (dar a luz) to give birth
aluminio M aluminum
alumnado M student body
alumno -na MF (de enseñanza primaria) pupil; (de enseñanza secundaria) student
alusión F allusion
aluvión M (de preguntas, pedidos) barrage; (de personas) flood
alza F appreciation; **— de precios** boost in prices
alzamiento M (acción de alzar) raising; (insurrección) uprising
alzaprima F crowbar
alzar[9] VT (la mano, la voz, una casa) to raise; (a un niño) to lift up; **— la vista** to look up; **—se** to rise up in rebellion; **—se con** to make off with
amabilidad F kindness; **¿tendría la — de...?** would you mind...?
amable ADJ kind, nice
amado -da MF beloved
amaestrador -ora MF trainer
amaestramiento M training
amaestrar VT to train
amagar[7] VI/VT **amagó que iba a llover** it looked like it was going to rain; **amagó con llover** it threatened to rain
amago M **hacer —** to make as if
amalgamar VT to amalgamate
amamantar VT to nurse, to breast-feed
amanecer[13] VI to dawn; **— enfermo** to wake up ill; **amanecí en Londres** I woke up in London; M dawn, sunrise, daybreak

amanerado ADJ effete

amansar VT to tame

amante MF lover; ADJ — **de** fond of

amañar VT (una elección) to rig; (un documento) to tamper with

amapola F poppy

amar VT to love

amargar[7] VT to embitter

amargo ADJ bitter

amargor M bitterness

amargura F bitterness

amarillear VI/VT to yellow, to turn yellow

amarillento ADJ yellowish

amarillo -lla ADJ yellow; MF (esquirol) scab

amarra F cable, rope; —**s** moorings; **soltar** —**s** to cast off

amarrar VT (un barco) to moor; (una cosa) to secure, to tie down

amartillar VT (pegar con martillo) to hammer; (un arma) to cock

amasar VT (masa) to knead; (una fortuna) to amass

amateur ADJ & MF amateur

amatista F amethyst

Amazonas M Amazon River

ambages M **hablar sin** — to not mince words, to speak plainly

ámbar M amber

ambición F ambition

ambicionar VT to have the ambition of

ambicioso ADJ ambitious; (codicioso) overambitious

ambidiestro ADJ ambidextrous

ambiental ADJ environmental; (temperatura) ambient

ambiente ADJ ambient; M (condiciones biológicas) environment; (atmósfera) atmosphere, ambiance; (sector social) milieu

ambigüedad F ambiguity

ambiguo ADJ ambiguous

ámbito M (ambiente) scene; (alcance) scope; (esfera) sphere

ambivalente ADJ ambivalent

ambos ADJ & PRON both

ambulancia F ambulance

ambulante ADJ itinerant

ameba F ameba

amedrentar VT to scare

amén INTERJ amen; **decir** — to approve without discussion; — **de** besides

amenaza F threat, menace

amenazador ADJ threatening

amenazar[9] VT to threaten; — **con** to threaten to

amenidad F (cualidad de ameno) pleasantness; (placer) pleasure

amenizar[9] VI to make entertaining

ameno ADJ enjoyable, entertainment

América F America

americano -na ADJ & MF American; F sport coat

ametrallador -ora MF gunner; F (arma) machine gun

ametrallar VT to strafe

amianto M asbestos

amigable ADJ friendly

amígdala F tonsil

amigdalitis F tonsillitis

amigo -ga ADJ friendly; — **de** fond of; — **de lo ajeno** thieving; MF friend

aminoácido M amino acid

aminorar VT to lessen

amistad F (relación) friendship; (amigo) friend; **trabar** — to strike up a friendship

amistoso ADJ friendly, amicable

amnesia F amnesia

amniocentesis F amniocentesis

amnistía F amnesty

amo -ma M (de esclavo, sirviente) master; (de animal) owner; F (de esclavo, de sirviente) mistress; (de animal) owner; **ama de leche** wet nurse; **ama de llaves** housekeeper; **ama de casa** homemaker

amodorrado ADJ drowsy

amodorrar VI to make drowsy; —**se** to become drowsy

amolar[2] VT to annoy

amoldar VT to mold

amonestación F admonition, warning

amonestar VT to admonish, to warn

amoníaco M ammonia

amontonamiento M pile

amontonar VT to pile up

amor M love; — **propio** self-esteem; **de mil** —**es** gladly; **hacerle el** — **a** to make love to; **por el** — **de Dios** for God's sake; **por** — **al arte** unremunerated

amoral ADJ amoral

amoratado ADJ (de golpes) black-and-blue; (de frío, por falta de oxígeno) blue

amordazar[9] VT (a una persona) to gag; (a un perro, a los críticos) to muzzle

amorfo ADJ amorphous

amorío M love affair

amoroso ADJ loving, amorous

amortajar VT to shroud

amortiguador M shock absorber

amortiguar[8] VT (un sonido) to muffle, to absorb; (un golpe) to cushion, to absorb; (un dolor) to deaden, to dull

amortizar[9] VT (recuperar a plazos) to amortize; (depreciar) to depreciate

amoscarse[6] VI to get peeved

amostazarse[9] VI to get peeved
amotinarse VI (en un barco) to mutiny; (en una ciudad) to riot
amparar VT (proteger) to protect; (refugiar) to shelter; **—se** to protect oneself
amparo M (protección) protection; (refugio) shelter; **al — de** under the protection of
amperio M ampere
ampicilina F ampicillin
ampliación F (de una foto) enlargement; (de una casa) extension
ampliar[16] VT (una foto) to enlarge; (una calle) to extend; (una explicación) to expand; (un volumen) to amplify
amplificador M amplifier
amplificar[6] VT (un sonido) to amplify; (una imagen) to magnify
amplio ADJ (información, tiempo) ample; (piso) spacious, roomy; (región, resonancia, sonrisa) broad; (vestido) full; **de amplias miras** open-minded
amplitud F (de comprensión) breadth; (de onda) amplitude
ampolla F (de la epidermis) blister; (vasija) vial
ampollar VT to blister
ampuloso ADJ bombastic
amputar VT to amputate
amueblar VT to furnish
amuleto M amulet, charm
anacronismo M anachronism
ánade M duck
anadear VI to waddle
anadeo M waddle
anaerobio ADJ anaerobic
anal ADJ anal
anales M PL annals
analfabetismo M illiteracy
analfabeto -ta ADJ & MF illiterate
analgésico ADJ & M analgesic
análisis M analysis
analítico ADJ analytical, analytic
analizar[9] VT to analyze
analogía F analogy
analógico ADJ (relativo a la analogía) analogical; (no digital) analog
análogo ADJ analogous
ananás M pineapple
anaquel M shelf
anaranjado ADJ & M (color) orange
anarquía F anarchy
anarquista MF anarchist
anatema M anathema
anatomía F anatomy
anatómico ADJ anatomical
anca F haunch, rump
ancho ADJ wide, broad; **a sus anchas** at his

ease; **me viene —** it's too wide for me; M width, breadth; **a lo —** widthwise; **tiene un metro de —** it's one meter wide
anchoa F anchovy
anchura F width, breadth
ancianidad F old age
anciano -na ADJ elderly, aged; MF old person
ancla F anchor
anclar VI/VT to anchor
andada F **volver a las —s** to backslide
andador -ora MF walker
Andalucía F Andalusia
andaluz -za ADJ & MF Andalusian
andamiaje M (para construcción) scaffolding; (fundamento) framework
andamio M scaffold
andanada F broadside
andante ADJ walking
andanzas F PL adventures
andar[20] VI to walk; (coche, motor, reloj) to run; (el tiempo) to pass; (un aparato) to work; **— con cuidado** to be careful; **— en coche** to travel by car, to ride in a car; **— mal** to be in bad shape, to be a mess; **— mal del corazón** to have heart trouble; **—se por las ramas / con vueltas** to beat around the bush; **no —se con rodeos** to make no bones about it; **en eso ando** that's what I'm up to; **¡andando!** move on! **¿dónde anda a estas horas?** where is he at this hour? **¡ándale!** *Méx* (apresúrate) come on! (de acuerdo) OK; M gait
andariego ADJ fond of walking
andas F **llevar en —** *RP* to carry on one's shoulders
andén M platform
Andes M PL Andes
andino ADJ Andean
Andorra F Andorra
andorrano -na ADJ & MF Andorran
andrajo M rag, tatter
andrajoso ADJ ragged, tattered
andrógino ADJ androgynous
anécdota F anecdote
anegar[7] VT to flood
anejo ADJ attached; M accompanying volume
anemia F anemia; **— falciforme** sickle cell anemia
anémico ADJ anemic
anestesia F (acción de anestesiar) anesthesia; (sustancia) anesthetic
anestésico ADJ & M anesthetic
anestesiología F anesthesiology
aneurisma M aneurysm
anexar VT to annex; (con una carta) to enclose

anexión F annexation
anexo ADJ attached; M (de un edificio) annex, extension; (a una ley) rider
anfeta F *fam* speed
anfetamina F amphetamine
anfibio ADJ & M amphibian
anfiteatro M amphitheater
anfitrión -ona M host; F hostess
ángel M angel; — **de la guarda** guardian angel
angelical ADJ angelic
angélico ADJ angelic
angina F —**s** tonsillitis; — **del pecho** angina pectoris
angioplastia F angioplasty
anglosajón -ona ADJ & MF Anglo-Saxon
Angola F Angola
angolano -na, angoleño -ña, angolés -esa ADJ & MF Angolan
angostar VT to narrow, to contract
angosto ADJ narrow
angostura F (cualidad de angosto) narrowness; (desfiladero) narrows
anguila F eel; — **eléctrica** electric eel
angular ADJ angular
ángulo M (figura geométrica, enfoque) angle; (rincón, esquina) corner; — **muerto** blind spot; — **recto** right angle
anguloso ADJ angular
angustia F (desasosiego) anguish, anxiety, distress; (congoja) heartache; (desazón existencial) angst
angustiado ADJ distraught
angustiante ADJ nerve-wracking
angustiar VT to distress; —**se** to feel distressed
angustioso ADJ distressing
anhelante ADJ longing
anhelar VT to long for, to yearn for
anhelo M longing, yearning
anidar VI to nest
anillas F PL gymnastics rings
anillo M ring; — **de boda** wedding ring; **me queda como — al dedo** it fits me like a glove
ánima F soul of the departed
animación F (viveza) animation, liveliness; (en películas) animation
animado ADJ (vivo) animate; (bullicioso) lively
animador -ora MF (de un espectáculo) host; (de un equipo) cheerleader
animal ADJ & M animal
animar VT (dar vida) to animate, to enliven; (incitar) to encourage, to urge on; (dar aliento) to cheer up; —**se** (alegrarse) to cheer up; (atreverse) to gather courage

ánimo M (espíritu) spirit; (aliento) encouragement; (humor) mood; (intención) intention; **no estoy de — para eso** I'm not in the mood for that; INTERJ hang in there!
animosidad F animosity
animoso ADJ spirited
aniñado ADJ childlike
aniquilar VT to annihilate, to wipe out
anís M anise
aniversario M anniversary
ano M anus
anoche ADV last night
anochecer[13] VI to get dark; **anochecimos en París** night found us in Paris; M nightfall, dusk
anomalía F anomaly
anómalo ADJ anomalous
anonadado ADJ dumbfounded
anonadar VT (aniquilar) to annihilate; (desconcertar) to dumbfound; —**se** to become dumbfounded
anónimo ADJ anonymous; M anonymous letter
anorak M anorak
anorexia F anorexia
anoréxico ADJ anorexic
anormal ADJ abnormal; MF freak
anotación F (nota) annotation, notation; (en fútbol) goal
anotar VT (apuntar) to note; (marcar un tanto) to score; —**se** to sign up
anquilosarse VT (las articulaciones) to become stiff; (una institución) to become stagnant
ansia F (deseo) eagerness; (congoja) anguish
ansiar[16] VT to covet
ansiedad F anxiety
ansioso ADJ anxious, eager
antagonismo M antagonism
antagonista MF antagonist
antagonizar[9] VT to antagonize
antaño ADV in the old days
antártico ADJ antarctic
Antártida F Antarctica
ante PREP before; — **este problema** in the face of this problem; — **todo** above all; M suede
anteanoche ADV night before last
anteayer ADV day before yesterday
antebrazo M forearm
antecedente ADJ & M antecedent; —**s** (profesionales) background; (criminales) record
antecesor -ora MF (antepasado) ancestor; (predecesor) predecessor
antedicho ADJ aforesaid

antelación LOC ADV **con** — beforehand
antemano LOC ADV **de** — beforehand
antena F (de radio) antenna, aerial; (de insecto) antenna, feeler
anteojera F blinder
anteojos M PL glasses, spectacles; — **de sol** sunglasses; — **bifocales** bifocals
antepasado -da MF ancestor, forebear
antepecho M sill
anteponer[39] VT (poner delante, poner antes) to place before; (dar preferencia) to give priority to
anterior ADJ (en el tiempo) previous; (en el espacio) anterior, front; — **a** prior to
antes ADV before; — **de** before; — **la muerte** I'd rather die; — **bien** rather
antiaborto ADJ antiabortion, right-to-life
antiácido ADJ & M antacid
antiaéreo ADJ antiaircraft
antibacteriano ADJ antibacterial
antibalas ADJ INV bulletproof
antibalístico ADJ antiballistic
antibiótico ADJ & M antibiotic
antibloqueo ADJ INV antilock
anticipación LOC ADV **con** — in advance
anticipado LOC ADV **por** — in advance
anticipar VT (una fecha) to move up; (dinero) to advance; (el porvenir) to anticipate; —**se a los acontecimientos** to jump the gun
anticipo M advance, deposit
anticoncepción F contraception
anticonceptivo ADJ & M contraceptive
anticongelante M antifreeze
anticuado ADJ antiquated, out-of-date, outdated
anticuerpo M antibody
antidepresivo ADJ & M antidepressant
antídoto M antidote
antieconómico ADJ wasteful
antiestético ADJ unsightly
antígeno M antigen
antigualla F old piece of junk
antiguano -na ADJ & MF Antiguan
Antigua y Barbuda F Antigua and Barbuda
antigüedad F (cualidad de antiguo) antiquity; (objeto) antique; (tiempo en un cargo) seniority
antiguo ADJ (era, historia) ancient; (ropa) old; (mueble) antique; **a la antigua** in the old style; **la antigua capital** the former capital; **más** — with more seniority
antihistamínico M antihistamine
antiinflamatorio ADJ & M anti-inflammatory
Antillas F PL West Indies

antílope M antelope
antimonio M antimony
antimonopolio ADJ antitrust
antioxidante ADJ & M antioxidant
antiparras F PL goggles
antipatía F antipathy
antipático ADJ unfriendly, unkind
antipoliomielítico ADJ antipolio
antisemitismo M anti-Semitism
antiséptico ADJ & M antiseptic
antisocial ADJ antisocial
antítesis F antithesis
antitranspirante M antiperspirant
antitrust ADJ antitrust
antojadizo ADJ whimsical
antojarse VI **se le antojó comer salchicha** he took a notion to eat sausage; **esa tarea se me antoja difícil** that task seems hard to me
antojo M (deseo) whim, craving; (mancha de nacimiento) birthmark
antología F anthology, reader
antónimo M antonym
antorcha F torch
antracita F anthracite
ántrax M anthrax
antro M (bar) dive, joint; — **de perdición** den of iniquity
antropología F anthropology
antropólogo -ga MF anthropologist
anual ADJ annual, yearly
anualidad F annuity
anuario M annual, yearbook
anudar VT to knot; **se le anudó la garganta** he got all choked up
anulación F (de un contrato) cancellation; (de un matrimonio) annulment
anular VT (un matrimonio) to annul; (un contrato, un evento) to cancel; (una sentencia) to overrule, to overturn; (un talón) to void; M ring finger
anunciador -ora MF announcer
anunciante MF advertiser
anunciar VT (información) to announce; (un producto) to advertise
anuncio M (de información) announcement; (de un producto) advertisement; — **clasificado** classified advertisement; — **publicitario** advertisement; **poner un** — to place an ad
anzuelo M fishhook; **morder / picar el** — to take the bait
añadidura F addition; **por** — in addition
añadir VT to add
añejo ADJ aged, vintage
añicos M **hacerse** — to break into a thousand pieces

añil M indigo, bluing

año M year; (de la escuela) grade; (de vino) vintage; — **bisiesto** leap year; — **luz** light-year; **de cuarenta —s** aged forty; **el — pasado** last year; **en los —s veinte** in the 1920s; **entrado en —s** getting on in years; **¿cuántos —s tienes?** how old are you?

añojo -ja MF yearling

añoranza F longing; (del hogar) homesickness

añorar VT to long for, to be homesick for

añoso ADJ old

añublo M blight

aorta F aorta

apabullar VT (impresionar) to bowl over; (derrotar) to crush

apacentar[1] VI to graze, to pasture

apacible ADJ good-natured

apaciguar[8] VT (pacificar) to pacify; (aplacar) to mollify, to appease; **—se** to calm down

apadrinar VT to sponsor; (en un bautismo) to act as godfather to; (en una boda) to act as best man for; (en un duelo) to second

apagado ADJ (no llamativo) flat; (no intenso) dull

apagar[7] VT (un fuego) to put out, to extinguish; (una luz) to turn off, to turn out; (motor) to turn off, to kill; (una vida) to kill, to snuff out; (la sed) to quench; **—se** (luz) to go out; (un color) to fade; (una voz) to trail off; (un volcán) to become extinct

apagón M blackout, outage

apalabrarse VI — **con** to make a verbal agreement with

apalear VT to thrash

aparador M sideboard, buffet, cupboard

aparato M (de gimnasia) apparatus; (de cocina) appliance; (teléfono) telephone; (máquina, dirigencia política) machine; (boato) pomp; — **circulatorio** circulatory system; — **de televisión** television set; — **ortodóntico** braces; — **ortopédico** leg brace

aparatoso ADJ pompous

aparcamiento M (lugar para aparcar) parking lot; (acción de aparcar) parking

aparcar[6] VI/VT to park; MF SG **aparcacoches** valet

aparcero -ra MF sharecropper

aparear VT (animales) to mate; (calcetines) to match, to pair; **—se** (animales) to mate; (en un baile) to pair off

aparecer[13] VI (ponerse a la vista, publicarse) to appear; (hacer acto de presencia) to show up; **se me apareció un ángel** an angel appeared to me

aparejar VT (un cuarto, un ejército) to prepare; (problemas) to entail; (una embarcación) to rig

aparejo M (de caballo) harness; (de buque) rigging; (para pescar) tackle; **—s** equipment

aparentar VT to feign; VI to show off; **aparenta la edad que tiene** she looks her age

aparente ADJ apparent; **un precio —** an acceptable price

aparición F (fantasma) apparition; (acción de aparecer) appearance

apariencia F (aspecto) appearance; (fingimiento) pretense, semblance; **las —s engañan** appearances are deceiving; **guardar las —s** to keep up appearances

apartado M section; — **postal** post office box; ADJ (recóndito) secluded; (distante) distant; **muy —** far apart

apartamento M apartment

apartamiento M separation

apartar VT **aparta las monedas de veinticinco centavos** set aside/sort out the quarters; **apartó la silla de la pared** he moved the chair away from the wall; **lo aparté para hablarle** I took him aside to talk to him; **apartó la cacerola del fuego** she took the pan off the fire; **lo apartó de un empujón** she pushed him away; **apartaron al ministro de su cargo** they removed the minister from his post; **apartó la vista** he looked away; VI **se apartaron del buen camino** they strayed from the straight and narrow; **los resultados se apartan de lo esperado** the results depart/deviate from the norm; **se apartó para que no lo atropellara el coche** he got out of the way so the car wouldn't hit him

aparte ADJ separate; ADV **bromas —** kidding aside; **dejar —** to exclude; **punto y —** new paragraph; M aside; PREP — **de** (además de) besides; (salvo) except for

apasionado ADJ (amor, hombre) passionate; (defensa, comentario) impassioned

apasionar VT **eso me apasiona** I love that; **—se por** to be passionate about

apatía F apathy

apático ADJ apathetic

apear VT to get down; **—se** to dismount

apechugar[7] VI — **con** to put up with

apedrear VT to stone

apegado ADJ attached

apegarse[7] VI to become attached
apego M attachment
apelación F appeal
apelar VI/VT to appeal
apellidarse VI to have the surname of
apellido M surname, last name
apelotonarse VI (una almohada) to ball up; (gente) to bunch together
apenado ADJ grieved
apenar VT to grieve, to pain; —**se** to be grieved
apenas ADV hardly, scarcely, barely; — **llegó, se desmayó** no sooner had he arrived than he fainted
apéndice M (órgano, parte de un libro) appendix; (añadido) appendage
apendicectomía F appendectomy
apendicitis F appendicitis
apercibir VT to warn; —**se de** to notice
aperitivo M appetizer
apero M farm implement
apertura F opening
apesadumbrado ADJ doleful
apestar VT (hacer heder) to stink up; (causar la peste) to plague; VI to stink, to reek
apestoso ADJ smelly
apetecer[13] VI **no me apetece ir contigo** I don't feel like going with you
apetecible ADJ appetizing
apetito M appetite
apetitoso ADJ appetizing
apiadarse VI — **de** to pity, to take pity on
ápice M apex; (de la lengua) tip; **no apartarse ni un** — not to diverge a jot
apio M celery
apisonadora F steamroller
apisonar VT to pack down
aplacamiento M appeasement
aplacar[6] VT (a una persona) to appease, to mollify; (miedo) to allay; (sed, pasión) to quench; —**se** to relent
aplanadora F steamroller
aplanamiento M flattening, leveling
aplanar VT (un terreno) to level, to flatten; (con una aplanadora) to roll
aplastado ADJ flattened
aplastamiento M crushing
aplastante ADJ (derrota) crushing; (victoria) sweeping
aplastar VT (achatar) to squash, to crush; (derrotar) to plaster, to stomp; (una revolución) to squelch, to smash, to crush; —**se** to crumple
aplaudir VI/VT to applaud
aplauso, aplausos M (PL) applause
aplazamiento M postponement; (de un proceso legal) continuance

aplazar[9] VT to postpone, to put off
aplicable ADJ applicable
aplicación F (acción de aplicarse) application; (de un castigo) administration
aplicado ADJ industrious
aplicar[6] VT to apply; —**se** to work hard, to apply oneself
aplomado ADJ (equilibrado) poised; (vertical) plumb
aplomar VT to plumb
aplomo M poise
apnea M apnea
apocado ADJ timid
apocalipsis MF apocalypse
apocamiento M timidity
apocarse[6] VT to become intimidated
apodar VT to nickname
apoderado -da MF proxy, agent
apoderarse VI — **de** to take possession of, to seize
apodo M nickname
apogeo M apogee; **en su** — (una fiesta) in full swing; (un estilo) in its heyday, at its peak
apolillado ADJ (comido por las polillas) moth-eaten; (anticuado) antiquated
apología F apology
aporrear VT to club, to cudgel
aportación F contribution
aportar VT (posibilidades, evidencia) to provide; (dinero) to contribute
aporte M contribution
aposento M chamber
apostador -ora MF bettor
apostar[2] VI/VT to bet, to wager; (a un centinela) to station, to post; — **por** (caballo) to bet on; (cambio) to commit to
apóstol M apostle
apóstrofe MF apostrophe, invocation
apóstrofo M apostrophe
apostura F bearing
apoyar VT (sostener) to rest; (respaldar) to support, to back; (votar por) to second; (respaldar un argumento) to buttress; —**se en** (recostarse contra) to lean on, to prop against; (basarse en) to be based on; M SG **apoyabrazos** armrest
apoyo M support
apreciable ADJ (digno de aprecio) esteemed; (perceptible) noticeable; (registrable) appreciable
apreciación F appreciation
apreciado ADJ dear
apreciar VT (reconocer la valía) to appreciate; (percibir) to notice; (registrar) to measure; (considerar) to take into consideration; (sentir afecto) to cherish;

—se (un fenómeno) to be noticeable; (moneda) to appreciate

aprecio M appreciation

aprehender VT (a un delincuente) to apprehend; (contrabando) to seize; (una idea) to grasp

aprehensión F (arresto) apprehension; (incautación) seizure

apremiante ADJ pressing

apremiar VT to pressure

apremio M pressure

aprender VI/VT to learn; **— de memoria** to memorize, to learn by heart

aprendiz -za MF (de un oficio) apprentice, trainee; (de una lengua, canto) learner

aprendizaje M (de un oficio) apprenticeship; (acto de aprender) learning

aprensión F apprehension, misgivings

aprensivo ADJ apprehensive

apresar VT (aprisionar) to imprison; (incautar) to seize

aprestar VT to prepare; **—se a** to get ready to

apresurado ADJ hasty, hurried

apresurar VT to hurry, to hasten

apretado ADJ (zapato) tight; (beso) hard; (racimo) compact; (síntesis) succinct; (jornada) busy; (situación) difficult, dangerous

apretar[1] VT (un botón) to press; (un gatillo) to squeeze; (un tornillo) to tighten; (los dientes, puños) to clench; (a un bebé) to clasp; **me apretó para que le diera dinero** he pressured me to give him money; **ese profesor nos aprieta mucho** that teacher demands a lot of us; VI (zapatos) to be tight, to pinch; (sol) to be intense; (esforzarse) to try hard, to bear down; **—se** to crowd together

apretón M squeeze; **— de manos** handshake

aprieto M jam, fix, predicament; **en —s** in need, hard-pressed, in dire straits; **estar en un —** to be in a tight spot, to be in trouble, to be in a pickle; **poner en —s** to embarrass

aprisa ADV quickly

aprisco M (para el ganado) fold

aprisionar VT to trap

aprobación F (aceptación) approval; (de una ley) passage, adoption; (nota) passing grade

aprobar[2] VT (una medida, una opinión) to approve of; (una ley) to pass, to approve; (un examen) to pass; VI to pass

aprontar VT to ready

apropiación F appropriation; **— indebida** embezzlement

apropiado ADJ appropriate, suitable

apropiarse VT to appropriate

aprovechable ADJ usable

aprovechado ADJ opportunistic

aprovechamiento M use

aprovechar VT (una ocasión) to take advantage of; (el espacio) to utilize; (la enseñanza) to profit from; VI to be useful; **—se de** to take advantage of; **¡que aproveche!** enjoy your meal!

aproximación F approach

aproximado ADJ approximate

aproximar VT to bring near; **—se** to approach; **— a** to approximate

aptitud F aptitude; **—es musicales** musical aptitude

apto ADJ apt, suitable; **— para menores** for general audiences

apuesta F bet, wager

apuesto ADJ good-looking

apuntalar VT to prop up, to shore up

apuntar VT (señalar) to point out; (dirigir a un blanco) to aim; (matricular) to enroll; (escribir) to write down, to note; (ayudar a un actor) to prompt; VI (una flecha) to point; (canas) to sprout; **—se** to score; **a un blanco** to aim at a target; **me apunto para ir con vosotros** I'm game to go with you

apunte M notation; **—s** notes; **tomar —s** to take notes; **llevar el — a alguien** to pay attention to someone

apuñalar VT to stab

apurado ADJ (situación) difficult; (persona) in dire straits; *Am* (apresurado) in a hurry

apurar VT (consumir) to drink up; (apremiar) to put under pressure

apuro M predicament, fix; *Am* (prisa) hurry; **estar en —s** to be in distress

aquejado ADJ stricken

aquejar VT to afflict, to trouble

aquel ADJ that; **aquella chica se llama María** that girl is named María; **aquellas ciudades son antiguas** those cities are old; PRON that one; **— es el mayor** that one is the oldest; **aquellos son mis hijos** those are my children; **de mis dos hijos, Juan y Pedro, este es gordo y — es flaco** of my two sons, Juan and Pedro, the latter is fat and the former is thin; **en / por — entonces** back then

aquí ADV here; **está por —** it is around here; **ven por —** come this way; **hasta —** this far; **de — a cuatro horas** four hours from now; **de — en adelante** from now on; **de — para allá** to and fro, back and forth; **— y ahora** here and now

aquietar VT to quiet; **—se** (los nervios) to calm down; (una tormenta) to subside

ara LOC ADV **en —s de** for the sake of

árabe MF (persona) Arab; (caballo) Arabian; (lengua) Arabic; ADJ Arabian; (costumbre, arte) Arab

Arabia Saudí, Arabia Saudita F Saudi Arabia

arácnido M arachnid

arado M plow

Aragón M Aragon

aragonés -esa ADJ Aragonese; MF (persona) Aragonese; M (dialecto) Aragonese

arancel M (impuesto) tariff; (lista de honorarios) list of fees

arancelario ADJ **acuerdo —** tariff agreement

arándano M cranberry

arandela F washer

araña F (arácnido) spider; (candelabro) chandelier

arañar VT (rayar) to scratch; (herir con garras) to claw, to scratch; (raspar) to scrape, to score

arañazo M scratch

arañero M warbler

arar VI/VT to plow, to till

arbitraje M arbitration

arbitrar VT (un desacuerdo) to arbitrate; (un partido) to referee, to officiate; (un partido de béisbol) to umpire

arbitrario ADJ arbitrary

arbitrio M (libre albedrío) free will; (capricho) whim; (decisión) discretion; (deseos) wishes

árbitro -tra MF (del buen gusto) arbiter; (de conflictos) arbitrator; (de encuentros deportivos) referee

árbol M tree; (mástil) mast; **— de Navidad** Christmas tree; **— de levas** camshaft; **— genealógico** family tree

arbolado ADJ woody, wooded

arboleda F grove, clump

arbóreo ADJ arboreal

arbusto M shrub, bush

arca F ark; **— de Noé** Noah's ark; **las —s municipales** municipal coffers

arcada F arcade, archway; **tener / dar —s** to gag

arcaico ADJ archaic

arcaísmo M archaism

arcano ADJ arcane

arce M maple (tree)

arcén M shoulder of a road

archienemigo -ga MF archenemy

archipiélago M archipelago

archisabido ADJ very well-known

archivador M filing cabinet

archivar VT (guardar en un archivo) to file; (arrinconar) to shelve

archivo M (lugar) archive; (fichero de ordenador) file; (acción de archivar) filing

arcilla F clay

arco M (curva, eléctrico) arc; (estructura arquitectónica) arch; (arma, varilla de violín) bow; **— iris** rainbow

arder VT to burn; **la cosa está que arde** things are really getting hot; **el trigo se ardió** the wheat spoiled

ardid M scheme, artifice

ardiente ADJ (de deseo) ardent; (de calor, fuego, deseo) burning

ardilla F squirrel; **— de tierra** gopher; **— listada** chipmunk

ardite M **no valer un —** not to be worth a penny

ardor M (de pasión) ardor; (de fuego) heat; **— de estómago** heartburn

arduo ADJ arduous, grueling

área F area

arena F (tierra) sand; (plaza) arena; **— movediza** quicksand

arenero M sandbox

arenga F harangue

arengar[7] VT to harangue

arenisca F sandstone

arenisco ADJ sandy

arenoso ADJ sandy

arenque M herring

arete M earring

argamasa F mortar

Argelia F Algeria

argelino -na ADJ & MF Algerian

Argentina F Argentina

argentino -na ADJ Argentine, Argentinian; (propio de la plata) silvery; MF Argentine, Argentinian

argolla F iron ring

argón M argon

argot M slang

argucias F PL trickery

argüir[31] VT to argue

argumentar VT to argue

argumento M (razonamiento) argument; (conjunto de sucesos) plot

aridez F dryness

árido ADJ (seco) arid, dry, barren; (aburrido) dry; **—s** dry goods

ariete M battering ram

arisco ADJ surly

arista F (borde) edge; (de trigo) beard; **limar —s** to overcome difficulties

aristocracia F aristocracy

aristócrata MF INV aristocrat

aristocrático ADJ aristocratic

aritmética F arithmetic
aritmético ADJ arithmetical
arma F (instrumento bélico) arm, weapon; (división del ejército) branch; — **blanca** sharp weapon; — **de fuego** firearm; **a las** — to arms; **de** —**s tomar** resolute; **tomar las** —**s** to take up arms
armada F armada, fleet
armado ADJ armed; **a mano armada** at gunpoint; M assembly, putting together
armador -ora MF shipowner
armadura F (piezas de hierro) armor; (de un edificio) framework; (de gafas) frame; (de música) key signature
armamento M armament
armar VT (proveer de armas) to arm; (abastecer una embarcación) to equip; (reforzar) to reinforce; (ensamblar) to assemble, to put together; (levantar una tienda de campaña) to pitch; — **jaleo** to whoop it up; — **relajo** to make a mess; —**se de** to arm oneself with; — **una pendencia** to pick a fight, to start a quarrel
armario M (de ropa) wardrobe, closet; (de cocina) cabinet, armoire
armatoste M unwieldy object
armazón MF framework, skeleton
Armenia F Armenia
armenio -nia ADJ & MF Armenian
armería F (depósito de armas) armory; (tienda de armas) gun shop
armiño M ermine
armisticio M armistice
armonía F harmony
armónico ADJ & M harmonic
armonioso ADJ harmonious
armonizar[9] VI/VT to harmonize, to blend
ARN (ácido ribonucleico) M RNA
arnés M harness
aro M (de baloncesto) hoop; (de rueda) rim
aroma M (olor agradable) aroma; (del vino) bouquet
aromático ADJ aromatic
arpa F harp
arpía F shrew
arpillera F burlap
arpón M harpoon
arponear VT to harpoon
arqueado ADJ arched
arquear VT to arch
arqueología F archaeology
arquetipo M archetype
arquitecto -ta MF architect
arquitectónico ADJ architectural
arquitectura F architecture
arrabal M outlying slum

arraigar[7] VT to take root
arrancar[6] VT (una planta) to uproot; (el pelo) to tear out; (un diente) to pull; (un vicio) to eradicate; (una flor) to pick; (una confesión) to extract; — **de** to wrest from; VI/VT (un vehículo) to start; **arrancó para el valle** he took off for the valley; **arrancó a sudar** he began to sweat; **sus problemas arrancan de su niñez** his problems are rooted in his childhood; —**se los cabellos** to tear one's hair (out)
arranque M (proceso de arrancar un coche) starting; (dispositivo para arrancar un coche) starter; (decisión, empuje) gumption; — **de ira** fit of rage
arrasar VT (destruir) to level, to raze; (derrotar) to crush; — **con** to obliterate; VI to win
arrastrado ADJ wretched
arrastrar VT (mover por el suelo) to drag; (llevarse consigo) to sweep away; (atraer) to draw; (soportar) to bear; (pronunciar lentamente) to draw out; — **los pies** (moverse con dificultades) to shuffle; (ser renuente) to stall; VI to hang down to the floor; —**se** (una serpiente) to slither; (una lagartija, un insecto) to crawl; (una persona) to grovel; M SG **arrastrapiés** shuffle
arrayán M myrtle
arrear VT to drive, to herd
arrebatar VT (quitar) to snatch away, to wrest away; (quemar) to burn on the outside; —**se** to have a fit
arrebatiña F mad scramble
arrebato M fit, outburst
arreciar VI to increase in intensity
arrecife M reef
arreglar VT (poner en orden, concertar, adaptar música) to arrange; (ordenar) to tidy up; (reparar) to fix, to repair; (resolver) to settle; — **cuentas** to settle accounts; **ya te arreglo** I'll fix you; —**se** (embellecerse) to fix oneself up; (llevarse bien con) to get along with; (entablar relaciones amorosas) to start dating; (reconciliarse) to make up; (conformarse) to make do; (despejarse) to clear up; —**se en** to agree on; **arreglárselas** to cope, to manage
arreglo M arrangement; **con** — **a** in accordance with; **no tiene** — it can't be helped; **llegar a un** — to settle; —**s** alterations
arrellanarse VI to lounge, to loll
arremangado ADJ turned up
arremangar[7] VT to roll up; —**se** to roll up

one's sleeves, to knuckle down

arremeter VI to attack; **— contra** to lunge at

arremetida F thrust, lunge

arremolinarse VT (viento) to whirl around; (agua) to eddy

arrendajo M bluejay

arrendamiento M rental

arrendar VI/VT to rent, to lease

arrendatario -ria MF tenant

arreo M adornment; **—s** tack, harness

arrepentido ADJ repentant, rueful

arrepentimiento M (contrición) repentance; (disgusto) regret

arrepentirse[3] VI (de los pecados) to repent; (de los errores) to regret

arrestar VT to arrest

arresto M arrest

arriar[16] VT (la bandera) to lower; (un cabo) to slacken

arriate M flower bed

arriba ADV above; **¡—!** get up! **¡— las manos!** stick 'em up! **¡— Juan!** long live Juan! **de — abajo** from top to bottom; **lleno hasta —** full to the brim; **te vas para —** you are doing well; **viven —** they live upstairs

arribar VI LIT to arrive; (buque) to put into port

arribista MF social climber

arribo M LIT arrival

arriendo M leasing, rental

arriero -ra MF animal driver

arriesgado ADJ (peligroso) risky; (valiente) daring

arriesgar[7] VT to risk; **—se** to take a chance

arrimar VT (acercar) to bring near; (golpear) to strike; **—se a** (apoyarse) to lean on; (acercarse) to get near

arrinconar VT (acorralar) to corner; (poner en un rincón) to put in a corner; (abandonar) to abandon

arritmia F arrhythmia

arrobamiento M rapture

arrobarse VI to be enraptured

arrodillarse VI to kneel

arrogancia F arrogance

arrogante ADJ arrogant

arrogarse[7] VT to assume

arrojadizo ADJ projectile

arrojar VT (lanzar) to throw, to hurl; (expulsar) to throw out; (botar) to throw away; (vomitar) to throw up, to vomit; (proyectar una luz) to shed, to throw; **— un saldo de** to show a balance of; **—se** to hurl oneself

arrojo M boldness, daring

arrollador ADJ overwhelming

arrollar VT (poner en forma de rollo) to roll up; (arrastrar) to run over; (derrotar) to defeat

arropar VT to wrap up; (en la cama) to tuck in; **—se** to pull up the covers

arroyo M stream, creek

arroz M rice; **— integral** brown rice

arrozal M rice field

arruga F wrinkle

arrugar[7] VT to wrinkle; **— el ceño** to knit one's brow; **—se** (pasar a tener arrugas) to get wrinkles; (asustarse) to be afraid

arruinar VT (estropear) to ruin; (destruir) to destroy, to ravage; (aguar) to spoil; (dejar en la quiebra) to bankrupt, to ruin; **—se** to go to ruin

arrullar VI (una paloma) to coo; VT (a un enamorado) to whisper sweet nothings to; (a un niño) to rock to sleep, to lull to sleep

arrullo M (de la tórtola) cooing; (del agua) babbling

arrumbar VT (arrinconar) to put aside; (marginalizar) to marginalize

arsenal M (depósito) arsenal; (astillero) navy yard

arsénico M arsenic

arte M SG art; F PL arts; M (destreza) skill, ability; (actividad técnica) craft; **bellas —s** fine arts; **el — por el —** art for art's sake; **malas —s** wiles; **no tener ni — ni parte en algo** to have nothing to do with something; **por — de** by means of

artefacto M (aparato útil) contrivance, device; (bomba) bomb

arteria F artery

arteriosclerosis F arteriosclerosis

artero ADJ artful, wily

artesanía F (trabajo, obra) craft; (habilidad) craftsmanship

artesano -na MF artisan, craftsman

ártico ADJ arctic

articulación F (acción de articular) articulation; (juntura) joint

articular VT (pronunciar) to articulate, to enunciate; (unir) to join

artículo M article; (entrada en un diccionario) article, entry; **— de fondo** editorial; **— definido** definite article; **hacer el —** to give a sales pitch

artífice MF (autor) architect; M (artesano) craftsman; F craftswoman

artificial ADJ artificial

artificio M artifice

artificioso ADJ affected, contrived

artillería F artillery

artillero -ra MF gunner
artimaña F trick, wile
artista MF artist
artístico ADJ artistic
artritis F arthritis
artroscópico ADJ arthroscopic
Aruba F Aruba
arveja F pea
arzobispo M archbishop
arzón M saddletree
as M ace (también atleta)
asa F handle
asado ADJ roasted; M (carne asada) roast; (acción de asar) roasting
asador -ora M spit; MF barbecue cook
asalariado -da MF wage-earner
asaltante MF mugger
asaltar VT (a una persona) to assault, to assail; (un banco) to hold up; (con preguntas) to assail; **—le a uno una idea** to be struck by an idea
asalto M (ataque) assault; (de un banco) holdup, stickup; **tomar por —** to storm
asamblea F assembly, gathering
asar VT to roast; **— a la parrilla** to grill; **— con adobo** to barbecue
asbesto M asbestos
ascendencia F ancestry
ascendente ADJ (que incrementa) ascending, rising; (hacia arriba) upward
ascender[1] VT (a un empleado) to promote; (una montaña) to climb; VI to ascend; **— a** to amount to
ascendiente MF ancestor
ascenso M (acción de ascender) ascent; (en el trabajo) promotion
ascensor M elevator
asceta MF INV ascetic
ascético ADJ ascetic
asco M disgust, revulsion; **hacer —s a** to reject; **me da —** it makes me sick, it disgusts me; **ese hombre está hecho un —** that man is a mess
ascórbico ADJ ascorbic
ascua F ember; **estar en —s** to be on pins and needles; **tener en —s** to string along
aseado ADJ well-groomed
asear VT to clean up
asediar VT to besiege
asedio M siege
asegurar VT (una victoria) to assure; (una frontera, una cerradura) to secure; (con un contrato de seguro) to insure; **—se (de)** to make sure (of); **te lo aseguro** I assure you
asemejarse VI **— a** to resemble
asentaderas F PL buttocks

asentar VT (datos) to enter; (una población) to establish; **—se** (posarse) to settle; (madurar) to settle down
asentimiento M assent, acquiescence
asentir[3] VI to assent, to acquiesce; **— con la cabeza** to nod
aseo M (acción de asearse) cleaning; (cualidad de aseado) cleanliness; (cuarto de baño) bathroom; (servicio) toilet, restroom
asequible ADJ (que se puede obtener) available; (que se puede pagar) affordable
aserción F assertion
aserradero M sawmill, lumber mill
aserrado ADJ serrated; M sawing
aserrar[1] VT to saw
aserrín M sawdust
aserto M assertion
asesinar VT to murder; (a una figura pública) to assassinate
asesinato M murder, killing; (de una figura pública) assassination
asesino -na ADJ murderous; MF killer, murderer; (de una figura pública) assassin
asesor -ora MF consultant, advisor
asesoramiento M consulting, advising
asesorar VT to advise
asestar VT **— un golpe** to inflict / deal a blow
aseveración F assertion
aseverar VT to assert
asexual ADJ asexual
asfalto M asphalt
asfixia F suffocation, asphyxiation
asfixiar VT to suffocate, to smother
así ADV so, thus, like this; **— —** so-so; **— como** in the same way that; **— de grande** that big; **— que** so that; **¿— que no vienes?** so you're not coming?
Asia F Asia
asiático -ca ADJ & MF Asian
asidero M hold; **eso no tiene — en la realidad** that has no basis in reality
asiduo ADJ (lector) assiduous; (cliente) steady
asiento M (lugar donde sentarse, parte de una silla, de válvula) seat; (de nóminas) entry, record; **tomar —** to take a seat
asignación F (acción de asignar) assignment; (acción de dar fondos) appropriation; (pago) allowance
asignar VT (una tarea) to assign; (fondos) to allot, to allocate
asignatura F subject
asilado -da MF inmate
asilar VT (a un político) to give asylum to; (un animal) to shelter
asilo M (para los perseguidos) asylum; (para huérfanos, ancianos) home

asimétrico ADJ asymmetric

asimilar VT (vitaminas, un grupo étnico) to assimilate; (información) to absorb

asimismo ADV likewise

asir[21] VT to grasp, to grip; **—se a** to hold onto

asistencia F (presencia, personas presentes) attendance; (ayuda) assistance, aid; (servicio para averías) roadside assistance; **— médica** health care; **— social** (ayuda) welfare; (profesión) social work

asistente -ta ADJ assistant; MF assistant, helper; **— social** social worker

asistir VT **— a** (estar presente) to attend; (ayudar) to help, to assist

asma F asthma

asmático ADJ asthmatic

asno M ass, donkey

asociación F association

asociado -da MF associate

asociar VT to associate; **—se** to join

asolamiento M desolation

asolar VT to desolate, to devastate

asomar VI to show; VT to poke out, to stick out; **—se a** to look out

asombrar VT to astonish, to amaze, to astound; **—se** to be astonished

asombro M astonishment, amazement

asombroso ADJ astonishing, amazing

asomo LOC ADV **ni por —** by no means

asonancia F assonance

aspa F (de hélice) blade; (de ventilador) vane

aspecto M (faceta) aspect, feature; (apariencia) looks

aspereza F roughness, harshness; **limar —s** to smooth over disagreements

áspero ADJ (terreno, mano) rough; (lucha) bitter; (tiempo, voz) harsh

aspiración F (ambición) aspiration, ambition; (respiración) breathing in; (succión) suction

aspiradora F vacuum cleaner

aspirante MF applicant, candidate

aspirar VT to breathe in, to inhale; **— a** to aspire to

aspirina F aspirin

asqueado ADJ disgusted

asquear VT to disgust

asquerosidad F nastiness; **¡estás hecho una —!** you're gross!

asqueroso ADJ nasty, disgusting, gross

asta F (de toro) horn; (de ciervo) antler; (de bandera) flagpole; (de lanza) shaft; **a media —** at half mast

asterisco M asterisk, star

asteroide M asteroid

astigmatismo M astigmatism

astilla F (de madera) chip, splinter; (de vidrio) sliver; **—s** kindling

astillar VT to chip, to splinter

astillero M shipyard

astringente ADJ & M astringent

astro M (del cielo) celestial body; (de cine) movie star

astrofísica F astrophysics

astrología F astrology

astronauta MF astronaut

astronáutica F astronautics

astronomía F astronomy

astrónomo -ma MF astronomer

astucia F (listeza) cunning, guile; (treta) trick

asturiano -na ADJ & MF Asturian

Asturias F SG Asturias

astuto ADJ shrewd, wily, cunning

asueto M time off

asumir VT (una responsabilidad) to assume, to shoulder; (una mala noticia) to accept; **— un cargo** to take office

asunto M (cuestión) matter; (de una obra artística) theme

asustadizo ADJ easily frightened, jumpy

asustado ADJ frightened

asustar VT to frighten, to scare; **—se** to become frightened

atacante ADJ attacking; MF assailant

atacar[6] VT to attack, to assault; **—se de risa** to have a laughing fit

atado M bundle

atadura F **sin —s** with no strings attached

atajador M tackle

atajar VT (interrumpir) to cut off; VI (tomar un atajo) to take a shortcut

atajo M shortcut

atalaya F watchtower

atañer[18, 50] VI to concern, to pertain to

ataque M (violento, de asma) attack; (de rabia, de tos) fit; (de epilepsia) seizure; **— cardíaco** heart attack; **— de nervios** nervous breakdown; **— relámpago** blitz

atar VT (sujetar) to tie, to bind; **— cabos** to make sense of something; **—se los zapatos** to tie one's shoes

atardecer[13] VI to get dark; M late afternoon, dusk, evening; **al —** at dusk

atareado ADJ busy

atarearse VI to busy oneself

atascadero M (lodazal) quagmire; (de tránsito) bottleneck

atascado ADJ stuck

atascar[6] VT (un tubo) to stop up; (una máquina) to jam; (el tráfico) to obstruct; **—se** (un vehículo) to get stuck; (una máquina) to get jammed

ataúd M coffin, casket

ataviar[16] VT to attire, to array; **—se** to dress up
atavío M attire, garb
ateísmo M atheism
atemorizar[9] VT to frighten
atención F attention; (médica) care; (acto de cortesía) courtesy; **a la — de** to the attention of; **llamar la —** (hacer notar) to call attention; (ser llamativo) to attract attention; (interesar) to interest; INTERJ watch out!
atender[1] VI **— a** to pay attention to; (el trabajo) to attend to, to take care of; VT (a un enfermo) to take care of, to look after; (una súplica) to heed; (a un cliente) to serve
atenerse[44] VI **— a los hechos** to bear the facts in mind; **— a la ley** to abide by the law
atentado M assassination; assassination attempt; **un — contra** an affront to
atentamente ADV (con atención) attentively; (despedida en cartas) yours truly / sincerely
atentar[1] VI **— contra la vida de alguien** to make an attempt on someone's life
atento ADJ (que presta atención) attentive; (amable) thoughtful
atenuar[17] VT (la violencia) to attenuate; (una luz) to dim; **—se** to abate
ateo -a MF atheist
aterciopelado ADJ velvety
aterido ADJ stiff with cold
aterirse[50] VI to become stiff with cold
aterrador ADJ terrifying
aterrar VT to terrify
aterrizaje M landing; **— forzoso** crash landing
aterrizar[9] VI/VT to land
aterrorizar[9] VT to terrify
atesorar VT (memorias) to treasure; (dinero) to hoard
atestado ADJ crowded, crammed
atestar VT (certificar) to attest to; (llenar) to jam, to pack
atestiguar[8] VT to bear witness, to testify
atiborrar VT to stuff; **—se** to stuff one's face
atiesar VT to stiffen
atildado ADJ spruced up
atinar VT (dar en el blanco) to hit the mark; (adivinar) to guess right; **no — a decir palabra** not to manage to get a word out
atisbar VT (mirar con disimulo) to peek at, to peep at; (vislumbrar) to catch a glimpse of; VI to peek
atisbo M glimpse, hint
atizar[9] VT (un fuego) to poke, to stake; (las pasiones) to stir up, to stoke

atlántico ADJ Atlantic; M **Océano Atlántico** Atlantic Ocean
atlas M atlas
atleta MF athlete
atlético ADJ athletic
atletismo M track and field
atmósfera F atmosphere
atmosférico ADJ atmospheric
atolladero M quagmire
atolondrado ADJ scatterbrained; (muchacha) ditsy
atómico ADJ atomic
atomizar[9] VT to atomize
átomo M atom
atónito ADJ dumbfounded
atontado ADJ stupefied
atontar VT to stupefy
atorar VT to jam; **—se** to choke
atormentar VT to torment; **—se por** to agonize over
atornillar VT to bolt
atracadero M dock
atracar[6] VT (amarrar) to dock; (robar) to hold up, to mug; **—se** to gorge oneself
atracción F attraction
atraco M holdup, stickup
atracón M **darse un —** to gorge
atractivo ADJ (capacidad de atraer) attractiveness, appeal; M (cosa que atrae) attraction; **— sexual** sex appeal
atraer[45] VT to attract
atragantarse VI to choke
atrancar[6] VT to bolt, to bar
atrapada F catch
atrapar VT (en una trampa) to trap, to ensnare, to catch; (una pelota, el interés) to catch
atrás ADV **— de la casa** behind the house; **cuatro años —** four years back; **hacia —** backward; **para —** back / backwards; **quedarse —** to fall behind
atrasado ADJ (pasado) late; (en el pago) in arrears, behind; (país) backward; (un libro de biblioteca) overdue; **tengo sueño —** I'm behind in my sleep; **el reloj anda —** the clock is slow; **feliz cumpleaños —** happy belated birthday
atrasar VT (un plazo) to delay; (una mesa) to push back; (un reloj) to turn back; VI (un reloj) to run slow; **—se** to fall behind, to lag
atraso M (condición de atrasado) backwardness; (pago) back payment; (de trabajo) backlog; **con dos meses de —** two months in arrears
atravesar[1] VT (cruzar) to cross; (ir de lado a lado) to span; (penetrar) to impale, to run

through; — **un momento difícil** to go through a difficult moment; **se me atravesó un caballo** a horse crossed in front of me; **—se en la cama** to lie crossways in bed

atreverse VI to dare

atrevido ADJ (audaz) bold, daring; (insolente) insolent

atrevimiento M (cualidad de atrevido) boldness, daring, audacity; (acción atrevida) daring act

atribución F attribution; **atribuciones** powers

atribuir[31] VT to attribute, to ascribe

atribular VT to distress; **—se** to be distressed

atributo M attribute

atril M stand

atrincherar VT to entrench

atrio M atrium

atrocidad F atrocity

atrofia F atrophy

atrofiar VT to atrophy, to stunt

atronador ADJ thunderous, deafening

atronar[2] VI to make a racket

atropellar VT (a un peatón) to run over, to run down; (los derechos de alguien) to trample upon

atropello M (de un peatón) running over; (ultraje) outrage; (de derechos) trampling

atroz ADJ (modales, crimen) atrocious; (dolor) excruciating; (ofensa) grievous

atuendo M getup

atún M tuna

aturdido ADJ bewildered; **estar —** to be in a daze

aturdimiento M bewilderment

aturdir VT to bewilder, to daze

atusar VT to smooth, to fix

audacia F audacity, boldness

audaz ADJ audacious, bold

audible ADJ audible

audición F audition

audiencia F (tribunal) court; (reunión, conjunto de oyentes) audience; (hecho de oír un pleito) hearing

audífono M (para los sordos) earphone; (para música) headphones

audio M audio; **—libro** book on tape; **—visual** audiovisual

audiología F audiology

auditar VI/VT to audit

auditivo ADJ auditory

auditor -ora MF auditor

auditoría F audit

auditorio M (público) audience; (local) auditorium

auge M (del mercado) boom; (de una moda) heyday; (de una carrera) peak

augurar VT to foretell; **no — nada bueno** not to bode well

aula F (de clase) classroom; (de conferencia) lecture hall

aullar VI to howl

aullido M howl

aumentar VT to augment, to increase; VI (los precios) to rise, to escalate; (población) to swell; (violencia) to escalate

aumento M increase; (de expectativas) buildup; (de población) growth; (de precios) rise, upturn; (de peso) gain

aun ADV even; **— así** even so; **— cuando** even though / if

aún ADV still

aunque CONJ though, although

aura F aura

áureo ADJ golden

aureola F halo

auricular M (de teléfono) receiver; **—es** headphones, earphones

aurora F dawn, aurora; **— boreal** aurora borealis, northern lights

auscultar VT to listen to with a stethoscope

ausencia F absence

ausentarse VT to absent oneself

ausente ADJ absent, missing

ausentismo M absenteeism

auspicios M PL auspices

austeridad F austerity

austero ADJ austere, stern

Australia F Australia

australiano -na ADJ & MF Australian

Austria F Austria

austríaco -ca ADJ & MF Austrian

autenticar[6] VT to authenticate

auténtico ADJ authentic

autismo M autism

auto M (coche) auto; (orden judicial) writ; **— de choques** bumper car

autoadhesivo M decal; (para el parachoques) bumper sticker

autoayuda F self-help

autobiografía F autobiography

autobomba M fire engine

autobús M bus

autocine M drive-in movie theater

autocompasión F self-pity

autocontrol M self-control

autócrata MF INV autocrat

autóctono ADJ indigenous

autodestructivo ADJ self-destructive

autodisciplina F self-discipline

autoestima F self-esteem

autogobierno M self-government

autógrafo M autograph

autoimagen F self-image
automático ADJ automatic
automatización F automation
automatizar[9] ADJ (mecanizar) to automate; (hacer automáticamente) to do automatically
automóvil M automobile
automovilista MF motorist
automovilístico ADJ automotive
autonomía F autonomy; (de un vehículo) range
autopista F freeway, turnpike
autopropulsado ADJ self-propelled
autopsia F autopsy
autor -ora MF author
autoridad F authority
autoritario ADJ (tiránico) authoritarian; (respetado) authoritative
autorización F authorization
autorizar[9] VT to authorize; (dar propiedad intelectual) to license
autosatisfacción F self-satisfaction
autoservicio M (sistema de venta) self-service; (tienda) convenience store
autosuficiente ADJ self-sufficient; (presumido) smug
autovía F freeway
auxiliar VT to help; ADJ auxiliary; MF assistant; **— de vuelo** (hombre) steward; (mujer) stewardess
auxilio M help
avalancha F avalanche
avalar VT to guarantee, to co-sign
avaluar[17] VT to appraise
avalúo M appraisal
avance M (acción de avanzar, adelanto) advance, headway; (sinopsis de película) trailer
avanzada F scouting party
avanzado ADJ advanced
avanzar[9] VI (ir hacia adelante) to advance; (progresar) to make headway; **a medida que avanzaba la mañana** as the morning progressed; VT to move forward; (una cinta) to fast-forward
avaricia F avarice
avariento ADJ avaricious, miserly
avaro ADJ miserly, avaricious
avasallar VT to subjugate
ave F bird; **— de corral** poultry; **— de rapiña** bird of prey; **— canora** songbird; **— zancuda** wading bird
avecindarse VI to take up residence
avellana F hazelnut
avellano M hazel
avena F oats
avenencia F agreement

avenida F avenue
avenir[47] VI to reconcile; **—se a** to come around; **—se bien** to get along
aventadora F fan, blower
aventajar VT (ser mejor) to be superior to; (sobrepasar) to get ahead of
aventón M **dar un —** *Méx* to give a lift
aventura F (suceso que implica riesgo) adventure; (relación amorosa) fling, affair
aventurado ADJ (arriesgado) risky; (atrevido) daring
aventurar VT (arriesgar) to risk; (sugerir) to venture; **—se a** to dare to
aventurero -ra ADJ adventurous; MF adventurer
avergonzado ADJ (tímido) abashed; (arrepentido) ashamed
avergonzar[2,9] VT to shame, to embarrass; **—se** to be ashamed / embarrassed
avería F (de frutas) damage; (de coche) breakdown, mechanical trouble
averiado ADJ (un coche) broken-down; (un televisor) on the blink
averiarse[16] VI (fruta) to become damaged; (un coche) to break down
averiguar[8] VT to find out, to ascertain
aversión F aversion, dislike
avestruz MF ostrich
avezado ADJ seasoned
aviación F aviation
aviador -ora MF aviator
aviar[16] VT to fix
avidez F eagerness
ávido ADJ eager, avid
avinagrado ADJ sour
avinagrar VT to sour; **—se** to become sour
avío M tidying up; **—s de pescar** fishing tackle
avión M (máquina) airplane; (ave) martin; **— comercial** airliner; **— a reacción** jet airplane; **— caza** fighter airplane
avisar VT (notificar) to advise; (a la policía) to alert
aviso M notice; **— publicitario** advertisement; **estar sobre —** to be forewarned; **poner sobre —** to forewarn; **sin previo —** without warning
avispa F wasp
avispado ADJ lively
avisparse VI to wise up
avispero M wasp's nest; **alborotar el —** to stir up a wasp's nest
avispón M hornet
avistar VT to catch sight of
avivar VT (una fiesta) to enliven; (un fuego, un debate) to fuel; (una llama) to fan
avizorar VT to spy on

axila F underarm
ay INTERJ (de dolor) ouch; (de decepción) oh, no; (de sorpresa desagradable) oh; — **de mí** poor me
ayer ADV yesterday
ayuda F help; (después de un desastre) relief
ayudante -ta MF assistant, helper; — **de médico** physician's assistant
ayudantía F assistantship
ayudar VT to help, to aid
ayunar VI to fast
ayunas F PL **en** — (antes de comer) without having eaten; (despistado) clueless; **estoy en** — I am fasting
ayuno M fast
ayuntamiento M (gobierno) municipal government; (edificio) city hall
azabache M jet; ADJ jet-black, raven
azada F hoe
azadón M hoe
azafato -ta MF (en aviones) flight attendant; (en ferias) host
azafrán M saffron
azahar M orange blossom
azar M chance; **al** — by chance, at random
azaroso ADJ (arriesgado) risky; (aleatorio) random
azerbaijano -na, azerbaiyano -na ADJ & MF Azerbaijani, Azerbaijanian
Azerbaiyán F Azerbaijan
azogar[7] VT to silver
azogue M (sustancia) quicksilver, mercury; (niño inquieto) restless child; **tener — en el cuerpo** to be restless
azorar VT to embarrass
azotaina F flogging
azotar VT (con azote) to whip, to lash, to flog; VI/VT (el viento) to whip, to buffet; (el sol) to beat down; (la lluvia) to sting
azote M (instrumento) whip; (golpe) lash; (aflicción) scourge; (golpe de viento) buffet
azotea F flat roof
azúcar MF sugar; — **moreno -na** brown sugar
azucarar VT to sugar
azucarera F (fábrica) sugar mill; (recipiente) sugar bowl
azucarero M sugar bowl
azucena F white lily
azufre M sulfur / sulphur
azul ADJ blue; — **acero** steel blue; — **celeste** sky-blue; — **claro** light blue; — **marino** navy blue
azulado ADJ bluish
azular VT to color blue
azulear VI (tener color azul) to be blue;

(ponerse azul) to become blue; VT (dar color azul) to color blue
azulejar VT to tile
azulejo M tile
azuzar[9] VT (a un perro) to sic; (a una persona) to egg on

Bb

baba F drivel, drool, slobber; (de un caracol, de agua estancada) slime; **se le cae la baba por el coche nuevo** he's drooling over the new car
babear VI to drivel, to drool
babero M bib
babor M portside
babosa F slug
babosear VI/VT to slobber (on)
baboso ADJ (caracol) slimy; (persona que babea) driveling; (persona tonta) idiotic; (adulador) fawning
babuino M baboon
baca F luggage rack
bacalao M cod
bache M pothole; (momento) bad time; (de aire) air pocket
bacheado ADJ bumpy
bachiller -ra M (graduado) high school graduate; (alumno) high school student
bachillerato M baccalaureate
bacilo M bacillus
backgammon M backgammon
bacteria F bacteria
bacteriología F bacteriology
badajo M bell clapper
badana F sheepskin
bagaje M baggage
bagatela F trifle
bagazo M pulp
Bahamas F PL Bahamas
bahameño -ña ADJ & MF Bahamian
bahía F bay
Bahrein M Bahrain
bahreiní ADJ & MF Bahraini
bailador -ora MF folk dancer; ADJ dancing
bailar VI/VT to dance; **me bailan los pantalones** my pants are falling off; **me tocó — con la más fea** I was left holding the bag; **que me quiten lo bailado** I enjoyed it anyway
bailarín -ina MF dancer
baile M (movimiento rítmico) dance; (fiesta) dance, ball; — **aeróbico** aerobic dance; —

de máscaras masked ball; — **folklórico** folk dance; — **zapateado** clog dance

bailongo M hop

bailotear VI to jig

baivel M bevel

baja F (caída barométrica) drop; (de precios) decline; (víctima de guerra) casualty; (del ejército) discharge, dismissal; (licencia) leave; **dar de** — to discharge; **darse de** — to call in sick

bajada F (acción de bajar, pendiente) descent; (de un caballo) dismount; — **contra-reloj** downhill ski race

bajar VI to go down; (corriendo) to run down; (de un árbol) to climb down; (de un caballo) to get down; (de un ómnibus) to step off, to get off; (empeorar) to worsen; (alcanzar) to reach down; (la marea) to ebb; (una creciente) to subside; VT (las escaleras) to go down; (un avión de un tiro) to shoot down; (comida con agua) to wash down; (la cabeza) to lower; (un cargamento) to let down; (el volumen) to turn down; (focos) to dim; (la voz) to lower, to soften; — **de categoría** to demote; — **el cursor** to scroll down; — **en picada** to dive; **—se los pantalones** to pull down one's pants

bajeza F (cualidad) baseness; (acción) vile act

bajío M shoal

bajista ADJ (bolsa) bearish

bajo ADJ (nubes, estante, precio, voz grave) low; (persona) short; (voz débil) soft; (río) lower; (vista, persianas) lowered; (acto) base; **baja espalda** small of the back; **de baja ley** base; PREP under; — **control** under control; — **cuerda** under-the-table; — **fianza** on bail; — **fuego** under fire; — **sospecha** under a cloud; — **tierra** underground; **poner** — **llave** to lock up; **por lo** — under one's breath; M (voz grave) bass; (de pantalón) cuff; **hacer los —s** to cuff; ADV low

bala F (de pistola) bullet; (de prueba olímpica) shot; (de cañón) ball

balada F ballad

baladí ADJ trivial

balance M (cálculo) balance; (documento) balance sheet; (de víctimas) toll; (movimiento) sway; **hacer un** — to take stock

balancear VT to swing; VI to sway; **—se** to sway

balanceo M (de un cuerpo) swinging, swing; (de un barco) rolling, roll

balancín M seesaw

balanza F scale; — **comercial** balance of trade; — **de pagos** balance of payments

balar VI to bleat

balasto M ballast

balaustrada F banister

balazo M (disparo) shot; (herida) bullet wound

balbucear VI to stammer; (un bebé) to babble

balbuceo M stammer; stammering; (de bebé) babble, babbling

balcón M balcony

balde M pail, bucket; **de** — gratis; **en** — in vain

baldear VT to flush

baldío ADJ (terreno) fallow; (acción) useless

baldosa F (en una casa) floor tile; (en una calle) flagstone

balido M bleat, bleating

balística F ballistics

balístico ADJ ballistic

ballena F whale; (hueso) whalebone

ballenato M whale calf

ballet M ballet

balneario M summer resort; (con aguas medicinales) spa

balón M ball; **baloncesto** basketball; **balonmano** European handball; F **balonvolea** volleyball

balsa F raft, balsa; (lago) pond

bálsamo M balsam, balm

baluarte M bulwark, stronghold

bambolear VT to sway, to swing; **—se** to sway, to swing

bamboleo M swinging, swaying

bambú M bamboo

banal ADJ banal; **una respuesta** — a pat answer

banana F banana

banano M banana tree

banca F (industria) banking; (en el juego) bank

bancario -ria ADJ bank, banking; MF banker

bancarrota F bankruptcy

banco M (establecimiento) bank; (asiento) bench; (de peces) school; (de arena) shoal, spit; — **de datos** data bank; — **de niebla** fog bank

banda F (musical) band; (cinta ancha) band, sash; (grupo) gang, band, ring; (dibujo) stripe; (de un neumático) tread; (lindero) side, edge, border; (de un barco) side; — **de frecuencia** frequency band; — **horaria** time slot; — **magnética** magnetic strip; — **sonora** sound track

bandada F (de aves) flock, flight; (de peces) school

bandeja F tray; **me lo sirvieron en** — (de

plata) they served it to me on a silver
platter
bandera F flag; **jurar la —** to pledge
allegiance to the flag
banderín M pennant
banderola F pennant
bandido -da MF bandit, outlaw; (como
epíteto) rascal
bando M (decreto) edict; (partido) camp
bandolero -ra MF bandit
Bangladesh M Bangladesh
banjo M banjo
banquero -ra MF banker
banqueta F (taburete) stool; (acera) *Méx*
sidewalk
banquete M banquet
banquetearse VI to feast
banquillo M bench
bañar VT to bathe; (una torta) to ice, to frost;
—se to take a bath, to bathe
bañera F bathtub
bañista MF bather
baño M (acción) bath; (cuarto) bathroom,
lavatory; (de torta) icing, frosting; **darse
un —** (bañarse) to take a bath; (nadar) to
take a swim; **— (de) María** double boiler;
— de sangre bloodbath
bar M bar
barahúnda F ruckus, racket
baraja F pack / deck of cards
barajada F shuffle
barajar VI/VT (naipes) to shuffle;
(alternativas) to weigh
baranda F railing, guard rail
barandal M banister
barandilla F rail, railing
barata F *Méx* sale
baratear VT to sell cheap
baratija F trinket, knickknack
barato ADJ cheap
baratura F cheapness
barba F beard; **—s** whiskers; **hacer algo en
las —s de alguien** to do something right
under someone's nose
barbacoa F barbecue
barbadense ADJ & MF Barbadian
barbado ADJ bearded
Barbados M Barbados
barbaridad F atrocity; **una — de** a lot of;
¡qué —! what nonsense!
barbarie F savagery
bárbaro -ra ADJ (salvaje) barbarous, barbaric;
(estupendo) cool, super; MF barbarian
barbecho M fallow land
barbería F barbershop
barbero -ra MF barber
barbilla F chin

barbitúrico M barbiturate
barbudo ADJ bearded
barca F rowboat
barcaza F barge
barco M boat
bardo M bard
bario M barium
barítono ADJ & M baritone
barlovento M windward
barniz M (para madera) varnish; (para
cerámica) glaze; (de cultura) veneer
barnizar[9] VT (madera) to varnish; (cerámica)
to glaze
barómetro M barometer
barón M baron
barquero -era M boatman; F boatwoman
barquillo M rolled wafer
barquinazo M **dar —s** to lurch
barra F (de hierro, arena, chocolate, en un
bar) bar; (en gimnasia) crossbar; (signo
ortográfico) slash; **— de jabón** bar of
soap; **— espaciadora** space bar
barrabasada F mischief
barraca F (en las fiestas) stall, stand;
(casucha) hovel
barracuda F barracuda
barranca M ravine
barranco M gully, ravine
barrena F (de un taladro) bit; (de un avión)
tailspin; **entrar en —** to go into a
tailspin
barrenar VT to drill
barrendero -ra MF street sweeper
barrer VI/VT to sweep; (derrotar) to defeat
decisively; M SG **barreminas** minesweeper
barrera F barrier; (valla) barrier, bar; **—
arancelaria** tariff barrier; **— de coral**
barrier reef; **— del sonido** sound barrier
barrica F vat
barricada F barricade
barrida F sweep
barrido M (acción de barrer) sweeping;
(movimiento) sweep
barriga F belly; (gorda) paunch; **rascarse la
—** to do nothing
barrigón ADJ pot-bellied
barril M barrel, keg, drum
barrio M neighborhood, quarter; **—
residencial** residential neighborhood; **—s
bajos** slums
barritar VI to trumpet
barro M (lodo) mud; (arcilla) clay; (acné)
pimple; **de —** earthen
barroco ADJ & M baroque
barroso ADJ muddy
barrote M bar

barruntar VT to suspect
barrunto M suspicion
bártulos M PL stuff
barullo M hubbub
basal ADJ basal
basalto M basalt
basar VT to base; **—se en** (depender de) to rely on; (fundamentar en) to be based on
basca F nausea
báscula F scale
base F (apoyo, área militar, química) base; (punto de partida) basis; (de maquillaje) foundation; (de una campaña) plank; **— de concurso** contest rules; **— de datos** database; **— de lanzamiento** launching pad; **con — en** on the basis of; **en — a** on the basis of; **las —s** (de un partido) grass roots; (de un sindicato) rank and file; **salario —** base salary; **tener una — sólida** to be on a strong footing
basic M (lenguaje de programación) basic
básico ADJ basic; (comida) staple
bastante ADJ & PRON enough, sufficient; ADV (suficientemente) enough; (mucho) quite a lot; (algo) quite, pretty
bastar VI to be enough, to suffice; **¡basta!** enough!
bastardilla F italics
bastardo -da ADJ & MF *ofensivo* bastard
bastedad F coarseness
bastidor M (de un teatro) wing; (para bordado) frame; (de un coche) chassis; (de una ventana) sash; **entre —es** (en teatro) offstage; (en privado) behind the scenes
bastimentos M PL provisions
basto ADJ coarse, crude; M suit in the Spanish deck of cards
bastón M (para andar) cane, walking stick; **— de esquí** ski pole
basura F rubbish, garbage, trash
basural M *Am* dump
basurero -ra MF (persona) garbage collector; M (lugar) dump
bata F (para llevar en casa) robe, housecoat; (de laboratorio) lab coat; (de pacientes) hospital gown; **— de baño** bathrobe
batahola F racket
batalla F battle; (de coches) wheelbase; **— naval** sea battle; **ropa de —** everyday clothing; **trabar —** to engage in battle
batallar VI to battle
batallón M battalion
batata F sweet potato
bate M baseball bat
batea F tray
bateador -ora MF batter
batear VI to bat

batería F (de coche, artillería) battery; (de cocina) pots and pans; (musical) drums
baterista MF drummer
batiburrillo M hodgepodge
batido M shake, milk shake
batidor M whisk, beater
batidora M mixer
batintín M gong
batir VT (una alfombra) to beat; (un terreno) to comb; (mantequilla) to cream, to churn; (un récord) to break; (huevos) to beat; (crema) to whip; (alas) to flap, to beat; **—se en duelo** to duel; **—se en retirada** to retreat; **— palmas** to clap, to applaud
batuta F baton; **llevar la —** to call the shots
baudio M baud
baúl M trunk
bautismo M baptism, christening; **— de fuego** baptism of fire
bautizar[9] VT to baptize, to christen
bautizo M christening, baptism
baya F berry
bayeta F cleaning cloth
bayo ADJ bay
bayoneta F bayonet
baza F card trick; **meter — en una conversación** to participate in a conversation
bazar M bazaar
bazo M spleen
bazofia F slop
bazuca F bazooka
beagle M beagle
beato ADJ (bendito) blessed; (piadoso) beatified; (santurrón) overly pious
bebé M baby, infant
bebedero M (recipiente) drinking trough; (lugar) watering hole
bebedor -ora MF drinker
beber VI/VT to drink
bebercio M *fam* booze
bebida F drink, beverage
beca F scholarship, fellowship
becario -ria MF scholar, fellow
becerro M calf; (piel) calfskin
becuadro M natural sign
befa F jeer
befar VT to jeer at
beicon M *Esp* bacon
beige ADJ INV & M beige
beldad F beauty
belga ADJ & MF Belgian
Bélgica F Belgium
Belice M Belize
beliceño -ña ADJ & MF Belizean
bélico ADJ warlike

belicoso ADJ (guerrero) bellicose; (agresivo) feisty

beligerante ADJ & MF belligerent

bellaco M rascal, scoundrel

bellaquería F mischief

belleza F beauty

bello ADJ beautiful

bellota F acorn

bemol ADJ & M flat; **tener —es** to be tricky

bencina F benzine

bendecir[26b] VT to bless

bendición F (parte de la misa) benediction; (acción y efecto de bendecir) blessing; (cosa excelente) boon, blessing

bendito ADJ (agua) holy; (alma) blessed; — **sea** may he be blessed; **dormir como un** — to sleep like a log; **es un** — he is a saint

benefactor -ora M benefactor, patron; F benefactress, patroness

beneficencia F charity; — **pública** welfare

beneficiar VT to benefit; **—se de** to benefit from

beneficiario -ria MF (de una herencia, perdón, acto de bondad) beneficiary; (de un cheque) payee

beneficio M benefit (también espectáculo)

beneficioso ADJ beneficial

benéfico ADJ beneficent

benemérito ADJ worthy of esteem

benevolencia F benevolence

benévolo ADJ benevolent

bengala F flare

benigno ADJ benign

Benín M Benin

beninés -esa ADJ & MF Beninese

benjamín -ina MF youngest child

beodo ADJ drunk

berbiquí M carpenter's brace

berenjena F eggplant

bermejo ADJ reddish

bermellón ADJ vermilion

berrear VI (animal) to bellow, to bawl; (bebé) to squall

berrido M (de animal) bellowing, bawling; (de bebé) squall, squalling

berrinche M tantrum

berro M watercress

berza F cabbage

besar VT to kiss

beso M kiss

bestia F beast

bestial ADJ bestial

best-seller ADV best seller

besuquear VT to kiss repeatedly; **—se** to make out

betabel M *Méx* beet

betún M shoe polish

Biblia F Bible

bíblico ADJ biblical

bibliografía F bibliography

biblioteca F library; (estante) bookcase

bibliotecario -ria MF librarian

bicarbonato M bicarbonate; — **de sosa** bicarbonate of soda

bíceps M SG bicep(s)

bicho M (insecto) bug (también en informática); (animal) *fam* critter; — **raro** odd bird; **mal** — creep; **¿qué** — **te ha picado?** what's gotten into you? **—s** vermin

bici F bike

bicicleta F bicycle; — **de montaña** mountain bike; — **estática** stationary bike

biela F connecting rod

Bielorrusia F Belarus

bien ADV well; **—aventurado** blessed; — **arreglado** well groomed; — **hecho** well-made, well-done; — **poco** very little; **agarrarse** — to hold on tight; **ahora** — now then; **apretar** — to press hard; **está** — she is fine; **más** — rather; **me doy** — **cuenta** I'm perfectly aware; **pues** — now; **qué** — how wonderful; **si** — although; **ya está** — that's enough; M good; **—es** property, assets; **—es inmuebles** real estate; **—es muebles** personal property; **—es raíces** real estate; **—estar** well-being, welfare; **—hechor** benefactor; **persona de** — a good person

bienio M biennium

bienvenida F welcome

bienvenido ADJ welcome

bifurcación F fork, forking; (en un programa de computadora) branch

bifurcarse[6] VI to fork, to branch off

bigamia F bigamy

bigote M mustache; (de animal) whisker

bikini M bikini

bilateral ADJ bilateral

bilingüe ADJ & MF bilingual

bilingüismo M bilingualism

bilis F bile

billar M billiards, pool; (mesa) pool table

billete M (de viaje, para espectáculos) ticket; (de banco) bill, banknote

billetera F billfold

billón M trillion

bimestral ADJ bimonthly

bimestre M two-month period

binario ADJ binary

bingo M bingo

binomial ADJ binomial

binomio M binomial
biodegradable ADJ biodegradable
biofeedback M biofeedback
biografía F biography
bioingeniería F bioengineering
biología F biology
biombo M folding screen
biopsia F biopsy
bioquímica F biochemistry
biorritmo M biorhythm
biotecnología F biotechnology
bipartidista ADJ bipartisan
bipolar ADJ bipolar
birlar VT *fam* to pinch, to swipe
Birmania F Burma
birmano -na ADJ & MF Burmese, from Myanmar
birrete M mortarboard
bis M encore
bisabuelo -la M great-grandfather; F great-grandmother
bisagra F hinge
bisecar[6] VT to bisect
bisel M bevel
biselar VT to bevel
bisexual ADJ bisexual
bisiesto ADJ **año** — leap year
bisnieto -ta M great-grandson; F great-granddaughter
bisonte M bison, buffalo
bistec M beefsteak
bisturí M scalpel
bisutería F costume jewelry
bit M bit
bizarría F gallantry
bizarro ADJ gallant
bizco ADJ cross-eyed
bizcocho M sponge cake
bizcochuelo M sponge cake
bizquear VI to be cross-eyed
black-jack M black-jack
blanca ADJ half note
blanco ADJ (color) white; (tez) fair; M (color) white (también de huevos, ojos); (de tiro) target; (de una burla) butt; — **fácil** sitting duck; **dar en el** — to hit the target; **en** — (hoja de papel, mente) blank; (sin dormir) sleepless; **en** — **y negro** in black and white
blancura F whiteness; (de tez) fairness
blancuzco ADJ whitish
blandir VT to brandish, to wield
blando ADJ soft; (sensiblero) mushy
blandura F softness
blanqueador M bleach
blanquear VT (una pared) to whitewash; (dinero) to launder; (verduras) to blanch;

— **se** to whiten
blanquecino ADJ whitish
blanqueo M whitening
blasfemar VI/VT to blaspheme
blasfemia F blasphemy
blasón M coat of arms
blasonar VI to boast
blazer M blazer
blindado ADJ armored
blindaje M armor
blindar VT to armor
bloc M writing tablet, pad of paper
bloque M block (también de motor, político); (edificio) building; **en** — together
bloquear VT (una carretera, un asalto, un pase) to block; (un puerto) to blockade; (cuentas bancarias) to freeze; —**se** to choke
bloqueo M block; (militar) blockade
blues M PL blues
bluff M bluff
blusa F blouse, top
boa F boa constrictor
boato M pomp
bobada F foolish act; (fruslería) trifle
bobalicón -ona ADJ goofy; MF nincompoop
bobear VI to fool around, to monkey around
bobería F (cualidad) foolishness; (dicho) foolish remark; (hecho) foolish act
bobina F (de hilo) bobbin; (de alambre, de coche) coil; (de película) reel
bobinar VT to reel
bobo -ba ADJ (tonto) dumb, dimwit, silly; (estupefacto) flabbergasted; MF booby, fool
boca F mouth (también de río); (de un arma de fuego) muzzle; (del estómago) pit; (de una cueva) opening; — **a** — mouth-to-mouth; — **abajo** face down; — **arriba** face up; —**calle** intersection; **a** — **de jarro** at close range; **callarse la** — to shut up
bocadillo M snack; *Esp* sandwich
bocado M bite, morsel, mouthful; (de una brida) bit
bocanada F (de líquido) mouthful; (de humo) puff; (de aire) sniff
bocazas MF SG loudmouth
boceto M sketch
bochorno M (calor) oppressive heat; (vergüenza) embarrassment
bochornoso ADJ (caluroso) sultry, oppressive, muggy; (vergonzoso) embarrassing
bocina F (de coche) horn; (megáfono) megaphone
bocinazo M honk, toot
boda F wedding; — **de oro** golden anniversary; — **de plata** silver

anniversary

bodega F (despensa subterránea) cellar; (para vinos) wine cellar; (vinería) winery; (espacio en un barco, avión) hold; (tienda de comestibles) *Caribbean, Central America* grocery store

bodeguero -ra MF wine producer; *Caribbean, Central America* grocer

bofe M (de animal) lung; **echar los — s** to tire oneself out

bofetada F slap

boga LOC ADV **en —** in vogue, fashion

bogar[7] VI/VT to row

bohemio -mia ADJ & MF Bohemian

boicot M boycott

boicotear VT to boycott

boicoteo M boycott

boina F beret

bol M bowl

bola F (pelota) ball; (canica) marble; (de helado) dip; **— blanca** cue ball; **en —s** in the buff; **no dar pie con —** to be lost; **no dar ni —** not to pay attention

bolera F bowling alley

boleta F (de lotería) ticket; (de votación) *Méx* ballot

boletín M bulletin

boleto M ticket

boliche M (juego) bowling; (bolera) bowling alley

bolígrafo M ballpoint pen

bolita F pellet

Bolivia F Bolivia

boliviano -na ADJ & MF Bolivian

bollo M bun, roll

bolo M bowling pin; **jugar a los —s** to bowl

bolsa F bag, purse; (de canguro) pouch; (de valores) stock market; **— de aire** airbag; **— de estudio** scholarship; **— de miseria** pocket of poverty; **hace —s** it pooches out

bolsillo M pocket; **de —** pocket-sized

bolsista MF stockbroker

bolso M (grande) bag; (pequeño) purse

bomba F (para agua, gasolina) pump; (noticia, mujer) *fam* bombshell; (artefacto explosivo) bomb; **— atómica** atomic bomb; **— de hidrógeno** hydrogen bomb; **— de neutrones** neutron bomb; **— de tiempo** time bomb; **— fétida** stink bomb; **— incendiaria** incendiary bomb; **— inteligente** smart bomb; **lo pasamos —** we had a blast

bombacha F *RP* panties, underpants

bombardear VT to bombard

bombardeo M bombardment, bombing

bombardero -era MF (tripulante)

bombardier; M (avión) bomber

bombear VT to pump

bombero -era MF firefighter

bombilla F lightbulb

bombo M bass drum; **dar —** to extol; **con — y platillo** with great fanfare

bombón M (dulce de chocolate) bonbon, candy; (mujer atractiva) *fam* dish

bombonería F candy store

bonachón ADJ (amable) good-natured; (inocente) naïve

bonanza F (buen tiempo) fair weather; (prosperidad) prosperity

bondad F goodness, kindness; **—es** virtues; **tenga la — de** would you please

bondadoso ADJ kind, kindly

boniato M sweet potato

bonito ADJ pretty; M tuna

bono M (financiero) bond; (vale) voucher

boñiga F dung

boqueada F gasp

boquear VI to gasp

boquete M opening

boquiabierto ADJ openmouthed, astonished

boquilla F (para cigarros) cigarette holder; (para una trompeta) mouthpiece; **defender de —** to pay lip-service to

bórax M borax

borbollar VI to bubble

borbollón M bubbling; (alboroto) *Am* commotion; **a borbollones** bubbling over

borbotar VI to bubble, to gurgle

borboteo M bubbling, gurgling

bordado M embroidery, needlework

bordar VI/VT to embroider

borde M edge, border; (de un vaso) rim, brim; (de un desastre) brink; (de una calle) *Méx* curb

bordear VT (rodear) to skirt, go along the edge of; (adornar) to trim

bordillo M curb

bordo LOC ADV **a —** on board

bordó, bordeaux ADJ & M maroon

borla F (de birrete) tassel; (algodón) powder puff

boro M boron

borra F dregs

borrachera F (estado) drunkenness; (juerga) drunken spree

borrachín -ina M drunkard

borracho -cha ADJ drunk, wasted; **no lo hago ni —** I would never do such a thing; MF drunkard, wino

borrador M (bosquejo) rough draft; (goma) eraser

borrar VT to erase; **—se de un club** to

withdraw from a club

borrasca F squall

borrego M lamb

borrico M donkey; (persona) *pey* ass

borrón M blot, blotch, smudge; **hacer — y cuenta nueva** to start over at square one

borronear VT to smudge

borroso ADJ blurry, fuzzy

boscaje M thicket

Bosnia-Herzegovina F Bosnia and Herzegovina

bosnio -nia ADJ & MF Bosnian

bosque M forest, woods

bosquecillo M grove

bosquejar VT to sketch, to outline

bosquejo M sketch, outline

bosta F dung

bostezar[9] VI to yawn

bostezo M yawn

bota F (calzado) boot; (bolsa) leather wine bag

botadura F launch

botánica F botany

botánico ADJ botanical

botar VT (una pelota) to bounce; (un buque) to launch; (a un borracho) to throw out

botarate M fool

bote M (jarro) can; (embarcación) boat; (rebote) bounce; **— de basura** garbage can; **— de remos** rowboat; **— de salvamento** lifeboat; **de — en —** filled to overflowing

botella F bottle

botero M boatman

botija F earthen jug

botijo M earthen jar

botín M (de guerra) booty, plunder; (de ladrón) loot, haul

botiquín M (en el baño) medicine cabinet; (de primeros auxilios) first-aid kit

botón M (de planta) bud; (de aparato, de camisa) button; (remache) stud; **botones** bellboy, page

Botsuana F Botswana

bouquet M bouquet

boutique F boutique

bóveda F (techo) arched roof, vault; **— celeste** the vault of heaven

bowling M bowling

box M pit

boxeador -ora MF boxer, prizefighter

boxear VI/VT to box

boxeo M boxing

bóxer M boxer

boya F (en el mar) buoy; (corcho) float

boyante ADJ buoyant

boyar VI to buoy

bozal M muzzle

bozo M fuzz on the lip

bracear VI to move one's arms

bracero -ra MF migrant worker

bragas F PL underpants, panties

bragueta F fly

brainstorming M brainstorming

bramar VI (ciervo, cochino) to bellow; (león, viento) to roar

bramido M (de ciervo, cochino) bellow; (de león, viento) roar

brandy M brandy

brasa F ember

brasero M brazier

Brasil M Brazil

brasileño -ña ADJ & MF Brazilian

brasilero -ra ADJ & MF Brazilian

bravata F act of bravado

bravío ADJ wild

bravo ADJ (animal, río) wild; (terreno) rugged; (persona) brave; (barrio) tough; INTERJ bravo!

bravucón -ona ADJ bullying; MF bully

bravuconería F bullying

bravura F (de bestia) fierceness; (de persona) courage

braza F fathom

brazada F (cantidad) armful; (en natación) stroke

brazalete M bracelet

brazo M arm (también de silla); (de cornamenta) branch; (de balanza) beam; **— de mar** sound; **— derecho** right-hand man; **—s** day laborers; **con los —s abiertos** with open arms; **con los —s cruzados** with crossed arms; **ir del — to** go arm in arm; **luchar a — partido** to fight to the end

brea F pitch, tar

brecha F breach, gap

brécol M broccoli

bregar[7] VI to struggle, to toil

breña F scrubland

breve ADJ brief, short; (bikini) scanty; **en —** shortly

brevedad F brevity, shortness; **a la —** as soon as possible

bribón -ona ADJ roguish; MF rascal, rogue, scoundrel

brida F bridle

brigada F brigade

brillante ADJ brilliant, bright; M brilliant, gem

brillantez F brilliance

brillantina F glitter

brillar VI to shine; (los ojos) to sparkle, to twinkle; (nieve) to glisten; **— por su**

ausencia to be conspicuous by its absence
brillo M shine, luster, sparkle; (de los ojos) twinkle; (de nieve) glistening; (del pelo, plumas) sheen; (de diamantes) sparkle; **dar** — to give luster; **sacar** — to polish
brilloso ADJ shiny
brincar[6] VI to hop, to skip
brinco M hop, skip
brindar VI to toast; — **por alguien** to toast someone; —**se a hacer algo** to volunteer to do something
brindis M toast
brío M spirit
brioso ADJ spirited
brisa F breeze
británico ADJ British
brizna F blade of grass
broca F drill bit
brocado M brocade
brocal M curb
brocha F paint brush; **de** — **gorda** coarse
broche M (alhaja) brooch; (sujetador) clasp, clip; (para el pelo) barrette; — **de oro** grand finale
brocheta F skewer
brócoli, bróculi M broccoli
broma F (chiste) joke; (réplica) jest, wisecrack; — **pesada** practical joke; —**s aparte** kidding aside; **en** — in jest; **gastar una** — to play a joke; **ni en** — no way; **no estoy para** —**s** I'm not in the mood for kidding
bromear VI to joke, to kid
bromista MF wag, joker
bromo M bromine
bromuro M bromide
bronca F row; **armar una** — to cause a disturbance, to raise a rumpus; **echarle** — **a alguien** to bawl someone out
bronce M bronze
bronceado ADJ (cubierto de bronce) bronzed; (piel) tanned; (de color bronce) bronze; M suntan
broncear VT (un objeto) to bronze; (a una persona) to tan; —**se** to get a tan
bronco ADJ (voz) gruff; (terreno) rough; (caballo) wild
bronquio M bronchial tube
bronquitis F bronchitis
brotar VI (planta) to sprout; (enfermedad eruptiva) to break out; (agua) to gush, to flow, to issue
brote M (de una enfermedad) outbreak; (retoño) sprout, spear
broza F brushwood
bruces LOC ADV **de** — face down

brujería F deviltry, witchcraft
brujo -ja M wizard, sorcerer; F witch
brújula F compass
bruma F mist
brumoso ADJ misty
brunch M brunch
bruneano -na ADJ & MF Bruneian
Brunéi M Brunei
bruñir[18] VT to burnish
brusco ADJ (descortés) brusque, curt; (repentino) sudden
brusquedad F (descortesía) brusqueness; (lo repentino) suddenness
brutal ADJ brutal
brutalidad F brutality
bruto -ta ADJ (ignorante) ignorant; (maleducado, burdo) uncouth; (violento) brutish; (no neto) gross; **a lo** — roughly; **en** — in the rough; **recaudar en** — to gross; MF (ignorante) blockhead; (persona violenta) brute; (mal educado) lout, brute
bucal ADJ oral
bucear VI to scuba-dive; (indagar) to explore
buceo M scuba diving
buche M (en las aves) crop; (bocado) mouthful
bucle M curl, ringlet; (en informática) loop
budín M pudding
bueno ADJ good; **buena voluntad** willingness; **a la buena de Dios** haphazardly; **de buenas a primeras** out of the blue; **estar** — to be sexy; **hace buen tiempo** it is fine weather; **lo** — the good thing; **por las buenas o por las malas** by hook or by crook; **ser** — **con los números** to be good at figures; INTERJ OK! —**s días** good day/morning; **buenas noches** good night/evening; **buenas tardes** good afternoon
buey M ox, steer
búfalo M buffalo, bison
bufanda F scarf, muffler
bufar VI to snort; **está que bufa** he is incensed
bufete M (despacho) lawyer's office; (negocio) practice
buffet M buffet
bufido M snort
bufón -ona MF buffoon, jester
bufonear VI to clown
buhardilla F (desván) attic, garret; (ventana) dormer
búho M owl
buhonero -ra MF peddler
buitre M vulture, buzzard
buje M bushing
bujía F spark plug

bulbo M bulb
buldog M bulldog
bulevar M boulevard
Bulgaria F Bulgaria
búlgaro -ra ADJ & MF Bulgarian
bulla F uproar, fuss, bustle
bulldozer M bulldozer
bullicio M uproar, racket, bustle
bullicioso ADJ boisterous, rowdy
bullir[19] VI (hervir) to boil; (hacer burbujas) to bubble; (ajetrearse) to bustle; (moverse) to stir
bullón M puff
bulto M (paquete) bundle; (tumor) lump, growth; (silueta) shape; (saliente) bulge; **a — ** approximately; **escurrir el —** to slack off
bungaló M bungalow
bungee M bungee jumping
búnker M bunker
buñuelo M fritter
buque M ship
burbuja F bubble
burdel M brothel, *fam* whorehouse
burdo ADJ coarse
burgués ADJ bourgeois
burla F ridicule, mockery; **hacer — a alguien** to mock someone
burlar VT to mock; **—se de** to scoff at, to make fun of
burlesco ADJ burlesque
burlón ADJ mocking
burocracia F bureaucracy
burócrata MF INV bureaucrat
burrez F stupidity
burro M (animal) donkey, ass; (persona) dunce; ADJ dense
burundés -esa ADJ & MF Burundian
Burundi M Burundi
bus M bus
busca LOC ADV **en — de** in search of
buscar[6] VT to seek, to look for, to search for; (datos, palabras) to look up; (provocar) to provoke; (la verdad) to seek after; (minerales) to prospect for; (talento) to scout for; **—se problemas** to invite trouble; **tú te lo buscaste** you asked for it; **ir a —** to fetch; M SG **buscapersonas** beeper
búsqueda F search; **— del tesoro** treasure hunt
busto M bust
butaca F armchair; (en el teatro) orchestra seat
Bután M Bhutan
butanés -esa ADJ & MF Bhutanese
butano M butane

buzo M diver
buzón M mailbox; **— de sugerencias** suggestion box
bypass M bypass operation
byte M byte

Cc

cabal ADJ (completo) complete; (exacto) exact; (honrado) upright; **estar uno en sus —es** to be in one's right mind
cabalgar[7] VI to ride horseback
caballa F mackerel
caballada F herd of horses
caballejo M nag
caballeresco ADJ chivalrous
caballería F (tropas a caballo) cavalry; (equino) equine; (condición de caballero) knighthood
caballeriza F stable
caballerizo M groom
caballero M (señor) gentleman; (hidalgo) knight, cavalier; **— andante** knight errant; ADJ gentlemanly
caballerosidad F chivalry
caballeroso ADJ chivalrous, gentlemanly
caballete M (soporte de madera) sawhorse; (de la nariz) bridge; (de pintor) easel; (de tejado) ridge
caballo M (animal) horse; (en ajedrez) knight; (heroína) *fam* smack; **a — ** on horseback; **— de carreras** racehorse; **— de batalla** hobbyhorse; **— de fuerza** horsepower; **— de Troya** Trojan horse
cabaña F (casa tosca) hovel; (casa de campo) cabin, cottage; (conjunto de ganado) livestock
cabaret M cabaret
cabecear VI (con la cabeza) to nod; (dormirse) to nod off; (un barco) to bob, to pitch
cabeceo M (de la cabeza) nodding; (de un barco) pitching
cabecera F (de cama) headboard; (de mesa) head
cabecilla MF INV ringleader
cabellera F head of hair
cabello M hair; **traido por los —s** far-fetched
caber[22] VI to fit; **no cabe duda** there is no doubt; **no cabe nadie más** there is no room for anybody else; **no — uno en sí** to be puffed up with pride; **no cabe en**

lo posible it is absolutely impossible; **¿en qué cabeza cabe?** who would believe that?

cabestrillo M sling

cabestro M halter

cabeza F head; **— de chorlito** scatterbrain, airhead; **— de playa** beachhead; **— de puente** bridgehead; **— de turco** scapegoat, fall guy; **— rapada** skinhead; **a la —** at the forefront; **caerse de —** to fall headfirst; **echarse de —** to plunge headlong; **ir a la —** to lead the way; **por — each; romperse la —** to rack one's brains; **se le fue la —** it went to his head; **sentar —** to settle down; **tiene la — cuadrada** she's a square

cabezada F nod; **dar —s** to nod off

cabezal M magnetic head

cabezazo M butt (with the head)

cabezón ADJ (de cabeza grande) big-headed; (testarudo) pig-headed; (fuerte) strong

cabezudo ADJ (de cabeza grande) big-headed; (testarudo) pig-headed

cabida F capacity; **dar —** to include; **tener — en** to fit in

cabina F (de pasajeros) cabin; (de piloto) cockpit; (de camión) cab; (de teléfono, control) booth

cabizbajo ADJ crestfallen, downcast

cable M cable

cableado M wiring

cablevisión F cable television

cabo M (parte extrema) end; (hilo) thread; (cuerda) rope; (saliente de la costa) cape; (rango militar) corporal; **— suelto** loose end; **al — de** at the end of; **atar —s** to make sense of; **de — a rabo** from beginning to end; **llevar a —** to carry out

cabotaje M coastal trade

Cabo Verde M Cape Verde

caboverdiano -na ADJ & MF Cape Verdean

cabra F goat; **— montés** mountain goat; **como una —** completely crazy

cabrearse VI to get mad

cabrestante M winch

cabrillas F PL whitecaps

cabrio M rafter

cabrío ADJ **macho —** he-goat

cabriola F caper

cabriolar VI to cavort

cabritilla F kid (leather)

cabrito M kid (goat)

cabrón -ona M (macho de cabra) he-goat; (hombre cuya mujer le engaña) cuckold; (hijo de puta) *ofensivo* bastard; F (hija de puta) *ofensivo* bitch; MF (cobarde) wimp

caca F poop; **hacer —** to poop

cacahuate M *Méx* peanut

cacahuete M *Esp* peanut

cacao M cocoa

cacarear VI to cackle, to squawk

cacareo M cackling, squawking

cacatúa F cockatoo

cacería F hunt; **— de brujas** witch hunt

cacerola F saucepan

cacha F (de navaja) handle; (nalga) hip; **hasta la —** completely

cachalote M sperm whale

cacharro M (vasija) earthen pot; (coche viejo) clunker, jalopy

cachaza F slowness

cachazudo ADJ slow

caché M (en informática) cache; (distinción) cachet

cachear VT to body-search, to frisk

cachet M artist's fee

cachetada F slap

cachete M cheek

cachiporra F blackjack

cachivaches M PL stuff, odds and ends

cacho M hunk

cachondo ADJ *fam* horny

cachorro M (de oso, lobo, tigre, león) cub; (de perro) puppy

cacique -ca M (de indios) chief, chieftain; MF (caudillo) political boss

cacofonía F cacophony

cacto M cactus

cactus M cactus

cada ADJ each; **— uno** each one; **— vez más** more and more; **— vez menos gente** fewer and fewer people; **— vez menos harina** less and less flour; **— vez peor** worse and worse; **doscientas pesetas — una** two hundred pesetas each / apiece

cadalso M gallows

cadáver M corpse; (para disecar) cadaver

cadavérico ADJ ghastly

caddie, caddy MF caddie

cadena F (serie de piezas) chain; (de televisión) network; (cordillera) mountain range; **— alimenticia** food chain; **— de montaje** assembly line; **— perpetua** life sentence; **—s** shackles; **tirar la —** to flush

cadencia F cadence

cadera F hip

cadete MF cadet

cadmio M cadmium

caducar[6] VI to lapse, to expire

caducidad F expiration

caduco ADJ (destinado a caer) deciduous; (decrépito) decrepit

caer[23] VI to fall; (perder el equilibrio) to fall down; (colgar) to hang; (ir a parar) to end up; **al — la noche** at nightfall; **— en desgracia** to fall into disfavor; **— en desuso** to fall into disuse; **— en cama** to fall ill; **— en cuenta** to catch on; **— en ruina** to fall into disrepair; **—le bien/mal a uno** (una persona) to make a good/bad impression; (una comida) to agree with; **—le en suerte a uno** to fall to one's lot; **— muy bajo** to fall so low; **caiga quien caiga** let fall who may; **dejar —** to drop; **está al —** he's about to show up; **—se** to fall down; **—se de culo** to fall on one's bottom

café M (bebida) coffee; (color) brown; (establecimiento público) coffee shop

cafeína F caffeine

cafetal M coffee plantation

cafetera F coffeepot

cafetería F snack bar, cafeteria, diner

cafetero -ra MF coffee dealer; ADJ **industria cafetera** coffee industry

cafeto M coffee bush

cagada F (acción de cagar) *vulg* dump; (desacierto) *vulg* screw-up; **este libro es una —** *fam* this book sucks

cagalera F *vulg* the trots, the shits

cagar[7] VI/VT *vulg* to shit, to take a crap; **—la** *vulg* to screw up, to fuck up; **me cago en diez/la mar** *fam* I'll be damned; **me cago en tu madre** *ofensivo* fuck you! **me cagué la chaqueta** *vulg* I fucked up my jacket; **—se de miedo** *vulg* to shit a brick

caída F (acción de caer) fall, tumble, spill; (de presión arterial) drop; (de un ordenador) crash; (de una cortina) hang; **— libre** free fall; **— del sol** sunset

caído ADJ (orejas) floppy; (arco del pie) fallen; **los —s** the fallen

caimán M alligator

caja F box; **— chica** petty cash; **— de ahorros** savings bank; **— de cambios** transmission; **— de escalera** stairwell; **— de fusibles** fuse box; **— de herramientas** tool kit; **— de jubilaciones** pension fund; **— de música** music box; **— de reloj** watchcase; **— fuerte** safe; **— registradora** (aparato) cash register, till; (lugar) checkout counter; **— tonta** idiot box; **— torácica** rib cage; **entrar en —** to get going

cajero -ra MF cashier; (en un banco) teller; **— automático** ATM

cajetilla F pack (of cigarettes)

cajilla F pack (of cigarettes)

cajón M (para transportes) crate; (parte de un mueble) drawer; **eso es de —** that's a

foregone conclusion

cajuela F *Méx* car trunk

cal F lime; **cerrar a — y canto** to close hermetically

calabacín M zucchini

calabaza F (grande y redonda) pumpkin; (pequeña y/o alargada) squash; (vaciado) gourd; **dar —s** to turn down

calabozo M dungeon

calado M draft

calamar M squid

calambre M cramp

calamidad F calamity

calamina F calamine

calandria F lark

calar VT (agujerear) to perforate; (empapar) to soak, to drench; **— a alguien** to see through someone; **— hondo** to resonate; **—se** to get drenched

calavera F skull; M libertine

calcar[6] VT (sobre papel) to trace; (imitar) to copy

calcetería F hosiery

calcetín M sock

calcinar VT to bake

calcio M calcium

calco M (acción de calcar) tracing; **es el — de su padre** he's the spitting image of his father

calcomanía F decal

calculador ADJ calculating

calculadora F calculator

calcular VT (averiguar una cantidad) to calculate, to figure; (sopesar) to weigh; (prever) to reckon

cálculo M (acción de calcular) calculation; (aritmética) arithmetic; (integral, diferencial) calculus; **— biliar** gallstone; **— renal** kidney stone

caldear VT to warm up; **— los ánimos** to get everyone upset

caldera F (en una máquina de vapor) boiler; (recipiente con asas) kettle; (de la calefacción) furnace

calderón M hold

caldo M broth, stock; **— de cultivo** culture medium

calefacción F heat, heating; **— central** central heating

calendario M calendar

caléndula F marigold

calentador M heater; **— de agua** water heater

calentamiento M warming; (en deportes) warm-up; **— global** global warming

calentar[1] VI/VT (poner caliente) to warm, to heat; **—se** (ponerse caliente, prepararse para un partido) to warm up, to heat up; (excitarse sexualmente) *fam* to get horny

calentura F (fiebre) fever; (excitación sexual) *fam* horniness

calesa F buggy

caletre M **no tener —** to have no brains

calibrador M caliper

calibrar VT to gauge, to calibrate

calibre M (de pistola, tubo) caliber; (de alambre) gauge; (instrumento para medir) caliper

calicó M calico

calidad F quality; **de —** of good quality; **estoy aquí en — de representante** I'm here in my capacity as representative

cálido ADJ warm

caliente ADJ (agradable) warm; (excesivo) hot; (excitado sexualmente) *fam* horny

calificación F (nota) grade, mark; (acción de asignar notas) grading; (juicio) rating; **le dieron la — de genio** they called him a genius

calificar[6] VT (expresar la calidad) to rate, to adjudge; (asignar nota) to grade; **—se como** to be characterized as

caligrafía F (calidad de letra) penmanship; (arte) calligraphy

calina F haze

callado ADJ silent, quiet; **estarse —** to keep quiet

callar VT (no manifestar, hacer que calle) to quiet; (no hablar) to remain silent; (dejar de hablar) to shut up; **—se la boca** to shut up, to pipe down

calle F street; (en un campo de golf) fairway; **— abajo** down the street; **— arriba** up the street; **— de sentido único** one-way street; **hacer la —** *fam* to cruise for Johns; **no pisar la —** to stay home

calleja F narrow street

callejear VI to walk the streets

callejero ADJ **perro —** stray dog; **caos —** chaos in the streets

callejón M alley; **— sin salida** blind alley, dead end

callo M callus, corn

calloso ADJ callous

calma F calm; **— chicha** absolute calm; **mantener la —** to keep one's temper; **tomar las cosas con —** to take things easy

calmante ADJ & M sedative

calmar VT (los nervios) to calm; (dolor) to sooth; (miedo) to allay, to quell; (sed) to quench; **—se** (una persona) to calm down; (una tormenta, la ira) to subside, to abate

calmo ADJ calm

calmoso ADJ easygoing

calor M heat, warmth; (actitud acogedora) warmth; **hace — hoy** it's hot today; **los —es** hot flashes; **tengo —** I'm hot

caloría F calorie

calumnia F calumny, slander

calumniar VT to slander, to malign

calumnioso ADJ slanderous

caluroso ADJ (día) hot; (recepción) warm

calva F bald spot

calvario M **mi vida es un —** *fam* my life is hell

calvo ADJ bald, baldheaded; **ni tanto ni tan — ** *fam* it ain't necessarily so; **quedarse —** to go bald

calza F long sock

calzada F pavement

calzado M footwear

calzador M shoehorn

calzar[9] VT (poner zapatos) to shoe; (hacer zapatos para) to make shoes for; **— a la familia** to buy shoes for the family; **calzo 42** I take size 10; **—se** to put on shoes

calzones M PL (de mujer) panties; (de hombre) shorts

calzonazos M SG *vulg* pussy-whipped man

calzoncillos M PL underpants, briefs; **— largos** long johns

cama F bed; **— de agua** waterbed; **— doble** double bed; **— elástica** trampoline; **— individual** twin bed; **guardar —** to be confined to bed; **meterse en la — con** to sleep with

camada F litter

camafeo M cameo

camaleón M chameleon

cámara F (espacio) chamber; (de neumático) inner tube; (fotográfica) camera; **— de comercio** chamber of commerce; **— de diputados** lower house; **— de gas** gas chamber; **— de oxígeno** oxygen tent; **— frigorífica** locker; **— legislativa** legislature; **en — lenta** in slow motion; MF INV (persona que maneja una cámara) camera operator

camarada MF INV comrade

camarero -ra M (en un restaurante) waiter, server; (en un coche cama) steward; F (en un restaurante) waitress, server; (en un coche cama) stewardess; (en un hotel) maid

camarilla F clique

camarógrafo -fa M cameraman; F camerawoman

camarón M shrimp

camarote M cabin, stateroom

cambalache M fraudulent swap

cambalachear VI/VT to swap fraudulently

cambiante ADJ (que cambia) changing; (propenso a cambiar) changeable; (temperamento) volatile

cambiar VI/VT to change; VT (una cosa por otra) to exchange, to swap, to trade; **— de marcha** to shift gears; **— de opinión / parecer** to change one's mind; **— de sitio** to move

cambio M (acción de cambiar) change; (marcha) gear; (cotización) exchange rate; (de ferrocarril) railway switch; **— de divisas** foreign exchange; **— para peor** a turn for the worse; **— y fuera** over and out; **a —(de)** in return (for); **en —** on the other hand

cambista MF money changer

Camboya F Cambodia

camboyano -na ADJ & MF Cambodian

camellear VT to push (drugs)

camello -lla M (animal) camel; (vendedor de droga) pusher; F (animal) female camel; (vendedora de droga) pusher

camerino M dressing room

Camerún M Cameroon

camerunés -esa ADJ & MF Cameroonian

camilla F stretcher, litter

camillero -ra MF hospital orderly

caminante MF walker, wayfarer

caminar VI/VT to walk

caminata F long walk; (por un lugar agreste) hike

camino M (carretera) road; (itinerario, dirección que hay que seguir) way; **— de** on the way to; **— de mesa** table runner; **— de rosas** bed of roses; **abrirse —** to make way; **a medio —** halfway; **en —(a)** on the way (to); **llevar por mal —** to lead astray; **mostrar el —** to lead the way; **ponerse en —** to set out; **señalar el —** to show the way

camión M truck; *Méx* bus; **— de la basura** garbage truck; **— de mudanzas** moving van; **— de remolque** tow truck, wrecker; **— de reparto** delivery truck; **— volteador** dump truck

camionero -ra MF truck driver; *Méx* bus driver

camioneta F (furgoneta) van, minivan; (camioncito) pickup truck; (coche sin maletero) station wagon

camisa F shirt; **— de fuerza** straitjacket; **meterse en — de once varas** to get into a jam

camiseta F (exterior) T-shirt; (interior) undershirt

camisón M nightgown

camorrista MF hell-raiser, rowdy

campamento M (de refugiados, exploradores) camp; (recreativo) campground

campana F bell; **tocar una —** to ring a bell

campanario M belfry, bell tower

campanilla F (campana pequeña) small bell; (flor) bluebell; (órgano en la boca) uvula

campanilleo M ringing

campánula F bellflower

campaña F campaign; **de —** on the front; **hacer —** to campaign

campechano ADJ straightforward

campeón -ona MF champion

campeonato M championship

campero ADJ **hombre —** a man from the country

campesino -na MF peasant; ADJ **casa —** peasant house

campestre ADJ rural

camping M (lugar) campground; (actividad) camping

campiña F open country

campista MF camper

campo M (fuera de la ciudad) country, countryside; (para cultivos, deportes, ámbito) field; (grupo en un conflicto) camp; **— abierto** range; **— de acción** field of action; **— de batalla** battlefield; **— de concentración** concentration camp; **— de golf** golf course; **— de tiro** shooting range; **— libre** free rein; **— magnético** magnetic field; **— minado** minefield; **—santo** churchyard; **— visual** visual field; **a — traviesa** cross-country

campus M campus

camuflaje M camouflage

camuflar VT to camouflage

can M dog

cana F white hair; **echar una — al aire** to go out for a good time

Canadá M Canada

canadiense ADJ & MF Canadian

canal M (cauce artificial de agua) canal; (estrecho marítimo, banda de frecuencia) channel; (emisora) station

canalé M ribbed fabric

canalizar[9] VT to channel

canalla MF *ofensivo* scum, lowlife

canalón M spout

canana F cartridge belt

canapé M divan

canario -ria M canary; ADJ of / from the Canary Islands; MF Canary Islander

canasta F basket

canasto M hamper

cancelación F cancellation
cancelar VT (un contrato, un sello) to cancel; (una deuda) to pay off; (una actividad) to call off
cáncer M cancer; **— de mama** breast cancer
cancerígeno ADJ carcinogen
canceroso -sa MF cancer patient
cancha F (de baloncesto, tenis) court; (de fútbol) field; **¡abran —!** gangway! **falta —** there's no room
canciller MF (de Alemania, de universidades) chancellor; (de EEUU) Secretary of State
canción F song; **— de cuna** lullaby
candado M padlock
candela F candle
candelabro M candelabrum
candelero M candlestick; **en —** in the limelight
candente ADJ red-hot
candidato -ta MF candidate
candidatura F (hecho de ser candidato) candidacy; (conjunto de candidatos en equipo) ticket
candidez F innocence
cándido ADJ naïve
candil M oil lamp
candilejas F PL footlights
candor M innocence
canela F (especia) cinnamon; (árbol) cinnamon tree
canesú M yoke of a shirt
cangrejo M crab
canguro M kangaroo; MF INV *Esp* baby-sitter
caníbal ADJ & MF cannibal
canica F toy marble
caniche M poodle; **— enano** toy poodle
canilla F (espinilla) shin; (pantorrilla) calf; (grifo) faucet
canino ADJ canine; **tener un hambre canina** to be ravenous; M canine (tooth)
canje M exchange
canjear VT (prisioneros, libros) to exchange; (un cupón) to redeem
cano ADJ gray-haired
canoa F canoe
canon M (regla, modelo) canon; (canción) round
canónigo M canon
canoso ADJ gray-haired
cansado ADJ (fatigado) tired, weary; (fatigoso) wearing, tiring
cansancio M weariness
cansar VT (fatigar) to tire, to tire out; (aburrir) to bore; **—se** to get tired
cantante MF singer
cantar VI/VT to sing; VT (anunciar) to call out; (confesar) to confess; **— a tono** to

sing on key; **—le a alguien las cuarenta** to give someone a piece of one's mind; **— victoria** to declare victory; **en menos que cante un gallo** before you can say Jack Robinson; M epic poem; **eso es otro —** that's another story
cántaro M pitcher; **llover a —s** to rain cats and dogs
cantera F quarry
cantero M *RP* flowerbed
cántico M chant
cantidad F quantity, amount; (de dinero) amount, sum; **— de gente** a lot of people
cantimplora F canteen
cantina F (lugar donde comer) mess hall, mess, canteen; (bar) tavern
cantinela F chant
cantinero -ra MF bartender
canto M (cosa cantada) song; (piedra) pebble; **— de cisne** swan song; **— llano** chant; **— rodado** rounded pebble; **de —** on edge
cantor -ora MF singer
canturrear VI to hum
canturreo M hum, humming
caña F (planta gramínea) reed; (de azúcar) cane; (cerveza) *Esp* beer; (vaso para cerveza) *Esp* beer glass; **— de pescar** fishing pole; **dale —** floor it
cañada F (barranco) ravine; (arroyo) brook
cáñamo M hemp
cañaveral M reed patch
cañería F (en la calle) piping; (en la casa) plumbing
caño M (tubo) pipe; (grifo) spout; (de arma) barrel; **de doble —** double-barreled
cañón M (arma) cannon; (pieza hueca) barrel; (cañada profunda) canyon; (de pluma, bolígrafo) shaft
cañonero M gunboat
caoba F mahogany
caos M chaos
caótico ADJ chaotic
capa F (prenda) cape, cloak; (de pintura, animal) coat; (de tierra) layer; (de hielo) sheet; **— de ozono** ozone layer; **— freática** water table; **de — y espada** cloak and dagger
capacidad F capacity; **—es** aptitude, ability, capability
capacitar VT (entrenar) to train; (habilitar) to qualify
capar VT to castrate
caparazón M shell
capataz -za MF boss, overseer
capaz ADJ (que puede hacer algo) capable, able; (apto) apt; (espacioso) spacious,

roomy; (competente) competent

capear VT to ride out; **— un temporal** to weather a storm

capellán M chaplain

caperuza F pointed hood

capilar ADJ & M capillary

capilla F chapel; **estar en —** (castigado) to be in the doghouse; (esperando una noticia) to be on pins and needles

capital M (dinero) capital; (de préstamo) principal; **— de riesgo** venture capital; **el gran —** big business; F capital (city); ADJ main

capitalino ADJ **atmósfera capitalina** capital city atmosphere

capitalismo M capitalism

capitalista MF capitalist; ADJ capitalistic

capitalización F capitalization

capitalizar[9] VT (aportar capital) to capitalize; (aprovechar) to capitalize on

capitán -ana MF captain

capitanear VT to captain

capitel M capital

capitolio M capitol

capitular VI to capitulate

capítulo M chapter

capó M hood (of a car)

capo M mafia boss

capota F top

capote M cloak; (de coche) *Méx* hood; **decir para su —** to say under one's breath

capricho M caprice, whim, notion

caprichoso ADJ (impredecible) capricious; (impulsivo) whimsical, fanciful; (malcriado) willful

cápsula F capsule

captar VT (un concepto) to grasp; (atención, interés) to capture; (una emisión) to receive; (una indirecta) to get; **— la onda** to get the drift

captor -ora MF captor

captura F (acción de capturar) capture; (pesca capturada) catch

capturar VT to capture; (pescado) to catch

capucha F (de cabeza) hood, cowl; (de lapicero) cap

capuchina F nasturtium

capuchino M cappuccino

capullo M (de insecto) cocoon; (de flor) bud; (tonto) *vulg* dickhead

caqui M khaki

cara F (rostro) face; (de cubo) surface; (de papel, moneda) side; (morro) nerve; **— a — face** to face; **— o cruz** heads or tails; **dar la —** to face up to things; **de — al sur** facing south; **decir en la —** to tell to one's face; **de dos —s** two-sided; **la otra**

— de la moneda the other side of the coin; **poner buena —** to put on a good face; **se le ve en la —** it's written all over his face; **tener — (dura)** to have a lot of nerve; **un ojo de la —** an arm and a leg; **volverle la — a** to snub

caracol M (molusco) snail; (concha) snail shell; **¡—es!** *fam* darn!

carácter M (temperamento, signo) character; (rasgo) characteristic; (índole) kind

característica F characteristic, feature

característico ADJ characteristic

caracterizar[9] VT to characterize

carajo INTERJ *vulg* shit! **irse al —** *vulg* to go to hell; **no sabe un —** *vulg* he doesn't know shit; **¿qué — quieres?** *vulg* what the fuck do you want? **un artista del —** *vulg* a shitty artist; M *Esp vulg* dick

caramba INTERJ *fam* darn! good grief! heck!

carámbano M icicle

carambola F carom; **por —** indirectly

caramelo M (azúcar fundido) caramel; (dulce pequeño) bonbon

caramillo M reed pipe

carátula F (máscara) mask; (portada) title page

caravana F (en el desierto, convoy) caravan; (remolque) trailer

caray INTERJ *fam* shoot!

carbohidrato M carbohydrate

carbón M (sustancia sólida) coal; (pedazo) piece of coal; **— de leña** charcoal

carboncillo M charcoal drawing

carbonera F coal bin

carbono M carbon

carburador M carburetor

carca MF INV *fam* fossil, old fogey

carcaj M quiver

carcajada F burst of laughter, guffaw

carcamal MF INV *fam* fossil, old fogey

cárcel F jail, prison

carcelero -ra MF jailer

carcinógeno M carcinogen

carcinoma M carcinoma; **— de célula basal** basal cell carcinoma

carcomido ADJ worm-eaten

carda F card, comb

cardán M universal joint

cardar VT (lana) to card, to comb; (pelo) to rat, to tease

cardenal M (pájaro, prelado) cardinal; (moretón) bruise

cardíaco -ca ADJ cardiac; MF heart patient

cardinal ADJ cardinal

cardiología F cardiology

cardiovascular ADJ cardiovascular

cardo M thistle

cardumen M school of fish
carear VT to bring face to face; **—se** to meet face to face
carecer[13] VI to lack
carencia F lack; (en la dieta) deficiency
carenciado ADJ disadvantaged
carente ADJ lacking; **— de** lacking in
carero ADJ expensive
carestía F (escasez) scarcity; (costo alto) high cost
careta F mask
carga F (cosa cargada) load, freight; (de la prueba, impuesto) burden; (hipoteca) lien; (de encendedor) refill; (de explosivo, electricidad) charge; **— de municiones** round of ammunition; **— útil** payload; **volver a la —** to insist
cargado ADJ (bebida) stiff; (pausa) pregnant; (cartucho) live; **— de deudas** deep in debt; **— de espaldas** stooping
cargador M (de batería) charger; (de arma de fuego) clip, magazine
cargamento M cargo, load, shipment
cargar[7] VT (cargamentos, dados, un arma, un programa de ordenador) to load; (una batería, a una cuenta) to charge; (de obligaciones) to burden with; (a un niño) to carry; (a un estudiante) *Esp* to flunk; (molestar) to bother; **— a alguien de responsabilidades** to saddle someone with responsibilities; **— al hombro** to shoulder; **— con la culpa** to saddle with blame; **— de combustible** to fuel; VI to charge; **— sobre** to charge, to attack
cargo M (función en una empresa) position; (en una factura, a una cuenta) charge; (acusación) count, charge; **— de conciencia** guilt feelings; **a mi —** under my charge; **hacerse — de** (responsabilizarse de) to take charge of; (ser consciente de) to understand; **investir de un —** to induct into office; **los niños están a — de la maestra** the children are under the care of the teacher; **la maestra está a(l) — de los niños** the teacher is in charge of the children
cargoso ADJ fussy
carguero ADJ freight-carrying
caribeño ADJ Caribbean
caricatura F (retrato) caricature; (con texto) cartoon
caricaturista MF cartoonist
caricaturizar[9] VT to caricature
caricia F caress
caridad F charity
caries F cavity, tooth decay
carillón M chimes

cariño M (amor) affection, fondness; (apodo) honey; **darle —s a alguien** to send love to someone; **ella y el perro se hacen —s** she and the dog nuzzle each other; **hacer con —** to do with great care; **tenerle — a alguien** to be fond of someone
cariñoso ADJ affectionate, loving
carisma M charisma
caritativo ADJ charitable
cariz M complexion
carmesí ADJ & M crimson
carmín M (carmesí) crimson; (lápiz de labios) lip gloss
carnal ADJ carnal
carnaval M carnival
carne F (para comer) meat; (de animal vivo, de persona, de tomate) flesh; **— de cañón** cannon fodder; **— de cerdo** pork; **— de cordero** mutton; **— de gallina** goose bumps; **— de res** beef; **— de venado** venison; **— y hueso** flesh and blood; **como — y uña** *fam* thick as thieves; **en — viva** raw; **metido en —s** overweight
carnear VT to butcher
carnero M ram
carnet M **— de conducir** driver's license; **— de identidad** identification card
carnicería F (tienda) butcher's shop; (matanza) carnage, bloodbath
carnicero -ra MF butcher; ADJ (carnívoro) carnivorous; (cruel) cruel
carnívoro ADJ carnivorous
carnoso ADJ fleshy
caro ADJ expensive, costly, high-priced; ADV at a high price
carona F saddle pad
carótida F carotid artery
carozo M *RP* pit
carpa F (pez) carp; (tienda de circo) circus tent
carpeta F (para documentos, también en ordenador) folder; (cartera) portfolio
carpintería F (oficio) carpentry; (taller) carpenter's shop
carpintero -ra MF carpenter
carraspear VI to clear one's throat
carraspera F scratchy throat
carrera F (conjunto de estudios, trayectoria profesional) career; (competición) race; (en las medias) run; (recorrido corto) run, dash; (de pistón) stroke; **— a pie** footrace; **— de caballos** horse race; **— de relevos** relay race; **a la —** running; **hacer —** to succeed in a profession; **tomar —** to get a running start

carreta F wagon

carrete M (de película) reel; (de hilo) bobbin; (de alambre) spool

carretera F highway; **— de circunvalación** bypass; **— de peaje** toll road

carretero ADJ **sistema —** highway system

carretilla F (de una rueda) wheelbarrow; (de más de una rueda) dolly; **de —** by memory

carretón M large wagon

carril M (de ferrocarril) rail; (de calle) lane

carrillo M cheek; **a dos / cuatro —s** voraciously

carrillón M chimes

carrizo M reed

carro M (vehículo de dos ruedas) cart; (automóvil) car; (de máquina de escribir) roll; **— alegórico** parade float; **— blindado** armored car; **— de guerra** chariot; **poner el — delante de los bueyes** to put the cart before the horse; **subirse al —** to get on the bandwagon

carrocería F auto body

carroña F carrion

carroza F (coche de caballos) coach; (de desfile) parade float; (fúnebre) hearse

carruaje M carriage, coach

carta F (misiva) letter; (naipe) card; (de restaurante) menu; (constitución) charter; (mapa) chart; **— blanca** free hand; **a la — ** à la carte; **echarle las —s a alguien** to do a card-reading for someone; **tomar —s en la situación** to take charge of a situation

cartearse VI to correspond

cartel M poster, placard; **en —** showing

cartelera F (de periódico) entertainment section; (publicitaria) billboard; (tablón para anuncios) bulletin board

cárter M oil pan

cartera F (para dinero) wallet, billfold; (para papeles) briefcase; (de alumnos) satchel; (bolsa) handbag; (de valores) portfolio

carterista MF pickpocket

cartero -ra MF letter carrier; M mailman, postman

cartílago M cartilage

cartilla F (libro para aprender a leer) reader; (librito de información) booklet; **— de racionamiento** ration book

cartografiar[16] VT to chart

cartón M cardboard, pasteboard; **— de cigarrillos** carton of cigarettes

cartuchera F cartridge belt

cartucho M (de arma de fuego) cartridge, shell; (de monedas) roll; (de dinamita) stick; **— de fogueo** blank cartridge;

quemar el último — to exhaust one's resources

cartulina F thin cardboard

casa F (edificio) house; (hogar) home; (negocio) business firm; **— de ancianos** old folks' home; **— de citas** cheap motel for rendezvous; **— de empeños** pawnshop; **— de la moneda** mint; **— de muñecas** dollhouse; **— de pompas fúnebres** funeral home; **— de putas** *vulg* whorehouse; **— de reposo** rest home; **— embrujada** haunted house; **— rodante** house trailer; **— solariega** manor house; **de — en —** from house to house; **en —** at home; **entró como Perico por su —** he made himself right at home; **estás en tu —** make yourself at home; **ir a —** to go home; **la — paga** on the house; **poner una —** to set up a household; **quedarse en —** to stay home; **tirar la — por la ventana** to live it up

casaca F riding jacket

casadero ADJ marriageable

casado ADJ married

casamentero -ra MF matchmaker

casamiento M wedding, marriage ceremony

casar VT to marry off; **—se** to get married, to wed; **—se con** to get married to; **no —se con nadie** to remain independent

cascabel M (cosa que tintinea) jingle bell; (de víbora) rattle; **ser un —** to be lively; **poner el — al gato** to stick one's neck out

cascada F cascade, waterfall

cascajo M old wreck

cascar[6] VT (quebrar) to crack; (dar bofetadas) to slap around; **—se** to crack open; M SG **cascanueces** nutcracker

cáscara F (de huevo, fruto seco) shell; (de granos, arvejas) husk; (de fruto seco) hull; (de fruta) rind; (de naranja, manzana) peel

cascarrabias MF SG crab, grouch; ADJ INV grouchy

casco M (de ciclista, militar) helmet; (de obrero) hard hat; (de barco) hull; (de naranja) shell; (uña del pie de caballería) hoof; **— urbano** limits of the city

cascote M rubble

caserío M (aldea) hamlet; (casa) *Esp* farmhouse

casero -ra ADJ (doméstico) domestic; (hecho en casa) homemade; MF caretaker; M landlord; F landlady

caseta F (en un mercado) booth, stall; (de guardia) guardhouse; (de perro) doghouse

casete MF cassette

casi ADV almost, nearly; **— diez mil** almost /

nearly ten thousand; — **lo hago** I almost did it; — **siempre** almost always; — **nadie** hardly anyone; — **nunca** hardly ever

casilla F (en el tablero de ajedrez) square; (en una tabla) box; (en un casillero) pigeonhole, cubbyhole; — **de perro** doghouse; **sacarle a alguien de sus —s** to drive someone up the wall

casino M (club) men's club; (lugar de recreo) casino

caso M case; **en —de** in the event of; **en — de que** in case that; **el — es que** the deal is that; **en todo —** in any case, at any rate; **en último —** as a last resort; **eso no viene al —** that is beside the point; **hacer — (de)** to pay attention (to); **hacer — omiso de** to disregard; **no hay —** there's no point; **pongamos por —** let's suppose that; **venir al —** to come to the point

caspa F dandruff

casquillo M (de bala) case; (de lámpara) socket

cassette MF cassette

casta F caste

castaña F chestnut; — **de cajú** cashew

castañetear VI to chatter; — **con los dedos** to snap one's fingers

castañeteo M (de dientes) chattering; (de dedos) snapping

castaño M (árbol) chestnut tree; (color, madera) chestnut; ADJ chestnut-colored, brown

castañuela F castanet

castellano ADJ & MF Castilian; M (lengua) Castilian

castidad F chastity

castigar[7] VT to chastise, to punish

castigo M chastisement, punishment; ¡**qué —!** what a nuisance!

Castilla F Castile

castillo M castle; — **de arena** sand castle; **—s en el aire** *fam* pie in the sky

casting M casting

castizo ADJ traditional

casto ADJ chaste

castor M beaver

castrar VT (a un hombre, animal) to castrate; (a una mascota) to neuter, to fix; (a mascotas hembras) to spay

casual ADJ chance, accidental

casualidad F chance, coincidence; **da la — que** it so happens that; **oír por —** to overhear; **por —** by chance

casucha F shack

cata F — **de vinos** wine-tasting

catalán -ana ADJ (del catalán) Catalan; (de Cataluña) Catalonian; MF Catalan; M (lengua) Catalan

catalejo M spyglass

catalizador M catalyst

catalogar[7] VT to catalog, catalogue

catálogo M catalog, catalogue

Cataluña F Catalonia

catar VT to taste

catarata F (cascada) cataract, waterfall; (de los ojos) cataract

catarí ADJ & MF Qatari

catarro M cold

catástrofe F catastrophe

catecismo M catechism

cátedra F (puesto de profesor) chair, professorship; (enseñanza) teaching; (división académica) department; **sentar —** to hold forth

catedral F cathedral

catedrático -ca MF (full) professor

categoría F category; **de —** important; **de — mundial** world-class; **de poca —** third-rate

caterpillar M caterpillar

catéter M catheter

cátodo M cathode

catolicismo M Catholicism

católico -ca ADJ Catholic; MF Catholic

catorce NUM fourteen

catre M cot

cátsup M catsup, ketchup

cauce M channel; — **de río** riverbed

cauchero -ra MF rubber gatherer; ADJ **industria cauchera** rubber industry

caucho M rubber; — **sintético** synthetic rubber

caución F security payment

caudal M (conjunto de bienes) wealth; (cantidad de agua) volume of water

caudaloso ADJ mighty

caudillo M leader

causa F cause; (proceso) case; — **noble** worthy cause; — **perdida** lost cause; **a — de** on account of, because of; **con conocimiento de —** wittingly; **hacer — común** to work together

causar VT to cause; — **problemas** to make trouble

cáustico ADJ caustic

cautela F caution

cauteloso ADJ cautious, wary

cauterizar[9] VT to cauterize

cautivar VT (tomar cautivo) to capture; (atraer la simpatía) to captivate

cautiverio M captivity

cautivo -va MF captive

cauto ADJ cautious, wary
cavar VT to dig
caverna F cavern, cave
cavidad F cavity
cavilar VI to muse
cayado M shepherd's crook, staff
cayo M key
caza F (acción de cazar) hunt, hunting; (conjunto de animales) wild game; — **mayor** big game; — **menor** small game; **andar a la — de** to hunt; **dar — a** to hunt down; M (avión) fighter
cazador -ora ADJ hunting; MF hunter; F windbreaker[tm]
cazar[9] VI/VT (buscar presas) to hunt; (matar presas) to shoot, to bag; (atrapar presas) to trap; MF SG **cazatalentos** talent scout; **cazatorpedero** destroyer, torpedo-boat
cazo M (cacerola) pan; (cucharón) ladle, dipper
cazoleta F pipe bowl
cazuela F (recipiente) casserole; (cazo) pan
CD M CD; — **ROM** CD-ROM
cebada F barley
cebador M pump primer
cebar VT (un animal) to fatten; (bombas) to prime; (anzuelos) to bait; **—se** to vent one's anger
cebo M (para peces) bait, lure; (para animales) feed
cebolla F onion
cebollar M onion patch
cebollino M scallion
cebra F (animal) zebra; (paso) crosswalk
cecear VI to lisp
ceceo M lisp
cecina F jerky
cedazo M sieve
ceder VT (propiedad) to cede, to assign; (un sitio) to yield, to give up; VI (disminuir) to diminish; (perder resistencia) to give way
cedro M cedar
cédula F — **de identidad** identification card
céfiro M zephyr
cegar[1,7] VT to blind
ceguera F blindness
ceja F (sobre el ojo) eyebrow; (en una encuadernación) tab; **quemarse las —** to cram for an exam
cejar VI to back down
cejijunto ADJ with thick eyebrows
celada F ambush
celador -ora MF school monitor
celar VT to watch over jealously
celda F cell
celebración F (fiesta) celebration; (acto solemne) performance
celebrar VT (festejar) to celebrate; (una

reunión) to hold; (un rito) to perform
célebre ADJ famous, noted
celebridad F celebrity
celeste ADJ (relativo al firmamento) celestial; (del color del cielo) azure, light blue
celestial ADJ celestial, heavenly
célibe ADJ celibate; MF unmarried person
cellisca F sleet; **caer —** to sleet
celo M (diligencia) zeal; (excitación sexual) heat; **estar en —** to be in heat; **—s** jealousy; **tener —s** to be jealous
celofán M cellophane
celosía F window lattice
celoso ADJ (que tiene celos) jealous; (diligente) zealous
célula F cell; — **adiposa** fat cell; — **estaminal embrional** stem cell
celular ADJ cellular; M mobile phone
celulitis F cellulite
celuloide M celluloid
celulosa F cellulose
cementar VT to cement
cementerio M cemetery, graveyard
cemento M cement; — **armado** reinforced concrete
cena F supper, dinner
cenagal M quagmire, swamp
cenagoso ADJ marshy, swampy
cenar VI to eat supper, to eat dinner; **vamos a — pescado** we're having fish for dinner
cencerro M cowbell
cenicero M ashtray
ceniciento ADJ ashen
cenit M zenith
cenizas F PL ashes, cinders
censar VI/VT to take a census (of)
censo M census
censor -ora MF censor; — **de cuentas** auditor
censura F (reprobación) censure; (control) censorship
censurador ADJ censuring
censurar VT (criticar) to censure; (examinar) to censor
centavo M cent
centella F sparkle; **pasar como una —** to go by in a flash
centelleante ADJ sparkling
centellear VI to sparkle, to scintillate
centelleo M sparkle
centenar M group of a hundred; **—es** hundreds
centenario M centennial; ADJ centenarian
centeno M rye
centésimo ADJ & M hundredth
centígrado ADJ centigrade
centímetro M centimeter

céntimo M cent
centinela MF INV sentry, sentinel
centrado ADJ true; M truing
central ADJ central; F plant; **— de teléfonos** telephone exchange; **— eléctrica** power plant; **— lechera** milk processing plant; **— nuclear** nuclear power plant
centralita F switchboard
centrar VT to center; **—se** to focus, to be focused
céntrico ADJ central
centrífugo ADJ centrifugal
centrípeto ADJ centripetal
centro M center; (de ciudad) downtown; **— comercial** shopping center; **— de gravedad** center of gravity; **— de mesa** centerpiece
Centroamérica F Central America
ceñido ADJ tight
ceñir[5,18] VT (rodear) to gird; (abrazar) to encircle; **— la corona** to be crowned; VI (estar apretado) to be tight; **—se a** (limitarse) to limit oneself to; (arrimarse) to get close to
ceño M **fruncir el —** to frown, to scowl
cepa F (de árbol) stump; (de viña) stock; (de bacteria) strain; **de pura —** of good stock
cepillar VT (dientes, pelo) to brush; (madera) to plane, to shave
cepillo M (para el pelo, los dientes) brush; (para madera) carpenter's plane; **— de dientes** toothbrush
cepo M (para cazar) trap; (para inmovilizar coches) boot
cera F wax; **— de oídos** earwax; **— para muebles** polish
cerámica F (arte) ceramics; (conjunto de artículos) pottery, earthenware
cerámico ADJ ceramic
cerbatana F blowpipe
cerca ADV near, nearby, close; **— de** near, close to; **de —** at close range; F fence
cercado M (terreno cercado) enclosure; (cerca) fence
cercanía F proximity, nearness, closeness
cercano ADJ (lugar) near, nearby; (pariente) close; **— Oriente** Near East
cercar[6] VT (rodear con una cerca) to fence, to enclose; (sitiar) to besiege
cercenar VT (cortar) to chop off; (reducir) to curtail, to encroach upon
cerciorarse VI **— (de)** to make sure (of)
cerco M (sitio) siege; (cerca) Am fence
cerda F bristle
cerdo -da M (animal, persona sucia) hog, pig; (carne) pork; F sow
cerdoso ADJ bristly

cereal M cereal; **—es** breakfast cereal; **cultivo —** cereal crop
cerebral ADJ cerebral
cerebro M brain (también genio); **lavarle el — a** to brainwash
ceremonia F ceremony
ceremonial ADJ & M ceremonial
ceremonioso ADJ ceremonious
cereza F cherry
cerezo M cherry tree
cerilla F match
cerner[1] VT to sift; **—se** (un ave) to hover; (un desastre) to loom
cernícalo M kestrel
cero M zero; (en deportes) nothing, goose egg, zip; (en tenis) love; **— absoluto** absolute zero; **partir de —** to start from scratch; **ser un — a la izquierda** to be a nobody
cerrado ADJ (no abierto) closed; (denso, tonto) dense; (poco comunicativo) reserved; (intransigente) closed-minded; (curva) sharp; M enclosure
cerradura F lock; **— de combinación** combination lock
cerrajería F locksmith's shop
cerrajero -ra MF locksmith
cerrar[1] VT (la puerta, un cajón) to close, to shut; (un trato) to close, to clinch; (un terreno) to enclose; (el gas, un grifo) to turn off; (una fábrica) to shut down, to close; **— filas** to close ranks; **— el paso** to block passage; VI to close; **—se** (una flor, una tienda) to close; (un plazo) to end; **—se el cielo** to become overcast
cerrazón F closed-mindedness
cerro M hill
cerrojo M bolt
certamen M contest; **— de belleza** beauty contest
certero ADJ sure
certeza F certainty
certidumbre F certainty
certificación F certification
certificado ADJ certified; M certificate; **— de nacimiento** birth certificate
certificar[6] VT (la autenticidad de algo) to certify; (una carta) to register
cervatillo M fawn
cervecera F brewery
cervecería F bar
cerveza F beer; **— de barril** draft beer
cérvix M (uterino) cervix
cerviz F (del cuello) cervix
cesar VI to cease; **— de trabajar** to stop working; **— en un cargo** to resign from a position; **— a** to dismiss

cesárea F Caesarean section
cese M cessation; **— el fuego** ceasefire; **— de actividades** shutdown
cesión F (de propiedad) assignment; (de derechos) waiver
césped M lawn, grass; (para deportes) turf
cesta F basket
cestería F basketry
cesto M (cesta) basket; (para ropa) hamper
cetrino ADJ olive-colored
chabacano ADJ (modales) crude; (gustos) tacky; M *Méx* apricot
chacal M jackal
chacha F servant girl
cháchara F small talk
chacota F joke; **tomarse algo a la —** to take lightly
chacra F small farm
Chad M Chad
chadiano -na ADJ & MF Chadian
chal M shawl, wrap
chala F *Am* husk; **quitar la —** to husk
chalán M horse trader
chalé M cottage
chaleco M waistcoat, vest; **— antibalas** bulletproof vest; **— de fuerza** straitjacket; **— salvavidas** life jacket
chalupa F small canoe; *Méx* tortilla with sauce
chamaco -ca M *Méx* boy; F *Méx* girl
chamarra F sheepskin jacket
chambergo M wide-brimmed hat
chambón ADJ clumsy
champán M champagne
champaña F champagne
champiñón M mushroom
champú M shampoo
chamuscadura F scorch
chamuscar[6] VT to scorch, to singe; **—se** to get scorched, to get singed
chamusquina F scorching, singeing
chance MF chance
chancearse VI **— de** to make fun of
chancho M hog
chanchullo M *fam* monkey business
chancleta F thong, flip-flop; **tirar la —** to kick up one's heels
chanclo M galosh, overshoe; **—s** rubbers
chándal M sweatsuit
chantaje M blackmail
chantajear VT to blackmail
chanza F jest
chao INTERJ bye-bye
chapa F (de metal) sheet metal; (identificación de policía) badge; (tapa de botella) bottle top; (cópula de prostituta) trick; (de madera) veneer; **— en la**

puerta shingle on the door; **hacer —s** to turn tricks; **hacerle — y pintura** to fix the bodywork and paint
chapado ADJ **— a la antigua** old-fashioned
chapalear VI to splash
chapar VT to plate
chaparro M scrub oak; ADJ *Méx* short
chaparrón M cloudburst
chaperón -ona MF chaperon(e); **ir de —** to chaperon(e)
chapitel M spire, steeple
chapotear VI to splash
chapoteo M splash, splashing
chapucear VT to botch, to bungle
chapucería F (cosa chapuceada) botched job; (cualidad de chapucero) sloppiness
chapucero ADJ shoddy, slipshod
chapurrear VT to speak a language poorly
chapuz M dive
chapuza F botched job
chapuzar[9] VI to dive
chaqueta F jacket; **— de sport** sport jacket
charada F charades
charca F pond
charco M puddle, pool; **cruzar el —** to cross the ocean
charcutería F (tienda) delicatessen; (industria) sausage-making
charla F chat, talk
charlar VI to chat, to gab
charlatán -ana ADJ talkative; MF (parlanchín) chatterbox, windbag; (curandero) charlatan, quack
charlotear VI to chatter, to jabber
charloteo M chatter, jabber
charol M (barniz) varnish; (cuero barnizado) patent leather
charolar VT to varnish
charqui M beef jerky
charro ADJ flashy, tawdry
chárter M charter flight
chascar VT (los nudillos, un hueso) to crack; (los labios) to smack; (la lengua) to click
chascarrillo M funny anecdote
chasco M (broma) prank; (decepción) dud; **llevarse un —** to be disappointed
chasis M frame, chassis
chasquear VI (decepcionar) to disappoint; (una cerradura, la lengua) to click; (un látigo) to crack; (los labios) to smack; (los dedos) to snap; **—se** to be disappointed
chasquido M (de látigo, madera, las articulaciones) crack; (de los labios) smack; (de la lengua, una cerradura) click; (de los dedos) snap
chata F bedpan
chatarra F scrap iron

chatarrería F junkyard
chato ADJ (nariz) snub-nosed; (zapatos, pecho) flat; **— como una tabla** as flat as a pancake
chaucha F green bean
chaval -la M *Esp* boy; F *Esp* girl
chaveta F cotter pin; **perder la —** *fam* to go bonkers
che INTERJ *RP* say! hey!
checo -ca ADJ & MF Czech
chef MF chef
cheque M check; **— de viajero** traveler's check
chequear VT to check
chequera F checkbook
chic ADJ & M chic
chicha F (bebida alcohólica) *Am* corn liquor; (carne) *Esp fam* meat; **de — y nabo** two-bit; **ni — ni limonada** neither fish nor fowl
chicharra F (insecto) cicada; (timbre eléctrico) buzzer
chiche M *Am vulg* tit, boob
chichi M *Am vulg* tit, boob; *Esp vulg* beaver, cunt
chichón M bump, lump, knot
chicle M chewing gum; **— de globo** bubblegum
chico -ca ADJ small, little; M boy; F girl; **mis —s** my kids
chicote M *Am* whip
chicotear VT *Am* to whip
chicoteo M *Am* whipping
chiflado ADJ *fam* nuts, cuckoo, loony
chifladura F craziness
chiflar VI (silbar) to whistle; VT (volver loco) to drive crazy; **—se** to go crazy
chiflido M whistle
chifón M chiffon
chile M chili
Chile M Chile
chileno -na ADJ & MF Chilean
chillar VI (persona) to shriek; (puerta, ratón) to squeak; (cerdo) to squeal
chillido M (de persona) shriek; (de puerta, ratón) squeak; (de cerdo) squeal
chillón ADJ (sonido) shrill; (color) loud, gaudy
chimenea F (de casa) chimney; (hogar) fireplace; (de volcán, baño, mina) vent; (de fábrica) smokestack
chimpancé M chimpanzee
china F (porcelana) china; (piedra) pebble
China F China
chinche MF (insecto) bedbug; (chincheta) thumbtack; (persona molesta) pain
chinchilla F chinchilla

chinchorro M rowboat
chingar[7] VT (fastidiar) *vulg* to screw with; (estropear) *vulg* to screw up; VI/VT *Méx vulg* to fuck
chino -na ADJ Chinese; M (lengua) Chinese; MF Chinese; **eso es —** that's Greek to me
chip M (de ordenador, en golf) chip; (de patata) potato chip
Chipre M Cyprus
chipriota ADJ & MF Cypriot(e)
chiquilín -ina M little boy; F little girl
chiquito ADJ tiny, wee
chiripa F stroke of good luck; **por / de —** by a fluke
chirivía F parsnip
chirona F jail
chirriante ADJ squeaky
chirriar[16] VI (puerta, freno) to squeak; (ave, freno) to screech
chirrido M (de puerta, freno) squeak; (de ave, freno) screech
chisgarabís M pipsqueak
chisguete M squirt
chisme M (noticia) gossip, piece of gossip; (objeto) *fam* gizmo, thingamajig
chismear VI to gossip
chismoso -sa ADJ gossipy; MF gossip
chispa F (partícula incandescente) spark; (ingenio) wit; **echar —s** to be furious; **pasar echando —s** to whiz by
chispeante ADJ (que echa chispas) sparkling; (ingenioso) witty
chispear VI (echar chispas) to spark; (lloviznar) to sprinkle
chisporrotear VI (leña) to sputter; (cigarrillo) to fizzle; (carne) to sizzle
chisporroteo M (de leña) sputter; (de carne) sizzle
chiste M (verbal) joke; (visual) cartoon; (ocurrencia) wisecrack; **— verde** dirty joke; **no le veo el —** I don't see the humor in it
chistera F top hat
chistoso ADJ funny, amusing, humorous
chivar VI/VT to snitch (on), to rat (on)
chivatar VI/VT to squeal (on), to snitch (on)
chivato -ta MF (delator) informer, snitch, stool pigeon; (chivito) kid
chivo M kid; **— expiatorio** scapegoat; **estar como un —** to be crazy as a loon
chocante ADJ shocking, jarring
chocar[6] VI (dar con) to bump, to collide; (estar en conflicto) to clash; VT (sorprender) to shock; (causar un accidente) to wreck; **— los cinco** to shake hands
chocarrería F coarseness

chochear VI to be in one's dotage
chochera F senility, dotage
chochez F senility, dotage
chocho ADJ senile; **estar —** to be in one's dotage; **estar — con** to dote on; M *vulg* cunt
choclo M ear of corn
chocolate M chocolate; (bebida) cocoa, hot chocolate; (hachís) *Esp* pot
chocolatera F chocolate pot
chocolatina F chocolate bar
chófer, chofer MF chauffeur, driver
cholo -la MF (mestizo) person of mixed race; (indio) Europeanized Indian
chopo M poplar
choque M (de objetos móviles) collision, bump, crash; (eléctrico, emocional, cultural) shock
chorizo M sausage
chorlito M plover
chorrear VI/VT (poco) to drip; (mucho) to gush
chorro M spurt, jet; **a —s** in buckets
chotearse VI **— de** to make fun of
choteo M mocking
chovinismo M chauvinism
choza F hut, shack, hovel
chubasco M squall, shower
chuchería F trinket, knick-knack
chueco ADJ *Am* crooked
chuleta F (papel para copiar) cheat sheet; **— de cerdo** pork chop; **— de ternera** veal cutlet
chulo -la M (proxeneta) pimp; (dandi) dandy, dude; (bravucón) tough guy; MF working-class resident of Madrid; ADJ (fanfarrón) boastful; (bonito) cute
chupada F (de cigarro) puff; (de bebida) sip
chupar VI/VT (succionar) to suck; (fumar) to puff (on); VT (absorber) to absorb; (vivir a costa de) to sponge off of; **chupársela** *vulg* to suck off; **chúpate esa** put that in your pipe and smoke it; M SG **chupasangre** leech
chupete M pacifier
chupetín M *RP* lollipop, sucker
churrasco M *Am* barbecued steak
churro M fritter
chusma F rabble, riffraff
chutar VI (drogas) to shoot up; (un balón) to shoot
chute M narcotic fix
chuzo M watchman's pike
CIA F CIA
cianotipo M blueprint
cianuro M cyanide
ciberespacio M cyberspace

cibernética F cybernetics
ciberpunk M cyberpunk
cicatero ADJ stingy
cicatriz F scar
cicatrizar VI to form a scar, to heal up
cíclico ADJ cyclical
ciclista MF bicycle rider, cyclist
ciclo M cycle; **—motor** moped; **— vital** life cycle
ciclón M cyclone
ciclotrón M cyclotron
cicuta F hemlock
ciego ADJ (que no ve) blind; (por borrachera) plastered; (por los efectos de drogas) high; **quedarse —** to go blind; **a ciegas** blindly
cielo M (firmamento) sky; (paraíso) heaven; **— abierto** open mining; **— raso** ceiling; **¡—s!** good heavens! **estar en el séptimo —** to be in seventh heaven; **me cayó del —** it's a godsend; **poner el grito en el —** *fam* to hit the ceiling
ciempiés M centipede
cien, ciento NUM hundred; **por ciento** percent
ciénaga F swamp, mire, marsh
ciencia F (campo de estudio) science; (conocimiento) knowledge; (arte) art; **— ficción** science fiction; **—s políticas** political science; **a — cierta** with certainty; **las — ocultas** the occult; **no tiene —** nothing to it
cieno M mud, mire, ooze
científico -ca ADJ scientific; MF scientist
cierre M (cosa para cerrar) clasp, fastener; (de cremallera) zipper; (acción de cerrar) closing, closure; **— patronal** lock-out; **al —** at press time
cierto ADJ certain; (verdadero) true; (seguro) sure; **en — sentido** in a sense; **hasta — punto** to a certain extent; **por —** by the way; INTERJ you're right!
ciervo -va M deer; (macho) stag; **— volante** stag beetle; F (hembra) doe, hind
cierzo M north wind
cifra F (0-9) digit; (número) figure; (clave) cipher, key; **poner en —** to encode
cifrar VT to write in code; **— la esperanza en** to place one's hopes on; **—se en** to amount to
cigarra F cicada
cigarrera F cigar case, cigarette case
cigarrillo M cigarette
cigarro M (de cigarette; (puro) cigar
cigoto M zygote
cigüeña F stork
cigüeñal M crankshaft

cilíndrico ADJ cylindrical
cilindro M cylinder
cima F summit
cimarrón -ona ADJ wild; MF runaway slave
címbalo M cymbal
cimbel M decoy
cimbrar VT to sway, to vibrate
cimentar VT (una casa) to lay the foundation of; (una victoria) to secure
cimiento M foundation
cinc M zinc
cincel M chisel
cincelar VT to chisel
cincha F cinch, girth
cinchar VT to cinch, to girth
cinco NUM five
cincuenta NUM fifty
cine M cinema, movies
cinematografiar VI/VT to film
cinematográfico ADJ **industria cinematográfica** motion-picture industry
cingalés -esa ADJ & MF Sri Lankan
cínico -ca ADJ cynical; MF cynic
cinismo M cynicism
cinta F (para adornar) ribbon; (adhesiva) tape; (cinematográfica) film; **— aislante** electrical tape; **— de vídeo** video tape; **— magnetofónica** recording tape; **— métrica** tape measure; **— rodante** treadmill; **— transportadora** conveyor belt
cinto M belt
cintura F (de persona) waist; (de cosa) middle
cinturón M belt; **— de seguridad** safety belt
ciprés M cypress
circo M circus
circonio M zirconium
circuitería F circuitry
circuito M circuit; **— cerrado** closed circuit; **— impreso** circuit board; **— integrado** integrated circuit
circulación F circulation; **poner en —** to circulate
circular VI to circulate; **hay que — por la derecha** you have to drive on the right; F circular letter
círculo M circle; **— vicioso** vicious circle
circuncidar VT to circumcise
circundante ADJ surrounding
circundar VT to surround
circunferencia F circumference
circunlocución F circumlocution
circunscribir[51] VT to circumscribe
circunspecto ADJ circumspect

circunstancia F circumstance
circunstancial ADJ circumstantial
cirio M candle
cirro M cirrus
cirrosis F cirrhosis
ciruela F plum; **— pasa** prune
ciruelo M plum tree
cirujano -na MF surgeon
cirujía F surgery; **— de corazón abierto** open-heart surgery; **— plástica / estética** plastic surgery
cisne M swan
cisterna F cistern
cita F (romántica) date; (con el médico) appointment; (textual) quotation, quote; **— a ciegas** blind date; **darse —** to meet
citación F citation, summons
citar VT (a un testigo) to summon; (a un autor) to cite, to quote; **—se con** (el médico) to make an appointment with; (un amigo) to make a date with
cítrico ADJ citric; M citrus
ciudad F city
ciudadanía F citizenship
ciudadano -na MF citizen
Ciudad del Vaticano F Vatican City
ciudadela F citadel
cívico ADJ civic
civil ADJ (no criminal, no religioso) civil; (no militar) civilian
civilidad F civility
civilización F civilization
civilizador ADJ civilizing
civilizar[9] VT to civilize; **—se** to become civilized
cizalla F metal shears
cizaña F **sembrar —** to sow discord
clamar VT to clamor for; **— por** to clamor for
clamor M clamor, outcry
clamorear VI/VT to shout
clamoreo M shouting
clamoroso ADJ clamorous
clan M clan
clandestino ADJ clandestine
claqué M tap dance
clara F egg white
claraboya F skylight
clarear VI (ponerse claro) to become clear; (amanecer) to grow light; (volverse menos espeso) to grow less dense; VT to illuminate; **—se** to grow light
claridad F clarity; (luz) brightness, lightness
clarificar[6] VT to clarify, to clear
clarín M bugle
clarinete M clarinet
clarividente ADJ & MF clairvoyant

claro ADJ clear; (franco) straightforward; (que tiene mucha luz) light, bright; **azul —** light blue; **a las claras** clearly; ADV clearly; INTERJ of course! M (espacio) gap; (en un bosque) clearing; **— de luna** moonlight

clase F (grupo social, sesión docente, conjunto de alumnos) class; (aula) classroom; (tipo) kind, sort; **— alta** upper class; **— obrera** working class; **— turista** economy class; **dar —** to teach a class; **toda — de** all sorts of

clasicismo M classicism

clásico ADJ (destacado, consabido) classic; (de un período histórico) classical; M classic

clasificación F classification; (deportiva) qualification

clasificado[6] M want ad

clasificar[6] VT to classify; (en deportes) to qualify; **—se para** to qualify for; **—se segundo** to come in second

claustro M cloister; **— de profesores** university faculty

claustrofobia F claustrophobia

claustrofóbico ADJ claustrophobic

cláusula F clause

clausura F closing

clavadista MF diver

clavado ADV exactly; M nailing

clavar VT to nail, to drive a nail into; (pinchar) to stick, to poke; **—le la mirada / los ojos a alguien** to stare at someone; **— los frenos** to stomp on the brakes; **me clavaron** I got a raw deal

clave F (sistema de signos) code; (tabla de correspondencias, base) key; (signo musical) clef; (clavicémbalo) harpsichord; (de mapa) legend; **— de fa** bass clef; **— de seguridad** password; **— de sol** treble clef; ADJ key

clavel M carnation

clavetear VT to put pegs on

clavicémbalo M harpsichord

clavícula F collarbone, clavicle

clavija F (de guitarra) peg; (de enchufe) pin

clavo M (pieza de metal) nail; (capullo) clove; (de zapato) spike; **dar en el —** to hit the nail on the head

claxon M car horn

clearing M clearing

clemencia F clemency, mercy

clemente ADJ forgiving

clerecía F (funciones de clérigo) ministry; (conjunto de clérigos) clergy

clerical ADJ clerical

clérigo M clergyman, minister

clero M clergy

clic M click; **hacer —** to click; **hacer doble —** to double-click

cliché M (placa fotográfica) photographic plate; (expresión muy usada) cliché

cliente MF (de un profesional) client; (de un negocio) customer; (de un restaurante) patron; (de un hotel) guest

clientela F clientele

clientelismo M patronage

clima M climate

climatización F air conditioning

clímax M climax

clinch M clinch

clínica F clinic

clip M paper clip

clítoris M clitoris

cloaca F sewer

clon M clone

clonación F cloning

clonaje M cloning

clonar VT to clone

cloquear VI to cluck

cloqueo M cluck, clucking

cloro M chlorine

clorofila F chlorophyll

cloroformo M chloroform

cloruro M chloride

club M club (también palo de golf); **— nocturno** nightclub

coacción F compulsion, coercion; **bajo —** under duress

coagular VI to coagulate; (sangre) to clot

coágulo M clot

coalición F coalition

coartada F alibi

coartar VT (una libertad) to restrict; (a una persona) to inhibit; (la creatividad) to strangle

cobalto M cobalt

cobarde ADJ cowardly; MF coward

cobardía F cowardice

cobertizo M shed

cobertor M cover

cobertura F (de nieve, aérea) cover; (de noticias, telecomunicativa) coverage

cobija F cover; (manta) blanket

cobijar VT to shelter; **—se** to seek shelter

cobra F cobra

cobrador -ora MF (persona que cobra) collector; M (perro) retriever

cobranza F collection

cobrar VT (impuestos) to collect; (una cuenta) to charge; (un cheque) to cash; (el sueldo) to earn; (víctimas) to claim; (adquirir) to gain; **— ánimo** to take heart; **— caro** to charge a lot; **— de más** to overcharge; **vas a —** you're in for it

cobre M (elemento) copper; (objetos de cobre) copper utensils

cobrizo ADJ copper-colored

cobro M collection

coca F (planta, hoja) coca; (cocaína) *fam* coke

cocaína F cocaine

cocear VI/VT to kick

cocer[2,10c] VI/VT (huevos) to boil; (verduras) to cook; (cerámica) to fire; **— al vapor** to steam; **a medio —** half-cooked; **romper a —** to break into a boil; **¿qué se cuece aquí?** what's up?

coche M (automóvil, vagón) car; (autobús) coach; (vehículo tirado por caballerías) carriage; **— bomba** car bomb; **— cama** sleeper; **—-comedor** dining car; **— de bebé** stroller, baby carriage; **— de bomberos** fire engine; **— de choque** bumper car; **— de línea** city bus; **— deportivo** sports car; **— fúnebre** hearse; **ir en —** to go by car, to drive; **pasear en —** to go on a drive

cochera F carport

cochinada F (acto asqueroso) filthy action; (acto perverso) dirty trick

cochinilla F woodlouse

cochino ADJ filthy; M pig

cocido M stew

cociente M quotient

cocina F (habitación) kitchen; (aparato para cocinar) range, stove; (arte de guisar) cuisine, cookery

cocinar VI/VT to cook; (tramar) to cook up

cocinero -ra MF cook

cócker MF cocker spaniel

coco M (fruto del cocotero) coconut; (cabeza) *fam* dome; (fantasma) bogeyman; **comerse el —** to get all worked up

cocodrilo M crocodile

cóctel M (fiesta) cocktail party; (bebida) cocktail, mixed drink

codazo M jab with the elbow; **dar —s to** elbow

codear VI/VT to elbow, to jab; **—se** to nudge one another; **—se con** to rub elbows with

codeína F codeine

codicia F (deseo de poseer) greed; (deseo sexual) lust

codiciar VT (una cosa) to covet; (sexualmente) to lust after

codicioso ADJ covetous, greedy

codificar[6] VT to codify, to encrypt

código M code; **— de barras** bar code; **— genético** genetic code; **— postal** zip code

codo M elbow; **— a —** side by side; **— de tenista** tennis elbow; **empinar el —** to

drink too much; **hablar por los —s** to talk one's head off; **hasta los —s** up to one's elbows

codorniz F quail

coeficiente M coefficient; **— de inteligencia** intelligence quotient

coerción F compulsion

coetáneo ADJ contemporary

coexistencia F coexistence; **— pacífica** peaceful coexistence

cofre M coffer

coger[11b] VT (a un criminal) to catch; (con las manos) to grasp; (flores) to gather; to pick; (a un empleado) to hire; (una emisora) to receive; (cosas del suelo) to pick up; (espacio) to take up; (un pez) to land, to catch; (un camino, tren, curso) to take; (poseer sexualmente) *Am vulg* to screw, to fuck; **— de sorpresa** to catch by surprise; **— el sueño** to fall asleep; **— hacia el castillo** to turn toward the castle; **—le miedo a algo** to get scared of something; **—le el tranquillo a algo** to get into the swing of things; **—se un resfriado** to come down with a cold; **coge y le dice** he ups and says

cognado ADJ & M cognate

cognitivo ADJ cognitive

cogollo M heart

cogote M neck

cohabitar VI to live (with); (sin casarse) to cohabitate

cohecho M bribe

coheredero -ra MF joint heir

coherencia F (consecuencia) consistency; (lógica) coherence

coherente ADJ (consecuente) consistent; (lógico) coherent

cohesión F cohesion

cohesivo ADJ coherent

cohete M rocket

cohetería F rocketry

cohibición F inhibition

cohibido ADJ inhibited, self-conscious

cohibir VT to inhibit

coincidencia F coincidence

coincidir VI to coincide

coito M coitus

cojear VI to limp; **saber de qué pie cojea alguien** to know someone's weaknesses

cojera F limp

cojín M cushion

cojinete M bushing; **— de bolas** ball bearing

cojo ADJ lame, crippled

cojones M PL (testículos) *vulg* balls, nuts; (valor) guts, grit; **estoy hasta los —** I've had it; **¿qué — quieres?** *vulg* what the hell do you want? **tener —** to be brave, to be impassive; **tu doctorado me lo paso por los —** *vulg* I don't give a shit about your doctorate

cojonudo ADJ (estupendo) cool; (valeroso) gutsy

cok M coke

col F cabbage; **— de Bruselas** Brussels sprouts

cola F (de perro, ave, avión) tail; (de vestido) train; (hilera de gente) line; (pegamento) glue; **— de caballo** ponytail; **hacer —** to stand in line; **no pegar ni con —** not to go together; **traer —** to have consequences

colaboración F collaboration

colaborador -ora MF (de periódico) contributor; (con el gobierno) collaborator

colaborar VI to collaborate; (con un periódico) to contribute

colación F **sacar a —** to bring up

colacionar VT to collate

colador M (para té) strainer; (para verduras) colander

colágeno M collagen

colapso M collapse

colar[2] VT (té) to strain; (metal líquido) to pour; VI to go through, to slip through; **esa excusa no va a —** that excuse won't wash; **—se en una fiesta** to crash a party

colateral ADJ collateral

colcha F bedspread

colchón M mattress; (recurso de emergencia) cushion

colchoneta F mat

colear VI (un perro) to wag the tail; (un tema) to be pending; (un auto) to fishtail

colección F collection

coleccionar VT to collect

coleccionista MF collector

colecta F charity collection

colectivo M (grupo) collective; (autobús) *Am* bus

colector M (de aguas negras) sewer; (eléctrico) collector; (de coche) manifold

colega MF INV colleague

colegio M (escuela privada) private school; (centro de enseñanza primaria) elementary school; (asociación de profesionales) association, college

colegir[5, 11] VI to gather

cólera F rage, wrath; **montar en —** to fly into a rage; M cholera

colérico ADJ irritable

colesterol M cholesterol

coleta F pigtail

coletilla F tag

coleto M **decir para su —** to say to oneself

colgadero M hanger; ADJ hanging

colgado ADJ high and dry

colgadura F drapery; **—s** hangings

colgante ADJ hanging; M pendant

colgar[2, 7] VT (suspender, ahorcar) to hang; (un teléfono, un abrigo) to hang up; VI (un espejo) to hang; (un andrajo) to dangle; (un asunto) to be pending; **esa falda te cuelga por atrás** that dress hangs down in the back; **—se (un ordenador)** to crash; **—se de** to get hooked on; **—se del teléfono** to tarry on the phone

colibrí M hummingbird

cólico M colic

coliflor F cauliflower

colilla F cigarette butt

colina F hill, knoll

colindante ADJ neighboring

colindar VI **— con** to border (on), to adjoin

coliseo M coliseum

colisión F collision

collage M collage

collar M (de perlas) necklace; (de perro) collar; **— antipulgas** flea collar

collera F horse collar

collie M collie

colmar VT (un vaso) to fill; (una demanda) to satisfy; **— de alabanzas** to lavish praise upon

colmena F beehive

colmillo M (de persona) eyetooth; (de elefante) tusk; (de víbora) fang

colmo M **— de la locura** height of folly; **¡eso es el —!** that takes the cake; **para —** to top it all

colocación F (ubicación) placement; (puesto) position

colocar[6] VT (poner, encontrar un puesto para) to place; (casar) to marry off; (invertir) to invest; **—se** (drogarse) to get stoned; (encontrarse empleo) to get a job

coloide M colloid

Colombia F Colombia

colombiano -na ADJ & MF Colombian

colon M colon

colón M (moneda de El Salvador y Costa Rica) colon

colonia F (territorio, grupo de insectos) colony; (comunidad de inmigrantes) community, settlement; (vivienda) development; (perfume) cologne

colonial ADJ colonial

colonización F colonization

colonizador -ora MF colonist

colonizar[9] VT to colonize, to settle

colono -na MF (habitante de una colonia) colonist, settler; (arrendatario) tenant farmer

coloquial ADJ colloquial

coloquio M colloquium

color M color; (pintura) paint; (maquillaje) rouge; (de naipes) flush; **—es primarios** primary colors; **a todo —** full color; **de —** of color

coloración F coloring

colorado ADJ & M red; **ponerse —** to blush

colorante ADJ & M coloring

coloreado ADJ colored; M coloring

colorear VT to color

colorete M rouge

colorido M (de un caballo) coloring; (de un comentario, paisaje) color; ADJ colorful

colosal ADJ (grande) colossal; (estupendo) wonderful

columbrar VT to glimpse

columna F column; **— de dirección** steering column; **— vertebral** spinal column, backbone

columnista MF columnist

columpiar VI/VT to swing

columpio M swing

colza F (planta) rape; (aceite) rapeseed oil

coma F (signo) comma; M (falta de conciencia) coma

comadre F (chismosa) gossip; (partera) midwife

comadreja F weasel

comadrona F midwife

comandancia F command

comandante M (rango militar) major; (militar que ejerce el mando) commander; **— en jefe** commander in chief

comandar VT to command; **— un avión** to pilot an airplane

comando M (militar) commando; (orden dada al ordenador) command

comarca F district

comatoso ADJ comatose

comba F (de una pared) bulge; (de madera) warp; **saltar a la —** to jump rope

combar VI (una pared) to sag; (madera) to warp

combate M combat; **fuera de —** out of the competition

combatiente MF combatant

combatir VI/VT to combat

combativo ADJ combative

combinación F combination; (billete) transfer ticket

combinar VT to combine; **—se para hacer algo** to agree to do something

combo M combo

combustible ADJ combustible; M fuel

combustión F combustion

comedero M trough

comedia F comedy; (farsa) farce; **— de situación** situation comedy, sitcom; **hacer la — de** to play the part of

comediante MF comedian

comedido ADJ moderate; *Am* obliging

comedirse[5] VI to show restraint; **— a hacer algo** *RP* to volunteer to do something

comedor M dining room; (de empresa) cantina

comensal MF fellow diner

comentador -ora MF commentator

comentar VI/VT to comment (on), to remark (on)

comentario M (análisis) commentary; (observación) comment, remark

comentarista MF commentator

comenzar[1,9] VI/VT to begin, to start; **— a comer** to begin to eat; **— comprando** to begin by buying

comer VI/VT to eat; (al mediodía) to eat lunch; (en ajedrez) to take; (en el juego de las damas) to jump; **dar de —** to feed; **sin —lo ni beberlo** through no fault of one's own; **—se** (ácido) to eat away; (completamente) to eat up; **—se las eses** to drop s; **—se las palabras** to eat one's words; **—se un semáforo rojo** to run a red light

comercial ADJ commercial

comercialización F marketing, merchandising

comercializar[9] VT (dar carácter comercial) to commercialize; (llevar al mercado) to market

comerciante MF merchant, trader, dealer

comerciar VI to trade

comercio M commerce, trade; **— exterior** foreign trade; **— minorista** retail trade

comestible ADJ edible; M **—s** groceries

cometa M (cuerpo celeste) comet; F (juguete) kite

cometer VT to commit

cometido M function

comezón F itch; **tener —** to itch

comic M comic book

comicios M PL polls

cómico -ca ADJ comic, comical; MF comedian

comida F (alimento que se toma de una vez) meal; (conjunto de cosas para alimentarse) food; (de mediodía) lunch; **— basura** junk food; **— macrobiótica** health food; **— rápida** fast food

comienzo M beginning; **a —s de** toward the beginning of; **al —** at first; **desde un / el**

— from the start

comilla F quotation mark; **entre —s** in quotes

comilón -ona MF big eater; F binge

comino M cumin seed; **me importa un —** *fam* I don't give a hoot; **no vale un —** *fam* it's not worth a hoot

comisaría F **— de policía** police station, precinct

comisario -ria MF (comisionado) commissioner; (jefe de policía) police chief

comisión F (acción de cometer, porcentaje ganado) commission; (conjunto de personas) committee

comisionar VT to commission

comistrajo M bad food

comisura F **— de los labios** corner of the mouth

comité M committee

comitiva F retinue

como ADV (del mismo modo que) as, like; **ella pinta — yo** she paints like I do; (aproximadamente) about; **pesa — diez kilos** it weighs about ten kilos; CONJ (puesto que) since; **— no tenemos dinero** since we have no money; **— no me pagues** if you don't pay me; **era — que muy viejo** he was, like, real old; **— que te voy a permitir** like I would let you; **— quieras** as you please; **— si** as if; **— si me lo fuera a creer** a likely story

cómo ADV INTERR & PRON (de qué manera) how; (¿perdón?) what? **¡— brillan las estrellas!** how the stars are shining! **¿— no?** of course; **¿a — me lo vende?** what does that cost?

cómoda F bureau, chest of drawers, dresser

comodidad F (cualidad de cómodo) comfort; (cosa cómoda) convenience; **—es** amenities

comodín M joker, wild card

cómodo ADJ (mueble) comfortable; (horario) convenient; (persona) lazy

Comoras F PL Comoros

compactar VT to compact

compacto ADJ compact

compadecer[13] VT to pity; **—se de** to take pity on

compadre M pal, crony

compañero -ra MF companion; (de un zapato) mate; **— de clase** classmate; **— de cuarto** roommate

compañía F company; **en — de** in the company of

comparable ADJ comparable

comparación F comparison

comparar VI/VT to compare; **—se con** to

compare with

comparativo ADJ comparative

comparecer[13] VI to appear

compartimiento M compartment

compartir VT (bienes) to share; (el tiempo) to divide

compás M (instrumento de dibujo) compass; (ritmo) beat; (espacio entre barras) measure, bar; (división de música en partes iguales) time signature; **marcar el —** to beat time

compasión F compassion

compasivo ADJ compassionate, sympathetic

compatible ADJ compatible

compatriota MF compatriot

compeler VT to compel

compendiar VT to summarize

compendio M digest, condensation

compenetración F bonding

compensación F compensation

compensar VT to compensate

competencia F (pugna, competición deportiva, conjunto de competidores) competition; (cualidad de competente) competence

competente ADJ competent

competición F athletic competition, meet

competidor -ora ADJ competing; MF competitor

competir[5] VI to compete, to vie

competitivo ADJ competitive

compilador M compiler

compilar VT to compile

compinche M chum, crony

complacencia F satisfaction

complacer[37] VT to please, to gratify; **—se (en)** to take pleasure (in)

complaciente ADJ (que complace) obliging; (que consiente) indulgent

complejidad F complexity

complejo ADJ complex; M complex; **— de inferioridad** inferiority complex

complementar VT to complement, to supplement

complemento M complement; **— alimenticio** dietary supplement; **— directo** direct object; **— indirecto** indirect object; **—s** fringe benefits

completar VT to complete; **—se** to be completed

completo ADJ complete; (baño, pensión, hotel) full; **hoy tenemos el —** today we have a full house; **por —** completely

complexión F build

complicación F complication

complicado ADJ complicated

complicar[6] VT to complicate; **—le a**

alguien la vida to give someone trouble
cómplice MF accomplice
complicidad F complicity
complot M plot
componenda F (arreglo provisional) quick fix; (arreglo ilegal) shady deal
componente ADJ & M component
componer[39] VT (un grupo) to compose, to make up; (imprenta) to set; (un coche descompuesto) to fix; (música) to compose; **—se de** to be composed of; **componérselas** to deal with one's problems alone
comportamiento M conduct, behavior
comportarse VI/VT to conduct oneself, to behave
composición F composition
compositor -ora MF composer
compostura F (arreglo) repair; (dignidad) composure
compra F purchase; **ir de —s** to go shopping
comprador -ora MF (persona que compra) buyer, purchaser; (persona que está de compras) shopper
comprar VT to buy, to purchase
comprender VT (entender) to understand, to comprehend; (abarcar) to cover, to include
comprensible ADJ comprehensible, understandable
comprensión F (intelectual) understanding, comprehension; (emocional) sympathy, understanding
comprensivo ADJ understanding
compresa F compress
compresión F compression
comprimido ADJ compressed; M tablet
comprimir VT to compress
comprobación F verification, check
comprobante M proof; **— de compra** proof of purchase
comprobar[2] VT (verificar) to verify, to check; (probar) to prove; (darse cuenta) to realize
comprometer VT (obligar) to commit; (poner en peligro) to jeopardize, to compromise; **—se** (prometer) to promise; (tomar partido) to commit oneself; (para casarse) to get engaged
compromiso M (ideología, obligación, promesa) commitment; (acuerdo) agreement; (cita) appointment, engagement; (de matrimonio) engagement; (solución) compromise; **no me pongas en —** don't compromise me; **sin — de compra** without obligation to buy
compuerta F sluice gate, floodgate
compuesto ADJ (ojos, tiempo, interés) compound; **estar — de** to be composed of; M compound
compulsión F compulsion
compulsivo ADJ compulsive
compungirse[11] VI to feel sorry
computación F computing
computadora F Am computer; **— personal** Am personal computer
computar VT to compute
computarizar[9] VT to computerize
cómputo M computation
comulgar[7] VI (recibir el sacramento) to take communion; (estar de acuerdo) to agree
común ADJ common; **en —** in common; **por lo —** generally; **el — de las gentes** the majority of the people
comuna F commune
comunicable ADJ communicable
comunicación F communication; (ponencia) presentation; **se nos cortó la —** we got disconnected
comunicar[6] VI/VT to communicate; **—se con** (entenderse) to communicate with; (tener acceso a) to open into; (ponerse en contacto con) to reach
comunicativo ADJ communicative
comunidad F community
comunión F communion
comunismo M communism
comunista ADJ & MF communist
con PREP with; **— lo que come, tendría que estar obesa** given what she eats, she should be obese; **— mucho** by far; **— que le digas alcanza** just telling him is enough; **— tal que** provided that; **— todo** all things considered
conato M minor problem
concavidad F hollow
cóncavo ADJ concave
concebible ADJ conceivable
concebir[5] VT (engendrar) to conceive; (explicarse) to conceive of
conceder VT (dar) to grant; (admitir) to concede, to allow
concejal MF councilor
concejo M council
concentración F concentration; (manifestación) rally, demonstration
concentrar VT to concentrate; **—se** (prestar atención) to concentrate; (manifestar) to rally
concepción F conception
concepto M concept; (literario) conceit
concernir[50] VT to concern
concertar[1] VT (arreglar) to arrange; (concretar) to finalize; (planear) to concert; **—se** to agree

concesión F (admisión) concession; (otorgamiento) grant; (permiso comercial) franchise

concha F shell; (genitales femeninos) *Am vulg* pussy

conchabarse VI to conspire

conciencia F (vida moral) conscience; (vida mental) consciousness; **tomar — de** to come to grips with

concienzudo ADJ conscientious, thorough

concierto M (música) concert; (armonía) harmony; (acuerdo) agreement

conciliar VT (personas) to conciliate; (ideas) to reconcile; **— el sueño** to get to sleep

concilio M council

concisión F conciseness

conciso ADJ concise, brief

conciudadano -na MF fellow citizen

concluir[31] VI/VT to conclude

conclusión F conclusion

concluyente ADJ conclusive

concomitante ADJ attendant

concordancia F agreement

concordar[2] VI to agree

concordia F concord

concretar VT (cerrar) to finalize; (especificar) to be specific about; (realizar) to realize; **—se a** to focus on

concreto ADJ concrete; **en—** specifically

concubina F concubine

concurrencia F gathering

concurrido ADJ well-attended

concurrir VI (confluir) to come together; (asistir) to attend

concursante MF contestant

concurso M (para un premio) contest; (como parte de una licitación) call for bids; (para un puesto de trabajo) competitive examination; **— de belleza** beauty pageant

concusión F graft

concusionario -ria MF grafter

condado M county

conde M count

condecoración F decoration

condecorar VT to decorate

condena F (castigo) sentence; (crítica) condemnation; **¡qué —!** what a pain!

condenación F condemnation

condenar VT (criticar) to condemn; (sentenciar) to sentence; **eso le condenó al fracaso** that doomed him to failure; **—se** to go to hell

condensación F condensation

condensar VI to condense

condesa F countess

condescendencia F (tolerancia) acquiescence; (superioridad) condescension

condescender[1] VI (acomodarse) to acquiesce; (dignarse) to condescend

condición F condition; **— social** social station; **a — de que** on the condition that; **condiciones** (físicas) condition; (de un contrato) terms, provisos

condicional ADJ & M conditional

condicionamiento M conditioning

condicionar VT to condition

condimentar VT to season

condimento M condiment, seasoning

condiscípulo -la MF classmate

condolencias F PL condolences; **dar las —** to offer one's condolences

condolerse[2] VI to offer one's condolences

condominio M condominium

condón M condom, rubber

cóndor M condor

conducente ADJ conducive

conducir[24] VT (a un grupo) to lead; (una orquesta, electricidad) to conduct; (un coche) to drive, to steer; **—se** to behave

conducta F (moral) conduct, behavior; (biológica) behavior

conducto M (de agua) conduit; (anatómico) duct; **por — de** through

conductor -ora M (de electricidad, calor) conductor; MF (de coches) driver

conectar VI/VT to connect

conejillo M **— de Indias** Guinea pig

conejo M rabbit; (genitales femeninos) *Esp vulg* pussy

conexión F connection

confabulación F collusion

confección F (fabricación) confection; (calidad) workmanship; **de —** ready-made

confeccionar VT to manufacture

confederación F confederation

confederado -da ADJ & MF confederate

confederar VI to form a confederacy

conferencia F (discurso) lecture; (reunión) conference; **— de prensa** press conference; **dar una —** to give a lecture

conferenciante MF lecturer

conferenciar VI to confer

conferencista MF lecturer, speaker

conferir[3] VT to confer, to bestow; (un título) to confer

confesar[1] VI/VT to confess

confesión F confession

confesionario M confessional

confesor -ora MF confessor

confiabilidad F reliability

confiable ADJ reliable

confiado ADJ (seguro de sí) confident;

(crédulo) trusting

confianza F confidence, trust; **en —** in confidence; **tener —** to be confident; **tener — en** to have confidence in; **tomar —s** to be overly familiar with

confianzudo ADJ over-familiar

confiar[16] VT (un secreto) to confide; (una cosa) to entrust; **— en** to rely on; **confío que Dios me proteja** I trust that God will protect me

confidencia F confidence

confidencial ADJ confidential

confidente MF confidant; M (mueble) love seat

configuración F configuration

confinamiento M confinement

confinar VT to confine

confines M PL bounds, confines

confirmación F confirmation

confirmar VT to confirm

confiscación F confiscation, seizure

confiscar[6] VT to confiscate

confitar VT to candy

confite M candy

confitería F confectionery

confitura F confection

conflicto M conflict

confluencia F (de calles) junction; (de ríos) confluence

conformar VT to adapt; **—se con** to settle for

conforme ADJ in agreement, content; **— a** in accordance with; **— amanece** as dawn breaks

conformidad F conformity, agreement; **estar de / en — con** to be in accordance with

conformismo M conformity

confort M comfort

confortable ADJ comfortable

confortar VT to comfort

confraternidad F fraternity, fellowship

confraternizar[9] VI to fraternize

confrontar VT (a un enemigo) to confront; (dos listas) to compare

confundido ADJ confused, mixed-up

confundir VT to confuse, to perplex, to baffle; **—se** (personas) to become confused; (cosas) to mingle

confusión F (mental) confusion; (de cosas) clutter, disarray

confuso ADJ (que no comprende, falto de orden) confused; (difícil de comprender) confusing

congelación F freezing

congelado ADJ frozen

congelador M freezer

congelar VT to freeze

congeniar VI **— con** to get along with

congénito ADJ congenital

congestión F congestion

conglomeración F conglomeration

conglomerado M conglomeration

Congo M Congo

congoja F anguish, grief

congoleño -ña ADJ & MF Congolese

congregación F congregation

congregar[7] VI to congregate

congresista MF (representante) member of Congress; (asistente a un congreso) conventioneer

congreso M (cuerpo legislativo, edificio) congress; (reunión periódica) convention

congresual ADJ congressional

congruencia F congruence

conífera F conifer

conjetura F conjecture, surmise

conjeturar VT to conjecture, to surmise

conjugación F conjugation

conjugar[7] VT to conjugate

conjunción F conjunction

conjuntivitis F conjunctivitis

conjunto M (grupo de cosas) set; (totalidad) total, aggregate; (de ropa) outfit; **— musical** ensemble; **en —** as a whole, all told; ADJ joint

conjuración F conspiracy

conjurado -da MF conspirator

conjurar VT (conspirar) to conspire, to plot; (alejar un daño) to ward off

conjuro M incantation, spell

conmemorar VT to commemorate

conmemorativo ADJ memorial

conmigo PRON with me

conmiseración F commiseration

conmoción F commotion; **— cerebral** brain concussion

conmovedor ADJ moving, touching

conmover[2] VT to move, to touch

conmovido ADJ moved, touched

conmutador M switch

conmutar VT to commute

connatural ADJ inborn

connotación F connotation

cono M cone

conocedor -ora ADJ who know(s); MF connoisseur, expert

conocer[13] VT to know (también en sentido carnal); (reconocer) to recognize; (tratar por primera vez) to meet; **— el paño** to know the ropes; **se conoce que** it is clear that

conocido -da ADJ well-known; MF acquaintance

conocimiento M knowledge, acquaintance; **— de embarque** bill of lading; **perder el —** to lose consciousness; **poner en —** to inform; **—s** knowledge

conque CONJ so

conquista F conquest

conquistador -ora MF conqueror; ADJ conquering

conquistar VT (un terreno) to conquer; (el amor de alguien) to win

consabido ADJ habitual

consagración F consecration

consagrar VT (declarar consagrado) to consecrate; (dedicar) to devote

consciente ADJ conscious; **— del problema** aware of the problem

consecución F attainment, achievement

consecuencia F (hecho que resulta de otro) consequence; (cualidad de consecuente) consistency; **a — de** as a result of

consecuente ADJ (que se sigue de) consequent, logical; (fiel en sus actos) consistent

consecutivo ADJ consecutive

conseguible ADJ obtainable

conseguir[5, 12] VT to get; (un objetivo) to achieve; (un puesto de trabajo) to land, to get; **— hacer algo** to manage to do something

consejero -ra MF (persona que da consejos) adviser; (miembro del consejo) board member

consejo M (opinión) counsel, advice; (comité) council; **— de guerra** court-martial

consenso M consensus

consentimiento M consent, acquiescence

consentir[3] VT (permitir) to consent to, to acquiesce to; (mimar) to pamper, to indulge; **— en** to permit

conserje MF (limpiador) janitor; (portero) superintendent; (recepcionista) hotel clerk

conserva F canned food; **en —** canned

conservación F conservation, preservation

conservador -ora MF (en política) conservative; (de museo) curator; ADJ (de las tradiciones) conservative; (de comida) preservative

conservadurismo M conservatism

conservante M preservative

conservar VT (guardar) to keep; (seguir teniendo) to retain; (no destruir) to preserve; (no malgastar) to conserve

conservatorio M conservatory

considerable ADJ considerable

consideración F consideration; **de —** considerable; **tomar / tener en —** to take into consideration

considerado ADJ considerate, thoughtful

considerar VT to consider

consigna F watchword

consignación F consignment

consignar VT to consign

consignatario -ria MF consignee

consigo PRON with oneself / himself / herself / themselves

consiguiente ADJ consequent; **por —** consequently

consistencia F consistency

consistente ADJ (que consiste) which consists; (firme) consistent

consistir VI **— en** to consist of

consocio -cia MF fellow member

consola F console

consolación F consolation

consolar[2] VT to console

consolidar VT to consolidate

consonante ADJ & F consonant

consorcio M consortium

consorte MF consort

conspicuo ADJ conspicuous

conspiración F conspiracy, plot

conspirador -ora MF conspirator, plotter

conspirar VI to conspire, to plot

constancia F (en el amor) constancy; (en el esfuerzo) perseverance; (en el trabajo) steadiness; (prueba) documentary proof

constante ADJ & F constant; **—s vitales** vital signs

constar VI to be stated; **— de** to consist of, to be composed of; **hacer —** to mention; **me consta que** I am aware that; **que conste** let it be known

constatar VT to verify

constelación F constellation

consternación F consternation, dismay

consternar VT to dismay

constipación F constipation

constipado ADJ *Esp* suffering from a cold; *Am* constipated; M *Esp* head cold

constitución F constitution

constitucional ADJ constitutional

constituir[31] VT to constitute

constitutivo ADJ (constituyente) constituent; (inherente) inherent; **— de un delito** which constitutes a crime

constituyente ADJ constituent

constreñimiento M constraint

constreñir[5, 18] VT (limitar) to constrain; (apretar) to constrict, to constrain

constricción F constriction

construcción F (acción y actividad de construir, cosa construida) construction, building; (gramatical) construction; **construcciones** building blocks

constructivo ADJ constructive
construir[31] VI/VT to construct, to build
consuelo M consolation, comfort, solace
consuetudinario ADJ (acción) habitual; (derecho) common
cónsul MF consul
consulado M consulate
consulta F (acción de consultar) consultation; (pregunta) question; (consultorio del médico) doctor's office
consultar VT to consult; **—lo con la almohada** to sleep on it
consultoría F consulting
consultorio M doctor's office
consumado ADJ consummate, accomplished
consumar VT to consummate
consumidor -ora MF consumer; ADJ consuming
consumir VT to consume; **—se** (agua) to boil off; (neumático) to wear out; **—se de** to be consumed by
consumismo M consumerism
consumo M consumption
consunción F consumption
contabilidad F accounting, bookkeeping
contable MF accountant, bookkeeper
contactar VI/VT to contact; **—(se) con** to get in contact with
contacto M contact; **en — con** in touch with
contado M **al —** in cash; ADJ **—s** few
contador -ora ADJ counting; M (de dinero) counter; (de electricidad) meter; **— Geiger** Geiger counter; MF accountant; **— público** certified public accountant
contaduría F accountant's office
contagiar VT to infect
contagio M contagion; (de ordenador) infection
contagioso ADJ contagious, catching, infectious
contaminación F (del agua, de la comida) contamination; (del medio ambiente) pollution
contaminante M contaminate
contaminar VT (agua, alimentos, cultura) to contaminate; (el medio ambiente) to pollute; **—se** (agua) to become contaminated; (medio ambiente) to become polluted
contar[2] VI/VT (medir una cantidad) to count; (decir historias) to tell; **el hotel cuenta con una piscina** the hotel has a swimming pool; **cuento con mi hermano** I count on my brother; **esto no cuenta** this doesn't count; **¿me lo vas a contar a mí?** you can say that

again; **mi padre cuenta 55 años** my father is 55 years old; **tienes que — con el tiempo** you have to watch the time; M SG **cuentakilómetros** (marcador de kilómetros) odometer; (velocímetro) speedometer
contemplación F contemplation
contemplar VT (mirar, tener en cuenta) to contemplate; (consentir) to spoil; VI to contemplate
contemporáneo ADJ contemporary
contender[1] VI to contend
contenedor M container
contener[44] VT (un líquido) to contain; (risa, lágrimas) to hold back; (entusiasmo) to restrain; (el aliento) to hold
contenido ADJ restrained; M content(s)
contentar VT to satisfy; **—se** to be satisfied
contento ADJ (conforme) content, contented; (feliz) happy; M contentment
contera F (de paraguas) tip; (de bolígrafo) cap
contestación F answer, reply
contestador M answering machine
contestar VT to answer; VI to talk back, to mouth off
contexto M context
contextura F makeup; (de persona) build
contienda F (guerra) conflict; (encuentro deportivo) competition
contigo PRON with you
contiguo ADJ contiguous; **estar — a** to adjoin
continental ADJ continental
continente M continent, mainland; ADJ continent
contingencia F contingency
contingente ADJ & M contingent
continuación F continuation; (de película) sequel; **a —** after that; **a — hubo una guerra** there ensued a war
continuar[17] VI/VT to continue
continuidad F continuity
continuo ADJ (ininterrumpido) continuous; (repetido) continual
contonearse VI (mujer) to swing one's hips; (hombre) to swagger
contoneo M (de mujer) swinging of the hips; (de hombre) swagger
contorno M (forma) outline, contour; (tamaño de árbol, persona) girth
contorsión F contortion
contra PREP against; M **el pro y el —** the pros and cons; **en —** against; F drawback; **llevar a alguien la —** to contradict someone
contraatacar[6] VI/VT to counterattack

contraataque M counterattack
contrabajo M double bass; MF INV double bass player
contrabandear VI/VT to smuggle
contrabandista MF smuggler
contrabando M (introducción de mercancías) smuggling; (mercancías introducidas) contraband; **hacer —** to smuggle
contracción F contraction
contrachapado M plywood
contractual ADJ contractual
contracultura F counterculture
contradecir[26b] VT to contradict
contradicción F contradiction
contradictorio ADJ contradictory
contraejemplo M counterexample
contraer[45] VT to contract; (limitar) to limit; **— matrimonio** to get married
contraespionaje M counterespionage
contrafuerte M (de muro) buttress; (de zapato) counter
contrahecho ADJ deformed
contralor -ora MF comptroller, controller
contralto M (voz) alto; MF (persona) alto
contramandar VT to countermand
contraoferta F counteroffer
contraorden F countermand
contrapartida F compensation
contrapelo LOC ADV **a —** against the grain
contrapesar VT to counterbalance
contrapeso M counterbalance
contraproducente ADJ counterproductive
contrariar[16] VT to annoy; **—se** to get annoyed
contrariedad F (fastidio) annoyance; (dificultad) snag
contrario ADJ (opuesto) opposite; (discrepante) conflicting; **al —** on the contrary; **de lo —** otherwise; **llevar la contraria** to be contrary; **por el —** on the contrary; **soy — al doblaje de películas** I'm against the dubbing of films; **todo lo —** just the opposite
contrarrestar VT to counteract
contrarrevolución F counterrevolution
contraseña F password, watchword
contrastar VI/VT to contrast
contraste M contrast
contrata F contract
contratación F hiring
contratar VT (a un empleado) to hire; (un servicio) to contract for; **—se** to be hired
contratiempo M mishap
contratista MF contractor, builder
contrato M contract
contravenir[47] VT to contravene

contraventana F shutter
contribución F (cosa contribuida) contribution; (impuesto) tax
contribuir[31] VT to contribute
contribuyente MF taxpayer
contrincante MF opponent
contrito ADJ contrite
control M (dominio, dirección) control; (médico) checkup; (vigilancia) check; (puesto) checkpoint; **— de calidad** quality control; **— de la natalidad** birth control; **— remoto** remote control; **bajo —** under control
controlador -ora MF comptroller
controlar VT (ejercer control) to control; (llevar a cabo un control) to check on
controversia F controversy
contumacia F obstinacy
contumaz ADJ stubborn
contusión F bruise
convalecer[13] VI to convalesce
convección F convection
convencer[10a] VT (por medio de la lógica) to convince; (por insistencia) to persuade
convencimiento M (creencia) conviction; (acción de convencer) convincing
convención F convention
convencional ADJ conventional
conveniencia F (lo cómodo) convenience; (lo aconsejable) desirability; **a su —** at your convenience
conveniente ADJ (cómodo) convenient; (aconsejable) advisable
convenio M agreement; **— colectivo** collective bargaining
convenir[47] VI (ser apropiado) to be suitable; (llegar a un acuerdo) to agree
convento M convent
converger[11b] VI to converge
conversación F conversation; **trabar — con** to engage in a conversation with
conversar VI to converse
conversión F conversion
converso -sa MF convert
convertible ADJ convertible
convertidor M converter
convertir[3] VT to convert; **—se en** to become
convexo ADJ convex
convicción F conviction
convicto -ta ADJ convicted; MF convict
convidar VT to invite; *Am* to offer
convincente ADJ convincing, compelling
convite M (invitación) invitation; (banquete) banquet
convocación F convocation
convocar[6] VT to convoke, to call together; (una reunión, un concurso) to convene

convoy M convoy
convoyar VT to convoy
convulsión F convulsion
conyugal ADJ conjugal, marital
cónyuge MF spouse
coñac M cognac, brandy
coñazo M (persona molesta, molestia) *vulg* pain in the butt; (cosa de mala calidad) *vulg* piece of crap
coño M *vulg* pussy, cunt; **en el quinto —** in the boondocks; INTERJ *fam* damn!
cooperación F cooperation
cooperar VI to cooperate
cooperativa F cooperative, co-op
cooperativo ADJ cooperative
coordenada F coordinate
coordinación F coordination
coordinado ADJ coordinate
coordinar VT to coordinate
copa F (vaso) goblet, wineglass; (de árbol) top; (de sombrero) crown; (palo de la baraja) card in the suit of copas; (trofeo, parte de un sujetador) cup; **ir de —s** to go for a drink
copete M (de pelo) tuft; (de plumas) crest; **estar hasta el —** to be fed up
copia F copy; (de foto) print; **— de seguridad** backup copy
copiadora F copy machine
copiar VT (reproducir) to copy; (en un examen) to cheat
copión -ona MF copycat
copioso ADJ copious, plentiful
copla F (canción) popular song; (estrofa) stanza
copo M (de nieve) snowflake; (masa de lana) wad; **—s de maíz** cornflakes
copropietario -ria MF joint owner
coprotagonista MF co-star
copular VI to copulate
copyright M copyright
coque M coke
coqueta F (mujer) coquette; (mueble) dressing table
coquetear VI to flirt
coquetería F flirtation
coqueto ADJ flirtatious
coraje M (valentía) courage; (enojo) anger
coral M (marino) coral; (musical) chorale
coralino ADJ coral
coraza F armor
corazón M heart; (de manzana) core; (vocativo) honey; **con el — en la boca** really tired; **de buen —** kindhearted; **de todo —** wholeheartedly; **romper el — a alguien** to break someone's heart
corazonada F hunch

corbata F necktie, tie, cravat
corcel M charger, steed
corchea F eighth note; **— con puntillo** dotted eighth note
corchete M (en costura) hook and eye; (paréntesis recto) square bracket; (llave) brace
corcho M (para botella) cork; (para pescar) float
corcova F hump, hunchback
corcovear VI to buck
cordel M string
cordero M lamb; (piel) lambskin
cordial ADJ cordial
cordillera F mountain range
cordón M cord; (al borde de la calle) *Am* curb; **— de apertura** rip cord; **— de zapatos** shoelace, shoestring; **— policial** police cordon; **— umbilical** umbilical cord
cordoncillo M ridge, rib
cordura F sanity
Corea F Korea; **— del Norte** North Korea; **— del Sur** South Korea
coreano -na ADJ & MF Korean
corear VI/VT to chant
coreografía F choreography
cornada F goring
cornear VT to gore
corneja F crow
corneta F cornet; M bugler
cornisa F cornice, ledge
corno M horn; **— francés** French horn
cornudo ADJ horned; M cuckold
coro M (grupo de cantantes) choir, chorus; (pieza de música) chorus; (parte de la iglesia) loft; **cantar a —** to sing in unison
corolario M corollary
corona F crown
coronación F coronation
coronar VT to crown
coronel M colonel
coronilla F crown of the head; **estar hasta la —** to be fed up
corpiño M bodice; (sujetador) *Am* bra
corporación F guild
corporal ADJ corporal, bodily
corpulento ADJ stout, corpulent
corpus M corpus
corpúsculo M corpuscle
corral M (de granja) barnyard, farmyard; (para ganado) corral, pen
correa F leather strap; (de ventilador) belt; (de perro) leash
corrección F (acción de corregir) correction; (cualidad de correcto) correctness
correcto ADJ (apropiado) correct, proper;

(acertado) right

corrector -ora MF editor; **— de pruebas** proofreader

corredizo ADJ sliding

corredor -ora ADJ running; MF (persona que corre) runner; (deportista automovilístico, ciclista) racer; (intermediario) broker, agent; M (pasillo) hallway, corridor

corregir[5,11] VT to correct; (exámenes) to grade; **—se** to mend one's ways

correlacionar VT to correlate

correlato M correlate

correo M mail; (edificio) post office; **— aéreo** air mail; **— certificado** certified mail; **— electrónico** e-mail; **echar al —** to mail

correoso ADJ tough

correr VI (persona, agua, calle) to run; (coche) to go fast; (una puerta) to slide; (dinero, tiempo) to pass; **— con los gastos** to take on the costs; VT (una cortina) to draw; (una carrera, un riesgo) to run; **—se** (moverse) to scoot over; (colores) to run, to bleed; (tinta) to smear; (tener orgasmo) *Esp fam* to come

correría F foray

correspondencia F correspondence

corresponder VI (ser adecuado, estar en consonancia) to correspond; (pertenecer) to belong; VT (amor, favores) to reciprocate; **a mí me corresponde llamarla** it's up to me to call her

correspondiente ADJ corresponding; MF correspondent

corresponsal MF correspondent

corretaje M broker's/agent's commission

corretear VI to run around

corrida F (acción de correr) running; (competición) race; (orgasmo) *Esp* orgasm; (de banco) run; **— de toros** bullfight; **de —** without stopping

corrido ADJ (que tiene mucha experiencia) worldly; (continuo) uninterrupted; **de —** without stopping; M ballad

corriente ADJ (que corre) running; (común) usual; (franco) frank; **el — mes** the current month; **estar al —** to be up-to-date; F (de agua, electricidad) current; (de dinero) flow; (de pesimismo) wave; (de aire) draft; **— alterna** alternating current; **— continua** direct current; **— del Golfo** Gulf Stream; **dejarse llevar por la —** to conform; **llevarle la — a alguien** to humor someone

corrillo M group of gossips

corro M circle of people

corroborar VT to corroborate

corroer[50] VT to corrode

corromper VT (a una persona) to corrupt; (un alimento) to rot; **—se** (una persona) to become corrupt; (un alimento) to rot

corrompido ADJ corrupt

corrosión F corrosion

corrupción F corruption

corrupto ADJ corrupt

corsé M corset

cortada F shortcut

cortador -ora MF (persona) cutter; F (aparato) cutter; **cortadora de césped** lawn mower

cortadura M cut

cortante ADJ (comentario, instrumento) cutting; (frío, viento) biting; (tono, instrumento) sharp

cortar VT to cut; (un vestido, el uso de algo) to cut out; (a un locutor, una rama, el gas) to cut off; (un árbol) to cut down; (las uñas) to clip; (el césped) to mow; **— el paso** to block; **— por lo sano** to take drastic action; M SG **cortacésped** lawn mower; **cortacircuitos** circuit breaker; **cortafuego** fire line; **cortapapeles** paper cutter; **cortaplumas** penknife; **cortauñas** nail cutter; VI (el frío) to bite; (la piel) to crack; **—se** (una persona) to be intimidated; (la leche) to curdle, to sour; **—se el pelo** to get a haircut

corte M (de un traje, herida) cut; (acción de cortar) cutting; (de televisión) commercial break; (estilo) style; **— de pelo** haircut; **— transversal** cross section; **— y confección** dressmaking; **eso me da —** that embarrasses me; F court; (séquito) retinue; **—s** Spanish parliament; **hacer la — to court**

cortedad F shortness

cortejar VT to court, to woo

cortejo M (séquito) entourage; (acción de cortejar) courtship

cortés ADJ courteous, polite

cortesano -na MF courtier

cortesía F courtesy

córtex M cortex

corteza F (de árbol) bark; (de pan, de la Tierra) crust; (de queso, fruta) rind; **— cerebral** cerebral cortex

cortijo M country house

cortina M (de ventana) curtain; (de lluvia) sheet; **— de humo** smokescreen

cortisona F cortisone

corto ADJ (bajo, no largo) short; (no inteligente) short on brains; (encogido) bashful; **—circuito** short circuit; **— de vista** short-sighted; **a — plazo** in the short run; **quedarse —** to come up short;

vestirse de — to wear a short dress; M short (film)

cosa F thing; **como quien no quiere la** — without realizing it; **como si tal** — as cool as a cucumber; **como son las —s** what a surprise; **decir una** — **por otra** to tell a lie; **esperamos** — **de cinco minutos** we waited about five minutes; **las —s como son** let's be honest; **las —s de la vida** that's life; **no es gran** — it's no big deal; **otra** — something else

cosecha F crop, harvest; **de su** — of his invention; **vino** — **1975** wine of 1975 vintage

cosechadora F combine

cosechar VT (cultivos) to harvest; (resultados) to reap

coser VI/VT to sew

cosignatario -ria MF cosigner

cosmético ADJ & M cosmetic

cósmico ADJ cosmic

cosmología F cosmology

cosmonauta MF cosmonaut

cosmopolita ADJ cosmopolitan

cosmos M cosmos

cosmovisión F worldview

coso M doodad

cosquillas F **hacer** — to tickle; **tener** — to be ticklish

cosquillear VT to tickle

cosquilleo M tickle

cosquilloso ADJ ticklish

costa F (del mar) coast, shore; **a toda** — at all costs; **—s** costs

Costa de Marfil F Ivory Coast

costado M side; **al** — alongside; **de** — edgewise; **por los cuatro —s** from all sides

costal M sack

costanero ADJ coastal

costar[2] VI/VT to cost; — **trabajo** to be difficult; — **un dineral** to cost a fortune; — **un ojo de la cara** to cost an arm and a leg

Costa Rica F Costa Rica

costarricense, costarriqueño -ña ADJ & MF Costa Rican

coste M cost; — **de (la) vida** cost of living

costear VT (pagar) to defray costs; VI to sail along the coast

costero ADJ coastal

costilla F rib; **lo hizo a —s de su padre** he did it at his father's expense

costo M cost; — **de (la) vida** cost of living

costoso ADJ costly

costra F (de pan) crust; (de herida) scab

costroso ADJ (de pan) crusty; (de heridas) scabby

costumbre F (manera habitual) habit; (uso tradicional) custom; **de** — habitual; **tener la** — **de** to be accustomed to

costura F (acción de coser) sewing; (línea de puntadas) stitching; (unión de dos piezas) seam; **alta** — high fashion

costurero -ra M (caja) sewing box; (sastre) tailor; F seamstress

costurón M large scar

cota F (nivel del agua) height above sea level; (estándar) benchmark

cotejar VT to check against

cotejo M comparison

cotidiano ADJ everyday

cotización F price quote / quotation

cotizar[9] VT to quote

coto M — **de caza** game preserve; **poner** — **a** to put an end to

cotorra F (loro) parrot; (persona) chatterbox

cotorrear VI to chatter

covacha F small cave

coyote M coyote

coyuntura F joint; **aprovechar la** — to take advantage of the situation

coz F kick; **dar coces** to kick

crack M (cocaína) crack; (deportista) ace

cráneo M cranium, skull

craso ADJ crass

cráter M crater

crayola® F crayon

creación F creation

creacionismo M creationism

creador -ora MF creator; ADJ creative

crear VI/VT to create

creativo ADJ creative

crecer[13] VI to grow; (masa, río) to rise; (madera, mar) to swell; (la luna) to wax

crecida F rise of a river

crecido ADJ (adulto) grown; (grande) large; (demasiado alto) overgrown

creciente ADJ (que crece) growing; (luna) crescent; M (luna) crescent; (marea) high tide

crecimiento M growth

credencial F credential

crédito M (solvencia, unidad de estudios) credit; (hecho de creer) credence; (fama) reputation; (préstamo) loan; **dar** — **a** to believe; **—s** film credits; **vender a** — to sell on credit

credo M creed

crédulo ADJ credulous, gullible

creencia F belief

creer[14] VI/VT (tomar como cierto) to believe; (opinar) to think, to feel; **—se** to fall for; **¿quién se cree que es?** who does he think he is? **se cree artista** he fancies himself an artist; **¡ya lo creo!** I should say so!

creíble ADJ credible, believable

crema F cream (también cosmético); **— de espárragos** cream of asparagus

cremallera F (de coche) rack; (de prenda) zipper; **— y piñón** rack and pinion

cremar VT to cremate

cremoso ADJ creamy

creosota F creosote

crepitación F crackle

crepitar VI to crackle

crepúsculo M twilight

crespo ADJ wiry, kinky

crespón M crepe

cresta F (de ola, montaña) crest; (de ave) tuft; (de gallo) comb

creyente MF believer; ADJ believing

cría F (acción de criar) breeding; (camada) litter; (animal joven) young

criadero M **— de peces** hatchery; **— de pollos** chicken farm

criado -da MF servant; F maid

criador -ora MF breeder

crianza F (de animales) breeding; (de hijos) upbringing; (modales) manners

criar[16] VT (animales) to breed; (hijos) to bring up, to rear, to raise; **estar criando malvas** *fam* to be pushing up daisies; **—se** to grow up

criatura F (ser extraño) creature; (bebé) baby

criba F sieve

cribar VT to sift

crimen M (delito grave) serious crime; (asesinato) murder; **— de guerra** war crime

criminal ADJ & MF criminal

criminalidad F crime

crin F mane

criollo ADJ (nacido en América) born in Spanish America; (tradicionalmente americano) traditionally Spanish American; M (lengua) Creole

críquet M cricket

crisálida F chrysalis

crisantemo M chrysanthemum

crisis F crisis

crisma F crown of the head

crisol M crucible, melting pot

crisparse VI (un músculo) to contract; (los puños) to clench; (los nervios) to be on edge

cristal M (mineral, vidrio de gran calidad) crystal; (vidrio de ventana) *Esp* glass, pane; (lente) lens; **— labrado** cut glass

cristalería F (objetos de cristal) glassware;

(establecimiento) glassware store; (fábrica) glassworks

cristalino ADJ (de cristal) crystalline; (transparente) crystal clear; M lens of the eye

cristalizar[9] VI/VT to crystallize

cristiandad F Christendom

cristianismo M Christianity

cristiano -na ADJ & MF Christian; **hablar en —** (claramente) to speak clearly; (español) to speak Spanish

criterio M criterion

crítica F criticism; (de un libro) review

criticar[6] VT to criticize

crítico -ca ADJ critical; MF critic; (de un libro) reviewer

criticón -ona ADJ critical; MF faultfinder

Croacia F Croatia

croar VI to croak

croata ADJ & MF INV Croatian

crocante ADJ crisp, crunchy

croché, crochet M crochet; **hacer —** to crochet

croissant M croissant

crol M crawl

cromado ADJ chroming

cromo M chromium, chrome

cromosoma M chromosome

crónica F (narración de eventos) chronicle; (reportaje) feature; **— policial** police report

crónico ADJ chronic

cronología F chronology

cronológico ADJ chronological

cronometrador -ora MF timer, timekeeper

cronometraje M timing

cronometrar VT to time

cronómetro M chronometer, stopwatch

croquet M croquet

croquis M rough sketch

cross M cross-country race

cruasán M croissant

cruce M (acción de cruzar, lugar donde cruzar) crossing; (de dos calles) crossroads, intersection; (de razas) crossbreeding; (animal procedente de una mezcla) cross; **— peatonal** crosswalk

crucero M (buque) cruiser; (viaje de placer) cruise

cruceta F crosspiece

crucial ADJ crucial

crucificar[6] VT to crucify

crucifijo M crucifix

crucigrama M crossword puzzle

crudo ADJ (comida, seda) raw; (tiempo, invierno, imágenes) harsh; (petróleo, lenguaje) crude; **agua cruda** hard water;

color — yellowish white
cruel ADJ cruel, mean
crueldad F cruelty, meanness
cruento ADJ grisly, gruesome
crujido M (de puerta, piso) creak; (de un tallo al quebrarse) crack; (de hojas) rustle; (de un fuego) crackle
crujiente ADJ (manzana, tocino) crisp, crispy; (nueces) crunchy
crujir VI (puerta, piso) to creak; (dientes) to grate; (hojas) to rustle; (nueces) to crunch; (fuego) to crackle
cruz F cross; (de moneda) tails; **hacerse cruces de** to dread
cruzada F crusade
cruzado -da MF crusader; ADJ (cheque) crossed; (fuego) cross; (traje) double-breasted
cruzamiento M (de piernas, razas) crossing; (de calles) crossroads; (de razas) cross
cruzar[9] VT to cross; (un cheque) to write across; **—le la cara a alguien** to backhand someone's face; **cruzo los dedos** I'll keep my fingers crossed; **—se con alguien** to bump into someone; **—se de brazos** to fold one's arms; **se me cruzó un ciervo** a deer crossed in front of me
cuaderno M notebook; **— de bitácora** logbook; **— de espiral** spiral notebook
cuadra F (establo) stable; (distancia entre calles) *Am* block
cuadrado ADJ square; **estar —** to be fat; M square; **es (un) —** he's a square; **dos al —** two squared; **elevar al —** to square
cuadrar VT (trabajar en ángulo recto) to square; VI (corresponder) to fit; (ser conveniente) to be convenient; (ser iguales) to balance, to add up; **— con** to be in agreement with
cuadricular VT to divide into squares
cuadrilátero ADJ quadrilateral; M (en boxeo) ring; (polígono) quadrilateral
cuadrilla F (de ladrones) gang; (de obreros) crew; (baile) square dance
cuadro M (cuadrado) square; (pintura) picture; (de bicicleta) frame; (de jardín) bed; (de tela) checker; (de fútbol) team; **— clínico** symptoms; **— sinóptico** table; **a / de —s** checked
cuadrúpedo ADJ & M quadruped
cuajada F curd
cuajar VI (leche) to curdle; (queso, cemento) to set; (gelatina) to jell; (un movimiento literario) to come about; **—se** to curdle; **la cosa no cuajó** that didn't pan out
cuajarón M clot

cual PRON REL which; **el / la —** (cosa) which; (persona) who; **lo —** which; **sea — sea** whichever it may be; ADV like; **— hoja al viento** like a leaf in the wind
cuál PRON INTERR which; **¿cuáles son los tuyos?** which ones are yours?
cualidad F quality
cualquiera ADJ INDEF any; **de cualquier manera / forma** anyhow; **en cualquier lado** anywhere; PRON INDEF (cosa) any; (persona) anyone; **— que sea su nacionalidad** whatever his nationality may be; **— que elijas** whichever one you choose; **— podría hacer eso** anyone could do that
cuando ADV REL when; **— la guerra** during the war; **— menos** at least; **— mucho** at most; **se rompió — lo usaba** it broke while she was using it
cuándo ADV INTERR & PRON when
cuantía F (cantidad) quantity; (importancia) importance
cuantificar[6] VT to quantify
cuantioso ADJ considerable
cuanto ADJ REL any; **lee — libro ve** she reads any book she sees; PRON REL **unos —s** a few; CONJ **hice — pude** I did as much as I could; ADV **— antes** as soon as possible; **más trabajo, menos consigo** the more I work, the less I accomplish; **en —** as soon as possible; **en — a** regarding; **en — que** as
cuánto ADJ, ADV & PRON INTERR (dinero, agua) how much; (personas, libros) how many; **¿cada —?** how often? **¿— piensas quedarte?** how long do you plan to stay?
cuarenta NUM forty; **cantarle las — a alguien** to bawl someone out
cuarentena F quarantine; **una — de libros** forty-odd books
cuarentón -ona MF person in his or her forties
cuaresma F Lent
cuarta F (marcha) fourth gear; (palmo) span of a hand
cuartear VT (una res) to quarter; (los labios) to chap; **—se** to chap
cuartel M barracks; **— general** headquarters; **no dar —** to give no quarter
cuartelada F military coup
cuartelazo M military coup
cuarteto M quartet
cuartilla F sheet of paper
cuarto ADJ one-fourth, quarter; M (cuarta parte) fourth, quarter; (habitación) room; (cantidad) quarter, one fourth; **— de**

baño bathroom; **— de estar** living room; **— de final** quarter finals; **— oscuro** darkroom; **¡ni que ocho —s!** no way! **tres —s** three fourths

cuarzo M quartz

cuásar M quasar

cuate M *Méx* pal, buddy

cuatrero -ra MF cattle rustler

cuatrillizo -za MF quadruplet

cuatro NUM four; **— ojos** four-eyes; **más de — ** a good number

cuba F (barril) cask, barrel; (tina) tub, vat

Cuba F Cuba

cubano -na ADJ & MF Cuban

cubeta F (recipiente triangular) tray; (balde) pail; **— de hielo** ice tray

cúbico ADJ cubic

cubículo M cubicle

cubierta F (de libro) cover; (cosa para cubrir) covering; (neumático) tire; (de buque) deck

cubierto M place setting; **— de plata** silverware; **a —** sheltered

cubismo M cubism

cubo M (cuerpo geométrico, tercera potencia) cube; (balde) bucket; (de rueda) hub; (juguete) building block; **— de basura** trash can

cubrir[51] VT to cover; (con carteles) to plaster; (una vacante) to fill; (con pintura) to coat; (con crema batida) to smother; (de niebla) to shroud; **—se** (nublarse) to fog up; (ponerse el sombrero) to put on one's hat

cucaracha F cockroach

cuchara F spoon; (de excavadora) bucket; (para helado) scoop; **— sopera** soup spoon; **meter la —** to butt in

cucharada F (lo que cabe en una cuchara) spoonful; (medida) tablespoonful; (de helado) dip

cucharadita F teaspoonful

cucharear VT to spoon

cucharita F teaspoon

cucharón M (para helado) scoop, dipper; (para sopa) ladle

cuchichear VI/VT to whisper

cuchicheo M whisper

cuchilla F (cuchillo grande) large knife, cleaver; (de afeitar, de licuadora) blade; (de patín) runner

cuchillada F (golpe) stab, slash; (herida) stab wound, gash

cuchillería F (conjunto de cuchillos) cutlery; (tienda) cutlery store

cuchillo M knife; **pasar a —** to kill with a knife

cuclillas LOC ADV **en —** squatting; **sentarse en —** to squat

cuclillo M cuckoo

cuco ADJ cute

cucú INTERJ cuckoo

cucurucho M (de papel) paper cone; (para helado) ice-cream cone; (capirote) hood

cuello M (parte del cuerpo) neck; (parte de una prenda) collar; **— de botella** bottleneck; **— uterino** cervix; **— vuelto** turtleneck; **estoy hasta el — en deudas** I'm up to my neck in debts

cuenca F (conjunto de tierras) basin; (cavidad del ojo) eye socket

cuenco M earthen bowl

cuenta F (cálculo) count, calculation; (factura) bill, check; (relación de ingresos y gastos) account; (bolita) bead; (depósito bancario) bank account; **— conjunta** joint account; **— corriente** checking account; **— de ahorros** savings account; **— de crédito** charge account; **— de gastos** expense account; **— regresiva / atrás** countdown; **abrir / cerrar una —** to open / close an account; **a fin de —s** when all is said and done; **ajustar —s** to settle old scores; **caí en (la) — de que** it just dawned on me that; **dar — de** to finish off; **dar —s** to give an accounting; **darse —** to realize; **en resumidas —s** in short; **eso corre por mi —** that is my responsibility; **habida — de** bearing in mind; **más de la —** more than necessary; **pasar la —** to call in a favor; **tomar / tener en —** to take into account; **trabajar por — propia** to freelance; M SG **cuentagotas** eyedropper

cuento M story, tale; **— chino** tall tale; **— de hadas** fairy tale; **— de nunca acabar** never-ending tale; **déjese de —s** come to the point; **traer a —** to bring up; **venir a —** to be to the point

cuerda F (soga) cord, rope; (parte de un arco) bowstring; (de guitarra) string; (de reloj) spring; **— floja** tight rope; **—s vocales** vocal cords; **bajo —** under-the-table; **contra las —s** on the ropes; **dar — a** to wind

cuerdo ADJ sane

cuerno M horn (también instrumento de viento); (de caracol) feeler; (de ciervo) antler; **— de la abundancia** horn of plenty; **coger el toro por los —s** to take the bull by the horns; **irse al —** *vulg* to go to hell; **poner —s a** to be unfaithful to

cuero M (piel de animal) hide; (piel curtida) leather; **— cabelludo** scalp; **en —s** naked

cuerpo M body; (torso) torso; **¡— a tierra!** hit the deck! **— de bomberos** fire department; **— de policía** police force; **— de prensa** press corps; **— docente** teaching staff; **a — de rey** in great luxury; **dar — a** to flesh out; **de — entero** through and through; **ganó por tres —s de ventaja** he won by three lengths; **ir de —** to have a bowel movement

cuervo M crow, raven

cuesta F slope; **— abajo** downhill; **— arriba** uphill; **a —s** piggyback

cuestión F question; **en — de** in a matter of; **poner en —** to question; **ser — de** to be a matter of

cuestionable ADJ questionable

cuestionador ADJ questioning

cuestionar VT to question

cuestionario M questionnaire

cueva F cave

cuidado M (atención) care; (preocupación) worry; **— con el perro** beware of the dog; **— de la casa** housekeeping; **al — de** in care of; **eso me trae sin —** I don't care about that; **tener —** to be careful; **un enfermo de —** a severely ill patient; INTERJ look out!

cuidador -ora MF caregiver, caretaker

cuidadoso ADJ careful

cuidar VT to take care of, to look after; **— de** to take care of; **— la casa** to keep house; **— niños** to babysit; **—se de** to beware of

culata F (anca) haunch; (de rifle) butt; (de motor) cylinder head

culatazo M (golpe) blow with the butt of a rifle; (rebote al disparar) recoil

culear VI/VT *Am vulg* to fuck, to screw

culebra F snake

culebrear VI to slither

culebrilla F shingles

culinario ADJ culinary

culminar VI to culminate

culo M (trasero) *vulg* ass, butt; (ano) anus; **— de botella** bottle bottom; **— del mundo** boondocks; **— veo, — quiero** I want everything I see; **caerse de —** to be astounded; **dar por el —** (fastidiar) to bother; (sodomizar) to sodomize; **hacer de —** to be lucky; **lamer —s** *fam* to suck up to someone, *vulg* to brown-nose; **rascarse el —** *vulg* to fart around; **romperse el —** *vulg* to bust one's ass

culpa F (responsabilidad) fault, blame; (sentimiento) guilt; **echar la — a** to blame; **por — de** because of; **tener la —** to be to blame

culpabilidad F guilt

culpable ADJ guilty; MF culprit

culpar VT to blame

cultivado ADJ (tierra) cultivated; (perlas) cultured

cultivador -ora MF (persona) cultivator; F (aparato) cultivator

cultivar VT (cosechas) to grow, to raise; (la tierra) to farm; (relaciones, inteligencia) to cultivate; (microbios) to culture

cultivo M (de plantas) growing; (de la tierra) farming; (de microbios) culture; (de relaciones) cultivation; **de —** cultured

culto ADJ educated, cultured; M worship; **libertad de —** freedom of religion

cultura F culture; **— general** general knowledge

cultural ADJ cultural

culturismo M body-building

cumbre F summit

cumplido ADJ (cortés) polite; (perfecto) perfect; M compliment; **hacer algo de —** to do something out of duty; **hacer un —** to pay a compliment

cumplimiento M (de un contrato) performance; (de una promesa, obligación) fulfillment; (de un plazo) expiration

cumplir VT (una obligación) to fulfill, to discharge; (una promesa) to keep; (una condena) to complete, to serve; **— diez años** to turn ten; **hacer —** to enforce; VI (acceder a las relaciones sexuales) to have sexual relations; (vencer) to expire; **— con** to meet a goal; **me cumple informarle que** it is my duty to inform you that

cúmulo M (grupo) host; (tipo de nube) cumulus

cuna F (que se puede mecer) cradle; (con barandas) crib

cundir VI (extenderse) to spread; (rendir) to go a long way

cuneta F roadside ditch; **en la —** out to pasture

cuña F (pieza para hender) wedge; (recipiente de excrementos) bedpan

cuñado -da M brother-in-law; F sister-in-law

cuño M die; **de — hispano** with a Hispanic stamp

cuota F (cantidad que le corresponde a uno) quota; (cantidad que hay que pagar) dues; (mensualidad) installment

cupé M coupé

cupo M (cantidad) quota; (capacidad) *Am* room

cupón M coupon

cúpula F dome

cura F cure, remedy; M priest
curable ADJ curable
curación F cure
curandero -ra MF healer
curar VT (una enfermedad, carne) to cure; (una herida) to heal; VI to heal; **—se** to heal; **—se en salud** to take precautionary measures
curiosear VI to look around; (en asuntos ajenos) to pry
curiosidad F curiosity
curioso ADJ curious
curita F *Am* adhesive bandage, Band-Aid™
currículum M résumé
curro M *Esp* job
curruca F warbler
curry M curry
cursar VT (un curso) to take; (un telegrama) to send
cursi ADJ (afectado) affected; (de mal gusto) tacky
cursivo ADJ cursive; **escribir en —** to write in cursive
curso M (de río, enfermedad, acontecimientos, moneda) course; (período docente) academic year; (grupo de estudiantes que siguen el mismo curso) class; (libro de texto) textbook; **— legal** legal currency; **el mes en —** the current month
cursor M cursor
curtiduría F tannery
curtiembre F tannery
curtir VT (cuero) to tan; (cutis) to weather; (hacer adquirir experiencia) to harden; **—se** (envejecerse) to get weathered; (acostumbrarse a las dificultades) to become accustomed to hardships
curva F curve
curvatura F curvature
curvo ADJ curved
cúspide F summit
custodia F custody, keeping; **en —** in escrow
custodiar VT to guard
custodio -dia MF guardian
cutícula F cuticle
cutis M facial skin
cuyo ADJ REL whose
cyborg M cyborg

Dd

dádiva F gift
dadivoso ADJ generous

dado ADJ given; M die; **jugar a los —s** to throw dice
dador -ora MF giver; **— de sangre** blood donor
daga F dagger
dalia F dahlia
daltónico ADJ color-blind
dama F lady; (en el juego de la dama) king; **jugar a las —s** to play checkers; **— de honor** bridesmaid
damajuana F demijohn
damasco M (fruta) apricot; (árbol) apricot tree
damisela F damsel
dandi M dandy
danés -esa ADJ Danish; MF Dane; M (lengua) Danish
danza F dance; **— del vientre** belly dance; **en —** in action
danzante MF dancer
danzar[9] VI/VT to dance
dañar VT to harm, to damage; **—se** to suffer harm
dañino ADJ harmful
daño M damage, harm; **— emergente** actual damage; **— físico** bodily harm; **—s y perjuicios** damages; **hacer —** to harm
dañoso ADJ harmful
dar[25] VT (un regalo) to give; (un golpe, naipes) to deal; (sal) to add; (una fiesta) to throw; (la hora) to strike; (un olor) to give off; (la alarma) to raise; (un paseo) to take; **— a** (un edificio) to face; (una calle) to lead to; **— a conocer** to announce; **— a entender** to intimate; **— con** to hit upon, to find; **— de alta** to discharge, to release from the hospital; **— de baja** to discharge; **— de comer** to feed; **— de sí** to perform at capacity; **esta tela da de sí** this fabric gives; **— en la pared** to hit the wall; **—le con** to scrub with; **lo misma da** it makes no difference; **¿qué más da?** what difference does it make? **dale que dale** on and on; **hoy no doy una** today I can't get anything right; **le doy cincuenta años** he must be about fifty; **me da rabia / miedo** that makes me angry / afraid; **no me da el tiempo para ir al cine** I don't have time to go to the movie; **que no le dé el sol** don't let the sun shine on it; **y dale** enough already; **—se** to be found; **—se a** to indulge in; **—se por conforme** to be satisfied; **dárselas de** to boast of being
dardo M dart
dársena F dock
datar VT to date; **— de** to date from

dátil M date

dato M piece of information; **—s** data

de PREP **— la familia** of the family; **— Madrid** from Madrid; **habló — la guerra** he talked about the war; **el hombre — gafas** the man with glasses; **el mejor estudiante — la clase** the best student in the class; **fácil — hacer** easy to do; **más — tres** more than three; **llevar — la mano** to lead by the hand; **— regreso a España** upon returning to Spain; **— venta en farmacias** on sale in pharmacies; **ancianos — respeto** older people to be respected; **— lo más lindo** really pretty; **tonto — mí** silly me

deambular VI to amble, to saunter

deán M dean

debacle M debacle

debajo ADV under, underneath; PREP **— de** under, below; **por — de** under

debate M debate

debatir VT to debate; **—se** to struggle

debe M debit

deber V AUX **deben apoyarme** they should support me; **debe de ser** it must be; **deberías sentarte** you should sit down; VT to owe; **me debes una** you owe me one; **me debo a mis alumnos** I'm devoted to my students; M duty; **—es** homework

debidamente ADV duly

debido ADJ due; **— a** due to, owing to; **a su — tiempo** in due time

débil ADJ (que tiene poca fuerza) weak; (endeble) frail, feeble; (sonido) faint

debilidad F weakness; (cualidad de endeble) frailty; (de un sonido) faintness

debilitamiento M weakening

debilitar VT to weaken, to debilitate

débito M debit

debutar VI to make a debut

década F decade

decadencia F (moral) decadence, decay; (cultural, económica) decline

decadente ADJ decadent

decaer[23] VI (fuerza) to weaken; (energía) to ebb; (salud) to fail; (ánimo) to flag

decaimiento M (decadencia) decline; (debilidad) weakness

decano -na ADJ senior; MF dean

decapitar VT to behead, to decapitate

decatlón M decathlon

decencia F decency

decenio M decade

decente ADJ decent; **muy —** rather good

decepción F disappointment

decepcionante ADJ disappointing

decepcionar VT to disappoint

decibelio M decibel

decidido ADJ resolute, determined; **una decidida preferencia** a decided preference

decidir VI/VT to decide; **—se** to make up one's mind; **—se a** to resolve to

deciduo ADJ deciduous

décima F tenth

decimal ADJ decimal

décimo ADJ & M tenth

decir[26] VT (palabras, oraciones) to say; (una mentira, un chiste, la verdad) to tell; **— tonterías** to talk nonsense; **con —te que** suffice it to say that; **este tipo no me dice nada** this guy leaves me cold; **¿que me lo digan a mí?** you're telling me that? VI to say; **diga** hello (al contestar el teléfono); **es —** that is to say; **he dicho** I have spoken; **no es prometedor que digamos** it's hardly promising; **no me digas** you don't say; **querer —** to mean; M saying

decisión F decision; **tomar una —** to make a decision

decisivo ADJ decisive

declaración F (de amor, independencia, guerra) declaration; (de un hecho) statement; (de un testigo) deposition; **— de derechos** bill of rights; **— de impuestos / de la renta** tax return; **— jurada** affidavit

declarar VT (amor, independencia, ingresos) to declare; (un hecho) to state; **— culpable** to find guilty; **os declaro marido y mujer** I pronounce you man and wife; VI (como testigo) to testify; **—se** (un amante) to declare one's love; **—se culpable** to plead guilty; **—se en huelga** to go on strike; **—se en quiebra** to declare bankruptcy

declinar VI/VT to decline

declive M (pendiente) slope, drop; (decadencia) decline

decoración F decoration; **— de interiores** interior decorating

decorado M (de una casa) decoration; (de un escenario) scenery

decorar VT to decorate

decorativo ADJ decorative

decoro M decorum, propriety

decoroso ADJ decorous, proper

decrépito ADJ decrepit

decretar VT to decree

decreto M (disposición ejecutiva) decree; (ley) act

dedal M thimble

dedicación F dedication

dedicar[6] VT (la vida) to dedicate, to devote; (un libro) to dedicate; **—se** to dedicate oneself; (a los estudios) to apply oneself

dedicatoria F dedication

dedo M (de la mano) finger; (del pie) toe; **— anular** ring finger; **— índice** index finger; **— mayor / del corazón** middle finger; **— meñique** little finger; **— pulgar** thumb; **chuparse el —** to be a fool; **chuparse los —s** to lick one's fingers; **cruzar los —s** to keep one's fingers crossed; **elegir a —** to appoint directly; **hacer —** to hitch a ride; **no mover un —** not to lift a finger

deducción F deduction

deducible ADJ deductible

deducir[24] VT (concluir) to deduce, to conclude; (descontar) to deduct

defecar[6] VI/VT to defecate

defección F defection

defecto M defect, flaw

defectuoso ADJ defective, faulty

defender[1] VT to defend; (una causa) to champion; (los derechos) to stand up for, to stick up for; **se defiende en francés** he can hold his own in French

defendible ADJ defensible

defensa F defense; **aprende — personal** he's learning self-defense; **lo dijo en — propia** he said it in self-defense

defensivo ADJ defensive; **a la defensiva** on the defensive

defensor -ora MF defender; (de una causa) champion

deferencia F deference

deficiencia F deficiency

deficiente ADJ deficient

déficit M deficit

definición F definition

definido ADJ definite

definir VT to define

definitivo ADJ (superior) definitive; (final) final; **en definitiva** all things considered

deflación F deflation

deflector M baffle

deforestación F deforestation

deformación F deformation

deformar VT to deform; **—se** to become deformed

deforme ADJ deformed

deformidad F deformity

defraudar VT (cometer fraude) to defraud; (decepcionar) to disappoint

defunción F death

degenerado -da ADJ & MF degenerate

degenerar VI to degenerate

degollar[2] VT to slash someone's throat

degradación F degradation

degradar VT (envilecer) to degrade, to debase; (rebajar el rango) to demote; **—se** to degrade

degüello M throat-slashing; **lucha a —** fight to the death

dehesa F pasture

deidad F deity

dejadez F slovenliness

dejado ADJ slovenly

dejar VT (abandonar, no comer, legar) to leave; (a un enamorado) to leave, to dump; (permitir) to let; (soltar) to let go; **— de** to stop; **— caer** to drop; **déjame en paz** leave me alone; **me dejó atónito** it left / rendered me speechless; **no dejes de venir** don't fail to come; **te lo dejo en mil dólares** I'll sell it to you for one thousand dollars; **—se** to let oneself go; **—se crecer la barba** to grow a beard; **déjate de joder** give me a break

deje M slight accent

dejo M (sabor) aftertaste; (acento) slight accent; (toque) hint; **tener un — de** to smack of

delantal M apron

delante ADV in front; **— de** in front of, ahead of

delantera F (de carrera) lead; (de vestido) front; **llevar la —** to be in the lead; **tomar la —** to take the lead

delantero ADJ (pata) front; (línea) forward; M front

delatar VT to inform against, to squeal on; **— la edad** to betray one's age

delator -ora MF accuser, informer

delegación F delegation

delegado -da MF delegate

delegar[7] VT to delegate

deleitar VT to delight; **—se en algo** to revel in something; **—se la vista con** to feast one's eyes on

deleite M delight

deletrear VT to spell; **— mal** to misspell

deleznable ADJ despicable

delfín M dolphin

delgadez F thinness

delgado ADJ thin, slender, slim

deliberación F deliberation

deliberado ADJ deliberate

deliberar VI/VT to deliberate

delicadeza F (tacto) gentleness; (fineza) delicacy; **con —** gently; **tuvo la — de llamar** he was kind enough to call

delicado ADJ (suave, fácil de romper, controvertido) delicate; (enfermizo) frail;

(exquisito) dainty; (quisquilloso) squeamish

delicatessen F PL delicacies

delicia F delight

delicioso ADJ delicious, delectable

delimitar VT to delimit

delincuencia F crime

delincuente ADJ & MF delinquent, criminal; **— juvenil** juvenile delinquent

delineador M eyeliner

delinear VT to delineate, to outline

delirante ADJ delirious, raving

delirar VI to be delirious, to rave

delirio M delirium; **— paranoico** paranoid delusion; **—s de grandeza** delusions of grandeur

delito M crime, offense

demacrado ADJ drawn, gaunt, haggard

demagogo -ga MF demagog

demanda F (de mercancías) demand; (de seguros) insurance claim; (pleito) lawsuit; **por —** on demand; **entablar una —** to file a lawsuit

demandado -da MF defendant

demandante MF plaintiff

demandar VT (pedir) to ask for; (poner pleito) to sue, to file a suit against

demarcar[6] VT to demarcate

demás ADJ (restante) remaining; PRON the others, the rest; **lo —** the rest; **y —** and whatnot; ADV **por lo —** moreover; **por —** useless

demasía LOC ADV **en —** excessively

demasiado ADV too; too much; **eso es — para mí** that's too much for me; **él es — alto** he's too tall; ADJ too much; too many; **— dinero** too much money; **demasiadas cosas** too many things

demencia F (locura) insanity; (senilidad) senility

demente ADJ demented, insane, deranged

democracia F democracy

demócrata MF INV democrat

democrático ADJ democratic

demografía F demographics

demográfico ADJ demographic

demoler[2] VT to demolish, to tear down

demonio M demon; **al — con los libros** vulg to hell with books; **mandar al —** vulg to tell someone to go to hell; **¿qué —s haces?** what the heck are you doing? **un frío de —s** bitter cold

demora F delay

demorar VT to delay; **—se** to linger

demostración F demonstration; **— de fuerza** show of force

demostrar[2] VT (mostrar) to demonstrate, to show; (hacer ver la verdad) to prove, to demonstrate

demostrativo ADJ demonstrative

demudar VT to change, to alter

denigrar VT to denigrate, to disparage

denodado ADJ untiring

denominación F (valor) denomination; (nombre) designation

denominar VT to designate, to term

denostar[2] VT to revile

denotación F denotation

denotar VT to denote

densidad F density

denso ADJ dense; (líquido) heavy

dentado ADJ (rueda) toothed; (montaña) ragged

dentadura F set of teeth; **— postiza** false teeth

dental ADJ dental

dentellada F (mordedura) bite; (señal de diente) tooth mark; **a —s** biting

dentífrico M dentifrice

dentista MF dentist

dentro ADV inside; PREP **— de la casa** inside the house; **— de la ley** within the law; **— de quince días** (en el plazo de) within two weeks; (al cabo de) in two weeks; **por — within**

denuncia F (acusación) denunciation; (de mina, de seguro) claim

denunciar VT (un hecho negativo) to denounce; (una mina) to claim; (un delito) to report

deparar VT to have in store for

departamento M (división) department; (piso) small apartment

departir VI lit to commune

dependencia F (hecho de depender) dependence; (habituación) dependency; (filial) branch office

depender VI to depend; **— de** to depend on

dependiente -ta ADJ dependent; MF clerk

depilar VT to remove hair

depilatorio ADJ & M depilatory

deplorable ADJ deplorable

deplorar VT to deplore

deponer[39] VT (las armas) to lay down; (a un ministro) to depose; VI to defecate

deportar VT to deport

deporte M sport; **me gusta el —** I like sports / athletics

deportista ADJ athletic; MF athlete

deportivo ADJ athletic; **revista deportiva** sports magazine

deposición F (de un testigo) deposition; (de un ministro) removal; (movimiento de

vientre) bowel movement
depositante MF depositor
depositar VT to deposit; **—se** to settle
depositario -ria MF repository
depósito M (en el banco) deposit; (de
gasolina) tank; (de agua) reservoir; (de
cadáveres) morgue; (de armas) depot,
dump; (de mercancías) stock room,
storehouse; **hacer un —** to make a
deposit; **en —** on consignment
depravado ADJ depraved
depreciar VI to depreciate
depredador -ora MF predator
depresión F depression
deprimente ADJ depressing
deprimido ADJ depressed
deprimir VT to depress
deprisa ADV quickly
depuración F purification; (de un programa)
debugging
depurar VT to purify; (un programa) to
debug
derby M derby
derecha F (política) right wing; **a la —** to
the right; **de —s** right-wing
derechista ADJ right-wing; MF rightist
derecho ADJ (no izquierdo) right; (recto)
straight; **ponerse —** to hold oneself erect;
ADV straight; **volver — a casa** to go
straight home; **todo —** straight ahead; M
(preceptos, disciplina) law; (posibilidad
legal) right; **— consuetudinario**
common law; **— de admisión** fee; **—
internacional** international law; **—s**
fees; **—s aduaneros** tax on imports; **—s
civiles** civil rights; **—s de autor**
copyright; **—s de la mujer** women's
rights; **—s de los animales** animal
rights; **estar en su —** to be entitled;
poner al — to put on right side out;
registrar los —s to copyright
derechura F straightness
deriva F drift; **ir a la —** to be adrift
derivación F derivation
derivado M (subproducto) by-product;
(palabra) derivative
derivar VT to derive
dermatología F dermatology
dermatólogo -ga MF dermatologist
derogación F repeal
derogar[7] VT to repeal
derramamiento M spill, spilling; **— de
sangre** bloodshed
derramar VT (un líquido) to spill; (sangre,
lágrimas) to shed; **—se** to spill over, to
run over
derrame M spill; **— cerebral** stroke, cerebral

hemorrhage
derredor LOC ADV **en —** all around
derrengar[7] VT (dañar la espalda) to sprain
one's back; (cansar) to exhaust
derretir[5] VT to melt; **—se por alguien** to
be crazy about someone
derribar VT (un edificio) to demolish, to tear
down; (a una persona) to knock down;
(un gobierno) to topple, to overthrow; (un
avión) to shoot down, to down
derrocamiento M overthrow
derrocar[6] VT (un gobierno) to overthrow, to
topple; (a un dictador) to depose
derrochador -ora ADJ extravagant; MF (de
dinero) spendthrift; (de recursos)
squanderer
derrochar VT (dinero) to squander; (salud) to
radiate
derroche M (de recursos) waste,
extravagance; (de color) profusion
derrota F defeat
derrotar VT to defeat
derrotero M course
derrubio M washout
derruido ADJ dilapidated
derrumbadero M precipice
derrumbamiento M collapse
derrumbar VT to demolish; **—se** (edificio) to
collapse; (túnel, caverna) to cave in
derrumbe M (de tierra) landslide; (de un
edificio) collapse
desabotonar VT to unbutton, to undo
desabrido ADJ (comida) tasteless; (persona)
Am dull; *Esp* surly
desabrigado ADJ exposed
desabrochado ADJ undone, unfastened
desabrochar VT to undo; (ganchos) to
unhook; (hebillas, cinturones) to
unbuckle; (botones) to unbutton; **—se** to
come undone
desacato M disrespect; **— al tribunal**
contempt of court
desacelerar VI to decelerate
desacierto M mistake
desaconsejable ADJ inadvisable
desaconsejar VT to caution against
desacoplar VT to uncouple, to disconnect
desacostumbrado ADJ unusual
desacostumbrar VT to break of a habit; **—se**
to lose a habit
desacreditar VT to discredit
desactivar VT (explosivo, situación) to
defuse; (mecanismo) to disable; (virus) to
deactivate
desacuerdo M disagreement; **estar en —** to
be at odds
desafiar[16] VT (retar) to challenge, to dare;

(enfrentar) to defy
desafilado ADJ dull
desafilar VT to dull; **—se** to become dull
desafinado ADJ out of tune, off-key
desafinar VT to be out of tune
desafío M (reto) challenge; (desobediencia) defiance
desafortunado ADJ unfortunate, unlucky
desafuero M (de un diputado) withdrawal of immunity; (ultraje) outrage
desagradable ADJ disagreeable, unpleasant
desagradar VT to displease
desagradecido ADJ ungrateful
desagrado M displeasure
desagraviar VI to make amends, to redress
desagravio M redress
desaguadero M drainpipe
desaguar[8] VI to drain
desagüe M (acción de desaguar) drainage; (de lavabo) drain, drainpipe; (en la azotea) gutter
desaguisado M mess
desahogado ADJ (cómodo) comfortable; (espacioso) spacious
desahogar[7] VT (aliviar) to relieve; (expresar) to pour out one's feelings
desahogo M relief; **vivir con —** to live an easy life
desairar VT to slight, to snub, to rebuff
desaire M slight, snub, rebuff
desajustar VT to loosen; **—se** to come loose
desalentado ADJ despondent
desalentador ADJ disheartening
desalentar[1] VT to discourage, to dishearten; **—se** to get discouraged
desaliento M discouragement, dismay
desaliñado ADJ disheveled, slovenly, unkempt
desaliño M slovenliness
desalmado ADJ heartless
desalojar VT (una piedra) to dislodge; (un tribunal) to clear; (por peligro) to evacuate; (por no pagar) to evict; (dejar vacío) to vacate
desamparado ADJ helpless, forlorn
desamparar VT to forsake
desamparo M abandonment, helplessness
desamueblado ADJ unfurnished
desangrar VT to bleed
desanimado ADJ (persona) discouraged; (jornada) dull
desanimar VT to discourage
desánimo M discouragement
desaparecer[13] VI to disappear, to vanish; (morir) to pass away
desaparición F disappearance; (muerte) demise

desapasionado ADJ dispassionate
desapego M detachment
desapercibido ADJ unnoticed
desaprobación F disapproval
desaprobar[2] VT to disapprove of
desarmado ADJ unarmed
desarmar VT (quitar las armas) to disarm; (desmontar) to take apart
desarme M disarmament
desarraigar[7] VT to uproot
desarreglar VT to disturb, to mess up
desarreglo M (nervioso) disorder; (falta de arreglo) mess
desarrollar VT (aumentar) to develop; (extender algo arrollado) to unroll; (llevar a cabo) to carry out; (aclarar) to elaborate, to flesh out; **—se** to unfold
desarrollo M development; (de una ecuación) expansion; **en —** developing
desarticulado ADJ disjointed
desaseado ADJ slovenly
desaseo M slovenliness
desasir[21] VT to let go of
desasosiego M uneasiness
desastrado ADJ (desaseado) untidy; (funesto) ill-fated
desastre M disaster
desastroso ADJ disastrous
desatado ADJ (ambición) unfettered; (zapatos) untied
desatar VT (un nudo) to untie, to loosen; (una ola de violencia) to unleash; **—se** to come untied; **—se en insultos** to let out a string of insults
desatascador M plunger
desatascar[6] VT (un inodoro) to unclog; (una cosa) to dislodge
desatención F lack of attention
desatender[1] VT (no ocuparse de algo) to neglect; (ignorar) to ignore
desatendido ADJ (descuidado) neglected; (ignorado) ignored
desatento ADJ inattentive
desatinado ADJ imprudent
desatornillar VT to unscrew
desatracar[6] VI/VT to shove off
desavenencia F discord
desayunar VT **desayuné huevos** I had eggs for breakfast; **—se** to have breakfast; **—se (con que)** to find out (that)
desayuno M breakfast
desazón F uneasiness
desbandarse VI to disband
desbaratar VT (un plan) to disrupt; (un hechizo) to break
desbocado ADJ (caballo) runaway; (collar) loose

desbordamiento M overflow
desbordante ADJ overflowing
desbordar VI (derramar) to overflow; VT (abrumar) to overwhelm; **—se** to overflow, to spill over
desbravar VT to break
descabalgar[7] VI to dismount
descabellado ADJ harebrained
descabezar[9] VT to behead; **— un sueño** to take a nap
descafeinado ADJ decaffeinated
descalabrar VT to split someone's head open
descalabro M disaster
descalificar VT to disqualify
descalzar[9] VT to take off someone's shoes; **—se** to take off one's shoes
descalzo ADJ barefoot
descaminado ADJ **andar / ir —** to be on the wrong track
descamisado ADJ (sin camisa) shirtless; (pobre) poor
descansar VI/VT to rest; **— en paz** to rest in peace; **—se en** to rely on
descanso M (acción de descansar) rest; (de escalera) staircase landing; (tiempo en que se descansa) break; **en —** at ease
descapotable ADJ & M convertible
descarado ADJ shameless, impudent, brazen; **a la descarada** shamelessly
descarga F (de batería, agua, armas) discharge; (de buques) unloading; (emocional) outpouring; (de electricidad) shock
descargar[7] VT (una batería, agua) to discharge; (un buque, un arma de fuego) to unload; (bombas) to drop; (un programa de computadora) to download; **—se** (una batería) to drain; (ira) to vent
descargo M **en su —** in his defense
descarnado ADJ (realidad) stark; (cara) emaciated
descaro M effrontery, impudence, nerve
descarriar[16] VT to lead astray; **—se** to go astray
descarrilarse VI to derail, to jump the track
descartar VT (un naipe) to discard; (una posibilidad) to dismiss, to discard
descarte M discard; **por —** by elimination
descascararse VI (en jirones) to peel; (en fragmentos) to chip, to flake
descendencia F (linaje) descent; (descendientes) descendants
descendente ADJ descending, downward
descender[1] VI to descend; **— de** to descend from
descendiente MF descendant
descenso M descent

descifrar VT to decipher
descodificar[6] VT to decode
descolgar[2,7] VT (una cortina) to take down; (un teléfono) to pick up; **—se con** to come up with; **—se de** to come down from
descollar[2] VI to excel
descolorido ADJ (persona) pale; (cosa) colorless
descomponer[39] VT (disgustar) to upset; (dar diarrea) to give diarrhea; (dar náuseas) to make nauseous; (productos químicos) to break down; (cadáveres) to decompose; (un reloj) to break; **— en factores** to factor; **—se** (productos químicos) to break down; (cadáveres) to decompose; (un reloj) to break; (sentir náuseas) to be nauseous; (tener diarrea) to have diarrhea; (disgustarse) to go to pieces
descomposición F (de cadáveres) decomposition; (de productos químicos) breaking down; (diarrea) diarrhea
descompuesto ADJ (roto) broken; (caótico) chaotic; (con diarrea) having diarrhea
descomunal ADJ enormous
desconcertado ADJ disconcerted
desconcertante ADJ disconcerting
desconcertar[1] VT to disconcert, to puzzle, to baffle; **—se** to become disconcerted
desconchar VT to chip
desconcierto M confusion
desconectado ADJ disconnected
desconectar VT to disconnect
desconexión F (acción de desconectar) disconnecting; (incomunicación) disconnect
desconfiado ADJ mistrustful, suspicious
desconfianza F mistrust
desconfiar[16] VT to distrust, to mistrust, to be wary of
descongelación F thawing
descongestionante M decongestant
desconocer[13] VT (no reconocer) to fail to recognize; (no saber) not to know
desconocido -da ADJ unknown; **un actividad desconocida** an unheard-of activity; MF stranger
desconocimiento M ignorance
desconsideración F thoughtlessness
desconsiderado ADJ thoughtless, inconsiderate
desconsolado ADJ disconsolate, dejected
desconsolador ADJ disheartening
desconsolar[2] VT to dishearten; **—se** to become disheartened
desconsuelo M dejection
descontar[2] VT (bajar el precio) to discount;

(excluir) to exclude; (quitar del sueldo) to dock

descontentadizo ADJ hard to please

descontentar VT to displease

descontento ADJ & M discontent

descorazonado ADJ disheartened

descortés ADJ discourteous, impolite

descortesía F discourtesy, impoliteness

descortezar[9] VT to strip the bark from

descoser VT to rip; **—se** to come unsewn

descosido ADJ unsewn; M unsewn place; **hablar como un —** to talk one's head off

descostrar VT to remove the crust from

descoyuntado ADJ dislocated, out of joint

descoyuntar VT to dislocate; **—se** to become dislocated

descrédito M discredit

descreído -da ADJ unbelieving; MF unbeliever

descreimiento M unbelief

describir[51] VT to describe

descripción F description

descriptivo ADJ descriptive

descuartizar[9] VT to quarter

descubierto ADJ (destapado) uncovered; (sin sombrero) hatless; **al —** in the open; **estar al —** to be exposed; **poner al —** to expose, to lay bare; **en —** overdrawn; M overdraft

descubridor -ora MF discoverer

descubrimiento M discovery

descubrir[51] VT (hallar) to discover; (destapar) to uncover; **—se** to take off one's hat; **— el pastel** to spill the beans

descuento M discount

descuidado ADJ (en lo que se hace) careless, negligent; (en el arreglo de su persona) slovenly

descuidar VT to neglect; **descuida, yo me ocupo de eso** don't worry, I'll take care of that; **—se** to be negligent

descuido M (falta de cuidado) neglect; (acción descuidada) oversight; **al —** off-hand; **por —** by chance

desde PREP (origen) from; (tiempo) since; **— Madrid** from Madrid; **— el martes** since Tuesday; **— luego** of course; **— el principio** from the start; **— el vamos** from the word go; **— entonces** ever since

desdecirse[26] VI (decir lo contrario) to contradict oneself; (negar lo dicho) to retract

desdén M disdain, scorn

desdentado ADJ toothless

desdeñar VT to disdain, to scorn

desdeñoso ADJ disdainful, scornful

desdicha F misfortune; **por —** unfortunately

desdichado ADJ wretched

desdoblamiento M division

desdoblar VT (desplegar) to unfold; (dividir) to divide

deseabilidad F desirability

deseable ADJ desirable

desear VT to desire

desecación F drying

desecar[6] VT to dry; **—se** to dry up

desechar VT (ropa vieja) to discard; (una oferta) to refuse; (una posibilidad) to dismiss

desecho M waste material; **—s** refuse, waste

desembalar VT to unpack

desembarazar[9] VT to rid of; **—se** to get rid of

desembarcadero M dock

desembarcar[6] VI (de un buque) to disembark, to go ashore; (de un avión) to deplane

desembarco M landing

desembarque M landing

desembocadura F mouth

desembocar[6] VI to flow; **— en** to flow into; **la calle Ocho desemboca en la Rambla** eighth street feeds into la Rambla

desembolsar VT to disburse, to pay out

desembolso M disbursement, outlay

desembragar[7] VI/VT to disengage (the clutch)

desempacar[6] VT to unpack

desempañar VT to wipe clean

desempeñar VT to redeem; **— un cargo** to perform the duties of a position; **— un papel** to play a part; **—se** to get out of debt

desempeño M (de un cargo o papel) performance; (de una cosa en prenda) redemption

desempleado ADJ unemployed

desempleo M unemployment

desempolvar VT to dust off

desencadenar VT (quitar las cadenas) to unchain; (producir algo) to trigger, to spark

desencajado ADJ (mandíbula) dislocated; (mirada) wild; **estaba — en el funeral** he was deeply disturbed at the funeral

desencajar VT (un cajón) to unstick; (la mandíbula) to dislocate

desencantar VT (desilusionar) to disillusion; (quitar un hechizo) to remove a spell from

desencanto M disillusion

desenchufar VI/VT to unplug

desenfadado ADJ uninhibited

desenfado M lack of inhibition

desenfrenadamente ADV with wild abandon

desenfrenado ADJ (sin moderación) unbridled, wanton, rampant; (muy rápido) reckless

desenganchar VT to unhook

desengañar VT to disabuse; —**se** (de un error) to become disabused; (de una ilusión) to become disillusioned

desengaño M disillusion

desengranar VT to take out of gear

desenmarañar VT to disentangle

desenmascarar VT to unmask, to expose

desenredar VT to disentangle

desenrollar VT to unroll

desenroscar VT to untwist

desentenderse[1] VI to pay no attention

desentendido ADJ **hacerse el —** to pretend not to notice / know

desenterrar[1] VT (una cosa) to unearth, to dig up; (un cadáver) to disinter

desentonado ADJ out of tune

desentonar VI (cantar mal) to sing off key; (estar fuera de lugar) to be out of place

desentrañar VT to unravel

desenvoltura F self-assurance

desenvolver[2,51] VT (desenrollar) to unroll; (quitar la envoltura) to unwrap; —**se** to behave

desenvuelto ADJ self-assured

deseo M desire, wish; (sexual) desire; **pedir un —** to make a wish

deseoso ADJ desirous

desequilibrado -da ADJ unbalanced; MF unbalanced person

desequilibrar VT to unbalance

desequilibrio M imbalance

deserción F desertion

desertar VI/VT to desert; **— de** to defect from

desértico ADJ desert

desertor -ora MF deserter

desesperación F desperation

desesperado ADJ desperate

desesperanza F despair, hopelessness

desesperanzado ADJ hopeless

desesperanzar[9] VT to discourage, to deprive of hope; —**se** to despair

desesperar VI to despair; VT to drive crazy

desestabilizar[9] VT to destabilize

desestimación F rejection

desestimar VT to reject

desfachatez F audacity

desfalcar[6] VT to embezzle

desfalco M embezzlement

desfallecer[13] VI (debilitarse) to grow weak; (desmayarse) to faint

desfallecimiento M (debilidad) weakness; (desmayo) faint

desfavorable ADJ unfavorable

desfibrilar VT to defibrillate

desfigurar VT (el rostro) to disfigure; (una estatua) to deface

desfiladero M narrow passage

desfilar VI to file by; (soldados, modelos) to parade

desfile M parade

desgana F (falta de apetito) lack of appetite; (falta de entusiasmo) lack of enthusiasm

desganado ADJ without enthusiasm

desgarbado ADJ ungainly, gawky

desgarrado ADJ (prenda) torn; (grito) heart-rending

desgarradura F tear

desgarrar VT (rasgar) to tear; (causar dolor) to break one's heart; —**se** to tear, to pull

desgarro M muscle pull

desgarrón M tear

desgastar VT to wear away; —**se** to get worn away

desgaste M wear and tear

desglosar VT (una suma) to itemize; (un documento) to separate out

desgracia F (infortunio) misfortune; (infelicidad) unhappiness; —**s personales** casualties; **caer en —** to fall into disgrace / disfavor

desgraciado -da ADJ (desafortunado) unfortunate; (infeliz) unhappy; MF (persona desafortunada) unfortunate person; (hombre despreciable) *vulg* bastard; F (mujer desgraciada) *vulg* bitch

desgranar VT (granos) to thrash, to thresh; (guisantes) to shell

desgravable ADJ tax-deductible

desgreñado ADJ disheveled, unkempt

desgreñar VT to dishevel; —**se** to muss up one's hair

desguazar[9] VT to scrap

deshabitado ADJ (territorio) uninhabited; (casa) vacant

deshacer[30] VT (una acción) to undo; (una cama) to strip; (una cosa) to destroy; (un sólido en un líquido) to dissolve; (un nudo) to untie; **— la maleta** to unpack the suitcase; —**se de** to get rid of; —**se en elogios** to rave about

desharrapado ADJ ragged

deshelar[1] VT to thaw

desheredar VT to disinherit

deshielo M thaw

deshierbar VT to weed

deshilachar VT to unravel

deshojado ADJ leafless

deshojar VT to strip of leaves; —**se** (un árbol)

to shed leaves; (un libro) to lose pages
deshonestidad F (falta de honradez) dishonesty; (falta de recato) immodesty
deshonesto ADJ (no honrado) dishonest; (no modesto) immodest
deshonra F dishonor, disgrace
deshonrar VT to dishonor, to disgrace
deshonroso ADJ dishonorable
deshora LOC ADV **a** — at an inopportune time; **comer a** — to eat between meals
deshuesar VT (un fruto) to stone; (un animal) to bone
deshumanizar[9] VT to dehumanize
desidia F indolence
desierto ADJ (lugar) deserted; (premio) unawarded; M (región árida) desert; (región poco fértil y no habitada) wilderness
designación F (acción de designar, nombre) designation; (nombramiento) appointment
designar VT to designate; (a un funcionario) to appoint
designio M design
desigual ADJ (pelea) one-sided; (actuación) uneven; (números) not equal; (rango) unequal; (terreno) uneven
desigualdad F inequality; (del terreno) roughness
desilusión F disillusion, disappointment
desilusionar VT to disillusion, to disappoint; **—se** to become disillusioned/disappointed
desinencia F ending
desinfectante ADJ & M disinfectant
desinfectar VT to disinfect
desinflado ADJ (globo, persona) deflated; (neumático) flat; M flat tire
desinflar VT to deflate
desinformación F disinformation
desinformar VT to misinform
desinhibido ADJ uninhibited
desintegración F disintegration; — **atómica** atomic decay
desintegrarse VI to disintegrate; (materia radiactiva) to decay
desinterés M (falta de interés) lack of interest; (generosidad) unselfishness
desinteresado ADJ (que no muestra interés) disinterested; (generoso) unselfish, selfless
desistir VI to desist
deslavado ADJ faded
deslavar VT (quitar color) to fade; (lavar ligeramente) to wash superficially
desleal ADJ (persona) disloyal, faithless; (competencia) unfair
desleír[15] VT to mix with a liquid

deslindar VT to mark off
desliz M slipup
deslizamiento M slide, glide
deslizar[9] VT (un patín) to slip, to slide, to glide; (una tarjeta) to swipe; **—se** (un patín) to slide, to glide; (un error) to slip by
deslucido ADJ (actuación) dull; (color) dingy
deslucir[13b] VT (un espectáculo) to tarnish; (color) to make dingy
deslumbramiento M dazzle
deslumbrante ADJ dazzling
deslumbrar VT to dazzle; **—se** to be dazzled
deslustrar VT to tarnish
deslustre M tarnish
desmadejado ADJ (fatigado) exhausted; (desgarbado) ungainly
desmadejar VT to exhaust
desmán M abuse
desmantelar VT to dismantle
desmañado ADJ awkward, clumsy
desmayar VI to lose courage; **—se** to faint, to pass out
desmayo M faint, swoon; **peleó sin** — he fought unflaggingly
desmedido ADJ excessive
desmejorar VI (empeorar el aspecto) to look worse; (debilitarse) to get worse
desmembrar VT to dismember
desmentido M denial
desmentir[3] VT to deny
desmenuzar[9] VT (pan) to crumble; (zanahorias) to mince
desmerecer[13] VI **no** — **de** to compare favorably with
desmesurado ADJ (esfuerzo) inordinate; (orejas) too large
desmigajar VT to crumb, to crumble
desmitificar[6] VT to debunk
desmochar VT to top, to cut the top off of
desmontar VT (limpiar un monte) to clear; (desarmar) to dismantle, to take apart; (derribar de una caballería) to throw; **—se** to dismount
desmoralizar[9] VT to demoralize; **—se** to become demoralized
desmoronar VT to crumble
desmovilizar[9] VT to demobilize
desnatar VT to skim
desnaturalizado ADJ (madre) unnatural; (aceite) denatured
desnudar VT to undress; **—se** to get undressed
desnudez F nakedness
desnudo ADJ nude, naked
desnutrición F malnutrition
desnutrido ADJ underfed, malnourished

desobedecer[13] VT to disobey
desobediencia F disobedience; **— civil** civil disobedience
desobediente ADJ disobedient
desocupación F (paro) unemployment; (abandono de vivienda) vacating
desocupado ADJ (asiento, casa) unoccupied, empty; (tiempo) idle; (que no trabaja) unemployed
desocupar VT to vacate; **—se** to get free
desodorante M deodorant
desoír[35] VT to turn a deaf ear to
desolación F desolation
desolado ADJ desolate, bleak
desolar VT to lay waste to, to desolate; **—se** to be desolated
desollar[2] VT to skin; **— vivo** to skin alive
desorbitado ADJ out of proportion; (ojos) bulging
desorden M disorder, disarray; **— público** public disturbance; **en —** in disarray
desordenado ADJ (persona, situación) messy; (niño, vida) wild; (cuarto) untidy, disorderly; (archivo) disorganized
desordenar VT to mess up
desorganización F disorganization
desorganizado ADJ disorganized
desorientar VT to disorient; (confundir) to confuse; **—se** to lose one's bearings, to become disoriented
desovar VT to spawn
desoxidar VT to deoxidize
despabilado ADJ (despierto) wide-awake; (listo) on the ball
despabilar VT (cortar el pabilo) to trim the wick of; (despertar) to awaken; **—se** to wake up
despachar VT (problemas) to dispatch; (una carta) to mail; (a un cliente) to take care of; (mercancías) to ship; (a una víctima) to bump off; (un pedido) to fill; **— al público** to sell to the public; **—se a su gusto** to speak one's mind
despacho M (oficina) office; (comunicación) dispatch; (envío de cartas) mailing; (envío de mercancías) shipping
despachurrar VT to squash
despacio ADV slow, slowly
desparasitar VT to worm
desparejo ADJ uneven
desparpajo M (desenvoltura) ease; (descaro) impudence
desparramar VT to scatter; **—se** to be scattered
desparramo M (lío) commotion; (de libros) clutter
despatarrarse VT (caerse) to sprawl; (abrirse de piernas) to spread one's legs
despecho M spite; **por —** out of spite
despectivo ADJ derogatory, pejorative
despedazar[9] VT to tear to pieces
despedida F farewell; **— de soltero** bachelor party
despedir[5] VT (acompañar a una persona que se va) to see off; (echar de un empleo) to fire, to dismiss; (emitir un dolor) to emit, to give off; **despídeme de tus padres** say good-bye to your parents for me; **—se (de)** to take leave (of), to say good-bye (to)
despegar[7] VT (dos cosas pegadas) to detach; VI (un avión) to take off; (un cohete) to blast off; **—se** to become detached
despegue M (de avión) takeoff; (de cohete) blastoff, liftoff
despeinado ADJ unkempt
despejado ADJ (el cielo) clear, cloudless; (un camino) clear; (la frente) with one's hair pulled back; (una persona) bright
despejar VT (el campo) to clear; VI (una duda, el cielo) to clear up; **—se** to sober up
despellejar VT to skin
despensa F pantry
despeñadero M cliff
despeñar VT to push off a precipice; **—se** to fall down a precipice
despepitar VT (una granada) to seed; (una manzana) to core; **—se por una cosa** to be crazy about something
desperdiciar VT to waste; **—se** to go to waste
desperdicio M waste; **—s** scraps
desperdigar[7] VT to scatter; **—se** to be scattered
desperezarse[9] VI to stretch
desperezo M stretch
desperfecto M damage; **— mecánico** mechanical breakdown
despertador M alarm clock
despertar[1] VT (a una persona) to awaken, to wake up; (sospecha) to arouse; (interés, deseo) to kindle; **—se** to wake up
despiadado ADJ merciless, heartless, ruthless
despido M dismissal, termination
despierto ADJ (no dormido) awake; (vivaracho) alert
despilfarrador ADJ wasteful
despilfarrar VT to squander
despilfarro M waste
despistado ADJ absent-minded
despistar VT to throw off the track; (a un perseguidor) to lose; **—se** to get confused
desplantador M trowel

desplante M rude remark

desplazar[9] VT to displace; **—se** to move

desplegar[1,7] VT (algo plegado) to unfold; (una bandera) to unfurl; (tropas) to deploy; (interés) to display

despliegue M display

desplomarse VI (edificio, precios) to collapse; (una persona) to slump

desplome M collapse

desplumar VT (un ave) to pluck; (a una víctima) to fleece

despoblado ADJ uninhabited; **— de árboles** treeless; M open country

despojar VT to despoil; **—se** to shed leaves

despojos M PL (de batalla) spoils; (mortales) remains

desportilladura F chip

desportillar VT to chip

desposeer VT to dispossess

déspota MF INV despot

despótico ADJ despotic

despotismo M despotism

despotricar[6] VI to rant

despreciable ADJ (vil) contemptible, despicable, worthless; (insignificante) negligible

despreciar VT (menospreciar) to despise, to look down on; (rechazar) to snub

desprecio M (menosprecio) contempt, disdain; (rechazo) snub

desprender VT (un cierre) to unfasten; (algo prendido) to detach; (gases) to give off; **—se de algo** to part with something; **—se la ropa** to undo one's clothes; **de lo dicho se desprende que** from what has been said it follows that

desprendimiento M (de retina) detachment; (de energía) release; (de tierra) landslide; (generosidad) generosity

despreocupado ADJ carefree

desprestigiar VT to discredit; **—se** to lose one's prestige

desprestigio M loss of prestige

desprevenido ADJ unprepared; **tomar —** to take by surprise

desproporcionado ADJ disproportionate, out of proportion

despropósito M nonsense

desprovisto ADJ **— de** lacking in

después ADV after, afterward; **— de** after; **— de todo** after all

despuntar VI/VT to blunt; **—se** to become blunt

desquiciar VT to unhinge; **—se** to come unhinged

desquitarse VI to get even

desquite M getting even

desregular VT to deregulate

destacado ADJ outstanding

destacamento M military detachment, military detail

destacar[6] VT (tropas) to detach; (una cualidad) to accentuate; VI to stand out; **—se** to stand out

destajo LOC ADV **a —** by the job

destapar VT (una cacerola) to take the top off of; (un plan, a un niño) to uncover; **—se** (en la cama) to uncover; (desnudarse) to bare all

destartalado ADJ dilapidated

destellar VI to flash

destello M flash

destemplado ADJ (persona) feverish; (sonido) out of tune

desteñido ADJ washed-out

desteñir[5,18] VI/VT to fade; VI to run; **—se** to fade

desternillarse VI **— de risa** to die laughing

desterrado -da ADJ exiled, banished; MF exile

desterrar[1] VT to exile, to banish

destetar VT to wean

destierro M exile, banishment

destilación F distillation

destilar VT to distill

destilería F distillery

destinar VT (determinar el destino) to destine; (dirigir) to address; (asignar) to commit

destinatario -ria MF addressee, recipient

destino M (hado) destiny, fate, lot; (uso) use; (lugar adonde se viaja) destination

destitución F dismissal

destituir[31] VT to dismiss

destornillador M screwdriver

destoxificación F detoxification

destrabar VT to untie

destreza F dexterity, skill

destripar VT to gut

destronar VT to dethrone

destrozar[9] VT (estropear) to ruin; (causar grandes daños) to destroy; (derrotar) to rout

destrozo M damage

destrucción F destruction

destructible ADJ destructible

destructivo ADJ destructive

destructor -ra ADJ destructive; M (buque) destroyer; MF (persona) destroyer

destruir[31] VT (reducir a pedazos) to destroy, to obliterate; (estropear) to ruin

desunir VT to divide; **—se** to come apart

desusado ADJ (no frecuente) unusual; (no usado) obsolete

desuso M disuse, obsolescence; **caer en —** to fall into disuse

desvaído ADJ faded

desvainar VT to hull, to husk

desvalido ADJ helpless

desvalijar VT (un cuarto) to ransack; (a una persona) to clean out

desvalimiento M helplessness

desván M attic

desvanecer[13] VT (un color) to fade; (un contorno) to blur; **—se** (una persona) to faint; (un color, arrugas) to fade; (un sonido) to trail off

desvanecido ADJ (una persona) fainted; (un color) faded; (un contorno) blurred

desvanecimiento M (de una persona) fainting; (de colores) fading; (de un contorno) blurring

desvariar[16] VI to rave

desvarío M raving

desvelado ADJ sleepless

desvelar VT to keep awake; **—se** to be sleepless

desvelo M (falta de sueño) sleeplessness; **—s** (esfuerzos) efforts

desvencijado ADJ dilapidated, rickety; **estoy —** I'm all beat up

desventaja F disadvantage; **estar en —** to be at a disadvantage

desventura F misfortune

desventurado ADJ unfortunate

desvergonzado ADJ shameless

desvergüenza F shamelessness

desvestir[5] VT to undress; **—se** to get undressed, to undress

desviación F (de una norma) deviation, divergence; (para coches) detour; (de fondos) diversion; (de la columna vertebral) curvature; **— estándar** standard deviation

desviar[16] VT (la vista) to avert; (fondos, tráfico) to divert; (un golpe) to ward off; (una conversación) to steer; (un tren) to sidetrack; **—se de** (un camino) to stray from; (una norma) to deviate from

desvío M (camino secundario) side road; (desviación) detour

desvirtuar[17] VT to distort; **—se** to become distorted

desvivirse VI **— por hacer algo** to bend over backward to do something; **— por alguien** to go out of one's way for someone

detallado ADJ detailed

detallar VT to detail, to go into detail about

detalle M (pormenor) detail; (venta al por menor) retail; (lista) list; **¡qué —!** how

thoughtful! **con / al / en —** in detail

detallista ADJ (cuidadoso) meticulous; (considerado) thoughtful; M (comercio) retail; MF retailer

detectar VT to detect

detective M detective; **— privado** private eye

detención F (arresto) detention, arrest; (de un vehículo) stop; **— domiciliaria** house arrest; **— ilegal** false arrest

detener[44] VT (arrestar) to detain, to arrest; (parar) to stop; **—se** to stop; **—se en** to linger on; **—se a pensar** to stop to think

detenido ADJ thorough

detenimiento LOC ADV **con —** with care

detergente ADJ & M detergent

deteriorar VT to deteriorate

deterioro M deterioration

determinación F determination

determinar VT to determine

detestable ADJ detestable

detestar VT to detest

detonación F detonation; **hacer detonaciones** to backfire

detonar VI/VT to detonate

detrás ADV behind; **— de** (en el espacio) behind; (en el tiempo) after; **por —** behind

detritus M debris

deuda F debt

deudor -ora ADJ & MF debtor; **— hipotecario** mortgagor

devaluación F devaluation

devanar VT to spool; **—se los sesos** to rack one's brain

devaneo M (acción de pasatiempo) idle pursuit; (amorío) fling

devastar VT to devastate

devengar[7] VT to earn

devoción F devotion

devolución F return

devolver[2,51] VT (volver al dueño) to return; VI (vomitar) to throw up

devorar VT to devour

devoto ADJ (pío) devout; (que muestra devoción) devoted

dextrosa F dextrose

día M day; **— a —** day-to-day; **— tras —** day after day; **al —** up-to-date; **al otro —** on the next day; **de —** by day; **de todos los —s** everyday; **el — de mañana** in the future; **hoy —** nowadays; **no veo el —** I can't wait; **ponerse al —** to catch up; **por —** by the day; **todo el —** all day; **todos los —s** every day; **un — sí y otro no** every other day; **vivir al —** to live from hand to mouth

diabetes F SG diabetes

diablo M devil; **irse al —** *vulg* to go to hell; **pobre —** poor devil; **¿por qué —s dices eso?** *fam* why the heck are you saying that?

diablura F deviltry, mischief

diabólico ADJ diabolic, devilish

diácono M deacon

diacrítico ADJ & M diacritic

diafragma M diaphragm

diagnosticar[6] VT to diagnose

diagonal ADJ & F diagonal

diagrama M diagram; **— de flujo** flow chart

dial M dial

dialéctica F dialectic

dialéctico ADJ dialectic

dialecto M dialect

dialectología F dialectology

diálisis F dialysis

dialogar[7] VI to dialog, to hold talks

diálogo M dialog, conversation; **— de sordos** conversation in which no one listens

diamante M diamond; **— en bruto** diamond in the rough

diámetro M diameter

diana F bull's eye

diapasón M tuning fork

diapositiva F slide

diario ADJ daily; M (periódico) newspaper; (de sucesos personales) journal, diary; (de navegación) log; **a —** every day; **de —** everyday; **llevar un —** to keep a diary

diarrea F diarrhea

diatriba F diatribe

dibujante MF illustrator

dibujar VT to draw; **—se** to appear, to loom

dibujo M (arte de dibujar, cosa dibujada) drawing; (diseño) design; **— al carbón** charcoal drawing; **—s animados** animated cartoon

dicción F diction

diccionario M dictionary

dicha F happiness

dicharachero ADJ witty

dicho ADJ aforementioned; M saying

dichoso ADJ happy; **todo el — día** the whole blessed day

diciembre M December

dicotomía F dichotomy

dictado M (ejercicio) dictation; (orden) dictate; **escribir al —** to take dictation

dictador -ora MF dictator

dictadura F dictatorship

dictamen M (opinión) report; (judicial) ruling

dictaminar VI (dar una opinión) to report; (fallar) to rule

dictar VT to dictate; **— clase** to teach class; **— sentencia** to rule

diecinueve NUM nineteen

dieciocho NUM eighteen

dieciséis NUM sixteen

diecisiete NUM seventeen

diente M (de persona, sierra) tooth; (de víbora) fang; (de rueda dentada) cog; (de tenedor) prong; **— de león** dandelion; **— de leche** baby tooth; **—s postizos** false teeth; **entre —s** under one's breath; **tener buen —** to have a good appetite

diesel M diesel

diestra F right hand

diestro -tra ADJ (habilidoso) skillful, deft; (no zurdo) right-handed; MF right-handed person; **a diestra y siniestra** on all sides

dieta F diet; **estar a —** to be on a diet

diez NUM ten

diezmar VT to decimate

diezmo M tithe; **pagar el —** to tithe

difamación F (oral) slander; (escrito) libel

difamar VT to defame, to malign; (oralmente) to slander; (por escrito) to libel

difamatorio ADJ slanderous

diferencia F difference; **a — de** unlike; **hacer —s entre** to treat differently; **partir la —** to split the difference

diferencial ADJ & M (distancia, pieza de coche) differential; F (matemática) differential

diferenciar VT to differentiate; **—se de** to differ from

diferente ADJ different

diferir[3] VT (aplazar) to defer; VI (ser diferente) to differ

difícil ADJ difficult, hard

dificultad F difficulty

dificultar VT to make difficult

dificultoso ADJ difficult

difteria F diphtheria

difundir VT (luz) to diffuse; (noticias) to broadcast

difunto -ta ADJ & MF deceased

difusión F (de luz) diffusion; (de noticias) broadcasting

difuso ADJ diffuse

digerible ADJ digestible

digerir[3] VT to digest

digestible ADJ digestible

digestión F digestion

digestivo ADJ digestive

digesto M digest

digital ADJ digital

dígito M digit

dignarse VI to deign
dignatario -ria MF dignitary
dignidad F dignity
digno ADJ (respetable) worthy; (orgulloso) dignified; **— de confianza** trustworthy; **— de elogio** praiseworthy
digresión F digression
dije M charm
dilación LOC ADV **sin —** without delay
dilatación F (de un metal, parte dilatada) expansion; (del ojo) dilation
dilatar VT (pupila, capilares, útero) to dilate; (metal, músculo) to expand; (posponer) to defer; **—se en un asunto** to dwell on a subject
dilema M dilemma
diletante MF dilettante
diligencia F (laboriosidad) diligence, industry; (vehículo) stagecoach
diligente ADJ diligent, industrious
dilucidar VT to elucidate
diluido ADJ dilute
diluir[31] VT (una solución) to dilute; (pintura, sopa) to thin
diluvio M deluge
dimensión F dimension
dimes M PL **— y diretes** gossip; **andar en — y diretes** to quibble
diminutivo ADJ & M diminutive
diminuto ADJ (tamaño) diminutive; (cantidad) minute
dimisión F resignation
dimitir VI to resign
Dinamarca F Denmark
dinámica F dynamics
dinámico ADJ dynamic
dinamismo M vigor
dinamita F dynamite
dinamitar VT to dynamite
dínamo M dynamo
dinastía F dynasty
dineral M fortune
dinero M money; **— contante y sonante** ready cash, hard cash; **— de plástico** plastic, credit card; **— sucio** dirty money
dinosaurio M dinosaur
diodo M diode; **— electroluminiscente** light-emitting diode
Dios M God; **dios** god; **— dirá** we'll see; **— los cría y ellos se juntan** birds of a feather flock together; **— mediante** God willing; **¡— mío!** my God! **— te lo pague** may God reward you; **— y su madre** everybody and their dog; **a la buena de —** any old way; **como — manda** as it should be; **¡por —!** oh, my! **que — te oiga** I hope you're right

diosa F goddess
diploma M diploma
diplomacia F diplomacy
diplomático -ca ADJ diplomatic; MF diplomat
diptongo M diphthong
diputación F council
diputado -da MF representative
dique M (presa) dike; (al lado de un río) levee; **— seco** dry dock
dirección F (sentido, rumbo) direction; (domicilio) address; (administración) management; (oficina de administración de una escuela) principal's office; (mecanismo para conducir, acción de conducir) steering; **— asistida** power steering
directiva F (orden) directive; (norma) guideline; (junta de directores) board of directors
directivo -va ADJ leadership; MF officer
directo ADJ (sin desviaciones, intermediarios) direct; (derecho) straight; **en —** live
director -ora MF (de una empresa) director, manager; (de una escuela) principal; (de orquesta) conductor; **— de correos** postmaster
directorio M (índice) directory; (junta directiva) board of directors
dirigente MF leader; **— sindical** union leader
dirigible M dirigible
dirigir[11] VT (una obra teatral) to direct; (una empresa) to manage; (una orquesta) to conduct; (a un turista) to guide; (un saludo, una carta, una pregunta, una crítica) to address; **—se a** (hablar con) to address; (ir a) to go to; (tratar de) to be aimed at
discar[6] VI/VT *Am* to dial
discernimiento M discernment, insight
discernir[1] VT to discern
disciplina F discipline
disciplinar VT to discipline
discípulo -la MF disciple
disco M (cartílago, objeto plano y circular) disk; (fonográfico) record; **— compacto** compact disk; **— duro** hard disk; **es un — rayado** he's a broken record
díscolo ADJ unruly
disconforme ADJ dissatisfied
discontinuo ADJ discontinuous
discordancia F discord
discordia F discord
discoteca F (lugar donde bailar) discotheque; (colección de discos) record collection
discreción F discretion; **a —** at one's own

discretion

discrepancia F discrepancy

discrepar VI to disagree; — **de** to take issue with

discreto ADJ (prudente) discreet; (de unidades indivisibles) discrete; **un partido** — a sorry game

discriminación F discrimination; — **positiva** affirmative action

discriminar VI to discriminate; — **a** to discriminate against

disculpa F (excusa) excuse; (perdón) apology

disculpable ADJ excusable

disculpar VT (excusar) to excuse; (perdonar) to forgive, to pardon; —**se** to apologize

discurrir VI (transcurrir) to pass; (exponer) to discourse

discursear VI to make speeches

discurso M (enunciado) discourse; (alocución pública) speech, address; — **de apertura** keynote address

discusión F (charla) discussion; (riña) argument

discutible ADJ debatable, questionable

discutir VT (hablar sobre) to discuss; (oponerse a) to dispute; VI (reñir) to argue

disecar[6] VT (cortar) to dissect; (preparar para conservar) to stuff

diseminación F dissemination

diseminar VT to disseminate

disensión F dissension, dissent

disenso M dissent

disentería F dysentery

disentir[3] VI to dissent, to disagree

diseñador -ora MF designer

diseñar VT to design

diseño M design; — **de interiores** interior design; — **gráfico** graphic design

disertación F lecture

disertar VI to lecture

disfraz M (para ocultarse) disguise; (de carnaval) costume

disfrazar[9] VT to disguise

disfrutar VI/VT to enjoy; — **de** to enjoy

disfrute M enjoyment

disfunción F dysfunction

disgustado ADJ (molesto) upset; (enojado) angry

disgustar VT to upset; —**se** (molestarse) to get upset; (enfadarse) to get angry

disgusto M (desagrado) unpleasantness; (discusión) quarrel; **a** — (con desgana) against one's will; (con incomodidad) uncomfortably; (en disconformidad) in conflict; **esa niña no da más que** —**s** that girl keeps us upset all the time

disidente ADJ & MF dissident

disimulado ADJ **hacerse el** — to pretend not to notice

disimular VI (fingir) to dissemble; (ocultar) to conceal

disimulo M (fingimiento) dissimulation; (ocultamiento) concealment

disipación F dissipation

disipar VT (niebla, calor) to dissipate; (dudas) to dispel; (miedo) to allay; (dinero) to squander; —**se** to dissipate; (miedo, dudas) to allay, to lift

dislocar[6] VT to dislocate; —**se** to get dislocated

disminuir[31] VT to diminish, to decrease, to lessen; (despreciar) to belittle

disolución F dissolution

disoluto ADJ dissolute, loose

disolvente M solvent; — **de pintura** paint thinner

disolver[2,51] VT to dissolve; (una reunión) to break up

disonancia F discord

dispar ADJ disparate

disparar VT (un arma de fuego) to shoot, to fire; (una cámara) to click; (la inflación) to trigger; VI (en fútbol) to shoot; —**le a alguien** to shoot at someone; —**se** (aumentar) to take off; (salir) to shoot out

disparatado ADJ absurd

disparatar VI to talk nonsense

disparate M absurdity, nonsense; **decir** —**s** to talk nonsense; **un** — **de plata** a ton of money; **puros** —**s** *vulg* pure bullshit

disparo M (acción de disparar) shooting; (tiro, herida) shot

dispensa F dispensation

dispensación F dispensation

dispensar VT to dispense; — **de** to exempt from

dispensario M dispensary

dispersar VT to disperse

dispersión F dispersal

display M display

displicencia F flippancy

displicente ADJ (comportamiento) flippant; (actitud) cavalier

disponer[39] VT (colocar) to arrange; (preparar) to prepare, to dispose; (mandar) to order; — **de** to have; —**se** to get ready; —**se a** to set about

disponible ADJ available

disposición F (voluntad) disposition; (colocación) arrangement; (de ánimo) mood; **a** — **de** at the disposal of

dispositivo M device; — **intrauterino** intrauterine device

dispuesto ADJ ready; **bien** — willing; **no**

estar — a to be unwilling to
disputa F (controversia) dispute; (riña) argument
disputar VI/VT to dispute; **—se el poder** to vie/challenge/contend for power; **—se la posición** to jockey for position
disquete M floppy disk
disquetera F disk drive
distancia F distance; **a —** at arm's length; **guardar —s** to keep at a distance; **¿a qué — está?** how far away is it?
distanciar VT to distance
distante ADJ distant
distar VI **dista mucho de** it's a far cry from; **dista diez kilómetros de** it's ten kilometers from
distender[1] VT (aflojar) to relax; (dilatar) to expand
distinción F distinction
distinguido ADJ distinguished
distinguir[12] VT to distinguish
distintivo ADJ distinctive, distinguishing; M distinguishing characteristic
distinto ADJ (diferente, no el mismo) different; (que se percibe con claridad) distinct
distorsión F distortion
distorsionar VT to distort
distracción F distraction
distraer[45] VT (la atención) to distract; (fondos, mano de obra) to divert; **—se** to entertain oneself
distraído ADJ distracted, absent-minded; **hacerse el —** to play dumb
distribución F distribution
distribuidor -ora MF (persona) distributor; M (pieza de un motor) distributor
distribuir[31] VT to distribute
distrito M district
Distrito de Columbia M District of Columbia
disturbio M disturbance, trouble
disuadir VT (mediante palabras) to dissuade; (mediante acciones) to deter
diurético ADJ & M diuretic
diurno ADJ (actividad) daytime; (animal) diurnal
divagación F rambling
divagar[7] VI to ramble on, to digress
diván M divan; (de psiquiatra) couch
divergencia F divergence
divergir[11] VI to diverge
diversidad F diversity
diversión F (pasatiempo) amusement, entertainment, fun; (hecho de distraer la atención) diversion
diverso ADJ diverse; **—s** various

divertido ADJ amusing, entertaining
divertir[3] VT to amuse, to entertain; **—se** to have a good time, to have fun
dividendo M dividend
dividir VT to divide; (un territorio conquistado) to partition
divieso M boil
divinidad F divinity
divino ADJ divine; **estuvo —** it was heavenly; **lo pasé —** I had a wonderful time
divisa F (señal) emblem; (moneda) currency; (moneda extranjera) foreign currency
divisar VT to make out, to catch sight of
división F division; (de un territorio conquistado) partition
divisorio ADJ dividing
divorciar VT to divorce; **—se** to get divorced
divorcio M divorce
divulgar[7] VT (un secreto) to divulge; (información) to disseminate
dobladillo M hem; **hacer —s** to hem
doblaje M dubbing
doblar VT (una sábana) to fold; (el capital) to double; (una esquina) to turn; (la voz de un actor) to dub; VI (un coche) to turn; (una campana) to knell; **—se** to bend over
doble ADJ double; **— agente** double agent; **— personalidad** split personality; **— visión** double vision; **de — caño** double-barreled; **de — filo** double-edged; **de — sentido** two-way; MF (persona muy parecida, actor sustituto) double; M (repique) knell; **—s** doubles; **el —** double
doblegar[7] VT to break
doblez M fold; F deceitfulness
doce NUM twelve
docena F dozen; **— del fraile** baker's dozen
docente ADJ teaching
dócil ADJ (persona, animal) docile, pliant; (pelo) manageable
docto ADJ learned
doctor -ora MF doctor
doctorado M doctorate
doctrina F doctrine
documental ADJ & M documentary
documentar VT to document
documento M document
dogma M dogma
dogmático ADJ dogmatic
dogo M pug
dólar M dollar
dolencia F ailment
doler[2] VI to ache, to hurt; **me duele el brazo** my arm aches, my arm is sore; **—se de** (compadecerse) to feel sorry for; (arrepentirse) to regret

doliente MF mourner
dolor M (físico) pain, ache; (espiritual)
  sorrow, pain; — **de barriga** bellyache; —
  de cabeza headache; — **de espalda**
  backache; — **de muela** toothache; — **de**
  oídos earache; — **de garganta** sore
  throat
dolorido ADJ aching, sore
doloroso ADJ painful
doma F (de caballos) breaking; (de leones)
  taming
domado ADJ (caballo) broken; (león) tamed
domador -ora MF (de perros) trainer; (de
  leones) lion tamer
domar VT (caballos, personas) to break;
  (leones) to tame
domesticar[6] VT to domesticate, to tame
doméstico -ca ADJ domestic; MF servant
domiciliarse VI to take up residence;
  ¿dónde se domicilia usted? where do
  you reside?
domicilio M (casa) dwelling; (dirección)
  address
dominación F domination
dominador ADJ (predominante) dominant;
  (tiránico) domineering
dominante ADJ (predominante) dominant;
  (tiránico) domineering, overbearing
dominar VT (tener bajo su autoridad, ser más
  alto) to dominate; (reprimir los impulsos)
  to control, to rein in; (tener sometido a su
  voluntad) to domineer
domingo M Sunday; — **de Ramos** Palm
  Sunday; — **de Pascua** Easter Sunday
Dominica F Dominica
dominicano -na ADJ & MF Dominican
dominio M (sobre una tierra, derecho de usar
  una cosa) dominion; (de sí mismo)
  control; (de una lengua) mastery,
  command; (hecho de dominar)
  domination; (ámbito, campo) domain; —
  público public domain
dominiqués -esa ADJ & MF Dominican
dominó M (pieza) domino; (juego) dominoes
domo M dome
don M (gracia) gift; (título, jefe mafioso) don;
  un — nadie a nobody
dona F *Méx* doughnut
donación F donation
donador -ora MF donor
donaire M grace
donante MF donor
donar MF to donate
doncella F *lit* maiden
donde ADV REL where; **de —** whence, from
  which; **ir — el herrero** to go to the
  blacksmith's shop; — **no** otherwise;

—**quiera** wherever
dónde ADV INTERR where
donoso ADJ graceful
doña F doña
dopar VT to dope
dorado ADJ (cubierto de oro) gilt; (del color
  de oro) golden; M dolphinfish
dorar VT to gild; — **la píldora** to sweeten
  the pill
dormido ADJ asleep
dormir[4] VI/VT to sleep; — **a** to put to bed; —
  a un paciente to anesthetize a patient;
  — **la mona** to sleep it off; — **la siesta** to
  take a nap; **se me ha dormido el brazo**
  my arm has fallen asleep; —**se** to fall
  asleep
dormitar VI to doze, to snooze
dormitorio M bedroom
dorso M back, reverse
dos NUM two; — **puntos** colon; — **veces**
  twice; **cada — por tres** constantly; **en**
  un — por tres in a jiffy; **los —** both of
  them
DOS M DOS
dosel M canopy
dosificar[6] VT to dose
dosis F (de medicamento) dose; (de droga) hit
dotación F (de fondos) endowment; (de
  personal) complement
dotar VT to endow
dote F dowry; —**s** talents
draga F dredge
dragado M dredging
dragar[7] VT (para limpiar) to dredge; (para
  buscar objetos) to drag; M SG
  dragaminas minesweeper
dragón M (animal fantástico) dragon;
  (planta) snapdragon
drama M drama
dramático ADJ dramatic
dramatizar[9] VT to dramatize
dramaturgo -ga MF playwright, dramatist
drapear VI to drape
drástico ADJ drastic
drenaje M drainage
drenar VI/VT to drain
dribbling M dribble, dribbling
driblar VI/VT to dribble
dril M drill
drive M drive
drive-in M drive-in
driver M (de golf) driver
droga F drug; — **de recreo** recreational
  drug; —**s de diseño** designer drugs;
  tomar —s to do drugs; MF **drogadicto**
  -ta drug addict
drogar[7] VT to drug

drogata MF INV junkie
drogota MF INV junkie
droguería F (tienda) drugstore; (industria) drug industry
droguero -ra MF druggist
ducado M dukedom
ducha F shower; **— vaginal** vaginal douche
ducharse VI to shower
ducho ADJ skillful
dúctil ADJ (metal) ductile; (persona) flexible, supple
duda F doubt; **en —** in doubt; **fuera de —** beyond doubt; **no cabe —** there's no doubt; **poner en —** to cast doubt on; **sin —** without a doubt, undoubtedly; **sin lugar a —s** without doubt; **tengo una —** I have a question
dudar VT to doubt; (vacilar) to hesitate; **— de** to have doubts about
dudoso ADJ doubtful; **de dudosa honestidad** of dubious honesty
duela F stave
duelo M (combate) duel; (luto) mourning; (pena) grief; (dolientes) mourners; **estar de —** to be in mourning
duende M (gnomo) goblin, gremlin; (gracia) charm
dueño -ña MF owner; **me sentí — de la situación** I felt like I was in control of the situation; M landlord; F landlady
dueto M duet
dulce ADJ (sabor, personalidad) sweet; (clima) pleasant; (agua) fresh; **—amargo** bittersweet; M (cosa dulce) sweet; (mermelada) preserves, conserve
dulcería F confectionery
dulcificar[6] VT to sweeten
dulzón ADJ unpleasantly sweet
dulzor M sweetness
dulzura F sweetness
duna F dune
dúo M duet; **decir a —** to say in unison
dúplex M duplex
duplicado ADJ & M duplicate; **por —** in duplicate
duplicar[6] VT to duplicate
duplicidad F duplicity
duque M duke
duquesa F duchess
durabilidad F durability
duración F duration; (de una película, vocal) length
duradero ADJ (ropa) durable, serviceable; (pilas) long-lasting
durante PREP during; **— el mandato de los demócratas** under the Democrats; **— muchos años** for/over many years

durar VI/VT to last
duraznero M peach tree
durazno M (fruto) peach; (árbol) peach tree
dureza F (de metal) hardness; (del clima, de la expresión, de una tempestad) severity; (del invierno) harshness; (de un boxeador) toughness; (del cuero) stiffness
durmiente ADJ sleeping; M railroad tie, sleeper
duro ADJ (metal, golpe, droga, agua) hard; (clima, tormenta) severe; (invierno, expresión, sonido) harsh; (soldado) tough; (grifo) stuck; (viento) strong; (autoridad) inflexible; (pan) stale; (cuero) stiff; **— de corazón** hard-hearted; **— de entendederas** slow on the uptake; **a duras penas** barely; M five peseta coin; **no tengo un —** I'm flat broke
DVD M DVD

Ee

e CONJ and
ebanista MF cabinetmaker
ébano M ebony
ebrio ADJ drunk, inebriated
ebullición F boiling
eccema M eczema
echar VT (una pelota, redes) to throw, to cast; (yemas, hojas) to sprout; (a un empleado) to fire; (humo, olor) to give off; (un líquido) to pour; (a un borracho) to throw out; **— abajo** to knock down; **— a la basura** to throw away; **— al mar** to put to sea; **— al correo** to mail; **— anclas** to drop anchor; **— a pique** to sink; **— carnes** to get fat; **— de menos** to miss; **— de ver** to notice; **— mano de** to seize upon; **— la culpa** to blame; **— por la borda** to jettison; **— raíces** to take root; **— sangre** to bleed; **— suertes** to draw lots; **— una carta** to mail a letter; **— una siesta** to take a nap; **— un vistazo a** to glance at, to take a look at; **te echo una carrera** I'll race you; **—le el muerto a alguien** to pass the buck to someone; **—se** to lie down; **—se a correr** to bolt; **—se a** to start to; **—se a perder** to spoil; **—se a reír** to burst out laughing; **—se a un lado** to dodge; **—se para atrás** to lean back; **—se atrás** to back down
ecléctico ADJ eclectic

eclesiástico ADJ & M ecclesiastic
eclipsar VT to eclipse; (superar) to eclipse, to outshine, to overshadow; **—se** to fade
eclipse M eclipse; **— de sol** solar eclipse; **— de luna** lunar eclipse
eco M echo; **hacer —** to echo; **hacerse — de** to repeat
ecología F (medio ambiente) environment; (ciencia) ecology
ecológico ADJ environmental
ecologista ADJ environmental; MF environmentalist
economato M commissary
economía F (conjunto de actividades de producción) economy; (ciencia) economics; (familiar) finances; **— doméstica** home economics; **—s** savings; **hacer —s** to be thrifty
económico ADJ (relativo a la economía) economic; (que gasta poco) frugal, thrifty; (que cuesta poco) economical
economista MF economist
economizar[9] VT to economize, to save
ecosistema M ecosystem
ecuación F equation
ecuador M equator
Ecuador M Ecuador
ecualizar[9] VT to equalize
ecuatoriano -na ADJ & MF Ecuadorian
ecuménico ADJ ecumenical
edad F age; **— avanzada** ripe old age; **— mental** mental age; **— de Piedra** Stone Age; **— Media** Middle Ages; **— de merecer** marriageable age
edición F (tienda, ejemplar) edition; (acción de editar) publication; **— de sobremesa** desktop publishing
edicto M edict
edificación F building
edificar[6] VT (construir) to build; (infundir sentimientos morales) to edify, to uplift
edificio M building
editar VT to edit, to publish
editor -ora ADJ publishing; MF editor
editorial ADJ publishing; F publishing house; M editorial
editorializar[9] VI to editorialize
edredón M comforter
educación F (en la escuela) education; (de normas sociales) breeding; **— a distancia** distance learning; **— cívica** civics; **— especial** special education; **— física** physical education
educado ADJ (cortés) well-bred; (instruido) educated
educador -ora MF educator
educar[6] VT (a una persona en la escuela) to educate; (a una persona en la casa, la voz) to train
educativo ADJ educational
edulcorante M sweetener
EEUU (Estados Unidos) M SG USA
efectivo ADJ (eficaz) effective; (real) actual; **hacer —** (un cheque) to cash; (una deuda) to pay off; (una amenaza) to make good on; M cash; **en —** in cash; **—s** troops
efecto M (resultado) effect, result; (letra comercial) bill of exchange; (rotación) English, spin; **en —** in fact; **llevar a —** to carry out; **surtir —** to work; **— invernadero** green house effect; **—s especiales** special effects; **—s personales** personal effects; **perder —** to wear off; **rebotar con —** to glance off; **a estos —s** to this effect; **para los —s** to all intents and purposes; **por — de** as a consequence of
efectuar[17] VT to effect; **—se** to be carried out
eficacia F efficacy; **— de una ley** force of law
eficaz ADJ effective
eficiencia F efficiency
eficiente ADJ efficient
efigie F effigy; **quemar en —** to burn in effigy
efímero ADJ ephemeral, fleeting
efusivo ADJ effusive
egipcio -cia ADJ & MF Egyptian
Egipto M Egypt
égloga F pastoral
ego M ego
egocéntrico ADJ egocentric, self-centered
egoísmo M selfishness
egoísta ADJ selfish; MF selfish person
egotismo M egotism
egresado -da MF graduate
eje M (de la Tierra) axis; (de un vehículo) axle; **— del pistón** piston rod; **eso me parte por el —** that messes me up
ejecución F (de un condenado) execution; (de un plan, una orden) carrying out, execution; (de una tarea) performance; (de una propiedad) foreclosure
ejecutar VT (a un condenado) to execute; (un plan, una orden) to carry out; (una tarea, música) to perform; (una propiedad) to foreclose on
ejecutivo -va ADJ & MF executive
ejemplar ADJ exemplary, model; M (libro) copy; (individuo) specimen
ejemplificar[6] VT to exemplify
ejemplo M (cosa típica) example; (modelo) model; **a — de** on the example of; **dar —** to set an example; **por —** for example

ejercer[10a] VT (una profesión) to practice; (influencia, fuerza) to exert; (poder) to wield

ejercicio M exercise; (de una profesión) practice; **hacer —** to take exercise; **— contable** accounting period; **— físico** physical exercise; **en —** active

ejercitar VT (la vista, los músculos) to exercise; (a soldados) to drill; (a alumnos) to train; **—se** to train

ejército M army; **el —** the military

ejido M common

ejote M *Méx* green bean

el ART DEF M the; **— de la derecha** the one on the right; **— que** the one that; **— que sepa** whoever knows

él PRON PERS M SG (como sujeto) he; **— dijo** he said; (como objeto) him; **para —** for him; **le di el libro a —** I gave the book to him; **estamos hablando de —** we're talking about him; **el libro de —** his book

elaboración F (de miel, comida) making; (de un método) development; (de un informe) drafting

elaborado ADJ elaborate

elaborar VT (un método) to elaborate, to develop; (comida) to make; (un informe) to draft

elasticidad F elasticity

elástico ADJ (sustancia) elastic; (cuerpo) supple; (horario) flexible; M elastic

elección F (votación) election; (selección) choice, selection; **no tuve —** I had no choice

electo ADJ elect

elector -ora ADJ electoral; MF elector

electoral ADJ electoral

electricidad F electricity; **— estática** static electricity

electricista MF electrician

eléctrico ADJ (aparato) electric; (instalación, corriente) electrical

electrificar[6] VT to electrify

electrizado ADJ electrified

electrizante ADJ electrifying

electrizar[9] VT (suministrar electricidad) to electrify; (emocionar) to galvanize, to electrify

electrocardiograma M electrocardiogram

electrocutar VT to electrocute

electrodo M electrode

electrodoméstico M electrical appliance

electroencefalograma M electroencephalogram

electroimán M electromagnet

electrólisis F electrolysis

electromagnético ADJ electromagnetic

electrón M electron

electrónica F electronics

electrónico ADJ electronic

elefante M elephant

elegancia F elegance

elegante ADJ (que tiene gracia) elegant; (en el vestir) stylish, smart

elegible ADJ eligible

elegir[5,11] VT to choose, to select; (votar) to elect

elemental ADJ (sencillo) elementary; (básico) elemental

elemento M element

elenco M cast

elevación F elevation; **tirar por —** to throw high in the air

elevado ADJ (pensamiento, estilo) elevated; (fiebre, montaña) high; (precios) high

elevador M elevator

elevar VT (en una jerarquía) to elevate; (precios, voz, objeto) to raise; (el espíritu) to uplift; **— la vista** to look up; **— al cuadrado** to square; **— al cubo** to cube; **—se a** to go up to, to rise to; **el rascacielos se eleva sobre la ciudad** the skyscraper towers over the city

elfo M elf

eliminación F elimination

eliminar VT to eliminate

eliminatoria F heat

elíptico ADJ elliptical

elite / élite F elite

elitista ADJ & MF elitist

ella PRON PERS F SG (como sujeto) she; **— dijo** she said; (como objeto) her; **para —** for her; **le di el libro a —** I gave the book to her; **el libro de —** her book

ellas PRON PERS F PL (como sujeto) they; **— dijeron** they said; (como objeto) them; **para —** for them; **les di el libro a —** I gave them the book; **el libro de —** their book

ello PRON it; **— es que** the fact is that

ellos PRON M PL (como sujeto) they; **— dijeron** they said; (como objeto) them; **para —** for them; **les di el libro a —** I gave them the book; **el libro de —** their book

elocuencia F eloquence

elocuente ADJ eloquent; **las estadísticas son —s** the statistics speak for themselves

elogiar VT to praise

elogio M praise

elote M *Méx* corn on the cob

elucidación F elucidation

elucidar VT to elucidate

eludir VT to elude, to avoid, to dodge
emanación F emanation, flow
emanar VI/VT to emanate
emancipación F emancipation
emancipar VT to emancipate; **—se** to become free
emascular VT to emasculate
embadurnar VT to daub
embajada F embassy
embajador -ora MF ambassador
embalador -ora MF packer
embalaje M packing
embalar VT to pack; VI to accelerate
embaldosar VT to tile
embalsamar VT (a un muerto) to embalm; (un animal) to stuff
embalse M reservoir
embanderar VT to adorn with flags
embarazada ADJ pregnant
embarazar[9] VT (impedir) to hamper; (fecundar) to make pregnant; **—se** to get pregnant
embarazo M (obstáculo) impediment; (estado de embarazada) pregnancy
embarazoso ADJ embarrassing, awkward
embarcación F boat, embarkation, craft
embarcadero M wharf, pier
embarcar[6] VT (pasajeros) to embark; (mercancías) to load; **—se** to embark, to go aboard; **—se en** to embark upon
embargar[7] VT to seize; **estar embargado de emoción** to be overcome with emotion
embargo M embargo; **— judicial** seizure; **imponer un —** to embargo; **sin —** nevertheless, however
embarque M (de mercancías) loading; (de pasajeros) embarkation
embarrado ADJ smeared with mud
embarrar VT to smear with mud, to muddy
embate M lashing
embaucador M confidence man
embaucar[6] VT to dupe
embeber VT to soak up; **—se** to be enraptured
embelesar VT to enrapture
embeleso M rapture
embellecer[13] VI/VT to beautify
embestida F charge
embestir[5] VI/VT to charge
embetunar VT to polish
emblanquecer[13] VI/VT to whiten
emblema M emblem
embobar VT to amaze; **—se** to be amazed
embolia F embolism
émbolo M piston, plunger
embolsar VT (dinero) to pocket; (una compra) to bag
emborrachar VT (a una persona) to intoxicate; (el carburador) to flood; **—se** to get drunk
emborronar VT (manchar) to blot; (hacer impreciso) to blur
emboscada F ambush
emboscar[6] VT to ambush; **—se** to lie in ambush
embotamiento M (efecto de embotar) dullness, bluntness; (acción de embotar) dulling
embotar VT to dull
embotelladora F bottling plant
embotellamiento M (acción de embotellar) bottling; (de tráfico) traffic jam, bottleneck
embotellar VT (cerveza) to bottle; (tráfico) to bottle up
embozar[9] VT to conceal
embragar[7] VI to engage the clutch
embrague M clutch
embriagado ADJ drunken
embriagar[7] VT to intoxicate; **—se** to become intoxicated
embriaguez F intoxication, drunkenness
embridar VT to bridle
embrión M embryo
embrollar VT to embroil
embrollo M muddle
embromar VT to kid
embrujar VT to bewitch
embrujo M spell
embrutecer[13] VT to stupefy
embudo M funnel
embuste M lie
embustero -ra MF liar, trickster
embutido M sausage
embutir VT to cram, to jam
emergencia F emergency
emerger[11b] VI to emerge; (del agua) to surface
emigración F (de personas) emigration; (de animales) migration
emigrante ADJ & MF emigrant
emigrar VI (personas) to emigrate; (animales) to migrate
eminencia F eminence; **— gris** gray eminence
eminente ADJ eminent
emisario -ria MF emissary; M outlet
emisión F (de acciones, billetes) issue; (de un olor) discharge; (de programas) broadcast; (de vapor) emission
emisor ADJ emitting; M transmitter
emisora F radio / television station
emitir VT (un olor, vapor) to emit; (juicios) to pronounce; (dinero, acciones) to issue;

VI/VT (programas) to broadcast; —**se** to be on the air

emoción F emotion; **¡qué** —**!** what a thrill!

emocional ADJ emotional

emocionante ADJ (conmovedor) touching; (apasionante) exciting

emocionar VT (apasionar) to excite; (conmover) to move, to touch; —**se** (estar apasionado) to be excited; (estar conmovido) to be touched

emotivo ADJ emotional

empacador -ora MF packer

empacar[6] VT (regalos, mercancías) to pack; (algodón) to bale

empachar VI to cause indigestion; —**se** to suffer indigestion; —**se de** to get sick on, to stuff oneself with

empacho M (indigestión) indigestion; (cohibición) inhibition; **no tener** — **en** to have no qualms about

empalagar[7] VI/VT to cloy

empalagoso ADJ cloying, saccharine

empalar VT to impale

empalizada F stockade, palisade

empalmar VT to splice; — **con** to join

empalme M (de caminos) junction; (de cuerdas) splice; — **genético** gene splicing

empanada F turnover, pie

empanar VT to bread

empañado ADJ (vidrio) misty, foggy; (metal, reputación) tarnished

empañar VT (vidrio) to fog up, to blur; (metal, reputación) to tarnish

empapado ADJ soggy, sopping wet

empapamiento M soaking

empapar VT (mojar) to soak, to drench; (recoger con algo) to soak up; —**se** (mojarse) to get soaked; (enterarse) to find out all about

empapelado M wallpapering

empapelar VT to paper, to wallpaper; — **las calles** to plaster the streets

empaque M (acción de empacar) packing; (envoltorio) packaging

empaquetadura F gasket

empaquetar VT to pack, to package; —**se** to get dolled up

emparedado M sandwich

emparejar VT (una carga, un partido) to even up; VI/VT (los enamorados) to pair up

emparentado ADJ akin, related

emparentarse VI to become related by marriage

empastar VT to fill

empaste M filling

empatar VI to tie

empate M tie

empatía F empathy

empecinado ADJ stubborn

empedernido ADJ (criminal) hardened; (mujeriego) incorrigible; (solterón) confirmed

empedernirse[50] VI to become hardened

empedrado M (acción) paving with stones; (cosa) cobblestone pavement; ADJ paved with stones

empedrar[1] VT to pave with stones

empeine M (del pie) instep; (del vientre) groin

empellón M shove; **a empellones** with shoves, shoving

empeñar VT to pawn; — **la palabra** to pledge; —**se** (endeudarse) to go into debt; (obstinarse) to insist; (esforzarse) to apply oneself; —**se en** to engage in

empeño M (prenda) pawn; (insistencia) insistence; (deseo) desire; (esfuerzo) exertion; **poner** — **en** to strive for

empeorar VT to make worse, to aggravate; VI to worsen; —**se** to get worse

empequeñecer[13] VT to make smaller; VI to get smaller

emperador -triz M emperor; F empress

emperifollarse VI to deck oneself out, to doll oneself up

empezar[1,9] VI/VT to begin, to start; — **a** to start to; — **de cero** to start from scratch; **para** — for starters; **no tengo ni para** — **con él** I can't touch him; — **por** to begin with; **empezamos mal** we got off to a bad start; **un tubo sin** — an unopened tube; **por algo se empieza** you have to start somewhere

empinado ADJ steep

empinar VT to raise; — **el codo** to drink; —**se** (una persona) to stand on tiptoes; (un caballo) to rear; (una torre) to tower

empírico ADJ empirical

empizarrar VT to cover with slate

emplastar VT to plaster

emplasto M plaster

empleado -da MF employee

emplear VT (usar) to employ, to use; (dar trabajo) to employ; —**se en** to be employed in

empleo M (ocupación) employment, work; (puesto de trabajo) job; (utilización) use

emplumado ADJ feathery

emplumar VT (poner plumas a algo) to adorn with feathers; (pegar plumas en el cuerpo) to tar and feather; VI (echar plumas) to grow feathers

empobrecer[13] VI/VT to impoverish

empollar VT (huevos) to hatch, to brood; VI/VT (para un examen) to cram

empollón -ona MF grind, egghead

empolvar VT to cover with dust; —**se** (con cosméticos) to powder oneself; (con polvo) to get dirty

emponzoñar VT to poison

empotrado ADJ built-in

emprendedor ADJ enterprising

emprender VT (una tarea) to undertake; (un viaje) to embark on; —**la con alguien** to attack someone

empresa F (cosa que se emprende) undertaking; (compañía) company, enterprise; — **libre** free enterprise; — **privada** private enterprise; — **pública** public company

empresario -ria MF entrepreneur

empréstito M loan

empujar VT to push; (con violencia) to shove; (apresurar) to hurry

empuje M (ánimo) drive; (fuerza de propulsión) thrust; (fuerza hacia arriba) lift

empujón M shove, push; **dar empujones** to jostle

empuñadura F (espada) hilt; (cuchillo) handle

empuñar VT to grasp

emular VT to emulate

en PREP in; — **Asturias** in Asturias; (sobre una superficie) on, upon; — **la mesa** on the table; **sentarse** — **el suelo** to sit down on the floor; **me lo vendió** — **mil pesetas** she sold it to me for a thousand pesetas; — **la parada del autobús** at the bus stop; — **la noche** at night; **ir** — **tren** to go by train

enaguas F PL petticoat

enajenación M (mental) insanity; (cambio de dueño) transfer

enajenar VT (trasladar) to transfer; (alienar) to alienate; —**se** (a los amigos) to alienate

enaltecer[13] VT to extol

enamorado -da ADJ in love; MF lover

enamoramiento M crush

enamorar VT to make fall in love; —**se (de)** to fall in love (with)

enano -na MF (de los cuentos de hada, persona deforme) dwarf; (de proporciones normales) midget

enarbolar VT (una bandera) to raise on high; (un garrote) to brandish

enardecer[13] VT to inflame; —**se** to become inflamed

enardecimiento M inflaming

encabezamiento M heading

encabezar[9] VT (una carta, una obra, un gobierno) to head; (un desfile) to lead

encabritarse VI (un caballo) to rear (up); (enfurecerse) to get furious

encadenar VT (poner en cadenas) to chain; (unir) to link

encajar VI/VT to fit; **el policía me encajó una multa** the policeman stuck me with a fine; **tu historia no encaja** your story doesn't hold water

encaje M (tejido) lace; (reserva bancaria) reserve; (acción de encajar) fitting together

encajonar VT (meter en una caja) to box; (apretar) to squeeze in

encallar VI to run aground, to strand; (una ballena) to beach; VT to ground

encamarse VI — **con** to go to bed with

encaminar VT to direct; —**se hacia** to head for

encanecer[13] VI to go gray; VT to cause to go gray

encanijado ADJ sickly

encanijarse VI to get sickly

encantado ADJ (a gusto) delighted; (hechizado) enchanted; — **de conocerla** pleased to meet you

encantador -ora ADJ charming, delightful; MF charmer

encantamiento M enchantment

encantar VT to enchant; **eso me encanta** I love that

encanto M (encantamiento) enchantment; (atractivo) charm; **un** — **de persona** a delightful person; **como por** — as if by magic

encapotado ADJ overcast

encapotarse VI to become overcast

encapricharse VI — **con / de / por** to become infatuated with

encapuchar VT (a una persona) to hood; (un bolígrafo) to put the top on

encaramar VT to raise; —**se** to climb up on; —**se al primer puesto** to rise to first place

encarar VT to face; **me encaró el fusil** he pointed the rifle at me; —**se con** to face

encarcelamiento M imprisonment

encarcelar VT to imprison, to jail, to incarcerate

encarecer[13] VI (subir de precio) to increase in price; VT (rogar) to beg

encarecidamente ADV earnestly

encargado -da MF person in charge; — **de curso** lecturer

encargar[7] VT (dar cargo) to put in charge; (pedir) to order; (mandar) to commission, to order; — **a alguien una tarea** to charge someone with a task; —**se de** to take care of

encargo M (pedido) order; (tarea)

assignment, charge, errand; **construido por / de** — custom-built; **hecho por** — made-to-order

encariñarse VI — **de** to become fond of

encarnado ADJ (rojo) red; (uña) ingrown

encarnar VT (un ideal) to embody; (a un personaje) to play; **se me encarnó una uña** one of my nails got ingrown

encarnizado ADJ fierce

encarnizarse[9] VI — **con alguien** to attack someone viciously

encarte M insert

encasillar VT to pigeonhole

encauzamiento M channeling

encauzar[9] VT to channel

encendedor M cigarette lighter

encender[1] VT (un cigarro, fuego) to light; (un fósforo) to strike; (una luz, radio) to switch on, to turn on; (pasión) to arouse; VI **—se** (una persona, sexualmente) to get aroused; (una lámpara) to turn on

encendido ADJ (rojo) bright; (sexualmente) aroused; M ignition

encerado M (pizarrón) blackboard; (acción de encerar) waxing; (capa de cera) wax coating; ADJ waxed

encerar VT to wax, to polish

encerrar[1] VT (palabras entre paréntesis) to enclose; (una oveja) to pen; (a una persona) to lock up; (un contenido) to contain; (un peligro) to involve; **—se** (aislarse) to isolate oneself; (obstinarse) to become fixated

enchapar VT (metal) to plate; (madera) to veneer

enchilada F enchilada

enchufar VT (un aparato eléctrico) to plug in; (a un protegido) to fix up; — **un tubo con otro** to fit one pipe into another

enchufe M (de aparatos eléctricos) socket, plug-in, electrical outlet; (situación ventajosa) connection

encías F PL gums

enciclopedia F encyclopedia

encierro M (confinamiento) confinement; (lugar) enclosure

encima ADV (arriba) on top; (además) in addition; — **de** on top of; **por** — **de** above; **sacar de** — to get rid of; **orinarse** — to urinate on oneself; **ya tenía el coche** — the car was already on top of me; **no lleves tanto dinero** — don't carry so much money on you; **los exámenes están** — the exams are upon us; **mi madre siempre me está** — my mother is always on me; **lo leí por** — I scanned it

encimera F counter

encina F oak

encinta ADJ pregnant

enclaustrar VT to cloister

enclavarse VI to be located

enclave M enclave

enclenque ADJ (endeble) sickly; (desvencijado) rickety

encoger[11b] VI/VT to shrink; **—se** (una prenda) to shrink; (una persona) to be intimidated; **—se de hombros** to shrug one's shoulders

encogido ADJ (tímido) shy; M (acción de encoger) shrinkage

encogimiento M (acción de encoger) shrinking; — **de hombros** shrug

encolar VT to glue

encolerizar[9] VT to incense; **—se** to become incensed, to lose one's temper

encomendar[1] VT to entrust; **—se** to commend oneself

enconar VT to inflame; VI **—se** (discusión) to become inflamed; (herida) to fester

encono M animosity

encontrado ADJ contrary, opposing

encontrar[2] VT (hallar) to find; (converger) to meet; — **a** to run into; **—se** (estar ubicado) to be located; (hallarse) to feel; **—se con** (verse, según plan) to meet with; (verse, por coincidencia) to run into; (enterarse) to find out; **vas a encontrarte la casa en obras** you'll find the house under construction

encontronazo M collision

encordar[2] VT to string

encorvado ADJ stoop-shouldered

encorvamiento M slouch, stoop

encorvar VT to stoop; **—se** to bend over

encostrarse VI to scab

encrespar VT (el pelo) to curl; (el mar) to make choppy; **—se** (el pelo) to get curly; (el mar) to get choppy

encrucijada F crossroads

encuadernación F (oficio) bookbinding; (lo encuadernado) binding

encuadernar VT to bind

encuadrar VT to frame; **la poesía de esta época se encuadra en tres tendencias** the poetry of this period can be classified into three tendencies

encubierto ADJ covert

encubrimiento ADJ (de un delincuente) concealment; (de un escándalo) cover-up

encubrir[51] VT (un secreto) to conceal; (un escándalo) to cover up, to hush up

encuentro M (casual) encounter; (planeado) meeting; (partido) game; (de atletismo) meet; **salir al — de** (ir a encontrar) to go out to meet; (prevenir) to counter

encuerar VT to strip

encuesta F survey, poll

encuestar VI/VT to survey, to poll

encumbrado ADJ elevated, lofty

encumbramiento M elevation

encumbrar VT to elevate

encurtido M pickle

encurtir VT to pickle

ende LOC ADV **por —** hence

endeble ADJ (persona) feeble; (material, argumento) flimsy; (mesa) rickety

endémico ADJ endemic

endemoniado ADJ (poseído por el diablo) possessed by the devil; (niño) devilish; (pregunta) tough

enderezar[9] VT to straighten; **enderézate** stand up straight; **la niña se enderezó con los años** the girl straightened out after a few years

endeudarse VI to get into debt

endiablado ADJ devilish

endócrino ADJ endocrine

endomingado ADJ dressed in one's Sunday best

endorfina F endorphin

endosante MF endorser

endosar VT to endorse

endoso M endorsement

endulzante M sweetener

endulzar[9] VT to sweeten; **se endulzó el tiempo** the weather became milder

endurecer[13] VT to harden; VI **—se** (músculos) to get hard; (cola) to set

endurecimiento M hardening

enebro M juniper

eneldo M dill

enema MF enema

enemigo -ga ADJ & MF enemy; **buques —s** enemy ships; **ser — de una cosa** to dislike a thing

enemistad F enmity

enemistar VT to cause enmity between; **—se con** to become an enemy of

energético ADJ (politica energética) energy policy

energía F energy; **— nuclear** nuclear energy; **— hidráulica** water power; **— solar** solar energy; **— térmica** thermal energy

enérgico ADJ (persona) energetic; (protesta, medida, tono) forceful

enero M January

enervar VT (debilitar) to enervate; (irritar) to irritate

enfadado ADJ angry

enfadar VT to anger; VI **—se** to get angry

enfado M anger

enfadoso ADJ annoying

enfardar VT to bale

énfasis M emphasis

enfático ADJ emphatic

enfatizar[9] VT to emphasize

enfermar VT to sicken; VI to become sick; **—se** to become ill

enfermedad F (estado de enfermo) sickness, illness; (cardiovascular, de Parkinson) disease; (social) ill; **— contagiosa** contagion; **— coronaria** heart disease; **— mental** mental illness; **— venérea** venereal disease

enfermería F infirmary

enfermero -ra M male nurse; F nurse

enfermizo ADJ (persona) sickly, infirm; (obsesión, aspecto) unhealthy; (imaginación) sick

enfermo -ma ADJ sick, ill; **me tiene — que vengan tarde** I'm sick of them coming late; MF patient; **— del corazón** person with a heart condition

enfisema M emphysema

enflaquecer[13] VI to get thin

enfocar[6] VT (los ojos) to focus; (un faro) to point; (una cámara) to train; (un tema) to approach

enfoque M approach

enfrentamiento M clash

enfrentar VT to confront; (una dificultad) to face, to tackle; **— a** to pit against; **—se con** to clash with

enfrente ADV opposite; **— de** in front of, opposite

enfriamiento M (del aire) cooling; (de una persona) chill; (de la economía, las relaciones) cooling off

enfriar[16] VT to cool, to chill; VI **—se** to cool off

enfundar VT to sheathe

enfurecer[13] VT to infuriate, to enrage; VI **—se** to become enraged, to rage

enfurruñado ADJ sulky

enfurruñarse VI to sulk

engalanar VT (una mesa) to decorate; (a una muchacha) to dress up; **—se** to dress up

enganchar VT (bueyes) to hitch; (una red) to snag; (un teléfono) to hook up; (a los televidentes, a un adicto) to hook; VI **—se** to get hooked

enganche M (del gas, teléfono) connection, hookup; (de drogas) addictiveness; (de vagones) coupling; (de caballos) team; (entrada) *Méx* down payment

enganchón M snag

engañador ADJ deceitful

engañar VT (mentir) to deceive; (ser infiel) to cheat on; — **el hambre** to ward off hunger; **—se** to deceive oneself

engaño M deceit, deception

engañoso ADJ deceitful

engastar VT to set

engaste M setting

engatusar VT to coax, to cajole

engendrar VT (emociones) to engender; (hijos) to procreate

englobar VT to encompass

engomar VT to glue

engordar VI to get fat, to put on weight; VT to make fat, to fatten; **esta semana he engordado dos kilos** I gained two kilos this week

engorroso ADJ irksome

engoznar VT to hinge

engranado ADJ meshed, interlocking; **estar — ** to be in gear

engranaje M gears, gearing; **el — del partido** the party apparatus

engranar VT (meter una marcha) to put in gear, to throw into gear; (encajar) to mesh; — **la marcha atrás** to put (the car) in reverse

engrandecer[13] VT (la fama) to aggrandize; (un palacio) to make more grandiose

engrapar VT to staple, to cramp

engrasar VT (untar) to grease; (manchar) to make greasy; (sobornar) to grease someone's palm; **—se** to get greasy

engrase M grease job

engreído ADJ conceited

engreírse[15] VI to get conceited

engrillar VT to shackle

engrosar VT (una manifestación) to swell; (un volumen) to grow; (una persona) to get fat

engrudo M paste

engullir[19] VT to gobble

enhebrar VT (un hilo) to thread; (cuentas) to string; — **idioteces** to string together a bunch of idiocies

enhorabuena F congratulation; INTERJ congratulations

enigma M (misterio) enigma, conundrum; (adivinanza) riddle; (problema) puzzle

enjabonar VT (poner jabón) to soap, to lather; (adular) to flatter

enjaezar[9] VT to harness

enjalbegar[7] VT to whitewash

enjambre M swarm

enjaular VT (un animal) to cage; (a una persona) to jail

enjuagar[7] VT to rinse; (ropa) to rinse out; (platos) to rinse off

enjuague M (limpieza) rinse, rinsing; (trama) scheme; — **bucal** mouthwash

enjugar[7] VT (la frente) to wipe; (lágrimas) to wipe away

enjuiciar VT to prosecute, to try

enjuto ADJ dry; (delgado) thin

enlace M (de trenes) link; (químico) bond; (boda) marriage; (persona) liaison

enladrillado M brick pavement

enladrillar VT to brick, to pave with bricks

enlatar VT to can

enlazar[9] VT (unir) to link; (sujetar con lazo) to rope, to lasso; VI to connect; **—se** to connect

enlodar VT to muddy; **—se** to get muddy

enloquecedor ADJ maddening

enloquecer[13] VT to drive crazy; VI to go crazy; **—se** to go crazy

enlosado M flagstone pavement

enlosar VT to pave with flagstones

enmantecar[6] VT to butter

enmarañar VT (pelo) to entangle; (problema) to complicate

enmarcar[6] VT (un cuadro) to frame; **se enmarca dentro de** it takes place in the context of

enmascarar VT to mask

enmendar[1] VT (una ley) to amend; (un texto) to revise; — **la situación** to mend matters; **no me enmiendes la plana** don't correct me; VI **—se** to mend one's ways

enmienda F (de una ley) amendment; (de un texto) revision

enmohecer[13] VT to mold; **—se** to get moldy, to mold

enmudecer[13] VT to silence; VI to go silent

ennegrecer[13] VI/VT to blacken

ennoblecer[13] VT to ennoble

enojadizo ADJ hotheaded

enojado ADJ angry, mad

enojar VT to anger; **—se** to get angry

enojo M anger

enojoso ADJ bothersome

enorgullecer[13] VT to fill with pride; **—se de** to take pride in

enorme ADJ enormous

enramada F bower

enrarecido ADJ thin, rare

enrarecimiento M rarity, thinness

enredadera F creeper

enredar VT (enmarañar) to entangle; (complicar) to complicate; (involucrar) to mix up; VI to cause trouble; **—se** to get tangled up; **—se con** to become involved with

enredijo M tangle, snarl
enredo M (enredijo) snarl; (lío) mess; (amancebamiento) affair
enredoso ADJ complicated
enrejado M (conjunto de rejas) grating, grate; (entrecruzamiento de varillas) lattice
enrejar VT to install a grate on
enrevesado ADJ involved
enriquecer[13] VT to enrich; —**se** to become rich
enrojecer[13] VI/VT to redden
enrollar VT (manga, alfombra) to roll up; (hilo, cuerda, cinta magnética) to wind up; —**se con** to become involved with
enronquecer[13] VT to make hoarse; VI to become hoarse
enroscar[6] VT (soga) to coil, to roll up; (tuerca) to screw in; (tapa) to screw on; —**se** (vid) to twine; (serpiente) to coil up
ensacar[6] VT to sack
ensalada F salad
ensalzar[9] VT to extol
ensanchar VT to widen; —**se** (una calle) to widen; (una falda) to flare
ensanche M (de una calle) widening; (de una ciudad) expansion
ensangrentado ADJ gory, bloody
ensangrentar VT to smear blood on; —**se** to get covered with blood
ensartar VT (cuentas) to string; (aguja) to thread; (con un pincho) to pierce; (historias) to rattle off
ensayar VT (probar) to try out; (intentar) to try; (analizar un metal) to assay; (practicar una obra teatral) to rehearse
ensayo M (intento) trial, attempt; (de teatro) rehearsal; (obra literaria) essay; (nuclear) testing; (de un metal) assay; — **general** dress rehearsal; **por — y error** by trial and error
ensenada F cove
enseña F ensign
enseñanza F teaching, education; —**s** teachings
enseñar VT (mostrar) to show; (instruir) to teach; — **a** to teach how to
enseres M PL household utensils
ensillar VT to saddle, to saddle up
ensimismarse VI to lose oneself in thought
ensoberbecer[13] VT to make haughty; —**se** to become haughty
ensombrecer[13] VT (oscurecer) to make shadowy; (entristecer) to sadden
ensoñación F dream
ensordecedor ADJ deafening
ensordecer[13] VT to deafen
ensortijar VT to curl

ensuciar VT to dirty, to sully; —**se** (ponerse sucio) to get dirty; (defecar) to soil oneself; —**se en** to defecate on
ensueño M reverie, dream
entablar VT (relaciones) to establish; (un conflicto) to start; (una conversación) to strike up; (una demanda) to file; (una pelea) to pick
entablillar VT to splint
entallar VT to take in
entarimar VT to floor with planks
ente M (ser) entity; (excéntrico) weirdo; (agencia) agency
enteco ADJ sickly
entender[1] VT to understand; (oír) to hear; (ser homosexual) *Esp* to be homosexual; — **de** to know about; —**se con** (comunicar) to communicate with; (llevarse bien) to get along with; **dar a** — to intimate; **yo me entiendo** I know what I'm doing; **se entiende** of course
entendido -da ADJ (comprendido) understood; (experto) expert; **tengo** — **que** I understand that; **caridad mal entendida** misguided charity; MF expert
entendimiento M understanding
enterado ADJ informed; **darse por** — to acknowledge; **estar** — **de** to be privy to
enterar VT to inform; —**se (de)** to find out (about); **recién me entero** I just found out; **para que te enteres** just so you know
entereza F fortitude
enternecedor ADJ touching
enternecer[13] VT to touch; —**se** to be touched
entero ADJ (completo) entire, whole; (número) whole; **se mantuvo** — **durante el funeral** he held himself together during the funeral; M integer, whole number
enterrar[1] VT to bury
entibiar VT to make lukewarm; —**se** to become lukewarm
entidad F entity; **de** — significant; — **bancaria** banking institution
entierro M burial, funeral
entintar VT to stain with ink
entoldar VT to cover with an awning
entomología F entomology
entonación F intonation
entonar VT to sing; VI to sing in tune; — **con** to go well with; —**se** to get tipsy
entonces ADV then; **desde** — ever since; **hasta** — until then; **el** — **presidente** the then president; CONJ (así que) so
entornado ADJ half-open

entornar VT (una puerta) to leave ajar; (los ojos) to partially close

entorpecer[13] VT (los sentidos) to dull; (el paso) to hinder; **—se** to become sluggish

entorpecimiento M (de los sentidos) dullness; (del paso) hindrance

entrada F (sitio por donde se entra, de un actor) entrance; (acción de entrar, artículo de diccionario) entry; (conjunto de personas que asisten) gate; (oportunidad para actuar) opening; (billete, derecho, precio de entrar) admission; (llegada) arrival; (primer plato) entrée; (pago inicial) down payment; (tiempo en béisbol) inning; **—s** cash receipts; **— de coches** driveway; **— por partida doble** double entry; **de —** from the start

entramado M lattice

entrante ADJ (alcalde, etc.) incoming; (año) next; M recess

entrañas F PL (intestinos) entrails, *fam* guts; (sentimientos) heart, core; **— de la tierra** bowels of the earth; **de mis —** of my own flesh and blood

entrar VI to enter; (a trabajar) to come in; (en un lugar) to fit; VT (datos) to enter, to input; **le entré dos pastillas** I brought in two pills for him; **me entró miedo** I became afraid; **me entró sueño** I got sleepy; **no sé cómo —le a esa chica** I don't know how to approach that girl; **la física no me entra** I can't learn physics; **no entra entre mis favoritos** it is not included among my favorites; **la semana que entra** next week; **este vestido no me entra** this dress doesn't fit me; **seis entra dos veces en doce** six goes into twelve two times; **dejar —** to let in; **hacer — en razón** to bring to reason; **hazle —** show him in; **— a medicina** to go into medicine; **— en calor** to warm up; **— en coma** to go into a coma; **— en / a un cuarto** to enter a room; **— en una discusión** to take part in a discussion; **— en materia** to get to the meat of a matter; **— en vigencia / vigor** to go into effect

entre PREP (dos) between; (muchos) among; **— vaso y vaso** between glasses; **— dientes** under one's breath

entreabierto ADJ ajar, half-open

entreabrir[51] VT (puerta) to crack open; (los ojos) to half-open

entreacto M intermission

entrecano ADJ graying

entrecejo M space between the eyebrows

entrecortado ADJ (voz) faltering; (respiración) irregular

entrecortarse VI to falter

entrecruzar[9] VT to interlace; **—se** to cross

entredicho LOC ADV **en —** in doubt

entrega F (de un paquete) delivery; (de un manuscrito) submission; (al vicio) surrender; (de una novela) installment; (de revista) issue; **por —s** serial; **— a domicilio** home delivery; **— de premios** presentation of awards; **— inicial** down payment

entregar[7] VT (un paquete) to deliver; (a un rehén, prisionero) to hand over; (a un delincuente) to turn in; (a una hija en matrimonio) to give; (premios) to hand out, to present; (los deberes) to hand in; (el coche) to trade in; **—se (a)** to surrender (to), to dedicate oneself to

entrelazar[9] VT to intertwine

entremés M (obra de teatro) interlude; (comida) hors d'oeuvre

entremeter VT to insert; **—se en** (meterse) to get mixed up in; (inmiscuirse) to meddle in

entremetido -da ADJ meddlesome, nosy; MF meddler

entremezclar VT to intermingle

entrenador -ora MF trainer, coach

entrenamiento M training

entrenar VI/VT to train

entrepierna F (de personas) crotch; (de pantalón) inseam

entrepiso M mezzanine

entresacar[6] VT (seleccionar) to cull; (hacer menos espeso) to thin

entresuelo M (de hotel) mezzanine; (de cine) balcony

entretanto ADV meanwhile

entretejer VT (el pelo, una tela) to weave; (una historia) to weave together

entretener[44] VT (hacer atrasar) to delay; (distraer) to distract; (divertir) to entertain; **—se** (divertirse) to amuse oneself; (detenerse) to delay

entretenido ADJ entertaining

entretenimiento M entertainment, amusement

entrever[48] VT (apenas) to catch a glimpse of; (a lo lejos) to make out

entreverar VT to intersperse; **—se** to meddle

entrevía F gauge

entrevista F interview

entrevistar VT to interview; **—se con** to have an interview with

entristecer[13] VT to sadden; **—se** to become sad

entrometerse VI to meddle, to interfere

entrometido -da ADJ meddlesome, nosy; MF meddler, busybody

entronque M (ferroviario) junction; (parentesco) relationship

entropía F entropy

entumecido ADJ (dedo, diente) numb; (músculo) stiff

entumecimiento M (de los dedos, dientes) numbness; (de los músculos) stiffness

enturbiar VT (el agua) to muddy; (una decisión) to muddle; (el juicio, la alegría) to cloud; —**se** (agua) to get muddy; (alegría) to be marred

entusiasmado ADJ enthusiastic

entusiasmar VT to excite; —**se** to be excited

entusiasmo M enthusiasm, excitement

entusiasta MF enthusiast; ADJ enthusiastic

enumerar VT to enumerate

enunciado M utterance

enunciar VT (palabras) to enunciate; (una teoría) to articulate, to enunciate

envainar VT to sheathe

envalentonar VT to make bold; —**se** to get bold

envanecer[13] VT to make vain; —**se** to become vain

envarado ADJ stiff

envaramiento M stiffness

envasar VT to package; — **al vacío** to vacuum-pack

envase M packaging

envejecer[13] VT to make old; **ese maquillaje te envejece** that makeup makes you look old; VI to grow old, to age

envenenamiento M poisoning

envenenar VT to poison

envergadura F (de un avión) wingspan; (de un ave) wingspread; (de un evento, proyecto) importance

envés M back

enviado -da MF (político) envoy; (periodístico) correspondent

enviar[16] VT to send

enviciar VT to corrupt; —**se con** to get hooked on

envidia F envy

envidiable ADJ enviable

envidiar VT to envy

envidioso ADJ envious, jealous

envilecer[13] VT to debase

envío M (de mercancías) shipment; (de un manuscrito) submission

envite M bet

envoltorio M (cosa envuelta) bundle; (envoltura) wrapper

envoltura F wrapping, wrapper

envolver[2, 51] VT (involucrar) to involve; (cubrir) to wrap; (atrapar) to entangle; (rodear) to surround; —**se** to become involved

enyesar VT (enlucir con yeso) to plaster; (escayolar) to put in a cast

enzima MF enzyme

épica F epic

epicentro M epicenter

épico ADJ epic

epidemia F epidemic

epidémico ADJ epidemic

epidermis F epidermis

epifanía F epiphany

epilepsia F epilepsy

epílogo M epilog

episódico ADJ episodic

episodio M episode

epitafio M epitaph

epítome M epitome

época F (momento) time, period; (período histórico) age; (temporada) season; (período geológico) epoch

epopeya F epic poem

equidad F equity

equidistante ADJ equidistant

equilibrar VT to balance

equilibrio M equilibrium, balance; **perder el** — to lose one's balance; **hacer** —**s** to do a balancing act

equino ADJ & M equine

equinoccio M equinox

equipaje M baggage, luggage

equipamiento M equipment

equipar VT to equip, to outfit

equiparar VT to equate

equipo M (materiales) equipment; (grupo de personas) team; — **de vida** life-support system; — **deportivo** sweatsuit; — **de esquí** ski gear

equitación F horsemanship

equitativo ADJ equitable

equivalente ADJ equivalent

equivaler[46] VI to be equivalent; **lo que equivale a decir** which amounts to saying

equivocación F mistake

equivocado ADJ mistaken, wrong; **estar** — to be wrong / mistaken

equivocar[6] VT to mistake; —**se** to be mistaken, to make a mistake; —**se de sala** to choose the wrong room; **si no me equivoco** unless I'm mistaken

equívoco ADJ (ambiguo) equivocal; (moralmente dudoso) questionable; M misunderstanding

era F (período) era, age; (lugar donde se trilla) threshing floor; (parcela) plot

erario M treasury
erección F erection
erecto ADJ (órgano) erect; (postura) upright
erguido ADJ erect, upright
erguir[3b] VT to lift, to raise; —**se** to rise
erial M uncultivated land
erigir[11] VT (construir) to erect; (fundar) to found; —**se en** to set oneself up as
Eritrea F Eritrea
eritreo -a ADJ & MF Eritrean
erizado ADJ bristly; — **de** bristling with
erizar[9] VT to set on end; —**se** to bristle
erizo M hedgehog; — **de mar** sea urchin; **ser un** — to be a grouch
ermitaño -ña MF (persona) hermit; M (cangrejo) hermit crab
erógeno ADJ erogenous
erosión F erosion
erótico ADJ erotic
erradicar[6] VT to eradicate, to root out
errado ADJ erroneous, in error
errante ADJ wandering
errar[27] VT to miss; — **el cálculo** to miscalculate; VI (estar equivocado) to be mistaken; (vagar) to roam, to rove, to wander
errata F misprint, typographical error
errático ADJ erratic
erróneo ADJ erroneous
error M error, mistake; — **de imprenta** misprint
eructar VI to belch, to burp
eructo M belch, burp
erudición F learning, scholarship
erudito -ta ADJ (persona) erudite; (obra) scholarly, learned; MF scholar
erupción F eruption; **hacer** — to erupt
esbelto ADJ slender
esbozar[9] VT to outline; — **una sonrisa** to give a hint of a smile
esbozo M sketch, outline; — **de una sonrisa** hint of a smile
escabechar VT to pickle
escabroso ADJ (agreste) rugged; (espinoso) thorny; (sórdido) lurid, sordid
escabullirse[19] VI (ladrones) to slip away, to steal away; (lagartijas) to scurry away / off; — **de** to wriggle out of
escafandra F (en el agua) scuba gear; (en el espacio) spacesuit
escala F (escalera, escalafón) ladder; (serie de grados, notas, relación de importancia) scale; (parada) stopover; **hacer** — **en** to stop over at; — **salarial** wage scale; **a** — **nacional** nationwide; **de gran** — large-scale; **sin** —**s** nonstop
escalada F (de una montaña) climb; (de violencia) escalation
escalador -ora MF climber
escalar VT to scale, to climb
escaldadura F scald
escaldar VT (la piel) to scald; (las verduras) to blanch; —**se** to get scalded
escalera F (en un edificio) stairs, staircase; (de mano) ladder; (de naipes) flush; — **mecánica** escalator; — **de caracol** spiral / winding staircase; — **de color** straight flush; — **de incendios** fire escape; — **real** royal flush
escalfar VT to poach
escalinata F grand staircase
escalofriante ADJ chilling, hair-raising
escalofrío M chill; —**s** the shivers
escalón M (peldaño) step, stair; (terraza) terrace; (de escalera de mano, de escalafón) rung; (formación militar) echelon
escalonar VT (distribuir) to stagger; (aterrazar) to terrace
escalope M scallop
escama F (de animal) scale; (de piel, de corteza) flake
escamar VT to scale
escamoso ADJ (animal) scaly; (piel) flaky
escamotear VT (esconder) to palm; (robar) to snatch; (eludir) to shirk
escampar VI to clear up
escandalizar[9] VT (chocar) to scandalize; (causar escándalo) to cause a scandal; —**se** to be shocked
escándalo M (suceso vergonzoso) scandal; (riña) uproar
escandaloso ADJ (chocante) scandalous, shocking; (ruidoso) raucous
escandir VT lit to scan
escanear VT to scan
escáner M scanner
escaño M seat in parliament
escapada F (escape) escape
escapar VI (de un lugar, una situación) to escape; (de una persona, responsabilidad) to run away; —**se** (persona) to escape; (gas) to leak; **se me escapó una sonrisa** I inadvertently smiled; **Matilde se me está escapando de las manos** Matilde is getting out of hand
escaparate M shop window
escapatoria F escape, way out
escape M (de fantasía, escapatoria) escape; (de motor) exhaust; (de gas, agua) leak
escarabajo M beetle
escaramuza F skirmish
escaramuzar[9] VI to skirmish
escarbar VI/VT to dig, to scratch; — **en los**

archivos to dig around in the files; —
los dientes to pick one's teeth
escarcha F frost
escarchar VI to frost
escardar VT to weed
escarlata ADJ & M (color) scarlet; F
(enfermedad) scarlet fever
escarlatina F scarlet fever
escarmentar[1] VI to learn one's lesson; VT to
teach a lesson
escarmiento M lesson; **que te sirva de —**
let that be a lesson to you
escarnecer[13] VT to deride
escarnio M derision
escarpa F steep slope
escarpado ADJ steep, precipitous; M steep
slope
escasear VI (estar escaso) to be scarce;
(acabarse) to grow scarce
escasez F (falta) shortage; (carestía) scarcity,
want
escaso ADJ sparse, scarce; **una docena
escasa** a scant dozen; **— de** short on; **—
de personal** short-handed
escatimar VT to skimp on; **no — gastos** to
spare no expense
escena F (fragmento de una obra de teatro,
episodio) scene; (escenario) stage; **montar
una —** to make a scene; **en —** on stage;
poner en — to stage; **entrar en —** to go
on stage
escenario M stage
escenificación F staging
escepticismo M skepticism
escéptico -ca ADJ skeptical; MF skeptic
escisión F split
esclarecer[13] VT to elucidate
esclavitud F slavery
esclavizar[9] VT to enslave
esclavo -va MF slave
esclerosis F sclerosis; **— múltiple** multiple
sclerosis
esclusa F (de un canal) lock; (de una presa)
floodgate, sluice gate
escoba F broom
escobilla F whisk broom
escocer[2, 10c] VI to sting
escocés -esa ADJ Scottish; **(cuadros)
escoceses** plaid; MF Scot; M (whisky)
Scotch; (lengua) Scottish
Escocia F Scotland
escoger[11b] VT to choose
escolar MF pupil; ADJ **año —** school year
escoliosis F scoliosis
escollo M (en el mar) reef; (obstáculo)
obstacle
escolta F (policial) escort; MF INV (persona)

escort
escoltar VT to escort
escombros M PL rubble, debris
esconder VT to hide; VI **—se** to hide
escondidas LOC ADV **a —** on the sly; **entrar
a —** to sneak in; **meter algo a —** to
sneak something in; **jugar a las —** to
play hide and seek
escondite M hiding place; (de ladrón)
hideout; (de cazador) blind; **jugar al —**
to play hide and seek
escondrijo M hiding place
escopeta F shotgun
escoplo M chisel
escora F listing
escorar VI to list
escoria F (de metales) slag; (de la sociedad)
scum, dregs
escorpión M scorpion
escotado ADJ low-cut
escote M (parte del vestido) neckline; (parte
del cuerpo) cleavage; **pagar a —** to go
Dutch
escotilla F hatch
escozor M smarting sensation
escribiente MF clerk
escribir[51] VI/VT to write; **¿cómo se escribe?**
how do you spell it? **— a máquina** to
type
escrito ADJ written; **— a máquina**
typewritten; **no —** unwritten; **por —** in
writing; M document
escritor -ora MF writer, author
escritorio M (mueble) desk; (oficina) office
escritura F (acción de escribir) writing;
(certificado de propiedad) deed; **— de
traspaso** conveyance; **— de venta** bill of
sale
escroto M scrotum
escrúpulo M scruple, qualm; **sin —s**
unscrupulous
escrupuloso ADJ scrupulous
escrutar VT (a una persona) to scrutinize; (el
horizonte) to scan; (votos) to count
escrutinio M (examen) scrutiny; (recuento)
vote count
escuadra F (de buques, soldados) squadron;
(instrumento) square
escuadrilla F (de aviones) flight of aircraft;
(de buques) squadron
escuadrón M squadron; **— de la muerte**
death squad
escualidez F (delgadez) skinniness; (suciedad)
squalor
escuálido ADJ (sucio) squalid; (delgado) thin
escuchar VT to listen to; (oír) to hear; VI to
listen; **— a hurtadillas** to eavesdrop

escudar VT to shield
escudo M (arma defensiva) shield; (moneda de Portugal) escudo; **— de armas** coat of arms
escudriñar VT (a una persona) to scrutinize, to peer at; (el horizonte) to scan
escuela F school; **— industrial** trade school; **— normal** school of education; **— pública** public school; **— primaria** elementary school; **— secundaria** secondary school; **tener —** to have good technique
escueto ADJ (explicación) succinct; (verdad) simple
esculpir VI/VT to sculpture, to sculpt
escultor -ora MF sculptor
escultura F sculpture
escupir VI/VT to spit
escupitajo M spit
escurridizo ADJ (acera) slippery; (ladrón) elusive, slippery
escurrir VI/VT (platos, verduras) to drain; (ropa) to wring out; **—se** to slink away
ese ADJ that, those; **esa chica se llama Matilde** that girl is named Matilde; **esas ciudades son antiguas** those cities are old; PRON that one, those; **ese es el mayor** that one is the oldest; **esos son mis hijos** those are my children
esencia F essence
esencial ADJ essential; **lo —** gist, bottom line, name of the game
esfera F (sólido) sphere; (espacio, ámbito) realm, sphere; (de reloj) face, dial
esférico ADJ spherical; M soccer ball
esforzado ADJ valiant
esforzarse[9] VI to try hard, to exert oneself; **— por** to strive to, to make an effort to
esfuerzo M effort
esfumar VT to tone down; **—se** to vanish
esgrima F fencing; **practicar —** to fence
esgrimir VT (armas) to brandish, to wield; (argumentos) to employ
eslabón M chain link; **— perdido** missing link
eslabonar VT to link
eslavo -va ADJ Slavic; MF Slav
eslogan M slogan
eslovaco ADJ & MF Slovakian; M (lengua) Slovakian
Eslovaquia F Slovakia
Eslovenia F Slovenia
esloveno -na ADJ & MF Slovene; M (lengua) Slovene
esmaltar VT to enamel
esmalte M enamel; **— de uñas** nail polish
esmerado ADJ painstaking, careful

esmeralda F emerald
esmerarse VI to take pains
esmerilado ADJ frosted; M frosting
esmerilar VT to frost
esmero M care
esmirriado ADJ scrawny
esmoquin M tuxedo
esnifar VT to snort
esnob M snob
esnórquel M snorkel
eso PRON DEM that; **— es** that's true; **— sí** granted; **a — de las tres** at about three o'clock; **de —, nada** no way! **en — llega y me dice** at that moment he arrives and says to me; **y — que le dije que viniese temprano** even when I told him to come early
esófago M esophagus
esotérico ADJ esoteric
espaciado M pitch, spacing
espacial ADJ spatial; **nave —** space ship
espaciar VT to space; **—se** to space out
espacio M (capacidad) space, room; (superficie) expanse; (separación entre líneas) space, spacing; (en un formulario) blank space; (porción de tiempo) span; **— aéreo** aerospace; **— exterior** outer space; **— noticioso** newscast; **a doble —** double-spaced; **a un —** single-spaced; **por — de una semana** for a week
espacioso ADJ spacious, roomy
espada F sword; **—s** (palo de naipes) swords; **— de doble filo** double-edged sword; **estar entre la — y la pared** to be between a rock and a hard place
espalda F back; **— mojada** pey wetback; **a —s de alguien** behind one's back; **caerse de —s** to fall on one's back; **nadar de —** to do the backstroke; **tener las —s anchas** to take a lot of abuse; **volver las —s** to turn one's back
espaldar M chair back
espantadizo ADJ easily scared
espantado ADJ frightened
espantajo M scarecrow
espantar VT to frighten, to scare; (ahuyentar) to frighten away, to scare away; **—se** to get scared; M SG **espantapájaros** scarecrow
espanto M fright, dread; **estás hecho un —** you look a sight; **estoy curado de —** nothing surprises me anymore
espantoso ADJ frightful, dreadful
España F Spain
español -ola ADJ Spanish; MF Spaniard; M (lengua) Spanish
esparadrapo M surgical tape

esparcimiento M (recreo) relaxation; (reparto) spreading

esparcir[10b] VT to scatter, to spread; **—se** to amuse oneself

espárrago M asparagus

espasmo M spasm, jerk

espasmódico ADJ jerky

espástico ADJ spastic

espátula F spatula

especia F spice

especial ADJ & M special; **en —** in particular

especialidad F specialty, specialization

especialista MF specialist

especialización F specialization

especializar[9] VT to specialize; **—se en** to specialize in

especie F (en ciencias naturales) species; (clase) kind; **—s en peligro de extinción** endangered species; **pagar en — to pay in kind; una — de** a kind of

especiero M spice rack

especificar[6] VT to specify

específico ADJ & M specific

espécimen M specimen

espectacular ADJ spectacular

espectáculo M (escándalo) spectacle; (actuación pública) show; (vista) sight; **dar el —** to make a spectacle of oneself

espectador -ora MF (de un espectáculo) spectator; (de un suceso) onlooker

espectro M (fantasma) specter; (de luz, medicina) spectrum

especulación F speculation

especulador -ora MF speculator

especular VT to speculate; ADJ mirror; **imagen —** mirror image

espejismo M (en el desierto) mirage; (ilusión) illusion

espejo M mirror; **— de cuerpo entero** full-length mirror; **— retrovisor** rearview mirror

espeluznante ADJ hair-raising

espeluznar VT to terrify; **—se** to be terrified

espera F (acción de esperar) wait; (aplazamiento) extension; **estar en — de** to be waiting for

esperanza F hope; **— de vida** life expectancy; **con una — de voto de 12,5%** expected to get 12.5% of the vote

esperanzado ADJ hopeful

esperanzador ADJ hopeful

esperanzar[9] VT to give hope to

esperar VT (tener esperanza) to hope; (llevar a un hijo, creer que sucederá algo) to expect; (aguardar) to wait for; VI to wait; **era de —** it was to be expected; **espera sentado** don't hold your breath; **estoy esperando un milagro** I'm hoping for a miracle; **todavía espera confirmación** it still awaits confirmation

esperma MF sperm

esperpento M grotesque person or thing

espesar VT to thicken

espeso ADJ (pelo, sopa, niebla) thick; (cejas) bushy

espesor M thickness

espesura F (espesor) thickness; (lugar poblado de matorrales) thicket

espetar VT (decir bruscamente) to blurt out; (atravesar con un espeto) to run a spit through

espía MF INV spy

espiar[16] VI to spy; VT to spy on

espichar VI *fam* to croak, to bite the dust

espiga F spike

espigar[7] VT to glean; VI to grow spikes; **—se** to grow tall

espina F (de planta) thorn; (de pez) fish bone; **— dorsal** spinal column; **me quedé con la —** I was left wondering

espinaca F spinach

espinal ADJ spinal

espinazo M spine, backbone

espinilla F (de persona) shin; (de animal) shank; (grano) blackhead

espino M thorny shrub

espinoso ADJ thorny

espionaje M espionage

espiración F expiration

espiral ADJ & F spiral

espirar VI/VT to exhale, to breathe out, to expire

espíritu M (ser no físico, fantasma, de una ley) spirit; (alma) soul; **— fuerte** free spirit; **— deportivo** sportsmanship; **— emprendedor** can-do attitude; **— Santo** Holy Spirit

espiritual ADJ & M spiritual

espita F spigot

espléndido ADJ (estupendo) splendid; (generoso) lavish

esplendor M splendor

esplendoroso ADJ magnificent

espliego M lavender

espolear VT to spur

espoleta F bomb fuse

espolón M (de gallo, planta, estímulo) spur; (de buque) ram

espolvorear VT to dust, to sprinkle

esponja F (animal, utensilio) sponge; (borracho) souse

esponjado ADJ spongy

esponjar VT to make spongy; **—se** to become spongy

esponjoso ADJ spongy

esponsales M PL betrothal

espontaneidad F spontaneity

espontáneo ADJ spontaneous

espora F spore

esposar VT to handcuff

esposo -sa M husband; F wife; **esposas** handcuffs

espuela F spur

espulgar[7] VT to delouse

espuma F (de cerveza) froth; (de jabón) suds, lather; (de la boca) foam; (de colchón) foam rubber; (de mar) foam, spray; **echar — por la boca** to foam at the mouth; **hacer —** to make suds

espumar VT (quitar la espuma) to skim; (formar espuma) to foam

espumarajo M foam; **echar —s por la boca** to foam at the mouth

espumillón M tinsel

espumoso ADJ foamy

esputo M sputum

esquela F note; **— mortuoria** death notice

esqueleto M (huesos) skeleton; (armazón) framework; **mover el —** (bailar) to dance; (moverse) to move

esquema M outline; **romperle los —s a alguien** (planes) to ruin one's plans; (conceptos) to shatter one's preconceptions

esquí M (tabla) ski; (deporte) skiing; **— acuático** (tabla) water ski; (deporte) water skiing; **hacer — acuático** to water-ski

esquiar[16] VI to ski

esquila F (cencerro) cowbell; (acción de esquilar) shearing

esquilador -ora MF sheep shearer

esquilar VT to shear, to clip

esquileo M shearing

esquimal ADJ & MF Eskimo; M (lengua) Eskimo

esquina F corner; **en cada —** everywhere

esquirol M strikebreaker; *pey* scab

esquivar VT (a una vecina) to avoid; (un golpe) to dodge

esquivo ADV (tímido) shy, coy; (huraño) aloof; (reservado) elusive

esquizofrenia F schizophrenia

estabilidad F stability

estabilizar[9] VT to stabilize

estable ADJ (mesa) stable; (precio) firm; (huésped) long-term

establecer[13] VT to establish; (averiguar) to ascertain; **— una cita** to set up an appointment; **—se** to settle

establecimiento M establishment

establishment M establishment

establo M stable

estaca F (con punta) stake; (gruesa) club

estacada F stockade; **dejar en la —** to leave in the lurch

estacar[6] VT (atar) to stake; (delimitar) to stake off

estación F (de tren, autobús, radio) station; (parte del año) season; **— bípeda** bipedal stance; **— de bomberos** fire station; **— de esquí** ski resort; **— de servicio** filling station; **— de trabajo** work station; **— espacial** space station

estacionamiento M (acción) parking; (lugar) parking lot

estacionar VT (tropas) to station; (un vehículo) to park; **—se** (un coche) to park; (precios) to level off

estacionario ADJ stationary

estadía F stay

estadio M (recinto con graderías) stadium; (fase) stage

estadista M statesman; F stateswoman

estadística F (ciencia) statistics; **—s** (datos numéricos) statistics

estado M (manera de estar, unidad política) state; **— civil** marital status; **— de cuenta** bank statement; **— de alarma** state of emergency; **— de ánimo** state of mind; **— de excepción** martial law; **— de guerra** state of war; **— de sitio** state of siege; **— mayor** chiefs of staff; **— policíaco** police state; **de — sólido** solid state; **en — interesante** expecting; **en — vegetativo** brain-dead

Estados Unidos M PL / SG United States

estadounidense ADJ & MF American

estafa F swindle, scam, racket

estafador -ora MF swindler

estafar VT to swindle

estalactita F stalactite

estalagmita F stalagmite

estallar VI (una bomba) to explode; (un globo) to burst; (una guerra) to break out; (una persona) to snap; **— de risa** to burst with laughter; **— en una carcajada** to burst out laughing; **hacer —** to set off

estallido M (de bomba, color) explosion; (ruido) bang, report

estampa F (de revista) illustration; (imagen) image; (apariencia) appearance; **de buena —** good-looking; **la viva — de la madre** the spitting image of her mother; **la viva — de la desolación** the very picture of desolation

estampado ADJ printed; M (tela) print; (acción) printing

estampar VT (en tela, papel) to print; (con

un molde, en metal) to stamp; —**le un beso a alguien** to plant a kiss on someone

estampida F stampede

estampido M bang

estampilla F stamp

estampillar VT to stamp

estancado ADJ stagnant

estancar[6] VT to stem; to dam; to block; —**se** to stagnate

estancia F (estadía) stay; (habitación) hall; (hacienda) *RP* cattle ranch

estanco ADJ waterproof; M government store

estándar ADJ INV & M standard

estandarización F standardization

estandarizar[9] VT to standardize

estandarte M standard, banner

estanque M pond

estante M (tabla) shelf; (mueble) bookcase

estantería F (mueble) bookcase; (en una biblioteca) stack

estañar VT to tin-plate

estaño M tin

estar[28] VI to be; — **a tres kilómetros de aquí** to be three kilometers from here; — **bien** to be all right; — **del corazón** to have heart trouble; — **de más** to be unnecessary; — **para** to be about to; — **por** (a favor de) to be in favor of; (a punto de) to be about to; — **trabajando duro** to be working hard; **¿a cuántos estamos?** what day of the month is it? **ahí está** that's it; **¿está Alice?** is Alice there? **están muy buenos tus zapatos nuevos** your new shoes are nice; **estáte tranquilo** don't worry; **no** — to be out; **cuarto de** — living room

estático ADJ static

estatua F statue

estatura F (importancia) stature; (altura de una persona) height

estatuto M (ley) statute; (de una sociedad) bylaw

este ADJ DEM this, these; **esta chica se llama Hilary** this girl is named Hilary; **estas ciudades son antiguas** these cities are old; PRON DEM this one, these; — **es el mayor** this one is the oldest; **estos son mis hijos** these are my children; M & ADJ east; **hacia el** — eastward

estela F (de una embarcación) wake; (de humo, polvo) trail; **dejar una** — to leave a trail

estelar ADJ stellar

estenotipista MF court reporter

estentóreo ADJ booming

estepa F steppe

estera F mat

estercolar VT to fertilize with manure

estercolero M dunghill

estéreo ADJ & M stereo; **en** — in stereo

estereotipo M stereotype

estéril ADJ sterile; (mujer) barren

esterilidad F sterility

esterilizar[9] VT to sterilize

esternón M sternum

esteroide M steroid

estertor M death rattle

estética F aesthetics

estético ADJ aesthetic

estetoscopio M stethoscope

estibador M longshoreman

estibar VT to stow

estiércol M manure

estigma M stigma

estigmatizar[9] VT to stigmatize

estilarse VI to be in style

estilo M (literario, estético) style; (de natación) stroke; — **de vida** lifestyle; — **espalda** backstroke; — **indirecto** reported speech; — **libre** freestyle; — **mariposa** butterfly stroke; — **pecho** breaststroke; — **perrito** dog paddle; **cosas por el** — things like that

estima F esteem, regard

estimación F (cálculo) estimate; (estima) estimation

estimado ADJ esteemed; — **Sr.** Dear Sir

estimar VT (apreciar) to esteem; (determinar el valor) to estimate; (opinar) to think

estimulación F stimulation

estimulante ADJ stimulating; M stimulant

estimular VT to stimulate; (alentar) to encourage

estímulo M stimulus

estío M *lit* summer

estipendio M stipend

estipulación F stipulation

estipular VT to stipulate

estirado ADJ stuck-up

estirar VT (alargar) to stretch; — **el cuello** to crane one's neck; — **la pata** *fam* to kick the bucket; (crecer) to grow; —**se** to stretch

estirón M growth spurt; **pegar un** — to have a growth spurt

estirpe F lineage

estival ADJ **vacaciones —es** summer vacation

esto ADJ & PRON this; — **es** that is to say; **a todo** — meanwhile; **en** — at this point

estocada F thrust; **lanzar una** — to thrust

estofa F type; **de baja** — low-class

estofado M stew

estofar VT to stew
estoico -ca ADJ & MF stoic
estolón M runner
estómago M stomach
Estonia F Estonia
estonio -nia ADJ & MF Estonian; M (lengua) Estonian
estopa F tow
estorbar VT (obstaculizar) to hinder, to impede; (ser una molestia) to be a nuisance
estorbo M (obstáculo) hindrance, impediment; (molestia) nuisance
estornino M starling
estornudar VI to sneeze
estornudo M sneeze
estrado M bench
estrafalario ADJ bizarre, outlandish
estragar[7] VT (físicamente) to devastate; (moralmente) to corrupt
estrago M havoc; **hacer —s** to wreak havoc
estrangular VT to strangle
estratagema F stratagem
estrategia F strategy
estratégico ADJ strategic
estrato M stratum, layer; **— social** social class
estratosfera F stratosphere
estrechamiento M constriction
estrechar VT (hacer más estrecho) to narrow; (abrazar) to embrace; **la estrechó en sus brazos** he held her in his arms; **—se** to get narrower; **—se la mano** to shake hands
estrechez F (cualidad de estrecho) narrowness; (estrechamiento) narrowing; (aprietos) dire straits
estrecho ADJ narrow; **la falda le quedaba estrecha** the skirt was too tight for her; M strait
estrella F star; **— binaria** binary star; **— de cine** movie star; **— de mar** starfish; **— fugaz** shooting star, falling star; **ver las —s** to see stars
estrellado ADJ (como una estrella) starlike; (cubierto de estrellas) starry
estrellar VT (aplastar) to smash; (romper) to crack; **—se** (avión) to crash; (intento) to fail; **—se contra** to smash into
estremecer[13] VT to make shudder; **el terremoto estremeció París** the earthquake rocked Paris; VI to shudder
estremecimiento M shudder
estrenar VT (un vestido) to wear for the first time; (una obra de cine, teatro) to debut; (una bicicleta) to try out for the first time; (un título) to use for the first time; **—se** to debut

estreno M (de una película) premiere; (de un objeto) first use; (de una actividad) debut
estreñido ADJ (constipado) constipated; (antipático) uptight
estreñimiento M constipation
estreñir[5,18] VT to constipate; **—se** to become constipated
estrépito M racket, clatter; **causar —** to clatter
estrepitoso ADJ noisy
estrés M stress
estresar VT to stress (out)
estría F (en la piel) stretch mark; (en una columna) flute
estriado ADJ (piel) covered with stretch marks; (columna) fluted; (piedra) streaked
estriar[16] VT to flute; **—se** to get stretch marks
estribación F spur
estribar VI **— en** (apoyarse en) to lean on; (radicar en) to lie in
estribillo M refrain
estribo M (de silla, oído) stirrup; (de coche) running board; **perder los —s** to fly off the handle
estribor M starboard
estricnina F strychnine
estricto ADJ strict
estridente ADJ strident
estrofa F verse, stanza
estrógeno M estrogen
estropajo M scrubber; **tengo la boca que es un —** my mouth is as dry as a bone
estropajoso ADJ sinewy
estropear VT to ruin
estructura F structure
estructural ADJ structural
estruendo M din, racket
estruendoso ADJ thunderous
estrujamiento M (para romper) crushing; (para sacar jugo) squeezing
estrujar VT (aplastar) to crush; (apretar) to squeeze
estrujón M squeeze
estuario M estuary
estucar[6] VT to stucco
estuche M (para joyas) jewelry box; (para pastillas) pill box; (para lentes) glasses case
estuco M stucco
estudiantado M student body
estudiante MF student
estudiantil ADJ **vida —** student life
estudiar VI/VT to study
estudio M (acción de estudiar, investigación, habitación de casa) study; (habitación de artista) studio; (apartamento pequeño)

studio apartment; **en —** understudy
estudioso -sa ADJ studious; MF scholar
estufa F (para calentar) heater, stove; (para cocinar) *Méx* stove
estupefaciente ADJ & M narcotic
estupefacto ADJ stunned, speechless
estupendo ADJ stupendous, terrific; **me la pasé — en la casa de Hilary** I had a great time at Hilary's house
estupidez F stupidity; **estupideces** nonsense
estúpido ADJ stupid
estupor M stupor
estupro M statutory rape
etapa F stage; **por —s** by stages
etcétera CONJ etcetera, and so forth
éter M ether
eternidad F eternity
eternizarse[9] VI to drag on
eterno ADJ eternal, everlasting
ética F ethics
ético ADJ ethical
etimología F etymology
etíope ADJ & MF Ethiopian
etiqueta F (normas de comportamiento) etiquette; (en una lata, botella) label; (en una prenda) tag; **— adhesiva** sticker; **— de identificación** name tag; **— de precio** price tag; **nos trataron con —** they treated us very formally; **vestirse de —** to dress formally
etiquetar VT (latas, botellas, personas) to label; (prendas) to tag
etnicidad F ethnicity
étnico ADJ ethnic
etnografía F ethnography
etnología F ethnology
ETS (enfermedad de transmisión sexual) F STD
eucalipto M eucalyptus
eufemismo M euphemism
euforia F euphoria
eunuco M eunuch
euro M euro
Europa F Europe
europeo -a ADJ & MF European
eutanasia F euthanasia
evacuación F (de un lugar) evacuation; (del vientre) bowel movement; (de agua) drainage
evacuar VT (un lugar, a una persona) to evacuate; (el vientre, los excrementos) to void; (agua) to drain
evadir VT to evade; **—se** to escape
evaluación F evaluation
evaluar[17] VT (analizar) to evaluate, to assess; (tasar) to estimate; (calificar) to test
evangélico ADJ evangelical

evangelio M gospel
evaporación F evaporation
evaporar VT to evaporate; **—se** to vanish
evasión F (fiscal) evasion; (de prisioneros, de la realidad) escape; **— de capitales** capital flight
evasiva F **salirse con —s** to beat around the bush
evasivo ADJ evasive
evasor -ora MF evader
evento M event
evidencia F evidence; **dejar / poner en —** to show up; **quedar / ponerse en —** to become apparent
evidenciar VT to make evident; **—se** to become evident
evidente ADJ evident, obvious
evitar VT (eludir) to avoid; (ahorrar) to spare
evocar[6] VT (una memoria) to evoke; (a los espíritus) to conjure up
evolución F evolution
evolucionar VI to evolve
ex MF *fam* ex
exacerbar VT (intensificar) to exacerbate; (irritar) to aggravate
exactitud F accuracy, precision
exacto ADJ exact, precise, accurate; INTERJ exactly
exageración F exaggeration
exagerado ADJ exaggerated; **Jorge es un —** Jorge always exaggerates
exagerar VI/VT to exaggerate
exaltar VT to exalt; **—se** to get excited
examen M (inspección) examination; (prueba) examination, test, exam; **— de ingreso** entrance examination; **— final** final examination; **— médico** checkup; **dar un —** to take a test; **poner un —** to give a test
examinar VT (inspeccionar) to examine; (someter a un examen) to test
exasperar VT to exasperate, to aggravate
excavación F excavation; (arqueológica) dig
excavador -ora MF (persona) excavator; F (aparato) excavator, earthmover
excavar VT to excavate, to dig
excedente ADJ & M surplus
exceder VT (sobrepasar) to exceed; (superar) to surpass; **— de** to go beyond
excelencia F excellence; **por —** par excellence
excelente ADJ excellent, great
excentricidad F eccentricity
excéntrico ADJ eccentric
excepción F exception; **a — de** with the exception of
excepcional ADJ exceptional

excepto ADV & PREP except
exceptuar[17] VT to except
excesivo ADJ excessive
exceso M excess; **— de equipaje** excess baggage; **beber en —** to drink to excess; **comer en —** to overeat
excitación F (de músculos) excitement; (sexual) arousal
excitante ADJ stimulating
excitar VT (un órgano) to excite; (sexualmente) to arouse; **—se** (sexualmente) to get aroused; (átomos) to be excited
exclamación F exclamation
exclamar VT to exclaim
excluir[31] VT to exclude
exclusión F exclusion
exclusivo ADJ exclusive
excomulgar[7] VT to excommunicate
excremento M excrement
excretar VT to excrete
excursión F excursion, outing
excusa F excuse
excusable ADJ excusable
excusado M *Méx* toilet
excusar VT to excuse
exención F exemption
exento ADJ exempt; **— de impuestos** tax-exempt
exequias F PL funeral rites
exhalar VI/VT (aire) to exhale, to breathe out; (un olor) to give off; **— un suspiro** to sigh
exhaustivo ADJ exhaustive, thorough
exhausto ADJ exhausted
exhibición F (manifestación) exhibition; (despliegue) display
exhibir VT (fotos) to exhibit; (mercancías) to display; (el carnet de identidad) to show; **—se** to be shown
exhortar VT to exhort, to urge
exigencia F demand
exigente ADJ demanding, exacting
exigir[11] VT to demand; **exigen a alguien que sepa inglés** they require someone who knows English
exiguo ADJ meager; **exigua mayoría** scant majority
exiliado -da MF exile
exiliar VT to exile
exilio M exile
eximio ADJ illustrious
eximir VT (de impuestos) to exempt; (de sospecha) to clear; (de una responsabilidad) to excuse
existencia F existence; **complicarle la — a alguien** to cause someone trouble; **la**

lucha por la — the fight for survival; **—s** stock on hand; **en —** in stock, on hand
existente ADJ extant, existing
existir VI to exist
éxito M success; (musical) hit; **— de taquilla** blockbuster; **tener —** to be successful; **tiene — con las mujeres** he's popular with women
exitoso ADJ successful
éxodo M exodus
exonerar VT to exonerate
exorbitante ADJ exorbitant
exorcisar VT to exorcise
exorcismo M exorcism
exótico ADJ exotic
expansión F (crecimiento) expansion; (diversión) relaxation
expansivo ADJ (que expande) expansive; (efusivo) effusive
expatriado -da MF expatriate
expatriar VT to expatriate, exile
expectación F anticipation
expectativa F (esperanza) expectation; (posibilidad) prospect; **estar en — de algo** to be on pins and needles; **— de vida** life expectancy
expectorar VI/VT to expectorate, to cough up
expedición F (viaje) expedition; (de documentos) issuing; (de mercancías) delivery
expedicionario -ria ADJ expeditionary; MF member of an expedition
expedidor -ora ADJ shipping; MF shipper
expediente M (administrativo) file, dossier; (policial, académico) record
expedir[5] VT (enviar) to dispatch; (emitir) to issue
expeler VT to expel
experiencia F experience
experimentado ADJ experienced
experimental ADJ experimental
experimentar VI (hacer experimentos) to experiment; VT (tener experiencia de) to experience
experimento M experiment
experto -ta ADJ & MF expert
expiación F atonement
expiar[16] VT to atone for
expirar VI to expire
explayarse VI to become extended; **— sobre** to enlarge upon
explicable ADJ explainable, explicable
explicación F explanation
explicar[6] VT to explain; **—se** to make oneself clear; **no me explico por qué** I can't figure out why
explicativo ADJ explanatory

explícito ADJ explicit
exploración F exploration
explorador -ora ADJ exploring; MF
(expedicionario) explorer; (militar) scout
explorar VI/VT to explore; (con fines
diagnósticos) to scan; (con fines militares)
to scout
explosión F explosion; **hacer —** to explode
explosivo ADJ & M explosive
explotación F exploitation
explotar VT (sacar provecho) to exploit;
(hacer explosión) to explode
exponente M exponent
exponer[39] VT (al sol, al peligro) to expose; (al
público) to exhibit, to display; (explicar)
to state, to set forth; **—se al peligro** to
expose oneself to danger
exportación F (acción) exportation, export;
(cosa) export
exportar VI/VT to export
exposición F (feria) exposition; (de arte)
exhibition; (explicación) explanation; (al
sol, a una influencia, al peligro) exposure
expresar VT to express
expresión F expression; **valga la —** so to
speak
expresivo ADJ expressive
expreso ADJ (explícito) express; (rápido) fast;
M express train
exprimidor M juicer
exprimir VT (naranjas) to squeeze; (zumo) to
squeeze out
expropiar VT to expropriate
expuesto ADJ exposed; **lo —** what has been
said
expulsar VT to expel; (de un bar) to throw
out; (de un partido) to eject
expulsión F expulsion
exquisito -ta ADJ exquisite; (comida)
delicious; MF effete snob
extasiado ADJ rapt
extasiarse[16] VI to be enraptured
éxtasis M ecstasy (también droga)
extender[1] VT (el brazo, radio de acción,
gratitud) to extend; (un tapete, una masa,
un idioma) to spread; (un cheque) to draw
up; **—se** to extend; (una masa) to enlarge
upon; **la fiesta se extendió hasta las 3**
the party lasted until 3 o'clock
extendido ADJ (brazos) outstretched;
(costumbre) widespread
extensión F (del antebrazo, semántica,
telefónica) extension; (de terreno)
expanse; (de un texto) length; (eléctrica)
extension cord; **por —** by extension;
tener mucha — to be widespread
extensivo ADJ extensive; **hacer —** to extend

extenso ADJ (calendario, plan, grupo)
extensive; (narración, programa de radio)
extended
extenuado ADJ exhausted
exterior ADJ (de fuera) exterior, outer;
(mundo) outside; (política) foreign; M
(parte de afuera) exterior, outside;
(aspecto) outward appearance; **en —es** on
location
exteriorizar[9] VT to externalize
exterminación F extermination
exterminar VT to exterminate
exterminio M extermination
externo ADJ external
extinción F extinction
extinguidor M fire extinguisher
extinguir[12] VT (un fuego) to extinguish, to
put out; (una especie) to make extinct, to
wipe out; **—se** (animal, volcán) to go
extinct
extinto ADJ extinct
extintor M fire extinguisher
extirpación F removal
extirpar VT to remove
extorsión F extortion
extorsionar VT to extort money from
extorsionista MF racketeer
extra ADJ extra; **horas —s** overtime; MF INV
(de película) extra; M (cosa accesoria)
extra; F (pago extraordinario) bonus
extracto M (resumen) abstract; (de café)
extract
extraditar VT to extradite
extraer[45] VT (esencia) to extract; (minerales)
to mine; (un diente) to pull
extramarital ADJ extramarital
extranjero -ra ADJ foreign; MF foreigner; **en
el —** abroad
extrañar VT (sorprender) to surprise; (echar
de menos) to miss; **no es de — que** it's
no wonder that; **no me extraña** it
doesn't surprise me; **—se** to be surprised
extrañeza F surprise
extraño -ña ADJ (persona, costumbre)
strange; (partícula) foreign; MF stranger
extraoficial ADJ unofficial
extraordinario ADJ extraordinary
extrapolar VI/VT to extrapolate
extrasensorial ADJ extrasensory
extraterrestre ADJ & M alien, extraterrestrial
extravagancia F (cualidad de extravagante)
extravagance; (comportamiento
extravagante) outrageous behavior
extravagante ADJ flamboyant, outrageous
extraviar[16] VT (perder) to misplace;
(confundir) to lead astray; **—se** to lose
one's way, to get lost

extravío M loss
extremado ADJ extreme
extremar VT to maximize
extremidad F extremity
extremo ADJ (máximo, mínimo, extraordinario) extreme; (más lejos) farthest; **con — cuidado** with utmost care; M (punto más alejado) extreme; (de una región) end; **llegar al — de** to go so far as to; **— Oriente** Far East; **extrema izquierda** far left; **extrema unción** last rites
extrovertido -da ADJ extroverted; MF extrovert
exuberante ADJ (vegetación, jóvenes) exuberant; (mujer) voluptuous
exudar VI/VT to exude
exultante ADJ exhilarated, exultant
exultar VI to exult
eyacular VI/VT to ejaculate
eyectar VT to eject

Ff

fábrica F factory, plant; (de acero, de textiles) mill
fabricación F manufacture, manufacturing
fabricante MF manufacturer; (de coches) maker
fabricar[6] VT (producir) to manufacture, to make; (construir) to build; (inventar) to concoct, to fabricate
fabril ADJ manufacturing
fábula F (relato) fable; (mentira) falsehood
fabuloso ADJ (imaginario) imaginary; (magnífico) awesome, fabulous
facción F faction; **facciones** facial features
faceta F facet
facha F **estaba hecho una —** he was a sight
fachada F façade
facial ADJ facial
fácil ADJ easy; (promiscuo) easy, loose; **— de entender** self-explanatory; **— de usar** user-friendly
facilidad F ease; (habilidad) facility, knack
facilitar VT (hacer más fácil) to facilitate; (proporcionar) to furnish
facsímil M fax
factible ADJ feasible
fáctico ADJ factual
factor M factor
factoría F trading post

factura F bill, invoice
facturable ADJ billable
facturación F billing
facturar VT to invoice; (equipaje) to check
facultad F (habilidad) faculty; (autoridad) authority; (división de una universidad) college
facundia F gift of gab
faena F (trabajo corporal) chore; (labor) task; (molestia) nuisance
fagot M bassoon
fairway M fairway
faisán M pheasant
faja F (en la cintura) sash; (prenda interior) girdle; (de tierra) ribbon, strip
fajar VT (ceñir) to gird; (envolver) to wrap up; (golpear) to thrash
fajo M (de dinero) wad; (de papel, paja) sheaf
falacia F fallacy
falaz ADJ fallacious
falda F (prenda de vestir) skirt (también mujer o mujeres); (de una montaña) slope
faldón M (de una camisa) tail, shirttail; (de un saco) coattail
falible ADJ fallible
falla F (en un argumento) flaw; (en un motor) miss; (de una máquina) failure; (geológica) fault; **las Fallas** Valencian holiday
fallar VI (no funcionar) to fail; (un motor) to miss; VI/VT (un juez) to find, to rule
fallecer[13] VI to pass away, to decease
fallecimiento M demise, decease
fallo M (de una computadora) bug, failure; (de la memoria) lapse; (de un juez) ruling, finding
falo M phallus
falsear VT to falsify
falsedad F (dicho falso) falsehood; (condición de falso) falseness
falsificación F (de dinero) counterfeit; (de un documento) forgery
falsificar[6] VT to falsify, to fake; (dinero) to counterfeit; VI/VT (una firma) to forge
falso ADJ (incorrecto) false, untrue; (no auténtico) fake, phony; (dinero) counterfeit; (promesa) hollow; (amigo) faithless, two-faced; (excusa) made-up; **falsa alarma** false alarm; **jurar en —** to perjure oneself; **paso en —** a false step; **salida en —** false start
falta F (defecto) fault; (carencia) lack, want; (ausencia) absence, miss; (jugada ilícita) foul; (de ortografía) mistake; **— de aire** shortness of breath; **— de respeto** disrespect; **a — de** for want of, in the absence of; **hacer —** to be necessary; **me**

hace — I need; **sin** — without fail
faltar VI (ausentarse) to be absent; (no haber) to be lacking; — **a la palabra** to break a promise; — **a la verdad** to misstate oneself; —**le el respeto a** to disrespect; — **poco para las cinco** to be almost five o'clock; **me falta tiempo** I don't have enough time; **¡no faltaba más!** (con indignación) that's the last straw; (no hay de qué) don't mention it! (no te molestes) I wouldn't hear of it
falto ADJ lacking; — **de esperanza** devoid of hope
fama F (condición de conocido) fame; (reputación) reputation
famélico ADJ ravenous
familia F family; — **nuclear** nuclear family; **en** — in the family; **jefe de** — head of household; **la señora de Juan tuvo** — John's wife had a baby
familiar ADJ (de familia) (of the) family; (amistoso, coloquial, conocido) familiar; (de tamaño grande) family-size; **coche** — family car; **vida** — family life; MF relative; —**es** next of kin
familiaridad F familiarity
familiarizar[9] VT to familiarize, to acquaint; —**se** to acquaint oneself, to become familiar with
famoso ADJ famous
fanático -ca ADJ fanatic; MF fanatic, zealot; (de deportes) freak
fanatismo M fanaticism
fanega F bushel
fanfarria F fanfare
fanfarrón -ona MF braggart, show-off; ADJ blustering
fanfarronear VI to bluster
fanfarronería F bluster, swagger
fango M mire
fangoso ADJ miry
fantasear VI to fantasize
fantasía F (imaginación) imagination; (imagen) fantasy; **de** — fake, artificial
fantasioso ADJ (niño) imaginative; (idea) fanciful
fantasma M ghost, phantom
fantasmagórico ADJ ghostly
fantástico ADJ fantastic
farándula F show business
fardo M (paquete) bundle; (de heno, algodón) bale
farfolla F husk
farfulla F jabber
farfullar VI to jabber
faringe F pharynx
faríngeo ADJ pharyngeal

farmacéutico -ca MF pharmacist, druggist; ADJ pharmaceutical
farmacia F pharmacy, drugstore
farmacología F pharmacology
faro M (torre) lighthouse; (luz) beacon; — **delantero** headlight
farol M (portátil) lantern; (del alumbrado público) street lamp, streetlight; (pie de hierro) lamppost; (jactancia, envite) bluff; **darse** — to show off, to put on airs
farra F spree; **ir de** — to go on a spree
farsa F (engaño) sham, hoax; (obra teatral, imitación ridícula) farce, mockery
farsante MF fraud, fake
fascículo M installment
fascinación F fascination
fascinante ADJ fascinating
fascinar VI/VT to fascinate
fascismo M fascism
fascista ADJ & MF fascist
fase F phase
fastidiado ADJ irked
fastidiar VT to irk
fastidio M annoyance
fastidioso ADJ annoying, wearisome
fatal ADJ (mortal) fatal; (terrible) terrible; **mujer** — femme fatale; ADV very badly
fatalidad F (desgracia) misfortune; (destino) destiny
fatídico ADJ ill-fated
fatiga F fatigue, exhaustion; —**s** hardships
fatigado ADJ tired, weary
fatigar[7] VT to tire out
fatigoso ADJ (cansado) tiring; (aburrido) tiresome
fauces F PL jaw
favor M favor; **a** — **de** in favor of; **por** — please
favorable ADJ favorable
favorecer[13] VT to favor
favoritismo M favoritism
favorito -ta ADJ favorite; MF favorite; (en una elección) front-runner; (de la maestra) pet
fax M fax
faxear VT to fax
faz F face
FBI M FBI
fe F faith; — **de bautismo** baptismal certificate; — **de erratas** list of errors; — **de nacimiento** birth certificate; **de buena** — in good faith; **dar** — **de** to vouch for
fealdad F ugliness
febrero M February
febril ADJ (con fiebre) feverish; (actividad) feverish, hectic
fecha F date

fechado ADJ dated
fechar VT to date
fechoría F misdeed
fecundar VT to fertilize; (una hembra) to impregnate
fecundo ADJ fertile
federación F federation
federal ADJ federal
felicidad F happiness; ¡—es! congratulations
felicitación F congratulation; ¡**felicitaciones!** congratulations!
felicitar VT to congratulate
feligrés -esa MF parishioner; **feligreses** congregation
felino ADJ feline; M cat
feliz ADJ happy
felpa F plush
felpudo M door mat
femenino ADJ (como una mujer, de género gramatical) feminine; (de la mujer) female
feminidad F femininity
feminismo F feminism
fémur M femur
fenómeno M phenomenon
feo ADJ ugly, homely; (dentadura) bad; (accidente) nasty
féretro M coffin
feria F (mercado) market; (exposición) fair; (espectáculo) carnival; (celebración) holiday
feriante MF trader at fairs
fermentación F fermentation
fermentar VT to ferment; (cerveza) to brew
fermento M ferment
ferocidad F ferocity
feroz ADJ ferocious, fierce
férreo ADJ iron; (disciplina) harsh
ferretería F (tienda) hardware store; (artículos) hardware
ferrocarril M railroad, railway
ferroviario -ria ADJ railroad; MF railroad employee
ferry M ferryboat
fértil ADJ fertile
fertilidad F fertility
fertilizante M fertilizer
fertilizar[9] VT to fertilize
ferviente ADJ fervent
fervor M fervor, zeal
fervoroso ADJ zealous
festejar VT to celebrate
festejo M celebration
festín M feast; **darse un —** to treat oneself
festival M festival
festividad F festivity
festivo ADJ festive, gay; **día —** holiday
festón M scallop

festonear VT to scallop
fetal ADJ fetal
fetiche M fetish
fétido ADJ foul-smelling
feto M fetus
feudal ADJ feudal
feudo M manor
fiabilidad F reliability
fiable ADJ reliable
fiador -ora MF guarantor, voucher; (prestamista) backer; (de un preso) bondsman
fiambre M (carne) cold cut; (cadáver) *fam* stiff
fianza F security, guaranty; (de un preso) bail
fiar[16] VT (garantizar) to vouch for; **—se de** to trust
fiasco M fiasco
fibra F fiber; **— de vidrio** fiberglass; **— óptica** optical fiber
fibroso ADJ fibrous
ficción F fiction
ficha F (pieza) token; (de dominó) domino; (de damas) checker; (en poker, ruleta) chip; (tarjeta) index card; MF INV (persona con antecedentes penales) delinquent
fichar VT to open a file on; VI to punch in
fichero M (de computadora) file; (archivador) filing cabinet
ficticio ADJ (no real) fictitious; (novelesco) fictional
fidedigno ADJ trustworthy
fideicomisario -ria MF trustee
fideicomiso M trusteeship
fidelidad F fidelity, faithfulness; (de una traducción) closeness; (a la bandera) allegiance
fideo M noodle
fiduciario -ria ADJ & MF fiduciary
fiebre F fever; **— aftosa** foot-and-mouth disease; **— amarilla** yellow fever; **— de candilejas** stage fight; **— del oro** gold rush; **— tifoidea** typhoid fever; **tener —** to run a fever
fiel ADJ faithful; (exacto) true, accurate; M pointer on a scale; **los —es** the congregation
fieltro M felt; (sombrero de fieltro) felt hat
fiera F beast; **ponerse hecho una —** to go berserk
fiereza F ferocity
fiero ADJ fierce; (muy grande) huge
fierro M piece of iron
fiesta F (festejo) party; (día feriado) holiday; **aguar una —** to ruin a party
fiestero -ra ADJ fond of parties; MF merrymaker, party animal

figura F figure
figurado ADJ figurative
figurar VI (aparecer) to feature; (lucirse) to be seen; (incluirse) to figure, to enter into; **—se** (imaginarse) to imagine; **¡figúrate!** imagine!
figurativo ADJ figurative
figurín M fashion plate
figurón M dummy
fijación F fixing
fijador M hairspray
fijar VT (un cartel) to fix, to fasten; (una fecha) to set; **—se en** (notar) to notice; (prestar atención) to pay attention to, to focus on
fijo ADJ (sujeto, que no cambia) fixed; (inmóvil) fixed, stationary; (firme) firm; (definitivo) definite; (permanente) permanent
fila F (uno detrás del otro) row, file; (hombro a hombro) rank; (de espera) line; **— india** single file; **cerrar —s** to close ranks; **romper —s** to break ranks
filamento M filament
filantropía F philanthropy
filarmónica F philharmonic
filarmónico ADJ philharmonic
filete M (de carne) fillet; (de un plato) rim
filetear VT to fillet
filial ADJ filial; F affiliate
filibusterismo M filibustering
filigrana F filigree
Filipinas F Philippines
filipino -na ADJ & MF Philippine
filmar VT to film, to shoot
filo M (de una navaja) cutting edge; (biológico) phylum; **de doble —** two-edged; **al — de las dos** at around two o'clock
filón M seam, vein, pocket
filoso ADJ sharp
filosofía F philosophy
filosófico ADJ philosophical
filósofo -fa MF philosopher
filtración F (acción de filtrar) filtration; (de información) leak
filtrar VT to filter; **—se** to leak through
filtro M filter; **— de aire** air filter; **— de amor** love potion
fin M (conclusión, objetivo) end; **— de año** New Year's Eve; **— del mundo** (lugar apartado) boondocks; **— de semana** weekend; **— de siglo** turn of the century; **al —** at last; **al — y al cabo** at any rate; **a — de que** so that; **a — de mes** toward the end of the month; **en —** in conclusion; **poner — a** to put an end to;

por — at last; **sin —** (ilimitado) myriad; (continuo) endless
finado ADJ late
final ADJ final, last; F (deportiva) final; M (de una historia) ending; (de un terreno) end; (de una carrera) finish; (de una filmación) wrap
finalista MF finalist
finalización F completion
finalizar[9] VT to finish
finalmente ADV at last
financiación F (para una compra) financing; (para un proyecto científico) funding
financiamiento M (para una compra) financing; (para un proyecto científico) funding
financiar VT (una compra) to finance; (un proyecto) to fund, to underwrite
financiero -ra ADJ financial; MF financier
finanza F finance; **—s** finances
finca F property
finés -esa MF Finn; M (lengua) Finnish; ADJ Finnish
fineza F (atención) courtesy; (suavidad) smoothness
fingir[11] VI/VT (sorpresa) to feign; (un ataque al corazón) to fake; **fingió que la quería** he pretended to love her
finiquito M settlement
finito ADJ finite
finlandés -esa MF Finn; M (lengua) Finnish; ADJ Finnish
Finlandia F Finland
fino ADJ (vino, arena, pelo, metal) fine; (sentidos) keen, sharp; (medias) sheer; (hielo, alambre, voz) thin; (modales) smooth, refined
firma F (compañía) firm; (rúbrica) signature
firmamento M sky
firmante MF signer
firmar VI/VT to sign
firme ADJ firm; (control) tight; (colores) fast; (amarras) secure; (mano) steady, sure; (resistencia) stiff; (apoyo, resistencia) strong, staunch, steadfast; **mantenerse —** to stand one's ground; **¡—s!** attention!
firmeza F firmness; (de la mano) steadiness; (de la resistencia) stiffness; (del apoyo) strength
fiscal ADJ fiscal; MF public prosecutor, district attorney
fiscalía F prosecution
fisgar[7] VI to snoop
fisgón -ona ADJ snooping; MF snoop
fisgonear VI to snoop
física F physics
físico -ca ADJ physical; MF (persona)

physicist; M (cuerpo) physique
fisiología F physiology
fisiológico ADJ physiological
fisonomía F features
fisura F fissure
fiyano ADJ Fijian
Fiyi M Fiji
flácido, fláccido ADJ (sin firmeza) limp; (gordo) flabby
flaco ADJ thin, skinny; **su lado —** his weakness
flacura F thinness
flagrante ADJ (injusticia) gross; **en — delito** in the act
flamante ADJ brand-new
flamear VI (llamear) to flame; (ondear) to flap
flamenco -ca ADJ Flemish; MF Flemish person; M (lengua) Flemish; (ave) flamingo; (baile) flamenco
flamígero ADJ flaming
flan M caramel custard
flanco M (de un animal, ejército) flank; (de un neumático) sidewall
flanquear VT to flank
flaquear VI (intención) to waver; (salud) to wane
flaqueza F weakness
flash M (noticias, visión) flash; (lámpara) flashbulb, flash
flashback M flashback
flatulencia F flatulence
flauta F flute; **— dulce** recorder
flautín M piccolo
flecha F arrow
flechar VT to wound with an arrow
flechazo M (herida) wound from an arrow; (enamoramiento) love at first sight
fleco M (de una alfombra) fringe; (de pelo) bangs
flema F phlegm
flequillo M bangs
fletamento M charter
fletar VT to charter
flete M (contratación) charter; (envío) transport; (precio de transporte) freight
flexibilidad F flexibility; (libertad) latitude
flexible ADJ flexible; (cuerpo humano) limber, supple; (opinión) pliant, pliable
flojear VT to slacken
flojedad F laxity, looseness; (debilidad) weakness
flojera F (debilidad) weakness; (pereza) laziness
flojo ADJ (no ajustado) loose, slack; (holgazán) lazy; (inferior) crummy; (débil) weak; (sin fundamento) flimsy

floppy M floppy disk
flor F flower, blossom, bloom; (cumplido) compliment; **— de la edad** prime of life; **— de Pascua** poinsettia; **— y nata** the cream of the crop; **a — de** flush with; **en — in bloom
floración F blooming, blossoming
floral ADJ flowery
floreado ADJ flowery
florear VT (adornar con flores) to decorate with flowers; (adornar) to adorn
florecer[13] VI (echar flores) to flower, to bloom; (prosperar) to flourish, to thrive
floreciente ADJ (que prospera) flourishing, prosperous; (que echa flores) blooming
florecimiento M flourishing
floreo M flourish
florería F florist's shop
florero M flower vase
florete M fencing foil
florido ADJ flowery
florista MF florist
floritura F flourish
flota F fleet
flotador M (cosa que flota) float; (de un avión) pontoon; ADJ floating
flotante ADJ floating, buoyant
flotar VI (estar suspendido, variar en valor) to float; (moverse en la superficie) to drift; (en el aire) to waft
flote M flotation; **a —** afloat; **poner a —** to set afloat
fluctuación F fluctuation; (amplitud de variación) range
fluctuar[17] VI to fluctuate
fluidez F (lo fluido) fluency; (lo aguado) thinness
fluido ADJ (que fluye) fluid, flowing; (no vacilante) fluent; M fluid
fluir[31] VI to flow
flujo M flow; (uterino) discharge; **— de caja** cash flow
flúor M (elemento gaseoso) fluorine; (sal) fluoride
fluorescente ADJ fluorescent
fluoruro M fluoride
flux M flush
fluyente ADJ flowing
fobia F phobia
foca F seal
foco M (punto central) focus; (bombilla) bulb; (lámpara potente) spotlight
fofo ADJ mushy
fogata F bonfire; (en un campamento) campfire
fogonazo M flash
fogonero M fireman

fogoso ADJ fiery, spirited
folclore M folklore
folio M folio
folíolo M leaflet
follaje M foliage
follar VT *vulg* to fuck, to screw
folleto M pamphlet, brochure
follón M (confusión) mess; (alboroto) ruckus
fomentar VT (estudio) to promote; (amistad) to foster; (discordia) to foment; (apoyo) to drum up
fomento M encouragement
fonda F inn
fondear VI to anchor
fondillos M PL seat of pants
fondista MF (posadero) innkeeper; (corredor) long-distance runner
fondo M (parte más profunda de algo) bottom; (de un salón) rear; (del mar) bed; (de un cuadro, foto) background; (de dinero) fund; (de una biblioteca) holdings; **— común** pool; **— físico** endurance; **— musical** background music; **— mutuo** mutual fund; **—s** funds; **a —** in depth; **carrera de —** long-distance race; **de cuatro en —** four abreast; **de —** in depth; **sin —** bottomless; **tocar —** to hit rock bottom
fonética F phonetics
fonógrafo M phonograph
fonología F phonology
fontanería F plumbing
fontanero -ra MF plumber
forajido -da MF outlaw
foráneo ADJ foreign; **influencia foranéa** outside influence
forastero -ra MF stranger, outsider
forcejear VI to struggle
forcejeo M struggle
fórceps M forceps
forense ADJ forensic; MF forensic scientist
forja F (fogón) forge; (acción de forjar) forging; (taller) blacksmith's shop
forjado ADJ wrought
forjar VT (metales, un acuerdo) to forge; (un acuerdo) to hammer out; (un documento) to frame
forma F (figura) form, shape; (manera) manner; **ponerse en —** to get in shape; **no hay —** no way; **dar — a** to shape
formación F formation
formal ADJ (que atañe a la forma) formal, serious; (fiable) reliable
formalidad F (convencionalidad) formality; (fiabilidad) reliability
formalismo M formality
formalizar[9] VT to make official; **—se** to settle down
formar VT to form; (reunir tropas) to muster; (entrenar) to train; **—se** (montañas) to form; (estudiantes) to be educated
formatear VT to format
formateo M formatting
formativo ADJ formative
formato M format
formidable ADJ formidable
formón M wood chisel
fórmula F formula
formular VT to formulate; (un plan, una pregunta) to frame; (un documento) to word
formulario M form
fornicar[6] VI to fornicate
fornido ADJ stout, sturdy
foro M forum; (de un escenario) back
forrado ADJ (con un forro) lined; (bien provisto) flush
forraje M forage, fodder
forrajear VI to forage
forrar VT (un saco) to line; **—se** to line one's pockets
forro M lining; (de un libro) jacket
fortalecer[13] VT to fortify, to strengthen
fortaleza F (construcción) fortress, fort; (fuerza) fortitude
fortificación F fortification
fortificar[6] VT to fortify
fortuito ADJ fortuitous, accidental
fortuna F fortune; **por —** fortunately; **probar —** to try one's luck; **hacer —** to become rich
forúnculo M boil
forzar[9] VT to force, to coerce; **— la entrada** to break into
forzoso ADJ (por la fuerza) forcible; (inevitable) necessary; (aterrizaje) forced
fosa F (sepultura) grave; (de la nariz) cavity; (en el fondo del mar) trench
fosfato M phosphate
fósforo M (sustancia) phosphorus; (cerilla) match
fósil ADJ & M fossil
foso M (de un castillo) moat; (de un taller, teatro) pit
foto F snapshot, photo
fotocopia F photocopy
fotocopiadora F photocopier
fotocopiar VI/VT to photocopy
fotoeléctrico ADJ photoelectric
fotogénico ADJ photogenic
fotografía F (foto) photograph; (arte) photography
fotografiar[16] VT to photograph
fotógrafo -fa MF photographer

fotón M photon
fotosíntesis F photosynthesis
foul M foul
frac M tails
fracasar VI to fail; (una película) to bomb; (una embarcación) to break up
fracaso M failure; (una película) flop, bomb
fracción F fraction
fractura F fracture, break
fracturar VT to fracture, to break; **se fracturó la cadera** she broke her hip
fragancia F fragrance
fragante ADJ fragrant; **en —** in the act
fragata F frigate
frágil ADJ (delicado) delicate; (que se quiebra) fragile, brittle; (una paz) tenuous
fragilidad F (condición de quebradizo) brittleness, delicacy; (debilidad) frailty
fragmento M fragment; (de metal, piedra) scrap; (de una conversación) snatch; (de un texto) extract, excerpt
fragoso ADJ rugged
fragua F (fogón) forge; (taller) blacksmith's shop
fraguar[8] VT to forge; (una trama) to hatch; VI (cemento, yeso) to set
fraile M friar
frambuesa F raspberry
frambueso M raspberry bush
francés -esa ADJ French; M (lengua) French; (hombre) Frenchman; F (mujer) Frenchwoman
franchute -uta MF *pey* frog
Francia F France
franco ADJ (sincero) frank, candid; (exento) free; **una franca mayoría** a clear majority; **un tratado —-americano** a Franco-American treaty
francotirador -ora MF sniper
franela F flannel
franja F ribbon
franquear VT (una frontera) to cross; (una carta) to frank; **—se** to be frank
franqueo M postage
franqueza F frankness
franquicia F (concesión) franchise; (exención) exemption
frasco M (recipiente de vidrio) flask; (de medicina, perfume) bottle; (de mermelada) jar
frase F phrase
frasear VI/VT to phrase
fraternal ADJ fraternal, brotherly
fraternidad F fraternity
fraternizar[9] VI fraternize
fraterno ADJ fraternal
fraude M fraud

fraudulento ADJ fraudulent
frazada F blanket
frecuencia F frequency; **con —** frequently
frecuentar VT to frequent; (una tienda) to patronize
frecuente ADJ frequent
fregadero M sink
fregado M scrubbing
fregar[7] VT to scour, to scrub
fregona F (persona) scrubwoman, drudge; (utensilio) mop
freír[15] VI/VT to fry
frenar VT (un coche) to brake; (la inmigración) to restrain; (los impulsos) to bridle; VI to brake, to apply the brakes
frenesí M frenzy; (de actividad) flurry
frenético ADJ frantic
freno M (de coche) brake; (de caballo) bit; (contra el contrabando) curb
frente F forehead; **el sudor de la —** the sweat of one's brow; M (parte delantera, zona de combate, zona meteorológica) front; (de un edificio) face; **— a** (ante) in the face of; (al otro lado) facing; **— a —** face to face; **de —** head-on; **en — de** in front of; **hacer —** to face; **pasar al —** to come to the fore
fresa F (fruta) strawberry; (herramienta) mill
fresadora F milling machine
fresar VT to mill
frescachona F buxom woman
fresco ADJ (que acaba de producirse, descansado) fresh; (frío) cool, brisk; (de poco abrigo) light; (no cocinado) raw; (pintura) wet; M (frío) coolness; (pintura) fresco
frescor M (de verduras) freshness; (del aire) coolness
frescura F (de verduras, del carácter) freshness; (del tiempo) coolness; (comentario) impudent remark
fresno M ash tree
friabilidad F looseness
frialdad F coldness, coolness
fricción F friction, rubbing
friccionar VT to rub
friega F rubbing, massage
frigorífico M (electrodoméstico) refrigerator; (cámara) refrigeration chamber
frijol M bean
frío ADJ cold; (muy frío) frigid; M cold; **tener — to** be cold
friolento ADJ sensitive to cold
friolera F **la — de $50,000** a trifling $50,000
fritada F dish of fried food
frito ADJ fried; M dish of fried food

fritura F (acción de freír) frying; (comida frita) dish of fried food
frivolidad F frivolity
frívolo ADJ frivolous
fronda F foliage
frondoso ADJ leafy
frontera F frontier, border
fronterizo ADJ frontier
frontón M (juego) jai alai; (pista) jai alai court
frotación F rubbing
frotar VI/VT to rub
frote M rub
frotis M smear
fructífero ADJ fruitful
fructificar[6] VI to bear fruit
fructosa F fructose
frugal ADJ frugal
frunce M (volante) ruffle; (defecto) pucker
fruncir[10b] VT to gather; — **el ceño** to frown, to knit one's brow; — **los labios** to purse one's lips
fruslería F trifle
frustración F frustration
frustrar VT (los planes) to frustrate, to thwart, to foil; (las esperanzas) to shatter, to dash; **—se** to fail, to miscarry
fruta F fruit
frutero -era MF fruit vendor; M fruit dish
fruto M fruit; **—s del mar** seafood
fuego M fire; (para un cigarro) light; — **antiaéreo** anti-artillery fire; **—s artificiales** fireworks; **abrir el** — to begin to fire; **alto el** — cease-fire; **bajo** — under fire; **arma de** — firearm; **entre dos —s** between a rock and a hard place; **hacer** — to fire; **poner / pegar / prender** — **a** to set fire to
fuelle M bellows
fuel-oil M fuel oil
fuente F (surtidor) fountain; (manantial, referencia) spring; (caracteres de imprenta) font; **de buena** — from the horse's mouth
fuera ADV outside, out; — **de** outside of; — **de borda** outboard; — **de combate** out of commission; — **de serie** one of a kind; INTERJ out!
fuero M (jurisdicción) jurisdiction; (privilegio) privilege, charter
fuerte ADJ strong; (ruido) loud; (cuero) tough; (personalidad) forceful; (estantería) sturdy; (comida) hearty; (castillo) fort; (talento especial) strong point; ADV (tirar) strongly; (respirar) heavily; (gritar) loud; **soplar** — to bluster; **pisar** — to stomp; **atar** — to tie tight

fuerza F (capacidad de mover algo) force; (de una persona, animal) strength; — **aérea** air force; — **bruta** brute force; — **de la naturaleza** force of nature; — **de tarea** task force; — **de voluntad** willpower; **—s armadas** armed forces; **a** — **de** by dint of; **hacer** — to press on; **por la** — by force; **sacar** — **de flaqueza** to pull oneself together
fuga F (escape) escape, flight; (de la cárcel) jailbreak; (de gas) leak; (de capitales) drain
fugarse[7] VI to flee, to escape; — **con** to abscond with
fugaz ADJ fleeting
fugitivo -va ADJ fugitive; MF fugitive
fulano -na MF so-and-so; —, **zutano y mengano** Tom, Dick and Harry; F tart, tramp
fulgor M radiance
fulgurar VI to flash
full M full house
fullero -ra MF (tramposo) cheat; (en naipes) card sharp
fulminante M cap; ADJ devastating
fulminar VT to strike with lightning; to thunder; **lo fulminó con la mirada** she gave him a withering look
fumadero M crackhouse
fumador -ora MF smoker
fumar VI/VT to smoke; **—se mucho dinero** to blow a lot of money
fumigar[7] VT to fumigate, to fog
función F (uso) function; (de una obra de teatro) performance; (cargo) office
funcionamiento M operation, working
funcionar VI to function, to work; (motor) to run
funcionario -ria MF government employee, official
funda F cover; (de una almohada) pillowcase, slip; (de navaja) sheath
fundación F foundation
fundador -ora MF founder
fundamental ADJ (básico) fundamental; (importante) crucial
fundamentarse VI to be based
fundamento M foundation, basis; **—s** fundamentals
fundar VT (un instituto) to found, to establish; (un argumento) to base
fundición F (fábrica) foundry; (acción de fundirse) fusing
fundido ADJ molten; M (en cinematografía) fade-in / out
fundidor -ora MF foundry worker
fundir VT (combinar) to fuse; (derretir) to melt; (moldear) to mold; **—se**

(combinarse) to fuse; (romperse una bombilla) to burn out

fúnebre ADJ funeral

funeral ADJ & M funeral

funerario -ria ADJ funeral; F funeral parlor; MF funeral director

funesto ADJ ill-fated, unlucky

funicular M cable car

funky ADJ funky

furgón M (vagón) boxcar; (camioneta de policía) police van; **— de cola** caboose

furia F fury

furibundo ADJ furious, livid

furioso ADJ furious; (tempestad) fierce

furor M fury; **hacer —** to be all the rage

furtivo ADJ furtive, stealthy

fuselaje M fuselage

fusible M electric fuse

fusil M rifle

fusilar VT to execute with firearms

fusión F (derretimiento) melting; (nuclear) fusion; (empresarial) merger

fusionar VT (metales) to fuse; (compañías) to merge

fusta F crop

fustigar[7] VT to lash, to whip; (criticar) to lash out at

fútbol M soccer; **— americano** football

fútil ADJ futile, trivial

futilidad F triviality

futuro ADJ future; M future; **—s** futures

Gg

gabacho -cha ADJ & MF (francés) *pey* frog; (americano) *pey* American

gabán M overcoat

gabardina F trench coat

gabinete M (ministerial) cabinet; (oficina) office

Gabón M Gabon / Gabun

gabonés -esa ADJ & MF Gabonese

gacela F gazelle

gaceta F gazette

gacetilla F short news item

gachas F PL **— de avena** oatmeal

gachí F bimbo

gacho ADJ (orejas) drooping; (cabeza) bowed; (ojos) lowered

gachupín -ina MF *Méx pey* Spaniard

gafar VT to jinx

gafas F PL glasses

gafe M jinx

gaffe M gaffe, faux pas

gag M gag

gaita F bagpipe

gaje M **—s del oficio** occupational hazards

gajo M (rama) branch; (de naranja) section

gala F (cena) banquet; **—s** finery; **hacer — de** to boast of, to flaunt; **vestirse de —** to dress up

galán M gallant, suitor; (en un drama) leading man

galante ADJ gallant

galantear VT to court

galanteo M courting

galantería F (caballerosidad) gallantry; (cumplido) compliment

galardón M award

galaxia F galaxy

galera F galley (también prueba de imprenta); *RP* top hat

galerada F galley proof

galería F gallery; (pasillo) corridor; (tiendas) mall, gallery; (de coro) loft; (subterráneo) tunnel; **—s** *Esp* department store

Gales M Wales

galés -esa ADJ & MF Welsh

galgo M greyhound

Galicia F Galicia

gallardete M pennant

gallardía F (elegancia) elegance; (valentía) bravery

gallardo ADJ (elegante) elegant; (valiente) brave

gallego -ga ADJ Galician; M (lengua) Galician; MF Galician

gallera F cockpit

galleta F (salada) cracker; (dulce) cookie

gallina F (pollo) chicken; (hembra) hen; MF coward; **— ciega** blind man's bluff; **la — de los huevos de oro** the goose that laid the golden egg

gallinero M (de gallinas) chicken coop; (de teatro) gallery; **alborotarse el —** to raise a ruckus

gallito ADJ cocksure, cocky

gallo M cock, rooster; (de la voz) break; **tener —s en la garganta** to have a frog in one's throat; **en menos que canta un —** before you can say Jack Robinson

galón M (de líquido) gallon; (de tela) stripe

galopar VI/VT to gallop

galope M gallop; **al —** at a gallop

galvanizar[9] VT to galvanize

gama F gamut, range

gamba F large shrimp

gamberro -rra MF punk, hoodlum

Gambia F Gambia

gambiano -na ADJ & MF Gambian

gamo M buck

gamuza F chamois (también piel); (piel de venado) buckskin, deerskin; (de vaca) suede

gana F urge; **con —s** with a vengeance; **de buena —** willingly; **tener —s de** to feel like; **tengo —s** I have to go (to the bathroom); **no me da la —** I absolutely don't want to

ganadero -ra M cattleman; F cattlewoman; ADJ **industria ganadera** cattle industry

ganado M livestock; **— ovino** sheep; **— porcino** swine; **— vacuno** cattle

ganador -ora MF winner; ADJ winning

ganancia F profit, gain, return; **—s** (recaudación de un evento) proceeds; (de un juego) winnings; (de un negocio) earnings

ganapán M (obrero) menial worker; (trabajo) bread-and-butter

ganar VI/VT (una guerra, la lotería) to win; (kilos, en eficacia) to gain; VT (un sueldo) to earn; (tiempo, espacio) to save; (tierra) to reclaim; **dejarse — por algo** to give in to something; **nos ganaron el partido** they beat us; **—se la vida** to make a living

ganchillo M crochet

gancho M hook (también en boxeo, baloncesto); (rama) snag; (para sujetar) clip; (atractivo) lure; **echar a uno el —** to hook someone; **tener —** to be attractive

gandul -la MF loafer

ganga F bargain, steal

gangoso ADJ twangy

gangrena F gangrene

gangrenarse VI to gangrene

gángster M gangster

ganguear VI to twang

ganso M (animal) goose; (macho) gander; (tonto) *fam* ding-a-ling

ganzúa F picklock

gañido M yelp

gañir[18] VI to yelp

garabatear VI to scribble

garabato M scribble; **hacer —s** to scribble

garaje M garage

garante MF voucher

garantía F (de producto) guarantee, warranty; (de promesa) security, guaranty; (de un derecho) guarantee

garantizar[9] VT (un producto) to guarantee, to warranty; (prometer) to warrant

garañón M stud, horse

garbanzo M chickpea

garbo M grace

garboso ADJ graceful

garfio M hook

garganta F (interno) throat; (todo) neck; (valle estrecho) gorge

gárgara F gargle; **hacer —s** to gargle

gargarismo M gargle

garita F sentry box

garito M gambling house

garra F (de ave) claw; (de león) paw with claws; **caer en las —s de alguien** to fall into someone's clutches

garrafa F decanter

garrapata F tick

garrapatear VI to scribble

garrapiñar VT to candy

garrocha F pole

garrote M club

garrucha F pulley

gárrulo ADJ garrulous

garza F heron

gas M gas; **—es** (de motor) fumes; (de intestino) gas; **— lacrimógeno** tear gas; **— mostaza** mustard gas; **— natural** natural gas; **— nervioso** nerve gas; **a todo —** at full speed

gasa F gauze; (para heridas) dressing

gaseosa F soda, soft drink

gaseoso ADJ gaseous

gasoducto M pipeline

gasolina F gasoline, gas

gasolinera F gas station

gastado ADJ (neumático) smooth; (ropa) worn-out, shabby

gastador -ora ADJ extravagant, wasteful; MF spendthrift

gastar VT (dinero, tiempo) to spend; (energía) to expend; (neumáticos, ropa) to wear out, to use up; **— una broma** to play a trick; **—se** to wear out

gasto M (dinero) expense, expenditure, outlay; (desgaste) wear

gástrico ADJ gastric

gastritis F gastritis

gastroenteritis F gastroenteritis

gastrointestinal ADJ gastrointestinal

gastronomía F gastronomy

gatas LOC ADV **a —** on all fours

gatear VI to creep, to crawl

gatillo M (en un arma de fuego) trigger; (de dentista) forceps

gatito M kitten

gato M (felino) cat; (aparato para levantar) jack; **aquí hay — encerrado** I smell a rat; **a gatas** on all fours; **dar — por liebre** to sell someone a pig in a poke

gaucho M gaucho

gaveta F small drawer
gavilán M hawk
gavilla F (de maíz) sheaf; (de maleantes) gang
gaviota F seagull
gayola F big house
gazmoñería F prudery
gazmoño -ña MF prude; ADJ prudish
gaznate M gullet
gazpacho M *Esp* cold vegetable soup
geco M gecko
géiser M geyser
gel M gel
gelatina F gelatin
gélido ADJ frigid
gema F gem, jewel
gemelo -la ADJ & MF twin; **—s** (mellizos) twins; (binoculares) binoculars, opera glasses; (de camisa) studs
gemido M (de dolor) moan, groan; (de queja) whine
gemir[5] VI (gruñir) to moan, to groan; (lloriquear) to whine
gen, gene M gene
genealogía F genealogy
generación F generation
generador M generator
general ADJ & M general; **por lo —** generally
generalidad F generality
generalizar[9] VI/VT to generalize; **—se** to become widespread
generar VT generate
genérico ADJ generic
género M (clase) kind; (gramatical) gender; (tela) material; (literario) genre; (biológico) genus; **— humano** human race; **—s** dry goods
generosidad F generosity
generoso ADJ generous
genética F genetics
genético ADJ genetic
genial ADJ brilliant
genio MF (persona inteligente) genius; M (inteligencia) genius, brilliance; (temperamento) temperament, nature; (mal humor) temper; **de mal —** mean; **de buen —** genial
genital ADJ genital; M PL **—es** genitals
geniudo ADJ quick-tempered
genocidio M genocide
genoma M genome
gente F (personas) people; **— de campo** country folk; **— de color** persons of color; **— joven** young people; **— menuda** small fry; **buena —** good person
gentil ADJ (cortés) gracious; (no judío)

gentile; MF gentile
gentileza F graciousness
gentío M crowd
gentuza F rabble, riffraff
genuino ADJ genuine
geocéntrico ADJ geocentric
geoestacionario ADJ geostationary
geofísica F geophysics
geografía F geography
geográfico ADJ geographical
geología F geology
geológico ADJ geological
geometría F geometry
geométrico ADJ geometric
Georgia F Georgia
georgiano -na ADJ & MF Georgian
geotérmico ADJ geothermal
geranio M geranium
gerencia F management
gerente -ta MF manager
geriátrico ADJ geriatric
germen M germ
germinar VI to germinate, to sprout
gerundio M gerund, present participle
gestación F gestation
gesticular VI to gesture; (exageradamente) to gesticulate
gestión F (acción) step, maneuver; (empresarial) management; (política) administration; **—es** negotiations; **hacer —es para** to take steps to
gestionar VT (negociar) to negotiate; (administrar) to administer
gesto M (con la cara) face; (con las manos) gesture; **hacer —s a** to make faces at
Ghana F Ghana
ghanés -esa ADJ & MF Ghanaian
giba F hump, hunch
gibón M gibbon
Gibraltar M Gibraltar
gibraltareño -ña ADJ & MF Gibraltarian
giga F jig
gigabyte M gigabyte
gigante ADJ giant, gigantic; MF giant
gigantesco ADJ gigantic
gilipollas MF *ofensivo* idiot, schmuck
gimnasia F gymnastics
gimnasio M gymnasium, gym
gimotear VI to whimper
gimoteo M whimper
ginebra F gin
ginecología F gynecology
ginecólogo -a MF gynecologist
gingivitis F gingivitis
gira F tour
girar VI/VT (una llave, un volante, un coche, a la derecha) to turn; VI (repetidas veces)

to revolve, to spin, to whirl; VT (dinero) to wire

girasol M sunflower

giratorio ADJ rotary, revolving

giro M (movimiento circular) rotation, spin; (cambio de dirección) turn; (expresión) turn of phrase; (monetario) draft, remittance; — **postal** money order

giroscopio M gyroscope

gitano -na ADJ & MF gypsy

glacial ADJ glacial, bitter

glaciar M glacier

gladiador M gladiator

glamoroso ADJ glamorous

glamour M glamour

glándula F gland

glandular ADJ glandular

glaseado M (de una torta) glaze; ADJ (papel) glossy

glasear VT to glaze

glaucoma M glaucoma

glicerina F glycerin

global ADJ (mundial) global; (de conjunto) blanket, overall

globo M (esfera) globe; (de árbol de Navidad) ball; (lleno de gas) balloon; (en tenis) lob; — **ocular** eyeball; — **terráqueo** globe

glóbulo M globule; (de sangre) corpuscle

gloria F glory

glorieta F (pérgola) arbor; (rotonda) traffic circle

glorificar[6] VT to glorify

glorioso M glorious

glosa F gloss

glosar VT to gloss

glosario M glossary

glotón -ona ADJ gluttonous; MF glutton

glotonería F gluttony

glucosa F glucose

gluglutear VI to gobble

gobernador -ora ADJ governing; MF governor

gobernante ADJ governing; MF ruler

gobernar[1] VI/VT to govern, to rule; (un buque) to steer

gobierno M government

goce M enjoyment

gofre M waffle

gol M goal

goleador -ora MF shooter

goleta F schooner

golf M golf

golfo -fa M (mar) gulf; (sinvergüenza) rascal; F tramp

gollería F delicacy

golondrina F swallow

golosina F sweet, goody, tidbit

goloso ADJ sweet-toothed

golpazo M bang, whack

golpe M (físico) blow, knock, whack; (emocional) blow; (estafa) sting; (robo) holdup; (de viento) buffet; (con el codo) to jab; (con los nudillos) rap; — **bajo** low blow; — **de calor** heat stroke; — **de estado** coup; — **de gracia** coup de grâce; — **de sol** sunstroke; **de** — suddenly; **de un** — all at once

golpear VI/VT to strike, to hit; (a la puerta) to knock, to rap; (dar una paliza a una persona) to beat, to batter; (con el codo) to jab

golpecito M tap

golpetear VI to tap; (lluvia) to patter; (motor) to knock; (algo suelto) to rattle

golpeteo M tap; (de lluvia) patter; (de un motor) knock; (de algo suelto) rattle

goma F (de mascar) gum; (caucho) rubber; (neumático) tire; — **de borrar** eraser; — **de mascar** chewing gum; — **elástica** rubber band; — **espuma** foam

gomero M rubber tree

gomoso ADJ slimy

góndola F gondola

gong M gong

gonorrea F gonorrhea, *fam* the clap

gordinflón ADJ *pey* fatso

gordito ADJ chubby

gordo ADJ fat; **se armó la gorda** all hell broke loose; **hacer la vista gorda** to turn a blind eye

gordura F (cualidad de gordo) fatness; (sebo) fat

gorgojo M weevil

gorila M gorilla; (en un bar) bouncer; (guardaespaldas) bodyguard

gorjear VI (ave) to warble, to chirp, to twitter; (niño) to gurgle

gorjeo M (de ave) warble, twitter, chirp; (de niño) gurgle

gorra F cap; **de** — at someone else's expense; **vivir de** — to sponge

gorrino M piglet

gorrión M sparrow

gorro M cap, bonnet

gorrón M sponge, sponger

gorronear VI/VT to mooch, to freeload

gospel M gospel

gota F (de líquido) drop; (de sudor) bead; (enfermedad) gout; — **a** — drop by drop; **ser dos —s de agua** to be like two peas in a pod; **sudar la** — **gorda** (sudar) to sweat profusely; (trabajar) to work hard

gotear VI (caer gota a gota) to drip; (rápidamente) to dribble, to trickle;

(salirse) to leak; (llover) to sprinkle

goteo M drip (también intravenoso); (rápido) dribble, trickle

gotera F leak

gotero M dropper

gótico ADJ Gothic; M (lengua) Gothic

gourmet ADJ & MF gourmet

gozar[9] VT to enjoy; **— de** to enjoy

gozne M hinge

gozo M pleasure, enjoyment

gozoso ADJ enjoyable

grabación F recording

grabado M engraving; (con ácido) etching

grabador -ora MF (persona) engraver; F (instrumento) tape recorder; (empresa) recording company

grabar VI/VT (marcar) to engrave; (con ácido) to etch; (en cinta magnetográfica) to record, to tape; **— en la memoria** to etch / imprint on one's memory

gracejo M wit

gracia F (garbo, desenvoltura) grace, gracefulness; (humor) humor; (monería) antic; (favor) favor; (indulto) pardon; **¡—s!** thanks! thank you! **—s a Dios** thank God; **caer en —** to please; **dar —s** to say the blessing; **dar las —s** to thank; **hacer —** to amuse; **tener —** to be funny

grácil ADJ supple, graceful

gracioso ADJ (chistoso) amusing, funny; (gentil) gracious

grada F step, bleachers

gradación F gradation

graderías F PL bleachers

grado M (de temperatura, de parentesco, de un ángulo, de universidad) degree; (militar) rank; (de alcohol) proof; **de buen —** willingly; **en alto —** to a great extent; **en mayor o menor —** to some extent; **quemadura de primer —** first-degree burn

graduación F (de una escuela) graduation, commencement; (rango militar) military rank; (de alcohol) proof; (de un lente óptico) correction

graduado -da MF graduate

gradual ADJ gradual

graduar[17] VT (ajustar) to adjust; (regular) to calibrate; **—se** to graduate, to get a degree

graffiti M graffiti

grafiar[16] VT to graph

gráfica F (arte) graphics; (representación) graph, chart

graficar[6] VT to chart

gráfico -ca ADJ graphic; **acento —** written accent; M (representación) graph, chart; MF (empleado) printer

grafito M graphite

grama F lawn

gramática F grammar

gramatical ADJ grammatical

gramo M gram

grana ADJ INV & F scarlet

granada F (fruta) pomegranate; (proyectil) grenade; **— de mano** hand grenade

Granada F Grenada

granadino -na ADJ & MF Grenadian

granado M pomegranate tree; ADJ notable

granate M garnet

Gran Bretaña F Great Britain

grande ADJ large, big; (importante) great; **un gran poeta** a great poet; **divertirse en —** to have a whale of a time; **a —s alturas** at high altitudes; **de gran alcance** far-reaching; **de gran escala** large-scale; **en gran parte** in large measure; **gran almacén** department store

grandeza F greatness; **delirios de —** delusions of grandeur

grandiosidad F grandeur

grandioso ADJ grandiose, grand

granero M (edificio) granary, grain barn; (recipiente) bin, crib

granito M granite

granizada F hailstorm

granizar[9] VI to hail

granizo M hail

granja F farm

granjearse VI to win for oneself

granjero -ra MF farmer

grano M (de una foto, arena, semilla) grain; (cereal) cereal, grain; (barrito) pimple; **— de café** coffee bean; **ir al —** to come to the point

granuja MF ragamuffin

granular VT to granulate; **—se** to become granulated

grapa F (para sujetar madera) clamp; (para sujetar papel) staple

grapadora F stapler

grasa F (aceite) grease; (animal) fat

grasiento ADJ greasy

grasoso ADJ greasy

gratificación F bonus

gratificar[6] VT to gratify

gratis ADV free

gratitud F gratitude, thankfulness

grato ADJ pleasant

gratuito ADJ (gratis) free; (arbitrario) wanton, gratuitous

grava F gravel

gravamen M (impuesto) tax, assessment; (carga sobre una propiedad) lien

gravar VT to tax, to assess

grave ADJ (enfermedad, decisión) grave, serious; (sonido) low, deep; (injuria) grievous; (de carácter) earnest

gravedad F (fuerza de atracción) gravity; (de una situación) seriousness; (de una tormenta) severity; (de un tono) depth; (de una personalidad) earnestness

gravitación F gravitation

gravoso ADJ burdensome

graznar VI (cuervo) to caw, to croak; (pato) to quack; (ganso) to honk

graznido M (de cuervo) caw, croak; (de pato) quack; (de ganso) honk

Grecia F Greece

greda F clay

green M (de golf) green

gregario ADJ gregarious

gremial ADJ **acuerdo —** union agreement

gremio M (conjunto de personas) trade; (asociación histórica) guild; (sindicato) trade union

greña F mop of hair

grey F flock, fold

griego -ga ADJ & MF Greek

grieta F crevice, crack

grifo M faucet, spigot, tap

grillete M fetter, shackle

grillo M (insecto) cricket; **—s** shackles

grima F uneasiness; **dar —** (disgustar) to be upsetting; (dar asco) to be disgusting

gringo -ga ADJ & MF *pey* American

gripe F flu, influenza

gris ADJ & M gray

grisáceo ADJ grayish

gritar VI/VT to shout, to yell; (chillar) to scream

gritería F shouting

grito M shout, cry; (chillido) scream; **el último —** the last word; **estar en un —** to be in agony; **pedir a —s** to clamor for; **poner el — en el cielo** to hit the ceiling

grosella F currant

grosellero M currant

grosería F (cualidad) rudeness; (hecho, dicho) profanity, something rude

grosero ADJ (descortés) rude, ill-mannered, boorish; (vulgar) vulgar, profane; (sin arte) coarse, unrefined

grosor M thickness

grotesco ADJ grotesque

grúa F (máquina) crane; (automóvil para remolcar coches) wrecker, tow truck

gruesa F gross

grueso ADJ (persona) thick-set, heavy; (tabla) thick; (palabra, arena) coarse; M (grosor) thickness; (parte más numerosa) majority

grulla F crane

grumo M lump

grumoso ADJ lumpy

gruñido M (de perro) growl, snarl; (de cerdo) grunt; (humano) grumble

gruñir[18] VI (el cerdo) to grunt; (el perro) to growl, to snarl; (el ser humano) to grumble

gruñón -ona ADJ grumpy; MF grumpy person

grupa F rump; **volver —s** to turn around

grupo M group; **— de apoyo** support group; **— de presión** lobby; **— étnico** ethnicity; **— paritario** peer group; **— sanguíneo** blood type

gruta F grotto, cavern

guacal M crate

guacamole M *Méx* guacamole

guacho M (cría de ave) chick; *Am* (animal huérfano) orphan

guadaña F scythe

guagua F (fruslería) trifle; *Caribbean* bus; MF *Chile* baby; LOC ADV **de —** for nothing, free

guaje -ja MF urchin

guano M guano, bird dung

guantada F slap

guante M glove; **— de boxeo** boxing glove; **arrojar el —** to challenge; **echarle el — a alguien** to capture someone; **te queda como un —** it fits you like a glove

guantelete M gauntlet

guantera F glove compartment

guapetón -ona MF *fam* fox

guapo ADJ (de hombre) good-looking, handsome; (de mujer) good-looking, pretty; (valiente) brave; **¡hola —!** hey, good-looking!

guarapo M cane syrup

guarda MF INV (guardián) guard; F (almacenamiento) storage

guardar VT (almacenar) to keep, to store; (observar) to observe; (datos) to save; (proteger) to guard; **— rencor** to hold a grudge; **— un secreto** to keep a secret; **—se de** to guard against; M SG **guardabarros** fender; **guardacostas** Coast Guard cutter; **guardaespaldas** bodyguard; **guardafangos** fender; **guardapelo** locket; **guardarropa** (armario, ropa) wardrobe; (en un local) cloakroom; MF SG **guardabosques** forest ranger, forester; **guardafrenos** brake operator; **guardagujas** switch operator; **guardameta** goalie

guardería F nursery, day-care center

guardia MF (persona) guard; **— civil** civil guard; F (vigilancia) guard; **bajar la —** to let down one's guard; **de** — on duty, on watch; **en** — en garde; **hacer / montar** — to stand guard

guardián -ana MF guardian, keeper

guarecerse[13] VT to take shelter

guarida F den, lair

guarismo M cipher

guarnecer[13] VT (un plato) to garnish; (un vestido) to trim; (una fortaleza) to man, to garrison

guarnición F (de tropas) garrison; (de comida) trimmings; **guarniciones** harness

guarro ADJ filthy; M pig

guasa LOC ADV **de / a** — in jest, as a joke

guasón -ona MF joker

guata F padding

Guatemala F Guatemala

guatemalteco -ca ADJ & MF Guatemalan

guau INTERJ woof

guay ADJ cool, great

guayaba F guava

guayabera F tropical pleated shirt

gubernamental ADJ governmental

gubernativo ADJ governmental

gubia F gouge

guedeja F shock of hair

guepardo M cheetah

guerra F war, warfare; **dar** — to aggravate; **en pie de** — at war; — **fría** cold war

guerrear VI to war

guerrero -rra MF warrior; **operación** — war operation; **espíritu** — warrior spirit

guerrilla F group of guerrillas

guerrillero -ra MF guerrilla

gueto M ghetto

guía MF (persona) guide, leader; F (cosa o animal) guide; — **telefónica** telephone directory

guiar[16] VT to guide, to lead; —**se por** to follow

guijarro M pebble

güinche M hoist

guinda F cherry

guindilla F *Esp* small hot pepper

Guinea F Guinea

guineano -na ADJ & MF Guinean

guingán M gingham

guiñada F wink

guiñapo M rag

guiñar VI/VT to wink

guiño M wink

guión M (ortografía) hyphen; (libreto) script, screenplay

guionista MF screenwriter

guirnalda F garland; (de Navidad) tinsel

guisa F **a** — **de** by way of

guisado M stew, hash

guisante M pea

guisar VI/VT to cook; (en guisado) to stew

guiso M stew, casserole

guitarra F guitar

gula F gluttony

gusano M worm; — **de seda** silkworm

gustar VT (agradar) to be pleasing to; **ella me gusta** I like her; **le gustan los perros** he likes dogs; **no me gustan las fiestas** I dislike parties; **te guste o no te guste** whether you like it or not; **cuando gustes** whenever you want; — **de** to be fond of; (saborear) to taste

gusto M (sentido, sabor, aprecio estético) taste; (agrado) pleasure; (preferencia personal) like; **a** — at ease; **a mi** — to my liking; **dar** — to be a pleasure; **darle** — **a alguien** to humor someone; **darse el** — to indulge oneself; **de mal** — in bad taste; **el** — **es mío** the pleasure is mine; **estar a** — to be comfortable; **mucho** — nice to meet you; **por** — for fun; **tener el** — **de** to have the pleasure of; **tomar el** — **a una cosa** to become fond of something

gustoso ADJ (que gusta de) fond of; (agradable) pleasant; ADV willingly

Guyana F Guyana

guyanés -esa ADJ & MF Guyanese

Hh

haba F bean; (verde) Lima bean

habano M cigar

haber[29] V AUX to have; — **comido cuatro veces en un día** to have eaten four times in a day; **habérselas con** (un problema) to grapple with; (una persona) to have it out with; **ha de llegar mañana** he is to arrive tomorrow; **hay** there is, there are; **hay viento** it is windy; **hubo** there was / were; **había** there was / were; **hay que** it is necessary to; **no hay de qué** don't mention it; **no hay forma** no way; **no hay problema** no problem; **¿qué hay?** what's up; **todo lo habido y por haber** everything possible; M (hacienda) assets; (columna en una cuenta) credit; —**es** earnings

habichuela F bean; — **verde** string bean

hábil ADJ adept, able; **día** — workday

habilidad F ability, skill

habilidoso ADJ deft, skillful
habilitar VT (equipar) to outfit; (autorizar) to authorize
habitación F (vivienda) dwelling; (cuarto) room
habitante MF inhabitant; (de un barrio) resident
habitar VT to inhabit
hábitat M habitat
hábito M habit (también vestimenta religiosa)
habitual ADJ habitual, usual
habituar[17] VT to accustom; **—se** to get used to
habla F (lenguaje) speech; (modalidad local) dialect; **— infantil** baby talk; **al —** in communication with; **quedarse sin —** to be left speechless
hablador ADJ talkative
habladurías F idle talk, gossip
hablar VI/VT to talk, to speak; **— de** to talk about; **— hasta por los codos** to talk one's head off; **— no cuesta nada** talk is cheap; **— por señas** to use sign language; **— por teléfono** to talk on the phone; **— sin rodeos** to speak one's mind; **— solo / para sí** to talk to oneself; **hablando mal y pronto** pardon my French; **no —se** not to be on speaking terms; **no me hagas —** don't get me started on it
hablilla F malicious tale
hacedor -ora MF maker
hacendado -da MF landowner
hacendoso ADJ industrious, diligent
hacer[30] VT (crear) to do, to make; (causar) to make; (decir) to go; (resolver) to do; **— frío / calor / viento** to be cold / hot / windy; **— una torta** to make a cake; **— un crucigrama** to do a crossword puzzle; **me hizo llorar** he made me cry; **la vaca hace 'mu'** the cow goes moo; **hace mucho tiempo** a long time ago; **hace poco** a short while ago; **hizo como si estuvieras presente** he acted as if you were here; **a lo hecho, pecho** you've got to face the music; **la hiciste buena** you've really screwed up; **¿qué le vamos a hacer?** that's life; **¿qué se hizo de Juan?** whatever became of Juan? **haz el trabajo** do the work; **—se rico** to become rich; **—se el tonto** to play the fool; **—se el listo** to pull a stunt; **—se pasar por el jefe** to pose as the boss; **—se a un lado** to step aside; **—se amigo de** to befriend; **—se a la oscuridad** to get used to the dark; **—se rogar** to play hard to get

hacha F (grande) ax(e); (pequeña) hatchet
hachís M hashish
hacia PREP (en dirección) toward; (aproximadamente) about; **— abajo** downward; **— adelante** forward; **— adentro** inward; **— afuera** outward; **— arriba** upward; **— atrás** backward; **— el este** eastward; **— la izquierda** to the left; **dar —** to face
hacienda F estate; (de ganado) ranch; (impositiva) Internal Revenue Service
hacina F shock
hacinar VT (liar) to shock; (atestar) to crowd in
hada F fairy
hado M fate
Haití M Haiti
haitiano -na ADJ & MF Haitian
halagar[7] VT to flatter
halago M flattery
halagüeño ADJ (palabras) flattering; (perspectiva) promising
halcón M falcon
hálito M breath
hallar VT to find; **—se** to be; **—se en un aprieto** to be in a pickle; **—se mal de salud** to be in a bad way
hallazgo M (resultado científico) finding; **ese documento fue un — sensacional** that document was a real find
halo M halo
halógeno ADJ & M halogen
halterofilia F weight training, weightlifting
hamaca F hammock
hambre F (deseo de comer) hunger; (hambruna) famine; **tener —** to be hungry; **pasar —** to hunger; **morirse de —** to starve
hambrear VI/VT to starve
hambriento ADJ (que tiene hambre) hungry; (que se muere de hambre) famished, starving
hambruna F famine
hamburguesa F hamburger
hampa F underworld
hámster M hamster
handicapar VT to handicap
hangar M hangar
haragán -ana ADJ indolent; MF loafer
haraganear VI to loaf
haraganería F laziness
harapiento ADJ ragged, tattered
harapo M rag, tatter
hardware M hardware
harén M harem
harina F (fino) flour; (grueso) meal; **— de avena** oatmeal; **— de maíz** cornmeal; **es**

— **de otro costal** that's another kettle of fish

hartar VT to satiate; —**se** (de comida) to have one's fill; (de aburrimiento) to get sick

hartazgo M surfeit, excess

harto ADJ (satisfecho) full; **estar** — to be fed up; **ese asunto me tiene** — I'm sick and tired of the whole business

hasta PREP (temporal) till, until; (espacial) (up) to; — **ahora** to date / so far; — **cierto punto** to a certain extent; — **luego** good-bye, see you later; — **pronto** see you later; **caminó** — **la esquina** he walked to the corner; **lo llenó** — **el borde** he filled it up to brim; **estar** — **la coronilla** to be fed up; ADV even; — **mi madre lo notó** even my mother noticed it; — **que** until

hastiado ADJ jaded

hastial M gable

hastiar[16] VT to cloy, to tire; —**se** to grow weary of

hastío M tedium

hato M (envoltorio) bundle; (rebaño) herd

hay *ver* haber

haya F beech

hayuco M beechnut

haz M (de leña) bundle; (de luz) beam; (de flechas) sheaf

hazaña F deed, exploit, feat

hazmerreír M laughingstock

he VT IMPERSONAL **he aquí la lista** here's the list

hebilla F buckle

hebra F (de hilo) thread; (vegetal) fiber

hebreo -a ADJ & MF Hebrew

heces F PL (de vino, cafe) dregs; (excremento) feces

hechicería F enchantment

hechicero -ra ADJ bewitching; M sorcerer; F sorceress

hechizar[9] VT to bewitch, to enchant; (al público) to enthrall

hechizo M charm, spell

hecho M fact; **los —s de la noche del 17** the events of the night of the 17th; **de** — in fact

hechura F cut

hectárea F hectare

heder[1] VI to stink, to reek

hediondez F stench

hediondo ADJ stinking, smelly

hedonismo M hedonism

hedor M stink, stench

hegemonía F hegemony

helada F (frente frío) freeze; (escarcha) frost

heladera F refrigerator

heladería F ice-cream parlor

helado ADJ (muy frío) frozen, freezing; (con hielo) icy; M ice cream

helar[1] VI/VT to freeze

helecho M fern

hélice F (espiral) helix; (de avión) propeller; (de barco) screw, propeller

helicóptero M helicopter

helio M helium

hematoma M hematoma

hembra F (de animal) female; (del venado) doe; (de la ballena, foca) cow; (ave) hen

hemisferio M hemisphere

hemofilia F hemophilia

hemoglobina F hemoglobin

hemorragia F hemorrhage

hemorroides F PL hemorrhoids

henchir[5,18] VT to swell

hender[1] VI/VT to cleave, to split

hendido ADJ cleft, split

hendidura F rift, rent

henil M hayloft

heno M hay; **fiebre de** — hay fever

hepatitis F hepatitis

heraldo M herald

herbicida M weedkiller, herbicide

herbívoro ADJ herbivorous; M herbivore

herboso ADJ grassy

heredad F homestead

heredar VI/VT (recibir en herencia) to inherit; (dar en herencia) to bequeath

heredero -ra M heir; F heiress

hereditario ADJ hereditary

hereje MF heretic

herejía F heresy

herencia F (económica) inheritance; (cultural) heritage; (genética) heredity

herida F injury; (abierta) wound; **respirar por la** — to reopen an old wound

herido ADJ injured; (con herida abierta) wounded

herir[3] VI/VT to injure; (con herida abierta) to wound; (sentimientos) to hurt

hermanastro -tra M stepbrother; F stepsister

hermandad F (de hombres) brotherhood; (de mujeres) sisterhood

hermanito -ta M little brother; F little sister

hermano -na M brother (también religioso); — **mayor** big brother; — **menor** little brother; F sister (también religiosa); — **mayor** big sister; — **menor** little sister

herméticamente ADV tight

hermético ADJ hermetic, airtight; (a prueba de agua) watertight; (que no revela secretos) secretive

hermosear VT to beautify

hermoso ADJ beautiful, lovely
hermosura F beauty
hernia F hernia
héroe M hero
heroico ADJ heroic
heroína F (droga) heroin; (personaje) heroine
heroísmo M heroism
herpes M herpes; (en la boca) cold sore
herradura F horseshoe
herraje M ironwork
herramienta F tool
herrar[1] VT (un caballo) to shoe; (una vaca) to brand
herrería F blacksmith's shop
herrero -ra MF blacksmith
herrumbre F rust
hervidero M swarm
hervidor M kettle
hervir[3] VI/VT to boil; **— a fuego lento** to simmer; **— de** to be swarming with; **me hervía la sangre** I was seething
hervor M (acción de hervir) boiling; **levantar el —** to come to a boil
heterodoxo ADJ unorthodox
heterogéneo ADJ heterogeneous
heterosexual ADJ heterosexual; *fam* straight
hexágono M hexagon
hiato M hiatus
hibernar VI to hibernate
híbrido ADJ & M hybrid
hidalgo M hidalgo
hidalguía F (nobleza) nobility; (generosidad) generosity
hidrato M hydrate
hidráulico ADJ hydraulic
hidroavión M hydroplane, seaplane
hidrocarburo M hydrocarbon
hidroeléctrico ADJ hydroelectric
hidrofobia F hydrophobia
hidrógeno M hydrogen
hiedra F ivy
hiel F gall
hielo M ice; **— seco** dry ice; **romper el —** to break the ice
hiena F hyena
hierba F (pasto) grass; (especia) herb; (marihuana) *fam* weed; **— buena** mint; **mala —** weed; **y otras —s** and so on
hierro M iron (también de golf); **— corrugado** corrugated iron; **— forjado** wrought iron; **— fundido** cast iron; **—s** handcuffs
hígado M liver; **malos —s** ill will
higiene F hygiene
higo M fig; **me importa un —** I couldn't care less
higuera F fig tree

hijastro -tra M stepson; F stepdaughter
hijo -ja M son; **— de perra** *ofensivo* son of a bitch; **— de puta** *ofensivo* son of a bitch; **— de su madre** *vulg* son of a gun; **John Smith, —s** John Smith, Jr.; **sin —s** childless; F daughter; **hija de puta** *ofensivo* bitch
hilachas F loose threads
hilado M spinning
hilandería F (fábrica) spinning mill; (técnica) spinning
hilandero -ra MF spinner
hilar VI/VT to spin; **— fino** to split hairs
hilaridad F mirth
hilera F row, line
hilo M (para coser) thread; (para tejer, hilar) yarn; (alambre) filament; **— de agua** trickle; **— de pensamiento** train of thought; **— de perlas** string of pearls; **— de voz** thin voice; **— dental** floss; **al —** in a row; **mover —s** to pull strings; **seguir el — de** to keep track of; **pender de un —** to be hanging by a thread; **perder el —** to lose track
hilván M basting
hilvanar VT to baste, to tack
himno M (religioso) hymn; (patriótico) anthem
hincapié M emphasis; **hacer —** to emphasize
hincar[6] VT **— los dientes en** to sink one's teeth into; **—se** to kneel
hincha MF INV (aficionado) supporter; F (antipatía) *Esp* grudge
hinchado ADJ (inflamado) swollen; (exagerado) inflated
hinchar VI to swell; (un globo) to blow up; **— por el equipo de Uruguay** to pull for the Uruguayan team; **—se** (cuerpo) to swell; (pulmones) to inflate; (las mejillas) to bulge; (de orgullo) to puff up; (el pan) to rise
hinchazón F swelling
hindi M Hindi
hindú ADJ & MF Hindu
hinojos LOC ADV **de —** on one's knees
hipar VI hiccup
hiperactivo ADJ hyperactive, overactive
hipermétrope ADJ farsighted
hipersensible ADJ hypersensitive; (a la crítica) touchy
hipertensión F high blood pressure
hiperventilar VI to hyperventilate
hipnosis F hypnosis
hipnotizar VI/VT to hypnotize, to mesmerize
hipo M (espasmo) hiccup; (sollozo) sob; **tengo —** I have the hiccups

hipoalérgico ADJ hypoallergenic
hipocondríaco -ca, hipocondriaco -ca
  ADJ & MF hypochondriac
hipocresía F hypocrisy
hipócrita ADJ INV hypocritical, two-faced; MF
  INV hypocrite
hipódromo M racetrack
hipogloso M halibut
hipoglucemia F hypoglycemia
hipopótamo M hippopotamus
hipoteca F mortgage
hipotecar[6] VT to mortgage
hipotecario ADJ **banco —** mortgage bank
hipótesis F hypothesis
hiriente ADJ hurtful; (comentario) nasty,
  catty
hirviente ADJ boiling
hisopo M swab
hispano -na ADJ Hispanic, Spanish-speaking;
  MF Spanish-speaking person
Hispanoamérica F Spanish America
hispanoamericano ADJ Spanish-American
histamina F histamine
histerectomía F hysterectomy
histérico ADJ hysterical
historia F (el pasado, estudio del pasado)
  history; (relato) story; **— clínica** case
  history; **dejarse de —s** to stop fooling
  around; **esa es otra —** that's another
  story; **la — se repite** history repeats
  itself; **pasar a la —** to be a thing of the
  past
historiador -ora MF historian
historial M record
histórico ADJ (de importancia histórica)
  historic; (pertinente a la historia) historical
historietas F PL funnies
histrionismo M histrionics
hito M landmark, milestone; **de — en —**
  fixedly; **marcar un —** to be a milestone
hobby M hobby
hocicar[6] VI/VT (un cerdo) to root; (un
  caballo) to nose
hocico M snout, muzzle
hockey M hockey
hogaño ADV LIT nowadays
hogar M (lumbre) hearth, fireplace; (casa,
  asilo) home
hogareño ADJ domestic; **persona hogareña**
  homebody
hoguera F bonfire, campfire
hoja F (de planta) leaf; (de mesa plegadiza)
  flap; (de papel) sheet; (de un libro) page;
  (de navaja) blade; **— de afeitar** razor
  blade; **— de metal** foil; **echar —s** to leaf;
  — de servicio record; **—lata** tin plate
hojaldre M puff pastry

hojarasca F fallen leaves
hojear VT to page through, to flip through,
  to browse
hojuela F flake; **—s de maíz** cornflakes
hola INTERJ hello
Holanda F Holland
holandés -esa ADJ Dutch; M (hombre)
  Dutchman; (lengua) Dutch; F
  Dutchwoman
holding M holding company
holgado ADJ (vida) comfortable; (pantalón)
  loose-fitting, baggy; (cuarto) roomy
holganza F (haraganería) idleness; (diversión)
  leisure
holgar[2,7] VI to loaf; **huelga decir** it is
  needless to say
holgazán -ana ADJ lazy, idle; MF idler, loafer,
  slouch
holgazanear VI to idle, to loaf
holgazanería F laziness
holgura F (de movimiento) ease; (financiera)
  comfort; (de la ropa) looseness
holístico ADJ holistic
hollejo M skin
hollín M soot, smut
holocausto M holocaust
hombre M man; **— anuncio** sandwich man;
  — de bien a man of good will; **— de
  familia** family man; **— de las cavernas**
  caveman; **— de la calle** man in the
  street; **— de negocios** businessman; **—
  del saco** bogeyman; **— de paja** straw
  man; **— lobo** werewolf; **— orquesta** one-
  man band; **— rana** frogman; **es bien —**
  he's a real he-man; INTERJ come on!
hombro M shoulder; **encogerse de —s** to
  shrug; **cargar al —** to shoulder; **en / a
  —s** piggyback; **poner el —** to lend a
  hand
hombruno ADJ mannish
homenaje M homage, tribute
homeopatía F homeopathy
homeopático ADJ homeopathic
homicida MF INV murderer
homicidio M homicide, murder
homogeneizar VT to homogenize
homogéneo ADJ homogeneous
homólogo -ga MF counterpart
homóplato M shoulder blade
homosexual ADJ homosexual; *fam* gay
honda F sling, slingshot
hondo ADJ deep; M hollow
hondonada F hollow, dell
hondura F depth; **meterse en —s** to get in
  over one's head
Honduras F Honduras
hondureño -ña ADJ & MF Honduran

honestidad F (castidad) chastity, modesty; (honradez) honesty

honesto ADJ chaste, modest; (honrado) honest, straightforward

hongo M (seta) mushroom; (moho) fungus; **aburrirse como un —** to be bored stiff

honor M honor; **con —es** with honors; **tener el — de** to have the honor of; **hacer los —es a** to be appreciative of

honorable ADJ honorable

honorario ADJ honorary; M **—s** fee

honra F honor

honradez F honesty

honrado ADJ honest

honrar VT to honor; (hacer más digno) to do credit to

honroso ADJ honorable

hora F hour; **— de dormir** bedtime; **— oficial** standard time; **—s extras** overtime; **a esta —** at this time; **¿a qué —?** at what time? **a todas —s** at all hours; **a última —** at the last minute; **decir la —** to tell time; **en —** on time; **es — de** it is time to; **es — de que me vaya** it's time for me to go; **kilómetros por —** kilometers per hour; **no ver la — de** to be dying to; **por —** by the hour; **¿qué — es?** what time is it? **ya era —** it was about time

horadar VT to bore

horario M schedule, timetable; (manecilla del reloj) hour hand

horca F (cadalso) gallows; (herramienta con púas) pitchfork; **— de ajos** string of garlic

horcajadas LOC ADV **a —** astraddle, astride

horda F horde

horizontal ADJ horizontal

horizonte M horizon; (de una ciudad) skyline

horma F (de zapato) shoe last; (de queso) wheel

hormiga F ant; **— blanca** termite

hormigón M concrete

hormigonera F cement mixer

hormiguear VI (moverse animales) to swarm; (sentir hormigueo) to tingle

hormigueo M tingle

hormiguero M anthill

hormona F hormone

hornada F batch

horneado M baking

hornear VI/VT to bake

hornilla F burner

horno M (industrial) furnace; (doméstico) oven; (para cerámica) kiln; **— de microondas** microwave oven; **alto —** blast furnace; **el — no está para bollos**

it's not a good time; **recién salido del —** brand-new

horóscopo M horoscope

horquilla F (para el pelo) hairpin; (horca) pitchfork

horrendo ADJ horrendous, horrid; (feo) hideous, ghastly

horrible ADJ horrible

horripilante ADJ gruesome, hair-raising

horror M (miedo, repulsión) horror; (cosa monstruosa) abomination; (espectáculo) sight; **tenerle — a** to be scared of

horrorizar[9] VT to horrify, to shock, to appall

horroroso ADJ appalling, awful

hortaliza F vegetable; **—s** produce, truck

hortera ADJ INV tacky, uncool, cheesy

horticultura F horticulture

hosco ADJ sullen, surly

hospedaje M lodging

hospedar VT to lodge, to accommodate; **—se** to lodge, to room

hospicio M (para peregrinos) hospice; (para huérfanos) orphanage

hospital M hospital

hospitalario ADJ hospitable

hospitalidad F hospitality

hostal M hostel

hostería F hostelry

hostia F (oblea) host, wafer; (golpe) whack; **¡—s!** vulg shit! **me cago en la —** vulg God damn it!

hostigar[7] VT to harass, to harry

hostil ADJ hostile

hostilidad F hostility

hotel M hotel

hotelero -ra MF hotel keeper

hoy ADV today; **— (en) día** nowadays; **de — en adelante** from now on; **— por —** at present

hoya F river basin

hoyo M hole (también de golf); (muy profundo) pit

hoyuelo M dimple

hoz F sickle

hozar[9] VI to root

HTML M HTML

hucha F piggy bank

hueco ADJ (vacío) hollow; (vanidoso) vain, affected; **palabras huecas** empty words; M (entre los dientes) gap; (cavidad) hollow; (del ascensor) shaft

huelga F strike, work stoppage; **— de hambre** hunger strike; **declararse en —** to strike; **en —** on strike

huelguista MF striker

huella F (señal dejada al pasar) trace, trail;

(de pie) footprint, track; (de rueda) track; **— dactilar / digital** fingerprint; **seguir las —s de alguien** to follow in someone's footsteps

huérfano -na ADJ & MF orphan

huerta F (de verduras) large vegetable garden; (de árboles frutales) large orchard; **la — valenciana** the farming region of Valencia

huerto M (de verduras) vegetable garden; (de árboles frutales) orchard

hueso M (de animal) bone; (de una fruta) stone, pit; **calado hasta los —s** soaked to the bone; **la sin —** the tongue; **no dejarle un — sano** to break someone's bones; **un — duro de roer** a hard pill to swallow

huésped MF (invitado) guest; (anfitrión) host (también de parásitos)

hueste F host

huesudo ADJ bony

hueva F spawn

huevo M egg; **— de Pascua** Easter egg; **— duro** hard-boiled egg; **— estrellado / frito** fried egg; **— pasado por agua** soft-boiled egg; **—s** (testículos, valentía) *vulg* balls; **—s revueltos** scrambled eggs; **ir pisando —s** to walk on eggshells; **me importa un —** *vulg* I don't give a shit; **¡y un —!** *vulg* my ass!

huída F flight

huir[31] VI to flee, to fly

hule M oilcloth

hulla F soft coal; **— blanca** hydroelectric power

humanidad F (cualidad y condición) humanity; (conjunto de los seres humanos) mankind; **—es** humanities

humanismo M humanism

humanitario ADJ (organización, ayuda) humanitarian; (generoso) humane

humano ADJ (del hombre) human; (generoso) humane; M human

humareda F cloud of smoke

humeante ADJ smoking

humear VI (echar humo) to give off smoke; (echar vapor) to give off steam

humedad F (del aire) humidity; (de un paño) dampness; (en la tierra) moisture; (mancha) moisture stain

humedal M wetland

humedecer[13] VT (sello, ojo) to moisten; (paño) to dampen; **se le humedecieron los ojos** his eyes grew teary

húmedo ADJ damp; (aire) humid; (tierra) moist; (tiempo) wet, soggy

humero M flue, funnel

humidificar[6] VT to humidify

humildad F (actitud de humilde) humility; (condición) lowliness

humilde ADJ (actitud) humble; (condición) low, lowly, mean

humillación F humiliation

humillar VT (dañar el amor propio) to humiliate; (hacer sentirse disminuido) to humble; **—se** to grovel

humo M smoke; (vapor) vapor; **—s** conceitedness; **bajarle los —s a alguien** to cut someone down to size; **echar —** to put out smoke; **estar que echa —** to be fuming; **hacerse —** to vanish into thin air

humor M (actitud risueña) humor; (estado de ánimo) mood

humorada F witty remark

humorismo M (humor) humor; (profesión) comedy

humorístico ADJ humorous

humoso ADJ smoky

hundimiento M (acción de hundirse) sinking; (hoyo) sinkhole

hundir VT (un barco) to sink, to scuttle; (arruinar) to destroy; (enterrar) to bury; **—se** (barco) to sink; (empresa, edificio, precios) to collapse; (tierra) to subside; (sol) to go down

húngaro -ra MF Hungarian

Hungría F Hungary

huracán M hurricane

huraño ADJ sullen, unsociable

hurgar[7] VI (en una bolsa) to rummage; (en la basura) to scavenge; **—se las narices** to pick one's nose

hurón M ferret

huronear VI to ferret out

hurra INTERJ hurrah

hurtadillas LOC ADV **a —** stealthily

hurtar VT to steal, to swipe; **— el cuerpo** to dodge; **—se** to hide

hurto M theft, larceny; **— con escalo** break-in

husky M (perro) husky

husmear VT (un pedazo de carne) to sniff at; (a un delincuente) to smell out; (peligro) to smell; (en los asuntos ajenos) to nose around in, to poke around in

husmeo M sniff

huso M spindle; **— horario** time zone

huy INTERJ (sorpresa) wow; (pena) oh

Ii

ibérico ADJ Iberian
iceberg M iceberg
ictericia F jaundice
ida F —**s y venidas** comings and goings
idea F (reflexión) idea, thought; (intuición) inkling
ideal ADJ & M ideal
idealismo M idealism
idealista ADJ idealistic; MF idealist
idear VT to devise, to think out, to plan; (un método) devise; (un plan) to conceive; (una solución) to engineer; (un complot) to hatch
ídem PRON & ADV ditto
idéntico ADJ identical
identidad F identity
identificación F identification
identificar[6] VT to identify
ideología F ideology
idilio M idyll
idioma M language
idiosincrasia F idiosyncrasy
idiota ADJ INV idiotic, lamebrained; MF INV *fam* idiot, dork, twerp
idiotez F idiocy
idolatrar VT to idolize
idolatría F idolatry
ídolo M idol
idóneo ADJ (calificado) expert; (ideal) ideal
iglesia F church
iglú M igloo
ignición F ignition
ignifugar[7] VT to fireproof
ignorancia F ignorance
ignorante ADJ ignorant, uneducated
ignorar VT (no saber) to be unaware of; (hacer caso omiso de) to ignore, to disregard; (despreciar) to shrug off, to discount
igual ADJ (idéntico) equal; (semejante) same, alike; (liso) even; **me da** — it's all the same to me; **al** — **que** just like; M equal sign
igualar VT (alisar) to level; (ser igual a) to equal; (hacer iguales) to equalize; (compararse con) to match
igualdad F equality
ijada F loin
ijar M loin
ilegal ADJ illegal, unlawful, lawless
ilegítimo ADJ illegitimate

ileso ADJ unharmed, unhurt
ilícito ADJ illicit
ilimitado ADJ unlimited; (energía) boundless; (horizonte) limitless
iluminación F illumination, lighting; (moral) enlightenment
iluminado ADJ lit
iluminar VT (un cuarto) to illuminate, to brighten; (moralmente) to enlighten
ilusión F (idea o imagen falsa) illusion; (deseo) dream, fond hope; (entusiasmo) thrill; — **óptica** optical illusion; **me da** — I'm looking forward to
iluso ADJ naive
ilusorio ADJ illusory
ilustración F illustration; **la** — the Enlightenment
ilustrador -ora MF illustrator
ilustrar VT illustrate; (intelectualmente) to enlighten
ilustre ADJ illustrious
imagen F (representación, reputación) image; (foto, televisión) picture; (unidad de película fotográfica) frame; — **especular** mirror image; **la** — **del tacto** the soul of tact; — **por resonancia magnética** magnetic resonance imaging
imaginable ADJ conceivable
imaginación F imagination
imaginar VT to imagine, to picture; (idear) to dream up
imaginario ADJ imaginary
imaginativo ADJ imaginative
imán M magnet
imantar VT to magnetize
imbatible ADJ unbeatable
imbécil ADJ idiotic; MF *ofensivo* imbecile, moron
imbuir[31] VT to imbue
imitación F imitation
imitador -ora MF (que imita) imitator; (que imita gestos y voces) mimic; **un** — **de Elvis** an Elvis wannabe
imitar VT to imitate; (en gestos y voces) to mimic, to impersonate
impaciencia F impatience
impaciente ADJ impatient; *fam* antsy
impactar VI/VT to impact
impacto M impact
impagado ADJ unpaid
impala M impala
impar ADJ odd, uneven
imparcial ADJ impartial, unbiased; (justo) evenhanded; (que no toma partido) nonpartisan
imparcialidad F impartiality
impartir VT to impart

impasible ADJ impassive
impasse M impasse
impávido ADJ undaunted
impeachment M impeachment
impecable ADJ (perfecto) flawless; (limpio) spick and span
impedimento M impediment, hindrance; (incapacidad) handicap
impedir[5] VT to impede, to prevent, to hinder; (acceso) to bar
impeler VT (empujar) to impel; (inducir) to drive
impenetrable ADJ impenetrable
impensable ADJ unthinkable
imperar VI to prevail
imperativo ADJ & M imperative
imperceptible ADJ imperceptible
imperdible M safety pin
imperecedero ADJ undying
imperfecto ADJ & M imperfect
imperial ADJ imperial
imperialismo M imperialism
impericia F lack of skill
imperio M (forma de gobierno) empire; (hecho de imperar) rule
imperioso ADJ (mandón) imperious; (necesario) imperative
impermeabilizar[9] VT to waterproof
impermeable ADJ (al agua) waterproof; (a la crítica) impervious; M raincoat, slicker
impersonal ADJ impersonal
impertinencia F (actitud) impertinence, impudence; (réplica) backtalk
impertinente ADJ impertinent, impudent
ímpetu M impetus
impetuoso ADJ impetuous, brash
impío ADJ godless
implacable ADJ implacable, relentless
implantar VT to implant
implante M implant
implementar VT to implement
implemento M implement
implicar[6] VT (involucrar) to implicate, to involve; (conllevar) to entail
implícito ADJ implicit
implorar VI/VT to implore
imponente ADJ (impresionante) imposing; (espantoso) forbidding
imponer[39] VT to impose, to force upon; (gravar) to assess; **—se** to get one's way
impopular ADJ unpopular
importación F import
importancia F importance
importante ADJ important; (cantidad) substantial; (tema, asunto) weighty; (suceso, ocasión) momentous
importar VI (ser de importancia) to matter;

me importa un comino I don't give a hoot; **no importa** it makes no difference; VT (introducir bienes) to import
importe M amount
importunar VT to besiege
importuno ADJ inopportune
imposibilidad F impossibility
imposibilitar VT to make impossible
imposible ADJ impossible
imposición F imposition; (de impuestos) assessment
impostor -ora MF impostor, fraud
impotencia F impotence
impotente ADJ powerless; (sexualmente) impotent
impreciso ADJ inaccurate
impredecible ADJ unpredictable
impregnar VT to impregnate
impremeditado ADJ unpremeditated
imprenta F (arte, oficio) printing; (máquina) press, printing press
imprescindible ADJ indispensable
impresión F (efecto en el ánimo) impression; (acción de imprimir) printing; (huella) imprint
impresionante ADJ (logro) impressive, imposing; (edificio) grand, imposing; (panorama) breathtaking
impresionar VT to impress; **—se** to be overwhelmed
impreso M printed matter
impresor -ora MF (persona) printer; F (aparato) printer; **impresora de inyección de tinta** ink-jet printer; **impresora gráfica** plotter; **impresora láser** laser printer
imprevisible ADJ unpredictable
imprevisto ADJ unforeseen; M unforeseen event
imprimir[51] VI/VT to print; (marcar con presión) to imprint
improbable ADJ improbable, unlikely
improductivo ADJ unproductive
impromptu M impromptu
impropio ADJ (inadecuado) unbecoming; (atípico) atypical
improvisación F improvisation, role-playing
improvisado ADJ impromptu
improvisando ADV ad lib
improvisar VI/VT to improvise
improviso LOC ADV **de —** all of a sudden
imprudencia F (actitud) recklessness; (acción) reckless act
imprudente ADJ imprudent, unwise
impublicable ADJ unprintable
impúdico ADJ immodest
impuesto M tax, duty; **— de sucesión**

inheritance tax; **—s** taxation; **— sobre ingresos** income tax; **— sobre las ventas** sales tax; **— sobre rentas** income tax

impugnar VT to contest, to dispute

impulsar VT (empujar) to propel, to drive; (estimular) to boost

impulsivo ADJ impulsive

impulso M (estímulo) boost; (deseo espontáneo) impulse, urge

impunidad F impunity

impureza F impurity

impuro ADJ (sustancia) impure; (pensamiento) impure, unclean

inacabado ADJ unfinished

inaccesible ADJ inaccessible

inaceptable ADJ unacceptable, inadequate

inacostumbrado ADJ unwonted

inactividad F inactivity

inactivo ADJ inactive

inadaptado -da ADJ maladjusted; MF misfit

inadecuado ADJ unsuitable

inadvertido ADJ unnoticed, unobserved

inagotable ADJ (recursos) inexhaustible; (optimismo) unfailing

inaguantable ADJ unbearable

inalámbrico ADJ cordless, wireless

inalterable ADJ unalterable, unchangeable

inalterado ADJ unchanged

inamovible ADJ immovable

inanición F starvation

inanimado ADJ inanimate

inapetencia F lack of appetite

inapreciable ADJ (invalorable) invaluable; (muy pequeño) too small to be seen

inapropiado ADJ unsuitable

inasequible ADJ inaccessible

inaudible ADJ inaudible

inaudito ADJ unheard-of, unprecedented; (sufrimiento) untold

inauguración F (de un gobierno) inauguration; (de una carretera, etc.) dedication

inaugurar VT (un gobierno) to inaugurate; (una carretera) to dedicate

incalculable ADJ untold

incandescencia F glow

incandescente ADJ incandescent, glowing

incansable ADJ untiring, tireless

incapacidad F inability

incapacitar VT to disable, to incapacitate

incapaz ADJ incapable

incautación F seizure

incauto ADJ unwary

incendiar VT to set fire to; VI/VT to burn; **—se** to catch fire, to burn down

incendiario -ria ADJ incendiary; MF arsonist

incendio M conflagration, fire, blaze; **— doloso** arson; **— forestal** forest fire

incentivo M incentive, inducement

incertidumbre F uncertainty, suspense

incesante ADJ incessant, ceaseless

incesto M incest

incidencia F incidence

incidental ADJ incidental

incidente M incident

incienso M incense

incierto ADJ uncertain

incinerar VT to incinerate

incipiente ADJ incipient

incisión F incision

incisivo ADJ incisive; M incisor

incitar VT to incite, to whip up

incivilizado ADJ uncivilized

inclemencia F **las —s del tiempo** foul weather

inclemente ADJ inclement, foul

inclinación F (de personalidad) inclination, bent, disposition; (acto de inclinar) tilting; (estado de inclinado) tilt; (de un techo) slant; (del terreno) slope; (sesgo) bias

inclinar VT (ladear) to tilt; (bajar la cabeza) to hang; **—se** (doblarse en la cintura) to bend over; (tener tendencia a) to tend; (hacer una reverencia) to bow

incluir[31] VT (incorporar) to include; (abarcar) to include, to comprise

inclusive ADV even

inclusivo ADJ inclusive

incluso ADJ even

incógnita F unknown (quantity)

incógnito LOC ADV **de —** incognito

incoherente ADJ incoherent

incoloro ADJ colorless

incomestible ADJ inedible

incomformista ADJ & MF nonconformist

incomible ADJ inedible

incomodar VT to inconvenience

incomodidad F uneasiness

incómodo ADJ (silla) uncomfortable; (situación) awkward, inconvenient; (baúl) cumbersome; (silencio) uneasy; (que siente molestia) ill at ease

incomparable ADJ incomparable, peerless

incompatible ADJ incompatible

incompetente ADJ incompetent

incompleto ADJ incomplete

incomprensible ADJ incomprehensible

incomunicación F disconnect

inconcebible ADJ inconceivable

inconcluso ADJ unfinished

incondicional ADJ unconditional, unqualified

inconexo ADJ disconnected

inconformista MF nonconformist
inconfundible ADJ unmistakable
inconsciente ADJ (sin sentido) unconscious, senseless; (ignorante) unaware, oblivious
inconsecuencia F inconsistency
inconsecuente ADJ inconsistent
inconsolable ADJ heartbroken
inconstancia F inconstancy
inconstante ADJ inconstant, changeable
inconstitucional ADJ unconstitutional
incontable ADJ countless
incontenible ADJ uncontrollable
incontinente ADJ incontinent
incontrolable ADJ uncontrollable
incontrovertible ADJ incontrovertible
inconveniencia F inconvenience
inconveniente ADJ improper; M inconvenience, downside
incorporado ADJ built-in
incorporar VT to incorporate, to build into; (incluir) to incorporate; —**se** (erguirse) to sit up
incorrecto ADJ incorrect, wrong
incorregible ADJ incorrigible
incredulidad F disbelief
incrédulo ADJ incredulous
increíble ADJ (que no puede creerse) incredible, unbelievable; (extraordinario) amazing
incrementar VT to augment
incremento M increment, increase
incriminar VT to incriminate
incrustación F inlay
incrustado ADJ (en piedra) embedded; (joyas) inlaid
incrustar VT to embed; (oro) to inlay; —**se en** to become embedded in
incubadora F incubator
incuestionable ADJ unquestionable
inculcar[6] VT to inculcate, to instill
inculto ADJ (sin modales) uncultured, unrefined; (sin instrucción) uneducated
incumbencia F **no es de tu —** it's none of your business
incurable ADJ incurable
incurrir VI **— en** (una deuda) to incur; (un error) to fall into
incursión F raid, foray
incursionar VI to foray
indagación F investigation, probe
indagar[7] VI/VT to investigate, to inquire into
indebido ADJ undue
indecencia F indecency
indecente ADJ indecent
indecible ADJ unspeakable
indecisión F indecision
indeciso ADJ (que no ha decidido)

undecided; (que suele vacilar) wishy-washy
indecoroso ADJ improper
indefendible ADJ indefensible
indefenso ADJ defenseless
indefinible ADJ indefinable
indefinido ADJ indefinite
indeleble ADJ indelible
indelicado ADJ indelicate
indemnización F indemnity; (de guerra) reparation; (de un pleito) recovery
indemnizar[9] VT to indemnify
independencia F independence; (de un individuo) self-reliance
independiente ADJ independent
indescriptible ADJ indescribable
indeseable ADJ undesirable, unwelcome
indestructible ADJ indestructible
indeterminado ADJ indeterminate
indexar VT to index
India F India
indicación F indication; (instrucción) instruction; **indicaciones** directions
indicador M pointer
indicar[6] VT to indicate, to point out; (aparato de medida) to read, to register; (mostrar) to show
indicativo ADJ & M indicative
índice M (lista alfabética) index; (tabla de materias) table of contents; (dedo) index finger
indicio M clue, sign
Indico M **Océano —** Indian Ocean
indiferencia F indifference; (frialdad) coolness
indiferente ADJ (apático) indifferent, unconcerned; (frío) cool; (sin entusiasmo) lukewarm; (no conmovido) unmoved; **esa chica me es —** I don't care about that girl
indígena ADJ INV indigenous; MF INV native
indigente ADJ destitute, indigent
indigestión F indigestion
indignación F indignation
indignado ADJ indignant
indignar VT to make indignant; —**se** to become indignant
indigno ADJ unworthy
índigo M indigo
indio -dia ADJ & MF Indian
indirecta F hint
indirecto ADJ indirect; (ruta) roundabout
indisciplinado ADJ unruly
indiscreción F indiscretion
indiscreto ADJ indiscreet
indiscutible ADJ unquestionable
indispensable ADJ indispensable

indisponer[39] VT to indispose; **—se** to become indisposed
indispuesto ADJ (disgustado) upset; (enfermo) indisposed
indistinto ADJ indistinct, vague
individual ADJ individual; (habitación) single
individualidad F individuality
individualismo M individualism
individualista MF individualist
individuo ADJ & M individual
indivisible ADJ indivisible
índole F type
indolencia F indolence
indolente ADJ indolent
indoloro ADJ painless
indomable ADJ indomitable
indomado ADJ unbroken
Indonesia F Indonesia
indonesio -sia ADJ & MF Indonesian
inducción F induction
inducir[24] VT to induce, to prompt
indudablemente ADV undoubtedly
indulgencia F indulgence
indulgente ADJ indulgent, lenient
indultar VT to pardon
indulto M pardon
indumentaria F apparel
industria F industry, trade
industrial ADJ industrial; MF industrialist
industrioso ADJ industrious
inédito ADJ unpublished
inefable ADJ ineffable
ineficaz ADJ ineffective, ineffectual
ineficiente ADJ inefficient
inelegible ADJ ineligible
inepto ADJ inept
inequívoco ADJ unequivocal
inercia F inertia
inerte ADJ inert
inescrutable ADJ inscrutable
inesperado ADJ unexpected
inestabilidad F instability
inestable ADJ unstable; (andar) unsteady
inestimable ADJ inestimable, invaluable
inevitable ADJ inevitable; (accidente) unavoidable
inexacto ADJ inaccurate
inexcusable ADJ inexcusable
inexorable ADJ inexorable
inexperto ADJ inexperienced, unskilled; (ojo) untrained
inexplicable ADJ inexplicable
inexpresivo ADJ inexpressive, wooden
infalible ADJ infallible, foolproof; (confiable) unfailing
infame ADJ infamous

infamia F infamy
infancia F childhood
infante -ta MF (hijo -ja del rey) infante -ta; M (soldado) infantrymen
infantería F infantry; **— de marina** marine corps
infantil ADJ (como niño) childlike; (aniñado) childish, infantile
infección F infection
infeccioso ADJ infectious
infectar VT to infect; **—se** to become infected
infecto ADJ foul, repugnant
infelicidad F misery
infeliz ADJ unhappy, wretched, miserable; MF poor wretch
inferencia F inference
inferior ADJ (en calidad) inferior; (en posición) lower
inferioridad F inferiority
inferir[3] VT to infer
infernal ADJ infernal; (ruido) unholy
infestar VT to infest
infiel ADJ unfaithful, faithless, untrue
infierno M hell; (lugar donde hace mucho calor) inferno; **en el quinto —** in the middle of nowhere
infinidad F infinity; **una — de** a large number of
infinitivo ADJ & M infinitive
infinito ADJ infinite; M infinity
inflación F inflation
inflado M inflation
inflamable ADJ flammable
inflamación F inflammation
inflamar VT to inflame; **—se** to become inflamed
inflar VT (neumáticos) to inflate, to pump up; (globos) to blow up; (precios) to balloon
inflexible ADJ (rígido) inflexible; (testarudo) unbending, adamant
infligir[11] VT to inflict
influencia F influence, pull, clout; (sobre las masas) sway
influir[31] VI **— en / sobre** to influence; (las masas) to sway
influjo M influence
influyente ADJ influential
infomercial M infomercial
información F information; (periodística) story
informal ADJ (no formal) informal, casual; (poco fiable) unreliable
informante MF (para un estudio) informant; (de la policía) informer
informar VT to inform, to appraise; (un

militar) to debrief; (un periodista) to
report; (un abogado) to advise; **—se** to
become informed
informática F computer science
informatizar[9] VT to computerize
informe M report; (militar) debriefing; **—s**
information; ADJ shapeless
infortunio M misfortune
infracción F (de reglamentos) infraction; (de
contrato) breach; (de tránsito) violation
infractor -ora MF lawbreaker
infraestructura F infrastructure
infrarrojo ADJ & M infrared
infrascrito -ta MF undersigned
infringir[11] VT to infringe, to breach, to
violate
infructuoso ADJ fruitless, unsuccessful
ínfulas F PL airs; **darse —** to put on airs
infundado ADJ groundless, unfounded
infundir VT to infuse, to imbue
infusionar VT to steep
ingeniar VT to contrive; **ingeniárselas
para** to contrive to
ingeniería F engineering; **— genética**
genetic engineering; **— química**
chemical engineering
ingeniero -ra MF engineer; **— civil** civil
engineer; **— electricista** electrical
engineer
ingenio M (mental) ingenuity, cleverness;
(verbal) wit; (artefacto) artifact; **— de
azúcar** (refinería) sugar refinery, sugar
mill; (plantación) sugar plantation
ingeniosidad F ingenuity
ingenioso ADJ ingenious, resourceful
ingenuo -nua ADJ (inocente) naive; (crédulo)
gullible; MF dupe
ingerir VI/VT to ingest
ingestión F ingestion
ingle F groin
inglés -esa ADJ English; M Englishman;
(lengua) English; F Englishwoman
ingobernable ADJ unruly
ingratitud F ingratitude
ingrato -ta ADJ thankless, ungrateful; MF
ingrate
ingrávido ADJ weightless
ingrediente M ingredient; **—s** makings
ingresar VT (datos) to input; (dinero en una
cuenta) to deposit; VI (a un hospital) to be
admitted
ingreso M (permiso para entrar) entrance,
entry; (depósito bancario) deposit; (renta)
income; **—s** (de una firma) earnings; (del
Estado) revenue
inhábil ADJ unskilled
inhabilidad F inability

inhabilitar VT to disqualify
inhalar VI/VT to breathe in, to inhale
inherente ADJ inherent
inhibición F inhibition
inhibir VT to inhibit
inhospitalario ADJ inhospitable
inhóspito ADJ inhospitable
inhumano ADJ inhuman
iniciación M initiation, induction
inicial ADJ initial; (pago) up-front; F initial
inicializar[9] VT to initialize
iniciar VT (comenzar) to initiate; (admitir) to
induct
iniciativa F initiative
inimitable ADJ inimitable
ininflamable ADJ fireproof
ininteligible ADJ unintelligible
ininterrumpido ADJ continuous, unbroken
injertar VT to graft
injuria F (insulto) insult, verbal abuse;
(daño) damage
injuriar VT to insult, to abuse verbally
injurioso ADJ insulting, injurious, verbally
abusive
injusticia F injustice; (acto injusto) wrong;
(error judicial) miscarriage of justice
injustificable ADJ unjustifiable
injustificado ADJ uncalled-for, unwarranted
injusto ADJ unjust, unfair
inmaculado ADJ immaculate, spotless
inmaduro ADJ immature
inmanejable ADJ unmanageable
inmaterial ADJ immaterial
inmediación F vicinity
inmediato ADJ immediate, instant; **de —** at
once
inmensidad F immensity, vastness
inmenso ADJ immense, vast
inmigración F immigration
inmigrante ADJ & MF immigrant
inmigrar VI to immigrate
inminente ADJ imminent, impending
inmiscuir[31] VI to mix; **—se** to meddle
inmoral ADJ immoral
inmoralidad F immorality
inmortal ADJ & MF immortal
inmortalidad F immortality
inmóvil ADJ motionless, immobile
inmovilizar[9] VT to immobilize; (en una
pelea) to pin
inmune ADJ immune
inmunidad F immunity
inmutable ADJ unchangeable, immutable
innato ADJ innate, inborn
innecesario ADJ unnecessary, needless
innegable ADJ undeniable
innoble ADJ ignoble

innocuo ADJ innocuous
innovación F innovation
innumerable ADJ innumerable, countless
inocencia F innocence
inocente ADJ innocent, guiltless; MF dupe
inocuo ADJ harmless
inodoro ADJ odorless; M toilet, commode
inofensivo ADJ inoffensive, harmless
inolvidable ADJ unforgettable
inoperable ADJ inoperable
inoportuno ADJ inopportune, untimely
inorgánico ADJ inorganic
inoxidable ADJ rustproof
inquietar VT to worry
inquieto ADJ (movedizo) restless; (preocupado) uneasy
inquietud F (intranquilidad) restlessness; (preocupación) alarm
inquilino -ina MF (de un apartamento) tenant, renter; (de una pensión) lodger
inquina F spite
inquirir[34] VI/VT to inquire
inquisición F inquisition
inquisitivo ADJ inquisitive
insaciable ADJ insatiable
insalubre ADJ unhealthy
insatisfactorio ADJ unsatisfactory
insatisfecho ADJ dissatisfied, unhappy
inscribir[51] VT (grabar) to inscribe; (matricular) to register, to enroll; —se to register, to enroll
inscripción F (grabado) inscription; (matriculación) registration, enrollment
insecticida M insecticide
insectívoro ADJ insectivorous
insecto M insect
inseguro ADJ (personalidad) insecure; (vehículo) unsafe; (el andar) unsteady
insensato -ta ADJ foolish; MF fool
insensibilizar[9] VT to desensitize
insensible ADJ (cruel) insensitive, callous; (imperturbable) unfeeling, thick-skinned; (entumecido) numb
inseparable ADJ inseparable
inserción F insertion
insertar VT to insert
inservible ADJ useless
insidioso ADJ insidious
insigne ADJ famous
insignia F insignia, badge
insignificante ADJ insignificant, unimportant
insincero ADJ insincere
insinuación F insinuation; (sexual) innuendo
insinuante ADJ suggestive
insinuar[17] VT to insinuate, to suggest; —se

to insinuate oneself
insípido ADJ insipid, flavorless
insistencia F insistence; (perseverancia) persistence
insistente ADJ insistent; (perseverante) persistent
insistir VI/VT to insist; (perseverar) to persist; — en to insist on; — sobre to harp on
insolación F (por sol) sunstroke; (por calor) heatstroke
insolencia F insolence; (comentario) smart remark
insolente ADJ insolent, sassy
insólito ADJ unusual; (accidente) freak, freakish
insoluble ADJ insoluble
insolvente ADJ insolvent
insomne ADJ wakeful, unable to sleep
insoportable ADJ unbearable, impossible; (dolor) excruciating
insospechado ADJ unsuspected
insostenible ADJ untenable
inspección F inspection; (encuesta) canvass
inspeccionar VT to inspect, to survey
inspector -ora MF inspector
inspiración F (idea) inspiration; (inhalación) inhalation
inspirar VI/VT to inspire; VI to inhale, to breathe in
instalación F installation
instalar VT to install; —se to take up residence
instancia LOC ADV a —s de at the request of
instantánea F snapshot
instantáneo ADJ instantaneous
instante M instant; al — right away
instar VT to enjoin
instigar[7] VT to instigate, to abet
instintivo ADJ instinctive
instinto M instinct; — suicida death wish
institución F institution; — benéfica charity
instituir[31] VT to institute
instituto M institute; (escuela secundaria) high school
institutriz F governess
instrucción F instruction, schooling
instructivo ADJ instructive
instructor -ora MF instructor
instruir[31] VT to instruct, to school
instrumental ADJ instrumental
instrumentar VT (un plan) to implement; (música) to do the instrumentation for
instrumento M instrument; — de metal brass instrument; — de viento wind instrument
insubordinado ADJ insubordinate

insuficiencia F insufficiency; (de los órganos) failure
insuficiente ADJ insufficient, inadequate
insufrible ADJ insufferable
insulina F insulin
insulso ADJ bland
insultar VT to insult
insulto M insult, put-down
insuperable ADJ (resultado) insuperable; (obstáculo) insurmountable
insurgente ADJ & MF insurgent
insurrección F insurrection
insurrecto -ta ADJ rebellious; MF rebel
intachable ADJ blameless
intacto ADJ intact, unbroken
intangible ADJ intangible
integral ADJ integral; (harina) whole-grain
integrante ADJ integral
integrar VT to form; (ser miembro de) to be a member of
integridad F integrity
íntegro ADJ whole; (moralmente) upright
intelecto M intellect
intelectual ADJ & MF intellectual
inteligencia F intelligence (también militar); (persona) mind; **— artificial** artificial intelligence
inteligente ADJ intelligent, bright, smart
inteligible ADJ intelligible
intemperie LOC ADV **a la —** exposed to the weather
intención F intention, intent
intencional ADJ intentional
intensidad F intensity
intensificar[6] VT to intensify; **—se** to intensify; (violencia) to escalate
intensivo ADJ intensive
intenso ADJ intense; (debate) fierce; (calor) severe
intentar VI/VT to try; VT to attempt
intento M (tentativa) try, attempt; (propósito) intention
interactivo ADJ interactive
interactuar[17] VI to interact
intercalación F insertion
intercalar VT to insert
intercambiador M interchange
intercambiar VI/VT to exchange
intercambio M exchange
interceder VI to intercede
interceptación F interception
interceptar VT to intercept
intercesión F intercession
intercesor -ora MF advocate
interés M (intelectual, financiero) interest; (preocupación) concern; (participación comercial) stake; **— compuesto**
compound interest
interesado ADJ interested; (preocupado) concerned; (egoísta) self-serving
interesante ADJ interesting
interesar VT to interest; **—se por** to become interested in
interestatal ADJ interstate
interestelar ADJ interstellar
interface MF interface
interfaz MF (electrónica / informática) interface
interferencia F interference; (en una transmisión) interference, static
interferir VT to jam; VI to interfere
ínterin M interim; **en el —** meanwhile
interino ADJ acting, interim
interior ADJ (de un edificio) interior; (no costeño) inland; (dentro de una organización) internal; (hacia dentro) inward; M interior
interiorizar[9] VT to internalize
interjección F interjection
interlineal ADJ interlinear
interlock M interlock
interlocutor -ora MF interlocutor
interludio M interlude
intermediario -ria M middleman; MF (mensajero) go-between
intermedio ADJ intermediate; M intermission; **por — de** through
interminable ADJ interminable, unending, endless
intermitente ADJ intermittent; M turn signal
internacional ADJ international
internado -da M (escuela) boarding school; (período de práctica) internship; MF (alumno) boarding student; (en un hospital) inmate
internalizar[9] VT to internalize
internar VT (en una cárcel) to intern; (en un hospital) to admit; (en un manicomio) to commit
internet M Internet
internista MF internist
interno -na ADJ internal; MF (alumno) boarding-school student; (prisionero, médico) intern
interpersonal ADJ interpersonal
interponer[39] VT to interpose; **—se** to intervene
interpretación F interpretation; (artístico) performance, rendition
interpretar VT to interpret; (música) to perform; (intenciones) to construe
intérprete MF interpreter; (músico) artist
interracial ADJ interracial
interrelacionado ADJ interrelated

interrogación F interrogation
interrogador -ora MF questioner; ADJ
　　questioning
interrogar[7] VI/VT (por la policía) to
　　interrogate; (con intensidad) to grill; (a un
　　testigo) to question, to cross-examine
interrogativo ADJ interrogative
interrogatorio M interrogation, questioning
interrumpir VI/VT to interrupt; VT (servicios)
　　to disrupt, to cut off; (producción de un
　　modelo) to discontinue; (en una
　　conversación) to intrude, to cut in
interrupción F interruption; (en una
　　conversación) intrusion; (de producción)
　　stoppage
interruptor M switch
intersección F intersection
intersticio M interstice
intervalo M interval; (en el teatro)
　　intermission, interlude
intervención F intervention; — **de**
　　teléfono wiretap
intervenir[47] VI to intervene; — **un**
　　teléfono to wiretap
interviú F interview
intestino ADJ & M intestine; — **delgado**
　　small intestine; **—s** bowels
intimar VI to become friendly
intimidad F intimacy
intimidar VT (una persona) to intimidate;
　　(una tarea) to daunt
íntimo ADJ intimate, close
intitular VT to entitle; **—se** to be entitled
intolerable ADJ intolerable
intolerancia F intolerance, bigotry
intolerante ADJ intolerant, narrow-minded
intoxicación F intoxication, poisoning; —
　　con plomo lead poisoning; — **por**
　　alimentos food poisoning
intoxicar[6] VT to poison, to intoxicate
intransigente ADJ intransigent,
　　uncompromising
intransitivo ADJ intransitive
intravenoso ADJ intravenous
intrepidez F fearlessness
intrépido ADJ (sin miedo) intrepid, fearless;
　　(aventurero) adventurous
intriga F intrigue
intrigante MF schemer; ADJ scheming
intrigar[7] VI/VT to intrigue, to scheme
intrincado ADJ intricate
intrínseco ADJ intrinsic
introducción F introduction
introducir[24] VT (incorporar) to introduce;
　　(colocar) to put in, to insert
introspección F introspection
introvertido -da ADJ introverted; MF

introvert
intrusión F intrusion
intrusivo ADJ intrusive
intruso -sa ADJ intruding; MF intruder
intuición F intuition
intuir[31] VT to sense
intuitivo ADJ intuitive
inundación F flood
inundar VI/VT to inundate, to flood; (de
　　regalos) to shower
inusitado ADJ unusual
inútil ADJ useless, pointless; (esfuerzo) futile;
　　(persona) worthless, good-for-nothing
inutilidad F uselessness; (de un esfuerzo)
　　futility
inutilizar[9] VT to render useless, to put out
　　of commission
invadir VI/VT to invade
invalidar VT to render invalid
inválido -da ADJ (discapacitado) invalid;
　　(nulo) void; MF invalid
invalorable ADJ priceless, invaluable
invariable ADJ invariable
invasión F invasion
invasor -ora MF invader; ADJ invading
invencible ADJ invincible
invención F invention (también mentira);
　　(mental) construct
inventar VT to invent; (una historia) to
　　fabricate, to make up
inventariar[16] VT to inventory
inventario M inventory
inventiva F ingenuity
inventivo ADJ inventive
invento M invention
inventor -ora MF inventor
invernadero M greenhouse, hothouse
invernal ADJ wintry
invernar[1] VI to winter
inverosímil ADJ unlikely, farfetched
inversión F (trueque) inversion; (financiero)
　　investment
inversionista MF investor
inverso ADJ inverse, reverse; **a la inversa**
　　the other way around
inversor -ora MF investor
invertir[3] VT to invert, to reverse; VI/VT
　　(dinero) to invest
investidura F inauguration, investment
investigación F (policial) investigation,
　　inquiry; (científico) research
investigador -ora MF investigator;
　　(científico) researcher
investigar[7] VI/VT to investigate, to look into;
　　(científico) to research
investir VI/VT to invest; — **de un cargo** to
　　induct into office

invicto ADJ unbeaten
invierno M winter
invisible ADJ invisible; (oculto) unseen
invitación F invitation
invitado -da MF guest
invitar VI/VT to invite
invocación F invocation
invocar[6] VT to invoke; (espíritus) to conjure
involucrar VT (implicar) to implicate; (consistir de) to involve
involuntario ADJ involuntary; (accidental) inadvertent
inyección F injection, shot; (en coches) fuel injection
inyectado ADJ — **de sangre** bloodshot
inyectar VT to inject
ión M ion
ionizar[9] VT to ionize
ir[32] VI to go; (deber estar situado) to belong; — **a caballo** to ride horseback; — **a pie** to walk; —**a por** to fetch; — **aprendiendo** to learn gradually; — **corriendo** to run; — **de mal en peor** to go from bad to worse; — **en coche** to drive / ride in a car; — **tirando** to scrape along; **no me va ni me viene** it's all the same to me; **¿cómo te va?** how are you? **¡vaya!** well now! **¡vaya a saber uno!** go figure! **¡vamos!** let's go! come on! **¡vaya hombre!** what a man! **¡ve a freír espárragos!** take a hike! **va por dos años que me casé** it's going on two years since I got married; **voy a comer** I'm going to eat; **va y se come un hongo venenoso** she goes and eats a poisonous mushroom; **en lo que va del año** since the beginning of the year; **ya van siete veces que me lo dice** that makes seven times that she's told me; **voy a ir de rojo** I'm going dressed in red; **para que no vayas a creer** lest you should think; **no vayas a caerte** don't fall; **¡qué va!** no way! —**se** to go away, to leave; —**se a la quiebra** to go broke; —**se a las manos** to come to blows; —**se a pique** to founder; —**se de vacaciones** to take a vacation
ira F ire, wrath
Irak M Iraq
Irán M Iran
iraní ADJ & MF Iranian
iraquí ADJ & MF Iraqi
irascible ADJ irascible, quick-tempered
iridiscente ADJ iridescent
iris M iris
Irlanda F Ireland
irlandés -esa MF Irish; ADJ Irish

ironía F irony
irónico ADJ ironic, wry
irracional ADJ irrational, unreasonable
irradiar VT to radiate, to irradiate
irreal ADJ unreal
irreconocible ADJ unrecognizable
irrecuperable ADJ irretrievable
irreflexivo ADJ thoughtless
irrefutable ADJ irrefutable
irregular ADJ irregular; (borde, filo) ragged; (pulso) unsteady; (superficie) rough, uneven; (comportamiento) erratic, haphazard
irremediable ADJ hopeless
irremplazable ADJ irreplaceable
irreparable ADJ irreparable
irreprochable ADJ irreproachable, flawless
irresistible ADJ irresistible
irrespetuoso ADJ disrespectful
irresponsable ADJ irresponsible
irreverente ADJ irreverent
irrevocable ADJ irrevocable
irrigación F irrigation
irrigar[7] VI/VT to irrigate
irritable ADJ irritable
irritación F irritation
irritante ADJ (molesto) irritating, grating; (agresivo) abrasive
irritar VI/VT to irritate, to aggravate
irrumpir VI to burst into
isla F island, isle; —**s Fiyi** Fiji Islands; —**s Malvinas** Falkland Islands; —**s Marshall** Marshall Islands; —**s Salomón** Solomon Islands; —**s Vírgenes** Virgin Islands
islamismo M Islam
islandés -esa MF Icelander; ADJ Icelandic
Islandia F Iceland
isleño -ña MF islander
isobara F isobar
isométrico ADJ isometric
isótopo M isotope
Israel M Israel
israelí ADJ & MF Israeli
istmo M isthmus
Italia F Italy
italiano -na ADJ & MF Italian
itálico ADJ italic
ítem M item
itinerante ADJ itinerant
itinerario M itinerary
IVA (impuesto al valor añadido / agregado) M sales tax
izar[9] VT to hoist, to raise
izquierda F left (también política); (mano) left hand; **a la —** to the left
izquierdista ADJ & MF leftist
izquierdo ADJ left

Jj

jab M jab
jabalí M (wild) boar
jabalina F javelin
jabón M soap
jabonera F soap dish
jabonoso ADJ soapy
jaca F nag
jacinto M hyacinth
jactancia F boastfulness
jactancioso ADJ boastful, blustering
jactarse VI to boast, to brag
jacuzzi M Jacuzzi[tm], hot tub
jade M jade
jadear VI to pant, to gasp
jadeo M panting, gasping
jaez M harness
jaguar M jaguar
jalar VI/VT to pull, to tug
jalea F jelly
jaleo M (lío) mess; (barahúnda) ruckus
jam M jam session
Jamaica F Jamaica
jamaicano -na ADJ & MF Jamaican
jamaiquino -na ADJ & MF Jamaican
jamás ADV never
jamelgo M hack
jamón M ham
jamona F buxom woman
Japón M Japan
japonés -esa ADJ & MF Japanese
jaque M check; — **mate** checkmate; **tener a uno en** — *fam* to have someone by the short hairs
jaqueca F migraine
jarabe M syrup
jarana F revelry; **ir de** — to paint the town red
jarcia F rigging
jardín M (de flores) garden; (de césped) yard; — **de niños** kindergarten; — **infantil** nursery
jardinero -ra MF gardener
jarra F (cántaro) jug, pitcher; (taza) mug; **en —s** akimbo
jarro M pitcher, jug
jarrón M vase
jaspe M jasper; (mármol) veined marble
jaula F cage, coop
jauría F pack
jazmín M jasmine
jazz M jazz

jeans M PL jeans
jefatura F headquarters
jefe -fa MF (en un lugar de trabajo) boss; (militar) commander; (departamental) chair, head; (policial) chief; — **del estado mayor** chief of staff
jején M gnat
jengibre M ginger
jerarquía F hierarchy
jerez M sherry
jerga F jargon, slang
jerigonza F gibberish, gobbledygook; (juego lingüístico) pig Latin
jeringa F syringe
jeringar[7] VT to annoy
jeroglífico ADJ & M hieroglyphic
jersey M sweater
jesuita ADJ INV & M Jesuit
Jesús INTERJ God bless you! gesundheit!
jeta F (hocico) snout; (cara) mug
jet-set M jet set
jilguero M goldfinch
jinete -ta MF rider
jinetear VI to ride horseback
jingle M jingle
jirafa F giraffe
jobar INTERJ holy cow! holy Moses! holy mackerel!
jockey M jockey
jocoso ADJ jocular
joder INTERJ *vulg* fuck! shit! VI/VT (tener relaciones sexuales) *vulg* to fuck; VT (dañar) *vulg* to fuck up; (fastidiar) *vulg* to jerk around
jodido ADJ (de mierda) *vulg* fucking; (estropeado) *vulg* fucked up
jofaina F basin
jolgorio M rumpus
Jordania F Jordan
jordano -na ADJ & MF Jordanian
jornada F (día laboral) workday; (coloquio) colloquium
jornal M daily wage
jornalero -ra MF day laborer
joroba F hump
jorobado -da ADJ & MF hunchback
jorobar VT (molestar) to hassle; (estropear) to gum up
jota F jay; **no saber ni** — to know zilch
joven ADJ young; M (muchacho) youth
jovial ADJ jolly
joya F jewel; (persona apreciada) gem; **—s** jewelry
joyería F jewelry store
joyero -ra MF jeweler
joystick M joystick
juanete M bunion

jubilación F retirement; (pagos) pension
jubilar VT to pension, to retire; **—se** to retire
jubileo M jubilee
júbilo M glee
jubiloso ADJ jubilant, joyous
judía F bean; **— blanca** navy bean; **—
    pinta** pinto bean; **— verde** green bean
judicial ADJ judicial
judío -ía ADJ Jewish; MF Jew
judo M judo
juego M (actividad recreativa) play; (partido
    de pelota) game; (conjunto de tazas) set;
    (conjunto de muebles) suite; **— de
    damas** checkers; **— de palabras** pun,
    play on words; **—s Olímpicos** Olympic
    Games; **estar en —** to be at stake; **hacer
    —** to match
juerga F binge; **irse de —** to go on a binge
juerguista MF merrymaker
jueves M Thursday
juez -za MF judge; (en deportes) referee; **—
    de paz** justice of the peace
jugada F play, move
jugador -ora MF player; (apostador) gambler
jugar³³ VI to play; (apostar) to gamble; **— a
    la baraja / a los naipes** to play cards; **—
    con fuego** to play with fire; **— limpio** to
    play fair; **—se** to risk
jugarreta F bad turn
jugo M juice
jugoso ADJ juicy
juguete M plaything, toy
juguetear VI to toy with, to fiddle with
juguetón -ona ADJ playful
juicio M (criterio) judgment; (proceso) trial;
    perder el — to lose one's mind; **a mi —**
    in my estimation
juicioso ADJ judicious
juke-box M jukebox
julio M July
jumbo ADJ jumbo; M jumbo jet
jumper M jumper
junco M rush, reed; (barco chino) junk
jungla F jungle
junio M June
junta F (reunión) meeting; (concejo) council;
    (juntura) joint; (pieza de coche) gasket
juntar VT (tubos) to attach; (valentía) to
    muster; (flores) to gather, to pick;
    (ganado) to round up, to wrangle; **—
    polvo** to gather dust; **— valor** to muster
    courage; **—se** (acumularse) to gather;
    (asociarse) to band together; (reunirse) to
    come together
junto ADJ together; LOC ADV **— a** next to; **—
    con** together with
juntura F (lugar) juncture; (articulación)

joint
jurado -da MF juror; M (conjunto de jurados)
    jury
juramentar VI/VT to swear in; **—se** to be
    sworn in
juramento M oath
jurar VI/VT to swear, to vow; **— en falso** to
    perjure oneself; **— la bandera** to pledge
    allegiance to the flag
jurisdicción F jurisdiction
jurisprudencia F (doctrina) jurisprudence;
    (derecho) law
justa F joust, tilt
justamente ADV precisely, fairly
justicia F justice
justificación F justification
justificar⁶ VT to justify
justo ADJ just; (equitativo) equitable; (pío)
    righteous, upright; **— después de** right
    after; **— en ese momento** exactly at that
    moment
juvenil ADJ (inmaduro) juvenile; (de
    apariencia joven) youthful
juventud F youth
juzgado M court
juzgar⁷ VI/VT to judge, to pass judgment
    (on); **— mal** to misjudge

Kk

kaki M khaki
kart M go-cart
kayak M kayak
Kazajstán M Kazakhstan
kazako -ka ADJ & MF Kazak(h)
Kenia F Kenya
keniata ADJ INV & MF INV Kenyan
kermés F bazaar
keroseno M kerosene
ketchup M catsup, ketchup
kilo M kilo
kilobyte M kilobyte
kilociclo M kilocycle
kilogramo M kilogram
kilometraje M mileage
kilómetro M kilometer
kilovatio M kilowatt; F **—-hora** kilowatt-
    hour
Kirguistán M Kyrgyzstan
Kiribati M Kiribati
kosher ADJ kosher
Kuwait M Kuwait
kuwaití ADJ & MF Kuwaiti

Ll

la ART DEF F the; **— de** the one with, that one with; PRON PERS it, her; PRON REL **— que** she who, the one that
laberinto M labyrinth, maze
labia F gift of gab
labio M lip; **— leporino** harelip
labor F (trabajo) labor; (tarea) task; (manualidad) handiwork
laboral ADJ **legislación —** labor legislation
laboratorio M laboratory
laborioso ADJ (trabajoso) laborious; (amante del trabajo) hard-working
labrado ADJ carved
labranza F plowing
labrar VT to till; **—se una carrera** to carve out a career
laca F lacquer
lacar[6] VT to lacquer
lacayo M lackey, flunky
laciar VT *RP* to straighten
lacio ADJ straight
lacónico ADJ (persona) laconic; (comentario) terse
lacra F (física) scar; (moral) blight
lacre M sealing wax
lacrimógeno ADJ tear-producing
lactar VT to nurse
lácteo ADJ (parecido a la leche) milky; (hecho de leche) dairy
ladeado ADJ (torcido) awry, askew; (asimétrico) lopsided
ladear VT to tilt; (la cabeza) to cock; (un avión) to bank; (ignorar) to snub, to ignore; **—se** to tilt, to lean
ladeo M tilt
ladera F hillside
ladillas F PL crabs
ladino ADJ artful
lado M side; **— a —** side by side; **al —** nearby; **¡a un —!** gangway! **de —** sideways; **hacerse a un —** to move over
ladrar VI to bark; VI/VT (hablar de modo áspero) to snap (at)
ladrido M bark, barking
ladrillo M brick
ladrón -ona MF (de casas) burglar; (con violencia) robber; (con astucia) thief
lagartija F lizard; (ejercicio) push-up
lagarto M alligator
lago M lake
lágrima F tear, teardrop

lagrimear VI to weep
laguna F lagoon; (de la memoria, conocimiento) gap; (legal) loophole
laico -ca MF layperson; ADJ lay
laja F slab
lamentable ADJ (desafortunado) lamentable, regrettable; (ruinoso) woeful
lamentación F lamentation
lamentar VT to lament, to regret; **—se** to lament, to wail
lamento M lament, lamentation
lamer VT to lick; **— culos** *fam* to brown-nose; VI/VT (el mar) to lap
lamida F lick
lámina F (de vidrio, metal) sheet; (de metal) plate; (grabado) print
laminar VT to laminate
lámpara F lamp
lamparilla F night-light
lampiño ADJ (sin pelo) hairless; (sin barba) beardless
lana F wool; **— de acero** steel wool
lanar ADJ wool-bearing
lance M incident
lancear VT to lance, to spear
lanceta F lancet, lance
lancha F launch, boat; **— a motor** motorboat
langosta F (crustáceo) lobster; (insecto) locust
langostino M prawn
languidecer[13] VI to languish, to wilt
languidez F languor
lánguido ADJ languid, listless
lanilla F flannel
lanolina F lanolin
lanudo ADJ wooly, shaggy
lanza F lance, spear; **romper una — por alguien** to stick one's neck out for someone; **— SG —llamas** flame thrower
lanzadera F shuttle
lanzador -ora MF pitcher
lanzamiento M (de un cohete, producto) launch; (de suministros) drop; (de una roca grande) heave; (de una pelota) pitch
lanzar[9] VT (un cohete, un producto) to launch; (una pelota) to throw; (una bala) to fire; (algo pesado) to heave; (lodo) to sling; VI/VT (vomitar) to puke; **—se** to launch forth / out
lanzazo M thrust with a lance
Laos M Laos
laosiano -na ADJ & MF Laotian
lápida F stone tablet; (de sepultura) gravestone, tombstone
lapidar VT to stone
lapidario ADJ & M lapidary

lápiz M pencil; — **de color** crayon; — **de labios** lipstick
lapso M lapse, span
lapsus M lapse, slip of the tongue
laptop M laptop
laquear VT to lacquer
largar[7] VI (soltar) to cough up; —**se** *fam* to scram, to buzz off, to shove off
largo ADJ long; (discurso) lengthy; ¡— **de aquí!** scram! —**metraje** feature film; **a la larga** in the long run; **a lo** — lengthwise; M length
largueza F generosity
larguirucho ADJ lanky
largura F length
laringe F larynx
laringitis F laryngitis
larva F larva
lascivia F (deseo) lust; (perversión) lewdness
lascivo ADJ (pervertido) lascivious, lewd; (cachondo) *fam* horny
láser M laser
lástima F (compasión) pity; ¡**qué** —! what a shame!
lastimadura F hurt
lastimar VT to hurt; (insultar) to hurt one's feelings; —**se** to get hurt
lastimoso ADJ pitiful
lastrar VT to ballast
lastre M ballast
lata F tin can, can; (con tapa) canister; (pesadez) bore; **dar la** — to be a nuisance
latente ADJ latent, dormant
lateral ADJ lateral, side
látex M latex
latido M (individual) beat, throb; (colectivo) beating; (del corazón) heartbeat
latifundio M large estate
latigazo M (golpe) lash; (chasquido) crack of a whip
látigo M whip
latín M Latin
latino -na ADJ (relativo a los hispanos) Latino; (relativo a la lengua latina) Latin; M Latino; F Latina
Latinoamérica F Latin America
latinoamericano ADJ Latin American
latir VI to beat, to throb
latitud F latitude (también flexibilidad)
latón M brass
latrocinio M larceny
laudable ADJ laudable
laurel M laurel; **dormirse sobre los** —**es** to rest on one's laurels
lava F lava
lavable ADJ washable
lavabo M (retrete) lavatory, toilet; (recipiente) sink
lavadero M laundry
lavado M wash, washing; — **de cerebro** brain washing; — **de dinero** money laundering; — **en seco** dry cleaning
lavadora F washing machine
lavanda F lavender
lavandera F washerwoman
lavandería F laundry
lavar VI/VT to wash; (ropa) to launder; —**se** to wash up; —**se las manos** to wash one's hands; M SG **lavaplatos / lavavajillas** dishwasher
lavativa F enema
lavatorio M washroom
laxante M laxative
laxitud F laxity
laxo ADJ lax
lazada F bowknot
lazar[9] VT to lasso
lazarillo M (persona) guide for the blind; (perro) guide dog
lazo M (soga) lasso, rope; (vuelta) loop; (nudo corredizo) noose; (relación) tie, bond
le PRON PERS — **dije** I told you / him / her; — **vi** *Esp* I saw him; **se** — **murió el perro** his / her dog died on him / her
leal ADJ loyal, trusty
lealtad F loyalty, allegiance
lección F lesson, assignment; **darle una** — **a alguien** to teach someone a lesson
lechada F whitewash
leche F (de vaca) milk; (semen) *vulg* come; — **desnatada** skim milk; — **en polvo** powdered milk; — **entera** whole milk; — **homogeneizada** homogenized milk; — **malteada** malted milk; ¿**qué** —**s quieres?** *Esp fam* what the hell do you want? **mala** — nasty disposition; **ir a toda** — to barrel along; **ese tío es la** — that guy's a case; **es un mala** — *Esp fam* he's a nasty creep
lechería F dairy
lechero -ra ADJ dairy; M milkman; F milkmaid
lecho M bed (también de río)
lechón M suckling pig
lechoso ADJ milky
lechuga F lettuce
lechuza F screech owl, barn owl
lector -ora MF reader
lectura F (acción) reading; (material) reading matter
leer[14] VI/VT to read
legación F legation
legado M legacy, bequest
legajo M file

legal ADJ legal, lawful
legalizar[9] VT to legalize
legar[7] VT to will, to bequeath
legendario ADJ legendary
leggings M PL leggings
legible ADJ legible
legión F legion
legislación F legislation
legislador -ora MF legislator, lawmaker
legislar VI/VT to legislate
legislativo ADJ legislative
legislatura F legislature
legítimo ADJ legitimate, lawful, rightful
lego -ga MF layperson; ADJ lay
legua F league
leguleyo -ya MF *pey* shyster
legumbre F legume
leído ADJ well-read
lejanía F distance
lejano ADJ distant, faraway; (parentesco) remote
lejía F (producto de limpieza) bleach; (de sosa) lye
lejos ADV far away, far; **a lo —** in the distance; **— de** far from; **desde —** from afar
lelo ADJ silly
lema M motto; (político) slogan
lencería F lingerie
lengua F (órgano) tongue; (idioma) language; **— materna** mother tongue
lenguado M sole
lenguaje M language (también en informática); **— corporal** body language; **— de máquina** machine language; **— de signos** sign language; **— ensamblador** assembly language
lenguaraz ADJ gossipy
lengüeta F (de un instrumento de viento) reed; (de un zapato) tongue
lengüetazo M lick
lente MF lens; **— filtrador** filter lens; **—s** eyeglasses; **—s de contacto** contact lenses; **—s negros / oscuros** sunglasses, shades
lenteja F lentil
lentitud F slowness
lento ADJ (no rápido) slow; (no inteligente) dull; (letárgico) sluggish
leña F firewood
leñador -ora MF woodcutter, lumberjack
leñera F woodshed
leño M log
leñoso ADJ woody
león M lion; **— marino** sea lion
León M Leon
leona F lioness

leonés ADJ Leonese
leopardo M leopard
lepra F leprosy
lerdo ADJ slow
lesbiano -na ADJ lesbian; F lesbian
lesión F injury, lesion
lesionar VT to injure; **—se** to get injured
Lesotho M Lesotho
letal ADJ lethal
letargo M lethargy
letón -ona ADJ & MF Latvian
Letonia F Latvia
letra F (del alfabeto) letter; (caligrafía) handwriting; (de una canción) lyrics, words; **— bastardilla / cursiva** italics; **— chica** fine print; **— de cambio** bill of exchange; **— de imprenta** block letter; **— manuscrita** longhand; **sin —s** uneducated
letrado ADJ learned, literate
letrero M sign
letrina F latrine
leucemia F leukemia
leudar VI to rise; VT to leaven
leva F (de tropas) levy; (de motor) cam
levadura F leaven, yeast
levantamiento M (revuelta) uprising; (suspensión) suspension; **— de pesas** weight-lifting
levantar VT (la mano) to raise; (una caja) to lift; (un interruptor) to switch; (algo caído) to pick up; (perdices) to flush; (a un dormido) to wake up, to rouse; (un edificio) to put up; **— el campamento** to break camp; **— falso testimonio** to bear false witness; **— la mesa** to clear the table; **— la sesión** to adjourn the meeting; **— vuelo** to take flight; **—se** (de la cama) to get up, to rise, to arise; (de una silla) to stand up, to get up; (un edificio) to go up
levar VT **— anclas** to weigh anchor
leve ADJ (brisa) light; (resfrío) mild; (problema) slight
levedad F (de una brisa) lightness; (de un resfrío) mildness
léxico M lexicon, dictionary; ADJ lexical
lexicografía F lexicography
ley F law, statute; **— de prescripción** statute of limitations; **— marcial** martial law; **de buena —** of good quality
leyenda F (mitología) legend; (texto que acompaña una figura) caption
liar[16] VT (paquetes) to bundle; (cigarros) to roll; **—se** to get involved
libanés -esa ADJ & MF Lebanese
Líbano M Lebanon

libelo M libel

libélula F dragonfly

liberación F liberation; (de pecados) deliverance; (de presos) release

liberal ADJ & MF liberal

liberalidad F liberality

liberalismo M liberalism

liberar VT (de un deber) to relieve; (a un pueblo) to liberate; (del sufrimiento) to deliver; (a un preso) to free, to release

Liberia F Liberia

liberiano -na ADJ & MF Liberian

libertad F liberty, freedom; **— condicional** parole; **— de expresión** free speech; **poner en —** to set free; **poner en — bajo fianza** to let out on bail; **poner en — condicional** to parole

libertador -ora MF liberator

libertar VT to liberate

libertinaje M licentiousness

libertino -na MF libertine

Libia F Libya

libido F libido

libio -bia ADJ & MF Libyan

libra F pound (también moneda británica)

librar VT to free, to set free; (de una obligación) to release; (un cheque) to write; (una letra de cambio) to draft; (una guerra) to wage; **—se de** to get rid of

libre ADJ free; (asiento) vacant; (camino) clear; (traducción) loose; (de una obligación) exempt; **— albedrío** free will; **— cambio / comercio** free trade; **— de impuestos** duty-free; **— pensador** free thinker

librería F bookstore

librero -ra MF bookseller

libresco ADJ bookish

libreta F small notebook

libreto M libretto

libro M book; **— de bolsa** pocket book; **— de cocina** cookbook; **— de texto** textbook; **— en rústica** paperback; **— mayor** ledger

licencia F (carnet de conducir, libertad poética) license; (permiso) leave

licenciado -da MF college graduate

licenciar VT to discharge; **—se** to graduate from college

licenciatura F bachelor's degree

licencioso ADJ licentious

liceo M high school

licitación F bid

lícito ADJ lawful, permissible

licor M liqueur, cordial

licuadora F blender

líder MF leader

lidiar VI/VT to contend, to grapple

liebre F hare; **levantar la —** to let the cat out of the bag

Liechtenstein M Liechtenstein

liechtensteiniano -na MF Liechtensteiner

lienzo M canvas

lifting M face-lift

liga F (alianza, grupo deportivo) league; (cinta elástica) garter; **— mayor** major league

ligado M slur

ligadura F ligature

ligamento M ligament

ligar[7] VT to bind; (conectar notas) to slur; (perseguir sexualmente) to hit on; (conquistar sexualmente) to score; VI **—se** to bind; **—se las trompas** to have one's tubes tied

ligereza F (de peso) lightness; (de temperamento) levity

ligero ADJ (poco pesado) light; (rápido) swift; (pequeño) slight; **a la ligera** lightly

ligue M (amistad casual) pickup; (conquista sexual) score

liguero M garter belt

lija F sandpaper

lijar VI/VT to sandpaper, to sand

lila ADJ & MF INV lilac

lima F (fruta) lime; (árbol) lime tree; **— de uñas** nail file

limar VI/VT to file

limero M lime tree

limitación F (restricción) limitation; (defecto) shortcoming

limitar VT to limit; (gastos) to curb; **—se a** to limit oneself to

límite M limit; (de una región) boundary; (de la paciencia) bounds; **— de velocidad** speed limit

limítrofe ADJ bordering

limo M slime

limón M lemon

limonada F lemonade

limonero M lemon tree

limosna F alms, handout

limpiador M cleanser

limpiar VI/VT to clean; VT (una superficie) to wipe; (la piel) to cleanse; (un camino, una pantalla de computadora, la reputación) to clear; (animales) to dress; (zapatos) to shine; (un derrame) to mop up, to wipe up; (dejar sin dinero) to clean out; M SG **limpiaparabrisas** windshield wiper; **limpiavidrios** squeegee

límpido ADJ limpid

limpieza F cleanliness, neatness; (operación militar) mop-up; **— étnica** ethnic

cleansing
limpio ADJ clean, neat; (piel, conciencia) clear; (juego) fair; (sin dinero) broke; **pasar en —** to make a clean copy
limusina F limousine
linaje M lineage, ancestry
linaza F linseed
lince M (animal) lynx; (persona astuta) sly fox; **con ojos de —** sharp-eyed
linchar VT to lynch
lindante ADJ neighboring
lindar VI to border, to adjoin
linde MF boundary
lindero ADJ adjoining; M boundary
lindo ADJ pretty; **un día —** a nice day; **de lo — a** lot
línea F line; **— de conducta** course of action; **— de crédito** credit line; **— de montaje** assembly line
lineal ADJ linear
linfa F lymph
lingüista MF linguist
lingüística F linguistics
lingüístico ADJ linguistic
linimento M liniment
lino M (tela) linen; (fibra) flax
linóleo M linoleum
linterna F flashlight; (de un faro) lantern
lío M (bulto) bundle; (enredo, molestia) mess, hassle; (amorío) affair, fling; **armar un —** to raise a rumpus; **meterse en un —** to get oneself into a mess
liposucción F liposuction
liquidación F (ajuste de cuentas, de bienes) settlement, liquidation; (rebaja) sale, clearance sale; (pago completo) payment in full
liquidar VT (bienes, mercancías) to liquidate; (una cuenta, herencia) to settle; (a una persona) *fam* to waste, to off
liquidez F liquidity
líquido ADJ & M liquid
lira F lira
lírico ADJ lyric, lyrical
lirio M iris; **— de los valles** lily of the valley
lirismo M lyricism
lisiado ADJ (descapacitado) handicapped; (lesionado) injured
lisiar VT to handicap
liso ADJ (neumático) bald; (camino) even, smooth; (terreno) flat; (pelo) straight; **azul —** solid blue
lisonja F flattery
lisonjear VI/VT to flatter
lisonjero -ra MF flatterer; ADJ flattering
lista F list; (de miembros) roster; (de alumnos) roll; (banda) stripe; (de precios)

schedule, list; **— de control** checklist; **— de espera** waiting list; **pasar —** to call the roll
listado ADJ striped; M listing, printout
listo ADJ (preparado) ready, set; (inteligente) clever, smart; **hacerse el —** to pull a stunt
listón M (tabla) board; (en salto de altura) crossbar
lisura F smoothness
litera F (cama en el tren, barco) berth; (cama superpuesta) bunk bed
literal ADJ literal
literario ADJ literary
literato -ta MF writer
literatura F literature
litigio M (pleito) lawsuit; (acción de litigar) litigation
litio M lithium
litoral ADJ seaside; M seaboard, seacoast
litro M liter
Lituania F Lithuania
lituano -na ADJ & MF Lithuanian
liviano ADJ (leve) light; (promiscuo) promiscuous
lívido ADJ livid
living M living room
llaga F sore
llama F (fuego) flame; (animal) llama
llamada F call; (grito) hail; (nota al pie) footnote; **— de cobro revertido / por cobrar** collect call
llamador M knocker
llamamiento M (conversación) call; (exhortación) appeal; **hacer un —** to appeal
llamar VT (un nombre, una huelga, por teléfono) to call; (a la puerta) to knock; (grito) to hail; **— la atención** to call attention; **me llamo Juan** my name is Juan
llamarada F blaze, flare
llamativo ADJ (impactante) striking, bold; (chabacano) gaudy, flashy
llameante ADJ flaming
llamear VI to flare, to flame
llana F trowel
llano ADJ (sencillo) plain; (liso) flat, smooth, level; (de poca profundidad) shallow; M plain
llanta F (reborde metálico) rim; (neumático) tire
llanto M crying, weeping
llanura F plain, prairie
llave F (para puertas) key; (de armas de fuego) lock; (en lucha libre) lock, hold; (grifo) faucet, tap; (interruptor) light

switch; (de gas) cock; **— de tuercas** wrench; **— inglesa** pipe wrench; **— maestra** master key

llavero M key ring

llegada F arrival

llegar[7] VI (arribar) to arrive, to get there/ here; (alcanzar) to reach; **— a las manos** to come to blows; **— a ser** to become; **— a un arreglo** to cut a deal; **— tarde** to be late

llenar VT to fill; (un formulario) to fill out; **— el tanque** to tank up, to gas up; **— el vacío** to take up the slack; **—se** to fill up; **—se de** to get filled with; **—se de oro** to make a killing

lleno ADJ full; **— de** full of; **de —** totally; **un — completo** a full house

llevadero ADJ bearable

llevar VT (transportar) to carry, to take; (transportar en coche) to drive; (tener puesto) to wear; (contener) to hold; (inducir) to lead, to drive; **— a cabo** to carry out; **— la cuenta** to keep score; **— la ventaja** to have an advantage; **— los libros** to keep the books; **— un mes aquí** to have been here one month; **le llevo dos años a mi hermano** I'm two years older than my brother; **llevo las de perder** the odds are against me; **—se** to carry away, to take away; **—se bien con** to get along with

llorar VI (con ruido) to cry, to bawl; (con lágrimas) to weep; VT (una pérdida) to lament; (una muerte) to mourn

lloriquear VI to whimper

lloriqueo M whimper

llorón -ona ADJ weeping; MF crybaby, whiner

lloroso ADJ tearful, weeping

llovedizo ADJ **agua llovediza** rainwater

llover[2] VI/VT to rain; **— a cántaros** to rain cats and dogs; **llueva o truene** rain or shine

llovizna F drizzle

lloviznar VI to drizzle, to mist

lluvia F rain; (de preguntas, críticas) barrage; (de protestas, flechas, piedras) volley; (de golpes, de chispas) shower; **— ácida** acid rain

lluvioso ADJ rainy

lo PRON PERS **— bueno** the good thing; **— de la protesta** the matter of the protest; **— que quiero** what I want; **sé — bueno que eres** I know how good you are; **yo — vi** I saw it/him/you

loable ADJ laudable, praiseworthy

loar VT to laud

lobato M wolf cub

lobbista, lobista MF lobbyist

lobby M lobby

lobezno M wolf cub

lobo M wolf

lobotomía F lobotomy

lóbrego ADJ gloomy

lóbulo M lobe

local ADJ local; M premises

localidad F (pueblo) town, locality; (en un teatro) seat

localización F location

localizar[9] VT (encontrar) to locate; (limitar) to localize

loción F lotion

loco -ca ADJ insane, mad, crazy; **— de remate** stark raving mad; MF lunatic, insane person; M madman

locomotora F locomotive, train engine

locuaz ADJ garrulous, loquacious

locura F madness, insanity

locutor -ora MF radio announcer

lodazal M quagmire

lodo M mud

lodoso ADJ muddy

logaritmo M logarithm

logia F lodge

lógica F logic

lógico ADJ logical; (bien fundado) sound

logística F logistics

lograr VT to achieve, to accomplish; **logré convencerle** I managed to/succeeded in convincing him

logro M accomplishment, achievement; (hazaña) feat

lola F (teta) *fam* boob

loma F knoll

lombriz F (de tierra) earthworm; (de estómago) tapeworm

lomo M (de animal) back ridge; (corte de carne) loin

lona F canvas

longaniza F cured sausage

longevidad F longevity

longevo ADJ long-lived

longitud F (distancia angular) longitude; (largo) length; **— de onda** wavelength

lonja F (mercado) commodity exchange; (loncha) slice of meat

loquería F *fam* booby hatch, funny farm

loquero -ra MF (psiquiatra) *fam* shrink; M (manicomio) *fam* funny farm

lord M lord

loro M parrot

losa F slab; (baldosa) flagstone

lote M lot

lotería F lottery

loza F (basto) crockery; (fino) china

lozanía F freshness, bloom
lozano ADJ fresh, blooming
LSD MF LSD
lubina F bass
lubricante ADJ & M lubricant
lubricar[6] VI/VT to lubricate
lucero M morning star; — **del alba** morning star
lucha F (de clases) struggle; (pelea) fight; — **libre** wrestling
luchador -ora MF fighter; (en lucha libre) wrestler
luchar VI/VT (contra un enemigo) to fight; (con un problema) to struggle; (en lucha libre) to wrestle; — **por** to strive for
lúcido ADJ lucid, clear-headed
luciérnaga F firefly, glowworm
lucio M pike
lucir[13b] VI (mostrarse) to look; VT (llevar) to model, to sport; (alardear de) to flaunt; —**se** (sobresalir) to excel; (ostentar) to show off
lucrativo ADJ lucrative, profitable
lucro M **sin fines de** — not for profit
luctuoso ADJ sad, mournful, dismal
luego ADV afterwards, then, next; — **de** after; **desde** — of course; **hasta** — so long
lugar M place; — **común** platitude; — **de nacimiento** birthplace; — **de trabajo** workplace; **dar** — **a** to give rise to; **no hay** — there's no room; **en** — **de** instead of
lúgubre ADJ mournful, gloomy
lujo M luxury; **darse un** — to indulge oneself; **con** — **de detalles** in great detail
lujoso ADJ luxurious; (hotel) plush
lujuria F lust
lujurioso ADJ lustful
lumbre F fire
luminosidad F brilliance
luminoso ADJ luminous
luna F moon; (espejo) large mirror; — **de miel** honeymoon; **estar en la** — to be distracted; — **llena** full moon
lunar ADJ lunar; M (en la piel) mole; (en una tela) polka dot
lunático -ca ADJ & MF lunatic
lunes M Monday
lupa F magnifying glass
lúpulo M hops
lustrar VT to shine, to polish
lustre M luster, shine
lustroso ADJ (revista) glossy; (pelo) shining, sleek
luto M mourning
Luxemburgo M Luxembourg

luxemburgués -esa MF Luxembourger; ADJ Luxembourgian
luz F light (también aparato); (del sol) sunshine; (abertura) aperture; — **trasera** tail light; — **verde** green light; **dar a** — to give birth; **sacar a** — to disclose

Mm

macabro ADJ grim
macanudo ADJ cool
Macao M Macao
macarrones M PL macaroni
Macedonia F Macedonia
macedonio -nia ADJ & MF Macedonian
maceta F flowerpot
machacar[6] VT (aplastar) to pound, to crush; (insistir) to harp on
machacón ADJ persistent
machetazo M hack with a machete
machete M machete
machismo M (male) chauvinism
macho M (animal masculino) male; (mulo) he-mule; (varón) man; (hombre muy varonil) he-man; — **cabrío** he-goat; — **y hembra** hook and eye; ADJ (masculino) male; (fuerte) strong; INTERJ man!
machote ADJ butch
machucar[6] VT to bruise
macilento ADJ pale
macizo ADJ massive; M plateau
Madagascar M Madagascar
madama F madam
madeja F skein
madera F wood; (árboles maderables) timber; (madera para construcción) lumber; — **contrachapada** plywood; — **flotante** driftwood; — **noble** hardwood; —**s** woodwinds; **tocar** — to knock on wood
maderaje M woodwork
madero M trunk
madrastra F stepmother
madre F mother; — **de alquiler** surrogate mother; — **patria** mother country; —**perla** mother-of-pearl; — **política** mother-in-law; —**selva** honeysuckle; **ciento y la** — everybody and their dog
madriguera F burrow, hole
madrileño -ña ADJ & MF (person) from Madrid
madrina F godmother
madrugada F early morning hours; **a las dos de la** — at two in the morning

madrugador -ra ADJ & MF early bird
madurar VI to mature, to grow up
madurez F (de personas) maturity; (de frutas) ripeness
maduro ADJ (de personas) mature; (de frutas) ripe
maestría F master's degree
maestro -tra MF (docente) (school)teacher; (artesano) master
mafia F mafia
mafioso -sa MF mafioso
magia F magic
mágico ADJ magic, magical
magistrado -da MF magistrate
magistral ADJ masterful, masterly
magma M magma
magnánimo ADJ magnanimous
magnate MF magnate, tycoon
magnesia F magnesia
magnesio M magnesium
magnético ADJ magnetic
magnetismo M magnetism
magnetizar[9] VT to magnetize
magnificar[6] VT to magnify
magnificencia F magnificence
magnífico ADJ magnificent; (día) glorious
magnitud F magnitude
magno ADJ great
magnolia F magnolia
magnolio M magnolia tree
mago M magician, wizard
magro ADJ lean
magulladura F bruise
magullar VI/VT (machucar) to bruise; (mutilar) to mangle
mahonesa F mayonnaise
maicena® F cornstarch
maíz M corn, maize
maizal M cornfield
majadería F stupidity
majadero ADJ stupid
majar VT to pound
majestad F majesty
majestuoso ADJ majestic, stately
majo ADJ (atractivo) good-looking; (agradable) charming
mal M (maldad) evil; (enfermedad) malady, affliction; (daño) harm; **— de altura** altitude sickness; **— de ojo** evil eye; ADV wrong, badly; **— aconsejado** misguided; **— adquirido** ill-gotten; **— hablado** foulmouthed; **hablar — de alguien** to speak ill of someone; **hacer —** to do wrong
malabarista MF juggler
malandanza F misfortune
malaria F malaria

Malasia F Malaysia
malasio -sia ADJ & MF Malaysian
Malawi M Malawi
malawiano -na ADJ & MF Malawian
malbaratar VT to undersell
malcontento ADJ discontented
malcriado ADJ spoiled
malcriar VT to spoil
maldad F evil, wickedness
maldecir[26b] VI/VT to curse
maldición F curse
maldito ADJ accursed; **¡— sea!** *fam* damn it!
Maldivas F PL Maldives
maldivo -va ADJ & MF Maldivian
maleable ADJ malleable
maleante MF gangster, hoodlum
malear VT to corrupt
maleducado ADJ ill-mannered, ill-bred
maleficio M evil spell
maléfico ADJ evil
malentendido M misunderstanding
malestar M (de estómago) upset; (físico) discomfort; (espiritual) malaise; (social) unrest
maleta F suitcase, bag; **hacer la —** to pack one's suitcase
maletero M car trunk
maletín M briefcase
malévolo ADJ malevolent; (comentario) snide
maleza F underbrush, scrub
malgache ADJ & MF Madagascan
malgastar VI/VT to waste, to throw away
malgasto M waste
malhechor -ora MF evildoer, criminal
malhumorado ADJ grumpy, ill-humored
Malí M Mali
malí ADJ & MF Malian
malicia F malice
malicioso ADJ malicious, spiteful
maligno ADJ vicious, evil; (tumor) malignant
malinterpretar VI/VT to misunderstand
malla F (de armadura) mail; (de metal) mesh
malo ADJ bad; (calidad, letra) poor; (enfermo) ill; **mal estado** disrepair; **mal humor** bad mood; **mala fama** ill repute; **mala hierba** weed; **mala pasada** bad turn; **mala racha** slump; **mala suerte** bad luck; **mala voluntad** ill will
malograr VT to spoil, to ruin; **-se** to miscarry
malpagar[7] VI/VT to underpay
malparto M miscarriage
malsano ADJ unhealthy, unwholesome
malta F malt
Malta F Malta
maltés -esa ADJ & MF Maltese
maltratar VT to mistreat, to abuse

maltrato M mistreatment, abuse
maltrecho ADJ battered
malvado ADJ wicked, evil
malversación F misuse, misappropriation
malversar VT to misuse, to embezzle
mamá F mama, mamma, mom
mamada F suck; (felación) *vulg* blow job
mamado ADJ drunk
mamar VI (un bebé) to suckle, to nurse; VI/VT
  to suck; **—la** *vulg* to blow
mamarracho M sight
mami F mommy
mamífero ADJ mammalian, mammal; M
  mammal
mamografía F mammography
mampara F partition
mamut M mammoth
manada F (de ballenas) pod; (de vacas) herd;
  (de lobos) pack
manantial M (naciente) spring; (cantidad
  inagotable de algo) wellspring
manar VI to stream out
mancha F (marca) stain, spot; (de tinta) blot;
  (cosa borrosa) blur; (aceitosa) smear,
  smudge; (menoscabo) tinge; (en la piel)
  blemish
manchado ADJ spotted
manchar VI/VT (ensuciar) to spot;
  (menoscabar) to stain, to blemish
manchón M large spot
mancilla F blemish
mancillar VT to defile, to sully
manco ADJ one-armed
mancuerna F dumbbell
mandado M errand
mandamiento M commandment
mandante MF principal
mandar VI/VT (dar órdenes) to command, to
  order; (enviar) to send; **— buscar a** to
  send for; **— decir** to send word; **¿quién
  manda?** who's in charge? **—se hacer un
  traje** to have a suit made
mandarina F tangerine
mandatario -ria MF (mediante contrato)
  agent; (de estado) head of state
mandato M (orden) command, order; (cargo
  político) term, mandate
mandíbula F jaw; (hueso) jawbone
mandil M apron
mandioca F manioc
mando M (de un estado) rule; (de un
  aparato) control; **— a distancia** remote
  control
mandolina F mandolin
mandón -ona ADJ bossy, domineering; MF
  bossy person, control freak
mandonear VI/VT to domineer, to boss

  around
manea F hobble
manear VT to hobble
manecilla F clock hand
manejable ADJ manageable
manejar VT (un vehículo) to drive, to steer;
  (un negocio) to run, to manage; (una
  máquina) to operate
manejo M (de un negocio) running,
  management; (de asuntos) handling; (de
  una máquina) operation
manera F manner, way; **a — de** like; **de
  alguna —** somehow; **de cualquier —**
  anyway; **de ninguna —** on no account;
  de — que so that
manga F (de una camisa) sleeve; (de una
  nave) beam; (de agua) hose; **— de viento**
  windsock; **en —s de camisa** not wearing
  a jacket; **ser de — ancha** to be broad-
  minded; **sacar algo de la —** to pull
  something out of a hat
manganeso M manganese
mangle M mangrove
mango M (agarradera) handle, grip; (fruta,
  árbol) mango
mangosta F mongoose
manguera F hose
manguito M muff
maní M peanut
manía F (moda, estado patológico) mania;
  (hábito) bad habit; (tic) tic
maníaco -ca ADJ maniacal; MF maniac
maníacodepresivo ADJ manic-depressive
maniatar VT to tie the hands; (manear) to
  hobble
maniático ADJ (que tiene manías) crotchety;
  (melindroso) fastidious
manicomio M insane asylum
manicura F manicure
manicurar VT to manicure
manido ADJ hackneyed
manifestación F (muestra) manifestation;
  (protesta) demonstration
manifestar[1] VT to manifest, to show;
  (expresar) to air; (protestar en público) to
  demonstrate; (declarar) to state
manifiesto ADJ & M manifest; **poner de —**
  to underscore; M (dogma) manifesto
manija F handle
maniobra F (militar) maneuver; (para llamar
  la atención) stunt
maniobrar VI/VT to maneuver
manipulación F (de la opinión pública)
  manipulation; (de alimentos) handling
manipular VT (influir) to manipulate; (tocar
  con las manos) to handle
maniquí M (muñeco) mannequin; MF

(modelo) model

manivela F crank

manjar M delicacy

mano F hand (también de naipes); (de pintura) coat; **— a —** one on one; **— de obra** workforce; **—s a la obra** let's get to work; **—s de mantequilla** butterfingers; **a —** (presente) at hand; (con la mano) by hand; **a — armada** at gunpoint; **dar una —** to lend a hand; **dar una — de pintura** to put on a coat of paint; **darle una — a alguien** to lend someone a hand; **darse la —** (saludo) to shake hands; (señal de afecto) to hold hands; **de primera —** firsthand; **de segunda —** secondhand; **estar a — con alguien** to be even with someone; **hecho a —** handmade; **poner las —s en el fuego por alguien** to go out on a limb for someone; **quedar a —** to break even; **se le fue la —** he got carried away; **ser —** to lead (in a card game); **tener buena — con / para algo** to have a knack for something; **tomarse de la —** to hold hands

manojo M handful; (de llaves) bunch

manómetro M pressure gauge

manopla F mitten

manosear VT (a una persona) to fondle, to grope; (tocar una cosa) to feel, to finger

manoseo M feel, grope

manotazo M swat; **tirarle un — a alguien** to take a swipe at someone

manotear VI to swat at

mansalva LOC ADV **a —** at will

mansedumbre F gentleness

mansión F mansion

manso ADJ (humilde) meek; (domesticado) tame; (apacible) gentle

manta F blanket, cover; (liviana) throw

manteca F lard, shortening; *RP* butter; **— de cacao** cocoa butter

mantecoso ADJ rich, buttery

mantel M tablecloth

mantener[44] VT (conservar, sostener) to maintain; (dejar prolongadamente) to keep; (alimentar, costear a alguien) to provide for; (apoyar a lo largo del tiempo) to sustain; **— a flote** to buoy up; **— el orden público** to keep the peace; **— en suspenso** to keep in suspense; **— la calma** to remain calm; **—se** (quedarse) to remain; (ganarse la vida) to support oneself; **—se al corriente** to keep abreast; **—se al tanto** to stay informed; **—se firme** to stand pat, to stick to one's guns

mantenimiento M maintenance, upkeep

mantequera F (platillo) butter dish; (aparato para hacer mantequilla) churn

mantequilla F butter; **— de maní** peanut butter

mantilla F mantilla

manto M mantle (también geológico); (de juez) robe

mantón M shawl

mantra M mantra

manual ADJ & M manual

manubrio M handlebar

manufactura F manufacture

manufacturar VT to manufacture

manufacturero -ra ADJ manufacturing; MF manufacturer

manuscrito ADJ written by hand; M manuscript

manutención F maintenance

manzana F (fruta) apple; (de calles) block; **— de discordia** bone of contention

manzanar M apple orchard

manzano M apple tree

maña F (destreza) skill, knack; (artimaña) cunning

mañana F (división del día) morning; (futuro) tomorrow; ADV tomorrow; **— por la —** tomorrow morning

mañanero -ra MF early bird

mañoso ADJ tricky

mapa M map; **— en relieve** relief map

mapache M raccoon

maple M maple

maqueta F mock-up

maquillaje M makeup

maquillarse VI to put on makeup

máquina F (aparato) machine; (motor) engine; **— de búsqueda** search engine; **— de coser** sewing machine; **— de escribir** typewriter; **— de lavar** washing machine; **— de vapor** steam engine; **— expendedora** vending machine; **— fotográfica** camera

maquinación F scheming, plotting

maquinador -ora MF schemer

maquinal ADJ automatic

maquinar VI/VT to plot, to scheme

maquinaria F machinery, apparatus; (de un gobierno) machine

maquinilla F clipper; **— de afeitar** razor

maquinista M (de locomotora) locomotive engineer; (obrero) machinist

mar MF sea; **— de fondo** undercurrent; **llover a mares** to rain cats and dogs; **en alta —** on the high seas; **un — de cosas** a lot of things; **hacerse a la —** to put to sea

maraca F maraca
maraña F tangle, snarl; (de pelo) mat
marañón M cashew
maratón M marathon
maravilla F wonder, marvel; (flor) marigold;
  a las mil —s wonderfully
maravillar VT to amaze; **—se** to be amazed,
  to marvel
maravilloso ADJ marvelous, wonderful
marca F (récord) record; (de ganado) brand;
  (de producto) brand, brand-name, label;
  (de coche) make; **— de fábrica**
  trademark; **— registrada** registered
  trademark; **de —** name-brand
marcado ADJ (acento) thick; (contraste)
  sharp, stark; (descenso) steep; (parecido)
  strong
marcador M marker; **— de libros**
  bookmark; **— genético** genetic marker
marcar[6] VT to mark; (ganado) to brand; (el
  ritmo) to beat; (la hora) to say; (un tanto)
  to score; (medida) to read, to show; (un
  número telefónico) to dial
marcha F (caminata, pieza musical) march;
  (partida) leaving; (progreso) course; (modo
  de andar) gait; (cambio en un coche) gear;
  (animación) nightlife; **— atrás** reverse;
  ponerse en — to get going; **puesta en**
  — beginning; **sobre la —** as you go
marchante MF (vendedor) art dealer;
  (cliente) customer
marchar VI (soldado) to march; (máquina,
  vehículo) to run; **—se** to go away
marchista MF walker
marchitar VT to wither; **—se** to wither, to
  shrivel up
marchito ADJ withered, shriveled up
marcial ADJ martial
marco M (de un cuadro, de una puerta, de
  referencia) frame; (moneda alemana) mark
marea F tide; **— baja** low tide
mareado ADJ (en una embarcación) seasick;
  (en un coche) carsick; (de alegría) giddy;
  (con vértigo) dizzy, lightheaded
marear VT to make dizzy; (en un barco) to
  make seasick; **—se** to get dizzy; (en un
  barco) to get seasick
marejada F tidal wave
maremoto M tidal wave
mareo M (en una embarcación) seasickness;
  (en un vehículo) motion sickness;
  (vértigo) dizziness
marfil M ivory
marfileño -ña ADJ & MF Ivorian
margarina F margarine
margarita F daisy; **echar —s a los cerdos**
  to cast pearls before swine

margen M margin; (de la sociedad) fringe; MF
  (de un río) bank; **al —** on the outside
marginado -da ADJ & MF outcast
marginal ADJ marginal
marginar VT to marginalize
mariachi M mariachi
marica ADJ (homosexual) *ofensivo* queer;
  (cobarde) sissy; M (cobarde) sissy, pansy;
  (homosexual) *ofensivo* queer, fruit
maricón ADJ (cobarde) sissy; (homosexual)
  ofensivo queer; M (cobarde) sissy;
  (homosexual) *ofensivo* queer, fruit
marido M husband
marihuana F marijuana; *fam* grass, pot
marimacho ADJ (niña) tomboyish; (mujer)
  butch; MF (niña) tomboy; (mujer) butch
  woman
marimba F marimba
marina F navy; **— mercante** merchant
  marine
marinar VT to marinate
marinero -ra ADJ (buque) seaworthy;
  (nación) seafaring; MF sailor
marino -na ADJ marine; MF sailor; (oficial)
  naval officer
marioneta F marionette
mariposa F (insecto) butterfly (también
  natación); (tuerca) wing nut; **—**
  nocturna moth
mariquita F ladybug
mariscal M marshal; **— de campo** field
  marshal
mariscos M PL shellfish
marítimo ADJ maritime
marketing M marketing
marmita F pot
mármol M marble
marmóreo ADJ marble
marmota F groundhog
maroma F rope
marrano M hog
marrón ADJ brown
marroquí ADJ & MF Moroccan
Marruecos M Morocco
marshalés -esa ADJ & MF Marshallese
marsopa F porpoise
martes M Tuesday
martillar VI/VT to hammer
martillo M hammer (también hueso del
  oído, pieza de revólver); (de juez) gavel; **—**
  neumático jackhammer
martinete M (martillo grande) pile driver;
  (pieza de piano) piano hammer
martini M martini
mártir MF martyr
martirio M martyrdom
martirizar[9] VT to martyr, to torment

marxismo M Marxism
marzo M March
mas CONJ but
más ADJ more; PREP plus; ADV more; (más tiempo) longer; — **allá de** beyond; — **bien** rather; — **de tres** more than three; — **o menos** more or less; — **que nunca** more than ever; — **que tú** more than you; **a lo** — at best; **a** — **tardar** at the latest; **de** — extra; **el** — **allá** the hereafter; **es de lo** — **simpático** he's really nice; **es** — furthermore; **está de** — it is superfluous; **otro** — yet another; **por** — **que** no matter how much; **y** — **todavía** and then some
masa F mass; (de agua) body; (harina líquida) batter; (harina para amasar) dough; **en** — en masse, in large numbers; **las** —**s** the masses; — **de hojaldre** puff pastry
masacrar VT to massacre, to slaughter
masacre M massacre
masaje M massage
masajear VT to massage
masajista M masseur; F masseuse
mascar[6] VI/VT to chew; (con ruido) to crunch
máscara F mask; — **de gas** gas mask
mascarada F masquerade
mascota F (animal doméstico) pet; (emblema de un equipo) mascot
masculino ADJ (como un hombre) masculine; (del hombre) male
mascullar VI/VT to mumble
masilla F putty
masivo ADJ massive
masón M mason
masonería F masonry
masoquismo M masochism
mastectomía F mastectomy
masticar[6] VT to chew
mástil M (en un barco) mast; (para una bandera) flagpole, flagstaff
mastín M mastiff
masturbar VI to masturbate
mata F bush; — **de pelo** head of hair
matadero M slaughterhouse
matador ADJ horrendous; M bullfighter
matanza F slaughter, killing
matar VT to kill; (animales) to butcher, to slaughter; — **a tiros** to gun down; — **con hambre** to starve; **matasellar** to cancel a stamp; M SG **matamoscas** flyswatter; **matasellos** postmark; **matasanos** quack (doctor)
mate M (en ajedrez) checkmate; (planta, bebida) mate; ADJ (pintura) flat
matemática, matemáticas F mathematics

matemático -ca ADJ mathematical; MF mathematician
materia F matter; (tema de estudio) school subject; (tema) topic; — **extraña** extraneous matter; — **fecal** fecal matter; — **gris** gray matter; — **prima** raw material
material ADJ (necesidades) material; (autor) real; M material
maternal ADJ (instinto) maternal; (amor) motherly
maternidad F (pertinente al nacimiento) maternity; (estado de ser madre) motherhood
materno ADJ maternal
matiné M matinee
matiz M (de un color) tint, shade, hue; (de ironía) tinge; (de sentido) nuance
matizar[9] VT (mezclar colores) to blend, to tinge; (moderar) to qualify
matón M (que intimida a los pequeños) bully; (pendenciero) thug
matorral M (mata) thicket; (región) bush
matraz M flask
matriarca F matriarch
matrícula F (de alumnos) enrollment, matriculation; (de un coche) registration; (placa) license plate; (en la universidad) tuition fees
matriculación F matriculation
matricular VT to matriculate, to enroll
matrimonio M matrimony, marriage; (pareja) married couple
matriz F (en matemáticas) matrix; (útero) womb; (plantilla) stencil; **casa** — main office
matrona ADJ frumpy; F matron
matutino ADJ of the morning
maullar VI to mew
maullido M mew
mauriciano -na ADJ & MF Mauritian
Mauricio M Mauritius
Mauritania F Mauritania
mauritano -na MF Mauritanian
maxilar M jawbone
máxima F maxim
máximo ADJ & M maximum; (autoridad) ultimate; (cuidado) utmost
mayo M May; (palo) maypole
mayonesa F mayonnaise
mayor ADJ (de tamaño) greater, larger; (de edad) older, elder; (rango, clave) major; **al por** — wholesale; **dedo** — middle finger; **el** — **número de votos** the most votes; M (adulto) adult
mayoral M boss
mayordomo M butler

mayoreo M wholesale
mayoría F majority; **— de edad** legal age, majority
mayorista M wholesale dealer
mayúsculo -la ADJ (letra) capital; (problema) major; F capital letter
mazmorra F dungeon
mazo M mallet
mazorca F ear of corn; (sin maíz) corncob
me PRON PERS **él — vio me** he saw me; **él — habló** he talked to me; **se — murió el perro** my dog died on me
meadero M *fam* john
mear VI/VT *fam* to pee, to piss
mecánico -ca ADJ mechanical; MF mechanic; F mechanics
mecanismo M mechanism; **— de seguridad** safety device
mecanografía F typewriting
mecanografiar[16] VI/VT to type
mecanógrafo -fa MF typist
mecedora F rocking chair, rocker
mecenas MF SG/PL patron, sponsor
mecenazgo M patronage
mecer[10a] VI/VT (cuna) to rock; (columpio) to swing
mecha F (de una vela) wick; (de explosivos) fuse; **—s** (en el pelo) highlights
mechar VT (rellenar con tocino) to lard; (robar) to shoplift
mechero -ra MF shoplifter; M burner; **— Bunsen** Bunsen burner
mechón M lock, strand
medalla F medal
médano M dune
media F (hasta el muslo) stocking; (hasta la cintura) pantyhose; (calcetín) sock; (promedio) mean
mediación F mediation
mediador -ra MF mediator
mediados LOC ADV **a — de mayo** in mid-May
mediana F median
mediano ADJ (intermedio en tamaño) medium; (intermedio en calidad) average; **de tamaño —** middle-sized; **de mediana edad** middle-aged
medianoche F midnight
mediante PREP by means of
mediar VI (intervenir en un asunto) to mediate, to intervene; (transcurrir tiempo) to intervene; **mediaba febrero** it was mid-February
medible ADJ measurable
medicación F medication
medicamento M medicine, drug
medicina F medicine

medición F measurement; (de un terreno) survey
médico -ca MF doctor, physician; **— forense** coroner; **— general** general practitioner; ADJ medical
medida F (dimensión) measure; (acto de medir) measurement; **— para áridos** dry measure; **a — que** as; **en la — en que** to the extent that; **hacer a la —** to make to measure; **hecho a la —** made-to-measure; **tomar —s** to take measures; **tomarle las —s a alguien** to measure someone
medidor M gauge, meter
medieval ADJ medieval
medio ADJ **—día** noon, midday; **— hermano** half brother; **a media asta** at half mast; **clase media** middle class; **el americano —** the average American; **hacer una cosa a medias** to do something halfway; **ir a medias** to go halves; **media hora** half an hour; **mi media naranja** my better half; **temperatura media** mean temperature; ADV half; **a — camino** halfway; **a — derretir** half-melted; **de — tiempo** part-time; M (centro) middle; (ambiente) medium; **— ambiente** environment; **— tiempo** halftime; **—s** means, resources; **en (el) — de** in the middle of; **en — de la calle** in the middle of the street; **meterse de por —** to intervene; **por — de** by means of; **—s de comunicación** the media; **por todos los —s** by all possible means
medioambiental ADJ environmental
mediocre ADJ mediocre; (actuación) lackluster
mediocridad F mediocrity
medir[5] VI/VT to measure; VT (consecuencias) to gauge; (terreno) to survey; **— a pasos** to step off; **—se** to be moderate
meditación F meditation
meditar VI to meditate, to ponder
médium MF medium, psychic
medroso ADJ fearful
médula F marrow, pith; **— espinal** spinal cord; **— ósea** bone marrow
medusa F jellyfish, man-of-war
megabyte M megabyte
megáfono M megaphone
megahercio, megahertz M megahertz
mejilla F cheek
mejor ADJ better; **el —** the best; **en el — de los casos** at best; **te deseo lo —** I wish you the best; ADV better; **a lo —** maybe; **tanto —** so much the better
mejora F improvement

mejoramiento M improvement

mejorar VT to improve, to improve upon; (las posibilidades de uno) to better; VI (ventas) to pick up; **—se** to get better / well

mejoría F improvement

melancolía F melancholy, gloom

melancólico ADJ melancholy, gloomy

melanoma M melanoma

melaza F molasses

melena F mane

melindre M affectation

melindroso ADJ affected, finicky

mella F notch; **hacer —** to make a dent

mellar VT to notch

mellizo -za ADJ & MF twin

melocotón M peach

melocotonero M peach tree

melodía F melody

melodioso ADJ melodious

melodrama M melodrama

melómano -na ADJ music-loving; MF music-lover

melón M melon, cantaloupe

membrana F membrane; (en los patos) web

membrete M letterhead

membrillo M (fruta) quince; (árbol) quince tree

membrudo ADJ stout

memorable ADJ memorable

memorándum M memorandum

memoria F (facultad de recordar, recuerdo) memory; (obra autobiográfica) memoir; (actas) proceedings; **— de acceso directo** random access memory (RAM); **— de sólo lectura** read only memory (ROM); **— intermedia** buffer; **— residente** internal memory; **de —** by heart; **hacer —** to try to remember / recollect

memorial M memorial

memorizar[9] VI/VT to memorize

mención F mention

mencionar VT to mention

mendigar[7] VI to beg

mendigo -ga MF beggar

mendrugo M large crumb

menear VT (las caderas) to wiggle, to wriggle, to shake; (la cola) to wag

meneo M (de las caderas) wiggle; (de la cola) wag

menesteroso ADJ needy, destitute

mengua F diminution, waning

menguante ADJ waning

menguar[8] VI (luna) to wane; (energía) to flag; (provisiones) to dwindle

meningitis F meningitis

menjurje M concoction

menopausia F menopause

menor ADJ (de tamaño) smaller; (de cantidad) lesser, smaller; (de edad) younger; (de importancia, en música) minor; **el —** (de tamaño) the smallest; (de cantidad) the least, the smallest; (de edad) the youngest; MF **— de edad** minor; **al por —** retail

menos ADV less; **— de** less than; **— mal** just as well; **a — que** unless; **al — at** least; **dar de —** to shortchange; **echar de —** to miss; **lo —** the least; **no es para menos** there is good reason; **por lo —** at least; **signo de menos** minus sign; **venir a —** to decline; **el que trabaja —** the one who works the least; **las cinco — cuarto** quarter to five; **no puede — de hacerlo** he cannot help doing it; **tienes — que yo** you have less than I; **trabaja — que yo** she works less than I; PREP (salvo) except, but; ADJ & PRON less, least; **— agua** less water; **— problemas** fewer problems; M minus

menoscabar VT to impair, to undermine

menoscabo M impairment

menospreciar VI/VT (despreciar) to despise; VT (burlarse de) to belittle, to demean

menosprecio M contempt

mensaje M message

mensajería F carrier

mensajero -ra MF messenger, courier

menstruación F menstruation

mensual ADJ monthly

mensualidad F (recibida) monthly allowance; (pagada) monthly installment

mensuario ADJ monthly

mensurable ADJ measurable

menta F mint, peppermint; **—verde** spearmint

mental ADJ mental

mentalidad F mentality

mente F mind

mentecato -ta ADJ foolish, simple; MF simpleton

mentir[3] VI to lie

mentira F lie, falsehood

mentirilla F fib, white lie

mentiroso -sa ADJ lying; MF liar

mentón M chin

mentor -ora MF mentor

menú M menu (también de computadoras); **— del día** daily special

menudeo LOC ADV **al —** retail

menudo ADJ (pequeño) small; (insignificante) insignificant; **a —** often; **dinero —** small change; **— perro** that's some dog; M (entrañas) entrails

meñique ADJ little (finger); M little finger, *fam* pinkie

meollo M (médula) marrow; (parte sustancial de un asunto) marrow, pith, core; (seso) brain

mequetrefe M runt, pipsqueak

mercachifle M peddler, huckster

mercadear VT to market

mercadeo M merchandising

mercader M merchant

mercadería F merchandise

mercado M market; **— alcista** bull market; **— bajista** bear market; **— de pulgas** flea market; **— de valores** stock market; **— libre** free market; **— negro** black market

mercadotecnia F marketing

mercancía F merchandise, goods

mercante ADJ merchant

mercantil ADJ mercantile

merced LOC ADV **— a** thanks to; **a (la) — de** at the mercy of

mercenario -ria ADJ & MF mercenary

mercería F notions

mercurio M mercury, quicksilver

merecedor ADJ deserving

merecer[13] VT to deserve, to merit

merecido M deserved punishment, due

merendar[1] VI to have a snack

merendero M picnic area

meridiano ADJ & M meridian

meridional ADJ southern; MF southerner

merienda F afternoon snack

mérito M merit

meritorio ADJ meritorious, worthy

merluza F hake

merma F decrease

mermar VI/VT to decrease, to dwindle

mermelada F jam; (de cítricos) marmalade

mero ADJ mere; **la mera idea** the very idea; M grouper

merodear VI to loiter

mes M month

mesa F table; (consejo) board; (formación geológica) mesa; **— de noche** nightstand; **levantar la —** to clear the table; **poner la —** to set the table

mesada F monthly allowance

mesero -ra M waiter; F waitress

meseta F plateau

mesón M inn, lodge

mesonero -ra MF innkeeper

mestizo -za ADJ (persona) *pey* half-breed; (perros) mongrel; MF *pey* half-breed; (mezcla de europeo e india) mestizo; (perro de raza mezclada) mongrel

mesura F moderation

mesurado ADJ moderate; (respuesta) measured

meta F (objetivo) goal; (en una carrera) finish line

metabolismo M metabolism

metafísica F metaphysics

metáfora F metaphor

metafórico ADJ metaphorical

metal M metal; **— precioso** precious metal

metálico ADJ metallic; M cash

metalurgia F metallurgy

metamorfosis F metamorphosis

metano M methane

metástasis F metastasis

meteorito M meteorite

meteoro M meteor

meteorología F meteorology

meteorólogo -ga M weatherman; F weatherwoman

meter VT to put (into), to stick (into); (un lío) to get (into); (invertir) to invest; **— el estómago** to suck in one's stomach; **— la pata** to make a mistake; **— miedo** to scare; **— ruido** to make noise; **— un gol** to score a goal; **—se** to meddle; **—se a bailar** to begin to dance; **—se con** to mess with; **—se en camisa de once varas** to get oneself into a fix

metódico ADJ methodical

método M method

metralleta F portable machine gun

métrico ADJ metric

metro M (medida) meter; (cinta de medir) measuring tape; (tren subterráneo) subway

metrónomo M metronome

metrópoli F metropolis

metropolitano ADJ metropolitan; M subway

mexicano -na ADJ & MF Mexican

México M Mexico

mezcla F mixture, mix; (en albañilería) mortar; (de café, especias) blend

mezclador -ora MF (persona) mixer; F (aparato) mixer

mezclar VT to mix, to blend; (naipes) to shuffle; (números) to scramble; **—se** (combinarse) to mix; (tener trato con) to mingle; (entrometerse) to meddle

mezcolanza F hodgepodge

mezquindad F (crueldad) meanness; (tacañería) stinginess

mezquino ADJ (cruel) mean, mean-spirited, petty; (insignificante) small, petty; (tacaño) tight, stingy

mezquita F mosque

mi ADJ POS my

mí PRON PERS me; **es para —** it's for me; **me vio a —** he saw me; **me la dio a —** he gave it to me

miau M meow
mico M long-tailed monkey
micra F micron
micro M (autobús) bus; (micrófono) microphone
microbio M microbe, germ
microcirugía F microsurgery
microcomputadora F microcomputer
microeconomía F microeconomics
microficha F microfiche
microfilm M microfilm
micrófono M microphone
Micronesia F Micronesia
micronesio -sia ADJ & MF Micronesian
microonda F microwave; M SG **—s** microwave oven
microordenador M microcomputer
microorganismo M microorganism
microprocesador M microprocessor
microscópico ADJ microscopic
microscopio M microscope; **— electrónico** electron microscope
miedo M fear; **— al escenario** stage fright; **tener —** to be afraid
miedoso ADJ fearful
miel F honey
miembro M member; (extremidad) limb; **— viril** penis
mientras CONJ (durante) while, as; (siempre y cuando) as long as; **— que** while; **— tanto** meanwhile; ADV in the meantime
miércoles M Wednesday
mierda F (excremento) *vulg* shit, crap; (droga) *vulg* shit; (persona o cosa despreciable) *vulg* piece of shit, piece of crap; **una — de coche** *vulg* a crappy / shitty car; **mandar a alguien a la —** *vulg* to tell somebody to go to hell; **¡—!** *vulg* shit!
mies F grain; **—es** fields of grain
miga F crumb; **hacer buenas —s** to get along well
migaja F crumb
migración F migration
migrante ADJ migrant
migraña F migraine
mil NUM thousand; **— millones** billion; **llegamos a las — y quinientas** we got there very late
milagro M miracle, wonder
milagroso ADJ miraculous
milano M kite
milenio M millennium
milicia F militia
miligramo M milligram
mililitro M milliliter
milímetro M millimeter

militante ADJ & MF militant
militar ADJ military; MF soldier; VI to militate
milla F mile
millaje M mileage
millar M thousand
millón M million
millonario -ria MF millionaire
millonésimo ADJ & M millionth
mimar VT to pamper, to spoil, to coddle
mimbre M wicker
mímico ADJ mimic; F mimicry
mimo M (trato cariñoso) caressing, cuddling; MF (actor) mime
mimoso ADJ cuddly
mina F (yacimiento) mine; (explosivo) (land) mine; (de un lápiz) lead; (fuente) storehouse
minado M mining
minar VT (sembrar minas) to mine; (socavar) to undermine; VI (cavar) to burrow
mineral M mineral; (de oro) ore; ADJ mineral
minería F mining
minero -ra MF miner; ADJ mining
mingitorio M urinal
miniatura F miniature
minicomputadora F minicomputer
minifalda F miniskirt
minifundio M subsistence farm
minimizar[9] VT (gastos) to minimize; (a una persona) to belittle; VI (un incidente) to play down
mínimo ADJ (cantidad) least; (tamaño) smallest; M minimum; **como —** at least; **en lo más —** at all
minino M kitty
miniordenador M minicomputer
ministerio M (religioso) ministry; (gubernamental) ministry, department
ministro -tra MF minister, secretary; **— de Justicia** Attorney General
minoría F minority
minoridad F minority
minorista MF retailer
minoritario ADJ minority
minucioso ADJ (detalle) minute; (trabajo) thorough; (persona) fastidious
minúsculo ADJ small, minuscule; **letra —** lowercase letter
minusválido ADJ disabled
minuta F (honorarios) lawyers' fees; (actas) minutes
minutero M minute hand
minuto M minute
mío PRON mine; **este libro es ——** this book is mine; **un amigo —** a friend of mine
miope ADJ shortsighted, nearsighted
miopía F near-sightedness, myopia

mira F (dispositivo de arma) gun sight; (intención) intention; **con —s a** with a view to

mirada F gaze, look; **— asesina** dirty look; **— de soslayo** side glance; **— fija** stare

mirador M vantage point, overlook

miramiento M consideration

mirar VI/VT to look (at); (un partido, televisión) to watch; **— de soslayo** to look askance (at); **— fijamente** to stare (at); **¡mira (tú)!** you don't say!

miríada F myriad

mirilla F peephole

mirlo M blackbird

mirón M onlooker; (erótico) voyeur

mirto M myrtle

misa F mass

misántropo -pa MF misanthrope

misceláneo ADJ miscellaneous

miserable ADJ (vil, pobre) wretched, unhappy; (insignificante) paltry; (tacaño) miserly

miseria F (desgracia) misery; (pobreza) poverty, squalor; (cantidad despreciable) trifle

misericordia F mercy

misericordioso ADJ merciful, gracious

mísero ADJ miserable

misil M missile; **— balístico** ballistic missile; **— crucero** cruise missile

misión F mission

misionero -ra MF missionary

mismo ADJ same; **ese — día** that very day; **se nombró a sí —** he named himself; **lo — the same thing; me da lo —** it's all the same to me; **yo —** I myself

misoginia F misogyny

misterio M mystery

misterioso ADJ mysterious

místico -ca ADJ mystical; MF mystic

mitad F half; **por la —** in half; **en la — de** in the middle of; **a — del camino** midway

mitigar[7] VT to mitigate

mitin M political meeting

mito M myth

mitología F mythology

mixto ADJ mixed; **escuela mixta** coed school

mobiliario M furniture

mocasín M (zapatilla de indio, culebra) moccasin; (zapato sin cordones) loafer

mochar VT to chop off

mochila F knapsack, backpack

moción F motion

moco M mucus; (líquido) *fam* snot

mocoso -sa ADJ snotty; MF *fam* brat, punk

moda F fashion; **de —** fashionable, in style; **ponerse de —** to catch on

modales M PL manners

modelar VI/VT to model

modelo ADJ & MF model

módem M modem

moderación F moderation, restraint

moderado -da ADJ moderate; (invierno) mild; (precio) reasonable; (respuesta) measured; (clima) temperate; MF moderate

moderar VT (restringir) to moderate, to restrain; (presidir) to moderate

moderno ADJ modern

modestia F modesty

modesto ADJ modest

módico ADJ moderate, reasonable

modificación F modification

modificar[6] VT to modify

modismo M idiom

modista MF dressmaker

modo M (manera) mode, manner, way; (categoría gramatical) mood; (de computadora / ordenador) mode; **a — de** by way of; **del mismo —** in like manner; **de ningún —** by no means; **de — que** so that; **de otro —** otherwise; **de ningún — not at all; de todos —s** anyway; **en cierto —** in a way; **ni — no dice; no hay —** no way

modorra F drowsiness

modular VT to modulate

mofa F jeer, ridicule

mofarse VT **— de** to make fun of, to scoff at

mofeta F skunk

moflete M fat cheek

mohair M mohair

mohín M grimace

moho M mold, mildew

mohoso ADJ moldy

mojado -da ADJ wet; MF (inmigrante ilegal) *pey* wetback

mojadura F wetting

mojar VT to wet; (impregnar) to dip; **—se** to get wet; *vulg* to get laid

mojigatería F prudery

mojigato -ta ADJ prudish; MF prude

mojo M dip

mojón M (hito) landmark; (zurullo) turd

molar ADJ molar

Moldavia F Moldova

moldavo -va ADJ & MF Moldovan

molde M (norma) mold, cast; (tortera) cakepan; (patrón) pattern; (de imprenta) die; **letras de —** block letters

moldeado M molding

moldear VT to mold, to cast

moldura F molding

mole F mass

molécula F molecule

moler[2] VI/VT to mill, to grind; **— a palos** to beat thoroughly

molestar VT to bother, to pester; **no te molestes** don't bother

molestia F bother, nuisance; **no te tomes la —** don't go to the trouble

molesto ADJ bothersome, irksome; (situación) uneasy

molibdeno M molybdenum

molienda F grinding

molinero -ra MF miller

molinete M (puerta) turnstile; (juguete) pinwheel

molinillo M mill, grinder

molino M mill; **— de viento** windmill

mollete M muffin

molusco M mollusk

momentáneo ADJ momentary

momento M (tiempo) moment; (movimiento) momentum; **al —** immediately; **a cada —** continually; **en todo —** all the time; **no veo el —** I can't wait; **se oscurecía por —s** it was getting darker by the minute

momia F mummy

Mónaco M Monaco

monada F (acción graciosa) antic; (persona atractiva) *fam* peach

monarca MF INV monarch

monarquía F monarchy

monasterio M monastery

mondar VT to pare; **—se los dientes** to pick one's teeth; M SG **mondadientes** toothpick

moneda F (dinero metálico) coin; (divisa) currency; **— corriente** common currency; **— de curso legal** legal tender; **— falsa** counterfeit money

monegasco -ca ADJ & MF Monegasque

monería F antic

monetario ADJ monetary

mongol -la ADJ & MF Mongolian

Mongolia F Mongolia

monigote M puppet

monitor -ora M (aparato) monitor; MF (persona) monitor

monja F nun

monje M monk

mono -na MF (simio) monkey; **— araña** spider monkey; M (mimo) mimic; (prenda de trabajo) overalls, coverall; (síndrome de abstinencia) withdrawal symptoms; **dormir la mona** to sleep it off; ADJ cute

monogamia F monogamy

monokini M topless swimsuit

monólogo M monolog, monologue

mononucleosis F mononucleosis

monopatín M skateboard; (con manillar) scooter; (de nieve) snowboard

monopolio M monopoly

monopolizar[9] VT to monopolize; (un mercado) to corner

monotonía F monotony

monótono ADJ monotonous

monserga F nonsense

monstruo M monster; (persona grotesca) freak

monstruosidad F monstrosity

monstruoso ADJ monstrous

monta F mount; **de poca —** of little value

montaje M (de un aparato) assembly, set up; (de una película) editing

montante M (total) total; (ventana de puerta) transom; (columna) upright

montaña F mountain; **— rusa** roller coaster

montañés -esa ADJ mountain; MF mountain dweller

montañismo M mountaineering

montañoso ADJ mountainous

montar VT (ir a caballo, en bicicleta) to ride; (un aparato) to assemble; (una película) to edit; (subirse al caballo) to mount, to get on; **— en cólera** to fly into a rage; **— una escena** to make a scene; **—se a caballo** to mount a horse

montaraz ADJ coarse

monte M (montaña) mount; (zona agreste) wilderness; **— de piedad** pawnshop

montés ADJ (salvaje) wild; (de la montaña) of the mountains

montículo M mound

montón M pile, heap; (de papel) stack; (de nieve) drift; (de flores) basketful; (de gente) bunch; **a montones** in abundance; **del —** run-of-the-mill

montura F (animal) mount; (silla) saddle; (armazón de gafas) frame, rim

monumental ADJ monumental

monumento M monument

moño M (de pelo) bun; (adorno) bow

mopa F mop

moquearse VI to be snotty

moquillo M distemper

mora F blackberry, mulberry; **en —** in default

morada F dwelling, abode

morado ADJ purple; **ojo —** black eye

morador -ora MF dweller

moral ADJ moral; F (principios éticos) morals; (estado de ánimo) morale; M mulberry tree

moraleja F moral

moralidad F morality

moralista MF moralist

moralizar[9] VI/VT to moralize
morar VI to dwell, to abide
mórbido ADJ morbid
morboso ADJ (mórbido) morbid; (atractivo) sexy
morcilla F black pudding
mordacidad F sharpness
mordaz ADJ (comentario) cutting, sharp; (persona) sharp-tongued
mordaza F (de la boca) gag; (de un torno) vise jaw
mordedor ADJ biting, snappy
mordedura F bite
morder[2] VI/VT to bite; —**se la lengua** to bite one's tongue
mordida F (mordisco) bite; (comisión ilegal) bribe, kickback
mordiscar[6] VI/VT to nibble; to nip
mordisco M nibble, nip
mordisquear VI/VT to nip; to nibble
mordisqueo M nibble
moreno ADJ (piel) dark, dark-skinned, swarthy; (pelo) dark, brunette
moretón M bruise
morfina F morphine
morgue F morgue
moribundo ADJ dying, moribund
morir[4,51] VI to die; (una calle) to end; —**se de envidia** to eat one's heart out; —**se de hambre** to starve; —**se de miedo** to die of fear; —**se de risa** to die laughing; —**se por algo** to crave something; —**se por alguien** to be crazy about someone
morisco ADJ Moorish
moro -ra ADJ Moorish; MF Moor; —**s y cristianos** beans and rice; **no hay —s en la costa** the coast is clear
morocho ADJ dark-haired, brunet, brunette
moroso ADJ delinquent, deadbeat
morrear VI to make out
morriña F homesickness
morro M (monte) knoll; (caradura) gall, nerve; (de un avión) nose; (de animal) snout
morrón M bell pepper
morsa F walrus
mortaja F shroud
mortal ADJ mortal, deadly; MF mortal
mortalidad F mortality
mortandad F death toll
mortecino ADJ fading
mortero M mortar
mortífero ADJ deadly
mortificación F chagrin
mortificar[6] VT to mortify, to chagrin
mortuorio ADJ **casa mortuaria** funeral home

mosaico M mosaic
mosca F fly; (dinero) dough; — **muerta** hypocrite; **no se oía volar una** — you could have heard a pin drop
mosquear VT (crear desconfianza) to cause distrust; (hacer enfadarse) to enrage; —**se** (desconfiar) to distrust; (enfadarse) to become enraged
mosquitero M (de ventana) window screen; (de tienda de campo) mosquito net
mosquito M mosquito
mostacho M mustache, moustache
mostaza F mustard
mostrador M counter
mostrar[2] VT to show; —**se reticente** to appear reticent
mostrenco ADJ stray
mota F speck, speckle
mote M nickname
moteado ADJ speckled, spotted
motear VT to speck, to speckle
motejar VI — **de** to brand as
motel M motel
motín M (en un barco) mutiny; (de prisioneros) riot
motivación F motivation
motivar VT (impulsar) to motivate; (causar) to cause
motivo M (causa) motive, reason; (figura repetida) motif, theme; **con** — **de** on the occasion of
moto F bike, motorcycle
motocicleta F motorcycle
motociclista MF biker, motorcyclist
motor ADJ of motion; M motor, engine; — **de reacción** jet engine; — **de búsqueda** search engine; — **de combustión interna** internal combustion engine; — **fuera de borda** outboard engine
motriz ADJ **fuerza** — motive power
movedizo ADJ restless
mover[2] VT to move; — **palancas** to pull strings; —**se** to move, to budge
movible ADJ movable
movido ADJ eventful; (foto) blurred
móvil M (motivo) motive; (teléfono) mobile telephone; (adorno, juguete) mobile; ADJ (que se mueve) mobile; (que puede ser movido) movable; **un blanco** — a moving target
movilizar[9] VI/VT to mobilize
movimiento M movement, motion; (organización, pieza de reloj) movement; (comercial) traffic; **los rojos tienen poco** — the red ones don't sell well; **un cuerpo en** — a moving body
Mozambique M Mozambique

mozambiqueño -ña ADJ & MF Mozambican
mozárabe ADJ Mozarabic
mozo -za ADJ young; **en mis años —s** in my youth; M (joven) young man; **buen —** handsome man; (siervo) servant; **— de cordel** porter; F (joven) young woman; (sierva) servant
mucama F chambermaid
muchacho -cha M boy, youngster; F girl; (de servicio) maid
muchedumbre F crowd, throng
mucho ADJ a lot of; (cosas contables) many; (cosas incontables, en oraciones interrogativas y / o negativas) much; **¿tienes — tiempo?** do you have much time? **no tenemos — tiempo** we don't have much time; **tenemos —s problemas** we have many problems; ADV much; (demasiado) too much; **hace — que no lo veo** I haven't seen him for a long time; **ni con —** not by a long shot; **ni — menos** not by any means; **por — que** no matter how much; PRON a lot, many; (en preguntas y oraciones negativas) much
mucoso ADJ mucous
muda F (de ropa, voz) change; (de plumas, piel de serpiente) molt
mudable ADJ fickle
mudanza F move
mudar VT to change; (el pelo) to shed; **— la piel** to molt; **— las plumas** to molt; **—se (de casa)** to move (house); **—se de ropa** to change clothes
mudez F dumbness, muteness
mudo -da ADJ mute, dumb; (por emoción) speechless; (película) silent; MF mute
mueble M piece of furniture; **—s** furniture
mueblería F (tienda) furniture store; (fábrica) furniture factory
mueca F grimace; **hacer —s** to grimace
muela F (diente) molar tooth; (piedra) grindstone; **— del juicio** wisdom tooth
muelle M (para embarcaciones) wharf, pier; (resorte) spring; **— en espiral** coil; **— real** mainspring
muérdago M mistletoe
muerte F death; **dar —** to kill; **sus clases son la —** his classes are unbearable; **de mala —** disreputable
muerto ADJ dead, lifeless; **— de cansancio** dead tired; **— de hambre** famished; **estoy — de sed** I'm parched; **echarle el — a uno** to pass the buck; **ni —** not in a million years
muesca F notch, indentation
muestra F (ejemplo) sample; (señal) sign, token; **— de orina** urine specimen; **dar —s de impaciencia** to show impatience
muestrear VT to sample
muestreo M sampling
mugido M moo, lowing
mugir[11] VI to moo, to low
mugre F dirt, grime, crud
mugriento ADJ grimy, dirty
mujer F woman; (esposa) wife
mujeriego ADJ womanizing; M womanizer
mujerzuela F *pey* slut
mulato -ta ADJ & MF mulatto
muleta F crutch
muletilla F cliché
mullido ADJ fluffy
mullir[19] VT to fluff
mulo -la MF mule (también en el tráfico de drogas)
multa F fine, penalty; (de tránsito) ticket
multar VT to fine; (en tránsito) to ticket
multicultural ADJ multicultural
múltiple ADJ multiple
multiplicación F multiplication
multiplicar[6] VI/VT to multiply; **—se** to breed
multiplicidad F multiplicity
múltiplo M multiple
multitarea F multitasking
multitud F multitude, throng
mundano ADJ mundane, worldly
mundial ADJ global, worldwide; **la guerra —** the world war
mundo M world; **todo el —** everybody; **tener —** to be worldly; **el tercer —** the third world; **el — al revés** the world upside-down
munición F ammunition, munition
municipal ADJ municipal; **servicios —es** city services
municipalidad F municipality
municipio M municipality; (ayuntamiento) city hall
muñeca F (juguete) doll; (articulación del brazo) wrist; **— de trapo** ragdoll
muñeco M (juguete) boy doll; (de ventrílocuo) dummy; **— de nieve** snowman
muñón M stump
mural ADJ & M mural
muralla F wall
murciélago M bat
murmullo M murmur; (de agua) babble
murmuración F gossip
murmurar VI/VT to murmur; VI (agua) to babble
muro M wall
murria F the blues; **tener —** to have the

blues
musa F muse
musaraña F shrew
muscular ADJ muscular
músculo M muscle
musculoso ADJ muscular
muselina F muslin
museo M museum
musgo M moss
musgoso ADJ mossy
música F music; **— de cámara** chamber
music; **— folclórica** folk music; **—
incidental** incidental music
musical ADJ & M musical
músico -ca ADJ musical; MF musician
musitar VI to mutter
muslo M thigh
mustio ADJ sad, humble; (marchito) limp;
(deslucido) faded
musulmán -ana ADJ & MF Moslem, Muslim
mutación F mutation
mutante ADJ & MF mutant
mutilar VT to mutilate, to mangle; (a un ser
vivo) to maim, to mutilate; (una estatua)
to deface
mutuo ADJ mutual
muy ADV very; **estás — grande para eso**
you're too big for that
Myanmar M Myanmar

Nn

nabo M turnip
nácar M mother-of-pearl
nacarado ADJ pearly
nacer[13] VI to be born; (una calle) to begin; **—
de** (río) to spring from; **— de nuevo** to
have a new lease on life
naciente ADJ (tendencia) incipient; (sol)
rising; M (de río) origin
nacimiento M birth; (pesebre) nativity scene;
(naciente) origin (of a river)
nación F nation
nacional ADJ national; MF national
nacionalidad F nationality
nacionalismo M nationalism
nacionalizar[9] VT to nationalize
nada PRON nothing; **— del otro mundo**
nothing special; **— en absoluto** nothing
at all; **como si —** as if nothing were
going on; **de —** you are welcome, don't
mention it; **no es por —, pero** I hope
you don't mind my saying this, but; **no**

sirve para — it's useless; **no tener —
que ver con** to have nothing to do with;
no tengo — de dinero I don't have any
money; **para —** in the least; **quedar en
la —** to fall through; **salir de la —** to
come out of nowhere; ADV not at all; **no
me gusta —** I don't like it at all; F
nothingness
nadador -ora MF swimmer
nadar VI/VT to swim; **— en la abundancia**
to be in the lap of luxury
nadería F trifle, nothing
nadie PRON nobody; **— más** no one else; **no
vi a — en el parque** I didn't see anyone
in the park; **un don —** a nobody
nafta F gasoline
nailón M nylon
naipe M playing card
nalgada F smack on the bottom
nalgas F PL buttocks
Namibia F Namibia
namibio -bia ADJ & MF Namibian
nana F (canción de cuna) lullaby;
(lastimadura) boo-boo; (niñera) baby-sitter
nanosegundo M nanosecond
napalm M napalm
napias F PL *fam* snout
naranja F (fruta) orange; ADJ & M (color)
orange; **— de ombligo** navel orange; **mi
media —** my better half
naranjal M orange grove
naranjo M orange tree
narcisismo M narcissism
narciso M narcissus, daffodil
narcolepsia F narcolepsy
narcótico ADJ & M narcotic
narcotizar[9] VT to drug
narcotráfico M narco-trafficking
nariz F nose; **— chata** pug nose; **sonarse la
—** to blow one's nose; F PL **narices**
nostrils; **se dio de narices contra la
ventana** he bumped his nose on the
window; **estoy hasta las narices** I've
had it up to here
narración F narration
narrador -ora MF narrator
narrar VT to narrate, to recount
narrativa F narrative
narrativo ADJ narrative
NASA F NASA
nasal ADJ nasal
nata F skin of boiled milk; *Esp* cream
natación F swimming
natal ADJ natal; (suelo) native
natillas F PL custard
nativo -va ADJ & MF native
nato ADJ **es un músico —** he's a born

musician

natural ADJ natural; (nacido en un lugar) native; (nacido fuera del matrimonio) illegitimate; M nature; **al —** unprocessed; (sin afectación) unaffected

naturaleza F nature; **— muerta** still life

naturalidad F naturalness

naturalista MF naturalist

naturalización F naturalization

naturalizar[9] VT to naturalize; **—se** to become naturalized

naturalmente ADV (de forma natural) naturally; (desde luego) of course

naufragar[7] VI to shipwreck; (una empresa) to fail

naufragio M shipwreck

náufrago -ga MF shipwrecked person

Nauru M Nauru

nauruano -na ADJ & MF Nauruan

náusea F nausea; **—s** morning sickness; **dar —s** to nauseate; **hasta la —** ad nauseam; **tener —s** to be nauseated, to be sick to one's stomach

nauseabundo ADJ nauseating

nauseoso ADJ queasy

náutica F navigation

náutico ADJ nautical

navaja F jackknife, pocketknife; (de barbero) razor

navajazo M (golpe) stab with a jackknife; (herida) stab wound

naval ADJ naval

nave F (embarcación) vessel; (parte de una catedral) nave; **— espacial** spaceship

navegable ADJ navigable

navegación F navigation; (deportiva) boating

navegador M computer browser

navegante MF navigator; ADJ navigating

navegar[7] VI/VT to navigate; (barco o vela) to sail; (en el Internet) to browse, to surf

Navidad F Christmas

navideño ADJ **fiesta navideña** Christmas party

navío M ship

neblina F mist

neblinoso ADJ misty

nebuloso ADJ (poco claro) nebulous; (que tiene niebla) foggy

necesario ADJ necessary

neceser M toiletry bag

necesidad F need; (cosa necesaria) necessity; **hacer sus —es** to relieve oneself; **de primera —** indispensable

necesitado ADJ needy

necesitar VT to need

necio -cia ADJ asinine, foolish; MF pey clod

necrología F necrology

néctar M nectar

nectarina F nectarine

nefasto ADJ unholy

nefritis F nephritis

negación F (que sirve para negar) negation; (que no acepta) denial

negar[1,7] VT (decir que no es verdad) to deny; (no dar a alguien algo que ha pedido) to refuse; (no reconocer públicamente) to disavow; **—se** to refuse; **—se a** to refuse to

negativa F (rechazo verbal) denial; (ausencia de cooperación) refusal

negativo ADJ negative; **signo —** minus sign; M (photographic) negative

negligencia F negligence, neglect; (médica) malpractice

negligente ADJ negligent, neglectful

negociación F negotiation

negociante MF business person

negociar VI/VT (tratar condiciones) to negotiate; (realizar un negocio) to trade

negocio M (tienda, actividad comercial) business; (transacción) business deal, business transaction; **hombre de —s** businessman; **mujer de —s** businesswoman; **hacer —** to make a profit

negrear VI to appear black; VT to blacken

negritas F boldface type

negro -ra ADJ black (también aplicado al café sin leche); (futuro) bleak; **pasarlas negras** to undergo hardships; F (nota) quarter note; MF (persona) person of color, black

negrura F blackness

negruzco ADJ blackish

némesis F nemesis

nene -na M baby boy; F baby girl

nenúfar M water lily

neologismo M neologism

neón M neon

neozelandés -esa MF New Zealander

Nepal M Nepal

nepalés -esa ADJ & MF Nepalese

nepalí ADJ & MF Nepalese

nepotismo M nepotism

nervado ADJ veined

nervio M nerve; **perder los —s** to lose one's cool; **tener los —s de punta** to be on edge

nerviosismo M nervousness

nervioso ADJ (relativo a los nervios) nervous; (inquieto) nervous, jumpy; (carne) sinewy

nervudo ADJ sinewy, wiry

neto ADJ (mejoría) distinct; (ganancia) net

neumático M tire; ADJ pneumatic

neural ADJ neural

neurona F nerve cell
neurosis F neurosis
neurótico -ca ADJ & MF neurotic
neutral ADJ neutral
neutralidad F neutrality
neutralizar[9] VT to neutralize
neutro ADJ neutral; (género) neuter
neutrón M neutron
nevada F snowfall
nevado ADJ snowy
nevar[1] VI to snow
nevera F icebox, refrigerator
nevisca F snow flurry
ni CONJ & ADV — **con mucho** not by a long
  shot; — **hablar** forget it; — **habló**
  conmigo he didn't even talk to me; —
  idea (it) beats me; — **modo** no way; —
  que esto fuera un hotel it's not like
  this is a hotel; — **siquiera** not even; —
  soñar fat chance; — **trabaja** — **estudia**
  he neither works nor studies; — **una**
  palabra not a word; **no tiene amigos**
  — **enemigos** he has no friends nor
  enemies; **no es rico** — **mucho menos**
  he's not even close to being rich
Nicaragua F Nicaragua
nicaragüense ADJ & MF Nicaraguan
nicho M niche, recess
nicotina F nicotine
nidada F (huevos) nest of eggs; (crías) hatch,
  brood
nido M nest
niebla F fog
nieto -ta M grandson; F granddaughter; —**s**
  grandchildren
nieve F snow (también cocaína, heroína)
Níger M Niger
Nigeria F Nigeria
nigeriano -na ADJ & MF Nigerian
nigerino -na ADJ & MF Nigerien
nigua F chigger
nihilismo M nihilism
nilón M nylon
nimio ADJ insignificant
ninguno PRON **no tengo** — I have none / I
  don't have any; **ningún amigo mío** no
  friend of mine; **no tengo ningún libro**
  I don't have any books; — **de los dos**
  neither one; **de ningún modo** in no way
niñera F (ocasional) baby-sitter;
  (permanente) nanny
niñería F childish act
niñez F childhood; (de niño) boyhood; (de
  niña) girlhood
niño -ña M child, kid, boy; F child, kid, girl;
  — **del ojo** pupil (of the eye); ADJ childish
níquel M nickel

niquelado ADJ nickel-plated
níspero M loquat
nitidez F sharpness
nítido ADJ sharp
nitrato M nitrate
nitrógeno M nitrogen
nitroglicerina F nitroglycerine
nivel M level (también herramienta); (grado
  jerárquico) echelon; — **de mar** sea level;
  — **de vida** standard of living; **a** —
  straight; **a** — **de** level with
nivelar VT to level; (un camino de tierra) to
  grade
níveo ADJ snowy
no ADV no; — **quiero** I don't want to; —
  bien llegaron no sooner had they
  arrived; — **sólo** not only; — **sea que** lest;
  a — **ser que** unless
noble ADJ noble; M nobleman; F noblewoman
nobleza F nobility
nócaut M knockout
noche F night; (horas de la noche) nighttime;
  —**buena** Christmas Eve; —**vieja** New
  Year's Eve; — **y día** day and night; **de** —
  at night; **de la** — **a la mañana**
  overnight; **esta** — tonight; **por la** — at
  night
noción F notion; **no tener ni** — to have no
  clue
nocivo ADJ harmful, noxious
nocturno ADJ (que actúa de noche)
  nocturnal; (que sucede todas las noches)
  nightly
nodo M node
nodriza F wet nurse
nódulo M node
nogal M walnut tree
nómada MF INV nomad
nombramiento M appointment; (militar)
  commission
nombrar VT to name, to appoint; (a un
  oficial militar) to commission
nombre M name; — **de pila** first name; —
  de soltera maiden name; **en** — **de** on
  behalf of; **eso no tiene** — that's unheard
  of; **hacerse un** — to make a name for
  oneself
nomenclatura F nomenclature
nomeolvides M SG forget-me-not
nómina F payroll
nominación F nomination
nominal ADJ nominal
nominar VT to nominate
non ADJ odd; M odd number
nopal M prickly pear
noquear VT to knock out
norcoreano -na ADJ & MF North Korean

nordeste ADJ & M northeast
nórdico ADJ Nordic
noreste ADJ & M northeast
norma F norm, standard
normal ADJ normal, standard; F (escuela) teacher's college; (línea) perpendicular line
normalizar[9] VT to normalize
noroeste ADJ & M northwest
norte ADJ & M north
norteamericano -na ADJ & MF (de América del Norte) North American; (de EEUU) American
norteño -ña ADJ northern; MF northerner
Noruega F Norway
noruego -ga ADJ & MF Norwegian
nos PRON us; **él — vio** he saw us; **— dio el libro** he gave us the book, he gave the book to us
nosotros -as PRON we; **para —** for us
nostalgia F nostalgia
nostálgico ADJ nostalgic
nota F (musical) note; (anotación) annotation; (calificación) grade, mark; **— al pie de página** footnote; **de —** of note; **exagerar la —** to overdo something
notable ADJ notable, noteworthy, remarkable
notación F notation
notar VT (percibir) to note, to notice; (señalar) to note
notariar VT to notarize
notario -ria MF notary
noticia F piece of news; **—s** news; **tener —s de alguien** to hear from someone
noticiario M newscast, news bulletin
noticiero M newscast
notificación F notification; (policial) summons
notificar[6] VT to notify
notorio ADJ (conocido públicamente) well-known; (evidente) obvious
novato -ta MF novice; (policía, atleta) rookie
novedad F novelty; **—es** news; **sin —** all's well
novedoso ADJ novel
novela F novel
novelesco ADJ fictional
novelista MF novelist
noveno ADJ ninth
noventa NUM ninety
noviazgo M engagement
novicio -cia MF novice
noviembre M November
novillo -lla M steer; **hacer —s** to play hooky; F heifer
novio -via M (comprometido) fiancé; (no formal) boyfriend; (de boda) bridegroom; F (comprometida) fiancée; (no formal) girlfriend; (de boda) bride
nubarrón M thunderhead
nube F cloud; (de humo) billow; **poner por las —s** to praise to the skies; **está en las —s** his head is in the clouds; **los precios están por las —s** prices have gone through the roof
nublado ADJ (cielo) cloudy, overcast; (los ojos, de emoción) misty; (los ojos, por falta de sueño) bleary
nublar VT to blur; **—se** (cielo) to become overcast; (ojos) to cloud over
nuboso ADJ cloudy
nuca F nape
nuclear ADJ nuclear
núcleo M nucleus; (de imán, reactor) core
nudillo M knuckle
nudismo M nudism
nudista ADJ & MF nudist
nudo M knot (también en la madera, medida de velocidad); (de una obra teatral) turning point; (en el pelo) tangle; (en plantas) node; (en la garganta) lump; **— corredizo** slipknot; **— de rizo** square knot
nudoso ADJ knotty, gnarled
nuera F daughter-in-law
nuestro ADJ POS our; **— hijo** our son; PRON ours; **esto es —** this is ours
nueve NUM nine
nuevo ADJ new; **de —** again; **¿qué hay de — ?** what's new?
nuez F walnut; **— de Adán** Adam's apple; **— moscada** nutmeg
nulidad F nonentity
nulo ADJ null and void, invalid
numeral ADJ & M numeral
numerar VT to number
numérico ADJ numerical
número M (dígito) number; (en un espectáculo) act; (de una revista) issue; (cifra) figure
numeroso ADJ numerous
nunca ADV never, not ever; **no viene —** he never comes, he doesn't ever come; **más que —** more than ever; **casi —** hardly ever; **peor que —** worse than ever
nupcial ADJ nuptial, bridal
nupcias F PL nuptials
nutria F otter
nutrición F nutrition
nutrido ADJ **el congreso tuvo una nutrida concurrencia** the conference was well attended
nutriente M nutrient
nutrir VT to nourish

nutritivo ADJ nutritious, nourishing

Ññ

ñandú M rhea
ñato ADJ *Am* pug-nosed
ñoño ADJ bland
ñu M gnu

Oo

o CONJ or; **— se casa — lo mato** either he
    gets married or I'll kill him; **— sea** that is
oasis M oasis
obedecer[13] VI/VT to obey; **esto obedece a**
    que this is due to the fact that
obediencia F obedience
obediente ADJ obedient
obertura F musical overture
obesidad F obesity
obeso ADJ obese
obispo M bishop
obituario M obituary
objeción F objection
objetar VI/VT to object, to take exception (to)
objetivo ADJ objective; M (lente) objective;
    (meta) aim, objective
objeto M object
oblea F wafer
oblicuo ADJ (inclinado) oblique; (sesgado)
    biased
obligación F (deber) obligation, duty; (título
    financiero) bond
obligar[7] VT to force, to compel, to oblige;
    —se (a) to obligate oneself (to)
obligatorio ADJ obligatory, compulsory
oboe M oboe
obra F (artística, literaria, de construcción)
    work; (lugar de construcción) construction
    site; **— maestra** masterpiece; **en —s**
    under construction
obrar VI to act; **obra en nuestro poder** we
    acknowledge receipt of
obrero -ra MF worker; ADJ working
obscenidad F obscenity; **—es** filth
obsceno ADJ obscene
obsequiar VT to present, to give; **me**
    obsequió perfume he gave me perfume
obsequio M gift

obsequioso ADJ obsequious
observación F observation; (comentario)
    remark
observador -ora MF observer; ADJ observant
observancia F observance
observar VI/VT to observe; (hacer un
    comentario) to remark, to observe
observatorio M observatory
obsesión F obsession
obsesionar VT to obsess; **—se con** to obsess
    over, to be obsessed with
obsesivo-compulsivo ADJ obsessive-
    compulsive
obstaculizar VT to impede
obstáculo M obstacle, hindrance,
    impediment; (en carreras) hurdle
obstante LOC PREP no **— tu oposición**
    notwithstanding your opposition; LOC ADV
    no —, voy a ir nevertheless, I am going
    to go
obstar VT to preclude
obstetricia F obstetrics
obstinación F obstinacy
obstinado ADJ obstinate, bullheaded
obstinarse VI to be obstinate
obstrucción F obstruction, blockage
obstruir[31] VT to obstruct, to block; (un
    aparato) to jam; VI **—se** to get jammed
obtención F acquisition
obtener[44] VT to obtain, to get; (permiso) to
    secure; (con dificultad) to procure
obturador M (de una cámara fotográfica)
    shutter; (de un coche) choke
obviar VT to circumvent
obvio ADJ obvious
ocasión F occasion; (oportunidad)
    opportunity; (ganga) bargain; **de —**
    reduced
ocasional ADJ occasional
ocasionar VT to occasion, to cause
ocaso M sunset, twilight
occidental ADJ occidental, western; MF
    westerner
occidente M west
océano M ocean
oceanografía F oceanography
ocelote M ocelot
ochenta NUM eighty
ocho NUM eight
ocio M (diversión) leisure; (inacción) idleness
ociosidad F idleness
ocioso ADJ (inactivo) idle; (no usado) unused
octágono M octagon
octano M octane
octava F octave
octavilla F tract
octavo ADJ & M eighth

octeto M byte
octógono M octagon
octubre M October
ocular M eyepiece; ADJ **infección —** eye infection
oculista MF oculist
ocultar VT to conceal; (información) to withhold
ocultismo M the occult
oculto ADJ unseen, occult
ocupación F occupation
ocupado ADJ busy; (asiento, aseo) occupied
ocupante MF occupant
ocupar VT to occupy; (contratar) to employ; **—se de** to take care of
ocurrencia F witticism, quip
ocurrente ADJ witty
ocurrir VI to occur
oda F ode
odiar VI/VT to hate
odio M hatred, hate
odioso ADJ (tarea) odious; (persona) hateful
odontología F dentistry
odre M wineskin
OEA (Organización de Estados Americanos) F OAS
oeste ADJ & M west
ofender VI/VT to offend; **—se** to get offended, to take offense
ofensa F offense
ofensiva F (militar) offensive; (deportiva) offense
ofensivo ADJ offensive, obnoxious
oferta F offer; (rebaja) special offer; **en —** on sale
offset M offset
oficial -la ADJ official; MF (militar) officer; (obrero calificado) skilled worker; **— general** high-ranking officer
oficiar VI to officiate; **— de** to serve as
oficina F office; (dependencia gubernamental) bureau
oficinista MF office worker
oficio M (actividad laboral) trade, craft; (comunicación oficial) official communication; **tiene mucho —** he knows his stuff; **buenos —s** good offices
oficioso ADJ (entrometedor) officious; (no oficial) unofficial
ofrecer[13] VT to offer; (en una subasta) to bid; (una cena) to give; **— resistencia** to put up resistance; **¿qué se le ofrece a Vd.?** how can I help you?
ofrecimiento M (acción de ofrecer) offering; (oferta) offer
ofrenda F offering
ofuscar[6] VT to bewilder

ogro M ogre
ohmio M ohm
oído M (facultad) hearing; (órgano) inner ear; (musical) ear; **— medio** middle ear; **al —** confidentially; **de —** by ear
oír[35] VI/VT (percibir) to hear; (atender) to listen; **— decir que** to hear that; **— hablar de** to hear about; **— misa** to attend mass; **¡oye!** listen! hey!
ojal M buttonhole
ojalá INTERJ **— estuviera aquí** I wish he were here; **— que venga** I hope that he comes
ojeada F glimpse
ojear VT to glimpse
ojera F dark circle under the eye
ojeriza F animosity
ojeroso ADJ with dark circles under the eyes
ojiva F (arco) pointed arch; (explosivo) warhead
ojo M (órgano, centro de huracán, instinto, yema de patata) eye; **¡—!** careful! look out! **a — de buen cubero** as a rule of thumb; **a —s vistas** clearly; **me costó un — de la cara** it cost me an arm and a leg; **¿no tienes —s en la cara?** are you blind? **dichosos los —s que te ven** you're a sight for sore eyes; **— de buey** porthole; **— de la cerradura** key hole; **— de lince** eagle-eye; **— morado** black eye; **— por —** an eye for an eye
ola F wave; (de un olor) waft; (de protesta) storm
oleada F wave, surge
oleaje M swell, surge
óleo M oil painting
oleoducto M pipeline
oleoso ADJ oily
oler[36] VI/VT to smell (también sospechar); **— a** to smell of
olfatear VI/VT to scent, to sniff
olfateo M sniff, sniffing
olfato M (facultad) sense of smell; (instinto) nose
olfatorio ADJ olfactory
olimpiada F Olympiad; **—s** Olympic games
olímpico ADJ Olympian
oliva F olive
olivar M olive grove
olivo M olive tree
olla F pot; **— de grillos** snake pit; **— podrida** stew of mixed vegetables and meat
olmo M elm
olor M smell, odor
oloroso ADJ odorous
olvidadizo ADJ forgetful

olvidar VI/VT to forget; **—se (de)** to forget;
   se me olvidó algo I forgot something
olvido M oblivion; **caer en el —** to be
   forgotten; **echar al —** to cast into
   oblivion; **tus —s** your forgetfulness
Omán M Oman
omaní ADJ & MF Omani
ombligo M navel
omisión F omission
omiso ADJ **hacer caso — (de)** to ignore
omitir VT to omit, to leave out; (no notar) to
   overlook
ómnibus M bus
omnipotencia F omnipotence
omnipotente ADJ omnipotent
omnisciencia F omniscience
omnisciente ADJ omniscient
omnívoro ADJ omnivorous
once NUM eleven
oncología F oncology
onda F wave; **— corta** short wave; **—**
   expansiva shock wave; **— sonora** sound
   wave; **agarrarle la — a algo** to get in
   the swing of things; **captar la —** to get
   the drift
ondeado ADJ wavy
ondeante ADJ flying
ondear VI to wave
ondulación F ripple, ruffle, roll
ondulado ADJ wavy
ondulante ADJ undulating
ondular VI to undulate; VI/VT to wave
ónix M onyx
onomatopeya F onomatopoeia
ONU (Organización de las Naciones
   Unidas) F UN
onza F ounce
opacar[6] VT (oscurecer) to dull; (eclipsar) to
   overshadow
opaco ADJ (no transparente) opaque; (no
   brillante) dull
ópalo M opal
opción F option; **opciones** stock options
opcional ADJ optional
OPEP (Organización de Países
   Exportadores de Petróleo) F OPEC
ópera F (composición) opera; (teatro) opera
   house
operable ADJ operable
operación F operation
operador -ora M (en matemáticas) operator;
   MF (de teléfono) operator
operar VI/VT to operate; VT (intervenir
   quirúrgicamente) to operate on; (llevar a
   cabo) to carry out; VI (hacer cuentas) to do
   mathematical operations
operario -ria MF operator, operative

opinar VI/VT to hold an opinion, to think
opinión F opinion, view, feeling; **cambiar**
   de — to change one's mind
opio M opium
oponer[39] VT to oppose; **—se** to conflict; **—se**
   a to oppose, to be against
oporto M port wine
oportunidad F opportunity, chance;
   (pretexto) opening
oportunista ADJ & MF opportunistic
oportuno ADJ (en el momento conveniente)
   opportune, timely; (adecuado) appropriate
oposición F opposition; **oposiciones**
   competitive examinations
opositor -ora MF opponent
opresión F oppression
opresivo ADJ oppressive
opresor -ora MF oppressor
oprimir VT (al pueblo) to oppress; (un
   botón) to press
optar VI to choose; **— por** to choose
optativo ADJ optional
óptico -ca ADJ optical; MF optician; F optics
optimismo M optimism
optimista ADJ optimistic; MF optimist
optometría F optometry
opuesto ADJ opposite, contrary; **se mostró**
   — al casamiento he was against the
   marriage; **dos fuerzas opuestas** two
   opposing forces; **lo —** the opposite;
   dirección opuesta the opposite / reverse
   direction
opulencia F opulence
opulento ADJ opulent; (sociedad) affluent
oración F (frase) sentence; (súplica) prayer
oráculo M oracle
orador -ora MF orator, speaker
oral ADJ oral
orangután M orangutan
orar VI/VT to pray
oratoria F oratory
oratorio M oratory
órbita F (de los cuerpos celestes) orbit; (de
   los ojos) eye socket
orbitador M orbiter
orbital ADJ orbital
orbitar VI/VT to orbit
orca F killer whale
orden M (limpieza, secuencia) order; **— del**
   día order of the day; **perturbar el —**
   público to disturb the peace; **sin — ni**
   concierto haphazard; F (mando)
   command, order; (de religiones) order; (de
   cateo) warrant; **a sus órdenes** at your
   service
ordenado ADJ orderly, neat
ordenador M computer

ordenanza F ordinance; M orderly

ordenar VT (arreglar) to put in order; (mandar) to order, to command; (conferir órdenes) to ordain; —**se** to become ordained

ordeñar VT to milk

ordeño M milking

ordinal ADJ ordinal

ordinariez F vulgarity

ordinario ADJ (corriente) ordinary; (vulgar) vulgar

orear VT to air out

orégano M oregano

oreja F (outer) ear; (de un martillo) claw; (en un utensilio) flap; **aguzar la —** to prick up one's ears; **sonreír de — a —** to smile from ear to ear; **estar hasta las —s en algo** to be up to one's neck in something

orejera F ear muff

orfanato M orphanage

orfebre MF (con oro) goldsmith; (con plata) silversmith

orgánico ADJ organic

organismo M organism

organista MF organist

organización F organization

organizador -ora MF organizer

organizar[9] VT to organize; (un ataque) to stage; (una fiesta) to give, to throw

órgano M organ

orgía F orgy

orgullo M pride; **es mi —** she's my pride and joy

orgulloso ADJ proud

orientación F orientation, guidance; (de velas) trim; (de estudios) track; (de un objeto) lie; (del terreno) lay

oriental ADJ oriental, eastern; MF oriental

orientar VT to orient; —**se** to get one's bearings

oriente M orient, east

orificio M orifice

origen M origin; (de un problema, conflicto) source; (antecedentes familiares) birth

original ADJ original; M original; (de una cinta magnética) master

originalidad F originality

originar VT to originate, to give rise to; —**se** to originate, to arise

orilla F (de un lago, mar) shore, bank; (de una cama) edge; (de una prenda) hem

orillar VT (una calle) to border; (una prenda) to hem

orín M rust; M PL **orines** urine

orina F urine

orinal M chamber pot

orinar VI/VT to urinate

oriundo ADJ ser — **de** (persona) to hail from; (cosa) to originate in

orla F (de un uniforme) trimming; (de una alfombra) fringe

orlar VT to fringe

orlón[tm] M Orlon[tm]

ornamental ADJ ornamental

ornamentar VT to ornament, to embellish

ornamento M ornament

ornar VT to adorn

ornitología F ornithology

oro M gold; — **blanco** white gold; — **en lingotes** gold bullion; — **negro** black gold; — **puro** solid gold; **prometer el — y el moro** to promise the moon

orondo ADJ self-satisfied

oropel M tinsel

oropéndola F oriole

orquesta F orchestra

orquestar VT to orchestrate

orquídea F orchid

ortiga F nettle

ortodoncia F orthodontics

ortodoxo ADJ orthodox

ortografía F orthography, spelling

oruga F caterpillar

orujo M rape

orzuelo M sty

osadía F boldness, daring

osado ADJ bold, daring

osamenta F skeleton

osar VI/VT to dare

oscilación F oscillation

oscilar VI to oscillate, to seesaw; — **entre** to range between

oscuridad F (lugar sin luz) dark, darkness; (condición de oscuro) darkness; (falta de claridad conceptual, anonimato) obscurity

oscuro ADJ (sin luz) dark; (nublado) murky; (poco claro, poco conocido) obscure; **lentes —s** dark glasses; **gris —** dark gray; **a oscuras** in the dark

óseo ADJ bony

osezno M bear cub

ósmosis F osmosis

oso -sa M bear; F she-bear; — **blanco / polar** polar bear; — **hormiguero** anteater

ostentación F ostentation, show, display; **hacer de —** to flaunt

ostentar VI/VT to display, to show off, to flaunt

ostentoso ADJ ostentatious, showy

osteoporosis F osteoporosis

ostión M large oyster

ostra F oyster

OTAN (Organización del Tratado del Atlántico Norte) F NATO

otero M hillock
otoñal ADJ autumnal
otoño M autumn, fall
otorgamiento M grant
otorgar[7] VT (permiso) to grant, to concede; (un premio) to award
otro ADJ (uno adicional) another; (uno diferente) other; **otra vez** again; **otra cosa** something else; **— más** another one; **al — día** the next day; **de — modo** otherwise; **en otra parte** somewhere else; **la otra cara de la moneda** the flip side; **por otra parte** on the other hand; PRON (uno más) another one; (una persona diferente) someone else; (una cosa diferente) something else
ovación F ovation, acclaim
oval ADJ oval
ovalado ADJ oval
óvalo M oval
ovario M ovary
oveja F sheep; (hembra) ewe
ovejero M sheepdog
overoles M PL overalls
ovillar VT to ball; **—se** to curl up into a ball
ovillo M ball of yarn; **hacerse un —** to curl up
OVNI (objeto volador no identificado) M UFO
ovular VI to ovulate
óvulo M egg
oxidado ADJ oxidized, rusty
oxidar VI/VT to oxidize, to rust
óxido M (cuerpo químico) oxide; (herrumbre) rust
oxígeno M oxygen
oyente MF (que oye) listener, hearer; (alumno no oficial) auditor
ozono M ozone

Pp

pabellón M (de feria) pavilion; (parte de un edificio) wing; (bandera) flag; (departamento de hospital) ward; **— de la oreja** outer ear
pabilo M wick
paca F bale
pacana F (fruto) pecan; (árbol) pecan tree
pacer[13] VI to pasture, to graze; VT to crop, to graze
paciencia F patience; **tener —** to be patient
paciente ADJ & MF patient

pacificar[6] VT to pacify
pacífico ADJ peaceful; M **Océano Pacífico** Pacific Ocean
pacifismo M pacifism
pacto M pact, covenant
paddock M (de caballos) paddock; (de coches) pit
padecer[13] VI/VT to suffer; **— de cáncer** to suffer from cancer
padecimiento M suffering
padrastro M (marido de la madre) stepfather; (uñero) hangnail
padre M father; **—s** parents, folks; **— de familia** male head of the household; **—nuestro** the Lord's Prayer; **John Smith, —** John Smith, senior; **ser —** to become a father; **un lío —** a real mess
padrino M (de bautizo) godfather; (de boda) best man; (en un duelo) second
paella F paella
paga F pay; (para un niño) allowance
pagadero ADJ payable, due
pagado ADJ **— de sí mismo** self-satisfied
pagador -ora MF payer
paganismo M paganism
pagano -na ADJ & MF pagan
pagar[7] VT (cuentas, deudas) to pay; (mercancías) to pay for; **—se de** to be proud of; **— el pato** to be left holding the bag; **pagan justos por pecadores** the just pay for the sins of others; **— a plazos** to pay in installments; **— al contado** to pay cash; **— con la misma moneda** to pay in kind; **— en especie** to pay in kind
pagaré M promissory note
página F page
paginar VT to paginate
pago M payment; **— en efectivo** cash payment
paila F large pan
país M country
paisaje M landscape, scenery
paisajismo M landscape architecture
paisano -na M countryman; F countrywoman
paja F straw (también para beber de un vaso); **a humo de —s** thoughtlessly; **hacerse una —** *vulg* to jack off; **no caberle a alguien una — por el culo** to be self-satisfied; **por un quítame allá esas —s** for a trifle
pajar M hayloft
pájaro M bird; **— carpintero** woodpecker; **— pinto** cautious person; **un — francés** a French guy
paje M page

pajizo ADJ straw-colored

pajonal M *Am* grassland

pala F (para cavar) shovel; (para recoger basura) dustpan; (de hélice, remo) blade; (de zapato) upper; (para remar, de ping-pong) paddle; **— mecánica** power shovel; **lo tuvimos que recoger con —** he was exhausted

palabra F (unidad léxica) word; (facultad) speech; **— clave** key word; **—s mayores** a big deal; **cuatro —s** a few words; **cumplir con la —** to keep one's word; **dejar con la — en la boca** to cut someone off in mid-sentence; **en pocas —s** in a nutshell; **faltar a la —** to break a promise; **la última —** the final say; **ni una —** not a word; **no dijo —** he didn't breathe a word; **un hombre de —** a man of his word; **tener la —** to have the floor; **tomar la —** to take the floor; **traducción — por —** word for word translation; **tragarse / comerse las propias —s** to eat one's words

palabrería M verbiage

palabrero ADJ long-winded

palabrota F curse word, four-letter word; **—s** profanity

palacio M palace

paladar M palate; **— hendido** cleft palate

paladear VT to relish

paladín M champion, crusader

palanca F (mecanismo para levantar algo) lever; (para abrir algo) crowbar; (fuerza) leverage; **— del cambio** gearshift lever; **— de juegos** joystick; **— del regulador** throttle lever; **hacer —** to use leverage

palangana F basin

Paláu M Palau

palco M box

palenque M fence

paleontología F paleontology

paleta F (de pintor) palette; (de albañil) trowel; (de ping-pong, para mezclar, batir) paddle; (hélice) blade; (pirulí) lollipop, sucker

paletilla F shoulder

paleto -ta MF hayseed, hick

paliar VT to alleviate

palidecer[13] VI to turn pale

palidez F pallor, paleness

pálido ADJ pallid, pale

palillo M (de dientes) toothpick; (de tambor) drumstick; (para comida china) chopstick; **tocar todos los —s** to try everything

palique M chit-chat

paliza F beating, whipping; **dar una —** to beat, to whip

palma F (árbol) palm (tree); (hoja) palm leaf; (de mano) palm (of the hand); **batir —s** to clap; **llevarse la —** to take the prize; **conocer como la — de la mano** to know like the back of one's hand

palmada F (en la espalda) slap; (aplauso) clap; (en el trasero) spank; **dar una —** (en la espalda) to slap; (en el trasero) to spank

palmear VT to slap on the back

palmera F palm tree

palmípedo M web-footed bird

palmo M span; **— a —** inch by inch

palmotear VT to slap on the back

palo M (de madera) stick; (de barco) mast; (de naipes) suit; **— de golf** golf club; **— de escoba** broomstick; **dar —s** to hit with a stick; **de tal — tal astilla** a chip off the old block

paloma F dove, pigeon

palomar M pigeon loft

palomilla F wing nut

palomitas F PL popcorn; **hacer —** to pop corn

palote M rolling pin

palpable ADJ palpable

palpar VT to feel

palpitación F palpitation

palpitante ADJ palpitating; **una cuestión —** a burning question

palpitar VI to palpitate

palta F *Am* avocado

paludismo M malaria

pampa F *Am* prairie

pamplinas F PL baloney, hogwash

pan M bread; (pieza) loaf of bread; **— comido** piece of cake, cinch; **— de cada día** everyday occurrence; **— rallado / molido** bread crumbs; **al —, — y al vino, vino** to call a spade a spade; **contigo, — y cebolla** love is all we need; **ganarse el —** to make a living

pana F corduroy

panacea F panacea, magic bullet

panadería F bakery

panadero -ra MF baker

panal M honeycomb

Panamá M Panama

panameño -ña ADJ & MF Panamanian

panamericano ADJ Pan-American

panceta F bacon

páncreas M pancreas

panda M panda bear

pandearse VT to buckle, to sag

pandeo M sag

pandereta F tambourine

pandilla F gang, band

panecillo M roll
panegírico M eulogy
panel M panel
panera F breadbasket
panfleto M pamphlet
pánico ADJ & M panic
panoja F ear of corn
panorama M panorama; (horizonte) outlook
panorámico ADJ panoramic
panqueque M pancake
pantaletas F PL panties
pantalla F (de lámpara) lampshade; (de monitor, para películas) screen; (para actividades ilícitas) cover, front; **la — grande** the silver screen; **— dividida** split screen; **— táctil** touchscreen
pantalón M trousers, pants; **— corto** shorts; **pantalones** trousers, pants; **llevar bien puestos los pantalones** to be master in one's own house
pantano M swamp, marsh
pantanoso ADJ swampy, marshy
panteón M vault
pantera F panther
pantomima F mime, pantomime
pantorrilla F calf
pantufla F slipper
panty M pantyhose
panza F paunch, belly
panzudo ADJ pot-bellied
pañal M diaper; **estar en —es** to be in infancy
paño M (trozo de tela) cloth; (de lana) woolen cloth; (para limpiar) rag; **— higiénico** sanitary napkin; **— mortuorio** pall; **— de manos** towel; **— de cocina** dishcloth; **— de mesa** tablecloth; **ella es mi — de lágrimas** I always cry on her shoulder; **—s menores** underwear
pañuelo M (para la nariz) handkerchief; (de cuello) scarf
papa M pope; F *Am* potato; **no saber ni —** not to know a thing; **—s fritas** French fries
papá M papa, dad
papacito M daddy
papada F double chin
papado M papacy
papagayo M parrot
papaíto M daddy
papar VT to eat; MF SG **papamoscas** (pájaro) flycatcher; (tonto) half-wit; **papanatas** twerp
paparruchas F PL baloney, bull
papaya F papaya
papel M paper; (dramático) role, part; **—**

aluminio aluminum foil; **— carbón** carbon paper; **— cuadriculado** graph paper; **— de cartas** stationery; **— de estaño** tin foil; **— de estraza** brown paper; **— de lija** sandpaper; **— de seda** tissue paper; **— encerado** wax paper; **— higiénico** toilet paper; **— moneda** paper money; **— tisú** tissue paper; **desempeñar un —** to play a role; **en el —** on paper; **hacer buen —** to cut a good figure
papelera F (fábrica) paper factory; (cubo) wastepaper basket
papelería F stationery store
papeleta F slip of paper; (para votar) ballot
paperas F PL mumps
papito M daddy
páprika F paprika
papú ADJ & MF Papua New Guinean
paquete M (envuelto) package; (atado) bundle; (conjunto de programas) package
Paquistán M Pakistan
paquistano -na ADJ & MF Pakistani
par ADJ even; M (de cosas idénticas) pair; (de cosas diferentes) couple; (título) peer; (en golf) par; **a la —** at par; **sin —** peerless; **de — en —** wide-open
para PREP in order to, for; **lo hice — ganar dinero** I did it in order to earn money; **demasiado — mí** too much for me; **trabajo — mi padre** I work for my father; **— ser perro es inteligente** for a dog he's smart; **— mi sorpresa** to my surprise; **voy — Madrid** I'm going to Madrid; **— las dos** by two o'clock; **— atrás** backwards; **— empezar** for starters; **— llevar** to go; **¿— qué?** what for? **— que** so that, so as to; **— siempre** forever; **habla — sí** he talks to himself; **— mis adentros** to myself; **— morirse de risa** hilarious; **no es — tanto** it's no big deal; **sin qué ni — qué** without rhyme or reason
parabién M congratulations; **dar el —** to congratulate
parada F (acción de parar) stop; (de perro de caza) point; (de taxis) stand; (militar) parade; (relevo de guardia) changing the guard; (de balón) parry
paradero M whereabouts
paradigma M paradigm
parado ADJ (que no se mueve) stationary; (que no tiene trabajo) unemployed, idle; **salir bien —** to come out on top
paradoja F paradox
paradójico ADJ paradoxical
parafernalia F paraphernalia

parafina F paraffin
parafrasear VI/VT to paraphrase
paráfrasis F paraphrase
paraguas M SG umbrella
Paraguay M Paraguay
paraguayo -ya ADJ & MF Paraguayan
paraíso M paradise
paraje M spot
paralela F parallel line; **—s** parallel bars
paralelo ADJ & M parallel; **hacer —s** to draw parallels
parálisis F paralysis
paralítico -ca ADJ & MF paralytic
paralización F (de tránsito) gridlock; (del cuerpo) paralysis
paralizar[9] VT to paralyze; (negociaciones) to stall; **—se** to gridlock
paramédico -ca ADJ & MF paramedic
parámetro M parameter
paramilitar ADJ & MF paramilitary
páramo M cold highland, moor
parangón M comparison; **sin —** incomparable
parangonar VT to compare
paraninfo M auditorium
paranoia F paranoia
paranoico -ca ADJ & MF paranoid
paranormal ADJ paranormal
parapsicología F parapsychology
parar VI/VT (detener) to stop; (motor) to stall; VT (un pase de pelota) to block; (un golpe) to parry; **— de hacer algo** to stop doing something; **y para de contar** and that's it; **— en seco** to stop short; **ir a —** to end up; **habló sin —** he talked non-stop; **—se** to stop; *Am* to stand up; **—se a pensar** to stop to think; M SG **parabrisas** windshield; **paracaídas** parachute; **paracaidismo** skydiving; **parachoques** bumper; **pararrayos** lightning rod; **parasol** parasol; MF **paracaidista** parachutist
parásito M parasite
parcela F parcel, plot
parcelación F subdivision
parcelar VT to parcel (out)
parche M (para remendar) patch; (de tambor) drum head; **— de ojo** eye patch
parcial ADJ partial
pardillo M linnet
pardo ADJ (color) gray-brown; (mulato) mulatto
pareado M couplet
parear VT to match
parecer[13] VI to seem; **— que** to seem like, to look like; **¿qué te parece?** what do you think? **—se a** to resemble, to look like; M

(opinión) opinion; (aspecto) appearance; **al —** apparently; **a mi —** to my mind / way of thinking; **del mismo —** like-minded
parecido ADJ alike, similar; **bien —** good-looking; M similarity, resemblance
pared F wall; **poner a alguien contra la —** to corner; **subirse por las —es** to be furious; **de — a —** wall-to-wall; **reloj de —** wall clock
paredón M execution wall
pareja F (de personas) couple; (de cosas) pair, match; (compañero) partner
parejo ADJ (hermanos) alike; (carrera) even; (dientes) straight; **correr al —** to go hand in hand
parental ADJ parental
parentela F kin
parentesco M kinship, relation
paréntesis M parenthesis
pargo M red snapper
paria MF INV pariah, outcast
paridad F parity
pariente -ta MF relative, relation; **— consanguíneo** blood relative
parir VI/VT to give birth (to)
parlamentar VI to parley
parlamentario -ria ADJ parliamentary; MF member of parliament
parlamento M (en una obra de teatro) speech; (negociación) parley; (cuerpo legislativo) parliament
parlanchín ADJ talkative
parlotear VI to chatter, to rattle on
parloteo M chatter
paro M (pequeña huelga) stoppage; (situación de no tener trabajo) unemployment; (ave) tit; **— cardiaco** cardiac arrest
parodia F parody
parodiar VT to parody
parpadear VI (un ojo) to blink; (una vela) to flicker; (una estrella) to twinkle
parpadeo M (del ojo) blink; (de una vela) flicker; (de una estrella) twinkle
párpado M eyelid
parque M park; **— automotor** fleet of cars; **— de atracciones** amusement park; **— zoológico** zoo
parra F grapevine
párrafo M paragraph; **echar un — con** to have a chat with
parral M grape arbor
parranda F binge, spree; **andar de —** to go on a spree
parrandear VI to revel
parrandero -ra MF party animal
parrilla F (sobre el fuego) grill; (en el horno)

broiler; (de calles) grid; (de coche) grille

parrillada F barbecue dish

párroco M parish priest

parroquia F (distrito) parish; (iglesia) parish church

parroquial ADJ parochial

parroquiano -na MF (de iglesia) parishioner; (de tienda) regular

parte F (sección) part; (lugar) place; (papel en un drama) lines; (persona) party; **—s pudendas** private parts; **a otra —** somewhere else; **a —s iguales** fifty-fifty; **de un tiempo a esta —** for some time; **de — de** on behalf of; **de — a —** completely; **echar a mala —** to take amiss; **en —** partly; **en gran —** in large measure; **en otra —** elsewhere; **en / por todas —s** everywhere; **formar — de** to be part of; **ir por —s** to proceed by steps; **la mayor — de** most of; **la — del león** the lion's share; **no está en ninguna —** it's nowhere to be found; **no va a ninguna —** it's going nowhere; **por otra —** on the other hand; **tomar — en** to take part in; M report; **dar — to** report; **dar — de enfermo** to report sick; **dar — de un crimen** to report a crime

partera F midwife

participación F participation; (en un negocio) interest; **— de nacimiento** birth announcement

participante MF participant; (en una carrera) entrant; (en un concurso) contestant

participar VI to participate; VT to announce; **— de / en** to participate in, to share in

partícipe MF participant

participio M participle

partícula F particle

particular ADJ (específico) particular; (poco usual) peculiar; (privado) private; **en —** in particular; **clases —es** private lessons; M (detalle) particular; (asunto) matter; MF private citizen

partida F (fondos) appropriation; (de caza) party; (cantidad de mercancía) parcel, lot; (de ajedrez) game; (acción de partir) departure; **— de nacimiento** birth record; **jugar una mala —** to play a mean trick; **por — doble** double-entry

partidario -ria MF (de una medida) supporter, advocate; (de partido político) partisan

partido M (grupo político) party; (de golf) round; (de tenis, fútbol) game, match; **es un buen —** he's a good match; **sacar — de** to take advantage of; **tomar —** to take sides; ADJ split, cleft

partir VT (dividir) to divide; (repartir) to share; (quebrar) to break; **eso me parte por el eje** that screws me up; **que te parta un rayo** go jump in the lake; VI (salir) to depart, to leave; **a — de entonces** since then; **a — del lunes** starting Monday; **—se de risa** to die of laughter

partisano -na MF partisan

partitura F musical score

parto M childbirth, delivery; **estar en trabajo de —** to be in labor

parvulario M kindergarten, nursery

párvulo -la MF nursery school child

pasa F raisin

pasable ADJ passable

pasada F (acción de pasar) passing; (con una máquina) pass; **una mala —** a mean trick; **de —** by the way

pasadizo M secret passage

pasado M past; ADJ (anterior) past; (demasiado maduro) overripe; **— mañana** day after tomorrow; **el año —** last year; **el — mes de septiembre** last September

pasador M pin

pasaje M (sitio por donde se pasa, fragmento de texto) passage; (billete) ticket; (pasajeros) passengers

pasajero -ra ADJ fleeting, transitory; MF passenger

pasaporte M passport

pasar VI (no querer jugar, ir de un lado a otro, seguir su proceso, transcurrir) to pass; (ocurrir) to happen; (mantenerse) to get by on; **— a ser** to become; **— de moda** to go out of style; **— por** to pass by; **—le por la cabeza a alguien** to occur to someone; **pasan de los 80 años** they're over 80 years old; **te pasaste la casa** you missed the house; **—se de la raya** to cross the line; **—se de sol** to get too much sun; **—se de listo** to outsmart oneself; **—se** to spoil; **se me pasó ir a buscarte** I totally forgot to pick you up; **me la paso bien** I have a good time; VT (la sal, una prueba, la plancha) to pass; (un sofocón) to endure; (una tarde) to spend; **—las de Caín** to go through hell; **— en limpio** to make a new copy; **— por alto** to overlook; **— los 50 kmh** to exceed 50 kmh; **— revista** to pass in review; **nos pasó un Volvo** a Volvo passed us; **no lo paso** I can't stand him; M **tienen un buen —** they have a comfortable life; **pasamano** (de barco) guard rail, gangway; (de escalera) banister, railing; **pasatiempo** pastime

pasarela F (en un barco) gangplank; (para modelos) runway

Pascua F Easter; (fiesta judía) Passover; **— Florida / de Resurrección** Easter Sunday; **— de Navidad** Christmas

pase M pass

pasear VI (a pie) to take a walk; (en bici, a caballo) to go on a ride; (en coche) to go for a drive, to go on a ride; **—se** to parade, to take a walk; **—se a caballo** to go horseback riding; VT (un perro) to walk a dog

paseo M (a pie) walk, stroll; (a caballo, en bicicleta) ride; (en coche) drive, ride; (lugar donde pasear) mall; **irse a —** to go jump in a lake; **dar un —** (a pie) to take a walk; (a caballo, en bicicleta) to go on a ride; (en coche) to go on a drive

pasillo M (de un teatro) aisle; (de un edificio) hallway, corridor; (para vuelo aéreo) corridor

pasión F passion

pasivo ADJ passive; **voz pasiva** passive voice; M SG (en un negocio) liabilities; (de una cuenta) debit side

pasmado ADJ astounded

pasmar VT to astound, to stun; **—se** to be astounded, to be stunned

pasmo M astonishment

pasmoso ADJ astonishing, stunning

paso M (acción de pasar, lugar donde pasar) pass; (de pie, de danza, distancia, de un proceso) step; (velocidad) pace; (de caballerías) walk; (de tornillo) pitch; (de coche) wheelbase; **— elevado** overpass; **— a nivel** grade crossing; **— de tortuga** snail's pace; **a paso** step by step; **dar —** (dejar pasar) to let pass; (dejar actuar) to make possible; **dar —s** to take steps; **de —** by the way, in passing; **estar de —** to be passing through; **marcar el —** to set the pace; **al — que** while; **salir del —** to get out of a difficulty; **dicho sea de —** incidentally; **a cada —** at every turn; **— del tiempo** passage of time; **abrir — para** to make way for; **abrirse —** to plow through, to press through; ADJ dried

pasta F (de almidón) paste; (de harina) dough; (de fideos) pasta; (de libro) hard cover, binding; (dinero) *fam* dough; **de buena —** of good disposition; **— dentífrica / dental** toothpaste

pastar VI/VT to pasture, to graze

pastel M (torta) cake; (tarta) pie; (pintura, cuadro) pastel; **— de cumpleaños** birthday cake; **— de limón** lemon pie; **— de carne** meat pie; **descubrir el —** to spill the beans; ADJ pastel

pastelería F (establecimiento) pastry shop; (conjunto de pasteles) pastry

pastelero -ra M pastry cook

pasterizar, pasteurizar[9] VT to pasteurize

pastilla F (de medicina) tablet, pill; (para la tos) drop; (de jabón) bar

pastizal M grassland

pasto M (terreno) pasture, grassland; (hierba) grass; **ser — de** to be a victim of

pastor -ora MF (de ovejas) shepherd; (sacerdote protestante) pastor, minister; M **— alemán** German shepherd

pastoral ADJ pastoral; F pastoral letter

pastoril ADJ pastoral

pastoso ADJ pasty

pastura F feed

pata F (de animal, mueble) foot, leg; (de pollo) drumstick; (de un enchufe) pin; **— palmada** webfoot; **— de gallo** crow's-foot; **en cuatro —s** on all fours; **a (la) coja** skipping on one leg; **estirar la —** *fam* to kick the bucket; **mala —** bad luck; **metedura de —** faux pas; **meter la —** to slip up; **—s arriba** upside down; ADJ **patihendido** cloven-hoofed; **patitieso** dumbfounded; **patizambo** (hacia adentro) knock-kneed; (hacia afuera) bow-legged

patada F kick; **libros a —s** tons of books; **en dos —s** in a jiffy; **dar —s** to kick; **echar a —s** to kick out

patalear VI (en el aire) to kick; (en el suelo) to stamp

pataleo M (en el aire) kick; (en el suelo) stamp

pataleta F fit; **dar una —** to throw a fit

patán M boor

patata F *Esp* potato; **—s fritas** French fries; **— caliente** hot potato

patear VT (algo, a alguien) to kick; (el suelo) to stamp; VI to tramp around

patentar VT to patent

patente ADJ & F patent; **se hizo — su ignorancia** he betrayed his ignorance; **— en trámite** patent pending

paternal ADJ (del padre) paternal; (como padre) fatherly

paternidad F paternity, fatherhood; **prueba de —** paternity test

paterno ADJ paternal

patético ADJ moving

patetismo M pathos

patíbulo M gallows scaffold, gallows

patilla F (de gafas) arm; **—s** sideburns

patín M skate; (de trineo) runner; **— de**

ruedas roller skate; **— de cuchilla / de hielo** ice skate

patinaje M skating

patinar VI (una persona) to skate; (un coche sobre hielo) to skid; (un embrague) to slip; (en un examen) to blank out

patinazo M (de embrague) slip; (de coche) skid

patio M (de casa) patio, courtyard; (de escuela) playground

pato M duck; (macho) drake; **pagar el —** to take the rap

patochada F blunder

patógeno M pathogen

patología F pathology

patológico ADJ pathological

patoso ADJ clumsy

patraña F tall tale

patria F fatherland, homeland

patriarca M patriarch

patriarcal ADJ patriarchal

patrimonio M patrimony; **— cultural** cultural heritage; **— personal** personal assets

patriota MF patriot

patriótico ADJ patriotic

patriotismo M patriotism

patrocinador -ora MF sponsor

patrocinar VT to sponsor

patrocinio M sponsorship

patrón -ona MF (protector) patron; (jefe) employer; (de navío) skipper; M (dueño de pensión) landlord; (de costura) pattern; (punto de referencia) yardstick, standard; (planta) stock; (de un parásito) host; **— de oro** gold standard; F (dueña de pensión) landlady

patronato M board of trustees

patrono -na MF patron

patrulla F (grupo de policías o soldados) patrol, squad; (coche) squad car

patrullar VI/VT to patrol

patrullero M patrol car, squad car

pausa F (musical) pause, rest; **trabajar con — **to work slowly; **hacer —** to pause

pauta F guideline

pavimentar VT to pave

pavimento M pavement

pavo M turkey; **— real** peacock; **— frío** cold turkey; ADJ silly

pavón M peacock

pavonearse VI to strut, to swagger

pavoneo M strut, swagger

pavor M dread

pavoroso ADJ frightful

payasada F clownish act or remark; **—s** antics, horseplay

payasear VI to clown around, to horse around

payaso M (de circo) clown; (persona poco seria) buffoon; **hacer el —** to clown around

paz F peace; **estamos en —** we are even; **en — descanse** may she rest in peace; **hacer las paces** to make up; **dejar en —** to leave alone

PC M PC

peaje M toll; (lugar donde se paga) tollbooth

peatón -ona MF pedestrian

peca F freckle

pecado M sin; **— mortal** mortal sin

pecador -ora MF sinner; ADJ sinful

pecaminoso ADJ sinful

pecar[6] VI to sin; **— contra** to transgress against; **— de bueno** to be too good; **— de generoso** to be too generous; **— de oscuro** to be exceedingly unclear

pecera F aquarium

pechera F (de camisa) front; (de delantal) bib

pecho M (parte del cuerpo) chest; (mama) breast; **dar el —** to nurse; **nadar —** to do the breaststroke; **tomar a —(s)** to take to heart; **sacar —** to puff out one's chest

pechuga F breast

pechugona ADJ buxom

pecio M flotsam and jetsam

pecoso ADJ freckled

pectoral ADJ & M pectoral

peculado M embezzlement

peculiar ADJ peculiar

peculiaridad F peculiarity

pedagogía F pedagogy, education

pedagogo -ga MF pedagogue

pedal M pedal

pedalear VI/VT to pedal

pedante ADJ pedantic; MF pedant

pedazo M piece; **— de idiota** absolute idiot; **él es un — de pan** he's a saint; **hacer —s** to tear to pieces; **caerse a —s** to fall to pieces; **— por —** piece by piece

pedernal M flint

pedestal M pedestal

pedestre ADJ pedestrian

pediatra MF INV pediatrician

pediatría F pediatrics

pedido M order, requisition; **hacer un —** to place an order; **— fijo** standing order; **— urgente** rush order

pedigrí M pedigree

pedigüeño ADJ **no seas —** stop asking me for things

pedir[5] VT (requerir) to ask for, to request; (exigir) to demand; (encargar) to order, to requisition; **— limosna** to beg; **—**

prestado to borrow; **— socorro** to cry for help; **— un deseo** to make a wish; **— que** to ask/pray that; **— la mano** to ask in marriage; **— por alguien** to ask to speak to someone

pedo M fart; **tener/cogerse un —** to be drunk; **tirarse —s** to fart

pedrada F **dar una —** to hit with a stone; **matar a —s** to stone to death

pedregal M rocky ground

pedregoso ADJ stony

pedrería F precious stones

pedrusco M boulder

pedúnculo M stem

pega F snag

pegadizo ADJ catchy

pegajoso ADJ sticky, tacky

pegamento M glue

pegar[7] VT (con el puño) to hit, to strike; (algo con pegamento) to stick, to glue; (botones) to sew on; (una devisa) to peg; **— con** to match; **— contra** to touch; **— un grito** to yell; **— un susto** to give a scare; **— un salto** to jump; **—le un tiro a alguien** to shoot someone; **—se** (adherir) to stick together, to cling; (contagiarse) to be contagious; **—se a** to latch onto; **no — un ojo** not to sleep a wink

pegote M glob

pegotear VT to gum up

peinado M (estilo) coiffure, hairdo; (acción) combing

peinador -ora MF hairdresser

peinar VT to comb (también registrar); (en una peluquería) to style; **— a contrapelo** to rub the wrong way

peine M comb

pelada F bald spot

pelado ADJ (pobre) poor; (sin cáscara) peeled; (sin pelo) hairless; (sin árboles) treeless; (sin plumas) plucked; (sin dinero) broke

pelador M peeler

pelaje M coat, fur

pelar VT (el pelo) to cut the hair of; (las plumas) to pluck the feathers from; (frutas, verduras) to peel; (a un jugador) to fleece; **duro de —** hard to deal with; **el agua está que pela** the water is really hot; **—se** to peel; M SG **pelagatos** nobody

peldaño M step, stair

pelea F (de palabra) fight, quarrel; (de obra) fight, scrape; (de boxeo) fight; **— a puñetazos** fistfight; **— de perros** dogfight

pelear VI (con palabras) to fight, to quarrel; (con obras) to fight, to scuffle; **—se con**

alguien to have a fight with someone

pelechar VI (perder la piel) to shed; (mejorar) to get better

pelele M (persona sin carácter) wimp; (muñeca) straw doll

peletería F (tienda) fur store; (comercio) fur trade

pelícano M pelican

película F film (también membrana); (obra cinematográfica) motion-picture film, movie; **de —** extraordinary; **dar una —** to show a film; **— muda** silent film

peligrar VI to be in danger

peligro M danger, peril; **ese muchacho es un —** that boy is dangerous; **en —** in danger; **poner en —** to imperil/ endanger/jeopardize

peligroso ADJ dangerous, perilous

pellejo M (piel de animal) hide, pelt; (odre) wineskin; **salvar el —** to save one's skin; **ser todo —** to be skin and bones; **jugarse el —** to risk one's life

pellizcar[6] VT to pinch

pellizco M pinching

pelma MF jerk

pelo M (de persona) hair; (de animal) fur; (de alfombra) pile; **con —s y señales** with every possible detail; **de medio —** low-class; **eso me viene al —** that suits me perfectly; **montar en —** to ride bareback; **ni un —** not at all; **no tener —s en la lengua** not to mince words; **se le ponen los —s de punta** his hair stands on end; **se salvó por un —** he was saved by the skin of his teeth; **tomar el — a** to make fun of; **traído de los —s** far-fetched; ADJ **pelirrojo** redheaded

pelón ADJ bald

pelota F (objeto) ball (también testículo); (juego) ball game; **— vasca** jai-alai; **en —s** naked; **pasar la —** to pass the buck

pelotera F brawl

pelotón M (pelota grande) large ball; (de tierra seca) clod; (de ciclistas) pack; (de soldados) platoon; (de fusilamiento) firing squad

peltre M pewter

peluca F wig

peludo ADJ (persona) hairy; (animal) furry; (perro) shaggy

peluquería F (para hombres) barbershop; (para mujeres) salon

peluquero -ra MF (de hombres) barber; (de mujeres) hairdresser

peluquín M toupee

pelusa F (de tela) lint; (de melocotón, cara) fuzz; (de plantas) hair; (de ropa) fluff, lint;

(de polvo) dust bunny
pelvis F pelvis
pena F (castigo) penalty; (tristeza) sorrow; **— de muerte** death penalty, capital punishment; **—s** hardships; **a duras —s** with great difficulty; **me da —** it grieves me; **hecho una —** in a mess; **sería una — perder** it would be a shame to lose; **so — de** on pain of; **valer la —** to be worthwhile
penacho M (de plumas) tuft, crest; (de humo) plume
penal ADJ penal; M penitentiary
penalidad F (penuria) hardship; (castigo) penalty
penalizar[9] VT to penalize
penalty M penalty kick
penar VI to suffer; VT to punish
penco M plug, nag
pendejo -ja MF (persona licenciosa) *pey* swine; (persona tonta) *fam* dummy; M (hombre despreciable) *pey* schmuck; (pelo púbico) pubic hair
pendencia F wrangle, fight
pendenciero ADJ quarrelsome
pender VI to hang, to dangle
pendiente F slope, incline; M *Esp* earring; ADJ (aretes) dangling; (negocio) pending, unfinished; (pago) outstanding; **vive — de su hija** she lives for her daughter
pendón M banner
péndulo M pendulum
pene M penis
penetración F penetration
penetrante ADJ (mirada, sonido) penetrating, piercing; (frío) biting; (comentario) cutting; (inteligencia) keen
penetrar VT (pasar al interior) to penetrate, to pierce; (comprender) to comprehend
penicilina F penicillin
península F peninsula
peninsular ADJ peninsular
penitencia F penance
penitenciaría F penitentiary
penitente ADJ & MF penitent
penoso ADJ (que produce tristeza) painful, grievous; (que lleva consigo penalidades) trying
pensador -ora MF thinker; ADJ reflective
pensamiento M (facultad, acción, efecto) thought; (flor) pansy
pensar[1] VI/VT to think; **— en** to think about/ over; **— hacer algo** to intend to do something; **eso da que —** that seems questionable; **no lo pienses dos veces** don't think twice
pensativo ADJ pensive, thoughtful

pensión F (asignación periódica) pension, allowance; (comidas) board; (hostal) boardinghouse; **— completa** room and board; **tener en —** to have as a boarder
pensionado M boarding school
pensionar VT to pension
pensionista MF (que vive en una pensión) boarder; (que cobra una pensión) pensioner
pentágono M pentagon
pentagrama M musical staff
penthouse M penthouse
penúltimo ADJ next to the last, penultimate
penumbra F semi-darkness, dimness
penuria F (escasez) shortage; (pobreza) poverty
peña F boulder; **— folklórica** folklore club
peñasco M crag
peñascoso ADJ craggy
peñón M crag
peón -ona MF (obrero) unskilled laborer, farm hand; **— caminero** road worker; M (en ajedrez) pawn; (en damas) piece
peonada F gang of laborers
peonaje M gang of laborers
peonza F toy top
peor ADJ worse, worst; **este libro es —** this book is worse; **el — libro** the worst book; ADV worse; **trabaja —** he works worse; **— que** worse than; **— que nunca** worse than ever; **en el — de los casos** if worst comes to worst; **lo —** the worst (thing); **tanto —** so much the worse
pepa F **es un viva la —** it's bedlam
pepino M cucumber
pepita F (simiente) seed; (tumor de gallina) pip; (masa de oro) nugget
pequeñez F (cualidad de pequeño) smallness; (cosa insignificante) trifle
pequeño -ña ADJ (de poco tamaño) small, little; (de corta edad) young; (de poca importancia) trivial
pera F pear; **pedirle —s al olmo** to ask the impossible
peral M pear tree
perca F perch; **— americana** black bass
percal M percale
percance M accident, mishap
percebe M barnacle
percepción F perception
perceptible ADJ perceptible, noticeable
perceptivo ADJ perceptive
percha F (para el armario) clothes hanger; (palo para colgar cosas) peg; (palo para aves) perch; (perchero) coat rack
perchero M coat rack
percibir VT (experimentar) to perceive, to

sense; (recibir) to collect

percudir VT to make grimy; **—se** to get grimy

percusión F percussion

percutor M firing pin

perdedor -ora MF loser

perder[1] VT (dejar de tener algo, extraviar) to lose, to mislay; (echar a perder) to spoil, to ruin; (ser derrotado) to lose; (no sacar el provecho debido) to waste; (no llegar a tiempo, no disfrutar) to miss; **— el conocimiento** to lose consciousness; **— el tiempo** to waste time; **— los estribos** to fly off the handle; **— hojas** to shed leaves; **— pie** to lose one's footing; **— terreno** to lose ground; **echarse a —** to spoil; **el vaso pierde agua** the glass leaks water; **llevo las de —** the odds are against me; **—se** (extraviarse) to lose one's way, to get lost; (pervertirse) to go astray, to go stray; **se han perdido las llaves** the keys have gotten lost; **—se de vista** to disappear; **—(se) una oportunidad** to pass up an opportunity

perdición F perdition, damnation

pérdida F (acción de perder, cosa perdida) loss; **entrar en —** to nosedive; **— de tiempo** waste of time

perdido -da ADJ (extraviado) lost, missing; (aislado) isolated; (promiscuo) promiscuous; **un borracho —** an utter drunkard; **estar — por alguien** to be crazy about someone; M degenerate; F slut

perdigón M (pollo de perdiz) young partridge; (grano de plomo) birdshot, buckshot

perdiz F partridge

perdón M forgiveness; (oficial) pardon; **con — de los presentes** present company excepted; **no tener —** to be unforgivable; INTERJ excuse me

perdonar VT to forgive; (oficial) to pardon

perdurable ADJ lasting

perdurar VI to last

perecedero ADJ perishable

perecer[13] VI to perish

peregrinación F pilgrimage

peregrinar VI to go on a pilgrimage

peregrino -na MF pilgrim; ADJ far-fetched

perejil M parsley

perenne ADJ perennial

pereza F laziness, idleness, sloth

perezoso ADJ lazy, idle; M (animal) sloth

perfección F perfection; **a la —** to perfection

perfeccionamiento M perfecting

perfeccionar VT to perfect

perfecto ADJ perfect, flawless; **es un —**

tarado he's an utter idiot

perfil M profile; **de —** from the side

perfilar VT to outline; **—se** (marcarse) to be outlined; (definirse) to become clear

perforación F perforation; (de un pozo) drilling

perforar VT (agujerear) to perforate; (para petróleo) to drill

perfumar VT to perfume, to scent

perfume M perfume, scent

perfumería F perfumery

pergamino M parchment

pérgola F arbor

pericia F expertness

perico M (loro) parakeet; (cocaína) *fam* snow

periferia F periphery, fringe

periférico ADJ & M peripheral

perilla F (adorno, remate) knob; (pelo de barbilla) goatee; **de —** apt

perímetro M perimeter

periódico M newspaper; **— mensual** monthly periodical; ADJ periodic

periodismo M journalism

periodista MF journalist

periodístico ADJ journalistic

período M period (también menstruación); (de materia radiactiva) half-life; **— glaciar** ice age

peripecia F vicissitude

peripuesto ADJ dressed up, dolled up, decked out

periquito M parakeet

periscopio M periscope

perito -ta ADJ expert, practiced; MF technician

peritonitis F peritonitis

perjudicar[6] VT to harm

perjudicial ADJ harmful, detrimental

perjuicio M harm

perjurar VT to swear; VI to commit perjury; **—se** to commit perjury

perjurio M perjury

perla F (de nácar) pearl; (persona) gem; (gota de sudor) bead; (de sabiduría) nugget; (frase desafortunada) blooper; **de —s** perfectly

perlado ADJ pearly

permanecer[13] VI to remain, to stay

permanencia F (carácter de permanente) permanence; (acción de permanecer) stay

permanente ADJ permanent

permeable ADJ permeable

permear VT to permeate

permisible ADJ permissible

permisivo ADJ permissive

permiso M permission; (para faltar al servicio militar) furlough; (para faltar al trabajo) leave; (licencia) license, permit; **con —** excuse me

permitir VT (dar posibilidad moral) to permit, to allow; (dar posibilidad física) to enable; **—se** (una libertad) to take the liberty of; (un lujo) to allow oneself; **¿me permite?** may I cut in?

permuta F exchange

permutación F permutation

permutar VT to exchange

pernetas LOC ADV **en —** barelegged

pernicioso ADJ pernicious

pernicorto ADJ short-legged

perno M bolt, pin

pero CONJ but; ADV **muy — muy lindo** very, very pretty; M objection; **no hay — que valga** no buts about it

perogrullada F platitude

perorar VI to hold forth

perorata F lecture

peróxido M peroxide

perpendicular ADJ perpendicular

perpetrar VT to perpetrate

perpetuar[17] VT to perpetuate

perpetuo ADJ perpetual

perplejidad F perplexity, bewilderment

perplejo ADJ perplexed, bewildered; VT **dejar —** to perplex

perrera F (lugar donde guardar perros) pound; (rabieta) tantrum

perrero -ra MF dogcatcher; ADJ dog-loving

perro M dog; **— caliente** hot dog; **— cobrador** retriever; **— de caza** hunting dog; **— faldero** lapdog; **— callejero** stray dog; **— de lanas** poodle; **— esquimal** husky; **— guía** guide dog; **— guardián** watchdog, guard dog; **— pastor** sheepdog; **— policía** police dog; **hijo de —** *vulg* son of a bitch; ADJ miserable; **en la perra vida** never

perruno ADJ canine

persa ADJ & MF Persian; M (lengua) Persian

persecución F (religiosa) persecution; (acción de seguir) pursuit, chase

perseguidor -ora MF (que sigue) pursuer; (que acosa) persecutor

perseguir[5,12] VT (seguir para alcanzar) to pursue, to chase; (seguir para encontrar) to track down; (acosar) to hound; (tratar de destruir) to persecute

perseverancia F perseverance

perseverar VI to persevere

persiana F blind, shade

persistencia F persistence

persistente ADJ persistent

persistir VI to persist

persona F person; **— legal** legal entity; **en**

— in person; — mayor adult

personaje M (persona importante) personage; (de obra literaria) character; **es todo un —** he's quite a character

personal ADJ personal; M personnel, staff

personalidad F personality

personificar[6] VT to personify, to embody

perspectiva F (punto de vista, distancia, técnica de representación) perspective; (panorama) view, vista; (posibilidad) prospect; **tener en —** to have planned

perspicacia F insight, sharpness

perspicaz ADJ perspicacious, perceptive

persuadir VT to persuade

persuasión F persuasion

persuasivo ADJ persuasive

pertenecer[13] VI to belong

perteneciente ADJ belonging

pertenencias F PL belongings

pértiga F pole

pertinente ADJ pertinent, relevant

pertrechos M PL military supplies

perturbación F disturbance

perturbar VT to perturb, to disturb

Perú M Peru

peruano -na ADJ & MF Peruvian

perversidad F (distorsión) perversity; (maldad) wickedness

perversión F perversion

perverso ADJ (distorsionante) perverse; (malvado) wicked

pervertido -da MF pervert

pervertir[3] VT (hacer vicioso) to pervert; (alterar negativamente) to distort; **—se** to become perverted

pesa F weight; **—s y medidas** weights and measures

pesadez F (cualidad de pesado) heaviness; (tedio) tiresomeness; (persona pesada) tiresome person

pesadilla F nightmare

pesado -da ADJ (que pesa mucho, difícil de digerir) heavy; (aburrido) tiresome; (robusto) heavy-set; (tardo) slow; MF bore, pest

pesadumbre F grief, sorrow

pésame M condolence, expression of sympathy

pesar VT (apenar) to sadden; (medir el peso de) to weigh; (recaer sobre) to weight down; VI (tener peso, importancia) to weigh; M grief, sorrow; LOC ADV **a — de** in spite of

pesaroso ADJ (triste) sad; (arrepentido) repentant

pesca F (acción de pescar) fishing; (lo pescado) catch; **ir de —** to go fishing

pescadería F fish market
pescado M fish
pescador -ora MF fisherman
pescar[6] VI/VT (capturar peces) to fish; (sacar del agua, coger, comprender, sorprender, pillar) to catch; (obtener) to land, to nail
pescozón M blow to the back of the head
pescuezo M neck
pesebre M (para pienso) manger, crib; (belén) nativity scene
peseta F peseta
pesimismo M pessimism
pesimista MF pessimist
pésimo ADJ dismal, wretched
peso M (fuerza, importancia) weight; (que oprime moralmente) burden; (cosa pesada) load; **vender al —** to sell by weight; **levantar en —** to lift off the ground
pesquería F fishery
pesquero ADJ fishing; M fishing boat
pesquisa F inquiry
pestaña F (del ojo) eyelash; (en costura) fringe; (de papel) tab; **quemarse las —s** to burn the midnight oil
pestañear VI to blink; **sin —** unflinchingly
pestañeo M blink
peste F (enfermedad) plague; (persona molesta) pest; (hedor) stench; **— bubónica** bubonic plague; **— negra** black death; **hablar —s de alguien** to speak badly of someone
pestilencia F pestilence
pestillo M deadbolt, latch
petaca F (para tabaco) tobacco pouch; (para whisky) flask
pétalo M petal
petardear VI to backfire
petardeo M backfire
petate M bundle; **liar el —** to pack up and go
petición F petition, request
peticionar VT to petition
petirrojo M robin
pétreo ADJ stony
petróleo M petroleum; **— crudo** crude oil
petrolera F oil company
petrolero M oil tanker
petulancia F smugness
petulante ADJ smug
petunia F petunia
peyorativo ADJ pejorative
peyote M peyote
pez M fish; **— dorado** goldfish; **— espada** sword fish; **— gordo** *fam* fat cat, big shot; **— vela** sail fish; **— volador** flying fish; **como — en el agua** perfectly at ease; F pitch

pezón M nipple
pezuña F hoof
piadoso ADJ pious, saintly
piafar VI to stamp
piano M piano; **— de cola** grand piano; **— vertical** upright piano
pianola F player piano
piar[16] VI to peep, to chirp
pica F (lanza) pike; (palo de baraja) spade
picada F (de insecto) bite; (de avión) nosedive; **bajar en —** to dive
picadillo M meat and vegetable hash
picado ADJ (mar) rough, choppy; (carne) chopped; (de viruela) pocked; M (de avión) nosedive
picador M picador; ADJ stinging
picadora F grinder
picadura F (de serpiente) bite; (de insecto) sting, bite
picante ADJ (obsceno) risqué; (especia) spicy, hot; (queso) sharp; M (especia fuerte) strong seasoning; (cualidad) spiciness
picar[6] VI/VT (un pez) to bite; (un ave) to peck; (comer en pequeñas cantidades) to nibble; VT (tomates) to chop up; (carne) to mince; (una vaca) to goad, to poke; (la curiosidad) to pique; (con espuelas) to spur; VI (una comida picante) to sting; (el sol) to burn; (la piel) to itch, to smart; (un avión) to dive; **— alto** to aim high; **— en** to border on; **—se** to spoil; **—se heroína** to shoot up heroin; **se pica el mar** the sea is getting rough; **se me picó un diente** I got a cavity; M SG **picapleitos** *pey* shyster; **picaporte** latch
picardía F mischief
picaresco ADJ picaresque
pícaro -ra MF rogue, rascal; ADJ roguish, mischievous
picazón F (en la piel) itch; (en la garganta) tickle
picea F spruce
pichi M jumper
pichón M (paloma) pigeon; (cría de ave) chick
picnic M picnic
pico M (de ave) beak, bill; (de montaña) peak; (herramienta) pick; (de tetera) spout; **cuarenta y —** forty-odd; **cerrar el —** to shut one's mouth; **tener el — de oro** to be very eloquent
pícolo M piccolo
picotazo M peck
picotear VI/VT (aves) to peck; (personas) to nibble
pídola F leapfrog
pie M (del cuerpo, de calcetín, de cama,

medida) foot; (de foto) caption; (de copa) stem; (de lámpara) stand; (de página) bottom; (para un actor) cue; (de árbol) trunk; (de mueble) leg; — **de atleta** athlete's foot; — **de autor** byline; — **de imprenta** printer's mark; **a** — on foot; **un soldado de** — a foot soldier; — **de banco** silly remark; **a** — **juntillas** firmly; **al** — **de la letra** to the letter; **caer de** — to have good luck; **con un** — **en el estribo** with one foot out of the door; **dar** — (a una crítica) to give rise to; (a un actor) to cue; **de / en** — standing; **en** — **de guerra** (enojado) on the warpath; (belicoso) on a war footing; **estar de** — to be standing; **estar en** — **de igualdad con** to be on a par with; **esto no tiene ni** —**s ni cabeza** I can't make heads or tails of this; **ir a** — to walk; **perder** — to lose one's footing; **ponerse de** — to stand up

piedad F (cualidad de pío) piety; (misericordia) mercy; **tener** — to show mercy

piedra F stone; — **angular** cornerstone, keystone; — **caliza** limestone; — **de afilar** whetstone; — **de toque** touchstone; — **pómez** pumice; — **preciosa** gemstone; **ser** — **de escándalo** to be an object of scandal

piel F (humana) skin; (animal) hide, pelt; (prenda de piel) fur; — **de gallina** goose bumps; — **de naranja** cellulite

pienso M feed; **ni por** — no way

pierna F leg; — **de ternera** leg of lamb; **dormir a** — **suelta** to sleep like a log

pieza F (de artillería, de tela, de música, de teatro, mueble) piece; (habitación) room; **de una** — astonished; **menuda** — a piece of work

pífano M fife

pifia F goof, miscue

pifiar VT to goof up, to miscue

pigmento M pigment

pigmeo -a MF pygmy

pija F *vulg* cock, dick

pijama M pajamas

pila F (recipiente) basin; (bautismal) baptismal font; (cúmulo) pile, heap, stack; (generador) battery; — **atómica** atomic reactor

pilar M pillar

píldora F pill; —**s para dormir** sleeping pills

pillaje M pillage, plunder

pillar VT (saquear) to pillage, to plunder; (atrapar, coger) to catch; (en el juego infantil) to tag

pillo -lla ADJ (travieso) naughty; (taimado) sly; MF (adulto) scoundrel; (niño) scamp

pilluelo -la MF urchin

pilón M (de fuente) large basin; (de puente) pylon

pilotar, pilotear VT to pilot, to fly

pilote M pile, stilt

piloto MF pilot; (llama pequeña de gas) pilot light; — **automático** autopilot; — **de pruebas** test pilot

pimentar VT to pepper

pimentero M pepper shaker

pimentón M paprika

pimienta F pepper; — **de cayena** red pepper; — **negra** black pepper

pimiento M pepper, bell pepper; — **verde** green pepper

pimpollo M (de rosa) rosebud; (de vid) shoot

PIN M PIN

pináculo M pinnacle

pinar M pine grove

pincel M artist's brush

pincelada F stroke; **dar las últimas** —**s** to put on the final touches

pinchadura F flat tire

pinchar VT to prick, to puncture; (apuñalar) to poke; (inyectar) to inject; (intervenir un teléfono) to wiretap; (provocar) to needle; VI to have a flat; **ni corta ni pincha** he doesn't count; M SG **pinchadiscos** disk jockey, DJ

pinchazo M (acción de pinchar) puncture, prick; (neumático) flat tire; (puñalada) stab; (de teléfono) wiretap

pincho M (palo afilado) spike; (de roticería) spit

pingajo M (harapo) tatter; (persona harapienta) person dressed in rags

ping-pong M ping-pong

pingüe ADJ abundant

pingüino M penguin

pino M (árbol) pine; (ejercicio) handstand; **en el quinto** — in the boondocks

pinta F (mancha) dot; (aspecto) looks; (medida de líquidos) pint

pintar VT (colorear) to paint; (describir) to depict; **este marcador no pinta** this marker won't write; **no** — **nada** to count for nothing; **las cosas no pintaban bien** things did not look well; —**se** to put on makeup

pintarrajear VT to daub, to smear with paint

pinto ADJ paint, dapple(d)

pintor -ora MF painter; — **de brocha gorda** house painter

pintoresco ADJ picturesque, colorful
pintorrear VT to smear with paint
pintura F (acción de pintar, obra) painting; (sustancia) paint; **— al óleo** oil painting; **— en aerosol** spray paint; **— fresca** wet paint
pinza F (de cangrejo) claw; (de vestido) dart; (instrumento) clothespin; **—s** tweezers
piña F (fruto del pino) pine cone; (ananás) pineapple; (bomba) hand grenade
piñata F piñata
piñón M (semilla del pino) pine nut; (rueda del engranaje) pinion; (de bicicleta) sprocket
pío ADJ pious; INTERJ peep; **ni —** not a word
piojo M louse; **como —s en costura** like sardines
piojoso ADJ lousy
pionero -ra MF pioneer
pipa F pipe; (semilla) sunflower seed; **pasarlo —** to have a great time
pipí M pee; **hacer —** *fam* to pee
pipiolo -la MF novice
pique M (rivalidad) rivalry; (desavenencia) falling-out; **echar a —** to sink; **irse a —** to capsize
piquete M picket
piragua F dugout canoe
pirámide F pyramid
pirata MF INV pirate
piratear VT to pirate
pirómano -na MF pyromaniac
piropo M compliment
pirotecnia F pyrotechnics
pirulí M sucker, lollipop
pisada F (paso) footstep; (huella) footprint; **seguir las —s de** to follow in the footsteps of
pisar VT (oprimir con el pie) to step on, to tread on; (apisonar) to mash; **jamás pisó una plaza de toros** he never set foot in a bullfight; **ir pisando huevos** to walk on eggshells; M SG **pisapapeles** paperweight; VI to step on; **— fuerte** to throw one's weight around
piscifactoría F fishery
piscina F swimming pool
piso M (suelo) floor; (planta) story; (vivienda) apartment; **de — a techo** from the ground up
pisotear VT to tramp on, to trample, to stomp on
pisotón M stamp; **dar un —** to stamp
pista F (rastro) track, scent; (noticia) clue; (de aterrizaje) runway; (de circo) arena, ring; (de patinaje) skating ring; (de tenis) court; (de baile) floor; (de carreras) track,

racetrack; **seguir la —** to track; **— para bicicletas** bike lane
pistola F pistol; (para pintura) gun
pistolera F holster
pistolero M gunman
pistón M piston; (explosivo) cap
pitada F drag, puff
pitar VI to toot, to whistle; VI/VT (rechiflar) to boo
pitazo M honk
pitido M whistle, toot
pitillo M cigarette
pito M (silbato) whistle; (pene) *fam* dick; **no vale un —** *fam* it is not worth a damn; **entre —s y flautas** when all is said and done; **¿qué —s toca?** what's his role here?
pitón M (serpiente) python; (punta de cuerno) tip of a bull's horn
pituitario ADJ pituitary
pivotar VI to pivot
pivote M pivot; **— central** kingpin
píxel M pixel
pizarra F (roca) slate; (tablero de escuela) blackboard, chalkboard
pizarrón M blackboard, chalkboard
pizca F (de sal) pinch, dash; (de evidencia) shred; (de verdad) grain; (de suciedad) speck; **no entiendo ni —** I don't understand a bit / jot
pizza F pizza
placa F (fotográfica) plate; (de policía) badge; (condecoración, dental) plaque; (de coche) license plate; (de computadora) board, card
placaje M tackle
placar[6] VI/VT to tackle
placebo M placebo
placenta F placenta, afterbirth
placentero ADJ pleasant
placer[37] M pleasure, enjoyment; VT *lit* to please
plácido ADJ placid
plaf INTERJ plop
plaga F plague; (persona, insecto) pest
plagar[7] VT to infest; **—se de** to become infested with
plagio M plagiarism
plan M (proyecto) plan; (ligue) pickup; **— de estudios** curriculum; **se vistió en — de vampiresa** she was dressed to kill
plana F newspaper page; **— mayor** top brass; **enmendar la — a uno** to correct a person's mistakes
plancha F (electrodoméstico) iron; (lámina) metal plate; (parrilla) griddle; **hacer la —** to float; **tirarse una —** to fall flat on

one's face
planchado M ironing
planchar VT to iron, to press; **me dejó
planchado** it left me speechless
plancton M plankton
planeador M glider
planear VI/VT to plan; VI (volar) to glide, to
plane; VT (madera) to plane
planeo M gliding
planeta M planet
planetario M planetarium
planificar[6] VI/VT to plan
planilla F payroll; *Am* — **de cálculo**
spreadsheet
plano ADJ flat, even; M (superficie) plane; (de
un edificio) plan; (de calles) map; —
inclinado inclined plane; **caer de** — to
fall flat; **de** — flatly; **primer** —
foreground
planta F (vegetal) plant; (del pie) sole; —
baja ground floor
plantación F plantation
plantar VT (una planta, cruz) to plant; (a un
novio) to dump; (a un colega) to make
wait; —**se** to stand firm, to refuse to
move; — **a alguien una bofetada** to
give someone a slap; **dejar plantado** to
stand up
plantear VT (presentar) to present; **me
planteó sus planes** she explained her
plans to me; (provocar) to give rise to; **eso
plantea un problema** that gave rise to
a problem; —**se** to occur to; **¿te has
planteado lo que pasa si te quedas
sin trabajo?** have you thought about
what will happen if you become
unemployed?
plantel M (personal) staff; (almáciga) nursery
plantilla F (pieza suelta) insole; (patrón)
pattern, stencil
plantío M grove
plasma M plasma
plasta ADJ INV tiresome; F (cosa informe)
lump; (persona) bore
plástico ADJ & M plastic
plata F (metal, color, objeto de plata) silver;
Am money; **hablar en** — to speak in
plain language
plataforma F platform (también política); —
de lanzamiento launching pad; —
petrolífera oil rig; — **continental**
continental shelf
platanar M banana grove
plátano M (fruta) banana; (bananero) banana
tree; (árbol ornamental) plane tree
platea F main floor of a theatre
plateado ADJ & M (color) silver; M (acción de

platear) silver-plating
platear VT to silver-plate
platero -ra MF silversmith
plática F chat
platicar[6] VI to chat
platija F flounder
platillo M (plato pequeño) saucer;
(instrumento musical) cymbal; —
volador flying saucer
platino M platinum
plato M (recipiente) plate; (comida) dish; —
fuerte main dish / course; — **hondo**
bowl; — **sopero** soup dish
plausible ADJ plausible
playa F beach
playboy M playboy
plaza F (espacio amplio) plaza, public square;
(puesto de trabajo) job; **de cuatro** —**s**
four-seater; — **de toros** bullring; —
mayor main square
plazo M term; **a corto** — short-term; **a
largo** — long-term; **a** — **fijo** fixed-term;
a —**s** on credit; **cumplir un** — to meet a
deadline
plazoleta F court
plazuela F court
pleamar F high tide
plebe F rabble
plebeyo -ya ADJ & MF plebeian
plegable ADJ folding
plegadera F paper folder
plegadizo ADJ folding
plegar[1,7] VT to fold; —**se (a)** to yield (to)
pleitesía F compliance
pleito M dispute; (judicial) litigation, lawsuit;
poner — to sue
plenario ADJ & M plenary
plenitud F — **de la vida** prime of life
pleno ADJ complete; **en** — **día** in broad
daylight; **en** — **invierno** in the dead of
winter; **en** — **rostro** right on the face; **en
— verano** in midsummer; **en plena
vista** in plain sight; M full session
pliego M leaflet
pliegue M (en papel) fold; (en tela) pleat
plomada F plumb
plomería F plumbing
plomero -ra MF plumber
plomizo ADJ leaden
plomo M (metal, color) lead; (pesos) lead
weight; (perdigón) shot; **a** — plumb; **caer
a** — to fall vertically; **sin** — unleaded; ADJ
tiresome
pluma F (de ave) feather, quill; (para escribir)
pen; — **fuente** fountain pen
plumaje M plumage
plumero M dust mop, duster

plumífero ADJ feathery
plumón M down
plural ADJ & M plural
pluralidad F plurality
pluscuamperfecto ADJ & N pluperfect
plutonio M plutonium
pluvial ADJ **aguas —es** rain water
pluviómetro M rain gauge
PNB (producto nacional bruto) M GNP
población F (conjunto de personas)
    population; (acción de poblar) settlement;
    (pueblo) town
poblado M hamlet
poblador -ora MF settler
poblar² VT (habitar) to populate; (colonizar)
    to settle; **—se** to become covered with
pobre ADJ poor; MF **los —s** the poor
pobrecito -ta MF poor thing
pobreza F poverty; (escasez) scarcity
pocilga F pigsty, pigpen
pocillo M cup
poción F potion
poco ADJ (no mucho) little; **poca paciencia**
    little patience; **al — rato** after a little
    while; (no muchos) few; **—s pasajeros**
    few passengers; **al — tiempo** shortly; **a**
    los —s meses after a few months; **como**
    — at least; **de pocas luces** stupid; **en**
    pocas palabras in a nutshell; ADV
    trabaja — he works little; **— caritativo**
    not very charitable; **— a —** little by little;
    — más o menos about; **hace —** a short
    while ago; **por — me caigo** I almost fell;
    tener en — to hold in low esteem; M a
    little, a bit; **un —** a little bit, a little while;
    unos —s a few
poda F trim
podadera F pruning hook
podar VT to prune, to trim
poder³⁸ VI to be able to; **no puedo llegar**
    antes de las cinco I can't get there
    before five; **¿puedo sentarme?** may I be
    seated? **puede que venga** she may come;
    a más no — to the utmost; **no puedo**
    más I can't go on; **nadie puede con**
    ella nobody can deal with her; **no puede**
    menos que venir he can't help but
    come; **no puede menos de hacerlo** he
    cannot help doing it; M (fuerza) power;
    (escrito que da autoridad) proxy, power of
    attorney; **— judicial** the judiciary
    branch; **por —** by proxy
poderío M power, might
poderoso ADJ powerful, mighty
podio M podium
podredumbre F rot
podrido ADJ rotten

podrir *ver* pudrir
poema M poem
poesía F poetry; (poema) poem
poeta -tisa MF poet
poética F poetics
poético ADJ poetic
polaco -ca ADJ Polish; M (lengua) Polish; MF
    Pole
polaina F legging
polar ADJ polar
polaridad F polarity
polarización F polarization
polca F polka
polea F pulley
polémica F polemic, controversy
polémico ADJ polemic
polen M pollen
poli MF cop; F cops
policía F (en conjunto) police; (mujer)
    policewoman; M policeman
policíaco ADJ police
poliéster M polyester
poliestireno M Styrofoam^tm
poligamia F polygamy
políglota ADJ & MF INV polyglot
polígrafo M polygraph
poliinsaturado ADJ polyunsaturated
polilla F moth
polímero M polymer
polinizar⁹ VT to pollinate
polio F polio
pólipo M polyp
política F (actividad relativa al gobierno)
    politics; (conjunto de orientaciones)
    policy; **— exterior** foreign policy
político -ca ADJ (relativo a la política)
    political; (diplomático) politic; MF
    politician
poliuretano M polyurethane
póliza F policy; **— de seguros** insurance
    policy
polizón -ona MF stowaway
polizonte M *pey* cop
polla F (cría de ave) pullet; (pene) *vulg* cock,
    dick; **y una —** *vulg* bullshit!
pollada F brood
pollera F woman who raises and sells
    chickens; *Am* skirt
pollo M (cría de ave) young chicken; (carne)
    chicken
polo M (extremo) pole; (juego) polo; **—**
    acuático water polo; **— de atención**
    focus of attention; **— Norte** North Pole
Polonia F Poland
poltrona F easy chair
polvareda F cloud of dust; **levantar una —**
    (causar escándalo) to raise a ruckus;

(causar una nube de polvo) to kick up the dust

polvera F compact

polvo M (suciedad) dust; (partículas) powder; (acto sexual) *vulg* screwing; **— de hornear** baking powder; **echarse un —** *fam* to get laid; **juntar —** to gather dust; **limpio de — y paja** net

pólvora F gunpowder

polvoriento ADJ dusty

polvorín M (almacén de pólvora) magazine; (situación explosiva) powder keg

pomada F salve

pomelo M grapefruit

pómez M pumice

pomo M doorknob

pompa F (boato) pomp; (burbuja) soap bubble; **—s fúnebres** funeral

pomposo ADJ pompous

pómulo M cheekbone

ponche M punch

ponchera F punch bowl

poncho M poncho

ponderación F (acción de ponderar) pondering; (valor relativo) weighting

ponderar VT (considerar) to ponder, to consider; (exagerar) to exaggerate; (ajustar estadísticas) to weight

ponencia F presentation

poner[39] VT to put, to place; (la mesa, un reloj) to set; (huevos) to lay; (azúcar) to add; (un examen) to give; (el televisor) to turn on; (un pleito) to file; **— a alguien a hacer algo** to have someone do something; **— en claro** to clarify; **— en limpio** to recopy, to make a clean copy; **— nombre a un niño** to name a child; **cada uno pone mil pesetas** each person contributes a thousand pesetas; **pongamos que** let us suppose that; **—se** (volverse) to become; (el sol) to set; (ropa) to put on; (sexualmente) to get turned on; **—se a** to begin to; **—se al corriente** to become informed; **—se de acuerdo** to come to an agreement; **—se de pie** to stand up

póney M pony

poniente M (oeste) west; (viento del oeste) west wind

pontón M pontoon

ponzoña F poison

ponzoñoso ADJ poisonous

pool M pool

popa F poop, stern

populacho M mob

popular ADJ (conocido y citado) popular; (del pueblo) folk

popularidad F popularity

populoso ADJ populous

popurrí M potpourri; (musical) medley

por PREP **— barco** by boat; **— casualidad** by chance; **— Dios** by God; **— etapas** by stages; **— las buenas o — las malas** by hook or by crook; **— litro** by the liter; **multiplicar —** to multiply by; **lo agarró por la mano** he grabbed him by the throat; **mi amor — ella** my love for her; **— poco tiempo** for a short time; **— primera vez** for the first time; **— vía de argumento** for the sake of argument; **— ejemplo** for instance; **— el momento** for the time being; **hazlo — mí** do it for my sake; **trabaja — mí** work on my behalf; **no me gustan — su olor** I don't like them because of their smell; **lo supe — él** I found out through him; **pasé — Londres** I passed through London; **un viaje — la costa** a trip along the coast; **— lo que cuentas** from what you're telling me; **— adelantado** in advance; **— escrito** in writing; **— la mañana** in the morning; **— lo general** in general; **— rachas** in spurts; **está — Badajoz** it's near Badajoz; **— fin** at last; **— el mes de marzo** around the month of March; **— ciento** percent; **— consiguiente** consequently; **— escrito** in writing; **— poco se muere** he almost died; **está — hacer** it is yet to be done; **él está — hacerlo** he is in favor of doing it; **recibir — esposa** to take as a wife; **tener —** to consider, to think of as; **¿— qué?** why? for what reason?

porcelana F porcelain, china

porcentaje M percentage

porche M porch, stoop

porcino ADJ **ganado —** swine; M pig

porción F (parte) portion, share; (de alimento) helping

pordiosear VT to panhandle

pordiosero -ra MF panhandler

porfía F obstinacy

porfiado ADJ willful

porfiar[16] VT to insist

pormenor M detail

pormenorizar[9] VT to detail, to go into detail about

pornografía F pornography

pornográfico ADJ pornographic

poro M pore

poroso ADJ porous

poroto M *Am* bean

porque CONJ because

porqué M why

porquería F (suciedad) filth; (acción despreciable) dirty trick; (cosa de mala calidad) crud; (comida de mala calidad) junk food; (persona despreciable) *pey* douchebag, dirtbag

porra F club, cudgel

porrista MF cheerleader

porro M joint

portada F title page

portador -ora MF (de enfermedad) carrier; (de cheque) bearer; **— del féretro** pallbearer

portal M portal, doorway

portar VT to carry; **—se** to behave; **—se mal** to misbehave; M SG **portaaviones** aircraft carrier; **portaequipajes** luggage bin; **portaestandarte** standard-bearer; **portafolio** briefcase; **portalámparas** socket; **portaligas** garter belt; **portamonedas** coin purse; **portaobjeto** slide

portátil ADJ portable

portavoz MF spokesperson

portazo M slam; **dar un —** to slam the door

porte M (envío) freight; (por correo) postage; (aspecto) bearing, carriage; (capacidad de carga) capacity; (tamaño) size; **— de armas** the carrying of arms; **enviar — pagado** to send prepaid

portear VT to carry

portentoso ADJ portentous

portería F (de un edificio) entrance area; (en fútbol) goal

portero -ra MF (de un edificio) doorkeeper, superintendent; (en fútbol) goalkeeper; M **— automático** intercom

portón M gate

Portugal M Portugal

portugués -esa ADJ & MF Portuguese; M (lengua) Portuguese

porvenir M future

pos LOC PREP **en — de** after

posada F inn, lodge

posaderas F PL *fam* rear end

posadero -ra MF innkeeper

posar VT (la mano, los ojos) to rest; VI (en el suelo) to sit down; (como modelo) to pose; **—se** (partículas) to settle; (mariposa) to alight; (pájaro) to perch

posdata F postscript

pose F pose

poseedor -ora MF possessor

poseer[14] VT to possess

posesión F possession

posesivo ADJ & M possessive

posibilidad F possibility

posible ADJ possible; **hacer lo —** to do one's best; **es —** it's possible

posición F position; (opinión) stance; (rango) standing; **— del misionero** missionary position; **— fetal** fetal position

positivo ADJ & M positive

poso M dregs; (de café) grounds

posponer[39] VT (aplazar) to postpone, to defer, to put off; (relegar) to put after

posta F (relevo) relay; (perdigón) buckshot

postal ADJ postal; F (tarjeta) postcard

poste M post; (de portería) upright

póster M poster

postergar[7] VT to neglect

posteridad F posterity

posterior ADJ (en el espacio) back, rear; (anatómico) posterior; (temporal) later; **nuestro divorcio fue posterior a nuestra boda** our divorce came after our wedding

postigo M shutter

postizo ADJ false; **familia postiza** adoptive family; M hairpiece

postrado ADJ prostrate, prone

postrar VT to prostrate

postre M dessert; **a la —** at last

postulado M postulate

postulante MF candidate

postular VT to postulate

póstumo ADJ posthumous

postura F posture (también opinión)

potable ADJ drinkable, potable

potasio M potassium

pote M (cilíndrico) jar; (panzudo) jug

potencia F (sexual) potency; (de una fuerza, nación) power; **es un asesino en —** he's a potential murderer; **— naval** sea power; **de alta —** high-powered; **segunda —** the second power

potencial ADJ & M potential

potentado -da MF potentate

potente ADJ potent, powerful

potranco -ca M colt; F filly

potrero M pasture; *Am* cattle ranch, stock farm

potro M (caballo) colt; (en gimnasia) vaulting horse; **— de tormento** rack

pozo M (de agua, petróleo) well; (hoyo profundo) pit; (minero) mine shaft; **sacar del —** to rescue; **— negro** sink; **— sin fondo** bottomless pit; **— séptico** septic tank

práctica F (repetición, costumbre) practice; (destreza) skill; **en la —** in practice; **poner en —** to put into practice

practicante ADJ practicing; MF (que practica) practitioner; (asistente de médico) physician's assistant

practicar[6] VI/VT to practice; (un agujero) to make
práctico ADJ practical; (adiestrado) skillful; M — **de puerto** harbor pilot
pradera F prairie, grassland
prado M meadow, pasture
pragmático ADJ pragmatic
preadolescente ADJ & MF preteen, preadolescent
preámbulo M preamble
precalentamiento M warmup
precario ADJ precarious
precaución F precaution
precaverse VT to take precautions
precavido ADJ cautious
precedencia F precedence
precedente ADJ preceding; M precedent; **sin** — unprecedented; **sentar** — to set a precedent
preceder VI/VT to precede
precepto M precept
preciado ADJ (estimado) prized; (valioso) valuable
preciarse VI — **de** to be proud of
precintar VT to seal
precinto M seal
precio M price; **poner** — **a** to put a price on; **no tener** — to be priceless; — **de lista** list price; — **de mercado** market price
preciosista ADJ precious
precioso ADJ (de gran valor, metal, piedra) precious; (muy bonito) beautiful, adorable
precipicio M precipice, cliff
precipitación F precipitation (también atolondramiento)
precipitado ADJ precipitate, hasty, rash; M precipitate
precipitar VI to precipitate; VT to hurl; —**se** (apresurarse) to be hasty; (arrojarse) to plunge, to plummet; (depositarse) to precipitate; (adelantarse) to come to a head
precisar VT (determinar) to determine precisely; (necesitar) to need
precisión F precision, accuracy; **precisiones** clarifications
preciso ADJ precise, accurate; **es** — **que vengas** you must come; **en este** — **instante** at this very moment
precoz ADJ (niño) precocious; (diagnóstico) early
precursor -ora MF precursor, forerunner
predecesor -ora MF predecessor
predecir[26b] VT to predict, to foretell
predestinar VT to predestine
predicación F preaching
predicado ADJ & M predicate

predicador -ora MF preacher
predicar[6] VI/VT to preach
predicción F prediction
predilección F predilection
predilecto ADJ favorite, pet
predisponer[39] VT to predispose
predominante ADJ predominant, prevailing
predominar VI to predominate
predominio M predominance
preeminente ADJ foremost
preescolar ADJ nursery; MF nursery school child
preestreno M preview
prefacio M preface
preferencia F preference; (en el tráfico) right of way; **de** — predominately
preferente ADJ preferential; (acciones) preferred
preferible ADJ preferable
preferido ADJ preferred, favorite
preferir[3] VT to prefer
prefijar VT to prefix
prefijo M prefix
pregonar VT (noticias) to make public; (mercancías) to hawk
pregunta F question; **hacer una** — to ask a question
preguntar VI/VT to ask, to inquire; — **por** (pedir información) to inquire about; (pedir para hablar) to ask for; —**se** to wonder
preguntón ADJ inquisitive
prehistórico ADJ prehistoric
prejuicio M prejudice, bias
prejuzgar[7] VT to prejudge
preliminar ADJ & M preliminary
preludiar VT to prelude
preludio M prelude
prematrimonial ADJ premarital
prematuro ADJ premature; (muerte) untimely
premeditado ADJ premeditated
premiar VT to reward; **las obras premiadas** the award-winning works
première M premiere
premio M (galardón) prize, award; (de la moneda) appreciation; **Juan Pérez,** — **nacional de poesía** Juan Pérez, winner of the national poetry award; — **gordo** jackpot
premisa F premise
premonición F premonition
prenatal ADJ prenatal
prenda F (fianza) pawn, pledge; (de vestir) article of clothing, garment; **dejar en** — to pawn; **en** — **de** as a token of
prendar VT to charm; —**se de** to fall in love

with

prendedor M brooch, pin

prender VT (agarrar) to grab; (sujetar) to clasp; (enganchar) to fasten; (detener) to arrest; (arraigar) to take root; (encender) to turn on, to switch on; — **fuego** to set on fire; **la vacuna no prendió** the vaccination didn't take

prensa F press; **tener mala** — to have bad press

prensar VT to press

prensil ADJ prehensile

prenupcial ADJ prenuptial

preñada ADJ pregnant

preñar VT *vulg* to knock up

preñez F pregnancy

preocupación F worry, concern

preocupado ADJ worried, concerned, anxious

preocupante ADJ worrisome

preocupar VT to worry, to concern; —**se de** to worry about; —**se por** to be concerned about

preocupón -ona MF worrywart

preparación F preparation

preparado ADJ ready; M preparation

preparar VT to prepare; —**se** to get ready, to brace oneself

preparativo ADJ preparatory; M preparation

preparatorio ADJ preparatory

preponderancia F preponderance

preponderante ADJ preponderant

preponderar VI to predominate

preposición F preposition

prepucio M foreskin

prerequisito M prerequisite

prerrogativa F prerogative

presa F (animal de caza) prey, quarry; (dique) dam

presagiar VT to forebode

presagio M omen, sign

présbita ADV & MF INV farsighted

prescindible ADJ dispensable

prescindir VI — **de** to dispense with

prescribir[51] VT to prescribe

prescripción F prescription

presencia F presence; — **de ánimo** presence of mind

presenciar VT to witness

presentable ADJ presentable

presentación F presentation; (a una persona) introduction

presentador -ora MF (de televisión) host; (de noticiero) anchor

presentar VT to present; (a una persona) to introduce; (la declaración de impuestos, una demanda) to file; (un informe) to submit; (documentos) to produce; (una

queja) to lodge; (una renuncia) to tender; —**se** (aparecer) to appear; (hacerse conocer) to introduce oneself

presente ADJ present; M (tiempo) present; (regalo) present, gift; **al** — at the present time; **tener** — to bear in mind; **en el** — **(contrato)** herein; **por la** — **(carta)** hereby

presentimiento M presentiment, foreboding, hunch

presentir[3] VT to have a presentiment of

preservación F (protección) preservation; (ahorro) conservation

preservar VT (proteger) to preserve; (ahorrar) to conserve

preservativo M condom

presidencia F presidency

presidencial ADJ presidential

presidente -ta MF (de un país) president; (de una reunión, junta) chair

presidiario -ria MF prisoner

presidio M prison

presidir VI to preside; VT to preside over

presilla F loop

presión F pressure; — **atmosférica** atmospheric pressure; — **arterial** blood pressure; — **de aire** air pressure

presionar VT (un botón) to press; (al gobierno) to lobby

preso -sa MF prisoner, inmate

prestación F provision; **prestaciones** benefits

prestador -ora MF lender

prestamista MF lender; (en un montepío) pawnbroker

préstamo M loan

prestar VT to loan, to lend; — **ayuda** to give help; — **atención** to pay attention; — **juramento** to take an oath; — **servicio** to render service

prestatario -ria MF borrower

prestidigitación F sleight of hand

prestigio M prestige

prestigioso ADJ prestigious

presumido ADJ conceited, presumptuous

presumir VT (suponer) to presume; VI (ostentar) to show off; — **de valiente** to boast of one's valor

presunción F presumption

presunto ADJ (autor) presumed; (asesino) alleged; — **heredero** heir apparent

presuntuoso ADJ presumptuous

presuponer[39] VT to presuppose

presupuesto M (de gastos e ingresos) budget; (de costo) estimate

presuroso ADJ hasty

pretencioso ADJ pretentious

pretender VI (sostener) to claim, to purport; — **ser** to claim to be; — **al trono** to pretend to the throne; VT (intentar) to attempt

pretendiente -ta MF (al trono) pretender; (a un puesto) aspirant; M (de una mujer) suitor, admirer

pretensión F pretension

pretérito ADJ past; M past tense; — **perfecto** present perfect

pretexto M pretext, pretense; **so — de** under pretense of

pretil M railing

pretina F waistband

prevalecer[13] VI to prevail

prevaleciente ADJ prevalent

prevención F (protección) prevention; (recelo) caution

prevenido ADJ forewarned

prevenir[47] VT (precaver) to prevent; (prever) to foresee; (advertir) to warn; — **contra** to protect oneself against

preventivo ADJ preventive

prever[48] VT to foresee, to anticipate

previo ADJ previous, prior; — **examen de salud** after undergoing a health examination

previsión F foresight, anticipation

prieto ADJ swarthy

prima F (cuota de seguro) premium; (recargo) surcharge; (pago extraordinario) bonus

primario ADJ primary

primate M primate

primavera F spring

primaveral ADJ springlike

primero ADJ & ADV first; **primer ministro** prime minister; — **piso** second floor; **primer plano** foreground; **primera enseñanza** primary education; **primera persona** first person; —**s auxilios** first aid; **a primera vista** at first sight; **de — grado** first degree; **de primera** top-notch; **de primera mano** firsthand; **por primera vez** for the first time; — **del mes** first of the month; F (marcha) first gear; (clase) first-class

primicia F (fruto primero) first fruit; (noticia) scoop

primitivo ADJ primitive

primo -ma MF (hijo de tío) cousin; (persona incauta) sucker, dupe; — **hermano** first cousin; — **segundo** second cousin; ADJ prime

primogénito -ta ADJ & MF firstborn

primogenitura F birthright

primor M (esmero) care; (cosa fina) lovely thing

primordial ADJ primordial

primoroso ADJ exquisite

princesa F princess

principal ADJ principal, main; **la causa — de muerte** the leading cause of death; **el dormitorio —** the master bedroom

príncipe M prince

principesco ADJ princely

principiante MF beginner; ADJ beginning

principiar VT to commence

principio M (fundamento, regla de conducta) principle, tenet; (hecho de empezar, tiempo, lugar) beginning, start; **a —s de** towards the beginning of; — **activo** active ingredient; **al —** at the beginning, at first; **de — a fin** from beginning to end; **desde el —** from the beginning; **en —** in principle

pringar[7] VT (ensuciar) to get greasy; (mojar) to dip

pringoso ADJ greasy

pringue MF grease

prioridad F (autoridad, preferencia) priority, precedence; (en el tráfico) right of way

prisa F haste, hurry; **a toda —** at full speed; **correr —** to be urgent; **darse —** to hurry; **las —s comienzan a la una** the rush starts at one; **tener —** to be in a hurry; **sin —** leisurely

prisión F prison; — **perpetua** life in prison

prisionero -ra MF prisoner; — **de guerra** prisoner of war

prisma M prism

prismáticos M PL binoculars

privacidad F privacy

privación F privation; **pasar privaciones** to suffer want

privado ADJ private; **en —** in private

privar VT to deprive; —**se de** to deprive oneself of

privativo ADJ exclusive

privilegiado ADJ privileged

privilegiar VT to favor, to give a privilege to

privilegio M privilege

pro M advantage; **en — de** in favor of; **en — y en contra** for and against

proa F prow, bow

proaborto ADJ pro-choice

probabilidad F probability; **tienes pocas —es de ganar** you have little chance of winning; **¿qué —es tiene?** what are her odds?

probable ADJ probable, likely

probador M dressing room

probar[2] VT (alimento, bebida) to taste, to try, to sample; (una hipótesis) to prove; (una guitarra) to try out; (un coche) to test-drive; **—se un vestido** to try on a dress; **prueba a venir más temprano** try to come earlier; **no — bocado** not to eat a bite; **— fortuna** to try one's luck

probeta F test tube

problema M problem; **él sólo da —s** he's nothing but trouble

problemático ADJ problematic

procedente ADJ **— de** from

proceder VI to proceed; **— de** to come from; **— a** to proceed to; **— contra** to take action against

procedimiento M procedure; **—s** proceedings

procesado -da MF accused; M processing

procesamiento M prosecution; **— de datos** data processing; **— de textos** word processing

procesar VT to prosecute, to try

procesión F procession; **la — va por dentro** he doesn't let it show

proceso M (conjunto de fases) process; (juicio) trial, legal proceedings

proclama F proclamation

proclamación F proclamation

proclamar VT to proclaim; **—se campeón** to be proclaimed winner

proclive ADJ prone

procrear VI/VT to procreate

procurador -ora MF attorney

procurar VT (intentar) to endeavor; (obtener) to procure, to obtain

prodigar[7] VT to lavish; **—se** to be lavish

prodigio M prodigy

prodigioso ADJ prodigious

pródigo -ga ADJ (derrochador) prodigal; (muy generoso) lavish; MF spendthrift

producción F (acción de producir) production; (cantidad producida) production, yield; **— masiva** mass production

producir[24] VT (efectos, mercancías, películas) to produce; (fruta, resultados) to yield, to bear; **—se** to happen

productivo ADJ productive

producto M product; **— interno bruto** gross national product

productor -ora MF producer; ADJ **un país — de petróleo** an oil-producing country

proeza F exploit

profanación F desecration

profanar VT to profane, to desecrate

profano ADJ profane

profecía F prophecy

proferir[3] VT to utter

profesar VT to profess

profesión F profession

profesional ADJ & MF professional

profesionista MF *Méx* professional

profesor -ora MF (universitario) professor; (de enseñanza secundaria) teacher; (de tenis, perros) instructor

profesorado M faculty

profeta MF INV prophet

profético ADJ prophetic

profetizar[9] VI/VT to prophesy

profilaxis F prevention

prófugo -ga ADJ & MF fugitive

profundidad F (del mar, de comprensión, de un armario) depth; (sabiduría) profundity

profundizar[9] VT to deepen; VI to do into deeply

profundo ADJ (trascendente) profound; (mar, pozo, armario, voz) deep

profuso ADJ profuse

progesterona F progesterone

programa M (de boxeo) card; (de televisión) show, program; (de un curso) syllabus

programación F programming

programador -ora MF programmer

programar VT (una computadora) to program; (un evento) to schedule

progresar VT to progress, to advance

progresista ADJ & MF progressive

progresivo -va ADJ & MF progressive

progreso M progress

prohibición F prohibition, ban

prohibido ADJ forbidden; **prohibida la entrada** no admittance

prohibir VT to prohibit, to ban; **se prohibe fumar** no smoking

prohijar VT to adopt

prójimo -ma MF fellow human

prole F offspring

proletariado M proletariat

proletario -ria ADJ & MF proletarian

proliferación F spread

prolífico ADJ prolific

prolijo ADJ (verboso) wordy; (esmerado) overly careful

prologar[7] VT to preface

prólogo M prologue, foreword, preface

prolongación F prolongation

prolongado ADJ extended

prolongar[7] VT to prolong; **—se** to wear on

promediar VT to average

promedio M average, mean; **de / en —** on average

promesa F promise; **romper una —** to break a promise; **un joven —** a promising young player

prometedor ADJ promising

prometer VT to promise; VI to show promise; **—se** to trust that

prometido -da ADJ engaged; M fiancé; F
  fiancée
prominente ADJ prominent
promiscuo ADJ promiscuous
promisorio ADJ promissory
promoción F promotion; (conjunto de
  personas) class
promocionar VT to promote
promontorio M promontory
promotor -ora MF promoter
promover[2] VT (ideas, producto, a un
  alumno) to promote; (mutua
  comprensión, una causa) to foster, to
  further
promulgación F enactment
promulgar[7] VT to promulgate, to enact
pronombre M pronoun
pronominal ADJ pronominal
pronosticar[6] VT to forecast
pronóstico M (del tiempo, de la economía)
  forecast; (de una enfermedad) prognosis
pronto ADJ (rápido) quick; (listo) ready; ADV
  soon, promptly; **de —** suddenly; **¡hasta
  —!** see you soon! **tan — como** as soon as
pronunciación F pronunciation
pronunciado ADJ pronounced
pronunciar VT (un sonido, una sentencia) to
  pronounce; (un discurso) to make, to
  deliver; **—se** (acusarse) to be pronounced;
  (expresarse) to declare one's opinion
propagación F propagation, spread
propaganda F (de ideas) propaganda; (de
  mercancías) advertising, publicity; **hacer
  —** to advertise
propagar[7] VT to propagate
propalar VT to spread
propano M propane
propasarse VI to go too far
propensión F propensity
propenso ADJ prone
propiciar VT to favor
propicio ADJ propitious, auspicious
propiedad F (cualidad, pertenencia, finca)
  property; (derecho de dueño) ownership;
  (corrección) precision; **—es** estate
propietario -ria M (de una tienda)
  proprietor, owner; (de un apartamento)
  landlord; F (de una tienda) owner; (de un
  apartamento) landlady
propina F tip, gratuity; **dar (una) —** to tip
propinar VT **— una paliza** to give a
  beating
propio ADJ (correcto) proper; **el significado
  —** the proper meaning; (típico) like; **no es
  — de él quejarse así** it's not like him to
  complain like that; (conveniente)
  appropriate; **una expresión propia** an
  appropriate expression; (que le pertenece)
  own; **su — hijo** his own son; **un hijo —**
  a son of his own; **por tu — bien** for your
  own good; (mismo) same; **al — tiempo**
  at the same time
proponente MF proponent
proponer[39] VT to propose; **—se** to set out to
proporción F proportion, ratio;
  proporciones dimensions
proporcionar VT (ajustar a proporción) to
  proportion; (brindar) to furnish, to
  provide
proposición F proposition; (de matrimonio)
  proposal; **proposiciones deshonestas**
  indecent proposals
propósito M purpose, intent; **a —** (adecuado)
  apropos; (voluntariamente) on purpose,
  intentionally; (además) by the way,
  incidentally; **a — de** apropos of
propuesta F proposal
propugnar VT to urge
propulsar VT to propel
propulsión F propulsion; **— a chorro** jet
  propulsion
propulsor -ora ADJ propelling; MF promoter
prorratear VT to prorate
prórroga F (plazo) extension of time; (de un
  préstamo) renewal; (de un encuentro
  deportivo) overtime
prorrogar[7] VT (un pago) to put off, to defer;
  (un tiempo) to extend; (un préstamo) to
  renew
prorrumpir VI to burst; **— en llanto** to
  burst into tears; **— en carcajadas** to
  burst out laughing
prosa F prose
prosaico ADJ prosaic
proscribir[51] VT to banish, to disenfranchise
proscripción F banishment
proseguir[5, 12] VI to proceed
prosódico ADJ prosodic
prospectar VT to prospect
prospector -ora MF prospector
prosperar VI to prosper, to flourish, to thrive
prosperidad F prosperity
próspero ADJ prosperous
próstata F prostate (gland)
prostituir[31] VT to prostitute
prostituta F prostitute
protagonista MF protagonist
protagonizar[9] VT to star in
protección F protection
proteccionista ADJ & MF protectionist
protector -ora ADJ protective; MF protector;
  — de tensión surge protector; **— solar**
  sunblock
protectorado M protectorate

proteger[11b] VT to protect; (a un artista) to sponsor

protegido -da MF protégé(e)

proteína F protein

prótesis F prosthesis

protesta F protest

protestante MF Protestant

protestar VI/VT to protest

protocolo M protocol

protón M proton

protoplasma M protoplasm

prototipo M prototype

protozoario M protozoan

protuberancia F protuberance, bulge, bump

protuberante ADJ bulging

provecho M (beneficio) benefit; (eructo) burp; **¡buen —!** bon appétit! **sacar — (de)** to benefit (from), to profit (from)

provechoso ADJ beneficial, advantageous

proveedor -ora MF provider

proveer[14,51] VT to provide; **— de** to provide with; **—se de** to provide oneself with

provenir[47] VI to arise; **— de** to stem from

proverbio M proverb

providencia F providence

providencial ADJ providential

provincia F province

provincial ADJ provincial

provinciano -na ADJ & MF provincial

provisión F provision, supply, store

provisional ADJ temporary, provisional

provisorio ADJ temporary

provocación F provocation

provocar[6] VT (ira) to provoke; (sexualmente) to excite; (un incendio) to start; (una respuesta) to elicit

provocativo ADJ provocative

proxeneta MF pander, pimp

proximidad F proximity, nearness; **en las —es** in the vicinity

próximo ADJ (después) next; (cercano) near, nearby; **el lunes — pasado** last Monday; **de próxima aparición** forthcoming

proyección F projection

proyectar VT to project; (una película) to screen; (una sombra) to cast; **—se** to overhang, to jut

proyectil M projectile

proyecto M project; (arquitectónico) plan; **— de ley** bill

proyector M (para películas) projector; (en el teatro) spotlight

prudencia F prudence

prudente ADJ prudent

prueba F (de imprenta, argumento irrefutable) proof; (argumento parcial) evidence; (intento, dificultad) trial, test;

(examen) examination; (de ropa) fitting; **a — de incendio** fireproof; **— de fuego** trial by fire; **poner — a** to put to the test

psicodélico ADJ & M psychedelic

psicología F psychology

psicológico ADJ psychological

psicólogo -ga MF psychologist

psicópata MF INV psychopath

psicosis F psychosis

psicosomático ADJ psychosomatic

psicoterapia F psychotherapy

psicótico ADJ psychotic

psiquiatra MF INV psychiatrist

psiquiatría F psychiatry

psíquico ADJ psychic

psoriasis F psoriasis

púa F (con punta aguda) spike; (de alambre) barb; (de guitarra) pick; (de erizo) quill; (de horca) prong

puaf, puaj INTERJ yuck, ugh

pubertad F puberty

publicación F publication

publicar[6] VT to publish; (revelar) to divulge

publicidad F publicity, advertising; **hacer —** to advertise

público ADJ public; M (la gente) public; (en un espectáculo) audience; **en —** in public

puchero M (vasija) pot; (gesto) pout; **hacer —s** to pout

puck M puck

pudiente ADJ wealthy

pudor M (sexual) modesty; (reserva) reserve

pudrir[5] VI to rot

pueblerino ADJ provincial

pueblo M (población) town; (nación) people, folk

puente M bridge (también dental, de gafas, de nariz); (fin de semana) long weekend; **— aéreo** (regular) shuttle; (de emergencia) airlift; **— colgante** suspension bridge; **— levadizo** drawbridge

puénting M bungee jumping

pueril ADJ childish

puerta F door; (de aeropuerto, de ciudad) gate; (medio de acceso) entrance; **vender de — en —** to sell door-to-door; **dar a alguien con la — en las narices** to slam the door in someone's face; **llamar a la —** to knock on the door; **— trasera** back door; **a — cerrada** behind closed doors

puerto M port (también en informática); **llegar a buen —** to bring to a satisfactory conclusion

puertorriqueño -ña ADJ & MF Puerto Rican

pues CONJ (puesto que) since, for; ADV (entonces) then; **— bien** well then, now

puesta F — **al día** update; — **del sol** sunset, setting of the sun; — **en marcha** (de un proyecto) setting in motion; (de un coche) starting; — **en libertad** freeing

puestero -ra MF vendor, seller

puesto ADJ **bien** — (casa) well-appointed; (persona) well made-up; **llevar** — to have on; M (posición) place; (de venta) booth, stand; (de trabajo) post, position; — **de socorros** first-aid station; **quedarse con lo** — to be left with only the clothes on one's back; CONJ — **que** since

pugilato M boxing

pugilista M boxer, prizefighter

pugna F struggle; **estar en** — **con** to be in conflict with

pugnaz ADJ feisty

puja F (del viento) push; (en una subasta) bid

pujanza F vigor

pujar VI (para dar a luz) to push; (en una subasta) to bid; — **por** to strive to

pujo M contraction

pulcritud F neatness

pulcro ADJ neat

pulga F flea; **tener malas** —s to be ill-tempered

pulgada F inch

pulgar M thumb

pulido ADJ polished; M polishing

pulimento M (de modales) refinement; (de metales) buffing; (sustancia) scouring powder

pulir VT (metal, oración) to polish; (madera) to sand

pulla F taunt, dig

pulmón M lung; — **de acero** iron lung

pulmonar ADJ **capacidad** — lung capacity

pulmonía F pneumonia

pulpa F pulp

púlpito M pulpit

pulpo M octopus

pulque M *Méx* pulque

pulquería F *Méx* pulque bar

pulsación F pulse

pulsar VT (una tecla) to hit; (cuerdas de guitarra) to pluck; (la opinión pública) to gauge

púlsar M pulsar

pulsera F bracelet; (de reloj) watchband; **reloj de** — wristwatch

pulso M pulse; (firmeza de mano) steadiness; **echar un** — to arm-wrestle; **tomar el** — to take the pulse; **a** — with great effort

pulular VI to swarm, to teem with

pulverizar[9] VT to pulverize

puma F mountain lion, cougar

puna F cold, arid tableland of the Andes

punitivo ADJ punitive

punk ADJ & M punk

punkero -ra MF punk

punta F (de cuchillo, lengua) point; (de espárrago, lápiz) tip; (de calcetín) toe; — **de lanza** spearhead; **una** — **de** a bunch of; **a** — **de cuchillo** at knifepoint; — **de flecha** arrowhead; **de** — on end; **iba caminando de** —s he was tiptoeing; **sacar** — **a un lápiz** to sharpen a pencil; **en la** — **de la lengua** on the tip of the tongue; **me pone los nervios de** — it makes me nervous; M —**pié** kick; ADJ **puntiagudo** sharp, pointed

puntada F stitch, prick

puntal M (de un edificio) prop; (de la economía) mainstay

puntear VT (una guitarra) to pluck; (un mapa) to make dots on; (una lista) to check off

puntería F aim; **tener buena** — to be a good shot

puntero M pointer

puntilla F point lace; **de** —s on tiptoe

punto M (puntuación) period; (de cinturón) notch; (signo) point, dot; (tanteo, tema, lugar) point; (puntada) stitch; — **álgido** fever pitch; — **de apoyo** foothold; — **de condensación** dewpoint; — **de congelación** freezing point; — **de ebullición** boiling point; — **de partida** point of departure; — **de referencia** point of reference, benchmark; — **de vista** viewpoint, point of view; — **muerto** (en un negocio) stalemate, deadlock; (en un coche) neutral; — **y coma** semicolon; **al** — at once; **a** — ready; **a** — **de** on the point / verge of; **cogerle el** — to figure out; **dos** —s colon; **el** — **medio** the halfway mark; **en** — on the dot; **hacer** — to knit; **hasta cierto** — to a certain extent; **poner los** —**s sobre las íes** to dot the i's and cross the t's

puntuación F punctuation

puntual ADJ punctual, prompt; (específico) specific

puntualidad F punctuality

puntualizar[9] VT to point out

puntuar[17] VT to punctuate

punzada F (de dolor) stab; (de remordimiento, hambre) pang, twinge

punzante ADJ sharp, piercing

punzar[9] VT to prick

punzón M (en papel) hole punch; (en cuero) awl

puñado M handful; **a** —s by the handful

puñal M dagger

puñalada F stab; **coser a —s** to stab to death

puñetazo M punch, slug; **dar un —** to punch; **dar un — en la mesa** to bang on the table

puño M (mano cerrada) fist; (en un mango) cuff; (de espada) handle; **arreglarlo con los —s** to duke it out; **de mi — y letra** by my own hand

pupa F *Esp* boo-boo

pupila F pupil

pupilo -la MF ward

pupitre M school desk

puré M purée; **— de patatas** mashed potatoes; **hacer —** to smash

pureza F purity

purga F (política) purge; (medicinal) purgative

purgación F atonement

purgante ADJ & M purgative, laxative

purgar[7] VT (el vientre, a un rival) to purge; (frenos) to bleed; (pecados) to atone for

purgatorio M purgatory

purificar[6] VT to purify

purista ADJ & MF purist

puritano ADJ puritanical

puro ADJ pure; **lo hizo de — bueno** he did it out of sheer kindness; **a pura fuerza** by sheer force; **la pura verdad** the plain truth; **son puras mentiras** that's a lot of bull; **de purasangre** thoroughbred; M cigar

púrpura ADJ & M purple

pus M pus

puta F (prostituta) *ofensivo* whore; (mujer fácil) *ofensivo* slut; **de — madre** *vulg* very good; **de la gran —** *vulg* huge

putañero M john

putón M *ofensivo* slut

putrefacto ADJ putrid

putter M putter

Qq

Qatar M Qatar

quásar M quasar

que PRON REL that; (antecedentes no humanos) which; (antecedentes humanos) who, whom; **el / la —** the one that; **lo tú dices** what you say; **vino la suegra, lo — complicó la visita** the mother-in-law came, which complicated the visit;

CONJ that; **no creo — haya tiempo** I don't think (that) there's time; **estoy — me muero** I feel like I'm about to die; **Carlos es más alto — Luis** Carlos is taller than Luis; **más (menos) —** more (less) than; **déjalo aquí — lo voy a necesitar después** leave it here because I will need it later; **por mucho —** no matter how much; **a — gana** I bet he'll win; **— yo sepa** as far as I know

qué ADJ INTERR & PRON what, which; **¿— libro vas a usar?** what / which book are you going to use? **¿— dices?** what are you saying? **no sé — dijo** I don't know what he said; **¡— bonito!** how beautiful! **¡— de gente!** what a lot of people! **y eso — —** so what! **no hay de —** don't mention it; **¿ — sé yo?** what do I know? **¿— tal?** how are you? **¡— más da!** what's the difference! **¡a mí —!** so what!

quebrada F ravine

quebradizo ADJ breakable, brittle

quebrado ADJ (roto) broken; (rajado) cracked; (sin dinero) broke; M fraction

quebrantar VT (una casa, la salud) to weaken; (la ley) to violate

quebranto M weakening

quebrar[1] VT (romper) to break; (rajar) to crack; VI (irse a bancarrota) to go bankrupt, to go under, to fail; **—se** to break (up); **se quebró la muñeca** he broke his wrist; **—se uno la cabeza** to rack one's brain

queda F curfew

quedar VI (permanecer) to remain; (no haberse terminado) to be left; (estar ubicado) to be located; (sentar bien la ropa) to suit; **queda leche en el vaso** there's milk in the glass; **la iglesia queda en la esquina** the church is located on the corner; **— bien** to come out well; **— en** to agree to; **—se** to remain, to stay; **—se con una cosa** to take (buy) something

quehacer M chore

queja F complaint; (oficial) grievance

quejarse VI to complain; (ruidosamente) to gripe, to squawk; (incesantemente) to whine

quejica ADJ INV whiny; MF INV nag, whiner

quejido M (de sonido grave) moan, groan; (agudo) squawk

quejoso ADJ whiny

quema F burning

quemado -da MF burn victim

quemador M burner

quemadura F (lugar quemado) burn;

(enfermedad de plantas) blight
quemar VT to burn; (del sol) to sunburn;
—**se** to burn up / down
quemazón F burning sensation
querella F lawsuit
querellante MF plaintiff
querellarse VI to file suit
querer[40] VI/VT (desear) to want; (amar) to
love; **como quieras** as you please;
cuando quieras whenever you want; **no
quiso hacerlo** he refused to do it;
quiere llover it is about to rain; **sin —**
unwillingly; — **decir** to mean
querido -da ADJ beloved, dear; MF
sweetheart; (como tratamiento) dear,
darling
queroseno M kerosene
quesería F dairy, cheese factory
queso M cheese; — **crema / de untar** cream
cheese; — **suizo** Swiss cheese
quiche M quiche
quicio M hinge; **sacar a uno de** — to drive
someone up the wall
quiebra F bankruptcy (también moral); (de
un mercado) crash; (de un comercio)
failure
quiebre M break
quien PRON REL who, whom; **Juan, —
recién cumplió cuarenta años** Juan,
who just turned forty; — **hizo eso**
whoever did that; **a — corresponda** to
whom it may concern; —**quiera**
whoever; **de —** whose; **con —** with
whom
quién PRON INTERR & PRON who; **¿— es?** who
is it? **no sé — entró** I don't know who
came in; **¿a — se lo diste?** who did you
give it to? to whom did you give it?
quieto ADJ still
quietud F stillness
quijada F jaw
quilate M carat
quilla F keel
química F chemistry
químico -ca ADJ chemical; MF chemist
quimioterapia F chemotheraphy
quince NUM fifteen
quincena F (de cosas) group of 15; (de días)
two-week period
quincha F thatch
quinchar VT to thatch
quingombó M okra
quinqué M oil lamp
quinta F (casa) villa; (reclutamiento) draft
quinto ADJ, ADV, & M fifth
quiosco M kiosk, newsstand
quiquiriquí INTERJ cock-a-doodle-doo

quirófano M surgery, operating room
quiropráctico -ca ADJ chiropractic; MF
chiropractor; F chiropractic
quirúrgico ADJ surgical
quisquilloso ADJ particular, fussy
quiste M cyst
quitar VT (una mancha) to remove; (una
prenda de vestir) to take off; (despojar de)
to take away; M SG **quitaesmalte** nail
polish remover; **quitanieves** snowplow;
quitamanchas spot remover; VI —**se** to
take off; —**se a alguien de encima** to
get rid of someone; **quítate de ahí** move
over
quite M **salir al — de** to go to the rescue of
quizá, quizás ADV perhaps, maybe

Rr

rabadilla F (coxis) tailbone; (de un ave)
rump
rábano M radish; **me importa un —** I
couldn't care less
rabia F (hidrofobia) rabies; (enojo) rage; **me
tiene —** he hates me; **dar —** to anger
rabiar VI to rage, to fume; **guapa a —** drop-
dead beautiful
rabieta F tantrum
rabino -na MF rabbi
rabioso ADJ (hidrofóbico, apasionado) rabid,
mad; (enojado) mad, furious
rabo M (cola) tail; (pene) *fam* dick; (cabo)
stem; **mirar con el — del ojo** to look
out of the corner of one's eye; **con el —
entre las piernas** with his tail between
his legs
rabón ADJ bobtail
racha F (de suerte) streak; (de viento) gust
racial ADJ racial
racimo M (de plátanos, personas) bunch; (de
uvas) cluster
raciocinio M reasoning
ración F ration, allowance; (de comida)
portion
racional ADJ rational (también número)
racionalizar[9] VT to rationalize
racionamiento M rationing
racionar VT to ration
racismo M racism
racista ADJ & MF racist
radar M radar
radiación F radiation
radiactivo ADJ radioactive

radiador M radiator

radial ADJ radial

radiante ADJ radiant

radiar VT to radiate; (por radio) to broadcast

radical ADJ (extremo) radical; (hojas, células) root; M (en ciencias) radical; (en gramática) root

radicalismo M radicalism

radicar[6] VI to be located; — **en** to lie in; **—se** to take up residence

radio M (hueso, segmento de un círculo) radius; (elemento radiactivo) radium; F (aparato, difusión) radio; (emisora) radio station; — **de acción** sphere of influence

radiodifusión F broadcasting

radiodifusora F radio station

radioescucha MF INV radio listener

radiofónico ADJ radio

radiografía F x-ray

radiografiar[16] VT to x-ray; (examinar con cuidado) to examine carefully

radiología F radiology

radiotelescopio M radio telescope

radiotransmisor M radio transmitter

radón M radon

raer[23] VI/VT to scrape (off); (un artículo de ropa) to wear out

ráfaga F (de viento) gust, blast; (de luz) flash; (de ametralladora) burst

raído ADJ threadbare

raigón M stump

raíz F root; — **cuadrada** square root; **a** — **de** due to; **arrancar de** — to uproot; **cortar de** — to nip in the bud; **echar raíces** to take root

raja F (de melón) slice; (de falda) slit; (del culo) *vulg* crack; (de leña) stick

rajadura F (en piedra, metal) crack; (en tela) rent, rip

rajar VT (una piedra) to crack; (un tronco) to split; **—se** (partir) to split open; (acobardarse) to chicken out, to blink; ADV **a rajatabla** strictly

ralea F ilk

ralear VI to thin out

ralentización F (de la economía) slump; (de un motor) idle

rallador M grater

rallar VT to grate, to shred

ralo ADJ sparse, thin

rama F branch, limb; (delgada) twig; **andarse por las —s** to beat around the bush; **algodón en** — raw cotton

ramaje M foliage

ramal M (de soga) strand; (de vía férrea) branch, spur

ramera F whore

ramificarse[6] VI to divide into branches, to branch off

ramillete M bouquet, bunch, spray

ramo M (de flores) bouquet; (de una ciencia) branch; (de una actividad) line; — **de olivo** olive branch

rampa F ramp

ramplón ADJ vulgar

rana F frog

ranchero -ra MF rancher

rancho M (comida para soldados) mess; (comida mala) swill; (finca) ranch; **hacer** — to keep to oneself

rancio ADJ (alimento) rancid; **de** — **abolengo** of ancient lineage

rango M (militar) rank; (categoría) standing

ranilla F frog (of a hoof)

ranura F (corte) groove; (para insertar monedas, cartas) slot

rapar VT (pelo) to shave off; (cabeza) to shave

rapaz ADJ (animal) predatory; (destructivo) rapacious

rape M **cortar al** — to crop

rapé M snuff

rapear VI to rap

rapidez F (de un coche) speed; (de un movimiento) rapidity, quickness

rápido ADJ (con mucha velocidad) fast; (en poco tiempo) quick; M rapids; ADV (con mucha velocidad) fast; (en poco tiempo) quickly

rapiña F pillage

raptar VT to kidnap, to abduct

rapto M (secuestro) abduction, kidnapping; (arrebato) fit

raqueta F racket

raquítico ADJ feeble, sickly

raramente ADV seldom

rareza F (escasez) rarity; (cosa rara) oddity; (cualidad de extraño) strangeness

raro ADJ (infrecuente, de gases, tierras) rare; (extraño) strange, funny; **rara vez** seldom; **sentirse** — to feel funny

ras LOC ADV **a** — **de la tierra** low to the ground

rascar[6] VT to scratch; **—se el culo** *vulg* to fart around; M SG **rascacielos** skyscraper

rasgado ADJ **ojos —s** slit eyes

rasgadura F tear, rip

rasgar[7] VT to tear, to rip

rasgo M (propiedad) trait, feature; **a grandes —s** in broad strokes

rasgón M tear

rasguñar VT to scratch

rasguño M scratch

raso ADJ (superficie) smooth; (cucharada)

level; **al** — in the open air; M satin
raspado M scrape
raspador M scraper
raspadura F scrape
raspar VT to scrape
raspón M scrape
rastra F harrow; **a —s** dragging, pulling
rastrear VT (a un animal) to trail, to track, to trace; (un terreno) to search
rastreo M sweep, search
rastrero ADJ (planta) creeping; (persona) contemptible
rastrillar VT to rake
rastrillo M rake
rastro M (huella) track, trail; (olor) scent; (mercado) flea market; **ni —s** no trace
rastrojo M stubble
rasurado M shave
rasurador -ora MF razor
rasurar VT to shave
rata F rat
ratear VT to pilfer
ratería F petty larceny
ratero -ra MF pickpocket
ratificar[6] VT to ratify
rato M while; **—s perdidos** leisure hours; **a cada** — frequently; **a —s** from time to time; **pasar el** — to kill time; **pasar un buen** — (divertirse) to have a pleasant time; (permanecer) to spend a long time; **un largo** — a great while
ratón M mouse; **— almizclero** muskrat
ratonera F mousetrap
raudal LOC ADV **a —es** in great quantities
raudo ADJ swift
raya F line; (linde) boundary; (lista) stripe; (en el pelo) part; (en un pantalón) crease; (ortografía) dash; (en un zapato) scuff; (pez marino) stingray; **tener a** — to hold in check; **pasarse de la** — to be out of line
rayado ADJ (papel) lined; (vestido) striped; **hablaba como disco** — he talked like a broken record
rayar VT (papel) to rule, to make lines on; (discos, espejo) to scratch; (zapatos) to scuff; **— el alba** to dawn; **— en** to border on
rayo M (de luz) ray, beam, streak; (de relámpago) flash of lightning; (de rueda) spoke; (de esperanza) ray, flicker; **—s infrarrojos** infrared rays; **—s X** X-rays
rayón M rayon
raza F (de personas) race; (de animal) breed
razón F (facultad) reason; (proporción) ratio; **— social** company name; **a — de** at the rate of; **¡con —!** no wonder! **entrar en**

— to listen to reason; **te doy la** — I admit you're right; **perder la** — to lose one's mind; **tener** — to be right
razonable ADJ reasonable
razonamiento M reasoning
razonar VI (pensar) to reason; (arguir) to argue
reabastecer[13] VT to replenish
reabrir[51] VT to reopen
reacción F reaction; **— en cadena** chain reaction; **— nuclear** nuclear reaction
reaccionar VI to react
reaccionario ADJ & MF reactionary
reacio ADJ averse, reluctant
reacondicionar VT to rebuild
reactivo M reagent
reactor M reactor; **— nuclear** nuclear reactor
readaptación F readjustment
readaptar VT to readjust
reagrupar VT to regroup
reajustar VT to readjust
reajuste M readjustment
real ADJ (verdadero) real, actual; (del rey) royal; M fairground
realce M **dar** — to enhance
realeza F royalty
realidad F reality, actuality; **en** — really, actually; **— virtual** virtual reality
realismo M realism
realista ADJ (auténtico) realistic; (partidario del rey) royalist; MF (no idealista) realist; (partidario del rey) royalist
realización F (de un sueño) realization, fulfillment; (de una tarea) realization; (de una película) production
realizar[9] VT (un sueño) to realize, to fulfill; (película) to produce
realzar[9] VT (mejorar) to enhance; (destacar) to accentuate; (intensificar) to heighten
reanimar VT (devolver fuerzas) to revive; (dar ánimos) to rally
reanudación F renewal
reanudar VT (una amistad) to renew; (una reunión) to resume
reaparecer[13] VI to reappear
reasumir VT to resume
reata F lariat, lasso
reavivar VT to revive
rebaja F markdown, price cut; **de —s** cut-rate
rebajar VT (precios) to cut, to lower, to slash; (una bebida) to water down; (una crítica) to tone down; VI/VT (los cambios) to downshift; **—se** to lower oneself; **—se a** to stoop to
rebanada F slice
rebanar VT to slice

rebaño M flock, fold

rebasar VT (un coche) to overtake; (un límite) to exceed

rebatir VT to refute

rebato M alarm

rebelarse VI to rebel, to revolt

rebelde ADJ rebellious; (pelo) unruly; MF rebel

rebeldía F rebelliousness, defiance; (no comparecencia) default

rebelión F rebellion

rebenque M whip

rebobinar VT to rewind

reborde M edge

rebosante ADJ (de líquido) brimming, overflowing; (de salud) flush, glowing

rebosar VI (líquido) to overflow, to brim over; (de alegría) to bubble over; (de salud) to glow

rebotar VI (botar para atrás) to rebound, to bounce; (chocar) to bounce; (cambiar de dirección una bala) to ricochet; (cambiar de dirección una pelota) to carom

rebote M rebound, bounce; (de bala) ricochet

rebozar[9] VT to cover with batter; **—se** to muffle up

rebozo M shawl; **sin —** frankly

rebullir[19] VI to stir

rebuscado ADJ (estilo) overly elaborate; (persona) affected

rebuscar[6] VT (espigar) to glean; VI **— en** (la memoria) to search through; (un cajón) to rummage in

rebuznar VI to bray

rebuzno M bray, braying

recabar VT to raise (money)

recado M (mensaje) message; (quehacer) errand; **— de escribir** writing materials

recaer[23] VI to relapse; **— sobre** to fall to

recaída F relapse

recalar VI to make a stop at

recalcar[6] VT to accentuate

recalcitrante ADJ obstinate

recalentar[1] VT (volver a calentar) to warm over; (calentar en exceso) to overheat

recamar VT to embroider

recámara F (de un arma de fuego) chamber; *Méx* bedroom

recapitular VI/VT to recapitulate, to sum up

recargado ADJ busy, fussy

recargar[7] VT to overload, to burden

recargo M (emocional) burden; (de precio) surcharge, premium

recatado ADJ (cauteloso) cautious; (modesto) modest

recato M (cautela) caution; (modestia) modesty

recaudación F collection, levy; **— de fondos** fund-raising

recaudador -ora MF tax collector

recaudar VT (impuestos) to collect, to levy; (fondos) to raise; **— en bruto** to gross; **lo recaudado** proceeds

recaudo M **estar a buen —** to be in a safe place

rección F government

recelar VT to suspect; **— de** to be suspicious of

recelo M misgivings

receloso ADJ mistrustful

recepción F reception

receptáculo M receptacle, holder

receptor M receiver

recesión F recession

receta F (de cocina) recipe; (de médico) prescription

recetar VT to prescribe

rechazar[9] VT to reject; (un ataque) to repel, to repulse; (una oferta) to decline, to turn down, to refuse; (una acusación) to deny; (a un amante) to spurn, to reject

rechazo M (de un amante) rejection; (de un ataque) repulse; (de una oferta) refusal; (de una acusación) denial

rechifla F whistling, booing

rechiflar VT to whistle, to boo

rechinamiento M (de una puerta) creaking, squeaking; (de los dientes) grinding

rechinante ADJ squeaky

rechinar VI (una puerta) to squeak, to creak; VI/VT (los dientes) to grind; **eso me rechina** that grates on my nerves

rechoncho ADJ plump, chubby, roly-poly

recibidor -ora MF receiver; M reception room

recibimiento M reception

recibir VT to receive, to get; (visitas) to receive, to welcome; (una noticia trágica) to take; **— noticias de** to hear from; **—se** to graduate; **—se de médico** to graduate from medical school

recibo M receipt; **de —** acceptable; **al — de** upon receipt of; **acusar —** to acknowledge receipt; **acuse de —** acknowledgment of receipt

reciclar VI/VT to recycle

recién ADV recently; **— casado** newlywed; **— comprado** brand-new; **— llegado** newly arrived; **— me entero** it's news to me; **— nacido** newborn

reciente ADJ recent

recinto M enclosure

recio ADJ strong, rugged

recipiente M container

recíproco ADJ reciprocal

recitación F recitation
recital M recital
recitar VT to recite, to speak
reclamación F (protesta) protest; (demanda) claim
reclamante MF claimant
reclamar VT (protestar) to protest; (demandar) to claim; VI (aves) to call
reclamo M (reclamación) claim; (voz de animal) call, cry; (dispositivo) bird call; (señuelo) decoy
reclinar VT to lean; **—se** to recline
recluir[31] VT to confine; **—se** to be a recluse
recluso -sa MF inmate
recluta F recruitment; M (voluntario) recruit; (forzoso) conscript
reclutamiento M (voluntario) recruitment; (forzoso) conscription
reclutar VT (voluntariamente) to recruit; (por la fuerza) to draft, to conscript
recobrar VI to recover, to recuperate; VT to recover, to regain
recodo M bend, turn
recoger[11b] VT (el cabello) to gather; (un cuarto) to tidy up; (citas en un texto) to collect; (la mesa) to clear; (polvo) to sweep up; (a un desamparado) to shelter; (los frutos del campo) to glean; **—se** (retirarse) to retire, to withdraw; (acumularse) to gather
recogida F (del cabello) gathering; (de un cuarto) tidying up; (de la mesa) clearing; (de un desamparado) sheltering
recogimiento M (aislamiento) seclusion; (meditación) meditation
recolección F (de frutos, datos) collecting, gathering; (de carga) pickup; (cosecha) harvest
recolectar VT to gather, to forage
recomendable ADJ advisable
recomendación F recommendation
recomendar[1] VT to recommend
recompensa F recompense, reward
recompensar VT to recompense, to reward
reconcentrar VI to concentrate intensely; **—se** to concentrate, to become absorbed in thought
reconciliación F reconciliation
reconciliar VT to reconcile
recóndito ADJ remote
reconfortante ADJ heart-warming, comforting
reconfortar VT to comfort
reconocer[13] VT (identificar) to recognize; (admitir) to admit, to acknowledge; (explorar) to reconnoiter
reconocimiento M (identificación)

recognition; (admisión, agradecimiento) acknowledgment; (exploración) scouting; **hacer un —** to reconnoiter
reconsiderar VT to reconsider
reconstrucción F reconstruction
reconstruir[31] VT to reconstruct, to rebuild
recopilar VT to compile
récord M record
recordar[2] VT (acordarse) to remember, to recollect, to recall; (hacer acordar) to remind
recordatorio M reminder
recorrer VT (andar una distancia) to cover; (examinar) to go over, to look over
recorrido M (ruta) run; (distancia) distance
recortado ADJ jagged
recortar VT (pelo, hilos, presupuesto) to trim; (uñas, periódicos) to clip; (una película) to shorten; **—se** to be outlined
recorte M (de pelos, hilos) trimming; (de uñas, periódicos) clipping; (de sueldo) cut; (sobrante) trimming
recostar[2] VT (sobre) to lay; (contra) to lean; **—se** to recline
recoveco M (en un camino) turn; (rincón) cranny
recreación F recreation
recrear VT to entertain; **—se** to amuse oneself
recreo M recreation, relaxation; (tiempo de descanso) recess; (lugar de juego) playground
recriminar VT to recriminate
recrudecer[13] VI to flare up
recrudecimiento M flareup
rectángulo M rectangle
rectificar[6] VT to rectify
rectitud F uprightness, righteousness
recto ADJ (no curvo) straight; (honrado) upright, righteous; (estricto) strict; **todo —** straight ahead; M rectum
rector -ora MF university president, chancellor
recua F herd
recuento M account; **— sanguíneo** blood count
recuerdo M (acción de recordar, cosa recordada) memory, recollection; (objeto que hace recordar) souvenir, token; **—s** regards
recular VI (ir hacia atrás) to move backward; (en un coche) to back up; (ante un desafío) to back down
recuperación F recovery
recuperar VT (una cosa perdida) to recover; (tiempo perdido) to make up; **—se** to recuperate

recurrir VT to appeal; — **a** to resort to, to have recourse to

recurso M (acción de recurrir) recourse; (reclamación) appeal; —**s** resources; —**s naturales** natural resources

recusar VT (a una persona) to reject; (a un juez) to challenge

red F (para pescar) net; (tejido de mallas) mesh; (conjunto de mallas) network; (para engañar) snare; (internet) World Wide Web, Internet

redacción F (ensayo) composition; (acción de redactar) drafting; (en un periódico) editorial department

redactar VT to draft; (en la escuela) to compose

redactor -ora MF editor

redada F (de peces) catch, haul; (por la policía) raid

redar VT to net

redecilla F hairnet

redención F redemption

redil M sheepfold, sheep pen; **volver al —** to come back into the fold

redimir VT (a un pecador) to redeem; (a un esclavo) to set free

rédito M (de ahorros) interest; (de acciones) yield

redituar[17] VT to yield

redoblar VT to double; VI/VT (un tambor) to roll

redoble M drumroll

redoma F flask

redonda F whole note; **a la —** all around

redondear VT to make round

redondel M ring

redondez F roundness

redondo ADJ round; **en —** all around; **caer — —** to collapse; **salir —** to turn our perfect

reducción F reduction, cutback; **hacer — de personal** to cut back on personnel

reducir[24] VT to reduce; (un hueso) to set; (actividades) to curtail, to cut down on; —**se** to limit oneself; —**se a** to boil down to

redundante ADJ redundant

reedificar[6] VT to rebuild

reelección F reelection

reelegir[11] VT reelect

reembolsar VT to reimburse, to refund

reembolso M reimbursement, refund

reemplazable ADJ replaceable

reemplazar[9] VT to replace

reemplazo M replacement, substitute

reencarnación F reincarnation

reescribir[51] VT to rewrite

reexpedir[5] VT to forward

referencia F reference

referéndum M referendum

referente LOC ADV — **a** relative to

referir[3] VT (narrar) to narrate; —**se a** to refer to

refinación F refinement

refinado ADJ refined, genteel

refinamiento M refinement

refinar VT to refine

refinería F refinery

reflector M (en una bicicleta) reflector; (en deportes) floodlight; (militar, policial) searchlight

reflejar VT (luz) to reflect; (imagen) to mirror; —**se** to be reflected

reflejo M (luz) reflection; (movimiento) reflex; —**s** frosting; ADJ reflex

reflexión F reflection

reflexionar VI to reflect; — **sobre** to think over

reflexivo ADJ (gramatical) reflexive; (pensativo) thoughtful

reflujo M ebb

reforma F (política) reform; (religiosa) reformation

reformador -ora MF reformer

reformar VT (un gobierno, a un delincuente) to reform; (ropa) to make alterations in; —**se** to mend one's ways

reformatorio M reformatory

reformista MF reformer

reforzar[2,9] VT to reinforce; (las defensas) to beef up; (un argumento) to bolster, to buttress

refracción F refraction

refractario ADJ refractory

refrán M proverb, saying

refrenar VT (un caballo) to rein in; (emociones) to restrain, to check

refrendar VT (una sentencia) to uphold; (un documento) to countersign, to endorse

refrendario -ria MF endorser

refrendo M endorsement

refrescante ADJ refreshing

refrescar[6] VT to refresh; (el tiempo) to get cool; —**se** to cool off

refresco M refreshment

refriega F fray, scuffle

refrigeración F refrigeration

refrigerador ADJ refrigerating; M refrigerator

refrigerante ADJ cooling; M coolant

refrigerar VT to cool, to refrigerate

refrigerio M refreshment

refrito ADJ (comida) refried; M (obra) rerun

refuerzo M (acción de reforzar) reinforcement; (de tela) backing; (de una vacuna) booster

refugiado -da MF refugee
refugiar VT to shelter; **—se** to take shelter
refugio M refuge, shelter; **— antiaéreo**
   bomb shelter; **— fiscal** tax shelter
refulgente ADJ resplendent
refundir VT to recast
refunfuñar VI to grumble, to mutter
refunfuño M grumbling, muttering
refunfuñón -ona ADJ grouchy, grumpy; MF
   grouch
refutar VT to refute
regadera F watering can
regadío M (tierra irrigada) irrigated land;
   (riego) irrigation
regalar VT (dar como presente) to give as a
   gift; (vender barato, donar) to give away;
   (agasajar) to regale
regaliz M licorice
regalo M (presente, cosa barata) present, gift;
   (para los sentidos) treat, delight
regañar VI (un perro) to snarl; VT (a un
   niño) to scold, to reprimand;
   (constantemente) to nag; **a**
   regañadientes reluctantly
regaño M scolding, reprimand
regañón -ona MF scold
regar[1,7] VT (campos) to irrigate; (flores) to
   water
regatear VI to haggle, to bargain
regateo M bargaining
regazo M lap
regente MF regent; ADJ ruling
reggae M reggae
régimen M (gobierno) regime; (dieta) diet; **—**
   de vida lifestyle
regimiento M regiment
regio ADJ regal
región F region
regir[5,11] VT to govern; VI to be in force; **—se**
   por to be guided by
registrar VT (buscar en) to search; (indicar)
   to record, to register
registro M (de la voz, lingüístico) register;
   (de nacimientos) record, register; (del
   equipaje) search; (de un órgano) stop
regla F (norma) rule; (utensilio para medir)
   ruler; (menstruación) period; **en —** in
   order; **por — general** as a general rule
reglamento M regulations
regocijar VT to gladden; **—se** to rejoice
regocijo M joy, rejoicing
regodearse VI (en la desgracia propia) to
   wallow; (en la desgracia ajena) to gloat
regodeo M (en la desgracia propia)
   wallowing; (en la desgracia ajena) gloating
regordete ADJ plump
regresar VI to return

regreso M return; **estar de —** to be back
reguero M trail; **correr como un — de**
   pólvora to spread like wildfire
regulación F (acción de regular) regulation;
   (de una máquina) adjustment
regulador M regulator, governor, throttle; **—**
   de voltaje dimmer
regular VT to regulate; (ajustar una máquina)
   to adjust; ADJ regular; **una paliza —**
   quite a beating; ADV so-so
regularidad F regularity
regularizar[9] VT to regulate; (formalizar) to
   formalize; **—se** to become regular
regurgitar VI/VT to regurgitate
rehabilitador ADJ remedial
rehacer[30] VT to remake; **—se** to recover
rehén MF hostage
rehuir[31] VT to shun; (responsabilidades) to
   shirk
rehusar VT to refuse; **—se a** to refuse to
reimpresión F reprint
reina F queen
reinado M reign
reinante ADJ prevailing
reinar VI to reign
reincidencia F relapse
reincidir VI to relapse
reino M (territorio de un rey) kingdom,
   realm; (período de reinado) reign;
   (división biológica) kingdom; (ámbito)
   realm
reintegrar VT to rebate; **—se a** to return to
reintegro M rebate
reír[15] VI to laugh; **—se de** to laugh at
reiterar VT to reiterate
reivindicar[6] VT to vindicate
reja F grate, grating; (pieza de arado)
   plowshare; **entre —s** behind bars
rejilla F (para equipaje) luggage rack; (de
   coche) grille
rejuvenecer[13] VT to rejuvenate; VI to become
   rejuvenated
relación F relation, connection;
   (interpersonal) relationship; (relato)
   account, report; (lista) list; **relaciones**
   (conocidos) connections; (trato) dealings;
   relaciones públicas public relations;
   con — a in relation to
relacionado ADJ related, germane
relacionar VT to relate, to connect; **—se con**
   to relate to
relajación F relaxation
relajamiento M relaxation
relajar VT to relax; **—se** to become lax
relajo M (aflojamiento) relaxation; (desorden)
   mess
relamerse VI to lick one's lips

relámpago M lightning
relampaguear VI to lightning; (los ojos, cosa reluciente) to flash
relampagueo M flash of lightning
relatar VT to relate, to recount
relativo ADJ relative; **— a** relative to
relato M (informe) account; (cuento) story, tale
relé M relay
relegar[7] VT to relegate
relevar VT to relieve
relevo M (soldado) relief; (carrera) relay
relicario M reliquary, locket
relieve M relief; **de —** (mapa) relief; (persona) prominent; **poner de —** to emphasize; **letras en —** raised letters
religión F religion
religioso -sa ADJ religious; M monk; F nun
relinchar VI to neigh
relincho M neigh
reliquia F relic
rellenado M filling
rellenar VT (un vaso) to refill, to replenish; (un tanque de gasolina) to fill, to fill up; (un formulario) to fill out; (un hueco) to fill in; (una almohada) to stuff
relleno ADJ (un pimiento) stuffed; (el cuerpo) full; M (de comida) stuffing, dressing; (de un colchón) padding
reloj M (de pared) clock; (de muñeca, bolsillo) watch; (de horno) timer; **— de pulsera** wristwatch; **— de sol** sundial; **— despertador** alarm clock; **contra —** against the clock; **como un —** regularly, like clockwork
relojería F (tienda) watch shop; (actividad) clock-making
relojero -ra MF watchmaker
reluciente ADJ shining
relucir[13b] VI to shine; **sacar a —** to bring up
relumbrar VI to glare
relumbre M glare
REM M REM
remachar VT (una victoria, un clavo) to clinch; (un remache) to rivet
remache M (acción de remachar) clinching; (clavo) clinching; (clavija) rivet
remanente M remainder
remar VI/VT to row, to paddle
rematador -ora MF auctioneer
rematar VT (acabar) to finish; (matar) to finish off; (perfeccionar) to give the finishing touches to; (patear un balón) to take a shot; (subastar) to auction
remate M (de una obra) finishing touch; (tiro) shot; (subasta) auction; **— de un**

chiste punch line; **loco de —** stark raving mad
remedador -ora MF mimic
remedar VT to mimic, to ape, to mock
remediar VT to remedy
remedio M remedy, cure; **sin —** unavoidable; **no tiene —** it can't be helped; **no tengo más —** I can't help it; **el — es peor que la enfermedad** the remedy is worse than the disease
remedo M mockery
remendar[1] VT to mend, to patch; (calcetines) to darn; (zapatos) to repair
remendón -ona MF cobbler
remero -ra MF rower
remesa F (de mercancías) shipment; (de dinero) remittance
remiendo M (de ropa) patch; (de zapatos) repair
remilgado ADJ fussy, prim
remilgo M fussiness, primness
reminiscencia F reminiscence
remisión F remission
remitente MF sender
remitir VT (enviar) to remit; (mandar a otra parte) to refer; **—se** to yield; **a las pruebas me remito** the evidence speaks for itself
remo M (pala) oar, paddle; (deporte) rowing
remodelar VI/VT to remodel
remojar VT to soak
remojo M soaking; **poner en —** to soak
remojón M soaking
remolacha F beet
remolcador M tugboat
remolcar[6] VT to tow
remolino M swirl, whirl; (de viento) whirlwind; (de agua) whirlpool, eddy; (de pelo) cowlick; (juguete) pinwheel; **— de gente** throng, crowd
remolón -ona ADJ dallying; MF dallier
remolonear VI to dally
remolque M (acción de remolcar) tow; (vehículo remolcado) towed vehicle; (vehículo que remolca) tow truck; (de camión) trailer; **llevar a —** to tow
remontar VT (una cometa) to fly; (una pendiente, un río) to go up; **—se** to rise; **el coche se remonta a los años 20** the car dates from the '20s; **para comprenderlo, debemos remontarnos a su juventud** in order to understand him, we must go back to his youth
remorder[2] VT to gnaw at
remordimiento M remorse
remoto ADJ remote, distant; **no tiene la**

más remota idea he doesn't have the slightest idea

remover[2] VT (un cargo, un obstáculo) to remove; (un asunto problemático) to stir up

remuneración F compensation

remunerado ADJ gainful

renacer[13] VI to be reborn

renacimiento M revival; (período histórico) Renaissance

renacuajo M tadpole; (hombre esmirriado) shrimp

rencilla F quarrel

rencor M rancor; **guardar —** to bear a grudge

rencoroso ADJ resentful

rendición F surrender

rendido ADJ exhausted

rendija F crack

rendimiento M (lo rendido) yield, output; (productividad) performance

rendir[5] VT (someter) to subdue; (producir) to yield; (fatigar) to fatigue; **— homenaje** to pay homage; **— cuentas a** to answer to; VI (obtener buenos resultados) to perform well; **—se** (darse por vencido) to surrender, to give in; (fatigarse) to become fatigued

renegado -da MF renegade

renegar[1,7] VT (negar) to deny insistently; (repudiar) to renounce; **— de** to gripe about

renglón M line; **a — seguido** immediately following

rengo ADJ lame

renguear VI to limp

renguera F limp

reno M reindeer

renombrado ADJ renowned

renombre M renown; **de —** of note

renovación F renewal; **— urbana** urban renewal

renovar[2] VT (un edificio) to renovate; (ataques, temores) to renew

renquear VT to limp

renta F (de una persona) income; (de un gobierno) revenue; (alquiler) rent; **— anual** annuity; **—s internas** internal revenue; **vivir de la —** to live on the interest

rentable ADJ profitable; (idea) viable

renuencia F reluctance

renuente ADJ reluctant, loath; **ser — a** to be loath to

renuevo M sprout

renuncia F (dimisión) resignation; (de un derecho) waiver; (de una herencia) renunciation

renunciar VI **— a** (un cargo) to resign; (la ciudadanía) to renounce; (un derecho) to relinquish, to waive

reñido ADJ contested

reñir[5,18] VI (discutir) to quarrel, to bicker, to argue; (pelear) to fight, to scuffle; (rezongar) to scold

reo -a MF defendant, accused

reojo M **mirar de —** to look out of the corner of one's eye

reorganizar[9] VT to reorganize, to regroup

repantigarse[7] VI to lounge

reparación F (compensación) reparation, redress; (arreglo) repair

reparador ADJ refreshing; M serviceman

reparar VT (arreglar) to repair; (compensar) to redress; **— en** to notice

reparo M **no tener —s en** to have no qualms about; **sin —s** freely; **hacer —s** to object

repartición F distribution

repartir VT (tierras, un botín) to distribute; (volantes) to hand out; (periódicos) to deliver; (naipes) to deal; (días libres) to space out

reparto M (de tierras) distribution; (entrega de periódicos) delivery; (de naipes) dealing; (ruta de entrega) route; (lista de actores) cast; **— proporcional** apportionment

repasar VT (una lección) to review, to go over again; (en la memoria) to retrace; (leer por encima) to skim

repaso M review

repelente ADJ repellent

repeler VT to repel, to repulse

repente M **de —** suddenly

repentino ADJ sudden

repercusión F repercussion

repercutir VI to have repercussions

repertorio M repertoire

repetición F repetition

repetido ADJ repeated; **repetidas veces** repeatedly

repetir[5] VI/VT to repeat; VI to belch; (tomar una segunda ración) to have seconds; **— como loro** to parrot; **—se** to recur

repicar[6] VI/VT to ring

repique M ringing, ring

repiquetear VI/VT to ring

repiqueteo M ringing

repisa F shelf

replegar[1,7] VT to fold; **—se** to retreat

repleto ADJ replete

réplica F (contestación) reply, comeback; (copia) replica; (temblor secundario)

aftershock
replicar[6] VI/VT to reply, to rejoin; (una célula) to replicate
repliegue M (pliegue marcado) crease; (retirada) retreat
repollo M cabbage
reponer[39] VT (reemplazar) to replace; (restituir) to restore; (replicar) to reply; (una obra de teatro) to revive; (una película) to show again; —**se** to recover one's health
reportaje M feature story
reportar VT (beneficios) to yield; VI (en una jerarquía) to answer to; —**se enfermo** to call in sick
reportero -ra MF reporter
reposado ADJ quiet, calm
reposar VI to repose, to rest; **dejar** — to let steep; M SG **reposacabezas** headrest
reposición F (reemplazo) replacement; (de una obra de teatro) revival
reposo M (descanso) repose, rest; (sosiego) calm
repostería F (establecimiento) pastry shop; (actividad) baking
repostero -ra MF pastry cook
reprender VT to reprimand, to scold, to rebuke
reprensión F rebuke
represa F (dique) dam; (reservorio de agua) reservoir
represalia F reprisal
represar VT to dam
representación F representation; (delegación) delegation; (de un papel) portrayal; (de una obra de teatro) performance
representante MF representative; (comercial) agent
representar VT to represent, to depict; (una obra de teatro) to perform; (un personaje) to portray; **tiene treinta años, pero no los representa** he's thirty years old, but he doesn't look it; **tu presencia representa mucho para mí** your presence means a lot to me
representativo ADJ representative
represión F (psicológica) repression; (política) suppression, crackdown
reprimenda F reprimand, rebuke
reprimido ADJ repressed, pent-up
reprimir VT (impulsos) to repress; (una tendencia) to check; (enemigos políticos) to suppress, to crack down on; (una rebelión) to quell
reprobación F reproof
reprobar[2] VT to reprove; VI/VT (no aprobar

un examen) to flunk, to fail
reprochar VT to reproach, to rebuke
reproche M reproach, rebuke
reproducción F reproduction
reproducir[24] VI/VT to reproduce; —**se** to reproduce, to breed
reproductor -ora ADJ breeding; MF breeding animal; F (aparato) VCR
reptar VI to crawl
reptil M reptile
república F republic
republicano -na ADJ & MF republican
repudiar VT (a la sociedad) to repudiate; (a un hijo) to disown; (una herencia) to renounce
repuesto M (pieza de reemplazo) spare part; **de** — spare
repugnancia F repugnance, disgust, revulsion
repugnante ADJ repugnant, disgusting, loathsome
repugnar VI to be repugnant; VT to disgust, to cloy
repulir VT to polish up
repulsa F rebuff, repulse
repulsar VT to repulse
repulsivo ADJ repulsive, creepy
repuntar VI to rally
reputación F reputation
reputado ADJ reputable
requemar VT to burn
requerimiento M request
requerir[3] VT to require
requesón M cottage cheese
requiebros M PL advances
requisa F requisition
requisar VT to commandeer, to requisition; (registrar) to search
requisito M requirement, requisite
res F animal; — **lanar** sheep; — **vacuna** cow
resabio M (dejillo) aftertaste; (vicio) bad habit
resaca F (de mar) undertow; (malestar físico) hangover
resaltar VI (sobresalir) to stand out; (poner de relieve) to highlight
resarcir[10b] VT to compensate for
resbaladizo ADJ slippery, slick
resbalar VI (deslizar) to slip; (ser / estar resbaladizo) to be slippery
resbalón M slip; **darse un** — to slip
resbaloso ADJ slippery; *Méx fam* sleazy
rescatar VT (a un secuestrado) to ransom; (a una persona en peligro) to rescue
rescate M (para un secuestrado) ransom; (de una persona en peligro) rescue

rescindir VT to rescind
rescoldo M embers
resecar[6] VT to dry; **—se** to dry out
reseco ADJ dried-up, parched
resentido ADJ resentful
resentimiento M resentment, grudge;
  guardar — to hold a grudge
resentirse[3] VI to hurt, to suffer; **— de** to
  resent
reseña F book review
reseñar VT to review
reserva F (de provisiones, de oro, de
  jugadores, del ejército) reserve; (de
  localidades, de hotel, de indios)
  reservation; (de animales) preserve; **sin
  —s** without reservations; **tener —s** to
  have reservations
reservación F *Am* reservation
reservado ADJ (distante) aloof; (discreto)
  reserved
reservar VT to reserve; **me reservo mi
  opinión** I'll spare you my opinion
resfriado M common cold; **estoy —** I've got
  a cold
resfriarse VI to catch cold
resfrío M cold, head cold
resguardar VT to shelter; **—se de** to seek
  shelter from
resguardo M (abrigo) shelter; (comprobante)
  deposit slip
residencia F residence
residencial ADJ residential; (en las afueras)
  suburban
residente ADJ & MF resident
residir VI to reside
residuo M residue
resignación F resignation
resignarse VI to resign oneself
resina F resin
resistencia F resistance; (de la calefacción)
  element; (aguante) endurance, stamina
resistente ADJ resistant, tough
resistir VT (una tentación) to resist; (un
  ataque) to withstand; **—se a un arresto**
  to resist arrest; VI to resist, to hold (up)
resollar[2] VI (por enfermedad) to wheeze;
  (después de un esfuerzo) to pant; (por
  alivio) to sigh
resolución F (acción de resolver) resolution;
  (ánimo) determination, resolve
resolver[2,51] VT (decidir) to decide;
  (solucionar) to solve; **—se a** to resolve to
resonancia F resonance
resonar[2] VI (sonidos) to resound, to boom;
  (una polémica) to resonate
resoplar VI (con enfado) to huff and puff;
  (un caballo) to snort

resoplido M (con enojo) puff; (de caballo)
  snort
resorte M spring
respaldar VT to back, to stand behind
respaldo M (parte de una silla) back; (apoyo)
  support, backing
respectivo ADJ respective
respecto LOC ADV **— a / de** with respect to,
  concerning; **a ese —** on that score; **con
  — a** with regard to, regarding, vis-à-vis
respetable ADJ respectable
respetar VT to respect
respeto M respect, regard; **con todo —** with
  all due respect; **faltar el / al —** to slight,
  to disregard
respetuoso ADJ respectful
respingar[7] VI (dar respingos) to buck;
  (asustarse) to shy away
respingo M (salto) buck; (susto) start
respiración F respiration, breathing; **— boca
  a boca** mouth-to-mouth resuscitation
respirar VI/VT to breathe; (sentir alivio) to
  breathe easy; **dejar —** to give a breather
respiro M (acto de respirar) breathing;
  (descanso) respite
resplandecer[13] VI (brillar) to glare; (de
  felicidad) to glow
resplandeciente ADJ resplendent, radiant
resplandor M brilliance, radiance
responder VI (reaccionar) to respond; VT
  (contestar) to answer; (corresponder) to
  correspond
respondón ADJ saucy
responsabilidad F (obligación de aceptar
  consecuencias) responsibility; (obligación
  de informar) accountability
responsable ADJ (que debe aceptar las
  consecuencias) responsible; (obligado
  legalmente) liable for; (que tiene que
  informar) accountable
respuesta F response, answer
resquebrajadura F crack
resquebrajar VI to crack
resquicio M (rendija) crack; (laguna legal)
  loophole
resta F subtraction
restablecer[13] VT to reestablish; (una
  costumbre) to revive; **—se** to recover
restante ADJ remaining
restañar VT to stanch / staunch
restar VT (sustraer) to subtract; (quitar) to
  take away from; (quedar) to remain; **—
  importancia a** to make light of
restauración F restoration
restaurante M restaurant
restaurar VT to restore; (muebles) to
  refurbish

restitución F restitution
restituir[31] VT to pay back, to give back
resto M (lo demás) rest; (sobrante) remainder; —**s** (de un edificio) remains; (de una comida) leftovers; **echar el —** to go all out
restorán M restaurant
restregar[1,7] VT to scrub, to scour
restricción F restriction
restringir[11] VT to restrict, to curtail
resucitación F resuscitation, revival
resucitar VT to resuscitate, to revive
resuello M (por enfermedad) wheeze; (por fatiga) panting
resuelto ADJ (de carácter decidido) resolute, strong-willed; (de actitud decidida) determined
resulta LOC ADV **de —s** as a result
resultado M result; (de un suceso) outcome; (de un partido) score; —**s científicos** findings; —**s electorales** returns; **como — as a result; dar buen —** to pan out; **dar por —** to result in
resultante ADJ resulting, consequent
resultar VI to result; (acabar siendo) to turn out, to prove; **— de** to result from; **resulta que** it turns out that
resumen M summary, abstract; **en —** in sum, in brief
resumir VT to summarize, to sum up; —**se a** to be condensed to, to boil down to
resurgimiento M revival
resurgir[11] VI to arise again
resurrección F resurrection
retablo M altarpiece
retaguardia F rear guard
retal M remnant
retama F broom
retar VT to challenge
retardar VI/VT to retard
retardo M lag
retazo M remnant
retén M (aparato) retainer; (de vigilancia) squad
retención F retention
retener[44] VT (una pelota, la atención) to hold; (salarios, fondos) to garnish, to withhold
retina F retina
retintín M (en los oídos) ringing; (de cascabeles) jingle
retirada F (de tropas) retreat, withdrawal; (de un diplomático, producto) recall
retirar VT (apartar) to move away; (dinero) to withdraw; (algo dicho) to take back, withdraw; (un producto) to recall; —**se** (para descansar, de un trabajo) to retire;

(un ejército) to retreat, to pull back
retiro M (refugio) retreat; (jubilación) retirement; (de fondos) withdrawal
reto M challenge
retocar[6] VT to retouch, to touch up
retoñar VI to sprout
retoño M sprout, shoot, bud
retoque M retouching
retorcer[2,10c] VT (una toalla mojada) to wring out; (la muñeca) to wrench, to twist; —**se** (de dolor) to writhe; (de inquietud) to squirm
retorcido ADJ (persona) devious; (rama) gnarled
retorcimiento M (de dolor) writhing; (de inquietud) squirming
retórica F rhetoric
retornar VT to return
retorno M return; (de una costumbre, moda) revival
retozar[9] VI to frolic, to romp; (en juegos eróticos) to cavort
retozo M frolic, romp
retractarse VI to take back one's words
retraer[45] VT (las garras) to retract; —**se** to withdraw
retraído ADJ shy
retraimiento M shyness
retrasado ADJ (falto de desarrollo) backward; (deficiente mental) retarded
retrasar VT to delay; (un reloj) to set back; —**se** to fall behind
retraso M delay, lag
retratar VT to portray; (pintar un retrato) to paint a portrait
retrato M (pintura) portrait; (descripción) portrayal
retreta F retreat
retrete M lavatory
retroactivo ADJ retroactive
retroalimentación F feedback
retroceder VI to step back; (de horror) to recoil, to shrink back; (en un coche) to back up; (al mecanografiar) to backspace; (dar marcha atrás) to backtrack; (tropas) to retreat, to fall back; (una inundación) to recede
retroceso M (de un arma de fuego) recoil; (económico) recession; (en un teclado) backspace
retrogradismo M backwardness
retrógrado ADJ backward
retroproyector M overhead projector
retrovirus M retrovirus
retrucar[6] VT to counter
retruécano M play on words
retumbar VI to rumble, to roll

retumbo M rumble
reubicar[6] VT to relocate
reuma M rheumatism
reumatismo M rheumatism
reunión F meeting; (informal) get-together; (de ex-alumnos) reunion
reunir VT (juntar) to gather; (hacer que acudan al mismo lugar) to reunite, to bring together; (coleccionar) to collect; (juntar coraje) to muster; (juntar dinero) to raise; **—se** (formal) to meet; (mucha gente) to gather; (informal) to get together
revancha F (venganza) revenge; (en deportes) return game
revelación F revelation
revelado M film development
revelador ADJ revealing
revelar VT to reveal; (película) to develop; (un escándalo) to expose; (información) to disclose; **—se** to show oneself
revendedor -ora MF (de mercadería) middleman; (de entradas) scalper
revender VT (vender de nuevo) to resell; (billetes) to scalp
reventar[1] VI/VT (estallar) to burst, to bust; (morir) to die; (fastidiar) to annoy
reventón M (acción de reventar) bursting; (de un neumático) blowout
reverberar VI to reverberate
reverdecer[13] VI (ponerse verde de nuevo) to become green again; (renovarse) to gain new strength
reverencia F reverence; (gesto) bow
reverenciar VT to revere
reverendo -da ADJ & MF reverend
reverente ADJ reverent
reverso M reverse
revertir[3] VI to revert; **— en beneficio de** to be of benefit to
revés M (cosa opuesta) reverse; (en tenis) backhand; (contratiempo) setback, downturn; **al —** (con lo de adelante hacia atrás) backwards; (con lo de arriba hacia abajo) upside down; **dar vuelta al —** to turn inside out
revestimiento M overlay
revestir[5] VT (un camino) to surface; (una pared) to cover; (conllevar) to be marked by
revisar VT (examinar) to review, to go over; (un coche) to service
revisión F review; (de una película vieja) revival
revisor -ora MF (en un tren, autobús) conductor
revista F (inspección) inspection; (de tropas) muster; (publicación) magazine, journal,

periodical; (espectáculo) revival; **— de historietas** comic book; **— electrónica** e-zine; **pasar —** to pass in review
revistar VT to inspect
revivir VI/VT to revive
revocación F revocation; (de una ley) repeal
revocar[6] VT (un fallo) to reverse; (una ley) to repeal; (una pared) to plaster
revolcar[6] VT (derribar) to knock over; **—se** (cerdos) to wallow; (niños) to roll around
revolear VT to roll
revolotear VI to flutter, to flit
revoltijo M (de cosas) jumble; (de pelo) muss
revoltoso -sa ADJ unruly, disorderly; MF troublemaker
revolución F (cambio radical) revolution; (giro) revolution, turn; **revoluciones por minuto** revolutions per minute
revolucionario -ria ADJ revolutionary, earthshaking; MF revolutionary
revolver[2, 51] VT (remover) to stir up; (registrar) to rummage in; (desordenar) to mess up; (huevos) to scramble; (ensalada) to toss; **eso me revuelve el estómago** that makes my stomach turn; **—se** to toss and turn
revólver M revolver, pistol
revuelo M stir, commotion
revuelta F revolt
revuelto ADJ (el mar) rough; (los ánimos) restless; (el pelo) disheveled; **huevos —s** scrambled eggs
rey M king; **los —es Magos** the Wise Men
reyerta F melee, squabble
rezagarse[7] VI to straggle behind, to lag behind
rezar[9] VI/VT (a Dios) to pray; (un letrero) to say
rezo M prayer
rezongar[7] VI/VT (murmurar) to grumble; (quejarse) to gripe
rezongón -ona ADJ grumpy; MF grouch
rezumar VT to ooze
riachuelo M brook
riada F flash flood
ribazo M steep bank
ribera F shore, bank; (de río) riverbank
ribereño ADJ on the bank
ribete M (de uniforme) trimming; (de alfombra) binding; (de ropa) piping; (de mosaico) border; **tener —s de** to have hints of
ribetear VT (un uniforme) to trim; (una alfombra) to bind; (un diseño) to border
ricacho ADJ very rich
rico ADJ (persona) rich, wealthy, affluent; (suelo) rich; (piso) exquisite; (manjar)

delicious; (niño) cute

ridiculizar[9] VT to ridicule, to deride

ridículo ADJ ridiculous; (medio absurdo) ludicrous; **hacer el —** to act the fool; **poner en —** to ridicule; **ponerse en —** to make a spectacle of oneself

riego M irrigation

riel M rail

rienda F rein; **dar — suelta** to give a free hand

riesgo M risk; **correr un —** to run a risk

rifa F raffle

rifar VT to raffle

rifirrafe M free-for-all

rifle M rifle

rigidez F rigidity

rígido ADJ rigid

rigor M (exactitud) rigor; (del invierno) harshness; **en —** in reality; **de —** indispensable

riguroso ADJ rigorous; (invierno) harsh

rima F rhyme

rimar VI/VT to rhyme

rimbombante ADJ grandiose

rímel M mascara

rin M rim

rincón M corner; (lugar retirado) nook, alcove

rinconera F (mueble) corner cupboard; (mesa) corner table

ring M boxing ring

ringlera F row

rinoceronte M rhinoceros

rinoplastia F *fam* nose job

rinovirus M rhinovirus

riña F (discusión) quarrel; (pelea) scrap, fight, spat

riñón M kidney; (región lumbar) lower back

río M river; **— abajo** downstream

ripio M rubble

riqueza F wealth; **—s** riches

risa F (carcajada) laugh; (acción, sonido de reír) laughter; **reventar / desternillarse de —** to burst with laughter; **morirse de —** to die laughing; **¡qué —!** what a joke!

risco M crag, bluff

risible ADJ laughable

risita F (burlona) snicker; (ahogada) chuckle

risotada F guffaw, gale of laughter

ristra F string

risueño ADJ (sonriente) smiling; (alegre) cheerful

rítmico ADJ rhythmical

ritmo M rhythm; **— cardíaco** heart rate; **— de vida** pace of life

rito M rite

ritual ADJ & M ritual

rival ADJ & MF rival

rivalidad F rivalry

rivalizar[9] VI to rival; **— con** to compete with

rizado ADJ curly; M curling

rizar[9] VT (pelo) to curl, to crimp; (agua) to ripple

rizo M (en el pelo) curl, ringlet; (en el agua) ripple, ruffle; (hecho por un avión) loop

robar VT (algo a una persona) to rob; (dinero) to steal

roble M oak tree

robledal M oak grove

robo M (violento) robbery; (furtivo) theft; **— con allanamiento** burglary

robot M robot

robótica F robotics

robusto ADJ robust; (grueso) stout, stocky; (sólido) sturdy

roca F rock

roce M (acción de rozar) graze; (en una prenda) rub; (conflicto) brush

rociada F (acción de rociar) sprinkling, spraying; (de insultos) volley

rociar[16] VI/VT to spray, to sprinkle; (carne) to baste

rocín M nag

rocío M (del alba) dew; (en aerosol) spray, mist

rock M rock

rocoso ADJ rocky

rodada F track; (profunda) rut

rodadura F rolling

rodaja F flat round slice

rodaje M (de un coche) running; (de una película) shoot

rodar[2] VI (girar) to roll; (caer) to tumble down; (vagar) to roam; (filmar) to shoot

rodear VT (cercar) to surround; (cubrir) to wrap around; (evitar) to go around

rodeo M (desvío) detour; (modo de expresarse) circumlocution; (fiesta) rodeo

rodilla F knee; **de —s** on one's knees; **hincarse de —s** to kneel down

rodillo M (para pintar) roller; (para cocinar) rolling pin; (para caminos) road roller

rododendro M rhododendron

roedor M rodent

roer[50] VI/VT to gnaw

rogar[2,7] VT to pray, to beg, to beseech; **hacerse —** to play hard to get; **se ruega no molestar** please do not disturb

rojez F redness

rojizo ADJ reddish

rojo ADJ & M red; **al — vivo** red-hot

rollizo ADJ plump; M log

rollo M (de papel, de película, de grasa) roll;

(de árbol) log; (de cuerda) reel; (de tela) bolt; (discurso aburrido) story; (mentira) lie; (lío) mess, hassle; (relación amorosa) affair; (manuscrito) scroll; (de alambre) coil; **dar el —** to hassle

ROM M ROM

romance ADJ Romance; M (lengua románica) Romance language; (español) Spanish language; (relación amorosa) romance; (composición métrica) ballad; **en buen —** in plain language

románico ADJ (arte) Romanesque; (lengua) Romance

romano -na ADJ & MF Roman

romanticismo M (corriente literaria) romanticism; (sentimentalismo) romance

romántico -ca ADJ & MF romantic

rombo M diamond

romería F pilgrimage

romero -ra MF (persona) pilgrim; M rosemary

romo ADJ (sin punta) blunt; (sin filo) dull

romper[51] VI/VT to break; VT (relaciones) to sever; **— a** to start to; **— con** to break up with; **— el alba** to dawn; **— filas** to break ranks; **rompió las aguas / la fuente** her water broke; **de rompe y rasga** coarse; M SG **rompecabezas** jigsaw puzzle; **rompehuelgas** strikebreaker; **rompeolas** breakwater

rompible ADJ breakable

rompientes M PL surf

rompimiento M (con el pasado) break; (de una promesa) breach

rompope M *Méx* eggnog

ron M rum

roncar[6] VI to snore

roncha F (de sarampión) spot; (de mosquito) bite

ronco ADJ hoarse, raspy

ronda F (de policía) patrol, beat; (de niños) circle; (de bebidas, de negociaciones) round

rondar VT (patrullar) to patrol; (acercarse por interés) to hang around; (cantar serenatas) to serenade; **rondaba los cuarenta** she was around forty years old

ronquera F hoarseness

ronquido M snore

ronronear VI to purr

ronroneo M purr

ronzal M halter

roña F (enfermedad de plantas) scab; (sorna) mange; MF INV (tacaño) skinflint

roñoso ADJ (planta) scabby; (animal) mangy; (persona) stingy

ropa F clothing, clothes; **— blanca** linen; **— vieja** stew made from leftover meat

ropaje M apparel

ropería F checkroom

ropero M (armario) wardrobe; (cuarto) closet

roque M castle

rorro M baby

rosa F (flor) rose; (marca) blemish; **— de los vientos** mariner's compass; ADJ (rosado) rose colored, pink; (homosexual) *fam* gay

rosado ADJ (saludable) rosy; (de color de rosa) rose-colored, pink; M rosé wine

rosal M rosebush

rosario M rosary

rosbif M roast beef

rosca F (de tornillo) screw; (pan) ring-shaped roll; **pasarse de —** to go off the deep end

rostro M (cara) face; (morro) nerve

rotación F rotation

rotar VI/VT to rotate

rotativo ADJ (movimiento) rotary; (cultivos) rotating; M *Esp* newspaper

rotatorio ADJ rotary

roto ADJ broken; (cansado) exhausted; (ropa, voz) ragged

rotor M rotor

rótula F kneecap

rotular VT to label

rótulo M (título) title; (etiqueta) label

rotundo ADJ resounding; **una negativa rotunda** a categorical denial

rotura F break; (de un órgano, tubo) rupture

roturar VT to plow

round M (asalto) round

rozadura F chafing

rozamiento M friction

rozar[9] VT (herir levemente) to graze; (arañar) to scrape; (irritar) to rub, to chafe; (limpiar un terreno) to clear; **—se con alguien** to have dealings with someone; **rozaba en los cuarenta** she was almost forty years old

Ruanda F Rwanda

ruandés -esa ADJ & MF Rwandan

rubí M ruby; (en un reloj) jewel

rubicundo ADJ (permanente) ruddy; (temporal) flush

rubio -a ADJ & MF blond

rubor M blush, flush; (de las mejillas) bloom, glow

ruborizarse[9] VI to blush

rúbrica F (trazo) flourish; (título) title

rucio ADJ gray

rudeza F rudeness, coarseness

rudo ADJ rude, coarse; **— golpe** hard blow

rueca F spinning wheel

rueda F (de coche) wheel; (de personas) circle; (rodaja) slice; **— de prensa** news conference; **ir sobre —s** to be smooth sailing

ruedo M ring; (de vestido) hem

ruego M prayer, plea, entreaty

rufián M (matón) ruffian; (proxeneta) pimp

rugby M rugby

rugido M roar

rugir[11] VI to roar; (estómago) to growl

rugoso ADJ rough

ruibarbo M rhubarb

ruido M noise; **mucho — y pocas nueces** much ado about nothing

ruidoso ADJ noisy, loud

ruin ADJ (persona, cosa) vile; (animal) puny

ruina F (acción de arruinar) destruction; (edificio, estado de pobreza) ruin; (persona) wreck; (perjuicio) downfall; **en —s** in ruins

ruindad F (actitud) vileness; (acto) vile act

ruinoso ADJ ruinous

ruiseñor M nightingale

rulero M *RP* roller, curler

ruleta F roulette

rulo M roller, curler

Rumania F Romania, Rumania

rumano -na ADJ & MF Romanian, Rumanian

rumba F rumba

rumbear VI to head in a certain direction

rumbo M course, route; **— a** toward

rumiar VI (meditar) to ruminate; (reflexionar) to ruminate, to mull over, to brood over

rumor M rumor

runrún M (rumor) rumor; (sonido sordo) humming

ruptura F (de relaciones) break; (de órganos internos) rupture

rural ADJ rural

Rusia F Russia

ruso -sa ADJ & MF (persona) Russian; M (lengua) Russian

rústico ADJ (rural) rustic, rural; (tosco) coarse; **en rústica** paperback

ruta F route; (carretera) highway

rutina F routine

Ss

sábado M Saturday

sábalo M shad

sábana F bed sheet

sabañón M chilblain

saber[41] VI/VT to know; **— nadar** to know how to swim; **supo la verdad** he found

out the truth; **— a** to taste like; **— a ciencia cierta** to know for sure; **— de biología** to know all about biology; **a —** namely; **hacer —** to let know; **las vacaciones me han sabido a poco** my vacation was too short; **para que sepas** for your information; **sabe bien** it tastes good; **sabérselas todas** to know the ropes; **vaya a —** who knows? M knowledge, learning; **a mi leal — y entender** as far as I know; **sabelotodo** know-it-all

sabiduría F wisdom

sabiendas LOC ADV **a —** knowingly

sabihondo -da ADJ & MF wise guy; know-it-all

sabio -bia ADJ wise, sage; MF (estudioso) scholar; (sabedor) sage, wise person

sable M saber

sabor M taste, flavor

saborear VT to savor, to relish

sabotaje M sabotage

sabotear VT to sabotage

sabroso ADJ (comida) savory, tasty; (cuento) juicy

sabueso M (perro) bloodhound; (detective) sleuth

sacar[6] VT (cosas de la maleta, a pasear) to take out; (manchas, dinero del banco) to get out; (los zapatos) to take off; (malas notas, carnet de conducir) to get; (una copia) to make; (una foto) to take; (una conclusión) to draw; (la lengua, la cabeza por la ventana) to stick out; (una pelota de tenis) to serve; (una asignatura escolar) *Esp* to pass; **— ampollas** to blister; **— brillo** to polish up; **— provecho (de)** to benefit (from); **— a bailar** to ask to dance; **— a colación** to broach; **— a luz** to divulge; **— de un apuro** to bail out; **me saca de quicio** he gets my goat, he gets on my nerves; **— el cuerpo** to dodge; **— el mejor partido de** to make the best of; **—le el jugo a algo** to make the most of; **— en limpio** to deduce; **— el sombrero** *Am* to take off one's hat; **¡sáquese de allí!** *Am* get out of there! **— punta** to sharpen; M SG **sacabocados** punch; **sacacorchos** corkscrew; **sacamuelas** quack dentist; **sacapuntas** pencil sharpener

sacarina F saccharine

sacerdocio M priesthood

sacerdote M priest

saciar VT to satiate; **—se** to be satiated

saco M (bolsa) sack; (prenda) blazer, sport coat; (de boxeo) punching bag; **— de**

dormir sleeping bag; **— de noche** overnight bag; **echar en — roto** to waste one's effort

sacramento M sacrament

sacrificar[6] VT to sacrifice; (una mascota) to put to sleep

sacrificio M sacrifice

sacrilegio M sacrilege

sacrílego ADJ sacrilegious

sacristán M sexton

sacudida F shake, jolt; (de terremoto) tremor; (de la cabeza) toss; (eléctrica) shock

sacudir VT to shake; (las alfombras) to beat; (el polvo) to dust; **ir sacudiéndose** to rattle along, to jolt along; **—se de alguien** to get rid of someone

sádico ADJ sadistic

sadismo M sadism

sadomasoquismo M sadomasochism

saeta F arrow

safari M safari

sagaz ADJ shrewd, astute

sagrado ADJ sacred, holy; **Sagrada Escritura** Holy Scripture

sahumar VT to perfume with incense

sahumerio M burning of incense

sainete M one-act farce; **esa familia es un — that** family is a complete mess

sal F (mineral) salt; (gracia) wit; **— gorda** cooking salt; **— yodada** iodized salt; **— de mesa** table salt; **dar —** to spice up; **— y pimienta** life, spark

sala F (de estar) parlor, living room; (grande) large room; **— de justicia** courtroom; **— de clase** classroom; **— de espera** waiting room; **— de directorio** boardroom; **— de lectura** reading room; **— de operaciones** operating room

salado ADJ salty; (gracioso) witty; M (acción) salting

salamandra F salamander

salar VT to salt; **—se** to become salty

salario M pay, wages; **— base** base pay; **— mínimo** minimum wage

salchicha F sausage

saldar VT to settle

saldo M (resultado final) balance; (venta especial) sale

salegar[7] VT to give salt to; M salt lick

salero M (dispensador) saltcellar, saltshaker; (gracia) charm

saleroso ADJ charming

salida F (partida) departure; (puerta) exit, way out; (de una carrera) start; (militar) sally; (eléctrica, computadora) output; (de una crisis) way out; **este artículo tiene mucha —** this article sells well; **dar la —**

to start a race; **— del sol** sunrise; **— de emergencia** emergency exit; **— en falso** false start

saliente ADJ (roca) salient, projecting; (gobierno) outgoing; M salient, projection, overhang

salina F salt mine

salino ADJ saline

salir[42] VI (del interior al exterior, para divertirse) to go out; (de un país) to depart, to leave; (del trabajo) to quit; (manchas de tinta) to come out; (un anillo del dedo) to come off; (el sol) to rise; (una publicación) to appear; (flores) to sprout; **trabajando no se puede — de pobre** you can't work your way out of poverty; **salió a su madre** she takes after her mother; **— a la luz** to surface; **— adelante** to overcome difficulties; **— bien** to turn out well; **— con** to date; **— ganando** to come out ahead; **— mal** to go wrong; **¿a cuánto sale?** how much is it? **no me sale ser amable con él** I can't bring myself to be nice to him; **—se** (gotear) to leak; (rebosar) to overflow; (proyectarse) to stick out

saliva F saliva

salmón M salmon

salmonela F salmonella

salmuera F brine

salobre ADJ salty

salomonense ADJ & MF Solomon Islander

salón M (de estar) living room, parlor; (de conferencias) hall; **— de belleza** beauty parlor; **— de clase** classroom; **— de exposición y ventas** showroom; **— de exhibición** exhibition hall; **— de té** tearoom

salpicadero M dashboard

salpicadura F spatter, splash, splatter

salpicar[6] VI/VT to sprinkle, to spatter, to splash; (adornar) to punctuate; (dispersar) to intersperse

salpicón M meat salad

salpimentar[1] VT to salt and pepper

salsa F sauce; **en su —** in her element; **— tártara** tartar sauce; **— de soya** soy sauce; **— de tomate** ketchup

saltar VI (brincar) to jump, to leap; (cinco metros) to jump; (una cerca) to jump over, to vault; (un renglón) to skip; VT (los fusibles) to trip; (una ley) to ignore; **— a la vista** to be obvious; **— sobre** to pounce on; **se le saltaron los ojos** his eyes bugged out; **se le saltó un botón** one of his buttons popped off; **se me saltaban las lágrimas** it brought tears

to my eyes; M SG **saltamontes**
grasshopper

salteador -ora MF bandit

saltear VT to stir-fry

salto M jump, leap; **—** **de agua** waterfall; **a
— de mata** from hand to mouth; **—** **de
cama** dressing gown; **dar un —** (saltar)
to jump; (el corazón) to skip a beat; **—
alto** high jump; **— con esquí** ski jump;
— con pértiga pole vault; **— de
longitud** broad jump; **— del ángel**
swan dive; **— mortal** somersault; **—
triple** triple jump

saltón ADJ jumping; (ojo) bulging; M
grasshopper

salubridad F sanitation

salud F health; **— mental** mental health;
curarse en — to take precautions; INTERJ
cheers!

saludable ADJ healthy, healthful

saludar VT (decir hola) to greet; (recibir bien)
to salute, to hail; (en el militar) to salute;
(hacer un gesto amistoso con la mano) to
wave

saludo M (hola) greeting, salutation; (gesto)
wave; (militar) salute; **retirar el — a
alguien** to stop speaking to someone; **—s**
best wishes, regards

salva F salvo

salvación F salvation

salvado M bran

salvador -ora MF savior; ADJ saving

salvadoreño -ña ADJ & MF Salvador(i)an

salvaguarda F safeguard

salvaguardar VT to safeguard

salvajada F (acción) savage act; (comentario)
savage remark

salvaje ADJ (feroz) savage; (no domesticado)
wild; MF savage

salvajismo M savagery

salvamento M (de gente) rescue; (de
propiedad) salvage

salvar VT (la vida, el alma) to save; (de un
peligro) to rescue; (propiedad) to salvage;
(un obstáculo) to clear; (un camino difícil)
to negotiate; **— el pellejo** to save one's
skin; **el puente salva el río** the bridge
spans the river; **—se** to pull through; **—se
por poco** to have a narrow escape;
sálvese quien pueda every man for
himself; M SG **salvavidas** (aparato) life
preserver, life jacket; MF (persona)
lifeguard

salvia F sage

salvo ADJ safe; **a —** safe; **—conducto** safe-
conduct; PREP save, except; **— en caso de
desastre** barring a disaster

Samoa F Samoa

samoano -na ADJ & MF Samoan

sanar VI/VT to heal; M **sanalotodo** cure-all

sanatorio M (para convalecientes)
sanitarium; (hospital) hospital

sanción F sanction

sancionar VT to sanction

sandalia F sandal

sandez F (acción) stupidity, foolishness;
(dicho) foolish remark

sandía F watermelon

saneamiento M sanitation

sanear VT to drain

sangrar VI/VT to bleed; VT (un árbol) to tap;
(un párrafo) to indent

sangre F blood; **— fría** coolness under
pressure; **a — fría** in cold blood; **hacerse
mala —** to get upset; **eso lo llevo en la
—** that's in my blood; **de — caliente**
warm-blooded; **— azul** blue blood; **sudar
—** to sweat bullets; **de pura —**
thoroughbred; **chupar la — a alguien**
to be a parasite on someone

sangría F (bebida) wine punch; (acción de
sangrar) bleeding; (espacio tipográfico)
indentation; (pérdida de recursos) drain

sangriento ADJ (manchado de sangre, que
provoca la pérdida de sangre) bloody;
(sanguinario) bloodthirsty

sanguijuela F leech

sanguinario ADJ bloody, vicious

sanidad F public health

sanitario ADJ sanitary; M **—s** bathroom
fittings

sanmarinense ADJ & MF San Marinese

sanmarinés -esa ADJ & MF San Marinese

sano ADJ (persona) healthy; (juicio) sound;
(dieta) healthful; (vaso) unbroken; **— y
salvo** safe and sound; **en su — juicio** of
sound mind

sánscrito M Sanskrit

sanseacabó INTERJ **te quedas y —** you're
staying and that's that

santalucense ADJ & MF St. Lucian

santiamén LOC ADV **en un —** in a jiffy,
lickety-split

santidad F sanctity, holiness

santificar[6] VT to sanctify

santiguarse[8] VI to cross oneself

santo -ta ADJ saintly, holy; **esperar todo el
— día** to wait the whole blessed day; MF
saint; **día del —** saint's day; **quedarse
para vestir —s** to be a spinster; **¿a — de
qué?** for what reason? **¡por todos los
—s!** my goodness!

santotomense ADJ & MF São Tomean

santuario M sanctuary

santurrón -ona ADJ & MF goody-goody
saña F fury
sañudo ADJ furious
sapo M toad (también hombre); **echar —s y culebras** to swear, to curse; **sentirse como un — de otro pozo** to feel like a fish out of water
saque M tennis serve, tennis service
saquear VT to sack, to plunder, to pillage
saqueo M sacking, plundering, pillaging
sarampión M measles
sarape M *Méx* serape
sarcasmo M sarcasm
sarcástico ADJ sarcastic
sarcófago M sarcophagus
sarcoma M sarcoma
sardina F sardine
sardo -da ADJ & MF Sardinian
sardónico ADJ sardonic
sargento -ta MF sergeant; F battle-ax(e)
sarmentoso ADJ gnarled
sarmiento M vine
sarna F mange
sarnoso ADJ mangy
sarpullido M rash
sarro M tartar, plaque
sarta F string
sartén F frying pan, skillet
sastre -tra MF tailor
sastrería F tailor shop
satánico ADJ satanic
satélite M satellite; **— artificial** man-made satellite
satén M satin
sátira F satire
satírico ADJ satirical
satirizar[9] VT to satirize
satisfacción F satisfaction
satisfacer[30, 51] VT to satisfy; (una deuda) to pay; **—se** to be satisfied
satisfactorio ADJ satisfactory
satisfecho ADJ contented, satisfied
saturar VT to saturate; (un mercado) to glut; (líneas de teléfono) to overload
sauce M willow; **— llorón** weeping willow
saudí, saudita ADJ & MF Saudi Arabian
savia F sap
saxofón M saxophone
sazón F season; **a la —** at that time; **en —** ripe
sazonar VT (condimentar) to season, to flavor; (llegar a su sazón) to ripen
scooter M scooter
scout MF scout
se PRON PERS **— coronó a sí mismo** he crowned himself; **— lavó la cara** he washed his face; **— besaron** they kissed

each other; **— habla español** Spanish is spoken; **— lo puede combatir** it can be fought
sebo M tallow, fat
secador M hair dryer
secadora F clothes dryer
secante ADJ drying
secar[6] VT to dry; (las manos) to dry off; **—se** (planta) to dry up; (río) to run dry; (madera) to season
sección F (militar) platoon; (de un almacén) department
seccionar VT to section
seco ADJ dry; (río) dried-up; (planta) withered; (respuesta) curt, brief; **en —** on dry land; **parar en —** to stop short; **quedar —** to fall dead; **estar —** to be broke; **lavar en —** to dry-clean; **a secas** plain
secreción F secretion
secretar VT to secrete
secretaría F secretariat
secretariado M (profesión) secretarial profession; (secretaría) secretariat; (conjunto de secretarias) secretarial pool
secretario -ria MF secretary; **— general** secretary general
secretear VI to whisper
secreto ADJ secret; (de policía sin uniforme) undercover; M (cosa oculta) secret; (condición de oculto) secrecy; **— a voces** open secret; **en —** in secret; **— bancario** client confidentiality
secta F sect
sector M sector
secuaz M henchman
secuela F consequence; **—s** aftermath
secuencia F sequence
secuenciar VT to sequence
secuestrador -ora MF kidnapper
secuestrar VT (a una persona) to kidnap, to abduct; (propiedad) to seize; (un avión) to hijack
secuestro M (de una persona) kidnapping; (de propiedad) seizure; (de un avión) hijacking
secular ADJ secular
secundar VT to second; (imitar) to imitate; (seguir) to follow suit
secundaria F secondary school
secundario ADJ secondary
sed F thirst; **tener —** to be thirsty
seda F silk; **como una —** (suave) soft as silk; (afable) sweet-tempered
sedación F sedation
sedán M sedan
sedante ADJ & M sedative
sedar VT to sedate

sedativo ADJ & M sedative
sede F (gubernamental) seat; (religiosa) see
sedentario ADJ sedentary
sedería F (conjunto de artículos de seda) silk goods; (tienda de sedas) silk shop
sedero -ra MF (que vende) silk dealer; (que fabrica) silk weaver; ADJ **industria sedera** silk industry
sedición F sedition
sediento ADJ thirsty; **estar — de** to thirst for
sedimento M sediment
sedoso ADJ silken, silky
seducción F seduction
seducir[24] VT (corromper) to seduce; (atraer) to entice; (persuadir con argucias) to lure
seductivo ADJ alluring
seductor -ora ADJ alluring; M seducer; F seductress
sefardí ADJ Sephardic; MF Sephardi; M (variedad del español) Sephardi
sefardita ADJ & MF Sephardi
segador -ora MF (persona) mower, reaper; F (máquina) mower, reaper
segar[1,7] VT (hierba) to mow; (mies) to reap
seglar ADJ secular; M layman; F laywoman
segmento M segment
segregar[7] VT (separar) to segregate; (producir una sustancia) to secrete
seguida LOC ADV **en —** at once, immediately
seguido ADJ in a row; **dos horas seguidas** two hours in a row; ADV straight through; **trabajaron —** they worked continuously
seguidor -ora MF follower
seguimiento M (persecución) pursuit; (atención continuada) follow-up
seguir[5,12] VT to follow; (estudios) to pursue; (progreso de un avión) to track; **sigue trabajando** he keeps on working; **sigue allí** he is still there; **de lo anterior se sigue que** from the preceding it follows that; **— los pasos de** to follow in the footsteps of; **—le la corriente a alguien** to play along with someone; **— el tren** to keep up; **— el hilo de** to keep track of; **— la pista de** to trail
según PREP according to; **— se mire** depending on how you see it; **— pasa el tiempo** as time goes by; **— tus instrucciones** per your instructions; CONJ as; **lo haré — me digas** I will do it as you tell me to
segundero M (de reloj) second hand
segundo -da ADV, ADJ & M second; **segunda intención** ulterior motive; **de —** second-rate; **de segunda mano** secondhand; MF second in command
segundón -ona MF (hijo) second-born child;

(persona mediocre) also-ran
seguridad F (contra el delito) security; (contra accidentes) safety; **— en sí mismo** self-confidence; **— social** social security
seguro ADJ (a prueba de delincuencia) secure; (que no ofrece, siente duda) sure, certain; (libre de peligro) safe; (firme) stable; **es — que** it is certain that; **su — servidor** yours truly; **— de sí mismo** self-assured; M (contrato contra riesgos) insurance; (dispositivo) safety device, restraint; **— contra daños a terceros** liability insurance; **— contra incendios** fire insurance; **— contra todo riesgo** comprehensive insurance; **— médico** health insurance; **— de vida** life insurance; **en —** in safety; **sobre —** without risk
seis NUM six
selección F selection, choice; **— natural** natural selection; **— nacional** national team
seleccionar VT to select, to choose
selectivo ADJ selective
selecto ADJ select, choice
sellar VT (poner sello) to stamp; (precintar) to seal
sello M (de correo) stamp; (de documento oficial) seal; (instrumento) seal, stamp; (de discos) label; **— de goma** rubber stamp; **— fiscal** revenue stamp
selva F forest; (tropical) jungle; **— virgen** virgin forest
semáforo M traffic light
semana F week; **entre —** during the week
semanal ADJ weekly
semanario M weekly publication
semántica F semantics
semblante M countenance
semblanza F biographical sketch
sembrado M sown ground
sembradora F planting machine
sembrar[1] VT (plantar) to sow, to plant; (esparcir) to scatter; (minas) to lay; (pánico, alegría) to spread
semejante ADJ similar, like; **— afirmación** such a statement; **un tipo —** such a guy; MF fellow human being
semejanza F resemblance, similarity; **a — de** in the manner of
semejar VT to resemble
semen M semen, sperm
semental ADJ stud; M stud, stallion
semestre M semester
semicírculo M semicircle
semiconductor M semiconductor

semifinal ADJ & F semifinal
semilla F seed
semillero M seedbed; **— de vicios** hotbed of vice
seminario M (religioso) seminary; (universitario) seminar
semítico ADJ Semitic
senado M senate
senador -ora MF senator
sencillez F simplicity
sencillo ADJ (no complicado, de clase humilde) simple; (fácil) easy, simple; (sin adornos) plain; (no afectado) straightforward
senda F (construida) path, pathway; (natural) track, trail
sendero M (construido) path, pathway; (natural) track, trail
sendos ADJ one for each
Senegal M Senegal
senegalés -esa ADJ & MF Senegalese
senil ADJ senile
senilidad F senility
seno M (pecho) breast; (hueco) sinus; (útero) womb; **— de la familia** bosom of the family
sensación F (física) sensation; (mental) feeling, impression; **tengo la — de que** I have the feeling that; **fue la — de la fiesta** she was the life of the party
sensacional ADJ sensational
sensatez F common sense
sensato ADJ sensible, level-headed
sensibilidad F (modo de pensar) sensibility; (percepción) sensitiveness
sensibilizar[9] VT to sensitize
sensible ADJ sensitive; (notable) perceptible; **tengo el brazo muy — por el accidente** my arm is very tender because of the accident; **Juana es muy — en estas ocasiones** Juana is very emotional on these occasions
sensiblería F sentimentality
sensiblero ADJ sentimental, mushy
sensitivo ADJ sensitive
sensor M sensor
sensorial ADJ sensory
sensual ADJ (carnal) sensual; (de los sentidos) sensuous
sensualidad F sensuality
sentada F sitting; (protesta) sit-in; **de una —** at one sitting
sentado ADJ **dar por —** to take for granted
sentar[1] VT to seat; **— bien** to agree with; **me sentó muy mal lo que dijo** what he said did not sit well with me; **este peinado no te sienta** this hairdo does

not become you; **no te sienta ese traje** that suit does not fit you; **— precedente** to set a precedent; **—se** to sit down
sentencia F maxim; (fallo) ruling; (condena) sentence; (indemnización) award
sentenciar VT (condenar) to sentence; (fallar) to rule
sentido ADJ heartfelt; M (facultad) sense; (significado) meaning; (dirección) way; **— común** common sense; **aguzar el —** to prick up one's ears; **de un sólo —** one-way; **de dos —s** two-way; **dejar sin —** to render unconscious; **en cierto —** in a sense; **perder el —** to faint; **quedar —** to have one's feelings hurt; **sin —** meaningless; **tener —** to make sense
sentimental ADJ sentimental
sentimentalismo M sentimentality
sentimiento M feeling, sentiment
sentir[3] VT to feel; (oír) to hear; (lamentar) to regret; **—se** to feel; **—se capaz de** to feel up to; **—se de los pies** to have pains in the feet
seña F (gesto) sign; (rasgo) trait; (marca) mark; **—s** name and address; **por mas —s** as an additional proof; **—s de vida** life signs; **hablar por —s** to use sign language; **hacer —s** to signal
señal F (de tráfico, violencia, vida, de la cruz) sign; (de violencia) mark; (de radio) signal; (pago anticipado) deposit; **en — de** in token of
señalar VT (marcar, señalar) to mark; (mostrar, mencionar) to point out; (fijar) to fix; **—se** to distinguish oneself
señor M (título) mister; (forma de tratamiento) sir; (dueño) lit master, lord; **el Señor** the Lord; **un gran —** a great man
señora F (dama) lady; (forma de tratamiento) madam, ma'am; (título) Mrs., Ms.; (esposa) wife
señorear VI to dominate
señoría F lordship; **su —** your honor
señorial ADJ lordly
señorío M (dominio) dominion; (dignidad) lordship
señorita F miss
señorito M (joven) master; (dandi) dandy
señuelo M decoy, lure
separación F separation
separado ADJ (apartado) separate; (estado civil) separated; **por —** separately
separar VT to separate; (clasificar) to sort out; (despedir de un cargo) to remove; **—se** to separate, to part company
separata F offprint, reprint

septentrional ADJ northern

septicemia F blood poisoning

septiembre, setiembre M September

séptimo ADJ & M seventh

sepulcro M tomb

sepultar VT to bury, to inter

sepultura F (acción) burial; (lugar) grave, tomb; **dar —** to bury

sepulturero -ra MF gravedigger

sequedad F dryness

sequía F drought

séquito M retinue, entourage

ser[43] VI to be; **— de Valencia** to be from Valencia; **— de madera** to be made of wood; **a no — que** unless; **así es** that's right; **érase una vez** once upon a time; **es decir** that is to say; **es de esperar** it is to be expected; **es más** what's more; **la boda es hoy** the wedding takes place today; **son las nueve** it is nine o'clock; **somos cuatro** there are four of us; V AUX to be; **fue elegido presidente** he was elected president; M (entidad viviente) being; (esencia) essence; (existencia) existence; **un — humano** a human being

serenar VI to quiet; **—se** (el alma) to become serene, to calm down; (el tiempo) to clear up

serenata F serenade; **dar —** to serenade

serenidad F serenity

sereno ADJ (mar, alma) serene; (cielo) clear; **al —** in the night air; M night watchman

serie F series; **en —** serial

seriedad F seriousness, earnestness

serio ADJ serious; (persona) earnest, serious; **en —** seriously

sermón M (prédica) sermon; (reprimenda) lecture

sermonear VI/VT (predicar) to preach; (reprender) to lecture

serpentear VI to wind, to meander

serpiente F snake

serrado ADJ serrated

serranía F mountainous region

serrano -na M mountain man; F mountain woman; ADJ **zona —** mountain region

serrín M sawdust

serrucho M handsaw

servicial ADJ helpful

servicio M service; (sirvientes) servants; (para un comensal) place setting; (aseo) rest room, facilities; **— militar** military service; **— de entrega** delivery service; **— a la habitación** room service; **poner en —** to commission, to put into service; **estar en —** to be in commission; **a su —** at your service

servidor -ora MF (persona) servant; **un —** yours truly; **su seguro —** yours truly; M (ordenador) server

servidumbre F servitude

servil ADJ (personalidad) servile; (trabajo) menial

servilleta F napkin

servir[5] VI to serve; **— de** to serve as; **— para** to be used for; **para —le** at your service; **no — para nada** to be of no use; **¿en qué le puedo —?** how can I help you? **—se de** to make use of; **sírvase usted hacerlo** please do it

sésamo M sesame; **¡abre —!** open sesame!

sesenta NUM sixty

sesgado ADJ biased

sesgar[7] VT (una tela) to cut on the bias; (una opinión) to slant; (las estadísticas) to skew

sesgo M (en la tela) bias; (de los ojos, de orientación) slant; **al —** obliquely

sesión F (reunión, periodo) session; (para fotografías) sitting; (de una película) showing

seso M brain; **de poco —** foolish; **devanarse los —s** to rack one's brain

sestear VI to take a nap

sesudo ADJ (persona) brainy; (explicación) intelligent; (testarudo) *Méx* stubborn

set M set

seta F mushroom

setenta NUM seventy

seto M hedge

sétter M setter

seudónimo M pseudonym, pen name

severidad F severity, harshness

severo ADJ severe, stern, harsh

sexar VT to sex

sexismo M sexism

sexo M sex; (órganos) genitals; **el — bello** the fair sex; **— seguro** safe sex

sexto ADV, ADJ & M sixth

sexual ADJ sexual

sexualidad F sexuality

sexy ADJ sexy

Seychelles F PL Seychelles

shock M shock

short, shorts M shorts

si CONJ if; **yo voy — tú vas** I'm going if you're going; **no sé — viene o no** I don't know whether she's coming or not; **¡— ya te lo dije!** but I already told you! **— bien** although; **por — acaso** just in case; **— Dios quiere** God willing; **— no me equivoco** unless I'm mistaken

sí ADV yes; **¿—?** really? **— que fui** I did go; **creo que —** I think so; M consent; **me dio el —** she said yes; PRON himself, herself, itself, oneself, themselves; **de por** — in itself; **estar sobre** — to be on the alert; **volver en** — to come to; **pagado de** — self-satisfied; **estar fuera de** — to be beside oneself; **hablar para** — to talk to oneself; **dio todo de** — she gave her all; **cada cual para** — every man for himself

sicario M hitman

sicomoro M sycamore

SIDA (síndrome de inmunodeficiencia adquirida) M AIDS

siderurgia F steel industry

sidra F cider

siega F (de la hierba) mowing; (de las mieses) reaping

siembra F (acción de sembrar) sowing; (época) sowing time

siempre ADV always; **desde** — since forever; **para / por** — forever; **por** — **jamás** forevermore; — **que** (en cualquier momento) whenever; (con tal que) provided that; — **y cuando** provided that; **como** — as usual; **hoy no eres el mismo de** — you're not yourself today

sien F temple

sierpe F *lit* serpent

sierra F saw; (cordillera) small mountain range; — **de cadena** chain saw

siesta F siesta, afternoon nap; **dormir la** — to take an afternoon nap

siete NUM seven

sífilis F syphilis

sifón M (para líquidos) siphon; (tubo) trap

sigilo M stealth

sigla F acronym

siglo M century

signatario -ria MF signer

significación F (sentido) meaning; (importancia) significance

significado M meaning, sense

significar[6] VT to mean, to signify

significativo ADJ significant

signo M sign; — **de admiración** exclamation point; — **de igual** equal sign; — **de interrogación** question mark; — **de más** plus sign; — **de menos** minus sign; — **de multiplicación** multiplication sign; —**s vitales** vital signs

siguiente ADJ following; **al día** — the next day

sílaba F syllable

silbar VI to whistle; (rechiflar) to hiss

silbato M whistle

silbido M whistle

silenciador M (de arma) silencer; (de coche) muffler

silenciar VT to silence

silencio M silence, quiet; **guardar** — to keep quiet

silencioso ADJ silent, quiet

silicio M silicon

silla F chair; (de montar) saddle; — **de ruedas** wheelchair; — **eléctrica** electric chair; — **plegadiza** folding chair

sillín M saddle, seat

sillón M armchair

silo M silo

silogismo M syllogism

silueta F silhouette

siluro M catfish

silvestre ADJ wild

silvicultura F forestry

sima F chasm

simbiosis F symbiosis

simbólico ADJ symbolic

simbolismo M symbolism

símbolo M symbol; — **de status** status symbol; — **sexual** sex symbol

simetría F symmetry

simétrico ADJ symmetrical

simiente F seed

símil M simile

similar ADJ similar

simio M ape

simpatía F friendliness; **no le tengo mucha** — I don't like him much

simpático ADJ (amistoso) nice, friendly, congenial; (sistema nervioso) sympathetic

simpatizar[9] VI (con alguien) to like; (con una idea) to be sympathetic toward

simple ADJ (no complicado) simple; (mero) mere; (tonto) simpleminded

simpleza F (sencillez) simplicity; (estupidez) stupidity

simplicidad F simplicity

simplificar[6] VT to simplify

simplista ADJ simplistic; (explicación) glib, simplistic

simplón -ona ADJ simpleminded; MF simpleton

simposio M symposium

simulacro M — **de batalla** mock battle; — **de incendio** fire drill

simular VT to simulate, to feign

simultáneo ADJ simultaneous

sin PREP without; — **aliento** out of breath; — **amueblar** unfurnished; — **azúcar** sugar-free; — **comentarios** no comment; — **compromiso** without obligation; — **duda** without doubt, undoubtedly; — **embargo** nevertheless; — **escrúpulos** unscrupulous; — **falta** without fail; — **sentido** meaningless

sinagoga F synagogue
sincerarse VI to clear the air
sinceridad F sincerity
sincero ADJ sincere; (opinión) candid; (agradecimiento) heartfelt, wholehearted
sincronización F timing
sincronizar[9] VT to synchronize
sindicar[6] VT to unionize, to syndicate
sindicato M syndicate, trade union, labor union
síndico -ca MF receiver, trustee
síndrome M syndrome; **— de Down** Down's syndrome; **— de abstinencia** withdrawal symptoms
sinfín M **un — de cosas** a lot of things
sinfonía F symphony
Singapur M Singapore
singapurense ADJ & MF Singaporean
singular ADJ (número) singular; (excepcional) unique
siniestro ADJ sinister; M disaster
sinnúmero M myriad
sino CONJ but; **no vino — que llamó** she didn't come, but instead called; **no tengo dos — tres** I don't have two but three; **no es — madera** it's only wood
sinónimo ADJ synonymous; M synonym
sinopsis F synopsis
sinrazón F injustice
sinsabor M trouble
sinsonte M mockingbird
sintaxis F syntax
síntesis F synthesis
sintético ADJ synthetic; (fibras) man-made
sintetizar[9] VT to synthesize
síntoma M symptom
sintonía F tuning
sintonizador M tuner
sintonizar[9] VT (una emisora) to tune in; (un sintonizador) to fine-tune; **los dos sintonizan bien** the two are on the same wavelength
sinuoso ADJ (camino) sinuous, winding; (comportamiento) devious
sinvergüenza MF creep
siquiera ADV at least; **dame — unos días** give me a few days at least; **ni —** not even
sirena F (ninfa, bocina) siren; (mitad mujer, mitad pez) mermaid
Siria F Syria
sirio -ria ADJ & MF Syrian
sirviente -ta MF servant
sisar VT to pilfer, to swipe
sisear VI to hiss
siseo M hiss, hissing
sísmico ADJ seismic

sistema M system; **— operativo** operating system; **— binario** binary system; **— mundial de posicionamiento** global positioning system; **— experto** expert system; **— inmune** immune system; **— nervioso central** central nervous system; **— solar** solar system
sistemático ADJ systematic
sistematizar[9] VI/VT to systematize
sistémico ADJ systemic
sitial M seat of honor
sitiar VT to besiege
sitio M (espacio vacío) room; (ubicación) place, site; (asedio) siege; **no hay —** there's no room; **esto no está en su —** this is out of place; **— web** website; **poner — a** to lay siege to; **poner a alguien en su —** to put someone in his place
sito ADJ situated
situación F situation; (legal, financiero, social) status
situado ADJ situated; **estar —** to be located
situar[17] VT to locate, to place; **—se** to be located
sketch M sketch, skit
slalom M slalom
smog M smog
smoking M dinner jacket
so PREP **— pena de** under penalty of; **— pretexto de** under the pretext of; INTERJ whoa; ADV **— tonto** you stupid idiot!
sobaco M armpit
sobar VT (la masa) to knead; (a una persona) to fondle; (un traje) to wear out
soberanía F sovereignty
soberano -na ADJ & MF sovereign
soberbia F pride, haughtiness
soberbio ADJ proud, haughty
sobornar VT to bribe
soborno M (acción) bribery; (mordida) bribe
sobra F surplus; **—s** leftovers, leavings; **de —** sabes you know full well; **está de —** it is superfluous; **las piezas de —** spare parts
sobrado ADJ more than enough
sobrante ADJ leftover; M surplus
sobrar VI (dinero, libros) to be left over, to remain; (personas) to be in the way
sobre PREP (encima de) above, over; (en contacto con) on, upon; (acerca de) about; **un préstamo — su coche** a loan on his car; **— todo** above all; **— las 9:30** at about 9:30; **marchar — Madrid** to march toward Madrid; M (para cartas) envelope; (de sopa) packet; **— manila** manila envelope; **irse al —** to hit the sack

sobreactuar[17] VI to ham it up
sobrealimentador M supercharger
sobrecalificado ADJ overqualified
sobrecarga F overload
sobrecargar[7] VT to overload
sobrecogedor ADJ awesome
sobrecoger[11b] VI/VT to awe; **—se** to be in awe; **—se de pánico** to be panic-stricken
sobrecogimiento M awe
sobredosis F overdose
sobreentenderse[1] VI to be understood
sobreentendido ADJ understood; M assumption
sobreexcitado ADJ overexcited, wired
sobreexcitar VT to overexcite
sobregirar VT to overdraw
sobregiro M overdraft
sobrehumano ADJ superhuman
sobrellevar VT to bear, to endure
sobremanera ADV beyond measure
sobremesa F after-dinner conversation
sobrenadar VI to float
sobrenatural ADJ supernatural
sobrenombre M nickname
sobrepasar VT to exceed
sobrepeso M overweight
sobreponerse[39] VT to superimpose; VI **— a** (valer más que) to outweigh; (recuperarse) to get over
sobreproteger[11b] VT to smother
sobrepujar VT to surpass
sobresaliente ADJ outstanding; MF understudy
sobresalir[42] VI (ser notable) to stand out; (estar en un plano más saliente) to project, to jut out; (ser excelente) to excel
sobresaltar VT to startle, frighten; **—se** to be startled, to start
sobresalto M start, scare
sobrestante M foreman
sobresueldo M extra pay
sobretodo M overcoat
sobrevenir[47] VI to happen unexpectedly
sobrevivencia F survival
sobreviviente MF survivor; ADJ surviving
sobrevivir VI/VT to survive
sobriedad F sobriety
sobrino -na M nephew; **— nieto** great-nephew; F niece
sobrio ADJ sober
socarrar VT to singe
socarrón ADJ sarcastic
socarronería F sarcasm
socavar VT (excavar por debajo) to dig under; (debilitar) to undermine, to undercut
socavón M sinkhole; shaft, tunnel
sociable ADJ sociable, gregarious

social ADJ social
socialismo M socialism
socialista ADJ & MF socialist
socializar[9] VT to socialize
sociedad F society; (firma) company, partnership; **— anónima** corporation; **— de consumo** consumer society; **alta —** high society
socio -ia MF (de una firma) partner; (de un club) member
socioeconómico ADJ socioeconomic
sociología F sociology
sociópata MF INV sociopath
socorrer VT to help
socorro INTERJ & M help; **acudir al — de** to go to the rescue of; **pedir —** to cry out for help
soda F soda
sodio M sodium
sodomía F sodomy
soez ADJ vulgar
sofá M sofa, couch; **—-cama** sleeper, sofa bed
sofisma M fallacy
sofisticado ADJ sophisticated
sofocante ADJ suffocating, oppressive
sofocar[6] VI/VT to suffocate; (una rebelión) to quash, to quell, to suppress; (un incendio) to put out
sofoco M suffocation
softball M softball
software M software
soga F rope; **estar con la — al cuello** to have a rope around one's neck
soja F (planta) soy; (semilla) soybean
sojuzgar[7] VT to subjugate, to subdue
sol M sun; **de — a —** from sunrise to sunset; **hace —** it is sunny; **tomar el —** to sunbathe; **ella es un —** she's a gem; **arrimarse al — que más calienta** to know which side one's bread is buttered on
solamente ADV only
solana F sunny place
solapa F lapel
solapado ADJ underhanded
solar M (terreno) lot; (casa ancestral) manor; ADJ solar
solaz M lit recreation
soldado M soldier; **— raso** private; **— de línea** regular soldier
soldador M soldering iron
soldadura F (acción, con estaño) soldering; (resultado) solder; (acción, sin estaño) welding; (resultado) weld; **— autógena** arc welding
soldar[2] VI/VT (con estaño) to solder; (sin

estaño) to weld; **—se** to mend

soleado ADJ sunny

solear VT to put in the sun; **—se** to sun oneself

soledad F solitude, loneliness

solemne ADJ solemn; **— disparate** downright foolishness

solemnidad F solemnity

solenoide M solenoid

soler[2,50] VI **suelo levantarme a las siete** I usually get up at seven; **solía acostarme tarde** I used to go to bed late

solferino ADJ reddish-purple

solicitante MF applicant

solicitar VT (permiso) to request; (un puesto, una beca) to apply for

solícito ADJ solicitous

solicitud F (para beca, puesto) application; (de información, permiso) request; **a — de** at the request of

solidaridad F solidarity

solidez F solidity

solidificar[6] VT to solidify

sólido ADJ solid; (mueble) sturdy; (argumento) strong; M solid

solista MF soloist

solitario -ria ADJ solitary; MF (persona) recluse; M (juego de cartas, brillante) solitaire; F tapeworm

sollozar[9] VI to sob

sollozo M sob

solo ADJ (desamparado) lonely, lonesome; (no acompañado) alone; **tengo un — coche** I only have one car; **a solas** alone; **habla solo** he talks to himself; **ni una sola palabra** not a single word; M solo

sólo ADV just, only; **— quiero saber** I just / only want to know

solomillo M sirloin

solsticio M solstice

soltar[2] VT (a un prisionero) to let go, to release; (el vientre) to loosen; (una carcajada) to let out; (bombas) to drop; (un disparate) to say; **— amarras** to cast off; **— el hervor** to come to a boil; **— tacos** to swear; **—se** to loosen up; **—se el pelo** to kick up one's heels

soltero -ra ADJ single, unmarried; M bachelor; F unmarried woman

solterón -ona M old bachelor; F *pey* spinster

soltura F ease; **hablar con —** to speak fluently

soluble ADJ soluble

solución F solution

solucionar VT to solve

solventar VT to settle

solvente ADJ & M solvent

somalí ADJ & MF Somalian

Somalia F Somalia

sombra F (de una figura) shadow; (protección del sol) shade; (para ojos) eye shadow; **hacer —** to overshadow; **dar —** to shade; **no fiarse ni de su propia —** to be scared of one's own shadow; **a la —** in the shade; **sin — de duda** without a shadow of a doubt

sombreado ADJ (con protección del sol) shady; (oscuro) shadowy

sombrear VT to shade

sombrerería F millinery

sombrerero -ra MF milliner

sombrero M hat; **— de copa** top hat; **— hongo** derby

sombrilla F parasol

sombrío ADJ (oscuro) dark; (triste) somber, gloomy

somero ADJ shallow

someter VT (proponer algo) to submit; (poner bajo dominio) to subject; **—se a** to undergo

sometimiento M (proposición) submission; (dominio) subjection

somnífero M sleeping pill

somnolencia F drowsiness, sleepiness

somnoliento ADJ drowsy

son LOC ADV **al — de** to the sound of; **venimos en — de paz** we come in peace

sonaja F rattle

sonajero M rattle

sonámbulo -la MF sleepwalker

sonar[2] VI (hacer un sonido) to sound; (mencionarse) to be mentioned; (ser familiar) to sound familiar; **— a** to sound like; VT (bocina) to sound; (tambor) to beat; (campana, timbre) to ring; **—se la nariz / los mocos** to blow one's nose; **suena que** it is rumored that; M sonar

sonda F (de médico) catheter; (cohete) probe; **tirar una —** to sound

sondear VT (medir la oportunidad) to sound, to fathom; (investigar la opinión) to sound out

sondeo M survey

soneto M sonnet

sonido M sound

sonoro ADJ sonorous

sonreír[15] VI to smile

sonriente ADJ smiling

sonrisa F smile

sonrojarse VI to blush

sonrojo M blush, flush

sonrosado ADJ rosy

sonsacar[6] VT to extract

soñador -ora MF dreamer

soñar[2] VI/VT to dream; **— con / en** to dream of; **— despierto** to daydream; **— que** to dream that; **ni —** *fam* fat chance

soñoliento ADJ sleepy

sopa F (líquido) soup; (pan mojado) sop; **estar hecho una —** to be sopping wet; **— crema** cream soup

sopapo M smack

sopera F soup tureen

sopesar VT to weigh

sopetón LOC ADV **de —** all of a sudden

soplador -ora MF blower

soplar VI/VT to blow; (la sopa) to blow on; (en un examen) to whisper; (a un amante) to steal

soplete M blowtorch

soplo M breath, puff; **en un —** in a jiffy; **— cardíaco** heart murmur

soplón -ona MF informer, snitch, stool pigeon

sopor M lethargy

soportar VT (apoyar) to support, to bear; (aguantar) to stand, to endure

soporte M support; (de una bicicleta) kickstand

soprano M (voz) soprano; F (cantante) soprano

sorber VI/VT to sip; **—se los mocos** to sniffle

sorbete M sherbet

sorbo M sip; **de un —** in one gulp

sordera F deafness

sórdido ADJ sordid, tawdry, sleazy

sordina F mute

sordo -da ADJ (que no oye) deaf; (dolor) dull; (sonido) dull, muffled; **hacerse oídos —s** to turn a deaf ear; MF deaf person; **hacerse el —** to pretend not to hear

sordomudo -da ADJ deaf and dumb; MF deaf-mute

sorna F irony

sorprendente ADJ surprising, startling

sorprender VT to surprise; **—se** to be surprised

sorpresa F surprise; **— de cumpleaños** party favor; **para mi —** to my surprise; **pillar por —** to catch by surprise

sortear VT (elegir al azar) to draw lots, to raffle; (esquivar) to dodge

sorteo M drawing, raffle

sortija F (anillo) ring; (de pelo) ringlet

sortilegio M spell, charm

SOS M SOS

sosa F soda

sosegado ADJ composed, sedate

sosegar[1,7] VT to calm, to quiet; **—se** to quiet down, to compose oneself

sosiego M quiet, calm

soslayo LOC ADV **de —** oblique, slanting; **mirar de —** to look at out of the corner of one's eye

soso ADJ tasteless, insipid; (persona) dull

sospecha F suspicion

sospechar VT to suspect

sospechoso -sa ADJ suspicious; MF suspect

sostén M (apoyo, sustento) support, prop; (persona que sostiene) supporter, provider; (prenda) brassiere; **— de la familia** breadwinner

sostener[44] VT (una nota musical) to hold, to sustain; (una familia) to support; (un peso) to support, to hold; (una opinión) to claim, to uphold

sostenido ADJ sustained; M sharp

sota F jack, knave

sótano M cellar, basement

soto M thicket

soya F (semilla) soybean; (planta) soy

squash M squash

Sr. M Mr.

Sra. F (casada) Mrs.; (sin indicación de estado civil) Ms.

S.R.C. (Se Ruega Contestar) LOC RSVP

status M status

stop M stop sign

strip-tease M striptease

striptisero -ra MF stripper

su ADJ POS (de él) his; (de ella) her; (de usted, ustedes) your; (de ellos, ellas) their

suave ADJ (pelo, piel) soft; (tiempo, droga) mild; (brisa, persona, animal) gentle; (coñac) smooth; **hablan —** they speak gently

suavidad F (pelo, piel) softness; (coñac) smoothness; (tiempo, droga) mildness; (brisa, persona, animal) gentleness

suavizante M fabric softener

suavizar[9] VT to soften

suazi ADJ & MF Swazi

Suazilandia F Swaziland

subalterno -na ADJ & MF subordinate

subarrendar VI/VT to sublet

subasta F auction

subastador -ora MF auctioneer

subastar VT to sell at auction, to auction

subconsciente ADJ subconscious

subcontratar VT to subcontract

subdesarrollado ADJ underdeveloped

súbdito -ta MF subject

subdivisión F subdivision

subempleado ADJ underemployed

subestimar VT to underestimate

subida F (de precios, de río) rise; (de montaña) climb; (de drogas) high; (cuesta) slope; **—s y bajadas** ups and downs

subido ADJ (color) bright; **— de tono** risqué
subir VI to rise, to go up; (la marea) to surge; (a un tren) to board; (a un autobús, coche) to get into; VT (algo del sótano) to bring up; (una montaña) to climb; (precios) to raise; **—se** to ride up; **el vino se me sube a la cabeza** the wine goes to my head; M **subibaja** seesaw
súbito ADJ sudden
subjetivo ADJ subjective
subjuntivo ADJ & M subjunctive
sublevación F revolt
sublevar VT to incite to rebellion; (indignar) to infuriate; **—se** to revolt
sublime ADJ sublime
submarino ADJ underwater; M submarine
subordinado -da ADJ & MF subordinate
subordinar VT to subordinate
subproducto M by-product
subproletariado M underclass
subrayar VT (con una línea) to underline; (enfatizar) to emphasize
subrepticio ADJ surreptitious
subrutina F subroutine
subsanar VT (una deficiencia) to remedy; (un error) to correct
subsecretario -ia MF undersecretary; **— de Justicia** Solicitor General
subsidiario ADJ subsidiary
subsiguiente ADJ subsequent
subsistencia F survival
subsistir VI to subsist, to survive
subteniente MF second lieutenant
subterfugio M subterfuge
subterráneo ADJ subterranean, underground; M subway
subtítulo M (de un capítulo, película) subtitle; (pie de foto) caption
suburbano -na ADJ of shantytowns; MF shantytown resident
suburbio M shantytown
subvaluar[17] VT to underestimate
subvención F subsidy
subvencionar VT to subsidize
subversivo ADJ subversive
subyacer[49] VI to underlie
subyugar[7] VT (dominar) to subjugate; (hechizar) to charm
succión F suction
sucedáneo -a MF substitute
suceder VI to happen, to occur; **— al trono** to succeed to the throne; VT to succeed
sucesión F succession; (heredero) descendant
sucesivo ADJ successive; **en lo —** in the future
suceso M (evento) event, occurrence; (incidente) incident

sucesor -ora MF successor
suciedad F (porquería) dirt, filth; (cualidad de sucio) filthiness
sucinto ADJ concise
sucio ADJ dirty, filthy; (trabajo, chiste) dirty; (conciencia) guilty; **blanco —** off-white; **este traje es —** this suit gets dirty easily
sucumbir VI to succumb
sucursal F branch, subsidiary
sudadera F sweatshirt
sudado ADJ sweaty
Sudáfrica F South Africa
sudafricano -na ADJ & MF South African
Sudamérica F South America
sudamericano -na ADJ & MF South American
Sudán M Sudan
sudanés -esa ADJ & MF Sudanese
sudar VT to sweat; **— la gota gorda** to sweat blood
sudeste ADJ southeast, southeastern; M southeast
sudoeste ADJ southwest, southwestern; M southwest
sudor M sweat
sudoroso ADJ sweaty
Suecia F Sweden
sueco -ca ADJ Swedish; M (lengua) Swedish; MF Swede; **hacerse el —** to pretend not to understand
suegro -a M father-in-law; F mother-in-law
suela F (de zapato) sole; (pez) flounder
sueldo M salary
suelo M (tierra) soil, ground; (piso) floor; **arrastrar por el —** to drag; **por los —s** at rock-bottom
suelto ADJ (no atado) loose, unattached; (flojo) loose; (libre) free; M loose change
sueño M (hecho de dormir) sleep; (hecho de soñar) dream; (ganas de dormir) sleepiness; **en —s** dreaming; **conciliar el —** to get to sleep; **tener —** to be sleepy; **ni en —(s)** never; **perder el —** to lose sleep; **— húmedo** wet dream; **— profundo** sound sleep; **estar en el séptimo —** to be deeply asleep
suero M serum; **— de leche** buttermilk; **— fisiológico** saline solution
suerte F (destino) fate; (fortuna) luck; (clase) kind; **de —** in luck; **dejar a su —** to leave to his own devices; **echar —s** to cast lots; **mala —** (desgracia) bad luck; (lo siento) too bad; **tener —** to be lucky; **tentar a la —** to court danger; **tocarle en —** to be one's lot
suertudo -da ADJ lucky; MF lucky devil
suéter M sweater

suficiencia F adequacy; **tiene una —** she's so arrogant

suficiente ADJ (adecuado) sufficient, adequate; (arrogante) smug; M (calificación mínima) lowest passing grade; PRON enough; **ser —** to be enough; **más que —** ample

sufijo M suffix

sufragar[7] VT to defray; **— los gastos** to meet the expenses

sufragio M suffrage

sufrido ADJ (madre) long-suffering; (pantalón) durable

sufrimiento M suffering

sufrir VI/VT to suffer; VT to stand; (una lesión) to sustain; (un cambio) to undergo; (una pena) to grieve; **— de** to suffer from; **— de los pies** to have foot pains

sugerencia F suggestion

sugerir[3] VT to suggest

sugestión F suggestion

suicida MF suicide

suicidarse VI to commit suicide

suicidio M suicide

suite F suite

Suiza F Switzerland

suizo -za ADJ & MF Swiss; M sweet roll

sujeción LOC ADV **con —a** subject to

sujetar VT (fijar) to attach; (unir) to hold; (someter) to subdue, to hold down; **—se** to hold on; M SG **sujetalibros** bookend; **sujetapapeles** paper clip

sujeto ADJ held by; **— a** subject to; M (de oración, de experimento) subject; (individuo) individual

sulfato M sulphate

sulfurarse VI to hit the roof

sulfúrico ADJ sulfuric

sulfuro M sulfide

suma F (resultado aritmético) sum; (operación aritmética) addition; (cantidad) amount, sum; **en —** in sum

sumadora F adding machine

sumar VT to add, to add up; **—se a** to join

sumario M brief; ADJ summary

sumergible ADJ waterproof

sumergir[11] VT to submerge, to dip; **—se** to dive; **—se en** to immerse oneself in

sumidero M (socavón) sinkhole; (desagüe) drain

suministrar VT to furnish, to supply with

suministros M PL supplies

sumir VT to immerse

sumisión F submission

sumiso ADJ submissive

súmmum M ultimate; **el — de la moda** the cat's meow

sumo ADJ utmost, paramount; **a lo —** at the most

suntuoso ADJ sumptuous, luxurious

superar VT (las expectativas) to surpass; (un límite) to exceed; (una dificultad) to overcome, to surmount; (una prueba) to pass; **—se** to improve oneself

superávit M surplus

supercomputadora F supercomputer

superdirecta F overdrive

superdotado ADJ gifted

superego M superego

superestrella F superstar

superficial ADJ (conocimiento, herida, persona) superficial; (persona) shallow

superficialidad F shallowness

superficie F (parte exterior) surface; (de una figura geométrica) area

superfluo ADJ superfluous

superintendente MF superintendent

superior ADJ (mejor) superior; (más alto) higher; (más grande, intenso) greater; MF superior

superioridad F superiority

superlativo ADJ & M superlative

supermercado M supermarket

superordenador M supercomputer

superponer[39] VT to superimpose

superpotencia F superpower

supersónico ADJ supersonic

superstición F superstition

supersticioso ADJ superstitious

supervisar VT to supervise

supervisión F supervision

supervisor -ora MF supervisor

supervivencia F survival; **la — del más apto** the survival of the fittest

superyó M superego

suplantar VT to supplant

suplementar VT to supplement

suplemento M supplement

suplente ADJ & MF substitute

súplica F entreaty, plea

suplicar[6] VT to plead, to beseech

suplicio M ordeal

suplir VT (sustituir) to substitute for; (compensar) to make up for

suponer[39] VT (dar por sentado) to suppose, to presume, to surmise; (implicar) to involve

suposición F supposition, surmise

supositorio M suppository

supremacía F supremacy

supremo ADJ supreme

supresión F (de una idea) suppression; (de una palabra) deletion

suprimir VT (una idea) to suppress; (la

esclavitud) to abolish; (una palabra) to delete

supuesto ADJ supposed; **— que** supposing that; **dar por —** to consider certain; **por —** of course; M supposition

supuración F discharge

supurante ADJ festering, running

supurar VI to fester, to discharge

sur ADJ & M south; **hacia el —** southward; **rumbo al —** southward

surcar[6] VT to plow

surco M (en la tierra) furrow; (en un camino) rut; (en un disco) groove; (en el rostro) wrinkle

surcoreano -na ADJ & MF South Korean

sureño -ña ADJ southern; MF southerner

sureste ADJ southeast, southeastern; M southeast

surfear VI/VT to surf (también en el internet)

surfing M surfing; **hacer —** to surf

surgimiento M rise

surgir[11] VI (situación) to arise; (manantial) to rise; (problema) to emerge, to crop up

Surinam M Surinam, Suriname

surinamés -esa ADJ & MF Surinamer

surmenage M burnout

suroeste ADJ southwest, southwestern; M southwest

surrealismo M surrealism

surtido M stock, assortment; ADJ assorted

surtidor M (bomba) pump; (chorro, pieza de carburador) jet

surtir VT to provide; **— efecto** to produce the desired effect; **— un pedido** to fill an order

susceptible ADJ susceptible

suscitar VT to stir up

suscribir[51] VT (una opinión) to subscribe to, to endorse; (un seguro) to underwrite; **—se a** to subscribe to

suscripción F subscription

suscriptor -ora MF subscriber

susodicho ADJ above-mentioned

suspender VT (colgar) to suspend, to hang; (interrumpir) to suspend, to stop; (cancelar) to cancel; (no dejar trabajar) to suspend; VI/VT (no aprobar) to fail, to flunk

suspense M suspense

suspensión F suspension

suspenso ADJ hanging; **quedarse —** to freeze; M (en un examen) failure; (en una película) suspense; **en —** in suspense

suspensorio M jock (strap)

suspicaz ADJ suspicious

suspirar VT to sigh; **— por** to yearn for

suspiro M sigh; **dame un —** give me a

breather

sustancia F substance

sustancial ADJ substantial

sustancioso ADJ substantial

sustantivo M noun; ADJ substantive

sustentar VT to sustain

sustento M (alimento) sustenance; (apoyo) support; **ganarse el —** to earn a living

sustitución F substitution

sustituible ADJ replaceable

sustituir[31] VI/VT to substitute for, to replace; **Juan sustituyó a María** John substituted for Mary; **sustituí la leche por agua** I substituted water for milk

sustituto -ta MF substitute

susto M scare, fright

sustracción F subtraction

sustraer[45] VT to take away; **—se a** to avoid

susurrar VI/VT (una persona, el viento) to whisper; (agua) to murmur, to ripple; (hojas) to rustle

susurro M (de una persona, del viento) whisper; (del agua) murmur; (de las hojas) rustle

sutil ADJ subtle

sutileza F subtlety; (exagerada) nicety, quibble

sutilizar[9] VT to quibble over

sutura F suture

suyo ADJ (de él) his; (de ella) her; (de usted, de ustedes) your; (de ellos, de ellas) their; PRON (de él) his; (de ella) hers; (de usted, de ustedes) yours; (de ellos, de ellas) theirs; **salirse con la suya** to get one's own way; **hacer de las suyas** to be up to one's tricks; **los —s** his / her / your / their family

swing M swing

Tt

tabaco M tobacco

tábano M horsefly

tabaquismo M smoking

taberna F tavern, saloon

tabernero -ra MF bartender

tabicar[6] VT to partition

tabique M partition

tabla F (tablero) board, plank; (teatro) stage; (pliegue) pleat; (gráfica) table, chart; **— de surf** surfboard; **— de planchar** ironing board; **—s** (escenario) stage; **—s de la ley** the tables of the law; **—s de multiplicar**

multiplication tables; — **periódica** periodic table; — **de contenidos** table of contents; — **de cortar** cutting board; **hacer —s** to tie

tablado M stage

tablero M (para juegos de mesa) board; (de instrumentos) panel, instrument panel; (de coche) dashboard; (pizarra) blackboard; (para noticias) bulletin board; — **de mando** control panel

tableta F (de aspirina) tablet; (de chocolate) bar

tablilla F (de arcilla) tablet; (de cama) slat; (para fracturas) splint

tabloide M tabloid

tablón M plank

tabú M taboo

tabulador M tab

tabular VT to tabulate, to chart

taburete M stool, footstool

TAC (tomografía axial computarizada) F CAT scan

tacañería F stinginess, tightness

tacaño -ña ADJ stingy, miserly; MF miser

tacha F blemish; (al honor) blot

tachar VT (borrar) to cross out, to delete; (atribuir una tacha) to accuse of

tachón M crossing out

tachonar VT to stud

tachuela F tack, thumbtack

tácito ADJ tacit

taciturno ADJ taciturn

taco M (de artillería) wad; (palo de billar) billiard cue; (comida ligera) snack; (palabrota) swear word; (comida mexicana) *Méx* taco; **soltar —s** *Esp* to swear

tacómetro M tachometer

tacón M heel

taconear VI to click the heels

taconeo M clicking

táctica F tactics

táctil ADJ tactile

tacto M (acción de tocar) touch; (sentido) sense of touch; (habilidad diplomática) tact

tahúr -ura MF gambler

tailandés -esa ADJ & MF Thai, Thailander

Tailandia F Thailand

taimado ADJ sly, devious

Taiwán M Taiwan

taiwanés -esa ADJ & MF Taiwanese

tajada F (de pan, carne) slice; (de carne) slab; **sacar —** to take one's cut

tajante ADJ (inequívoco) unequivocal; (cortante) sharp

tajar VT to slice

tajear VI/VT to slash

tajo M (corte) slash, hack; (cañón) gorge; (separación) gap

tal ADJ such; — **cual** just so; — **vez** perhaps; **un — García** a certain García; **a — grado** to such an extent; **de — palo — astilla** a chip off the old block; **en — caso** in such a case; CONJ — **como** like, just as; **con — (de) que** provided that; ADV **¿qué —?** how is it going? PRON **y — and so on; **como si — as if nothing had happened

taladrar VT to bore, to drill

taladro M drill

talante M temperament

talar VT (un árbol) to chop down; (un bosque) to lumber

talco M talcum

talento M talent

talentoso ADJ talented, gifted

talismán M charm

talla F (altura) height; (moral, intelectual) stature; (de ropa) size; (de madera) carving

tallado M carving

tallar VT to carve; (madera) to whittle, to carve; (naipes) to deal

tallarín M noodle

talle M (cintura) waist, waistline; **tiene buen —** she has a good figure; **corto de —** short-waisted

taller M (para trabajo manual, para enseñanza artística) workshop; (de artista plástico) studio; (de mecánico) garage, shop

tallo M stalk, stem

talón M (de pie, calcetín) heel; (de cheque) stub; — **de Aquiles** Achilles' heel; **girar sobre los talones** to turn on one's heels; **pisarle los talones a alguien** to be hot on someone's heels

talonario M checkbook

talonear VI to walk briskly

tamal M *Méx* tamale

tamaño M size; — **mediano** medium-sized; **de — natural** life-sized; ADJ such a big, so big a

tambalearse VI (un borracho) to stagger; (un boxeador) to reel; (un viejo) to dodder

tambaleo M stagger

también ADV also, too, as well

tambor M (instrumento musical, pieza de máquina) drum; (músico) drummer; (cilindro) cylinder; **a — batiente** with fanfare

tamborilear VI to drum, to tap

tamborilero -ra MF drummer

tamiz M sieve

tamizar[9] VT to sift
tampoco CONJ either; **no lo hizo —** he did not do it either; **ni yo —** me either
tampón M tampon
tan ADV **es — rica** she is so rich; **— alto como Juan** as tall as Juan; **— pronto como** as soon as; **es — idiota** he's such an idiot; **vecinos — simpáticos** such nice neighbors
tanda F (de personas) group; (de galletas) batch; (de ejercicios) set
tándem M tandem
tanga F thong
tangente ADJ & F tangent; **salirse por la —** (irse de tema) to go off on a tangent; (evadir) to beat about the bush
tangerina F tangerine
tangible ADJ tangible
tango M tango
tanque M tank
tantán M African drum
tantear VT (calcular) to estimate roughly; (averiguar) to sound out, to feel out; (apuntar) to score; (palpar) to grope
tanteo M (cálculo) estimate; (número de tantos) score; **al —** approximately
tanto ADJ, PRON & ADV **lloró — que se le enrojecieron los ojos** he cried so much his eyes got red; **yo tengo — como tú** I have as much as you do; **me quiere —** he loves me so; **no te quiero —** I don't love you that much; **a cada —s pasos** every so many steps; **cuarenta y —s** forty-odd; **a — el kilo** at so much per kilo; **el — por ciento** at such and such a percentage; **estar al —** to be in the know; **no es para —** it's not such a big deal; **— da** it's all the same; **— como** as much as; **— en la ciudad como en el campo** both in the city and in the country; **entre / mientras —** meanwhile; **mantenerse al —** to stay informed; **otros —s** just so many more; **por lo —** therefore; **a las tantas** until late at night; M (en los juegos) points
Tanzania F Tanzania
tanzano -na ADJ & MF Tanzanian
tañer[18] VT *lit* (una guitarra) to play; VI (una campana) to ring, to toll
tañido M (de guitarra) twang; (de campanas) toll
tapa F (de botella) cap; (de libro) cover; (de coche) hood; (de olla, bote) lid, top; *Esp* bar snack
tapadera F (de recipiente) lid; (de un fraude) cover
tapar VT (una olla) to cover; (una salida) to block; (un caño) to plug up, to stop up; (encubrir) to cover up for; M SG

tapacubos hubcap; **tapajuntas** flashing; **taparrabos** loincloth
tapete M runner
tapia F garden wall
tapiar VT to board up
tapicería F (para paredes) tapestry; (para muebles) upholstery; (tienda de textiles de decoración) tapestry shop; (arte de hacer tapices) tapestry making; (tienda de tapicero) upholstery shop
tapioca F tapioca
tapir M tapir
tapiz M tapestry, wall hanging
tapizar[9] VT to upholster
tapón M stopper; (de lavabo) plug; (de corcho) cork; **— de oídos** earplug
taponazo M pop of a cork
taquigrafía F shorthand
taquígrafo -fa MF stenographer
taquilla F ticket office, box office
tarambana MF INV dork, knucklehead
tarántula F tarantula
tararear VI/VT to hum
tarareo M hum, humming
tarascada F (mordedura) snap, bite; (réplica) rude answer
tardanza F lateness
tardar VI to take time; **¿cuánto tarda el trámite de divorcio?** how long does it take to get divorced? **—se** to take a long time; **tu padre se tarda** your father is taking a long time; **a más —** at the latest
tarde F afternoon; (hacia el anochecer) evening; **buenas —s** good afternoon; ADV late; **ya es —** it is late; **— o temprano** sooner o later; **más —** later on; **llegar —** to be late
tardío ADJ late
tardo ADJ *lit* slow
tarea F task, chore; (escolar) homework
tarifa F (impuesto) tariff; (lista de precios) list of prices; (de transporte) fare; (precio estipulado) rate
tarima F platform
tarjeta F card (también dispositivo de computadora); **— comercial** business card; **— postal** postcard; **— de cobro automático / de débito** debit card; **— de crédito** credit card; **— de Navidad** Christmas card; **marcar —** to punch in
tarro M jar
tarta F tart, pie
tartajear VI to stutter
tartamudear VI to stutter, to stammer
tartamudeo M stammer, stutter

tartamudez F stuttering
tartamudo -da MF stutterer, stammerer; ADJ stuttering, stammering
tártaro M tartar
tartera F round baking pan
tarugo M (trozo de madera) piece of wood; (tonto) blockhead
tasa F (índice) rate; (impuesto) tax; **— de desempleo** rate of unemployment; **— de interés** interest rate; **— de mortalidad** death rate; **— de natalidad** birth rate; **— prima** prime rate
tasación F valuation, appraisal
tasajo M jerky
tasar VT to appraise, to assess
tatarabuelo -la M great-great-grandfather; F great-great-grandmother
tataranieto -ta M great-great-grandson; F great-great-granddaughter
tatuaje M tattoo
tatuar[17] VT to tattoo
tauromaquia F bullfighting
taxi M taxi, taxicab
taxidermia F taxidermy
taxista MF taxi driver, cab driver
taxonomía F taxonomy
Tayikistán M Tajikistan
tayiko -ka ADJ & MF Tajik
taza F (de té, café) cup; (del inodoro) bowl
tazón M (para beber) mug; (de comida) bowl
té M (bebida) tea; (fiesta) tea party
te PRON you; **yo — amo** I love you; **— digo mañana** I'll tell you tomorrow; **no — mires en el espejo** don't look at yourself in the mirror
teatral ADJ theatrical
teatro M theater; **— de títeres** puppet show; **no hagas —** don't make such a production
techado M (techo) roof; (acción de techar) roofing
techar VT to roof
techo M (exterior) roof; (interior) ceiling
techumbre F roof
tecla F key; **— para mayúsculas** capital letter key; **— de cambio** shift key; **— de control** control key; **— de función** function key; **— de retroceso** backspace key; **— de tabulación** tab key; **dar uno en la —** to hit the nail on the head
teclado M keyboard; **— numérico** keypad
teclear VT (pulsar las teclas) to key in; (hacer ruido) to click
tecleo M keying in, clicking
técnica F (método) technique; (tecnología) technology
técnico -ca ADJ technical; MF technician

tecnología F technology
tectónica F tectonics
tedio M boredom
tedioso ADJ tedious
tee M tee
teja F (de cerámica) tile; (de madera u otros materiales) shingle
tejado M roof
tejar M tile factory; VT to cover with tiles
tejedor -ora MF weaver
tejer VI/VT (cesta, tela) to weave; (suéter) to knit; M **tejemaneje** (fraude) hanky-panky; (actividad) goings-on
tejido M (tela) textile, fabric; (de células) tissue; (acción de tejer tela) weaving; (acción de tejer un suéter) knitting
tejo M disk
tejón M badger
tela F (paño) cloth, fabric; (lienzo para pintar) canvas; (de araña) web; (dinero) money; (película) film; **— adhesiva** adhesive tape; **— de cebolla** onion skin; **en —** hardbound; **poner en — de juicio** to call into question
telar M loom
telaraña F cobweb, spider's web
tele F TV
telebobo -ba MF couch potato
telecomunicaciones F PL telecommunications
teleconferencia F teleconference
teledifusión F telecast
teledirección F remote guidance
teleférico M cable car
telefonazo M buzz, ring
telefonear VI/VT to telephone, to phone
telefónico ADJ **llamada telefónica** telephone call
telefonista MF telephone operator
teléfono M telephone, phone; (número) telephone number
telegrafiar[16] VI/VT to telegraph, to wire
telegráfico ADJ telegraphic
telégrafo M telegraph
telegrama M telegram
telemarketing M telemarketing
telemercadeo M telemarketing
telémetro M range finder
telenovela F soap opera
teleobjetivo M zoom lens
telepatía F telepathy
telescopio M telescope
telesquí M ski lift
teletipo M Teletype[tm]
televidente MF television viewer
televisión F television
televisor M television set; **— a / en color**

color television

telón M theater curtain; **— de acero** iron curtain

tema M (de una obra literaria, musical) theme; (de conversación) topic, subject; (de un CD) song

temario M agenda

temático ADJ thematic

temblar[1] VI (la mano, la tierra) to tremble; (la voz) to shake, to quaver; (de frío) to shiver; (de miedo) to shudder; (la luz) to flicker

temblequear VI to dodder

temblón ADJ trembling

temblor M (acción de temblar) trembling; (de tierra) tremor; (de una llama) flicker; (de la voz) quaver; (de frío) shiver; (de miedo) shudder; **— de tierra** earthquake

tembloroso ADJ (mano) shaky; (llama) flickering; (voz) quavering; (de miedo) shuddering; (de frío) shivering

temer VI/VT to fear, to be afraid (of); **— por** to fear for; **mucho me temo que** I fear that

temerario ADJ rash, reckless

temeridad F temerity, recklessness

temeroso ADJ fearful

temible ADJ dreadful, dread

temor M fear

témpano M (bloque de hielo) block of ice; (persona fría) cold fish

temperamento M temperament, disposition

temperancia F temperance

temperatura F temperature

tempestad F tempest, storm; **una — en un vaso de agua** a tempest in a teapot

tempestuoso ADJ tempestuous, stormy

templado ADJ (clima) moderate, temperate; (ánimo) serene; (actitud) moderate

templanza F temperance

templar VT (moderar, dar fuerza) to temper; (calentar) to warm up; (una guitarra) to tune

temple M (dureza) temper; (coraje) mettle; **de mal —** in a bad mood

templo M temple

temporada F season; **— baja** off-season; **— de caza** hunting season

temporal ADJ (del tiempo) temporal; (secular) worldly; (no permanente) temporary; M storm; **capear el —** to weather the storm

tempranero -ra ADJ early rising; MF early riser

temprano ADJ & ADV early

tenacidad F tenacity

tenaz ADJ tenacious

tenazas F PL (de cangrejo) pincers; (de mecánico) pliers; (de dentista) forceps; (para hielo) tongs

tendedero M clothesline

tendencia F tendency; (orientación) orientation; (de la moda) trend; **de — mayoritaria** mainstream; **— a la baja** downturn; **— al alza** upturn

tender[1] VT (un mantel) to spread out; (la ropa) to hang out; (la mano) to extend; (un cable) to lay; (una trampa) to set; VI **— a** to tend to; **—se** to stretch out

tendero -ra MF storekeeper; (de comestibles) grocer

tendido M (de cables) laying; (de ropa mojada) hanging out; (conjunto de cables) cables

tendinitis F tendonitis

tendón M tendon, sinew; **— de Aquiles** Achilles' tendon

tenebroso ADJ (oscuro) dark; (sombrío) gloomy

tenedor -ora M (utensilio) table fork; MF holder, payee; **— de libros** bookkeeper

teneduría F **— de libros** bookkeeping

tener[44] VT to have; **tiene el pelo castaño** she has brown hair, her hair is brown; **— en mucho** to esteem highly; **— por** to consider; **— que** to have to; **— ganas** to feel like; **tengo escrita la carta** I have the letter written; **— éxito** to be successful; **— miedo** to be afraid; **— sueño** to be sleepy; **— frío** to be cold; **— hambre** to be hungry; **tiene cinco años** she is five years old; **—se** to stand straight; **no — más remedio** to have no other choice; **— que ver con** to have to do with

tenería F tannery

tenia F tapeworm

teniente MF lieutenant

tenis M (juego) tennis; (zapatos) sneakers, tennis shoes

tenista MF tennis player

tenor M (voz, estilo) tenor; (tono) tone, tenor; ADJ **saxofón —** tenor saxophone

tensión F tension

tenso ADJ tense; (extendido) taut

tentación F temptation

tentáculo M tentacle

tentador ADJ tempting

tentar[1] VT to tempt; **— a la suerte** to court danger; **— por todos los medios** to try everything

tentativa F attempt, try

tentativo ADJ tentative

tentempié M snack

tenue ADJ (tela) delicate; (luz) tenuous, dim, faint; (sonido) feeble

tenuidad F faintness, softness

teñir[5,18] VT (de color) to dye; (de tristeza) to tinge

teología F theology

teoría F theory

teórico ADJ theoretical

tepe M sod

tequila M tequila

terabyte M terabyte

terapeuta MF INV therapist

terapéutico ADJ therapeutic

terapia F therapy

tercero ADJ third; **tercera persona** third person; **tercera edad** old age; **tercer mundo** third world; M third party

terciar VI/VT to arbitrate

tercio M third

terciopelo M velvet

terco ADJ obstinate, stubborn

tergiversación F distortion, misrepresentation

tergiversar VT (palabras) to distort; (datos) to skew

termal ADJ thermal

terminación F termination, completion; (de una palabra, cuento) ending; (de un piso) finish

terminal ADJ terminal; MF (de aeropuerto, de omnibus) terminal; M (de computadora, eléctrico) terminal

terminante ADJ (negativa) flat; (prohibición) absolute

terminar VI/VT (completar) to finish, to conclude; VI (tener como final) to end; **— por** to end up; **no termino de entender** I still can't understand; **terminó con las ratas** he got rid of the rats; **sin —** unfinished

término M (final) end; (período de tiempo) period; (límite) boundary; (palabra) term; **a —** with a deadline; **estar en buenos —s** to be on good terms; **por — medio** on average; **— medio** medium; **en primer —** first of all; **poner —** to end; **en —s generales** in general terms; **en último —** as a last resort

terminología F terminology

termita F termite

termo M thermos

termodinámico ADJ thermodynamic

termómetro M thermometer

termonuclear ADJ thermonuclear

termostato M thermostat

ternero -ra MF (animal) calf; F (carne) veal

terneza F tenderness

terno M three-piece suit

ternura F tenderness

terquedad F obstinacy, stubbornness

terraplén M embankment

terrateniente MF landholder

terraza F (terreno) terrace; (de casa) veranda; (delante de un bar) deck; (azotea) flat roof

terremoto M earthquake

terrenal ADJ earthly

terreno M (campo) piece of land, tract of land; (lote) lot; (formación geológica) terrain; (campo científico) field; **todo —** with four-wheel drive; **ganarle — a alguien** to gain on someone; **tantear el —** to put out feelers; **perder —** to lose ground

terrestre ADJ terrestrial, earthly

terrible ADJ terrible, awful

terrier M terrier

territorio M territory

terrón M (de tierra) clod; (de azúcar) lump

terror M terror, dread

terrorismo M terrorism

terrorista MF INV terrorist

terso ADJ (liso) smooth; (pulido) polished

tersura F smoothness

tertulia F social gathering

tesis F thesis; **— doctoral** dissertation

tesón M determination

tesonero ADJ determined

tesorería F treasury

tesorero -ra MF treasurer

tesoro M treasure; (público) treasury

test M test

testaferro M straw man

testamentaría F (gestiones) execution; (bienes) estate

testamento M testament, will

testarudez F stubbornness

testarudo ADJ stubborn, headstrong

testículo M testicle

testificar[6] VI to testify

testigo MF witness; **— de cargo** witness for the prosecution; **— ocular** eyewitness; M proof

testimoniar VI to give testimony

testimonio M testimony, proof, evidence; **levantar falso —** to bear false witness; **en — de su amor** as a testament to his love

testosterona F testosterone

teta F (de animal) teat; (de mujer) *vulg* tit, jug

tétanos M tetanus

tetera F teapot, teakettle

tetilla F nipple

tetina F nipple

tetrapléjico -ca ADJ & MF quadriplegic

tétrico ADJ gloomy
teutónico ADJ Teutonic
textil ADJ & M textile
texto M text; (libro de texto) textbook
textual ADJ verbatim
textura F texture
tez F complexion
ti PRON PERS you; **para —** for you; **te lo doy a —** I give it to you
tibieza F (poco fervor, afecto) lukewarmness; (calor) warmth
tibio ADJ (ni caliente ni frío) tepid, lukewarm; (templado) warm
tiburón M shark
tic M twitch, tic
tictac M **hacer —** to tick
tiempo M (cronológico) time; (climático) weather; (gramatical) tense; (de un partido de cuatro tiempos) quarter; (de un partido de dos tiempos) half; **— completo** full time; **— extra** overtime; **— y medio** time and a half; **— libre** leisure hours, free time; **— pretérito** past tense; **a —** on time; **al mismo —** at the same time; **antes de —** ahead of time; **a su —** in due course; **a un —** at the same time; **con —** in advance; **de medio —** part-time; **en aquel —** back then; **en mis —s** in my day; **hace buen —** the weather is nice; **hace mucho —** a long time ago; **mal —** rough weather; **motor de dos —s** two-stroke motor; **perder el —** to goof off, to waste time; **tener — de sobra** to have time to spare; **todo el —** all the time; **tomar el —** to clock
tienda F (de venta) store; (de campaña) tent
tientas LOC ADV **a —** blindly; **andar a —** to feel one's way
tiento M care; **coger el —** to get the hang of something
tierno ADJ (fácil de cortar) tender; (joven) young; (cariñoso) affectionate
tierra F (planeta) earth; (superficie seca) land; (país) country; (suelo) soil; **— adentro** inland; **—s altas** highlands; **—s bajas** lowlands; **— de nadie** no-man's land; **— firme** mainland; **—s raras** rare earths; **bajo —** underground; **caer a —** to fall to the ground; **dar en — con alguien** to overthrow someone; **echar por —** to knock down; **por —** overland; **tomar —** to land
tieso ADJ stiff; (persona) erect; **quedarse —** *fam* to kick the bucket
tiesto M flowerpot
tiesura F stiffness
tifoideo -a ADJ & F typhoid

tifón M typhoon
tifus M typhoid fever
tigre M tiger
tijeretada F snip
tijeretazo M snip
tijeretear VT to snip
tildar VT to brand
tilde F (en la ñ) tilde; (en las vocales) accent (mark)
tilín M *fam* ding-a-ling
timador M confidence man
timbrar VT to stamp
timbrazo M ring
timbre M (aparato) buzzer, doorbell; (cualidad de la voz) timbre; (sello) stamp; (insignia heráldica) crest
timidez F timidity, shyness
tímido ADJ timid, shy, bashful
timo M confidence game, scam
timón M helm, rudder
timonear VT to steer
timonel M pilot
timorato ADJ timorous, faint-hearted
tímpano M eardrum
tina F (bañera) tub; (de tintorero) vat
tinaja F large earthen jar
tinglado M (armazón) shed; (plataforma) platform
tinieblas F PL darkness; **en —** in the dark
tino M (buen juicio) good judgment; (puntería) marksmanship
tinta F ink; **medias —s** wishy-washiness
tinte M (sustancia) dye, stain; (matiz) tint
tintero M inkwell; **eso se me quedó en el —** I never got to that
tintín M clink
tintinear VI to tinkle, to clink
tintineo M tinkle, tinkling
tinto ADJ red
tintorería F dry cleaner
tintorero -ra MF dry cleaner
tintura F (medicina) tincture; (tinte) dye, tint
tiñoso ADJ scabby
tío -a M (hermano de madre o padre) uncle; **— abuelo** great uncle; (tipo) guy; F (hermana de madre o padre) aunt; (tipa) woman, gal; (prostituta) *pey* whore
tíovivo M merry-go-round
típico ADJ typical
tiple M treble
tipo -pa M (especie, imprenta) type; (tío) *fam* guy, dude; *Am* rate of interest; *Am* **— de cambio** rate of exchange; **— de interés** interest rate; **un buen —** a good-looking fellow, a regular guy; **tiene buen —** he's good looking; F (tía) woman, gal

tipografía F printing
tipología F typology
tira F (de papel, tocino, tela) strip; (de cuero, zapato) strap; **— cómica** comic strip
tirada F (de una pelota) throw; (de una publicación) issue, print run; (distancia) stretch; **de una —** all at once
tirador -ora MF (persona que dispara) shooter; M (tirachinas) slingshot; (pomo) knob
tiranía F tyranny
tiránico ADJ tyrannical
tirano -na ADJ tyrannical; MF tyrant
tirante ADJ (cable) taut; (relaciones) strained; M (de caballería) trace; (de vestido) strap; (apoyo) brace, strut; **—s** suspenders
tirantez F tension, strain
tirar VT (pelota) to throw, to toss, to pitch; (derechos, dinero) to throw away; (una bala) to shoot; (una moneda) to flip, to toss; (dados) to cast; (una cuerda) to pull, to tug; **— la cadena** to flush; **— la casa por la ventana** to live it up; **— la chancleta** to kick up one's heels; **no me tira la política** I'm not attracted to politics; **el coche tira a un lado** the car pulls to one side; **— al suelo** to throw down; **— a** to tend toward; **— abajo** to knock over; **— de** to tug at; **ir tirando** to get along; **—se** to lie down; **—se pedos** to fart; **—se solo** to go it alone; **tirárselas de** to pretend to be; **trabajar con él es un constante tira y afloja** working with him is a roller-coaster; M **tirabuzón** (sacacorchos) corkscrew; (espiral) coil; M SG **tirachinas** slingshot
tiritar VI (de frío) to shiver; (de miedo) to shudder
tiro M (lanzamiento) throw; (disparo) shot; (deporte) shooting; (de cocaína) hit; (de dados) roll; (de caballos) team; (de chimenea) draft; **— al arco** archery; **— al blanco** target practice; **— de penalidad** penalty kick; **errar el —** to miss the mark; **matar a —s** to gun down; **ni a —s** absolutely not; **pegarle un — a alguien** to shoot someone; **me salió el — por la culata** the plan backfired on me
tiroides ADJ & M thyroid
tirón M jerk, tug, pull; (atracción fuerte, lesión de un músculo) pull; **de un —** all at once; **un — de orejas** a slap on the wrist
tironear VI/VT to jerk, to tug at
tirotear VI to shoot; **—se** to exchange shots
tiroteo M shooting, gunfire
tirria F dislike; **tenerle — a una persona** to have a strong dislike for someone
tisana F herbal tea
tísico ADJ consumptive
tisis F consumption
titánico ADJ titanic
titanio M titanium
títere M (marioneta) puppet; (persona) puppet, dupe; **—s** puppet show; **no dejar — sin cabeza** to leave no one standing
titilación F flicker
titilar VI to flicker, to twinkle
titileo M twinkle
titubear VI (vacilar) to hesitate, to waver; (oscilar) to totter, to dodder
titubeo M hesitation
titular VT to entitle; **—se** to graduate; ADJ permanent; M (de periódico) headline; MF (de cargo) incumbent
titularidad F tenure
título M (de una obra, persona, liga) title; (derecho) claim, legal right; (universitario) degree, diploma; **—s de crédito** credits; **— de propiedad** title deed; **a — de** by way of
tiza F chalk
tiznado ADJ sooty
tiznar VT to smear with soot
tizne M soot
tizón M (leña) burning log; (parásito) smut
TNT M TNT
toalla F towel; **tirar la —** to throw in the towel
toallero M towel rack
tobillo M ankle
tobogán M slide
tocado M headdress; ADJ touched
tocador M (mueble) dressing table, vanity table; (habitación) *lit* boudoir
tocante a PREP concerning
tocar[6] VT (con los dedos) to touch; (un instrumento musical) to play; (una campana) to ring; (un timbre) to buzz; (a la puerta) to knock; (la bocina) to honk, to blast; (una alarma) to sound; (mencionar) to touch upon; **— en** to stop over in; **—le a uno** to be one's turn; **— fondo** to hit bottom; M SG **tocadiscos** record player
tocayo -ya MF namesake
tocino M bacon
tocón M stump
todavía ADV still, as yet, yet; **— está aquí** she's still here; **¿— no has comido?** have you not eaten yet? **— no ha llegado** she still has not arrived, as yet she has not arrived; **me dio — más** she gave me even more

todo ADJ all; (cada uno) every, each; — **hombre** every man; **—s los días** every day; **a — correr** at top speed; **a toda costa** at all costs; **a toda marcha** in high gear; **a toda vela** under full sail; **a toda velocidad** at full speed; **a — volumen** at full blast; **de — corazón** whole-heartedly; **de —s modos** still, anyway, all the same; **del —** entirely; **en — caso** in any case, at any rate, in any event; **es — un personaje** he's quite a character; **por — lados** everywhere; **— el día** all day; **— el tiempo** all the time; **— el mundo** everyone; **todas las noches** nightly; **toda la noche** all through the night; **toda clase de** all sorts of; **en / por todas partes** everywhere, for and wide; **con toda el alma** from the bottom of one's heart; **con toda sinceridad** in all earnestness; PRON **de una vez por todas** once and for all; **— se vale** anything goes; **—s** everybody; **—s juntos** all together; ADV **— derecho** straight ahead; **— lo contrario** quite the opposite; **— recto** straight ahead; **— sucio** all dirty; **ante —** first of all; **así y — in** spite of that; **con — in** spite of that; **del — completely**; **sobre — especially**; M whole; **—poderoso** almighty

toga F (de catedrático) gown; (de juez) robe

Togo M Togo

togolés -esa ADJ & MF Togolese

toldería F Indian village

toldo M awning, canopy

tolerancia F tolerance

tolerante ADJ tolerant, broad-minded

tolerar VT to tolerate; **no lo puedo —** I can't stand it

tolete M oarlock

toma F (de una ciudad) taking; (cinematográfica) take; (de juramento) administration; (de teléfono) jack; **— de agua** faucet; **— de corriente** electric outlet; **— de poder** takeover; **toma y daca** give and take

tomar VT to take; (un juramento) to administer; (un vestido) to take in; (a un criado) to hire; (una bebida) to drink; **— a pecho** to take to heart; **— asiento** to take a seat; **— desprevenido** to take by surprise; **— el sol** to sunbathe; **—lo a mal** to take the wrong way; **— el pelo a** to make fun of, to kid, to pull someone's leg; **— medidas** to take action; **— una decisión** to make a decision; **—le las medidas a alguien** to measure someone for clothes; **—se de la mano** to hold

hands; **—se la molestia** to bother to

tomate M tomato

tomillo M thyme

tomo M volume

tomografía F scan; **— axial computarizada** CAT scan

ton LOC ADV **sin — ni son** for no reason

tonada F tune

tonel M (barril) barrel; (persona) *pey* fatso

tonelada F ton

tóner M toner

Tonga F Tonga

tongano -na ADJ & MF Tongan

tongo M setup

tónica F (tono) tone; (agua) tonic (water)

tónico ADJ & M tonic

tono M tone; (tono musical) pitch; (intervalo musical) step; **— de ocupado** busy signal; **— menor** low key; **a — on** key; **bajar el —** to lower the volume; **darse — to** put on airs; **de buen — in** good taste; **fuera de — out** of place; **subido de — risqué**

tontear VI to fool around

tontería F (cualidad de tonto) stupidity; (hecho o dicho) foolishness, nonsense

tonto -ta ADJ (ingenuo) foolish; (de poca inteligencia) stupid, dumb; **a tontas y a locas** haphazardly; MF (persona ingenua) fool; (persona de poca inteligencia) *fam* dummy, blockhead, dimwit; **— de capirote** dunce; **hacer(se) el —** to play the fool

topacio M topaz

topar VT to butt; **—se con** to bump into

tope M (de precios) ceiling, cap; (de tren) bumper; (de puerta) doorstop; **a — a** lot; **hasta el — to** the maximum; **estar hasta el — to** be completely full

topetazo M butt

tópico M (lugar común) cliché; (tema) topic; ADJ topical

topless ADJ topless

topo M mole (también espía)

toque M (con la mano) touch; (de campana) ringing; (de tambor) beat; (de trompeta) blare; (de pintura) dab; **— de queda** curfew; **dar los últimos —s** to put the finishing touches on; **dar —s** to dab; **un — femenino** a woman's touch

toquetear VI/VT (mercancías) to finger; (por placer sexual) *vulg* to grope, to feel up / off

toqueteo M feel

tórax M thorax

torbellino M whirlwind

torcedura F twist, sprain, strain

torcer[2,10] VT to twist; (una articulación) to sprain, to strain; (tergiversar) to distort;

—le el pescuezo a alguien to wring someone's neck; VI (un río) to bend
torcido ADJ crooked
tordo M thrush
torear VT (lidiar) to fight a bull; (provocar) to provoke
torero -ra MF bullfighter
tormenta F storm; **— de arena** sandstorm; **— eléctrica** electrical storm
tormento M torment
tormentoso ADJ stormy
tornadizo ADJ changeable
tornado M tornado, twister
tornar VI (regresar) to return; VT (cambiar) to turn; **— a hacer algo** to do something again
tornasolado ADJ iridescent
tornear VT to turn on a lathe
torneo M tournament
tornillo M screw; **— de banco** vise; **faltarle a uno un —** to have a screw loose
torniquete M (eje giratorio) turnstile; (contra hemorragia) tourniquet
torno M (para levantar pesos) hoist, winch; (para cerámicas) lathe, pottery wheel; **en —** around
toro M bull; **coger / agarrar el — por los cuernos** to take the bull by the horns
toronja F grapefruit
torpe ADJ (poco habilidoso) clumsy, awkward; (lento) slow, sluggish
torpedear VT to torpedo
torpedero M (barco) torpedo boat; (avión) torpedo plane
torpedo M torpedo
torpeza F (falta de habilidad) clumsiness; (lentitud) slowness, sluggishness
torpor M torpor
torrar VT to roast
torre F (de castillo) tower; (de buque de guerra) turret; (en ajedrez) castle; **— de control** control tower; **— de marfil** ivory tower; **— de perforación** oil derrick; **— de vigilancia** watch tower
torrencial ADJ torrential
torrente M torrent; **— de lágrimas** flood of tears; **— sanguíneo** bloodstream
torreón M large tower
torreta F turret
tórrido ADJ torrid
torsión F torsion
torso M torso
torta F (postre) cake; (bofetada) slap
tortícolis F kink
tortilla F (de huevo) omelet; (de harina) *Méx* tortilla; **se dio vuelta la —** the tables

have turned
tortillera F *ofensivo* dyke
tórtola F turtledove
tortuga F tortoise, turtle; **— marina** sea turtle; **a paso de —** at a snail's pace
tortuoso ADJ (camino) tortuous; (carácter) devious
tortura F torture
torturante ADJ torturous
torturar VT to torture
torvo ADJ fierce
tos F cough; **— ferina** whooping cough
tosco ADJ coarse, crude
toser VI to cough
tosquedad F coarseness, crudeness
tostada F toast
tostado ADJ (pan) toasted; (café) roasted; M (acción de tostar pan) toasting; (color, bronceado) tan; (acción de tostar café) roasting
tostador -ora MF toaster
tostar² VT (el pan) to toast; (la piel) to tan; (el café) to roast
total ADJ & M total; **en —** altogether; **—, a mí no me importa** anyway, I don't care
totalidad F **la — del dinero** all the money; **en su —** as a whole
totalitario ADJ totalitarian
tour M tour
tóxico ADJ toxic
toxina F toxin
traba F (estorbo) hindrance; (de caballo) hobble
trabajador -ora ADJ (esforzado) hard-working; (proletario) working; MF worker
trabajar VI/VT to work; **— un taxi** to drive a taxi; VI (una tienda) to be open; **— duro** to work hard
trabajo M work; (acción de trabajo) working; (puesto) job; (informe académico) paper; **da mucho —** it's a lot of work; **sin —** unemployed
trabajoso ADJ laborious
trabar VT (una puerta) to jam; (un caballo) to hobble; (a un boxeador) to clinch; (una salsa) to thicken; (negociaciones) to impede; **— amistad con alguien** to strike up a friendship with someone; **— batalla** to join battle; **— conversación** to strike up a conversation; M SG **trabalenguas** tongue twister
tracción F traction
tractocamión M tractor-trailer
tractor M tractor
tradición F tradition
tradicional ADJ traditional
traducción F translation

traducir[24] VI/VT to translate
traductor -ora MF translator
traer[45] VT to bring; (llevar puesto) to have on; (contener) to feature; — **a colación** to bring up; — **a mal a alguien** to mistreat someone; **este niño se las trae** this child is something else; **¿qué te traes entre manos?** what are you up to? —**se secretos** to have secrets
tráfago M bustle
traficante MF dealer
traficar[6] VI to traffic, to trade
tráfico M traffic
tragar[7] VI/VT to swallow; (comer) *fam* to feed one's face; (consumir gasolina) to guzzle; (aguantar) to stand; (hacer desaparecer) to engulf; —**se algo** to swallow (accidentally); **no me lo trago** I don't buy that; M **tragaluz** skylight; MF SG **tragamonedas / tragaperras** slot machine
tragedia F tragedy
trágico ADJ tragic
trago M swallow; (bebida alcohólica) shot, slug; **a —s** (bebiendo) in sips; (poco a poco) little by little; **echar / tomar un —** to take a drink; **pasar un mal —** to suffer a difficulty
traición F (política) treason; (personal) betrayal; (acto desleal) treachery; **a —** by treachery
traicionar VT to double-cross
traicionero ADJ treacherous
traidor -ora ADJ treacherous; MF (político) traitor; (personal) betrayer
trailer M trailer
traílla F leash
traje M (conjunto) suit; (de fiesta) gown; — **de baño** swimsuit
trajeado ADJ **bien —** well-dressed
trajín M hustle and bustle
trajinar VI to rush around
trama F (argumento) plot; (intriga) scheme; (conjunto de hilos) woof
tramador -ora MF plotter
tramar VT (con hilos) to weave; (intrigar) to plot, to scheme
tramitar VT to take steps to obtain
trámite M procedure, paperwork
tramo M (de carretera) stretch; (de puente) span; (de hielo) patch; (de escalera) flight
tramoyista MF stagehand
trampa F (de caza) trap, snare; (engaño) trick; **hacer —** to cheat, to trick; **tender una —** to set a trap
trampear VI to cheat
trampilla F trap door

trampolín M (de piscina) springboard; (de circo) trampoline
tramposo -sa ADJ deceitful; MF cheat
tranca F crossbar
trance M (momento difícil) pass, difficult moment; (estado de suspensión) trance; **el último —** the last moment of life; **a todo —** at any cost
tranco M stride; **a —s** hurriedly; **en dos —s** in a jiffy
tranquera F wooden fence
tranquilidad F tranquility, calm, quiet
tranquilizante M tranquilizer
tranquilizar[9] VT to quiet, to calm down; —**se** to calm down, to wind down
tranquilo ADJ (no ruidoso) quiet, peaceful; (no excitado) calm, cool; (no preocupado) calm, at ease; (no excitable) sedate; (mar) smooth, tranquil
transacción F transaction; — **comercial** business transaction
transar VI to compromise
transatlántico ADJ transatlantic; M transatlantic liner
transbordar VI to transfer
transbordo M transfer
transcribir[51] VT to transcribe
transcripción F transcript
transcultural ADJ cross-cultural
transcurrir VI to elapse
transcurso M passing, passage; **en el — de un año** in the course of a year
transeúnte MF passer-by, transient
transexual ADJ & MF transsexual
transferencia F transfer
transferible ADJ transferable
transferir[3] VT to transfer
transformación F transformation
transformador M transformer
transformar VT to transform
transfusión F transfusion
transgredir[50] VT to transgress
transgresión F transgression
transgresor -ora MF lawbreaker
transición F transition
transigir[11] VI to compromise
transistor M transistor
transitable ADJ passable
transitar VI/VT to travel
transitivo ADJ transitive
tránsito M (acción de viajar) transit, passage; (tráfico) traffic; **de / en —** in transit
transitorio ADJ transitory
transmisible ADJ communicable
transmisión F transmission; — **automática** automatic transmission
transmisor M transmitter; ADJ transmitting

transmitir VI/VT to transmit; (una enfermedad) to communicate; (por radio o televisión) to broadcast

transparencia F transparency

transparente ADJ transparent

transpiración F perspiration

transpirar VI/VT to transpire, to perspire

transportación F transportation, transport

transportar VT (mercancías, gente) to transport; (mercancías) to ship, to haul

transporte M (acción) transport, transportation; (vehículo de transporte) transport (vessel); **— de locura** fit of madness; **— público** mass transit

transportista MF teamster, trucker

transversal ADJ transverse; F transversal

transverso ADJ transverse

tranvía M (transporte urbano) streetcar, trolley; (tren de cercanías) local train

trapacería F racket

trapacero -ra MF racketeer

trapeador M mop

trapear VT *Am* to mop

trapecio M trapeze

trapezoide ADJ & M trapezoid

trapiche M sugar mill

trapisonda F trick

trapo M rag; **—s** *fam* duds; **a todo —** at full speed; **tratar a alguien como un —** to treat someone like dirt; **—s sucios** dirty laundry

tráquea F trachea, windpipe

traquetear VI (hacer sonido) to rattle, to clatter; (llevar a todos lados) to drag from place to place

traqueteo M rattle, clatter

tras PREP (temporal) after; (espacial) after, behind, in back of; **correr —** to run after; **día — día** day after day; **una vez — otra** time after time

trascendencia F transcendence

trascendental ADJ transcendental; (importante) momentous

trascendente ADJ transcendental

trascender VT to transcend; VI (surgir) to emerge; (extender) to extend

trasegar[1,7] VT (vino) to pour from one container to another; (objetos) to move around; (papeles) to shuffle

trasero ADJ (punto, asiento) rear, back; (pata) hind; M (de persona) *fam* rear, rear end, bottom

traslación F transfer

trasladar VT (a un empleado) to transfer; (una reunión) to postpone; **—se** to travel

traslado M transfer

traslapo M overlap

trasnochar VI to stay up late

traspapelar VT to mislay, to misplace; **—se** to become mislaid

traspasar VT (pasar por) to transfix; (ir más allá de) to go beyond; (pasar un límite) to transgress, to cross over; (una propiedad) to transfer

traspaso M transfer

traspié M stumble, slip; **dar un —** to stumble

trasplantar VT to transplant

trasplante M transplant

trasponer[39] VT to transpose

trasquilar VT (una oveja) to shear; (a una persona) to fleece

trastabillar VI to stumble

trastazo M bump

traste M (de guitarra) fret, stop; (trasero) buttocks; **dar al — con** to destroy; **irse al —** to go down the drain

trasto M piece of junk; **—s** stuff

trastocar[6] VT to disrupt

trastornar VT (alterar psíquicamente) to disturb; (alterar el funcionamiento) to disrupt; **—se** to go crazy

trastorno M (molestia) trouble; (patología) disorder; **— bipolar** bipolar disorder; **— de personalidad múltiple** multiple personality disorder

trasudar VI/VT to perspire

trata F trade

tratable ADJ (curable) treatable; (amistoso) approachable

tratado M (acuerdo) treaty; (libro) treatise

tratamiento M (acción de tratar) treatment; (fórmula de cortesía) form of address; **— de textos** *Esp* word processing

tratante MF dealer, trader

tratar VT (una enfermedad, a un paciente, un asunto) to treat; VI (intentar) to try; **— como** to treat like; **— con** to have dealings with; **— de** to try to, to attempt; **— sobre** to be about; **lo trató de imbécil** she called him an idiot; **—le a uno de** to address someone as; **— en** to deal in; **—se con** to have to do with; **—se de** to be a question of, to be

trato M (acuerdo) treatment; (acción de tratar) dealings; (convenio) deal; (comercio) trade; (modales) manners; **¡— hecho!** it's a deal! **tener buen —** to have good manners; **cerrar un —** to strike a bargain

trauma M trauma

traumático ADJ traumatic

traumatismo M trauma

través LOC ADV **a / al — de** through, across;

a — de las declaraciones throughout the declarations; **de —** across; **mirar de —** to look askance (at)

travesaño M crossbar

travesía F crossing, sea voyage, passage

travestí, travesti MF cross-dresser, transvestite

travestido -da MF transvestite

travesura F mischief, prank; **hacer —s** to play pranks

traviesa F railway tie

travieso ADV mischievous, naughty

trayecto M course, route

trayectoria F (de proyectil) trajectory, path; (profesional) career

traza F (huella) trace; (aspecto) appearance; **tiene —s de no acabar nunca** it looks as if it will never end

trazado M (de ciudad) layout; (de edificio) blueprint; (de un plan) outline

trazador M **— gráfico** plotter

trazar[9] VT to trace, to sketch; (un plan) to outline; (un edificio) to blueprint; **— el curso** to plot a course

trébol M clover

trece NUM thirteen

trecho M (distancia) stretch; **a —s** at intervals; **de — en —** at intervals

tregua F (de guerra) truce; (descanso) lull, respite

treinta NUM thirty

tremendo ADJ (extraordinario) tremendous; (terrible) terrible

trementina F turpentine

tremolar VI (bandera) to flutter; (voz) to trill

trémolo M quaver

trémulo ADJ tremulous, trembling

tren M train; **— de aterrizaje** landing gear; **— de carga / de mercancías** freight train; **— de cercanías** local train; **— de vida** lifestyle; **— expreso** express train; **a todo —** at top speed; **perder el —** to miss the boat; **seguir el —** to keep up

trenza F braid

trenzar[9] VT to braid

trepador ADJ (planta) climbing; (ciclista) climber

trepadora F climbing plant

trepar VI to climb

trepidar VI to tremble

tres NUM three

treta F trick, wile

triaje M triage

triangular ADJ triangular

triángulo M triangle; **— recto** right triangle

tribu F tribe

tribulación F tribulation

tribuna F (de orador) rostrum; (de un público) grandstand

tribunal M (judicial) tribunal, court; (cuerpo de jueces) body of judges

tributar VT to pay tribute with; VI to pay taxes

tributario ADJ & M tributary

tributo M (pago obligatorio) tribute; (impuesto) tax

triceps M triceps

triciclo M tricycle

tridimensional ADJ three-dimensional

trifulca F fight

trigo M wheat

trigueño ADJ (tez) swarthy; (pelo) dark-blond

trillado ADJ trite

trilladora F threshing machine

trillar VT to thresh

trillizo -za ADJ & MF triplet

trilogía F trilogy

trimestral ADJ quarterly

trimestre M quarter

trinar VI to trill; **está que trina** she is furious

trinchante M carving knife

trinchar VT to carve

trinche M pitchfork

trinchera F trench; (gabardina) trench coat

trinchero M carving table

trineo M sleigh, sled

trinitense ADJ & MF Trinidadian

trino M trill

trinquete M ratchet

trío M trio

tripas F PL guts; **hacer de — corazón** to pluck up one's courage

triple ADJ triple

triplicar[6] VT to triple, to treble

trípode M tripod

triptongo M triphthong

tripulación F crew

tripular VT to man

triquiñuela F caper

triquitraque M firecracker

triscar[6] VI to frisk

triste ADJ sad, sorrowful

tristeza F sadness, sorrow

tristón ADJ glum

tritón M newt

trituradora F (para desechos) garbage disposal unit; (para papel) paper shredder

triturar VI/VT (documentos) to shred; (granos) to grind

triunfal ADJ triumphal

triunfante ADJ triumphant

triunfar VT to triumph

triunfo M triumph

trivial ADJ trivial, commonplace, trite
trizas F PL **hacer —** to tear into shreds
trocar[2,6] VT (transformar) to change into;
    (cambiar una cosa por otra) to exchange
trocear VT to divide into pieces
trocha F trail
trofeo M trophy
troje M granary
trola F whopper
trole M trolley
trolebús M trolley bus
tromba F waterspout; **salir en —** to storm
    out
trombón M trombone
trompa F (de elefante) trunk; (instrumento
    musical) horn; **— de Falopio** Fallopian
    tube
trompada F blow with the fist
trompeta F trumpet
trompetazo M trumpet blast
trompetear VI to trumpet
trompo M spinning top
tronada F thunderstorm
tronar[2] VI to thunder
tronchar VT to chop off
tronco M (de árbol) trunk, log; (del cuerpo)
    trunk, torso; **dormir como un —** to
    sleep like a log
tronera F (de buque) gun port; (de mesa de
    billar) pocket
trono M throne (también wáter)
tropa F (grupo) troop; (oficiales) rank and
    file; **—s de asalto** storm troops; **—s de**
    choque shock troops
tropel LOC ADV **en —** in droves
tropezar[1,9] VI to stumble, to trip; **—(se) con**
    alguien to meet up with someone; **—**
    con algo to come across something
tropezón M stumble, trip; **salir a**
    tropezones to stumble out; **darse un —**
    to stumble
tropical ADJ tropical
trópico M tropic
tropiezo M stumble
troquel M die
trotar VI to trot
trote M trot; **al —** at a trot; **no estoy para**
    estos —s I'm too old for this
troza F log
trozar[9] VT to cut up
trozo M (de roca, madera, torta) piece; (de un
    texto) section; (de carbón) lump; (de
    carne) slab
trucha F trout
truco M clever trick
truculento ADJ gruesome
trueno M thunder

trueque M barter
truhán -ana MF scoundrel
truja F cigarette
trust M trust
tu ADJ POS your
tú PRON PERS you
tuba F tuba
tuberculosis F tuberculosis
tubería F (tubo) pipe; (conjunto de tubos)
    piping
tubo M (cilindro hueco) tube; (de agua,
    órgano) pipe; (digestivo) tract; **— de**
    ensayo test tube; **— de escape** tailpipe
tubular ADJ tubular
tuerca F nut
tuerto ADJ one-eyed
tuétano M marrow; **hasta los —s** through
    and through
tufillo M whiff
tufo M (humo) fumes; (hedor) stench
tugurio M hovel; **—s** slums
tulipán M tulip
tullido -da ADJ crippled; MF pey cripple
tullir VT to cripple; **—se** to become crippled
tumba F (panteón) tomb; (sepultura) grave;
    soy una — my lips are sealed
tumbar VT to knock down, to flatten; **—se**
    to lie down, to stretch out
tumbo M tumble, somersault; **dar —s**
    (persona) to stagger; (coche) to bump
    along
tumor M tumor
tumulto M (alboroto) tumult, uproar;
    (muchedumbre) mob
tumultuoso ADJ tumultuous
tuna F prickly pear; *Esp* minstrel group
tunante -ta MF scamp
tunda F thrashing
túnel M tunnel
tunesino -na ADJ & MF Tunisian
Túnez M Tunisia
tungsteno M tungsten
túnica F tunic; **— de laboratorio** lab gown
tupido ADJ dense, compact
tupir VT (hacer tupido) to compact; (cubrir)
    to cover; **—se** to stuff oneself
turba F (muchedumbre) mob; (carbón fósil)
    peat
turbación F confusion
turbamulta F throng
turbante M turban
turbar VT to disturb; **—se** to become
    disturbed
turbina F turbine
turbio ADJ (pasado, secreto) dark; (agua,
    materia) murky
turbocompresor M turbocharger

turborreactor M turbojet
turbulento ADJ turbulent
turco -ca ADJ Turkish; MF Turk; M (lengua) Turkish
turcomano -na ADJ & MF Turkmen
turismo M (actividad) tourism; (conjunto de turistas) tourists; **hacer —** to go sightseeing
turista MF tourist
Turkmenistán M Turkmenistan
turnarse VI to take turns
turno M turn; (de trabajo) shift
turquesa F turquoise
Turquía F Turkey
turrón M nougat
tutear VT to address as "tú"
tutela F guardianship
tutelar VT to have charge of
tutor -ora MF (de un menor) guardian; M (de planta) prop
Tuvalu M Tuvalu
tuvaluano -na ADJ & MF Tuvaluan
tuyo PRON your, yours; **el amigo —** your friend; **esto es —** this is yours
tweed M tweed

Uu

u CONJ or
ubicación F location
ubicar[6] VT (situar) to locate; (identificar) to place; **—se** to be located
ubicuo ADJ ubiquitous
ubre F udder
UCP (unidad central de proceso) F CPU
Ucrania F Ukraine
ucraniano -na ADJ & MF Ukrainian
ufanarse VI to glory (in), to be proud (of)
ufano ADJ proud
Uganda F Uganda
ugandés -esa ADJ & MF Ugandan
ujier M bailiff
úlcera F (lesión superficial) sore; (en el estómago) sore; (en la boca) canker, sore
ulterior ADJ ulterior
últimamente ADV of late
ultimar VT to finalize
ultimátum M ultimatum
último ADJ last, final; (destino) ultimate; (más reciente) latest; **estar en las últimas** to be on one's last legs; **la última palabra** the last word; **en los —s tiempos** lately; **a última hora** at

the last moment
ultrajante ADJ outrageous
ultrajar VT to outrage
ultraje M outrage, indignity
ultraligero M ultralight
ultramar LOC ADV **de —** overseas
ultramoderno ADJ ultramodern
ultratumba LOC ADV **de —** from beyond the grave
ultravioleta ADJ INV & M ultraviolet
ulular VI to howl, to hoot
ululato M hoot
umbral M threshold, doorstep
umbrío ADJ shady
un, uno, una ART INDEF a, an; **un hombre** a man; **un actor** an actor; **una mujer** a woman; **una manzana** an apple; NUM one; **de a —** one at a time; **es la una** it is one o'clock; **yo tengo —** I have one; PRON one; **— por —** one by one; **—s** some; **—s cuantos** some; **— tiene que cuidarse** you've got to take care of yourself; **— tras otro** one after the other; **— al lado del otro** side by side; **los —s a los otros / el — al otro** one another / each other
unánime ADJ unanimous
unanimidad F unanimity
uncir[10b] VT to yoke; (a un carro) to hitch
ungüento M ointment, salve
único ADJ only; (extraordinario) unique
unidad F (indivisibilidad) unity; (ejemplar) unit; (fracción militar) unit, outfit; **— central de proceso** central processing unit
unificar[6] VT to unify
uniformar VT (estandarizar) to standardize; (dar uniformes) to furnish with uniforms
uniforme ADJ & M uniform
uniformidad F uniformity
unilateral ADJ unilateral
unión F (acción de unir, cosas unidas) union; (lugar en que se unen dos cosas) junction; (indivisibilidad) unity
unir VT to unite; (dos construcciones) to join; (cinta magnética, genes) to splice; (caños) to couple; VI/VT (con lazos) to bind
unisex ADJ unisex
unísono ADJ unison; **al —** in unison
universal ADJ universal
universidad F (de enseñanza e investigación) university; (de enseñanza) college
universitario ADJ university; (relativo a los deportes) collegiate
universo M universe
untar VT (la piel con crema) to oil; (pan con

mantequilla) to spread on; (la cara con pintura) to smear; **— la mano a alguien** to grease someone's palm

untuoso ADJ (graso) oily; (zalamero) slick, unctuous

uña F fingernail; (de gato) claw; **como — y carne** thick as thieves; **con —s y dientes** tooth and nail

uranio M uranium

urbanidad F refinement, polish

urbanización F development

urbanizar[9] VT to build up

urbano ADJ (relativo a la ciudad) urban; (refinado) suave; **autobus —** city bus

urbe F metropolis

urdimbre F warp

urdir VT (una tela) to weave; (una historia) to concoct; (un plan) to devise, to work out

uretra F urethra

urgencia F (prisa) urgency; (crisis médica) emergency; **con —** urgently; **—s** emergency room

urgente ADJ urgent, pressing

urgir[11] VT to urge; VI to be urgent

úrico ADJ uric

urinario ADJ urinary; M urinal

URL M URL

urna F (para cenizas) urn; (electoral) ballot box; **acudir a las —** s to go to the polls

urólogo -ga MF urologist

urraca F (ave) magpie; (persona acaparadora) packrat

urticaria F hives

Uruguay M Uruguay

uruguayo -ya ADJ & MF Uruguayan

usado ADJ used; (desgastado) worn

usar VT to use; (ropa) to wear; **—se** to be in use; **sin —** unused

uso M (empleo) use; (costumbre) usage, custom; **al — de la época** according to the custom of the time

usted PRON PERS you; **—es** you, you all, y'all

usual ADJ usual

usuario -ria MF user; (en una biblioteca) borrower

usufructo M enjoyment

usufructuar[17] VT to enjoy the use of

usura F usury

usurero -ra MF usurer, loan shark

usurpar VT to encroach upon, to usurp

utensilio M utensil

útero M uterus, womb

útil ADJ useful, helpful; M PL **—es** utensils

utilidad F usefulness, utility

utilitario ADJ utilitarian

utilización F use, utilization

utilizar[9] VT to utilize; (explotar) to use

utopía F utopia

uva F grape

úvula F uvula

uvular ADJ uvular

Uzbekistán M Uzbekistan

uzbeko -ka ADJ & MF Uzbek

Vv

vaca F cow; **— marina** sea cow

vacaciones F PL vacation

vacante ADJ vacant; F vacancy, opening

vaciar[16] VT to empty; (una naranja) to hollow out; (una estatua) to cast

vacilación F hesitation

vacilante ADJ vacillating, hesitating; (tembloroso) shaky

vacilar VI to vacillate, to hesitate, to waver; **— (con)** *Esp fam* to make fun (of)

vacío ADJ empty; (casa) vacant; (comentarios) idle; (expresión) blank; M (condición) emptiness; (lugar) void; (espacio sin aire) vacuum; **envasado al —** vacuum-packed; **hacer el —** to give the cold shoulder

vacuna F vaccine

vacunación F vaccination

vacunar VI/VT to vaccinate

vadear VT to ford

vado M ford, crossing

vagabundear VI to wander idly

vagabundo -da ADJ vagabond, vagrant; MF (pordiosero) tramp, bum; (trabajador errante) drifter, transient; (en la playa) beachcomber

vagancia F vagrancy

vagar[7] VI to wander, to roam

vagina F vagina

vago -ga ADJ (idea) vague; (silueta) shadowy; (impresión) faint, vague; (persona) lazy; MF vagrant, tramp

vagón M railway car; **— restaurante** dining car

vaguedad F faintness

vahído M dizzy spell

vaho M steam

vaina F (de una espada) sheath; (de legumbres) pod, shell; (molestia) nuisance

vainilla F vanilla

vaivén M swaying, swinging; **vaivenes** ups and downs

vajilla F tableware, dishes; **— de barro** earthenware; **— de porcelana** chinaware

vale M voucher
valedero ADJ valid
valentía F courage, valor, bravery
valentón -ona ADJ cocky; MF cocky person
valer[46] VT (tener un determinado valor) to be worth; VI (ser válido) to be valid; (estar permitido) to be allowed; (ser de utilidad) to be useful; — **la pena** to be worthwhile; — **más que** to outweigh; **—se de** to avail oneself of; **—se por sí mismo** to be self-sufficient; **¿cuánto vale?** how much is it? **hacer — los derechos** to assert one's rights; **hacerse** — to stand up for oneself; **le valió una paliza** that earned him a beating; **más vale sólo que mal acompañado** better alone than in poor company; **no hay pero que valga** no buts about it; **no vale ni un comino** it's not worth a hoot; **no vale** that's not fair; **¡vale!** OK; **¡válgame Dios!** gracious! **todo —** anything goes
valeroso ADJ valorous, brave
valía F worth
validez F validity
válido ADJ valid; (cheque) good; (argumento) solid
valiente ADJ valiant, brave, courageous
valija F valise, suitcase; (para el correo) pouch
valioso ADJ valuable
valla F fence; (en carreras) hurdle
vallar VT to fence
valle M valley, vale
valor M (precio) value, worth; (valentía) valor, mettle; — **contable** book value; **—es** securities; **—es en cartera** holdings; — **nominal** face value; **armarse de** — to muster up one's courage
valoración F valuation
valorar VT (apreciar el valor) to value; (determinar el valor) to appraise
valorizar[9] VT to make more valuable; **—se** to become more valuable
vals M waltz
valsar VI to waltz
valuación F valuation, appraisal
valuar[17] VT to appraise
valva F valve
válvula F valve; — **reguladora de aceleración** throttle
vampiresa F vamp
vampiro M vampire
vanagloria F boastfulness
vanagloriarse VI to boast
vanaglorioso ADJ boastful
vándalo -la MF vandal

vanguardia F vanguard; **a la** — at the forefront
vanidad F vanity, conceit
vanidoso ADJ vain
vano ADJ vain; **en** — in vain
Vanuatu M Vanuatu
vanuatuense ADJ & MF Vanuatuan
vapor M (de agua) vapor, steam; (buque) steamship; **—es** fumes; **cocer al** — to steam; **echar** — to give off steam
vapulear VT to thrash
vapuleo M thrashing
vaquería F cowshed
vaqueriza F cowshed
vaquero -ra M cowboy; **—s** blue jeans; F cowgirl; ADJ **botas —s** cowboy boots
vaqueta F cowhide
vaquilla F heifer
vara F (rama) stick; (palo) rod
varadero M dry dock
varano M monitor lizard
varar VT to beach, to strand; VI to run aground
varear VT to whip with a stick
variable ADJ variable, changeable; F variable
variación F variation
variado ADJ varied
variante F variant
variar[16] VI/VT to vary
varicela F chicken pox
várices, varices F PL varicose veins
varicoso ADJ varicose
variedad F variety, assortment
varilla F small rod; (para azotar) switch; (de paraguas) rib
vario ADJ varied; **—s** various, several
variopinto ADJ variegated
varita F wand
varón M male (person)
varonil ADJ manly; (hombruno) mannish
vasco -ca ADJ & MF Basque; M (lengua) Basque
vascuence ADJ Basque; M (lengua) Basque
vascular ADJ vascular
vasectomía F vasectomy
vaselina F Vaseline[tm]
vasija F vessel
vaso M (de vidrio) glass; (de papel, plástico) cup; (corto y grueso) tumbler; (sanguíneo) vessel; — **de precipitado** beaker
vástago M (de planta) shoot, sprout; (de persona) offspring; (de motor) rod
vasto ADJ vast
vataje M wattage
vaticinar VT to foretell
vaticinio M prediction
vatio M watt

vecindad F (cercanía) vicinity; (barrio) neighborhood

vecindario M neighborhood

vecino -na MF (de al lado) neighbor; (residente) resident; ADJ neighboring

vedar VT to prohibit

vega F fertile plain

vegan ADJ & MF INV vegan

vegetación F vegetation

vegetal ADJ vegetable; M plant; MF (persona paralizada) vegetable

vegetar VI to vegetate

vegetariano -na ADJ & MF vegetarian

vehemencia F vehemence

vehemente ADJ vehement

vehículo M vehicle

veinte NUM twenty

veintena F (aproximadamente) group of (about) twenty; (exactamente) score

veintiuno NUM twenty-one; M (juego de naipes) blackjack

vejancón -ona M codger; F old woman

vejar VT to humiliate

vejestorio -ria M codger; F old woman

vejete M codger

vejez F old age

vejiga F bladder; (ampolla) blister

vela F (período de vigilancia) vigil, watch; (de cera) candle; (de un navío) sail; **a toda —** under full sail; **en —** without sleep; **hacerse a la —** to set sail

velada F (noche) evening; (fiesta) evening party

velador M nightstand

velar VI (no dormir) to keep vigil, to stay awake; (cubrir con velo) to veil; (exponer a la luz una película fotográfica) to expose; **— por** to look after

velatorio M wake

veleidoso ADJ fickle

velero M sailboat; ADJ swift-sailing

veleta F weathervane; MF INV fickle person

vello M (del cuerpo) body hair; (de frutas) fuzz

vellón M fleece

velloso ADJ fuzzy

velludo ADJ hairy

velo M veil; **— del paladar** soft palate

velocidad F velocity, speed; **a toda —** at full speed

velocímetro M speedometer

velorio M wake

veloz ADJ swift, fast

vena F (vaso sanguíneo, veta) vein; (estado de ánimo) mood; (de locura) streak; **estar en —** to be in the mood, to be inspired

venado M deer; (macho) stag; (carne de venado) venison

vencedor -ora ADJ winning; MF winner, victor

vencer[10a] VT (a un enemigo) to conquer, to vanquish; (a un equipo) to defeat, to beat; (obstáculos) to overcome; (en valor, inteligencia) to surpass; VI **—se** (un plazo) to expire; (el asiento de una silla) to cave in

vencido ADJ (derrotado) defeated; (a pagar) due, overdue; **darse por —** to give up, to surrender

vencimiento M (de una deuda) maturity; (de un contrato) expiration

venda F bandage; (sobre los ojos) blindfold

vendaje M bandage

vendar VT (una herida) to bandage; (los ojos) to blindfold

vendaval M gale

vendedor -ora MF vendor, seller, salesperson; **— mayorista** wholesaler

vender VI/VT to sell; (traicionar) to betray; **—se a** to go over to; **se vende** for sale

vendetta F vendetta

vendible ADJ marketable

vendimia F vintage

veneciana F venetian blind

veneno M poison; (de víboras) venom

venenoso ADJ poisonous; (de víboras) venomous

venerable ADJ venerable

veneración F veneration, reverence

venerar VT (a una persona) to venerate, to revere; (a Dios) to worship

venéreo ADJ venereal

venezolano -na ADJ & MF Venezuelan

Venezuela F Venezuela

vengador -ora ADJ avenging; MF avenger

venganza F vengeance, revenge

vengar[7] VT to avenge; **—se de** to retaliate for, to avenge, to take revenge

vengativo ADJ vindictive, vengeful

venida F coming

venidero ADJ forthcoming

venir[47] VI to come; **— a colación** to come up (in conversation); **— al caso / a cuento** to be relevant; **— bien** to be convenient; **—le a uno bien** to be suitable to someone; **—se** *fam* to come (sexually); **—se abajo** to collapse; **¿a qué viene eso?** what is the point of that? **el año que viene** next year; **lo mejor esta por —** the best is yet to come; **no me vengas con excusas** no excuses; **venga lo que venga** come what may

venta F sale; **— al por mayor** wholesale; **— al por menor** retail; **en —** for sale;

poner a la — to put up for sale
ventaja F advantage; (en una carrera) head start
ventajoso ADJ advantageous
ventana F window; **tirar por la** — to throw out the window
ventanilla F (de coche, avión) window; (de la nariz) nostril
ventarrón M gale, high wind
ventear VI to sniff the wind
ventilación F ventilation; (hueco para el aire) vent
ventilado ADJ airy
ventilador M (abertura) ventilator; (aparato) electrical fan
ventilar VT to ventilate, to air out; (una cuestión) to air
ventisca F blizzard
ventisquero M (lugar ventoso) place prone to blizzards; (lugar nevado) snowfield
ventolera F gust of wind; **darle a uno la — de** to take a notion to
ventosear VI to break wind
ventoso ADJ windy, breezy
ventrículo M ventricle
venturoso ADJ **futuro** — bright future
ver[48] VI/VT to see; (televisión, espectáculos) to watch; **a** — let's see; **eso aún está por —se** that is still to be seen; **no lo puedo** — I can't stand him; **no — la hora de** to be dying for something to happen; **no tener nada que — con** not to have anything to do with; **te veo preocupado** you look worried; **a mi modo de** — in my opinion; **—se obligado a** to be obliged to; **vérselas con algo** to confront something; **vérselas negras** to have a hard time
vera LOC ADV **a la** — beside
veracidad F truthfulness
veranear VI to spend the summer
veraneo M summer vacation
veraniego ADJ summer
verano M summer
veras LOC ADV **de** — really
veraz ADJ truthful
verbal ADJ verbal
verbena F carnival
verbo M verb
verborrágico ADJ long-winded
verboso ADJ verbose, wordy
verdad F truth; **¿—?** really? **de** — indeed; **una pistola de** — a real pistol; **faltar a la** — to fib
verdadero ADJ true, real
verde ADJ green (también inmaduro, sin experiencia, ecologista); (chiste) off-color;

— **oliva** olive-green; **ponerse** — to stuff oneself; M green; **poner — a alguien** to run someone down
verdear VI/VT to turn green
verdín M scum
verdor M greenness
verdoso ADJ greenish
verdugo M executioner, hangman
verdugón M welt
verdulero -ra MF vegetable vendor
verduras F PL produce
vereda F *Am* sidewalk; **entrar en** — to toe the line
veredicto M verdict
verga F (percha para vela) yard; (pene) *vulg* dick
vergonzoso ADJ (que da vergüenza) shameful, disgraceful; (que siente vergüenza) sheepish, bashful
vergüenza F (humillación) shame; (incomodidad) embarrassment; (escándalo) disgrace; **tener** — to be ashamed; **es una** — it's a shame
vericueto M twists and turns
verídico ADJ truthful, true
verificación F verification, cross-check
verificar[6] VT to verify, to check; **—se** to take place
verja F grate
vermú M vermouth
vernáculo ADJ & M vernacular
verruga F wart; — **genital** genital wart
versado ADJ versed
versar VI — **sobre** to deal (with), to treat
versátil ADJ versatile
versículo M Bible verse
versión F version; (traducción) translation; (de una canción) rendition; — **original** original (of a film)
verso M line (of poetry); — **libre** free verse; — **suelto / blanco** blank verse
versus PREP versus
vértebra F vertebra
vertebrado ADJ & M vertebrate
vertebral ADJ spinal
vertedero M dump, landfill
verter[1] VT (echar líquido) to pour; (vaciar) to pour out; (derramar) to spill; — **en** to empty into; **—se** to spill
vertical ADJ vertical; (erguido) upright; (empinado) sheer
vertiente F (pendiente) slope; (cuenca) watershed; ADJ flowing
vertiginoso ADJ dizzy, giddy
vértigo M (falta de equilibrio) vertigo; (frenesí) hectic pace
vertigoso ADJ dizzy, giddy

vesícula F gall bladder
vestíbulo M (de un edificio) vestibule, lobby; (de una casa) hallway
vestido M dress; — **de noche** evening gown; — **de novia** bridal dress
vestidura F attire
vestigio M vestige, trace, remnant
vestimenta F attire, dress; (estrafalaria) get-up
vestir[5] VT to dress, to clothe; —**se** to get dressed; —**se de gala** to dress up
vestuario M wardrobe; (en el teatro) costumes; (lugar para vestirse) changing room
veta F (de minerales) vein, seam; (de madera) grain; (de humor) strain
vetar VT to veto
veteado ADJ veined
veterano -**na** ADJ & MF veteran
veterinario -**ria** MF veterinarian; ADJ veterinary; F veterinary medicine
veto M veto
vetusto ADJ ancient
vez F time; **a la** — at the same time; **a su** — in turn; **a veces** sometimes; **cada** — **más** more and more; **cada** — **que** whenever; **de** — **en cuando** from time to time; **de una** — (por entero) all at once; (por fin) one and for all; **de una** — **por todas** once and for all; **en** — **de** instead of; **por primera** — for the first time; **otra** — again; **una** — **(que)** once; **una** — **tras otra** one and over; **una y otra** — over and over again; **raras veces** seldom; **hacer las veces de** to take the place of
vía F (camino) road; (de ferrocarril) track; (medio de acceso) avenue; — **Láctea** Milky Way; — **navegable** waterway; **por** — **de** by means of; **en** —**s de** in the process of; PREP via
viable ADJ viable
viaducto M tunnel
viajante MF traveler; — **de comercio** traveling salesman / saleswoman
viajar VI to travel, to journey; (por mar) to voyage; (con drogas) to trip
viaje M trip, journey; (por mar) voyage; (en coche, caballo) ride; (por efecto de las drogas) trip; — **de ida y vuelta** round trip; **buen** — have a nice trip; **de** — out of town
viajero -**ra** MF traveler
viandante MF passer-by
viático M (de viaje) per diem; (religioso) last rites
víbora F viper; — **de cascabel** rattlesnake
vibración F vibration; (de la lengua) trill

vibrador M vibrator
vibrante ADJ vibrating
vibrar VI/VT to vibrate
vicegobernador -**ora** MF lieutenant governor
vicepresidente -**ta** MF vice-president
vicerrector -**ora** MF provost
viceversa ADV vice versa
viciado ADJ (aire) stale; (costumbre) stuffy; (corrupto) foul
viciar VT to foul; (corromper) to corrupt
vicio M (mala costumbre) vice, bad habit; **de** — unjustifiably; **quitarse el** — **de** to wean oneself of
vicioso ADJ (persona) having bad habits; (gasto) unjustifiable; (gramática) faulty
vicisitud F vicissitude
víctima F victim; (en un accidente) casualty, victim
victimizar[9] VT to victimize
victoria F victory
victorioso ADJ victorious
vid F vine, grapevine
vida F life; — **mía** sweetheart; — **nocturna** night life; — **sentimental** love life; **así es la** — that's life; **de toda la** — lifelong; **de** — **o muerte** life and death; **en la** — **voy a hacer eso** I would never do that; **esto es** — this is the life; **ganarse la** — to earn a living; **mujer de mala** — *fam* hooker; **sin** — lifeless
vidente MF seer; ADJ seeing
vídeo, video M (aparato) VCR; (técnica) video; (cinta) videocassette
videocasete F videocassette
videoconferencia F videoconference
videojuego M video game
vidriado M glaze; ADJ glazed
vidriar VT to glaze
vidriera F show window
vidriero -**ra** MF glazier, glassmaker
vidrio M (sustancia) glass; (en una ventana) pane; **pagar los** —**s rotos** to be left holding the bag
vidrioso ADJ glassy
vieira F scallop
viejo -**ja** ADJ old; (chiste) stale; M old man; (padre) father; — **verde** dirty old man; **los** —**s** the old folks; F old woman; (madre) mother
viento M wind; **hace** — it is windy; **a los cuatro** —**s** in all directions
vientre M abdomen; (barriga) belly; (de mujer) womb
viernes M Friday
Vietnam M Vietnam
vietnamita ADJ & MF INV Vietnamese

viga F (de madera) beam, rafter; (de metal) girder

vigencia F **entrar en —** to go into effect; **estar en —** to be in force

vigente ADJ effective, in force

vigía F lookout, reef; MF INV lookout

vigilancia F vigilance; (en una tienda) surveillance

vigilante ADJ vigilant; M watchman; F watchwoman

vigilar VI/VT to keep watch (over); VT to keep an eye on; (policía) to stake out

vigilia F vigil, watch

vigor M vigor; **en —** in force; **entrar en —** to become effective

vigorizar[9] VT to invigorate

vigoroso ADJ vigorous

VIH (virus de inmunodeficiencia humana) M HIV

vil ADJ vile, base, low

vileza F villainy, baseness

vilipendiar VT to revile

villa F village

villancico M Christmas carol

villanía F villainy

villano -na ADJ villainous; MF villain

vilo LOC ADV **en —** (en el aire) suspended; (en ascuas) in suspense

vinagre M vinegar

vincular VT to link; **—se** to link up

vínculo M link, tie

vindicar[6] VT to vindicate

vinilo M vinyl

vino M wine; **— blanco** white wine; **— espumoso** sparkling wine; **— rosado** rosé wine; **— tinto** red wine

viña F vineyard

viñatero -ra MF winegrower

viñedo M vineyard

viola F viola

violación F violation; (sexual) rape

violado ADJ violet; M violet

violar VT (una ley) to violate, to break; (una mujer) to rape, to ravish; (una promesa) to breach; (una cerradura) to pick; (derechos) to infringe upon; (mandamientos) to trespass against

violencia F violence; **— doméstica** domestic violence

violentar VT (a una persona) to manhandle; (una casa) to break into; **—se** to get mortified

violento ADJ violent, rough; (marido) abusive; (entrada) forcible; (ataque) vicious

violeta ADJ INV & M violet

violín M violin; (para música folklórica) fiddle

violinista MF violinist

violonchelo M cello

virada F veer

viraje M swerve

virar VI/VT (vehículo) to swerve, to veer; VI (barco) to tack

virgen ADJ & MF virgin; ADJ (cassette) blank; (selva) undisturbed

virginal ADJ virginal

viril ADJ virile, manly

virilidad F virility, manhood

virreinato M viceroyalty

virrey M viceroy

virtual ADJ virtual

virtud F (moral) virtue; (práctica) asset

virtuoso -sa ADJ (moral) virtuous; ADJ & MF (artístico) virtuoso

viruela F smallpox

virulento ADJ virulent

virus M virus (también de computadoras)

viruta F wood shaving

visa F visa

visado M visa

visar VT to endorse

visceral ADJ visceral

viscoso ADJ viscous

visera F visor

visible ADJ visible

visigodo -da ADJ Visigothic; MF Visigoth

visillo M window shade

visión F vision; (persona fea) sight

visionario -ria ADJ & MF visionary

visita F (acción de visitar) visit; (persona) visitor, caller; (a un edificio) tour; **— de médico** house call

visitación F visitation

visitador -ora MF visitor, caller; (inspector) inspector; (vendedor de medicamentos) pharmaceutical sales representative

visitante MF caller, visitor; ADJ visiting

visitar VT to visit; (un médico) to make a house call

vislumbrar VT to make out

viso M slip

visón M mink

víspera LOC ADV **en —s de** on the eve of

vista F (panorama) view, vista; (visión) eyesight; **a la —** in sight; **a primera —** at first sight; **a simple —** with the naked eye; **bajar la —** to lower one's eyes; **conocer de —** to know by sight; **con —s a** with a view to; **en — de** considering; **hacer la — gorda** to look the other way; **¡hasta la —!** good-bye; **perder de —** to lose sight of; **tener a la —** to have before one's eyes; **tener — a** to look out on

vistazo M glance, glimpse, look; **dar / echar**

un — a to glance over
visto ADJ **bien —** well thought of; **mal —** looked down upon; **— que** whereas; M **— bueno** approval; **dar el — bueno** to approve
vistoso ADJ showy
visual ADJ visual
visualizador M display
visualizar[9] VT to visualize; (en pantalla) to display
vital ADJ vital; **fuerzas —es** life force
vitalicio ADJ life; M lifetime pension
vitalidad F vitality
vitamina F vitamin
viticultor -ora MF winegrower
vítor M cheer
vitorear VI/VT to cheer
vitral M stained-glass window
vitrina F (ventana) shop window; (armario) showcase
vituperación F vituperation
vituperar VT to revile
vituperio M vituperation
viudo -da M widower; F widow; **viuda negra** black widow spider
vivacidad F vivacity
vivaracho ADJ vivacious
vivaz ADJ vivacious, lively
víveres M PL provisions
vivero M nursery
viveza F (vivacidad) liveliness; (inteligencia) cleverness
vívido ADJ vivid
vivienda F (casa) dwelling; (alojamiento) housing
viviente ADJ living
vivir VI/VT to live; **vive una vida normal** he leads a normal life; **¡viva!** hurrah! long live!
vivisección F vivisection
vivo ADJ (no muerto) alive, living; (ágil) lively; (vistoso, intenso) vivid; (listo) clever; **en —** before a live audience; **en — y en directo** live; **de viva voz** by word of mouth
vocablo M word
vocabulario M vocabulary
vocación F vocation, calling; (religioso) call
vocal ADJ vocal; (no consonántico) vowel; F vowel; MF member
vocálico ADJ vocalic
vocear VI/VT to cry out; (anunciar) to page
vocerío M clamor
vocero -ra MF spokesperson
vociferante ADJ vociferous
vociferar VI to clamor
vodevil M vaudeville

vodka M vodka
volado ADJ (drogado) high; (escrito arriba) superscript
volador ADJ flying
volante ADJ flying; M (en un vestido) ruffle, frill; (en un coche) steering wheel; (en un motor) flywheel; (folleto) leaflet, handbill
volar[2] VI/VT to fly; **— por su cuenta** to fly solo; **ir volando** to hurry; VT (un puente) to blow up; VI (hojas) to blow; **—se** (hacer explosión) to blow up; (enojarse) to lose one's temper; (irse volando) to fly away; (drogarse) *fam* to get stoned
volátil ADJ volatile
volcán M volcano
volcánico ADJ volcanic
volcar[2,6] VT (voltear) to tip over, to knock over; (derramar) to spill; (vaciar) to empty; VI to roll over; **—se** to tip over, to overturn
volea F volley
volear VI/VT to volley
voleibol M volleyball
volición F volition
volquete M dump truck
voltaje M voltage
voltear VT (una lámpara) to knock over, to turn over; (la cara) to turn away
voltereta F somersault, tumble; **dar una —** to somersault; **dar —s** to tumble
voltio M volt
voluble ADJ (malhumorado) moody; (mercado de valores) volatile
volumen M volume
voluminoso ADJ voluminous, bulky
voluntad F will; **a —** at will; **buena —** good will, willingness; **mala —** ill will; **por su propia —** of his own volition
voluntario -ria ADJ (por la propia voluntad) voluntary; MF volunteer
voluntarioso ADJ (bien dispuesto) willing; (testarudo) willful
voluptuoso ADJ voluptuous
voluta F scroll; **—s de humo** spirals of smoke
volver[2,51] VI (ir al punto de partida) to return, to come back; (ir de nuevo) to return, to go back, to go again; **— a comer** to eat again; **— del revés** to turn inside out; **— en sí** to regain consciousness; **—se** (regresar) to go back; (ponerse) to become; **—se contra** to turn against; **—se atrás** to turn back; **—se hacia** to go toward; **—se loco** to go crazy; VT (la cara) to turn away; **— las espaldas** to turn one's back
vomitar VI/VT to vomit, to throw up

vómito M vomit

voraz ADJ voracious, ravenous

vórtice M vortex

vosotros -as PRON PERS you, you guys; (sur de EEUU) you all, y'all

votación F vote

votante MF voter

votar VI to vote; VT (elegir) to vote for; (aprobar) to vote into law; — **a** / **por** to vote for

voto M (opinión) vote; (promesa) vow; — **de confianza** vote of confidence

voz F (sonido, aptitud, voto) voice; (cabeza de entrada) headword; **a — en cuello** at the top of one's lungs; **alzar la —** to raise one's voice; **correr la —** to be rumored; **en — alta** aloud; **a voces** shouting; **dar voces** to shout

vozarrón M loud voice

vudú M voodoo

vuelco M **todo daría un —** everything would change radically; **me dio un — el corazón** my heart skipped a beat; **dar un —** to overturn, to turn over

vuelo M flight; (de una falda) flare; **al —** on the fly; **de alto —** prestigious; **levantar** / **alzar el —** to fly away

vuelta F (movimiento circular) turn; (regreso, devolución) return; (carrera ciclista) tour; (en una pista) lap; (curva) twist; (de un collar) loop; (en deportes) round; (dinero) change; — **de tuerca** unforeseen event; **a la — de la esquina** around the corner; **a — de correo** by return mail; **dar —** to turn upside down; **dar — al revés** to turn inside out; **dar — a una página** / **una llave** to turn a page / a key; **dar —s** to spin; **dar —s en la cama** to toss and turn; **dar — a algo** to turn something upside down; **dar la —** to turn around; **dar una —** to take a walk, to take a spin; **darse —** to roll over; **estar de —** (de regreso) to be back; (desencantado) to be jaded; **me da —s la cabeza** my head is spinning; **no tiene — de hoja** there are no two ways about it

vuelto M *Am* change

vuestro ADJ POS — **hermano** your bother; **un amigo —** a friend of yours; PRON **el — yours**

vulgar ADJ (común) ordinary; (tosco) vulgar

vulgo M common people

vulnerable ADJ vulnerable

vulva F vulva

Ww

wafle M waffle

waflera F waffle iron

wáter M toilet

web F World Wide Web

whisky M whisk(e)y; — **escocés** scotch

windsurf M windsurfing

wok M wok

Xx

xenofobia F xenophobia

xilofón, xilófono M xylophone

Yy

y CONJ and

ya ADV (desde antes) already; (ahora) now; (pronto) soon; ¡—! enough! — **era hora** it was about time; ¡— **lo creo!** I should say so! — **no** no longer; — **que** since; — **sea que** whether; — **te arreglo** I'll fix you; — **verás** mark my words; — **voy** I am coming

yacer[49] VI to lie

yacimiento M (de minerales) deposit; (de petróleo) field

yanqui ADJ & MF *pey* American

yarda F yard

yate M yacht

yegua F mare

yelmo M helmet

yema F (de huevo) egg yolk; (de una planta) bud, shoot; — **del dedo** fingertip

Yemen M Yemen

yemení ADJ & MF Yemeni

yen M yen

yermo ADJ (estéril) barren; (desolado) bleak, stark

yerno M son-in-law

yesca F tinder

yeso M (mineral) gypsum; (en construcción, medicina) plaster (of Paris); (escayola) cast

Yibuti M Djibouti

yibutiano -na ADJ & MF Djiboutian
yo PRON PERS I; M (ego) ego
yodo M iodine
yoduro M iodide
yoga M yoga
yogur M yogurt
yo-yo M yo-yo
yuca F (ornamental) yucca; (comestible) manioc
yugo M yoke
Yugoslavia F Yugoslavia
yugoslavo -va ADJ & MF Yugoslavian
yugular ADJ & F jugular
yunque M anvil
yunta F yoke
yuppie MF yuppie
yuxtaponer[39] VT juxtapose

Zz

zafar VT to release; —se (soltarse) to slip off; (no cumplir) to cop out; —se de un aprieto to squirm out of a difficulty
zafio ADJ boorish
zafiro M sapphire
zafra F (sugar) harvest
zaga LOC ADV a la — behind; F ir a la — to be behind; quedar a la — to fall behind
zaguán M vestibule, hall
zaino ADJ chestnut-colored
zalamería F (tacto) smoothness; (lisonja) flattery
zalamero -ra MF flatterer; ADJ (empalagoso) smooth, unctuous; (lisonjero) flattering
Zambia F Zambia
zambiano -na ADJ & MF Zambian
zambo ADJ knock-kneed
zambullida F dive, plunge
zambullir[19] VT to plunge, to dip; —se to dive, to plunge
zanahoria F carrot
zanca F leg of a wading bird
zancada F stride; dar —s to stride
zancadilla F intentional tripping; hacer una — to trip
zanco M stilt
zancudo ADJ long-legged, lanky; M Am mosquito
zángano M drone (también holgazán)
zangolotear VI/VT to jiggle
zangoloteo M jiggle
zanja F ditch, trench
zanjar VT to settle

zapapico M pickax(e)
zapata F brake shoe
zapatear VI to tap the feet in dancing
zapateo M tapping with the feet in dance
zapatería F shoe store
zapatero -ra MF (que fabrica) shoemaker; (que vende) shoe dealer; (que remienda) cobbler
zapatilla F (pantufla) slipper; (de vestir) pump; —s sneakers
zapato M shoe
zar M czar
zarandear VT to jiggle; —se to flop around
zarandeo M jiggle
zarcillo M (arete) earring; (de planta) tendril
zarigüeya F opossum
zarpa F claw
zarpar VI to sail, to set sail
zarpazo M blow with a claw; dar —s to claw
zarza F bramble, briar
zarzamora F blackberry
zepelín M blimp, zeppelin
zigoto M zygote
zigzag M zigzag
zigzaguear VI to zigzag, to weave one's way
Zimbabue M Zimbabwe
zimbabuo -ua ADJ & MF Zimbabwean
zirconio M zirconium
zócalo M baseboard
zodíaco M zodiac
zombi M zombie
zona F (área) zone; (culebrilla) shingles; — gris gray area; — tampón buffer zone
zonzo ADJ silly, foolish
zoo M zoo
zoología F zoology
zoológico ADJ zoological; M zoo
zoom M zoom lens
zopenco -ca MF dolt, numbskull
zorrillo M skunk
zorro -a MF fox; F (hembra) vixen; (prostituta) pey prostitute; ADJ (astuto) foxy, cunning; (promiscuo) loose
zorzal M thrush
zozobra F anxiety, worry
zozobrar VI to founder
zueco M clog
zumbar VI (hacer sonidos los insectos) to buzz, to drone, to hum; (hacer ruidos las máquinas) to whir, to whiz; (tintinear los oídos) to ring; (dar golpe) to sock
zumbido M (sonido de insectos) buzz, drone, hum; (sonido de máquinas) whir, whiz; (sonido en los oídos) ring
zumo M fruit juice
zurcido M (remiendo) darn; (acción de remendar) darning

zurcir[10b] VT to darn
zurdo ADJ left-handed, southpaw
zuro M corncob
zurra F whipping
zurrar VT to whip, to thrash
zurullo M turd
zutano -na M so-and-so, what's-his-name; F
    what's-her-name

Inglés–Español · English–Spanish

Lista de abreviaturas / List of Abbreviations

adj	adjective	adjetivo
adv	adverb, adverbial	adverbio, adverbial
Am	America	América
art	article	artículo
conj	conjunction	conjunción
def	definite	definido
dem	demonstrative	demostrativo
f	feminine	femenino
fam	familiar	familiar
indef	indefinite	indefinido
interj	interjection	interjección
interr	interrogative	interrogativo
inv	invariable	invariable
lit	literary	literario
loc	locution	locución
m	masculine	masculino
Mex	Mexico	México
n	noun	sustantivo
num	numeral	numeral
pej	pejorative	peyorativo
pl	plural	plural
poss	possessive	posesivo
prep	preposition, prepositional	preposición, preposicional
pron	pronoun	pronombre
rel	relative	relativo
RP	River Plate	Río de la Plata
sg	singular	singular
Sp	Spain, Spanish	España
v aux	auxiliary verb	verbo auxiliar
vi	intransitive verb	verbo intransitivo
vt	transitive verb	verbo transitivo
vulg	vulgar	vulgar

Pronunciación inglesa

I. VOCALES

Símbolo fonético	Ortografía inglesa	Explicación
[i]	see, pea	como la *i* en hilo
[ɪ]	bit	el sonido más aproximado es la *i* en *virtud,* pero la [ɪ] inglesa es más abierta, tirando a *e*
[e]	late, they	equivale aproximadamente a *ei*
[ɛ]	set	semejante a la *e* de *perro,* pero más abierta
[ɝ]	work, bird	como la *u* de *cud* (ver abajo) pero articulada simultáneamente con una *r*
[æ]	sat	sonido intermedio entre *e* y *a*
[ɑ]	hot	como la vocal de *pan*
[ɔ]	saw, laud	sonido intermedio entre *a* y *o*
[o]	low, mode	equivale aproximadamente a *ou*
[ʊ]	book, pull	como la *u* de *turrón,* pero más abierta
[u]	June, moon	como la *u* de *uno*
[ʌ]	cud	una *e* muy relajada
[ə]	adept	una *e* muy relajada y átona
[ɚ]	teacher	una *e* átona relajada articulada simultáneamente con una *r*

II. DIPTONGOS

Símbolo fonético	Ortografía inglesa	Explicación
[aɪ]	pie, aisle	como *ai* en *aire*
[aʊ]	now, foul	como *au* en *causa*
[ɔɪ]	boy	como *oy* en *hoy*
[ju]	use	como *iu* en *ciudad*

III. CONSONANTES

Símbolo fonético	Ortografía inglesa	Explicación
[b]	bat	semejante a la *b* española, pero seguida de aspiración
[d]	day	semejante a la *d* española, pero articulada en los alvéolos y con más tensión
[f]	fun, photo	como la *f* española
[g]	go	como la *g* de *goma,* pero con más tensión

[h]	hat	muy suave como la *j* de los dialectos caribeños del español
[j]	year	como la *i* del diptongo de *hielo*
[k]	cat, kill	como la *c* de *carro,* pero seguida de aspiración
[l]	let	como la *l* de *lado*
[ɫ]	ball	como la *l* final catalana
[m]	much	como la *m* española
[n]	no	como la *n* española
[p]	pea	como la *p* española, pero seguida de aspiración
[r]	red	no tiene equivalente en español; se pronuncia con la punta de la lengua enrollada hacia arriba, sin tocar el paladar
[s]	sea	como la *s* hispanoamericana (no la castellana)
[t]	tea	como la *t* española pero articulada en los alvéolos y seguida de aspiración
[v]	very	se articula con los dientes incisivos superiores colocados en el labio inferior
[w]	weed	equivale a la *u* del diptongo de *fui*
[z]	zero, rose	como la *s* de *mismo* cuando se sonoriza, pero aun más sonora
[D]	latter, ladder	como la *r* de *para*
[θ]	thin	como la *z* del español castellano en *zagal*
[ð]	this	como la *d* de *cada*
[ʃ]	sheet, machine, notation	una *s* muy palatal como en francés *chapeau* o italiano *lasciare*
[ʒ]	measure, beige	como la *ll* argentina en *valle,* cuando es sonora
[tʃ]	church	como la *ch* de *charla*
[ʤ]	judge	como la *y* de *inyectar*
[ṇ]	eaten, button	representa la *n* silábica, articulada sin la vocal anterior
[ŋ]	ring	como la *n* española en *mango* y *banco*
[ḷ]	able	representa la *l* silábica, articulada sin la vocal anterior
[hw]	where	combinación de los sonidos [h] y [w] arriba descritos

Notas sobre gramática inglesa

El sustantivo

Género. En la gramática inglesa el género solo desempeña un papel importante en el sistema pronominal, p. ej. **he runs** 'él corre', **she runs** 'ella corre', **I see him** 'lo veo', **I see her** 'la veo'. En los sustantivos que designan a personas, se emplean varios métodos para distinguir entre los sexos, v. gr. por el agregado de un sufijo, como en **actor** 'actor', **actress** 'actriz', por el agregado de una palabra, como en **baby boy** 'niño', **baby girl** 'niña', **she-bear** 'osa', **male nurse** 'enfermero', o utilizando palabras completamente distintas, como en **uncle** 'tío', **aunt** 'tía'.

Número. Generalmente se forma el plural añadiendo -s al singular: **paper, papers** 'papel, papeles', **books, books** 'libro, libros', **chief, chiefs** 'jefe, jefes'.

Los sustantivos que terminan en **-ss, -x, -sh, -z,** y **-o** añaden **-es** para formar el plural: **kiss, kisses** 'beso, besos', **box, boxes** 'caja, cajas', **dish, dishes** 'plato, platos', **buzz, buzzes** 'zumbido, zumbidos', **hero, heroes** 'héroe, héroes'. Esto vale también por **-ch** cuando se pronuncia [č], como en **arch, arches** 'arco, arcos', pero no cuando se pronuncia [k], como en **monarch, monarchs** 'monarca, monarcas'.

Los sustantivos que terminan en **-fe,** y ciertos sustantivos que terminan en **-f,** cambian estas letras en **v** y añaden **-es** en el plural: **leaf, leaves** 'hoja, hojas', **life, lives** 'vida, vidas', **wife, wives** 'esposa, esposas', **knife, knives** 'cuchillo, cuchillos' (pero **reef, reefs** 'arrecife, arrecifes').

Para formar el plural de los sustantivos terminados en **-y** precedida de consonante se cambia la **-y** en **-ies: fly, flies** 'mosca, moscas', **family, families** 'familia, familias'. En cambio, los sustantivos terminados en **-y** precedida de vocal forman el plural añadiendo **-s** al singular: **day, days** 'día, días'.

Ciertos sustantivos forman el plural de una manera irregular: **man, men** 'hombre, hombres', **woman, women** 'mujer, mujeres', **mouse, mice** 'ratón, ratones', **louse, lice** 'piojo, piojos', **goose, geese** 'ganso, gansos', **tooth, teeth** 'diente, dientes', **foot, feet** 'pie, pies', **ox, oxen** 'buey, bueyes'.

Ciertos sustantivos que terminan en **-is** forman el plural cambiando la **i** de la terminación en **e: axis, axes** 'eje, ejes', **crisis, crises** 'crisis' (sg., pl.).

El adjetivo

El adjetivo inglés es invariable en cuanto a género y número. Normalmente se coloca delante del sustantivo: **an interesting woman** 'una mujer interesante', **a large man** 'un hombre grande', **beautiful birds** 'aves hermosas'.

Los comparativos y superlativos. Aunque no hay una regla general, por lo común los adjetivos monosílabos, los adjetivos acentuados en la última sílaba y algunos bisílabos comunes forman el comparativo de aumento y el superlativo añadiendo **-er** y **-est** (como en **tall**). Los demás adjetivos van precedidos de **more** (para el comparativo) y **most** (para el superlativo) (como en **careful**). Nótese que (1) si la palabra termina en **-e** muda, se añaden **-r** y **-st** en vez de **-er** y **-est** (ver **wise**), (2) los adjetivos terminados en **-y** cambian esta letra en **i** (ver **happy**), (3) los adjetivos terminados en consonante precedida de vocal doblan la consonante (ver **fat**):

Positivo	*Comparativo*	*Superlativo*
tall alto	**taller** más alto	**the tallest** el más alto
careful cuidadoso	**more careful** más cuidadoso	**the most careful** el más cuidadoso
wise sabio	**wiser** más sabio	**the wisest** el más sabio
happy feliz	**happier** más feliz	**the happiest** el más feliz
fat gordo	**fatter** más gordo	**the fattest** el más gordo

Los adjetivos siguientes forman el comparativo y el superlativo de una manera irregular:

good	**better**	**best**
bad, ill	**worse**	**worst**
much	**more**	**most**

El adverbio

Muchos adverbios se forman añadiendo **-ly** al adjetivo: **courteous** 'cortés', **courteously** 'cortésmente', **bold** 'atrevido', **boldly** 'atrevidamente'. Existen las irregularidades ortográficas siguientes en la formación de los adverbios que terminan en **-ly**: (1) los adjetivos terminados en **-ble** cambian la **-e** en **-y: possible, possibly**, (2) los terminados en **-ic** añaden **-ally: poetic, poetically**, (3) los terminados en -**ll** añaden sólo **-y: full, fully**, (4) los terminados en **-ue** pierden la **-e** final: **true, truly**, (5) los terminados en **-y** cambian la **-y** en **i: happy, happily.**

La mayor parte de los adverbios forman el comparativo y el superlativo con los adverbios **more** 'más' y **most** 'el/la más'. Asimismo los adverbios monosílabos añaden **-er** y **-est:**

Positivo	*Comparativo*	*Superlativo*
boldly	**more boldly**	**most boldly**
generously	**more generously**	**most generously**
soon	**sooner**	**soonest**
early	**earlier**	**earliest**
late	**later**	**latest**
fast	**faster**	**fastest**

Los adverbios siguientes forman el comparativo y el superlativo de una manera irregular:

well	**better**	**best**
badly	**worse**	**worst**
little	**less**	**least**
far	**farther, further**	**farthest, furthest**

Sufijos comunes del inglés

-dom   a partir de bases nominales, forma sustantivos con los sentidos de dominio, jurisdicción, estado, condición: **kingdom** 'reino' (**king** 'rey'), **martyrdom** 'martirio' (**martyr** 'mártir'), **freedom** 'libertad' (**free** 'libre')

-ee   a partir de verbos, forma sustantivos indicando a la persona que recibe una acción: **addressee** 'destinatario' (**to address** 'dirigir'), **employee** 'empleado' (**to employ** 'emplear').

-eer   a partir de bases diversas, forma sustantivos que denotan oficio u ocupación: **auctioneer** 'subastador' (**to auction** 'subastar'), **puppeteer** 'titiritero' (**puppet** 'títere')

-en   *a.*   forma adjetivos que denotan la sustancia de que está hecha una cosa: **golden** 'dorado' (**gold** 'oro'), **wooden** 'de madera' (**wood** 'madera')

    b.   forma verbos a partir de adjetivos: **to whiten** 'blanquear' (**white** 'blanco'), **to darken** 'oscurecer' (**dark** 'oscuro')

-er   *a.*   forma sustantivos a partir de verbos para indicar agente: **player** 'jugador' (**to play** 'jugar'), **speaker** 'hablante' (**to speak** 'hablar'), **baker** 'panadero' (**to bake** 'hornear')

    b.   forma sustantivos a partir de sustantivos para denominar al residente de un lugar: **New Yorker** 'neoyorkino' (**New York** 'Nueva York'), **islander** 'isleño' (**island** 'isla')

-ess   se usa para formar el género femenino de ciertos sustantivos: **princess** 'princesa' (**prince** 'príncipe'), **countess** 'condesa' (**count** 'conde')

-fold   indica el número de veces que se repite algo: **twofold** 'dos veces' (**two** 'dos'), **hundredfold** 'cien veces' (**hundred** 'cien')

-ful   *a.*   forma adjetivos a partir de sustantivos para indicar la presencia de una cualidad: **hopeful** 'esperanzado' (**hope** 'esperanza'), **careful** 'cuidadoso' (**care** 'cuidado'), **willful** 'voluntarioso' (**will** 'voluntad')

    b.   forma adjetivos a partir de verbos para indicar tendencia: **forgetful** 'olvidadizo' (**to forget** 'olvidar')

    c.   forma sustantivos a partir de sustantivos indicando la capacidad: **handful** 'puñado' (**hand** 'mano'), **spoonful** 'cucharada' (**spoon** 'cuchara')

-hood   forma abstractos a partir de sustantivos concretos: **motherhood** 'maternidad' (**mother** 'madre'), **childhood** 'niñez' (**child** 'niño'), **likelihood** 'probabilidad' (**likely** 'probable')

-ing   *a.*   forma adjetivos a partir de verbos: **running water** 'agua corriente' (**to run** 'correr'), **drinking water** 'agua potable' (**to drink** 'beber'), **waiting room** 'sala de espera' (**to wait** 'esperar'), **washing machine** 'máquina lavadora' (**to wash** 'lavar')

    b.   se usa para formar sustantivos que denominan la acción de un verbo: **understanding** 'entendimiento' (**to understand** 'entender'), **supplying** 'abastecimiento' (**to supply** 'abastar')

    c.   se usa para formar sustantivos que denominan una cosa que desempeña una acción: **clothing** 'ropa' (**to clothe** 'vestir'), **covering** 'cobertura' (**to cover** 'cubrir')

-ish   forma adjetivos a partir de sustantivos indicando semejanza o atenuación: **boyish** 'como un niño' (**boy** 'niño'), **womanish** 'como mujer, mujeril' (**woman** 'mujer'), **whitish** 'blancuzco' (**white** 'blanco')

-less   se agrega a sustantivos para indicar falta de algo: **childless** 'sin hijos' (**child** 'hijo'), **penniless** 'sin dinero' (**penny** 'centavo'), **endless** 'interminable, sin fin' (**end** 'fin')

-like   se añade a sustantivos para indicar semejanza: **lifelike** 'que parece vivo' (**life** 'vida'), **childlike** 'infantil' (**child** 'niño'), **tigerlike** 'como un tigre' (**tiger** 'tigre')

-ly
  a.   se añade a adjetivos para formar adverbios: **slowly** 'lentamente' (**slow** 'lento'), **happily** 'felizmente' (**feliz** 'happy')
  b.   deriva adjetivos a partir de sustantivos indicando manera: **motherly** 'maternal' (**mother** 'madre'), **gentlemanly** 'caballeroso' (**gentleman** 'caballero'), **friendly** 'amistoso' (**friend** 'amigo')
  c.   deriva adjetivos o adverbios de tiempo a partir de sustantivos: **daily** 'diario', 'diariamente' (**day** 'día'), **weekly** 'semanal', 'semanalmente' (**week** 'semana')

-ness   forma sustantivos abstractos a partir de adjetivos: **goodness** 'bondad' (**good** 'bueno'), **darkness** 'oscuridad' (**dark** 'oscuro'), **foolishness** 'tontería' (**fool** 'tonto')

-ship   se emplea para derivar sustantivos a partir de sustantivos y verbos para denotar
  a.   cualidades abstractas: **friendship** 'amistad' (**friend** 'amigo')
  b.   arte o destreza: **horsemanship** 'equitación' (**horseman** 'jinete')
  c.   dignidad, oficio, cargo, o título: **professorship** 'cátedra' (**professor** 'catedrático'), **lordship** 'señoría' (**lord** 'señor')
  d.   la duración de una acción: **courtship** 'cortejo' (**to court** 'cortejar')

-some   se añade a verbos para formar adjetivos que expresan tendencia excesiva: **tiresome** 'aburrido' (**to tire** 'aburrir'), **quarrelsome** 'pendenciero' (**to quarrel** 'discutir')

-th   es el sufijo que forma números ordinales a partir de los cardinales: **fifth** 'quinto' (**five** 'cinco'), **tenth** 'décimo' (**ten** 'diez')

-ward   se añade a sustantivos y adverbios para indicar movimiento hacia un lugar: **homeward** 'hacia casa' (**home** 'casa'), **downward** 'hacia abajo' (**down** 'abajo')

-wise,	se añaden a sustantivos para indicar dirección o posición: **edgewise**
-ways	'de lado' (**edge** 'borde'), **lengthwise** 'a lo largo' (**length** 'largo'),
	sideways 'de lado' (**side** 'lado')

-y	*a.*	es un sufijo diminutivo: **doggy** 'perrito' (**dog** 'perro'), **Johnny** 'Juanito' (**John** 'Juan')
	b.	se añade a sustantivos para formar adjetivos que indican abundancia: **rocky** 'rocoso' (**rock** 'roca'), **rainy** 'lluvioso' (**rain** 'lluvia'), **hairy** 'peludo' (**hair** 'pelo'), **angry** 'enojado' (**anger** 'enojo')
	c.	se añade a sustantivos para formar adjetivos que expresan semejanza: **rosy** 'rosado' (**rose** 'rosa')

Verbos irregulares de la lengua inglesa

Se denominan verbos irregulares los que no forman el pretérito o el participio pasivo con la adición de **-d** o **-ed** al presente. Obsérvese que en ciertos verbos (aquí señalados con asterisco) coexiste la forma regular al lado de la irregular. Las formas poco usadas aparecen entre paréntesis.

Presente	*Pretérito*	*Participio pasivo*
*abide	(abode)	abode
am, is, are	was, were	been
arise	arose	arisen
*awake	awoke	awoke, awoken
bear	bore	borne
beat	beat	beat, beaten
become	became	become
befall	befell	befallen
beget	begat	begotten
begin	began	begun
behold	beheld	beheld
bend	bent	bent
beseech	(besought)	(besought)
beset	beset	beset
bet	bet	bet
bid 'offer'	bid	bid
bid 'command'	bade	bidden
bind	bound	bound
bite	bit	bitten, bit
bleed	bled	bled
blow	blew	blown
break	broke	broken
breed	bred	bred
bring	brought	brought
build	built	built
*burn	burnt	burnt

Presente	*Pretérito*	*Participio pasivo*
burst	burst	burst
buy	bought	bought
cast	cast	cast
catch	caught	caught
choose	chose	chosen
cling	clung	clung
*clothe	(clad)	(clad)
come	came	come
cost	cost	cost
creep	crept	crept
*crow	crew	crowed
cut	cut	cut
deal	dealt	dealt
dig	dug	dug
*dive	dove	dived
do	did	done
draw	drew	drawn
*dream	dreamt	dreamt
drink	drank	drunk
drive	drove	driven
*dwell	dwelt	dwelt
eat	ate	eaten
fall	fell	fallen
feed	fed	fed
feel	felt	felt
fight	fought	fought
find	found	found
*fit	fit	fit
flee	fled	fled
fling	flung	flung
fly	flew	flown
forbear	forbore	forborne
forbid	forbade	forbidden
foresee	foresaw	foreseen
foretell	foretold	foretold
forget	forgot	forgotten, forgot
forgive	forgave	forgiven
forsake	forsook	forsaken
freeze	froze	frozen
get	got	got, gotten
*gild	gilt	gilt
*gird	girded	girt
give	gave	given
go	went	gone
grind	ground	ground

Verbos irregulares

Presente	Pretérito	Participio pasivo
grow	grew	grown
hang[1]	hung	hung
have, has	had	had
hear	heard	heard
*hew	hewed	hewn
hide	hid	hidden, hid
hit	hit	hit
hold	held	held
hurt	hurt	hurt
keep	kept	kept
*kneel	knelt	knelt
*knit	knit	knit
know	knew	known
lay	laid	laid
lead	led	led
*lean	(leant)	(leant)
*leap	leapt	leapt
*learn	(learnt)	(learnt)
leave	left	left
lend	lent	lent
let	let	let
lie[2]	lay	lain
*light	lit	lit
lose	lost	lost
make	made	made
mean	meant	meant
meet	met	met
mistake	mistook	mistaken
*mow	mowed	mown
pay	paid	paid
*plead	pled	pled
put	put	put
quit	quit	quit
read [rid]	read [rɛd]	read [rɛd]
rend	rent	rent
*rid	rid	rid
ride	rode	ridden
ring	rang	rung
rise	rose	risen
run	ran	run
*saw	sawed	sawn
say	said	said
see	saw	seen
seek	sought	sought

1. Es regular cuando significa 'ahorcar'.
2. Es regular cuando significa 'mentir'.

Presente	Pretérito	Participio pasivo
sell	sold	sold
send	sent	sent
set	set	set
*sew	sewed	sewn
shake	shook	shaken
*shave	shaved	shaven
*shear	sheared	shorn
shed	shed	shed
shine[3]	shone	shone
shoe	shod	shod
shoot	shot	shot
*show	showed	shown
*shred	shred	shred
shrink	shrank (shrunk)	shrunk (shrunken)
shut	shut	shut
sing	sang	sung
sink	sank	sunk
sit	sat	sat
slay	slew	slain
sleep	slept	slept
slide	slid	slid, slidden
sling	slung	slung
slink	slunk	slunk
slit	slit	slit
*smell	(smelt)	(smelt)
smite	smote	smitten
*sneak	snuck	snuck
*sow	sowed	sown
speak	spoke	spoken
*speed	sped	sped
*spell	(spelt)	(spelt)
spend	spent	spent
*spill	spilt	spilt
spin	spun	spun
spit	spat, spit	spat, spit
split	split	split
*spoil	(spoilt)	(spoilt)
spread	spread	spread
spring	sprang, sprung	sprung
stand	stood	stood
*stave	stove	stove
steal	stole	stolen
stick	stuck	stuck
sting	stung	stung
stink	stank	stunk

3. Suele ser regular cuando es transitivo, en el sentido 'pulir, dar brillo'.

Verbos irregulares

Presente	Pretérito	Participio pasivo
*strew	strewed	strewn
stride	strode	stridden
strike	struck	struck, stricken
string	strung	strung
*strive	strove	striven
swear	swore	sworn
*sweat	sweat	sweat
sweep	swept	swept
*swell	swelled	swollen
swim	swam	swum
swing	swung	swung
take	took	taken
teach	taught	taught
tear	tore	torn
tell	told	told
think	thought	thought
throw	threw	thrown
thrust	thrust	thrust
tread	trod	trodden
understand	understood	understood
undertake	undertook	undertaken
undo	undid	undone
uphold	upheld	upheld
upset	upset	upset
*wake	woke	woken
wear	wore	worn
weave	wove	woven
*wed	wed	wed
weep	wept	wept
*wet	wet	wet
win	won	won
wind	wound	wound
withdraw	withdrew	withdrawn
withhold	withheld	withheld
withstand	withstood	withstood
wring	wrung	wrung
write	wrote	written

Aa

a [ə, e] INDEF ART un *m*, una *f*; **what — fool!** ¡qué tonto! **such — fool** tan tonto; **I'm — teacher / Catholic** soy maestro / católico

aback [əbǽk] ADV **to be taken —** estar desconcertado

abandon [əbǽndən] VT abandonar; N **with wild —** desenfrenadamente

abandonment [əbǽndənmənt] N abandono *m*, desamparo *m*

abashed [əbǽʃt] ADJ humillado, avergonzado

abate [əbét] VI/VT disminuir, mitigar(se); (storm) calmarse, atenuarse

abbey [ǽbi] N abadía *f*

abbot [ǽbət] N abad *m*

abbreviate [əbríviet] VT abreviar

abbreviation [əbriviéʃən] N (act of abbreviating) abreviación *f*; (short form) abreviatura *f*

abdicate [ǽbdɪket] VI/VT abdicar

abdomen [ǽbdəmən] N abdomen *m*, vientre *m*

abdominal [æbdámənəɫ] ADJ abdominal

abduct [æbdʌ́kt] VT secuestrar, raptar

abduction [æbdʌ́kʃən] N rapto *m*, secuestro *m*

aberration [æbəréʃən] N anomalía *f*, aberración *f*

abet [əbét] VT instigar

abeyance [əbéəns] ADV LOC **in —** pendiente, en suspenso

abhor [əbhɔ́r] VT aborrecer

abhorrence [əbhɔ́rəns] N aborrecimiento *m*

abhorrent [əbhɔ́rənt] ADJ aborrecible

abide [əbáɪd] VT (tolerate) soportar; VI (dwell) morar, permanecer; **to — by** acatar, atenerse a

ability [əbílɪDi] N (skill) habilidad *f*; (aptitude) capacidad *f*

abject [ǽbdʒékt] ADJ abyecto; **in — poverty** en extrema miseria

ablaze [əbléz] ADV en llamas

able [ébəɫ] ADJ hábil, capaz; **—-bodied** de cuerpo sano; **to be — to** (be capable of) poder; (have an acquired skill) saber

abnegate [ǽbnɪget] VT renunciar

abnormal [æbnɔ́rməɫ] ADJ anormal

aboard [əbɔ́rd] ADV a bordo; **all —!** (train) ¡viajeros al tren! (ship) ¡pasajeros a bordo! **to go —** embarcarse

abode [əbód] N morada *f*; **place of —** domicilio *m*

abolish [əbálɪʃ] VT abolir, suprimir

abolition [æbəlíʃən] N abolición *f*

abominable [əbámənəbəɫ] ADJ abominable

abomination [əbaménéʃən] N (action) abominación *f*; (condition, habit) horror *m*

aboriginal [æbərídʒənəɫ] ADJ aborigen

aborigine [æbərídʒəni] N aborigen *mf*; **Australian —** aborigen australiano -na *mf*

abort [əbɔ́rt] VT (fetus) abortar; VI/VT (mission) suspender

abortion [əbɔ́rʃən] N aborto *m*

abortionist [əbɔ́rʃənɪst] N abortador -ra *mf*, abortero -ra *mf*

abortive [əbɔ́rDɪv] ADJ frustrado

abound [əbáʊnd] VI abundar; **to — with** abundar en

about [əbáʊt] PREP (concerning) acerca de, tocante a; (near, surrounding) alrededor de, por; **to be — one's business** atender a su negocio; ADV más o menos, alrededor de; **at — ten o'clock** a eso de las diez, sobre las diez; **to be — to do something** estar por / para hacer algo, estar a punto de hacer algo

above [əbʌ́v] PREP **you could see the towers — the buildings** se veían las torres sobre los edificios; **everyone — five years of age** todos los de más de cinco años; **he's — me in the company** es mi superior en la compañía; **to be — suspicion** estar libre de toda sospecha; **I thought you were — such things** no pensaba que te rebajarías a eso; ADV **the apartment —** el apartamento de arriba; **books of fifty pages and —** libros de cincuenta páginas y más; **the remark quoted —** la observación anteriormente citada; **— all** sobre todo; **—-mentioned** susodicho, ya mencionado; **from —** de arriba, del cielo, de Dios

abrasion [əbréʒən] N abrasión *f*

abrasive [əbrésɪv] ADJ (material) abrasivo; (person, tone) irritante

abreast [əbrést] ADV al lado; **to keep —** manteneral corriente; **four —** de cuatro en fondo

abridge [əbrídʒ] VT abreviar

abroad [əbrɔ́d] ADV en el extranjero; **to go —** ir al extranjero

abrupt [əbrʌ́pt] ADJ abrupto

ABS (antilock braking system) [ebiés] N SFA *m*

abscess [ǽbsɛs] N absceso *m*

abscond [æbskánd] VI fugarse

absence [ǽbsəns] N (nonpresence) ausencia *f*; (lack) falta *f*; **in the — of** a falta de

absent [ǽbsənt] ADJ ausente; **—-minded** distraído, despistado; **to be — from school** faltar a la escuela

absentee [æbsəntí] N ausente *mf*

absenteeism [æbsəntíízəm] N ausentismo *m*

absolute [ǽbsəlút] ADJ absoluto; (prohibition) terminante

absolutely [æbsəlútli] ADV **— not** en absoluto; INTERJ **—!** ¡sí, señor!

absolve [æbzáɫv] VT absolver

absorb [əbzɔ́rb] VT (emission) absorber; (shock) amortiguar; (people, information) asimilar

abstain [æbstén] VI abstenerse; **— from** abstenerse de

abstinence [ǽbstənəns] N abstinencia *f*

abstract [ǽbstrækt] ADJ abstracto; N resumen *m*, extracto *m*; **in the —** en abstracto

abstraction [æbstrǽkʃən] N abstracción *f*

absurd [əbsɚ́d] ADJ absurdo, disparatado

absurdity [əbsɚ́-DIDi] N (quality) absurdo *m*; (action) disparate *m*

abundance [əbʌ́ndəns] N abundancia *f*

abundant [əbʌ́ndənt] ADJ abundante

abuse [əbjús] N (of privileges) abuso *m*; (of authority) desmán *m*; (physical) maltrato *m*; (verbal) injuria *f*; [əbjúz] VT (privileges) abusar de; (physically) maltratar; (verbally) injuriar

abusive [əbjúsɪv] ADJ (physically) violento; (verbally) injurioso

abysmal [əbízməɫ] ADJ abismal; **— ignorance** ignorancia supina *f*; **— results** resultados desastrosos *m pl*

abyss [əbís] N abismo *m*

A/C (air conditioning) [esí] N aire acondicionado *m*

academic [ækədémɪk] ADJ (university) académico; (school) escolar; N profesor -ra universitario -ria *mf*

academy [əkǽɒəmi] N academia *f*

accede [æksíd] VI acceder; **to — to** acceder a

accelerate [ækséləret] VI/VT acelerar

acceleration [ækseləréʃən] N aceleración *f*

accelerator [ækséləreɒɚ] N acelerador *m*

accent [ǽksent] N (pronunciation) acento *m*; (written) tilde *f*, acento escrito *m*; [æksént] VT (stress, syllable) acentuar

accentuate [ækséntʃuet] VT (differences, facts) acentuar, recalcar; (beauty) realzar

accept [æksépt] VT aceptar

acceptable [ækséptəbəɫ] ADJ aceptable

acceptance [ækséptəns] N (action) aceptación *f*; (approval) aprobación *f*

access [ǽksɛs] N acceso *m*

accessible [æksésəbəɫ] ADJ accesible

accessory [æksésəri] ADJ accesorio; N accesorio *m*; (to a crime) cómplice *mf*

accident [ǽksɪɒənt] N accidente *m*; (mishap) percance *m*; **by —** por casualidad

accidental [æksɪdéntɫ] ADJ (injury) accidental; (discovery, meeting) casual, fortuito

acclaim [əklém] VT aclamar; N aclamación *f*, ovación *f*

acclamation [ækləméʃən] N aclamación *f*

acclimate [ǽkləmet] VI/VT (to physical conditions) aclimatar(se); (to an ambiance) acostumbrar(se)

accolade [ǽkəled] N elogio *m*

accommodate [əkámədet] VT (adjust) tener en cuenta; (lodge) hospedar, alojar; (contain) tener capacidad para; VI **to — oneself** adaptarse

accommodation [əkɑmədéʃən] N (adjustment) acomodación *f*, adaptación *f*; **—s** (lodging) alojamiento *m*; (facilities) comodidades *f pl*

accompaniment [əkʌ́mpənɪmənt] N acompañamiento *m*

accompanist [əkʌ́mpənɪst] N acompañante *mf*

accompany [əkʌ́mpəni] VI/VT acompañar

accomplice [əkámplɪs] N cómplice *mf*

accomplish [əkámplɪʃ] VT (objective) lograr; (mission) completar

accomplished [əkámplɪʃt] ADJ (actor, athlete) consumado; (musician) talentoso

accomplishment [əkámplɪʃmənt] N (achievement) logro *m*; (skill) habilidad *f*; (completion) realización *f*

accord [əkɔ́rd] N acuerdo *m*, convenio *m*; **of one's own —** voluntariamente; VT otorgar, conceder

accordance [əkɔ́rdn̩s] ADV LOC **in — with** de acuerdo con, de conformidad con

according [əkɔ́rDɪŋ] ADV LOC **— to** según

accordingly [əkɔ́rDɪŋli] ADV (therefore) por consiguiente; (correspondingly) como corresponde

accordion [əkɔ́rDiən] N acordeón *m*

accost [əkɔ́st] VT abordar

account [əkáʊnt] N (bill) cuenta *f*; (story) relato *m*, relación *f*; **to open (close) an —** abrir (cerrar) una cuenta; **on — of** a causa de, debido a; **on my —** por mí; **on one's own —** por cuenta propia; **on no —** de ninguna manera; **of no —** de ningún valor; **to take into —** tener en cuenta; VI **to — for** dar cuenta de; **how do you — for that?** ¿cómo se explica eso?

accountable [əkáʊntəbəɫ] ADJ responsable

accountant [əkáʊntn̩t] N *Am* contador -ra *mf*; *Sp* contable *mf*

accounting [əkáʊntɪŋ] N contabilidad *f*; — **firm** empresa de contadores públicos *f*; — **period** ejercicio contable *m*

accredit [əkrɛ́dɪt] VT acreditar

acculturate [əkʌ́ɫtʃəret] VI/VT aculturar(se)

accumulate [əkjúmjəlet] VI/VT acumular(se)

accumulation [əkjumjəléʃən] N acumulación *f*

accuracy [ǽkjəəsi] N precisión *f*, exactitud *f*

accurate [ǽkjəɪt] ADJ (measure, instrument) preciso, exacto; (translation) fiel

accursed [əkə́ːsɪd] ADJ maldito

accusation [ækjuzéʃən] N acusación *f*

accuse [əkjúz] VT acusar

accused [əkjúzd] ADJ acusado; N acusado -da *mf*, reo -a *mf*, procesado -da *mf*

accuser [əkjúzəˈ] N acusador -ra *mf*

accustom [əkʌ́stəm] VT acostumbrar, habituar; **to — oneself** acostumbrarse, habituarse; **to be —ed to** tener la costumbre de, estar acostumbrado a

AC/DC (alternating current / direct current) [ésidísi] ADJ (electricity) alterna y continua; (sexuality) bisexual

ace [es] N (cards, athlete, aviator) as *m*; VT sacarse la máxima nota en

acetone [ǽsəton] N acetona *f*

ache [ek] N dolor *m*; **—s and pains** achaques *m pl*; VT doler; **my stomach —s** me duele el estómago

achieve [ətʃív] VT (a goal) conseguir, lograr; (a level) alcanzar

achievement [ətʃívmənt] N (attainment) consecución *f*; (success) logro *m*, realización *f*

achy [éki] ADJ dolorido

acid [ǽsɪd] ADJ ácido; N ácido *m*; (hallucinogen) LSD *m*; — **rain** lluvia ácida *f*; — **test** prueba de fuego *f*

acidic [əsídɪk] ADJ ácido

acidity [əsídɪdi] N acidez *f*

acknowledge [æknálɪʤ] VT (merits) reconocer; (faults) admitir, reconocer; **to — receipt** acusar recibo

acknowledgment [æknálɪʤmənt] N (of merits) reconocimiento *m*; (of merits, faults) reconocimiento *m*, admisión *f*; (gratefulness) agradecimiento *m*; — **of receipt** acuse de recibo *m*

acme [ǽkmi] N súmmum *m*

acne [ǽkni] N acné *m*

acorn [ékɔrn] N bellota *f*

acoustics [əkústɪks] N acústica *f*

acquaint [əkwént] VT informar, familiarizar; **to — oneself with** informarse de, familiarizarse con; **to be —ed with** (a person, city, country) conocer; (a piece of news) estar enterado de

acquaintance [əkwéntn̩s] N (with facts) conocimiento *m*; (a person) conocido -a *mf*

acquiesce [ækwiés] VT asentir, condescender; (unwillingly) consentir

acquiescence [ækwiésəns] N asentimiento *m*, consentimiento *m*, condescendencia *f*

acquire [əkwáɪr] VT (knowledge, skill, purchase) adquirir; (fortune, information) obtener; (disease) contraer

acquisition [ækwəzíʃən] N (knowledge, skill, purchase) adquisición *f*; (fortune, information) obtención *f*

acquisitive [əkwízɪdɪv] ADJ codicioso

acquit [əkwít] VT absolver

acquittal [əkwídɫ] N absolución *f*

acre [ékəˈ] N acre (0,405 hectáreas) *m*

acrid [ǽkrɪd] ADJ acre

acrimony [ǽkrəmoni] N acritud *f*

acrobat [ǽkrəbæt] N acróbata *mf*

acrobatic [ækrəbǽdɪk] ADJ acrobático; **—s** acrobacia *f*

acronym [ǽkrənɪm] N acrónimo *m*, sigla *f*

acrophobia [ækrəfóbiə] N acrofobia *f*

across [əkrɔ́s] PREP **to lay one stick — the other** poner dos palos cruzados; **there's a bridge — that river** hay un puente sobre ese río; **he came — his old love letters** encontró sus viejas cartas de amor; **the library is — the street** la biblioteca está al otro lado de la calle; ADV **cut the boards —** corta los tablones a lo ancho; **five hundred miles —** de quinientas millas de ancho; **the meaning doesn't come —** el significado no se entiende; **to come / run —** encontrarse con, tropezar con

acrylic [əkrílɪk] ADJ & N acrílico *m*

act [ækt] N (deed, part of play) acto *m*; (part of show) número *m*; (law) ley *f*, decreto *m*; VI (behave) actuar, comportarse; (take measures) obrar; (play a part, chemical process) actuar; (on someone's behalf) representar; (mechanism) funcionar; **to — up** (child) portarse mal; (car) funcionar mal; **to — out** (event) representar; (feelings) exteriorizar

acting [ǽktɪŋ] N actuación *f*; (in a drama) representación *f*; ADJ (interim) interino; (substitute) suplente

action [ǽkʃən] N (practical measure, plot of a play) acción *f*; (deed) acto *m*; (mechanism) funcionamiento *m*; **to take —** tomar

medidas
activate [ǽktɪvet] VT activar
active [ǽktɪv] ADJ activo
activism [ǽktɪvɪzəm] N activismo *m*
activist [ǽktɪvɪst] N activista *mf*
activity [æktívɪɪ] N actividad *f*
actor [ǽktɚ] N actor *m*
actress [ǽktrɪs] N actriz *f*
actual [ǽktʃuəł] ADJ verdadero, real
actually [ǽktʃuəli] ADV en realidad
actuary [ǽktʃueri] N actuario -ria *mf*
acuity [əkjúɪɪ] N agudeza *f*
acumen [ǽkjəmən] N perspicacia *f*, agudeza *f*
acupuncture [ǽkjupʌŋktʃɚ] N acupuntura *f*
acupuncturist [ǽkjupʌŋktʃɚɪst] N acupuntor -ra *mf*
acute [əkjút] ADJ (pain, illness) agudo; (observation) perspicaz, penetrante
A.D. [edí] ADV d.C.
adamant [ǽdəmənt] ADJ inflexible, firme
adapt [ədǽpt] VT adaptar; VI **to — to** adaptar(se) a, acomodar(se) a
adaptation [æDæptéʃən] N adaptación *f*
add [æd] VT añadir, agregar; (sum) sumar; **to — to** aumentar; **to — up** (sum) sumar; (make sense) cuadrar; N **—-on** accesorio *m*
addict [ǽDɪkt] N adicto -ta *mf*
addicted [ədíktɪd] ADJ adicto
addiction [ədíkʃən] N adicción *f*
addition [ədíʃən] N (of numbers) suma *f*; (to a collection, staff) adición *f*, adquisición *f*; (to a building) anexo *m*; **in — (to)** además (de)
additional [ədíʃənəł] ADJ adicional
additive [ǽDɪɪv] N aditivo *m*
address [ədrés] N (street) dirección *f*, domicilio *m*; (speech) discurso *m*; **form of —** tratamiento *m*; VT (write the address) dirigir; (speak to) dirigirse a; (deal with) vérselas con
addressee [ædrɛsí] N destinatario -ria *mf*
adept [ədépt] ADJ hábil
adequacy [ǽDɪkwəsi] N suficiencia *f*
adequate [ǽDɪkwɪt] ADJ (sufficient) suficiente; (acceptable) aceptable
adhere [ædhír] VI adherirse; **to — to** adherirse a
adherence [ædhírəns] N adhesión *f*
adhesion [ædhíʒən] N (thing or tissue that adheres) adherencia *f*; (act of sticking together) adhesión *f*
adhesive [ædhísɪv] ADJ adhesivo; **— tape** cinta adhesiva *f*
adjacent [ədʒésənt] ADJ adyacente
adjective [ǽdʒɪktɪv] ADJ & N adjetivo *m*
adjoin [ədʒɔ́ɪn] VT lindar con, colindar con; VI estar contiguo a

adjourn [ədʒɚ́n] VT **to — the meeting** levantar la sesión; **meeting —ed** se levanta la sesión
adjournment [ədʒɚ́nmənt] N levantamiento de la sesión *m*
adjudge [ədʒʌ́dʒ] VT (declare) declarar; (deem) calificar
adjudicate [ədʒúDɪket] VI arbitrar; VT declarar
adjunct [ǽdʒʌŋkt] ADJ adjunto; N agregado -da *mf*
adjust [ədʒʌ́st] VT (fix) ajustar, graduar; (adapt a machine) regular; VI ajustarse, adaptarse
adjustment [ədʒʌ́stmənt] N ajuste *m*; (on a machine) regulación *f*
ad lib [ædlíb] ADV improvisando
administer [ædmínɪstɚ] VT (control) administrar, gestionar; (punishment) aplicar; (oath) tomar
administration [ædmɪnɪstréʃən] N administración *f*; (period in power) gestión *f*; (of punishment) aplicación *f*; (of an oath) toma *f*
administrative [ædmínɪstreDɪv] ADJ administrativo
administrator [ædmínɪstreDɚ] N administrador -ra *mf*
admirable [ǽdmɚəbəł] ADJ admirable
admiral [ǽdmɚəł] N almirante *m*
admiration [ædmɚéʃən] N admiración *f*
admire [ædmáɪr] VT admirar
admirer [ædmáɪrɚ] N admirador -ra *mf*; (suitor) pretendiente *mf*
admissible [ædmísəbəł] ADJ admisible
admission [ædmíʃən] N (acceptance) admisión *f*; (access, ticket price) entrada *f*; (confession) confesión *f*
admit [ædmít] VT (allow entry) admitir; (to a hospital) internar; (acknowledge) reconocer, admitir
admittance [ædmítns] N entrada *f*; **no —** prohibida la entrada
admonish [ædmánɪʃ] VT amonestar; **to — for** amonestar por
admonition [ædməníʃən] N (warning) amonestación *f*; (reproof) advertencia *f*
adobe [ədóbi] N (mud) adobe *m*; (house) casa de adobe *f*
adolescence [ædlésəns] N adolescencia *f*
adolescent [ædlésənt] ADJ & N adolescente *mf*
adopt [ədápt] VT (child, custom) adoptar; (suggestion) aprobar
adoption [ədápʃən] N (of a child, custom) adopción *f*; (of a suggestion) aprobación *f*
adoptive [ədáptɪv] ADJ adoptivo
adorable [ədɔ́rəbəł] ADJ adorable, precioso
adoration [ædəréʃən] N adoración *f*

adore [ədɔ́r] VT adorar; **I — playing tennis** me encanta jugar al tenis

adorn [ədɔ́rn] VT adornar, ornar

adornment [ədɔ́rnmənt] N adorno *m*

adrenal [ədrínḷ] ADJ — **gland** glándula suprarrenal *f*

adrenalin [ədrénəlın] N adrenalina *f*

adrift [ədríft] ADJ & ADV a la deriva

adult [ədʌ́łt] ADJ & N adulto -ta *mf*

adulterate [ədʌ́łtəret] VT adulterar

adulterer [ədʌ́łtərɚ] N adúltero -ra *mf*

adultery [ədʌ́łtəri] N adulterio *m*

advance [ædvǽns] VI (move forward) avanzar; (make progress) avanzar, progresar; (bring forward) adelantar; VT (promote) promover; (propose) proponer; (pay beforehand) adelantar, anticipar; N (movement) avance *m*; (progress) adelanto *m*; (loan) adelanto *m*, anticipo *m*; **—s** (sexual) requiebros *m pl*; **in —** por adelantado, con anticipación

advanced [ædvǽnst] ADJ (idea, stage) avanzado; (country) adelantado

advancement [ædvǽnsmənt] N (movement) avance *m*; (rank) ascenso *m*; (knowledge) progreso *m*

advantage [ædvǽntıʤ] N ventaja *f*; **it would be to your —** te convendría; **to take — of** aprovecharse de

advantageous [ædvæntéʤəs] ADJ ventajoso, provechoso

advent [ǽdvɛnt] N advenimiento *m*

adventure [ædvɛ́ntʃɚ] N aventura *f*

adventurer [ædvɛ́ntʃərɚ] N aventurero -ra *mf*

adventuresome [ædvɛ́ntʃɚsəm] ADJ osado

adventurous [ædvɛ́ntʃɚəs] ADJ (seeking adventure) aventurero, intrépido; (daring) atrevido, audaz

adverb [ǽdvɚb] N adverbio *m*

adversary [ǽdvɚsɛri] N adversario -ria *mf*

adverse [ǽdvɚs] ADJ adverso

adversity [ædvɚ́sıdi] N adversidad *f*

advertise [ǽdvɚtaız] VT anunciar, hacer publicidad / propaganda para; VI hacer propaganda / publicidad; **to — for a cook** poner un anuncio buscando cocinero

advertisement [ædvɚtáızmənt] N anuncio publicitario *m*, aviso *m*

advertiser [ǽdvɚtaızɚ] N anunciante *mf*

advertising [ǽdvɚtaızıŋ] N publicidad *f*

advice [ædváıs] N consejo *m*; (expert) asesoramiento *m*

advisable [ædváızəbəł] ADJ aconsejable, recomendable

advise [ædváız] VI/VT (counsel) aconsejar, advertir; VT (inform) avisar, informar;

(expertly) asesorar

adviser, advisor [ædváızɚ] N consejero -ra *mf*, asesor -ora *mf*

advocacy [ǽdvəkəsi] N defensa *f*

advocate [ǽdvəkıt] N (promoter) partidario -ria *mf*; (defender) defensor -ra *mf*, intercesor -ra *mf*; (lawyer) abogado -da *mf*; [ǽdvəket] VT abogar por, defender

aerial [ériəł] ADJ aéreo; N antena *f*

aerobic [ɛróbık] ADJ (exercise) aeróbico; (air-breathing) aerobio; **—s** aeróbic *m*

aerodynamic [ɛrodaınǽmık] ADJ aerodinámico; **—s** aerodinámica *f*

aeronautics [ɛrənɔ́dıks] N aeronáutica *f*

aerosol [érəsɑł] N aerosol *m*

aerospace [érospes] N espacio aéreo *m*; ADJ aeroespacial

aesthetic [ɛsθɛ́dık] ADJ estético; N **—s** estética *f*

affable [ǽfəbəł] ADJ afable

affair [əfɛ́r] N (social) acontecimiento social *m*; (business) asunto *m*, negocio *m*; (love) aventura amorosa *f*, affaire *m*

affect [əfɛ́kt] VT (have effect on) afectar; (move) conmover; (feign) fingir

affectation [æfɛktéʃən] N afectación *f*, melindre *m*

affected [əfɛ́ktıd] ADJ (moved) afectado, conmovido; (feigned) fingido, artificioso, melindroso

affection [əfɛ́kʃən] N afecto *m*, cariño *m*

affectionate [əfɛ́kʃənıt] ADJ afectuoso, cariñoso

affidavit [æfıdévıt] N declaración jurada *f*

affiliate [əfíliet] VT afiliar; VI afiliarse, asociarse; [əfíliıt] N filial *f*

affinity [əfínıdi] N afinidad *f*

affirm [əfɚ́m] VT afirmar

affirmation [æfɚméʃən] N afirmación *f*

affirmative [əfɚ́mədıv] ADJ afirmativo; N — **action** discriminación positiva *f*; **reply in the —** dar una respuesta afirmativa

affix [əfíks] VT fijar; **to — one's signature** poner su firma, firmar

afflict [əflíkt] VT aquejar; **to be —ed with** padecer de, sufrir de

affliction [əflíkʃən] N (misery) aflicción *f*; (ailment) achaque *m*, mal *m*

affluent [ǽfluənt] ADJ (society) opulento; (person) rico

afford [əfɔ́rd] VT **I cannot — a car** no me alcanza el dinero para un coche; **he cannot — to waste time** no puede darse el lujo de perder tiempo; **I cannot — the risk** no me puedo permitir ese riesgo; **we will — you every opportunity** se te darán todas las oportunidades

affordable [əfɔ́rɒəbəł] ADJ asequible

affront [əfrʌ́nt] N afrenta *f*

Afghan, Afghani [ǽfgæn / æfgǽni] ADJ & N afgano -na *mf*

Afghanistan [æfgǽnɪstæn] N Afganistán *m*

afire [əfáɪr] ADJ & ADV en llamas

afloat [əflót] ADJ & ADV flotando, a flote

afraid [əfréd] ADJ asustado; **to be — (of)** temer, tener miedo (de)

afresh [əfréʃ] ADV de nuevo, desde el principio

Africa [ǽfrɪkə] N África *f*

African [ǽfrɪkən] ADJ & N africano -na *mf*

African-American [ǽfrɪkənəmérɪkən] ADJ & N afroamericano -na *mf*

after [ǽftɚ] PREP (temporal) después de, tras; (spatial) detrás de; **— all** después de todo; ADV después; CONJ después (de) que

afterbirth [ǽftɚbɝθ] N placenta *f*

afterlife [ǽftɚlaɪf] N el más allá

aftermath [ǽftɚmæθ] N secuelas *f pl*

afternoon [ǽftɚnún] N tarde *f*; INTERJ **good — buenas tardes**

aftershave [ǽftɚʃev] N loción para después del afeitado *f*

aftershock [ǽftɚʃɑk] N réplica *f*

aftertaste [ǽftɚtest] N (in the mouth) dejo *m*; (bad memory) resabio *m*

aftertax [ǽftɚtæks] ADJ **— profit** ganancia neta *f*

afterthought [ǽftɚθɔt] N **it was just an —** se nos ocurrió después

afterward, afterwards [ǽftɚwɚd(z)] ADV después, luego

again [əgén] ADV otra vez, de nuevo; (on the other hand) por otra parte; **— and —** repetidas veces; **to fall —** volver a caerse

against [əgénst] PREP contra; **— the grain** a contrapelo; **— all odds** a pesar de todo

age [edʒ] N (of a person) edad *f*; (era) era *f*, época *f*; **of —** mayor de edad; **old —** vejez *f*; **to come of —** llegar a la mayoría de edad; **under —** menor de edad; VI/VT envejecer

aged [edʒd] ADJ (wine) añejo; **— forty** de cuarenta años; [édʒɪd] anciano

ageless [édʒlɪs] ADJ (everlasting) eterno; (not showing age) siempre joven; (classic) clásico

agency [édʒənsi] N agencia *f*; **through the — of** por mediación de

agenda [ədʒéndə] N temario *m*, orden del día *m*

agent [édʒənt] N agente *mf*; (commercial) representante *mf*; (legal) apoderado -da *mf*

aggrandize [əgrǽndaɪz] VT engrandecer

aggravate [ǽgrəvet] VT (worsen) exacerbar, agravar; (annoy) irritar, exasperar, exacerbar

aggregate [ǽgrɪgɪt] N conjunto *m*; (rock) agregado *m*; ADJ total, global

aggression [əgréʃən] N agresión *f*

aggressive [əgrésɪv] ADJ (violent) agresivo; (dynamic) emprendedor

aggressor [əgrésɚ] N agresor -ra *mf*

aghast [əgǽst] ADJ horrorizado

agile [ǽdʒəł] ADJ ágil

agility [ədʒílɪɾi] N agilidad *f*

agitate [ǽdʒɪtet] VT (shake) agitar; (perturb) turbar; (campaign) alborotar

agitation [ædʒɪtéʃən] N agitación *f*

agitator [ǽdʒɪteɾɚ] N agitador -ra *mf*

agnostic [ægnástɪk] ADJ & N agnóstico -ca *mf*

ago [əgó] ADV **many years —** hace muchos años; **long —** hace mucho tiempo

agog [əgág] ADJ planchado, boquiabierto

agonize [ǽgənaɪz] VI sufrir angustiosamente; **to — over** atormentarse

agony [ǽgəni] N (pain) dolor *m*, tormento *m*; (anguish) angustia *f*

agoraphobia [ægɚəfóbiə] N agorafobia *f*

agrarian [əgrériən] ADJ agrario

agree [əgrí] VI (be in agreement) estar de acuerdo; (in grammar, mathematics) concordar; (color, food) sentarle bien a uno; **they —d to buy the car** quedaron en comprar el coche

agreeable [əgríəbəł] ADJ (nice) agradable; (willing) conforme

agreement [əgrímənt] N (concord, document) acuerdo *m*, convenio *m*; (grammatical) concordancia *f*; **to be in —** estar de acuerdo; **to come to an —** ponerse de acuerdo

agricultural [ægrɪkʌ́ltʃɚəł] ADJ (related to crops) agrícola; (related to crops and cattle) agropecuario

agriculture [ǽgrɪkʌłtʃɚ] N agricultura *f*

aground [əgráʊnd] ADV **to run —** encallar, varar

ahead [əhéd] ADV delante; **— of time** adelantado, antes de tiempo; **to go —** ir adelante, adelantarse; **to get —** prosperar; **our team is —** nuestro equipo va primero; **the years —** los años venideros

aid [ed] N (help) asistencia *f*; (assistant) ayudante *mf*; VT ayudar; **to — and abet** instigar

AIDS (acquired immune deficiency syndrome) [edz] N SIDA *m*

ail [eł] VI/VT **what —s you?** ¿qué tienes? ¿qué te aflige? **he's —ing** está enfermo

aileron [élərɑn] N alerón *m*

ailment [éɫmənt] N achaque *m*, dolencia *f*
aim [em] N (with a weapon) puntería *f*; (objective) objetivo *m*; VT (a weapon) apuntar; (a question, blow) dirigir; **to — to please** tratar de agradar
aimless [émlɪs] ADJ (purposeless) sin propósito; (directionless) sin rumbo
air [ɛr] N aire *m*; **up in the —** en el aire, incierto; **in the open —** al aire libre; **to be on the —** estar en el aire, emitirse; **to put on —s** presumir, darse ínfulas; **to vanish into thin —** evaporarse; ADJ aéreo; **—bag** airbag *m*, bolsa de aire *f*; **—borne** (troops) aerotransportado; (particles) transportado por el aire; **—brake** freno neumático *m*; **— conditioned** con aire acondicionado; **— conditioner** acondicionador de aire *m*; **— conditioning** aire acondicionado *m*, climatización *f*; **—craft** aeronave *f*; **—craft carrier** portaaviones *m sg*; **—field** aeródromo *m*; **— Force** Fuerza Aérea *f*; **—head** cabeza de chorlito *mf*; **—lift** puente aéreo *m*; **—line** línea aérea *f*; **— mail** correo aéreo *m*; **—plane** avión *m*; **— piracy** piratería aérea *f*; **—port** aeropuerto *m*; **— power** fuerza aérea *f*; **— pressure** presión de aire *f*; **— raid** ataque aéreo *m*; **— rifle** escopeta de aire comprimido *f*; **—ship** dirigible *m*; **— strike** bombardeo aéreo *m*; **—strip** pista de aterrizaje *f*; **—tight** hermético; **—-to-—** aire-aire; **— traffic control** control del tráfico aéreo *m*; VT (an opinion) manifestar; **to —lift** aerotransportar; **to — out** orear, ventilar
aisle [aɪɫ] N pasillo *m*; (of a church) nave lateral *f*
ajar [ədʒár] ADJ entornado, entreabierto
akin [əkín] ADJ (related) emparentado; (similar) semejante
à la mode [ɑlɑmód] ADV con helado
alarm [əlárm] N (warning) alarma *f*; (worry) inquietud *f*; **— clock** despertador *m*; **to sound an —** tocar a rebato; VT (worry) alarmar; (frighten) asustar
Albania [æɫbéniə] N Albania *f*
Albanian [æɫbéniən] ADJ & N albanés -esa *mf*
albatross [ǽɫbətrɑs] N albatros *m*
albino [æɫbáɪno] N albino -na *mf*
album [ǽɫbəm] N álbum *m*
alcohol [ǽɫkəhɔɫ] N alcohol *m*
alcoholic [æɫkəhɔ́lɪk] ADJ & N alcohólico -ca *mf*
alcoholism [ǽɫkəhɔlɪzəm] N alcoholismo *m*
alcove [ǽɫkov] N rincón *m*
ale [eɫ] N cerveza inglesa *f*

alert [əlɜ́·t] ADJ (vigilant) alerta; (awake) despierto; **to be —** (on guard) estar alerta; (lively) ser despierto; N alerta *f*; VT alertar, avisar
alfalfa [æɫfǽɫfə] N alfalfa *f*
algae [ǽɫdʒi] N algas *f pl*
algebra [ǽɫdʒəbrə] N álgebra *f*
Algeria [æɫdʒíriə] N Argelia *f*
Algerian [æɫdʒíriən] ADJ & N argelino -na *mf*
algorithm [ǽɫgərɪðəm] N algoritmo *m*
alias [éliəs] N alias *m sg*
alibi [ǽləbaɪ] N coartada *f*
alien [éliən] N (visitor from space) extraterrestre *mf*; (foreigner) extranjero -ra *mf*; ADJ ajeno
alienate [éliənet] VT (people) ofender, ganarse la antipatía de; (property) enajenar
alight [əláɪt] VI (rider) apearse; (bird, insect) posarse
align [əláɪn] VI/VT alinear(se)
alignment [əláɪnmənt] N alineación *f*
alike [əláɪk] ADJ parecido, igual; **to be —** parecerse, ser iguales; ADV del mismo modo
alimony [ǽləmoni] N pensión alimenticia *f*
alive [əláɪv] ADJ (living) vivo; **— with** lleno de; **the symphony came — under his direction** la sinfonía cobró vida bajo su dirección
alkali [ǽɫkəlaɪ] N álcali *m*
alkaline [ǽɫkəlɪn] ADJ alcalino
all [ɔɫ] ADJ todo; **— the time** todo el tiempo; N todo *m*; **he gave his —** dio todo de sí; PRON todo; **is that —?** ¿eso es todo? ADV completamente, todo; **— at once** (uninterrupted) de una vez; (sudden) de repente; **— told** en conjunto; **he's — dirty** está todo sucio; **it is — over** se acabó; **not at —** de ninguna manera; **nothing at —** nada en absoluto; **once (and) for —** de una vez por todas; **she's — right** está bien; INTERJ **— right** bueno
allay [əlé] VT (fear, doubt) calmar, disipar; (anger) aplacar
allegation [æɫɪgéʃən] N acusación *f*
allege [əlédʒ] VT afirmar
allegiance [əlídʒəns] N lealtad *f*, fidelidad *f*; **to pledge — to the flag** jurar la bandera
allegory [ǽɫɪgɔri] N alegoría *f*
allergic [əlɜ́·dʒɪk] ADJ alérgico
allergist [ǽɫə·dʒɪst] N alergólogo -ga *mf*
allergy [ǽɫə·dʒi] N alergia *f*
alleviate [əlíviet] VT (suffering) aliviar; (hunger) paliar
alley [ǽli] N callejón *m*; **right up her —** ideal para ella

alliance [əláɪəns] N alianza f

allied [əláɪd, ǽlaɪd] ADJ aliado

alligator [ǽlɪgeɪɚ] N caimán m; *Am* lagarto m

alliterate [əlíɾəret] VI hacer aliteración

allocate [ǽləket] VT asignar

allot [əlát] VT asignar

allow [əláu] VI/VT (permit) permitir; (admit) admitir; **— an hour to change trains** date una hora para cambiar de trenes; **to — for** tener en cuenta

allowable [əláuəbəɫ] ADJ admisible, permisible

allowance [əláuəns] N (regular payment) asignación f, pensión f; (monthly payment) mensualidad f; (for a child) paga f, mesada f; (payment for a particular purpose) pago m; (food) ración f; **to make — for** tener en cuenta

alloy [ǽlɔɪ] N aleación f; [əlɔ́ɪ] VT alear

allude [əlúd] VI aludir; **to — to** aludir a

allure [əlúr] VI/VT seducir, atraer; N atractivo m

alluring [əlúrɪŋ] ADJ seductivo, atractivo

allusion [əlúʒən] N alusión f

ally [ǽlaɪ] N aliado -da mf; [əláɪ] VT **to — oneself with** aliarse con

almanac [ɔ́lmənæk] N almanaque m

almighty [ɔlmáɪɾi] ADJ todopoderoso

almond [ɔ́mənd] N almendra f; **— tree** almendro m

almost [ɔ́lmost] ADV casi; **I — fell down** por poco me caigo

alms [ɔmz] N limosna f

aloe vera [ǽlovírə] N áloe m

alone [əlón] ADJ solo; **— among his contemporaries** único entre sus contemporáneos; ADV sólo, solamente; **she — knew that** sólo ella sabía eso; **all — a** solas; **to leave —** no tocar, dejar en paz

along [əlɔ́ŋ] PREP **he was walking — the street** andaba por la calle; **all — the coast** a lo largo de toda la costa; **— with** junto con; **all —** desde el principio; **to carry — with oneself** llevar consigo; **to go — with** acceder a; **to get — with** llevarse bien con

alongside [əlɔ́ŋsaɪd] PREP al lado de; **— the boat** al lado del bote; ADV al lado, al costado; **the dog ran —** el perro corría al costado

aloof [əlúf] ADJ reservado, esquivo; ADV apartado

aloud [əláud] ADV en voz alta

alphabet [ǽlfəbɛt] N alfabeto m, abecedario m

alphanumeric [ælfənumérɪk] ADJ alfanumérico

alpine [ǽlpaɪn] ADJ alpino

already [ɔlrédi] ADV ya

also [ɔ́lso] ADV también, además; **—-ran** (horse, candidate) caballo / candidato vencido m; (loser) nulidad f, segundón -ona mf

altar [ɔ́ltɚ] N altar m; **—piece** retablo m

alter [ɔ́ltɚ] VI/VT (change) alterar; (neuter) capar, castrar

alteration [ɔltəréʃən] N (change) alteración f, cambio m; **—s** arreglos m pl, reformas f pl

altercation [ɔltɚkéʃən] N altercado m

alternate [ɔ́ltɚnɪt] ADJ alternativo, alterno; **— route** ruta alternativa f; **— spelling** ortografía alterna f; **he visits us on — Mondays** nos visita un lunes sí y otro no; N suplente mf; [ɔ́ltɚnet] VI/VT alternar

alternative [ɔltɚ́nəɾɪv] ADJ alternativo; N alternativa f

alternator [ɔ́ltɚneɾɚ] N alternador m

although [ɔlðó] CONJ aunque, si bien

altimeter [æltímɪɾɚ] N altímetro m

altitude [ǽltɪtjud] N altura f, altitud f; **— sickness** mal de altura m

alto [ǽlto] N contralto mf; ADJ alto

altogether [ɔltəgéðɚ] ADV (completely) completamente; (all included) en total

altruism [ǽltruɪzəm] N altruismo m

aluminum [əlúmənəm] N aluminio m; **— foil** papel de aluminio m

always [ɔ́lwez] ADV siempre

a.m. [eém] ADV de la mañana

amalgamate [əmǽlgəmet] VI/VT (metals) amalgamar(se); (companies) fusionar(se)

amass [əmǽs] VT acumular, amasar

amateur [ǽmətʃɚ] ADJ amateur; N aficionado -da mf

amaze [əméz] VT maravillar, asombrar

amazement [əmézmənt] N asombro m

amazing [əmézɪŋ] ADJ asombroso, increíble

Amazon [ǽməzɑn] N (region) Amazonia f; (river) Amazonas m sg

ambassador [æmbǽsəɾɚ] N embajador -ra mf

amber [ǽmbɚ] N ámbar m; ADJ (quality) ambarino; (material) de ámbar; (color) (de) color ámbar

ambiance [ǽmbɪəns] N ambiente m

ambidextrous [æmbɪdékstrəs] ADJ ambidiestro

ambient [ǽmbɪənt] ADJ ambiental; **— temperature** temperatura ambiente f

ambiguity [æmbɪgjúɪɾi] N ambigüedad f

ambiguous [æmbígjuəs] ADJ ambiguo

ambition [æmbíʃən] N ambición f,

ambitious [æmbíʃəs] ADJ ambicioso
ambivalent [æmbívələnt] ADJ ambivalente
amble [ǽmbəł] VI deambular
ambulance [ǽmbjələns] N ambulancia f
ambush [ǽmbuʃ] N emboscada f, celada f; **to lie in —** acechar; VT emboscar
ameliorate [əmíliəret] VI/VT mejorar
amen [ámén] INTERJ amén
amenable [əménəbəł] ADJ bien dispuesto
amend [əménd] VT enmendar; **to make —s (for)** compensar (por)
amendment [əméndmənt] N enmienda f
amenities [əménɪDiz] N PL comodidades f pl
America [əmérɪkə] N América f
American [əmérɪkən] ADJ & N (continental) americano -na mf; (USA) americano -na mf, norteamericano -na mf, estadounidense mf
amethyst [ǽməθɪst] N amatista f
amiable [émiəbəł] ADJ amable
amicable [ǽmɪkəbəł] ADJ amistoso
amid [əmíd] PREP en medio de
amino acid [əmínoǽsɪd] N aminoácido m
amiss [əmís] ADV **something is —** algo anda mal
ammonia [əmónjə] N amoníaco m
ammunition [æmjəníʃən] N munición f
amnesia [æmníʒə] N amnesia f
amnesty [ǽmnɪsti] N amnistía f
amniocentesis [ǽmniosɪntísɪs] N amniocentesis f
amoeba [əmíbə] N ameba f
among [əmʌ́ŋ] PREP entre
amoral [emɔ́rəł] ADJ amoral
amorous [ǽmərəs] ADJ (sexually aroused) excitado; (loving) amoroso
amorphous [əmɔ́rfəs] ADJ amorfo
amortize [ǽməˑtaɪz] VT amortizar
amount [əmáunt] N cantidad f; (of money) suma f, importe m; VI ascender (a); **that —s to stealing** eso equivale a robar
ampere [ǽmpír] N amperio m
amphetamine [æmféDəmin] N anfetamina f
amphibian [æmfíbiən] N anfibio m
amphibious [æmfíbiəs] ADJ anfibio
amphitheater [ǽmfəθiəDəˑ] N anfiteatro m
ampicillin [æmpɪsílɪn] N ampicilina f
ample [ǽmpəł] ADJ (in quantity) suficiente; (in size) amplio
amplifier [ǽmpləfaɪəˑ] N amplificador m
amplify [ǽmpləfaɪ] VT (an explanation) ampliar; (a sound) amplificar
amplitude [ǽmplɪtud] N amplitud f
amputate [ǽmpjətet] VT amputar
amuck, amok [əmʌ́k] ADV **to run —** (kill people) perpetrar un ataque homicida; (go

crazy) volverse loco
amulet [ǽmjəlɪt] N amuleto m
amuse [əmjúz] VT (make laugh) divertir; (help pass time) entretener; **to — oneself** divertirse, entretenerse, recrearse
amusement [əmjúzmənt] N diversión f, entretenimiento m
amusing [əmjúzɪŋ] ADJ (entertaining) divertido; (funny) gracioso, chistoso
an [ən, æn] INDEF ART un m, una f
anachronism [ənǽkrənɪzəm] N anacronismo m
anaerobic [ænəróbɪk] ADJ anaerobio
anal [énəł] ADJ anal
analgesic [ænəłʤízɪk] N & ADJ analgésico m
analog [ǽnəlɔg] ADJ analógico
analogical [ænəláʤɪkəł] ADJ analógico
analogous [ənǽləgəs] ADJ análogo
analogy [ənǽləʤi] N analogía f
analysis [ənǽlɪsɪs] N análisis m
analytic [ænəlídɪk] ADJ analítico
analytical [ænəlídɪkəł] ADJ analítico
analyze [ǽnəlaɪz] VT analizar
anarchist [ǽnəˑkɪst] N anarquista mf
anarchy [ǽnəˑki] N anarquía f
anathema [ənǽθəmə] N anatema m
anatomical [ænətámɪkəł] ADJ anatómico
anatomy [ənǽDəmi] N anatomía f
ancestor [ǽnsɛstəˑ] N antepasado -da mf, ascendiente mf
ancestral [ænséstrəł] ADJ de los antepasados; **— home** casa solariega f
ancestry [ǽnsɛstri] N linaje m, ascendencia f, abolengo m
anchor [ǽŋkəˑ] N ancla f; **— man** presentador m; **—woman** presentadora f; **to drop —** anclar, echar anclas; VT (a boat) anclar; (an argument) basar; VI echar anclas, fondear
anchovy [ǽntʃovi] N anchoa f
ancient [énʃənt] ADJ antiguo; pej vetusto
and [ænd] CONJ y; (before i, hi) e; **— so forth** etcétera, y así sucesivamente; **more — more** cada vez más
Andalusia [ændəlúʒə] N Andalucía f
Andalusian [ændəlúʒən] ADJ & N andaluz -za mf
Andes [ǽndiz] N Andes m pl
Andorra [ændɔ́rə] N Andorra f
Andorran [ændɔ́rən] ADJ & N andorrano -na mf
androgynous [ændráʤənəs] ADJ andrógino
anecdote [ǽnɪkdot] N anécdota f
anemia [ənímiə] N anemia f
anemic [ənímɪk] ADJ anémico
anesthesia [ænɪsθíʒə] N anestesia f
anesthesiology [ænɪsθiziáləʤi] N

anestesiología *f*

anesthetic [ænɪsθέDɪk] ADJ anestésico; N (substance) anestesia *f*

aneurysm [ǽnjərɪzəm] N aneurisma *m*

anew [ənjú] ADV otra vez

angel [éndʒəɫ] N ángel *m*

angelic [ændʒélɪk] ADJ angélico, angelical

anger [ǽŋgɚ] N enojo *m*, enfado *m*; VT enojar, enfadar

angina [ændʒáɪnə] N — **pectoris** angina de pecho *f*

angioplasty [ǽndʒiəplæsti] N angioplastia *f*

angle [ǽŋgəɫ] N (geometrical) ángulo *m*; (point of view) punto de vista *m*, perspectiva *f*; VI pescar

Anglo-Saxon [ǽŋglosǽksən] ADJ & N anglosajón -na *mf*

Angola [æŋgólə] N Angola *f*

Angolan [æŋgólən] ADJ angolano -na *mf*, angoleño -ña *mf*

angry [ǽŋgri] ADJ enojado, enfadado

angst [áŋkst] N angustia *f*

anguish [ǽŋgwɪʃ] N angustia *f*, ansia *f*, congoja *f*

angular [ǽŋgjələ] ADJ angular; (face) anguloso

animal [ǽnəməɫ] ADJ & N animal *m*; — **rights** derechos de los animales *m pl*

animate [ǽnəmɪt] ADJ animado; [ǽnəmet] VT (enliven) animar; (encourage) alentar; —**d cartoon** dibujo animado *m*

animation [ænəméʃən] N animación *f*

animosity [ænəmásɪDi] N animosidad *f*, ojeriza *f*, encono *m*

anise [ǽnɪs] N anís *m*

ankle [ǽŋkəɫ] N tobillo *m*

annals [ǽnɫz] N anales *m pl*

annex [ǽnɛks] N anexo *m*; [ənéks] VT anexar

annexation [ænɛkséʃən] N anexión *f*

annihilate [ənáɪəlet] VT aniquilar

anniversary [ænəvɚ́səri] N aniversario *m*

annotate [ǽnətet] VT anotar

annotation [ænətéʃən] N (action, result) anotación *f*; (result) nota *f*

announce [ənáʊns] VT anunciar; (an engagement, birth) participar

announcement [ənáʊnsmənt] N anuncio *m*; (of an engagement, birth) participación *f*

announcer [ənáʊnsɚ] N anunciador -ra *mf*; (on radio) locutor -ra *mf*

annoy [ənɔ́ɪ] VI/VT fastidiar, contrariar

annoyance [ənɔ́ɪəns] N fastidio *m*, contrariedad *f*

annual [ǽnjuəɫ] ADJ anual; N (book) anuario *m*; (plant) planta anual *f*

annuity [ənjúɪDi] N anualidad *f*, renta anual *f*

annul [ənʌ́ɫ] VT anular

annulment [ənʌ́ɫmənt] N anulación *f*

anomalous [ənáməlҙs] ADJ anómalo

anomaly [ənáməli] N anomalía *f*

anonymous [ənánəmҙs] ADJ anónimo

anorak [ǽnəræk] N anorak *m*

anorexia [ænəréksiə] N anorexia *f*

anorexic [ænəréksɪk] ADJ anoréxico

another [ənʌ́ðɚ] ADJ otro; — **day** otro día; PRON otro; **I want** — quiero otro; **one** — el uno al otro, los unos a los otros

answer [ǽnsɚ] N (to a question) respuesta *f*, contestación *f*; (to a problem) solución *f*; VI contestar, responder; **to** — **for** ser responsable de / por; VT contestar

answering [ǽnsɚɪŋ] ADJ — **machine** contestador automático *m*; — **service** servicio telefónico contratado *m*

ant [ænt] N hormiga *f*; —**eater** oso hormiguero *m*; —**hill** hormiguero *m*

antacid [æntǽsɪd] N & ADJ antiácido *m*

antagonism [æntǽgənɪzəm] N antagonismo *m*

antagonist [æntǽgənɪst] N antagonista *mf*

antagonize [æntǽgənaɪz] VT antagonizar

antarctic [æntárktɪk] ADJ antártico

Antarctica [æntárktɪkə] N Antártida *f*

antecedent [æntəsídn̩t] ADJ & N antecedente *m*

antelope [ǽntəlop] N antílope *m*

antenna [ænténə] N antena *f*

anterior [æntíriɚ] ADJ anterior

anthem [ǽnθəm] N himno *m*

anthology [ænθálədʒi] N antología *f*

anthracite [ǽnθrəsaɪt] N antracita *f*

anthrax [ǽnθræks] N ántrax *m*

anthropologist [ænθrəpálədʒɪst] N antropólogo -ga *mf*

anthropology [ænθrəpálədʒi] N antropología *f*

anthropomorphize [ænθrəpəmɔ́rfaɪz] VI/VT antropomorfizar

antiabortion [æntiəbɔ́rʃən] ADJ antiaborto *inv*

antiaircraft [æntiérkræft] ADJ antiaéreo

antibacterial [æntibæktíriəɫ] ADJ antibacteriano

antiballistic [æntibəlístɪk] ADJ antibalístico

antibiotic [æntibaɪáDɪk] N & ADJ antibiótico *m*

antibody [ǽntɪbaDi] N anticuerpo *m*

anticipate [æntísəpet] VI/VT prever, calcular

anticipation [æntɪsəpéʃən] N previsión *f*; **with great** — con gran expectación

anticlimactic [æntɪkləmǽktɪk] ADJ decepcionante

antics [ǽntɪks] N payasadas *f pl*, monerías *f*

pl, monadas *f pl*

antidepressant [æntidıprésənt] ADJ & N
antidepresivo *m*

antidote [ǽntıdot] N antídoto *m*

antifreeze [ǽntıfriz] N anticongelante *m*

Antigua and Barbuda [æntígəændbɑrbúɒə]
N Antigua y Barbuda *f*

Antiguan [æntígən] ADJ & N antiguano -ana
mf

antihistamine [æntihístəmin] N
antihistamínico *m*

anti-inflammatory [æntiınflǽmətɔri] ADJ &
N antiinflamatorio *m*

antilock [ǽntılɑk] ADJ antibloqueo

antimony [ǽntəmoni] N antimonio *m*

antioxidant [æntiáksıɒənt] N antioxidante
m

antipathy [æntípəθi] N antipatía *f*

antiperspirant [æntipɚ́spɚ-ənt] N
antitranspirante *m*

antiquated [ǽntıkweɒıd] ADJ anticuado;
(words) desusado

antique [æntík] ADJ antiguo; N antigüedad *f*

antiquity [æntíkwıɒi] N antigüedad *f*

anti-Semitism [æntisémıtızəm] N
antisemitismo *m*

antiseptic [æntıséptık] ADJ & N antiséptico *m*

antisocial [æntisófeł] ADJ antisocial

antithesis [æntíθəsıs] N antítesis *f*

antitrust [æntitrást] ADJ antimonopolio,
antitrust

antler [ǽntlɚ-] N asta *f*, cuerno *m*

antonym [ǽntənım] N antónimo *m*

antsy [ǽntsi] ADJ (impatient) impaciente;
(anxious) ansioso

anus [énəs] N ano *m*

anvil [ǽnvəł] N yunque *m*

anxiety [æŋzáıɒi] N ansiedad *f*, angustia *f*

anxious [ǽŋkʃəs] ADJ (worried) ansioso,
preocupado; (desirous) ansioso, deseoso

any [éni] ADJ & PRON cualquier(a),
cualesquier(a); **— woman** cualquier
mujer, una mujer cualquiera; **— man**
cualquier hombre, un hombre cualquiera;
— houses unas casas cualesquiera; *lit*
cualesquiera casas; **in — case** en todo
caso; **do you have — money?** ¿tienes
dinero? **I don't have —** no tengo

anybody [énibɑɒi] PRON alguien, cualquiera;
— could do that cualquiera podría hacer
eso; **is — here?** ¿hay alguien aquí? **he
does not know —** no conoce a nadie

anyhow [énihau] ADV de todos modos

anymore [énimɔ́r] ADV **he doesn't work —**
ya no trabaja, no trabaja más

anyone [éniwʌn] PRON alguien, cualquiera; **—
could do that** cualquiera podría hacer

eso; **is — here?** ¿hay alguien aquí? **he
does not know —** no conoce a nadie

anyplace [éniples] ADV en cualquier parte /
lugar; **you can buy it —** se puede
comprar en cualquier lugar; **he's not
going —** no va a ninguna parte

anything [éniθıŋ] PRON cualquier cosa, algo;
— is fine cualquier cosa me viene bien;
— you wish todo lo que quieras; **do you
have — for a cough?** ¿tienes algo para
la tos? **I don't know —** no sé nada

anytime [énitaım] ADV en cualquier
momento

anyway [éniwe] ADV de todos modos, de
cualquier manera

anywhere [énihwɛr] ADV en cualquier parte /
lugar; **you can buy it —** se puede
comprar en cualquier lugar; **he's not
going —** no va a ninguna parte

aorta [eɔ́rɒə] N aorta *f*

apart [əpárt] ADV **they are three miles —**
están a tres millas de distancia; **they
kept him — from the group** lo
apartaron del grupo; **each factor
viewed —** cada factor visto por separado;
to take — desarmar, desmontar; **to tear
—** despedazar, hacer pedazos; **to tell —**
distinguir

apartment [əpártmənt] N apartamento *m*; *Sp*
piso *m*

apathetic [æpəθéɒık] ADJ apático

apathy [ǽpəθi] N apatía *f*, abulia *f*

ape [ep] N simio *m*; VT remedar

aperture [ǽpɚ-tʃɚ-] N abertura *f*; (of a pipe)
luz *f*

apex [épɛks] N (of tongue) ápice *m*; (of a
mountain) cumbre *f*

aphasia [əféʒə] N afasia *f*

aphrodisiac [æfrədíziæk] N afrodisíaco *m*

apiece [əpís] ADV cada uno

apnea [ǽpniə] N apnea *f*

apocalypse [əpákəlıps] N apocalipsis *m*

apogee [ǽpəʤi] N apogeo *m*

apologetic [əpɑləʤéɒık] ADJ lleno de
disculpas

apologize [əpálɚʤaız] VI disculparse

apology [əpálɚʤi] N disculpa(s) *f (pl)*;
(justification) apología *f*

apostle [əpásəł] N apóstol *m*

apostrophe [əpástrəfi] N (punctuation)
apóstrofo *m*; (invocation) apóstrofe *m*

appall [əpáł] VT horrorizar

appalling [əpálıŋ] ADJ horroroso

apparatus [æpəréɒəs] N (single) aparato *m*;
(group) maquinaria *f*

apparel [əpǽrəł] N indumentaria *f*, ropa *f*;
(fine) ropaje *m*

apparent [əpǽrənt] ADJ (visible) visible; (clear) obvio, evidente; (seeming) aparente

apparition [æpəríʃən] N aparición f, fantasma m

appeal [əpíł] N (legal) apelación f, recurso m; (request) ruego m, llamamiento m; (attraction) atractivo m; VT apelar, recurrir (contra); VI **to — to** atraer

appear [əpír] VI (show up) aparecer(se); (seem) parecer, aparentar; (a publication) salir; (before a judge) comparecer

appearance [əpírəns] N (looks) apariencia f, traza f, estampa f; (act of appearing) aparición f

appease [əpíz] VT aplacar, apaciguar

appeasement [əpízmənt] N aplacamiento m, apaciguamiento m

appellate [əpélɪt] N — **court** tribunal de apelaciones m

append [əpénd] VT adjuntar

appendage [əpéndɪʤ] N apéndice m

appendectomy [æpɪndéktəmi] N apendicectomía f

appendicitis [əpendəsáɪdɪs] N apendicitis f

appendix [əpéndɪks] N apéndice m

appetite [ǽpɪtaɪt] N apetito m

appetizer [ǽpɪtaɪzɚ] N aperitivo m

appetizing [ǽpɪtaɪzɪŋ] ADJ apetecible, apetitoso

applaud [əplɔ́d] VI/VT aplaudir

applause [əplɔ́z] N aplauso(s) m (pl)

apple [ǽpəł] N manzana f; — **grove** manzanar m; — **of my eye** niña de mis ojos f; —**sauce** compota de manzana f; — **tree** manzano m; **Adam's —** nuez de Adán f

appliance [əpláɪəns] N aparato m; (electric) (aparato) electrodoméstico m

applicable [ǽplɪkəbəł] ADJ aplicable

applicant [ǽplɪkənt] N aspirante mf, solicitante mf

application [æplɪkéʃən] N (act of applying) aplicación f; (form) solicitud f, formulario f

apply [əpláɪ] VT aplicar; **to — for** solicitar, pedir; **are you —ing for the scholarship?** ¿te presentas para la beca? ¿estás solicitando la beca? **to — oneself** aplicarse, dedicarse

appoint [əpɔ́ɪnt] VT (designate) nombrar, designar; (furnish) amueblar, equipar; **a well —ed house** una casa bien amueblada

appointee [əpɔɪntí] N persona nombrada f

appointment [əpɔ́ɪntmənt] N (designation) nombramiento m, designación f; (engagement) cita f; **doctor's —** cita / hora con el médico f; —**s** mobiliario m sg, accesorios m pl

apportion [əpɔ́rʃən] VT repartir proporcionalmente

apportionment [əpɔ́rʃənmənt] N reparto proporcional m

appraisal [əpréz əł] N tasación f, valuación f

appraise [əpréz] VT avaluar, valorar, tasar

appreciable [əpríʃəbəł] ADJ apreciable

appreciate [əpríʃiet] VT (value) apreciar, estimar; (recognize) darse cuenta, percibir; (thank) agradecer; **to — in value** apreciarse

appreciation [əpriʃiéʃən] N (esteem) aprecio m; (thanks) agradecimiento m; (monetary value) apreciación f, alza f

apprehend [æprɪhénd] VT (arrest) aprehender; (understand) comprender

apprehension [æprɪhénʃən] N (arrest) aprehensión f; (worry) aprensión f

apprehensive [æprɪhénsɪv] ADJ aprensivo

apprentice [əpréntɪs] N aprendiz -iza mf; VT poner de aprendiz

apprenticeship [əpréntɪsʃɪp] N aprendizaje m

apprise [əpráɪz] VT informar

approach [əprótʃ] N (act of approaching) aproximación f; (method) enfoque m, aproximación f, acercamiento m; (means of access) acceso m, entrada f; VI acercarse, aproximarse; VT (a problem) abordar, enfocar; **to — someone about a problem** plantearle a alguien un problema

approachable [əprótʃəbəł] ADJ tratable

approbation [æprəbéʃən] N aprobación f

appropriate [əpróprɪɪt] ADJ apropiado, adecuado; [əprópriet] VT apropiarse; (funds) asignar

appropriation [əpropriéʃən] N (act of appropriation) apropiación f; (assignment of funds) asignación f; (assigned funds) partida f

approval [əprúvəł] N aprobación f

approve [əprúv] VI/VT aprobar

approximate [əpráksəmɪt] ADJ aproximado; [əpráksəmet] VT aproximarse a

apricot [ǽprɪkɑt] N albaricoque m; Am damasco m; Mex chabacano m

April [éprəł] N abril m

apron [éprən] N (for a cook) delantal m; (for a workman) mandil m

apropos [ǽprəpó] ADV a propósito; ADJ oportuno, pertinente; — **of** a propósito de

apt [æpt] ADJ (prone, able) capaz; (suited) pertinente; **is he — to be at home?** ¿estará en casa?

aptitude [ǽptɪtud] N aptitud f, capacidad f

aquamarine [ɑkwəmərín] N aguamarina *f*
aquarium [əkwériəm] N (tank) acuario *m*, pecera *f*; (building) acuario *m*
aquatic [əkwɑ́ɖɪk] ADJ acuático
aqueduct [ǽkwɪdʌkt] N acueducto *m*
Arab [ǽrəb] ADJ & N árabe *mf*
Arabic [ǽrəbɪk] ADJ árabe, arábigo; N (language) árabe *m*
Aragonese [ærəgəníz] ADJ & N aragonés -esa *mf*
arbiter [ɑ́rbɪɖɚ] N árbitro -ra *mf*
arbitrary [ɑ́rbɪtrɛri] ADJ arbitrario
arbitrate [ɑ́rbɪtret] VI/VT (mediate) arbitrar (en), terciar (en); (submit to mediation) someter al arbitraje
arbitration [ɑrbɪtréʃən] N arbitraje *m*
arbitrator [ɑ́rbɪtreɖɚ] N árbitro *mf*
arbor [ɑ́rbɚ] N pérgola *f*, glorieta *f*
arboreal [ɑrbɔ́riəł] ADJ arbóreo
arc [ɑrk] N arco *m*
arcade [ɑrkéd] N (series of arcs) arcada *f*; (shops) galería *f*; (of video games) sala de juegos electrónicos *f*
arcane [ɑrkén] ADJ arcano
arch [ɑrtʃ] N arco *m*; (curved roof) bóveda *f*; **—way** arcada *f*; VI/VT arquear(se)
archaeology [ɑrkiɑ́ləʤi] N arqueología *f*
archaic [ɑrkéɪk] ADJ arcaico
archaism [ɑ́rkeɪzəm] N arcaísmo *m*
archbishop [ɑrtʃbíʃəp] N arzobispo *m*
archenemy [ɑ́rtʃénəmi] N archienemigo -ga *mf*
archery [ɑ́rtʃəri] N tiro al arco *m*
archetype [ɑ́rkɪtaɪp] N arquetipo *m*
archipelago [ɑrkəpéləgo] N archipiélago *m*
architect [ɑ́rkɪtɛkt] N arquitecto -ta *mf*; (creator) artífice *mf*
architectural [ɑrkɪtéktʃɚəł] ADJ arquitectónico
architecture [ɑ́rkɪtɛktʃɚ] N arquitectura *f*
archive [ɑ́rkaɪv] N archivo *m*
arctic [ɑ́rktɪk] ADJ ártico
ardent [ɑ́rdn̩t] ADJ ardiente
ardor [ɑ́rɖɚ] N ardor *m*, fervor *m*
arduous [ɑ́rʤuəs] ADJ arduo
area [ériə] N área *f*; (region) zona *f*; (of a geometric figure) superficie *f*, área *f*
arena [ərínə] N estadio *m*; (in circus) pista *f*
Argentina [ɑrʤəntínə] N Argentina *f*
Argentinian [ɑrʤəntíniən] ADJ & N argentino -na *mf*
argon [ɑ́rgɑn] N argón *m*
argue [ɑ́rgju] VT (reason) argüir, argumentar; VI (bicker) discutir, reñir
argument [ɑ́rgjəmənt] N (reason) argumento *m*; (altercation) disputa *f*, discusión *f*
arid [ǽrɪd] ADJ árido

arise [əráɪz] VI (get up) levantarse; (appear) surgir; (result) provenir, resultar
aristocracy [ærɪstɑ́krəsi] N aristocracia *f*
aristocrat [ərístəkræt] N aristócrata *mf*
aristocratic [ərɪstəkrǽɖɪk] ADJ aristocrático
arithmetic [əríθmətɪk] N aritmética *f*; ADJ aritmético
ark [ɑrk] N arca *f*; **Noah's —** arca de Noé *f*
arm [ɑrm] N brazo *m*; **—chair** sillón *m*, butaca *f*; **—pit** sobaco *m*, axila *f*; **—rest** (in a car) apoyabrazos *m sg*; (on a sofa) brazo *m*; **— in —** del brazo; **at —'s length** a distancia; **with open —s** con los brazos abiertos; **—s** armas *f pl*
armada [ɑrmɑ́də] N armada *f*, flota *f*
armament [ɑ́rməmənt] N armamento *m*
Armenia [ɑrmíniə] N Armenia *f*
Armenian [ɑrmíniən] ADJ & N armenio -nia *mf*
armful [ɑ́rmfuł] N brazada *f*
armistice [ɑ́rmɪstɪs] N armisticio *m*
armoire [ɑrmwɑ́r] N armario *m*
armor [ɑ́rmɚ] N (of a knight) armadura *f*; (on a vehicle) blindaje *m*; (on insects) coraza *f*; VT (a car) blindar; (a tank) acorazar
armored [ɑ́rmɚd] ADJ (van) blindado; (tank) acorazado
armory [ɑ́rmɚi] N armería *f*
army [ɑ́rmi] N ejército *m*; (multitude) muchedumbre *f*
aroma [ərómə] N aroma *m*
aromatic [ærəmǽɖɪk] ADJ aromático
around [əráʊnd] ADV **there were books all — ** había libros por todos lados; **there is a supermarket — here** hay un supermercado por aquí; **it was the only farm for miles —** era la única granja en millas a la redonda; **the tree is forty centimeters —** el árbol tiene cuarenta centímetros de circunferencia; **we drove — the block** dimos vuelta a la manzana; **I'll show you —** te enseño el lugar; **the wheels turned —** las ruedas giraban; **turn —** date la vuelta; **she finally came —** al final la convencimos; **he hasn't been —** no ha estado por aquí; **a town with mountains — it** un pueblo rodeado de montañas; **we walked — town** dimos una vuelta por el pueblo; **— five o'clock** a eso de las cinco; PREP **a ribbon — her wrist** una cinta alrededor de su muñeca; **tie a string — your finger** atate un hilo al dedo; **stay — the house** quédate cerca de la casa; **he wandered — the park** deambuló por el parque; **the church — the corner** la

iglesia a la vuelta de la esquina; **motion — its axis** movimiento en torno a su eje; **—-the-clock** veinticuatro horas al día

arouse [əráuz] vi despertar; vt (suspicion) despertar; (sexual response) excitar

arraign [ərén] vt hacer comparecer ante un juez

arrange [əréndʒ] vt arreglar

arrangement [əréndʒmənt] N arreglo *m*; (of objects) disposición *f*; (agreement) acuerdo *m*; **to make —s (for)** hacer arreglos (para)

array [əré] N (arrangement) abanico *m*, selección *f*; (of troops) orden *m*; (attire) gala *f*; vt (troops) formar; (attire) ataviar

arrears [ərírz] ADV LOC **in —** atrasado

arrest [ərést] N arresto *m*, detención *f*; vi/vt arrestar, detener

arrhythmia [əríðmiə] N arritmia *f*

arrival [əráivəł] N llegada *f*; *lit* arribo *m*; **the new —s** los recién llegados

arrive [əráiv] vi llegar; *lit* arribar

arrogance [ǽrəgəns] N arrogancia *f*

arrogant [ǽrəgənt] ADJ arrogante

arrow [ǽro] N flecha *f*; *lit* saeta *f*; **—head** punta de flecha *f*

arsenal [ársənḷ] N arsenal *m*

arsenic [ársənɪk] N arsénico *m*

arson [ársən] N incendio doloso *m*

art [art] N arte *m (sg) f (pl)*; (works) obras *f pl*; (skill) destreza *f*; **fine —s** bellas artes *f pl*; **master of —s** maestría en humanidades *f*; **— deco** art déco *m*

arteriosclerosis [artiriosklərósɪs] N arteriosclerosis *f*

artery [árɾəri] N arteria *f*

artful [ártfəł] ADJ (esthetic) artístico; (deceitful) artero, ladino

arthritis [arθráɪdɪs] N artritis *f*

arthroscopic [arθrəskápɪk] ADJ artroscópico

artichoke [árɾɪtʃok] N alcachofa *f*

article [árɾɪkəł] N artículo *m*; **— of clothing** prenda de vestir *f*

articulate [artíkjəlɪt] ADJ (clear) claro; (eloquent) elocuente; **he's very —** se expresa muy bien; [artíkjəlet] vi/vt (pronounce, join) articular; (express) enunciar

articulation [artɪkjəléʃən] N articulación *f*

artifact [árɾəfækt] N artefacto *m*, ingenio *m*

artifice [árɾəfɪs] N artificio *m*

artificial [arɾəfíʃəł] ADJ artificial; (affected) afectado; **— insemination** inseminación artificial *f*; **— intelligence** inteligencia artificial *f*

artillery [artíləri] N artillería *f*

artisan [árɾɪzən] N artesano -na *mf*,

artífice *mf*

artist [árɾɪst] N artista *mf*; (performer) intérprete *mf*

artistic [artístɪk] ADJ artístico

Aruba [ərúbə] N Aruba *f*

as [æz] CONJ **— for me** en lo que a mí respecta; **— if** como si; **— it were** por decirlo así; **— large —** tan grande como; **— long — you wish** todo el tiempo que quieras; **— much —** tanto como; **— of** a partir de; **— per** según; **— well** también; **— the illness worsened** a medida que empeoraba la enfermedad; **— yet** hasta ahora, todavía; **the same —** lo mismo que; **it broke — I was using it** se rompió cuando lo usaba; **she knitted — we talked** tejía mientras conversábamos; **he played — never before** jugó como nunca; PREP **— a child, I always felt loved** de niño, siempre me sentí querido; **— a teacher, I must be tough** como maestro, tengo que ser estricto; ADV tan, tanto; **it's not — important** no es tan importante

asbestos [æzbéstəs] N asbesto *m*, amianto *m*

ascend [əsénd] vi ascender

ascent [əsént] N ascenso *m*

ascertain [æsəˌtén] vt averiguar, establecer

ascetic [əsɛ́dɪk] ADJ ascético; N asceta *mf*

ascorbic [əskɔ́rbɪk] ADJ ascórbico

ascribe [əskráɪb] vt atribuir, imputar

asexual [əsékʃuəł] ADJ asexual

ash [æʃ] N (residue, remains) ceniza *f*; (species of tree) fresno *m*; **—tray** cenicero *m*; **— Wednesday** miércoles de ceniza *m*

ashamed [əʃémd] ADJ avergonzado; **to be —** tener vergüenza, avergonzarse

ashen [ǽʃən] ADJ ceniciento

ashore [əʃɔ́r] ADV (movement) a tierra; (location) en tierra; **to go —** desembarcar

Asia [éʒə] N Asia *f*

Asian [éʒən] ADJ & N asiático -ca *mf*

aside [əsáɪd] ADV **all kidding —** bromas aparte; **his father took him —** su padre lo llamó aparte; **he threw his coat —** tiró su saco a un lado; PREP **— from** aparte de, además; N (theater) aparte *m*

asinine [ǽsənaɪn] ADJ necio

ask [æsk] vt (inquire) preguntar; (request) pedir; **to — a question** hacer una pregunta; **to — about** preguntar por; **to — for** pedir; **to — for someone** pedir para hablar con alguien; **to — out** invitar a salir; **what's your —ing price?** ¿cuánto pides? **you —ed for it** te lo has buscado

askance [əskǽns] ADV **to look —** (obliquely)

mirar de soslayo / través / reojo;
(suspiciously) mirar con recelo
askew [əskjú] ADJ ladeado
asleep [əslíp] ADJ dormido; **to fall —**
dormirse; **my arm is —** se me ha
dormido / entumecido el brazo
asparagus [əspǽrəgəs] N espárrago *m*
aspect [ǽspɛkt] N aspecto *m*
aspen [ǽspən] N álamo temblón *m*
asphalt [ǽsfɑɫt] N asfalto *m*
aspiration [æspəréʃən] N aspiración *f*
aspire [əspáɪr] VI aspirar
aspirin [ǽsprɪn] N aspirina *f*
ass [æs] N (animal) asno *m*, burro *m*, borrico
m; (fool) *fam, pej* borrico -ca *mf*, idiota *mf*;
(body part) *vulg* culo *m*; **—hole** *vulg* hijo
de puta *m*; **to bust one's —** *vulg*
romperse el culo
assail [əséɫ] VT (physically) asaltar, atacar;
(verbally) atacar
assailant [əsélənt] N atacante *mf*, agresor -ra
mf
assassin [əsǽsɪn] N asesino -na *mf*
assassinate [əsǽsənet] VT asesinar
assassination [əsæsənéʃən] N asesinato *m*
assault [əsáɫt] N asalto *m*, agresión *f*; **— rifle**
rifle de asalto *m*; **— and battery** agresión
con lesiones *f*; VT asaltar, agredir;
(sexually) violar
assay [æsé] VT (situation) examinar, analizar;
(metal) ensayar; [ǽse] N ensayo *m*
assemble [əsémbəɫ] VI/VT (call together)
reunir(se), congregar(se); VT (put together)
armar, montar
assembly [əsémbli] N (meeting) asamblea *f*,
reunión *f*; (putting together) montaje *m*,
armado *m*; **— language** lenguaje
ensamblador *m*; **— line** cadena de
producción *f*, línea de montaje *f*
assent [əsént] N asentimiento *m*; VI asentir
assert [əsɝ́t] VT (declare) aseverar; **to —**
one's rights hacer valer los derechos de
uno; **to — oneself** obrar con firmeza
assertion [əsɝ́ʃən] N (declaration)
aseveración *f*, afirmación *f*, aserto *m*; **an**
— of ownership una afirmación de los
derechos de propiedad
assess [əsés] VT (evaluate for tax purposes)
tasar; (impose tax) gravar, imponer
assessment [əsésmənt] N (estimate) avalúo *m*,
tasación *f*; (tax) imposición *f*, gravamen
m; (testing) evaluación *f*
asset [ǽset] N (useful thing) ventaja *f*; (useful
quality) virtud *f*; **—s** activo *m*, bienes *m pl*;
(on balance sheet) haber *m*, activo *m*;
personal —s bienes muebles *m pl*; **real**
—s bienes inmuebles *m pl*

assiduous [əsídʒuəs] ADJ (constant) asiduo;
(industrious) diligente
assign [əsáɪn] VT (give out) asignar; (appoint,
designate) designar; (transfer property)
ceder
assignment [əsáɪnmənt] N (act of assigning)
asignación *f*; (task) encargo *m*; (mission)
misión *f*; (transfer of property) cesión (de
bienes) *f*; (homework) tarea *f*; (lesson)
lección *f*
assimilate [əsíməlet] VI/VT asimilar(se)
assist [əsíst] VI/VT ayudar, asistir
assistance [əsístəns] N ayuda *f*, asistencia *f*
assistant [əsístənt] N ayudante *mf*, asistente
mf; ADJ auxiliar
assistantship [əsístəntʃɪp] N ayudantía *f*
associate [əsóʃiɪt] ADJ asociado; N
(acquaintance) compañero -ra *mf*; (co-
worker) colega *mf*; (employee) empleado
-da *mf*; [əsóʃiet] VI/VT asociar(se)
association [əsosiéʃən] N asociación *f*
assonance [ǽsənəns] N asonancia *f*
assorted [əsɔ́rdɪd] ADJ variado, surtido
assortment [əsɔ́rtmənt] N (act of assorting)
clasificación *f*; (of wares) surtido *m*; (of
tools, etc.) colección *f*
assume [əsúm] VT (responsibility, role)
asumir; (right) arrogarse; (suppose) dar por
sentado, suponer
assumption [əsʌ́mpʃən] N (premise)
suposición *f*; (unstated belief)
sobreentendido *m*; (seizure) toma *f*
assurance [əʃúrəns] N (promise) promesa *f*,
palabra *f*; (reassurance) palabras de apoyo
f pl; (certainty) certeza *f*; (confidence)
confianza *f*
assure [əʃúr] VT asegurar; (encourage)
infundir confianza
assuredly [əʃúrɪdli] ADV seguramente, sin
duda
asterisk [ǽstərɪsk] N asterisco *m*
asteroid [ǽstərɔɪd] N asteroide *m*
asthma [ǽzmə] N asma *f*
asthmatic [æzmǽdɪk] ADJ asmático
astigmatism [əstígmətɪzəm] N astigmatismo
m
astonish [əstánɪʃ] VT asombrar, pasmar
astonishing [əstánɪʃɪŋ] ADJ asombroso,
pasmoso
astonishment [əstánɪʃmənt] M asombro *m*,
pasmo *m*
astound [əstáund] VT pasmar, asombrar
astraddle [əstrǽdl] ADV a horcajadas
astray [əstré] ADV **to go —** perderse,
extraviarse; **to lead —** (seduce) llevar por
mal camino, seducir; (perplex) confundir
astride [əstráɪd] ADV a horcajadas

astringent [əstríndʒənt] ADJ & N astringente *m*

astrology [əstrálədʒi] N astrología *f*

astronaut [ǽstrənɔt] M astronauta *mf*

astronautics [æstrənɔ́DIks] N astronáutica *f*

astronomer [əstránəmə-] N astrónomo -ma *mf*

astronomy [əstránəmi] N astronomía *f*

astrophysics [æstrofízıks] N astrofísica *f*

Asturian [æstúriən] ADJ & N asturiano -na *mf*

Asturias [æstúriəs] N Asturias *f sg*

astute [əstút] ADJ astuto, sagaz

asylum [əsáiləm] N asilo *m*

asymmetric [esimétrik] ADJ asimétrico

at [æt] PREP — **the end of the story** al final de la historia; — **five o'clock** a las cinco; — **high altitude** a grandes alturas; — **the table** a / en la mesa; — **five dollars a kilo** a cinco dólares el kilo; — **Easter** en Pascua; — **home** en casa; — **war** en guerra; **wait** — **the door** espera en la puerta; **he is** — **peace with himself** está en paz consigo mismo; **the children are** — **play** los niños están jugando; **look** — **that** mira eso; **amazed** — pasmado por; **he laughed** — **me** se rió de mí; — **last** por fin, al fin

atheism [éθiizəm] N ateísmo *m*

atheist [éθiist] N ateo -a *mf*

athlete [ǽθlit] N deportista *mf*; (track and field) atleta *mf*; —'**s foot** pie de atleta *m*

athletic [æθléDIk] ADJ deportivo; (concerning track and field; well-built) atlético

athletics [æθléDIks] N deporte *m*; (track and field) atletismo *m*

Atlantic [ætlǽntik] ADJ atlántico; N — **Ocean** Océano Atlántico *m*

atlas [ǽtləs] N atlas *m*

atmosphere [ǽtməsfir] N (air) atmósfera *f*; (mood) ambiente *m*

atmospheric [ætməsfírik] ADJ atmosférico

atom [ǽDəm] N átomo *m*; — **bomb** bomba atómica *f*

atomic [ətámik] ADJ atómico; — **age** era atómica *f*; — **energy** energía atómica *f*; — **number** número atómico *m*; — **weight** peso atómico *m*

atomize [ǽDəmaiz] VT atomizar

atone [ətón] VI **to** — **for** expiar, purgar

atonement [ətónmənt] N expiación *f*, purgación *f*

atrium [étriəm] N (of office building, hotel) vestíbulo *m*, patio central *m*; (of church) atrio *m*

atrocious [ətróʃəs] ADJ atroz

atrocity [ətrásıDi] N atrocidad *f*, barbaridad *f*

atrophy [ǽtrəfi] N atrofia *f*; VI/VT atrofiar(se)

attach [ətǽtʃ] VI/VT (pipe, cable) unir(se), juntar; (paper) sujetar; (wages) retener; (significance) atribuir; **to be** —**ed to someone** estar apegado a alguien

attaché [ætæʃé] N agregado -da *mf*

attachment [ətǽtʃmənt] N (act of attaching) unión *f*; (pipe, cable) conexión *f*; (affection) apego *m*, cariño *m*; (of wages) retención *f*; (significance) atribución *f*; (accessory) accesorio *m*

attack [ətǽk] N ataque *m*, acometida *f*; VI/VT atacar, acometer

attain [ətén] VT alcanzar; VI llegar a

attainment [əténmənt] N (act) alcance *m*; (accomplishment) logro *m*, consecución *f*

attempt [ətémpt] N tentativa *f*, intento *m*; (murder) atentado *m*; VT tratar (de), intentar

attend [əténd] VT (meeting) asistir a, acudir a; VI **to** — **to** (a sick person) atender, cuidar; (a speaker) prestar atención

attendance [əténdəns] N asistencia *f*

attendant [əténdənt] N (at a gas station) encargado -da *mf*; (servant) sirviente -ta *mf*; ADJ concomitante

attention [əténʃən] N atención *f*; (courtesy) atenciones *f pl*; **to pay** — prestar atención; **to pay** — **to** atender a; **to call** — llamar la atención; INTERJ —! ¡firmes!

attentive [əténtıv] ADJ (focused) atento; (courteous) cortés

attenuate [əténjuet] VT atenuar

attest [ətést] VT (bear witness to) atestiguar; (manifest) demostrar; VI certificar, dar fe, atestar

attic [ǽDIk] N desván *m*, altillo *m*

attire [ətáir] N atavío *m*, vestidura *f*; VT ataviar

attitude [ǽDItud] N (mental) actitud *f*; (physical) postura *f*; (insolence) insolencia *f*, descaro *m*

attorney [ətɝ́ni] N abogado -da *mf*; — **General** Ministro -tra de Justicia *mf*

attract [ətrǽkt] VT atraer; **to** — **attention** llamar la atención

attraction [ətrǽkʃən] N (act, power) atracción *f*; (charm) atractivo *m*

attractive [ətrǽktıv] ADJ atractivo; (beautiful) atractivo, agraciado

attractiveness [ətrǽktıvnıs] N atractivo *m*

attribute [ǽtrəbjut] N atributo *m*; [ətríbjut] VT atribuir

attribution [ætrəbjúʃən] N atribución *f*

attrition [ətríʃən] N (wearing out) desgaste *m*; (casualties) bajas *f pl*; **war of** — guerra de agotamiento *f*

auburn [ɔ́bɚn] N & ADJ castaño rojizo *m*

auction [ɔ́kʃən] N subasta *f*, remate *m*; VI/VT subastar, rematar

auctioneer [ɔkʃənír] N subastador -ra *mf*, rematador -ra *mf*

audacious [ɔdéʃəs] ADJ audaz, atrevido

audacity [ɔdǽsɪDi] N desfachatez *f*, atrevimiento *m*

audible [ɔ́Dəbəɫ] ADJ audible

audience [ɔ́Diəns] N público *m*, auditorio *m*; (TV, radio) audiencia *f*

audio [ɔ́Dio] ADJ de audio; **— book** audiolibro *m*; **— frequency** audiofrecuencia *f*; **—visual** audiovisual; **—visuals** audiovisuales *m pl*; N audio *m*

audiology [ɔDiáləʤi] N audiología *f*

audit [ɔ́Dɪt] VI/VT (class) asistir de oyente; (accounts) auditar; N auditoría *f*

audition [ɔdíʃən] N audición *f*

auditor [ɔ́DIDɚ] N (of accounts) auditor -ra *mf*, censor -ora *mf*; (of a class) oyente *mf*

auditorium [ɔDɪtɔ́riəm] N auditorio *m*, paraninfo *m*

auditory [ɔ́DItɔri] ADJ auditivo

augment [ɔgmént] VT incrementar, aumentar

August [ɔ́gəst] N agosto *m*

aunt [ænt] N tía *f*

aura [ɔ́rə] N aura *f*

aurora [ərɔ́rə] N aurora *f*; **— borealis** aurora boreal *f*

auspices [ɔ́spɪsɪz] N auspicios *m pl*

auspicious [ɔspíʃəs] ADJ propicio

austere [ɔstír] ADJ austero

austerity [ɔstérɪDi] N austeridad *f*

Australia [ɔstréljə] N Australia *f*

Australian [ɔstréljən] ADJ & N australiano -na *mf*

Austria [ɔ́striə] N Austria *f*

Austrian [ɔ́striən] ADJ & N austríaco -ca *mf*

authentic [ɔθéntɪk] ADJ auténtico

authenticate [ɔθéntɪket] VT autenticar

author [ɔ́θɚ] N (professional) escritor -ra *mf*; (creator) autor -ra *mf*

authoritarian [əθɔrɪtériən] ADJ autoritario

authoritative [əθɔ́rɪteDIV] ADJ (official) autorizado; (dictatorial) autoritario

authority [əθɔ́rɪDi] N autoridad *f*; (permission) autorización *f*; **to have on good —** saber de buena fuente; **it's not within your —** no está dentro de tus facultades

authorization [ɔθɚɪzéʃən] N autorización *f*

authorize [ɔ́θərɑɪz] VT autorizar, habilitar

autism [ɔ́tɪzəm] N autismo *m*

autobiography [ɔDobɑɪágrəfi] N autobiografía *f*

autocrat [ɔ́Dəkræt] N autócrata *mf*

autograph [ɔ́Dəgræf] N autógrafo *m*

autoimmune [ɔDoɪmjún] ADJ autoinmune

automated [ɔ́DəmeDɪd] ADJ automatizado

automatic [ɔDəmǽDɪk] ADJ automático; (response) maquinal; **— pilot** piloto automático *m*; **— transmission** transmisión automática *f*

automation [ɔDəméʃən] N automatización *f*

automobile [ɔ́Dəməbiɫ] N automóvil *m*

automotive [ɔDəmódIV] ADJ (sport) automovilístico; (industry) automotor -ra, automotriz

autonomy [ɔtánəmi] N autonomía *f*

autopilot [ɔ́Dopɑɪlət] N piloto automático *m*

autopsy [ɔ́tɑpsi] N autopsia *f*

autumn [ɔ́Dəm] N otoño *m*

autumnal [ɔtámnəɫ] ADJ otoñal

auxiliary [ɔgzíləri] ADJ & N auxiliar *mf*

avail [əvéɫ] VI/VT servir; **to — oneself of** aprovechar; N **of no —** de ninguna utilidad; **to no —** en vano

available [əvéləbəɫ] ADJ disponible, asequible

avalanche [ǽvəlæntʃ] N avalancha *f*, alud *m*

avarice [ǽvərɪs] N avaricia *f*

avaricious [ævəríʃəs] ADJ avaro, avariento

avenge [əvénʤ] VT vengar

avenger [əvénʤɚ] N vengador -ra *mf*

avenue [ǽvənu] N avenida *f*; (means of access) vía *f*

aver [əvɚ́] VT afirmar

average [ǽvrɪʤ] N promedio *m*; **on —** de promedio; ADJ medio, mediano; **just —** (person) del montón; (thing) nada del otro mundo; VT promediar; **he —s 20 miles an hour** hace un promedio de 20 millas por hora

averse [əvɚ́s] ADJ reacio; **he's not — to a glass of wine** no se opone a una copa de vino

aversion [əvɚ́ʒən] N aversión *f*

avert [əvɚ́t] VT (eyes) desviar; (danger) evitar

aviation [eviéʃən] N aviación *f*

aviator [évieDɚ] N aviador -ra *mf*

avid [ǽvɪd] ADJ ávido

avocado [ævəkáDo] N aguacate *m*; *RP* palta *f*

avocation [ævəkéʃən] N pasatiempo *m*

avoid [əvɔ́ɪd] VI/VT (stay away from) evitar; (dodge) esquivar

avow [əváU] VT confesar

avowal [əváUəɫ] N confesión *f*

avuncular [əvʌ́ŋkjələ] ADJ propio de un tío; **— attitude** actitud paternal y amistosa

await [əwét] VT aguardar

awake [əwék] ADJ despierto; VI/VT despertar(se)

awaken [əwékən] VI/VT despertar(se)

award [əwɔ́rd] N premio *m*, galardón *m*; (judicial) adjudicación *f*; VT otorgar

aware [əwér] ADJ consciente, enterado; **I'm — of that** eso me consta

away [əwé] ADV **far —** lejos; **— from his family** lejos de su familia; **she looked —** apartó la vista; **she's —** no está; **he's been painting — all day** se ha pasado todo el día pintando; **right —** ahora mismo, ahorita; **ten miles —** a diez millas de distancia; **to give —** regalar; **to go —** irse; **to take —** quitar; **to blow —** (hacer) volar

awe [ɔ] N sobrecogimiento *m*; **to be in —** sobrecogerse; VT sobrecoger

awesome [ɔ́səm] ADJ (awe-inspiring) sobrecogedor; (impressive) fabuloso

awestruck [ɔ́strʌk] ADJ pasmado

awful [ɔ́fəɫ] ADJ terrible, horroroso; ADV espantoso; **it's — hot here** hace un calor horrible

awhile [əhwáɪɫ] ADV un rato

awkward [ɔ́kwə-d] ADJ (clumsy) torpe, desmañado; (embarrassing) embarazoso; (unwieldy) incómodo

awl [ɔɫ] N punzón *m*

awning [ɔ́nɪŋ] N toldo *m*

awry [əráɪ] ADJ (clothes) mal puesto; (hat) ladeado; **my plans went —** mis planes fracasaron rotundamente

ax, axe [æks] N hacha *f*; VT eliminar

axis [ǽksɪs] N eje *m*

axle [ǽksəɫ] N eje *m*

Azerbaijan [æzə-baɪdʒán] N Azerbaiyán *m*

Azerbaijani, Azerbaijanian [æzə-baɪdʒáni(ən)] ADJ & N azerbaijano -na *mf*, azerbaiyano -na *mf*

azure [ǽʒə-] ADJ (azul) celeste; N azul celeste *m*

Bb

babble [bǽbəɫ] N (baby talk) balbuceo *m*; (chatter) parloteo *m*; (murmur) murmullo *m*; VI (to talk like a baby) balbucear; (to chatter) parlotear; (to murmur) murmurar

baboon [bæbún] N babuino *m*

baby [bébi] N bebé *mf*; **who's the — in your family?** ¿quién es el menor / benjamín en tu familia? **— blue** celeste *m*; **— boomer** persona nacida entre 1946 y 1965 *f*; **— carriage** cochecito de bebé *m*; **— food** comida para bebés *f*; **— girl** nena *f*; **— sister** hermanita *f*; **— sitter** niñera *f*; **— talk** habla infantil *f*; **—**

tooth diente de leche *m*; **to —sit** cuidar niños; **she had a —** dio a luz; VT mimar

baccalaureate [bækəlɔ́riət] N bachillerato *m*

bachelor [bǽtʃələ-] N soltero *m*; **—'s degree** licenciatura *f*; **— of Arts** (degree) licenciatura en filosofía y letras *f*; (person) licenciado -da en filosofía y letras *mf*

bacillus [bəsíləs] N bacilo *m*

back [bæk] N (human body part) espalda *f*; (animal body part) lomo *m*; (opposite side) dorso *m*; (of chair) respaldo *m*, espaldar *m*; **—ache** dolor de espalda *m*; **—bone** columna vertebral *f*, espinazo *m*; **—pack** mochila *f*; **behind one's —** a espaldas de uno; **he has no —bone** no tiene carácter; **in — of** detrás de, tras; **in the — of the house** atrás de la casa; **to fall on one's —** caer de espaldas; **to turn one's —** volver las espaldas; ADJ **— door** puerta trasera *f*; **— issues** números atrasados *m pl*; **on the — burner** en suspenso; VT respaldar, apoyar; VI dar marcha atrás; **to — down** echarse (para) atrás, recular, cejar; ADV (look) atrás / para atrás; (fall) de espaldas; **— and forth** de aquí para allá; **—-and-forth movement** movimiento de vaivén *m*; **he ran — to the house** volvió corriendo a la casa; **he's — from work** está de vuelta del trabajo

backbite [bǽkbaɪt] VI/VT difamar

backer [bǽkə-] N (financial) fiador -ra *mf*; (political) partidario -ria *mf*

backfire [bǽkfaɪr] VI (automobile) petardear, hacer detonaciones; (plan) ser contraproducente; N petardeo *m*

backgammon [bǽkgæmən] N backgammon *m*

background [bǽkgraʊnd] N (of a picture) fondo *m*; (experience) antecedentes *m pl*; **I have a — in computers** tengo conocimientos de informática; **I know what goes on in the —** sé lo que pasa entre bastidores; **a humble —** orígenes humildes *m pl*

backhand [bǽkhænd] N revés *m*

backing [bǽkɪŋ] N respaldo *m*, apoyo *m*; (fabric) refuerzo *m*

backlash [bǽklæʃ] N reacción violenta *f*

backlog [bǽklɑg] N atraso *m*

backseat [bǽksít] N asiento trasero *m*

backslide [bǽkslaɪd] VI volver a las andadas, reincidir

backspace [bǽkspes] N retroceso *m*; VI retroceder

backstage [bækstédʒ] ADV entre bastidores

backtrack [bǽktræk] VI retroceder, dar

marcha atrás

backup [bǽkʌp] N (support) respaldo *m*; (software) copia de seguridad *f*

backward [bǽkwəd] ADV hacia atrás, para atrás; **to go** — recular; ADJ (underdeveloped) atrasado; (reactionary) retrógrado

backwardness [bǽkwədnɪs] N (underdevelopment) atraso *m*; (conservatism) retrogradismo *m*; (timidity) timidez *f*

backyard [bǽkjárd] N patio trasero *m*

bacon [békən] N tocino *m*, *Sp* beicon *m*

bacteria [bæktíriə] N bacteria(s) *f (pl)*

bacteriology [bæktiriáləʤi] N bacteriología *f*

bad [bæd] ADJ malo; (man) perverso; (teeth) feo; (drug) dañoso; (flood) grave; (fruit) podrido; (very good) *vulg* de puta madre; — **blood** enemistad *f*; **to go from** — **to worse** ir de mal en peor; **he has a** — **heart** está enfermo del corazón; **to** —**mouth** difamar (a); **to look** — tener mal aspecto; *fam* quedar mal; ADV mal; **not** — no está nada mal; **too** — ¡qué pena!

badge [bæʤ] N insignia *f*, chapa *f*

badger [bǽʤə] N tejón *m*; VT acosar

baffle [bǽfəl] VT (confuse) confundir; (frustrate) desconcertar; N deflector *m*

bag [bæg] N bolsa *f*, bolso *m*; (baggage) maleta *f*; — **lady** vagabunda *f*; —**pipe** gaita *f*; VT empacar, embolsar; (hunting) cazar

baggage [bǽgɪʤ] N (suitcases) equipaje *m*; (impediments) bagaje *m*; — **car** vagón de equipajes *m*; — **check** contraseña de equipajes *f*; — **tag** etiqueta *f*; — **inspection** revisión de equipaje *f*

baggy [bǽgi] ADJ flojo, holgado

Bahamas [bəhάməz] N Bahamas *f pl*

Bahamian [bəhémiən] ADJ & N bahameño -ña *mf*

Bahrain [bɑrén] N Bahréin *m*

Bahraini [bɑréni] ADJ & N bahreiní *mf*

bail [bel] N fianza *f*; **to let out on** — poner en libertad bajo fianza; VT pagar la fianza; **to** — **someone out** pagarle la fianza a alguien; **to** — **someone out of a predicament** sacar a alguien de un apuro; **to** — **out water** achicar, vaciar; VI **to** — **out** (of a plane) tirarse con paracaídas de un avión; (of a situation) abandonar

bailiff [bélɪf] N ujier *m*

bait [bet] N cebo *m*; VT (prepare hook) cebar; (attract customers) seducir; (harass) acosar

bake [bek] VI/VT hornear; (sun) calcinar,

abrasar; **I'm baking in this heat** me estoy asando, me muero de calor

baker [békə] N panadero -ra *mf*; — **'s dozen** la docena del fraile *f*

bakery [békəri] N panadería *f*

baking [békɪŋ] N (act of baking) horneado *m*; (activity) repostería *f*; — **powder** polvo de hornear *m*; — **soda** bicarbonato de sodio *m*

balance [bǽləns] N (instrument) balanza *f*; (equilibrium) equilibrio *m*; (debit, credit) saldo *m*, balance *m*; — **of payments** balanza de pagos *f*; — **of trade** balanza comercial *f*; — **sheet** balance *m*; **to lose one's** — perder el equilibrio; VT equilibrar, hacer equilibrio con; **to** — **the risks with the benefits** sopesar los riesgos y los beneficios; VI cuadrar

balcony [bǽlkəni] N balcón *m*; (in a theater) palco *m*, entresuelo *m*

bald [bɔld] ADJ (person) calvo, pelón; (mountain) pelón; (tire) liso; — **eagle** águila americana de cabeza blanca *f*; —**headed** calvo; — **spot** calva *f*; **he went** — se quedó calvo

bale [bel] N paca *f*, fardo *m*; VT empacar, enfardar

balk [bɔk] VI oponerse, rehusarse a

ball [bɔl] N (tennis, baseball, golf) pelota *f*; (basketball, football, soccer) balón *m*; (of string, thread) ovillo *m*; (cannon) bala (de cañón) *f*; (dance) baile *m*; — **and chain** grillete *m*; — **bearing** cojinete de bolas *m*; — **game** juego de pelota *m*; (baseball) partido de béisbol *m*; —**s** (testicles) *vulg* pelotas *f pl*, *vulg* huevos *m pl*; *Sp vulg* cojones *m pl*; VT (string) ovillar; (have sex) *Sp vulg* follar; *Am vulg* coger, culear

ballad [bǽləd] N balada *f*; (historical) romance *m*

ballast [bǽləst] N lastre *m*; (railroad) balasto *m*; VT lastrar

ballerina [bælərínə] N bailarina de ballet *f*

ballet [bælé] N ballet *m*

ballistic [bəlístɪk] ADJ balístico; — **missile** misil balístico *m*; N —**s** balística *f*

balloon [bəlún] N globo *m*; VI (travel in a balloon) pasear en globo; VI/VT (grow) inflar(se)

ballot [bǽlət] N (system of voting) votación *f*; (paper) papeleta *f*; *Mex* boleta *f*; — **box** urna *f*

balm [bɑm] N bálsamo *m*

balmy [bάmi] ADJ templado

baloney [bəlóni] N pamplinas *f pl*, paparruchas *f pl*

balsa [bɔ́lsə] N (wood) madera balsa *f*; (raft)

balsa *f*
balsam [bɔ́łsəm] N (resin) bálsamo *m*; (tree) especie de abeto *m*
bamboo [bæmbú] N bambú *m*
ban [bæn] N prohibición *f*; (church) excomunión *f*; VT prohibir
banal [bénəł] ADJ banal
banana [bənǽnə] N plátano *m*, banana *f*; — **grove** platanar *m*; — **split** banana split *m*; — **tree** plátano *m*, banano *m*
band [bænd] N (group) banda *f*, pandilla *f*; (musicians) banda *f*, conjunto *m*; (cloth) banda *f*; (ribbon) cinta *f*; (leather) tira *f*; **to join the —wagon** subirse al carro/ tren; **—width** amplitud de banda *f*; VI/VT **to — together** unirse, juntarse
bandage [bǽndɪʤ] N venda *f*, vendaje *m*; VT vendar
bandit [bǽndɪt] N bandido -da *mf*, bandolero -ra *mf*, salteador -ora *mf*
bang [bæŋ] N (blow) golpe *m*, golpazo *m*; (sound) estampido *m*, estallido *m*; **—s** fleco *m*, flequillo *m*; **I get a — out of seeing my grandkids** me emociona ver a mis nietos; VI/VT (hit) golpear; (make noise) hacer estrépito; (screw) *Sp vulg* follar; *Am vulg* coger, culear
Bangladesh [bæŋglədéʃ] N Bangladesh *m*
Bangladeshi [bæŋglədéʃi] ADJ & N bangladeshí *mf*
banish [bǽnɪʃ] VT desterrar
banishment [bǽnɪʃmənt] N destierro *m*, proscripción *f*
banister [bǽnɪstɚ] N barandal *m*, pasamano(s) *m*, balaustrada *f*
banjo [bǽnʤo] N banjo *m*
bank [bæŋk] N (financial institution) banco *m*; (in gambling) banca *f*; (of a body of water) orilla *f*, ribera *f*, margen *m*; (slope) escarpa *f*; — **statement** estado de cuenta *m*; — **vault** cámara *f*; ADJ bancario, de banco; VT (money) depositar en un banco; VI (snow, sand) amontonar; (airplane) ladear; **to — on** contar con; **to —roll** financiar
banker [bǽŋkɚ] N (bank owner) banquero -ra *mf*; (bank employee) bancario -ria *mf*
banking [bǽŋkɪŋ] N (activity) actividad bancaria *f*; (industry) banca *f*; ADJ bancario, de banco
banknote [bǽŋknot] N billete *m*
bankrupt [bǽŋkrʌpt] ADJ en bancarrota; VT arruinar, quebrar
bankruptcy [bǽŋkrʌptsi] N bancarrota *f*, quiebra *f*; **to go into** — declararse en quiebra
banner [bǽnɚ] N estandarte *m*, pendón *m*;

ADJ sobresaliente
banquet [bǽŋkwɪt] N banquete *m*, gala *f*
baptism [bǽptɪzəm] N (sacrament) bautismo *m*; (action) bautizo *m*
baptize [bǽptaɪz] VT bautizar
bar [bɑr] N (of iron, sand, of a tavern) barra *f*; (of chocolate) barra *f*, tableta *f*; (vertical rod) barrote *m*; (obstacle) barrera *f*, obstáculo *m*; (in music) compás *m*; (saloon) bar *m*; **—bell** barra para pesas *f*; **—code** código de barras *m*; — **graph** gráfica de barras *f*; **—keeper** tabernero -ra *mf*, cantinero -ra *mf*; **—room** bar *m*; **—room brawl** pelea de borrachos *f*; **—tender** tabernero -ra *mf*, cantinero -ra *mf*; **behind —s** tras las rejas; **to be admitted to the** — recibirse de abogado; VT (door, exit) atrancar; (access) impedir; (from a group) excluir; — **none** sin excepción; **—ring a disaster** salvo en caso de desastre
barb [bɑrb] N púa *f*; **—ed wire** alambre de púas *m*; *Sp* alambre de espino *m*
Barbadian [bɑrbédiən] ADJ & N barbadense *mf*
Barbados [bɑrbédos] N Barbados *m*
barbarian [bɑrbériən] ADJ & N bárbaro -ra *mf*
barbaric [bɑrbérɪk] ADJ bárbaro
barbarous [bárbəəs] ADJ bárbaro
barbecue [bárbɪkju] N (meat dish) barbacoa *f*, asado *m*, parrillada *f*; — **sauce** adobo de barbacoa *m*; VI/VT asar con adobo
barber [bárbɚ] N peluquero *m*, barbero *m*; **—shop** peluquería *f*, barbería *f*
barbiturate [bɑrbítʃɚɪt] N barbitúrico *m*
bard [bɑrd] N bardo *m*
bare [bɛr] ADJ (legs, walls) desnudo; (cabinet) vacío; **—back** a pelo; **—faced** descarado; **—foot** descalzo; **the — necessities** lo imprescindible; **—headed** con la cabeza descubierta; **—legged** con las piernas desnudas; — **majority** escasa mayoría *f*; **to lay —** poner al descubierto; **with his — hands** con las propias manos
barely [bérli] ADV apenas
bargain [bárgɪn] N (agreement) trato *m*; (inexpensive purchase) ganga *f*, ocasión *f*; — **basement** sección de ofertas *f*; **into the** — por añadidura; **to strike a** — cerrar un trato; VI (haggle) regatear; (expect) contar con
barge [bárʤ] N barcaza *f*; VI **to — in** interrumpir; **to — into** irrumpir en
baritone [bǽrɪton] N & ADJ barítono *m*
barium [bériəm] N bario *m*
bark [bɑrk] N (of a dog) ladrido *m*; (on a tree) corteza *f*; VI/VT ladrar; **to — out an**

order gritar una orden
barley [bárli] N cebada *f*
barn [bɑrn] N (for animals) establo *m*; (for grain) granero *m*; — **owl** lechuza *f*; —**yard** corral *m*
barnacle [bárnəkəɫ] N percebe *m*
barometer [bərámɪdə·] N barómetro *m*
baron [bǽrən] N barón *m*
baroque [bərók] ADJ & N barroco *m*
barracks [bǽrəks] N cuartel *m*
barracuda [bærəkúdə] N barracuda *f*
barrage [bərɑʒ] N (of artillery fire) barrera de fuego *f*; (of questions) lluvia *f*, aluvión *m*
barrel [bǽrəɫ] N barril *m*, tonel *m*; (gun) cañón *m*, caño *m*; **he's a — of laughs** es un payaso; **he is scraping the bottom of the —** está desesperado; **to — along** ir disparado
barren [bǽrən] ADJ (land) árido, yermo; (female) estéril
barrette [bərét] N broche *m*
barricade [bærɪkéd] N barricada *f*; VT cerrar con barricadas; VI atrincherarse
barrier [bǽriə·] N barrera *f*; — **reef** barrera de coral *f*
barrio [bário] N barrio hispano *m*
barter [bárDə·] VI hacer trueque; VT trocar; N trueque *m*
basal cell carcinoma [bésəɫsɛɫkɑrsɪnómə] N carcinoma de célula basal *m*
basalt [bésɔɫt] N basalto *m*
base [bes] N base *f*; — **pay** salario base *m*; —**ball** béisbol *m*; —**board** zócalo *m*; ADJ bajo, vil; (metal) de baja ley; VI/VT basar, fundar; **to be —d on** fundamentarse en; **the general is —d in Berlin** el general está estacionado en Berlín
baseless [béslɪs] ADJ sin fundamento
basement [bésmənt] N sótano *m*
baseness [bésnɪs] N bajeza *f*, vileza *f*
bash [bæʃ] VT golpear
bashful [bǽʃfəɫ] ADJ tímido, vergonzoso
bashfulness [bǽʃfəɫnɪs] N timidez *f*
basic [bésɪk] ADJ básico
basin [bésɪn] N (bowl) palangana *f*, jofaina *f*; (of a fountain) pilón *m*; (geographical formation) cuenca *f*; (pond) estanque *m*
basis [bésɪs] N fundamento *m*, base *f*; **on the — of** en base a, con base en; **on a regular —** regularmente
bask [bæsk] VI (in the sun) asolearse; (in praise) deleitarse
basket [bǽskɪt] N canasta *f*, cesta *f*, cesto *m*; —**ball** baloncesto *m*, básquetbol *m*
basketful [bǽskɪtfʌɫ] N (contents of a basket) canasto *m*; (large amount) montón *m*
basketry [bǽskɪtri] N cestería *f*

Basque [bæsk] ADJ & N (person) vasco -ca *mf*; (language) vascuence *m*, vasco *m*
bass [bes] N (voice, bass guitar) bajo *m*; (double bass) contrabajo *m*; — **clef** clave de fa *f*; — **drum** bombo *m*; — **horn** tuba *f*; [bæs] (marine fish) lubina *f*; (freshwater fish) perca *f*
bassoon [bæsún] N fagot *m*
bastard [bǽstə·d] N & ADJ (illegitimate) bastardo -da *mf*; N (mean person) *offensive* hijo de puta *m*, cabrón *m*
baste [best] VT (fabric) hilvanar; (meat) rociar
bat [bæt] N (baseball, cricket) bate *m*; (animal) murciélago *m*; VT golpear; **not to — an eye** no pestañear; VI (baseball) batear
batch [bætʃ] N (of cookies) hornada *f*; (of cement) tanda *f*; (of data) colección *f*
bath [bæθ] N baño *m*; —**robe** bata (de baño) *f*; *Sp* albornoz *m*; —**room** (in a house) baño *m*, cuarto de baño *m*; (public) *Sp* aseo *m*; *Am* servicio *m*, baño *m*; —**tub** bañera *f*
bathe [beð] VI/VT bañar(se); **bathing beauty** muchacha en traje de baño *f*; **bathing suit** traje de baño *m*
bather [béðə·] N bañista *mf*
baton [bətán] N batuta *f*
battalion [bətǽljən] N batallón *m*
batter [bǽDə·] N pasta *f*, masa *f*; (baseball) bateador *m*; VT golpear
battery [bǽDəri] N (of car, artillery) batería *f*; (of electronic devices) pila *f*; (of tests) serie *f*; (assault) asalto *m*
battle [bǽdɫ] N batalla *f*; —**-ax(e)** (weapon) hacha de guerra *f*; (woman) sargenta *f*; — **cry** grito de guerra *m*; —**field** campo de batalla *m*; —**ship** acorazado *m*; VI batallar; **to — cancer** luchar contra el cáncer
bawl [bɔɫ] VI berrear; **to — somebody out** echarle bronca a uno; **to — out orders** bramar órdenes
bay [be] N (body of water) bahía *f*; (howl) aullido *m*; — **leaf** hoja de laurel *f*; — **window** ventana saliente *f*; **to hold at —** tener a raya; ADJ bayo; VI aullar
bayonet [beənét] N bayoneta *f*
bazaar [bəzár] N (market place) bazar *m*; (benefit) kermés *f*
bazooka [bəzúka] N bazuca *f*
be [bi] VI **I am from Uruguay** soy de Uruguay; **there were four of us** éramos cuatro; **he is a doctor** es médico; **it's her** es ella; **sugar is sweet** el azúcar es dulce; **London is in England** Londres está en Inglaterra; **this water is cold** esta agua está fría; **the windows were**

open las ventanas estaban abiertas; **there is a problem** hay un problema; **to — cold / warm / hungry / right / in a hurry** tener frío / calor / hambre / razón / prisa; **it is cold / hot / windy** hace frío / calor / viento

beach [bitʃ] N playa *f;* **—comber** vagabundo -da *mf;* **—head** cabeza de playa *f;* VT varar, encallar

beacon [bíkən] N faro *m*

bead [bid] N cuenta *f;* (of sweat) gota *f,* perla *f;* **to get a — on somebody** apuntarle a alguien; **to tell one's —s** rezar el rosario; VT (string) enhebrar / ensartar cuentas; (decorate) adornar con cuentas

beagle [bígəɫ] N beagle *m*

beak [bik] N pico *m*

beaker [bíkɚ] N vaso de precipitados *m*

beam [bim] N (of light) rayo *m,* haz *m;* (in a building) viga *f;* (of a ship) manga *f;* (of a scale) brazo *m;* **broad in the —** ancho de caderas; VI/VT (light, radio) emitir; (smile) estar radiante

bean [bin] N judía *f,* habichuela *f; Sp* alubia *f; Am* frijol *m, Am* poroto *m;* **Lima —** haba *f;* **—stalk** tallo de habas / frijol *m;* **Jack and the —stalk** Juanito y las habichuelas; **I don't know —s about that** no sé ni papa / jota de eso

bear [bɛr] N oso *m;* **— hug** abrazo fuerte *m;* **— market** mercado bajista *m;* VT (hold up, tolerate) soportar, aguantar; (suffer) sobrellevar; (have a child) dar a luz; (produce young) parir; (produce fruit) producir; **to — down** (mash) apretar; (push) pujar; **to — a grudge** guardar rencor; **to — in mind** tener en cuenta; **to — oneself with dignity** portarse con dignidad; **to — out** confirmar; **to — testimony** dar testimonio; **to — interest** devengar interés; **to — gifts** traer regalos; **to — a resemblance** parecerse; **to — the cost of something** asumir el costo de algo; **it doesn't — repeating** no merece repetirse

bearable [bérəbəɫ] ADJ llevadero

beard [bird] N (on a man) barba *f;* (of wheat) aristas *f pl*

bearded [bírdɪd] ADJ barbado, barbudo

bearer [bérɚ] N portador -ra *mf*

bearing [bérɪŋ] N porte *m;* **to lose one's —s** perder el rumbo, desorientarse; **it has no — on our situation** no tiene relación con nuestra situación

bearish [bérɪʃ] ADJ (of bears) osuno; (of stock market) bajista

beast [bist] N bestia *f*

beat [bit] VT (wings, eggs) batir; (a person) golpear; (a drum) tocar; (an opponent) vencer; (tempo) marcar; VI (heart) latir; (drum) sonar; **to — around the bush** andarse por las ramas; **to — off** (repulse) rechazar; (masturbate) *vulg* hacerse una paja; **to — up** dar una paliza; **—s me!** ¡ni idea! N (blow) golpe *m;* (drum) toque *m;* (heart) latido *m;* (tempo) compás *m;* (policeman's territory) ronda *f*

beaten [bítn̩] ADJ (mixed) batido; (defeated) vencido; (tired) fatigado; **— path** camino trillado *m*

beater [bídɚ] N batidor *m*

beating [bídɪŋ] N (whipping) paliza *f;* (pulsation) latido *m*

beau [bo] N pretendiente *m*

beautiful [bjúdəfəɫ] ADJ hermoso; **— people** jet set *mf*

beautify [bjúdəfaɪ] VT embellecer, hermosear

beauty [bjúdi] N belleza *f,* hermosura *f;* (woman) beldad *f;* **— contest** concurso / certamen de belleza *m;* **— pageant** concurso / certamen de belleza *m;* **— parlor** salón de belleza *m*

beaver [bívɚ] N (animal) castor *m;* (vagina) *vulg* chichi *m,* conejo *m*

because [bɪkɔ́z] CONJ porque; **— of** por, a causa de

beckon [békən] VT llamar por señas

become [bɪkʌ́m] VT (through effort) hacerse; **he became rich** se hizo rico; (emotional or physical condition) ponerse; **she became ill** se puso enferma; (long process) llegar a ser; **he became a doctor** llegó a ser médico; (turn into) convertirse en; **the water became ice** el agua se convirtió en hielo; (drastic change) volverse; **he became crazy** se volvió loco; (suit) sentar bien; **to — angry** enojarse; **to — frightened** asustarse; **to — old** envejecer(se); **what has — of him?** ¿qué ha sido de él?

becoming [bɪkʌ́mɪŋ] ADJ (appropriate) propio; **that dress is — to you** te sienta bien ese vestido

bed [bɛd] N (furniture) cama *f; lit* lecho *m;* (of a river) cauce *m;* (of the sea) fondo *m;* (in a garden) cuadro *m;* **—bug** chinche *mf;* **—clothes** ropa de cama *f;* **—pan** cuña *f,* chata *f;* **—ridden** postrado en cama; **—rest** reposo *m;* **—rock** lecho de roca *m;* **—room** alcoba *f,* dormitorio *m; Mex* recámara *f;* **at the —side** al lado de la cama; **—side table** mesita de noche *f;* **—side manner** manera agradable de tratar a los pacientes *f;* **—sore** llaga *f;*

—**spread** colcha *f*; —**spring** resorte del colchón *m*; —**time** hora de dormir *f*; —**wetting** enuresis nocturna *f*; **to go to** — acostarse; **to put to** — acostar

bedding [bέdɪŋ] N ropa de cama *f*

bee [bi] N (insect) abeja *f*; (social gathering) tertulia *f*; **to have a** — **in one's bonnet** tener una idea metida en la cabeza; —**hive** colmena *f*; — **sting** picadura de abeja *f*

beech [bitʃ] N haya *f*; —**nut** hayuco *m*

beef [bif] N (meat) carne de vaca / res *f*; (complaint) queja *f*; — **jerky** cecina *f*; —**steak** bistec *m*; VI quejarse; **to** — **up** reforzar

beep [bip] N pitazo *m*; VI/VT **the alarm is** —**ing** la alarma está sonando; **he** —**ed his horn** tocó el claxón

beeper [bípɚ] N buscapersonas *m sg*

beer [bɪr] N cerveza *f*

beet [bit] N remolacha *f*

beetle [bídl̩] N escarabajo *m*

befall [bɪfɔ́l] VT acontecerle a

befit [bɪfít] VT convenir

before [bɪfɔ́r] ADV (temporal) antes; (spatial) delante; PREP (temporal) antes de; (spatial) delante de; *lit* ante; CONJ antes (de) que, antes de; — **beginning** antes de que comiences, antes de comenzar

beforehand [bɪfɔ́rhænd] ADV de antemano

befriend [bɪfrɛ́nd] VT hacerse amigo de

beg [bɛg] VT **to** — **for mercy** implorar misericordia; **she** —**ged me to do it** me rogó que lo hiciera; **to** — **the question** dar por sentado lo mismo que se arguye; VI mendigar, pedir limosna

beget [bɪgét] VT engendrar; **money** —**s money** la plata llama a la plata

beggar [bégɚ] N mendigo -ga *mf*

begin [bɪgín] VI/VT comenzar, empezar; **the ten dollars won't** — **to cover the expense** los diez dólares ni siquiera cubren los gastos

beginner [bɪgínɚ] N principiante *mf*

beginning [bɪgínɪŋ] N principio *m*; (temporal only) comienzo *m*; — **with** comenzando con / por; **at the** — al / por el principio

begrudge [bɪgrʌ́dʒ] VT aceptar de mala gana

behalf [bɪhǽf] PREP LOC **in / on** — **of** (in place of) por, en nombre de; (in favor of) a favor de

behave [bɪhév] VI portarse, comportarse; — **yourself!** ¡pórtate bien!

behavior [bɪhévjɚ] N comportamiento *m*, conducta *f*

behead [bɪhéd] VT decapitar, descabezar

behind [bɪháɪnd] ADV detrás; (in payments, schedule) atrasado; **he fell** — **his competitors** quedó a la zaga de sus competidores; **an hour** — una hora de retraso; **from** — desde atrás; **to fall** — atrasarse; **to leave something** — dejar atrás algo; PREP detrás de, tras; **we're all** — **you** todos te apoyamos; **who's** — **this evil plot?** ¿quién está detrás de este plan macabro? — **one's back** a espaldas de uno

behold [bɪhóɫd] VT contemplar; — **the future king!** ¡he aquí el futuro rey!

behoove [bɪhúv] VI corresponderle a uno

beige [beʒ] ADJ & N beige *m*

being [bíɪŋ] N ser *m*; **for the time** — por ahora

Belarus [bɛlərús] N Bielorrusia *f*

belated [bɪlédɪd] ADJ atrasado

belch [bɛɫtʃ] VI eructar, repetir; **to** — **from** salir de; N eructo *m*

belfry [bέɫfri] N campanario *m*

Belgian [bέɫdʒən] ADJ & N belga *mf*

Belgium [bέɫdʒəm] N Bélgica *f*

belief [bɪlíf] N creencia *f*; (strong opinion) convicción *f*

believable [bɪlívəbəɫ] ADJ creíble

believe [bɪlív] VI/VT creer

believer [bɪlívɚ] N creyente *mf*; (proponent) partidario -ria *mf*

belittle [bɪlídl̩] VT (a person) menospreciar, disminuir; (a situation) minimizar

Belize [bəlíz] N Belice *m*

Belizean [bəlíziən] ADJ & N beliceño -ña *mf*

bell [bɛɫ] N campana *f*; (small) campanilla *f*; —**boy** botones *m sg*; —**flower** campanilla *f*, campánula *f*; —**hop** botones *m sg*; — **jar** campana de cristal *f*; — **pepper** pimiento *m*, morrón *m*; — **tower** campanario *m*; **with all the** —**s and whistles** con todos los accesorios

bellicose [bέlɪkos] ADJ belicoso

belligerent [bəlídʒɚənt] ADJ & N beligerante *mf*

bellow [bélo] VI/VT bramar, berrear; N bramido *m*; —**s** fuelle *m*

belly [béli] N barriga *f*, vientre *m*; —**ache** dolor de barriga *m*; — **button** ombligo *m*; — **dance** danza del vientre *f*; — **laugh** carcajada *f*

belong [bɪlɔ́ŋ] VI (ownership) pertenecer; **this car** —**s to me** este coche me pertenece; (correspondence) corresponder; **this key** —**s to this door** esta llave corresponde a esta puerta; (placement) ir; **this** —**s on the shelf** esto va en el estante

belongings [bɪlɔ́ŋɪŋz] N pertenencias *f pl*

beloved [bɪlʎvɪd] ADJ querido; N amado -da *mf*

below [bɪló] ADV abajo; **five — (zero)** cinco bajo cero; PREP bajo, debajo de, abajo de

belt [bɛɫt] N (for the waist) cinturón *m*, cinto *m*; (for a machine) correa *f*; (region) zona *f*; **— line** cintura *f*; VT pegar; **to — out a song** cantar una canción a voz en cuello

bemoan [bɪmón] VT lamentarse de, quejarse de

bench [bɛntʃ] N banco *m*; (without a back) banqueta *f*; (in sports) banquillo *m*; (in court) estrado *m*; **—mark** (upper limit) cota *f*; (parameter) punto de referencia *m*; **opinion of the —** opinión del tribunal *f*

bend [bɛnd] VI/VT (make curved) doblar(se); (force) someter; **to — over** inclinarse; **to — over backward** desvivirse; **to — the rules** hacer una excepción; N (road) curva *f*, recodo *m*; **—s** enfermedad de los buzos *f*

beneath [bɪníθ] ADV abajo; PREP debajo de, bajo; (in rank) inferior a; **— contempt** totalmente despreciable; **that's — me** no es digno de mí

benediction [bɛnɪdíkʃən] N bendición *f*

benefactor [bɛnəfæktɚ] N benefactor -ra *mf*; *lit* bienhechor -ra *mf*

beneficent [bənéfɪsənt] ADJ benéfico

beneficial [bɛnəfíʃəɫ] ADJ beneficioso

beneficiary [bɛnəfíʃɪɛri] N beneficiario -ria *mf*

benefit [bénəfɪt] N beneficio *m*; **— performance** función de beneficencia *f*; VI/VT beneficiar(se), sacar provecho; **he —ed by the medicine** le hizo bien la medicina

benevolence [bənévələns] N benevolencia *f*

benevolent [bənévələnt] ADJ benévolo

benign [bɪnáɪn] ADJ benigno

Benin [benín] N Benín *m*

Beninese [benɪníz] ADJ & N beninés -esa *mf*

bent [bɛnt] N inclinación *f*; **to be — on** estar resuelto a

benzine [bénzin] N bencina *f*

bequeath [bɪkwíð] VT legar, heredar

bequest [bɪkwést] N legado *m*

berate [bɪrét] VT reprender

bereaved [bɪrívd] ADJ de luto

beret [bəré] N boina *f*

berry [béri] N baya *f*

berserk [bɚrzɝ́k] ADJ fuera de sí; **he went —** se puso hecho una fiera, se enfureció

berth [bɝθ] N litera *f*; **to give a wide — to** mantener una distancia prudencial de

beseech [bɪsítʃ] VT suplicar, rogar

beset [bɪsét] VT (attack) acosar; (surround) rodear

beside [bɪsáɪd] PREP al lado de; **sit down —**

me siéntate a mi lado; **to be — oneself** estar fuera de sí; **that is — the point** eso no viene al caso; ADV al lado

besides [bɪsáɪdz] ADV además; **they have a table but not much —** tienen una mesa pero poca cosa más; PREP además de, aparte de

besiege [bɪsídʒ] VT (lay siege) sitiar, cercar; (importune) importunar, asediar

best [bɛst] ADJ mejor; **—-case scenario** la mejor situación; **— man** padrino de boda *m*; **— seller** bestseller *m*; **she's the —** ella es la mejor; ADV mejor; **at —** a lo más, en el mejor de los casos; N **the — is still to come** lo mejor está por venir; **to do one's —** hacer lo mejor posible; **to get the — of a person** ganarle a una persona; **to make the — of** sacar el mejor partido de

bestial [béstʃəɫ] ADJ bestial

bestow [bɪstó] VT conferir; **to — gifts upon** dar regalos a

bet [bɛt] N apuesta *f*; VI/VT apostar; **to — on** apostar por

betray [bɪtré] VT (a person) traicionar; (a secret) revelar; (a feeling) traslucir, delatar; **to — one's ignorance** hacer patente su ignorancia

betrayal [bɪtréəɫ] N traición *f*

betrayer [bɪtréɚ] N traidor -ra *mf*

betrothal [bɪtróðəɫ] N esponsales *f pl*

better [béɾɚ] ADJ mejor; **— half** media naranja *f*; **the — part of a year** la mayor parte de un año; ADV mejor; **he lives — than a mile away** vive a más de una milla; **so much the —** tanto mejor; **—-off** en mejor posición económica; **to be — off** estar mejor así; **to change for the —** cambiar para bien; **to get —** mejorar(se), aliviarse; VT mejorar; **to — oneself** mejorarse, mejorar de situación; N **the — of the two** el / la mejor de los dos; **don't contradict your —s** no contradigas a tus superiores

better, bettor [béɾɚ] N apostador -ra *mf*

between [bɪtwín] PREP entre; ADV en medio

bevel [bévəɫ] N bisel *m*; VT biselar

beverage [bévrɪdʒ] N bebida *f*

bevy [bévi] N (of birds, people) bandada *f*; (of deer) manada *f*

beware [bɪwér] VI cuidarse (de); **— of the dog** cuidado con el perro

bewilder [bɪwíɫdɚ] VT dejar perplejo, ofuscar, aturdir; **to be —ed** estar perplejo

bewilderment [bɪwíɫdɚmənt] N perplejidad *f*, aturdimiento *m*

bewitch [bɪwítʃ] VT hechizar, embrujar

beyond [bɪjánd] ADV más allá de; — **my reach** fuera de mi alcance; N **the great** — el más allá

Bhutan [bután] N Bután *m*

Bhutanese [butṇíz] ADJ & N butanés -esa *mf*

bias [báɪəs] N (prejudice) prejuicio *m*; (in fabric) sesgo *m*; ADJ sesgado, oblicuo; VT predisponer

bib [bɪb] N babero *m*; (of an apron) pechera *f*

Bible [báɪbəl] N Biblia *f*

biblical [bíblɪkəl] ADJ bíblico

bibliography [bɪbliágrəfi] N bibliografía *f*

bicarbonate [baɪkárbənɪt] N bicarbonato *m*

bicep, biceps [báɪsep(s)] N bíceps *m sg*

bicker [bíkɚ] VI reñir

bicycle [báɪsɪkəl] N bicicleta *f*; VI andar en bicicleta

bid [bɪd] N (in an auction, contest) licitación *f*, puja *f*; (in card games) apuesta *f*; (attempt) tentativa *f*; VI/VT (offer) ofrecer; (command) mandar; (invite) rogar; (enter a bid in cards) apostar; **to — good-bye** despedirse; **to — up** pujar el precio

bidding [bídɪŋ] N (in auction) puja *f*; **at someone's —** por orden de alguien; **to do someone's —** cumplir con los deseos de alguien

bide [baɪd] VI/VT **to — one's time** esperar una oportunidad

biennium [baɪéniəm] N bienio *m*

bifurcate [báɪfɚket] VI/VT bifurcar(se)

big [bɪg] ADJ grande; — **Bang theory** teoría del Big Bang *f*; — **brother** hermano mayor *m*; — **bucks** mucha plata *f*; — **business** el gran capital; — **deal** asunto importante *m*; — **deal!** ¡no es para tanto! — **Dipper** Osa Mayor *f*; —-**headed** cabezón, cabezudo; —-**hearted** magnánimo; — **house** *fam* gayola *f*; — **name** personalidad prominente *f*; — **picture** panorama general *m*; — **shot** pez gordo *m*; — **sister** hermana mayor *f*; —-**ticket** caro; —**wig** pez gordo *m*; — **with child** embarazada; **jazz was — in the 1920s** el jazz era popular en los años veinte; **she's a — deal** es una persona importante; **a — problem** un gran problema; ADV —**time** un montón; **she wants to go —time** se muere por ir; **to talk —** jactarse; *Am* lucirse; **to go over —** tener éxito; **to be — on** ser entusiasta de

bigamy [bígəmi] N bigamia *f*

bigot [bígət] N intolerante *mf*

bigotry [bígətri] N intolerancia *f*

bike [baɪk] N bici *f*

biker [báɪkɚ] N motociclista *mf*

bikini [bɪkíni] N bikini *m*

bilateral [baɪlǽDəɚl] ADJ bilateral

bile [baɪl] N (secretion) bilis *f*; (ill temper) mal genio *m*; — **duct** conducto biliar *m*

bilingual [baɪlíŋgwəl] ADJ & N bilingüe *mf*

bilingualism [baɪlíŋgwəlɪzəm] N bilingüismo *m*

bill [bɪl] N (statement) factura *f*; (in a restaurant) cuenta *f*; (poster) cartel *m*; (bank note) billete *m*; (for movies, theater) programa *m*; (of a bird) pico *m*; (legislative) proyecto de ley *m*; —**board** cartelera *f*; —**fold** cartera *f*, billetera *f*; — **of exchange** letra de cambio *f*; — **of lading** conocimiento de embarque *m*; — **of rights** declaración de derechos *f*; — **of sale** escritura de venta *f*; —**s payable** efectos a pagar *m pl*; VT cobrar, mandar la factura a

billable [bíləbəl] ADJ facturable

billiards [bíljɚdz] N billar *m*

billing [bílɪŋ] N (theater) orden de importancia en espectáculos *m*; (business) facturación *f*

billion [bíljən] NUM mil millones *m pl*

billow [bílo] N (of smoke) nube *f*; (of water) ola *f*; VI ondular, hacer olas

bimbo [bímbo] N gachí *f*, *pej* putilla *f*, *pej* putón *m*

bin [bɪn] N (for clothes, food) cajón *m*, recipiente *m*; (on an airplane) portaequipajes *m sg*; (for coal) carbonera *f*; (for grain) granero *m*

binary [báɪneri] ADJ binario; — **star** estrella binaria *f*

bind [baɪnd] VI/VT (unite) unir; (connect) ligar; (tie) atar; (put a cover on a book) encuadernar; (press tightly) apretar; (oblige by contract) obligar

binding [báɪndɪŋ] N (of a book) encuadernación *f*; (on a rug) ribete *m*; ADJ obligatorio

binge [bɪndʒ] N (alcoholic) juerga *f*, parranda *f*; (food) comilona *f*; VI (on alcohol) emborracharse; (on food) atiborrarse

bingo [bíŋgo] N bingo *m*

binoculars [bənákjəlɚz] N gemelos *m pl*, prismáticos *m pl*

binomial [baɪnómiəl] N binomio *m*; ADJ binomial

biochemistry [baɪokémɪstri] N bioquímica *f*

biodegradable [baɪodɪgréDəbəl] ADJ biodegradable

bioengineering [baɪoɛndʒəníriŋ] N bioingeniería *f*

biofeedback [baɪofídbæk] N biofeedback *m*, retroalimentación biológica *f*

biography [baɪágrəfi] N biografía f

biology [baɪálədʒi] N biología f

biopsy [báɪɑpsi] N biopsia f

biorhythm [báɪoɪɪðəm] N biorritmo m

biotechnology [baɪotɛknálədʒi] N biotecnología f

bipartisan [baɪpárⅮɪzən] ADJ bipartidista

bipolar [baɪpólɚ] ADJ bipolar; **— disorder** trastorno bipolar m

birch [bɜtʃ] N abedul m

bird [bɜd] N ave f; (small) pájaro m; **— of prey** ave de rapiña f; **— seed** alpiste m; **odd —** persona peculiar f

birth [bɜθ] N (act of being born) nacimiento m; (act of giving birth) parto m; (lineage) linaje m; (origin) origen m; **— certificate** certificado de nacimiento m, fe / acta de nacimiento f; **— control** (policy) control de la natalidad m; (devices) anticonceptivos m pl; **—day** cumpleaños m sg; **in his / her —day suit** como Dios lo / la trajo al mundo; **—mark** antojo m; **—place** lugar de nacimiento m; **—rate** tasa de natalidad f; **—right** derechos de nacimiento m pl; (of oldest child) primogenitura f; **to give —** dar a luz, parir, alumbrar; **by —** de nacimiento

biscuit [bískɪt] N panecillo m

bisect [báɪsɛkt] VT bisecar

bisexual [baɪsékʃuəł] ADJ bisexual

bishop [bíʃəp] N obispo m; (in chess) alfil m

bison [báɪsən] N bisonte m, búfalo m

bit [bɪt] N (small piece) pedacito m, trocito m; (some) poquito m; (of a bridle) bocado m, freno m; (of a drill) broca f, barrena f; (computer) bit m; **I don't care a —** no me importa en absoluto

bitch [bɪtʃ] N (dog) perra f; (woman) *offensive* hija de puta f, cabrona f; (situation) plomazo m; *Sp vulg* coñazo m

bite [baɪt] VI/VT morder; (be duped) dejarse engañar; (insect, fish, snake) picar; **to — off** arrancar de un mordisco; N (act, wound) mordedura f, dentellada f; (morsel, small meal) bocado m, bocadito m; (of an insect) picadura f, roncha f

bitter [bíⅮɚ] ADJ (taste) amargo; (cold) glacial; (enemy) acérrimo; **—sweet** dulceamargo, agridulce; **to fight to the — end** luchar hasta morir; N **—s** cerveza amarga f

bitterness [bíⅮɚnɪs] N (taste) amargor m; (feelings) amargura f; (anger) rencor m, resentimiento m

bizarre [bɪzár] ADJ (event) extraño; (appearance) estrafalario

blab [blæb] VI parlotear; VT descubrir el pastel

black [blæk] ADJ (color, ethnicity) negro; (night) oscuro; **—-and-blue** lleno de moretones, amoratado; **— bean** frijol negro m; **—berry** zarzamora f, mora f; **—bird** mirlo m; **—board** pizarrón m, pizarra f; **— death** peste negra f; **— eye** ojo amoratado / morado m; **—head** espinilla f; **— hole** agujero negro m; **—jack** (weapon) cachiporra f; (card game) black-jack m, veintiuno m; **— magic** magia negra f; **—mail** chantaje m; **— mark** mancha f; **— market** mercado negro m; **—out** apagón m; **— pepper** pimienta negra f; **— pudding** morcilla f; **— sheep** oveja negra f; **—smith** herrero m; **—smith's shop** herrería f, forja f; **—top** asfalto m; **— widow spider** viuda negra f; N negro -a mf; **to put down in — and white** poner por escrito; VT **to —mail** chantajear; VI **to — out** desmayarse

blacken [blǽkən] VT ennegrecer, negrear; VI (sky) oscurecerse

blackness [blǽknɪs] N negrura f

bladder [blǽⅮɚ] N vejiga f

blade [bled] N (of a knife) hoja f; (of grass) brizna f; (of a sword) espada f; (of an oar) pala f, paleta f; (of a propeller) aspa f

blame [blem] VT culpar, echar la culpa a, achacar la culpa a; **to be to —** tener la culpa; N (responsibility) culpa f; (reproof) reproche m

blameless [blémlɪs] ADJ intachable

blanch [blæntʃ] VI palidecer; VT (whiten) blanquear; (scald) escaldar

bland [blænd] ADJ insulso

blank [blæŋk] ADJ (not written on) en blanco; (not recorded on) virgen; (unadorned, expressionless) vacío; (confused) desconcertado; **— cartridge** cartucho de fogueo m; **— check** cheque en blanco m; **— verse** verso libre m; N (place to be filled in on a form) espacio (en blanco) m; (gap) vacío m; VI **to — out** quedarse en blanco

blanket [blǽŋkɪt] N manta f, frazada f; *Am* cobija f; ADJ global; VT cubrir

blare [blɛr] VI hacer un ruido estruendoso; N estruendo m; (of a trumpet) toque m

blaspheme [blæsfím] VI/VT blasfemar (contra)

blasphemy [blǽsfəmi] N blasfemia f

blast [blæst] N (of wind) ráfaga f; (of criticism) lluvia f; (of a trumpet) trompetazo m; (explosive charge) carga f; (explosion) explosión f; **— furnace** alto horno m; **—off** despegue m; **we had a —** lo pasamos bomba; **at full —** a todo volumen; VI/VT (blow horn) pitar, tocar; (shatter) volar; (criticize) criticar duramente; (blow hard) azotar; **to — off** despegar

blatant [blétn̩t] ADJ descarado

blaze [blez] N (flame) llamarada *f;* (fire) incendio *m;* (glow) resplandor *m;* (mark) señal *f;* **— of anger** arranque de ira *m;* VI (burn) arder; (shine) resplandecer; **to — a trail** marcar una senda

blazer [bléza-] N blazer *m,* saco *m*

bleach [blitʃ] VI/VT (intentional) blanquear(se); (accidental) desteñir(se); N blanqueador *m; Sp* lejía *f*

bleachers [blítʃa-z] N gradas *f pl*

bleak [blik] ADJ (terrain) yermo, desolado; (winter) crudo; (wind) helado; (future) negro

bleary [blíri] ADJ nublado

bleat [blit] N balido *m;* VI balar

bleed [blid] VI (lose blood) sangrar; (run, as in colors) correrse, desteñir(se); **my heart —s for the poor** los pobres me dan lástima; VT (let blood) desangrar; (extort) extorsionar; (clean brakes) purgar

blemish [blémɪʃ] N mancha *f,* tacha *f;* VT manchar

blend [blɛnd] VI/VT (intermix) mezclar, entremezclar; (have no separation) fundirse; (harmonize voices) armonizar; N mezcla *f*

blender [blénda-] N licuadora *f*

bless [blɛs] VT bendecir; INTERJ **— you!** ¡salud!

blessed [blésɪd] ADJ (beatified) beato; (happy) bienaventurado, feliz; **— event** feliz acontecimiento *m;* **the whole — day** todo el santo día; **not a — drop of rain** ni una bendita gota de agua; [blɛst] **— with** dotado de

blessing [blésɪŋ] N bendición *f;* **to say the —** dar gracias

blight [blaɪt] N (plant disease) quemadura *f,* añublo *m;* (scourge) lacra *f;* VT (cause to wither) marchitar; (ruin) arruinar

blimp [blɪmp] N zepelín *m*

blind [blaɪnd] ADJ ciego; **— alley** callejón sin salida *m;* **— date** cita a ciegas *f;* **—fold** venda para los ojos *f;* **to —fold** vendar los ojos a; **— man's bluff** juego de la gallina ciega *m;* **— spot** ángulo muerto *m;* **to fly —** volar a ciegas; **to go —** quedarse ciego; N (shade) persiana *f;* (hunter's hiding place) escondite *m;* VT (make blind) cegar; (darken) oscurecer

blinder [blaínda-] N anteojera *f*

blindly [blaíndli] ADV a ciegas

blindness [blaíndnɪs] N ceguera *f*

blink [blɪŋk] VI/VT (move eyelids) pestañear, parpadear; (go on and off, as of a light) parpadear; (ignore) pasar por alto; (flee a challenge) rajarse; N parpadeo *m,* pestañeo *m;* **on the —** averiado

blip [blɪp] N (on radar) punto *m;* (of a movie) interrupción *f;* (moment) bache *m*

bliss [blɪs] N dicha *f,* felicidad absoluta *f*

blister [blísta-] N ampolla *f;* (small) vejiga *f;* VT sacar ampollas; VI ampollarse

blitz [blɪts] N ataque relámpago *m*

blizzard [blíza-d] N ventisca *f*

bloat [blot] VI hinchar(se), abotagar(se)

blob [blɑb] N pedazo de algo sin forma *m*

block [blɑk] N (piece of stone, cement) bloque *m;* (piece of wood) trozo de madera *m;* (toy) cubo *m;* (sports play) bloqueo *m;* (length from one street to the next) cuadra *f;* (square block) manzana *f;* (obstacle) obstáculo *m;* (group of tickets) sección *f;* **—buster** éxito de taquilla *m;* **—head** tarugo -ga *mf,* alcornoque *m;* VT (obstruct) bloquear, tapar; (stop a pass) parar; **to — out** (an essay) esbozar, bosquejar; (the sun) ocultar

blockade [blɑkéd] N bloqueo *m;* VT bloquear

blockage [blákɪdʒ] N obstrucción *f*

blond [blɑnd] ADJ & N rubio -a *mf*

blood [blʌd] N sangre *f;* **—bank** banco de sangre *m;* **—bath** carnicería *f,* baño de sangre *m;* **— count** recuento sanguíneo *m;* **— group** grupo sanguíneo *m;* **—hound** sabueso *m;* **— plasma** plasma sanguíneo *m;* **— poisoning** septicemia *f;* **— pressure** presión arterial *f;* **— relative** pariente consanguíneo *mf;* **—shed** derramamiento de sangre *m;* **— vessel** vaso sanguíneo *m;* **in cold —** a sangre fría; ADJ **—shot** inyectado de sangre; **—thirsty** sanguinario, sangriento

bloody [blʌ́di] ADJ (violent) sangriento; (smeared) ensangrentado

bloom [blum] N (flower) flor *f;* (flowering) floración *f;* (youthfulness) lozanía *f;* (flush) rubor *m;* **in —** en flor; VI florecer

blooming [blúmɪŋ] ADJ (flowering) floreciente; (thriving) lozano

blooper [blúpa-] N perla *f*

blossom [blásəm] N (flower) flor *f;* (flowering) floración *f;* VI florecer

blot [blɑt] N (on paper) mancha *f,* borrón *m;* (on honor) tacha *f;* VI/VT manchar(se), emborronar(se); **to — out** (obscure) borrar, tachar; (obliterate) destruir

blotch [blɑtʃ] VT borronear, manchar, cubrir con manchas; N mancha *f,* borrón *m*

blouse [blaʊs] N blusa *f*

blow [blo] VI (wind) soplar; (leaf) volar; (siren) sonar; (horse) resoplar; VT (play a horn) sonar; **to — a fuse** quemar un fusible; **to — away** dejar atónito; **to — down** tirar abajo; **to —-dry** secar con secador; **to — one's nose** sonarse las narices / la nariz; **to — on the soup** soplar la sopa; **to — one's brains out** levantarse la tapa de los sesos; **to — out** reventar(se); **to — over** (knock down) derribar; (dissipate) disiparse; **to — up** (a balloon) inflar, hinchar; (a bridge) volar; N (stroke, shock) golpe m; (wind) tempestad f; (breath) soplo m; **— job** vulg mamada f; **—out** (tire failure) reventón m; (party) fiestón m; **—pipe** cerbatana f; **—torch** soplete m; **—up** (fight) pelea f, riña f; (photo) ampliación f; **to come to —s** irse a las manos

blower [blóɚ] N (artisan) soplador m; (machine) aventadora f

blue [blu] ADJ azul; (sad) triste, melancólico; (from cold) amoratado; **—bell** campanilla f; **—bird** pájaro azul m; **—blood** sangre azul f; **— book** lista de precios de mercado f; **—-chip** de primera línea; **—-collar** de clase obrera; **—jay** arrendajo m; **— jeans** vaqueros m pl; **—print** (of a building) cianotipo m; (of a project) plan m, trazado m; **—-ribbon** distinguido; **— whale** ballena azul f; N azul m; **light —** (azul) celeste m; **the —s** (sadness) melancolía f, murria f; (genre of music) blues m pl; VI ponerse azul, azulear; VT azular, teñir de azul; **to —print** trazar

bluff [blʌf] N (cliff) acantilado m, risco m; (false boast) bluff m; (in poker) farol m; VT hacer un bluff; **to call a —** poner en evidencia

bluffer [blʌ́fɚ] N bluff m

bluing [blúɪŋ] N añil m

bluish [blúɪʃ] ADJ azulado

blunder [blʌ́ndɚ] N disparate m, patochada f; VI meter la pata; **to — upon / into** tropezar con

blunt [blʌnt] ADJ (not sharp) romo; (frank) directo, franco; VT despuntar

blur [blɝ] VT (to obscure) emborronar, desvanecer; (to make vision blurry) nublar; VI empañarse, nublarse; N (indistinct sight) mancha f; **it's a — in my mind** sólo tengo un recuerdo vago de eso

blurry [blɝ́i] ADJ borroso

blurt [blɝt] VT **to — (out)** espetar

blush [blʌʃ] VI sonrojarse, ponerse colorado, ruborizarse; N (act of blushing) sonrojo m; (effect of blushing) rubor m; **at first —** a primera vista

bluster [blʌ́stɚ] VI (blow hard) soplar fuerte, rugir; (boast) fanfarronear; N (noise) ventarrón m; (attitude) fanfarronería f

blustering [blʌ́stɚɪŋ] ADJ fanfarrón, jactancioso; **— wind** ventarrón m

boa constrictor [bóəkənstríktɚ] N boa f

boar [bɔr] N jabalí m

board [bɔrd] N (wood) tabla f, listón m; (game) tablero m; (meals) pensión f; (of directors) directorio m, mesa f; (for bulletins) cartelera f; **—ing school** pensionado m, internado m; **—inghouse** pensión f; **— of trustees** patronato m; **—room** sala de directorio f; **on —** a bordo; **to go by the —** irse por la borda; VI (lodge) alojarse; **to — up** tapiar, cerrar con tablas; VT (boat, plane, train) abordar; (provide lodging) alojar

boarder [bɔ́rDɚ] N pensionista mf

boast [bost] N alarde m; VI jactarse, vanagloriarse, blasonar; VT **the town —s two new schools** el pueblo ostenta dos escuelas nuevas

boastful [bóstfəł] ADJ jactancioso, vanaglorioso

boastfulness [bóstfəłnɪs] N jactancia f, vanagloria f

boat [bot] N (any water vessel) embarcación f; (open and small) bote m, lancha f; (closed, larger) barco m; **—house** cobertizo para botes m; **—man** barquero m, botero m

boating [bóDɪŋ] N navegación f; **to go —** navegar

bob [bab] N (of horsetail) cola cortada f; (of the head) sacudida f; (haircut) meˈlena corta f; (of a pendulum) pesa f, plomada f; **—tail** rabón m; VI sacudirse; (a ship) cabecear; VT **to — one's hair** cortarse el pelo en melena

bobbin [bábɪn] N carrete m, bobina f

bobcat [bábkæt] N lince rojo m

bode [bod] VI **that doesn't — well** eso no augura nada bueno

bodice [bádɪs] N corpiño m

bodily [bádl̩i] ADJ corporal; **— harm** daño físico m

body [bádi] N (of a person, animal, wine, fabric) cuerpo m; (torso) tronco m; (corpse) cadáver m; (of a text, army, etc.) parte principal f; (of water) masa f; (of a car) carrocería f; (of an airplane) fuselaje m; **— bag** bolsa para cadáveres f; **—-building** culturismo m; **— count** número de muertos m; **—guard** guardaespaldas m sg; **— language**

lenguaje corporal *m*; **— temperature** temperatura *f*; **to —search** cachear; **— shop** taller de carrocería *m*

bog [bɑg] N pantano *m*; VI hundir(se); **to get —ged down** atascarse

bogeyman [búgimæn] N coco *m*; *RP* cuco *m*

bogus [bógəs] ADJ falso

Bohemian [bohímiən] ADJ & N bohemio -a *mf*

boil [bɔɪɫ] VI/VT (water) hervir; (eggs) cocer; (ocean) bullir; (angry person) echar chispas; **to — down to** reducirse a; **to — over** derramarse; **—ing point** punto de ebullición *m*; N (inflammation) forúnculo *m*, divieso *m*; (act of boiling) hervor *m*; **to come to a —** soltar/romper el hervor

boiler [bɔ́ɪlɚ] N caldera *f*

boisterous [bɔ́ɪstɚəs] ADJ bullicioso

bold [boɫd] ADJ (not fearful) atrevido, osado; (unconventional) audaz; (visually striking) llamativo; **—-faced** descarado; **—face type** negrita *f*

boldness [bóɫdnɪs] N (courage) atrevimiento *m*, osadía *f*, arrojo *m*; (unconventional attitude) audacia *f*

Bolivia [bəlíviə] N Bolivia *f*

Bolivian [bəlíviən] ADJ & N boliviano -na *mf*

bolster [bóɫstɚ] N cojín cilíndrico *m*; VT reforzar; **to — someone's courage** alentar a alguien

bolt [boɫt] N (door lock) pestillo *m*, cerrojo *m*; (crossbar) aldaba *f*; (pin) perno *m*, tornillo grande *m*; (of cloth) rollo *m*; **it came as a — from the blue** cayó como bomba; VT (fasten) atornillar; (lock door) cerrar con tranca, atrancar; (devour) engullir; (break with) romper con; VI echarse a correr

bomb [bɑm] N bomba *f*; **—shell** bomba *f*; **— shelter** refugio antiaéreo *m*; VT (attack with bombs) bombardear; VI (fail) fracasar

bombard [bɑmbárd] VT bombardear

bombardier [bɑmbɚdír] N bombardero -ra *mf*

bombardment [bɑmbárdmənt] N bombardeo *m*

bombastic [bɑmbǽstɪk] ADJ grandilocuente, ampuloso

bomber [bámɚ] N bombardero *m*, avión de bombardeo *m*

bona fide [bónəfaɪd] ADJ genuino; **— offer** oferta seria *f*

bonbon [bánbɑn] N caramelo *m*; (chocolate) bombón *m*

bond [bɑnd] N (tie) lazo *m*; (fetter) cadenas *f pl*; (financial instrument) bono *m*, obligación *f*; (adhesion) adherencia *f*;

(chemical) enlace *m*; VI/VT (stick to) adherirse; (connect) establecer vínculos

bondage [bándɪdʒ] N (slavery) servidumbre *f*, esclavitud *f*; (sexual practice) prácticas sadomasoquistas *f pl*

bonding [bándɪŋ] N (mother-child) lazos afectivos *m pl*; (male) compenetración *f*

bondsman [bándzmən] N fiador -ra *mf*

bone [bon] N hueso *m*; (of fish) espina *f*; **— china** porcelana fina *f*; **—head** estúpido -da *mf*; **—yard** cementerio *m*; **— of contention** manzana de discordia *f*; **to make no —s about it** no andarse con rodeos; VT deshuesar; (fish) quitar las espinas; **to — up on something** estudiar algo

bonfire [bánfaɪr] N hoguera *f*, fogata *f*

bonnet [bánɪt] N gorro *m*

bonus [bónəs] N (extra salary) gratificación *f*, prima *f*; (at Christmas) aguinaldo *m*

bony [bóni] ADJ (with large bones) huesudo; (made of bones) óseo

boo [bu] VI/VT abuchear, rechiflar; INTERJ ¡bu! N rechifla *f*, abucheo *m*

boob [bub] N *fam* teta *f*; *Am fam* chiche *m*; *Mex fam* chichi *f*; *RP fam* lola *f*

boo-boo [búbu] N lastimadura *f*; *Sp fam* pupa *f*; *Am* nana *f*; **to make a —** meter la pata

booby [búbi] N (fool) bobo -a *mf*; (bird) bobo *m*; **— hatch** *fam* loquería *f*; **— prize** premio al peor competidor *m*; **— trap** trampa explosiva *f*

book [bʊk] N libro *m*; **—binding** encuadernación *f*; **—case** estante *m*, estantería *f*, biblioteca *f*; **—end** sujetalibros *m sg*; **—keeper** tenedor -ra de libros *mf*; *Sp* contable *mf*; **—keeping** teneduría de libros *f*, contabilidad *f*; **—mark** marcador de libros *m*; **—mobile** biblioteca móvil *f*; **— review** reseña *f*; **—seller** librero -ra *mf*; **—shelf** estante *m*; **—store** librería *f*; **— value** valor contable *m*; **by the —** según las reglas; **on the —s** registrado en los libros; **to keep —s** llevar los libros; VT (reserve) reservar; (hire) contratar; (record charges against) fichar

bookish [bʊ́kɪʃ] ADJ (person) estudioso; (allusion) libresco

booklet [bʊ́klɪt] N cartilla *f*

boom [bum] VI (resound) resonar; (prosper) prosperar; N (noise) explosión *f*; (increase) auge *m*

boon [bun] N (blessing) bendición *f*; (favor) favor *m*

boondocks [búndɑks] ADV LOC **(out) in the —** *fam* en los quintos infiernos, en el quinto pino

boondoggle [búndɑgəł] N despilfarro *m*

boor [bur] N patán -ana *mf*

boorish [búrɪʃ] ADJ grosero, zafio

boost [bust] VT (to shove) empujar (desde abajo o detrás); (to promote) estimular, impulsar; N (shove) empujón (desde abajo) *m*; (aid) estímulo *m*, impulso *m*; **— in prices** alza de precios *f*

booster [bústə-] N (person) animador -ra *mf*; (rocket) acelerador *m*; (electronic device) amplificador *m*; (vaccination) refuerzo *m*

boot [but] N (shoe) bota *f*; (trunk of a car) cajuela *f*; (clamp for cars) cepo *m*; **—black** limpiabotas *m sg*; **—legger** contrabandista de licores *m*; **—licker** *vulg* lameculos *mf*; **to —** por añadidura; **to give the —** poner de patitas en la calle; VT dar una patada a; **to — (out)** echar a patadas

booth [buθ] N (telephone) cabina *f*; (stand) puesto *m*; (ticket) taquilla *f*

booty [búDi] N botín *m*

booze [buz] N *fam* bebercio *m*, bebida alcohólica *f*

borax [bɔ́ræks] N bórax *m*

border [bɔ́rDə-] N (line between countries) frontera *f*; (edge, brink) borde *m*; (bed of flowers) ariete *m*; (design) ribete *m*; **—line** (on a border) fronterizo; (not up to standards) dudoso; VI/VT (make a design) ribetear; **to — on** colindar con; **it —s on madness** raya en la locura

bordering [bɔ́rDə-ɪŋ] ADJ limítrofe

bore [bɔr] N (hole) agujero *m*; (of a gun, cylinder) calibre *m*; (uninteresting person) aburrido -da *mf*, pesado -da *mf*; (uninteresting thing) lata *f*; VT (make a hole) taladrar, horadar; (fail to interest) aburrir; **to — a hole** hacer un agujero

bored [bɔrd] ADJ aburrido; **I'm —** estoy aburrido

boredom [bɔ́rDəm] N aburrimiento *m*, tedio *m*

boric acid [bɔ́rɪk ǽsɪd] N ácido bórico *m*

boring [bɔ́rɪŋ] ADJ aburrido; **he's —** es aburrido

born [bɔrn] ADJ nacido; **he's a — dancer** es un bailarín nato; **she's a — liar** es una mentirosa de nacimiento; **to be —** nacer

boron [bɔ́rɑn] N boro *m*

borrow [bɑ́ro] VT pedir prestado; **I —ed money from Fred** le pedí dinero prestado a Fred; **may I — your car?** ¿me prestas tu coche? **I —ed these books from the library** saqué estos libros de la biblioteca

borrower [bɑ́roə-] N (money) prestatario -ria

mf; (books) usuario -ria *mf*

Bosnia and Herzegovina [bázniəændhə-rtsəgəvínə] N Bosnia-Herzegovina *f*

Bosnian [bázniən] ADJ & N bosnio -nia *mf*

bosom [búzəm] N pecho *m*, seno *m*; **in the — of the family** en el seno de la familia; **— buddy** amigo -ga íntimo -ma *mf*

boss [bɔs] N jefe -fa *mf*; (on a plantation) mayoral *m*, capataz *m*; (political) dirigente *m*; (mafia) capo *m*; VT **to — around** mandonear

bossy [bɔ́si] ADJ mandón

botanical [bətǽnɪkəł] ADJ botánico

botany [bátn̩i] N botánica *f*

botch [bátʃ] VT chapucear, estropear; N chapucería *f*, chapuza *f*

both [boθ] ADJ & PRON ambos, los dos

bother [báðə-] VT molestar, fastidiar; VI molestarse, tomarse la molestia; N molestia *f*

bothersome [báðə-səm] ADJ (activity) molesto, enojoso; (person) enfadoso, molesto

Botswana [batswánə] N Botsuana *f*

bottle [bádl̩] N botella *f*; (for medicine, perfume) frasco *m*; **—neck** atascadero *m*, embotellamiento *m*; **— top** chapa de botella *f*; VT embotellar; **to — up** atascar, embotellar

bottom [bádəm] N (of a hole) fondo *m*; (of a hall, pile, page, bed) pie *m*; (lower part) base *f*, parte de abajo *f*; (buttocks) trasero *m*; **to be at the — of the class** ser el último de la clase; **to hit —** tocar fondo; **to — out** tocar fondo; **who is at the — of all this?** ¿quién está detrás de todo esto? ADJ de abajo; **— line** (business) balance final *m*; (essential element) lo esencial

bottomless [bádəmlɪs] ADJ sin fondo; **— supply** recursos ilimitados *m pl*; **— accusation** acusación infundada *f*; **he's a — pit** es un barril sin fondo

boudoir [búdwɑr] N tocador *m*

bough [baʊ] N rama *f*

bouillon [búljɑn] N caldo *m*

boulder [bóɫdə-] N peña *f*, pedrusco *m*

boulevard [búləvɑrd] N bulevar *m*

bounce [baʊns] N (of a ball) bote *m*, rebote *m*; (vitality) vitalidad *f*; VT echar, botar; **to — a check** rebotar un cheque; VI rebotar; **to — back** recuperarse

bouncer [baʊnsə-] N gorila *m*

bound [baʊnd] N (jump) salto *m*; **—s** límite *m*, confín *m*; ADJ (tied up) atado; (confined) confinado; (obliged) obligado;

(as a book) encuadernado; **to be — for** ir rumbo a; **to be — up in one's work** estar absorto en su trabajo; **it is — to happen** es seguro que pasará; **I am — to do it** estoy resuelto a hacerlo; VI (jump) saltar; (be contiguous) lindar

boundary [báʊndri] N (of a country, city) límite *m*, término *m*; (of a property) linde *mf*, lindero *m*

boundless [báʊndlɪs] ADJ ilimitado, sin límites

bountiful [báʊntəfəł] ADJ abundante

bounty [báʊnti] N (abundance) abundancia *f*; (reward) recompensa *f*

bouquet [bukél] N (flowers) ramo *m*; (small) ramillete *m*; (of wine) aroma *m*, bouquet *m*

bourgeois [burʒwá] ADJ & N burgués -sa *mf*

bout [baʊt] N encuentro *m*; **a — of flu** una gripe

boutique [butík] N boutique *f*

bow [baʊ] N (gesture) reverencia *f*; (prow) proa *f*; VI (bend at the waist) hacer una reverencia; (yield) someterse; **to — out** retirarse; VT inclinar; [bo] N (for arrows, violin) arco *m*; (curve) curva *f*; (decoration) moño *m*; **—knot** lazada *f*; **—-legged** patizambo; **—-string** cuerda de arco *f*; VI/VT (bend) arquear(se); (play with a bow) tocar con arco

bowel [báʊəł] N **—s** intestinos *m pl*; **—s of the earth** entrañas de la tierra *f pl*; **— movement** evacuación del vientre *f*

bower [báʊɚ] N enramada *f*

bowl [boł] N (container) bol *m*, tazón *m*; (dish) plato hondo *m*; (depression) cuenco *m*; (of a toilet) taza *f*; (of a pipe) cazoleta *f*; VT **to — over** apabullar, deslumbrar

bowling [bólɪŋ] N boliche *m*, bowling *m*; **let's go —** vamos al boliche; **— alley** boliche *m*, bolera *f*

box [bɑks] N caja *f*; (for jewelry) estuche *m*; (in the theater) palco de teatro *m*; (for the jury) tribuna *f*; (on a page) cuadro *m*; **— car** vagón de carga *m*; **— office** taquilla *f*; **— seat** asiento de palco *m*; VT (put in a box) meter en una caja; (hit) abofetear; (engage in sport) boxear

boxer [bɑ́ksɚ] N boxeador -ra *mf*, pugilista *mf*; (breed of dog) bóxer *m*; **— shorts** calzoncillo *m*

boxing [bɑ́ksɪŋ] N boxeo *m*, pugilato *m*; **— glove** guante de boxeo *m*; **— ring** ring *m*, cuadrilátero *m*

boy [bɔɪ] N (baby) niño *m*; (young man) muchacho *m*, chico *m*; **— scout** boy scout *m*; **—friend** novio *m*

boycott [bɔ́ɪkɑt] VT boicotear; N boicoteo *m*, boicot *m*

boyhood [bɔ́ɪhʊd] N niñez *f*, juventud *f*

boyish [bɔ́ɪʃ] ADJ de muchacho

brace [bres] N (in construction) tirante *m*; (pair) par *m*; (printed character) corchete *m*; (of a carpenter) berbiquí *m*; **—s** (for teeth) aparato ortodóntico *m*; (for a leg) aparato ortopédico *m*; VT (against a shock) agarrarse; (support) asegurar; (with alcohol) animarse

bracelet [bréslɪt] N brazalete *m*, pulsera *f*

bracket [brǽkɪt] N (support) soporte *m*, sostén *m*; (typographic sign) paréntesis recto *m*, corchete *m*; (division) banda *f*; VT (fix with brackets) fijar con soportes; (write in brackets) colocar entre paréntesis rectos; (associate) agrupar

brag [bræg] VI jactarse (de), hacer alarde (de)

braggart [brǽgɚt] ADJ & N fanfarrón -na *mf*

braid [bred] N trenza *f*; VT trenzar

brain [bren] N cerebro *m*; (food) seso *m*; **she blew out his —s** le levantó la tapa de los sesos; **he's short on —s** es corto de inteligencia; **he is the —s in this operation** él es el cerebro en esta operación; **to rack one's —s** devanarse los sesos, romperse la cabeza; **— drain** fuga de cerebros *f*; **— trust** grupo de expertos *m*; **—storming** brainstorming *m*; VT **to — someone** romperle la crisma a alguien; **to —wash** lavarle el cerebro a; **—-dead** clínicamente muerto, en estado vegetativo

brainy [bréni] ADJ sesudo

brake [brek] N freno *m*; **— drum** tambor del freno *m*; **— fluid** líquido para frenos *m*; **—man** guardafrenos *m sg*; **— shoe** zapata *f*; **to apply the —s** frenar; VI/VT frenar

bramble [brǽmbəł] N zarza *f*

bran [bræn] N salvado *m*; (for birds) afrecho *m*

branch [bræntʃ] N (of a plant, of a family) rama *f*; (of a train) ramal *m*; (of antlers) brazo *m*; (of a science) ramo *m*; (of a business) sucursal *f*; (of the armed forces) arma *f*; (in a computer program) bifurcación *f*; (of a river) tributario *m*; VI/VT ramificar(se)

brand [brænd] N (make, mark) marca *f*; (of humor, etc.) tipo *m*; (mark of disgrace) estigma *m*; **— name** marca *f*; **—-new** flamante, recién comprado; VT (burn) herrar, marcar; (stigmatize) estigmatizar; **to — as** tildar de, tachar de

brandish [brǽndɪʃ] VT blandir, esgrimir

brandy [brǽndi] N (fine) brandy *m*; (cheap)

aguardiente *m*

brash [bræʃ] ADJ (impudent) descarado; (impetuous) impetuoso

brass [bræs] N (metal) latón *m*; (attitude) descaro *m*; (high-ranking officers) la plana mayor; — **instrument** instrumento de metal *m*; **to get down to — tacks** ir al grano; ADJ de latón

brassiere [brəzír] N sostén *m*

brat [bræt] N mocoso -sa *mf*

bravado [brəváDO] N alarde *m*

brave [brev] ADJ valiente, gallardo; N guerrero indio *m*; VT desafiar

bravery [brévəri] N valentía *f*, gallardía *f*

brawl [brɔł] N reyerta *f*, riña *f*, pelotera *f*; VI reñir

bray [bre] N rebuzno *m*; VI rebuznar

brazen [brézən] ADJ (impudent) descarado; (made of brass) de latón

brazier [bréʒɚ] N brasero *m*

Brazil [brəzíł] N Brasil *m*

Brazilian [brəzíljən] ADJ & N brasileño -ña *mf*, brasilero -ra *mf*

breach [britʃ] N (opening) brecha *f*; (infraction) infracción *f*; (severance) ruptura *f*; — **of contract** incumplimiento de contrato *m*; — **of faith** abuso de confianza *m*; VT abrir una brecha; (violate a law) violar, infringir

bread [brɛd] N pan *m*; — **basket** panera *f*; — **box** panera *f*; —**winner** sostén de la familia *m*; ADJ —**-and-butter** básico; VT empanar

breadth [brɛdθ] N anchura *f*, ancho *m*; (size) extensión *f*; (perspective) amplitud *f*

break [brek] VI (fracture) romperse; (pause) parar; VT (a record) batir; (a code) descifrar; (a law) violar; (news) dar, divulgar; (a bone) fracturar; (a horse) domar, desbravar; (a habit) quitar(se) (una costumbre); (one's spirit) quebrar, doblegar; (cause to go bankrupt) arruinar; **to — a promise** romper una promesa, faltar a la palabra; **to — a ten-dollar bill** conseguir cambio para un billete de diez dólares; **to — away** escaparse; **to — down** (a person) descomponerse; (a car) averiarse; (resistance) vencer; (continuity) interrumpir; **to — even** quedar a mano; **to — into** violentar; **to — loose** liberarse; **to — out** (war) estallar; (one's face) brotarse; (from prison) escaparse; **to — up** (into pieces) quebrarse; (a relationship) romper con; —**-in** hurto con escalo *m*; —**down** (analysis) análisis *m*; (automotive) avería *f*; —**through** adelanto *m*; (military) penetración *f*;

—**water** rompeolas *m sg*; N (weather) cambio *m*; (from work) descanso *m*; (with tradition) quiebre *m*, rompimiento *m*; (of a bone) fractura *f*; (from prison) fuga *f*; (opportunity) oportunidad *f*; **give me a** —! *vulg* ¡déjate de joder! **lucky** — golpe de suerte *m*

breakable [brékəbəł] ADJ quebradizo, rompible

breaker [brékɚ] N rompiente *f*

breakfast [brékfəst] N desayuno *m*; VI desayunar

breast [brɛst] N seno *m*, pecho *m*; *fam* teta *f*; (bird) pechuga *f*; — **cancer** cáncer de mama *m*; —**stroke** (estilo) pecho *m*; VI/VT **to —-feed** amamantar, dar de mamar

breath [brɛθ] N aliento *m*; *lit* hálito *m*; (current of air) soplo *m*; —**taking** impresionante; **in the same** — al mismo tiempo; **out of** — sin aliento; **to catch one's** — recobrar el aliento; **to hold one's** — aguantar la respiración; **to take a** — inhalar; **to take a deep** — respirar hondo; **under one's** — entre dientes, por lo bajo

breathe [brið] VI/VT respirar; **to — in** inspirar, aspirar; **to — into** infundir; **to — out** exhalar, espirar; **he did not — a word** no dijo palabra

breathing [bríðɪŋ] N respiración *f*

breathless [bréθlɪs] ADJ sin aliento

breed [brid] VT (mate) criar; (bring up) educar; (give rise to) engendrar; VI reproducirse, multiplicarse; N (species) raza *f*; (type) clase *f*

breeder [bríDɚ] N (person who breeds) criador -ra *mf*; (animal used for breeding) (animal) reproductor *f*

breeding [bríDɪŋ] N (of animals) cría *f*; (people) educación *f*, modales *m pl*

breeze [briz] N brisa *f*

breezy [brízi] ADJ (windy) ventoso; (jaunty) ameno

brevity [brévɪDi] N brevedad *f*

brew [bru] VT (coffee) hacer; (mischief) fomentar, tramar; (beer) fabricar; VI (storm) armarse una tormenta; **let the tea** — deja reposar el té; N (mixture) mezcla *f*; (beer) cerveza *f*

brewery [brúari] N cervecera *f*, fábrica de cerveza *f*

briar [bráɪɚ] N zarza *f*

bribe [braɪb] N soborno *m*, cohecho *m*; *Mex* mordida *f*; VT sobornar

bribery [bráɪbəri] N soborno *m*

brick [brɪk] N ladrillo *m*; —**bat** (piece of brick) pedazo de ladrillo *m*; (insult) insulto *m;* —**layer** albañil *m;* —**laying** albañilería *f;* VT (adorn with bricks) revestir de ladrillo; (pave with bricks) enladrillar

bridal [bráɪdl̩] ADJ nupcial; — **dress** vestido de novia *m*

bride [braɪd] N novia *f;* —**groom** novio *m;* —**smaid** dama de honor *f*

bridge [brɪʤ] N puente *m;* (of the nose) caballete *m;* (card game) bridge *m;* VT tender un puente sobre; **to — a gap** llenar un vacío, salvar un obstáculo

bridle [bráɪdl̩] N (harness) brida *f;* (restraint) freno *m;* VT (put on a bridle) embridar; (restrain) frenar; VI (be insulted) ofenderse

brief [brif] ADJ (short) breve, escueto; (concise) conciso, escueto; (curt) seco; N sumario *m,* resumen *m;* (report) expediente *m;* —**case** portafolio(s) *m sg,* maletín *m;* —**s** calzoncillos *m pl;* **in —** en suma; VT informar

briefing [brífɪŋ] N reunión para dar instrucciones *f*

brigade [brɪgéd] N brigada *f*

bright [braɪt] ADJ (shining) brillante; (full with light) iluminado; (smart) inteligente; (future) venturoso, prometedor; (smile) radiante; (color) subido

brighten [bráɪtn̩] VT (a room) iluminar; VI **to — up** (become cheerful) animar(se); (sky) despejarse

brightness [bráɪtnɪs] N (light) claridad *f;* (cheerfulness) viveza *f;* (intelligence) inteligencia *f*

brilliance [brílj̩əns] N (of hair, of a historical period) brillantez *f;* (intelligence) genio *m*

brilliant [bríljənt] ADJ (shining) brillante; (intelligent) genial; (splendid) espléndido; N brillante *m,* diamante *m*

brim [brɪm] N borde *m;* (hat) ala *f;* **to fill to the —** llenar hasta el borde; **to be filled to the —** estar de bote en bote; **to be —ming with** estar rebosante de; VI **to — over** rebosar

brine [braɪn] N salmuera *f*

bring [brɪŋ] VT traer; (cause) ocasionar, causar; **to — about** producir, ocasionar; **to — down** (kill) bajar; (depress) deprimir; **to — forth** (give birth) dar a luz; (produce) producir; **to — to a stop** parar; **to — together** reunir, juntar; — **oneself to do something** poder hacer algo; **to — a good price** redituar una buena ganancia; **to — up** (raise children) criar, educar; (mention) mencionar

brink [brɪŋk] N borde *m;* **on the — of** al borde de

brisk [brɪsk] ADJ (walk) rápido; (weather) fresco; (trading) activo

bristle [brɪsəl̩] N cerda *f;* VI erizar(se); **to — with** estar erizado de

bristly [brísli] ADJ (with bristles) erizado, cerdoso; (irascible) irascible

Britain [brítn̩] N Gran Bretaña *f*

British [brídɪʃ] ADJ británico

brittle [brídl̩] ADJ quebradizo, frágil

brittleness [brídl̩nɪs] N fragilidad *f*

broach [brotʃ] VT sacar a colación

broad [brɔd] ADJ (wide) ancho; (vast) vasto; (ample) amplio; —**cast** emisión *f;* —**cast station** emisora *f;* —**casting** (radio) radiodifusión *f;* (TV) transmisión por televisión *f;* **to —cast** (communicate electronically) transmitir, emitir, radiar; — **hint** insinuación clara *f;* — **jump** salto de longitud *m;* —**-minded** tolerante; —**side** andanada *f;* **in — daylight** en pleno día; N *pej* tipa *f*

brocade [brokéd] N brocado *m*

broccoli [brákəli] N brócoli *m,* brécol *m*

brochure [broʃúr] N folleto *m*

broil [brɔɪl] VI/VT asar(se) (a la parrilla)

broiler [brɔ́ɪlɚ] N (oven) parrilla *f;* (chicken) pollo (para asar) *m*

broke [brok] ADJ **to be —** estar limpio, estar pelado; **to go —** irse a la quiebra

broken [brókən] ADJ (fragmented) roto, quebrado; (tamed) domado; (not functioning) descompuesto; (not continuous) interrumpido; —**-down** averiado, descompuesto; — **English** inglés chapurrado / chapurreado *m;* —**hearted** deshecho, con el corazón destrozado

broker [brókɚ] N (intermediary) agente *mf;* (stock salesman) corredor -ra de bolsa *mf*

brokerage [brókɚɪʤ] N agencia de corredores de bolsa *f*

bromide [brómaɪd] N bromuro *m*

bromine [brómin] N bromo *m*

bronchial [bráŋkiəl̩] ADJ bronquial; — **tube** bronquio *m*

bronchitis [brɑŋkáɪdɪs] N bronquitis *f*

bronco [bráŋko] N caballo no domado *m*

bronze [branz] N bronce *m;* VT broncear

brooch [brutʃ] N broche *m,* prendedor *m*

brood [brud] N pollada *f,* nidada *f;* VI/VT empollar; **to — over** rumiar

brook [brʊk] N riachuelo *m,* cañada *f;* VT tolerar

broom [brum] N (tool) escoba *f;* (plant) retama *f;* —**stick** palo de escoba *m*

broth [brɔθ] N caldo *m*

brothel [bráθəl̩] N burdel *m*

brother [bráðɚ] N hermano *m*; —**-in-law** cuñado *m*; **Oh —!** ¡caray!

brotherhood [bráðɚhʊd] N hermandad *f*

brotherly [bráðɚli] ADJ fraternal

brow [braʊ] N (ridge of eye) arco superciliar *m*; (eyebrow) ceja *f*; (forehead) frente *f*

brown [braʊn] ADJ (skin) moreno; (eyes, shoes, clothes) café, marrón; (hair) castaño; (dun) pardo; (tanned) bronceado; VI/VT dorar(se); **to —-nose** *vulg* lamer culos; **—-noser** *vulg* lameculos *mf pl*, adulón -ona *mf*; N (color) café *m*, castaño *m*, moreno *m*, pardo *m*; **— bear** oso pardo *m*; **— rice** arroz integral *m*; **— sugar** azúcar moreno -na *mf*

brownie [bráuni] N bizcocho de chocolate *m*

browse [braʊz] VT (leaf through) hojear; VI (graze) pacer, pastar; (surf the web) *Sp* navegar (la web); *Am* navegar (en la red)

browser [bráʊzɚ] N navegador *m*

bruise [bruz] N (skin) moretón *m*, cardenal *m*, contusión *f*; (fruit) magulladura *f*, cardenal *m*; VI/VT magullar(se), machucar(se)

brunch [brʌntʃ] N brunch *m*, desayuno tardío *m*

Brunei [brunái] N Brunéi *m*

Bruneian [brunáiən] ADJ & N bruneano -na *mf*

brunet, brunette [brunét] ADJ & N moreno -na *mf*, morocho -cha *mf*; *Cuba* trigueño -ña *mf*

brunt [brʌnt] N impacto *m*

brush [brʌʃ] N (tooth, clothes) cepillo *m*; (paint, shaving) brocha *f*; (artist's) pincel *m*; (vegetation) maleza *f*; (contact) roce *m*; **—-off** despedida brusca *f*; **—wood** (dead) broza *f*; (live) maleza *f*; VT (clean with a brush) cepillar; (touch lightly) rozar; **to — aside** echar a un lado; **to — up on** repasar; **to — off** (clean) quitar con cepillo; (reject) despedir bruscamente a alguien

brusque [brʌsk] ADJ brusco

Brussels sprouts [brásəɫspraʊts] N coles de Bruselas *f pl*, repollitos de Bruselas *m pl*

brutal [brúdl̩] ADJ brutal

brutality [brutǽlɪɾi] N brutalidad *f*

brute [brut] N (animal) bestia *f*; (person) bruto -ta *mf*; ADJ bruto

bubble [bábəɫ] N burbuja *f*; (in soap) pompa *f*; (in boiling water) borbollón *m*; (illusion) encanto *m*; **— bath** baño de burbujas *m*; **—gum** chicle de globo *m*; VI (make bubbles) borbotar, borbollar; (boil) bullir, hervir; **to — over with joy** rebosar de alegría

bubonic plague [bubánɪkplég] N plaga bubónica *f*

buck [bʌk] N (goat) macho cabrío *m*; (deer) gamo *m*; (male of other animals) macho *m*; (leap of horse) respingo *m*; **— private** soldado raso *m*; **—shot** posta *f*, perdigón *m*; **—skin** gamuza *f*; **—toothed** de dientes salidos; **—wheat** trigo sarraceno *m*; **to pass the —** echarle el muerto a uno; VI (horse) respingar, corcovear; **to — a trend** oponerse; **to — up** cobrar ánimo

bucket [bákɪt] N cubo *m*, balde *m*; (of a loader) cuchara *f*; **— seat** asiento delantero individual *m*

buckle [bákəɫ] N (clasp) hebilla *f*; (kink in a board) torcedura *f*; VT (to clasp) abrocharse; (to bend) torcerse, pandearse; **to — down** esforzarse; **to — up** abrocharse

bud [bʌd] N botón *m*, retoño *m*; VI (make buds) echar retoños

buddy [bádi] N camarada *mf*

budge [bʌdʒ] VI moverse

budget [bádʒɪt] N presupuesto *m*; VT (money) presupuestar; (time, personal resources) administrar

buff [bʌf] N (leather) gamuza *f*; (tan color) color beige *m*; (wheel for polishing) pulidor *m*; (devotee) aficionado *m*; **in the —** en cueros; ADJ (beige) de color beige; (muscular) musculoso; VT pulir

buffalo [báfəlo] N bisonte *m*, búfalo *m*; **— wings** alitas *f pl*

buffer [báfɚ] N (in a computer) memoria intermedia *f*; (shock absorber) amortiguador *m*; (polishing device) pulidor -ra *mf*; **— zone** zona tampón *f*

buffet [báfɪt] N (blow) golpe *m*, puñetazo *m*; (shock) azote *m*; VT (hit) golpear; (hit repeatedly) azotar; [bəfé] N (cabinet) aparador *m*; (meal) buffet *m*

buffoon [bəfún] N payaso -a *mf*, bufón -ona *mf*

bug [bʌg] N bicho *m*; (disease-causing) microbio *m*, virus *m*; (for eavesdropping) micrófono oculto *m*; (in a computer program) fallo *m*, bicho *m*; VT (bother) molestar; (install microphones) colocar micrófonos ocultos; **his eyes —ged out** se le saltaron los ojos

buggy [bági] N (cart) calesa *f*; (baby carriage) cochecillo *m*

bugle [bjúgəɫ] N clarín *m*; VI tocar el clarín

build [bɪɫd] VT (construct) construir, edificar; (manufacture) fabricar; **to — into** incorporar; **to — up** (make stronger) fortalecer; (accumulate) acumular;

(enhance) desarrollar; (urbanize) urbanizar; **—-up** (of military forces) concentración *f*; (of substance) acumulación *f*; (of anticipation) aumento *m*; N (of human body) complexión *f*
builder [bíɫdə-] N contratista *mf*
building [bíɫdɪŋ] N (thing built) edificio *m*, construcción *f*, edificación *f*; (act of building) construcción *f*, edificación *f*; (unit in a housing complex) bloque *m*; — **block** (solid mass) bloque (de construcción) *m*; (toy) cubo *m*; (essential element) elemento fundamental *m*
built [bɪɫt] ADJ **—-in** (furniture appliance) empotrado; (feature) incorporado; **—-up** urbanizado
bulb [bʌɫb] N (plant) bulbo *m*; (light) bombilla *f*; *Am* foco *m*
bulbous [bʌ́ɫbəs] ADJ bulboso
Bulgaria [bʌɫgériə] N Bulgaria *f*
Bulgarian [bʌɫgériən] ADJ & N búlgaro -ra *mf*
bulge [bʌɫʤ] N bulto *m*, protuberancia *f*; VI abultar, hincharse
bulgy [bʌ́ɫʤi] ADJ abultado
bulk [bʌɫk] N (mass) cantidad *f*, volumen *m*; (greater part) mayor parte *f*; **in — a** granel; VI **to — up** echar músculos
bulky [bʌ́ɫki] ADJ voluminoso
bull [buɫ] N toro *m*; **—dog** buldog *m*; **—dozer** bulldozer *m*; **—fight** corrida de toros *f*; **—fighter** torero *m*; **—fighting** tauromaquia *f*; **—frog** rana grande *f*; **—market** mercado alcista *m*; **—shit** disparates *m pl*, mentiras *f pl*; **that's —shit** y una polla (como una olla); **—'s eye** diana *f*; **to hit the —'s-eye** dar en el blanco; ADJ **—headed** terco, obstinado
bullet [búlɪt] N bala *f*; ADJ **—proof** antibalas *inv*
bulletin [búlɪtn̩] N boletín *m*; **— board** tablero *m*, cartelera *f*
bullion [búljən] N oro en lingotes *m*
bully [búli] N matón -ona *mf*, bravucón -ona *mf*; VT intimidar
bulwark [búɫwə-k] N baluarte *m*
bum [bʌm] N (lazy person) holgazán -ana *mf*; (hobo) vagabundo -da *mf*; (sports fan) fanático -ca *mf*; ADJ (accusation) falso; **my — knee** vulg mi rodilla jodida; VI holgazanear; VT gorronear
bumblebee [bʌ́mbəɫbi] N abejorro *m*, abejón *m*
bummer [bʌ́mə-] N *vulg* cagada *f*
bump [bʌmp] VT chocar; **to — along** ir dando tumbos; **to — off** despachar; **to — into** toparse con; N (blow) choque *m*, trastazo *m*; (lump) protuberancia *f*; (lump

on a person) chichón *m*
bumper [bʌ́mpə-] N parachoques *m sg*, tope *m*; **— car** coche de choque *m*, autito chocador *m*; **— crop** cosecha abundante *f*; **—-to-— traffic** caravana de autos *f*; **— sticker** autoadhesivo *m*
bumpy [bʌ́mpi] ADJ bacheado, lleno de baches
bun [bʌn] N (bread) bollo *m*; (in hair) moño *m*; **—s** *fam* nalgas *f pl*
bunch [bʌntʃ] N (group of things) manojo *m*; (group of people) montón *m*, grupo *m*; (of grapes, bananas) racimo *m*; (of flowers) ramillete *m*; VI/VT juntar(se), agrupar(se)
bundle [bʌ́ndl̩] N paquete *m*, fardo *m*, envoltorio *m*; (of clothes) lío *m*, atado *m*; (of belongings) hato *m*, petate *m*; (of firewood) haz *m*; VT (tie together) liar, atar; **to — up** abrigarse; **to — off** despachar
bungalow [bʌ́ŋgəlo] N bungaló *m*
bungee jumping [bʌ́nʤiʤʌmpɪŋ] N bungee *m*, puénting *m*
bungle [bʌ́ŋgəɫ] VT estropear; VI chapucear
bunion [bʌ́njən] N juanete *m*
bunk [bʌŋk] N (place to sleep) litera *f*; (nonsense) tonterías *f pl*; **— bed** litera *f*; VI dormir en una litera
bunker [bʌ́ŋkə-] N búnker *m*
bunny [bʌ́ni] N conejito *m*
buoy [búi] N boya *f*; VI boyar; **to — up** mantener a flote, animar
buoyant [bɔ́ɪənt] ADJ (floating) boyante, flotante; (mood) optimista
bur [bɝ] N abrojo *m*
burden [bɝ́dn̩] N (load) carga *f*; (responsibility) peso *m*; **— of proof** carga de la prueba *f*; VT (heavily) recargar; (oppressively) agobiar
burdensome [bɝ́dn̩səm] ADJ agobiante, gravoso
bureau [bjúro] N (government department) oficina *f*, agencia *f*; (chest of drawers) cómoda *f*
bureaucracy [bjurákrəsi] N burocracia *f*
bureaucrat [bjúrəkræt] N burócrata *mf*
burglar [bɝ́glə-] N ladrón -ona *mf*; **— alarm** alarma antirrobo *f*; **— proof** a prueba de robos
burglary [bɝ́gləri] N robo con allanamiento *m*
burial [bériəɫ] N entierro *m*; **— place** lugar de sepultura *m*
Burkina Faso [bə-kínəfáso] N Burkina Faso *m*
burlap [bɝ́læp] N arpillera *f*
burlesque [bə-lésk] ADJ burlesco; N

espectáculo de variedades *m*
burly [bɜ́ˑli] ADJ corpulento
Burma [bɜ́ˑmə] N Birmania *f*
Burmese [bə·míz] ADJ & N birmano -na *mf*
burn [bɜˑn] N quemadura *f*; **—out** surmenage *m*; VI/VT quemar(se), abrasar(se); (a house) incendiar(se); (food) quemar(se), requemar(se); **he got —ed in the transaction** lo estafaron en el negocio; **the bulb is still —ing** la bombilla sigue prendida; **the house is —ing** la casa se está quemando; **the iodine —ed his skin** el yodo le quemó la piel; **to — a hole** hacer un agujero con algo; VI (by heat, passion) arder, abrasar; **my skin —s** me arde la piel; **he's —ing with desire** arde en deseos; **to — down** incendiarse; **to — off** (fog) disiparse; **to — out** (to fuse) fundirse; (to be exhausted) agotarse; **to — up** quemarse completamente
burner [bɜ́ˑnə·] N (person or thing that burns something) quemador -ra *mf*; (on stove) hornilla *f*; **Bunsen —** mechero Bunsen *m*
burning [bɜ́ˑnɪŋ] ADJ (desire) ardiente, abrasador; (question) urgente
burnish [bɜ́ˑnɪʃ] VT bruñir
burp [bɜˑp] N eructo *m*; VI eructar, repetir
burrow [bɜ́ˑo] N madriguera *f*; VI (dig) hacer madrigueras; (live) vivir en una madriguera
burst [bɜˑst] VI reventar(se); **to — into** irrumpir en; **to — into tears** romper en llanto; **to — out** salir disparado; **to — with laughter** estallar / reventar de risa; N **— of activity** explosión de actividad *f*; **— of laughter** carcajada *f*; **— of machine-gun fire** ráfaga de ametralladora *f*; **— of speed** aceleración *f*
Burundi [bʊrúndi] N Burundi *m*
Burundian [bʊrúndiən] ADJ & N burundés -esa *mf*
bury [béri] VT enterrar; (in sand) hundir; (corpse only) sepultar; **to be buried in thought** estar absorto / meditabundo
bus [bʌs] N autobús *m*, ómnibus *m*; *Mex* camión *m*; *RP* colectivo *m*; *Chile* micro *m*; *Cuba* guagua *f*; (in a computer) bus *m*; VT transportar en autobús
bush [bʊʃ] N (plant) arbusto *m*, mata *f*; (region) matorral *m*; **to beat around the —** andarse por las ramas
bushed [bʊʃt] ADJ fatigado
bushel [bʊ́ʃəɫ] N fanega *f*
bushing [bʊ́ʃɪŋ] N buje *m*, cojinete *m*
bushy [bʊ́ʃi] ADJ (whiskers) espeso; (plants) poblado de arbustos
business [bíznɪs] N (trade, store) negocio *m*;

(occupation) ocupación *f*; (commercial activity) comercio *m*; **— card** tarjeta comercial *f*; **— day** día hábil *m*; **— hours** horas hábiles *f pl*, horario de atención al público *m*; **— is booming** el negocio florece; **—man** hombre de negocios *m*, negociante *m*; **— suit** traje *m*; **— transaction** negocio *m*, transacción comercial *f*; **—woman** mujer de negocios *f*, negociante *f*; **I'm tired of the whole —** este asunto me tiene harto; **I mean —** hablo en serio; **to do — with** comerciar con; **he has no — doing it** no tiene derecho a hacerlo; **it's none of your —** no es asunto tuyo; **mind your own —** no te metas en lo que no te importa
businesslike [bíznɪslaɪk] ADJ (efficient) eficiente; (cold) impersonal
bust [bʌst] N (statue, body part) busto *m*; VI/VT (burst, hit, break) reventar; (force into bankruptcy) hacer quebrar; (lower in rank) degradar
bustle [bʌ́səɫ] N (noise) bullicio *m*; (movement) ajetreo *m*, tráfago *m*; VI (move busily) ajetrear(se); (be crowded) bullir
busy [bízi] ADJ ocupado, atareado; (overdecorated) recargado; **—body** entrometido -da *mf*; **— signal** señal de ocupado *f*; VI **to — oneself** ocuparse
but [bʌt] CONJ (on the contrary) pero; (excepting) sino; PREP menos; **any day — today** cualquier día menos hoy; **he's nothing — trouble** sólo da problemas; ADV **— for you** si no fuera por ti
butane [bjúten] N butano *m*
butch [bʊtʃ] ADJ (of a woman) marimacha, camionera; (of a man) machote
butcher [bútʃə·] N carnicero -ra *mf*; **—'s shop** carnicería *f*; VT (cattle) matar; (people) masacrar; (performance) estropear
butchery [bútʃəri] N carnicería *f*
butler [bátlə·] N mayordomo *m*
butt [bʌt] N (body part) *fam* culo *m*; (rifle part) culata *f*; (of a cigarette) colilla *f*; (blow with head) topetazo *m*, cabezada *f*, cabezazo *m*; **the — of ridicule** el blanco de las burlas; VT embestir, topar; **to — in** entrometerse; **to — into a conversation** meter baza; *Am* meter la cuchara
butter [bʌ́Də·] N mantequilla *f*; VT (bread) untar con mantequilla; (a cakepan) enmantecar; **—cup** botón de oro *m*; **— dish** mantequera *f*; **—fingers** manos de mantequilla *mf sg*; **—milk** suero de leche *m*; **—scotch** dulce de azúcar y mantequilla *m*

butterfly [bʌ́Dɚ-flaɪ] N mariposa *f*; — **stroke** estilo mariposa *m*

buttery [bʌ́Dəri] ADJ mantecoso

buttocks [bʌ́Dəks] N nalgas *f pl*, asentaderas *f pl*, cachas *f pl*

button [bʌ́tn̩] N botón *m*; —**hole** ojal *m*; VI/VT abotonar(se); VT **to** —**hole** hacer ojales; **to** —**hole someone** detener a alguien

buttress [bʌ́trɪs] N apoyo *m*, sostén *m*; (of a building) contrafuerte *m*; VT apoyar, reforzar

buxom [bʌ́ksəm] ADJ (full-bosomed) pechugona; (fat and cheerful) frescachona, jamona

buy [baɪ] VT comprar; **to** — **into** dejarse convencer; **I don't** — **that** no me lo trago; **to** — **on credit** comprar a crédito; **to** — **off** sobornar; **to** — **in installments** comprar a plazos; **to** — **out** comprar la parte de; **to** — **up** acaparar; N (purchase) compra *f*; (bargain) ganga *f*

buyer [báɪɚ] N comprador -ra *mf*

buzz [bʌz] N zumbido *m*; (feeling of intoxication) borrachera *f*; (phone call) telefonazo *m*; **to give someone a** — pegarle / echarle un telefonazo a alguien; — **saw** sierra circular *f*; VI zumbar; (group) murmurar; VT hacer zumbar; **to** — **the bell** tocar el timbre; **to** — **off** largarse

buzzard [bʌ́zɚd] N buitre *m*

buzzer [bʌ́zɚ] N timbre *m*, chicharra *f*

by [baɪ] PREP por; **we drove** — **the church** pasamos por la iglesia; **a 4** — **3 room** un cuarto de 4 por 3; **multiply 2** — **2** multiplica 2 por 2; — **the liter** por litro; **we live** — **the church** vivimos al lado de la iglesia; **she had a son** — **him** tuvo un hijo con él; — **and** — a la larga; — **dint of** a fuerza de; — **far** con mucho; — **night** de noche; — **the way** a propósito; — **chance** por casualidad; **piece** — **piece** pedazo a / por pedazo; — **this time tomorrow** mañana a esta hora; — **two o'clock** para las dos; ADV **the factory is close** — la fábrica está cerca; **the bus drove** — pasó el autobús

bye-bye [báɪbáɪ] INTERJ ¡adiós! ¡chaucito!

bygones [báɪgɔnz] N **let** — **be** — lo pasado pisado

bylaw [báɪlɔ] N estatuto *m*

by-line [báɪlaɪn] N pie de autor *m*

bypass [báɪpæs] VT evitar; N desvío *m*; — **operation** bypass *m*

by-product [báɪprɑDəkt] N subproducto *m*; (chemical) derivado *m*

bystander [báɪstændɚ] N persona presente *f*

byte [baɪt] N byte *m*, octeto *m*

Cc

cab [kæb] N (taxi) taxi *m*; (of a truck) cabina *f*; — **driver** taxista *mf*

cabaret [kæbəré] N cabaret *m*

cabbage [kǽbɪdʒ] N col *f*, repollo *m*, berza *f*

cabin [kǽbɪn] N (hut) cabaña *f*; (in an airplane) cabina *f*; (in a ship) camarote *m*

cabinet [kǽbnɪt] N (for dishes) armario *m*; (for medicines) botiquín *m*; (for display) vitrina *f*; (department heads) gabinete *m*; —**maker** ebanista *mf*

cable [kébəł] N cable *m*; (on ships) amarra *f*; (telegram) telegrama *m*; — **car** funicular *m*, teleférico *m*; — **television** televisión por cable *f*, cablevisión *f*; VI/VT telegrafiar

caboose [kəbús] N furgón de cola *m*

cache [kæʃ] N (of weapons) alijo *m*; (in a computer) caché *m*

cachet [kæfé] N caché *m*

cackle [kǽkəł] VI cacarear; (talk) parlotear; N cacareo *m*; (talk) parloteo *m*

cacophony [kəkáfəni] N cacofonía *f*

cactus [kǽktəs] N cacto *m*, cactus *m*

cad [kæd] N *pej* canalla *mf*

cadaver [kədǽvɚ] N cadáver *m*

caddie [kǽDi] N caddy *m*, caddie *m*

cadence [kédn̩s] N cadencia *f*

cadet [kədét] N cadete *mf*

cadmium [kǽdmiəm] N cadmio *m*

Caesarian section [sɪzériənsékʃən] N cesárea *f*

café [kæfé] N (coffee only) café *m*; (coffee and food) cafetería *f*

cafeteria [kæfɪtíriə] N cafetería *f*; (in school, factory) cantina *f*

caffeine [kæfín] N cafeína *f*

cage [kedʒ] N jaula *f*; VT enjaular

cahoots [kəhúts] ADV LOC **in** — arreglados

cajole [kədʒół] VI/VT engatusar, persuadir con halagos

cake [kek] N pastel *m*, torta *f*; (sponge) bizcocho *m*; (soap) pastilla *f*; **a piece of** — pan comido; **to take the** — ser el colmo; VI/VT apelmazar(se)

calamine [kǽləmaɪn] N calamina *f*

calamity [kəlǽmɪDi] N calamidad *f*

calcium [kǽłsiəm] N calcio *m*

calculate [kǽłkjəlet] VI/VT calcular; **his actions were** —**d to fool us** con sus acciones trataba de engañarnos

calculating [kǽɫkjələɒɪŋ] ADJ calculador
calculation [kæɫkjəléʃən] N cálculo *m*
calculator [kǽɫkjəléɒɚ] calculadora *f*
calculus [kǽɫkjələs] N cálculo *m*
calendar [kǽlɪndɚ] N calendario *m*, almanaque *m*; — **year** año civil *m*
calf [kæf] N (animal) ternero -ra *mf*, becerro -rra *mf*; (of leg) pantorrilla *f*, canilla *f*; — **skin** piel de becerro *f*
caliber [kǽləbɚ] N calibre *m*
calibrate [kǽləbret] VT calibrar, graduar
calico [kǽlɪko] N calicó *m*
caliper [kǽləpɚ] N (on brakes) calibrador *m*; (for measuring) calibre *m*
call [kɔɫ] N (bird call, device for calling birds) reclamo *m*; (telephone call) llamada *f*; (summons) llamamiento *m*; (to the ministry) vocación *f*; — **girl** prostituta de cita *f*; **there's no — for panic** no hay motivo de alarma; **it's your —** tú decides; **within —** al alcance de la VOZ; VT (summon, by telephone, a name, a strike) llamar; (cry out) gritar; (a meeting) convocar; **she —ed me a liar** me llamó mentiroso; — **me back** llámame tú; **to — a meeting to order** abrir la sesión; VI/VT (birds) reclamar; **to — roll** pasar lista; VI (call out) gritar; **to — at a port** hacer escala en un puerto; **to — for** pedir; **to — off** cancelar; **to — on** (visit) visitar; (depend on) acudir a; **to — together** convocar; **to — up** llamar por teléfono
caller [kɔ́lɚ] N visita *f*, visitante *mf*; (by telephone) persona que llama *f*; — **ID** identificador de llamadas *m*
calligraphy [kəlígrəfi] N caligrafía *f*
calling [kɔ́lɪŋ] N vocación *f*
callous [kǽləs] ADJ (having calluses) calloso; (insensitive) insensible
callus [kǽləs] N callo *m*
calm [kɑm] ADJ tranquilo, reposado, calmo; N calma *f*, tranquilidad *f*, sosiego *m*; VT calmar, tranquilizar, sosegar; **to — down** calmar(se)
calmness [kámnɪs] N calma *f*, tranquilidad *f*
calorie [kǽləri] N caloría *f*
calumny [kǽləmni] N calumnia *f*
cam [kæm] N leva *f*
Cambodia [kæmbóɒɪə] N Camboya *f*
Cambodian [kæmbóɒɪən] ADJ & N camboyano -na *mf*
camel [kǽməɫ] N camello *m*
cameo [kǽmio] N camafeo *m*; — **appearance** actuación especial *f*
camera [kǽmrə] N cámara fotográfica *f*; —**man** cámara *m*, camarógrafo *m*; —**woman** cámara *f*, camarógrafa *f*

Cameroon [kæmərún] N Camerún *m*
Cameroonian [kæmərúniən] ADJ & N camerunés -esa *mf*
camouflage [kǽməflɑʒ] N camuflaje *m*; VT camuflar
camp [kæmp] N (campsite) campamento *m*; (faction) bando *m*; —**fire** fogata *f*, hoguera *f*; —**ground** campamento *m*, cámping *m*; —**site** campamento *m*; **the Republican —** el campo republicano; VI/VT acampar
campaign [kæmpén] N campaña *f*; VI hacer campaña
camper [kǽmpɚ] N acampante *mf*, campista *mf*
camphor [kǽmfɚ] N alcanfor *m*
camping [kǽmpɪŋ] N cámping *m*, acampada *f*; **let's go —** vamos de camping / acampada
campus [kǽmpəs] N campus *m*
can [kæn] N lata *f*, bote *m*; — **of worms** caja de Pandora *f*; — **opener** abrelatas *m sg*; VT enlatar; V AUX — **you come tomorrow?** ¿puedes venir mañana? — **you see me?** ¿me ves? **I — ride a bicycle** sé andar en bicicleta; **a —-do attitude** un espíritu emprendedor
Canada [kǽnəɒə] N Canadá *m*
Canadian [kənéɒiən] ADJ & N canadiense *mf*
canal [kənǽɫ] N canal *m*
canary [kənéri] N canario *m*
Canary Islands [kənériáɪlənz] N Islas Canarias *f pl*
cancel [kǽnsəɫ] VT cancelar; (a stamp) matasellar; (an order) anular; (writing) tachar
cancellation [kænsəléʃən] N cancelación *f*; (of an order) anulación *f*
cancer [kǽnsɚ] N cáncer *m*; — **patient** canceroso -sa *mf*; ADJ — **causing** cancerígeno
candelabrum, candelabra [kændəlábrəm -brə] N candelabro *m*
candid [kǽndɪd] ADJ franco, sincero
candidacy [kǽndɪɒəsi] N candidatura *f*
candidate [kǽndɪɒɪt] N (for office) candidato -ta *mf*; (for a job) aspirante *mf*, postulante *mf*
candle [kǽndl̩] N vela *f*, candela *f*; (on the altar) cirio *m*; —**stick** candelero *m*
candor [kǽndɚ] N franqueza *f*
candy [kǽndi] N dulce *m*, caramelo *m*, confite *m*; (with chocolate) bombón *m*; — **store** bombonería *f*; VT confitar, acaramelar; (nuts) garapiñar; VI (syrup) cristalizarse
cane [ken] N (sugar) caña *f*; (walking) bastón

m; — **chair** silla de mimbre *f;* **to beat with a** — bastonear, apalear

canine [kénaɪn] ADJ canino, perruno; N (canid) can *m;* (tooth) canino *m*

canister [kǽnɪstə⋅] N lata *f*

canker [kæŋkə⋅] N úlcera *f*

cannery [kǽnəri] N fábrica de conservas *f*

cannibal [kǽnəbəɬ] N caníbal *m*

cannon [kǽnən] N cañón *m;* — **fodder** carne de cañón *f*

canny [kǽni] ADJ sagaz, astuto

canoe [kənú] N canoa *f*

canon [kǽnən] N (rule, melody) canon *m;* (priest) canónigo *m*

canopy [kǽnəpi] N (of a bed) dosel *m;* (of a building) toldo *m*

cantaloupe [kǽntḷop] N melón *m*

canteen [kæntín] N (snack bar) cantina *f;* (container) cantimplora *f*

canvas [kǽnvəs] N (fabric) lona *f;* (for painting) lienzo *m*

canvass [kǽnvəs] VI/VT (poll) encuestar; (solicit votes) solicitar votos en; (solicit sales) buscar pedidos comerciales en; N solicitud *f*

canyon [kǽnjən] N cañón *m*

cap [kæp] N (head covering without visor) gorro *m;* (head covering with visor) gorra *f;* (of a bottle) tapa *f;* (of a pen) capucha *f,* contera *f;* (limit) tope *m;* (for capgun) fulminante *m,* pistón *m;* VT (to cover, put a cap on) tapar; (to complete) rematar; (to limit) limitar

capability [kepəbílɪɖi] N capacidad *f*

capable [képəbəɬ] ADJ capaz

capacious [kəpéʃəs] ADJ amplio

capacity [kəpǽsɪɖi] N capacidad *f*

cape [kep] N (clothing) capa *f;* (promontory) cabo *m*

caper [képə⋅] N (skipping) cabriola *f;* (prank) treta *f,* triquiñuela *f;* (crime) delito *m;* (food) alcaparra *f;* VI retozar

Cape Verde [kepvɝ́⋅d] N Cabo Verde *m*

Cape Verdean [kepvɝ́⋅ɖiən] ADJ & N caboverdiano -na *mf*

capillary [kǽpəleri] N & ADJ (vaso) capilar *m*

capital [kǽpɪḍl] N (city) capital *f;* (wealth) capital *m;* (of a column) capitel *m;* (letter) mayúscula *f;* **to make — of** sacar partido de, aprovecharse de; ADJ (city) capital; (financial) de capital; — **gains** ganancias en bienes de capital *f pl;* — **investment** inversión de capital *f;* — **punishment** pena de muerte *f*

capitalism [kǽpɪḍlɪzəm] N capitalismo *m*

capitalist [kǽpɪḍlɪst] N capitalista *mf*

capitalistic [kæpɪḍlístɪk] ADJ capitalista

capitalization [kæpɪḍlɪzéʃən] N capitalización *f*

capitalize [kǽpɪḍlaɪz] VT (finance) capitalizar; (write) escribir con mayúscula; **to — on** sacar provecho de

capitol [kǽpɪḍl] N capitolio *m*

capitulate [kəpítʃəlet] VI capitular

cappuccino [kæpətʃíno] N capuchino *m*

caprice [kəprís] N capricho *m*

capricious [kəpríʃəs] ADJ caprichoso

capsize [kǽpsaɪz] VI/VT volcar(se)

capsule [kǽpsəɬ] N cápsula *f*

captain [kǽptɪn] N capitán *m;* VT capitanear

caption [kǽpʃən] N (with illustration) pie *m;* (subtitle) subtítulo *m*

captivate [kǽptəvet] VT cautivar

captive [kǽptɪv] ADJ & N cautivo -va *mf;* — **animals** animales en cautiverio *m pl*

captivity [kæptívɪɖi] N cautiverio *m*

captor [kǽptə⋅] N captor -ra *mf*

capture [kǽptʃə⋅] VT (apprehend, record data) capturar; (attract) cautivar; (conquer) tomar; N captura *f*

car [kɑr] N (automobile) coche *m,* automóvil *m; Am* carro *m,* auto *m;* (railroad) vagón *m,* coche *m;* (elevator) cabina *f; Am* elevador *m;* — **bomb** coche bomba *m;* —**fare** pasaje *m;* —**jacking** secuestro de vehículo *m;* —**load** carga de un coche *f;* —**port** cochera *f;* —**sick** mareado; **he got —sick** se mareó en el coche; — **wash** túnel de lavado *m*

caramel [kǽrəməɬ] N caramelo *m*

carat [kǽrət] N quilate *m*

caravan [kǽrəvæn] N caravana *f*

carbohydrate [kɑrbəháɪdret] N carbohidrato *m,* hidrato de carbono *m*

carbon [kárbən] N carbono *m;* — **copy** copia en papel carbón *f;* — **dioxide** dióxido de carbono *m;* — **monoxide** monóxido de carbono *m;* — **paper** papel carbón *m*

carburetor [kárbəreɖə⋅] N carburador *m*

carcass [kárkəs] N (of an animal) cuerpo muerto *m;* (human) cadáver *m;* (of a ship) casco *m*

carcinogen [kɑrsínəʤən] N cancerígeno *m,* carcinógeno *m*

carcinoma [kɑrsənómə] N carcinoma *m*

card [kɑrd] N (piece of stiff paper) tarjeta *f;* (playing) naipe *m,* carta *f;* (for boxing events) programa *m;* (for textiles) carda *f;* (witty person) gracioso -sa *mf;* (in a computer) tarjeta *f,* placa *f;* —**board** (thick) cartón *m;* (thin) cartulina *f;* — **sharp** fullero -ra *mf;* **pack of —s** baraja *f;* **to play —s** jugar a la baraja, jugar a los naipes; **he's holding all the —s** tiene todas las ventajas; VT (comb) cardar; (ask for identification) pedir identificación

cardiac [kárɒɪæk] ADJ cardiaco, cardíaco

cardinal [kárdn̩l] ADJ (number, main) cardinal; (colored red) rojo, bermellón; N (bishop, bird) cardenal *m*

cardiology [kɑrɒɪáləʤi] N cardiología *f*

cardiovascular [kɑrɒɪovǽskjələ˞] ADJ cardiovascular

care [kɛr] N (worry) preocupación *f*; (attention) cuidado *m*, atención *f*, tiento *m*; (extreme attention) esmero *m*, primor *m*; **—free** despreocupado; **—giver** cuidador -ra *mf*; **to take — of** cuidar de, atender; (of a house) casero -ra *mf*; VI (be concerned, object) importarle a uno; **to — about** interesarle a uno, importarle a uno; **to — for** (look after) cuidar de; (love) tenerle cariño a; **to — to** tener ganas de; **I couldn't — less** me importa un rábano; **what does he —?** ¿a él qué le importa? **would you — for a drink?** ¿te puedo ofrecer algo?

careen [kərín] VI ladearse a toda velocidad

career [kərír] N carrera *f*, trayectoria *f*

careful [kérfəɫ] ADJ (cautious) cuidadoso, cauteloso; (painstaking) esmerado; **to be — tener** cuidado

carefulness [kérfəɫnɪs] N cuidado *m*

careless [kérlɪs] ADJ descuidado

caress [kərés] N caricia *f*; VT acariciar

cargo [kárgo] N cargamento *m*

Caribbean [kærəbíən] N Caribe *m*; ADJ caribeño

caricature [kérɪkətʃə˞] N caricatura *f*; VT caricaturizar

caries [kériz] N caries *f*

carnage [kárnɪʤ] N carnicería *f*

carnal [kárn̩l] ADJ carnal

carnation [kɑrnéʃən] N (flower) clavel *m*; (color) rosado *m*

carnival [kárnəvəɫ] N carnaval *m*; (traveling) feria *f*

carnivorous [kɑrnívɚəs] ADJ carnívoro, carnicero

carol [kérəɫ] N villancico *m*; VI cantar villancicos

carom [kérəm] N carambola *f*; VI rebotar

carotid artery [kərádɪdárɒəri] N (arteria) carótida *f*

carouse [kəráuz] VI andar de parranda

carp [kɑrp] N carpa *f*; VI (complain) quejarse

carpenter [kárpəntə˞] N carpintero -ra *mf*

carpentry [kárpəntri] N carpintería *f*

carpet [kárpɪt] N alfombra *f*; **—bagger** político -ca oportunista *mf*; VT alfombrar

carriage [kérɪʤ] N (wheeled vehicle) carruaje

m, coche *m*; (posture) porte *m*

carrier [kériɚ] N (one who carries) portador -ra *mf*; (postal worker) cartero -ra *mf*; (transport company) mensajería *f*

carrion [kériən] N carroña *f*

carrot [kérət] N zanahoria *f*

carry [kéri] VT llevar; **do you — Italian wine?** ¿venden vino italiano? **the bill carried** se aprobó el proyecto de ley; **you — yourself well** te comportas bien; **he can't — a tune** no puede seguir una tonada; **this suitcase carries a lot** esta maleta es espaciosa; **to — away** llevarse; **he got carried away** se le fue la mano; **to — on** continuar; **to — out** (complete) llevar a cabo, ejecutar; (take out) sacar; **—-on** de mano

cart [kɑrt] N carro *m*; VT acarrear

cartilage [kárdlɪʤ] N cartílago *m*

carton [kártn̩] N caja de cartón *f*

cartoon [kɑrtún] N (drawing) caricatura *f*; (strip) tira cómica *f*; (film) dibujo animado *m*

cartoonist [kɑrtúnɪst] N caricaturista *mf*

cartridge [kártrɪʤ] N cartucho *m*; **— belt** cartuchera *f*, canana *f*

carve [kɑrv] VI/VT (piece of wood) tallar; (a career) labrarse; (turkey) trinchar

carving [kárvɪŋ] N (action) tallado *m*; (figure) talla *f*; **— knife** trinchante *m*

cascade [kæskéd] N cascada *f*

case [kes] N caso *m*; (box) caja *f*; (of a pillow) funda *f*; **in — (that)** en caso de que; **in — it rains** por si llueve; **in any —** en todo caso; **just in —** por si acaso; **get off my —!** ¡déjame en paz!

cash [kæʃ] N efectivo *m*; **— advance** anticipo en efectivo *m*; **— and carry** al contado y sin entrega a domicilio; **— flow** corriente en efectivo *f*; **— on delivery** entrega contra reembolso *f*; **— payment** pago en efectivo *m*; **— register** caja registradora *f*; **to pay —** pagar al contado; VT cobrar

cashew [kǽʃu] N marañón *m*, castaña de cajú *f*, *Sp* anacardo *m*

cashier [kæʃír] N cajero -ra *mf*; **—'s check** cheque de caja *m*

casino [kəsíno] N casino *m*

cask [kæsk] N tonel grande *m*

casket [kǽskɪt] N ataúd *m*

casserole [kǽsəroɫ] N (container) cazuela *f*; (food) guiso *m*

cassette [kəsét] N cassette *mf*, casete *mf*

cast [kæst] VT (throw) tirar, echar; (adapt) adaptar; (form an object) moldear, vaciar; (give out dramatic roles) repartir papeles; **to — a ballot** votar; **to — about** buscar;

to — **a glance** echar un vistazo; **to —
aside** desechar; **to — doubt** poner en
duda; **to — light on** aclarar; **to — lots**
echar suertes; **to — off** (a ship) soltar
amarras; (something rejected) deshacerse
de; **to — out** exiliar; **to be — down**
estar abatido; N (form) molde m; (in
theater) reparto m, elenco m; — **iron**
hierro fundido m

castanet [kǽstənet] N castañuela f

caste [kæst] N casta f

castigate [kǽstɪget] VT (criticize) criticar,
reprender; (punish) castigar

Castile [kæstíł] N Castilla f

Castilian [kæstíljən] N & ADJ castellano -na
mf

casting [kǽstɪŋ] N (throwing) tiro m; (piece
of metal) pieza fundida f; (selection of
actors) cásting m

castle [kǽsəł] N castillo m; (chess piece) torre
f, roque m

castor oil [kǽstə-ɔɪł] N aceite de ricino m

castrate [kǽstret] VT castrar; (animals) capar

casual [kǽ-ʒuəł] ADJ (informal) informal;
(offhand) al pasar

casualty [kǽʒuəłti] N (of war) baja f; (in an
accident) víctima f

cat [kæt] N (domestic) gato -ta mf; (others)
felino m; —'**s meow** súmmum m; —**fish**
siluro m; —**house** burdel m

Catalan [kǽdlæn] ADJ & N catalán -ana mf;
(language) catalán m

catalog, catalogue [kǽdlɔg] N catálogo m;
VT catalogar

Catalonia [kædlóniə] N Cataluña f

Catalonian [kædlóniən] ADJ catalán

catalyst [kǽdlɪst] N catalizador m

cataract [kǽdərækt] N catarata f

catastrophe [kətǽstrəfi] N catástrofe f

catch [kætʃ] VT (a criminal, ball) atrapar; Sp,
Cuba coger; (a fish) pescar, capturar;
(someone in an act) pillar; (a bus) agarrar;
(what someone said) comprender, agarrar;
to — a glimpse of vislumbrar; **to —
cold** resfriarse; **to — fire** prenderse fuego;
to — on (understand) caer en cuenta;
(become popular) ponerse de moda; **to —
oneself** contenerse; **to — one's eye**
llamarle a uno la atención; **to — sight of**
avistar; **to — unawares** sorprender; **to —
up** (with a person) alcanzar; (on work)
ponerse al día; VI (get entangled)
enredarse; (snap into place) agarrar; N (act
of catching prey, quantity caught) captura
f, redada f, pesca f; (prey) presa f; (device)
pestillo m; (act of catching a ball) atrapada
f; —**phrase** eslogan m; **he is a good —**

es un buen partido; **to play —** jugar a la
pelota; **what's the —?** ¿cuál es la treta?

catching [kǽtʃɪŋ] ADJ contagioso

catchy [kǽtʃi] ADJ pegadizo

catechism [kǽdɪkɪzəm] N catecismo m

category [kǽdɪgɔri] N categoría f

cater [kédə-] VI/VT abastecer de alimentos
(banquetes, fiestas, etc.); **to — to** atender
a

caterpillar [kǽdəpɪlə-] N (insect) oruga f;
(tractor) tractor oruga m, caterpillar m

cathedral [kəθídrəł] N catedral f

catheter [kǽθɪdə-] N catéter m, sonda f

cathode [kǽθod] N cátodo m; — **rays** rayos
catódicos m pl

Catholic [kǽθlɪk] N & ADJ católico -ca mf

Catholicism [kəθálɪsɪzəm] N catolicismo m

CAT scan [kǽtskæn] N TAC f, tomografía
axial computadorizada f

catsup [kǽtʃəp] N cátsup m, ketchup m

cattle [kǽdl] N ganado (vacuno) m; —**man**
ganadero m; — **rustler** cuatrero m; —
rustling abigeato m

catty [kǽdi] ADJ hiriente

cauliflower [kɔ́lɪflauə-] N coliflor f

cause [kɔz] N causa f; — **for celebration**
motivo de celebración m; **the
democratic —** la causa democrática;
without — sin motivo; VT causar,
ocasionar; (involving volition) motivar; **to
— to flee** hacer huir; **the heat —d her
to faint** el calor la hizo desmayar

caustic [kɔ́stɪk] ADJ cáustico

cauterize [kɔ́dəraɪz] VT cauterizar

caution [kɔ́ʃən] N (prudence) cautela f, recato
m; (warning) advertencia f; —**!** ¡cuidado!
¡atención! VT advertir; **to — against**
desaconsejar

cautious [kɔ́ʃəs] ADJ cauto, cauteloso,
precavido

cavalier [kævəlír] N caballero m, galán m; ADJ
(disdainful) desdeñoso; (overly casual)
displicente

cavalry [kǽvəłri] N caballería f

cave [kev] N cueva f, caverna f; —**man**
hombre de las cavernas m; VI **to — in**
ceder, derrumbarse, desplomarse

cavern [kǽvə-n] N caverna f, gruta f

cavity [kǽvɪdi] N cavidad f; (in a tooth)
caries f; (nasal) fosa f

cavort [kəvɔ́rt] VI cabriolar, retozar

caw [kɔ] N graznido m; VI graznar

CD (compact disc) [sidí] N CD m, disco
compacto m; — **player** reproductor de
discos compactos m; —**-ROM** CD-ROM m

cease [sis] VI cesar; VT interrumpir; —**-fire**
alto el fuego m; Am cese el fuego m

ceaseless [síslıs] ADJ incesante
cedar [sídɚ] N cedro *m*
cede [sid] VT ceder
ceiling [sílıŋ] N techo *m*, cielo raso *m*; (cap) tope *m*; (sky) altura máxima *f*
celebrate [séləbret] VI/VT celebrar, festejar
celebrated [séləbreɪd] ADJ célebre
celebration [seləbréʃən] N (action) celebración *f*, festejo *m*; (festivities) fiesta *f*
celebrity [səlébrɪɾi] N celebridad *f*
celery [séləri] N apio *m*
celestial [səléstʃəł] ADJ celeste; (heavenly) celestial; — **body** astro *m*
celibate [séləbɪt] ADJ célibe
cell [sɛł] N (room) celda *f*; (structural) célula *f*
cellar [sélɚ] N sótano *m*; (for wine) bodega *f*
cello [tʃélo] N violonchelo *m*
cellophane [séləfen] N celofán *m*
cellular [séljələ˞] ADJ celular; — **phone** celular *m*; *Sp* móvil *m*
cellulite [séljəlaɪt] N celulitis *f*
celluloid [séljəlɔɪd] N celuloide *m*
cellulose [séljəlos] N celulosa *f*
cement [sɪmént] N cemento *m*; (glue) adhesivo *m*; — **mixer** hormigonera *f*; VI/VT cementar
cemetery [sémɪteri] N cementerio *m*
censor [sénsɚ] N censor -ora *mf*; VT censurar
censorship [sénsɚʃɪp] N censura *f*
censure [sénʃɚ] N censura *f*; VT censurar
census [sénsəs] N censo *m*; **to take a —** censar
cent [sɛnt] N centavo *m*, céntimo *m*
centennial [senténiəł] ADJ & N centenario *m*
center [séntɚ] N centro *m*; — **of gravity** centro de gravedad *m*; VI/VT centrar(se)
centigrade [séntɪgred] ADJ centígrado
centimeter [séntəmiɾɚ] N centímetro *m*
centipede [séntəpid] N ciempiés *m*
central [séntrəł] ADJ central; (downtown) céntrico; N centro de teléfonos *f*; — **heating** calefacción central *f*; — **nervous system** sistema nervioso central *m*; — **processing unit** unidad central de proceso *f*
Central [séntrəł] ADJ — **African Republic** República Centroafricana *f*; — **America** Centroamérica *f*
centralize [séntrəlaɪz] VI/VT centralizar(se)
centrifugal [sentrífəgəł] ADJ centrífugo
centripetal [sentrípɪdl̩] ADJ centrípeto
century [séntʃəri] N siglo *m*
ceramic [sərǽmɪk] ADJ cerámico; N **—s** cerámica *f*
cereal [sírıəł] N (breakfast food) cereal *m*; (the grain itself) grano *m*; ADJ cereal
cerebral [səríbrəł] ADJ cerebral; — **cortex** corteza cerebral *f*

ceremonial [sɛrəmóniəł] ADJ & M ceremonial
ceremonious [sɛrəmóniəs] ADJ ceremonioso
ceremony [sérəmoni] N ceremonia *f*
certain [sɝ́ tn̩] ADJ seguro; — **rules are inviolable** ciertas reglas son inviolables; **death are taxes are** — lo único seguro son los impuestos y la muerte; **he's — to come** seguro que viene; **it is — that it rained** es cierto que llovió
certainly [sɝ́ tn̩li] ADV (without doubt) sin duda; **she — gets her way** no cabe duda de que se sale con la suya; INTERJ ¡cómo no!
certainty [sɝ́ nti] N certeza *f*, certidumbre *f*
certificate [sətífıkɪt] N certificado *m*; — **of baptism** fe de bautismo *f*; — **of deposit** certificado de depósito *m*
certification [sɝ˞ Dəfıkéʃən] N certificación *f*
certify [sɝ́ Dəfaɪ] VT certificar; **certified check** cheque certificado *m*; **certified mail** correo certificado *m*; **certified public accountant** contador -ora público -ca *mf*
cervix [sɝ́ vɪks] N (neck) cerviz *f*; (uterine) cérvix *m*, cuello uterino *m*
cessation [seséʃən] N cese *m*
cesspool [séspuł] N pozo séptico *m*, fosa séptica *f*
Chad [tʃæd] N Chad *m*
Chadian [tʃǽDiən] ADJ & N chadiano -na *mf*
chafe [tʃef] VI/VT rozar(se); N rozadura *f*
chaff [tʃæf] N ahechaduras *f pl*
chagrin [ʃəgrín] N mortificación *f*; VT mortificar
chain [tʃen] N cadena *f*; — **reaction** reacción en cadena *f*; — **saw** sierra *f*; — **smoker** persona que fuma como una chimenea *f*; — **store** tienda de cadena *f*; VI/VT encadenar(se)
chair [tʃɛr] N silla *f*; (academic) cátedra *f*; (of a meeting) presidente -ta *mf*; (of a department) jefe -fa *mf*; —**man** presidente *m*, director *m*, jefe *m*; —**manship** dirección *f*; —**person** presidente -ta *mf*, jefe -fa *mf*; —**woman** presidenta *f*, jefa *f*
chalk [tʃɔk] N (substance) caliza *f*; (piece) tiza *f*; —**board** pizarrón *m*, pizarra *f*; VT marcar con tiza; **to — up** (attribute) atribuir; (score) marcar
chalky [tʃɔ́ki] ADJ de / con / como tiza
challenge [tʃǽlındʒ] N desafío *m*, reto *m*; (of a jury) recusación *f*; VT (defy) desafiar, retar; (take exception) cuestionar, disputar; (recuse) recusar; **to be vertically —d** ser muy bajito
chamber [tʃémbɚ] N (legislative) cámara *f*;

(in a palace) aposento *m*; (of a cannon) recámara *f*; —**maid** camarera *f*, mucama *f*; — **music** música de cámara *f*; — **of commerce** cámara de comercio *f*; — **pot** orinal *m*; —**s** (of a judge) despacho *m*

chameleon [kəmíljən] N camaleón *m*

chamois [ʃǽmi] N gamuza *f*

champagne [ʃæmpén] N champán *m*, champaña *mf*

champion [tʃǽmpiən] N campeón -ona *mf*; (of a cause) defensor -ra *mf*, paladín *m*; VT defender

championship [tʃǽmpiənʃip] N campeonato *m*

chance [tʃæns] N (opportunity) oportunidad *f*; (probability) probabilidad *f*; (unpredictable element) casualidad *f*, azar *m*; **by** — por casualidad; **game of** — juego de azar *m*; **to take a** — correr riesgo, arriesgarse; ADJ casual; VI arriesgarse; **we** —**d to meet him at the bar** nos encontramos con él en el bar por casualidad

chancellor [tʃǽnsələ] N (chief minister) canciller *m*; (of a university) rector -ora de universidad *mf*

chandelier [ʃændəlír] N araña de luces *f*

change [tʃendʒ] VT cambiar; **to** — **clothes** cambiarse de ropa; **to** — **into** transformar; **to** — **trains** cambiar de tren; N cambio *m*; (money returned) vuelta *f*, *Am* vuelto *m*; (fresh clothes) muda de ropa *f*; — **of heart** cambio de opinión *m*

changeable [tʃéndʒəbəɫ] ADJ (variable) cambiante, variable; (fickle) inconstante, tornadizo; — **silk** seda tornasolada *f*

channel [tʃǽnəɫ] N canal *m*; (bed of stream) cauce *m*; VT canalizar, encauzar

chant [tʃænt] N (plain song) canto llano *m*; (hymn) cántico *m*; (repeated slogan) cantinela *f*; VI/VT (sing) cantar; (repeat a slogan) corear

chaos [kéɑs] N caos *m*

chaotic [keɑ́dɪk] ADJ caótico

chap [tʃæp] VI/VT cuartear(se), agrietar(se); N tipo *m*

chapel [tʃǽpəɫ] N capilla *f*

chaperon, chaperone [ʃǽpəron] N chaperón -ona *f*; VI ir de chaperón -ona

chaplain [tʃǽplɪn] N capellán *m*

chapter [tʃǽptə] N capítulo *m*

char [tʃɑr] VI/VT (reduce to ashes) carbonizar(se); (scorch) chamuscar(se)

character [kǽrɪktə] N carácter *m*; (of a novel) personaje *m*; — **actor** actor de carácter *m*; **Chinese** —**s** caracteres chinos

m pl; **he's quite a** — es todo un personaje; **that's out of** — **for him** eso no es característico de él

characteristic [kærɪktərístɪk] ADJ característico; N característica *f*; (genetic) carácter *m*

characterize [kǽrɪktəraɪz] VT (describe) caracterizar; (attribute) calificar

charade [ʃəréd] N farsa *f*; —**s** charada *f*

charcoal [tʃɑ́rkoɫ] N carbón de leña *m*; — **drawing** dibujo al carbón *m*

charge [tʃɑrdʒ] VT (ask price) cobrar; (load) cargar; (buy on credit) cargar a cuenta; (attack) embestir; **to** — **off a loss** restar una pérdida; **to** — **with a task** encargarle a alguien una tarea; **to** — **with murder** acusar de homicidio; N (mission) misión *f*, encargo *m*; (accusation) cargo *m*, acusación *f*; (charge in account) cargo *m*, débito *m*; (explosives, electricity) carga *f*; (attack) embestida *f*; — **account** cuenta de crédito *f*; — **card** tarjeta de crédito *f*; **there will be a** — **for delivery** se cobra entrega a domicilio; **to be in** — **of** estar a cargo de; **under my** — a mi cargo

charger [tʃɑ́rdʒə] N (for a battery) cargador *m*; (horse) corcel *m*

chariot [tʃǽriət] N carro de guerra *m*

charisma [kərízmə] N carisma *m*

charitable [tʃǽrɪDəbəɫ] ADJ caritativo

charity [tʃǽrɪDi] N (virtue, aid to the poor) caridad *f*; (institution) institución benéfica *f*, institución de beneficencia *f*; **to give to** — dar dinero a las instituciones benéficas; **to live on** — vivir de la caridad

charlatan [ʃɑ́rlətən] N charlatán -ana *mf*

charm [tʃɑrm] N (attractiveness) encanto *m*, salero *m*; (trinket) dije *m*; (spell) sortilegio *m*, hechizo *m*; (amulet) talismán *m*, amuleto *m*; (delight) encanto *m*; (influence) hechizar, subyugar

charming [tʃɑ́rmɪŋ] ADJ encantador, salero; *Sp* majo

chart [tʃɑrt] N (table) tabla *f*; (graph) gráfica *f*; (marine map) carta *f*; (of musical hits) lista de éxitos *f*; VT (in a table) tabular; (in a graph) graficar; (a region) cartografiar; **to** — **a course** trazar una ruta

charter [tʃɑ́rDə] N (of a city) fuero *m*; (of an organization) estatuto *m*; (document granting rights) constitución *f*, carta *f*; (hire) flete *m*; — **flight** (vuelo) chárter *m*; — **member** socio fundador *mf*; VT (a corporation) aprobar los estatutos; (a flight) fletar

chase [tʃes] VT (hunt) cazar; (follow rapidly) perseguir; **to** — **after** correr tras; **to** —

away ahuyentar; N caza *f*, persecución *f*

chasm [kǽzəm] N sima *f*

chassis [tʃǽsi] N chasis *m*, bastidor *m*

chaste [tʃest] ADJ casto, honesto

chastise [tʃǽstaɪz] VT (punish) castigar; (criticize) criticar

chastisement [tʃæstáɪzmənt] N (punishment) castigo *m*; (criticism) crítica *f*

chastity [tʃǽstɪDi] N castidad *f*, honestidad *f*

chat [tʃæt] N charla *f*; *Mex* plática *f*; **— room** chat *m*; VI charlar; *Mex* platicar

chattel [tʃǽdl] N (movable property) bien mueble *m*; (slave) esclavo -va *mf*

chatter [tʃǽDə] VI (jabber) cotorrear, parlotear; VT (click rapidly) castañetear; N (of speech) cotorreo *m*, parloteo *m*; (of teeth) castañeteo *m*; **—box** charlatán -ana *mf*, cotorra *f*

chauffeur [ʃofə] N chófer *m*

chauvinism [ʃóvənɪzəm] N (nationalist) chovinismo *m*; (sexist) machismo *m*

cheap [tʃip] ADJ (costs little) barato; (stingy) avaro; **life is — there** la vida no vale nada allí; **talk is —** hablar no cuesta nada; **to feel —** sentirse despreciable; **— shot** golpe bajo *m*; **—skate** tacaño -ña *mf*

cheapen [tʃípən] VI/VT (lower in price) abaratar(se); VT (lower in esteem) desvalorizar

cheapness [tʃípnɪs] N (low price) baratura *f*; (stinginess) avaricia *f*

cheat [tʃit] N tramposo -sa *mf*, fullero -ra *mf*; VT engañar; **to — at cards** hacer trampa en / a las cartas, trampear; **to — on a test** copiar; **to — on one's spouse** engañar a la pareja de uno

check [tʃɛk] VT (stop) refrenar; (restrain) reprimir; (hand over luggage) facturar; (hand over coat) dejar; (verify) comprobar, verificar; *Am* chequear; (in chess) dar jaque; **to — against** cotejar con; **to — into a hotel** registrarse; **to — into something** averiguar algo; **to — off** puntear; **to — out a book** sacar (prestado) un libro; **to — up on** controlar; **—-up** examen / control médico *m*; **—out counter** caja *f*; **—point** control *m*; **—room** guardarropa *m*; **that —s out** lo hemos comprobado; N (bank) cheque *m*; (means of restraint) control *m*; (ticket) ficha *f*; (mark) marca *f*; (in a restaurant) cuenta *f*; (in fabric) cuadro *m*; (checked fabric) tela a cuadros *f*; (examination) comprobación *f*; (in chess) jaque *m*; **—book** chequera *f*, talonario *m*; **—ing account** cuenta corriente *f*; **—list** lista de control *f*; **—mate** jaque mate *m*; **— stub** talón *m*

checker [tʃékə] N (on a fabric) cuadro *m*; (on a checkerboard) casilla *f*; (game piece) ficha *f*; (cashier) cajero -ra *mf*; (person who checks) verificador -ra *mf*; **— board** tablero *m*; **—s** juego de damas *m*; VT cuadricular; **—ed cloth** tela a cuadros *f*; **—ed past** pasado oscuro *m*

cheek [tʃik] N (on face) mejilla *f*; *Am* cachete *m*; (impudence) descaro *m*; (of buttocks) nalga *f*; **— bone** pómulo *m*

cheer [tʃɪr] N (shout) viva *m*, vítor *m*; (applause) aplausos *m*; (encouragement) ánimo *m*; (joy) alegría *f*; **—leader** animador -ra *mf*; *Am* porrista *mf*; INTERJ **—s!** ¡salud! VI/VT vitorear; **to — on** dar ánimo; **to — up** animar(se)

cheerful [tʃírfəɫ] ADJ (person) risueño, alegre; (room, etc.) alegre

cheerfulness [tʃírfəɫnɪs] N alegría *f*

cheerless [tʃírlɪs] ADJ triste, sombrío

cheese [tʃiz] N queso *m*; **—burger** hamburguesa con queso *f*; **—cake** tarta de queso *f*

cheesy [tʃízi] ADJ (of cheese) de queso; (cheap) barato; (uncool) *Sp* hortera

cheetah [tʃíDə] N guepardo *m*

chef [ʃef] N chef *mf*

chemical [kémɪkəɫ] ADJ químico; **— engineering** ingeniería química *f*; **— warfare** guerra química *f*; N producto químico *m*

chemist [kémɪst] N químico -ca *f*

chemistry [kémɪstri] N química *f*

chemotheraphy [kimoθérəpi] N quimioterapia *f*

cherish [tʃérɪʃ] VT apreciar; **I — the memory of him** tengo muy buenos recuerdos de él

cherry [tʃéri] N cereza *f*; **— tree** cerezo *m*

chess [tʃes] N ajedrez *m*; **—board** tablero de ajedrez *m*

chest [tʃest] N (box) arca *f*; (body part) pecho *m*; **— of drawers** cómoda *f*

chestnut [tʃésnʌt] N castaña *f*; **— tree** castaño *m*; ADJ castaño; (horse) zaino

chew [tʃu] VT (food) masticar; (non-food) mascar; **—ing gum** goma de mascar *f*; *Am* chicle *m*; **to — a hole** hacer un agujero a mordiscones; **to — out** reprender; **to — over** meditar sobre; **to — up** romper a mordiscones; N mascada *f*, bocado *m*

chewy [tʃúi] ADJ correoso

chic [ʃik] ADJ & N chic *m*

chick [tʃik] N (young chicken) pollito *m*; (young bird) pichón *m*; (young woman) *fam* chavala *f*; **—pea** garbanzo *m*

chicken [tʃíkɪn] N gallina *f*; (flesh) pollo *m*; — **coop** gallinero *m*; —-**hearted** cobarde; — **pox** varicela *f*

chicory [tʃíkəri] N achicoria *f*

chide [tʃaɪd] VT regañar

chief [tʃif] N jefe *m*; (of a tribe) cacique *m*; ADJ principal; — **justice** presidente de la Suprema Corte de los Estados Unidos *m*; — **of staff** (military) jefe del estado mayor *m*; (of a division) secretario -ria general *mf*

chieftain [tʃíftən] N cacique *m*

chiffon [ʃɪfán] N chifón *m*

chigger [tʃígɚ] N nigua *f*

chilblain [tʃɪ́tblen] N sabañón *m*

child [tʃaɪld] N (young person) niño -ña *mf*; (offspring) hijo -ja *mf*; —**bearing** en edad de procrear; —**birth** parto *m*, alumbramiento *m*; —**like** infantil, aniñado; —**proof** a prueba de niños; —'**s play** cosa de niños *f*; **to be with** — estar embarazada

childhood [tʃáɪldhʊd] N niñez *f*, infancia *f*

childish [tʃáɪldɪʃ] ADJ infantil, pueril

childless [tʃáɪldlɪs] ADJ sin hijos

Chile [tʃíli] N Chile *m*

Chilean [tʃílɪən] ADJ & N chileno -na *mf*

chili, chile [tʃíli] N (pepper) chile *m*, ají *m*; (meat dish) chile con carne *m*

chill [tʃɪt] N (coldness) frío *m*; (fear, cold with shivering) escalofrío *m*; **it had a —ing effect on the group** le cayó al grupo como un baldazo de agua fría; VI/VT enfriar(se); **to — out** tranquilizarse

chilly [tʃíli] ADJ frío

chime [tʃaɪm] N (sound) repique *m*; (instrument) carillón *m*, carrillón *m*; VI repicar; VT tañer; **to — in** intervenir (en una conversación)

chimney [tʃímni] N chimenea *f*

chimpanzee [tʃɪmpænzí] N chimpancé *m*

chin [tʃɪn] N barbilla *f*, mentón *m*

china [tʃáɪnə] N (material) porcelana *f*, china *f*; (dishes) vajilla de porcelana *f*, china *f*; —**ware** vajilla de porcelana *f*

China [tʃáɪnə] N China *f*

Chinese [tʃaɪníz] ADJ chino; N (inhabitant of China) chino -na *mf*; (language) chino *m*

chink [tʃɪŋk] N grieta *f*

chip [tʃɪp] N (of wood) astilla *f*; (in glass) desportilladura *f*; (in gambling) ficha *f*; (in computers) chip *m*; **he's a — off the old block** de tal palo, tal astilla; **he has a — on his shoulder** guarda resentimientos; VI/VT (wood) astillar(se); (glass, plaster) desportillarse, desconchar(se); (paint) descascarar(se); **to — in** contribuir; **to —**

a tooth romperse un diente

chipmunk [tʃípmʌŋk] N ardilla listada *f*

chiropractic [kaɪrəpræktɪk] ADJ quiropráctico; N quiropráctica *f*

chiropractor [káɪrəpræktɚ] N quiropráctico -ca *mf*

chirp [tʃɝp] N gorjeo *m*; VI/VT piar, gorjear

chisel [tʃízəl] N escoplo *m*; (for stone) cincel *m*; (for wood) formón *m*; VT cincelar; (swindle) estafar

chiseler [tʃízlɚ] N estafador -ra *mf*

chit-chat [tʃíttʃæt] N palique *m*; VI charlar

chivalrous [ʃívəɬrəs] ADJ (of knights) caballeresco; (courteous to women) caballeroso

chivalry [ʃívəɬri] N caballerosidad *f*

chloride [klɔ́raɪd] N cloruro *m*

chlorine [klɔ́rin] N cloro *m*

chloroform [klɔ́rəfɔrm] N cloroformo *m*

chlorophyl, chlorophyll [klɔ́rəfɪɬ] N clorofila *f*

chocolate [tʃáklɪt] N chocolate *m*; (piece) chocolatina *f*; — **pot** chocolatera *f*

choice [tʃɔɪs] N (act of selecting, thing selected) selección *f*; (alternative) opción *f*; **to have no other —** no tener más remedio; ADJ selecto

choir [kwaɪr] N coro *m*

choke [tʃok] VI/VT (suffocate) ahogar(se); (strangle) estrangular(se); (on food) atragantarse, atorarse; (obstruct) tapar(se); VI (in sports) bloquearse; **I'm all —d up** estoy muy conmovido; **to — back / down** contener; N (act of choking on something) atragantamiento *m*; (act of choking someone) estrangulación *f*; (device in cars) obturador *m*; (in sports) bloqueo *m*

cholera [kálə·ə] N cólera *m*

cholesterol [kəléstərɔ̀ɬ] N colesterol *m*

choose [tʃuz] VI/VT elegir, seleccionar, escoger; **to — to** optar por

choosy [tʃúzi] ADJ quisquilloso

chop [tʃap] VI/VT cortar; **to — down** talar; **to — off** mochar, tronchar; **to — up** picar; N (act of chopping) golpe *m*; (cut of meat) chuleta *f*; —**s** morro *m*; —**stick** palillo *m*

choppy [tʃápi] ADJ picado, agitado

choral [kɔ́rəɬ] ADJ coral

chord [kɔrd] N (mathematical) cuerda *f*; (musical) acorde *m*; **it struck a — in me** me conmovió

chore [tʃɔr] N tarea *f*, faena *f*, quehacer *m*; **it's such a —** es un trabajo asqueroso

choreography [kɔriágrəfi] N coreografía *f*

chorus [kɔ́rəs] N coro *m*

chosen [tʃózən] ADJ **my — profession** la profesión de mi preferencia; **the — one** el elegido, la elegida

christen [krísən] VT bautizar

Christendom [krísəndəm] N cristianismo *m*

christening [krísənɪŋ] N bautizo *m*, bautismo *m*

Christian [krístʃən] ADJ & N cristiano -na *mf*; **— name** nombre de pila *m*

Christianity [krɪstʃiǽnɪɒi] N cristianismo *m*

Christmas [krísməs] N Navidad *f*, Pascua de Navidad *f*; ADJ navideño; **— card** tarjeta de Navidad *f*; **— Eve** Nochebuena *f*; **— gift** regalo de Navidad *m*; **— tree** árbol de Navidad *m*

chrome [krom] N cromo *m*; ADJ cromado

chromium [krómiəm] N cromo *m*

chromosome [króməsom] N cromosoma *m*

chronic [kránɪk] ADJ crónico

chronicle [kránɪkəł] N crónica *f*; VT registrar

chronological [kranłádʒɪkəł] ADJ cronológico

chronology [krənáləʤi] N cronología *f*

chronometer [krənámɪɒə-] N cronómetro *m*

chrysalis [krísəlɪs] N crisálida *f*

chrysanthemum [krɪsǽnθəməm] N crisantemo *m*

chubby [tʃʌ́bi] ADJ rechoncho, gordito

chuck [tʃʌk] N (cut of meat) paletilla *f*; VT (to throw) lanzar; (to discard) tirar, botar

chuckle [tʃʌ́kəł] N risita *f*; VI reírse levemente

chum [tʃʌm] N compinche *mf*

chunk [tʃʌŋk] N trozo *m*, pedazo *m*; **a — of cash** un montón de plata

church [tʃɝtʃ] N iglesia *f*; **—man** clérigo *m*

churn [tʃɝn] N mantequera *f*; VI/VT (make butter) batir; (agitate) agitar, revolver

CIA (Central Intelligence Agency) [siaɪé] N CIA *f*

cicada [sɪkéɒə] N chicharra *f*

cider [sáɪɒə-] N (alcoholic) sidra *f*; (non-alcoholic) *Am* jugo de manzana *m*; *Sp* zumo de manzana *m*

cigar [sɪgár] N puro *m*, habano *m*; **— store** tabaquería *f*; **close, but no —** bien, pero te quedaste corto

cigarette [sɪgərét] N cigarrillo *m*; *Sp* pitillo *m*; *Am* cigarro *m*; **— case** cigarrera *f*; *Sp* pitillera *f*; **— holder** boquilla *f*; **— lighter** encendedor *m*

cinch [sɪntʃ] N (for a saddle) cincha *f*; (something easy) pan comido *m*; (favorite) favorito -ta *mf*; VT cinchar

cinder [síndə-] N ceniza *f*, rescoldo *m*

cinema [sínəmə] N cine *m*

cinnamon [sínəmən] N canela *f*; **— tree** canelo *f*

cipher [sáɪfə-] N cifra *f*, guarismo *m*; VI/VT cifrar(se)

circle [sɝ́kəł] N círculo *m*; (literary) ámbito *m*, círculo *m*; VT (draw a circle) encerrar en un círculo; VI (go around) dar una vuelta

circuit [sɝ́kɪt] N circuito *m*; **— board** circuito impreso *m*; **— breaker** cortacircuitos *m*

circuitry [sɝ́kɪtri] N circuitería *f*

circular [sɝ́kjələ-] ADJ circular; **— saw** sierra circular *f*; N circular *f*

circulate [sɝ́kjəlet] VI circular; VT (to pass around) poner en circulación

circulation [sɝkjəléʃən] N circulación *f*

circulatory system [sɝ́kjələtɔrisɪstəm] N aparato circulatorio *m*

circumcise [sɝ́kəmsaɪz] VT circuncidar

circumference [sɚkámfə-əns] N circunferencia *f*

circumlocution [sɝkəmlokjúʃən] N circunlocución *f*, rodeo *m*

circumscribe [sɝkəmskráɪb] VT circunscribir

circumspect [sɝ́kəmspɛkt] ADJ circunspecto

circumstance [sɝ́kəmstæns] N circunstancia *f*; **—s** condiciones financieras *f pl*

circumstantial [sɝkəmstǽnʃəł] ADJ circunstancial; **— evidence** pruebas circunstanciales *f pl*

circumvent [sɝkəmvént] VT evitar, obviar

circus [sɝ́kəs] N circo *m*

cirrhosis [sɪrósɪs] N cirrosis *f*

cirrus [sírəs] N cirro *m*

cistern [sístə-n] N cisterna *f*, aljibe *m*

citadel [síɒəɒəł] N ciudadela *f*

citation [saɪtéʃən] N (summons) citación *f*; (quote, quotation) cita *f*; (commendation for bravery) mención *f*

cite [saɪt] VT (quote, summon) citar; (comment on) mencionar

citizen [síɒɪzən] N (of a nation) ciudadano -na *mf*; (of a city or region) habitante *mf*

citizenship [síɒɪzənʃɪp] N ciudadanía *f*

citrus [sítrəs] ADJ & N cítrico *m*

city [síɒi] N ciudad *f*; ADJ municipal, urbano; **— council** concejo *m*; **— hall** ayuntamiento *m*; **— planning** urbanismo *m*

civic [sívɪk] ADJ cívico; N **—s** educación cívica *f*

civil [sívəł] ADJ (civilian) civil; (polite) cortés; **— disobedience** desobediencia civil *f*; **— engineer** ingeniero -ra civil *mf*; **— rights** derechos civiles *m pl*; **— service** administración pública *f*; **— war** guerra civil *f*

civilian [sɪvíljən] ADJ & N civil *mf*

civility [sɪvílɪɒi] N civilidad *f*, cortesía *f*

civilization [sıvəlızéʃən] N civilización *f*

civilize [sívəlaız] VT civilizar

clad [klæd] ADJ vestido

claim [klem] VT (demand) reclamar, reivindicar; (assert) sostener, pretender; (notify of the existence of) denunciar; **to — to be** pretender ser; N (demand) reclamación *f*, reclamo *m*; (assertion) afirmación *f*; (right) derecho *m*, título *m*; (on insurance) demanda *f*, denuncia *f*

claimant [klémənt] N demandante *mf*, reclamante *mf*; (to the throne) pretendiente *mf*

clairvoyant [klɛrvóıənt] ADJ & N clarividente *mf*

clam [klæm] N almeja *f*; VI **to — up** callarse

clamber [klǽmbə-] VI/VT (climb with effort) trepar con dificultad; (climb on all fours) subir gateando

clammy [klǽmi] ADJ frío y húmedo

clamor [klǽmə-] N clamor *m*, vocerío *m*; VI clamar, vociferar

clamorous [klǽmə-əs] ADJ clamoroso

clamp [klæmp] N (support) grapa *f*; (vice) tornillo *m*; (wrap-around) abrazadera *f*; VT sujetar; **to — down on** reprimir

clan [klæn] N clan *m*

clandestine [klændéstın] ADJ clandestino

clang [klæŋ] VI sonar; N sonido metálico *m*

clap [klæp] N (tap) palmada *f*; (blow) golpe seco *m*; (gonorrhea) gonorrea *f*; **— of thunder** trueno *m*; VT (on the back) palmear; (in approval) aplaudir; (a book) cerrar de golpe; **to — in jail** meter en la cárcel

clapper [klǽpə-] N badajo *m*

clarification [klærəfıkéʃən] N aclaración *f*

clarify [klǽrəfaı] VT aclarar, clarificar

clarinet [klærənét] N clarinete *m*

clarity [klǽrıɾi] N claridad *f*

clash [klæʃ] N (noise) estruendo metálico *m*; (collision) choque *m*; (conflict) conflicto *m*, enfrentamiento *m*; VI/VT (collide) chocar; (oppose, fight) enfrentarse a; (not go with) no combinar, no pegar

clasp [klæsp] N (fastener) broche *m*, cierre *m*; (grip) apretón *m*; VT (fasten) abrochar; (grip) apretar; (embrace) abrazar, prender

class [klæs] N clase *f*; (graduation class) promoción *f*, graduación *f*; **in a — by itself** único; **—mate** compañero -ra de clase *mf*, condiscípulo -la *mf*; **—room** salón de clase *m*, aula *f*; **— struggle** lucha de clases *f*; VI/VT clasificar(se)

classic [klǽsık] ADJ & N clásico -ca *mf*

classical [klǽsıkəł] ADJ clásico

classicism [klǽsəsızəm] N clasicismo *m*

classification [klæsəfıkéʃən] N clasificación *f*

classify [klǽsəfaı] VT clasificar; N **classified ad** anuncio clasificado *m*

clatter [klǽɾə-] N (noise) estrépito *m*; (movement) traqueteo *m*; VI (make noise) causar estrépito; (move) traquetear

clause [klɔz] N cláusula *f*

claustrophobia [klɔstrəfóbiə] N claustrofobia *f*

claustrophobic [klɔstrəfóbık] ADJ claustrofóbico

clavicle [klǽvıkəł] N clavícula *f*

claw [klɔ] N (of a bear) garra *f*, zarpa *f*; (of a cat) uña *f*; (of a crab) pinza *f*; (of a hammer) orejas *f pl*; VI/VT arañar; **they —ed their way through** se abrieron paso con las uñas

clay [kle] N arcilla *f*; (for ceramics) greda *f*

clean [klin] ADJ limpio; (free from impurities, not ornate) puro; (honorable) decente; **—-cut** (person) acicalado; (concept) bien definido; **— joke** broma inocente *f*; **—-shaven** afeitado; **—up** limpieza *f*; **he has a — record** no tiene antecedentes; **you'd better come —** deberías confesar; VI/VT limpiar; **he —ed me out** me limpió, me desvalijó; **to — out something** vaciar algo; **to — up** (a room) limpiar, asear; (a document) pasar en limpio; (get rich) forrarse

cleaner [klínə-] N limpiador -ra *mf*; **—s** tintorería *f*

cleanliness [klénlinıs] N limpieza *f*; (personal) aseo *m*

cleanse [klɛnz] VT limpiar

cleanser [klénzə-] N limpiador *m*

clear [klir] ADJ claro; (skin, conscience) limpio; (sky) despejado; (path) libre; **—-cut** (clearly defined) bien definido; (obvious) claro; **—-headed** lúcido; **— profit** ganancia neta *f*; **to be in the — estar libre de culpa; **to keep — of someone** evitar a alguien; **to pass — through** pasar de lado a lado; VT (the mind, confusion, voice) aclarar(se); (a road, one's reputation, computer screen) limpiar; (of criminal charges) absolver; (of suspicion) eximir; (liquid) clarificar; (a legislative bill, plan) aprobar, obtener autorización para; (land for farming) desmontar; (a hurdle) salvar; (a net gain) sacar; **to — the air** sincerarse; **to — the table** levantar la mesa; **to — up** (a mystery) aclarar(se); (the sky) despejar(se)

clearance [klírəns] N (space) espacio libre *m*; (vertical) margen de altura *m*; (permission) autorización *f*; **— sale** liquidación *f*

clearing [klírɪŋ] N (terrain) claro *m*; (of checks) clearing *m*; — **house** banco de compensación *m*

cleavage [klívɪʤ] N (cut) hendidura *f*; (in dress) escote *m*

cleave [kliv] VT hender(se); **to** — **to** adherirse a

cleaver [klívɚ] N cuchilla *f*

clef [klɛf] N clave *f*

cleft [klɛft] N hendidura *f*; ADJ hendido, partido; — **palate** paladar hendido *m*

clemency [klɛ́mənsi] N clemencia *f*

clench [klɛntʃ] VT agarrar, asir; (teeth, fist) apretar

clergy [klɝ́ʤi] N clero *m*, clerecía *f*; —**man** clérigo *m*, pastor *m*; —**woman** pastora *f*

clerical [klɛ́rɪkəł] ADJ (of the clergy) clerical, eclesiástico; (of office personnel) de oficina; — **error** error de copia *m*; — **work** trabajo de escritorio *m*

clerk [klɝk] N (sales) dependiente -ta *mf*; (office) empleado -da de oficina *mf*; (court) escribiente *mf*, actuario -ria *mf*; VI trabajar como actuario -ria

clever [klɛ́vɚ] ADJ (ingenious) ingenioso; (smart) listo, vivo; (dexterous) habilidoso

cleverness [klɛ́vɚnɪs] N (intelligence) inteligencia *f*, viveza *f*; (ingenuity) ingenio *m*; (dexterity) habilidad *f*

cliché [kliʃé] N cliché *m*, muletilla *f*; *Sp* tópico *m*

click [klɪk] N clic *m*, chasquido *m*; (sound of heels) taconeo *m*; VI chascar; (on a computer) hacer clic; (heels) taconear; VT chascar, chasquear

client [kláɪənt] N (of professional or store) cliente -ta *mf*; (of social service) beneficiario -ria *mf*

clientele [klaɪəntéł] N clientela *f*

cliff [klɪf] N precipicio *m*, despeñadero *m*; (by the sea) acantilado *m*

climate [kláɪmɪt] N clima *m*

climax [kláɪmæks] N clímax *m*; VI culminar, alcanzar el clímax

climb [klaɪm] N (ascent) subida *f*; (in alpinism) escalada *f*; VI/VT (ascend) subir; (ascend with effort) trepar(se) (a), encaramar(se) (a); VT (a mountain, wall) escalar; **to** — **down** bajar

climber [kláɪmɚ] N (in alpinism) escalador -ora *mf*; (plant) trepadora *f*

clinch [klɪntʃ] VT (resolve) rematar; (hammer down) remachar; (hug, in boxing) trabar; (secure) sujetar; (finalize) cerrar; N (nail) remache *m*; (embrace) abrazo *m*; (in boxing) clinch *m*

cling [klɪŋ] VI (to stick to) pegarse; (to hold onto) aferrarse

clinic [klínɪk] N clínica *f*; (workshop) taller *m*

clink [klɪŋk] N tintín *m*; VI tintinear

clip [klɪp] VT (cut) cortar; (trim) recortar; (shear) esquilar; (shorten) acortar; (hit) tocar; (fasten) abrochar; (attach paper) sujetar con un clip; N (fastener) gancho *m*; (for paper) clip *m*; (of cartridge) cargador *m*; (brooch) broche *m*

clipper [klípɚ] N (shearer) esquilador -ra *mf*; —**s** (scissors) tijeras *f pl*; (hair trimmer) maquinilla *f*

clipping [klípɪŋ] N recorte *m*

clique [klɪk] N (political) camarilla *f*; (in school) pandilla *f*

clitoris [klítəɹɪs] N clítoris *m*

cloak [klok] N capa *f*; (military) capote *m*; —**room** guardarropa *m*; VT (put a cloak on) vestirse con una capa; (hide) encubrir

clock [klɑk] N reloj *m*; —-**making** relojería *f*; — **radio** radio reloj *f*; —**work** maquinaria de reloj *f*; **like** —**work** con precisión, sin falta; VT **you swim and I'll** — **you** tú nadas y yo te tomo el tiempo; **the police** —**ed him at 90 mph** la policía lo pescó haciendo noventa millas por hora

clockwise [klákwaɪz] ADV en el sentido de las manecillas de reloj

clod [klɑd] N (piece of dirt) terrón *m*, pelotón *m*; (dolt) tonto -ta *mf*, necio -cia *mf*

clog [klɑg] VI/VT obstruir(se), tapar(se); N (shoe) zueco *m*; — **dance** baile zapateado *m*

cloister [klɔ́ɪstɚ] N claustro *m*; (monastery) monasterio *m*; VT enclaustrar

clone [klon] N clon *m*; VT clonar

cloning [klónɪŋ] N clonaje *m*, clonación *f*

close [kloz] VI/VT cerrar(se); VT (a hole) tapar; **to** — **an account** cerrar una cuenta; **to** — **a meeting** levantar una sesión; **to** — **in upon** (oppress) oprimir; (approach) cercar a uno; **to** — **out** liquidar; N fin *m*; (act of closing) cierre *m*; —**out** saldo *m*; [klos] ADJ (near) cercano; (dense) tupido; (intimate) íntimo; — **attention** mucha atención *f*; —-**fought** reñido; —-**knit** muy unido; — **questioning** interrogatorio minucioso *m*; — **translation** traducción fiel *f*; —**up** primer plano *m*; **at** — **range** de cerca; **that was a** — **call** nos salvamos por poco; ADV cerca

closed [klozd] ADJ cerrado; — **circuit** circuito cerrado *m*; —-**minded** cerrado; —-**mindedness** cerrazón *f*

closeness [klósnɪs] N cercanía *f*; (friendship)

intimidad *f*; (correctness) fidelidad *f*

closet [klázɪt] N ropero *m*, armario *m*; VI enclaustrarse; ADJ a escondidas

closure [klóʒɚ] N (conclusion) cierre *m*; (sense of completeness) clausura *f*

clot [klɑt] VI/VT coagular(se); N coágulo *m*, cuajarón *m*

cloth [klɔθ] N tela *f*, tejido *m*; (wool) paño *m*; ADJ de tela; — **bound** encuadernado en tela; **man of the** — clérigo *m*

clothe [kloð] VT vestir; N —**s** ropa *f*; —**sline** tendedero *m*; —**spin** pinza *f*

clothier [klóðjɚ] N comerciante en ropa o paño *mf*

clothing [klóðɪŋ] N ropa *f*

cloud [klaʊd] N nube *f*; —**burst** chaparrón *m*, aguacero *m*; VT nublar, anublar; (make indistinct, place under suspicion) enturbiar; **to** — **up** nublarse, anublarse; **to be on** — **nine** estar en el séptimo cielo; **under a** — bajo sospecha

cloudless [kláʊdlɪs] ADJ despejado

cloudy [kláʊdi] ADJ nublado; *Sp* nuboso; (gloomy) sombrío

clout [klaʊt] N influencia *f*

clove [klov] N clavo *m*; — **of garlic** diente de ajo *m*

cloven [klóvən] ADJ hendido; —-**hoofed** patihendido

clover [klóvɚ] N trébol *m*; —**leaf** trébol *m*; **to be in** — vivir en el lujo

clown [klaʊn] N payaso *m*; VI payasear, bufonear

cloy [klɔɪ] VI/VT (to satiate) hastiar; (to be too sweet for) repugnar

club [klʌb] N (society, nightclub) club *m*; (stick) porra *f*, garrote *m*; (suit of cards) basto *m*; —**house** casa de club *f*; VT aporrear

cluck [klʌk] VI cloquear; N cloqueo *m*

clue [klu] N pista *f*, indicio *m*; **to have no** — no tener ni noción

clueless [klúlɪs] ADJ (absent-minded) despistado; (uninformed) en ayunas

clump [klʌmp] N (of bushes) matorral *m*; (of trees) arboleda *f*; VI/VT apiñar(se)

clumsiness [klámzinɪs] N torpeza *f*

clumsy [klámzi] ADJ torpe, desmañado, chambón; *Sp* patoso

clunker [klʌ́ŋkɚ] N cacharro *m*

cluster [klʌ́stɚ] N grupo *m*; (of grapes) racimo *m*; VI/VT agrupar(se), arracimar(se)

clutch [klʌtʃ] N (in a car) embrague *m*; — **pedal** pedal del embrague *m*; **to step on the** — pisar el embrague; —**es** garras *f pl*; VT (seize) asir; (hold) apretar

clutter [klʌ́Dɚ] VT **books —ed her desk**

tenía libros desparramados por todo el escritorio; N desparramo *m*, desorden *m*, confusión *f*

coach [kotʃ] N (carriage) coche *m*, carruaje *m*, carroza *f*; (bus) autobús *m*; (trainer) entrenador -ra *mf*; (in air travel) clase turista *f*; (tutor) profesor -ra particular *mf*; —**man** cochero *m*; VI/VT entrenar

coagulate [koǽgjəlet] VI/VT coagular(se)

coal [kołl] N carbón *m*; — **bin** carbonera *f*; — **tar** alquitrán *m*

coalition [koəlíʃən] N coalición *f*

coarse [kɔrs] ADJ (fabric) burdo, basto; (sand) grueso; (manners, language) grosero, tosco, rudo

coarseness [kɔ́rsnɪs] N (fabric) bastedad *f*; (language, manners) tosquedad *f*, rudeza *f*; (of a joke) chocarrería *f*

coast [kost] N costa *f*; — **Guard** Guardia Costera *f*; —**line** costa *f*; —-**to**-— de costa a costa; VI (on a sled) deslizar(se); (in a car, on a bike) tirarse por una bajada; **he —ed through medical school** la Facultad de Medicina le resultó muy fácil

coastal [kóstəł] ADJ costero

coat [kot] N abrigo *m*; (of paint) capa *f*, mano *f*; (on animals) pelaje *m*; — **of arms** escudo de armas *m*, blasón *m*; — **rack** percha *f*, perchero *m*; —**tail** faldón *m*; VT cubrir; (with paint) dar una mano a; (with grease) engrasar; (with soap) enjabonar; (with sugar) bañar

coax [koks] VT persuadir con halagos, engatusar

cob [kɑb] N mazorca *f*, panoja *f*; —**web** telaraña *f*

cobalt [kóbɔłt] N cobalto *m*

cobbler [kɑ́blɚ] N (person who repairs shoes) zapatero -ra *mf*, remendón -ona *mf*; (dessert) budín de bizcocho y fruta *m*

cobblestone [kɑ́bəłston] N adoquín *m*

cobra [kóbrə] N cobra *f*

cocaine [kokén] N cocaína *f*

cock [kɑk] N (rooster) gallo *m*; (male bird) macho de ave de corral *m*; (faucet) llave *f*; (gun part) martillo *m*; (penis) *vulg* polla *f*, pija *f*; —**fight** riña de gallos *f*; —**pit** (for cockfights) gallera *f*; (in an airplane) cabina *f*; —**scomb** cresta de gallo *f*; —**sure** gallito; VT (a gun) amartillar; (one's head) ladear

cock-a-doodle-doo [kákədudłdú] INTERJ quiquiriquí

cockatoo [kákətu] N cacatúa *f*

cocker spaniel [kákɚspǽnjəł] N cócker *m*

cockroach [kákrotʃ] N cucaracha *f*

cocktail [kákteł] N cóctel *m*; — **party**

cóctel *m*

cocky [káki] ADJ gallito, valentón

cocoa [kóko] N (powder) cacao *m*; (drink) chocolate *m*

coconut [kókənʌt] N coco *m*

cocoon [kəkún] N capullo *m*

cod [kɑd] N *Sp* abadejo *m*; *Am* bacalao *m*; **—-liver oil** aceite de hígado de bacalao *m*

coddle [kádļ] VT mimar

code [kod] N código *m*; **— switching** alternancia de códigos *f*

codeine [kódin] N codeína *f*

codger [kádʒɚ] N vejete *m*, vejancón *m*

codify [kádəfaɪ] VT codificar

coed [kóɛd] ADJ mixto; N alumna universitaria *f*

coefficient [koəfíʃənt] N coeficiente *m*

coerce [koɚ́s] VT forzar, obligar

coercion [koɚ́ʒən] N coacción *f*

coexistence [koɪgzístəns] N coexistencia *f*

coffee [kɔ́fi] N café *m*; **— bean** grano de café *m*; **— break** descanso para tomar el café *m*; **— bush** cafeto *m*; **— maker** máquina de café *f*, cafetera *f*; **—pot** cafetera *f*; **— shop** (for coffee) café *m*; (for coffee and light meals) cafetería *f*; **— table** mesa baja *f*

coffer [kɔ́fɚ] N cofre *m*

coffin [kɔ́fɪn] N ataúd *m*, féretro *m*

cog [kɑg] N diente *m*; **—wheel** rueda dentada *f*

cogent [kódʒənt] ADJ convincente

cognac [kánjæk] N coñac *m*

cognate [kágnet] ADJ & N cognado *m*

cognitive [kágnɪdɪv] ADJ cognitivo

cohabitate [kohǽbɪtet] VI cohabitar

coherent [kohírənt] ADJ coherente; (sticking together) cohesivo

cohesion [kohíʒən] N cohesión *f*

coiffure [kwɑfjúr] N peinado *m*

coil [kɔɪl] VI/VT arrollar(se), enrollar(se); (snake) enroscar(se); N (roll) rollo *m*; (spiral) tirabuzón *m*; (electric) bobina *f*; **— spring** muelle en espiral *m*

coin [kɔɪn] N moneda *f*; **—-operated** de monedas; VT acuñar (also words)

coinage [kɔ́ɪnɪdʒ] N acuñación *f* (also of words)

coincide [koɪnsáɪd] VI coincidir

coincidence [koínsɪdəns] N coincidencia *f*, casualidad *f*

coitus [kóɪdəs] N coito *m*

coke [kok] N (coal) cok *m*, coque *m*; (cocaine) *fam* coca *f*

cola [kólə] N gaseosa *f*

colander [káləndɚ] N colador *m*

cold [koɫd] ADJ frío; **— cream** cold cream *m*;

— cuts fiambres *m pl*; **— fish** *fam* témpano *m*; **— snap** ola de frío *f*; **— sore** herpes *m sg*; **— war** guerra fría *f*; **to be —** tener frío; **to be out —** quedar seco; **it is — today** hace frío hoy; **he gave me the — shoulder** me hizo el vacío; **he quit — turkey** dejó de un día para otro; **he got — feet** se acobardó; N frío *m*; (illness) resfrío *m*, resfriado *m*, catarro *m*; **to catch a —** resfriarse

coldness [kóɫdnɪs] N frialdad *f*

colic [kálɪk] N cólico *m*

coliseum [kɑlɪsíəm] N coliseo *m*

collaborate [kəlǽbəret] VI colaborar

collaboration [kəlæbəréʃən] N colaboración *f*

collaborator [kəlǽbəreɾɚ] N colaborador -ora *mf*

collage [kəláʒ] N collage *m*

collagen [kálədʒən] N colágeno *m*

collapse [kəlǽps] VI (fold into sections) plegarse; (cave in) hundirse, derrumbarse; (fail) fracasar; (faint) desmayarse; (empty of air, decline in value) colapsar(se); N (falling in) derrumbe *m*, derrumbamiento *m*, desplome *m*; (breakdown) colapso *m*

collar [kálɚ] N (for restraining dogs, marking on an animal, necklace) collar *m*; (of a shirt) cuello *m*; **—bone** clavícula *f*; VT acollarar; (grab by the neck) agarrar por el cuello; **I was —ed by the boss** el jefe me agarró de charla

collate [kólet] VT (put in order) colacionar; (compare) cotejar

collateral [kəlǽɾɚəɫ] ADJ (on the side) colateral; (auxiliary) subsidiario; N garantía subsidiaria *f*

colleague [kálig] N colega *mf*

collect [kəlékt] VT (gather) recoger; (make a collection) coleccionar; (receive taxes) recaudar; VI/VT (receive payment) cobrar, percibir; (assemble) reunir(se); (accumulate) acumular(se); **to — oneself** calmarse; **— on delivery** pago contra reembolso *m*; **— call** llamada de cobro revertido *f*, llamada por / a cobrar *f*

collection [kəlékʃən] N (set of collectibles, clothes) colección *f*; (for charity) colecta *f*; (of taxes) recaudación *f*, cobranza *f*, cobro *m*; (of data, fruit) recolección *f*

collective [kəléktɪv] N & ADJ colectivo *m*; **— bargaining** convenio colectivo *m*

collector [kəléktɚ] N (of taxes) recaudador -ra *mf*; (of collectibles) coleccionista *mf*; (of other things) colector -ora *mf*

college [kálɪdʒ] N (institution) universidad *f*; (division) facultad *f*; (association) colegio *m*; **let's give it the old — try** vamos a hacer un esfuerzo supremo

collegial [kəlíʤəł] ADJ cooperador

collegiate [kəlíʤɪt] ADJ universitario

collide [kəláɪd] VI/VT chocar

collie [káli] N collie *m*

collision [kəlíʒən] N colisión *f*, choque *m*

colloid [kálɔɪd] N coloide *m*

colloquial [kəlókwiəł] ADJ coloquial; **—expression** frase familiar *f*

colloquium [kəlókwiəm] N coloquio *m*, jornada *f*

collusion [kəlúʒən] N confabulación *f*

cologne [kəlón] N colonia *f*

Colombia [kəlámbiə] N Colombia *f*

Colombian [kəlámbiən] ADJ & N colombiano -na *mf*

colon [kólən] N (punctuation) dos puntos *m pl*; (bowels) colon *m*; [kəlón] (currency of El Salvador and Costa Rica) colón *m*

colonel [kə́·nəł] N coronel *m*

colonial [kəlóniəł] ADJ colonial

colonist [kálənɪst] N (settler) colono *m*; (colonizer) colonizador -ra *mf*

colonization [kalənɪzéʃən] N colonización *f*

colonize [kálənaɪz] VT colonizar

colony [káləni] N colonia *f*

color [kálə˞] N color *m*; (colorfulness) colorido *m*; **the —s** la bandera; **he showed his true —s** se mostró tal cual era; **persons of —** gente de color *f*; **a — TV** un televisor en / a color; ADJ **—-blind** daltónico; **—fast** de colores firmes; VT (give color) colorear; (make colorful) dar colorido; (taint) teñir; (blush) ruborizarse

colored [kálə˞d] ADJ coloreado; (biased) sesgado

colorful [kálə˞fəł] ADJ (full of color) colorido; (eccentric) pintoresco

coloring [kálə˞ɪŋ] N (tone) colorido *m*; (action) coloración *f*; (substance) colorante *m*

colorless [kálə˞lɪs] ADJ (without color) incoloro; (bleached) descolorido

colossal [kəlásəł] ADJ colosal

colt [kołt] N potro *m*

column [káləm] N columna *f*

columnist [káləmnɪst] N columnista *mf*

coma [kómə] N coma *m*

comatose [kámətos] ADJ comatoso

comb [kom] N (for hair) peine *m*; (of a rooster) cresta *f*; (for wool) carda *f*; (for horses) almohaza *f*; (of honey) panal *m*; VT (hair) peinar; (wool) cardar; (search an area) peinar, batir; **to — one's hair** peinarse

combat [kámbæt] VI/VT combatir; N combate *m*

combatant [kəmbǽtn̩t] ADJ & N combatiente *mf*

combative [kəmbǽDɪv] ADJ combativo

combination [kambənéʃən] N combinación *f*; **— lock** cerradura de combinación *f*

combine [kəmbáɪn] VI/VT combinar(se); [kámbaɪn] N cosechadora *f*

combo [kámbo] N combo *m*

combustible [kəmbástəbəł] ADJ & N combustible *m*

combustion [kəmbástʃən] N combustión *f*

come [kʌm] VI venir; (have an orgasm) *fam* venirse; *Sp fam* correrse; **an idea came to me** se me ocurrió una idea; **Christmas is coming** llega la Navidad; **milk —s from cows** la leche se saca de las vacas; **no harm will — to you** no te va a pasar nada; **the dress —s to her knees** el vestido le llega a las rodillas; **to — about** suceder; **to — across** (find) encontrar; (make an impression) parecer; **to — along** (accompany) acompañar; (appear) surgir; **how's your paper coming along?** ¿cómo va tu trabajo? **to — again** volver, volver a venir; **to — at** venirse encima; **to — back** volver; **to make a —back** resurgir; (in sports) recuperarse; **to — down with a cold** cogerse un resfriado; **to — downstairs** bajar; **to — from** ser de; **to — in** entrar; **to — off** salir(se); **to — out** salir; **to — over** venir para acá; **to — to** volver en sí; **to — together** (meet) juntarse, unirse; (reach agreement) ponerse de acuerdo; **to — up** subir; **your name came up** tu nombre vino a colación; N (semen) *vulg* leche *f*; **—back** (reply) réplica *f*; (in sports) recuperación *f*

comedian [kəmíɾiən] N cómico -ca *mf*, comediante *m*

comedy [kámədi] N (genre) comedia *f*; (profession) humorismo *m*

comet [kámɪt] N cometa *m*

comfort [kámfə˞t] VT reconfortar; N (feeling of ease) comodidad *f*, confort *m*, holgura *f*; (solace) consuelo *m*

comfortable [kámfə˞Dəbəł] ADJ cómodo, confortable; **— income** buen pasar *m*; **— life** vida holgada / desahogada *f*

comforter [kámfə˞Də˞] N edredón *m*

comic [kámɪk] ADJ cómico, chistoso, gracioso; **— book** revista de historietas *f*, comic *m*; **—s** tiras cómicas *f pl*, historietas *f pl*; **— strip** tira cómica *f*

comical [kámɪkəł] ADJ cómico, gracioso

coming [kámɪŋ] N venida *f*; **— of Christ** advenimiento de Cristo *m*; **—s and**

goings idas y venidas *f pl*; ADJ que viene, próximo

comma [kámə] N coma *f*

command [kəmǽnd] VT (order) mandar; (have authority over) comandar; **to —respect** inspirar respeto, imponerse; N (order) mandato *m*, orden *f*; (post) comandancia *f*; (dominance) dominio *m*; (on a computer) comando *m*; **he has a good — of English** domina bien el inglés; **to be in — of** estar al mando de; **to be under the — of** estar al mando de; **at your —** a sus órdenes

commandeer [kaməndír] VT apoderarse de; (for the military) requisar

commander [kəmǽndə] N (leader) jefe -fa *mf*; (army officer) comandante *mf*; (navy officer) capitán de fragata *m*; **— in chief** comandante en jefe *mf*

commandment [kəmǽndmənt] N mandamiento *m*

commemorate [kəmémərət] VT conmemorar

commence [kəméns] VI/VT comenzar, principiar

commencement [kəménsmənt] N (beginning) comienzo *m*; (graduation) graduación *f*, colación *f*

commend [kəménd] VT (praise) alabar; (entrust) encomendar

commendation [kaməndéʃən] N (praise) alabanza *f*; (mention) mención de honor *f*

commensurate [kəménsəɹɪt] ADJ proporcional, acorde

comment [kámɛnt] N comentario *m*; **no —** sin comentarios; VI/VT comentar

commentary [kámənteri] N comentario *m*

commentator [kámənteɒ] N (person who describes) comentador -ra *mf*; (on radio, etc.) comentarista *mf*

commerce [kámɚs] N comercio *m*

commercial [kəmɚ́ʃəł] ADJ comercial; N (on radio or television) anuncio *m*

commercialize [kəmɚ́ʃəlaɪz] VT comercializar

commiserate [kəmízəret] VI/VT compadecerse de

commiseration [kəmɪzəréʃən] N conmiseración *f*

commissary [kámɪseri] N economato *m*

commission [kəmíʃən] N (act, committee, payment) comisión *f*; (of a broker) corretaje *m*; (charge) encargo *m*; (mission) misión *f*; (title) nombramiento *m*; **to be in —** estar en servicio; **to be out of —** estar fuera de servicio; **to put out of —** (object) inutilizar; (person) retirar de servicio; VT (authorize) comisionar; (order)

encargar; (appoint) nombrar; (get ready) poner en servicio; **—ed officer** oficial *m*

commissioner [kəmíʃənə] N comisario -ria *mf*

commit [kəmít] VT (perpetrate) cometer; (entrust) encargar; (direct) destinar; **to — to an asylum** internar; **to — to memory** aprender de memoria; **to — to paper** poner por escrito; **to — to prison** encarcelar

commitment [kəmítmənt] N compromiso *m*

committee [kəmíɾi] N comité *m*, comisión *f*

commode [kəmód] N wáter *m*, inodoro *m*

commodity [kəmáɒɪɾi] N (product) mercancía *f*, artículo *m*, producto *m*; (raw material) materia prima *f*

common [kámən] ADJ (shared, frequent) común; (general) general; (vulgar) ordinario; (unremarkable) simple; **— cold** resfriado *m*; **— denominator** denominador común *m*; **— law** derecho consuetudinario *m*; **—place** trivial; **— sense** sentido común *m*, sensatez *f*; **— soldier** soldado raso *m*; **— stock** acciones ordinarias *f pl*; **—wealth** (state) estado *m*; (republic) república *f*; N **—s** (land) ejido *m*

commotion [kəmóʃən] N conmoción *f*, revuelo *m*

commune [kəmjún] VI (communicate) comunicarse, departir; (take communion) comulgar; [kámjun] N comuna *f*

communicable [kəmjúnɪkəbəł] ADJ comunicable; (disease) transmisible

communicate [kəmjúnɪket] VI/VT comunicar(se); (disease) transmitir(se)

communication [kəmjunɪkéʃən] N comunicación *f*

communicative [kəmjúnɪkəɒɪv] ADJ comunicativo

communion [kəmjúnjən] N comunión *f*

communism [kámjənɪzəm] N comunismo *m*

communist [kámjənɪst] N & ADJ comunista *mf*

community [kəmjúnɪɾi] N comunidad *f*

commute [kəmjút] VT (reduce a sentence) conmutar; VI viajar diariamente al trabajo

commuter [kəmjúɒ] N persona que viaja diariamente al trabajo *f*

Comoros [káməroz] N Comoras *f pl*

compact [kampǽkt] ADJ compacto; (dense) tupido, apretado; (concise) conciso; **— disk** disco compacto *m*; VT compactar; (make denser) tupir; [kámpækt] N (agreement) pacto *m*; (case for powder) polvera *f*

compactness [kampǽktnɪs] N densidad *f*; (conciseness) concisión *f*

companion [kəmpǽnjən] N (comrade, partner) compañero -ra *mf*; (caregiver) acompañante *mf*

companionship [kəmpǽnjənʃɪp] N compañía *f*

company [kʌ́mpəni] N compañía *f*; **to keep — with** codearse con, frecuentar

comparable [kʌ́mpəɹəbəɫ] ADJ comparable

comparative [kəmpǽɹəDɪv] ADJ comparativo

compare [kəmpéɹ] VI/VT comparar(se); **beyond —** incomparable, sin parangón

comparison [kəmpǽɹɪsən] N comparación *f*; **in — with** comparado con

compartment [kəmpártmənt] N compartimiento *m*

compass [kʌ́mpəs] N (for drawing) compás *m*; (for directions) brújula *f*

compassion [kəmpǽʃən] N compasión *f*

compassionate [kəmpǽʃənɪt] ADJ compasivo

compatible [kəmpǽDəbəɫ] ADJ compatible (also computer term)

compatriot [kəmpétriət] N compatriota *mf*

compel [kəmpéɫ] VT (force) obligar; (demand) exigir

compelling [kəmpélɪŋ] ADJ (argument) convincente; (story) emocionante

compensate [kʌ́mpənset] VT (make up for) compensar, resarcir; (pay) remunerar

compensation [kɑmpənséʃən] N (making up for) compensación *f*; (remuneration) remuneración *f*

compete [kəmpít] VI/VT competir

competence [kʌ́mpɪDəns] N competencia *f*

competent [kʌ́mpɪDənt] ADJ competente

competition [kɑmpɪtíʃən] N competencia *f*; (sports match) competición *f*, contienda *f*

competitive [kəmpéDIDɪv] ADJ competitivo; **— examination** *Sp* oposición *f*; *Am* concurso *m*; **— sports** deportes de competición *m pl*

competitor [kəmpéDIDɚ] N competidor -ra *mf*

compile [kəmpáɪɫ] VT recopilar, compilar

compiler [kəmpáɪlɚ] N compilador *m*

complacency [kəmplésənsi] N confianza infundada *f*

complacent [kəmplésənt] ADJ confiado

complain [kəmplén] VI quejarse

complaint [kəmplént] N queja *f*; (civil charge) demanda *f*; (ailment) dolencia *f*

complement [kʌ́mpləmənt] N complemento *m*; (of staff) dotación *f*; [kʌ́mpləmɛnt] VT complementar

complete [kəmplít] ADJ completo, pleno; **a — stranger** un perfecto desconocido; VT completar

completion [kəmplíʃən] N finalización *f*,

terminación *f*; **she brought the project to —** completó el proyecto

complex [kɑmpléks] ADJ complejo; [kʌ́mplɛks] N complejo *m*

complexion [kəmplékʃən] N (skin) cutis *m*; (color) tez *f*; (perspective) cariz *m*

complexity [kəmpléksɪDi] N complejidad *f*

compliance [kəmpláɪəns] N (obedience) conformidad *f*, acatamiento *m*; (meek agreement) pleitesía *f*; **in — with** en conformidad con

complicate [kʌ́mplɪket] VT complicar

complicated [kʌ́mplɪkeDɪd] ADJ complicado

complication [kɑmplɪkéʃən] N complicación *f*

complicity [kəmplísɪDi] N complicidad *f*

compliment [kʌ́mpləmənt] N cumplido *m*; (on looks) piropo *m*; (from a suitor) galantería *f*; **to pay someone a —** hacerle un cumplido a alguien; **to send one's —s** enviar saludos; [kʌ́mpləmɛnt] VI/VT elogiar

comply [kəmpláɪ] VI obedecer; **to — with** cumplir con, acatar

component [kəmpónənt] ADJ & N componente *m*

compose [kəmpóz] VI/VT componer; **to — oneself** sosegarse

composed [kəmpózd] ADJ sosegado; **to be — of** estar compuesto de, componerse de, constar de

composer [kəmpózɚ] N compositor -ra *mf*

composite [kəmpázɪt] ADJ compuesto; N amalgama *f*

composition [kɑmpəzíʃən] N (make-up, musical piece) composición *f*; (aggregate material) compuesto *m*; (school essay) composición *f*, redacción *f*

composure [kəmpóʒɚ] N compostura *f*

compound [kʌ́mpaʊnd] ADJ & N compuesto *m*; **— fracture** fractura expuesta *f*; **— interest** interés compuesto *m*; [kɑmpáʊnd] VT (combine) combinar; (worsen) empeorar

comprehend [kɑmprɪhénd] VT comprender

comprehensible [kɑmprɪhénsəbəɫ] ADJ comprensible

comprehension [kɑmprɪhénʃən] N comprensión *f*

comprehensive [kɑmprɪhénsɪv] ADJ exhaustivo; **— insurance** seguro contra todo riesgo *m*

compress [kəmprés] VT comprimir; [kʌ́mprɛs] N compresa *f*

compression [kəmpréʃən] N compresión *f*

comprise [kəmpráɪz] VT comprender, incluir; **to be —d of** comprender, incluir

compromise [kámprəmaɪz] N (arrangement) arreglo por concesiones mutuas *m*, compromiso *m*; (intermediate thing) cruce *m*, término medio *m*; VI/VT (make agreement) transigir; *Am* transar; (jeopardize) comprometer

comptroller [kəntrólɚ] N controlador -ra *mf*; *Am* contralor -ora *mf*

compulsion [kəmpʌ́ɫʃən] N (impulse) compulsión *f*, coacción *f*; (coercion) coerción *f*

compulsive [kəmpʌ́ɫsɪv] ADJ compulsivo

compulsory [kəmpʌ́ɫsəri] ADJ obligatorio

computation [kɑmpjʊtéʃən] N cómputo *m*, cálculo *m*

compute [kəmpjút] VI/VT computar, calcular

computer [kəmpjúdɚ] N *Am* computadora *f*; *Sp* ordenador *m*; — **graphics** gráficos por computadora/ordenador *m pl*; — **science** informática *f*; — **virus** virus de computadora/ordenador *m*

computerize [kəmpjúdəraɪz] VI/VT informatizar, computarizar

comrade [kámræd] N camarada *mf*

concave [kánkev] ADJ cóncavo

conceal [kənsíɫ] VT encubrir, ocultar, disimular

concealment [kənsíɫmənt] N encubrimiento *m*, disimulo *m*

concede [kənsíd] VI/VT (recognize) conceder; (yield) otorgar

conceit [kənsít] N (vanity) vanidad *f*; (literary device) concepto *m*

conceited [kənsíɾɪd] ADJ engreído, presumido

conceivable [kənsívəbəɫ] ADJ imaginable, concebible

conceive [kənsív] VI/VT concebir; (a plan) concebir, idear

concentrate [kánsəntret] VI/VT concentrar(se)

concentration [kansəntréʃən] N concentración *f*; — **camp** campo de concentración *m*

concept [kánsɛpt] N concepto *m*

conception [kənsɛ́pʃən] N concepción *f*

concern [kənsɚ́n] N (interest) interés *m*; (affair) asunto *m*; (worry) preocupación *f*; (company) compañía *f*; **to be of no** — no tener consecuencia; VT (be of interest) concernir, atañer; (worry) preocupar; **to** — **oneself with** ocuparse de; **to whom it may** — a quien corresponda

concerned [kənsɚ́nd] ADJ (involved) involucrado; (anxious) preocupado; **as far as I am** — en lo que a mí respecta; **to be** — **about** preocuparse por

concerning [kənsɚ́nɪŋ] PREP tocante a, respecto a

concert [kánsɚt] N concierto *m*; [kənsɚ́t] VT concertar

concession [kənsɛ́ʃən] N concesión *f*

conciliate [kənsíliet] VI/VT (make compatible) conciliar; (appease) aplacar

concise [kənsáɪs] ADJ conciso, sucinto

conciseness [kənsáɪsnɪs] N concisión *f*

conclude [kənklúd] VI/VT concluir, terminar; (deduce) deducir

conclusion [kənklúʒən] N conclusión *f*

conclusive [kənklúsɪv] ADJ concluyente

concoct [kənkákt] VT (contrive) fabricar, urdir; (prepare by cooking) preparar

concoction [kənkákʃən] N menjurje *m*

concord [kánkɔrd] N (peace) concordia *f*; (agreement) convenio *m*, acuerdo *m*

concrete [kankrít] ADJ concreto; (made of concrete) de hormigón; [kánkrit] N hormigón *m*

concubine [kánkjəbaɪn] N concubina *f*

concur [kənkɚ́] VI estar de acuerdo

concussion [kənkʌ́ʃən] N (brain injury) conmoción cerebral *f*; (shock) concusión *f*

condemn [kəndém] VT condenar; (acquire public ownership) expropiar; (declare unsafe) declarar ruinoso

condemnation [kandɛmnéʃən] N condenación *f*, condena *f*

condensation [kandɛnséʃən] N condensación *f*; (of a book) compendio *m*

condense [kəndéns] VI/VT condensar(se)

condescend [kandəsénd] VI condescender a

condescension [kandəsénʃən] N condescendencia *f*

condiment [kándəmənt] N condimento *m*, aliño *m*

condition [kəndíʃən] N condición *f*; **he's got a heart** — sufre del corazón, tiene una afección cardíaca; **he's in good physical** — está en buen estado físico; **the patient is in critical** — el paciente está en estado crítico; **on** — **that** a condición de que; VT (restrict on a condition, establish a conditioned response) condicionar; (accustom oneself) acostumbrarse

conditional [kəndíʃənəɫ] ADJ & N condicional *m*

conditioning [kəndíʃənɪŋ] N condicionamiento *m*

condolences [kəndólənsɪz] N pésame *m*, condolencias *f*; **to express one's** — dar las condolencias

condom [kándəm] N condón *m*, preservativo *m*

condominium [kandəmíniəm] N

condominio *m*
condone [kəndón] VT tolerar
conducive [kəndúsɪv] ADJ conducente
conduct [kándʌkt] N conducta *f*,
comportamiento *m*; [kəndʌ́kt] VI/VT
(behave) conducirse, comportarse; (carry
out) llevar a cabo; (direct, lead) dirigir;
(serve as channel for) conducir
conductor [kəndʌ́ktɚ] N (substance that
conducts) conductor *m*; (of an orchestra)
director -ra *mf*; (of a train) revisor -ra *mf*
conduit [kánduɪt] N conducto *m*
cone [kon] N cono *m*; (container) cucurucho
m
confection [kənfékʃən] N (of clothes)
confección *f*; (of candy) confitura *f*
confectionery [kənfékʃənɛri] N confitería *f*;
(shop) dulcería *f*; (candies) dulces *m pl*
confederacy [kənféDə-əsi] N confederación *f*
confederate [kənféDə-ɪt] ADJ & N
confederado -da *mf*; [kənféDəret] VI/VT
confederar(se)
confederation [kənfeDəréʃən] N
confederación *f*
confer [kənfɝ] VT (grant) conferir; (consult)
consultar; (negotiate) conferenciar
conference [kánfɚəns] N (consultation)
consulta *f*; (professional meeting) congreso
m; (legislative) asamblea general *f*; (sports
league) liga *f*; — **call** llamada en
conferencia *f*
confess [kənfés] VI/VT confesar(se)
confession [kənféʃən] N confesión *f*
confessional [kənféʃənəɫ] N confesionario *m*
confessor [kənfésɚ] N confesor *m*
confidant [kánfɪdɑnt] N confidente *mf*
confide [kənfáɪd] VI/VT (entrust) confiar; VI
(tell secrets to) hacer confidencias a
confidence [kánfɪDəns] N confianza *f*;
(certainty) seguridad *f*; (secret
communication) confidencia *f*; — **game**
timo *m*; — **man** timador *m*, embaucador
m; **in** — en confianza
confident [kánfɪDənt] ADJ seguro; **he's a —
person** tiene mucha confianza
confidential [kanfɪdénʃəɫ] ADJ confidencial;
(secretary, etc.) de confianza
configuration [kənfɪgjəréʃən] N
configuración *f* (also computer term)
confine [kənfáɪn] VT confinar, recluir; **to —
oneself to** limitarse a; [kánfaɪn] N confín
m
confinement [kənfáɪnmənt] N
confinamiento *m*
confirm [kənfɝm] VT confirmar
confirmation [kanfɚméʃən] N confirmación
f

confiscate [kánfɪsket] VT confiscar
confiscation [kanfɪskéʃən] N confiscación *f*
conflagration [kanfləgréʃən] N incendio *m*
conflict [kánflɪkt] N conflicto *m*, contienda *f*;
— **of interest** conflicto de intereses *m*;
[kənflíkt] VI oponerse
confluence [kánfluəns] N confluencia *f*
conform [kənfɔrm] VI/VT conformar(se)
conformity [kənfɔ́rmiDi] N (agreement)
conformidad *f*; (passive acquiescence)
conformismo *m*
confound [kənfáund] VT (bewilder)
desconcertar; (mix) confundir; — **it!** *fam*
¡caramba!
confront [kənfrʌnt] VT (set face to face,
fight) confrontar; (face up to) enfrentarse
a
confuse [kənfjúz] VT confundir
confused [kənfjúzd] ADJ (person)
confundido; (situation) confuso; **to
become —** confundirse
confusing [kənfjúzɪŋ] ADJ confuso
confusion [kənfjúʒən] N confusión *f*
congeal [kəndʒíɫ] VI/VT cuajar(se)
congenial [kəndʒínjəɫ] ADJ agradable,
simpático; **to be — with** congeniar con
congenital [kəndʒénɪdɫ] ADJ congénito
congestion [kəndʒéstʃən] N congestión *f*
conglomeration [kənglaməréʃən] N (unit)
conglomeración *f*; (mass) conglomerado *m*
Congo [káŋgo] N Congo *m*
Congolese [kaŋgəlíz] ADJ & N congoleño -ña
mf
congratulate [kəngrǽtʃəlet] VI/VT felicitar(se)
congratulation [kəngrætʃəléʃən] N
felicitación *f*, parabién *m*; —**s!**
¡enhorabuena! ¡albricias!
congregate [káŋgrɪget] VI/VT congregar(se)
congregation [kaŋgrɪgéʃən] N (worshippers)
fieles *m pl*, feligreses *m pl*; (act of
congregating, committee of cardinals)
congregación *f*
congress [káŋgrɪs] N (professional) congreso
m; (political) asamblea legislativa *f*; (US)
congreso *m*
congressional [kəngréʃənəɫ] ADJ congresual
congressman [káŋgrɪsmən] N representante
m; (US) congresista *m*
congresswoman [káŋgrɪswumən] N
representante *f*; (US) congresista *f*
congruence [kəngrúəns] N congruencia *f*
conifer [kánəfɚ] N conífera *f*
conjecture [kəndʒéktʃɚ] N conjetura *f*; VI
conjeturar
conjugal [kándʒəgəɫ] ADJ conyugal
conjugate [kándʒəget] VI/VT conjugar(se)
conjugation [kandʒəgéʃən] N conjugación *f*

conjunction [kəndʒʌ́ŋkʃən] N conjunción *f*
conjunctivitis [kəndʒʌ́ŋktəváɪdɪs] N
conjuntivitis *f*
conjure [kándʒɚ] VT invocar; **to — up**
evocar; VI hacer hechizos
connect [kənékt] VI/VT (join) conectar(se),
enlazar(se); (buildings, callers)
comunicar(se); (concepts) relacionar(se);
(pipes) acoplar(se); **—ing rod** biela *f*
connection [kənékʃən] N (act of connecting,
electrical device) conexión *f*; (of
telephone) comunicación *f*, enganche *m*;
(of concepts) relación *f*; (of pipes) acople
m; (affinity) afinidad *f*; (supplier) contacto
m; **—s** contactos *m pl*, enchufe *m*
connive [kənáɪv] VI conspirar
connoisseur [kanəsɝ] N conocedor -ra *f*
connotation [kanətéʃən] N connotación *f*
conquer [káŋkɚ] VT (win) conquistar;
(overcome) vencer
conqueror [káŋkərɚ] N conquistador -ra *mf*;
(one who overcomes) vencedor -ra *mf*
conquest [káŋkwest] N conquista *f*
conscience [kánʃəns] N conciencia *f*
conscientious [kanʃiéntʃəs] ADJ concienzudo
conscious [kánʃəs] ADJ consciente
consciousness [kánʃəsnɪs] N conciencia *f*; **to
lose —** perder el conocimiento
conscript [kənskrípt] VT reclutar; [kánskrɪpt]
N recluta *mf*
conscription [kənskrípʃən] N reclutamiento
m
consecrate [kánsɪkret] VT consagrar
consecration [kansɪkréʃən] N consagración *f*
consecutive [kənsékjədɪv] ADJ consecutivo
consensus [kənsénsəs] N consenso *m*
consent [kənsént] N consentimiento *m*; VI
consentir
consequence [kánsɪkwens] N consecuencia *f*;
(negative) secuela *f*
consequent [kánsɪkwənt] ADJ consiguiente,
resultante; N (in mathematics)
consecuente *m*; (in logic) consiguiente *m*
consequently [kánsɪkwəntli] ADV por
consiguiente, en consecuencia
conservation [kansɚvéʃən] N conservación *f*,
preservación *f*
conservatism [kənsɝvətɪzəm] N
conservadurismo *m*
conservative [kənsɝvədɪv] ADJ & N
conservador -ra *mf*
conservatory [kənsɝvətɔri] N conservatorio
m
conserve [kənsɝv] VT conservar, preservar;
[kánsɝv] N dulce *m*
consider [kənsídɚ] VT considerar
considerable [kənsídɚəbəł] ADJ considerable

considerate [kənsídɚɪt] ADJ considerado
consideration [kənsɪdəréʃən] N
consideración *f*; (tolerance) miramiento *m*;
(payment) remuneración *f*
considering [kənsídɚɪŋ] PREP en vista de,
teniendo en cuenta; **she cooks well, —**
para ser ella, cocina bien
consign [kənsáɪn] VT consignar
consignee [kənsaɪní] N consignatario -ria *mf*
consignment [kənsáɪnmənt] N consignación
f; **on — a** consignación
consist [kənsíst] VI consistir (en)
consistency [kənsístənsi] N (adherence to
principles) coherencia *f*, consecuencia *f*;
(density) consistencia *f*
consistent [kənsístənt] ADJ (adherent to
principles) consecuente, coherente;
(cohering) consistente
consolation [kansəléʃən] N consuelo *m*,
consolación *f*
console [kənsółł] VT consolar; [kánsoł] N
consola *f*
consolidate [kənsálɪdet] VI/VT consolidar(se)
consonant [kánsənənt] N consonante *f*; ADJ
consonante, conforme
consort [kánsɔrt] N consorte *mf*; [kənsɔ́rt] VI
to — with asociarse con
consortium [kənsɔ́rʃiəm] N consorcio *m*
conspicuous [kənspíkjuəs] ADJ evidente
conspiracy [kənspírəsi] N conspiración *f*,
conjura *f*
conspirator [kənspírəDɚ] N conspirador -ora
mf, conjurado -da *mf*
conspire [kənspáɪr] VI conspirar, conjurar
constable [kánstəbəł] N oficial de policía *mf*;
(keeper of fortress) condestable *m*
constancy [kánstənsi] N constancia *f*
constant [kánstənt] ADJ & N constante *f*
constellation [kanstəléʃən] N constelación *f*
consternation [kanstɚnéʃən] N
consternación *f*
constipate [kánstəpet] VT estreñir
constipated [kánstəpeDɪd] ADJ estreñido
constipation [kanstəpéʃən] N estreñimiento
m
constituent [kənstítʃuənt] ADJ componente,
constitutivo; N (component) componente
m; (voter) votante *mf*; (part of a sentence)
constituyente *m*
constitute [kánstɪtut] VT constituir
constitution [kanstɪtúʃən] N constitución *f*
constitutional [kanstɪtúʃənəł] ADJ
constitucional; N caminata *f*
constrain [kənstrén] VT constreñir
constraint [kənstrént] N constreñimiento *m*
constrict [kənstríkt] VT constreñir
constriction [kənstríkʃən] N (action)

constricción *f*; (place) estrechamiento *m*

construct [kənstrʌ́kt] VT construir; [kánstrʌkt] N invención *f*

construction [kənstrʌ́kʃən] N construcción *f*

constructive [kənstrʌ́ktɪv] ADJ constructivo

construe [kənstrú] VT interpretar

consul [kánsəł] N cónsul *mf*

consulate [kánsəlɪt] N consulado *m*

consult [kənsʌ́łt] VI/VT consultar; VI (serve as a consultant) asesorar

consultant [kənsʌ́łtənt] N asesor -ra *mf*

consultation [kansəłtéʃən] N consulta *f*

consulting [kənsʌ́łtɪŋ] N asesoramiento *m*, consultoría *f*

consume [kənsúm] VI/VT consumir

consumer [kənsúmɚ] N consumidor -ra *mf*

consumerism [kənsúmərɪzəm] N consumismo *m*

consuming [kənsúmɪŋ] ADJ **a — need** una necesidad imperiosa; **a — drive** un deseo abrasador

consummate [kánsəmet] VT consumar; [kánsəmɪt] ADJ consumado

consumption [kənsʌ́mpʃən] N (using up) consumo *m*; (wasting of the body) consunción *f*; (tuberculosis) tisis *f*

consumptive [kənsʌ́mptɪv] ADJ tísico

contact [kántækt] N contacto *m*; **— lens** lente de contacto *mf*; VI/VT (touch) tocar; (communicate with) contactar

contagion [kəntéʤən] N (spread) contagio *m*; (disease spread) enfermedad contagiosa *f*

contagious [kəntéʤəs] ADJ contagioso

contain [kəntén] VI/VT contener

container [kənténɚ] N recipiente *m*; (on a ship) contenedor *m*; **—ship** buque portacontenedores *m*

contaminate [kəntǽmənet] VT contaminar

contamination [kəntæmənéʃən] N contaminación *f*

contemplate [kántəmplet] VT (observe) contemplar; (consider) considerar

contemplation [kantəmpléʃən] N (observation) contemplación *f*; (consideration) consideración *f*

contemporary [kəntémpəreri] ADJ contemporáneo

contempt [kəntémpt] N desprecio *m*, menosprecio *m*; **— of court** desacato al tribunal *m*

contemptible [kəntémptəbəł] ADJ despreciable, rastrero

contemptuous [kəntémptʃuəs] ADJ desdeñoso

contend [kənténd] VI (struggle) contender, lidiar; (argue) disputar; VT afirmar

content, contents [kántɛnt(s)] N contenido *m*

content [kəntént] ADJ (happy) contento; (resigned) conforme; N **to one's heart's — a** discreción

contented [kənténtɪd] ADJ contento, satisfecho

contention [kənténʃən] N (opinion) opinión *f*; **in —** (disputed) en discusión; (with possibilities) con posibilidades *mf*

contentment [kənténtmənt] N contento *m*

contest [kántest] N (competition) concurso *m*, certamen *m*; (struggle) contienda *f*; [kəntést] VT (compete) contender; (dispute) disputar; (challenge) impugnar

contestant [kəntéstənt] N concursante *mf*, participante *mf*

context [kántɛkst] N contexto *m*

contiguous [kəntígjuəs] ADJ contiguo

continent [kántənənt] N continente *m*; ADJ (sexually) continente; (of bodily functions) capaz de controlar los esfínteres

continental [kantṇéntł] ADJ continental

contingency [kəntínʤənsi] N contingencia *f*

contingent [kəntínʤənt] ADJ & N contingente *m*

continual [kəntínjuəł] ADJ continuo

continuance [kəntínjuəns] N continuación *f*; (delay) aplazamiento *m*

continuation [kəntɪnjuéʃən] N continuación *f*

continue [kəntínju] VI/VT continuar

continuity [kantṇúɪDi] N continuidad *f*

continuous [kəntínjuəs] ADJ (uninterrupted in time) continuo; (uninterrupted in space) ininterrumpido

contortion [kəntɔ́rʃən] N contorsión *f*

contour [kántur] N contorno *m*

contraband [kántrəbænd] N contrabando *m*

contraception [kantrəsépʃən] N anticoncepción *f*

contraceptive [kantrəséptɪv] ADJ & N anticonceptivo *m*

contract [kántrækt] N contrato *m*; **— killer** asesino -na a sueldo *mf*; [kəntrǽkt] VI/VT contraer(se); (assign by contract) contratar

contraction [kəntrǽkʃən] N contracción *f*; (in childbirth) contracción *f*, pujo *m*

contractor [kántræktɚ] N contratista *mf*

contractual [kəntrǽktʃuəł] ADJ contractual

contradict [kantrədíkt] VI/VT contradecir

contradiction [kantrədíkʃən] N contradicción *f*

contradictory [kantrədíktəri] ADJ contradictorio

contraption [kəntrǽpʃən] N chisme *m*, coso *m*

contrary [kántrɛri] ADJ contrario, opuesto; (obstinate) testarudo; N lo contrario; **on the —** al contrario

contrast [kántræst] N contraste *m*; [kəntrǽst] VI/VT contrastar

contravene [kɑntrəvín] VT contravenir

contribute [kəntríbjut] VI contribuir; (to a newspaper) colaborar; VT contribuir con, aportar

contribution [kɑntrəbjúʃən] N (donation, article) contribución *f*; (scientific) aporte *m*, aportación *f*

contributor [kəntríbjəDɚ] N colaborador -ra *mf*

contrite [kəntráit] ADJ contrito

contrivance [kəntráivəns] N artefacto *m*

contrive [kəntráiv] VI/VT ingeniar; **he —d to get their money** se las ingenió para sacarles el dinero

contrived [kəntráivd] ADJ artificioso

control [kəntróɫ] VI/VT controlar; N control *m*; (of a machine) mando *m*; **who's in —?** ¿quién manda? **under —** bajo control; **— freak** mandón -ona *mf*; **— key** tecla de control/mando *f*; **— tower** torre de control *f*

controller [kəntrólɚ] N (comptroller) controlador -ora *mf*; *Am* contralor -ora *mf*; (device) regulador *m*

controversy [kántrəvɝsi] N controversia *f*, polémica *f*

conundrum [kənándrəm] N (riddle) adivinanza *f*, acertijo *m*; (mystery) enigma *m*

convalesce [kɑnvəlés] VI convalecer

convection [kənvékʃən] N convección *f*

convene [kənvín] VT convocar; VI reunirse

convenience [kənvínjəns] N (practicality) conveniencia *f*; (appliance) comodidad *f*; **— store** autoservicio *m*; **at your —** cuando le venga bien

convenient [kənvínjənt] ADJ conveniente, oportuno; (at hand) accesible

convent [kánvɛnt] N convento *m*

convention [kənvénʃən] N (political assembly) convención *f*; (professional assembly) congreso *m*; (pact) convenio *m*; (international agreement, acceptable usage) convención *f*

conventional [kənvénʃənəɫ] ADJ (not original) convencional; (traditional) clásico

conventioneer [kənvɛnʃənír] N congresista *mf*

converge [kənvɝʤ] VI converger

conversant [kənvɝsənt] ADJ **— with** versado en

conversation [kɑnvɚséʃən] N conversación *f*; **— piece** tema de conversación *m*

converse [kənvɝs] VI conversar

conversion [kənvɝʒən] N conversión *f*

convert [kənvɝt] VI/VT convertir(se); [kánvɚt] N converso -sa *mf*

converter [kənvɝDɚ] N convertidor *m*

convertible [kənvɝDəbəɫ] ADJ convertible; (car) descapotable; N descapotable *m*

convex [kánvɛks] ADJ convexo

convey [kənvé] VT (carry) llevar; (transfer a title) transferir; (transmit) transmitir; (communicate) comunicar; **to — thanks** expresar agradecimiento

conveyance [kənvéəns] N (vehicle) vehículo *m*; (transfer of property) transferencia *f*; (document) escritura de traspaso *f*

conveyer, conveyor [kənvéɚ] N transmisor -ra *mf*; **— belt** cinta transportadora *f*

convict [kánvɪkt] N convicto -ta *mf*; [kənvíkt] VI/VT declarar culpable

conviction [kənvíkʃən] N (belief) convicción *f*, convencimiento *m*; (act of convicting) declaración de culpabilidad *f*; (on one's record) condena *f*

convince [kənvíns] VT convencer

convincing [kənvínsɪŋ] ADJ convincente

convocation [kɑnvəkéʃən] N (act) convocación *f*; (group of people) asamblea *f*

convoke [kənvók] VT convocar

convoluted [kɑnvəlúDɪd] ADJ retorcido

convoy [kánvɔi] N convoy *m*; VT convoyar

convulse [kənváɫs] VI/VT convulsionar(se)

convulsion [kənváɫʃən] N convulsión *f*

coo [ku] VI arrullar; N arrullo *m*

cook [kʊk] N cocinero -ra *mf*; VT cociʔar, guisar; **—book** libro de cocina *m*; **to — up a plan** urdir un plan

cookery [kúkəri] N cocina *f*

cookie [kúki] N galletita dulce *f*

cool [kuɫ] ADJ (not hot) fresco; (indifferent) frío, indiferente; (calm) tranquilo; (good) excelente; *Caribbean* chévere; *RP* macanudo; *Sp* guay; *Sp vulg* cojonudo; **that's not —** eso no se hace; N (cold) fresco *m*; (composure) tranquilidad *f*; VT (make cooler) enfriar; (air condition) refrigerar; **to — off** (get cold) enfriarse; (get cooler) refrescar(se); (calm down) calmarse; **—ing-off period** tregua *f*

coolant [kúlənt] N refrigerante *m*

cooler [kúlɚ] N (room) cámara frigorífica *f*; (container) nevera portátil *f*

coolness [kúɫnɪs] N (cold weather) fresco *m*, frescor *m*; (indifference) frialdad *f*, indiferencia *f*

coon [kun] N (raccoon) mapache *m*; **a —'s age** una eternidad

co-op [kóap] N cooperativa *f*

coop [kup] N jaula *f*; (for chickens) gallinero *m*; VT enjaular; **to — up** encerrar

cooperate [koápəret] VI cooperar

cooperation [koapəréʃən] N cooperación *f*

cooperative [koápəˈədɪv] ADJ cooperativo; N cooperativa *f*

coordinate [koˈɔrdn̩ɪt] ADJ coordinado; N coordenada *f*; **—s** conjunto *m*; [koˈɔrdnet] VI/VT coordinar

coordination [koɔrdn̩éʃən] N coordinación *f*

cop [kap] N *fam* poli *mf*, polizonte *m*; VI **to — out** zafarse

cope [kop] VI **to — with** arreglárselas con; **I cannot — with this** no puedo con esto

copious [kópiəs] ADJ copioso

copper [kápəˈ] N cobre *m*; (cop) *fam* poli *mf*; ADJ de cobre

copulate [kápjəlet] VI copular

copy [kápi] N (reproduction) copia *f*; (specimen, example) ejemplar *m*; (news story) texto *m*; **—cat** copión -ona *mf*; **— machine** copiadora *f*; **—right** copyright *m*, derechos de autor *m pl*; **this material is —righted** reservados todos los derechos; VT copiar; **to —right** registrar los derechos

coquette [kokét] N coqueta *f*

coral [kɔ́rəɫ] N coral *m*; ADJ (related to coral) coralino; (made of coral) de coral; **— reef** arrecife de coral *m*

cord [kɔrd] N (thread) cuerda *f*; (for shoes) cordón *m*; (firewood measure) medida de leña *f*; **—s** pantalones de pana *m pl*

cordial [kɔ́rdʒəɫ] ADJ cordial; N licor *m*

cordless [kɔ́rdlɪs] ADJ inalámbrico

corduroy [kɔ́rɒərɔɪ] N pana *f*; **—s** pantalones de pana *m pl*

core [kor] N (of fruit) corazón *m*; (of a problem) meollo *m*; (of a magnet, reactor) núcleo *m*; VT despepitar

cork [kɔrk] N (woody material) corcho *m*; (stopper, buoy) tapón *m*; **—screw** sacacorchos *m sg*, tirabuzón *m*; **— tree** alcornoque *m*; VT tapar con un corcho

corn [kɔrn] N (plant) maíz *m*; (painful growth) callo *m*; **—bread** pan de maíz *m*; **—cob** mazorca *f*; *Sp* zuro *m*; **— on the cob** choclo *m*; *Mex* elote *m*; **—ed beef** corned beef *m*; **—field** maizal *m*; *Mex* milpa *f*; **—flakes** copos de maíz *m pl*; **—meal** harina de maíz *f*; **—starch** maicena® *f*

corner [kɔ́rnəˈ] N (angle) ángulo *m*; (of a room, of a country) rincón *m*; (of two streets) esquina *f*; (monopoly) monopolio *m*; **—stone** piedra angular *f*; **— table** mesa rinconera *f*; VT (trap) arrinconar, acorralar; (monopolize) monopolizar; VI doblar; *Sp* girar

cornered [kɔ́rnəˈd] ADJ (animal) acorralado; (person) arrinconado

cornet [kɔrnét] N corneta *f*

cornice [kɔ́rnɪs] N cornisa *f*

corny [kɔ́rni] ADJ sensiblero; (joke) viejo

corollary [kɔ́rəlɛri] N corolario *m*

coronation [kɔrənéʃən] N coronación *f*

coroner [kɔ́rənəˈ] N médico -ca forense *mf*

corporal [kɔ́rpəˈəɫ] ADJ corporal; N (rank) cabo *m*

corporation [kɔrpəréʃən] N sociedad anónima *f*

corps [kor] N cuerpo *m*

corpse [kɔrps] N cadáver *m*

corpulent [kɔ́rpjələnt] ADJ corpulento

corpus [kɔ́rpəs] N corpus *m*

corpuscle [kɔ́rpʌsəɫ] N corpúsculo *m*; (of blood) glóbulo *m*

corral [kərǽɫ] N corral *m*; VT acorralar

correct [kərékt] VT corregir; ADJ correcto; **that is —** es cierto

correction [kərékʃən] N corrección *f*; (for glasses) graduación *f*

correctness [kəréktnɪs] N corrección *f*

corrector [kəréktəˈ] N corrector -ra *mf*

correlate [kɔ́rəlet] VI/VT correlacionar; [kɔ́rəlɪt] N correlato *m*

correspond [kɔrəspánd] VI (be in agreement) corresponder, responder; (exchange letters) cartearse, escribirse

correspondence [kɔrəspándəns] N correspondencia *f*

correspondent [kɔrəspándənt] ADJ correspondiente; N (writer of letters) correspondiente *mf*; (news gatherer) corresponsal *mf*, enviado -da *mf*

corresponding [kɔrəspándɪŋ] ADJ correspondiente; (secretary, etc.) encargado de la correspondencia

corridor [kɔ́rɪdɔr] N corredor *m*, pasillo *m*

corroborate [kərábəret] VT corroborar

corrode [kəród] VI/VT corroer(se)

corrosion [kəróʒən] N corrosión *f*

corrupt [kərápt] ADJ (dishonest) corrupto; (rotten) corrompido; **to become —** corromperse; VT corromper, viciar

corruption [kərápʃən] N corrupción *f*

corset [kɔ́rsɪt] N corsé *m*

cortex [kɔ́rtɛks] N córtex *m*, corteza cerebral *f*

cortisone [kɔ́rdɪzon] N cortisona *f*

cosigner [kósaɪnəˈ] N cosignatario -ria *mf*

cosmetic [kazmédɪk] ADJ & N cosmético *m*

cosmic [kázmɪk] ADJ cósmico

cosmology [kazmáləʤi] N cosmología f

cosmonaut [kázmənɔt] N cosmonauta mf

cosmopolitan [kɑzməpálɪtṇ] ADJ cosmopolita

cosmos [kázmos] N cosmos m

cost [kɔst] N costo m; Sp coste m; **—s** (court costs) costas f pl; **at all —s** a toda costa; **— effective** económico; **— of living** costo / coste de vida m; **to sell at —** vender al costo / al coste; VT costar; **how much does this —?** ¿cuánto vale / cuesta esto?

co-star [kóstɑr] N coprotagonista mf

Costa Rica [kóstəríkə] N Costa Rica f

Costa Rican [kóstəríkən] ADJ & N costarricense mf

costly [kɔ́stli] ADJ costoso, caro

costume [kástum] N (style of clothing) vestimenta f; (in the theater) vestuario m; (disguise) disfraz m; **— jewelry** bisutería f

cot [kɑt] N catre m

cottage [kádɪʤ] N (small house) casita f; (vacation house) cabaña f, chalé m; **— cheese** requesón m

cotter pin [kádɚpɪn] N chaveta f

cotton [kɑtṇ] N algodón m; **— candy** algodón de azúcar m; **— gin** desmontadora de algodón f; **—seed** semilla de algodón f; **—wood** álamo (de Virginia) m; **— wool** algodón en rama m

couch [kautʃ] N sofá m; (psychiatrist's) diván m; **— potato** telebobo -ba mf; VT expresar

cougar [kúgɚ] N puma f

cough [kɔf] VI toser; **to — up** (spit) expectorar; (hand over) soltar, largar; N tos f; **— drop** pastilla para la tos f; **— syrup** jarabe para la tos m

could [kʊd] V AUX **I — do it if I wanted** podría hacerlo si quisiera; **— you arrive early?** ¿podrías llegar temprano? **— I leave early?** ¿puedo salir temprano? **you — be right** quizá tengas razón

council [káʊnsəɫ] N (religious) concilio m; (advisory) consejo m, junta f; (provincial) diputación f; (municipal) concejo m; **—man** concejal m; **—woman** concejal f, concejala f

councilor [káʊnsələɚ] N concejal mf

counsel [káʊnsəɫ] N (advice) consejo m; (lawyer) abogado -da mf; VI/VT (give advice) aconsejar

counselor [káʊnsələɚ] N consejero -ra mf; (lawyer) abogado -da mf

count [kaʊnt] VI/VT contar; **to — in** incluir; **to — on** contar con; **to — oneself lucky** considerarse dichoso; **to — out**

excluir; **—down** cuenta regresiva f; N (reckoning) cuenta f; (charge) cargo m; (noble) conde m

countenance [káʊntṇəns] N (expression) semblante m; (face) cara f; VT (tolerate) tolerar; (approve) aprobar

counter [káʊntɚ] N (in a kitchen) Sp encimera f; Am mostrador m; (in a store) mostrador m; (in a bar) barra f; (in board games) tablero m; (counting device) contador m; (in a shoe) contrafuerte m; **over the —** sin receta; ADJ contrario, opuesto; ADV **— to** contra; **to run — to** ser contrario a; VT (an argument) retrucar; (a blow) devolver; VI/VT replicar

counteract [kaʊntɚǽkt] VT contrarrestar

counterattack [káʊntɚətæk] N contraataque m; VI/VT contraatacar

counterbalance [kaʊntɚbǽləns] VI/VT contrapesar; [káʊntɚbæləns] N contrapeso m

counterculture [káʊntɚkʌɫtʃɚ] N contracultura f

counterespionage [kaʊntɚéspiɑnɑʒ] N contraespionaje m

counterexample [káʊntɚɪgzæmpəɫ] N contraejemplo m

counterfeit [káʊntɚfɪt] N falsificación f; ADJ falso; **— money** moneda falsa f; VT falsificar

countermand [kaʊntɚmǽnd] VT contramandar; [káʊntɚmænd] N contraorden f

counteroffer [káʊntɚɔfɚ] N contraoferta f

counterpart [káʊntɚpɑrt] N homólogo -ga mf

counterproductive [kaʊntɚprədákᵗɪv] ADJ contraproducente

counterrevolution [kaʊntɚrɛvəlúʃən] N contrarrevolución f

countersign [káʊntɚsaɪn] N contraseña f; VT refrendar

countess [káʊntɪs] N condesa f

countless [káʊntlɪs] ADJ incontables, innumerables

country [kántri] N (nation) país m; (territory) territorio m; (homeland) patria f; (rural area) campo m; ADJ (of the countryside) rural; (uncouth) rústico; **— club** club campestre m; **—man** compatriota m; **— music** música country f; **—side** campo m; (scenery) paisaje m; **—woman** compatriota f

county [káʊnti] N condado m; **— fair** feria (de ganado) f; **— seat** capital de condado f

coup [ku] N (success) golpe maestro m;

(putsch) golpe de estado *m*; — **d'état** golpe de estado *m*

coupe [kup] N cupé *m*

couple [kápəł] N (of times, of forces, of people) par *m*; (romantic) pareja *f*; VI/VT (pair up) formar parejas; VT (connect) acoplar; VI (copulate) copular

couplet [káplɪt] N pareado *m*

coupling [káplɪŋ] N (action) acoplamiento *m*, enganche *m*; (device) acople *m*, enganche *m*

coupon [kjúpɑn] N cupón *m*

courage [kɚ́ɪʤ] N valentía *f*, valor *m*, coraje *m*

courageous [kərédʒəs] ADJ valiente

courier [kúriɚ] N mensajero -ra *mf*

course [kɔrs] N (of a river, of study, of a disease) curso *m*; (of a road, route) trayecto *m*; (of a ship, plane) derrotero *m*; (progression of time) marcha *f*; (dish) plato *m*; — **of action** línea de conducta *f*, proceder *m*; **in the — of a year** en el transcurso de un año; **in due —** a la larga; INTERJ **of —** claro, por supuesto, naturalmente; VI correr, fluir

court [kɔrt] N (courtyard) patio *m*; (atrium) patio interior *m*; (in sports) cancha, pista *f*; (in a city) plazuela *f*, plazoleta *f*; (tribunal) juzgado *m*, tribunal *m*; (session) audiencia *f*; (royal residence, retinue) corte *f*; —**-martial** consejo de guerra *m*; — **of law** tribunal de justicia *m*; — **reporter** estenotipista *mf*; —**yard** patio *m*; **to settle out of —** llegar a un arreglo extrajudicial; **to pay — to** cortejar; VT cortejar, galantear; **to — danger** tentar a la suerte; **to —-martial** someter a consejo de guerra; VI estar de novios

courteous [kɚ́ɾiəs] ADJ cortés

courtesy [kɚ́ɾɪsi] N (attitude) cortesía *f*; (act) fineza *f*, atención *f*

courtier [kɔ́rɾiɚ] N (member of the court) cortesano -na *mf*; (sycophant) adulador -ra *mf*

courtship [kɔ́rtʃɪp] N cortejo *m*

cousin [kázən] N primo -ma *mf*; **first —** primo -ma hermano -na *mf*

counterclockwise [kaʊntɚklákwaɪz] ADV en el sentido opuesto al de las manecillas del reloj

cove [kov] N ensenada *f*

covenant [kávənənt] N pacto *m*; (religious) alianza *f*

cover [kávɚ] VI/VT cubrir; (with lid, screen) tapar; (replace) sustituir; (include, deal with) comprender; (traverse) recorrer; (sing) hacer una versión; **to — one's ass**

cuidarse la retaguardia; **to — up** (wrap up) tapar bien; (hide) ocultar; —**all** mono *m*; —**-up** encubrimiento *m*; N (lid) tapa *f*; (book) cubierta *f*, tapa *f*; (blanket) manta *f*; (for appliances, furniture) funda *f*; (front for activity) tapadera *f*, pantalla *f*; (shelter) resguardo *m*, abrigo *m*; — **charge** entrada *f*; —**girl** modelo de portada *f*; **to send under separate —** enviar por separado; **to take —** resguardarse; **under —** de incógnito; **under — of dark** bajo el manto de la noche

coverage [kávɚɪʤ] N cobertura *f*; (of a cell phone) alcance *m*

covering [kávɚɪŋ] N cubierta *f*

covert [kovɚ́t] ADJ encubierto

covet [kávɪt] VT (desire wrongfully) codiciar; (want) ansiar

covetous [kávɪɾəs] ADJ codicioso

cow [kaʊ] N (bovine female) vaca *f*; (female of other animals) hembra *f*; —**bell** cencerro *m*, esquila *f*; —**boy** vaquero *m*; —**hide** cuero de vaca *m*, vaqueta *f*; —**lick** remolino *m*; —**shed** vaquería *f*, vaqueriza *f*; **to have a —** tener una pataleta; VT intimidar

coward [káʊɚd] N cobarde *mf*

cowardice [káʊɚdɪs] N cobardía *f*

cowardly [káʊɚdli] ADJ cobarde

cower [káʊɚ] VI achicarse

cowl [kaʊł] N capucha *f*

coy [kɔɪ] ADJ (coquettish) remilgado; (evasive) esquivo

coyote [kaɪóɾi, káɪot] N coyote *m*

cozy [kózi] ADJ (warm) acogedor; (beneficial) conveniente; **to — up to** adular

CPU (central processing unit) [sipijú] N UCP *f*

crab [kræb] N cangrejo *m*; (mechanism) carro corredizo *m*; (grouch) cascarrabias *mf*; —**apple** manzana silvestre *f*; —**s** ladillas *f pl*; VI (fish) pescar cangrejos; (complain) quejarse

crack [kræk] VI (single fissure) rajarse; (multiple fissures) resquebrajarse, agrietarse; (psychological breakdown) sufrir un ataque de nervios; (of voice) quebrarse; VT (knuckles) hacer un chasquido con, chascar, chasquear; (nuts) cascar; (jokes) contar; (a prisoner) quebrar; (a case) resolver; (a code) descifrar; (a door) entreabrir; **to — down on** reprimir; **that —s me up** esto me hace desternillar de risa; N (fissure) rajadura *f*, grieta *f*, resquebrajadura *f*; (sound) chasquido *m*; (joke) pulla *f*, chanza *f*; (of the butt) *vulg* raja *f*; — **cocaine** crack *m*; —**down**

represión f; **—house** fumadero m; **—pot** excéntrico -ca mf; **at the — of dawn** al romper el alba; **I'd like a — at the championship** me gustaría poder participar en el campeonato

cracked [krækt] ADJ rajado, quebrado; (crazy) chiflado; **it's not all it's — up to be** no es para tanto

cracker [krǽkɚ] N galleta f

crackle [krǽkəł] N (of paper) crujido m; (of fire) crepitación f; VI crujir, crepitar

cradle [krédl] N cuna f

craft [kræft] N (skill) destreza f; (cunning) astucia f; (occupation) arte m, oficio m; (boat) embarcación f; **—sman** artesano m; **—swoman** artesana f; VT fabricar

crafty [krǽfti] ADJ astuto, taimado

crag [kræg] N risco m, peñasco m, peñón m

craggy [krǽgi] ADJ peñascoso

cram [kræm] VT (pack in) embutir; VI (study intensely) memorizar; Sp empollar; **the bar was —med with people** el bar estaba atestado

cramp [kræmp] N (spasm) calambre m; (staple) grapa f; VI/VT (to suffer a spasm) acalambrar(se); VT (to staple) engrapar; **you're —ing my style** me estorbas

cranberry [krǽnbɛri] N arándano agrio m

crane [kren] N (bird) grulla f; (machine) grúa f; VT **to — one's neck** estirar el cuello

cranium [kréniəm] N cráneo m

crank [kræŋk] N (mechanism) manivela f; (grouch) cascarrabias mf sg; (overzealous advocate) fanático -ca mf; **—case** cárter superior del aceite m; **—shaft** cigüeñal m; VI/VT arrancar con manivela

cranky [krǽŋki] ADJ (irritable) irritable; (eccentric) excéntrico

cranny [krǽni] N (crevice) rendija f; (corner) recoveco m

crap [kræp] N (excrement) vulg mierda f; (nonsense) estupideces f pl; **to take a —** vulg cagar; **—s** dados m pl; VI vulg cagar

crappy [krǽpi] ADJ vulg de mierda

crash [kræʃ] VI (collide) estrellarse; (market) quebrar; (overnight with someone) quedarse a dormir; (hang up, as with a computer) colgarse; (sleep) dormir; VT **to — a car** chocar un coche; **to — a party** colarse en una fiesta; N (noise) estallido m; (collision) choque m; (financial) quiebra f; **— landing** aterrizaje forzoso m

crass [kræs] ADJ craso

crate [kret] N cajón m, guacal m; VT poner en cajones

crater [krédɚ] N cráter m

cravat [krəvǽt] N corbata f

crave [krev] VT anhelar; **I — chocolate** me muero por un chocolate

craving [krévɪŋ] N antojo m

crawl [krɔł] VI (on hands and knees) gatear; (on the belly) arrastrarse, reptar; (proceed slowly) avanzar a paso de tortuga; **to be —ing with** hormiguear de; N (swimming stroke) crol m; **traffic is going at a —** el tráfico va a paso de tortuga

crayon [kréɑn] N lápiz de color m, crayola[tm] f

craze [krez] N (vogue) moda f; VI/VT enloquecer(se)

craziness [krézɪnɪs] N locura f, chifladura f

crazy [krézi] ADJ & N loco -ca mf; **I'm — about you** estoy loco por ti; **that's —!** ¡qué locura! **to go —** volverse loco, enloquecerse

creak [krik] N (of wooden floor) crujido m; (of a hinge) rechinamiento m; VI (a wooden floor) crujir; (a hinge) rechinar

cream [krim] N (milk product) crema f; Sp nata f; (medicament) crema f; **— cheese** queso de untar m; **— of tomato soup** sopa crema de tomate f; **the — of the crop** la flor y nata; VT (decream) desnatar; (butter, sugar) batir; (vegetables) preparar con salsa blanca; (defeat) aplastar

creamy [krími] ADJ cremoso

crease [kris] N (in trousers) raya f, repliegue m; (wrinkle) arruga f; VT (trousers) planchar la raya; (wrinkle) arrugar

create [kriét] VI/VT crear

creation [kriéʃən] N creación f

creationism [kriéʃənɪzəm] N creacionismo m

creative [kriéDɪv] ADJ creativo

creator [kriéDɚ] N creador -ra mf

creature [krítʃɚ] N (being) ser m; (animal) animal m; **a — of your imagination** un producto de tu imaginación

credence [krídn̩s] N crédito m

credentials [krɪdéntʃəłz] N credenciales f pl

credible [krédəbəł] ADJ creíble

credit [krédɪt] N crédito m; (commendation) reconocimiento m; **— card** tarjeta de crédito f; **— line** línea de crédito f; **—s** créditos m pl; **— underwriters** aseguradores de crédito m pl; **— union** banco cooperativo m; **—worthy** solvente; **on —** a crédito; **to give — to** (believe) dar crédito; (ascribe) acreditar; VT (believe) creer; (enter as credit) acreditar; (attribute) atribuir

creditor [krédIDɚ] N acreedor -ra mf

credulous [krédʒələs] ADJ crédulo

creed [krid] N credo m

creek [krik] N arroyo m

creep [krip] VI (crawl on belly) arrastrarse;

(crawl on all fours) gatear; (grow upward) trepar; (go slowly) andar a paso de tortuga; **to — up on** acercarse furtivamente a; N (obnoxious person) *pej* repulsivo -va *mf*, sinvergüenza *mf*; **that gives me the —s** eso me da asco; *Sp* eso me da grima

creeper [krípɚ] N enredadera *f*, planta trepadora *f*

creepy [krípi] ADJ repulsivo

cremate [krímet] VT cremar

Creole [krííol] ADJ & N criollo -lla *mf*

creosote [kríəsot] N creosota *f*

crepe [krep] N (fabric) crespón *m*; (band of fabric) crespón negro *m*

crescent [krésənt] N media luna *f*; ADJ creciente

crest [krest] N (of a wave, rooster) cresta *f*; (of feathers) penacho *m*, copete *m*; (of mountain) cima *f*, cumbre *f*; (of heraldic arms) timbre *m*; **—fallen** alicaído, cabizbajo; VI **the river —ed at two meters above flood-level** el río creció hasta dos metros por encima de lo normal

crevice [krévɪs] N grieta *f*

crew [kru] N (for ships, etc.) tripulación *f*; (of workers) cuadrilla *f*

crib [krɪb] N (bed) cuna *f*; (manger) pesebre *m*; (bin for grain) granero *m*; (cheat notes) hoja para copiar *f*; VI copiar

cricket [kríkɪt] N (insect) grillo *m*; (game) criquet *m*

crime [kraɪm] N (illegal act) delito *m*; (act of violence against people) crimen *m*; (criminal activity) delincuencia *f*, criminalidad *f*

criminal [krímənəl] ADJ & N delincuente *mf*, malhechor -ora *mf*; (violent crimes) criminal *mf*

crimp [krɪmp] VT rizar; N rizo *m*

crimson [krímzən] ADJ & N carmesí *m*, carmín *m*

cringe [krɪndʒ] VI **he makes me —** me da asco

cripple [krípəl] N *offensive* tullido -da *mf*; (in the legs) *offensive* cojo -ja *mf*; (in the arms) *offensive* manco -ca *mf*; VT tullir

crisis [kráɪsɪs] N crisis *f*

crisp [krɪsp] ADJ (apple, bacon, etc.) crocante, crujiente; (weather) fresco y despejado; (hair) crespo; VI/VT volver crujiente

crispy [kríspi] ADJ crocante, crujiente

criterion [kraɪtíriən] N criterio *m*

critic [krídɪk] N crítico -ca *mf*

critical [krídɪkəl] ADJ crítico

criticism [krídɪsɪzəm] N crítica *f*

criticize [krídɪsaɪz] VT criticar

croak [krok] VI (make the sound of a frog) croar; (make the sound of a crow) graznar; (die) *fam* espichar; N (sound made by frogs) canto de ranas *m*; (sound made by crows) graznido *m*

Croatia [kroéʃə] N Croacia *f*

Croatian [kroéʃən] ADJ & N croata *mf*

crochet [kroʃé] N ganchillo *m*, croché *m*, crochet *m*; **— hook** aguja de croché *f*; VI hacer ganchillo, hacer croché

crock [krɑk] N (pot) vasija *f*; (lies) pamplinas *f pl*

crockery [krákəri] N loza *f*

crocodile [krákədaɪl] N cocodrilo *m*

croissant [krəsánt] N cruasán *m*, croissant *m*

crony [króni] N compinche *mf*, compadre *m*, comadre *f*

crook [krʊk] N (criminal) delincuente *mf*; (curve) curva *f*; (hook) gancho *m*; (staff) cayado *m*

crooked [krúkɪd] ADJ (bent) torcido; *Am* chueco; (dishonest) deshonesto

crop [krɑp] N (harvest) cosecha *f*; (group of contemporaries) promoción *f*; (of a bird) buche *m*; (horse whip) fusta *f*; **— rotation** rotación de cultivos *f*; VT (graze) pastar, pacer; (trim) recortar; **to — up** surgir

croquet [kroké] N cróquet *m*

cross [krɔs] N (symbol) cruz *f*; (street intersection) cruce *m*; (act of mixing) cruzamiento *m*; (in boxing) cruzado *m*; **—bar** (soccer) travesaño *m*; (gymnastics) barra *f*; (high jump) listón *m*; (of a door) tranca *f*; **—-check** verificación *f*; **—piece** cruceta *f*; **to bear one's —** cargar la cruz; VI/VT (intersect, form a cross, breed, meet) cruzar(se); (make sign of the cross) santiguarse; **to —-dress** transvestir(se); VT (betray) traicionar; (pass) cruzar, franquear; **to — out** tachar; **to — over** (change allegiance) cambiar de bando; (go to the other side) traspasar; **you've —ed the line** se te fue la mano; **to —-check** verificar; ADJ (transverse) transversal; (angry) enojado; **—-country** a campo traviesa; **—-cultural** transcultural; **—-dresser** travesti *mf*, travestí *mf*; **to — examine** interrogar; **—-eyed** bizco; **to be —-eyed** bizquear; **—-fertilization** fecundación cruzada *f*; **—-reference** referencia cruzada *f*; **to —-reference** hacer una referencia cruzada; **—road** encrucijada *f*; **— section** corte transversal *m*; **—walk** cruce peatonal *m*, cebra *f*; **—word puzzle** crucigrama *m*

crossing [krɔ́sɪŋ] N (street or railroad

intersection, pedestrian path) cruce *m*; (hybridization, act of mixing) cruzamiento *m*; (of ocean) travesía *f*; (of a border) paso *m*; (of a river) vado *m*

crotch [krɑtʃ] N entrepierna *f*

crotchety [krátʃɪDi] ADJ cascarrabias

crouch [krautʃ] VI (stoop) agacharse; (prepare to spring) agazaparse

croup [krup] N tos *f*, croup *m*

crow [kro] N (bird) cuervo *m*; (sound of rooster) canto del gallo *m*; **—bar** alzaprima *f*; **—'s-foot** pata de gallo *f*; **to eat —** comerse sus propias palabras; VI cantar; (gloat, brag) jactarse

crowd [kraud] N (group of people) muchedumbre *f*, gentío *m*, aglomeración *f*; (at a performance) público *m*; (clique) pandilla *f*; VI (push forward) agolparse; VI/VT (gather in large numbers) apiñar(se), amontonar(se), aglomerar(se); (gather in a confined space) hacinar(se)

crowded [kráuDɪd] ADJ **it is — in here** hay demasiada gente aquí; **the restaurant is —** el restaurante está lleno

crown [kraun] N corona *f*; (of head) coronilla *f*, crisma *f*; (of a hat) copa *f*; **— jewels** joyas de la corona *f pl*; VT coronar; (hit on head) dar un coscorrón

crucial [krúʃəł] ADJ (element) fundamental; (moment) crucial

crucible [krúsəbəł] N crisol *m*

crucifix [krúsəfɪks] N crucifijo *m*

crucify [krúsəfaɪ] VT crucificar

crud [krʌd] N (filth) mugre *f*; (worthless thing, sickness, despicable person) *fam* porquería *f*

crude [krud] ADJ (vulgar, unpolished) basto, tosco; **— oil** petróleo crudo *m*; **— sugar** azúcar sin refinar *mf*

cruel [krúəł] ADJ cruel

cruelty [krúəłti] N crueldad *f*

cruise [kruz] VI (take a cruise) tomar un crucero; (patrol) patrullar; (seek sexual partners) salir a buscar plan; **— missile** misil crucero *m*; **cruising speed** velocidad de crucero *f*; N crucero *m*; **— control** control de crucero *m*

cruiser [krúzɚ] N crucero *m*

crumb [krʌm] N (small) miga *f*, migaja *f*; (large) mendrugo *m*; VT (break into crumbs) desmigajar; (remove crumbs) sacar las migas

crumble [krámbəł] VI/VT (bread) desmigajar(se); (clods of dirt) desmenuzar(se); (house) desmoronar(se)

crummy [krámi] ADJ (place) *fam* de mala muerte; (object) *fam* de porquería; (show)

flojo

crumple [krámpəł] VI/VT (crush) arrugar(se); VI (collapse) aplastarse

crunch [krʌntʃ] VI/VT (eat noisily) mascar; N (sound) crujido *m*; (shortage) crisis *f*; **—es** abdominales *m pl*

crunchy [krántʃi] ADJ crocante, crujiente

crusade [kruséd] N cruzada *f*; VI (engage in a campaign) hacer una campaña

crusader [kruséDɚ] N cruzado -da *mf*; **a — for human rights** un paladín de los derechos humanos

crush [krʌʃ] VI/VT aplastar, machacar; (stone) demoler; N (act of crushing) aplastamiento *m*; (crowd) tumulto *m*; (infatuation) enamoramiento *m*

crust [krʌst] N (of bread, earth) corteza *f*; (of bread) costra *f*; (of pie) tapa *f*

crusty [krásti] ADJ (with a crust) costroso; (grouchy) irascible

crutch [krʌtʃ] N muleta *f*

cry [kraɪ] N (shout) grito *m*; (weeping) llanto *m*; (call of an animal) reclamo *m*; **a far — from** muy distante de, muy lejos de; VI (shout) gritar; (weep) llorar; **—baby** llorón -ona *mf*; **to — over spilt milk** hacer como la lechera; **to — for attention** reclamar atención; **to — for help** pedir socorro; **to — out** vocear

crystal [krístł] N cristal *m*; **— ball** bola de cristal *f*; **— clear** cristalino

crystalline [krístlɪn] ADJ cristalino

crystallize [krístlaɪz] VI/VT cristalizar(se)

cub [kʌb] N (lion) cachorro *m*; (bear) osezno *m*; (whale) ballenato *m*; (wolf) lobato *m*, lobezno *m*; **— reporter** reportero -ra novato -ta *mf*

Cuba [kjúbə] N Cuba *f*

Cuban [kjúbən] ADJ & N cubano -na *mf*

cubbyhole [kábihoł] N casilla *f*

cube [kjúb] N cubo *m*; **— root** raíz cúbica *f*; VT (cut) cortar en cubos; (raise to the third power) elevar al cubo

cubic [kjúbɪk] ADJ cúbico

cubicle [kjúbɪkəł] N cubículo *m*

cubism [kúbɪzəm] N cubismo *m*

cuckold [kákəłd] N cornudo *m*, cabrón *m*; VT poner los cuernos a

cuckoo [kúku] N cuco *m*, cuclillo *m*; **— clock** reloj de cucú *m*; ADJ & N chiflado -da *mf*; INTERJ cucú

cucumber [kjúkʌmbɚ] N pepino *m*

cud [kʌd] N **to chew the —** rumiar

cuddle [kádł] VI/VT hacer(se) mimos; N mimo *m*

cuddly [kádli] ADJ mimoso

cudgel [kádʒəł] N porra *f*; VT aporrear

cue [kju] N (in theater) pie *m*; (stimulus) estímulo *m*; — **ball** bola blanca *f*; — **stick** taco de billar *m*; VT dar pie, dar la señal

cuff [kʌf] N (of sleeve, glove) puño *m*; (of pants) bajo *m*; (handcuffs) esposas *f pl*; (blow) bofetada *f*; VT (pants) hacer los bajos; (with handcuffs) esposar; (hit) abofetear

cuisine [kwɪzín] N cocina *f*

cul-de-sac [kʌ́ɫdəsæk] N callejón sin salida *m*

culinary [kjúlənɛri] ADJ culinario

cull [kʌɫ] VT (choose) seleccionar, entresacar; (collect) recoger

culminate [kʌ́ɫmənet] VI/VT culminar

culprit [kʌ́ɫprɪt] N culpable *mf*

cult [kʌɫt] N (sect) secta religiosa *f*; (worship) culto *m*

cultivate [kʌ́ɫtəvet] VT cultivar

cultivated [kʌ́ɫtəveDɪd] ADJ (land) cultivado; (plant) de cultivo; (educated) culto

cultivation [kʌɫtəvéʃən] N (tillage) cultivo *m*; (education) cultura *f*

cultivator [kʌ́ɫtəveDɚ] N (person) cultivador -ra *mf*; (implement) cultivadora *f*

cultural [kʌ́ɫtʃɚəɫ] ADJ cultural

culture [kʌ́ɫtʃɚ] N cultura *f*; (microorganisms) cultivo *m*; — **shock** choque cultural *m*; VT (microorganisms) cultivar

cultured [kʌ́ɫtʃɚd] ADJ (person) culto; (pearl) cultivado, de cultivo

cumbersome [kʌ́mbɚsəm] ADJ (bulky) voluminoso; (unwieldy) incómodo

cumulative [kjúmjələDɪv] ADJ acumulativo

cumulus [kjúmjələs] N cúmulo *m*

cunning [kʌ́nɪŋ] ADJ (sly) astuto, zorro; N astucia *f*, maña *f*

cunt [kʌnt] N *Sp vulg* coño *m*; *Mex vulg* chocho *m*; *RP vulg* concha *f*

cup [kʌp] N (with handle) taza *f*, pocillo *m*; (without handle) vaso *m*; (measure) taza *f*; (trophy, brassiere part) copa *f*; —**board** armario *m*, aparador *m*

cur [kɚ] N (dog) perro *m*; (villain) *pej* villano -na *mf*

curable [kjúrəbəɫ] ADJ curable

curator [kjúreDɚ] N conservador -ra *mf*

curb [kɚb] N (of a street) *Sp* bordillo *m*; *Mex* borde *m*; *RP* cordón *m*; (of a well) brocal *m*; (restraint) freno *m*, restricción *f*; VT (emotions) refrenar; (spending) limitar

curd [kɚd] N cuajada *f*; VI/VT cuajar(se), coagular(se)

curdle [kɚdɫ] VI/VT cuajar(se), coagular(se); **my blood** —**d** se me heló la sangre

cure [kjur] N (healing, preserving meat) cura *f*, curación *f*; (method) tratamiento *m*; VI/VT curar(se); —**-all** sanalotodo *m*

curfew [kɚ́fju] N toque de queda *m*, queda *f*

curio [kjúrio] N curiosidad *f*

curiosity [kjuriásɪDi] N curiosidad *f*

curious [kjúriəs] ADJ curioso

curl [kɚɫ] VI/VT (form ringlets) rizar(se), ensortijar(se); (coil) enroscar(se); (smoke) alzarse en espirales; **to** — **up** ovillar(se); N (of hair) rizo *m*, bucle *m*; (of smoke) espiral *f*

curler [kɚ́lɚ] N *Sp* rulo *m*; *Mex* tubo *m*; *RP* rulero *m*

curly [kɚ́li] ADJ rizado

currant [kɚ́ənt] N (fruit) grosella *f*; (tree) grosellero *m*

currency [kɚ́ənsi] N (money) moneda *f*, divisa *f*; (acceptance) aceptación *f*

current [kɚ́ənt] ADJ (commonly used) corriente; (prevalent) actual; **the** — **issue of a magazine** el último número de una revista; **the** — **month** el corriente mes; N corriente *f*

curriculum [kəríkjələm] N plan de estudios *m*

curry [kɚ́ri] N curry *m*

curse [kɚs] N (ill wish) maldición *f*; (swear word) palabrota *f*; VI/VT (wish ill) maldecir; (swear) decir palabrotas

cursive [kɚ́sɪv] ADJ cursivo; N cursiva *f*

cursor [kɚ́sɚ] N cursor *m*

curt [kɚt] ADJ (abrupt) seco, brusco; (brief) breve

curtail [kətéɫ] VT restringir, cercenar

curtain [kɚ́tn̩] N cortina *f*; (theater) telón *m*; VT ponerle cortinas a

curvature [kɚ́vətʃur] N curvatura *f*; (of the spine) desviación *f*

curve [kɚv] N curva *f*; **he threw me a** — me agarró desprevenido; VI/VT encorvar(se); (road) torcer(se), desviar(se); VI **the ball** —**s** la pelota tiene efecto

curved [kɚvd] ADJ curvo

cushion [kúʃən] N (pad) almohadilla *f*; (emergency resources, pad of air) colchón *m*; (pillow) almohadón *m*; (decorative pillow) cojín *m*; VT (put pads) poner almohadones; (soften a blow) amortiguar

cuss [kʌs] VI decir palabrotas; N —**word** *fam* palabrota *f*; **strange old** — *fam* bicho raro *m*

custard [kʌ́stɚd] N flan *m*, natillas *f pl*

custodian [kʌstódiən] N (caretaker) cuidador -ra *mf*; (guardian) custodio -dia *mf*

custody [kʌ́stədi] N custodia *f*; **to take into** — detener

custom [kʌ́stəm] N costumbre *f*, uso *m*;

—-**built** construido por encargo;
—-**made** hecho a medida; —**s**
(government department) aduana *f*;
(taxes) derechos de aduana *m pl*;
—**(s)house** aduana *f*
customary [kástəmɛri] ADJ acostumbrado
customer [kástəmə-] N cliente -ta *mf*
customize [kástəmaɪz] VT adaptar por
encargo
cut [kʌt] VI/VT cortar; (shorten) acortar; (trees)
talar; (prices) rebajar; —! ¡corte(n)! **to — a
deal** llegar a un arreglo; **to — across**
(take a shortcut) cortar por; (transcend)
trascender; **to — back** reducir; **to —
class** faltar a clase; **to — down on**
reducir; **to — in** (interrupt) interrumpir;
(in traffic) atravesarse; **may I — in?** ¿me
permite? **to — off** (interrupt) interrumpir;
(intercept) interceptar; **to — out** omitir;
to be — out for estar hecho para; **to —
up** (divide) trozar; (misbehave) portarse
mal; —-**and-dried** predeterminado;
—**back** reducción *f*; — **glass** cristal
labrado *m*; —**off date** fecha límite *f*;
—-**rate** de rebajas; —**throat** despiadado;
N corte *m*; (in salary) recorte *m*; (of prices)
rebaja *f*; (of a suit) hechura *f*, corte *m*;
(insult) desaire *f*
cute [kjut] ADJ mono, rico; **to act —** ser
afectado, ser melindroso
cuticle [kjúDɪkəl] N cutícula *f*
cutlery [kátləri] N (knives, knife store)
cuchillería *f*; (eating utensils) cubiertos *m
pl*
cutlet [kátlɪt] N filete *m*
cutter [káDə-] N (person) cortador -ra *mf*;
(device) cortadora *f*; (sleigh) trineo *m*;
Coast Guard — guardacostas *m sg*
cutting [káDɪŋ] ADJ (sharp) cortante; (cold)
penetrante; (sarcastic) mordaz, sarcástico;
— **board** tabla de cortar *f*; — **edge** filo *m*
cyanide [sáɪənaɪd] N cianuro *m*
cybernetics [saɪbə-néDɪks] N cibernética *f*
cyberpunk [sáɪbə-pʌnk] N ciberpunk *m*
cyberspace [sáɪbə-spes] N ciberespacio *m*
cyborg [sáɪbɔrg] N cyborg *m*
cycle [sáɪkəl] N ciclo *m*
cyclical [síklɪkəl] ADJ cíclico
cyclone [sáɪklon] N ciclón *m*
cyclotron [sáɪklətran] N ciclotrón *m*
cylinder [sílɪndə-] N cilindro *m*; (of a gun)
tambor *m*; — **head** culata *f*
cylindrical [sɪlíndrɪkəl] ADJ cilíndrico
cymbal [símbəl] N címbalo *m*, platillo *m*
cynic [sínɪk] N cínico -ca *mf*
cynical [sínɪkəl] ADJ cínico
cynicism [sínɪsɪzəm] N cinismo *m*

cypress [sáɪprɪs] N ciprés *m*
Cypriot, Cypriote [síprɪət] ADJ & N chipriota
mf
Cyprus [sáɪprəs] N Chipre *m*
cyst [sɪst] N quiste *m*
czar [zɑr] N zar *m*
Czech [tʃɛk] ADJ & N checo -ca *mf*
Czech Republic [tʃékrɪpáblɪk] N República
Checa *f*

Dd

dab [dæb] VT (pat) dar toques; (apply) aplicar
con golpecitos; N toque *m*
dabble [dǽbəl] VI (splash) chapotear; (be
interested superficially) ser aficionado a
dachshund [dáksənd] N perro salchicha *m*
dad [dæd] N papá *m*
daddy [dǽDi] N papaíto *m*, papito *m*,
papacito *m*
daffodil [dǽfədɪl] N narciso *m*
dagger [dǽgə-] N daga *f*, puñal *m*; **to look
—s at** traspasar con la mirada
dahlia [dǽljə] N dalia *f*
daily [déli] ADJ diario; — **wage** jornal *m*,
salario *m*; N diario *m*
dainty [dénti] ADJ (delicate) delicado,
exquisito; (finicky) remilgado
dairy [déri] N (milk) lechería *f*; (cheese)
quesería *f*; ADJ (industry) lechero;
(product) lácteo
daisy [dézi] N margarita *f*; **to be pushing
up daisies** *fam* estar criando malvas
dale [del] N valle *m*
dally [dǽli] VI (risk danger) jugar con fuego;
(waste time) remolonear
dam [dæm] N presa *f*, represa *f*; VT represar
damage [dǽmɪdʒ] N daño *m*, destrozo *m*; —**s**
daños y perjuicios *m pl*; **to pay —s**
indemnizar *m*; VI/VT dañar(se)
damaging [dǽmɪdʒɪŋ] ADJ perjudicial
dame [dem] N (noblewoman) dama *f*;
(woman) *pej* tipa *f*
damn [dæm] VT condenar; **it's not worth a
—** no vale un comino; INTERJ *vulg* ¡maldito
sea!
damnation [dæmnéʃən] N condenación *f*,
perdición *f*
damp [dæmp] ADJ húmedo; N humedad *f*; VT
(wet) humedecer; (deaden) amortiguar;
(extinguish) apagar
dampen [dǽmpən] VT (wet) humedecer;
(depress) deprimir; (deaden) amortiguar

dampness [dǽmpnɪs] N humedad *f*

damsel [dǽmzəł] N damisela *f*

dance [dæns] N (act of dancing, party, activity) baile *m*; (artistic activity, animal courtship movements) danza *f*; — **music** música bailable *f*; VI/VT (at a party) bailar; (in ballet, of animals) danzar; **she —d her way to stardom** llegó al estrellato bailando

dancer [dǽnsɚ] N bailarín -ina *mf*, danzante *mf*

dancercise [dǽnsɚsaɪz] N baile aeróbico *m*

dandelion [dǽndlaɪən] N diente de león *m*

dandruff [dǽndrəf] N caspa *f*

dandy [dǽndi] N (affected man) dandi *m*, señorito *m*; ADJ estupendo

Dane [den] N danés -esa *mf*

danger [déndʒɚ] N peligro *m*

dangerous [déndʒɚəs] ADJ peligroso

dangle [dǽŋgəł] VI/VT (hang) colgar; (sway) bambolear(se); (tempt) tentar con; **her legs were dangling off the bench** sus piernas pendían del banco

Danish [dénɪʃ] ADJ danés; N bollo dulce *m*

dapple, dappled [dǽpəl(d)] ADJ pinto, moteado

dare [dɛr] VI/VT (be brave) atreverse (a), osar; (challenge) desafiar; **how — you?** ¿cómo te atreves? N desafío *m*; —**devil** temerario -ria *mf*

daring [dérɪŋ] N atrevimiento *m*, osadía *f*; ADJ atrevido, osado, arriesgado

dark [dɑrk] ADJ (in color) oscuro; (of hair) moreno, morocho, trigueño; (gloomy) sombrío, tenebroso; (evil, ignorant) oscuro; (hidden) turbio; — **Ages** (Alta) Edad Media *f*; —**room** cuarto oscuro *m*; —-**skinned** moreno; N oscuridad *f*; **after** — después de que oscurece

darken [dárkən] VI/VT oscurecer(se)

darkness [dárknɪs] N (complete) oscuridad *f*, tinieblas *f pl*; (partial) penumbra *f*

darling [dárlɪŋ] ADJ & N amado -da *mf*, querido -da *mf*; **my —** vida mía, amor mío

darn [dɑrn] VT zurcir, remendar; —**ing needle** aguja de zurcir *f*; N zurcido *m*; **it is not worth a —** no vale un comino; INTERJ ¡caramba! ¡caracoles!

dart [dɑrt] N (missile) dardo *m*; (tuck) pinza *f*; (swift movement) movimiento rápido *m*; —**board** diana *f*; **to play —s** jugar a los dardos; VI disparar; **to — out** salir disparado

dash [dæʃ] VI/VT (of waves, porcelain) estrellar(se); VT (plans) frustrar; VI (hopes) desplomarse; **to — by** pasar corriendo; **to**

— **off / out** salir disparado; **to — off a letter** escribir de prisa una carta; N (line) raya *f*; (run) corrida *f*; (race) carrera *f*; (small amount) pizca *f*; (splash) salpicadura *f*; **the one-hundred-meter** — la carrera de los cien metros llanos / planos; —**board** tablero *m*, salpicadero *m*

data [déɾə,dǽɾə] N datos *m pl*; —**base** base de datos *f*; —**bank** banco de datos *m*; — **processing** procesamiento de datos *m*

date [det] N (time) fecha *f*; (appointment) cita *f*; (person) acompañante *mf*; (fruit) dátil *m*; **out of —** anticuado; **to —** hasta ahora; **up to —** al día; VI (be dated) estar fechado; (go out socially) salir; VT (write the date) fechar; (show to be old-fashioned) delatar la edad; (go out socially) salir con; **to — from** datar de, remontarse a

dated [déɾɪd] ADJ (having a date) fechado; (old-fashioned) anticuado

daub [dɔb] VT (smear) embarrar, embadurnar; (apply unskillfully) pintarrajear

daughter [dɔ́ɾɚ] N hija *f*; —-**in-law** nuera *f*

daunt [dɔnt] VT (intimidate) intimidar; (dishearten) desanimar

dauntless [dɔ́ntlɪs] ADJ intrépido

davenport [dǽvənport] N sofá grande *m*

dawn [dɔn] N alba *f*, amanecer *m*, aurora *f*; **the — of civilization** los albores de la civilización; VI amanecer, aclarar; **it just —ed on me that** caí en (la) cuenta de que

day [de] N día *m*; — **after tomorrow** pasado mañana *m*; — **before yesterday** anteayer *m*; —**break** amanecer *m*; **at —break** al amanecer; —**care** guardería *f*; —**dream** fantasía *f*; **to —dream** soñar despierto; — **laborer** jornalero -ra *mf*; —**light** luz del día *f*; —**time** día *m*; —**time activity** actividad diurna *f*; —-**to-** día a día; **by —** de día; **by the** — por día; **eight-hour —** jornada de ocho horas *f*; **in my —** en mis tiempos; **in the old —s** antaño; **make my —** dame el gusto; **New Year's —** Año Nuevo *m*; ADJ diurno

daze [dez] VT aturdir; N **to be in a —** estar aturdido

dazzle [dǽzəł] VI/VT deslumbrar

deacon [díkən] N diácono *m*

deactivate [diǽktəvet] VI/VT desactivar

dead [dɛd] ADJ muerto; — **air** aire viciado *m*; —**beat** moroso -sa *mf*; —**bolt** pestillo *m*; **he's a — duck** está muerto; — **end** callejón sin salida *m*; —-**end job** puesto sin perspectivas *m*; — **letter** letra muerta *f;* **—line** fecha límite *f;* **—lock** punto muerto *m;* **to —lock** trancarse; **—pan** de palo; **— ringer** fiel retrato *m;* **— sure** completamente seguro; **— tired** muerto de cansancio; **—wood** (person) persona inútil *f;* (thing) cosa inútil *f;* N **the —** los muertos; **in the — of the night** en el silencio de la noche; **in the — of winter** en pleno invierno

deaden [dédn̩] VT amortiguar

deadly [dédli] ADJ (enemy) mortal; (poison) letal; (weapon) mortífero; ADV mortalmente; **— dull** sumamente aburrido

deaf [dɛf] ADJ sordo; **—-mute** sordomudo -da *mf*

deafen [défən] VT (make deaf) ensordecer; (deaden) amortiguar

deafening [défənɪŋ] ADJ ensordecedor, atronador

deafness [défnɪs] N sordera *f*

deal [diɫ] VT (cards) dar, repartir; (drugs) vender; (a blow) dar, asestar; **to — in** comerciar en; **biology —s with the study of life** la biología se ocupa del estudio de la vida; **I have to — with all kinds of people** tengo que vérmelas con todo tipo de gente; N (business transaction) trato *m,* negocio *m;* (shady transaction) componenda *f;* (act of dealing) reparto *m;* **a great — of** una gran cantidad de; **it's a —** ¡trato hecho! **I got a raw —** me clavaron

dealer [dílɚ] N (in cars, antiques) comerciante *mf;* (in drugs, arms) traficante *mf;* (of cards) el / la que reparte *mf*

dealings [dílɪŋz] N trato *m,* relaciones *f pl;* (business) negocios *m pl*

dean [din] N (of university, professional group) decano -na *mf;* (in church) deán *m*

dear [dɪr] ADJ (beloved) querido; (expensive) caro; (cherished) apreciado; **— Sir / Madam** Estimado señor / Estimada señora; **my —est wish** mi deseo más ferviente; N **he's such a —!** ¡es un amor! **my —** querido mío *m* / querida mía *f;* ADV caro; **that cost me —** eso me costó caro; **— me!** ¡Dios mío! **oh —!** ¡Dios mío!

dearth [dɝθ] N escasez *f*

death [dɛθ] N muerte *f;* **—bed** lecho de muerte *m;* **— certificate** partida de defunción *f;* **— penalty** pena de muerte *f;* **— rate** tasa de mortalidad *f;* **— row** pabellón de los condenados a muerte *m;* **— squad** escuadrón de la muerte *m;* **— toll** mortandad *f;* **—trap** trampa mortal *f;* **— wish** instinto suicida *m;* **to put to —**

ejecutar; **we have discussed this to —** hemos discutido esto hasta el hartazgo; **I'm sick to — of this job** estoy harto de este trabajo

debacle [dɪbákət] N debacle *f*

debase [dɪbés] VT degradar, envilecer

debatable [dɪbédəbət] ADJ discutible

debate [dɪbét] N debate *m;* VI/VT (discuss) debatir, discutir; (weigh a decision) considerar

debilitate [dɪbílɪtet] VT debilitar

debit [débɪt] N débito *m,* adeudo *m;* (column in an account) debe *m;* (total sum owed) pasivo *m;* **— card** tarjeta de cobro automático *f;* VT adeudar, cargar a la cuenta

debriefing [dibrífɪŋ] N informe *m*

debris [dəbrí] N (ruins) escombros *m pl;* (detritus) detritus *m (pl)*

debt [dɛt] N deuda *f;* **bad —** cuenta incobrable *f;* **to get into —** endeudarse

debtor [dédɚ] N deudor -ra *mf*

debug [dibág] VT depurar

debugging [dibágɪŋ] N depuración *f*

debunk [dibáŋk] VT (ideas, beliefs) desacreditar; (myths) desmistificar

debut [debjú] N (of a play or film) estreno *m;* (in society) presentación en sociedad *f;* **to make a —** (an actor) debutar; (in society) presentarse en sociedad; VI/VT (a film) estrenar(se); (a product) lanzar(se) al mercado

decade [déked] N década *f,* decenio *m*

decadence [dékəɖəns] N decadencia *f*

decadent [dékəɖənt] ADJ decadente

decaffeinated [dɪkǽfɪneɖɪd] ADJ descafeinado

decal [díkæɫ] N calcomanía *f,* autoadhesivo *m*

decanter [dɪkǽntɚ] N garrafa *f*

decapitate [dɪkǽpɪtet] VT decapitar

decathlon [dɪkǽθlɑn] N decatlón *m*

decay [dɪké] VI/VT (biological matter) descomponer(se); (teeth) cariar(se); VI (health) deteriorarse; (radioactive matter) desintegrarse; N (of morals) decadencia *f;* (of biological matter) descomposición *f;* (nuclear) desintegración *f;* (tooth) caries *f*

decease [dɪsís] N muerte *f,* fallecimiento *m;* VI morir, fallecer

deceased [dɪsíst] ADJ & N difunto -ta *mf*

deceit [dɪsít] N engaño *m,* trampa *f*

deceitful [dɪsítfət] ADJ tramposo, engañoso

deceive [dɪsív] VI/VT engañar

decelerate [diséləret] VI desacelerar

December [dɪsémbɚ] N diciembre *m*

decency [dísənsi] N decencia *f*

decent [dísənt] ADJ decente

deception [dɪsέpʃən] N engaño *m*
decibel [désəbəɫ] N decibelio *m*
decide [dɪsáɪd] VT (make a decision) decidir; (award victory) fallar; **what —d you to come?** ¿qué te motivó a venir?
decided [dɪsáɪDɪd] ADJ (resolute) decidido; (clear) claro
deciduous [dɪsíʤuəs] ADJ deciduo, caduco; **— tooth** diente de la primera dentición *m*
decimal [désəməɫ] ADJ decimal
decimate [désəmet] VT diezmar
decipher [dɪsáɪfɚ] VT descifrar
decision [dɪsíʒən] N decisión *f*; (in court) fallo *m*
decisive [dɪsáɪsɪv] ADJ decisivo
deck [dɛk] N (of a boat) cubierta *f*; (of a house) terraza *f*; (of playing cards) baraja *f*; VT (knock down) tumbar; (decorate) decorar; **to — oneself out** emperifollarse; **hit the —!** ¡cuerpo a tierra!
declaration [dɛkləréʃən] N declaración *f*
declare [dɪklér] VI/VT declarar, afirmar
decline [dɪkláɪn] N (deterioration) decadencia *f*; (slope) declive *m*; (reduction in prices) baja *f*; VI/VT declinar; (an offer) rechazar; **to — to do something** negarse a hacer algo
decode [dikód] VT descodificar
decompose [dikəmpóz] VI/VT descomponer(se)
decongestant [dikənʤéstənt] N descongestionante *m*
decorate [dékəret] VT decorar; (award medals) condecorar
decoration [dɛkəréʃən] N (embellishment) adorno *m*; (interior decorating) decoración *f*; (medal of honor) condecoración *f*
decorative [dékəɚəDIV] ADJ decorativo
decorous [dékɚəs] ADJ decoroso
decorum [dɪkɔ́rəm] N decoro *m*
decoy [díkɔɪ] N (artifact) señuelo *m*, reclamo *m*; (live animal or person) cimbel *m*; VT atraer con señuelo / cimbel
decrease [díkris] N disminución *f*, merma *f*; [dɪkrís] VI/VT disminuir, mermar
decree [dɪkrí] N decreto *m*; VI/VT decretar
decrepit [dɪkrépɪt] ADJ decrépito
decry [dɪkráɪ] VT condenar
dedicate [déDɪket] VI/VT dedicar(se); VT (mark opening of a highway, etc.) inaugurar
dedication [dɛDɪkéʃən] N (act of dedicating) dedicación *f*; (in a book) dedicatoria *f*; (of a highway, etc.) inauguración *f*
deduce [dɪdús] VT deducir
deduct [dɪdʌ́kt] VT deducir
deductible [dɪdʌ́ktəbəɫ] ADJ deducible, desgravable; N deducible *m*

deduction [dɪdʌ́kʃən] N deducción *f*
deed [did] N (action) acción *f*; (exploit) hazaña *f*; (certificate of ownership) escritura *f*
deem [dim] VT considerar
deep [dip] ADJ (extending down) hondo, profundo; (dark) oscuro; (of a voice) grave; **— freeze** congelador *m*; **— in debt** cargado de deudas; **— in thought** absorto; **—-sea** de altura; **he's got — pockets** es un ricachón; **he went off the — end with his hobby** se le fue la mano con el pasatiempo; **ten meters —** de diez metros de profundidad; **to —-six** hacer desaparecer; **in the —** el piélago, el abismo; ADV **to dive —** bucear en las profundidades
deepen [dípən] VI/VT ahondar, profundizar
deer [dir] N ciervo *m*, venado *m*; **—skin** gamuza *f*
deface [dɪfés] VT (disfigure) desfigurar; (smear with paint) pintarrajear; (mutilate) mutilar
defame [dɪfém] VT difamar
default [dɪfɔ́ɫt] N (negligence) negligencia *f*; (failure to appear in court) rebeldía *f*; (computer setting) opción por defecto *f*; **in —** en mora; **by —** en ausencia de alternativa; (in sports) por abandono de los contrincantes; VI (on a loan) no pagar; (in a sports match) no comparecer
defeat [dɪfít] VT vencer, derrotar; N derrota *f*
defecate [défɪket] VI defecar
defect [dífɛkt] N defecto *m*; [dɪfɛ́kt] VI desertar
defection [dɪfɛ́kʃən] N defección *f*
defective [dɪfɛ́ktɪv] ADJ defectuoso
defend [dɪfɛ́nd] VI/VT defender
defendant [dɪfɛ́ndənt] N (criminal) acusado -da *mf*, reo -a *mf*; (civil) demandado -da *mf*
defender [dɪfɛ́ndɚ] N defensor -ora *mf*
defense [dɪfɛ́ns] N defensa *f*
defenseless [dɪfɛ́nslɪs] ADJ indefenso
defensible [dɪfɛ́nsəbəɫ] ADJ defendible
defensive [dɪfɛ́nsɪv] ADJ defensivo; **on the —** a la defensiva
defer [dɪfɚ́] VT (a meeting) diferir, posponer; (a payment) prorrogar; (an appointment) dilatar; (from military service) eximir; **to — to another's opinion** remitirse a la opinión de otro
deference [défɚəns] N deferencia *f*
defiance [dɪfáɪəns] N (challenge) desafío *m*; (resistance to authority) rebeldía *f*; **in — of** en abierta oposición a
defibrillate [difíbrəlet] VT desfibrilar
deficiency [dɪfíʃənsi] N deficiencia *f*

deficient [dɪfíʃənt] ADJ deficiente

deficit [défɪsɪt] N déficit *m*; **— spending** gastos deficitarios *m pl*

defile [dɪfáɪɫ] VT (violate) mancillar; (desecrate) profanar; (to make dirty) ensuciar

define [dɪfáɪn] VI/VT definir

defining [dɪfáɪnɪŋ] ADJ decisivo

definite [défənɪt] ADJ (clearly defined) definido; (certain) seguro; **she was — in her demands** ella fue terminante es sus exigencias; **— article** artículo definido *m*

definitely [défənɪtli] ADV sin duda

definition [dɛfəníʃən] N definición *f*

definitive [dɪfínɪDɪv] ADJ (final) definitivo; (authoritative) de mayor autoridad

deflate [dɪflét] VI/VT desinflar(se)

deflation [dɪfléʃən] N deflación *f*

deflect [dɪflékt] VI/VT desviar(se)

deforestation [difɔrɪstéʃən] N deforestación *f*

deform [dɪfɔrm] VI/VT deformar(se)

deformed [dɪfɔrmd] ADJ deforme

deformity [dɪfɔrmɪDi] N (body part) deformidad *f*; (act or result of deforming) deformación *f*

defraud [dɪfrɔd] VT defraudar

defray [dɪfré] VT sufragar, costear

defrost [difrɔst] VI/VT descongelar(se)

deft [dɛft] ADJ diestro, habilidoso

defunct [dɪfʌŋkt] ADJ caduco; **the Whig party is now —** el partido de los whigs se disolvió

defuse [difjúz] VT (bomb) desactivar; (situation) distender

defy [dɪfáɪ] VT (challenge) desafiar; (resist) resistir

degenerate [dɪdʒénəɪt] ADJ & N degenerado -da *mf*; [dɪdʒénəret] VI degenerar(se)

degradation [dɛgrədéʃən] N degradación *f*

degrade [dɪgréd] VI/VT degradar(se)

degree [dɪgrí] N (stage) grado *m*; (academic) título *m*; **by —s** gradualmente; **to a —** hasta cierto punto; **to get a —** graduarse

dehumanize [dihjúmənaɪz] VI/VT deshumanizar

dehydrate [diháɪdret] VI/VT deshidratar(se)

deign [den] VI dignarse

deity [díɪDi] N deidad *f*

déjà vu [deʒavú] N deja vu *m*

dejected [dɪdʒéktɪd] ADJ abatido, desconsolado

dejection [dɪdʒékʃən] N abatimiento *m*, desconsuelo *m*

delay [dɪlé] N demora *f*, retraso *m*; VT demorar, retrasar; VI demorar, retrasarse

delectable [dɪléktəbəɫ] ADJ delicioso; N delicia *f*

delegate [délɪgɪt] N delegado -da *mf*; [délɪget] VT delegar

delegation [dɛlɪgéʃən] N delegación *f*, representación *f*

delete [dɪlít] VT (omit) suprimir; (cross out) tachar

deletion [dɪlíʃən] N supresión *f*

deliberate [dɪlíbəɪt] ADJ (intentional) deliberado; (careful) cuidadoso; [dɪlíbəret] VI/VT deliberar

deliberation [dɪlɪbəréʃən] N deliberación *f*

delicacy [délɪkəsi] N (fineness, precision, sensitivity) delicadeza *f*; (food) manjar *m*, delicatessen *f pl*, gollería *f*; (breakability) fragilidad *f*

delicate [délɪkɪt] ADJ delicado, tenue; (breakable) frágil; (acute) fino

delicatessen [dɛlɪkətésən] N (store) tienda de fiambres *f*, charcutería *f*; *RP* rotisería *f*; (foods) delicatessen *f pl*

delicious [dɪlíʃəs] ADJ delicioso, rico

delight [dɪláɪt] N (pleasure) deleite *m*, regalo *m*; (source of pleasure) delicia *f*; VI/VT deleitar(se)

delighted [dɪláɪDɪd] ADJ encantado; **to be — to** alegrarse de; **I'm — to meet you** me alegro de conocerla; **I'd be — to dance with you** me encantaría bailar contigo

delightful [dɪláɪtfəɫ] ADJ encantador

delimit [dɪlímɪt] VT delimitar

delineate [dɪlíniet] VT delinear

delinquent [dɪlíŋkwənt] ADJ & N (debtor) moroso -sa *mf*; (wrong-doer) delincuente *mf*; (juvenile) delincuente juvenil *mf*

delirious [dɪlíriəs] ADJ delirante; (happy) contentísimo; **to be —** delirar

delirium [dɪlíriəm] N delirio *m*

deliver [dɪlívɚ] VT (hand over) entregar; (hand out) repartir; (liberate) liberar; (pronounce a speech) pronunciar; (administer a blow) dar; (have a baby) dar a luz; (assist a birth) atender en un parto; **— the goods** cumplir

deliverance [dɪlívɚəns] N liberación *f*

delivery [dɪlívəri] N (handing out) entrega *f*, expedición *f*; (things to be delivered) pedido *m*; (birth) parto *m*; (speaking) ejecución *f*, expresión oral *f*; **— service** servicio de entrega *m*; **— truck** camión de reparto *m*

dell [dɛɫ] N hondonada *f*

delude [dɪlúd] VT engañar

deluge [déljudʒ] N diluvio *m*; VT abrumar

delusion [dɪlúʒən] N (act of deluding, state of being deluded) engaño *m*; **—s of grandeur** delirios de grandeza *m pl*

deluxe [dɪlʌ́ks] ADJ de lujo

demagog, demagogue [démǝgɑg] N demagogo -ga *mf*

demand [dɪmǽnd] VT (ask for) exigir; (require) requerir, exigir; N demanda *f*, exigencia *f*; **on —** por demanda

demanding [dɪmǽndɪŋ] ADJ exigente

demarcate [dɪmárket] VT demarcar

demean [dɪmín] VT menospreciar

demeanor [dɪmínɚ] N conducta *f*, comportamiento *m*

demented [dɪméntɪd] ADJ demente

demijohn [démiʤɑn] N damajuana *f*

demise [dɪmáɪz] N fallecimiento *m*, desaparición *f*

demobilize [dimóbǝlaɪz] VT desmovilizar

democracy [dɪmákrǝsi] N democracia *f*

democrat [démǝkræt] N demócrata *mf*

democratic [dɛmǝkrǽDɪk] ADJ democrático

demographics [dɛmǝgrǽfɪks] N demografía *f*

demolish [dɪmálɪʃ] VT demoler, derrumbar

demon [dímǝn] N demonio *m*

demonstrate [démǝnstret] VT (prove) demostrar; (show a product) hacer una demostración; VI manifestar

demonstration [dɛmǝnstréʃǝn] N (proof, exhibition) demostración *f*; (protest) manifestación *f*, concentración *f*

demonstrative [dɪmánstrǝDɪv] ADJ demostrativo

demoralize [dɪmɔ́rǝlaɪz] VT desmoralizar

demote [dɪmót] VT degradar, bajar de categoría

den [dɛn] N (of an animal) guarida *f*; (room in a house) cuarto de estar *m*; (cave) cueva *f*; **— of iniquity** antro de perdición *m*

denial [dɪnáɪǝɫ] N (refusal to recognize) negación *f*; (act of denying) negativa *f*, rechazo *m*; (assertion that an allegation is false) desmentido *m*; **he is in —** no lo quiere aceptar

denigrate [dénɪgret] VT denigrar

denim [dénɪm] N tela de vaquero *f*

Denmark [dénmɑrk] N Dinamarca *f*

denomination [dɪnɑmǝnéʃǝn] N (name, monetary value) denominación *f*; (sect) secta religiosa *f*

denotation [dinotéʃǝn] N denotación *f*

denote [dɪnót] VT denotar

denounce [dɪnáʊns] VT denunciar

dense [dɛns] ADJ (compacted) denso, tupido, cerrado; (stupid) *fam* burro, duro de entendederas

density [dénsɪDi] N densidad *f*

dent [dɛnt] N abolladura *f*; **to make a — in a task** hacer mella en una tarea; VI/VT abollar(se)

dental [déntɫ] ADJ dental; **— floss** hilo dental *m*; **— hygienist** higienista dental *mf*

dentifrice [déntǝfrɪs] N dentífrico *m*, pasta dental *f*

dentist [déntɪst] N dentista *mf*

dentistry [déntɪstri] N odontología *f*

dentures [déntʃɚz] N dientes postizos *m pl*

denunciation [dɪnʌnsiéʃǝn] N denuncia *f*, acusación *f*

deny [dɪnáɪ] VT (state that something is false) negar, desmentir; (refuse to approve) rechazar; **to — oneself** abstenerse

deodorant [dióDǝǝnt] N desodorante *m*

deoxidize [diáksɪdaɪz] VT desoxidar

depart [dɪpárt] VI (leave) salir, partir; (deviate) desviarse, apartarse; (die) dejar de existir

departed [dɪpárDɪd] ADJ & N difunto -ta *mf*

department [dɪpártmǝnt] N (of company, school, country) departamento *m*; (of government) ministerio *m*; (of a store) sección *f*; (of knowledge, expertise) especialidad *f*; **— store** gran almacén *m*

departure [dɪpártʃɚ] N (scheduled) salida *f*; (not scheduled) partida *f*; (deviation) desviación *f*

depend [dɪpénd] VI depender; **to — on** (be conditioned by) depender de; (rely on) contar con

dependable [dɪpéndǝbǝɫ] ADJ confiable, fiable

dependence [dɪpéndǝns] N dependencia *f*

dependency [dɪpéndǝnsi] N dependencia *f*

dependent [dɪpéndǝnt] ADJ dependiente; **success is — on perseverance** el éxito depende de la perseverancia; N familiar a cargo *mf*

depict [dɪpíkt] VT (verbally) describir; (visually) representar

depilate [dépǝlet] VT depilar(se)

depilatory [dɪpílǝtɔri] ADJ & N depilatorio *m*

deplane [diplén] VI desembarcar

deplete [dɪplít] VT agotar

depletion [dɪplíʃǝn] N agotamiento *m*

deplorable [dɪplɔ́rǝbǝɫ] ADJ deplorable

deplore [dɪplɔ́r] VT deplorar

deploy [dɪplɔ́ɪ] VT desplegar

deport [dɪpórt] VT deportar; VI comportarse

deportment [dɪpɔ́rtmǝnt] N comportamiento *m*, conducta *f*

depose [dɪpóz] VT (overthrow) deponer, derrocar; (testify) declarar; (take testimony) tomar declaración

deposit [dɪpázɪt] VT (add to an account) depositar; *Sp* ingresar; (place) colocar; N (amount added to an account) depósito *m*; *Sp* ingreso *m*; (of a mineral) yacimiento *m*; (earnest money) señal *f*, anticipo *m*

deposition [dɛpəzíʃən] N (removal from office) deposición f; (testimony) declaración f

depositor [dɪpázɪDɚ] N depositante mf

depot [dípo] N (of trains) estación f; (of buses) terminal mf; (for storage) almacén m, depósito m; (for military training) cuartel m

depraved [dɪprévd] ADJ depravado

deprecate [dɛ́prɪket] VT despreciar

depreciate [dɪpríʃiet] VT (currency) depreciar(se); (goods) desvalorizar(se), amortizar(se)

depress [dɪprés] VT deprimir

depressed [dɪprést] ADJ deprimido

depressing [dɪprésɪŋ] ADJ deprimente

depression [dɪpréʃən] N depresión f

deprive [dɪpráɪv] VT privar

depth [dɛpθ] N (of hole, feeling) profundidad f, hondura f; (of the voice) gravedad f; **in the —s** en las profundidades; **in — a** fondo; **what is the — of that bookshelf?** ¿cuánto miden estos estantes de fondo? **he has sunk to such —s** ha caído muy bajo; **in the — of the night** bien entrada la noche; **in the — of winter** en lo más crudo del invierno

deputation [dɛpjətéʃən] N delegación f

deputy [dɛ́pjəDi] N (elected official) diputado -da mf; (substitute) suplente mf

derail [dɪréɫ] VI/VT descarrilar(se)

deranged [dɪréndʒd] ADJ trastornado, demente

derby [dɝ́bi] N (hat) sombrero hongo m; (race) derby m

deregulate [dɪrégjəlet] VT desregular

derelict [dɛ́rəlɪkt] ADJ (deserted) abandonado; (negligent) negligente; N (ship) buque abandonado m; (person) vagabundo -da mf

deride [dɪráɪd] VT escarnecer, ridiculizar

derision [dɪríʒən] N escarnio m

derivation [dɛrəvéʃən] N derivación f

derivative [dɪrívəDɪv] ADJ & N derivado m

derive [dɪráɪv] VI/VT derivar(se); **to — pleasure from** disfrutar de

dermatology [dɝmətáləɡi] N dermatología f

derogatory [dɪrágətɔri] ADJ despectivo

derrick [dɛ́rɪk] N torre de perforación f

descend [dɪsénd] VI/VT descender; **to — upon** caer sobre

descendant [dɪséndənt] ADJ & N descendiente mf

descent [dɪsént] N (act of descending, decline) descenso m; (slope) bajada f; (lineage) descendencia f

describe [dɪskráɪb] VT describir

description [dɪskrípʃən] N descripción f; **of all —s** de todas clases

descriptive [dɪskríptɪv] ADJ descriptivo

desecrate [dɛ́sɪkret] VT profanar

desecration [dɛsɪkréʃən] N profanación f

desegregate [diségrɪget] VI/VT eliminar la segregación racial

desensitize [disénsɪtaɪz] VT insensibilizar

desert [dɛ́zɚt] ADJ (barren, empty) desierto; (of the desert) desértico; N desierto m; [dɪzɝt] VI/VT (a person, place) abandonar; (military service) desertar

deserter [dɪzɝ́Dɚ] N desertor -ra mf

desertion [dɪzɝ́ʃən] N (of a person or place) abandono m; (from the military) deserción f

deserve [dɪzɝ́v] VT merecer

deserving [dɪzɝ́vɪŋ] ADJ merecedor

design [dɪzáɪn] VI/VT (prepare a sketch of) diseñar, trazar; (plan) planear, idear; N (model, pattern) diseño m; (sketch) esbozo m; **he has —s on her** le ha echado el ojo

designate [dɛ́zɪgnet] VT designar, denominar

designation [dɛzɪgnéʃən] N denominación f, designación f

designer [dɪzáɪnɚ] N diseñador -ra mf; **— drugs** drogas de diseño f pl

desirability [dɪzaɪrəbílɪDi] N deseabilidad f, conveniencia f

desirable [dɪzáɪrəbəɫ] ADJ deseable

desire [dɪzáɪr] VT desear; **I — your cooperation** requiero tu cooperación; N deseo m

desirous [dɪzáɪrəs] ADJ deseoso

desist [dɪsíst] VI desistir

desk [dɛsk] N escritorio m; (school) pupitre m; **—top publishing** edición de sobremesa f

desolate [dɛ́səlɪt] ADJ (barren) desolado; [dɛ́səlet] VT desolar, asolar

desolation [dɛsəléʃən] N desolación f, asolamiento m

despair [dɪspér] N desesperanza f; VI desesperarse, perder la esperanza

despairing [dɪspérɪŋ] ADJ de desesperación

desperate [dɛ́spɚət] ADJ desesperado; **— illness** enfermedad gravísima

desperation [dɛspɚéʃən] N desesperación f

despicable [dɪspíkəbəɫ] ADJ despreciable, deleznable

despise [dɪspáɪz] VT despreciar, menospreciar

despite [dɪspáɪt] N despecho m; PREP a pesar de

despoil [dɪspɔ́ɪɫ] VT despojar

despondency [dɪspándənsi] N abatimiento m, desaliento m

despondent [dɪspándənt] ADJ abatido, desalentado

despot [déspət] N déspota *mf*
despotic [dıspáɒık] ADJ despótico
despotism [déspətızəm] N despotismo *m*
dessert [dızə́t] N postre *m*
destabilize [distébəlaız] VT desestabilizar
destination [destənéʃən] N destino *m*
destine [déstın] VT destinar; **she's —d for greatness** promete grandes cosas
destiny [déstəni] N destino *m*
destitute [déstıtut] ADJ menesteroso, indigente; **— of** falto de, desprovisto de
destroy [dıstrɔ́ı] VT (demolish) destruir, deshacer; (kill) sacrificar; (ruin a reputation) arruinar
destroyer [dıstrɔ́ıə] N (person who destroys) destructor -ra *mf*; (ship) destructor *m*
destructible [dıstrʌ́ktəbəɬ] ADJ destructible
destruction [dıstrʌ́kʃən] N (act of demolishing) destrucción *f*; (act of killing) matanza *f*; (act of ruining a reputation) ruina *f*
destructive [dıstrʌ́ktıv] ADJ destructivo, destructor
detach [dıtǽtʃ] VT separar, desprender; (troops) destacar
detachment [dıtǽtʃmənt] N (physical) separación *f*; (emotional) desapego *m*; (of troops) destacamento *m*; (of the retina) desprendimiento *m*
detail [díteɬ] N detalle *m*, pormenor *m*; (military) destacamento *m*; **to go into —** detallar, pormenorizar; [dıtéɬ] VT detallar, pormenorizar; (assign duties) destacar
detain [dıtén] VT detener
detect [dıtékt] VT detectar
detective [dıtéktıv] N detective *mf*
detector [dıtéktə] N detector *m*
detention [dıténʃən] N detención *f*
deter [dıtə́] VT (dissuade) disuadir; (prevent) prevenir
detergent [dıtə́ʤənt] N detergente *m*
deteriorate [dıtíriəret] VI deteriorar(se)
deterioration [dıtiriəréʃən] N deterioro *m*
determination [dıtəmənéʃən] N determinación *f*; (resolution) resolución *f*; (persistence) tesón *m*, perseverancia *f*
determine [dıtə́mın] VT determinar; **to — to do something** decidirse a hacer algo
determined [dıtə́mınd] ADJ decidido, resuelto; (persistent) tesonero
detest [dıtést] VT detestar, abominar de
detestable [dıtéstəbəɬ] ADJ detestable
dethrone [diθrón] VT destronar
detonate [détṇet] VI/VT detonar
detonation [detṇéʃən] N detonación *f*
detour [dítur] N desvío *m*; VI/VT desviar(se)
detoxification [ditaksəfıkéʃən] N

destoxificación *f*
detract [dıtrǽkt] VT distraer; VI **to — from** disminuir
detrimental [detrəméntɬ] ADJ perjudicial
devaluation [divæljuéʃən] N devaluación *f*
devastate [dévəstet] VT devastar, asolar
develop [dıvéləp] VI/VT (mature, elaborate) desarrollar(se); (build houses on) construir, edificar; (treat film) revelar; **she —ed an allergy** le vino una alergia; **—ing countries** países en desarrollo *m pl*
development [dıvéləpmənt] N (evolution) desarrollo *m*; (buildings) urbanización *f*, colonia *f*; (of a photograph) revelado *m*
deviate [díviet] VI/VT desviar(se)
deviation [diviéʃən] N desviación *f*
device [dıváıs] N (gadget) artefacto *m*; (literary convention) recurso *m*; (emblem) divisa *f*; **they left me to my own —s** me dejaron que me las arreglara sola
devil [dévəɬ] N diablo *m*; **lucky —!** ¡suertudo! **what the — are you saying?** ¿qué diablos dices? **—'s advocate** abogado del diablo *m*
devilish [dévəlıʃ] ADJ (evil) diabólico; (large, extreme) endiablado, endemoniado
deviltry [dévəɬtri] N (mischief) diablura *f*; (witchcraft) brujería *f*
devious [dívias] ADJ (roundabout) sinuoso, tortuoso; (crafty) taimado, retorcido
devise [dıváız] VT idear, urdir
devoid [dıvɔ́ıd] ADJ **— of** falto de, desprovisto de
devote [dıvót] VT dedicar; (consecrate) consagrar
devoted [dıvódıd] ADJ (friend) leal; (parent) dedicado; (worshipper) devoto
devotion [dıvóʃən] N devoción *f*
devour [dıváur] VT devorar
devout [dıváut] ADJ devoto
dew [dju] N rocío *m*; **—drop** gota de rocío *f*; **—point** punto de condensación *m*
dexterity [dεkstérıɒı] N destreza *f*
dextrose [dékstros] N dextrosa *f*
diabetes [daıəbídiz] N diabetes *f*
diabolic [daıəbálık] ADJ diabólico
diacritic [daıəkrídık] ADJ & N diacrítico *m*
diagnose [daıəgnós] VT diagnosticar
diagonal [daıǽgənəɬ] ADJ & N diagonal *f*
diagram [dáıəgræm] N diagrama *m*
dial [dáıəɬ] N (of a watch, clock) esfera *f*; (of radio) dial *m*; VI/VT (telephone number) *Sp* marcar; *Am* discar; **— tone** *Sp* señal de marcar *f*; *Am* tono de discar *m*
dialect [dáıəlεkt] N dialecto *m*
dialectic [daıəléktık] ADJ dialéctico; N dialéctica *f*

dialectology [daɪəlɛktáləʤi] N dialectología f
dialog, dialogue [dáɪəlɑg] N diálogo m; VI dialogar
dialysis [daɪǽlɪsɪs] N diálisis f
diameter [daɪǽmɪDɚ] N diámetro m
diamond [dáɪəmənd] N (stone) diamante m; (shape) rombo m
diaper [dáɪpɚ] N pañal m; VT poner pañales
diaphragm [dáɪəfræm] N diafragma m
diarrhea [daɪəríə] N diarrea f
diary [dáɪəri] N diario m
diatribe [dáɪətraɪb] N diatriba f
dice [daɪs] N PL dados m pl; VT cortar en cubos; VI jugar a los dados; **no —!** (impossibility) no hay forma; *Mex* ¡ni modo! (refusal) de ninguna manera
dichotomy [daɪkáDəmi] N dicotomía f
dick [dɪk] N (penis) *vulg* polla f, pija f, verga f, rabo m; (detective) sabueso -sa mf; **—head** *offensive* capullo m; VI **to — somebody around** fastidiar a alguien
dicker [díkɚ] VI regatear
dictate [díktet] VI/VT dictar; N dictado m, precepto m
dictation [dɪktéʃən] N dictado m; **to take —** escribir al dictado
dictator [díkteDɚ] N dictador -ra mf
dictatorship [dɪktéDɚʃɪp] N dictadura f
diction [díkʃən] N dicción f
dictionary [díkʃəneri] N diccionario m
didactic [daɪdǽktɪk] ADJ didáctico
die [daɪ] VI morir(se); **—hard** intransigente mf; **to — down / away** disminuir; **to — off** irse muriendo; **to — out** morirse, extinguirse; **my car —d** se me murió el coche; N (game piece) dado m; (press) molde m; (stamp) cuño m, troquel m
diesel [dízəɬ] N diesel m; **— engine** motor diesel m
diet [dáɪɪt] N (food) dieta f; (controlled intake of food) dieta f, régimen m; **to be / go on a —** estar a dieta / régimen; **to put on a —** poner a dieta; VI estar a dieta
differ [dífɚ] VI diferir; **to — with** disentir, no estar de acuerdo con; **to — from** ser diferente de
difference [dífɚəns] N diferencia f; **it makes no —** no importa, da igual
different [dífɚənt] ADJ diferente, distinto
differential [dɪfərénʃəɬ] ADJ & N (difference, car part) diferencial m; **— equation** diferencial f
differentiate [dɪfərénʃiet] VI/VT diferenciar(se), distinguir(se)
difficult [dífɪkəɬt] ADJ difícil
difficulty [dífɪkʌti] N dificultad f
diffident [dífɪdənt] ADJ tímido

diffuse [dɪfjúz] VI/VT difundir; [dɪfjús] ADJ difuso
diffusion [dɪfjúʒən] N difusión f
dig [dɪg] VI/VT cavar; (by machine) excavar; (superficially) escarbar; **to — in the files** escarbar en los archivos; **to — under** socavar; **to — up** desenterrar; **he dug his heels into the ground** clavó los talones en el suelo; **I — your new shoes** están muy buenos tus zapatos nuevos; N (archaeological site) excavación f; (sarcastic remark) pulla f; **a — in the ribs** un codazo
digest [dɪʤést] VI/VT digerir; [dáɪʤest] N (summary) compendio m; (legal) digesto m
digestible [dɪʤéstəbəɬ] ADJ digerible, digestible
digestion [dɪʤéstʃən] N digestión f
digestive [dɪʤéstɪv] ADJ digestivo
digit [díʤɪt] N dígito m
digital [díʤɪd] ADJ digital
dignified [dígnəfaɪd] ADJ digno
dignitary [dígnɪteri] N dignatario -ria mf
dignity [dígnɪDi] N dignidad f
digress [dɪgrés] VI divagar
digression [dɪgréʃən] N digresión f
dike [daɪk] N dique m
dilapidated [dɪlǽpɪdeɪD] ADJ (machine) destartalado; (furniture) desvencijado; (house) derruido, venido abajo
dilate [dáɪlet] VI/VT dilatar(se)
dilation [daɪléʃən] N dilatación f
dilemma [dɪlémə] N dilema m
dilettante [dílɪtɑnt] N diletante mf
diligence [díləʤəns] N diligencia f
diligent [díləʤənt] ADJ diligente, hacendoso
dill [dɪɬ] N eneldo m; **— pickle** pepinillo en vinagre con eneldo m
dilute [dɪlút] VI/VT diluir(se); ADJ diluido
dim [dɪm] ADJ (light) tenue; (outline) difuso; (room) oscuro, en penumbras; (person) *fam* de pocas luces; **—wit** *fam* tonto, bobo; VI/VT (make less bright) atenuar; VT (switch to low beam) bajar
dime [daɪm] N moneda de diez centavos f; **English teachers are a — a dozen** sobran los profesores de inglés
dimension [dɪménʃən] N dimensión f
diminish [dɪmínɪʃ] VI/VT disminuir, menguar; **the law of —ing returns** la ley de los rendimientos decrecientes
diminution [dɪmənúʃən] N disminución f, mengua f
diminutive [dɪmínjətɪv] ADJ (small) diminuto; N diminutivo m
dimmer [dímɚ] N regulador de voltaje m

dimness [dímnɪs] N oscuridad *f*, penumbra *f*

dimple [dímpəł] N hoyuelo *m*; VT formar hoyuelos

din [dɪn] N estruendo *m*, estrépito *m*

dine [daɪn] VI cenar; **to — out** cenar afuera

diner [dáɪnɚ] N (restaurant) cafetería *f*; (on a train) coche-comedor *m*; (person) comensal *mf*

ding-a-ling [díŋəlɪŋ] N (silly person) ganso -sa *mf*; (eccentric person) excéntrico -ca *mf*; (sound) tilín *m*

dingy [díndʒi] ADJ deslucido

dining [dáɪnɪŋ] ADJ **— car** coche-comedor *m*; **— room** comedor *m*

dinner [dínɚ] N (main meal) comida *f*; (at midday) almuerzo *m*; (in the evening) cena *f*; **— jacket** smoking *m*; **—time** hora de la comida *f*

dinosaur [dáɪnəsɔr] N dinosaurio *m*

dint [dɪnt] ADV LOC **by — of** a fuerza de

dip [dɪp] VT (make wet) mojar; (scoop) sacar; (immerse) sumergir; (in insecticide) bañar; (in sauce, coffee) pringar, mojar; VI (sun) hundirse; (stocks) bajar; (road) hacer una bajada; (airplane) descender súbitamente; N (act of wetting) mojada *f*; (of ice-cream) bola *f*, cucharada *f*; (sauce) mojo *m*; (decrease) bajada *f*; (in a road) declive *m*; (in the land) hondonada *f*; (swim) baño *m*; (air travel) descenso rápido *m*; (irritating person) *pej* pesado -da *mf*

diphtheria [dɪpθíriə] N difteria *f*

diphthong [dípθɔŋ] N diptongo *m*

diploma [dɪplómə] N diploma *m*

diplomacy [dɪplóməsi] N diplomacia *f*

diplomat [dípləmæt] N diplomático -ca *mf*

diplomatic [dɪpləmǽdɪk] ADJ diplomático

dipper [dípɚ] N cucharón *m*, cazo *m*

dire [daɪr] ADJ terrible, espantoso; **— need** necesidad acuciante *f*; **— predictions** predicciones funestas *f pl*; **— situation** situación extrema *f*

direct [dɪrɛ́kt] ADJ directo; **— current** corriente continua *f*; **— object** complemento directo *m*; **— quotation** cita textual *f*; ADV directo, directamente; VI/VT dirigir; **he —ed me to leave** me mandó irme

direction [dɪrɛ́kʃən] N dirección *f*; **—s** indicaciones *f pl*; **I'm thinking in that — me** inclino por eso

directive [dɪrɛ́ktɪv] ADJ directivo; N directiva *f*

director [dɪrɛ́ktɚ] N director -ra *mf*

directory [dɪrɛ́ktəri] N directorio *m* (also computer term)

dirigible [dərídʒəbəł] ADJ & N dirigible *m*

dirt [dɚt] N (filth) suciedad *f*; (foul substance) mugre *f*; (vile person) *offensive* mierda *f*; (earth) tierra *f*; **—bag** *offensive* porquería *f*; **— cheap** baratísimo; **—-poor** pobrísimo; **I've got some — on him** le conozco los trapos sucios

dirty [dɚ́di] ADJ sucio, mugriento; **— joke** chiste verde *m*; **— look** mirada asesina *f*; **— money** dinero sucio *m*; **— shame** pena horrible *f*; **— trick** trampa *f*; **— word** palabrota *f*; *Sp* taco *m*; **— work** trabajo sucio *m*; VI/VT ensuciar; ADV **to talk —** decir cosas obscenas

disability [dɪsəbílɪdi] N incapacidad *f*

disable [dɪsébəł] VT (person) incapacitar; (device) desactivar

disabled [dɪsébəłd] ADJ minusválido

disabuse [dɪsəbjúz] VT desengañar

disadvantage [dɪsɪdvǽntɪdʒ] N desventaja *f*; **to be at a —** estar en desventaja

disadvantaged [dɪsɪdvǽntɪdʒd] ADJ carenciado

disagree [dɪsəgrí] VI (differ) diferir; (differ in opinion) disentir, no estar de acuerdo; **pizza —s with me** no me cae bien la pizza

disagreeable [dɪsəgríəbəł] ADJ desagradable

disagreement [dɪsəgrímənt] N (lack of agreement, argument) desacuerdo *m*; (discrepancy) discrepancia *f*

disallow [dɪsəláu] VT desaprobar; (in sports) anular

disappear [dɪsəpír] VI desaparecer

disappearance [dɪsəpírəns] N desaparición *f*

disappoint [dɪsəpɔ́ɪnt] VI/VT decepcionar, desilusionar; **to be —ed** estar desilusionado

disappointing [dɪsəpɔ́ɪntɪŋ] ADJ decepcionante

disappointment [dɪsəpɔ́ɪntmənt] N decepción *f*, desilusión *f*

disapproval [dɪsəprúvəł] N desaprobación *f*

disapprove [dɪsəprúv] VI/VT desaprobar

disarm [dɪsárm] VI/VT desarmar(se)

disarmament [dɪsárməmənt] N desarme *m*

disarray [dɪsəré] VT desordenar; N confusión *f*, desorden *m*; **in —** en desorden

disaster [dɪzǽstɚ] N desastre *m*

disastrous [dɪzǽstrəs] ADJ desastroso

disavow [dɪsəváu] VT negar

disband [dɪsbǽnd] VT disolver; VI desbandarse

disbelief [dɪsbɪlíf] N incredulidad *f*

disbelieve [dɪsbɪlív] VI/VT descreer de

disburse [dɪsbɚ́s] VT desembolsar

disbursement [dɪsbɚ́smənt] N desembolso *m*

discard [dɪskárd] VT (a card) descartar; (garbage) desechar; [dískard] N (card) descarte *m*; (garbage) desecho *m*

discern [dɪsɔ́·n] VT (distinguish mentally) discernir; (perceive) percibir

discernment [dɪsɔ́·nmənt] N discernimiento *m*

discharge [dɪstʃárdʒ] VI/VT (battery, load, firearm) descargar(se); (obligation) cumplir; (prisoner) poner en libertad, soltar; (odor) despedir; (soldier) dar de baja; (patient) dar de alta; (a debt) pagar; (pus) supurar; [dístʃardʒ] N (of a battery, load, firearm) descarga *f*; (of an obligation) cumplimiento *m*; (from a job) despido *m*; (of a soldier) baja *f*; (of a patient) alta *f*; (of a debt) pago *m*; (of an odor) emisión *f*; (of a prisoner) puesta en libertad *f*; (of oil) pérdida *f*; (of pus) supuración *f*; (uterine, vaginal) flujo *m*

disciple [dɪsáɪpəɫ] N discípulo -la *mf*

discipline [dísəplɪn] N disciplina *f*; VT disciplinar

disclaimer [dɪsklémɚ] N descargo de responsabilidad *m*

disclose [dɪsklóz] VT revelar

disco [dísko] N discoteca *f*

discolor [dɪskʌ́lɚ] VI/VT descolorar(se)

discomfort [dɪskʌ́mfɚt] N malestar *m*

disconcert [dɪskənsɔ́·t] VT desconcertar

disconnect [dɪskənékt] VI/VT desconectar; N desconexión *f*

disconnected [dɪskənéktɪd] ADJ (broken) desconectado; (incoherent) inconexo

disconsolate [dɪskánsəlɪt] ADJ desconsolado

discontent [dɪskəntént] N descontento *m*

discontinue [dɪskəntínju] VT suspender, interrumpir; VI abandonar

discontinuous [dɪskəntínjuəs] ADJ discontinuo

discord [dískɔrd] N (lack of concord) discordia *f*, desavenencia *f*; (dissonance) disonancia *f*, discordancia *f*

discotheque [dískotɛk] N discoteca *f*

discount [dískaunt] VT (deduct from a charge, take into account in advance) descontar; (sell at a reduced price) rebajar; (disregard) ignorar; N descuento *m*

discourage [dɪskɔ́·ɪdʒ] VT desanimar, desalentar; **to — from** disuadir de

discouragement [dɪskɔ́·ɪdʒmənt] N desánimo *m*, desaliento *m*

discourse [dískɔrs] N (conversation, talk) discurso *m*; (treatise) disertación *f*; [dɪskɔ́rs] VI (talk) discurrir; (treat a subject) disertar

discourteous [dɪskɔ́·ɾiəs] ADJ descortés

discourtesy [dɪskɔ́·ɾɪsi] N descortesía *f*

discover [dɪskʌ́vɚ] VT descubrir

discoverer [dɪskʌ́vərɚ] N descubridor -ra *mf*

discovery [dɪskʌ́vəri] N descubrimiento *m*

discredit [dɪskrédɪt] VT (injure the reputation of) desacreditar; (give no credence to) no creer; N descrédito *m*

discreet [dɪskrít] ADJ discreto

discrepancy [dɪskrépənsi] N discrepancia *f*

discrete [dɪskrít] ADJ discreto

discretion [dɪskréʃən] N discreción *f*; **at your own —** a discreción; **at the judge's —** al arbitrio del juez

discriminate [dɪskrímənet] VI/VT distinguir; **to — against** discriminar a

discuss [dɪskʌ́s] VT discutir

discussion [dɪskʌ́ʃən] N discusión *f*

disdain [dɪsdén] N desdén *m*, desprecio *m*; VT (treat with contempt) desdeñar; (think unworthy of a response) no dignarse a

disdainful [dɪsdénfəɫ] ADJ desdeñoso

disease [dɪzíz] N enfermedad *f*

diseased [dɪzízd] ADJ enfermo

disembark [dɪsɪmbárk] VI/VT desembarcar

disenfranchise [dɪsɪnfrǽntʃaɪz] VT (politician) proscribir; (minorities) privar de derechos, desheredar

disengage [dɪsɪngédʒ] VI/VT (a clutch) soltar(se); (from a situation) distanciar(se)

disentangle [dɪsɪntǽŋgəɫ] VT desenredar, desenmarañar

disfavor [dɪsfévɚ] N **to fall into —** (a person) caer en desgracia; (a fashion) caer en desuso; VT mirar con malos ojos

disfigure [dɪsfígjɚ] VT desfigurar

disgrace [dɪsgrés] N (dishonor) deshonra *f*; (shame) vergüenza *f*; **to fall into —** caer en desgracia; VT deshonrar

disgraceful [dɪsgrésfəɫ] ADJ vergonzoso

disgruntled [dɪsgrʌ́nt̩ld] ADJ descontento, resentido

disguise [dɪsgáɪz] VT disfrazar(se); N disfraz *m*

disgust [dɪsgást] VT (repel) asquear, repugnar; (displease) disgustar; N asco *m*, repugnancia *f*

disgusted [dɪsgástɪd] ADJ asqueado, repugnado

disgusting [dɪsgástɪŋ] ADJ asqueroso, repugnante

dish [dɪʃ] N (plate, food, quantity) plato *m*; (serving container) fuente *f*; (attractive person) *fam* bombón *m*; **—es** vajilla *f*; **—cloth / towel** paño de cocina *m*, repasador *m*; **—washer** lavaplatos *m sg*, lavavajillas *m sg*; **—water** agua de fregar *f*; VI/VT (serve food) servir; **to — out** repartir

dishearten [dɪshártn̩] VT desanimar, descorazonar, desalentar

disheartening [dɪshártn̩ɪŋ] ADJ desalentador

dishevel [dɪʃévəł] VT desgreñar
disheveled [dɪʃévəłd] ADJ (hair) desgreñado, revuelto; (clothes) desaliñado
dishonest [dɪsánɪst] ADJ deshonesto
dishonesty [dɪsánɪsti] N deshonestidad *f*
dishonor [dɪsánɚ] N deshonra *f*; VT deshonrar; (a check) no pagar
dishonorable [dɪsánəəbəł] ADJ deshonroso
disillusion [dɪsɪlúʒən] N desilusión *f*, desencanto *m*; VT desilusionar, desencantar
disinfect [dɪsɪnfékt] VT desinfectar
disinfectant [dɪsɪnféktənt] N desinfectante *m*
disinformation [dɪsɪnfɚméʃən] N desinformación *f*
disinherit [dɪsɪnhérɪt] VT desheredar
disintegrate [dɪsíntɪgret] VI/VT desintegrar(se)
disintegration [dɪsɪntɪgréʃən] N desintegración *f*
disinterested [dɪsíntrɪstɪd] ADJ desinteresado
disjointed [dɪsʤɔ́ɪntɪd] ADJ desarticulado
disk, disc [dɪsk] N disco *m*; (in certain games) tejo *m*; (in a computer) disco *m*, disquete *m*; — **brake** freno de disco *m*; — **drive** disquetera *f*; — **jockey** pinchadiscos *mf sg*
diskette [dɪskét] N disquete *m*
dislike [dɪsláɪk] N aversión *f*, tirria *f*; VT I — **parties** no me gustan las fiestas
dislocate [dɪslóket] VT dislocar, descoyuntar
dislodge [dɪsláʤ] VT (force out) desatascar; (displace) desprender
disloyal [dɪslɔ́ɪəł] ADJ desleal
dismal [dízməł] ADJ pésimo; **a — failure** un fracaso rotundo
dismantle [dɪsmǽntl̩] VT (a factory) desmantelar; (a car, watch, etc.) desmontar
dismay [dɪsmé] VT (disappoint) consternar; (daunt) desalentar; (alarm) alarmar; N (disappointment) consternación *f*; (loss of courage) desaliento *m*; (alarm) alarma *f*
dismember [dɪsmémbɚ] VT desmembrar
dismiss [dɪsmís] VT (fire a private employee) despedir; (fire a public employee) destituir, cesar; (reject a possibility) desechar, descartar; (discharge from military service) dar de baja; (reject a claim) desestimar; **class —ed!** ¡pueden retirarse!
dismissal [dɪsmísəł] N (firing) destitución *f*, despido *m*; (of a possibility) rechazo *m*; (from military service) baja *f*; (of a claim) desestimación *f*
dismount [dɪsmáʊnt] VI (get off a horse) desmontarse, apearse; (take apart) desarmar; N bajada *f*
disobedience [dɪsəbíɾiəns] N desobediencia *f*

disobedient [dɪsəbíɾiənt] ADJ desobediente
disobey [dɪsəbé] VI/VT desobedecer
disorder [dɪsɔ́rɾɚ] N (confusion) desorden *m*; (public disturbance) desorden público *m*; (illness) trastorno *m*, desarreglo *m*
disorderly [dɪsɔ́rɾɚli] ADJ (untidy) desordenado; (unruly) revoltoso; — **conduct** alteración del orden público *f*
disorganization [dɪsɔrgənɪzéʃən] N desorganización *f*
disorganized [dɪsɔ́rgənaɪzd] ADJ desorganizado
disown [dɪsón] VT repudiar
disparage [dɪspǽrɪʤ] VT denigrar
disparate [díspɚɪt] ADJ dispar
dispassionate [dɪspǽʃənɪt] ADJ desapasionado
dispatch [dɪspǽtʃ] VT despachar; N (sending off) envío *m*; (putting to death) ejecución *f*; (news story, official communication) despacho *m*
dispel [dɪspéł] VT disipar
dispensable [dɪspénsəbəł] ADJ prescindible
dispensary [dɪspénsɚi] N dispensario *m*
dispensation [dɪspɛnséʃən] N (relaxation of law) dispensa *f*; (act of handing out) dispensación *f*
dispense [dɪspéns] VT (goods) dispensar; (justice) administrar; **to — from an obligation** eximir de una obligación; **to — with** prescindir de
dispersal [dɪspɚ́səł] N dispersión *f*
disperse [dɪspɚ́s] VI/VT dispersar(se)
displace [dɪsplés] VT (evict) desalojar; (take up space, remove from office) desplazar; **—d person** expatriado -da *mf*
display [dɪsplé] VT (exhibit) exhibir, exponer; (unfold, flaunt) desplegar, ostentar; (show on a computer screen) visualizar; N (of wares, etc.) exhibición *f*, despliegue *m*; (advertisement) cartel *m*; (flaunting) ostentación *f*; (computer) visualizador *m*, display *m*
displease [dɪsplíz] VT contrariar, desagradar, descontentar; VI molestar
displeasure [dɪspléʒɚ] N disgusto *m*, desagrado *m*
disposal [dɪspózəł] N (arrangement) disposición *f*; (disposing of) eliminación *f*
dispose [dɪspóz] VT (give inclination) predisponer; (set in order, make ready) disponer; **to — of** descartar, eliminar
disposition [dɪspəzíʃən] N (attitude) temperamento *m*; (inclination) inclinación *f*, tendencia *f*; (arrangement, disposal) disposición *f*
dispossess [dɪspəzés] VT desposeer

disproportionate [dɪsprəpɔ́rʃənɪt] ADJ desproporcionado

disprove [dɪsprúv] VT refutar

dispute [dɪspjút] N disputa *f*; VI disputar; VT discutir, impugnar

disqualify [dɪskwáləfaɪ] VT (deprive of rights) inhabilitar; (exclude from a sport event) descalificar

disregard [dɪsrɪgárd] VT hacer caso omiso de, ignorar; N (neglect) descuido *m*; (disrespect) falta de respeto *f*

disrepair [dɪsrɪpér] N mal estado *m*; **to fall into** — caer en ruina

disreputable [dɪsrépjəɒəbəɫ] ADJ (of bad reputation) de mala reputación; (shabby) de mala muerte

disrespect [dɪsrɪspékt] N desacato *m*, falta de respeto *f*; VT faltar el respeto

disrespectful [dɪsrɪspéktfəɫ] ADJ irrespetuoso

disrobe [dɪsrób] VI/VT desvestir(se)

disrupt [dɪsrápt] VT (cause disorder) trastornar, trastocar; (interrupt) interrumpir

dissatisfied [dɪssǽDɪsfaɪd] ADJ insatisfecho, disconforme

dissatisfy [dɪssǽDɪsfaɪ] VT no satisfacer

dissect [daɪsékt] VT (cut apart) disecar; (analyze argument) analizar minuciosamente

dissemble [dɪsémbəɫ] VI/VT (hide) disimular; (feign) fingir

disseminate [dɪsémənet] VT (spread out) diseminar; (publicize) divulgar

dissemination [dɪsemənéʃən] N diseminación *f*

dissension [dɪsénʃən] N disensión *f*, disenso *m*

dissent [dɪsént] VI disentir; N disenso *m*

dissertation [dɪsɚtéʃən] N (formal discourse) disertación *f*; (doctoral treatise) tesis de doctorado *f*

dissident [dísɪdənt] N disidente *mf*

dissimilar [dɪssímələ] ADJ diferente

dissimulation [dɪsɪmjəléʃən] N disimulo *m*

dissipate [dísəpet] VI/VT disipar(se)

dissipation [dɪsəpéʃən] N disipación *f*

dissolute [dísəlut] ADJ disoluto

dissolution [dɪsəlúʃən] N disolución *f*

dissolve [dɪzáɫv] VI/VT disolver(se)

dissuade [dɪswéd] VT disuadir

distance [dístəns] N distancia *f*, recorrido *m*; **— learning** educación a distancia *f*; **in the** — a lo lejos, en la lejanía; VT distanciarse de, distanciar

distant [dístənt] ADJ (far away, aloof) distante; (remote) lejano, remoto; **to be — from** distar de

distaste [dɪstést] N aversión *f*

distasteful [dɪstéstfəɫ] ADJ desagradable

distemper [dɪstémpɚ] N moquillo *m*

distend [dɪsténd] VI/VT distender(se)

distill [dɪstíɫ] VI/VT destilar(se)

distillation [dɪstəléʃən] N destilación *f*

distillery [dɪstíləri] N destilería *f*

distinct [dɪstíŋkt] ADJ (different) distinto; (clear) bien delineado, neto

distinction [dɪstíŋkʃən] N distinción *f*; **he passed with** — aprobó con sobresaliente

distinctive [dɪstíŋktɪv] ADJ distintivo

distinguish [dɪstíŋgwɪʃ] VI/VT distinguir

distinguished [dɪstíŋgwɪʃt] ADJ distinguido

distinguishing [dɪstíŋgwɪʃɪŋ] ADJ distintivo

distort [dɪstɔ́rt] VT (an object) deformar; (reports, sound) distorsionar

distortion [dɪstɔ́rʃən] N (object) deformación *f*; (image, sound) distorsión *f*; (of a statement) tergiversación *f*

distract [dɪstrǽkt] VT distraer, entretener

distraction [dɪstrǽkʃən] N distracción *f*; **to drive to** — volver loco

distraught [dɪstrɔ́t] ADJ angustiado

distress [dɪstrés] N (anxiety) angustia *f*; (pain) dolor *m*, congoja *f*; **to be in** — (a person) estar en apuros; (a ship, plane) estar en peligro; VT (cause anxiety) angustiar, atribular; (cause pain) acongojar, afligir

distribute [dɪstríbjut] VT distribuir, repartir

distribution [dɪstrəbjúʃən] N distribución *f*, reparto *m*

distributor [dɪstríbjəɒɚ] N distribuidor *m*

district [dístrɪkt] N distrito *m*, comarca *f*; **— attorney** fiscal de distrito *mf*

District of Columbia [dístrɪktəvkəlámbiə] N Distrito de Columbia *m*

distrust [dɪstrást] N desconfianza *f*; VT desconfiar de

distrustful [dɪstrástfəɫ] ADJ desconfiado

disturb [dɪstɚ́b] VI/VT (interrupt, interfere, perplex) perturbar; (trouble) turbar; (alter mentally) trastornar; (mess up) desarreglar; **do not** — se ruega no molestar

disturbance [dɪstɚ́bəns] N disturbio *m*; (weather) perturbación *f*

disuse [dɪsjús] N desuso *m*; **to fall into** — caer en desuso

ditch [dɪtʃ] N (trench) zanja *f*; (roadside) cuneta *f*; (for irrigation) acequia *f*; VT (make ditches) abrir zanjas; (get rid of) deshacerse de; (crash-land an airplane on water) hacer un amarizaje; **to — someone** dejar a alguien

dither [díðɚ] VI (hesitate) titubear; N **it threw her into a** — se puso muy nerviosa

ditsy [dítsi] ADJ atolondrado, cabeza de chorlito

ditto [díɾo] PRON & ADV ídem *m*

diuretic [daɪəréɾɪk] ADJ & N diurético *m*

diurnal [daɪ'ɚnəɫ] ADJ diurno

divan [dɪvǽn] N diván *m*, canapé *m*

dive [daɪv] VI (into water) zambullirse, chapuzar; (into an activity) zambullirse; (with scuba equipment) bucear; (airplane) bajar en picada; (submarine) sumergirse; N (of a person) zambullida *f*, chapuz *m*; (of an airplane) picada *f*; (cheap bar) antro *m*

diver [dáɪvɚ] N saltador -ra *mf*; (high-dive) clavadista *mf*; (scuba) buzo *mf*

diverge [dɪvɚ́ʤ] VI (branch off, differ in opinion) divergir; VI/VT (deviate) desviar

divergence [dɪvɚ́ʤəns] N (separation, difference in opinion) divergencia *f*; (deviation) desviación *f*

diverse [dɪvɚ́s] ADJ (of various kinds) diverso; (different) diferente

diversify [dɪvɚ́səfaɪ] VI/VT diversificar(se)

diversion [dɪvɚ́ʒən] N (entertainment) entretenimiento *m*; (distraction) distracción *f*; (military) diversión *f*; (turning aside) desvío *m*, desviación *f*

diversity [dɪvɚ́sɪɾi] N diversidad *f*

divert [dɪvɚ́t] VI/VT (turn aside) desviar, distraer; (distract) entretener

divest [dɪvést] VT (strip) despojar; (get rid of) deshacerse de

divide [dɪváɪd] VI/VT dividir(se); (classify) clasificar(se); N línea divisoria *f*

dividend [dívɪdɛnd] N dividendo *m*

divine [dɪváɪn] ADJ divino; VI/VT adivinar

divinity [dɪvínɪɾi] N divinidad *f*; (theology) teología *f*

division [dɪvíʒən] N división *f*

divorce [dɪvɔ́rs] N divorcio *m*; VI/VT divorciar(se)

divulge [dɪváɫʤ] VT divulgar, publicar

dizziness [dízinɪs] N mareo *m*

dizzy [dízi] ADJ (person) mareado; (height) vertigoso; (speed) vertiginoso; **— spell** vahido *m*

DJ (disc jockey) [díʤe] N pinchadiscos *mf sg*

Djibouti [ʤɪbúti] N Yibuti *m*

Djiboutian [jɪbúɾiən] ADJ & N yibutiano -na *mf*

DNA (deoxyribonucleic acid) [diɛné] N ADN *m*

do [du] VI/VT hacer; **to — away with** eliminar; **to — one's hair** arreglarse el pelo; **to — the dishes** lavar los platos; **to — drugs** tomar drogas; **to — in** matar; **to — time** cumplir una condena; **we were —ing 100 kph** íbamos a cien kph;

to — well prosperar; **to — without** prescindir de; **to have nothing to — with** no tener nada que ver con; **that will —** basta; **that won't —** eso no sirve; **I'm —ing well** estoy bien; **I did her last night** *fam* me la tiré anoche; **this will have to —** habrá que conformarse con esto; **—-it-yourself** hágalo usted mismo; V AUX **I feel as you —** pienso igual que tú; **how — you —?** ¿cómo estás? — **you hear me?** ¿me oyes? **yes, I —** sí; **— come again** vuelve por favor; N (hairstyle) peinado *m*; (party) fiesta *f*

DOA (dead on arrival) [dioé] ADJ muerto -ta antes de ingresar al hospital *mf*

docile [dásəɫ] ADJ dócil

dock [dɑk] N (pier) muelle *m*; (for landing) desembarcadero *m*, atracadero *m*; (water between piers) dique *m*, dársena *f*; **dry —** dique seco *m*; VI/VT (a boat) atracar; (a space ship) acoplar(se); (wages) descontar

doctor [dáktɚ] N (physician) médico -ca *mf*; (Ph.D., scholar) doctor -ra *mf*; (expert) especialista *mf*; VT (treat) atender; (cure) curar; (restore) restaurar; (counterfeit) alterar; **I —ed up this recipe** le hice unos retoques a esta receta

doctorate [dáktɚɪt] N doctorado *m*

doctrine [dáktrɪn] N doctrina *f*

document [dákjəmənt] N documento *m*; [dákjəmɛnt] VT documentar

documentary [dɑkjəméntɚi] N documental *m*

dodder [dáɾɚ] VI (stumble along) tambalearse, titubear; (shake) temblequear

dodge [dɑʤ] VT esquivar, sortear; VI (be evasive) dar rodeos; (move sideways) apartarse, echarse a un lado; N evasiva *f*

doe [do] N cierva *f*; (female of various animals) hembra *f*

dog [dɔg] N perro -rra *mf*; **—catcher** perrero -ra *mf*; **— collar** collar de perro *m*; **—-eared** sobado, muy gastado; **—fight** (dogs) pelea *f* de perros; (aircraft) combate aéreo *m*; (people) reyerta *f*; **—gone** maldito -ta *mf*; **—house** casilla de perro *f*; *Sp* caseta *f*; **to be in the —house** haber caído en desgracia, estar en capilla; **— paddle** nado estilo perrito *m*; **to —-paddle** nadar estilo perrito; **—sled** trineo para perros *m*; **— tag** placa de identificación *f*; **—wood** cornejo *m*; **to go to the —s** venirse abajo; VT (follow) seguir la pista de; (harass) hostigar

doggy [dɔ́gi] N perrito -ta *mf*; **— bag** bolsa para las sobras *f*

dogma [dɔ́gmə] N dogma *m*
dogmatic [dɔgmǽdɪk] ADJ dogmático
doily [dɔ́ili] N mantelito *m*
doings [dúɪŋz] N acciones *f pl*
dole [dołf] N (alms) limosna *f*; **to be on the** — estar cobrando el seguro de desempleo / paro; **to** — **out** repartir
doleful [dólfəł] ADJ apesadumbrado, triste
doll [dɑł] N (toy) muñeco -ca *mf*; (attractive female) muñeca *f*; —**house** casa de muñecas *f*; VI **to get** —**ed up** emperifollarse, empaquetarse
dollar [dálɚ] N dólar *m*; — **diplomacy** diplomacia del dólar *f*; — **sign** signo del dólar *m*
dolly [dáli] N (doll) muñeca *f*; (cart) carretilla *f*
dolphin [dɔ́łfɪn] N (mammal) delfín *m*; (fish) dorado *m*
dolt [dołt] N zopenco -ca *mf*
domain [domén] N dominio *m*
dome [dom] N (roof) cúpula *f*, domo *m*; (head) coco *m*, pelada *f*; **the** — **of the sky** la bóveda celeste
domestic [dəméstɪk] ADJ (appliance, pet, chore) doméstico; (devoted to homemaking) hogareño; (home-loving) casero; (of a country) interno, nacional; — **violence** violencia doméstica *f*; N doméstico -ca *mf*
domesticate [dəméstɪket] VI/VT (animals) domesticar; (plants) aclimatar
domicile [dáməsaɪł] N domicilio *m*
dominant [dámənənt] ADJ dominante
dominate [dámənet] VI/VT dominar; VI señorear
domination [damənéʃən] N (act of dominating) dominación *f*; (rule) dominio *m*
domineer [damənír] VI/VT dominar, mandonear
domineering [damənírɪŋ] ADJ tiránico, mandón
Dominica [dəmínɪkə] N Dominica *f*
Dominican [dəmínɪkən] ADJ & N (of Dominica) dominiqués -esa *mf*; (of the Dominican Republic) dominicano -na *mf*
Dominican Republic [dəmínɪkənɹɪpáblɪk] N República Dominicana *f*
dominion [dəmínjən] N dominio *m*, señorío *m*
domino [dáməno] N (game, costume) dominó *m*; (piece) ficha *f*
don [dɑn] N (title, form of address, mafia boss) don *m*; (lecturer) profesor -ra universitario -ria *mf*; VT ponerse, vestirse
donate [dónet] VI/VT donar

donation [donéʃən] N donación *f*
done [dʌn] ADJ terminado, acabado; **when you are** — cuando termines; **to be all** — **in** estar muerto de cansancio; **the meat is well** — está bien asada la carne; **that sort of thing just isn't** — eso no se hace
donkey [dáŋki] N burro *m*, asno *m*, borrico *m*
donor [dónɚ] N donante *mf*, donador -ora *mf*
doodad [dúdæd] N (trinket) chuchería *f*; (device) chisme *m*, coso *m*
doohickey [dúhɪki] N chisme *m*, coso *m*
doom [dum] N perdición *f*; —**sday** día del juicio final *m*; VT condenar; **to be** —**ed to failure** estar condenado al fracaso
door [dɔr] N puerta *f*; —**-to-** — de puerta a puerta; —**bell** timbre *m*; —**keeper** portero -ra *mf*; —**knob** pomo *m*; —**man** portero *m*; —**mat** felpudo *m*; —**step** umbral *m*; —**way** puerta *f*, portal *m*; **I showed him the** — lo eché
dope [dop] N (narcotic) droga *f*; (stimulant) estimulante *m*; (information) chismes *m pl*; **he is a** — *fam* es un zopenco; VT dopar; **to** — **oneself up** medicarse en exceso
dork [dɔrk] N *fam* idiota *mf*, tarambana *mf*
dorky [dɔ́rki] ADJ **that's a** — **dress** *fam* pareces una idiota con ese vestido
dormant [dɔ́rmənt] ADJ latente
dormitory [dɔ́rmɪtɔri] N residencia estudiantil *f*
DOS (Disk Operating System) [dɑs] N DOS *m*
dose [dos] N dosis *f*; VT dosificar
dossier [dɔ́sie] N expediente *m*
dot [dɑt] N punto *m*; (on a tie) pinta *f*; —**-com** punto com; —**-matrix printer** impresora de matriz de puntos *f*; —**ted eighth note** corchea con puntillo *f*; **on the** — en punto; VT marcar con puntos
dotage [dódɪʤ] N chochez *f*, chochera *f*; **to be in one's** — chochear, estar chocho
dote [dot] VI **to** — **on** estar chocho con
double [dábəł] ADJ doble; — **agent** doble agente *mf*; —**-barreled** de doble caño; — **bass** contrabajo *m*; — **bed** cama doble *f*; — **bind** dilema *m*; — **boiler** baño de María *m*; —**-breasted** cruzado; — **chin** papada *f*; —**-click** hacer doble clic; — **cross** traición *f*; **to** —**-cross** traicionar; **to** —**-date** salir dos parejas juntas; — **dealing** duplicidad *f*; — **entry** entrada por partida doble *f*; — **sided** de dos caras; — **shift** turno doble *m*; — **standard** trato discriminatorio *m*; — **vision** doble

visión *f*; **to do a — take** quedar atónito; N doble *m*; **—s** juego de dobles *m*; ADV **to sleep —** dormir de a dos; **to —-check** verificar; **to —-talk** salirse con evasivas; VI/VT duplicar(se); (an effort) redoblar(se); (fold, be twice as old, challenge a bid) doblar(se); **to — up** (bend over) doblarse; (crowd) amontonarse; **this sofa —s as a bed** este sofá sirve también de cama

doubt [daʊt] VI/VT dudar; (not trust) desconfiar; N duda *f*; **beyond a —** indudablemente; **in —** en duda; **no —!** ¡sin duda!

doubtful [dáʊtfəł] ADJ dudoso

doubtless [dáʊtlɪs] ADV (certainly) sin duda; (probably) probablemente

douche [duʃ] N ducha vaginal *f*; **—bag** *offensive* porquería *f*

dough [do] N pasta *f*, masa *f*; (money) pasta *f*, mosca *f*; **—nut** rosquilla *f*; *Mex* dona *f*; *Sp* donut *m*

douse [daʊs] VI/VT empapar; (a flame) apagar (con agua)

dove [dʌv] N paloma *f*

dowdy [dáʊDi] ADJ (article of clothing) pasado de moda; (person) sin gracia

dowel [dáʊəł] N clavija *f*

down [daʊn] ADV abajo; **two blocks —** dos calles más abajo; **to turn — the volume** bajar el volumen; **to water — a drink** rebajar una bebida con agua; **to get — to work** aplicarse al trabajo; **to fall —** caerse; **to go / come —** bajar; **to come — with a cold** caer con gripe; *Sp* cogerse un resfriado; **to lie —** tumbarse, echarse; **to write —** anotar; **to put — someone** denigrar a alguien; **slow —!** ¡anda más despacio! **the wind died —** amainó el viento; PREP **— the street** calle abajo; ADJ (depressed) abatido; **one — and two to go** hicimos uno y nos quedan dos por hacer; **prices are —** han bajado los precios; **they're — on me** están mal conmigo; N (turn for the worse) revés *m*; (feathers) plumón *m*; VT (knock down, shoot down) derribar; (drink quickly) despachar de un solo trago; (defeat) vencer

down-and-dirty [dáʊnɪndɝ́Di] ADJ sucio

down-and-out [dáʊnɪnáʊt] ADJ tirado

downcast [dáʊnkæst] ADJ abatido, cabizbajo

downfall [dáʊnfɔ́ł] N ruina *f*

downgrade [dáʊngred] N declive *m*, pendiente *f*; VT quitarle importancia a

downhill [dáʊnhíł] ADV cuesta abajo; **his health is going —** su salud se deteriora; [dáʊnhíł] ADJ **a — slope** una pendiente; N

bajada contra-reloj *f*

download [dáʊnlod] VT descargar

down payment [dáʊnpémənt] N entrega inicial *f*, entrada *f*

downplay [dáʊnple] VT quitar la importancia a

downpour [dáʊnpɔr] N aguacero *m*

downright [dáʊnraɪt] ADJ absoluto; **— foolishness** reverenda tontería *f*; **he was — angry** echaba chispas

downshift [dáʊnʃɪft] VI rebajar (el cambio)

downside [dáʊnsaɪd] N inconveniente *m*

downsize [dáʊnsaɪz] VI (cut back) hacer reducción de personal; VT (make smaller) reducir el tamaño de; **he got —d** perdió el trabajo cuando hicieron reducción de personal

downstairs [dáʊnstérz] ADV abajo; (in the apartment one floor lower) en el piso de abajo; [dáʊnstɝz] ADJ de abajo; N planta baja *f*

downstream [dáʊnstrím] ADV río abajo

downtime [dáʊntaɪm] N (of a machine) tiempo de inactividad *m*; (of a person) horas de ocio *f pl*

down-to-earth [dáʊntəɝ́-θ] ADJ sensato, práctico

downtown [dáʊntáʊn] ADV (toward) al centro; (in) en el centro; ADJ del centro, céntrico; N centro *m*

downturn [dáʊntɝ-n] N tendencia a la baja *f*

down under [dáʊnándɚ] ADV en / a Australia

downward [dáʊnwɚd] ADJ descendente; **— mobility** descenso social *m*; **—s** hacia abajo

downwind [dáʊnwínd] ADV en la dirección del viento

downy [dáʊni] ADJ sedoso, suave

dowry [dáʊri] N dote *f*

doze [doz] VI dormitar; N siesta *f*

dozen [dázən] N docena *f*

drab [dræb] ADJ triste; N pardo *m*

draft [dræft] N (of air) corriente *f*; (drink) trago *m*; (bank) giro *m*; (outline) esbozo *m*; (military) conscripción *f*, quinta *f*; (of a ship) calado *m*; **— beer** cerveza de barril *f*; **— horse** caballo de tiro *m*; **—sman** dibujante *m*; VT (to sketch) esbozar; (to compose) redactar; (to select for military service) reclutar

drag [dræg] VI/VT (haul slowly) arrastrar(se); (search a body of water) dragar; **don't — me into this** no me metas en esto; **to — on and on** eternizarse; **to — out** estirar; N (dredge) draga *f*; (boring person) pesado -da *mf*; (hassle) lata *f*; (counterforce)

resistencia *f*; (on a cigarette) pitada *f*; —
race carrera de dragsters *f*; — **strip** pista
de dragsters *f*; **in** — vestido de mujer

dragon [drǽgən] N dragón *m*; —**fly** libélula *f*

drain [dren] N (channel) desagüe *m*,
sumidero *m*; (depletion of resources)
sangría *f*, fuga *f*; — **pipe** desaguadero *m*,
desagüe *m*; **to go down the** — irse por la
borda; VI/VT (empty a sink) desagotar(se),
desaguar(se); (exhaust) agotar(se); VT
(wetlands) drenar, sanear; VI (a battery)
descargarse

drainage [drénɪʤ] N (act of draining)
desagüe *m*, drenaje *m*; (system) drenaje *m*;
—**pipe** tubo de desagüe *m*

drake [drek] N pato (macho) *m*

drama [drámə] N drama *m*

dramatic [drəmǽDɪk] ADJ dramático

dramatist [drámətɪst] N dramaturgo -ga *mf*

dramatize [drámətaɪz] VI/VT dramatizar

drape [drep] VI (hang in folds) colgar,
drapear; VT (cover) cubrir; N cortina *f*

drapery [drépəri] N cortinado *m*, colgadura *f*

drastic [drǽstɪk] ADJ drástico

draw [drɔ] VT (a picture) dibujar; (lines,
shapes) trazar; (a cart) tirar de; (a curtain)
correr; (cards, blood, water, conclusion,
strength) sacar; (a crowd) atraer;
(withdraw money) retirar, sacar; (receive
money) cobrar; (comparison, distinction)
hacer; (sword) desenvainar; VI (of a boat)
tener calado; (of a fireplace) tirar; (in
sports, have the same score) empatar; **to**
— **aside** apartar(se); **to** — **away**
separar(se); **to** — **a breath** aspirar, tomar
aliento; **to** — **a blank** quedarse en
blanco; **to** — **in** involucrar; **to** — **lots /
straws** echar a la suerte, sortear; **to** —
near acercarse; **to** — **off** irse, retirarse; **to**
— **on** (be based on) basarse en; (have
recourse to) recurrir a; **to** — **out** (remove)
sacar; (prolong) alargar, prolongar; **to** —
up (approach) acercar(se); (write) redactar;
(shrink) encoger; N (tie) empate *m*; (lot)
número sorteado *m*; (attraction) atracción
f; —**back** inconveniente *m*; —**bridge**
puente levadizo *m*

drawer [drɔ] N cajón *m*; (small) gaveta *f*;
—**s** calzones *m pl*

drawing [drɔ́ɪŋ] N (picture) dibujo *m*; (raffle)
sorteo *m*; — **room** sala (de recibo) *f*

drawn [drɔn] ADJ demacrado; —**-out**
interminable

dread [drɛd] N pavor *m*, terror *m*, espanto *m*;
VT **I** — **going to the dentist** me aterra ir
al dentista

dreadful [drédfəɫ] ADJ horrendo, espantoso,

temible

dream [drim] N sueño *m* (also aspiration);
(reverie) ensueño *m*, ensoñación *f*; (fancy)
ilusión *f*; —**land** tierra del ensueño *f*; VI/
VT soñar; **to** — **of** soñar con; **I wouldn't**
— **of stealing** no se me ocurriría robar;
to — **that** soñar que; **to** — **up** imaginar;
ADJ **a** — **holiday** unas vacaciones
perfectas; — **team** dream team *m*, equipo
de estrellas *m*; — **world** mundo de
ensueño *m*

dreamer [drímə] N (impractical person)
soñador -ora *mf*; (visionary) visionario -ria
mf

dreary [dríri] ADJ sombrío, deprimente

dredge [drɛʤ] N draga *f*; VT dragar

dregs [drɛgz] N heces *f pl*, poso *m*; — **of
society** escoria de la sociedad *f*

drench [drɛntʃ] VT empapar, calar; —**ed in
blood** bañado en sangre

dress [drɛs] N (article of clothing for women)
vestido *m*; (attire) ropa *f*; (formal) traje de
etiqueta *m*, ropa de etiqueta *f*; (costume)
vestimenta *f*; —**maker** modista *mf*; —
rehearsal ensayo general *m*; — **shirt**
camisa para traje *f*; VI/VT vestir(se); VT
(store window) arreglar; (slaughtered
animals) limpiar; (salad) aderezar; (hides)
adobar; (a wound) vendar; **to** — **down**
(scold) regañar; (wear casual clothes)
ponerse ropa informal; **to** — **up** (wear
fine clothes) vestirse de gala; (make more
appealing) embellecer

dresser [drésə] N cómoda *f*; **she is a good**
— se viste con elegancia

dressing [drésɪŋ] N (act, result) vestir(se) *m*;
(for salad) aderezo *m*; (for fowl) relleno *m*;
(for wounds) gasa *f*, vendaje *m*; —**-down**
regaño *m*; — **gown** bata *f*; — **room** (in a
theater) camerino *m*; (in a store) probador
m; — **table** tocador *m*

dribble [dríbəɫ] VI (trickle) gotear; (sliver)
babear; VT (a ball) driblar; (liquid) rociar; N
(trickle) goteo *m*; (small quantity) chorrito
m; (of a ball) dribbling *m*

dried [draɪd] ADJ seco; — **fig** higo paso / seco
m; —**-up** (without water) seco; (wizened)
arrugado

drift [drɪft] N (direction) deriva *f*; (current)
corriente *f*; (meaning) sentido *m*, tenor *m*;
(pile) montón *m*, acumulación *f*; **do you
get my** —? ¿me captas la onda? VI (float)
flotar; (be adrift) ir a la deriva; (wander)
errar; **he** —**ed off** se durmió; VI/VT
(deviate) desviar(se); (accumulate)
amontonar(se), acumular(se); —**wood**
madera flotante *f*

drifter [dríftɚ] N (wanderer) vagabundo -da *mf*; (of a worker) itinerante *mf*

drill [drɪł] N (tool) taladro *m*; (training) ejercicios *m pl*; (procedure) procedimiento *m*; (rehearsal) simulacro *m*; (cloth) dril *m*; VI/VT (make a hole) taladrar, perforar, barrenar; (train) entrenar(se), adiestrar(se); VI (train) hacer ejercicios; (practice) practicar; VT hacer practicar

drink [drɪŋk] VI/VT (person) beber; (animal) abrevar; (absorb, take in) absorber; **to — up** apurar el trago; **to — to someone's health** brindar por alguien; N bebida *f* (also alcoholic); (a measure of beverage) trago *m*

drinkable [dríŋkəbəł] ADJ potable

drip [drɪp] N goteo *m*; (a bore) plasta *mf*; VI gotear; VT dejar caer gotas

drive [draɪv] VI/VT (a car) conducir, manejar; VI (go in a vehicle) ir en coche; VT (move forth) impulsar, impeler; (an animal) arrear; (convey) llevar (en coche); (force labor) forzar a trabajar; (a nail) clavar; (a ball) tirar, golpear; **to — a hard bargain** regatear mucho; **to — away** ahuyentar; **to — someone mad** volver loco a alguien; **what are you driving at?** ¿qué quieres decir con eso? **—-by shooting** tiroteo desde un coche *m*; **—-in** drive-in *m*, establecimiento en que el cliente es atendido en el coche *m*; **—-in movie theater** autocine *m*; **—way** camino de entrada *m*, entrada de coches *f*; N (ride) paseo (en coche) *m*; (of an animal) arreo *m*; (urge) impulso *m*; (military offensive) ofensiva *f*; (road) carretera *f*; (driveway) camino *m*; (campaign) campaña *f*; (energy) empuje *m*; (propulsion system) propulsión *f*; (of a ball) tiro *m*; (in tennis and golf) drive *m*; **front wheel —** tracción delantera *f*

drivel [drívəł] N (saliva) baba *f*; (idiocy) tontería *f*; VI babearse

driveling [drívəlɪŋ] ADJ baboso; **he's a — idiot** es un oligofrénico

driver [dráɪvɚ] N (chauffeur) chofer *mf*, conductor -ra *mf*; (of animals) arriero -ra *mf*; (golf club) driver *m*

drizzle [drízəł] VI lloviznar; N llovizna *f*

drone [dron] N (male bee; idler) zángano *m*; (remote-controlled vehicle) nave teledirigida *f*; (drudge) esclavo *m*; (sound) zumbido *m*; VI/VT (make a sound) zumbar; (talk) hablar monótonamente

drool [druł] N baba *f*; VI babearse

droop [drup] VI doblarse; (sag) colgarse; (flag) languidecer; (wither) marchitarse; **his shoulders —** tiene los hombros caídos; **—ing ears** orejas gachas *f pl*

drop [drɑp] N (liquid quantity) gota *f*; (descent) caída *f*; (incline) declive *m*; (in value) baja *f*; (lozenge) pastilla *f*; (of mail, etc.) buzón *m*, punto de recolección *m*; (of supplies) lanzamiento *m*; VI caer; (let fall) dejar caer, descargar; **to — a line** mandar unas líneas; **to — from sight** desaparecer; **to — in** caer de sorpresa; **to — out** (sports) retirarse; (school) abandonar; **—out** (student) estudiante que abandona *mf*; (marginalized person) marginado -da *mf*; **to — the curtain** bajar el telón; **why don't you — by?** ¿por qué no pasas por aquí? **—-dead beautiful** hermosísima

dropper [drɑpɚ] N gotero *m*

drought [draʊt] N sequía *f*

drove [drov] N tropel *m*

drown [draʊn] VI/VT ahogar(se)

drowse [draʊz] VI (be half-asleep) dormitar; (feel drowsy) estar amodorrado

drowsiness [dráʊzɪnɪs] N modorra *f*, somnolencia *f*

drowsy [dráʊzi] ADJ amodorrado, somnoliento; **to become —** amodorrarse

drudge [drʌdʒ] N esclavo del trabajo *m*, fregona *f*; VI trabajar como un esclavo

drug [drʌg] N (chemical substance, narcotic) droga *f*; (medicine) medicamento *m*; **to be a — on the market** ser invendible; **— addict** drogadicto -a *mf*; **—store** (drugs) farmacia *f*; (non-drug items) droguería *f*; perfumería *f*; VT (stupefy with drugs) drogar; (mix with a drug) adulterar con droga

druggist [drʌgɪst] N farmacéutico -ca *mf*, droguero -ra *mf*

drum [drʌm] N (musical instrument) tambor *m*; (eardrum) tímpano *m*; (receptacle for storing liquids) barril *m*; **—head** parche *m*; **—stick** (music) palillo de tambor *m*; (fowl) pata *f*; VI (play a drum) tocar el tambor; (beat rhythmically) tamborilear; **to — out** expulsar; **to — up** fomentar; **I'm trying to — this idea into his head** le estoy repitiendo esta idea con insistencia

drummer [drʌmɚ] N (classical) tambor *m*; (folk) tamborilero -ra *mf*; (rock & roll) baterista *mf*; (sales person) viajante de comercio *mf*

drunk [drʌŋk] ADJ & N borracho -cha *mf*; *fam* mamado -da *mf*; **to get —** emborracharse

drunkard [drʌŋkɚd] N borracho -cha *mf*, borrachín -ina *mf*

drunken [dráŋkən] ADJ borracho, embriagado

drunkenness [dráŋkənnɪs] N borrachera *f*, embriaguez *f*

dry [draɪ] ADJ seco; (sober) sobrio; (topic, book) árido, aburrido; — **land** tierra firme *f*; — **cleaner** (business) tintorería *f*; (owner of business) tintorero -ra *mf*; — **cleaning** limpieza en seco *f*; — **county** condado seco *m*; — **wit** humor agudo *m*; — **goods** géneros *m pl*; — **measure** medida para áridos *f*; — **run** prueba *f*; — **ice** hielo seco *m*; — **dock** dique seco *m*, varadero *m*; VI/VT (wet clothes) secar(se); (leather) resecar(se); **to — up** secarse, resecarse; **to — out** desintoxicar(se)

dryer [dráɪɚ] N (hair) secador *m*; (clothes) secadora *f*

dryness [dráɪnɪs] N (skin, etc.) sequedad *f*; (land, lecture) aridez *f*

dual [dúəł] ADJ (function) doble; (ownership) compartido

dub [dʌb] VT doblar

dubious [dúbiəs] ADJ dudoso

duchess [dátʃɪs] N duquesa *f*

duck [dʌk] N (species) pato *m*; (downward dodge) agachada *f*; VI/VT (plunge under water) hundir(se); (bend down) agachar(se); VT (avoid) esquivar

duckling [dáklɪŋ] N patito *m*

duct [dʌkt] N conducto *m*; — **tape** cinta aislante *f*

ductile [dáktḷ] ADJ dúctil

dud [dʌd] N (disappointing thing) chasco *m*; (unexploded bomb) bomba que no estalla *f*; —**s** (clothes) ropa *f*, *fam* trapos *m pl*; (belongings) pertenencias *f pl*

dude [dud] N (dandy) chulo *m*; (fellow) tipo *m*

due [du] ADJ (payable) pagadero; (immediately owed) vencido; (fitting, rightful) debido; (adequate) suficiente; **in — time / course** a su debido tiempo; **the train is — at two o'clock** se supone que el tren llega a las dos; ADV — **east** hacia el este; N (punishment) merecido *m*; **give Mary her —**; **she's honest** tienes que reconocer que María es honrada; —**s** cuota *f*

duel [dúəł] N duelo *m*; VI/VT batirse en / a duelo (con alguien)

duet [duét] N (played) dúo *m*; (sung) dueto *m*

dugout [dágaʊt] N (canoe) piragua *f*; (underground refuge) trinchera *f*

DUI (driving under the influence) [dijuáɪ] N conducir en estado de ebriedad *m*

duke [duk] N duque *m*; **to put up one's —s** levantar los puños; VT **to — it out** arreglarlo con los puños

dukedom [dúkdəm] N ducado *m*

dull [dʌł] ADJ (lackluster) opaco; (listless, muted) apagado; (boring) aburrido, soso, desanimado; (blunt) romo, desafilado; (sluggish, stupid) lento; (pain) sordo; VI/VT (a knife) desafilar(se); (color) opacar(se); (sound, impact) amortiguar(se); (pain) aliviar(se); (senses) embotar(se), entorpecer(se)

duly [dúli] ADV debidamente

dumb [dʌm] ADJ (mute) mudo; (dull) tonto; —**bell** (handweight) mancuerna *f*; (stupid person) bobo -ba *mf*; —**founded** patitieso, atónito; VT **to — down** simplificar demasiado

dumbness [dámnɪs] N (muteness) mudez *f*; (foolishness) estupidez *f*

dummy [dámi] N (figure) muñeco *m*; (fool) tonto -ta *mf*; *offensive* pendejo -ja *mf*; (front) hombre de paja *m*; ADJ (fake) falso; **a — president** un títere

dump [dʌmp] VT (unload) descargar; (empty) botar; (dismiss) echar, despedir; (discard) tirar la basura, descargar desechos; (flood a market) hacer dumping; (abandon) plantar; **to — on** (criticize) criticar; (unload problems) descargarse; N (place for waste) vertedero *m*, basural *m*, basurero *m*; (of weapons) depósito *m*; (act of discarding) vertido *m*; (act or effect of defecating) *vulg* cagada *f*; —**truck** camión volteador *m*, volquete *m*; **to be in the —s** estar deprimido, estar depre; **to take a —** *vulg* cagar

dunce [dʌns] N burro -rra *mf*, tonto -ta de capirote *mf*

dune [dun] N duna *f*, médano *m*

dung [dʌŋ] N boñiga *f*, bosta *f*; —**hill** estercolero *m*

dungeon [dánʤən] N mazmorra *f*

dupe [dup] N (gullible person) ingenuo -nua *mf*, inocente *mf*; *Sp* primo -ma *mf*; (manipulated person) títere *m*; VT embaucar

duplex [dúplɛks] N & ADJ dúplex *m*

duplicate [dúplɪkɪt] ADJ & N duplicado *m*; **in — por duplicado; [dúplɪket] VT duplicar(se)

duplicity [duplísɪɖi] N duplicidad *f*

durability [dʊrəbílɪɖi] N durabilidad *f*

durable [dúrəbəł] ADJ (long-lasting) duradero; (serviceable) sufrido

duration [dʊréʃən] N duración *f*

duress [dʊrés] N coacción *f*

during [dúrɪŋ] PREP durante

dusk [dʌsk] N atardecer *m*, anochecer *m*; **at**

— al atardecer

dusky [dʌ́ski] ADJ (dark) oscuro; (gloomy) sombrío

dust [dʌst] N polvo *m*; **—pan** pala *f*; **to bite the —** (die) *fam* espichar; (lose) morder el polvo de la derrota; **cloud of —** polvareda *f*; VI/VT (remove dust) quitar / sacudir el polvo (a); VT (sprinkle with powder) espolvorear; VI (become dusty) empolvarse; **to — off** desempolvar

duster [dʌ́stɚ] N plumero *m*

dusty [dʌ́sti] ADJ polvoriento

Dutch [dʌtʃ] ADJ & N holandés -esa *mf*; **to go — pagar a escote**

Dutchman [dʌ́tʃmən] N holandés *m*

duty [dúᴅi] N deber *m*, obligación *f*; (tax on imports) derechos aduaneros *m pl*; (any tax) impuesto *m*; **to be on —** estar de guardia; **to be off —** no estar de guardia; **—-free** libre de impuestos

DVD (digital versatile disc) [dívidí] N DVD *m*

dwarf [dwɔrf] ADJ & N enano -na *mf*; VT hacer parecer pequeño

dwell [dwɛɫ] VI morar, habitar; **to — on a subject** dilatarse en un asunto

dweller [dwɛ́lɚ] N habitante *mf*, morador -ra *mf*

dwelling [dwɛ́lɪŋ] N vivienda *f*, domicilio *m*

DWI (driving while intoxicated) [didʌbəljuái] N conducir en estado de ebriedad *m*

dwindle [dwíndḷ] VI/VT menguar, mermar

dye [daɪ] N tinte *m*, tintura *f*; VT teñir

dying [dáɪɪŋ] ADJ moribundo

dyke [daɪk] N *offensive* tortillera *f*

dynamic [daɪnǽmɪk] ADJ dinámico; N **—s** dinámica *f*

dynamite [dáɪnəmaɪt] N dinamita *f*; VT dinamitar; ADJ fabuloso

dynamo [dáɪnəmo] N dínamo *m*

dynasty [dáɪnəsti] N dinastía *f*

dysentery [dísn̩teri] N disentería *f*

dysfunction [dɪsfʌ́ŋkʃən] N disfunción *f*

Ee

each [itʃ] ADJ cada; **— person** cada persona; PRON cada uno; **— receives a prize** cada uno recibe un premio; **they looked at — other** se miraron el uno al otro

eager [íɡɚ] ADJ (enthusiastic) ansioso; (avid) ávido

eagerness [íɡɚnɪs] N (enthusiasm) ansia *f*, afán *m*; (strong desire) avidez *f*

eagle [íɡəɫ] N águila *f*; **—-eye** ojo de lince *m*

eaglet [íɡlɪt] N aguilucho *m*

ear [ir] N (outer organ) oreja *f*; (inner organ, sense of hearing, musical aptitude) oído *m*; (of corn) mazorca *f*; *Am* elote *m*; **—ache** dolor de oídos *m*; **—drops** gotas para los oídos *f pl*; **—drum** tímpano *m*; **—lobe** lóbulo de la oreja *m*; **— muff** orejera *f*; **— of wheat** espiga *f*; **—phone** audífono *m*; **—ring** pendiente *m*, zarcillo *m*; **by —** de oído; **within —shot** al alcance del oído; **he has the — of the governor** el gobernador le presta mucha atención

earful [írfʊɫ] N **I got an —** (scolding) me echó un rapapolvo; (gossip) me dio la lata

early [ɝ́li] ADJ temprano; **— man** hombre primitivo *m*; **— reply** respuesta rápida *f*; **— riser / bird** madrugador -ra *mf*, mañanero -ra *mf*; **the — bird gets the worm** al que madruga, Dios lo ayuda

earn [ɝn] VI/VT (money, admiration, etc.) ganar; (salary) cobrar, ganar; (interest) devengar; **to — a living** ganarse la vida

earnest [ɝ́nɪst] ADJ (sincere) serio, formal; (grave) grave; **in —** en serio; **— money** señal *f*; *Mex* enganche *m*

earnestness [ɝ́nɪstnɪs] N (sincerity) seriedad *f*, formalidad *f*; (gravity) gravedad *f*; **in all —** con toda sinceridad

earnings [ɝ́nɪŋz] N (of a person) ingresos *m pl*, haberes *m pl*; (of a business) ganancias *f pl*

earth [ɝθ] N tierra *f*; **—mover** excavadora *f*; **—quake** terremoto *m*, temblor de tierra *m*; **—shaking** revolucionario; **—worm** lombriz *f*; **the —** la Tierra

earthen [ɝ́θən] ADJ (wall) de tierra; (pot) de barro; **—ware** vajilla de barro *f*, cerámica *f*

earthly [ɝ́θli] ADJ terrenal; **— possessions** bienes terrenales *m pl*; **to be of no — use** no servir para nada

earthy [ɝ́θi] ADJ natural; (person) campechano; (sense of humor, joke) basto; **— smell** olor a tierra *m*

ease [iz] N (facility) facilidad *f*; (unaffectedness) soltura *f*, desparpajo *m*; (comfort) comodidad *f*; (lack of worry) tranquilidad *f*; (fullness of a garment) holgura *f*; **at —** (military) en descanso; (comfortable) tranquilo, a gusto; **a life of —** una vida desahogada; **ill at —** incómodo; VT (make easier) facilitar; VI/VT (relieve pain) aliviar(se); (release from tension) aflojar(se); (relieve anxiety) tranquilizar(se); **to — up** aflojar

easel [ízəɫ] N caballete *m*

east [ist] N este *m*, oriente *m*; ADJ del este, oriental; ADV **— of here** al este (de aquí); **to go —** ir al / hacia el este; **back —** en el este

Easter [ístə-] N Pascua *f*; **— egg** huevo de Pascua *m*; **— Sunday** Domingo de Pascua *m*

eastern [ístə-n] ADJ oriental, del este

eastward [ístwə-d] ADV & ADJ hacia el este

easy [ízi] ADJ (simple) fácil, sencillo; (compliant) fácil; (comfortable) cómodo; (informal) desenvuelto; (unworried) tranquilo; **— chair** poltrona *f*; **—-going** calmoso; **— terms** facilidades de pago *f pl*; **at an — pace** a paso moderado; **within — reach** al alcance de la mano; **go — on me** sea bueno; **he's on — street** vive en la abundancia

eat [it] VI/VT comer(se); VT (costs) absorber; **to — away** corroer, comer; **to — breakfast** desayunar(se); **to — dinner** (midday) comer; (evening) cenar; **to — lunch** comer, almorzar; **to — one's heart out** morirse de envidia; **to — one's words** tragarse las palabras; **to — supper** cenar; **to — up** comerse todo; **what's —ing you?** ¿qué bicho te picó?

eating [íDɪŋ] N (act) comer *m*; (food) comida *f*; **— utensils** cubiertos *m pl*; **— apples** manzanas para comer *f pl*

eaves [ivz] N PL alero *m*

eavesdrop [ívzdrɑp] VI escuchar sin ser visto

ebb [ɛb] N (flowing back) reflujo *m*; (decay) decadencia *f*; **— tide** reflujo *m*; **to be at a low —** estar en un punto bajo; VI (tide) bajar; (energy) decaer

ebony [ébəni] N ébano *m*

eccentric [ɛksɛ́ntrɪk] ADJ & N excéntrico -ca *mf*

ecclesiastic [ɪkliziǽstɪk] ADJ & N eclesiástico *m*

echelon [éʃəlɑn] N (military formation) escalón *m*; (rank) nivel *m*, estrato *m*

echo [éko] N eco *m*; VI hacer eco; **the gym —ed with laughter** el gimnasio resonó de risas; VT repetir

eclectic [ɪklɛ́ktɪk] ADJ ecléctico

eclipse [ɪklíps] N eclipse *m*; VT eclipsar

ecology [ɪkáləʤi] N ecología *f*

e-commerce [íkámə-s] N comercio electrónico *m*

economic [ɛkənámɪk] ADJ económico; **—s** economía *f*

economical [ɛkənámɪkəɫ] ADJ económico

economist [ɪkánəmɪst] N economista *mf*

economize [ɪkánəmaɪz] VI economizar

economy [ɪkánəmi] N economía *f* (also thrift); ADJ **— car** coche económico *m*; **— class** clase turista *f*

ecosystem [íkosɪstəm] N ecosistema *m*

ecstasy [ɛ́kstəsi] N éxtasis *m* (also drug)

Ecuador [ɛ́kwədɔr] N Ecuador *m*

Ecuadorian [ɛkwədɔ́riən] ADJ & N ecuatoriano -na *mf*

ecumenical [ɛkjəménɪkəɫ] ADJ ecuménico

eczema [ɛ́gzəmə] N eccema *m*

eddy [éDi] N remolino *m*; VI arremolinarse

edge [ɛʤ] N borde *m*, canto *m*; (of a knife) filo *m*; (of a cube) arista *f*; **to be on —** estar nervioso; **her voice has an — to it** tiene la voz penetrante; **a competitive —** una ventaja sobre la competencia; VT (make an edge) hacerle el borde; (sharpen) afilar; (move sideways) meterse de costado; **to — out** ganar por un pelito; **to — up** aproximarse; ADV **—wise** de costado

edgy [éʤi] ADJ nervioso

edible [éDəbəɫ] ADJ & N comestible *m*

edict [íDɪkt] N edicto *m*, bando *m*

edifice [éDəfɪs] N edificio *m*

edify [éDəfaɪ] VT edificar

edit [éDɪt] VT (revise, correct) corregir; (serve as editor) editar; (film) montar; **to — out** eliminar; N corrección *f*

edition [ɪdíʃən] N edición *f*

editor [éDɪtə-] N (director of a publication) redactor -ra *mf*; (compiler, radio or film worker) editor -ra *mf*; (proofreader) corrector -ra *mf*

editorial [ɛDɪtɔ́riəɫ] ADJ editorial; N editorial *f*

editorialize [ɛDɪtɔ́riəlaɪz] VI editorializar

educate [éʤəket] VT educar

education [ɛʤəkéʃən] N educación *f*, enseñanza *f*; (academic subject) pedagogía *f*; **school of —** escuela normal *f*

educational [ɛʤəkéʃənəɫ] ADJ educativo

educator [éʤəkeDə-] N educador -ra *mf*

eel [iɫ] N anguila *f*

eerie [íri] ADJ misterioso

effect [ɪfɛ́kt] N efecto *m*; **—s** efectos *m pl*; **to go into —** entrar en vigencia, ponerse en operación; **I wrote a letter to that —** le escribí una carta en ese sentido; VT efectuar

effective [ɪfɛ́ktɪv] ADJ efectivo, eficaz; (a law) vigente; **— date** fecha de vigencia *f*

effectively [ɪfɛ́ktɪvli] ADV (well) eficazmente; (in fact) de hecho, en efecto

effectual [ɪfɛ́ktʃuəɫ] ADJ eficaz

effeminate [ɪfémənət] ADJ afeminado

efficacy [ɛ́fɪkəsi] N eficacia *f*

efficiency [ɪfíʃənsi] N eficiencia *f*; — **apartment** estudio *m*

efficient [ɪfíʃənt] ADJ eficiente; (motor) económico

effigy [ɛ́fədʒi] N efigie *f*; **to burn in** — quemar en efigie

effort [ɛ́fɚt] N (exertion) esfuerzo *m*; (work of art) obra *f*; (campaign) campaña *f*

effrontery [ɪfrʌ́ntəri] N descaro *m*

effusive [ɪfjúsɪv] ADJ efusivo

egg [ɛg] N huevo *m*; (female gamete) óvulo *m*; (fellow) tipo *m*; **—beater** batidor de huevos *m*; **—head** empollón -na *mf*; **—nog** rompopo *m*, rompope *m*, ponche de huevo *m*; **—plant** berenjena *f*; **—shell** cáscara de huevo *f*; **to have — on one's face** estar avergonzado, quedar mal; **to lay an** — (of a hen) poner un huevo; (fail) fracasar; **to walk on —shells** ir pisando huevos; VT **to — on** incitar

ego [ígo] N (self) yo *m*, ego *m*; (vanity) ego *m*; (self-esteem) amor propio *m*; **winning the prize was an — trip for him** ganar el premio le aceitó el ego

egocentric [igosɛ́ntrɪk] ADJ egocéntrico

egotism [ígətɪzəm] N egotismo *m*

Egypt [ídʒɪpt] N Egipto *m*

Egyptian [ɪdʒípʃən] ADJ & N egipcio -cia *mf*

eight [et] NUM ocho

eighteen [ettín] NUM dieciocho

eighth [etθ] ADJ, N & ADV octavo *m*; **— note** corchea *f*

eighty [éɪ̯di] NUM ochenta

either [íðɚ] ADJ & PRON **— will do** cualquiera de los dos está bien; **choose — suit** elige uno de los dos trajes; **choose —** elige uno (u otro) de los dos; **there were flowers on — side of the road** había flores a ambos lados de la carretera; ADV **if you don't, I won't —** si tú no lo haces, yo tampoco; **I'll — go by bus or by car** voy (o) en autobús o en auto

ejaculate [ɪdʒǽkjələt] VI/VT eyacular; (exclaim) exclamar

eject [ɪdʒɛ́kt] VT (throw out) echar, expulsar; VI/VT (from a plane) eyectar(se)

ejection [ɪdʒɛ́kʃən] N expulsión *f*

elaborate [ɪlǽbɚɪt] ADJ (ornate) elaborado; (detailed) detallado; [ɪlǽbəret] VI/VT (create) elaborar; (develop) desarrollar

elapse [ɪlǽps] VI transcurrir, pasar

elastic [ɪlǽstɪk] ADJ elástico; N elástico *m*; (rubber band) goma elástica *f*

elasticity [ɪlæstísɪdi] N elasticidad *f*

elated [ɪléɪdɪd] ADJ encantado

elbow [ɛ́ɬbo] N codo *m*; **to be within —**
reach estar a la mano; VI/VT codear, dar codazos; **to — one's way through** abrirse paso a codazos

elder [ɛ́ɬdɚ] ADJ (older) mayor; N (older person) mayor *mf*; (old person) anciano -na *mf*; (in a church) miembro del consejo de una iglesia *m*; **our —s** nuestros mayores *m pl*

elderly [ɛ́ɬdɚli] ADJ anciano

elect [ɪlɛ́kt] ADJ (elected) electo; (chosen by God) elegido -da *mf*; VI/VT elegir

election [ɪlɛ́kʃən] N elección *f*

elector [ɪlɛ́ktɚ] N elector -ra *mf*

electoral [ɪlɛ́ktɚəɬ] ADJ electoral

electric [ɪlɛ́ktrɪk] ADJ eléctrico; (exciting) electrizante; (excited) electrizado; **— chair** silla eléctrica *f*; **— eel** anguila eléctrica *f*; **— eye** célula fotoeléctrica *f*; **— meter** contador eléctrico *m*; **— storm** tormenta eléctrica *f*

electrical [ɪlɛ́ktrɪkəɬ] ADJ eléctrico; **— engineer** ingeniero electricista *mf*; **— engineering** ingeniería eléctrica *f*; **— tape** cinta aislante *f*

electrician [ɪlɛktríʃən] N electricista *mf*

electricity [ɪlɛktrísɪdi] N electricidad *f*

electrify [ɪlɛ́ktrəfaɪ] VT (apply electricity) electrificar; (thrill) electrizar

electrocardiogram [ɪlɛktrokárɒiəgræm] N electrocardiograma *m*

electrocute [ɪlɛ́ktrəkjut] VT electrocutar

electrode [ɪlɛ́ktrod] N electrodo *m*

electroencephalogram [ɪlɛktroɛnsɛ́fələgræm] N electroencefalograma *m*

electrolysis [ɪlɛktrálɪsɪs] N electrólisis *f*

electromagnet [ɪlɛktromǽgnɪt] N electroimán *m*

electromagnetic [ɪlɛktromægnɛ́ɒɪk] ADJ electromagnético

electron [ɪlɛ́ktrɑn] N electrón *m*; **— microscope** microscopio electrónico *m*

electronic [ɪlɛktránɪk] ADJ electrónico; **— banking** banca electrónica *f*; **— mail** correo electrónico *m*; **—s** electrónica *f*; **— signature** firma electrónica *f*

elegance [ɛ́lɪgəns] N elegancia *f*, gallardía *f*

elegant [ɛ́lɪgənt] ADJ elegante, gallardo; (gift) de lujo

element [ɛ́ləmənt] N elemento *m*; (component part) componente *m*, pieza *f*; (for heating) resistencia *f*; **the —s** los elementos

elemental [ɛləmɛ́ntɬ] ADJ elemental; **— forces** fuerzas de la naturaleza *f pl*

elementary [ɛləmɛ́ntri] ADJ elemental; **— school** escuela primaria *f*

elephant [ɛ́ləfənt] N elefante -ta *mf*

elevate [éləvet] VT elevar
elevation [ɛləvéʃən] N elevación f; (altitude) altura f
elevator [éləvɛɾə‑] N ascensor m; Am elevador m; (for grain) elevador m
eleven [ɪlévən] NUM once
elf [ɛłf] N elfo m; (child) pillo -lla mf
elicit [ɪlísɪt] VT provocar; **to — admiration** despertar admiración; **to — applause** suscitar el aplauso
eligible [élɪʤəbəł] ADJ elegible; **an — bachelor** un buen partido; **you are — for a scholarship** tienes derecho a solicitar una beca
eliminate [ɪlímənet] VT eliminar
elimination [ɪlɪmənéʃən] N eliminación f
elite [ɪlít] N elite f, élite f
elitist [ɪlídɪst] ADJ & N elitista mf
elk [ɛłk] N alce m
elliptical [ɪlíptɪkəł] ADJ elíptico
elm [ɛłm] N olmo m
elongate [ɪlóŋget] VI/VT alargar(se)
elope [ɪlóp] VI fugarse para casarse a escondidas
eloquence [éləkwəns] N elocuencia f
eloquent [éləkwənt] ADJ elocuente
El Salvador [ɛłsæłvədor] N El Salvador m
else [ɛłs] ADJ & ADV **who — was there?** ¿quién más estaba? **someone —'s son** el hijo de otro; **somebody —** (algún) otro; **or —** si no; **leave town or —** vete del pueblo o sufre las consecuencias / o verás lo que es bueno; **nobody —** nadie más; **nothing —** nada más; **how —?** ¿de qué otra forma? ADV **—where** (location) en otra parte / en otro lado; (movement) a otra parte / a otro sitio
elucidate [ɪlúsɪdet] VI/VT dilucidar, esclarecer
elucidation [ɪlusɪdéʃən] N elucidación f
elude [ɪlúd] VT eludir
elusive [ɪlúsɪv] ADJ (slippery) escurridizo; (evasive) esquivo; (difficult to understand) difícil de entender
emaciated [ɪméʃiedɪd] ADJ escuálido, descarnado
e-mail, E-mail [ímeł] N correo electrónico m
emanate [émənet] VI/VT emanar
emanation [emənéʃən] N emanación f
emancipate [ɪmǽnsəpet] VT emancipar
emancipation [ɪmænsəpéʃən] N emancipación f
emasculate [ɪmǽskjəlet] VT castrar; (remove testicles) castrar, emascular
embalm [ɪmbám] VT embalsamar
embankment [ɪmbǽŋkmənt] N terraplén m
embargo [ɪmbárgo] N embargo m; VT imponer un embargo

embark [ɪmbárk] VI/VT embarcar(se)
embarrass [ɪmbǽrəs] VT (shame) hacerle pasar vergüenza a; (discomfit, financial difficulties) poner en aprietos; VI avergonzarse
embarrassing [ɪmbǽrəsɪŋ] ADJ (shameful) vergonzoso; (impeding) embarazoso
embarrassment [ɪmbǽrəsmənt] N (shame) vergüenza f, bochorno m; (act of embarrassing) vergüenza f; (financial difficulty) aprieto m; **he's an — to the company** siempre deja mal a la compañía; **we have an — of riches** nadamos en la abundancia
embassy [émbəsi] N embajada f
embattled [ɪmbǽdḷd] ADJ hostigado, agobiado
embed [ɪmbéd] VT incrustar
embedded [ɪmbédɪd] ADJ incrustado
embellish [ɪmbélɪʃ] VT adornar, ornamentar
ember [émbə‑] N ascua f, brasa f
embezzle [ɪmbézəł] VT desfalcar, malversar
embezzlement [ɪmbézəłmənt] N desfalco m, peculado m
embitter [ɪmbídə‑] VT amargar
emblem [émbləm] N emblema m, divisa f
embody [ɪmbádi] VT (personify) personificar; (to provide with a body) encarnar
embolism [émbəlɪzəm] N embolia f
embrace [ɪmbrés] VI/VT (hug, adopt) abrazar(se); (include) abarcar; N abrazo m
embroider [ɪmbróɪdə‑] VI/VT bordar, recamar
embroidery [ɪmbróɪdəri] N bordado m
embroil [ɪmbróɪł] VT (involve in a conflict) meterse en un lío; (throw into confusion) embrollar
embryo [émbrio] N embrión m
emerald [émə‑əłd] N esmeralda f
emerge [ɪmɝ́ʤ] VI (come into view) emerger; (arise, as a question, problem) surgir
emergency [ɪmɝ́ʤənsi] N emergencia f; **— brake** freno de emergencia m; **— exit** salida de emergencia f; **— room** urgencias f pl
emigrant [émɪgrənt] ADJ & N emigrante mf
emigrate [émɪgret] VI emigrar
emigration [emɪgréʃən] N emigración f
eminence [émənəns] N eminencia f
eminent [émənənt] ADJ eminente
emissary [émɪseri] N emisario -ria mf
emission [ɪmíʃən] N emisión f
emit [ɪmít] VT (light, sound, etc.) emitir; (smells) despedir; (sparks) echar
emotion [ɪmóʃən] N emoción f
emotional [ɪmóʃənəł] ADJ (of the emotions) emocional; (arousing or expressing emotions) emotivo; (easily moved)

sensible
empathy [émpəθi] N empatía *f*
emperor [émpərɚ] N emperador *m*; —
  penguin pingüino emperador *m*
emphasis [émfəsɪs] N énfasis *m*, hincapié *m*
emphasize [émfəsaɪz] VT enfatizar, hacer
  hincapié en, subrayar
emphatic [ɪmfǽDɪk] ADJ enfático
emphysema [ɛmfɪsímə] N enfisema *m*
empire [émpaɪr] N imperio *m*
empirical [ɛmpírɪkəł] ADJ empírico
employ [ɪmplɔ́ɪ] VT emplear; (hire) emplear,
  ocupar; N empleo *m*; **to be in someone's
  —** trabajar a las órdenes de alguien
employee [ɪmplɔɪí] N empleado -da *mf*
employer [ɪmplɔ́ɪɚ] N patrón -na *mf*
employment [ɪmplɔ́ɪmənt] N empleo *m*;
  (occupation) ocupación *f*; —
  opportunities oportunidades laborales *f*
  pl; **place of —** lugar de trabajo *m*
empower [ɪmpáʊɚ] VT (authorize) autorizar;
  (give strength) dar poder
empress [émprɪs] N emperatriz *f*
emptiness [émptɪnɪs] N vacío *m*
empty [émpti] ADJ vacío; (devoid of activity)
  desocupado; VI/VT vaciar(se), volcar(se);
  (debouch) desembocar; **—-handed** con
  las manos vacías; **to run on —** (of a car,
  person) quedarse sin combustible
emulate [émjəlet] VT emular (also computer
  term)
enable [ɪnébəł] VT permitir
enact [ɪnǽkt] VT (a law) promulgar; (a role)
  desempeñar
enamel [ɪnǽməł] N esmalte *m*; VT esmaltar
enamor [ɪnǽmɚ] VT enamorar; **to be —ed
  of** estar enamorado de
encamp [ɪnkǽmp] VI acampar
enchant [ɪntʃǽnt] VT (bewitch) hechizar;
  (delight) encantar
enchanting [ɪntʃǽntɪŋ] ADJ encantador
enchantment [ɪntʃǽntmənt] N
  encantamiento *m*, encanto *m*, hechicería *f*
encircle [ɪnsɚ́kəł] VT cercar, ceñir
enclave [ánklev] N enclave *m*
enclose [ɪnklóz] VT (confine someone or
  something) encerrar; (fence in) cercar; (put
  in the same envelope) adjuntar, anexar
enclosure [ɪnklóʒɚ] N (wall or fence) cerca *f*;
  (enclosed area) cercado *m*, recinto *m*;
  (enclosed document) documento adjunto
  m; (act of enclosing) encierro *m*
encompass [ɪnkámpəs] VT (include) abarcar,
  englobar; (surround) circundar
encore [ánkɔr] N bis *m*; INTERJ ¡otra!
encounter [ɪnkáʊntɚ] VI/VT encontrar(se);
  they —ed the enemy army se

enfrentaron con el ejército enemigo; N
  (meeting) encuentro *m* (also sports);
  (battle) enfrentamiento *m*
encourage [ɪnkɚ́ɪʤ] VT (inspire with
  confidence) alentar, animar; (promote)
  fomentar, estimular
encouragement [ɪnkɚ́ɪʤmənt] N aliento *m*;
  (inspiration) ánimo *m*; (promotion)
  estímulo *m*, fomento *m*
encroach [ɪnkrótʃ] VT **to — upon** (liberties)
  cercenar; (territory) usurpar; (time) quitar
encrypt [ɪnkrípt] VT codificar
encumber [ɪnkámbɚ] VT (block) impedir;
  (burden) agobiar
encyclopedia [ɪnsaɪkləpíɒiə] N enciclopedia *f*
end [ɛnd] N (temporal) fin *m*, término *m*;
  (limit, boundary) final *m*, extremo *m*; (tip)
  cabo *m*; (aim) fin *m*; **— to —** uno tras
  otro; **— table** mesa pequeña *f*; **at the —
  of the movie** al final de la película; **the
  north — of town** el barrio norte; **no —
  of things** un sinfín de cosas; **at the —
  of the day** al fin y al cabo; **on —** de
  punta; **for days on —** día tras día; **to
  put an — to** poner fin a; VI/VT terminar;
  (a street) morir; **he —ed his life** puso fin
  a su vida; **a prayer —s the class** la clase
  termina con una oración; **a war to — all
  wars** una guerra que supera a todas las
  anteriores
endanger [ɪndénʤɚ] VT poner en peligro;
  —ed species especie en peligro de
  extinción *f*
endear [ɪndír] VI **to — oneself** congraciarse;
  his humor —ed him to her se ganó la
  simpatía de ella gracias a su humor
endeavor [ɪndévɚ] VT (try) tratar de,
  intentar, procurar; VI (strive) esforzarse
  por; N esfuerzo *m*
endemic [ɪndémɪk] ADJ endémico
ending [éndɪŋ] N final *m*; (derivational,
  inflectional) terminación *f*; (inflectional)
  desinencia *f*
endless [éndlɪs] ADJ interminable;
  (continuous) sin fin; (infinite) eterno
endocrine [éndəkrɪn] ADJ endócrino
endorphin [ɪndɔ́rfɪn] N endorfina *f*
endorse [ɪndɔ́rs] VT (sign a check) endosar;
  (support) respaldar; (authorize a
  document) refrendar, visar
endorsement [ɪndɔ́rsmənt] N (signature)
  endoso *m*; (backing) respaldo *m*;
  (authorization) refrendo *m*
endorser [ɪndɔ́rsɚ] N (check signer)
  endosante *mf*; (supporter) partidario -ria
  mf; (authorizer) refrendario -ria *mf*
endow [ɪndáʊ] VT (grant funds) hacer un

legado; (furnish powers) dotar

endowment [ɪndáʊmənt] N (funds granted) legado *m*, dotación *f*; (power) dote *f*; **— annuity** anualidad dotal *f*; **— fund** fondo de un legado *m*

endurance [ɪndúrəns] N (stamina) resistencia *f*, fondo *m*; (power of bearing pain) aguante *m*

endure [ɪndúr] VT (undergo) sobrellevar, soportar, pasar; VI (live on) durar; (bear up) aguantar

enema [énəmə] N enema *m*, lavativa *f*

enemy [énəmi] N enemigo -ga *mf*

energetic [enəʤɛ́Dɪk] ADJ enérgico

energy [énəʤi] N energía *f*; **— policy** política energética *f*

enervate [énəvet] VT enervar, debilitar

enforce [ɪnfɔ́rs] VT hacer cumplir

enforcement [ɪnfɔ́rsmənt] N **law —** autoridades *f pl*; **the sheriff is responsible for the — of the law** el alguacil es responsable de hacer cumplir la ley

engage [ɪngéʤ] VT (hire) contratar; (attract) captar, atraer; (interlock) engranar; **to — the brake** poner el freno; **to — someone in conversation** trabar conversación con alguien; **to — in battle** trabar batalla; **to be —d in something** estar ocupado en algo; **to be —d to be married** estar comprometido (para casarse), estar prometido

engagement [ɪngéʤmənt] N (commitment) compromiso *m*; (betrothal) compromiso *m*, noviazgo *m*; (employment) empleo *m*; (battle) batalla *f*; (gear interlocking) engranaje *m*

engender [ɪnʤéndə] VT engendrar

engine [énʤɪn] N (machine) máquina *f*; (in a vehicle) motor *m*; (locomotive) locomotora *f*; **— block** bloque del motor *m*

engineer [enʤənír] N ingeniero -ra *mf*; (of locomotive) maquinista *mf*; VT (create) idear; (plot) maquinar

engineering [enʤənírɪŋ] N ingeniería *f*

English [ɪ́nglɪʃ] ADJ inglés; N (spin) efecto *m*; **the —** los ingleses; **—man, —woman** inglés -esa *mf*

engrave [ɪngrév] VI/VT grabar

engraver [ɪngrévə] N grabador -ora *mf*

engraving [ɪngrévɪŋ] N grabado *m*

engross [ɪngrós] VT absorber

engrossed [ɪngróst] ADJ absorto

engulf [ɪngʌ́lf] VT (swallow) tragar; (overwhelm) abrumar

enhance [ɪnhǽns] VT (intensify) realzar;

(improve) mejorar

enigma [ɪnígmə] N enigma *m*

enjoin [ɪnʤɔ́ɪn] VT instar; **to — from** prohibir

enjoy [ɪnʤɔ́ɪ] VI/VT (take pleasure) disfrutar (de), gozar (de); (benefit from) gozar (de); **—!** ¡Que lo disfrutes! **to — oneself** divertirse; **to — the use of** usufructuar

enjoyable [ɪnʤɔ́ɪəbəł] ADJ (pleasant) agradable, gozoso; (fun) ameno

enjoyment [ɪnʤɔ́ɪmənt] N (act of enjoying) goce *m*, disfrute *m*; (right of use) usufructo *m*; (pleasure) placer *m*, gozo *m*

enlarge [ɪnlárʤ] VI/VT agrandar(se); VT (blow up a photo) ampliar; VI **to — upon** explayarse sobre, extenderse sobre

enlargement [ɪnlárʤmənt] N (photo, building) ampliación *f*; (act of enlarging) agrandamiento *m*; (temporary swelling) dilatación *f*

enlighten [ɪnláɪtṇ] VT (morally) iluminar; (intellectually) explicar, ilustrar

enlightenment [ɪnláɪtṇmənt] N (moral) iluminación *f*; (intellectual) explicación *f*; **The —** La Ilustración

enlist [ɪnlíst] VI/VT (for the army) alistar(se); (for a campaign) conseguir el apoyo

enlistment [ɪnlístmənt] N alistamiento *m*

enliven [ɪnláɪvən] VT animar, avivar

enmity [énmɪDi] N enemistad *f*

ennoble [ɪnnóbəł] VT ennoblecer

enormous [ɪnɔ́rməs] ADJ enorme, descomunal

enough [ɪnʌ́f] ADJ suficiente; ADV **he's tall —** tiene altura suficiente; N lo suficiente; **we have — to live comfortably** tenemos lo suficiente como para vivir cómodamente; **that is —** con eso basta; **more than —** bastante; INTERJ ¡basta!

enrage [ɪnréʤ] VT enfurecer

enrapture [ɪnrǽptʃə] VT embelesar

enrich [ɪnrítʃ] VT enriquecer

enroll [ɪnrół] VI/VT matricular(se), inscribir(se); (in army) alistar(se)

enrollment [ɪnrółmənt] N matrícula *f*, inscripción *f*; **what is your —?** ¿Cuántos alumnos tienes matriculados?

ensemble [ɑnsámbəł] N conjunto *m*

ensign [énsɪn] N (naval rank) alférez de fragata *mf*; (flag) enseña *f*; (badge) insignia *f*

enslave [ɪnslév] VT esclavizar

ensnare [ɪnsnér] VT atrapar, coger en una trampa

ensue [ɪnsú] VI (follow) ocurrir después, suceder; (result from) resultar; **the ensuing events** los sucesos subsiguientes

ensure [ɪnʃúr] VT asegurar
entail [ɪntéɫ] VT implicar, traer aparejado; (an inheritance) vincular
entangle [ɪntǽŋgəɫ] VT enredar
enter [éntɚ] VT entrar en / a; (join) ingresar en / a; (write) escribir; (put data in a computer) dar entrada a; (put data in account books) asentar; VI/VT (register for a competition) inscribir(se); **to — into** (make an agreement) concertar; (form part of) figurar; VI salir / entrar a escena
enterprise [éntɚpraɪz] N empresa f
enterprising [éntɚpraɪzɪŋ] ADJ emprendedor
entertain [entɚtén] VI/VT (amuse) divertir, recrear; (host) invitar; **we — a lot** tenemos invitados muy a menudo; (consider) contemplar; (harbor) abrigar
entertainer [entɚténɚ] N artista mf
entertaining [entɚténɪŋ] ADJ (fun) divertido; (serving as pastime) entretenido; (pleasant) ameno
entertainment [entɚténmənt] N (source of fun) diversión f; (pastime) entretenimiento m; (of guests) agasajo m
enthrall [ɪnθrɔ́ɫ] VT (captivate) cautivar, hechizar; (make a slave of) esclavizar
enthusiasm [ɪnθúziæzəm] N entusiasmo m
enthusiast [ɪnθúziɪst] N entusiasta mf
enthusiastic [ɪnθuziǽstɪk] ADJ entusiasta inv; **I'm very — about the trip** estoy muy entusiasmado con el viaje
entice [ɪntáɪs] VI/VT (attract) atraer; (lure) tentar; (seduce) seducir
entire [ɪntáɪr] ADJ (unbroken) entero; (complete) completo; **the — crew** toda la tripulación, la tripulación entera
entirety [ɪntáɪrɪDi] N totalidad f
entitle [ɪntáɪdɫ] VT (give a title) titular, intitular; (give a right) dar derecho
entitlement [ɪntáɪdɫmənt] N derecho m
entity [éntɪDi] N (institution) entidad f; (being) ente m, ser m
entomology [entəmáləʤi] N entomología f
entourage [ánturɑʤ] N séquito m, cortejo m
entrails [éntreɫz] N entrañas f pl
entrance [éntrəns] N (act, point of entering) entrada f; (permission to enter) ingreso m; **— examination** examen de ingreso m; [ɪntrǽns] VT embelesar
entrant [éntrənt] N participante mf; **—s in the law profession** abogados recién recibidos m pl
entrap [ɪntrǽp] VT (ensnare) coger con una trampa; (deceive) embaucar
entreaty [ɪntríDi] N súplica f, ruego m
entrench [ɪntréntʃ] VT (establish) afianzar(se); (dig trenches) atrincherar; **a deeply —ed**

habit un hábito muy arraigado
entrepreneur [ɑntrəprənúr] N empresario -ria mf
entropy [éntrəpi] N entropía f
entrust [ɪntrÁst] VT confiar, encomendar
entry [éntri] N (act, point of entry) entrada f; (permission to enter) ingreso m; (record) anotación f; (contestant) participante mf; (dictionary definition) entrada f, artículo m; (computer) entrada f; (in bookkeeping) asiento m; **double —** contabilidad por partida doble f
enumerate [ɪnúməret] VT enumerar
enunciate [ɪnÁnsiet] VI/VT articular; (state a theory) enunciar; (proclaim) proclamar
envelop [ɪnvéləp] VT envolver
envelope [énvəlop] N sobre m
enviable [énviəbəɫ] ADJ envidiable
envious [énviəs] ADJ envidioso
environment [ɪnváɪɚnmənt] N ambiente m, medio ambiente m; (biological) medio ambiente m, ecología f; ADJ ambiental; (biological) medioambiental, ecológico
environmental [ɪnvaɪɚnméntɫ] ADJ ambiental; (biological) medioambiental, ecológico
environmentalist [ɪnvaɪɚnméntɫɪst] N ecologista mf
envisage [ɪnvízɪʤ] VT anticipar, prever
envision [ɪnvíʒən] VT imaginar
envoy [ánvɔɪ] N enviado -da mf
envy [énvi] N envidia f; VI/VT envidiar
enzyme [énzaɪm] N enzima f
ephemeral [ɪféməɚɫ] ADJ efímero
epic [épɪk] N (poem) epopeya f; (genre) épica f; ADJ épico
epicenter [épɪsentɚ] N epicentro m
epidemic [epɪdémɪk] ADJ epidémico; N epidemia f
epidermis [epɪdɚ́mɪs] N epidermis f
epilepsy [épələpsi] N epilepsia f
epilog, epilogue [épəlɔg] N epílogo m
epiphany [ɪpífəni] N epifanía f
episode [épɪsod] N episodio m
episodic [epɪsádɪk] ADJ (sporadic) episódico; (serial) en episodios
epitaph [épɪtæf] N epitafio m
epitome [ɪpíDəmi] N epítome m
epoch [épək] N época f; **—-making** trascendental
equal [íkwəɫ] ADJ igual; **— rights** igualdad de derechos f; **an — contest** una competición pareja; **to be — to a task** capaz de cumplir una tarea; N igual m; **— sign** signo de igual m; VT igualar
equality [ɪkwálɪDi] N igualdad f
equalize [íkwəlaɪz] VT igualar; (electronically)

ecualizar
equate [ɪkwét] VT equiparar
equation [ɪkwéʒən] N ecuación f
equator [ɪkwédɚ] N ecuador m
Equatorial Guinea [ɛkwətɔ́riəɫgíni] N
Guinea Ecuatorial f
equidistant [ikwɪdístənt] ADJ equidistante
equilibrium [ikwəlíbriəm] N equilibrio m
equine [íkwaɪn] ADJ & N equino m
equinox [íkwənɑks] N equinoccio m
equip [ɪkwíp] VT equipar
equipment [ɪkwípmənt] N (supplies) equipo
m; (act of equipping) equipamiento m
equitable [ékwɪdəbəɫ] ADJ equitativo, justo
equity [ékwɪDi] N equidad f, valor libre de
hipoteca de una propiedad m; **equities**
acciones f pl
equivalent [ɪkwívələnt] ADJ & N equivalente
m
equivocal [ɪkwívəkəɫ] ADJ equívoco
era [írə] N era f
eradicate [ɪrǽDɪket] VT (extirpate) erradicar;
(pull up by roots) arrancar
erase [ɪrés] VI/VT borrar(se)
eraser [ɪrésɚ] N (pencil) goma de borrar f;
(blackboard) borrador m
erasure [ɪréʃɚ] N (act of erasing) borrado m;
(smudge) borrón m
erect [ɪrɛ́kt] ADJ (of an organ) erecto;
(posture) erguido; VT erigir
erection [ɪrɛ́kʃən] N erección f
Eritrea [ɛɪtríə] N Eritrea f
Eritrean [ɛɪtríən] ADJ & N eritreo -a mf
ermine [ɚ́mɪn] N armiño m
erode [ɪród] VI/VT erosionar(se)
erogenous [ɪráʤənəs] ADJ erógeno
erosion [ɪróʒən] N erosión f
erotic [ɪráDɪk] ADJ erótico
err [ɛr] VI errar
errand [érənd] N mandado m, recado m; —
boy mandadero m
errant [érənt] ADJ errante
erratic [ɪrǽDɪk] ADJ (unpredictable) irregular,
errático; (eccentric) excéntrico;
(wandering) errante
erroneous [ɪróniəs] ADJ erróneo, errado
error [érɚ] N error m; **to be in** — estar
errado
erudite [érjədaɪt] ADJ erudito
erupt [ɪrʌ́pt] VI (volcano) hacer erupción;
(anger) estallar; (pimples) salir
eruption [ɪrʌ́pʃən] N erupción f
escalate [éskəlet] VI (prices) aumentar;
(violence) intensificarse, aumentar
escalator [éskəleDɚ] N escalera mecánica f
escapade [éskəped] N (adventure) aventura f;
(prank) travesura f

escape [ɪskép] N (of gas) escape m (also
computer term); (from reality) escape m,
evasión f; (of prisoners) fuga f, evasión f;
(means of escaping) escapatoria f; VI
escapar(se), evadirse; VT (elude) eludir; **his
name —s me** no me acuerdo de su
nombre
escort [éskɔrt] N (people who accompany)
escolta mf; (male companion)
acompañante m; (paid female companion)
señorita de compañía f; [ɪskɔ́rt] VT
(protect) escoltar; (accompany) acompañar
escrow [éskro] ADV LOC **in** — en custodia
escudo [ɪskúdo] N escudo m
Eskimo [éskəmo] N esquimal mf
esophagus [ɪsáfəgəs] N esófago m
esoteric [esətérɪk] ADJ esotérico
especial [ɪspéʃəɫ] ADJ especial
espionage [éspiənɑʒ] N espionaje m
espouse [ɪspáuz] VT defender, abrazar
essay [ése] N ensayo m; [ɛsé] VT ensayar
essence [ésəns] N esencia f; **time is of the
** — el tiempo apremia
essential [ɪsénʃəɫ] ADJ esencial
establish [ɪstǽblɪʃ] VT establecer; (a
university) fundar
establishment [ɪstǽblɪʃmənt] N
establecimiento m; (authority)
establishment m
estate [ɪstét] N (piece of land) hacienda f;
(possessions) bienes m pl; (property)
propiedades f pl; (of a dead person)
testamentaría f; — **tax** impuesto de
sucesión m
esteem [ɪstím] VT (regard highly) estimar;
(consider) considerar; N estima f
estimate [éstəmet] VT estimar, evaluꝰr; VI
hacer una estimación; [éstəmɪt] N
(calculation) estimación f; (approximate
charge) presupuesto m
estimation [estəméʃən] N (opinion) juicio m;
(esteem) estima f; (estimate) estimación f;
in my — a mi juicio
Estonia [stóniə] N Estonia f
Estonian [estóniən] ADJ & N estonio -nia mf
estrange [ɪstréndʤ] VT (alienate) enajenar; **to
become —d** separarse
estrogen [éstrəʤən] N estrógeno m
estuary [éstʃueri] N estuario m
etcetera [ɛtsétrə] ADV etcétera
etch [etʃ] VI/VT (engrave) grabar; (outline)
perfilar(se)
etching [étʃɪŋ] N grabado m
eternal [ɪtɚ́nəɫ] ADJ eterno
eternity [ɪtɚ́nɪDi] N eternidad f
ether [íθɚ] N éter m
ethical [éθɪkəɫ] ADJ ético

ethics [éθɪks] N ética *f*
Ethiopia [iθiópiə] N Etiopía *f*
Ethiopian [iθiópiən] ADJ & N etíope *mf*
ethnic [éθnɪk] ADJ étnico; (dances, clothes) tradicional; — **Chinese** de ascendencia china; — **cleansing** limpieza étnica *f*
ethnicity [εθnísɪDi] N etnicidad *f*; (group) grupo étnico *m*
ethnography [εθnágrəfi] N etnografía *f*
ethnology [εθnálədʒi] N etnología *f*
ethyl alcohol [éθəlǽɫkəhɑɫ] N alcohol etílico *m*
etiquette [éDɪkɪt] N etiqueta *f*
etymology [εDəmálədʒi] N etimología *f*
eucalyptus [jukəlíptəs] N eucalipto *m*
eulogy [júlədʒi] N (praise) elogio *m*; (at a funeral) panegírico *m*
eunuch [júnək] N eunuco *m*
euphemism [júfəmɪzəm] N eufemismo *m*
euphoria [jufɔ́riə] N euforia *f*
euro [júro] N euro *m*
Europe [júrəp] N Europa *f*
European [jurəpíən] ADJ & N europeo -a *mf*
euthanasia [juθəné̩ʒə] N eutanasia *f*
evacuate [ɪvǽkjuet] VI/VT (remove due to danger, defecate) evacuar; (empty a building) desalojar
evade [ɪvéd] VT (taxes, responsibilities) evadir, burlar; (questions) eludir
evaluate [ɪvǽljuet] VT (assess) evaluar; (appraise) avaluar, tasar
evangelical [ivændʒélɪkəɫ] ADJ evangélico
evaporate [ɪvǽpəret] VI/VT evaporar(se); VI (vanish) esfumarse
evaporation [ɪvæpəréʃən] N evaporación *f*
evasion [ɪvéʒən] N (escape) evasión *f*; (subterfuge) evasiva *f*
evasive [ɪvésɪv] ADJ evasivo
eve [iv] N (day before) víspera *f*; (evening) atardecer *m*; **on the — of** en vísperas de
even [ívən] ADJ (flat) plano, llano; (smooth) liso; (parallel) paralelo; (without fluctuation) parejo; (equal) igual; (divisible by two) par; (placid) tranquilo; —**handed** imparcial; —**-tempered** apacible; **an — dozen** una docena exacta; **to be — with someone** estar a mano con alguien; **to get — with someone** desquitarse de alguien; ADV (still, yet) aun; (for extreme case) hasta, inclusive, incluso; — **if / though** aun cuando; — **my mother went** hasta mi madre fue; — **so** aun así; **it's — more expensive** es aun más caro; **not —** ni siquiera; VI/VT (make a surface even) nivelar(se); (make accounts even) emparejar
evening [ívnɪŋ] N tarde *f*, velada *f*; (dusk) atardecer *m*; — **gown** vestido de fiesta *m*, vestido de noche *m*; — **party** velada *f*; — **star** lucero de la tarde *m*; **good —!** ¡buenas noches!
event [ɪvént] N (happening) hecho *m*, evento *m*; (of importance) acontecimiento *m*, suceso *m*; **in any —** en todo caso; **in the — of** en caso de
eventful [ɪvéntfəɫ] ADJ agitado, movido
eventual [ɪvéntʃuəɫ] ADJ (later) posterior; (final) final
eventuality [ɪventʃuǽlɪDi] N eventualidad *f*
eventually [ɪvéntʃuəli] ADV a la larga
ever [évɚ] ADV alguna vez; —**green** (planta de hoja) perenne *f*; —**lasting** eterno; —**more** para siempre; — **since** desde entonces; **have you — studied French?** ¿alguna vez has estudiado francés? **how did you — do this?** ¿cómo pudiste hacer esto? **for — and —** por / para siempre jamás; **hardly —** casi nunca; **if —** si alguna vez; **more than —** más que nunca; **the best friend I — had** el mejor amigo que he tenido jamás; **for—more** para / por siempre jamás
every [évri] ADJ (each) cada; — **child is different** cada niño es diferente; (all) todo(s); **we go — Friday** vamos todos los viernes; —**body** todos -das *mf pl*, todo el mundo *m*; — **day** todos los días; —**day** (of clothes) de diario, de todos los días; (of occurrences) cotidiano; — **once in a while** de vez en cuando; —**one** todos -das *mf pl*, todo el mundo *m*; — **other day** cada dos días, un día sí y otro no; —**thing** todo; **you are —thing to me** eres todo para mí; —**where** (location) por / en todas partes; (direction) a todas partes
evict [ɪvíkt] VT desalojar
evidence [évɪDəns] N evidencia *f*; (data in court) prueba *f*; **to be in —** ser evidente; VI/VT evidenciar(se), demostrar(se)
evident [évɪDənt] ADJ evidente
evil [ívəɫ] ADJ (wicked) malo, malvado; (harmful) maligno; —**doer** malhechor -ora *mf*; — **eye** mal de ojo *m*; N (force of nature) mal *m*; (wickedness) maldad *f*; **the lesser of two —s** el mal menor
evoke [ɪvók] VT (call up) evocar; (elicit) provocar
evolution [εvəlúʃən] N evolución *f*
evolve [ɪváɫv] VI/VT desarrollar(se); VI evolucionar
ewe [ju] N oveja *f*
ex [εks] N ex *mf*
exacerbate [ɪgzǽsɚbet] VI/VT exacerbar

exact [ɪgzǽkt] ADJ exacto; VT exigir

exacting [ɪgzǽktɪŋ] ADJ exigente

exaggerate [ɪgzǽdʒəret] VT exagerar

exalt [ɪgzɔ́lt] VT exaltar

exam [ɪgzǽm] N examen *m*

examination [ɪgzæmənéʃən] N examen *m* (also medical)

examine [ɪgzǽmɪn] VT (inspect) examinar; (analyze) analizar

example [ɪgzǽmpəl] N ejemplo *m*

exasperate [ɪgzǽspəret] VT exasperar

excavate [ékskəvet] VT excavar

excavator [ékskəvedə-] N (person) excavador -ora *mf*; (machine) excavadora *f*

exceed [ɪksíd] VT (go beyond) exceder, rebasar; (be superior) superar, sobrepasar

exceedingly [ɪksídɪŋli] ADV sumamente, extremadamente

excel [ɪksél] VI sobresalir, lucirse, descollar

excellence [éksələns] N excelencia *f*

excellent [éksələnt] ADJ excelente

except [ɪksépt] PREP excepto, menos; **all the students — Pam** todos los estudiantes menos Pam; CONJ excepto, salvo; **the cars are identical — that one is older** los coches son idénticos salvo que uno es más viejo; **we would go to the beach, — for the inclement weather** iríamos a la playa si no fuera por el mal tiempo; VT exceptuar

excepting [ɪkséptɪŋ] PREP exceptuando

exception [ɪksépʃən] N excepción *f*; **with the — of** con / a excepción de; **to take — (object)** objetar; (resent) ofenderse

exceptional [ɪksépʃənəl] ADJ (unusual) excepcional; (gifted) superdotado; (handicapped) con necesidades especiales

excerpt [éksɚpt] N fragmento *m*; VT seleccionar fragmentos

excess [éksɛs] N exceso *m*, hartazgo *m*; **— baggage** exceso de equipaje *m*; **— profits tax** impuesto sobre ganancias excesivas *m*; **— weight** exceso de peso *m*; **in — of twenty pounds** más de veinte libras; **to drink to —** beber en exceso

excessive [ɪksésɪv] ADJ excesivo, desmedido

exchange [ɪkstʃéndʒ] VT (replace with something similar) cambiar; (give mutually) intercambiar; (trade political prisoners, books, CDs) canjear; (barter) permutar; **to — greetings** saludarse; N (replacement) cambio *m*; (interchange) intercambio *m*; (barter) permuta *f*; (of prisoners, books, etc.) canje *m*; (for stock trading) bolsa *f*; (for commodity trading) lonja *f*; (telephone) central de teléfonos *f*; **— student** estudiante de intercambio *mf*;

rate of — tipo de cambio *m*

excise [éksaɪz] N impuesto sobre bienes de consumo *m*

excite [ɪksáɪt] VT excitar, alborotar; (enthuse) entusiasmar

excited [ɪksáɪdɪd] ADJ (agitated, aroused) excitado; (enthusiastic) entusiasmado; **to get — (enthused)** entusiasmarse; (aroused) excitarse

excitement [ɪksáɪtmənt] N (arousal) excitación *f*; (enthusiasm) entusiasmo *m*

exciting [ɪksáɪdɪŋ] ADJ (stimulating) excitante; (thrilling) emocionante

exclaim [ɪksklém] VI exclamar

exclamation [ɛkskləméʃən] N exclamación *f*; **— point** signo de admiración *m*

exclude [ɪksklúd] VT excluir

exclusion [ɪksklúʒən] N exclusión *f*

exclusive [ɪksklúsɪv] ADJ exclusivo; **— of** sin incluir

excommunicate [ɛkskəmjúnɪket] VT excomulgar

excrement [ékskrəmənt] N excremento *m*

excrete [ɪkskrít] VI/VT excretar

excruciating [ɪkskrúʃiedɪŋ] ADJ insoportable, atroz

excursion [ɪkskɚ́ʒən] N excursión *f*

excusable [ɪkskjúzəbəl] ADJ excusable, disculpable

excuse [ɪkskjúz] VT (release from a duty, seek exemption) excusar, eximir; (forgive) disculpar, perdonar; **— me!** (forgive me) disculpe; (let me pass) con permiso; [ɪkskjús] N excusa *f*, disculpa *f*; **it's a poor — for a car** no merece llamarse un coche

execute [éksɪkjut] VT ejecutar (also computer term); (by firing squad) fusilar

execution [ɛksɪkjúʃən] N ejecución *f*; **— wall** paredón *m*

executioner [ɛksɪkjúʃənɚ] N verdugo *mf*

executive [ɪgzékjədɪv] ADJ ejecutivo; N (person) ejecutivo -va *mf*; (branch of government) poder ejecutivo *m*

executor [ɪgzékjədə-] N albacea *mf*

exemplary [ɪgzémpləri] ADJ ejemplar

exemplify [ɪgzémpləfaɪ] VT ejemplificar

exempt [ɪgzémpt] VT eximir, dispensar; ADJ exento, libre

exemption [ɪgzémpʃən] N exención *f*, franquicia *f*

exercise [éksɚsaɪz] N ejercicio *m*; **—s** ceremonia *f*; VT ejercer; VI hacer ejercicio; **to be —d about something** estar disgustado por algo

exert [ɪgzɚ́t] VT ejercer; **to — oneself** esforzarse, empeñarse

exertion [ɪgzɚ́ʃən] N (use of powers,

faculties) ejercicio *m*; (vigorous action) esfuerzo *m*, empeño *m*

exhale [ɛkshéɫ] VT exhalar; VI espirar

exhaust [ɪgzɔ́st] VT agotar, desmadejar; (a topic) tratar exhaustivamente; N (from a car) escape *m*

exhausted [ɪgzɔ́stɪd] ADJ rendido, agotado

exhaustion [ɪgzɔ́stʃən] N (act or process of exhausting) agotamiento *m*; (weakness, tiredness) fatiga *f*

exhaustive [ɪgzɔ́stɪv] ADJ exhaustivo

exhibit [ɪgzíbɪt] VI/VT (manifest) exhibir; (put on view) exponer; N exposición *f*

exhibition [ɛksəbíʃən] N (manifestation, show of skills) exhibición *f*; (public display of objects) exposición *f*

exhilarated [ɪgzíləreɪɾɪd] ADJ exultante

exhort [ɪgzɔ́rt] VT exhortar

exile [égzaɪɫ] N exilio *m*, destierro *m*; (person exiled) exiliado -da *mf*, desterrado -da *mf*; VT exiliar

exist [ɪgzíst] VI existir

existence [ɪgzístəns] N existencia *f*

exit [égzɪt] N salida *f*; VI/VT salir (de); (theater) hacer mutis; **he —ed the building** salió del edificio

exodus [éksəɒəs] N éxodo *m*

exonerate [ɪgzánəret] VT exonerar

exorbitant [ɪgzɔ́rbɪɒənt] ADJ exorbitante

exorcise [éksɔrsaɪz] VT exorcisar

exorcism [éksɔrsɪzəm] N exorcismo *m*

exotic [ɪgzáɒɪk] ADJ exótico

expand [ɪkspǽnd] VI/VT expandir(se), ampliar(se); (an equation, an idea) desarrollar(se); (through heat) dilatar(se)

expanse [ɪkspǽns] N extensión *f*

expansion [ɪkspǽnʃən] N expansión *f*; (of an equation, of an idea) desarrollo *m*; (through heat) dilatación *f*

expansive [ɪkspǽnsɪv] ADJ expansivo

expatriate [ɛkspétriet] VI/VT expatriar(se); [ɛkspétriɪt] N expatriado -da *mf*

expect [ɪkspékt] VT esperar; **we — guests** esperamos visita(s); **I — you to be on time** cuento con que vengas puntualmente; **I'm —ed to work fifty hours a week** tengo que trabajar cincuenta horas por semana; **I — you're tired** estarás cansado; **she's —ing** está embarazada / encinta

expectation [ɛkspɛktéʃən] N (anticipation) expectación *f*; (expected thing) expectativa *f*; **he has great —s** tiene grandes expectativas

expectorate [ɪkspéktəret] VI/VT expectorar

expedient [ɪkspíɒiənt] ADJ conveniente, expeditivo

expedite [ékspɪdaɪt] VT (speed up) acelerar; (deal with promptly) despachar

expedition [ɛkspɪdíʃən] N expedición *f*

expeditionary [ɛkspɪdíʃəneɾi] ADJ expedicionario

expel [ɪkspéɫ] VT (discharge) expeler; (throw out) expulsar

expend [ɪkspénd] VT gastar, agotar

expenditure [ɪkspéndɪtʃɚ] N gasto *m*

expense [ɪkspéns] N gasto *m*; **— account** cuenta de gastos *f*; **they had fun at my —** se divirtieron a mi costa

expensive [ɪkspénsɪv] ADJ caro

experience [ɪkspíriəns] N experiencia *f*; VT experimentar; **—d** experimentado

experiment [ɪkspérəmənt] N experimento *m*; VI experimentar

experimental [ɪkspɛrəméntɫ] ADJ experimental

expert [ékspɚt] N experto -ta *mf*; ADJ experto, idóneo, perito; **— system** sistema experto *m*

expertise [ɛkspɚtíz] N pericia *f*

expiration [ɛkspəréʃən] N (of a contract) vencimiento *m*, caducidad *f*; (breathing out) espiración *f*

expire [ɪkspáɪr] VI (die, terminate) expirar; (breathe out) espirar; (lapse) vencer, caducar

explain [ɪksplén] VT explicar; **he tried to — away his absence** trató de justificar su ausencia

explainable [ɪksplénəbəɫ] ADJ explicable

explanation [ɛksplənéʃən] N explicación *f*

explanatory [ɪksplǽnətɔri] ADJ explicativo

expletive [ékspliɒɪv] N palabrota *f*

explicable [ɪksplíkəbəɫ] ADJ explicable

explicit [ɪksplísɪt] ADJ explícito

explode [ɪksplód] VI/VT estallar, hacer explosión, explotar; VT (a theory) hacer añicos; VI (population) dispararse

exploit [éksplɔɪt] N hazaña *f*, proeza *f*; [ɪksplɔ́ɪt] VT explotar

exploitation [ɛksplɔɪtéʃən] N explotación *f*

exploration [ɛkspləréʃən] N exploración *f*

explore [ɪksplɔ́r] VI/VT explorar; (a topic) bucear

explorer [ɪksplɔ́rɚ] N explorador -ra *mf*

explosion [ɪksplóʒən] N explosión *f*, estallido *m*

explosive [ɪksplósɪv] ADJ & N explosivo *m*

exponent [ɪkspónənt] N exponente *m*

export [ɪkspɔ́rt] VI/VT exportar; [ékspɔrt] N exportación *f*

exportation [ɛkspɔrtéʃən] N exportación *f*

expose [ɪkspóz] VT (to lay open to danger, exhibit, subject to light) exponer; (to

make known) revelar; (to unmask)
desenmascarar

exposition [ɛkspəzíʃən] N exposición *f*

exposure [ɪkspóʒɚ] N (to danger, to light, act
of exposing) exposición *f*; (disclosure)
revelación *f*; **to die of** — morir de frío

expound [ɪkspáʊnd] VI/VT exponer, explicar

express [ɪksprés] VT expresar; (send by mail)
enviar por correo expreso; (squeeze out)
exprimir; ADJ (clearly indicated) expreso;
— **train** tren expreso *m*; ADV por expreso;
N expreso *m*

expression [ɪkspréʃən] N expresión *f*

expressive [ɪksprésɪv] ADJ expresivo

expropriate [ɛksprópriet] VT expropiar

expulsion [ɪkspʌ́lʃən] N expulsión *f*

exquisite [ɛkskwízɪt] ADJ exquisito,
primoroso; (pain) penetrante

extant [ɛ́kstənt] ADJ existente

extemporaneous [ɪkstɛmpəréniəs] ADJ
improvisado

extend [ɪksténd] VI/VT extender(se); (a street)
ampliar(se); **he —ed his hand to her** le
tendió la mano

extended [ɪksténdɪd] ADJ (extensive) extenso;
(prolonged) prolongado; (folded out)
extendido

extension [ɪksténʃən] N extensión *f*; (of a
deadline) prórroga *f*; (phone line)
extensión *f*; (addition) anexo *m*,
ampliación *f*; — **cord** extensión *f*

extensive [ɪksténsɪv] ADJ extenso;
(agriculture) extensivo

extent [ɪkstént] N extensión *f*; **to a great** —
en alto grado; **to such an** — **that** a tal
grado que; **to the** — **that you are able**
en la medida en que seas capaz; **up to a
certain** — hasta cierto punto

extenuate [ɪksténjuet] VT atenuar

exterior [ɪkstíriɚ] ADJ exterior; N exterior *m*

exterminate [ɪkstɚmənet] VT exterminar

extermination [ɪkstɚmənéʃən] N exterminio
m, exterminación *f*

external [ɪkstɚnəɫ] ADJ externo; (concerned
with foreign countries) exterior; N exterior *m*

extinct [ɪkstíŋkt] ADJ extinto

extinguish [ɪkstíŋgwɪʃ] VT apagar, extinguir

extol [ɪkstóɫ] VT ensalzar, enaltecer

extort [ɪkstɔ́rt] VT extorsionar

extortion [ɪkstɔ́rʃən] N extorsión *f*

extra [ɛ́kstrə] ADJ de más, adicional; **make
some** — **cakes** haz unos pasteles de más /
adicionales / extras; ADV extra; N extra *m*
(including newspaper, actor); —**marital**
extramarital; —**ordinary** extraordinario;
—**sensory** extrasensorial

extract [ɛ́kstrækt] N (something extracted)

extracto *m*; (passage from a book)
fragmento *m*; [ɪkstrǽkt] VT extraer; (a
secret) sonsacar

extradite [ɛ́kstrədaɪt] VT extraditar

extraneous [ɪkstréniəs] ADJ superfluo

extrapolate [ɪkstrǽpəlet] VI/VT extrapolar

extravagance [ɪkstrǽvəgəns] N (unnecessary
expense) despilfarro *m*, derroche *m*;
(excess) exceso *m*; (oddity) extravagancia *f*

extravagant [ɪkstrǽvəgənt] ADJ (shopper)
gastador, derrochador; (price) exorbitante;
(praise, demand) excesivo

extreme [ɪkstrím] ADJ extremo; N extremo *m*;
to go to —**s** exagerar, llegar a extremos;
to the — sumamente, extremadamente

extremity [ɪkstrémɪDi] N extremidad *f*

extricate [ɛ́kstrɪket] VT sacar; VI **to** —
oneself from conseguir salir de

extrovert [ɛ́kstrəvɚt] N extrovertido -da *mf*

extroverted [ɛ́kstrəvɚDɪd] ADJ extrovertido

exuberant [ɪgzúbəənt] ADJ exuberante

exude [ɪgzúd] VI/VT (liquid) exudar;
(cheerfulness, confidence) emanar

exult [ɪgzʌ́ɫt] VI exultar

eye [aɪ] N ojo *m* (also of hurricane, needle,
tools); (look) mirada *f*; —**ball** globo ocular
m; —**brow** ceja *f*; —**dropper** cuentagotas
m sg; —**glass** (of a telescope, microscope)
ocular *m*; —**glasses** anteojos *m pl*, lentes
m pl; —**lash** pestaña *f*; —**lid** párpado *m*;
—**liner** delineador *m*; —**-opener**
revelación *f*; —**piece** ocular *m*; —**sight**
vista *f*; —**sore** monstruosidad *f*; —
shadow sombra para ojos *f*; — **socket**
órbita *f*; —**tooth** colmillo *m*; —**witness**
testigo ocular *mf*; **my** —**s are bad** tengo
mala vista; **in the twinkling of an** —
en un abrir y cerrar de ojos; **her dress
caught his** — su vestido le llamó la
atención; **to keep an** — **on** cuidar,
vigilar; **to see** — **to** — estar de acuerdo;
in the —**s of the law** ante la ley; **to
give someone the** — hacerle ojito a
alguien; **to have** —**s for someone** estar
prendado de alguien; **to keep one's** —
open tener cuidado; VT mirar

eyeful [áɪfʊɫ] N **we got an** — vimos más
que suficiente

e-zine [ízin] N revista electrónica *f*

Ff

fable [fébəɫ] N fábula *f*

fabric [fǽbrɪk] N tela *f*, tejido *m*; (wool) paño

m; (of society) estructura *f*; — **softener** suavizante *m*

fabricate [fǽbrɪket] VT (goods) fabricar; (a story) inventar

fabulous [fǽbjələs] ADJ fabuloso

façade [fəsád] N fachada *f*

face [fes] N (front part of head, coin, cube, facial expression) cara *f*; (of a building) frente *m*; (of a watch) esfera *f*; (of the Earth) faz *f*; —**cloth** toalla para la cara *f*; —**lift** lifting *m*; —-**to**-— cara a cara; — **value** valor nominal *m*; **in the — of** ante, frente a; **on the — of** aparentemente; **she put on a brave —** se comportó con entereza; **to make —s** hacer muecas; **to lose —** quedar mal; **to save —** quedar bien; **to show one's —** aparecerse; VT (stand opposite to) encarar; (meet defiantly) enfrentar, enfrentarse con, afrontar; (look forward) mirar a / hacia; (to have the front toward) dar a / hacia; (to put on facing) ribetear; **about —!** ¡media vuelta! **left —!** ¡a la izquierda! **to — down** intimidar; **to — the music** dar la cara; **to — with marble** revestir de mármol

faceless [féslɪs] ADJ (anonymous) anónimo; (without a face) sin cara

facet [fǽsɪt] N faceta *f*

facetious [fəsíʃəs] ADJ gracioso

facial [féʃəł] ADJ facial; N limpieza de cutis *f*

facilitate [fəsílɪtet] VT facilitar

facility [fəsílɪDi] N (skill) facilidad *f*; **facilities** (of a building) instalación *f*; (restroom) aseo *m*, servicio *m*

fact [fækt] N hecho *m*; **hard —s** datos concretos *m pl*; **is that a —!** ¡no me digas! **as a matter of —** de hecho; **in —** de hecho; **it's a — of life** así son las cosas

faction [fǽkʃən] N facción *f*

factor [fǽktɚ] N factor *m*; VT descomponer en factores; VI **to — in** tener en cuenta

factory [fǽktəri] N fábrica *f*

factual [fǽktʃuəł] ADJ (of facts) fáctico; (based on facts) objetivo

faculty [fǽkəłti] N (ability) facultad *f*; (in a college) profesorado *m*, cuerpo docente *m*, claustro *m*

fad [fæd] N moda pasajera *f*

fade [fed] VI/VT (cloth) decolorar(se), desteñir(se); (color) deslavar(se); VI (strength) disminuir; (lights) apagarse; (feelings, colors) desvanecerse

fag [fæg] N *offensive* marica *m*, maricón *m*

faggot [fǽgət] N (male homosexual) *offensive* marica *m*, maricón *m*; (bundle) haz *m*

fail [feł] VI (faculties, organs, machinery, structure) fallar; (experiment, plan) fracasar, frustrarse; (health) decaer; (business) quebrar, hacer bancarrota; VI/VT (exam, student) suspender, reprobar; **he —ed to remember their anniversary** no se acordó de su aniversario; **don't — to come** no dejes de venir; **without —** sin falta

failure [féljɚ] N (of a plan, a person) fracaso *m*; (of organs) insuficiencia *f*; (of faculties) deterioro *m*; (of machinery) falla *f*; *Sp* fallo *m*; (of business) quiebra *f*, bancarrota *f*; (in an exam) suspenso *m*; **her — to respond puzzled me** su falta de respuesta me confundió

faint [fent] ADJ (sound) débil; (light) tenue; (image) vago; **to feel —** sentirse mareado; —-**hearted** timorato, cobarde; N desmayo *m*, desfallecimiento *m*; VI desmayarse, desfallecer

faintness [féntnɪs] N (of sound) debilidad *f*; (of light) tenuidad *f*; (of an image) vaguedad *f*

fair [fer] ADJ (just) justo; (by the rules) limpio; (large) considerable; (of weather) bueno; (of sky) despejado; (of wind) propicio; (of complexion) blanco; — **play** juego limpio *m*; — **chance of success** buena probabilidad de éxito *f*; **the — sex** el sexo bello; **that's not —!** ¡no vale! ¡no es justo! ADV **to play —** jugar limpio; N feria *f*; —**ground** real de la feria *m*; —**way** calle *f*, fairway *m*

fairly [férli] ADV (justly) justamente; (moderately) medianamente; — **difficult** bastante difícil

fairness [férnɪs] N (justice) justicia *f*; (whiteness) blancura *f*

fairy [féri] N hada *f*; (male homosexual) *offensive* maricón *m*; — **godmother** hada madrina *f*; —**land** país de las hadas *m*; — **tale** cuento de hadas *m*

faith [feθ] N fe *f*; (fidelity) fidelidad *f*; — **healing** cura por la fe *f*; **in good —** de buena fe; **to have — in someone** tener confianza en alguien; **to keep —** cumplir con la palabra

faithful [féθfəł] ADJ fiel

faithfulness [féθfəłnɪs] N fidelidad *f*

faithless [féθlɪs] ADJ (disloyal) desleal, falso; (lacking in faith, fidelity) infiel

fake [fek] N (object) objeto falso *m*; (person who fakes) farsante *mf*; ADJ falso; — **pearls** perlas de fantasía *f pl*; VT (render false, counterfeit) falsificar; VI/VT (feign) fingir

falcon [fǽɫkən] N halcón *m*

Falkland Islands [fɔ́kləndáɪləndz] N Islas Malvinas *f pl*

fall [fɔɫ] VI (drop) caer(se); (light upon) detenerse; (slope downward) bajar; (be assigned to) tocar a, recaer sobre; **—ing out** desavenencia *f*, pique *m*; **—ing star** estrella fugaz *f*; **to — asleep** dormirse; **to — back** retroceder; **to — back on** recurrir a; **to — behind** atrasarse, retrasarse; **to — down** (drop) caerse; (fail) fallar; **to — in love** enamorarse; **to — off** disminuir; **he —s for blondes** se enamora de las rubias; **to — out with** reñir con; **to — through** quedar en la nada; **you — for it** te dejas engañar; N (drop) caída *f*; (of a terrain) declive *m*; (season) otoño *m*; **— guy** cabeza de turco *mf*; **—s** catarata *f*, salto de agua *m*

fallacious [fəléʃəs] ADJ falaz

fallacy [fǽləsi] N (false notion) falacia *f*; (false argument) sofisma *m*

fallible [fǽləbəɫ] ADJ falible

fallout [fɔ́laʊt] N (particle-settling) precipitación radiactiva *f*; (consequences) repercusiones *f pl*

fallow [fǽlo] ADJ baldío, en barbecho; N barbecho *m*; VT dejar en barbecho

false [fɔɫs] ADJ falso; **to bear — witness** jurar en falso; **— alarm** falsa alarma *f*; **— arrest** detención ilegal *f*; **— pretense** estafa *f*; **— start** salida en falso *f*; **— step** paso en falso *m*; **— teeth** postizo *m*

falsehood [fɔ́ɫshʊd] N falsedad *f*, mentira *f*

falseness [fɔ́ɫsnɪs] N falsedad *f*

falsify [fɔ́ɫsəfaɪ] VT falsificar, falsear

falter [fɔ́ɫtɚ] VI (hesitate) vacilar, entrecortarse; (stutter) titubear

fame [fem] N fama *f*

famed [femd] ADJ afamado

familiar [fəmíljɚ] ADJ (generally known) familiar, conocido; (informal) familiar; (too friendly) confianzudo; (closely personal) íntimo; **to be — with a subject** conocer bien un tema

familiarity [fəmɪljǽrɪɾi] N familiaridad *f*

family [fǽmli] N familia *f*; **— doctor** médico general *m*; **— jewels** *vulg* cojones *m pl*; **— man** hombre de familia *m*; **— name** apellido *m*; **— planning** planificación familiar *f*; **— room** cuarto de estar *m*; **— tree** árbol genealógico *m*; **— values** valores tradicionales *m pl*

famine [fǽmɪn] N (lack of food) hambruna *f*, hambre *f*; (scarcity) escasez *f*

famished [fǽmɪʃt] ADJ hambriento, muerto de hambre; **to be —** morirse de hambre

famous [fémǝs] ADJ famoso

fan [fæn] N (handheld) abanico *m*; (electrical) ventilador *m*; (for cleaning grain) aventadora *f*; (of sports) aficionado -da *mf*; (of a person) admirador -ra *mf*; VT (blow air) abanicar; (enliven) avivar; **to — out** abrirse en abanico; **— belt** correa del ventilador *f*; **— mail** correo de admiradores *m*

fanatic [fənǽdɪk] ADJ & N fanático -ca *mf*

fanaticism [fənǽdɪsɪzəm] N fanatismo *m*

fanciful [fǽnsɪfəɫ] ADJ (whimsical) caprichoso; (imaginary) imaginario; (led by fancy) fantasioso

fancy [fǽnsi] N fantasía *f*; (whim) capricho *m*; **to strike one's —** gustarle a alguien; **to take a — to** aficionarse a; **he took a — to his teacher** se enamoró de su maestra; ADJ (luxurious) de lujo; (elaborate) elaborado; (strange) estrafalario; **— free** despreocupado; **— work** bordado fino *m*; VT imaginar(se); **he fancies himself an artist** se cree artista; **just — the idea!** ¡figúrate!

fanfare [fǽnfɛr] N fanfarria *f*; **with great —** con bombo y platillo

fang [fæŋ] N colmillo *m*

fantasize [fǽntəsaɪz] VI fantasear

fantastic [fæntǽstɪk] ADJ fantástico

fantasy [fǽntəsi] N fantasía *f*

far [fɑr] ADV lejos; **— and away** sin duda; **— and wide** por todas partes; **— away / off** lejos, lejano; **—fetched** (implausible) inverosímil, peregrino; (forced) traído por los cabellos; **—flung** remoto; **—off** distante; **—out** radical, poco convencional; **—-reaching** de gran alcance; **—sighted** (with defective vision) présbita, hipermétrope; (seeing the future) con visión de futuro; **— be it from me to complain** no es mi intención quejarme; **— more money** mucho más dinero; **— off we could see land** a lo lejos divisábamos tierra; **as — as I know** que yo sepa; **as — as I'm concerned** en lo que a mí respecta; **by —** con mucho; **how — do I need to walk?** ¿cuánto tengo que caminar? **how — is the church?** ¿a cuánto queda la iglesia? **so — hasta ahora; we talked — into the night** hablamos hasta entrada la noche; **we traveled as — as Chicago** viajamos hasta Chicago; ADJ lejano; **the — corner** la esquina de más allá; **it is a — cry from what you said** dista mucho de lo que dijiste

farce [fɑrs] N farsa *f*

fare [fer] N (ticket) billete *m*; (price of transport) tarifa *f*; (food) comida *f*; VI **I —d well in the course** me fue bien en el curso; **—well** despedida *f*; **to bid —well to** despedirse de; **—well!** ¡adiós!

farm [fɑrm] N (large) hacienda *f*; (small) granja *f*; **—hand** peón *m*; **—house** alquería *f*, caserío *m*; **— produce** productos agrícolas *m pl*; **—yard** (enclosed) corral *m*; (open) patio *m*; VI/VT cultivar; **to — out** (lease) dar en arriendo; (distribute) repartir; (subcontract) subcontratar; (exhaust) agotar

farmer [fɑrmɚ] N agricultor -ra *mf*; (small) granjero -ra *mf*; (large) hacendado -da *mf*

farming [fɑrmɪŋ] N agricultura *f*; ADJ agrícola *mf*

fart [fɑrt] N *vulg* pedo *m*; **old — fam, pej** viejo pesado *m*; VI *vulg* tirarse pedos; **to — around** *vulg* rascarse el culo

farther [fɑrðɚ] ADV más lejos; **it's an even — distance** es una distancia mayor todavía; **the concept was extended —** el concepto se extendió más; **— on** más adelante; ADJ más lejano

farthest [fɑrðɪst] ADJ el más lejano; ADV lo más lejos

fascinate [fǽsənet] VI/VT fascinar, alucinar

fascination [fæsənéʃən] N fascinación *f*

fascism [fǽʃɪzəm] N fascismo *m*

fascist [fǽʃɪst] N fascista *mf*

fashion [fǽʃən] N (style) moda *f*; (way) manera *f*, modo *m*; **— plate** figurín *m*; **after a —** más o menos; **to be in —** estar de moda; VT hacer; (metal) forjar; (character) formar; (putty, etc.) moldear

fashionable [fǽʃənəbəɫ] ADJ de moda

fast [fæst] ADJ (quick) rápido, veloz; (ahead, of a watch) adelantado; (firm, permanent) firme; (closed) atrancado; (loyal) fiel; (dissolute) disipado; **— food** comida rápida *f*; **to —-forward** avanzar; **life in the — lane** vida loca *f*; **— money** dinero mal habido *m*; **— woman** mujer ligera de cascos *f*; ADV (quickly) rápido; (firmly) firmemente; **— asleep** profundamente dormido; N ayuno *m*; VI ayunar

fasten [fǽsən] VT (with buckles, buttons, hooks) abrochar(se), prender; (with ribbon, thread) atar; (door) atrancar

fastener [fǽsənɚ] N cierre *m*

fastidious [fæstídiəs] ADJ (hard to please) maniático; (painstaking) minucioso

fat [fæt] ADJ gordo; **— cat** pez gordo *m*; **— cell** célula adiposa *f*; **— chance** ¡ni soñar! **—head** idiota *mf*; **— job** trabajo lucrativo *m*; **— profits** pingües ganancias *f pl*; **to**

get — engordar; N (oily substance) grasa *f*; (animal tissue) gordura *f*, sebo *m*; **the — of the land** la abundancia de la tierra

fatal [fédɫ] ADJ fatal

fatality [fətǽlɪɾi] N víctima fatal *f*

fate [fet] N (lot) destino *m*, fatalidad *f*, hado *m*; (outcome) suerte *f*; VT destinar

father [fáðɚ] N padre *m*; **— figure** figura paterna *f*; **—-in-law** suegro *m*; **—land** patria *f*

fatherhood [fáðɚhʊd] N paternidad *f*

fatherly [fáðɚli] ADV paternal

fathom [fǽðəm] N braza *f*; VT (measure) sondear; (understand) comprender

fatigue [fətíg] N fatiga *f*; **—s** ropa de faena *f*; VI/VT fatigar(se), rendir(se)

fatness [fǽtnɪs] N gordura *f*

fatso [fǽtso] N *pej* gordinflón *m*, tonel *m*

fatten [fǽtn̩] VT engordar, cebar

fatty [fǽɾi] ADJ adiposo; N (insult for fat people) *pej* gordito -ta *mf*

faucet [fɔ́sɪt] N grifo *m*, llave *f*

fault [fɔɫt] N (defect, misdeed) falta *f*; (responsibility) culpa *f*; (geological) falla *f*; **—finder** criticón -ona *mf*; **to a —** demasiado cuidadoso; **to be at —** ser culpable; **to find — with** criticar a

faultless [fɔ́ɫtlɪs] ADJ perfecto

faulty [fɔ́ɫti] ADJ defectuoso; (grammar) vicioso

faux pas [fopá] N gaffe *f*, metedura de pata *f*

favor [févɚ] N (kind act, goodwill) favor *m*, gracia *f*; (popularity) popularidad *f*; (party gift) sorpresa *f*; VT (give help, show preference) favorecer; (foster) propiciar; (approve of) estar a favor de; **they are —ed to win** son los favoritos; **she —s her mother** se parece a su madre

favorite [févɚɪt] ADJ & N preferido -da *mf*, favorito -ta *mf*, predilecto -ta *mf*

favoritism [févɚɪtɪzəm] N favoritismo *m*

fawn [fɔn] N cervatillo *m*; VI **to — (over)** adular

fax [fæks] N fax *m*, facsímil *m*; VT faxear

FBI (Federal Bureau of Investigation) [ɛfbiáɪ] N FBI *m*

fear [fir] N miedo *m*, temor *m*; **— of God** temor de Dios *m*; VI/VT (be afraid of) temer, tenerle miedo a; (suspect) temerse; **to — for** temer por

fearful [fírfəɫ] ADJ (causing fear) terrible, espantoso; (showing fear) temeroso, miedoso, medroso

fearless [fírlɪs] ADJ intrépido

fearlessness [fírlɪsnɪs] N intrepidez *f*

feasible [fízəbəɫ] ADJ factible

feast [fist] N (party, religious celebration)

fiesta *f*; (abundant meal) festín *m*,
banquete *m*; VI **to — on** darse un festín
de; **to — one's eyes on** deleitarse la vista
con

feat [fit] N (heroic act) hazaña *f*; (trick) logro
m

feather [féðɚ] N pluma *f*; **a — in one's cap**
un triunfo personal; **—weight** peso
pluma *m*; **birds of a — flock together**
Dios los cría y ellos se juntan; VI/VT (grow
feathers, cover with feathers) emplumar;
(change blade angle) poner horizontal

feature [fítʃɚ] N (characteristic) aspecto *m*,
característica *f*; (newspaper article)
reportaje *m*; (facial) facción *f*, fisonomía *f*,
rasgo *m*; **— article** artículo principal *m*;
— film largometraje *m*; VT (give
prominence to) destacar; (depict) mostrar;
this film —s John Smith esta película
cuenta con la actuación de John Smith; **—
that!** ¡imagínate! VI figurar

February [fébjuɛri] N febrero *m*

feces [físiz] N PL heces *f pl*

federal [féDɚəl] ADJ federal

federation [feDəréʃən] N federación *f*

fee [fi] N (professional) honorarios *m pl*;
(artist) cachet *m*; (admission) derecho de
admisión *m*; **—s** (university) matrícula *f*

feeble [fíbəl] ADJ (person) débil, endeble;
(sound, light) tenue; **—-minded**
(retarded) *pej* retrasado; (stupid) tonto

feed [fid] VI/VT (supply with food, materials)
alimentar(se); (prompt lines) apuntar;
(broadcast) transmitir; **he —s sugar
cubes to his horse** le da terrones de
azúcar a su caballo; **I fed him a lie** le
dije una mentira; **to be fed up** estar
harto, estar hasta la coronilla; VI **to —
into** desembocar en; **—back**
retroalimentación *f*; (response) respuesta *f*,
reacción *f*; **—ing frenzy** (of the press)
escándalo periodístico *m*; (of sharks, etc.)
carnicería *f*; N (fodder) pienso *m*, cebo *m*;
(transmission) transmisión *f*

feel [fil] VI/VT (perceive, experience)
sentir(se); (examine with the hands)
palpar, manosear; (suffer) sufrir; (have an
opinion) creer; VI (grope, check out)
tantear; (seem) parecer; **to — one's way**
tantear el camino, andar a tientas; **I —
for you** te compadezco; **to — up / off**
toquetear, manosear; **it —s soft** está
suave al tacto; **I — like a coffee** tengo
ganas de tomar un café; **to — up to
something** sentirse capaz de algo; N
(feeling) sensación *f*; (sense) tacto *m*;
(ability) don *m*; (groping) manoseo *m*,

toqueteo *m*

feeler [fílɚ] N (of insects) antena *f*; (of snails)
cuerno *m*; (person who feels) persona
emotiva *f*; **to put out —s** tantear el
terreno

feeling [fílɪŋ] N (sense of touch) tacto *m*;
(instance of physical perception) sensación
f; (emotion) sentimiento *m*; (opinion)
opinión *f*; (compassion) compasión *f*; **a —
of sadness** un sentimiento de tristeza;
with — con sentimiento; **to hurt
someone's —s** herirle los sentimientos a
alguien; ADJ sensible

feign [fen] VI/VT fingir, simular, aparentar

feisty [fáisti] ADJ (aggressive) pugnaz,
belicoso; (energetic) vivaz

feline [fílain] ADJ felino

fell [fɛł] VT (an animal) derribar; (a tree) talar;
N (pelt) piel de animal *f*; **in one —
swoop** de un golpe

fellow [félo] N (member) miembro *m*;
(scholar) becario -ria *mf*; (man or boy) tipo
m; **— citizen** conciudadano -na *mf*; **—
man** prójimo *m*; **— student** compañero
-ra de clase *mf*

fellowship [féloʃɪp] N (friendly relations)
amistad *f*; (community of interest)
confraternidad *f*; (scholarship) beca *f*

felony [féləni] N delito grave *m*

felt [fɛłt] N fieltro *m*; ADJ de fieltro

female [fímeł] N (animal) hembra *f*; (person)
mujer *f*; ADJ (animal, fastener) hembra;
(person) femenino

feminine [fémənin] ADJ femenino

femininity [feməníniti] N feminidad *f*

feminism [fémənizəm] N feminismo *m*

femur [fímɚ] N fémur *m*

fence [fɛns] N (barrier) cerca *f*, cerco *m*, valla
f; (person who deals in stolen goods)
vendedor -ra de artículos robados *mf*;
(store for stolen goods) tienda de artículos
robados *f*; **to be sitting on the —** estar
indeciso; VT (enclose) cercar, vallar; **to —
in** cercar; **to — off** dividir con una cerca;
VI (sport) practicar esgrima

fencing [fénsɪŋ] N (barrier) cerca *f*; (sport)
esgrima *f*

fender [féndɚ] N guardabarro(s) *m*,
guardafango *m*; **— bender** choquecito *m*

ferment [fɝment] N fermento *m*; [fɚmént]
VI/VT fermentar(se)

fermentation [fɝmentéʃən] N fermentación
f

fern [fɝn] N helecho *m*

ferocious [fərófəs] ADJ feroz, fiero

ferocity [fərásiDi] N ferocidad *f*, fiereza *f*

ferret [férit] N hurón *m*; VI **to — out**

huronear

Ferris wheel [férıshwił] N rueda gigante *f*

ferry [féri] N ferry *m*; **— boat** ferry *m*; VT transportar de una orilla a otra; VI viajar en ferry

fertile [fɜ́·dl̩] ADJ fértil, fecundo

fertility [fə·tílıDi] N fertilidad *f*

fertilize [fɜ́·dl̩aɪz] VT fertilizar; (female, egg) fecundar; (land) abonar

fertilizer [fɜ́·dl̩aɪzə·] N fertilizante *m*, abono *m*

fervent [fɜ́·vənt] ADJ ferviente

fervor [fɜ́·və·] N fervor *m*

fester [féstə·] VI (form pus) supurar; (rankle) enconarse

festival [féstəvəł] N festival *m*

festive [féstɪv] ADJ festivo

festivity [festívıDi] N festividad *f*

fetal [fídl̩] ADJ fetal; **— position** posición fetal *f*

fetch [fetʃ] VT *Sp* ir a por; *Am* ir a buscar; **the ring —ed a fancy price** nos dieron una buena suma por el anillo; VI/VT (dog) buscar

fetish [féDıʃ] N fetiche *m*

fetter [féDə·] N grillete *m*; VT engrillar

fetus [fíDəs] N feto *m*

feud [fjud] N enemistad hereditaria *f*; VI pelear

feudal [fjúdl̩] ADJ feudal

fever [fívə·] N fiebre *f*, calentura *f*; **— pitch** punto álgido *m*

feverish [fívə·ıʃ] ADJ (related to fever) febril; (having a fever) afiebrado, destemplado

few [fju] ADJ & PRON pocos; **a —** unos pocos, algunos; **the —** una minoría

fiancé [fiansé] N novio *m*, prometido *m*; **—e** novia *f*, prometida *f*

fiasco [fiǽsko] N fiasco *m*

fib [fıb] N mentirilla *f*; VI decir mentirillas

fiber [fáɪbə·] N (textile) fibra *f*; (animal, vegetable) hebra *f*; **—-optic** de fibra óptica; **—glass** fibra de vidrio *f*

fibrous [fáıbrəs] ADJ fibroso

fickle [fíkəł] ADJ veleidoso, mudable

fiction [fíkʃən] N ficción *f*

fictional [fíkʃənəł] ADJ novelesco

fictitious [fıktíʃəs] ADJ ficticio

fiddle [fídl̩] N violín *m*; VI (play the violin) tocar el violín; **to — around** perder el tiempo; **to — with** juguetear con; **stop fiddling with the computer** deja de juguetear con la computadora

fidelity [fıdélıDi] N fidelidad *f*; **high —** alta fidelidad *f*

fidget [fídʒıt] VI estar inquieto; **stop —ing!** ¡deja de moverte!

fiduciary [fıdúʃiɛri] ADJ & N fiduciario -ria *mf*

field [fiłd] N (land) campo *m* (also in computers, heraldry, optics); (in sports) campo *m*; *Am* cancha *f*; (of oil) yacimiento *m*; (group of competitors) participantes *mf pl*; (of knowledge) campo *m*, terreno *m*; **— artillery** artillería de campaña *f*; **— day** (day for outdoor activity) día de campo *m*; (for military maneuvers) día de maniobras *m*; (unrestrained enjoyment) festín *m*; **— glasses** binoculares *m pl*; **— mouse** ratón de campo *m*; **— trip** (in school) paseo escolar *m*; (in science) viaje de estudio *m*; **—work** trabajo de campo *m*; VT (catch) atrapar; (answer) contestar

fiend [find] N (devil) demonio *m*, diablo *m*; (fanatic) fanático -ca *mf*

fierce [firs] ADJ (animals) feroz, fiero; (illness) espantoso; (storms, etc.) furioso, espantoso; (competition, debate) intenso, encarnizado; (a look) torvo

fierceness [fírsnıs] N ferocidad *f*, bravura *f*

fiery [fáıəri] ADJ (passionate) fogoso; (hot, causing burning sensation) ardiente

fife [faɪf] N pífano *m*

fifteen [fıftín] NUM quince

fifth [fıfθ] ADJ & N quinto *m*; (measure of liquor) tres cuartos de un litro *m pl*

fifty [fífti] NUM cincuenta; **to go —— on something** ir a medias; **a —— chance** un cincuenta por ciento de probabilidades

fig [fıg] N higo *m*; **— leaf** hoja de higuera *f*; **— tree** higuera *f*; **it's not worth a —** no vale ni un pepino / pito

fight [faɪt] N (combat) lucha *f*, pelea *f*; **the — against AIDS** la lucha contra el SIDA; (argument) pelea *f*, riña *f*; VI/VT (combat) luchar (con), pelear (con); VI (argue) pelear, reñir; **to — a duel** batirse a duelo; **to — back** (to hold back) contener; (resist) resistir; **to — it out** arreglarlo a los golpes; **to — off** rechazar; **to — one's way through** abrirse camino a la fuerza

fighter [fáıDə·] N (boxer) boxeador -ra *mf*; (someone who fights) luchador -ra *mf*; (dog, cock) animal de pelea / riña *m*; **— airplane** avión caza *m*

fighting [fáıDıŋ] N (fight) lucha *f*; ADJ combativo; **— chance** posibilidad remota *f*; **— words** palabras incendiarias *f pl*

figurative [fígjə·əDıv] ADJ (art) figurativo; (language) figurado

figure [fígjə·] N (number, amount) cifra *f*; (form, bodily shape, representation, dance move, syllogism) figura *f*; (character) personaje *m*; **—head** figurón de proa *m*;

— **of speech** figura retórica *f*; —**s** (written symbols) números *m pl*; — **skating** patinaje artístico *m*; **to be good at** —**s** ser bueno con los números; **to cut a poor** — dar una mala impresión; VI (appear) figurar; VI/VT (think) imaginar(se), figurar(se); **to** — **in** tener en cuenta; **to** — **on** contar con; **to** — **out** (solve) resolver; (calculate) calcular; **it** —**s!** no me extraña, era de esperar; VT calcular

Fijian [fíʤiən] N fijiano -na *mf*

Fiji Islands [fíʤiáiləndz] N Islas Fiji *f pl*

filament [fíləmənt] N filamento *m*

file [faɪɫ] N (documents) archivo *m*; (for computers) archivo *m*, fichero *m*; (official report) expediente *m*, legajo *m*; (line) fila *f*; (tool) lima *f*; —**name** nombre de archivo *m*; — **server** servidor *m*; **filing cabinet** fichero *m*, archivador *m*; VT (papers) archivar; (news story) entregar; (tax return, claim, etc.) presentar; **to** — **a suit** entablar una demanda, querellarse; VI (for a job) presentarse; (walk in a line) desfilar; VI/VT (smooth) limar

filial [fíliəɫ] ADJ filial

filibuster [fíləbʌstɚ] VI/VT practicar obstrucción parlamentaria; N filibusterismo *m*, obstrucción *f*

filigree [fíligri] N filigrana *f*

fill [fɪɫ] VI/VT (glass, container) llenar(se); (a hole, a pastry, land) rellenar; **the smell** —**ed the room** la habitación se llenó del olor; **the airline** —**ed the position** la compañía aérea llenó el cargo; **the new employee** —**ed the vacancy** el nuevo empleado ocupó el cargo vacante; VT (a tooth) empastar; (prescription, order) despachar; (a need) satisfacer; VI (sails) hinchar; **to** — **out** llenar; **to** — **in** (inform) informar; (fill out) llenar; (replace) sustituir; **to** — **up** llenarse hasta el tope

fillet [fɪlé] N filete *m*; VT filetear; [fɪlɪt] N cinta *f*; (on a book) filete *m*

filling [fílɪŋ] N (act) rellenado *m*; (filler) relleno *m*; (of a tooth) empaste *m*; — **station** estación de servicio *f*, gasolinera *f*

filly [fíli] N potranca *f*

film [fɪlm] N película *f* (also thin coating); (material) película *f*, cinta *f*; — **industry** industria cinematográfica *f*; VI/VT filmar, cinematografiar

filter [fíltɚ] N filtro *m*; VI/VT filtrar(se)

filth [fɪlθ] N (dirt, despicable person) mugre *f*, suciedad *f*; (moral impurity) porquería *f*; (vulgar material) obscenidades *f pl*

filthiness [fílθinɪs] N suciedad *f*

filthy [fílθi] ADJ (dirty) cochino, mugriento; (obscene, vile) puerco, cochino; *Sp* guarro; — **rich** riquísimo

filtration [fɪltréʃən] N filtración *f*

fin [fɪn] N aleta *f*

final [fáɪnəɫ] ADJ (result, conclusion) final; (last) último; (conclusive) definitivo; N (in sports) final *f*; (exam) examen final *m*

finalist [fáɪnəlɪst] N finalista *mf*

finalize [fáɪnəlaɪz] VT completar, ultimar

finance [fáɪnæns] N finanza *f*; —**s** finanzas *f pl*; VI/VT (to fund) financiar; (to purchase on credit) comprar financiado

financial [fɪnǽnʃəɫ] ADJ financiero

financier [fɪnænsír] N financiero -ra *mf*

financing [fáɪnænsɪŋ] N financiamiento *m*; *Am* financiación *f*

find [faɪnd] VT hallar, encontrar; (discover) descubrir; (determine innocence or guilt) declarar; VI (determine officially) fallar; **to** — **fault with** criticar a, censurar a; **to** — **out** (discover) descubrir; (verify) averiguar; N hallazgo *m*

finding [fáɪndɪŋ] N fallo *m*; —**s** resultados *m pl*

fine [faɪn] ADJ (wine, sand, hair, precious metal) fino; (thread) delgado; (cloth) delicado; (artist, athlete) consumado; (manners) refinado; (good-looking) atractivo, guapo; (weather) bueno; (distinction) sutil; — **arts** bellas artes *f pl*; — **print** letra pequeña *f*, letra chica *f*; **to** —**-tune** (a receiver) sintonizar; (an engine) ajustar; (a plan) afinar; **I'm** — estoy bien; **to feel** — sentirse muy bien de salud; **to have a** — **time** pasarlo bien; N multa *f*; VT multar

finery [fáɪnəri] N galas *f pl*

finesse [fɪnés] N (subtlety) sutileza *f*; (tact) diplomacia *f*; VI usar artimañas; VT conseguir por artimañas

finger [fíŋgɚ] N dedo *m*; —**food** canapé *m*, aperitivo *m*; —**nail** uña *f*; —**print** huella dactilar / digital *f*; —**tip** punta del dedo *f*; **at one's** —**tips** al alcance de la mano; **little** — dedo meñique *m*; **middle** — dedo del corazón *m*; VI/VT toquetear, manosear; VT (guitar) tañer; (squeal on) delatar; **to give someone the** — hacerle un gesto obsceno a alguien; **I'll keep my** —**s crossed** cruzo los dedos; **to wrap someone around one's** — meterse a alguien en el bolsillo; **I can't put my** — **on it** no se me ocurre una solución

finicky [fíniki] ADJ melindroso, dengoso

finish [fíniʃ] VI/VT (end) terminar(se), finalizar(se); VT (polish) pulir; (varnish) barnizar; (kill) liquidar; — **line** meta *f*; **to — off** acabar con, rematar; **to — up** terminar; N (ending) final *m*; (decisive end) fin *m*; (polish, treatment) acabado *m*; (varnish) barniz *m*; (coat of paint) última mano *f*; **with a rough —** sin pulir

finished [fínɪʃt] ADJ (doomed) acabado; (polished) pulido

finite [fáɪnaɪt] ADJ finito

Finland [fínlənd] N Finlandia *f*

Finn [fɪn] N finlandés -esa *mf*, finés -esa *mf*

Finnish [fínɪʃ] ADJ finlandés, finés

fir [fɜ˞] N abeto *m*

fire [faɪr] N (flame) fuego *m*; (conflagration) incendio *m*; (passion) ardor *m*; (for cigarettes, hearths) lumbre *f*; **— alarm** alarma contra incendios *f*; **—cracker** triquitraque *m*; **— drill** simulacro de incendio *m*; **— department** cuerpo de bomberos *m*; **— engine** coche de bomberos *m*, autobomba *f*; **— escape** escalera de incendios *f*; **— extinguisher** extinguidor (de incendios) *m*, extintor *m*; **—fly** luciérnaga *f*; **— hydrant** boca de incendio *f*; **— insurance** seguro contra incendios *m*; **—man** (who extinguishes) bombero *m*; (stoker) fogonero *m*; **—place** hogar *m*, chimenea *f*; **—proof** ininflamable, a prueba de incendio; **to —proof** hacer incombustible, ignifugar; **—side** hogar *m*; **— station** estación de bomberos *f*; **— trap** edificio sin medios de escape en caso de incendio *m*; **—wood** leña *f*; **—works** fuegos artificiales *m pl*; **when he finds out, there will be —works** cuando se entere, se va a armar la gorda; **to be on —** estar quemándose; **to catch —** incendiarse, prenderse fuego; **to set — to** prender fuego a, incendiar; **under —** bajo fuego; **to play with —** jugar con fuego; **firing pin** percutor *m*; **firing squad** pelotón de fusilamiento *m*; VT (pottery) cocer; (an employee) despedir; (a projectile) lanzar; VI/VT (a gun) disparar; VI **to — up** entusiasmar; **to — off** (gun) disparar; (letter) despachar

firm [fɜ˞m] ADJ (solid, unwavering) firme; (fixed) fijo; (not fluctuating, as prices) estable; VI/VT **to — up** (finalize) concretar; (harden) endurecer; N firma *f*

firmness [fɜ˞mnɪs] N firmeza *f*

first [fɜ˞st] ADJ primero; **— aid** primeros auxilios *m pl*; **— base** primera base *f*; **to get to — base** comenzar con éxito; **—born** primogénito -ta *mf*; **— chapter** capítulo primero *m*, primer capítulo *m*; **— class** primera clase *f*; **—-class** de primera clase; **— cousin** primo hermano; **—-degree** (burn) de primer grado; (murder) en primer grado; **— floor** (ground floor) planta baja *f*; **for the — time** por primera vez; **—-hand** de primera mano; **— lady** primera dama *f*; **— name** nombre de pila *m*; **— person** primera persona *f*; **—-rate** de primera clase; ADV (before anything else) primero; **I'd die —** antes la muerte; **at — al** principio; **— off** al principio; N (first in series) primero -ra *mf*; (low gear) primera *f*

fiscal [fískəl] ADJ fiscal; **— period** año fiscal *m*

fish [fɪʃ] N (in water) pez *m*; (out of water) pescado *m*; **—hook** anzuelo *m*; **— market** pescadería *f*; **— story** patraña *f*; **like a — out of water** como sapo de otro pozo; **neither — nor fowl** ni chicha ni limonada; **I have other — to fry** tengo otras cosas mejores que hacer; VI/VT pescar; **to — out** sacar, rebuscar; **to — for compliments** buscar cumplidos; **to —tail** colear

fisherman [fíʃə˞mən] N pescador *m*

fishery [fíʃəri] N (for breeding) piscifactoría *f*; (for fishing) pesquería *f*; (industry) industria pesquera *f*

fishing [fíʃɪŋ] N pesca *f*; **— pole / rod** caña de pescar *f*; **— tackle** aparejos de pescar *m pl*; **to go —** ir de pesca

fishy [fíʃi] ADJ (of smell, taste) a pescado; (suspicious) sospechoso

fissure [fíʃə˞] N fisura *f*

fist [fɪst] N puño *m*; **—fight** pelea a puñetazos *f*

fit [fɪt] ADJ (suited) apto; (healthy) en buen estado físico; **are you — for driving?** ¿estás en condiciones de manejar? **he was — to be tied** estaba que trincha; **he didn't see — to greet her** no se le antojó saludarla; N (process of fitting) prueba *f*; (mechanical union) encaje *m*; (attack of a disease) ataque *m*; (sudden outburst) rapto *m*; (of anger, coughing) acceso *m*; **to throw a —** tener una pataleta; **by —s and starts** a trompicones; **that suit is a good —** ese traje le queda bien; VT (be suitable for) adecuarse a; (be in agreement with) cuadrar con, ajustarse a; (measure for clothes) tomarle las medidas a; (make suitable) capacitar, preparar; **to — in with** acomodarse a; **I tried to — you in** traté de incluirte; VI (conform to contours of a person) quedarle bien a alguien; (conform to the contours of a mechanism) encajar

fitness [fítnɪs] N (suitability) aptitud *f*; (health) buen estado físico *m*

fitting [fíɾɪŋ] ADJ apropiado; N ajuste *m*; (trying on) prueba *f*

five [faɪv] NUM cinco

fix [fɪks] VT (repair, arrange) arreglar, aviar; **he —ed his eyes on me** me miró fijamente; (place permanently, determine) fijar; (prepare food) preparar; **to — up** arreglar, aviar; **to get an animal —ed** castrar a un animal; **I was —ing to call** estaba a punto de llamar; **I'll — you!** ¡ya te arreglo! N (predicament) apuro *m*, aprieto *m*; (temporary repair) arreglo provisorio *m*; (narcotic injection) chute *m*; **to get a — on** localizar

fixed [fɪkst] ADJ (stationary) fijo; (arranged in advance) arreglado

fixture [fíkstʃɚ] N (thing) artefacto *m*; **she's a permanent — in this office** está siempre en la oficina

fizzle [fízəɫ] VI (fail) fracasar; **to — (out)** (make a noise) apagarse chisporroteando

flabby [flǽbi] ADJ flácido

flag [flæg] N bandera *f*; **—pole** mástil *m*; **—staff** mástil *m*; **—stone** losa *f*, baldosa *f*; VT (adorn with flags) embanderar; (mark) marcar con banderas; **to — (down)** hacer parar; VI (diminish) menguar

flagrant [flégrənt] ADV flagrante

flair [flɛr] N (aptitude) aptitud *f*, facilidad *f*; (style) estilo *m*

flak [flæk] N (anti-artillery fire) fuego antiaéreo *m*; (criticism) crítica *f*

flake [flek] N (snow) copo *m*; (small thin piece) escama *f*; (eccentric person) chiflado -da *mf*; VI descascararse

flamboyant [flæmbɔ́iənt] ADJ (clothes) llamativo; (behavior) extravagante

flame [flem] N llama *f*; **— thrower** lanzallamas *m sg*; **old —** viejo amor *m*; VI llamear, flamear, encenderse

flaming [flémɪŋ] ADJ (emitting flames) llameante; (like a flame) flamígero; (ardent) ardiente; **— red** rojo encendido

flammable [flǽməbəɫ] ADJ inflamable

flank [flæŋk] N (of a bastion or army) flanco *m*; (of an animal) ijar *m*; VT flanquear

flannel [flǽnəɫ] N franela *f*, lanilla *f*

flap [flæp] VI (wings) aletear; (flag) flamear; VT (wings) batir; (arms) sacudir; N (of a jacket, pocket) cartera *f*; (of a saddle, table) hoja *f*; (of an airplane) alerón *m*; (action of flapping) aleteo *m*

flare [flɛr] VI (burn unsteadily) llamear; (skirt) ensancharse; **to — up** (fire) avivarse; (activity) recrudecer; **the illness —d up** recrudeció la enfermedad; VT (a skirt) levantar; (a flame) avivar; (a pipe) abocinar; (signal by flare) señalar con bengala; N (flaring light, burst of flame) llamarada *f*; (signal light) bengala *f*; (sudden emotional outburst) arranque *m*; (outward curvature) vuelo *m*; **—up** recrudecimiento *m*

flash [flæʃ] N (of light) destello *m*, ráfaga *f*; (of explosion) fogonazo *m*; (news, camera, vision) flash *m*; **— of hope** rayo de esperanza *m*; **— of lightning** relampagueo *m*, rayo *m*; **in a —** en un instante; VI/VT (shine) destellar (sobre); (expose) exhibir(se); VI (gleam) relucir, fulgurar, relampaguear; (appear) aparecer; VT (display) ostentar; **—back** flashback *m*, escena retrospectiva *f*; **—bulb** flash *m*; **—flood** riada *f*; **—light** linterna *f*; **to — by** pasar como un relámpago

flashing [flǽʃɪŋ] ADJ destellante

flashy [flǽʃi] ADJ (colorful) llamativo; (ostentatious) ostentoso; (tasteless) *Am* charro

flask [flæsk] N (glass container) frasco *m*; (in a laboratory) matraz *m*, redoma *f*; (for alcoholic beverages) petaca *f*

flat [flæt] ADJ (of surfaces) plano; (of land) llano; (smooth) liso; (horizontal) horizontal, acostado; (flattened) arrasado, aplastado; (of shoes, nose) chato; (deflated) desinflado, pinchado; (dull of color) apagado; (without effervescence) sin gas; (lifeless) soso; (without gloss) mate; (absolute) terminante; (of a photo) sin contraste; (of a painting) sin volumen; (too low in pitch) demasiado grave; (of a musical note) bemol; **—footed** con pie plano; **— rate** tarifa fija *f*; **trading was —** hubo poco movimiento económico; **to be — broke** estar completamente pelado; **to fall —** (of a body) caer de plano / redondo; (of a joke) caer mal; (of a plan) fracasar; N (shoe) zapato sin tacón *m*; (flat tire) desinflado *m*, pinchadura *f*, pinchazo *m*; (wooden box) caja para plantas *f*; (musical note) bemol *m*; **—iron** plancha *f*; ADV **—out** (directly) absolutamente; (at full speed) a toda velocidad; **in two minutes —** en dos minutos exactos

flatten [flǽtn̩] VI/VT (make flat) achatar(se), aplanar(se); VT (knock down) tumbar, voltear; (raze) arrasar

flatter [flǽɾɚ] VI/VT lisonjear, adular, halagar; **this picture —s you** esta foto te favorece; **I was —ed by his attentions** me halagaron sus atenciones

flatterer [fláɛDərɚ] N lisonjero -ra *mf*, adulador -ora *mf*

flattering [fláɛDɚɪŋ] ADJ (comment) lisonjero, halagüeño; (person) adulón

flattery [fláɛDəri] N lisonja *f*, adulación *f*, halago *m*

flatulence [fláɛtʃələns] N flatulencia *f*

flaunt [flɔnt] VI/VT ostentar, lucir(se)

flavor [flévɚ] N (taste, quality) sabor *m*; (flavoring) condimento *m*; VT sazonar

flavorless [flévɚlɪs] ADJ insípido

flaw [flɔ] N (in character, in construction) defecto *m*; (in an argument) falla *f*

flawless [flɔ́lɪs] ADJ (logic) impecable; (behavior) intachable, irreprochable; (appearance) perfecto

flax [flæks] N lino *m*

flea [fli] N pulga *f*; **— collar** collar antipulgas *m*; **— market** *Sp* rastro *m*; *Am* mercado de (las) pulgas *m*

flee [fli] VI huir; VT huir de

fleece [flis] N vellón *m*; VT (shear) trasquilar, esquilar; (defraud) estafar; (in card games) pelar, desplumar

fleet [flit] N (of boats, buses) flota *f*; (of cars) parque *m*; ADJ veloz

fleeting [flíDɪŋ] ADJ fugaz, efímero, pasajero

Flemish [flémɪʃ] ADJ & N flamenco -ca *mf*

flesh [flɛʃ] N carne *f*; (of a fruit) pulpa *f*; **— and blood** carne y hueso; **of my own — and blood** de mi propria sangre; **in the —** en persona; VI/VT **to — out** (a character) dar cuerpo a; (an argument) desarrollar

fleshy [fléʃi] ADJ (succulent) carnoso; (fat) metido en carnes

flexibility [flɛksəbílɪDi] N flexibilidad *f*

flexible [fléksəbəɫ] ADJ flexible

flicker [flíkɚ] VI (stars) titilar; (candle) parpadear; (of wings, etc.) temblar; N (of light) parpadeo *m*, titilación *f*; (of hope) rayo *m*

flier [fláɪɚ] N (one who flies) volador -ra *mf*; (aviator) aviador -ra *mf*; (leaflet) volante *m*

flight [flaɪt] N (act of flying, trip) vuelo *m*; (trajectory) trayectoria *f*; (flock of birds) bandada *f*; (group of military aircraft) escuadrilla *f*; (escape) fuga *f*, huida *f*; **— attendant** azafato -ta *mf*; **— plan** plan de vuelo *m*; **— school** escuela de aviación *f*; **a — of fancy** una fantasía; **— of stairs** tramo de escalera *m*; **to put to —** poner en fuga; **to take —** darse a la fuga

flimsy [flímzi] ADJ (structure, argument) endeble; (excuse) flojo, pobre

flinch [flɪntʃ] VI pestañear

fling [flɪŋ] VT arrojar, lanzar; **she flung herself at the attacker** se le tiró arriba al atacante; **he flung himself into his work** se dedicó de lleno a su trabajo; **he flung open the door** abrió la puerta de golpe; N (act of flinging) lanzamiento *m*; (sexual affair) aventura *f*; **he had a — at selling cars** intentó vender coches

flint [flɪnt] N pedernal *m*

flip [flɪp] VT (a coin) tirar; (a switch) (up) levantar, (down) bajar; (a pancake) dar vuelta; VI (head over heels) dar una voltereta; **to — through** hojear; **—-flop** (reversal of opinion) giro de 180 grados *m*; (backward somersault) voltereta para atrás *f*; (slipper) chancleta *f*; **— side** la otra cara de la moneda

flippant [flípənt] ADJ (frivolous) frívolo, displicente; (impudent) impertinente

flipper [flípɚ] N aleta *f*

flirt [flɝt] VI coquetear; N coqueto -ta *mf*

flirtation [flɝtéʃən] N coquetería *f*, coqueteo *m*

flit [flɪt] VI revolotear; **a smile —s across her face** una sonrisa le cruza la cara

float [flot] VI (rest on water, air, etc., fluctuate freely) flotar; (in soup) sobrenadar; (drift) errar, ir a la deriva; **she —ed down the stairs** se deslizó por la escalera; VT (set afloat) poner a flote; (start a company, scheme) lanzar; (emit shares) emitir; (let fluctuate) dejar flotar; (try out an idea) proponer; N (thing that floats) flotador *m*; (on a line) corcho *m*, boya *f*; (in a parade) carro alegórico *m*, carroza *f*; (with soda) gaseosa con helado *f*

flock [flɑk] N (birds, children) bandada *f*; (sheep) rebaño *m*; (worshipers) grey *f*; (people) muchedumbre *f*; VI acudir en masa, afluir; **to — around someone** rodear a alguien; **to — together** andar juntos

flog [flɑg] VT azotar

flood [flʌd] N inundación *f*; **— of tears** torrente de lágrimas *m*; **the —** El Diluvio Universal; (of tides) creciente *f*; **—gate** (of a dam) compuerta *f*; (of a canal lock) esclusa *f*; **—light** reflector *m*; VI/VT inundar(se), anegar(se); (car) ahogar(se), emborrachar(se)

floor [flɔr] N (surface of a room, vehicle) suelo *m*, piso *m*; (story) piso *m*; (of sea) fondo *m*; (dance) pista *f*; (minimum level) mínimo *m*; **to have the —** tener la palabra; VT (topple over) tumbar, derribar;

(stun, surprise) asombrar; — **it!** ¡acelera! *Sp* ¡mete caña!

flop [flɑp] VI (flail) zarandearse; (fish) dar coletazos; (drop) dejarse caer; (fail) fracasar; **to — down** dejarse caer, desplomarse; **to — over** voltear(se) flojamente; N (failure) fracaso *m*; (sound) ruido sordo *m*

floppy [flɑpi] ADJ caído; — **disk** disquete *m*, floppy *m*

florist [flɔ́rɪst] N florista *mf*; —**'s** (shop) florería *f*

floss [flɔs] N (silk) seda floja *f*; (for embroidery) hilo de seda *m*; (dental) hilo dental *m*; VI/VT pasar hilo dental (por)

flounder [fláʊndɚ] VI (in mud, etc.) andar/ moverse con dificultades; (for an answer) quedarse sin saber qué decir, perder pie; N platija *f*

flour [flaʊr] N harina *f*

flourish [flɝ́ɪʃ] VI (prosper) florecer, prosperar; VT (brandish) blandir; N (ornament, florid language, brandishing) floreo *m*; (of music) floritura *f*; (of a signature) rúbrica *f*; **in full —** en plena eclosión

flow [flo] VI (run) fluir, correr; (issue forth) surgir, brotar; (come and go) circular; (fall loosely) caer; (abound) abundar; (rise) crecer; **to — into** desembocar en, afluir a; N (liquid) flujo *m*; (electricity) corriente *f*; (of traffic, blood, air) circulación *f*; —**chart** diagrama de flujo *m*; — **of words** torrente de palabras *m*

flower [fláʊɚ] N flor *f*; (paragon) flor y nata *f*; **in —** en flor; — **bed** *Mex, Sp* arriate *m*; *RP* cantero *m*; —**pot** maceta *f*, tiesto *m*; — **vase** florero *m*; VI florecer

flowery [fláʊəri] ADJ (of a garden, language) florido; (of a pattern) floreado; (of a fragrance) floral

flowing [flóɪŋ] ADJ (liquid) fluyente; (clothing) suelto

flu [flu] N gripe *f*

fluctuate [flʌ́ktʃuet] VI fluctuar

fluctuation [flʌktʃuéʃən] N fluctuación *f*

fluency [flúənsi] N fluidez *f*

fluent [flúənt] ADJ fluido; **he is — in French** habla francés con fluidez/soltura

fluff [flʌf] VT mullir; (blunder) pifiar; N pelusa *f*; (blunder) pifia *f*; **this book is pure —** este libro es insustancial

fluffy [flʌ́fi] ADJ (airy) mullido; (covered with fluff) peludo

fluid [flúɪd] ADJ & N fluido *m*; — **ounce** onza líquida (29,42 mililitros) *f*

fluke [fluk] N (of whale) aleta *f*; (chance)

chiripa *f*; **by a —** por chiripa

flunk [flʌŋk] VI/VT reprobar, suspender; VI **to — out** abandonar

flunky [flʌ́ŋki] N (lackey, servant) lacayo *m*; (yes-man) adulón *m*

fluorescent [flʊrésənt] ADJ fluorescente; — **light** tubo fluorescente *m*

fluoride [flɔ́raɪd] N (chemical) fluoruro *m*; (dental aid) flúor *m*

fluorine [flɔ́rin] N flúor *m*

flurry [flɝ́i] N (of snow) nevisca *f*; (of activity) frenesí *m*

flush [flʌʃ] N (rosy glow, heat) rubor *m*; (of anger) arranque *m*; (of youth, color) resplandor *m*; (of embarrassment) sonrojo *m*; (in poker) color *m*; **did you hear the — of the toilet?** ¿oíste el sonido de la cisterna? ADJ (well supplied, rich) forrado; (ruddy, reddish) rubicundo; (full) rebosante; — **with** a(l) ras de; — **against** pegado a; VI/VT (make or turn red) sonrojar(se), ruborizar(se); (activate toilet) tirar la cadena; (rinse) baldear; VT **to — out** levantar

fluster [flʌ́stɚ] VI/VT agitar(se), poner(se) nervioso

flute [flut] N (musical instrument) flauta *f*; (of a column) estría *f*; VT estriar

flutter [flʌ́dɚ] VI (wings) aletear; (butterfly) revolotear; (flag) tremolar; (heart) palpitar; VT (agitate) agitar; N (of wings) aleteo *m*; (of excitement) agitación *f*; (of a fly) tremolar *m*; (of the heart) palpitación *f*

flux [flʌks] N flujo *m*; **a state of —** un estado de cambio continuo

fly [flaɪ] VI (through air) volar; (from danger) huir; (flag) ondear; (kite) remontar; VT (aircraft) pilotar; (air cargo) transportar en avión; **to — at** abalanzarse sobre; **to — away** volarse; **to — into a rage** montar en cólera; **to — off the handle** perder los estribos; **to — open (shut)** abrirse (cerrarse) de un golpe; **to — out of a room** salir disparado de un cuarto; **that idea won't —** esa idea no va a ser aceptada; **he flew the coop** se escapó; N (insect) mosca *f*; (over a zipper) bragueta *f*; —**catcher** papamoscas *m sg*; —**leaf** solapa *f*; —**swatter** matamoscas *m sg*; —**wheel** volante *m*; **on the —** al vuelo

flying [fláɪɪŋ] ADJ (passing through the air) volador; (fluttering) ondeante; **with — colors** con distinción; — **saucer** platillo volador *m*; **I hate —** no me gusta viajar en avión

foam [fom] N (suds, padding) espuma *f*; — **rubber** goma espuma *f*; VI hacer espuma;

to — at the mouth echar espuma por la boca

focus [fókəs] N foco *m*; VI/VT (bring into or be in focus) enfocar(se); (concentrate) centrarse; **to — on** fijarse en

fodder [fáDə-] N forraje *m*

foe [fo] N enemigo -ga *mf*

fog [fɑg] N niebla *f*; **to be in a —** estar confundido; **—horn** sirena de niebla *f*; VI/VT (confuse) ofuscar; (spray with insecticide) fumigar; (film) velar(se); **to — up** (window) empañar(se); (one's sight) nublar(se); **the airport was —ged in** el aeropuerto estaba cerrado por niebla

foggy [fági] ADJ (weather) brumoso, nebuloso; (window) empañado; (confused) confuso; (blurred, as a photograph) velado

foil [fɔɪł] N (any metal) hoja de metal *f*; (aluminum) papel de aluminio *m*; (on mirrors) azogue *m*; (rapier) florete *m*; (thing contrasted) contraste *m*; VT frustrar

fold [fołd] VI/VT (sheets) doblar(se); (paper, folding chairs) plegar(se); (wings, flag) replegar(se); (in cards) abandonar; (close a business) cerrar(se); (performance) bajar de cartel; **to — in** (in cooking) incorporar; **to — one's arms** cruzarse de brazos; N (pleat, hollow) pliegue *m*; (crease) doblez *m*; (enclosure) redil *m*, aprisco *m*; (sheep) rebaño *m*; (congregation) grey *f*; **to rejoin the —** volver al redil; **three—** tres veces

folder [fóɫdə-] N (file) carpeta *f*; (instrument for folding) plegadera *f*

folding [fóɫdɪŋ] ADJ plegadizo, plegable; **— chair** silla plegadiza *f*; **— screen** biombo *m*

foliage [fóliɪdʒ] N follaje *m*, fronda *f*, ramaje *m*

folic acid [fólɪkǽsɪd] N ácido fólico *m*

folio [fólio] N (page) folio *m*; (book) libro en folio *m*

folk [fok] N (people) gente *f*; (nation) pueblo *m*; ADJ popular; **— dance** baile folclórico *m*; **—lore** folclore *m*; (traditional stories) leyendas tradicionales *f pl*; **— medicine** medicina tradicional *f*; **— music** música folclórica *f*; **old —s** los viejos; **—s** (relatives) parientes *m pl*; (parents) padres *m pl*, viejos *m pl*; **— song** canción tradicional *f*

follow [fálo] VI/VT seguir; VI (be a consequence) seguirse; (come next) ir a continuación; **to — suit** seguir el ejemplo, secundar; **to — through** llevar a cabo; **—-through** continuación del movimiento; **to — up (on)** (pursue) obtener más detalles sobre; (develop) desarrollar; **—-up** seguimiento *m*

follower [fáloə-] N seguidor -ra *mf*

following [fáloɪŋ] N seguidores -ras *mf pl*; **the —** lo siguiente; ADJ siguiente

foment [fomént] VT fomentar

fond [fand] ADJ **I'm — of strolls** soy amigo de los paseos, soy gustoso de los paseos; **I'm — of Chinese food** me gusta la comida china; **I'm — of John** le tengo cariño a Juan; **— hopes** ilusión *f*; **to become — of** encariñarse de

fondle [fándɫ] VI/VT (touch affectionately) acariciar; (grope) manosear, sobar

fondness [fándnɪs] N (affection) cariño *m*, afecto *m*; (liking or weakness) afición *f*

font [fant] N (of water) pila *f*; (of characters) fuente *f*

food [fud] N comida *f*, alimento *m*; **— chain** cadena alimenticia *f*; **— poisoning** intoxicación por alimentos *f*; **—stuff** producto alimenticio *m*; **— for thought** algo para reflexionar

fool [fuł] N (foolish person) tonto -ta *mf*, bobo -ba *mf*, necio -cia *mf*; (jester) bufón *m*; **to make a — of someone** hacer quedar como un tonto; **to play the —** hacer el tonto; **I'm a card-playing —** soy loco por los naipes; VI bromear; **to — around** tontear; VT engañar; ADJ **—proof** (plan) infalible; (device) a prueba de tontos

foolish [fúlɪʃ] ADJ tonto, necio

foolishness [fúlɪʃnɪs] N tontería *f*, bobería *f*, sandez *f*

foot [fʊt] N pie *m*; (of an animal) pata *f*; **on — a** pie; **to put one's — in it** meter la pata; **—-and-mouth disease** fiebre aftosa *f*; **—ball** (American) fútbol americano *m*; (soccer) fútbol *m*; (ball) balón (de fútbol) *m*, pelota (de fútbol) *f*; **—hill** pie de la montaña *m*; **—hold** punto de apoyo *m*; **he has a —hold in the computer business** ha logrado establecerse en el negocio de la informática; **—lights** candilejas *f pl*; **—man** lacayo *m*; **—note** nota al pie de página *f*, llamada *f*; **—path** senda *f*; **—print** huella *f*, pisada *f*; **—race** carrera a pie *f*; **— soldier** soldado de infantería *m*; **—step** pisada *f*, paso *m*; (footprint) huella *f*, pisada *f*; **to follow in the —steps of** seguir los pasos de; **—stool** taburete *m*; **—wear** calzado *m*; **—work** (in sports) juego de piernas *m*; **it'll take some pretty fancy —work to get out of this** va a ser difícil zafar de esto; VI **to — it** andar a pie; VT **to — the bill** pagar la cuenta

footing [fÚDɪŋ] N (basis) base *f*; (foothold) punto de apoyo *m*; **to be on a friendly — with** tener relaciones amistosas con; **to lose one's —** perder pie

for [fɔr] PREP para; **this gift is — John** este regalo es para John; **we're headed — the beach** vamos para la playa; **this is a device — sorting letters** este es un aparato para clasificar cartas; **they gave me enough food — three people** me dieron comida (como) para tres personas; **she's studying — the bar** está estudiando para el examen de abogación; **the party is planned — Saturday** la fiesta está organizada para el sábado; **he has a good eye — talent** tiene buen ojo para descubrir talento; **he works — IBM** trabaja para IBM; **smoking is bad — your health** fumar es perjudicial para la salud; **he's mature — his age** es maduro para su edad; por; **I've come — the money** he venido por el dinero; **she asked — you** pidió por ti; **I walk to work — the exercise** voy al trabajo andando por el ejercicio; **we went to Spain — a month** fuimos a España por un mes; **she did it — the first time** lo hizo por primera vez; **my wife signed — me** mi esposa firmó por mí; **mothers feel love — their children** las madres sienten amor por sus hijos; **they fired him — arriving late** lo echaron por llegar tarde; **run — your life!** ¡corre por tu vida! **she took me — a fool** me tomó por tonto; **thanks — the help** gracias por la ayuda; **I paid ten dollars — the book** pagué diez dólares por el libro; **I'm — gun control** estoy por el control de armas; **— all her intelligence** a pesar de su inteligencia; **that's not — you to decide** a ti no te toca decidir esto; **as — him** en cuanto a él; **it's time — me to go** es hora de que me vaya; **to know — a fact** saber a ciencia cierta; CONJ porque, pues; **I wish to eat, — I'm hungry** quiero comer, pues tengo hambre

forage [fɔrɪʤ] N (feed) forraje *m*; (searching) recolección *f*; VI (gather food) forrajear; VT (feed) dar forraje a; (collect) recolectar

foray [fɔre] N incursión *f*, correría *f*; VI (explore) incursionar; (maraud) saquear

forbear [fɔrbér] VT abstenerse de; VI contenerse; [fɔrber] N antepasado -da *mf*

forbid [fə-bíd] VT prohibir

forbidden [fə-bídn̩] ADJ prohibido

forbidding [fə-bídɪŋ] ADJ (strict) severo; (daunting) imponente

force [fɔrs] N fuerza *f*; **in —** (effective) en vigor, vigente; (in large numbers) en masa; **armed —s** fuerzas armadas *f pl*; VT (oblige, compel) obligar; (rape, break open) forzar; **she —d a laugh** soltó una risa forzada; **to — upon** imponer; **to — one's way** abrirse paso a la fuerza; **to — out** echar a la fuerza

forced [fɔrst] ADJ forzado; (of a landing) forzoso

forceful [fɔrsfəɫ] ADJ (of personality) fuerte; (of arguments) convincente; (of behavior) enérgico

forceps [fɔrsəps] N (in obstetrics) fórceps *m*; (in dentistry) tenazas *f pl*, gatillo *m*

forcible [fɔrsəbəɫ] ADJ (done by force) forzoso; (effective) convincente; (by force) violento; **— entry** allanamiento de morada *m*

ford [fɔrd] N vado *m*; VT vadear

fore [fɔr] ADJ delantero; (of a ship) de proa; N frente *m*; **to come to the —** ponerse en evidencia; INTERJ ¡cuidado!

forearm [fɔrarm] N antebrazo *m*

forebode [fɔrbód] VT (foretell) presagiar; (have a presentiment) presentir

foreboding [fɔrbóDɪŋ] N (omen) presagio *m*; (presentiment) presentimiento *m*

forecast [fɔrkæst] N pronóstico *m*; VI/VT pronosticar

foreclose [fɔrklóz] VI ejecutar una hipoteca

foreclosure [fɔrklóʒə-] N ejecución *f*

forefather [fɔrfɑðə-] N antepasado *m*

forefront [fɔrfrʌnt] ADV LOC **at the —** a la cabeza, a la vanguardia

forego [fɔrgó] VT abstenerse de

foregone [fɔrgɔn] ADJ **it's a — conclusion** eso es de cajón

foreground [fɔrgraund] N primer plano *m*

forehead [fɔrɪd] N frente *f*

foreign [fɔrɪn] ADJ extranjero; (not local) foráneo; (alien) ajeno; **— affairs** relaciones exteriores *f pl*; **— aid** ayuda exterior *f*; **—-born** nacido en el extranjero; **— currency** divisa *f*; **— debt** deuda exterior *f*; **— exchange** cambio de divisas *m*; **— matter** materia extraña *f*; **— policy** política exterior *f*; **— trade** comercio exterior *m*

foreigner [fɔrənə-] N extranjero -ra *mf*

foreman [fɔrmən] N (in a factory) capataz *m*, sobrestante *m*; (of a jury) presidente *m*

foremost [fɔrmost] ADJ principal, preeminente

forensic [fərénzɪk] ADJ forense

forerunner [fɔrrʌnə-] N (precursor) precursor -ora *mf*; (omen) presagio *m*; (harbinger) mensajero -ra *mf*

foresee [fɔrsí] VT prever, prevenir

foresight [fɔ́rsaɪt] N previsión *f*

foreskin [fɔ́rskɪn] N prepucio *m*

forest [fɔ́rɪst] N (temperate) bosque *m*; (tropical) selva *f*; **— fire** incendio forestal *m*; **— ranger** guardabosques *m sg*

forestall [fɔrstɔ́ɫ] VT bloquear

forester [fɔ́rɪstɚ] N (forest ranger) guardabosques *m sg*; (forest animal) animal silvícola *m*

forestry [fɔ́rɪstri] N silvicultura *f*

foretell [fɔrtéɫ] VT predecir, vaticinar

forever [fɔrévɚ] ADV para siempre; **I'm — having to pick up after him** siempre tengo que estar juntando sus cosas; **we can't go on like this —** no podemos seguir así por toda la vida

foreword [fɔ́rwɚd] N prólogo *m*

forfeit [fɔ́rfɪt] VT perder; N (fine) multa *f*; (loss) pérdida *f*

forge [fɔrdʒ] N fragua *f*, forja *f*; VT (plans) fraguar; (metal, agreement) forjar; VI/VT (signature, legal document) falsificar; **to — ahead** abrirse paso

forgery [fɔ́rdʒəri] N falsificación *f*

forget [fɚgét] VI/VT olvidar, olvidarse de; **I forgot my keys** se me olvidaron las llaves; **to — oneself** meter la pata; N **—-me-not** nomeolvides *mf*

forgetful [fɚgétfəɫ] ADJ olvidadizo; **— of** negligente de

forgetfulness [fɚgétfəɫnɪs] N falta de memoria *f*

forgive [fɚgív] VI/VT perdonar (also a debt), disculpar

forgiveness [fɚgívnɪs] N perdón *m*

forgiving [fɚgívɪŋ] ADJ clemente

fork [fɔrk] N (for eating) tenedor *m*; (for hay) horca *f*, trinche *m*; (for tuning) diapasón *m*; (in a road) bifurcación *f*; **—lift** montacargas de horquilla *m sg*; VI bifurcarse; **to — over** soltar

forlorn [fɔrlɔ́rn] ADJ desamparado, abandonado

form [fɔrm] N forma *f*; (physical condition) condiciones físicas *f pl*; (document to be filled in) formulario *m*; VI/VT formar(se)

formal [fɔ́rməɫ] ADJ formal; **— attire** ropa de etiqueta *f*; **— dance** baile de etiqueta *m*

formality [fɔrmǽlɪdi] N (conventionality) formalidad *f*; (rigidity) formalismo *m*; (legal step) trámite *m*

format [fɔ́rmæt] N formato *m*; VT formatear

formation [fɔrméʃən] N formación *f*

formative [fɔ́rməDɪv] ADJ formativo

formatting [fɔ́rmæDɪŋ] N formateo *m*

former [fɔ́rmɚ] ADJ **the — capital** la antigua capital; **my — husband** mi ex-marido; **the — president** el ex-presidente, el ex-presidente; **in — times** antiguamente; PRON aquel (aquella, etc.), ese (esa, etc.)

formidable [fɔ́rmɪDəbəɫ] ADJ formidable

formula [fɔ́rmjələ] N fórmula *f*; (for babies) preparado para biberón *m*

formulate [fɔ́rmjəlet] VT formular

fornicate [fɔ́rnɪket] VI fornicar

forsake [fɔrsék] VT abandonar, desamparar

fort [fɔrt] N fuerte *m*, fortaleza *f*; **to hold (down) the —** quedarse cuidando

forth [fɔrθ] ADV (time) en adelante; (space) hacia adelante; **to go —** irse; **and so —** etcétera, y así sucesivamente

forthcoming [fɔrθkámɪŋ] ADJ (approaching) venidero, próximo; (available) disponible; **help wasn't —** no había ayuda disponible; (frank, friendly) abierto; (soon to be published) de próxima aparición

forthright [fɔ́rθraɪt] ADJ directo

forthwith [fɔrθwíθ] ADV en seguida, al punto

fortification [fɔrDəfɪkéʃən] N fortificación *f*

fortify [fɔ́rDəfaɪ] VT (building, body) fortificar; (food) enriquecer; (hair, mind) fortalecer; (argument) reforzar

fortitude [fɔ́rDɪtud] N fortaleza *f*, entereza *f*

fortress [fɔ́rtrɪs] N fortaleza *f*

fortuitous [fɔrtúɪDəs] ADJ (coincidental) fortuito; (lucky) afortunado

fortunate [fɔ́rtʃənɪt] ADJ afortunado

fortune [fɔ́rtʃən] N fortuna *f*; **— teller** adivino -na *mf*; **it cost me a —** me costó un dineral; **to tell someone's —** decirle la buenaventura a alguien

forty [fɔ́rDi] NUM cuarenta

forum [fɔ́rəm] N foro *m*

forward [fɔ́rwɚd] ADJ (toward the front) hacia adelante; (leading, in the front) delantero; (pushy) descarado; ADV adelante, en adelante; **to bring —** presentar; VT reexpedir; N delantero -ra *mf*

fossil [fásəɫ] N fósil *m*; (old fogey) carcamal *m*, carca *mf*; **— fuel** combustible fósil *m*

foster [fɔ́stɚ] VT (promote) fomentar, promover; (bring up) criar; ADJ adoptivo

foul [faʊɫ] ADJ (dirty, illicit) sucio; (disgusting) asqueroso; (of a smell) fétido; (of weather) inclemente; (of winds) adverso; (morally offensive) vil; (of air) viciado; **—mouthed** mal hablado; **the police suspect — play** la policía sospecha que fue un crimen; N falta *f*, foul *m*; **—-up** desastre *m*; VT (make dirty)

ensuciar; (pollute) viciar; (tarnish)
manchar; VI cometer una falta; **to — up**
estropear

found [faʊnd] VT (establish) fundar; (build)
cimentar

foundation [faʊndéʃən] N (establishment,
institution) fundación *f*; (of a building)
cimiento *m*; (of an argument) fundamento
m; (cosmetic) base *f*

founder [fáʊndɚ] N (establisher) fundador
-ra *mf*; (smith) fundidor -ra *mf*; VI (sink)
zozobrar, irse a pique; (fail) fracasar

foundry [fáʊndri] N fundición *f*

fountain [fáʊntṇ] N fuente *f*; **— pen** pluma
fuente *f*

four [fɔr] NUM cuatro; **—-eyes** *fam* cuatro
ojos *m sg*; **—-letter word** palabrota *f*;
—score ochenta; **—some** grupo de cuatro
m

fourteen [fɔrtín] NUM catorce

fourth [fɔrθ] ADJ cuarto; N cuarta parte *f*; **the
Fourth of July** el cuatro de julio

fowl [faʊɫ] N (domestic) ave de corral *m*;
(wild) ave *m*

fox [fɑks] N zorro -rra *mf*; (crafty person)
persona astuta *f*; (attractive person)
guapetón -na *mf*; **—hole** madriguera *f*;
(military) trinchera *f*

foxy [fáksi] ADJ (crafty) zorro; (attractive) sexy

foyer [fɔ́ɪɚ] N vestíbulo *m*

fraction [frǽkʃən] N fracción *f*, quebrado *m*

fracture [frǽktʃɚ] N fractura *f*; VI/VT
fracturar(se)

fragile [frǽdʒəɫ] ADJ frágil

fragment [frǽgmənt] N fragmento *m*;
[frægmént] VI/VT fragmentar(se)

fragrance [frégrəns] N fragancia *f*

fragrant [frégrənt] ADJ fragante

frail [freɫ] ADJ frágil, débil

frailty [fréɫti] N fragilidad *f*, debilidad *f*

frame [frem] N (of a building, airplane,
furniture) armazón *m*; (of eyeglasses)
montura *f*, armadura *f*; (of a car) chasis *m*;
(of a person's body) estatura *f*; (of a
picture, door) marco *m*; (for embroidery)
bastidor *m*; (on a strip of film) imagen *f*;
— of mind disposición *f*; **—work** (of a
house, structure) armazón *m*; (of
reference) marco *m*, esquema *m*; VT (a
document) forjar; (a question, plan)
formular; (a picture) enmarcar; (a person)
tenderle una trampa

franc [fræŋk] N franco *m*

France [fræns] N Francia *f*

franchise [frǽntʃaɪz] N (license) concesión *f*,
franquicia *f*; (voting privilege) derecho al
voto *m*; VT conceder en franquicia, dar la
concesión

frank [fræŋk] ADJ franco, abierto; VT
franquear; N salchicha alemana *f*

frankfurter [frǽŋkfɚDɚ] N salchicha
alemana *f*

frankness [frǽŋknɪs] N franqueza *f*

frantic [frǽntɪk] ADJ (wild) frenético;
(desperate) desesperado

fraternal [frətɚ́nəɫ] ADJ fraternal, fraterno

fraternity [frətɚ́nɪDi] N (relationship)
fraternidad *f*, confraternidad *f*; (student
association) asociación estudiantil *f*

fraternize [frǽDɚnaɪz] VI confraternizar,
fraternizar

fraud [frɔd] N (deceit) fraude *m*; (impostor)
farsante *mf*, impostor -ra *mf*

fraudulent [frɔ́dʒələnt] ADJ (of a business,
etc.) fraudulento; (of a person) engañoso

fray [fre] N (fight) reyerta *f*, riña *f*; (harsh
debate) refriega *f*; VI/VT (rub, wear out)
desgastar(se); (strain) crispar(se)

freak [frik] N (anomaly) anomalía *f*;
(monster) monstruo *m*, anormal *mf*;
(enthusiast) fanático -ca *mf*; (pervert)
pervertido -da *mf*; ADJ (unusual) insólito;
VT chiflar, flipar; **to — out** chiflar(se),
flipar(se)

freakish [fríkɪʃ] ADJ insólito

freckle [frékəɫ] N peca *f*; VI/VT cubrir(se) de
pecas

freckled [frékəɫd] ADJ pecoso

free [fri] ADJ (having liberty, unrestricted,
loose, uncombined chemically,
independent) libre; (unobstructed,
unoccupied) libre, despejado; (without
charge) gratis, gratuito; (generous)
generoso; (unstinted) sin límites,
descontrolado; (frank) franco, abierto; **—
and easy** despreocupado; **— enterprise**
empresa libre *f*; **— fall** caída libre *f*;
—-for-all rifirrafe *m*; **—lance** freelance
m; **— lunch / ride** algo gratis *m*; **—
market** mercado libre *m*; **— radical**
radical libre *m*; **— speech** libertad de
expresión *f*; **— spirit** espíritu fuerte *m*;
—style estilo libre *m*; **— thinker** libre
pensador -ra *mf*; **— trade** libre cambio *m*;
— verse verso libre *m*; **—way** autopista *f*,
autovía *f*; **— will** libre albedrío *m*; **to
give someone a — hand** dar rienda
suelta a alguien; **to set —** poner en
libertad; **for —** gratis; **sugar-—** sin
azúcar; ADV libremente; **— lance** por
cuenta propia; VT (liberate) liberar;
(deliver, rid) librar; (untie a knot)
desenredar; (drain) desatascar; **to —load**
gorronear; **to — up** (time) dejar libre

freedom [fríDəm] N libertad *f*; — **of speech** libertad de expresión *f*; **we all want — from fear** todos queremos vivir libres de miedo; **I want — from having to go to work every day** no quiero tener que ir a trabajar todos los días

freeze [friz] VI/VT (of food, water) congelar(se); (of accounts) bloquear(se), congelar(se); **he froze to death** murió congelado; **my computer froze up** se me colgó la computadora / el ordenador; VI (of temperature) helar; N (action or state of being frozen) congelación *f*; (cold snap) helada *f*

freezer [frízɚ] N congelador *m*

freezing [frízɪŋ] ADJ helado; — **cold** frío glacial *m*; — **point** punto de congelación *m*

freight [fret] N (load) carga *f*; (charge) flete *m*, porte *m*; — **train** tren de carga *m*, tren de mercancías *m*; **by** — por carga

French [frentʃ] ADJ francés; — **dressing** salsa francesa *f*; — **fries** *Am* papas fritas *f pl*; *Sp* patatas fritas *f pl*; — **horn** corno francés *m*; — **kiss** beso francés *m*; **(to)** -**kiss** besar en la boca; —**man** francés *m*; —**woman** francesa *f*; N **the** — los franceses

frenzy [frénzi] N frenesí *m*; **he worked himself into a** — se puso histérico

frequency [fríkwənsi] N frecuencia *f*

frequent [fríkwənt] ADJ frecuente; VT frecuentar

fresh [freʃ] ADJ (pure, cool, not stale, not frozen, not tired) fresco; (new) nuevo; (bold) impertinente, atrevido; (healthy) lozano; — **out of school** recién salido de la escuela; — **paint** pintura fresca *f*; — **water** agua dulce *f*; **we're — out of ideas** se nos acabaron las ideas

freshen [fréʃən] VI/VT refrescar(se); **to — up** arreglarse, lavarse

freshman [fréʃmən] N (student) estudiante de primer año *mf*; (novice) novato -ta *mf*

freshness [fréʃnɪs] N (of food, of temperature) frescor *m*, frescura *f*; (of skin, flowers, youth) lozanía *f*; (of an idea) originalidad *f*; (impudence) descaro *m*

fret [fret] VI/VT (worry) preocupar(se); (irritate) irritar(se); N traste *m*

fretful [frétfəɫ] ADJ preocupado

friar [fráɪɚ] N fraile *m*

friction [fríkʃən] N fricción *f*, rozamiento *m*

Friday [fráɪDe] N viernes *m*

fried [fraɪd] ADJ frito

friend [frend] N amigo -ga *mf*

friendliness [fréndlɪnɪs] N afabilidad *f*, simpatía *f*

friendly [fréndli] ADJ amistoso, simpático, amigable; — **advice** consejo de amigo *m*; **user-**— fácil de usar

friendship [fréndʃɪp] N amistad *f*

frigate [frígɪt] N fragata *f*

fright [fraɪt] N (fear) espanto *m*, susto *m*; (grotesque thing or person) espantajo *m*, esperpento *m*; **to take** — asustarse

frighten [fráɪtn̩] VI/VT espantar(se), asustar(se); **to — away** ahuyentar, espantar; **to get —ed** espantarse

frightened [fráɪtn̩d] ADJ asustado, espantado

frightful [fráɪtfəɫ] ADJ espantoso, pavoroso; **we had a — time** lo pasamos horrible; **he's a — flatterer** es un adulón espantoso

frigid [frídʒɪd] ADJ (of weather) gélido; (of sexual response) frígida; (of personal relations) frío

frill [frɪɫ] N (trimming) volante *m*; (something superfluous) adorno *m*; **with no —s** sin lujos, sencillo

fringe [frɪndʒ] N (of a rug, etc.) fleco *m*, orla *f*; (of a city) periferia *f*; (of a political party) extremo *m*; (of society) margen *m*; — **benefits** prestaciones *f pl*, complementos *m pl*; VT orlar, poner un fleco

frisk [frɪsk] VI/VT (frolic) retozar, triscar; (search) cachear

frisky [fríski] ADJ retozón

fritter [fríDɚ] VI/VT desmenuzar(se); VT **to — away** malgastar; VI irse gastando de poco a poco; N buñuelo *m*, churro *m*

frivolity [frɪváɫɪDi] N frivolidad *f*

frivolous [frívələs] ADJ frívolo

fro [fro] ADV **to and** — de aquí para allá

frock [frɑk] N (dress) vestido *m*; (habit) hábito *m*

frog [frɑg] N (animal) rana *f*; (fastener) alamar *m*; (of a hoof) ranilla *f*; (French person) *pej* franchute -ta *mf*; **to have a — in one's throat** tener gallos en la garganta; —**man** hombre rana *m*

frolic [fráɫɪk] N retozo *m*; VI retozar

from [frʌm] PREP desde; — **here to there** desde aquí hasta allá; — **two to four** de las dos a las cuatro; — **what I can tell** por lo que yo veo; **four hours — now** de aquí a cuatro horas, dentro de cuatro horas; **different — the other one** diferente del otro; **to come — Minnesota** ser de Minesota; **death — starvation** muerte por inanición *f*

front [frʌnt] N frente *m*; (cover for illegal activity) pantalla *f*; **in — of** en frente de, delante de; **—-runner** favorito -ta *mf*; **—-wheel drive** tracción delantera *f*; ADJ delantero; VI/VT (face) dar a; (cover up) servir de pantalla

frontier [frʌntír] N frontera *f*; ADJ fronterizo; **— spirit** espíritu pionero *m*; **— town** pueblo fronterizo *m*

frost [frɔst] N helada *f*, escarcha *f*; VI/VT helar, escarchar; VT (a cake) bañar; (glass) esmerilar; (hair) hacer rayitos / reflejos; **—bite** necrosis por congelación *f*

frosting [frɔ́stɪŋ] N (of a cake) baño *m*; (for glass) esmerilado *m*; (of hair) rayos *m pl*, reflejos *m pl*

frosty [frɔ́sti] ADJ (cold, unfriendly) helado; (covered with frost) escarchado

froth [frɔθ] N espuma *f*; VI echar espuma; VT batir

frown [fraʊn] VI fruncir el ceño; **to — on** desaprobar; N ceño *m*

frozen [frózən] ADJ congelado

fructose [frúktos] N fructosa *f*

frugal [frúgəɫ] ADJ (economical) económico, ahorrativo; (meager) frugal

fruit [frut] N (food) fruta *f*; (plant part, product of labor) fruto *m*; (male homosexual) *offensive* maricón *m*; **—cake** (food) torta de frutas secas *f*; (crazy person) *fam* chiflado -da *mf*

fruitful [frútfəɫ] ADJ fructífero

fruitless [frútlɪs] ADJ infructuoso

frumpy [frʌ́mpi] ADJ matrona

frustrate [frʌ́stret] VT frustrar; **to get —d** frustrar(se)

frustration [frʌstréʃən] N frustración *f*

fry [fraɪ] VI/VT (cook, also execute by electrocution) freír(se); **—ing pan** sartén *f*; N (fried potato) papa / patata frita *f*; (gathering with fried food) fiesta con comida frita *f*; (young fish) alevín *m*; **small —** gente menuda *f*

fuck [fʌk] VI/VT (have intercourse) *Sp vulg* follar; *Am vulg* coger, culear; (treat harshly) *vulg* joder; **—!** *vulg* ¡mierda! ¡coño! **— off!** *vulg* ¡vete a la mierda! **— you!** *vulg* ¡vete a la mierda! **to — around** (be idle) *vulg* rascarse las bolas; (be promiscuous) *vulg* coger / follar con todo el mundo; **to — up** *vulg* cagar, joder; **she's —ed up** (mentally ill, in trouble) *vulg* está jodida; (under the influence) está colocada; (confused) está confundida; **—up** *offensive* pendejo -ja *mf*; N (sexual act) *fam* polvo *m*; **he's a good —** *vulg* folla / coge muy bien; **what the — do you want?** *vulg* ¿qué carajo quieres? ¿qué demonios quieres?

fucker [fʌ́kɚ] N (person who fucks) *vulg* follador -ra *mf*; (annoying person) *offensive* hijo -ja de puta *mf*

fucking [fʌ́kɪŋ] ADJ *vulg* jodido, de mierda; **the whole — day** *fam* todo el maldito día

fudge [fʌʤ] N turrón blando de chocolate *m*; VI (cheat) hacer trampa; (avoid an issue) dar rodeos

fuel [fjúəɫ] N (combustible) combustible *m*; (topic) tema *m*; **— injection** inyección *f*; **— oil** fuel-oil *m*; VT (a vehicle) llenar el tanque, cargar de combustible; (fire, debate) avivar

fugitive [fjúʤɪDɪv] ADJ (fleeing) fugitivo; (transitory) fugaz; N fugitivo -va *mf*, prófugo -ga *mf*

fulfill [fʊɫfíɫ] VT (promise, order) cumplir; (need) satisfacer; **she doesn't feel —ed** no se siente realizada

fulfillment [fʊɫfíɫmənt] N (of a promise, order) cumplimiento *m*; (of a need) satisfacción *f*; (of a person) realización *f*

full [fʊɫ] ADJ (completely filled) lleno; (complete) completo; (a dress) amplio; (a person's figure) relleno; (sated) harto; **—-blooded** de raza; **—-blown** (of disease) declarado; (complete) auténtico; **—-bodied** con cuerpo; **—-fledged** verdadero; **—-grown** adulto; **— house** full *m*; **—-length** (movie) de largometraje; (mirror) de cuerpo entero; **— moon** luna llena *f*; **—-scale** (model, etc.) de tamaño natural; (war) total; (investigation) exhaustivo; **—-service** de servicio completo; **—-size** (bed) de matrimonio; (model, etc.) de tamaño natural; **— time** tiempo completo *m*, de tiempo completo; **to pay in —** pagar el total de la deuda; ADV **you know — well** sabes perfectamente; **it hit him — in the chest** le pegó en pleno pecho

fully [fúli] ADV (entirely) completamente; (at least) al menos

fumble [fʌ́mbəɫ] VI (search for) buscar a tientas; (move clumsily) andar a tientas; (blunder) meter la pata; **he —d his way into the living room** entró a tientas a la sala

fume [fjum] VI (be angry) rabiar; (emit vapors, smoke) emitir humo; N **—s** gases *m pl*, vapores *m pl*, tufo *m*

fumigate [fjúmɪget] VT fumigar

fun [fʌn] N diversión *f*; **for —** por gusto; **to make — of** burlarse de; **to have —** divertirse; ADJ divertido

function [fʌ́ŋkʃən] N (systems, computers,

etc.) función *f*; VI (work) funcionar; (serve) oficiar

fund [fʌnd] N (of money) fondo *m*; (of knowledge) acervo *m*; **—-raising** recaudación de fondos *f*; VT financiar

fundamental [fʌndəméntl̩] ADJ fundamental; N fundamento *m*

fundamentalism [fʌndəméntl̩ɪzəm] N fundamentalismo *m*

funding [fʌ́ndɪŋ] N financiamiento *m*, financiación *f*

funeral [fjúnəəɫ] N funeral *m*, entierro *m*, exequias *f pl*; **— director** director -ora de pompas fúnebres *mf*; **— home** casa de pompas fúnebres *f*, funeraria *f*; **— service** funeral *m*; **it's your —** te estás cavando tu propia tumba; ADJ (march, procession) fúnebre; (pyre) funerario; (expenses) de entierro

fungus [fʌ́ŋgəs] N hongo *m*

funky [fʌ́ŋki] ADJ (of music) funky; (strange) estrafalario, raro; (smelly) hediondo

funnel [fʌ́nəɫ] N (for liquids) embudo *m*; (in a chimney) humero *m*; VT canalizar, encauzar

funny [fʌ́ni] ADJ (amusing) cómico, chistoso, gracioso; (strange) raro; **— farm** *fam* loquero *m*, loquería *f*; **that's not —** eso no tiene gracia; **don't get — with me** no te pases de listo; N **funnies** historietas *f pl*, tiras cómicas *f pl*; ADV raro

fur [fɝ] N (hair) pelo *m*; (coat) pelaje *m*; (hide) piel *f*; **— store** peletería *f*; VT forrar de piel

furious [fjúriəs] ADJ (angry) furioso, sañudo, rabioso; (fight, storm) feroz; (activity) febril

furlough [fɝlo] N licencia *f*, permiso *m*; VT dar licencia

furnace [fɝnɪs] N (for heating) caldera *f*; (in industry) horno *m*

furnish [fɝnɪʃ] VT (put in furniture) amueblar; (equip) equipar; (provide) proporcionar, suministrar, facilitar

furniture [fɝnɪtʃɚ] N muebles *m pl*, mobiliario *m*; **— store** mueblería *f*

furrow [fɝo] N surco *m*; VT (soil) arar; (face) fruncir

furry [fɝi] ADJ peludo

further [fɝ́ðɚ] ADV **we want to go —** queremos ir más lejos; **I refuse to discuss this —** me niego a seguir discutiendo esto; (furthermore) (lo que) es más; ADJ (more distant) más lejano; (additional) adicional; VT (promote) promover; ADV **—more** además

furthest [fɝ́ðɪst] ADJ (el) más lejano, (el) más remoto; ADV más lejos

furtive [fɝ́DIV] ADJ furtivo; (shifty) sospechoso

fury [fjúri] N furia *f*, furor *m*, saña *f*

fuse [fjuz] N (in an explosive) mecha *f*; (in a circuit) fusible *m*; **he has a short —** tiene pocas pulgas; **he blew a —** estalló; VT (to join) fusionar; VI/VT (to merge) fusionar(se); (to blend metals) fundir(se)

fuselage [fjúsəlɑʒ] N fuselaje *m*

fusion [fjúʒən] N fusión *f*

fuss [fʌs] N (bustle) alboroto *m*, bulla *f*; (uproar) escándalo *m*, alharaca *f*; (argument) discusión *f*; VI (worry about trifles) preocuparse por naderías; (complain) quejarse

fussiness [fʌ́sinɪs] N remilgo *m*, ñoñería *f*

fussy [fʌ́si] ADJ (particular) quisquilloso, remilgado; (overdecorated) recargado; (whiny) quejica, cargoso

futile [fjúdl̩] ADJ inútil

futility [fjutílɪDi] N inutilidad *f*

future [fjútʃɚ] N futuro *m*, porvenir *m*; **—s** futuros *m pl*; ADJ futuro

fuzz [fʌz] N (fluff) pelusa *f*; (fine hair) vello fino *m*; (on the lip) bozo *m*

fuzzy [fʌ́zi] ADJ (fluffy) cubierto de pelusa; (hairy) velloso; (blurred) borroso; (muddled) confuso

Gg

gab [gæb] VI parlotear, charlar; N parloteo *m*, charla *f*; **gift of —** labia *f*, facundia *f*

gable [gébəɫ] N hastial *m*; **— roof** tejado de dos aguas *m*; **— window** buhardilla *f*

Gabon, Gabun [gəbón] N Gabón *m*

Gabonese [gæbəníz] ADJ & N gabonés -esa *mf*

gad [gæd] VI **to — about** callejear

gadget [gǽdʒɪt] N adminículo *m*

gaffe [gæf] N gaffe *f*, metedura de pata *f*

gag [gæg] VT (stop up mouth, silence) amordazar; (cause to choke) dar arcadas; VI tener arcadas; N (thing stuffed into mouth) mordaza *f*; (joke) gag *m*, burla *f*; **— order** orden de supresión de la libertad de expresión *f*

gaiety [géɪDi] N alegría *f*; **gaieties** festejos *m pl*

gain [gen] VT ganar; VI **to — on** irse acercando a; VI/VT (watch) adelantar; N (profit, act of gaining) ganancia *f*; (in weight) aumento *m*

gainful [génfəɫ] ADJ remunerado

gait [get] N marcha *f*, paso *m*

galaxy [gǽləksi] N galaxia *f*

gale [geɫ] N ventarrón *m*, vendaval *m*; **—-force winds** vientos huracanados *m pl*; **— of laughter** risotada *f*

Galicia [gəlíʃə] N Galicia *f*

Galician [gəlíʃən] ADJ & N gallego -ga *mf*

gall [gɔɫ] N (bile, bitterness) hiel *f*; (impudence) morro *m*; (of a plant) agalla *f*; **— bladder** vesícula (biliar) *f*; **—nut** agalla *f*; **—stone** cálculo biliar *m*; VT (irritate) irritar

gallant [gǽlənt] ADJ (brave) valiente; (attentive to women) galante; [gəlánt] N galán *m*

gallantry [gǽləntri] N (courage) valentía *f*, bizarría *f*; (chivalrous attention) galantería *f*

gallery [gǽləri] N (art, shopping) galería *f*; (theater) paraíso *m*, gallinero *m*; (golf) público *m*

galley [gǽli] N (kitchen) cocina *f*; (boat) galera *f*; **— proof** galerada *f*

gallium [gǽliəm] N galio *m*

gallon [gǽlən] N galón (3.7853 liters) *m*

gallop [gǽləp] VI galopar; N galope *m*

gallows [gǽloz] N horca *f*, cadalso *m*

galore [gəlɔ́r] ADV en abundancia

galoshes [gəláʃɪz] N chanclos *m pl*

galvanize [gǽɫvənaɪz] VT (metals) galvanizar; (a crowd) electrizar

Gambia [gǽmbiə] N Gambia *f*

Gambian [gǽmbiən] ADJ & N gambiano -na *mf*

gamble [gǽmbəɫ] VI jugar; VT jugarse; **I'll — my whole fortune on this venture** voy a jugarme todo en este negocio; **to — away** perder en el juego; N (risk) riesgo *m*; (bet) apuesta *f*

gambler [gǽmblɚ] N apostador -ora *mf*, tahúr *m*

game [gem] N juego *m*; (match of chess, etc.) partida *f*; (sports match) partido *m*; (wild animals and their meat) caza *f*; **— show** programa concurso *m*; **to be fair —** ser blanco legítimo; ADJ **I'm — for some tennis** me apunto para jugar al tenis; **he has a — knee from years of rugby** tiene la rodilla lisiada después de años de jugar al rugby

gamut [gǽmət] N gama *f*

gander [gǽndɚ] N ganso (macho) *m*; **to take a — at** echarle un vistazo a

gang [gǽŋ] N (of youths, thieves, etc.) pandilla *f*, gavilla *f*, banda *f*; (group of friends) grupo *m*; **—plank** pasarela *f*;

—way (passage way) pasillo *m*; (on a ship) pasamano *m*; **—way!** ¡abran cancha! VI **to — up on** conspirar contra, conspirar en masa

gangrene [gǽŋgrin] N gangrena *f*; VI/VT gangrenar(se)

gangster [gǽŋstɚ] N gángster *m*, maleante *m*

gap [gǽp] N (breach) brecha *f*, hueco *m*; (of memory) laguna *f*; (of time) intervalo *m*; **she has a — between her teeth** tiene los dientes separados; VT espaciar (correctamente)

gape [gep] VI mirar boquiabierto

garage [gəráʒ] N (for parking) garaje *m*; (for repairing) taller mecánico *m*; **— sale** venta de garaje *f*; VT estacionar en un garaje

garb [gɑrb] N vestimenta *f*, atavío *m*; VT vestir, ataviar

garbage [gárbɪdʒ] N basura *f*; **— can** bote de basura *m*; **— disposal unit** trituradora *f*; **—man** basurero *m*; **— truck** camión de la basura *m*; **what a lot of —!** ¡qué montón de mentiras!

garden [gárdn̩] N jardín *m*; **— of Eden** jardín del Edén *m*; VI cultivar un jardín

gardener [gárdnɚ] N jardinero -ra *mf*

gargle [gárgəɫ] VI hacer gárgaras; VT hacer gárgaras con; N (liquid) gargarismo *m*; (sound) gárgara *f*

garland [gárlənd] N guirnalda *f*

garlic [gárlɪk] N ajo *m*

garment [gármənt] N prenda *f*

garner [gárnɚ] VT cosechar

garnet [gárnɪt] N granate *m*

garnish [gárnɪʃ] VT (decorate) decorar; (decorate food) aderezar, guarnecer; (withhold wages) retener; N (decoration) adorno *m*, decoración *f*

garret [gǽrɪt] N desván *m*, buhardilla *f*

garrison [gǽrɪsən] N guarnición *f*; VT guarnecer

garrulous [gǽrələs] ADJ locuaz, gárrulo

garter [gárDɚ] N liga *f*; **— belt** liguero *m*, portaligas *m sg*; **— snake** culebra de jaretas *f*; VT sujetar con ligas

gas [gǽs] N (vapor) gas *m*; (fuel) gasolina *f*; (flatulence) gases *m pl*; **— chamber** cámara de gas *f*; **— mask** máscara de gas *f*; **— pedal** acelerador *m*; **— station** gasolinera *f*; **we had a —** lo pasamos bomba; VT asfixiar con gas, matar en la cámara de gas; **to step on the —** acelerar; **to — up** llenar el tanque

gaseous [gǽʃəs] ADJ gaseoso

gash [gǽʃ] N tajo *m*; VT hacer un tajo en

gasket [gǽskɪt] N junta (de culata) *f*

gasoline [gǽsəlin] N gasolina *f*, nafta *f*
gasp [gæsp] N (cry) grito sofocado *m*; (pant)
    jadeo *m*, boqueada *f*; VI (cry out) dar un
    grito sofocado; (in surprise) quedar
    boquiabierto; (for breath) jadear, boquear
gastric [gǽstrɪk] ADJ gástrico; — **ulcer** úlcera
    gástrica *f*
gastritis [gæstráɪdɪs] N gastritis *f*
gastroenteritis [gæstroɛntəráɪdɪs] N
    gastroenteritis *f*
gastrointestinal [gæstrointéstɪnəł] ADJ
    gastrointestinal
gastronomy [gæstránəmi] N gastronomía *f*
gate [get] N (to a garden) portón *m*; (to a
    city) puerta *f*; (at an airport) puerta de
    embarque *f*; —**way** (entrance, access)
    puerta (de entrada) *f*; (in computers)
    portal *m*
gather [gǽðɚ] VT (bring together) reunir,
    allegar; (pick) recolectar; (pick up, sort
    out) juntar; (deduce) deducir, colegir;
    (sew) fruncir; VI (come together) reunirse;
    (collect) juntarse; (contract into folds)
    fruncirse; **to** — **dust** juntar polvo / tierra;
    to — **speed** acelerar; N frunce *m*
gathering [gǽðɚɪŋ] N (meeting) asamblea *f*;
    (social) tertulia *f*; (assemblage of people)
    concurrencia *f*, reunión *f*; (act of gathering
    fruit, etc.) recolección *f*
gaudy [gɔ́di] ADJ (of bright color) chillón;
    (ostentatious) llamativo
gauge [geʤ] VT (measure) medir; (estimate)
    estimar; (calibrate) calibrar; N
    (measurement standard) medida *f*;
    (caliber) calibre *m*; (measuring device)
    medidor *m*; (track width) entrevía *f*
gaunt [gɔnt] ADJ demacrado
gauntlet [gɔ́ntlɪt] N (glove) guante *m*;
    (mailed glove) guantelete *m*; **to throw
    down the** — retar, desafiar; **to run the**
    — sufrir acosos
gauze [gɔz] N gasa *f*
gavel [gǽvəł] N martillo *m*
gawk [gɔk] VT mirar boquiabierto
gawky [gɔ́ki] ADJ torpe, desgarbado
gay [ge] ADJ (happy) alegre, festivo;
    (homosexual) homosexual; N *fam*
    homosexual *m*
gaze [gez] VI mirar fijamente, contemplar; N
    mirada fija *f*
gazelle [gəzéł] N gacela *f*
gazette [gəzét] N gaceta *f*
gear [gir] N (equipment) equipo *m*; (cog)
    rueda dentada *f*; (assembly of cogs)
    engranaje *m*; (speed) marcha *f*, cambio *m*;
    (personal property) pertenencias *f pl*;
    —**box** caja de cambios *f*; —**shift lever**

palanca de cambios *f*; **to be in** — estar
    engranado; **to change** —**s** cambiar de
    marcha, poner el cambio; **to put into** —
    engranar; **to put out of** — desengranar;
    to — **up** prepararse
gearing [gírɪŋ] N engranaje *m*
gecko [gɛ́ko] N geco *m*
Geiger counter [gáɪgɚkáʊntɚ] N contador
    Geiger *m*
gel [ʤɛł] VI/VT cuajar(se)
gelatin [ʤélətɪn] N gelatina *f*
gem [ʤɛm] N (precious stone) gema *f*;
    (valuable person) joya *f*; —**stone** piedra
    preciosa *f*
gender [ʤɛ́ndɚ] N género *m*; — **gap**
    diferencias entre los sexos *f pl*; —**-specific**
    propio de un solo sexo
gene [ʤin] N gen *m*; — **marker** marcador
    genético *m*; — **pool** conjunto de genes de
    una población *m*; — **splicing** empalme
    genético *m*; — **therapy** terapia genética *f*
genealogy [ʤiniálədʒi] N genealogía *f*
general [ʤɛ́nɚəł] ADJ & N general *mf*; **in** —
    por lo general; — **practitioner** médico
    -ca general *mf*
generality [ʤɛnɚǽlɪDi] N generalidad *f*
generalize [ʤɛ́nɚəlaɪz] VI/VT generalizar
generate [ʤɛ́nɚet] VT generar
generation [ʤɛnɚéʃən] N generación *f*; —
    gap brecha generacional *f*, abismo
    generacional *m*
generator [ʤɛ́nɚeɪDɚ] N generador *m*
generic [ʤənérɪk] ADJ genérico
generosity [ʤɛnɚásɪDi] N generosidad *f*,
    larguez a *f*
generous [ʤɛ́nɚəs] ADJ generoso
genetic [ʤənédɪk] ADJ genético; — **code**
    código genético *m*; — **engineering**
    ingeniería genética *f*; — **fingerprinting**
    identificación genética *f*; — **marker**
    marcador genético *m*; —**s** genética *f*
genial [ʤínjəł] ADJ afable, de buen genio
genital [ʤénɪdl̩] ADJ genital; N — **herpes**
    herpes genital *m*; — **wart** verruga genital
    f; —**s** genitales *m pl*, sexo *m*
genius [ʤínjəs] N genio *m*
genocide [ʤɛ́nəsaɪd] N genocidio *m*
genome [ʤínom] N genoma *m*
genre [ʒánrə] N género *m*
genteel [ʤentíł] ADJ refinado
gentile [ʤéntaɪł] ADJ & N gentil *mf*
gentle [ʤéntl̩] ADJ (kindly) amable; (mild,
    slow, gradual) suave; (tame) manso
gentleman [ʤéntl̩mən] N caballero *m*
gentlemanly [ʤéntl̩mənli] ADJ caballeroso
gentleness [ʤéntl̩nɪs] N (kindness)
    amabilidad *f*; (mildness) suavidad *f*;

(tameness) mansedumbre *f*

genuine [ʤénjuɪn] ADJ genuino

genus [ʤínəs] N género *m*

geocentric [ʤiosɛ́ntrɪk] ADJ geocéntrico

geographical [ʤiəgrǽfɪkəɬ] ADJ geográfico

geography [ʤiágrəfi] N geografía *f*

geological [ʤiəláʤɪkəɬ] ADJ geológico

geology [ʤiáləʤi] N geología *f*

geometric [ʤiəmétrɪk] ADJ geométrico

geometry [ʤiámɪtri] N geometría *f*

geophysics [ʤiofízɪks] N geofísica *f*

Georgia [ʤɔ́rʤə] N Georgia *f*

Georgian [ʤɔ́rʤən] ADJ & N georgiano -na *mf*

geostationary [ʤiostéʃənɛri] ADJ geoestacionario

geothermal [ʤioθɝ́məɬ] ADJ geotérmico

geranium [ʤəréniəm] N geranio *m*

geriatric [ʤɛriǽtrɪk] ADJ geriátrico

germ [ʤɝm] N (microorganism) microbio *m*, germen *m*; (bud, embryo, rudiment) germen *m*; **— warfare** guerra biológica *f*

German [ʤɝ́mən] ADJ & N alemán -na *mf*; **— measles** rubeola, rubéola *f*; **— shepherd** pastor alemán *m*

germane [ʤɝmén] ADJ pertinente, relacionado

Germany [ʤɝ́məni] N Alemania *f*

germinate [ʤɝ́mənet] VI germinar; VT hacer germinar

gerund [ʤérənd] N gerundio *m*

gestate [ʤéstet] VI/VT gestar(se)

gestation [ʤestéʃən] N gestación *f*

gesticulate [ʤestíkjəlet] VI gesticular

gesture [ʤéstʃɚ] N gesto *m*, ademán *m*; (token) muestra *f*; VI gesticular

gesundheit [gəzúnthaɪt] INTERJ ¡salud! *Sp* ¡Jesús!

get [gɛt] VT (receive, earn) recibir; (obtain) obtener; (reach by phone, etc.) comunicarse con; (hear, understand) entender; (seize) agarrar; *Sp* coger; (prevail) conseguir, lograr; (affect) afectar; (strike) pegar, dar; (catch disease) pescar; *Sp* coger; **to — across** comunicar; **to — ahead** prosperar; **to — along (with)** llevarse bien (con); **to — angry** enojarse; **to — around** (skirt) esquivar, evitar; (go out) salir mucho; **to — away** escapar(se); **to — away with** quedar impune; **—away** (escape) escape *m*; (vacation) escapada *f*; **to — back** (return) volver; (recover) recuperar; **to — back at** vengarse de; **to be —ting on in years** ponerse viejo; **to — by** (go past) pasar; (survive) ir tirando; **to — down** (lower oneself) bajar; (depress) deprimir; (swallow) tragar; **to —**

down to business / brass tacks ir al grano; **from the —-go** desde el principio; **to — going** ponerse en marcha; **to — in** (enter) entrar; (arrive) llegar; (a vehicle) subir a; **to — it** captar, entender; **to — married** casarse; **to — nowhere** no llegar a ningún lado; **to — off** (dismount, get down) bajar; (not receive punishment) salir impune; (leave work) salir; **to — off on** enloquecerse por; **to — off someone's back** dejar de fastidiar; **to — old** envejecer; **to — on** montarse a; **to — out** (take out) sacar; (exit) salir; **to — over** (recuperate) recuperarse, sobreponerse a; (forgive) olvidar; **to — ready** preparar(se); **to — rich** enriquecerse; **to — rid of** deshacerse de; **to — sick** enfermarse; **to — somewhere** tener resultado; **to — through** (survive an ordeal) sobrevivir; (reach by phone, be understood) comunicarse; (complete) lograr terminar; **to — to someone** afectar a alguien; **to — together** reunirse; **—-together** reunión *f*; **to — up** (arise) levantarse; (prepare) montar; **—up** disfraz *m*, atuendo *m*; **I got him to do it** conseguí / logré que lo hiciera; **I have got to do it** tengo que hacerlo; **we got our house painted** pintamos la casa; **he got a year in jail** le dieron un año de cárcel; **we — to stay up late in summer** en el verano nos dejan quedarnos despiertos hasta tarde; **that —s my goat** eso me fastidia

geyser [gáɪzɚ] N géiser *m*

Ghana [gánə] N Ghana *f*

Ghanaian [gánəjən] ADJ & N ghanés -esa *mf*

ghastly [gǽstli] ADJ (horrible) horrendo, espantoso; (cadaverous) cadavérico

ghetto [géɖo] N gueto *m*

ghost [gost] N fantasma *m*; **not a — of a chance** ni la menor posibilidad; **— town** pueblo fantasma *m*; **—writer** colaborador -ora anónimo -ma *mf*

ghostly [góstli] ADJ fantasmagórico

ghoul [guɬ] N fantasma *m*

giant [ʤáɪənt] N & ADJ gigante -ta *mf*

gibberish [ʤíbɚɪʃ] N jerigonza *f*

gibbon [gíbən] N gibón *m*

Gibraltar [ʤɪbrɔ́ɬtɚ] N Gibraltar *m*

Gibraltarian [ʤɪbrɔɬtériən] ADJ & N gibraltareño -ña *mf*

giddy [gíɖi] ADJ (dizzy) mareado; (of heights) vertiginoso; (of speed) vertiginoso

gift [gɪft] N (thing given, act of giving) regalo *m*, presente *m*; (special ability) don *m*; **— certificate** vale por un regalo *m*;

—**-wrap** envolver para regalo; VT regalar

gifted [gíftɪd] ADJ (artist) talentoso; (child) superdotado

gigabyte [gígəbaɪt] N gigabyte *m*

gigantic [dʒaɪgǽntɪk] ADJ gigantesco, gigante

giggle [gígəł] VI reír tontamente; N risita tonta *f*

gild [gɪłd] VT dorar

gill [gɪł] N agalla *f*

gilt [gɪłt] ADJ & N dorado *m*

gimmick [gímɪk] N treta *f*, estratagema *f*

gin [dʒɪn] N (liquor) ginebra *f*; — **rummy** gin rummy *m*

ginger [dʒíndʒɚ] N jengibre *m*; — **ale** ginger ale *m*; —**bread** pan de jengibre *m*

gingham [gíŋəm] N guingán *m*

gingivitis [dʒɪndʒəváɪdɪs] N gingivitis *f*

giraffe [dʒəræf] N jirafa *f*

gird [gɜˑd] VT ceñir; **to — oneself** prepararse

girder [gɜˑDɚ] N viga *f*

girdle [gɜˑdl] N faja *f*; VT rodear

girl [gɜˑł] N (female child) niña *f*; (young female) muchacha *f*, joven *f*, chica *f*; (servant) muchacha *f*, chacha *f*; —**friend** novia *f*

girlhood [gɜˑłhʊd] N niñez *f*

girlish [gɜˑlɪʃ] ADJ de niña

girth [gɜˑθ] N (of things) circunferencia *f*; (of persons) contorno *m*; (of horses) cincha *f*; VT cinchar

gist [dʒɪst] N esencia *f*, lo esencial

give [gɪv] VT dar; (present as a gift) regalar; (organize a party) organizar; (assign a name) poner; (donate) donar; **I don't — a hoot** me importa un comino; VI dar; (yield) ceder; (break) romperse; **to — away** (a gift) regalar, donar; (the bride) entregar; (the truth) revelar; **to — back** devolver; **to — in** (acknowledge defeat) rendirse; (hand in) entregar; **to — off** emitir, despedir, desprender; **to — out** (announce) anunciar; (distribute) repartir; (become exhausted) rendirse; (run out) acabarse; **to — over** entregar; **to — up** (surrender) darse por vencido; (stop) dejar (de); **we'll work on this two years, — or take a month** vamos a trabajar en esto dos años, un mes más, un mes menos; N elasticidad *f*; — **and take** toma y daca *m*

given [gívən] ADJ (stated, fixed) dado; (bestowed) regalado; — **name** nombre de pila *m*; — **that she's not here** dado que ella no está; — **to** propenso a; N premisa *f*

giver [gívɚ] N dador -ora *mf*, donador -ora *mf*

gizmo [gízmo] N coso *m*, chisme *m*

glacial [gléʃəł] ADJ glacial

glacier [gléʃɚ] N glaciar *m*

glad [glæd] ADJ contento; **I'm — to see you** me alegro de verte; **I'd be — to help** sería un placer ayudarte

gladden [glǽdn̩] VT alegrar, regocijar, alborozar

gladiator [glǽDieDɚ] N gladiador *m*

glamorous [glǽmə-əs] ADJ glamoroso, encantador

glamour [glǽmɚ] N (charm) glamour *f*, encanto *m*; (excitement) atractivo *m*

glance [glæns] VI echar un vistazo; **to — off** rebotar con efecto; N (look) vistazo *m*; (bounce) rebote oblicuo *m*

gland [glænd] N glándula *f*

glandular [glǽndʒələ-] ADJ glandular

glare [glɛr] N (bright light) relumbre *m*; (stare) mirada furiosa *f*; VI (shine) relumbrar; (stare fiercely) lanzar una mirada hostil

glaring [glérɪŋ] ADJ (blinding) deslumbrante; (obvious) evidente; (hostile) hostil

glass [glæs] N (substance) vidrio *m*; (window pane) vidrio *m*, cristal *m*; (tumbler) vaso (de vidrio) *m*; (mirror) espejo *m*; (glassware) cristalería *f*; (magnifier) lupa *f*; —**blowing** soplado de vidrio *m*; — **cutter** cortavidrio *m*; —**es** anteojos *m pl*, lentes *m pl*, gafas *f pl*; — **eye** ojo de vidrio *m*; —**maker** vidriero -ra *mf*; —**ware** cristalería *f*

glassy [glǽsi] ADJ vidrioso

glaucoma [glɔkómə] N glaucoma *m*

glaze [glez] VT (a window) poner vidrios a; (ceramic) vidriar; (food) glasear; (varnish) barnizar; VI vidriarse; N (pottery) vidriado *m*, barniz *m*; (food) glaseado *m*

glazier [gléʒɚ] N vidriero -ra *mf*

gleam [glim] N reflejo *m*, brillo *m*; **a — of hope** un rayo de esperanza; VI brillar, relucir

glean [glin] VT (grain) espigar; (information) extraer, deducir

glee [gli] N regocijo *m*, júbilo *m*; — **club** coro *m*

glib [glɪb] ADJ (fluent) de mucha labia; (superficial) simplista, superficial

glide [glaɪd] VI (slide) deslizarse; (fly) planear; N (sliding movement) deslizamiento *m*; (flight) planeo *m*

glider [gláɪDɚ] N planeador *m*

glimmer [glímɚ] N luz trémula *f*; **a — of hope** un destello de esperanza; **the — of an idea** el atisbo de una idea; VI guiñar, emitir una luz trémula

glimpse [glɪmps] N (look) ojeada *f*, vistazo *m*; (hint) atisbo *m*; VT ojear

glint [glɪnt] N destello *m*; VI destellar
glisten [glísən] VI brillar, relucir
glitch [glɪtʃ] N problema técnico *m*
glitter [glíDɚ] VI destellar; N (light) destello *m*; (showiness) brillo *m*; (sparkling powder) brillantina *f*
gloat [glot] VI regodearse; N regodeo *m*
glob [glɑb] N pegote *m*
global [glóbəɫ] ADJ global, mundial; — **positioning system** sistema mundial de posicionamiento *m*; — **warming** calentamiento global *m*
globe [glob] N globo *m*; (map of the Earth) globo terráqueo *m*
globule [glábjuɫ] N glóbulo *m*
gloom [glum] N (darkness) oscuridad *f*; (melancholy) melancolía *f*, tristeza *f*
gloomy [glúmi] ADJ (dark, depressing) sombrío, lúgubre, tenebroso; (melancholic) melancólico, deprimido
glorify [glɔ́rəfaɪ] VT glorificar
glorious [glɔ́riəs] ADJ (wonderful) magnífico, excelente; (related to glory) glorioso
glory [glɔ́ri] N gloria *f*; VI **to — in** regocijarse con
gloss [glɔs] N (shine) brillo *m* (also cosmetics); (marginal note) glosa *f*; (in a dictionary) acepción *f*; VT (polish) lustrar, dar brillo a; (explain) glosar; **to — over** disfrazar, encubrir
glossary [glɔ́səri] N glosario *m*
glossy [glɔ́si] ADJ lustroso; (paper) glaseado
glove [glʌv] N guante *m*; — **compartment** guantera *f*
glow [glo] N incandescencia *f*; (of cheeks) rubor *m*; (of emotion) calor *m*; VI resplandecer; (of metal) estar al rojo vivo; (of cheeks) ruborizarse; **to — with health** estar rebosante de salud; —**worm** luciérnaga *f*
glowing [glóɪŋ] ADJ (with light) incandescente; (colors) vivo; (with health) rebosante; (report, etc.) favorable
glucose [glúkos] N glucosa *f*
glue [glu] N cola *f*, pegamento *m*; VT (put glue on) engomar; (stick together) pegar; (stick wood together) encolar
glum [glʌm] ADJ tristón
glut [glʌt] VI/VT (with food) hartar(se); VT (with products) saturar; N exceso *m*
glutton [glʌ́tṇ] N glotón -ona *mf*
gluttonous [glʌ́tṇəs] ADJ glotón
gluttony [glʌ́tṇi] N glotonería *f*, gula *f*
glycerin [glísəɪn] N glicerina *f*
gnarled [nɑrɫd] ADJ (knotty) nudoso, sarmentoso; (twisted) retorcido
gnash [næʃ] VI/VT rechinar

gnat [næt] N jején *m*
gnaw [nɔ] VI/VT (bite, corrode) roer; (torment) remorder; **to — a hole** hacer un agujero a mordiscos
GNP (gross national product) [dʒiɛnpí] N PNB *m*
gnu [nu] N ñu *m*
go [go] VI (move) ir; (function) andar, marchar; **to — against** oponerse a; **to — ahead** seguir adelante; —**-ahead** visto bueno *m*; **to — all out** dar todo de sí; **to — along** estar de acuerdo; **to — around** (circumvent) dar la vuelta a; (circulate) circular; (be sufficient) alcanzar; **to — around with** andar con; **to — away** irse; **to — back** volver; **to — back on one's word** faltar a la palabra; —**-between** intermediario -ria *mf*; **to — beyond** traspasar; **to — by** (pass) pasar; (be guided by) guiarse por; **to — by another name** usar otro nombre; **to — crazy** enloquecerse; —**-cart** kart *m*; **to — down** (descend) bajar; (fall) caer, estrellarse; (lose) perder; (be accepted) gustar; **to — down on** practicar sexo oral; **to — for** (attack) atacar; **pizza to —** pizza para llevar; **to — in with** participar; **to — it alone** tirarse solo; **to — off** (explode) estallar; (happen) suceder; (leave) irse; **to — on** (happen) pasar; (continue) seguir; **to — out** (extinguish) apagarse; (socialize) salir; **to — over** (review) repasar, revisar; (be accepted) gustar; (read) leer; (cross) cruzar; **to — through** (suffer) sufrir; (examine) examinar; (be approved) ser aprobado; (spend) gastar; **to — through with** llevar a cabo; **to — to sleep** dormirse; **to — under** (go bankrupt) quebrar; (sink) hundirse; **to — up** (building) levantarse; (prices) subir; **to let —** soltar(se); **the car went for a good price** el coche se vendió a un buen precio; **he's smart, as dogs —** para ser perro, es inteligente; **that old couch has got to —** hay que deshacernos de ese sofá viejo; **cows — "moo"** las vacas hacen "mu"; **she went straight for the pizza** se fue derechito a la pizza; **she's —ing to buy a house** va a comprar una casa; **anything —es** todo vale; **what I say —es** lo que yo digo, vale; **don't — to any trouble** no te molestes; **— figure!** ¡vaya a saber uno! **I've got to — (to the bathroom)** tengo que ir al baño; N (energy) energía *f*; (attempt) intento *m*; **in one —** de una vez; **on the —** a las corridas; **at the first**

— de primera; **they made a — of it** tuvieron éxito; **it's a —** ¡trato hecho! **from the word —** desde el vamos

goad [god] N aguijada *f*; VT aguijonear

goal [goł] N (objective) meta *f*; (score) gol *m*; **—keeper** portero -ra *mf*

goalie [góli] N guardameta *mf*

goat [got] N cabra *f*; **—herd** cabrero -ra *mf*; **he gets my —** me saca de quicio

goatee [gotí] N perilla *f*

gobble [gábəł] VI/VT (devour) engullir; VI (turkey) gluglutear; **to — up** engullir

gobbledygook [gábəłdiguk] N jerigonza *f*

gobbler [gáblɚ] N pavo *m*

goblet [gáblɪt] N copa *f*

goblin [gáblɪn] N duende *m*

god, God [gɑd] N dios *m*, Dios *m*; **God bless you!** ¡que Dios te bendiga! (after a sneeze) ¡salud! ¡Jesús! **—child** ahijado -da *mf*; **—damned** *vulg* maldito; **—father** padrino *m*; **—forsaken** de mala muerte; **—given** divino; **—mother** madrina *f*; **—send** bendición *f*; **God willing** si Dios quiere; **by God** por Dios; **my God!** ¡Dios mío!

goddess [gádɪs] N diosa *f*

godless [gádlɪs] ADJ impío

godly [gádli] ADJ piadoso

goggles [gágəłz] N gafas protectoras *f pl*, antiparras *f pl*

going [góɪŋ] ADJ que marcha bien; **—s-on** tejemaneje *m*

gold [gołd] N oro *m*; **a heart of —** un corazón de oro; **— digger** mujer cazafortunas *f*; **—finch** jilguero *m*; **—fish** pez dorado *m*; **— medal** medalla de oro *f*; **—smith** orfebre *m*

golden [gółdən] ADJ (made of gold) de oro, áureo; (of gold color) dorado; **— eagle** águila dorada *f*; **— retriever** golden retriever *m*; **— rule** regla de oro *f*

golf [gałf] N golf *m*; **— ball** pelota de golf *f*; **— club** (stick) palo de golf *m*; (place) club de golf *m*; **— course** campo de golf *m*

gondola [gándələ] N (boat, basket under a balloon) góndola *f*; (cable car) cabina *f*

gone [gɔn] ADJ **my computer is —** desapareció mi computadora; **the candy is all —** se acabaron los dulces

gong [gɑŋ] N batintín *m*, gong *m*

gonorrhea [gɑnəríə] N gonorrea *f*

good [gud] ADJ bueno; (valid) válido; **—-for-nothing** inútil, zanguango; **—-looking** guapo, apuesto; **—-natured** apacible, bonachón; **for —** para siempre; **a — hour** una hora larga; **a — many** muchos; **to have a — time** divertirse; **to**

make — cumplir; **to smell —** oler bien; N (moral act, benefit) bien *m*; **— for two burritos** vale por dos burritos; **—s** mercancías *f pl*; **—s and services** bienes y servicios *m pl*; **for your own —** por tu propio bien; **to deliver the —s** cumplir lo prometido; INTERJ ¡bien! **— afternoon** buenas tardes; **—bye** adiós; **— day** buenos días; **— evening** buenas noches; **— morning** buenos días; **— night** buenas noches

goodly [gúdli] ADJ (considerable) considerable; (of fine appearance) de buen aspecto

goodness [gúdnɪs] N bondad *f*; (of food) calidad *f*; INTERJ ¡Dios mío!

goody [gudi] N golosina *f*; **—-—** santurrón -ona *mf*; INTERJ ¡qué bien!

goof [guf] VI pifiar; **to — off** perder el tiempo; **to — up** pifiarla; N pifia *f*

goofy [gúfi] ADJ (person) bobalicón; (idea) tonto

goose [gus] N ganso -sa *mf* (also fool); VT sorprender a alguien tocándole entre las nalgas; **—berry** (berry) grosella espinosa *f*; (bush) grosellero *m*; **—bumps** carne de gallina *f*; **— egg** cero *m*

GOP (Grand Old Party) [ʤiopí] N Partido Republicano *m*

gopher [gófɚ] N ardilla de tierra *f*

gore [gɔr] N sangre derramada *f*; VT cornear

gorge [gɔrʤ] N (body part) garganta *f*; (ravine) garganta *f*, tajo *m*; VI **to — one's self (on)** atracarse (de), darse un atracón (de)

gorgeous [gɔ́rʤəs] ADJ (woman, outfit) precioso; (weather) espléndido

gorilla [gərílə] N gorila *mf*; (thug) matón *m*

gory [gɔ́ri] ADJ (of a battle) sangriento; (of a surface) ensangrentado

gospel [gáspəł] N evangelio *m*; (music) gospel *m*; **— truth** pura verdad *f*

gossip [gásəp] N (rumor) chismorreo *m*, murmuración *f*, habladurías *f pl*; (person) chismoso -sa *mf*; (woman) comadre *f*; **a piece of —** us chisme; VI chismear, murmurar

gossipy [gásəpi] ADJ chismoso, lenguaraz

Gothic [gáθɪk] ADJ gótico (also literature); N (language) gótico *m*; (style) estilo gótico *m*

gouge [gauʤ] N gubia *f*; VT (scoop) sacar con gubia; (overcharge) cobrar de más; **to — someone's eyes out** arrancarle los ojos a alguien

gourd [gɔrd] N calabaza *f*

gourmet [gɔrmé] N & ADJ gourmet *mf*; **— cheese** queso fino *m*

gout [gaʊt] N gota *f*

govern [gΛ́vɚn] VI/VT gobernar, regir; VT (in grammar) regir

governess [gΛ́vɚnɪs] N institutriz *f*

government [gΛ́vɚnmənt] N gobierno *m*; (in grammar) rección *f*

governmental [gΛvɚnméntl̩] ADJ gubernamental, gubernativo

governor [gΛ́vɚnɚ] N (leader) gobernador -ora *mf*; (of an engine) regulador *m*

gown [gaʊn] N (woman's dress) vestido *m*; (for sleeping) camisón *m*; (in hospital) bata *f*; (for graduation) toga *f*

grab [græb] VT agarrar, prender; **how does that idea — you?** ¿qué te parece esa idea? VI **to — at** tratar de agarrar; N agarrón *m*; **up for —s** a la rebatiña

grace [gres] N gracia *f*; (of movement) garbo *m*; (of expression) donaire *m*; **to say —** decir la oración; **to be in the good —s of someone** gozar del favor de alguien, disfrutar de la gracia de alguien; VT (adorn) adornar; (honor) honrar, agraciar

graceful [grésfəɫ] ADJ (of movement) grácil, garboso; (of behavior) donoso

gracefulness [grésfəɫnɪs] N gracia *f*, donaire *m*

gracious [gréʃəs] ADJ (kind) gentil, cortés; (elegant) elegante; (merciful) misericordioso; **—!** ¡válgame Dios!

graciousness [gréʃəsnɪs] N gentileza *f*

gradation [gredéʃən] N gradación *f*

grade [gred] N (degree) grado *m*; (category) calidad *f*; (year in school) año *m*, curso *m*; (marks) nota *f*, calificación *f*; (slope) declive *m*; **to make the —** alcanzar el nivel deseado; **— point average** promedio de notas *m*; VT (classify) clasificar; (assign grades) calificar, corregir; (level) nivelar

gradual [grǽdʒuəɫ] ADJ gradual

graduate [grǽdʒuɪt] N (advanced student) estudiante de posgrado *mf*; (degree-holder) graduado -da *mf*, egresado -da *mf*; ADJ de posgrado; **— school** programa de posgrado *m*; [grǽdʒuet] VI graduarse, titularse; VT (confer a degree) dar un diploma a; (mark a scale) graduar

graduation [grædʒuéʃən] N graduación *f*

graffiti [grəfíDi] N graffiti *m*

graft [græft] N (of plant, tissue) injerto *m*; (corruption) concusión *f*, corrupción *f*; VI/VT injertar(se)

grain [gren] N (cereal, seed) grano *m*, mies *f*; (photographic texture) grano *m*; (of gold) pepita *f*; (of wood, meat, stone) veta *f*; (texture) textura *f*; (small amount) pizca *f*;

against the — a / al redopelo, a contrapelo

gram [græm] N gramo *m*

grammar [grǽmɚ] N gramática *f*

grammatical [grəmǽDɪkəɫ] ADJ gramatical

granary [grénəri] N granero *m*, troje *m*

grand [grænd] ADJ (splendid) grandioso, espléndido; (lofty) elevado; (impressive) impresionante; **—child** nieto -ta *mf*; **—children** nietos *m pl*; **—daughter** nieta *f*; **—father** abuelo *m*; **— jury** jurado de acusación *m*; **—mother** abuela *f*; **—ma** abuelita *f*; **—pa** abuelito *m*; **—parent** abuelo *m*; **—parents** abuelos *m pl*; **— piano** piano de cola *m*; **—son** nieto *m*; **—stand** tribuna *f*; **a — old man** un gran señor; **the — total** el total

grandeur [grǽndʒɚ] N grandiosidad *f*

grandiose [grǽndios] ADJ (complex) complejo; (of speech) grandilocuente, rimbombante; (imposing) grandioso

granite [grǽnɪt] N granito *m*

grant [grænt] VT (give) conceder, otorgar, dispensar; (accept) admitir; (transfer) ceder; **to take for —ed** (an assumption) dar por sentado; (a person) no valorar; N (something granted) concesión *f*; (act of granting) concesión *f*, otorgamiento *m*; (subsidy) subvención *f*

granulate [grǽnjəlet] VI/VT granular(se)

grape [grep] N uva *f*; **—fruit** pomelo *m*, toronja *f*; **—vine** vid *f*; (ornamental) parra *f*; **I heard it through the —vine** me lo contó un pajarito

graph [græf] N (curve) gráfica *f*; VT grafiar; **— paper** papel cuadriculado *m*

graphic [grǽfɪk] ADJ gráfico; **— design** diseño gráfico *m*; N gráfico *m*; **—s** gráfica *f*

graphite [grǽfaɪt] N grafito *m*

grapple [grǽpəɫ] VI/VT (hold) aferrar; (struggle) luchar, lidiar

grasp [græsp] VT (seize) agarrar, asir, aferrar; (understand) comprender; VI **to — at / for** tratar de agarrar; N (hold) agarre *m*, asidero *m*; (comprehension) comprensión *f*; **within one's —** al alcance; **to have a good — of a subject** dominar una materia

grass [græs] N (plant) hierba *f*; (lawn) césped *m*; (pasture) pasto *m*; (marijuana) marihuana *f*, maría *f*; **—hopper** saltamontes *m sg*, saltón *m*; **—land** pradera *f*, pastizal *m*; **— roots** las bases *f pl*

grassy [grǽsi] ADJ herboso

grate [gret] N (of a fireplace) parrilla *f*; (partition, guard) reja *f*, verja *f*; VT (install a grate) enrejar; (mince) rallar; (rub teeth together) crujir, rechinar; VI **to — on** rechinar

grateful [grétfəł] ADJ agradecido

grater [grédə-] N rallador *m*

gratification [græDəfɪkéʃən] N gratificación *f*

gratify [grǽDəfaɪ] VT complacer, gratificar

grating [gréDɪŋ] N reja *f*, enrejado *m*, rejilla *f*; ADJ (discordant) rechinante; (irritating) irritante

gratitude [grǽDɪtud] N gratitud *f*

gratuitous [grətúɪDəs] ADJ gratuito

gratuity [grətúɪDi] N propina *f*

grave [grev] ADJ grave; N fosa *f*, sepultura *f*; **—digger** sepulturero *m*; **—stone** lápida *f*; **—yard** cementerio *m*; **—yard shift** turno de la noche *m*; **to have one foot in the —** *fam* estar por reventar

gravel [grǽvəł] N grava *f*; VT cubrir con grava

gravitation [grævɪtéʃən] N gravitación *f*

gravity [grǽvɪDi] N gravedad *f* (also seriousness)

gravy [grévi] N jugo de carne *m*; **the rest is —** el resto es fácil

gray [gre] ADJ gris; (hair) canoso; (horses) rucio; **— area** zona gris *f*; **—-haired** cano, canoso; **— matter** materia gris *f*; N gris *m*; VI/VT agrisar; (hair) encanecer

grayish [gréɪʃ] ADJ grisáceo

graze [grez] VI/VT (feed) pacer, pastar, apacentar; (brush) rozar; N roce *m*

grease [gris] N grasa *f*; VT engrasar; **to — someone's palm** untarle la mano a alguien, engrasar a alguien

greasy [grísi, grízi] ADJ grasiento, grasoso

great [gret] ADJ (large, numerous) grande; **a — tree blocked the path** un árbol grande bloqueaba el camino; (good, excellent, considerable) gran; **she's a — friend** es una gran amiga; (long) largo; **a — while** un largo rato; (skillful) excelente; **she's — at tennis** juega muy bien al tenis; **a — deal of** mucho; ADV muy bien, excelente; **she did —** le fue muy bien; N **the —s** los/las grandes *mf*; **—-grandchild** bisnieto -ta *mf*; **—-grandfather** bisabuelo *m*; **—-grandmother** bisabuela *f*; **—-grandchild** tataranieto -ta *mf*; INTERJ ¡qué bien!

greatness [grétnɪs] N grandeza *f*

Greece [gris] N Grecia *f*

greed [grid] N codicia *f*

greedy [gríDi] ADJ (covetous) codicioso; (voracious) voraz; (eager) ávido

Greek [grik] ADJ & N griego -ga *mf*; **that's — to me** eso es chino

green [grin] ADJ verde; (verdant, unripe, inexperienced, nauseated, environmentally conscious) verde; N (color) verde *m*; (lawn) césped *m*; (pasture) prado *m*; (in golf) green *m*; (commons) ejido *m*; **—back** dólar *m*; **— bean** *Sp* judía verde *f*; *Mex* ejote *m*; *RP* chaucha *f*; **— card** tarjeta verde *f*; **—horn** novato -ta *mf*; **—house** invernadero *m*; **—house effect** efecto invernadero *m*; **— light** luz verde *f*; **— pepper** pimiento verde *m*; **—s** verduras de hoja verde *f pl*

greenish [gríniʃ] ADJ verdoso

greenness [grínnɪs] N verdor *m*

greet [grit] VT (say hello) saludar; (welcome) dar la bienvenida; (receive) recibir

greeting [gríDɪŋ] N saludo *m*; **— card** tarjeta de felicitación *f*; **—s!** ¡saludos!

gregarious [grɪgériəs] ADJ (animal) gregario; (person) sociable

gremlin [grémlɪn] N duende *m*

Grenada [grənéDə] N Granada *f*

grenade [grənéd] N granada *f*

Grenadian [grənéDiən] ADJ & N granadino -na *mf*

greyhound [gréhaʊnd] N galgo *m*

griddle [grídł] N plancha *f*

gridlock [grídlɑk] N paralización *f*; VI paralizarse

grief [grif] N congoja *f*, pesar *m*, pesadumbre *f*; **to come to —** sufrir una desgracia; **to give someone —** meterse con alguien, jorobar a alguien; **good —!** ¡caramba!

grievance [grívəns] N (complaint) queja *f*; (cause for complaint) motivo de queja *m*

grieve [griv] VI estar de duelo; **to — for / over** llorar (la muerte de alguien); **he's grieving over the loss of his dog** lamenta la muerte de su perro; VT **that —s me** eso me apena

grieved [grivd] ADJ apenado

grievous [grívəs] ADJ (painful) doloroso, penoso; (atrocious) grave, atroz; (sorrowful) dolido

grill [grɪł] N (metal grid, restaurant fixture) parrilla *f*; (dish) parrillada *f*; VI/VT asar a la parrilla; (interrogate) interrogar

grille [grɪł] N parrilla *f*

grim [grɪm] ADJ (news, situation) desalentador; (war) cruento; (joke) macabro

grimace [grímɪs] N mueca *f*, mohín *m*; VI hacer muecas

grime [graɪm] N mugre *f*, suciedad *f*

grimy [gráɪmi] ADJ mugriento, sucio; **to make —** percudir; **to get —** percudirse

grin [grɪn] VI sonreír; N sonrisa *f*; **wipe that**

— off your face deja de reírte

grind [graɪnd] VI/VT (mill finely) moler; (mill coarsely) triturar; (make shiny) pulir; (rub harshly) rechinar; (study hard) estudiar mucho; *Sp* empollar; **to — to a halt** pararse con un chirrido; N (drudgery) trabajo pesado *m*; (overzealous student) empollón -ona *mf*; **the daily —** la lucha diaria; **—stone** muela *f*; **to keep one's nose to the —stone** matarse trabajando / estudiando

grinder [gráɪndə] N (for coffee, pepper) molinillo *m*; (for meat) picadora *f*; (for sharpening tools) afilador *m*

grip [grɪp] N (hold) agarre *m*; (control) control *m*; (handle) mango *m*; **he had a firm — on the tool** tenía bien agarrada la herramienta; **get a — on yourself** contrólate, cálmate; VT (seize) agarrar, asir; (take hold, interest) atrapar

gripe [graɪp] VI quejarse, rezongar, renegar; N queja *f*

grisly [grízli] ADJ cruento, espantoso

gristle [grísəł] N cartílago *m*

grit [grɪt] N (sand) arena *f*; (pluck) firmeza *f*, *fam* cojones *m pl*; **—s** sémola de maíz *f*; VT apretar

gritty [gríɖi] ADJ (sandy) arenoso; (plucky) resuelto, *fam* cojonudo

grizzly [grízli] ADJ (grayish) grisáceo; **— bear** oso pardo *m*

groan [gron] N quejido *m*, gemido *m*; VI quejarse, gemir; (creak) crujir

grocer [grósə] N tendero -ra *mf*; *Mex* abarrotero -ra *mf*; *Caribbean* bodeguero -ra *mf*; *RP* almacenero -ra *mf*

grocery [grósəri] N tienda de comestibles *f*; *Mex* tienda de abarrotes *f*; *Caribbean* bodega *f*; *RP* almacén *m*; **groceries** comestibles *m pl*

groin [grɔɪn] N ingle *f*

groom [grum] N (in a wedding) novio *m*; (in a stable) mozo de cuadra *m*, caballerizo *m*; VT (a horse) almohazar; (prepare for a position) preparar; **to — oneself** arreglarse; **well--ed** bien arreglado

groove [gruv] N (narrow cut) estría *f*, ranura *f*; (on a record, road) surco *m*; (routine) rutina *f*; VT estriar, acanalar

grope [grop] VI (feel one's way) andar a tientas; (search) buscar a tientas; VT manosear, toquetear; N manoseo *m*, toqueteo *m*

gross [gros] ADJ (before deductions) bruto; (flagrant) flagrante; (indecent) grosero; (overall) general; (disgusting) asqueroso; **— domestic product** producto interno

bruto *m*; N gruesa *f*; VT recaudar en bruto; **to — out** dar asco, asquear

grotesque [grotésk] ADJ grotesco

grotto [gráɖo] N gruta *f*

grouch [grautʃ] N cascarrabias *mf sg*, refunfuñón -ona *mf*, rezongón -ona *mf*; VI refunfuñar

grouchy [gráutʃi] ADJ cascarrabias, refunfuñón

ground [graʊnd] N (land) tierra *f* (also electrical); (soil) suelo *m*; (basis) fundamento *m*; **—s** (reason) motivo *m*; (dregs) borra *f*, poso *m*; (tract of land) terreno *m*; **— floor** planta baja *f*; **—hog** marmota *f*; **to gain / lose —** ganar / perder terreno; **to stand one's —** ponerse firme; **from the — up** de piso a techo; VT (a wire) conectar a tierra; (a ship) hacer encallar; (punish) poner en penitencia; **the 747 was —ed** se prohibió volar en el 747

groundless [gráʊndlɪs] ADJ infundado

group [grup] N grupo *m*; **— therapy** terapia de grupo *f*; VI/VT agrupar(se)

grouper [grúpə] N mero *m*

groupie [grúpi] N admirador -ra *mf*

grove [grov] N arboleda *f*, plantío *m*; **orange —** naranjal *m*

grovel [grávəł] VI arrastrarse, humillarse

grow [gro] VI (naturally increase in size) crecer; (increase) aumentar, acrecentarse; (expand) desarrollarse; VT (crops) cultivar; (beard) dejarse crecer; **to — old** envejecer; **to — up** madurar; **Thai food —s on you** la comida tailandesa acaba gustándote

growl [graʊł] VI gruñir; (of thunder) retumbar; (of stomach) rugir; N gruñido *m*

grown [gron] ADJ adulto; **— man** hombre hecho y derecho *m*; **— up** adulto *m*; **—-up** para adultos

growth [groθ] N (increase in size) crecimiento *m*; (increase in number) aumento *m*, acrecentamiento *m*; (tumor) bulto *m*; (expansion) desarrollo *m*; **a — industry** una industria en expansión

grudge [grʌdʒ] N resentimiento *m*

grueling [grúəlɪŋ] ADJ arduo

gruesome [grúsəm] ADJ cruento, truculento

gruff [grʌf] ADJ (manner) bronco; (voice) ronco

grumble [grʌ́mbəł] VI/VT refunfuñar, rezongar; N refunfuño *m*, gruñido *m*

grumpy [grʌ́mpi] ADJ refunfuñón, gruñón, rezongón

grunt [grʌnt] VI/VT gruñir; N gruñido *m*

guarantee [gærəntí] N (promise, pledge)

garantía *f*; (guaranty) fianza *f*; VT (promise, pledge) garantizar; (warrant) dar fianza, avalar

guarantor [gǽrəntɔr] N fiador -ora *mf*

guaranty [gǽrənti] N (guarantee) garantía *f*; (thing taken as security) fianza *f*; (guarantor) fiador -ora *mf*

guard [gɑrd] VT custodiar; (watch over) vigilar; (protect) proteger; VI protegerse; **to — against** guardarse de; N (person that guards) guardia *mf*, guarda *mf*; (of a machine) dispositivo protector *m*; **to be on —** estar alerta / estar en guardia; **— dog** perro guardián *m*; **—rail** baranda *f*, pasamano *m*

guardian [gárᴅiən] N guardián -ana *mf*; (legal) tutor -ora *mf*; **— angel** ángel de la guarda *m*

guardianship [gárᴅiənʃɪp] N tutela *f*

Guatemala [gwɑᴅəmálə] N Guatemala *f*

Guatemalan [gwɑᴅəmálən] ADJ & N guatemalteco -ca *mf*

guava [gwávə] N guayaba *f*

guess [ges] VT (hazard, conjecture) adivinar; (suppose) suponer; N (conjecture) conjetura *f*; (supposition) suposición *f*; **I'll give you three —es** te doy tres oportunidades para adivinar

guest [gest] N (to a party, function) invitado -da *mf*; (to a restaurant) cliente *mf*; (overnight) huésped *mf*

guffaw [gəfɔ́] N carcajada *f*, risotada *f*

guidance [gáɪdn̩s] N (act of guiding) dirección *f*; (counsel) orientación *f*; (in a missile) teledirección *f*

guide [gaɪd] VT guiar; (force to move) dirigir; (counsel) orientar; N (person) guía *mf*; (publication, mechanism) guía *f*; **—book** guía *f*; **— dog** perro guía *m*; **—d missile** misil guiado *m*; **—lines** directivas *f pl*, pautas *f pl*

guild [gɪld] N gremio *m*, corporación *f*

guile [gaɪl] N astucia *f*

guilt [gɪlt] N culpa *f*; **— trip** manipulación por acusaciones falsas *f*

guiltless [gíltlɪs] ADJ inocente

guilty [gílti] ADJ culpable; **we find the defendant not —** hallamos al acusado inocente

Guinea [gíni] N Guinea *f*; **— pig** conejillo de Indias *m*; **—-Bissau** Guinea-Bissau *f*

Guinean [gíniən] ADJ & N guineano -na *mf*

guise [gaɪz] ADV LOC **under the — of** so / bajo pretexto de; **in the — of** a manera de

guitar [gɪtár] N guitarra *f*

gulf [gʌlf] N (body of water) golfo *m*; (abyss, gap) abismo *m*; **— Stream** corriente del Golfo *f*

gull [gʌl] N (bird) gaviota *f*; (dupe) crédulo -la *mf*; *Sp* primo -ma *mf*

gullet [gálɪt] N gaznate *m*

gullible [gáləbəl] ADJ crédulo, ingenuo

gully [gáli] N barranco *m*, barranca *f*; (gutter) alcantarilla *f*

gulp [gʌlp] VT tragar saliva; N trago *m*

gum [gʌm] N goma *f*; (for chewing) chicle *m*; **—s** encías *f pl*; VT **to — up** (ruin) jorobar; (stick) pegotear

gumption [gámpʃən] N (initiative) iniciativa *f*, arranque *m*; (courage) agallas *f pl*

gun [gʌn] N (firearm) arma de fuego *f*; (revolver) revólver *m*; (rifle) rifle *m*; (shotgun) escopeta *f*; (cannon) cañón *m*; (for painting, nailing) pistola *f*; VT (an engine) acelerar; **to — down** matar a tiros; **to — for** andar a la caza de; **to stick to one's —s** mantenerse firme; **don't jump the —** no te precipites; **to be under the —** estar bajo mucha presión; **—boat** cañonero *m*; **—fire** tiroteo *m*; **—man** pistolero *m*; **at —point** a mano armada; **—powder** pólvora *f*; **—shot** disparo *m*

gung-ho [gáŋhó] ADJ fanático, entusiasta

gunner [gánɚ] N (shooting artillery) artillero -ra *mf*; (shooting a machine gun) ametrallador -ora *mf*

gurgle [gɝgəl] VI (water) borbotar; (baby) gorjear; N (of water) borboteo *m*; (of a baby) gorjeo *m*

gush [gʌʃ] VI (liquids) chorrear, brotar; (talk effusively) hablar con efusividad

gust [gʌst] N ráfaga *f*; **— of wind** racha / ráfaga de viento *f*, ventolera *f*; VI soplar en ráfagas

gusto [gásto] N (pleasure) placer *m*; (enthusiasm) entusiasmo *m*

gut [gʌt] N tripa *f*; (belly) barriga *f*; **— feeling** corazonada *f*; **—s** (intestines) entrañas *f pl*; (courage) *fam* cojones *m pl*; VT (eviscerate) destripar; (destroy the insides of) destrozar el interior de; (strip) desarmar

gutsy [gátsi] ADJ *fam* cojonudo

gutter [gáɖɚ] N (in the street) alcantarilla *f*; (on the roof) canaleta *f*, desagüe *m*; (squalor) miseria *f*

guy [gaɪ] N (man) tipo *m*; *Sp* tío *m*; **you —s** *Sp* vosotros / vosotras, ustedes; **— wire** cable *m*

Guyana [gaɪánə] N Guyana *f*

Guyanese [gaɪəníz] ADJ & N guyanés -esa *mf*

gym [ʤɪm] N gimnasio *m*

gymnasium [dʒɪmnézɪəm] N gimnasio *m*
gymnastics [dʒɪmnǽstɪks] N gimnasia *f*
gynecology [gaɪnəkáləʤi] N ginecología *f*
gyp [dʒɪp] VT estafar, timar; N estafa *f*, timo *m*
gypsum [dʒípsəm] N yeso *m*
gypsy [dʒípsi] N & ADJ gitano -na *mf*
gyrate [dʒáɪret] VI girar
gyroscope [dʒáɪrəskop] N giroscopio *m*

Hh

habit [hǽbɪt] N (custom) hábito *m*, costumbre *f*; (clerical dress) hábito *m*; (vice) vicio *m*; —**-forming** que genera dependencia
habitat [hǽbɪtæt] N hábitat *m*
habitual [həbítʃuəɫ] ADJ habitual
hack [hæk] N (cut) tajo *m*, machetazo *m*; (cough) tos seca *f*; (horse for hire) caballo de alquiler *m*; (nag) jamelgo *m*; (writer) escritor -a mercenario -ria *mf*; VI/VT tajar, cortar a machetazos; VI toser con tos seca; —**saw** sierra para metales *f*
hag [hæg] N (witch) bruja *f*; (ugly old woman) vieja fea *f*
haggard [hǽgəd] ADJ demacrado
haggle [hǽgəɫ] VI regatear
hail [heɫ] N (precipitation) granizo *m*; (greeting) saludo *m*; (shout) llamada *f*; — **Mary** Ave María *f*; —**storm** granizada *f*; VI (precipitate) granizar; VT (greet) saludar; (call out) llamar; (acclaim) aclamar; **to — from** ser oriundo de
hair [hɛr] N pelo *m*; (of the head only) cabello *m*; (of the body only) vello *m*; (on plants) pelusa *f*; —**brush** cepillo para el cabello *m*; —**cut** corte de pelo *m*; **to get a —cut** cortarse el pelo; —**do** peinado *m*; —**dresser** peluquero -ra *mf*, peinador -ora *mf*; — **follicle** folículo capilar *m*; —**piece** postizo *m*; —**pin** horquilla *f*; —**-raising** horripilante, espeluznante; —**spray** fijador *m*
hairless [hérlɪs] ADJ (deprived of hair) pelado; (growing no hair) lampiño
hairy [héri] ADJ (including head) peludo; (body only) velludo
Haiti [héɪti] N Haití *m*
Haitian [héʃən] ADJ & N haitiano -na *mf*
hake [hek] N merluza *f*
half [hæf] N mitad *f*; — **an apple** media manzana *f*; ADJ medio; —**-baked** (not fully cooked) a medio cocer; (not fully

developed) mal concebido; —**-breed** mestizo -za *mf*; — **brother** medio hermano *m*; —**-cocked** mal preparado; **he went off half-cocked** actuó precipitadamente; —**-cooked** a medio cocer; —**-dozen** media docena *f*; —**-hearted** desganado; —**-hour** media hora *f*; —**-moon** media luna *f*; — **note** blanca *f*; —**-open** entreabierto, entornado; — **past one** la una y media; —**time** medio tiempo *m*; —**way** a medio camino; —**way measures** medidas parciales *f pl*; —**way point** punto medio *m*; —**-wit** *pej* imbécil *mf*, papamoscas *mf*; **at —-mast** a media asta; **to do something —way** hacer algo a medias; **to go halves** ir a medias
halibut [hǽləbət] N hipogloso *m*
hall [hɔɫ] N (corridor) corredor *m*, pasillo *m*; (large room) salón *m*; (building) edificio *m*; —**mark** distintivo *m*; —**way** (corridor) corredor *m*, pasillo *m*; (entrance) zaguán *m*, vestíbulo *m*
Halloween [hæləwín] N víspera del día de Todos los Santos *f*, noche de brujas *f*
hallucinate [həlúsənet] VI alucinar
halo [hélo] N halo *m*, aureola *f*
halogen [hǽləʤən] ADJ halógeno
halt [hɔɫt] N **to come to a —** detenerse; VI/VT parar, detener(se); —! ¡alto!
halter [hɔ́ɫtə] N cabestro *m*
halting [hɔ́ɫtɪŋ] ADJ vacilante
halve [hæv] VT partir por la mitad
ham [hæm] N (meat) jamón *m*; (attention getter) payaso *m*; —**string** (human) ligamento de la corva *m*; (horse) tendón del jarrete *m*; **to — it up** sobreactuar, exagerar
hamburger [hǽmbɚgɚ] N (meat) carne picada de vaca *f*; (sandwich or patty) hamburguesa *f*
hamlet [hǽmlɪt] N aldea *f*, poblado *m*, caserío *m*
hammer [hǽmɚ] N martillo *m*; VI/VT martillar, amartillar; **to — out** (an agreement) forjar; (differences) negociar
hammock [hǽmək] N hamaca *f*
hamper [hǽmpɚ] N canasto *m*, cesto *m*; VT impedir, embarazar
hamster [hǽmstɚ] N hámster *m*
hand [hænd] N mano *f*; (of a clock) aguja *f*, manecilla *f*; (farm helper) peón *m*; —**bag** (purse) bolsa *f*, cartera *f*; (valise) maletín *m*; —**ball** (American) pelota *f*, frontón *m*; (European) balonmano *m*; —**bill** volante *m*; —**cuffs** esposas *f pl*; — **grenade** granada de mano *f*, bomba de piña *f*;

—gun revólver *m*; **—held** de mano; **— in — **(cogidos) de la mano; **—kerchief** pañuelo *m*; **—made** hecho a mano; **—out** (notes) repartido *m*, notas *f pl*; (alms) limosna *f*; **—saw** serrucho *m*; **—shake** apretón de manos *m*; **—s-on** práctico; **—stand** pino *m*, paro de manos *m*; **—work** trabajo manual *m*; **—writing** letra *f*; **at —** (within reach) al alcance; (about to happen) cerca; **on —** disponible, a mano; **on the other —** en cambio, por otra parte; **to have one's —s full** estar ocupadísimo; VT entregar, dar; **to —cuff** esposar; **to — down** (a thing) pasar; (a judgment) pronunciar; **to — in** entregar; **to — over** entregar

handful [hǽndfʊɫ] N manojo *m*, puñado *m*

handicap [hǽndikæp] N (physical disability) impedimento *m*; (mental disability) retardo *m*; (disadvantage) desventaja *f*; **physically —ped** minusválido físico; **— race** carrera de hándicap *f*; VT (hinder) perjudicar, handicapar; (injure) lisiar

handiwork [hǽndiwɝk] N labor *f*

handle [hǽndl̩] N (straight) mango *m*; (curved) asa *f*; (of a drawer) manija *f*; (of a knife) empuñadura *f*, puño *m*; **—bar** manubrio *m*; VT (manage) manejar; (touch) manipular, tocar; (deal in) comerciar en; **the car —s easily** el coche tiene buena maniobrabilidad

handling [hǽndlɪŋ] N (dealing) manejo *m*; (touching) manipulación *f*; (charge) porte *m*; (of a car) maniobrabilidad *f*

handsome [hǽnsəm] ADJ guapo, bien parecido; **a — sum** una suma considerable

handy [hǽndi] ADJ (near) a (la) mano; (practical) práctico; (skillful) hábil, diestro; **—man** hombre habilidoso *m*

hang [hæŋ] VI/VT colgar, suspender; **— glider** ala delta *f*; **—man** verdugo *m*; **—nail** padrastro *m*; **—out** sitio frecuentado *m*; **—over** resaca *f*; **—-up** complejo *m*; VT (door) colocar; (one's head) inclinar; VI pender; **— in there!** ¡ánimo! **to — around** quedarse por ahí, rondar; **to — on** (hold tight) agarrarse bien; (persevere) aguantar; (wait) esperar; **to — out** (be outside) estar fuera; (hang around with) andar (con); **to — over** sobresalir; **to — paper on a wall** empapelar una pared; **to — up** colgar; **sentenced to —** condenado a la horca; N caída *f*; **to get the — of something** agarrarle la onda a algo

hangar [hǽŋɝ] N hangar *m*

hanger [hǽŋɝ] N colgadero *m*; (for clothes) percha *f*

hanging [hǽŋɪŋ] N muerte en la horca *f*; **—s** colgaduras *f pl*, tapiz *m*; ADJ colgante

hanky-panky [hǽŋkipǽŋki] N (deceit) tejemaneje *m*; (illicit sexual activity) aventuras *f pl*

haphazard [hæphǽzɝd] ADV a la buena de Dios; ADJ irregular

happen [hǽpən] VI suceder, pasar, acontecer; **I — to know** da la casualidad de que sé; **to — to pass by** acertar a pasar; **to — upon** encontrarse con, toparse con

happening [hǽpənɪŋ] N acontecimiento *m*, suceso *m*

happiness [hǽpɪnɪs] N felicidad *f*, dicha *f*

happy [hǽpi] ADJ (satisfied) feliz, dichoso; (pleased) contento; (lucky) afortunado; **— ending** final feliz *m*; **to be — to** hacer algo de buena gana

harangue [hərǽŋ] N arenga *f*; VT arengar

harass [hərǽs] VT acosar, hostigar

harbor [hárbɝ] N (for ships) puerto *m*; (refuge) refugio *m*; VT (refugees, suspicions) albergar; (hopes) abrigar

hard [hɑrd] ADJ (firm) duro; (erect) tieso; (difficult) difícil; (arduous) arduo; **to play —ball** ser despiadado; **— cash** dinero contante y sonante *m*; **— coal** antracita *f*; **— copy** copia *f*; **— core** núcleo resistente *m*; **—-core** (pornography) duro; (politics) radical; **— disk** disco duro *m*; **— hat** casco *m*; **—headed** testarudo; **—hearted** duro de corazón; **— liquor** bebida alcohólica fuerte *f*; **— luck** mala suerte *f*; **— of hearing** medio sordo; **—-on** erección *f*; **he had a —-on** la tenía dura; **—-pressed** en aprietos; **—ware** (metal articles) ferretería *f*; (computer) hardware *m*; **—ware store** ferretería *f*; **—wood** madera noble *f*; **— water** agua dura *f*; **— winter** invierno crudo *m*; **—-wired** programado; **—-working** trabajador; ADV (fall, push) con fuerza; (work) duro, con ahinco

harden [hárdn̩] VI/VT (make or become hard) endurecer(se); (make or become experienced) curtir(se)

hardening [hárdnɪŋ] N endurecimiento *m*

hardly [hárdli] ADV (scarcely) apenas; (at all) en absoluto; **— anyone** casi nadie; **— surprising** nada sorprendente

hardness [hárdnɪs] N dureza *f*

hardship [hárdʃɪp] N penuria *f*, penalidad *f*

hardy [hárdi] ADJ robusto

hare [hɛr] N liebre *f*; **—brained** descabellado; **—lip** labio leporino *m*

harem [hérəm] N harén *m*

harm [hɑrm] N daño *m*, mal *m*, perjuicio *m*; VT (object) dañar; (person) hacer daño; (chances) perjudicar

harmful [hɑ́rmfəł] ADJ perjudicial, dañino, nocivo

harmless [hɑ́rmlɪs] ADJ inocuo, inofensivo

harmonic [hɑrmɑ́nɪk] ADJ & N armónico *m*

harmonious [hɑrmóniəs] ADJ armonioso

harmonize [hɑ́rmənaɪz] VI/VT armonizar

harmony [hɑ́rməni] N armonía *f*

harness [hɑ́rnɪs] N arnés *m*, jaez *m*, guarnición *f*; VT (put on a harness) enjaezar; (utilize) aprovechar

harp [hɑrp] N arpa *f*; VI (play the harp) tocar el arpa; (insist) machacar; **to — on** insistir sobre

harpoon [hɑrpún] N arpón *m*; VT arponear

harpsichord [hɑ́rpsɪkɔrd] N clavicémbalo *m*

harrowing [hǽroɪŋ] ADJ angustioso; — **adventure** aventura espeluznante *f*

harry [hǽri] VT acosar, hostigar

harsh [hɑrʃ] ADJ (words) duro; (surface) áspero; (discipline) severo, férreo; (winter) crudo, riguroso

harshness [hɑ́rʃnɪs] N (of words) dureza *f*; (of a surface) aspereza *f*; (of character) severidad *f*; (of a winter) rigor *m*

harvest [hɑ́rvɪst] N cosecha *f*; (of sugar) zafra *f*; VT cosechar

hash [hæʃ] N guisado *m*, picadillo *m*

hashish [hǽʃíʃ] N hachís *m*

hassle [hǽsəł] N rollo *m*, lío *m*; VT jorobar

haste [hest] N prisa *f*; **in —** de prisa; **to make —** darse prisa, apresurarse; *Am* apurarse

hasten [hésən] VI apresurarse; *Am* apurarse; VT acelerar, adelantar

hasty [hésti] ADJ apresurado, precipitado, presuroso; *Am* apurado; **to be —** precipitarse, apresurarse

hat [hæt] N sombrero *m*

hatch [hætʃ] VI/VT (chicks) empollar; (plot, scheme) fraguar, maquinar; N (chicks) nidada *f*; (opening) escotilla *f*; — **way** escotilla *f*

hatchet [hǽtʃɪt] N hacha *f*; — **job** crítica feroz *f*; — **man** sicario *m*; **to bury the —** hacer las paces

hate [het] N odio *m*; VI/VT odiar; **I — to admit it** me molesta admitirlo; **I — eating leftovers** detesto comer restos

hateful [hétfəł] ADJ odioso, aborrecible

hatred [hétrɪd] N odio *m*

haughtiness [hɔ́ɔɪnɪs] N altivez *f*, altanería *f*, soberbia *f*

haughty [hɔ́ɔi] ADJ altivo, altanero, soberbio

haul [hɔł] VT (transport) transportar; (drag) arrastrar; VI (pull) jalar (de), tirar (de); N (quantity transported) carga *f*; (tug) tirón *m*; (catch of fish) redada *f*; (stolen goods) botín *m*; **long —** distancia larga *f*

haunch [hɔntʃ] N anca *f*

haunt [hɔnt] VI/VT (frequent) frecuentar; (enchant) rondar; **that idea —s me** me obsesiona esa idea; **—ed house** casa embrujada *f*; N (of animals, criminals) guarida *f*; (of people socializing) sitio frecuentado *m*

have [hæv] V AUX haber; VT tener; **to — to** tener que; **to — a baby** dar a luz; **to — a look at** echar una mirada a; **to — a suit made** mandarse hacer un traje; **— him come later** dile que venga más tarde; **what did she — on?** ¿qué tenía puesto? **we've been had** nos estafaron

haven [hévən] N abrigo *m*, refugio *m*

havoc [hǽvək] N estrago *m*; **to wreak —** hacer estragos

hawk [hɔk] N gavilán *m*; VT pregonar

hay [he] N heno *m*; — **fever** alergia al polen *f*; — **loft** henil *m*; **—seed** paleto -ta *mf*; **—stack** almiar *m*; **to look for a needle in a —** buscar una aguja en un pajar

hazard [hǽzəd] N (chance) azar *m*; (danger) peligro *m*; VT arriesgar, aventurar

hazardous [hǽzədəs] ADJ peligroso

haze [hez] N neblina *f*, calina *f*; VT atormentar (como parte de un rito de iniciación)

hazel [hézəł] N avellano *m*; **—nut** avellana *f*; ADJ de avellano

hazy [hézi] ADJ (weather) brumoso; (idea) confuso, vago

he [hi] PRON él; **—-goat** macho cabrío *m*; — **who** el que, quien

head [hɛd] N (of body) cabeza *f*; (of bed) cabecera *f*; (chief) jefe -fa *mf*; **—ache** dolor de cabeza *m*; — **cold** resfrío *m*; **—dress** tocado *m*, adorno para la cabeza *m*; **—gear** (hat) sombrero *m*; (helmet) casco *m*; (for a horse) cabezada *f*; **—land** cabo *m*, promontorio *m*; **—light** faro delantero *m*; **—line** titular *m*; **—long** (head first) de cabeza; (hastily) precipitadamente; **— of hair** cabellera *f*; **—-on** de frente; **—phone** audífono *m*, auricular *m*; **—quarters** (military) cuartel general *m*; (police) jefatura *f*; (corporation) oficina central *f*; **—rest** reposacabezas *m sg*; **—set** auriculares *m pl*; **—s or tails** cara o cruz; **I can't make —s or tails of it** esto no tiene ni pies ni cabeza; **— start** ventaja *f*; **— stone** lápida *f*; **—strong**

testarudo; **—way** avance *m*; **—word** voz *f*; **to make —way** avanzar, progresar; **to be out of one's —** desvariar; **to come to a —** (a crisis) precipitarse; (an abscess) supurar; **to keep one's —** mantener la calma; VT (lead) encabezar; (steer) dirigir; VI dirigirse; **to — off** atajar; **it went to his —** se le fue a la cabeza

heading [hédɪŋ] N encabezamiento *m*

heal [hil] VT curar; VI (get well) sanar, curarse; (form a scar) cicatrizarse

health [hɛlθ] N salud *f*; **— care** asistencia médica *f*; **— food** comida macrobiótica *f*; **— insurance** seguro de salud *m*

healthful [hélθfəl] ADJ saludable, sano

healthy [hélθi] ADJ sano, saludable

heap [hip] N montón *m*, pila *f*; VT amontonar; VI apilar; **to — up** amontonarse

hear [hir] VI/VT (perceive) oír; VT (listen) escuchar; **to — about / of someone / something** oír hablar de alguien / algo; **to — from someone** tener noticias de alguien; **I won't — of your leaving** no quiero saber de que te vayas

hearer [hírɚ] N oyente *mf*

hearing [hírɪŋ] N (sense) oído *m*; (trial) audiencia *f*; **within —** al alcance del oído; **— aid** audífono *m*; **—-impaired** sordo

hearsay [hírse] N testimonio de oídas *m*; **by —** de oídas

hearse [hɚs] N coche fúnebre *m*, carroza *f*

heart [hɑrt] N (organ) corazón *m*; (spirit) ánimo *m*; **—ache** angustia *f*; **— attack** ataque cardíaco *m*; **—beat** latido *m*; **I would do it in a —beat** lo haría sin pestañear; **—broken** inconsolable; **—burn** acidez de estómago *f*; **— disease** enfermedad coronaria *f*; **—felt** sincero, sentido; **— murmur** soplo cardíaco *m*; **my —felt sympathy** mi más sentido pésame; **—-warming** reconfortante; **at —** en realidad, en el fondo; **from the bottom of one's —** de corazón, con toda el alma; **to learn by —** aprender de memoria; **to take —** cobrar ánimo; **to take to —** tomar a pecho

hearten [hɑrtn̩] VT animar

hearth [hɑrθ] N hogar *m*

heartless [hɑrtlɪs] ADJ despiadado, desalmado

hearty [hɑrɖi] ADJ (cordial) cordial; (strong) fuerte; **— appetite** apetito saludable *m*; **a — laugh** una risa desbordante; **— meal** una comida abundante

heat [hit] N (warmth) calor *m*; (passion) ardor *m*; (estrus) celo *m*; (source of heat) calefacción *f*; (preliminary race) eliminatoria *f*; **—stroke** insolación *f*; VI/VT calentar(se); **to — up** acalorarse

heater [híɖɚ] N calentador *m*

heating [híɖɪŋ] N calefacción *f*

heave [hiv] VT (raise) levantar; (throw) arrojar, lanzar; (sigh) exhalar; (pull) jalar; VI (pant) jadear; (vomit) hacer arcadas; N (throw) lanzamiento *m*; (pull) tirón *m*

heaven [hévən] N cielo *m*

heavenly [hévənli] ADJ celestial; **— bodies** cuerpos celestes *m pl*; **it was —** estuvo divino

heaviness [hévɪnɪs] N pesadez *f*

heavy [hévi] ADJ (weighty) pesado; (thick) grueso, pesado; (dense) denso; (oppressive) opresivo; **— artillery** artillería pesada *f*; **— breathing** jadeos *m pl*; **—-duty** para uso industrial; **—-handed** severo, autoritario; **with a — heart** abatido; **— rain** lluvia fuerte *f*; **— schedule** agenda cargada *f*; **—weight** peso pesado *m*; N villano -na *mf*

Hebrew [híbru] N & ADJ hebreo -a *mf*; (language) hebreo *m*

heck [hɛk] INTERJ ¡caramba! **what the — are you doing?** ¿qué demonios haces? **that was a — of a good game** fue un partidazo

hectare [hékter] N hectárea *f*

hectic [héktɪk] ADJ febril, agitado

hedge [hɛʤ] N (row of bushes) seto *m*; (precaution) precaución *f*; VI/VT (a bet) cubrir(se); VT (a question) evadir

hedgehog [héʤhɑg] N erizo *m*

hedonism [hídn̩ɪzəm] N hedonismo *m*

heebie-jeebies [híbiʤíbiz] N **it gives me the —** me pone los pelos de punta

heed [hid] VT atender; N atención *f*, cuidado *m*; **to pay — to** prestar atención a

heel [hil] N (of foot or sock) talón *m*; (of shoe) tacón *m*; **kick up one's —s** tirar la chancleta, soltarse el pelo; VT poner tacón a; VI/VT seguir de cerca

hegemony [hɪʤéməni] N hegemonía *f*

heifer [héfɚ] N novilla *f*, vaquilla *f*

height [haɪt] N (of a building, mountain) altura *f*; (of a person) estatura *f*; (utmost point) colmo *m*

heighten [háɪtn̩] VI/VT (increase) aumentar(se); (intensify) realzar

heinous [hénəs] ADJ aborrecible

heir [ɛr] N heredero -ra *mf*; **— apparent** presunto heredero *m*, presunta heredera *f*

heiress [érɪs] N heredera *f*

helicopter [hélɪkɑptɚ] N helicóptero *m*

helium [híliəm] N helio *m*

helix [hílɪks] N hélice *f*

hell [hɛɫ] N infierno *m*; —**-raiser** camorrista *mf*

hello [hɛló] INTERJ ¡hola! (on the telephone) hola; *Sp* diga; *Mex* bueno; *RP* olá

helm [hɛɫm] N timón *m*

helmet [hɛ́ɫmɪt] N (for bikes, etc.) casco *m*; (armor) yelmo *m*

help [hɛɫp] N (aid) ayuda *f*; (rescue) auxilio *m*; (remedy) remedio *m*; (employee) empleado -da *mf*; INTERJ ¡auxilio! ¡socorro! VI/VT (aid) ayudar, asistir; (rescue) auxiliar, socorrer; — **yourself** sírvete; **he cannot** — **it** no puede evitarlo; **he cannot** — **but come** no puede menos que venir; **may I** — **you?** ¿en qué le puedo servir?

helper [hɛ́ɫpɚ] N ayudante *mf*, asistente *mf*

helpful [hɛ́ɫpfəɫ] ADJ (useful) útil; (willing to help) servicial

helping [hɛ́ɫpɪŋ] N porción *f*

helpless [hɛ́ɫplɪs] ADJ desamparado, desvalido

helplessness [hɛ́ɫplɪsnɪs] N desamparo *m*, desvalimiento *m*

hem [hɛm] N dobladillo *m*, orillo *m*; (of a skirt) ruedo *m*; VT hacer dobladillos en, orillar; **to** — **in** arrinconar; **to** — **and haw** vacilar

hematoma [himətómə] N hematoma *m*

hemisphere [hɛ́mɪsfɪr] N hemisferio *m*

hemlock [hɛ́mlɑk] N cicuta *f*

hemoglobin [hímɑglobɪn] N hemoglobina *f*

hemophilia [himəfíliə] N hemofilia *f*

hemorrhage [hɛ́mɑrɪʤ] N hemorragia *f*

hemorrhoids [hɛ́mɑrɔɪdz] N hemorroides *f pl*

hemp [hɛmp] N cáñamo *m*

hen [hɛn] N (chicken) gallina *f*; (female bird) ave hembra *f*; —**pecked** dominado por su mujer

hence [hɛns] ADV de ahí; **a week** — de aquí a una semana

henceforth [hɛ́nsfɔrθ] ADV de aquí en adelante, de hoy en adelante

hepatitis [hɛpətáɪDɪs] N hepatitis *f*

her [hɝ] PRON **I see** — la veo; **I talk to** — le hablo (a ella); **I went with** — fui con ella; POSS ADJ **this is** — **dog** este es su perro, este es el perro de ella

herald [hɛ́rəɫd] N heraldo *m*; VT anunciar, proclamar

herb [ɝb] N hierba *f*

herbal [ɝ́bəɫ] ADJ de hierbas; — **tea** tisana *f*

herbicide [ɝ́bɪsaɪd] N herbicida *m*

herbivore [ɝ́bəvɔr] N herbívoro *m*

herbivorous [hɝbívɑrəs] ADJ herbívoro

herd [hɝd] N (of animals) manada *f*; (of goats) hato *m*; (of sheep) rebaño *m*; (of horses, donkeys) recua *f*; **the common** — el populacho, la chusma; —**sman** pastor *m*; VT arrear; VI ir en manada

here [hir] ADV aquí, acá; — **it is** aquí está; **that is neither** — **nor there** eso no viene al caso; —**after** en adelante; **the** —**after** el más allá; —**by** (in writing) por la presente; **I** —**by pronounce you husband and wife** los declaro marido y mujer; —**in** en el presente; —**'s to you!** ¡a tu salud! —**tofore** hasta ahora; —**with** (hereby) por la presente; (attached) adjunto; **the** — **and now** el presente

hereditary [hɑrɛ́DɪtɛrI] ADJ hereditario

heredity [hɑrɛ́DɪtI] N herencia *f*

heresy [hɛ́rɪsI] N herejía *f*

heretic [hɛ́rɪtɪk] N hereje *mf*

heritage [hɛ́rɪtɪʤ] N herencia *f*, patrimonio *m*

hermetic [hɝmɛ́DɪK] ADJ hermético

hermit [hɝ́mɪt] N ermitaño -ña *mf*; — **crab** ermitaño *m*

hernia [hɝ́niə] N hernia *f*; —**ted** herniado; —**ted disk** hernia de disco *f*

hero [híro] N (brave man) héroe *m*; (main character) protagonista *mf*

heroic [hɪróɪk] ADJ heroico

heroin [hɛ́roɪn] N heroína *f*

heroine [hɛ́roɪn] N heroína *f*

heroism [hɛ́roɪzəm] N heroísmo *m*

heron [hɛ́rən] N garza *f*

herpes [hɝ́piz] N herpes *m*

herring [hɛ́rɪŋ] N arenque *m*

hers [hɝz] PRON **this book is** — este libro es suyo / de ella; **these things are** — estas cosas son suyas; — **is bigger** el suyo / la suya es más grande; **a friend of** — un amigo suyo / de ella

herself [hɝsɛ́ɫf] PRON ella misma; **she** — **wrote the letter** ella misma escribió la carta; **she's not** — **today** hoy no es la misma de siempre; **she was sitting by** — estaba sentada sola; **she** — **did it** lo hizo sola, lo hizo ella misma; **she talks to** — ella habla para sí, habla sola; **she looked at** — **in the mirror** se miró en el espejo; **she bought** — **a house** se compró una casa

hesitant [hɛ́zɪtənt] ADJ vacilante

hesitate [hɛ́zɪtet] VI (pause) vacilar; (stutter) titubear; (doubt) dudar

hesitating [hɛ́zɪteDɪŋ] ADJ vacilante

hesitation [hɛzɪtéʃən] N (pause) vacilación *f*; (stammer) titubeo *m*; (doubt) duda *f*

heterogeneous [hɛDə·ɑʤíniəs] ADJ heterogéneo

heterosexual [hɛDərosɛ́kʃuəɫ] ADJ heterosexual

hexagon [héksəgɑn] N hexágono *m*
hey [he] INTERJ ¡oiga!
heyday [héde] N auge *m*
hiatus [haiéɒəs] N hiato *m*
hibernate [háibə‑net] VI hibernar
hiccup, hiccough [híkʌp] N hipo *m*; VI
    hipar, tener hipo
hick [hɪk] N & ADJ paleto -ta *mf*
hickory [híkəri] N nogal americano *m*
hide [haid] VI/VT ocultar(se), esconder(se); —
    and seek *Sp* escondite *m*; *Am* escondidas
    f pl; **—out** escondite *m*; N cuero *m*, piel *f*,
    pellejo *m*
hideous [hídiəs] ADJ horrendo, espantoso
hierarchy [háiərɑrki] N jerarquía *f*
hieroglyphic [haiɾəglífɪk] ADJ & N jeroglífico
    m
high [hai] ADJ alto; (intoxicated) ebrio; (on
    drugs) volado; **— and dry** (ship) en seco;
    (person) colgado; **— blood pressure**
    hipertensión *f*; **—brow** culto; **—class** de
    clase; **—er-up** superior; **— explosive**
    explosivo de alta potencia *m*; **— fever**
    fiebre elevada *f*; **— fidelity** alta fidelidad
    f; **—-grade** de calidad superior;
    —-handed arbitrario; **— jump** salto alto
    m; **—lands** tierras altas *f pl*; **—light** lo
    más destacado *m*; **—lights** claritos *m pl*,
    mechas *f pl*; **to —light** resaltar;
    —-minded idealista; **—-pitched** agudo;
    —-powered de alta potencia; **—-priced**
    caro; **—-rise** de muchos pisos; **— school**
    escuela secundaria *f*; *Sp* instituto *m*; **—
    seas** alta mar *f*; **—-sounding** altisonante;
    —-speed de alta velocidad; **— spirits**
    buen ánimo *m*; **—-strung** nervioso;
    —-tech alta tecnología *f*; **—
    temperature** temperatura máxima *f*; **—
    tide** pleamar *f*; **—way** carretera *f*, ruta *f*;
    — wind ventarrón *m*; **in — gear** a toda
    marcha; **two feet —** dos pies de altura; **it
    is — time that** ya era hora de que; **to
    look — and low** buscar por todas partes;
    N flash *m*, subida *f*
highly [háili] ADV **— amusing** sumamente
    divertido; **— paid** muy bien pagado; **he
    spoke — of her** habló muy bien de ella
highness [háinɪs] N alteza *f*
hijack [háidʒæk] VT secuestrar (un vehículo)
hike [haik] N caminata *f*; VI salir a caminar;
    take a —! ¡ve a freír espárragos!
hilarious [hɪlériəs] ADJ graciosísimo, para
    morirse de risa
hill [hɪɫ] N (elevated area) colina *f*, cerro *m*;
    (pile) montón *m*; **—billy** paleto -ta *mf*;
    —side ladera *f*; **—top** cumbre *f*, cima *f*
hillock [hílək] N otero *m*

hilly [híli] ADJ accidentado
hilt [hɪɫt] N empuñadura *f*; **to the —** al
    máximo
him [hɪm] PRON **I see —** lo veo; *Sp* le veo; **I
    talk to —** le hablo; **I went with —** fui
    con él
himself [hɪmséɫf] PRON él mismo; **he —
    wrote the letter** el mismo escribió la
    carta; **he's not — today** hoy no es el
    mismo de siempre; **he was sitting by —**
    estaba sentado solo; **he talks to —** el
    habla para sí / solo; **he looked at — in
    the mirror** se miró en el espejo; **he
    bought — a house** se compró una casa
hind [haind] ADJ trasero; **—most** último; **in
    —sight** a posteriori; N cierva *f*
hinder [híndɚ] VT impedir, entorpecer,
    estorbar
Hindi [híndi] N hindi *m*
hindrance [híndrəns] N obstáculo *m*,
    impedimento *m*, traba *f*
Hindu [híndu] ADJ & N hindú *mf*
hinge [hɪndʒ] N gozne *m*, quicio *m*; VT
    engoznar, poner goznes; VI **to — on**
    depender de
hint [hɪnt] N (clue) indirecta *f*, pista *f*; (trace)
    dejo *m*; **to take the —** darse por
    enterado; VT insinuar
hip [hɪp] N cadera *f*
hippopotamus [hɪpəpáɒəməs] N
    hipopótamo *m*
hire [hair] VT (engage for work) contratar; VI/
    VT (rent) alquilar(se); **to — out** dar en
    alquiler, alquilar; N (engagement)
    contratación *f*; (employee) nuevo -va
    empleado -da *mf*; (rent) alquiler *m*
his [hɪz] POSS ADJ **this is — dog** este es su
    perro / el perro de él; PRON **these things
    are —** estas cosas son suyas; **— is right
    here** el suyo / la suya está aquí; **a friend
    of —** un amigo suyo / una amiga suya
Hispanic [hɪspǽnɪk] ADJ hispánico, hispano;
    N hispano -na *mf*
hiss [hɪs] VI sisear; (to boo) silbar; N siseo *m*
histamine [hístəmin] N histamina *f*
historian [hɪstɔ́riən] N historiador -ra *mf*
historic [hɪstɔ́rɪk] ADJ histórico
historical [hɪstɔ́rɪkəɫ] ADJ histórico
history [hístəri] N historia *f*
histrionics [hɪstriánɪks] N histrionismo *m*
hit [hɪt] VT (a target) dar en; (a car) chocar
    con; (a key) pulsar, tocar; **they — it off
    well** se llevaron bien desde el principio;
    to — the mark acertar, dar en el blanco;
    to — upon dar con; **to — on** ligar (con);
    N (blow) golpe *m*; (success) éxito *m*; (dose)
    dosis *f*; **that was a — with me** me

encantó; **—-and-run** que se da a la fuga después de atropellar a alguien; **—man** sicario *m*; **—-or-miss** al azar

hitch [hɪtʃ] VT atar, amarrar; (pants) levantar; (yoke) uncir, enganchar; **to get —ed** casarse; **to —hike** *Sp* hacer autostop; *Am* hacer dedo; N (knot) nudo *m*; (difficulty) dificultad *f*; (period) período *m*

hither [híðɚ] ADV acá; **— and thither** acá y allá; **—to** hasta ahora

HIV (human immunodeficiency virus) [etʃaɪví] N VIH *m*

hive [haɪv] N (shelter for bees) colmena *f*; (colony of bees) enjambre *m*; **—s** urticaria *f*

hoard [hɔrd] N reserva *f*; VI/VT acaparar

hoarse [hɔrs] ADJ ronco; (of alcoholics) aguardentoso

hoarseness [hɔ́rsnɪs] N ronquera *f*

hoax [hoks] N engaño *m*

hobble [hábəł] VI (limp) cojear; VT (tie to impede walking) manear; (hinder) trabar; N cojera *f*; (rope) traba *f*, manea *f*

hobby [hábi] N hobby *m*

hobo [hóbo] N vagabundo *m*

hockey [háki] N hockey *m*

hodgepodge [háʤpɑʤ] N mezcolanza *f*, batiburrillo *m*

hoe [ho] N azada *f*, azadón *m*; VI/VT limpiar con azadón

hog [hɑg] N puerco *m*, cerdo *m*, marrano *m*; *Am* chancho *m*; **—wash** pamplinas *f pl*; **to live high on the —** vivir en la abundancia; VT acaparar, adueñarse de

hoist [hɔɪst] VT izar; N torno *m*, guinche *m*

hokey [hóki] ADJ sensiblero

hold [hołd] VT (bear) llevar, sujetar; (contain) contener; (detain) detener; (decide legally, sustain a note) sostener; (opine) opinar; VI (remain fast) aguantar, resistir; (occupy a position) ocupar; (be valid) ser válido; **to — back** detener; **to — down** sujetar; **to — forth** perorar; **to — hands** tomarse de la mano; **to — in place** sujetar; **to — a meeting** celebrar una reunión; **to — off** mantener(se) a distancia; **to — on** (not let go) agarrar(se), sujetar(se); (stop) esperar; (persist) persistir; **— the pickles on that burger!** una hamburguesa sin pepinillos, por favor; **to — someone responsible** hacerle a uno responsable; **to — someone to his word** obligar a uno a cumplir con su palabra; **to — oneself erect** ponerse derecho; **to — one's own** defenderse; **to — one's tongue** callarse, morderse la lengua; **to — out** tender; **to — still** quedarse / estarse quieto; **to —**

tight agarrarse; **to — to one's promise** cumplir con la palabra; **to — up** (raise) alzar; (detain) detener; (rob) atracar, asaltar; (persevere) aguantar; **how much does it — ?** ¿Qué capacidad tiene? N (grip) agarro *m*; (thing to grasp) asidero *m*; (dominion) dominio *m*; (wrestling move) llave *f*; (in music) calderón *m*; (of a ship) bodega *f*; **—up** golpe *m*, atraco *m*; **to get — of** agarrar; **to take — of** *Sp* coger, agarrar; **to have a good — on something** agarrarse bien de algo

holder [hółdɚ] N (person) tenedor -ra *mf*, poseedor -ra *mf*; (device) receptáculo *m*

holding [hółdɪŋ] N propiedad *f*; **— company** holding *m*; **—s** (financial) valores en cartera *m pl*; (of a library) fondos *m pl*

hole [hoł] N agujero *m*; (in a wall) boquete *m*; (of an animal) madriguera *f*; (in ground only, golf included) hoyo *m*; **to be in a —** hallarse / estar en un apuro / aprieto

holiday [hálɪde] N día de fiesta *m*; **—s** vacaciones *f pl*

holiness [hólɪnɪs] N santidad *f*

holistic [holístɪk] ADJ holístico

Holland [hálənd] N Holanda *f*

hollow [hálo] ADJ (empty) hueco; (concave) cóncavo; (sunken) hundido; (insincere) falso; N (cavity) hueco *m*, concavidad *f*; (valley) hondonada *f*, hondo *m*; VT **to — out** ahuecar, vaciar

holly [háli] N acebo *m*

holocaust [háləkɔst] N holocausto *m*

holster [hółstɚ] N pistolera *f*, funda de pistola *f*

holy [hóli] ADJ santo, sagrado; **— Bible** Santa Biblia *f*; **— cow / Moses / mackerel!** ¡jobar! **— Ghost** Espíritu Santo *m*; **— Spirit** Espíritu Santo *m*; **— war** guerra santa *f*; **— water** agua bendita *f*

homage [hámɪʤ] N homenaje *m*; **to pay —** rendir homenaje, honrar

home [hom] N casa *f*, hogar *m*; (for old people, orphans) asilo *m*, hogar *m*; **at —** en casa; ADJ doméstico; **— economics** economía doméstica *f*; **— game** partido en casa *m*; **—land** patria *f*; **—less** sin techo; **—made** casero; **— office** oficina central *f*; **—owner** propietario -ria de un bien inmueble *mf*; **— page** página de inicio *f*; **— rule** autonomía *f*; **— run** jonrón *m*; **to be —sick** echar de menos / extrañar (a la familia); **—sickness** morriña *f*, añoranza *f*; **— stretch** último trecho *m*; **—work** tarea domiciliaria *f*, deber *m*; ADV (direction) a casa; (location) en casa; **to strike** — dar en el blanco

homely [hómli] ADJ (ugly) feo; (familiar) familiar, doméstico

homeopathic [homiopǽθɪk] ADJ homeopático

homeopathy [homiápəθi] N homeopatía *f*

homestead [hómstɛd] N heredad *f*, casa de la familia *f*

homeward [hómwəd] ADV a casa; — **bound** camino a casa

homicide [hámɪsaɪd] N homicidio *m*

homogeneous [homədʒíniəs] ADJ homogéneo

homogenize [həmádʒənaɪz] VT homogeneizar

homonym [hámənɪm] N homónimo *m*

homosexual [homosékʃuəł] ADJ & N homosexual *mf*

Honduran [hɑndúrən] ADJ & N hondureño -ña *mf*

Honduras [hɑndúrəs] N Honduras *f*

hone [hon] VT afilar; **to — one's skills** desarrollar las destrezas; N piedra de afilar *f*

honest [ánɪst] ADJ honrado, honesto; **I'll be — with you** voy a ser franco contigo; —! ¡de veras!

honesty [ánɪsti] N (integrity) honradez *f*, honestidad *f*; (sincerity) franqueza *f*

honey [háni] N (sweet substance) miel *f*; (endearment) querido -da *mf*; **—bee** abeja *f*; **—comb** panal *m*; **—suckle** madreselva *f*

honeymoon [hánimun] N luna de miel *f*; VI pasar la luna de miel

honk [hɑŋk] N (car) bocinazo *m*, pitazo *m*; (goose) graznido *m*; VI/VT tocar la bocina; VI graznar

honor [ánə] N (respect, privilege) honor *m*; (good reputation) honra *f*; (title) señoría *f*; **with —s** con honores; VT (revere) honrar; (accept invitation, check) aceptar

honorable [ánərəbəł] ADJ honorable

honorary [ánəreri] ADJ honorario

hood [hʊd] N (of a coat) capucha *f*, caperuza *f*; (of a car) capó *m*; *Am* tapa *f*; VT encapuchar

hoodlum [húdləm] N maleante *mf*, gamberro -rra *mf*

hoof [hʊf] N casco *m*, pezuña *f*; VI **to — it** ir andando

hook [hʊk] N (for lifting) gancho *m*, garfio *m*; (for fishing) anzuelo *m*; **— and eye** alamar *m*, macho y hembra *m*; **by — or by crook** por las buenas o por las malas; **—up** conexión *f*, enganche *m*; VT (snag) enganchar; (a dress) abrochar; **to — up**

conectar, enganchar

hooked [hʊkt] ADJ (shaped like a hook) ganchudo; (addicted) enganchado

hooky [húki] N **to play —** hacer novillos

hoop [hup] N aro *m*

hoot [hut] VI/VT (of owl) ulular; (in derision) abuchear; N (of an owl) ululato *m*; (cry of derision) abucheo *m*; **I don't give a —** no me importa un comino; **it's a —** es para morirse de risa

hop [hɑp] VI saltar, brincar; **to — on** subirse a montar; N (short jump) saltito *m*, brinco *m*; (dance) bailongo *m*; **—s** lúpulo *m*

hope [hop] N esperanza *f*; VI/VT esperar; **to — for** esperar; **to — against —** esperar lo imposible

hopeful [hópfəł] ADJ (having hopes) esperanzado; (giving hopes) esperanzador, alentador

hopefully [hópfəli] ADV — **she'll come** ojalá (que) venga

hopeless [hóplɪs] ADJ (without hope) desesperanzado; (with no solution) irremediable; (unattainable) inalcanzable; **— cause** causa perdida *f*; **it is —** no tiene remedio; **the new secretary is — with numbers** el nuevo secretario es un desastre con los números

hopelessness [hóplɪsnɪs] N desesperanza *f*

horde [hɔrd] N (of people) horda *f*; (of animals) plaga *f*

horizon [həráɪzən] N horizonte *m*

horizontal [hɔrɪzántł] ADJ horizontal

hormone [hɔ́rmon] N hormona *f*

horn [hɔrn] N (of an animal, substance) cuerno *m*, asta *f*; (of an automobile) bocina *f*, claxon *m*; (musical) corno *m*, trompa *f*; **— of plenty** cuerno de la abundancia *m*; **to toot one's own —** darse autobombo; VI **to — in** entremeterse

hornet [hɔ́rnɪt] N avispón *m*; **—'s nest** avispero *m*

horny [hɔ́rni] ADJ (with hard skin) calloso; (sexually excited) *Sp fam* cachondo; *Am fam* caliente

horoscope [hɔ́rəskop] N horóscopo *m*

horrendous [hɔréndəs] ADJ horrendo

horrible [hɔ́rəbəł] ADJ horrible

horrid [hɔ́rɪd] ADJ horrendo

horrify [hɔ́rəfaɪ] VT horrorizar

horror [hɔ́rə] N horror *m*

hors d'oeuvre [ɔrdɔ́v] N entremés *m*

horse [hɔrs] N caballo *m*; **—back** lomo de caballo *m*; **to ride —back** montar a caballo, cabalgar; **—fly** tábano *m*; **—laugh** carcajada *f*; **—man** jinete *m*;

—**manship** equitación *f*; —**play** payasadas *f pl*; —**power** caballo de fuerza *m*; — **race** carrera de caballos *f*; —**radish** rábano picante *m*; — **sense** sentido común *m*; —**shoe** herradura *f*; **hold your** —**s!** ¡para el carro! vi **to** — **around** payasear

horticulture [hɔ́rdɪkʌɫtʃɚ] N horticultura *f*

hose [hoz] N (for legs) medias *f pl*; (for irrigation) manguera *f*, manga *f*

hosiery [hóʒəri] N (stockings) medias *f pl*; (shop for stockings) calcetería *f*

hospice [háspɪs] N (inn) hospicio *m*; (hospital) hospital para enfermos terminales *m*

hospitable [hɑspídɔbɔɫ] ADJ hospitalario, acogedor

hospital [háspɪd]] N hospital *m*

hospitality [hɑspɪtǽlɪdi] N hospitalidad *f*

host [host] N anfitrión *m*; (at home, also for a parasite) huésped *m*; (on television) presentador -ra *mf*; (army) hueste *f*; (multitude) multitud *f*, cúmulo *m*; (wafer) hostia *f*

hostage [hástɪʤ] N rehén *m*

hostel [hástəɫ] N hostal *m*

hostelry [hástəɫri] N hostería *f*

hostess [hóstɪs] N (at home) anfitriona *f*; (on airplanes) azafata *f*

hostile [hástəɫ] ADJ hostil

hostility [hɑstílɪdi] N hostilidad *f*

hot [hɑt] ADJ (at high temperature) caliente; (sweltry) caluroso; (spicy) picante; (sexy) bueno; (sexually aroused) *Sp* cachondo; *Am* caliente; (stolen) robado; (recent) de último momento; (popular) popular; — **and heavy** apasionadamente; —**bed** semillero *m*; — **dog** perro caliente *m*; —**headed** impetuoso, exaltado; —**house** invernadero *m*; — **potato** patata caliente *f*; — **seat** situación embarazosa *f*; —**shot** estrella *f*; — **tub** jacuzzi *m*; **(to)** —-**wire** hacerle un puente a; **it is** — **today** hace calor hoy; — **under the collar** enojado

hotel [hotéɫ] N hotel *m*; —**keeper** hotelero -ra *mf*

hound [haʊnd] N perro de caza *m*, sabueso *m*; VT acosar, perseguir

hour [aʊr] N hora *f*; — **hand** horario *m*; **his finest** — su mejor momento *m*

hourly [áʊrli] ADV (by the hour) por horas; (on the hour) cada hora; — **wages** salario por hora *m*

house [haʊs] N (residence) casa *f*; (legislature) cámara legislativa *f*; — **arrest** detención domiciliaria *f*; —**boat** casa flotante *f*; —**cleaning** limpieza de la casa *f*; —**hold**

casa *f*, familia *f*; —**keeper** (in a house) ama de llaves *f*; (in a home) encargado -da de limpieza *mf*; —**keeping** mantenimiento del hogar *m*; —-**to**-— puerta a puerta; —**top** techo *m*, tejado *m*; —**wife** ama de casa *f*; —**work** trabajo de casa *m*, quehaceres domésticos *m pl*; **on the** — la casa paga; **to keep** — cuidar la casa; [haʊz] VI/VT alojar

housing [háʊzɪŋ] N (place to live) vivienda *f*; (protective covering) caja *f*

hovel [hávəɫ] N (hut) choza *f*, cabaña *f*, tugurio *m*; (open shed) cobertizo *m*

hover [hávɚ] VI (bird) cernerse; (hang in air) estar suspendido; (linger) rondar; —**craft** aerodeslizador *m*

how [haʊ] ADV cómo; — **about your mom?** ¿y tu mamá? — **beautiful!** ¡qué hermoso! — **come?** ¿por qué? — **early (late, soon)?** ¿cuándo? ¿a qué hora? — **far is it?** ¿a qué distancia está? ¿cuánto dista de aquí? — **long?** ¿cuánto tiempo? — **many?** ¿cuántos? — **much is it?** ¿cuánto vale? — **old are you?** ¿cuántos años tienes? **no matter** — **much it rains** por mucho que llueva; **he knows** — **difficult it is** él sabe lo difícil que es

however [haʊévɚ] CONJ sin embargo, no obstante; ADV como quieras; — **difficult it may be** por muy difícil que sea; — **much it rains** por mucho que llueva

howl [haʊɫ] VI aullar; (wind) ulular; (with laughter) reír a carcajadas; N aullido *m*, alarido *m*

HTML (HyperText Markup Language) [etʃtiɛméɫ] N HTML *m*

hub [hʌb] N (center of wheel) cubo *m*; (center of activity) núcleo *m*; —**cap** tapacubos *m sg*

hubbub [hábʌb] N alboroto *m*, barullo *m*

huckster [hákstɚ] N (peddler) vendedor ambulante *m*; (promoter) mercachifle *m*

huddle [hádɫ] VI/VT (a group) apiñar(se); (curl up) acurrucar(se); (consult) conferenciar; N tropel *m*; (group meeting for consultation) reunión *f*; **to be in a** — estar agrupados; **to get in a** — agruparse

hue [hju] N matiz *m*

huff [hʌf] N **to get into a** — enojarse; **to** — **and puff** resoplar

hug [hʌg] VI/VT abrazar(se); **to** — **the coast** costear; N abrazo *m*

huge [hjuʤ] ADJ enorme, fiero

hull [hʌl] N (of a ship, airplane) casco *m*; (of beans, peas) vaina *f*; (of fruits, nuts) cáscara *f*; VT (beans, peas) desvainar; (nuts) cascar

hum [hʌm] VI/VT (person) tararear; (insect, machine) zumbar; (place of activity) hervir; **to — to sleep** arrullar; N (of voice) tarareo *m*; (of insect, machine) zumbido *m*

human [hjúmən] ADJ & N humano *m*; — **being** ser humano *m*

humane [hjumén] ADJ humano, humanitario

humanism [hjúmənɪzəm] N humanismo *m*

humanitarian [hjumænɪtériən] ADJ humanitario

humanity [hjumǽnɪɾi] N humanidad *f*; **humanities** humanidades *f pl*

humble [hʌ́mbəł] ADJ humilde; VT humillar

humid [hjúmɪd] ADJ húmedo

humidify [hjumídəfaɪ] VT humidificar

humidity [hjumíɾɪɾi] N humedad *f*

humiliate [hjumíliet] VT humillar, vejar

humiliation [hjumɪliéʃən] N humillación *f*

humility [hjumílɪɾi] N humildad *f*

hummingbird [hʌ́mɪŋbɜ˞d] N colibrí *m*

humor [hjúmɚ] N humor *m*, humorismo *m*; **out of** — de mal humor, malhumorado; VT complacer a

humorous [hjúmɚəs] ADJ gracioso, chistoso

hump [hʌmp] N joroba *f*, giba *f*, corcova *f*; **we're over the** — ya pasamos lo peor; VI/VT *Sp vulg* follar; *Am* coger, culear

humpback [hʌ́mpbæk] N jorobado -da *mf*; — **whale** ballena jorobada *f*, yubarta *f*

hunch [hʌntʃ] N presentimiento *m*, corazonada *f*; **—back** (person) jorobado -da *mf*; (hump) corcova *f*; VI encorvar

hundred [hʌ́ndrɪd] NUM cien(to); **a — people** cien personas; **a — and fifty people** ciento cincuenta personas; N cien / ciento *m*; **—s** centenares *m pl*, cientos *m pl*

hundredth [hʌ́ndrɪdθ] ADJ centésimo

Hungarian [hʌŋgériən] ADJ & N húngaro -ra *mf*

Hungary [hʌ́ŋgəri] N Hungría *f*

hunger [hʌ́ŋgɚ] N hambre *f*; VI pasar hambre; **to — for** ansiar, anhelar

hungry [hʌ́ŋgri] ADJ hambriento; **to be —** tener hambre

hunk [hʌŋk] N pedazo *m*, cacho *m*; **he's a real —** es un cacho de hombre

hunt [hʌnt] VI/VT (seek prey) cazar; **to — down** dar caza a; **to — for** buscar; N (activity of hunting) caza *f*; (instance of hunting) cacería *f*; (search) búsqueda *f*

hunter [hʌ́ntɚ] N (who captures game) cazador -ra *mf*; (seeker) buscador -ra *mf*; (dog) perro de caza *m*

hunting [hʌ́ntɪŋ] N caza *f*; — **knife** cuchillo de caza *m*

huntsman [hʌ́ntsmən] N cazador *m*

hurdle [hɜ˞dl̩] N (impediment) obstáculo *m*; (in races) valla *f*; VT saltar

hurl [hɜ˞ł] VI/VT arrojar, lanzar, precipitar

hurrah [hərá] INTERJ ¡hurra!

hurricane [hɜ˞ɪken] N huracán *m*

hurried [hɜ˞id] ADJ apresurado; *Am* apurado

hurry [hɜ˞i] VI darse prisa, apresurarse; *Am* apurarse; VT apresurar; *Am* apurar; **to — in (out)** entrar (salir) de prisa; **to — up** apresurar(se), dar(se) prisa; *Am* apurar(se); N prisa *f*; *Am* apuro *m*; **to be in a —** tener prisa; *Am* estar apurado

hurt [hɜ˞t] VI/VT (to injure) lastimar(se), hacer(se) daño; (damage) dañar(se); (harm) perjudicar(se); VI (suffer pain) doler; **to get —** lastimarse; **to — someone's feelings** lastimar a uno; **my tooth —s** me duele la muela / el diente; N (damage) daño *m*; (wound) herida *f*, lastimadura *f*

hurtful [hɜ˞tfəł] ADJ hiriente

husband [hʌ́zbənd] N marido *m*, esposo *m*; VT administrar

hush [hʌʃ] VI/VT aquietar(se), callar(se); —! ¡chitón! ¡silencio! **to — up a scandal** encubrir un escándalo; N silencio *m*

husk [hʌsk] N (shell) cáscara *f*; (pod) vaina *f*; (of corn) chala *f*; *Sp* farfolla *f*; VT (corn) quitar la chala / farfolla a; (beans, peas) desvainar

husky [hʌ́ski] ADJ (voice) ronco; (strong) recio; N husky *m*, perro esquimal *m*

hustle [hʌ́səł] VI (work energetically) afanarse; (swindle) estafar; VT (hurry along) empujar; N (bustle) ajetreo *m*; (scheme) timo *m*; — **and bustle** ajetreo *m*, trajín *m*

hut [hʌt] N choza *f*, cabaña *f*

hyacinth [háɪəsɪnθ] N jacinto *m*

hybrid [háɪbrɪd] ADJ híbrido

hydrate [háɪdret] N hidrato *m*; VI/VT hidratar(se)

hydraulic [haɪdrɔ́lɪk] ADJ hidráulico

hydrocarbon [háɪdrəkarbən] N hidrocarburo *m*

hydroelectric [haɪdroɪléktrɪk] ADJ hidroeléctrico

hydrogen [háɪdrədʒən] N hidrógeno *m*; — **bomb** bomba de hidrógeno *f*; — **peroxide** peróxido de hidrógeno *m*, agua oxigenada *f*

hydrophobia [haɪdrəfóbiə] N hidrofobia *f*

hydroplane [háɪdrəplen] N hidroavión *m*

hyena [haɪínə] N hiena *f*

hygiene [háɪdʒin] N higiene *f*

hymn [hɪm] N himno *m*

hype [haɪp] N exageración *f*; VT promocionar (exageradamente)

hyper [háɪpɚ] ADJ hiperactivo

hyperactive [haɪpɚǽktɪv] ADJ hiperactivo
hypersensitive [haɪpɚsénsɪDɪv] ADJ
  hipersensible
hyperventilate [haɪpɚvéntlet] VI
  hiperventilar
hyphen [háɪfən] N guión m
hypnosis [hɪpnósɪs] N hipnosis f
hypnotize [hípnətaɪz] VT hipnotizar
hypoallergenic [haɪpoælɚʤénɪk] ADJ
  hipoalérgico
hypochondriac [haɪpokándriæk] N
  hipocondríaco mf, hipocondriaco mf
hypocrisy [hɪpákrɪsi] N hipocresía f
hypocrite [hípəkrɪt] N hipócrita mf
hypocritical [hɪpəkríDɪkəł] ADJ hipócrita
hypoglycemia [haɪpoglaɪsímiə] N
  hipoglucemia f
hypothesis [haɪpáθɪsɪs] N hipótesis f
hysterectomy [hɪstəréktəmi] N histerectomía
  f
hysterical [hɪstérɪkəł] ADJ (out of control)
  histérico; (funny) desternillante

Ii

I [aɪ] PRON yo
I-beam [áɪbim] N viga doble f
Iberian [aɪbíriən] ADJ ibérico
ice [aɪs] N hielo m; — **age** periodo glaciar m;
  —**berg** iceberg m; —**box** Sp nevera f; Am
  refrigerador m; — **cream** helado m; —
  cream cone cucurucho de helado m;
  —**-cream parlor** heladería f; — **hockey**
  hockey sobre hielo m; — **skates** patines
  de cuchilla m pl; —**d tea** té helado m; —
  water agua helada f; **to break the** —
  romper el hielo; **on** — en suspenso; VI/VT
  (freeze) helar(se); (cover with ice)
  cubrir(se) de hielo; VT (cover with icing)
  bañar; (insure a deal) cerrar; **to** —**-skate**
  patinar sobre hielo
Iceland [áɪslənd] N Islandia f
Icelander [áɪsləndɚ] N islandés -esa mf
Icelandic [aɪslǽndɪk] ADJ islandés
icicle [áɪsɪkəł] N carámbano m
icing [áɪsɪŋ] N (frosting) baño m; (formation
  of ice) formación de hielo f
icon [áɪkɑn] N icono m, ícono m (also
  computer term)
icy [áɪsi] ADJ helado
idea [aɪdíə] N idea f
ideal [aɪdíəł] N ideal m; ADJ ideal, idóneo
idealism [aɪdíəlɪzəm] N idealismo m

idealist [aɪdíəlɪst] N idealista mf
idealistic [aɪdiəlístɪk] ADJ idealista
identical [aɪdéntɪkəł] ADJ idéntico
identification [aɪdɛntəfɪkéʃən] N
  identificación f; — **card** carnet de
  identidad m, cédula de identidad f
identify [aɪdéntəfaɪ] VI/VT identificar(se)
identity [aɪdéntɪDi] N identidad f
ideology [aɪdiáləʤi] N ideología f
idiocy [íDiəsi] N idiotez f
idiom [íDiəm] N modismo m
idiosyncrasy [ɪDiosínkrəsi] N idiosincrasia f
idiot [íDiət] N idiota mf, gilipollas mf sg
idiotic [ɪDiáDɪk] ADJ idiota
idle [áɪdl] ADJ (not active) ocioso; (lazy)
  perezoso, holgazán; (of a machine,
  worker) parado; (of an engine) en ralentí;
  (meaningless) vacío; VI (person)
  holgazanear; (motor) girar en vacío; VT
  (cause to be idle) dejar parado/
  desocupado
idleness [áɪdl̩nɪs] N (inactivity) ociosidad f,
  ocio m, holganza f; (sloth) pereza f
idler [áɪdlɚ] N holgazán -ana mf, zanguango
  -ga mf
idol [áɪdl̩] N ídolo m
idolatry [aɪdálətri] N idolatría f
idolize [áɪdl̩aɪz] VT idolatrar
idyll [áɪdl̩] N idilio m
if [ɪf] CONJ si; — **I were you** en tu lugar/yo
  que tú; — **only I had known** de haber
  sabido/ojalá hubiera sabido; **he's tall,** —
  a bit stooped es alto, aunque un poco
  encorvado; N —**s** condiciones f pl; **no** —**s,
  ands, or buts** no hay pero que valga
igloo [íglu] N iglú m
ignite [ɪgnáɪt] VI/VT encender(se), prender
  fuego (a)
ignition [ɪgníʃən] N ignición f, encendido m;
  — **switch** llave de contacto f
ignoble [ɪgnóbəł] ADJ innoble
ignorance [ígnərəns] N ignorancia f
ignorant [ígnərənt] ADJ ignorante
ignore [ɪgnór] VT ignorar
ilk [ɪłk] N ralea f, calaña f
ill [ɪł] ADJ enfermo, malo; — **fortune** mala
  suerte f; — **nature** mal genio m, mala
  índole f; — **repute** mala fama f; — **will**
  mala voluntad f; N (unfavorable
  statement) mal m; (sickness) enfermedad f;
  (calamity) calamidad f; ADV — **at ease**
  incómodo; —**-bred** maleducado; —**-fated**
  fatídico, funesto, desastrado; —**-gotten**
  mal adquirido; —**-humored**
  malhumorado; —**-mannered**
  maleducado, grosero; —**-natured** de mal
  genio; **we can** — **afford to stop now**

de ninguna manera podemos detenernos ahora; **you would be —-advised to invest** sería desaconsejable que invirtieras

illegal [ɪlígəɫ] ADJ ilegal

illegitimate [ɪlɪʤíɾəmɪt] ADJ ilegítimo

illicit [ɪlísɪt] ADJ ilícito

illiteracy [ɪlíɾərəsi] N analfabetismo *m*

illiterate [ɪlíɾərɪt] ADJ & N analfabeto -ta *mf*

illness [íɫnɪs] N enfermedad *f*

illuminate [ɪlúmənet] VI/VT iluminar(se)

illumination [ɪlumənéʃən] N iluminación *f*

illusion [ɪlúʒən] N ilusión *f*

illusory [ɪlúzəri] ADJ ilusorio

illustrate [íləstret] VI/VT ilustrar

illustration [ɪləstréʃən] N ilustración *f*, estampa *f*

illustrator [íləstreɾɚ] N ilustrador -ra *mf*, dibujante *mf*

illustrious [ɪlÁstriəs] ADJ ilustre, eximio

image [ímɪʤ] N imagen *f*

imagery [ímɪʤri] N conjunto de imágenes *m*

imaginary [ɪmǽʤəneri] ADJ imaginario, fabuloso

imagination [ɪmæʤənéʃən] N imaginación *f*, fantasía *f*

imaginative [ɪmǽʤənəɾɪv] ADJ imaginativo, fantasioso

imagine [ɪmǽʤɪn] VI/VT imaginar(se); — **that!** ¡figúrate!

imbalance [ɪmbǽləns] N desequilibrio *m*

imbecile [ímbəsəɫ] N imbécil *mf*

imbibe [ɪmbáɪb] VI/VT beber

imbue [ɪmbjú] VT imbuir, infundir

imitate [ímɪtet] VT imitar

imitation [ɪmɪtéʃən] N imitación *f*; ADJ — **leather** imitación de cuero *f*

imitator [ímɪteɾɚ] N imitador -ra *mf*

immaculate [ɪmǽkjəlɪt] ADJ inmaculado

immaterial [ɪmətíriəɫ] ADJ inmaterial; **it is — to me** me es indiferente

immature [ɪmətʃúr] ADJ inmaduro

immediate [ɪmíɾiɪt] ADJ inmediato

immense [ɪméns] ADJ inmenso

immensity [ɪménsɪɾi] N inmensidad *f*

immerse [ɪmɝ́s] VT (submerge) sumergir; (absorb) sumir

immigrant [ímɪgrənt] ADJ & N inmigrante *mf*

immigrate [ímɪgret] VI inmigrar

immigration [ɪmɪgréʃən] N inmigración *f*

imminent [ímənənt] ADJ inminente

immobile [ɪmóbəɫ] ADJ inmóvil

immobilize [ɪmóbəlaɪz] VT inmovilizar

immodest [ɪmáɾɪst] ADJ impúdico, deshonesto

immodesty [ɪmáɾɪsti] N deshonestidad *f*

immoral [ɪmɔ́rəɫ] ADJ inmoral

immorality [ɪmɔrǽlɪɾi] N inmoralidad *f*

immortal [ɪmɔ́rdl̩] ADJ & N inmortal *mf*

immortality [ɪmɔrtǽlɪɾi] N inmortalidad *f*

immovable [ɪmúvəbəɫ] ADJ inamovible

immune [ɪmjún] ADJ inmune; — **system** sistema inmune *m*

immunity [ɪmjúnɪɾi] N inmunidad *f*

immutable [ɪmjúɾəbəɫ] ADJ inmutable

impact [ímpækt] N impacto *m*; VI/VT impactar

impair [ɪmpér] VT dañar, deteriorar, menoscabar

impairment [ɪmpérmənt] N daño *m*, deterioro *m*, menoscabo *m*

impala [ɪmpálə] N impala *m*

impale [ɪmpéɫ] VT empalar

impart [ɪmpárt] VT (bestow knowledge) impartir; (reveal) revelar

impartial [ɪmpárʃəɫ] ADJ imparcial

impartiality [ɪmpɑrʃiǽlɪɾi] N imparcialidad *f*

impasse [ímpæs] N impasse *m*

impassioned [ɪmpǽʃənd] ADJ apasionado

impassive [ɪmpǽsɪv] ADJ impasible

impatience [ɪmpéʃəns] N impaciencia *f*

impatient [ɪmpéʃənt] ADJ impaciente

impeach [ɪmpítʃ] VT acusar formalmente; **to — a person's honor** poner en tela de juicio el honor de uno

impeachment [ɪmpítʃmənt] N impeachment *m*

impede [ɪmpíd] VT obstaculizar, estorbar, trabar

impediment [ɪmpéɾəmənt] N impedimento *m*, obstáculo *m*; (of speech) defecto *m*

impel [ɪmpéɫ] VT impeler

impending [ɪmpéndɪŋ] ADJ inminente

impenetrable [ɪmpénɪtrəbəɫ] ADJ impenetrable

imperative [ɪmpéɾəɾɪv] ADJ (like a command) imperativo; (necessary) imperioso; N (command, grammatical mood) imperativo *m*; (obligation) obligación *f*

imperceptible [ɪmpɚséptəbəɫ] ADJ imperceptible

imperfect [ɪmpɝ́fɪkt] ADJ & N imperfecto *m*

imperial [ɪmpíriəɫ] ADJ imperial

imperialism [ɪmpíriəlɪzəm] N imperialismo *m*

imperil [ɪmpérəɫ] VT poner en peligro

imperious [ɪmpíriəs] ADJ imperioso

impersonal [ɪmpɝ́sənəɫ] ADJ impersonal

impersonate [ɪmpɝ́sənet] VT (assume traits of) hacerse pasar por; (mimic) imitar

impertinence [ɪmpɝ́tn̩əns] N impertinencia *f*

impertinent [ɪmpɝ́tn̩ənt] ADJ impertinente

impervious [ɪmpɔ́˞viəs] ADJ impermeable; (to reason) refractario
impetuous [ɪmpétʃuəs] ADJ impetuoso
impetus [ímpəɒəs] N ímpetu *m*, empuje *m*
impious [ímpiəs] ADJ impío
implacable [ɪmplǽkəbəɫ] ADJ implacable
implant [ɪmplǽnt] VT implantar; [ímplænt] N implante *m*
implement [ímpləmənt] N implemento *m*, utensilio *m*; [ímpləmɛnt] VT implementar, instrumentar
implicate [ímplɪket] VT implicar, involucrar
implicit [ɪmplísɪt] ADJ implícito
implore [ɪmplɔ́r] VI/VT implorar
imply [ɪmpláɪ] VT dar a entender
impolite [ɪmpəláɪt] ADJ descortés
import [ɪmpɔ́rt] VT (bring in) importar; [ímpɔrt] N (act of importing, thing imported) importación *f*; (significance) significado *m*
importance [ɪmpɔ́rtn̩s] N importancia *f*
important [ɪmpɔ́rtn̩t] ADJ importante
impose [ɪmpóz] VT imponer; **to — (upon)** abusar (de)
imposing [ɪmpózɪŋ] ADJ imponente, impresionante
imposition [ɪmpəzíʃən] N (act of imposing, burden) imposición *f*; (abuse) abuso *m*
impossibility [ɪmpɑsəbílɪɒi] N imposibilidad *f*
impossible [ɪmpásəbəɫ] ADJ (not possible) imposible; (unbearable) insoportable; **to make —** imposibilitar
impostor [ɪmpástɔ˞] N impostor -ra *mf*
impotence [ímpətəns] N impotencia *f*
impotent [ímpətənt] ADJ impotente
impoverish [ɪmpávə˞ɪʃ] VT empobrecer
impregnate [ɪmprégnet] VT (cause to be permeated) impregnar; (make pregnant) fecundar
impress [ɪmprés] VT (make a mark by pressing) estampar; VI/VT (affect deeply) impresionar
impression [ɪmpréʃən] N impresión *f*; (feeling) impresión *f*, sensación *f*
impressive [ɪmprésɪv] ADJ impresionante
imprint [ímprɪnt] N (indentation) impresión *f*, marca *f*; (printer's mark) pie de imprenta *m*; [ɪmprínt] VT (impress on) imprimir; (fix firmly in mind) grabar
imprison [ɪmprízən] VT (in jail) encarcelar; (anywhere) apresar
imprisonment [ɪmprízənmənt] N encarcelamiento *m*
improbable [ɪmprábəbəɫ] ADJ improbable
impromptu [ɪmprámptu] ADJ improvisado; **he gave the speech —** improvisó el discurso; N impromptu *m*
improper [ɪmprápə˞] ADJ indecoroso, inconveniente
improve [ɪmprúv] VI/VT mejorar(se); **to — upon** mejorar
improvement [ɪmprúvmənt] N (act & effect of improving) mejora *f*; (in health) mejoría *f*
improvisation [ɪmprɑvɪzéʃən] N improvisación *f*
improvise [ímprəvaɪz] VI/VT improvisar
imprudent [ɪmprúdn̩t] ADJ imprudente, desatinado
impudence [ímpjədəns] N impertinencia *f*, descaro *m*, desparpajo *m*
impudent [ímpjədənt] ADJ impertinente, descarado
impulse [ímpʌɫs] N impulso *m*; **to act on —** obrar impulsivamente
impulsive [ɪmpʌ́ɫsɪv] ADJ impulsivo
impunity [ɪmpjúnɪɒi] N impunidad *f*
impure [ɪmpjúr] ADJ impuro
impurity [ɪmpjúrɪɒi] N impureza *f*
in [ɪn] PREP en; **— London** en Londres; **— haste** de prisa; **— the morning** por / en la mañana; **— writing** por escrito; **she was walking — the street** andaba por la calle; **to arrive — London** llegar a Londres; **the books — the box** los libros de la caja; **at two — the morning** a las dos de la mañana; **dressed — white** vestido de blanco; **the tallest — his class** el más alto de su clase; **to come — a week** venir dentro de una semana; ADV adentro, dentro; **is she — or out?** ¿está adentro o afuera? **to be all —** estar rendido; **to be — with someone** estar bien con alguien; **to come —** entrar; **to have it — for someone** tenerle ojeriza a una persona; **to put —** meter; **the doctor is —** el doctor está; **hats are —** los sombreros están de moda; **—patient** paciente internado -da *mf*; **—seam** entrepierna *f*; **—step** empeine *m*; ADJ **the — place to eat** el restaurante de moda; **an — joke** una broma para un grupo selecto
inability [ɪnəbílɪɒi] N inhabilidad *f*, incapacidad *f*
inaccessible [ɪnæksésəbəɫ] ADJ inaccesible, inasequible
inaccurate [ɪnǽkjə˞ɪt] ADJ (not precise) inexacto, impreciso; (wrong) incorrecto
inactive [ɪnǽktɪv] ADJ inactivo
inactivity [ɪnæktívɪɒi] N inactividad *f*
inadequate [ɪnǽɒɪkwɪt] ADJ (insufficient) insuficiente; (unacceptable) inaceptable

inadvertent [ɪnədvɝ́·tn̩t] ADJ (unintentional) involuntario; (careless) descuidado, negligente

inadvisable [ɪnədváɪzəbəɫ] ADJ desaconsejable

inane [ɪnén] ADJ necio

inanimate [ɪnǽnəmɪt] ADJ inanimado

inasmuch as [ɪnəzmʌ́tʃæz] CONJ puesto que

inattentive [ɪnəténtɪv] ADJ desatento

inaudible [ɪnɔ́Dəbəɫ] ADJ inaudible

inaugurate [ɪnɔ́gjəret] VT (initiate) inaugurar; (induct into office) investir de un cargo

inauguration [ɪnɔgjəréʃən] N (initiation) inauguración f; (induction) investidura f

inboard [ínbɔrd] ADJ dentro del casco

inborn [ɪnbɔ́rn] ADJ innato

incandescence [ɪnkændésəns] N incandescencia f

incandescent [ɪnkændésənt] ADJ incandescente

incantation [ɪnkæntéʃən] N conjuro m

incapable [ɪnképəbəɫ] ADJ incapaz

incapacitate [ɪnkəpǽsɪtet] VT incapacitar

incarcerate [ɪnkársəret] VT encarcelar

incendiary [ɪnséndiɛri] ADJ & N incendiario -ria mf; — **bomb** bomba incendiaria f

incense [ínsɛns] N incienso m; [ɪnséns] VT encolerizar

incentive [ɪnséntɪv] N incentivo m, acicate m

inception [ɪnsépʃən] N comienzo m

incessant [ɪnsésənt] ADJ incesante

incest [ínsɛst] N incesto m

inch [ɪntʃ] N pulgada (2.54 centímetros) f; **to be within an — of** estar a un punto de; VI avanzar poco a poco

incidence [ínsɪdəns] N incidencia f

incident [ínsɪdənt] N incidente m, lance m; (crime, accident) suceso m

incidental [ɪnsɪdéntl̩] ADJ (happening in accordance with) accesorio; N — **music** música incidental f; —**s** gastos imprevistos m pl

incidentally [ɪnsɪdéntl̩i] ADV a propósito

incinerate [ɪnsínəret] VT incinerar

incipient [ɪnsípiənt] ADJ incipiente, naciente

incision [ɪnsíʒən] N incisión f

incisive [ɪnsáɪsɪv] ADJ incisivo

incite [ɪnsáɪt] VT incitar

inclement [ɪnklémənt] ADJ inclemente

inclination [ɪnklənéʃən] N (slope) inclinación f; (tendency) afición f, inclinación f

incline [ɪnkláɪn] VI/VT inclinar(se); [ínklaɪn] N declive m, pendiente f

include [ɪnklúd] VT incluir

inclusive [ɪnklúsɪv] ADJ inclusivo; **from Monday to Friday** — de lunes a viernes inclusive

incoherent [ɪnkohírənt] ADJ incoherente

income [ínkʌm] N Sp renta f; Am ingreso m; — **tax** Sp impuesto sobre la renta m; Am impuesto sobre ingresos m

incoming [ínkʌmɪŋ] ADJ entrante

incomparable [ɪnkámpə·əbəɫ] ADJ incomparable, sin parangón

incompatible [ɪnkəmpǽDəbəɫ] ADJ incompatible

incompetent [ɪnkámpɪtənt] ADJ incompetente

incomplete [ɪnkəmplít] ADJ incompleto

incomprehensible [ɪnkəmprɪhénsəbəɫ] ADJ incomprensible

inconceivable [ɪnkənsívəbəɫ] ADJ inconcebible

inconclusive [ɪnkənklúsɪv] ADJ no concluyente

inconsiderate [ɪnkənsíDɝ·ɪt] ADJ desconsiderado

inconsistency [ɪnkənsístənsi] N (condition) inconsecuencia f; (instance) incoherencia f

inconsistent [ɪnkənsístənt] ADJ inconsecuente

inconspicuous [ɪnkənspíkjuəs] ADJ poco llamativo; **to be —** pasar inadvertido

inconstancy [ɪnkánstənsi] N inconstancia f

inconstant [ɪnkánstənt] ADJ inconstante

incontinent [ɪnkántənənt] ADJ incontinente

incontrovertible [ɪnkɑntrəvɝ́·Dəbəɫ] ADJ incontrovertible

inconvenience [ɪnkənvínjəns] N (state of being inconvenient) inconveniencia f; (thing that is inconvenient) molestia f, inconveniente m; VT incomodar, molestar

inconvenient [ɪnkənvínjənt] ADJ (bothersome) incómodo; (untimely) inoportuno

incorporate [ɪnkɔ́rpəret] VI/VT (include) incorporar(se); (form a corporation) constituir(se) en sociedad

incorrect [ɪnkərékt] ADJ incorrecto

incorrigible [ɪnkɔ́rɪdʒəbəɫ] ADJ incorregible

increase [ɪnkrís] VI/VT aumentar(se), incrementar(se); [ínkris] N aumento m, incremento m

increasingly [ɪnkrísɪŋli] ADV cada vez más

incredible [ɪnkréDəbəɫ] ADJ increíble

incredulous [ɪnkrédʒələs] ADJ incrédulo

increment [ínkrəmənt] N incremento m

incriminate [ɪnkrímənet] VT incriminar

incubator [íŋkjəbeDɝ·] N incubadora f

inculcate [ɪnkʌ́ɫket] VT inculcar

incumbent [ɪnkʌ́mbənt] ADJ **a duty — upon me** un deber que me incumbe; N

titular *m*
incur [ɪnkə́-] VT incurrir en
incurable [ɪnkjúrəbəł] ADJ incurable
indebted [ɪndɛ́Dɪd] ADJ endeudado; **I'm — to you for your kindness** estoy en deuda contigo por tu amabilidad
indebtedness [ɪndɛ́DɪDnɪs] N endeudamiento *m*, adeudo *m*
indecency [ɪndísənsi] N indecencia *f*
indecent [ɪndísənt] ADJ indecente; **— exposure** delito de exhibicionismo *m*
indecision [ɪndɪsíʒən] N indecisión *f*
indeed [ɪndíd] ADV de verdad; INTERJ (ironically) ¡no me digas! (sincerely) ¡tienes razón!
indefensible [ɪndɪfɛ́nsəbəł] ADJ indefendible
indefinite [ɪndɛ́fənɪt] ADJ indefinido
indelible [ɪndɛ́ləbəł] ADJ indeleble
indelicate [ɪndɛ́lɪkɪt] ADJ (tactless) indelicado; (offensive) indecoroso
indemnify [ɪndɛ́mnəfaɪ] VT indemnizar
indemnity [ɪndɛ́mnɪDi] N indemnización *f*
indent [ɪndɛ́nt] VI/VT sangrar
indentation [ɪndɛntéʃən] N (notch) muesca *f*; (blank space) sangría *f*
independence [ɪndɪpɛ́ndəns] N independencia *f*
independent [ɪndɪpɛ́ndənt] ADJ independiente
indestructible [ɪndɪstráktəbəł] ADJ indestructible
indeterminate [ɪndɪtə́-mənɪt] ADJ indeterminado
index [índɛks] N índice *m*; **— card** ficha *f*; **— finger** índice *m*; VT (incorporate into an index) poner en el índice; (make the index) poner un índice; (adjust wages) indexar
India [índiə] N India *f*
Indian [índiən] ADJ & N indio -a *mf*; **— Ocean** Océano Indico *m*
indicate [índɪket] VT indicar
indication [ɪndɪkéʃən] N indicación *f*
indicative [ɪndíkəDɪV] ADJ & N indicativo *m*
indict [ɪndáɪt] VT acusar
indictment [ɪndáɪtmənt] N acusación *f*
indifference [ɪndífrəns] N indiferencia *f*
indifferent [ɪndífrənt] ADJ indiferente
indigenous [ɪndíʤənəs] ADJ (person) indígena; (plant, animal) autóctono
indigent [índɪʤənt] ADJ & N indigente *mf*
indigestion [ɪndɪʤéstʃən] N indigestión *f*
indignant [ɪndígnənt] ADJ indignado
indignation [ɪndɪgnéʃən] N indignación *f*
indignity [ɪndígnɪDi] N ultraje *m*, afrenta *f*
indigo [índɪgo] N índigo *m*, añil *m*; **— blue** azul añil *m*

indirect [ɪndɪrɛ́kt] ADJ indirecto; **— object** complemento ⁄ objeto indirecto *m*
indiscreet [ɪndɪskrít] ADJ indiscreto
indiscretion [ɪndɪskréʃən] N indiscreción *f*
indispensable [ɪndɪspɛ́nsəbəł] ADJ indispensable, imprescindible
indispose [ɪndɪspóz] VT indisponer
indisposed [ɪndɪspózd] ADJ indispuesto; **to become —** indisponerse
indistinct [ɪndɪstíŋkt] ADJ indistinto
individual [ɪndəvíʤuəł] ADJ individual; N individuo *m*, persona *f*; *pej* sujeto *m*, individuo *m*
individualism [ɪndəvíʤuəlɪzəm] N individualismo *m*
individualist [ɪndəvíʤuəlɪst] N individualista *mf*
individuality [ɪndəvɪʤuǽlɪDi] N individualidad *f*
indivisible [ɪndəvízəbəł] ADJ indivisible
indoctrinate [ɪndáktrɪnet] VT adoctrinar
indolence [índələns] N indolencia *f*, desidia *f*
indolent [índələnt] ADJ indolente, haragán
indomitable [ɪndámɪDəbəł] ADJ indomable
Indonesia [ɪndəníʒə] N Indonesia *f*
Indonesian [ɪndəníʒən] ADJ & N indonesio -sia *mf*
indoor [índɔr] ADJ interior; [ɪndɔ́rz] ADV **—s** dentro; **to go —s** entrar, ir para adentro
induce [ɪndús] VT inducir
inducement [ɪndúsmənt] N aliciente *m*, incentivo *m*
induct [ɪndákt] VT (initiate) admitir, iniciar; (draft) reclutar
induction [ɪndákʃən] N (philosophical, electrical) inducción *f*; (into an organization) admisión *f*, iniciación *f*
indulge [ɪndáłʤ] VT mimar, consentir; VI **to — in** darse a, entregarse a; **to — oneself (in)** darse el gusto (de)
indulgence [ɪndáłʤəns] N (act or state of indulging, religious) indulgencia *f*; (thing indulged in) exceso *m*, lujo *m*
indulgent [ɪndáłʤənt] ADJ indulgente; (toward a child) complaciente
industrial [ɪndástriəł] ADJ industrial
industrialist [ɪndástriəlɪst] N industrial *mf*
industrious [ɪndástriəs] ADJ (student) aplicado, diligente; (worker) industrioso
industry [índəstri] N (manufacturing) industria *f*; (hard work) diligencia *f*
inebriated [iníbrieDɪd] ADJ ebrio
inedible [ɪnɛ́dəbəł] ADJ incomestible, incomible
ineffable [ɪnɛ́fəbəł] ADJ inefable
ineffective [ɪnɪfɛ́ktɪv] ADJ (measure) ineficaz; (person) ineficiente

ineffectual [ɪnɪféktʃuəł] ADJ ineficaz
inefficient [ɪnɪfíʃənt] ADJ ineficiente
ineligible [ɪnélɪʤəbəł] ADJ inelegible
inept [ɪnépt] ADJ inepto
inequality [ɪnɪkwálɪDi] N desigualdad *f*
inert [ɪnɝt] ADJ inerte
inertia [ɪnɝ́ʃə] N inercia *f*
inescapable [ɪnɪsképəbəł] ADJ inevitable
inestimable [ɪnéstəməbəł] ADJ inestimable
inevitable [ɪnévɪDəbəł] ADJ inevitable
inexcusable [ɪnɪkskjúzəbəł] ADJ inexcusable
inexhaustible [ɪnɪgzɔ́stəbəł] ADJ inagotable
inexorable [ɪnéksɚəbəł] ADJ inexorable
inexpensive [ɪnɪkspénsɪv] ADJ económico,
  barato
inexperienced [ɪnɪkspíriənst] ADJ inexperto
inexplicable [ɪnɪksplíkəbəł] ADJ inexplicable
infallible [ɪnfǽləbəł] ADJ infalible
infamous [ínfəməs] ADJ infame, de mala
  fama
infamy [ínfəmi] N infamia *f*
infancy [ínfənsi] N primera infancia *f*
infant [ínfənt] N bebé *mf*
infantile [ínfəntaɪł] ADJ infantil
infantry [ínfəntri] N infantería *f*; **—man**
  infante *m*
infatuated [ɪnfǽtʃueDɪd] ADJ enamorado
infect [ɪnfékt] VT (cause disease) infectar;
  (spread a mood) contagiar
infection [ɪnfékʃən] N infección *f*
infectious [ɪnfékʃəs] ADJ (disease) infeccioso,
  contagioso; (mood) contagioso
infer [ɪnfɝ] VT inferir, deducir
inference [ínfɚəns] N inferencia *f*, deducción
  f
inferior [ɪnfíriɚ] ADJ inferior
inferiority [ɪnfiriɔ́rɪDi] N inferioridad *f*; **—
  complex** complejo de inferioridad *m*
infernal [ɪnfɝnəł] ADJ infernal
inferno [ɪnfɝno] N (fire) incendio *m*; (hot
  place) infierno *m*
infest [ɪnfést] VT infestar, plagar
infiltrate [ɪnfíłtret] VI/VT infiltrar(se); **to —
  an organization** infiltrarse en una
  organización
infinite [ínfənɪt] ADJ & N infinito *m*
infinitive [ɪnfínɪDɪv] ADJ & N infinitivo *m*
infinity [ɪnfínɪDi] N (large number) infinidad
  f; (space) infinito *m*
infirm [ɪnfɝm] ADJ enfermizo, achacoso
infirmary [ɪnfɝməri] N enfermería *f*
infirmity [ɪnfɝmɪDi] N enfermedad *f*,
  achaque *m*
inflame [ɪnflém] VT (with infection)
  inflamar(se); (with passion) enardecer(se);
  (with fire) encender(se)
inflammation [ɪnfləméʃən] N inflamación *f*

inflate [ɪnflét] VI/VT (fill with air) inflar(se),
  hincharse; (exaggerate) exagerar
inflation [ɪnfléʃən] N (rise in prices) inflación
  f; (introduction of air) inflado *m*
inflexible [ɪnfléksəbəł] ADJ inflexible
inflict [ɪnflíkt] VT (impose on) infligir; **to —
  a blow** asestar un golpe
influence [ínfluəns] N influencia *f*, influjo *m*;
  VT influir en / sobre; **— peddling** tráfico
  de influencias *m*
influential [ɪnfluénʃəł] ADJ influyente
influenza [ɪnfluénzə] N gripe *f*
influx [ínflʌks] N (of fluid, goods) entrada *f*;
  (of people) afluencia *f*
infomercial [ínfomɝʃəł] N infomercial *m*
inform [ɪnfɔ́rm] VI/VT (give knowledge)
  informar(se); VT (inspire) inspirar; **to —
  against / on** delatar a, denunciar a
informal [ɪnfɔ́rməł] ADJ informal
informant [ɪnfɔ́rmənt] N informante *mf*
information [ɪnfɚméʃən] N (service)
  información *f*; (details) informes *m pl*
informer [ɪnfɔ́rmɚ] N informante *mf*, delator
  -ora *mf*, *pej* soplón -ona *mf*
infraction [ɪnfrǽkʃən] N infracción *f*
infrared [ɪnfrəréd] ADJ & N infrarrojo *m*
infrastructure [ínfrəstrʌktʃɚ] N
  infraestructura *f*
infringe [ɪnfrínʤ] VT infringir; VI **to —
  upon** violar
infuriate [ɪnfjúriet] VT enfurecer, sublevar
infuse [ɪnfjúz] VT infundir
ingenious [ɪnʤínjəs] ADJ ingenioso
ingenuity [ɪnʤənúɪDi] N ingenio *m*,
  inventiva *f*
ingest [ɪnʤést] VI/VT ingerir
ingrate [íngret] N ingrato -ta *mf*
ingratitude [ɪngrǽDɪtud] N ingratitud *f*
ingredient [ɪngrídiənt] N ingrediente *m*
ingrown [íngron] ADJ encarnado
inhabit [ɪnhǽbɪt] VT habitar
inhabitant [ɪnhǽbɪtənt] N habitante *mf*
inhale [ɪnhél] VI/VT inhalar, aspirar
inherent [ɪnhérənt] ADJ inherente
inherit [ɪnhérɪt] VI/VT heredar
inheritance [ɪnhérɪDəns] N herencia *f*
inhibit [ɪnhíbɪt] VT inhibir, cohibir
inhibition [ɪnɪbíʃən] N inhibición *f*,
  cohibición *f*
inhospitable [ɪnhɑspíDəbəł] ADJ (person)
  inhospitalario; (place) inhóspito
inhuman [ɪnhjúmən] ADJ inhumano
inimitable [ɪnímɪDəbəł] ADJ inimitable
initial [ɪníʃəł] ADJ & N inicial *f*; VT firmar las
  iniciales
initialize [ɪníʃəlaɪz] VT inicializar
initiate [ɪníʃiet] VT iniciar

initiative [ɪníʃəDɪv] N iniciativa *f*

inject [ɪndʒékt] vɪ/vᴛ inyectar(se), pinchar(se)

injection [ɪndʒékʃən] N inyección *f*

injunction [ɪndʒʌ́ŋkʃən] N mandato judicial *m*, orden judicial *f*

injure [índʒɚ] vɪ/vᴛ herir(se); (sports) lesionar(se)

injurious [ɪndʒúriəs] ADJ (harmful) perjudicial; (defamatory) injurioso

injury [índʒəri] N herida *f*, lesión *f*

injustice [ɪndʒʌ́stɪs] N injusticia *f*

ink [ɪŋk] N tinta *f*; vᴛ (mark with ink) entintar; (sign) firmar; **—-jet printer** impresora de inyección de tinta *f*; **—pad** almohadilla *f*; **—well** tintero *m*

inkling [íŋklɪŋ] N idea *f*

inlaid [ínled] ADJ incrustado; **— work** incrustación *f*

inland [ínlənd] ADJ interior; ADV tierra adentro

inlay [ɪnlé] vᴛ incrustar; [ínle] N incrustación *f*

inmate [ínmet] N (in a prison) preso -sa *mf*, recluso -sa *mf*; (in an asylum) internado -da *mf*; (in a hospital) paciente *mf*

inn [ɪn] N posada *f*, fonda *f*; **—keeper** posadero -ra *mf*, fondista *mf*

innate [ɪnét] ADJ innato

inner [ínɚ] ADJ (inside) interior; (intimate) íntimo; **— city** zona céntrica empobrecida *f*; **— ear** oído interno *m*; **—most** más recóndito; **— tube** cámara *f*

inning [íŋɪŋ] N entrada *f*

innocence [ínəsəns] N (absence of guilt) inocencia *f*; (naivety) candidez *f*, candor *m*

innocent [ínəsənt] ADJ & N inocente *mf*

innocuous [ɪnákjuəs] ADJ innocuo

innovation [ɪnəvéʃən] N innovación *f*

innuendo [ɪnjuéndo] N insinuación *f*

innumerable [ɪnúmərəbəɫ] ADJ innumerables

inoculate [ɪnákjəlet] vɪ/vᴛ inocular(se)

inoffensive [ɪnəfénsɪv] ADJ inofensivo

inoperable [ɪnápɚəbəɫ] ADJ inoperable

inopportune [ɪnapɚtún] ADJ inoportuno

inordinate [ɪnɔ́rdn̩ɪt] ADJ desmesurado

inorganic [ɪnɔrgǽnɪk] ADJ inorgánico; **— chemistry** química inorgánica *f*

input [ínput] N (electric, computer) entrada *f*; (opinion) opinión *f*; vᴛ ingresar / entrar datos

inquire [ɪnkwáɪr] vɪ/vᴛ inquirir, preguntar; **to — about / after** preguntar por; **to — into** indagar, investigar

inquiry [íŋkwari] N (scientific) investigación *f*; (police) pesquisa *f*; **we made — about hotels** hicimos averiguaciones acerca de hoteles

inquisition [ɪnkwɪzíʃən] N inquisición *f*

inquisitive [ɪnkwízɪDɪv] ADJ (curious) inquisitivo, curioso; (asking many questions) preguntón

insane [ɪnsén] ADJ demente, loco; **— asylum** manicomio *m*

insanity [ɪnsǽnɪDi] N locura *f*, demencia *f*

insatiable [ɪnséʃəbəɫ] ADJ insaciable

inscribe [ɪnskráɪb] vᴛ (mark) inscribir; (engrave) grabar; (dedicate) dedicar

inscription [ɪnskrípʃən] N (marks, engraving) inscripción *f*; (dedication) dedicatoria *f*

inscrutable [ɪnskrúDəbəɫ] ADJ inescrutable

insect [ínsɛkt] N insecto *m*

insecticide [ɪnsɛ́ktɪsaɪd] N insecticida *m*

insectivorous [ɪnsɛktívɚəs] ADJ insectívoro

insecure [ɪnsɪkjúr] ADJ inseguro

insensible [ɪnsénsəbəɫ] ADJ insensible

insensitive [ɪnsénsɪDɪv] ADJ insensible

inseparable [ɪnsépɚəbəɫ] ADJ inseparable

insert [ɪnsɚ́t] vᴛ insertar, introducir; (into a text) intercalar; [ínsɚt] N encarte *m*

insertion [ɪnsɚ́ʃən] N inserción *f*; (into a text) intercalación *f*

inside [ɪnsáɪd] PREP dentro de; ADV dentro, adentro; [ínsaɪd] N interior *m*; **to turn out** volver del revés; **—s** entrañas *f pl*; **he passed me on the —** me pasó por la derecha; ADJ (interior) interior; **— job** delito cometido por un empleado *m*; **— track** pista interior *f*

insider [ɪnsáɪDɚ] N privilegiado -da *mf*; **— trading** abuso de información privilegiada *m*

insidious [ɪnsíDiəs] ADJ insidioso

insight [ínsaɪt] N (intuition) perspicacia *f*; (discernment) discernimiento *m*

insignia [ɪnsígniə] N insignia *f*

insignificant [ɪnsɪgnífɪkənt] ADJ insignificante, menudo, nimio

insincere [ɪnsɪnsír] ADJ insincero

insinuate [ɪnsínjuet] vᴛ insinuar

insinuation [ɪnsɪnjuéʃən] N insinuación *f*

insipid [ɪnsípɪd] ADJ insípido, soso

insist [ɪnsíst] vɪ/vᴛ insistir; **to — on** insistir en

insistence [ɪnsístəns] N insistencia *f*

insistent [ɪnsístənt] ADJ insistente

insole [ínsoɫ] N plantilla *f*

insolence [ínsələns] N insolencia *f*

insolent [ínsələnt] ADJ insolente, atrevido

insoluble [ɪnsáljəbəɫ] ADJ insoluble

insolvent [ɪnsáɫvənt] ADJ insolvente

inspect [ɪnspékt] vᴛ inspeccionar; **to — the troops** pasar revista a la tropa, revistar la tropa

inspection [ɪnspékʃən] N inspección *f*; (of troops) revista *f*

inspector [ɪnspéktɚ] N inspector -ra *mf*

inspiration [ɪnspəréʃən] N inspiración *f*

inspire [ɪnspáɪr] VI/VT inspirar

instability [ɪnstəbílɪDi] N inestabilidad *f*

install [ɪnstɔ́ł] VT instalar (also computer term)

installation [ɪnstəléʃən] N instalación *f* (also computer term)

installment [ɪnstɔ́łmənt] N (payment of debt) cuota *f*; (of a book) entrega *f*, fascículo *m*; **to pay in —s** pagar a plazos

instance [ínstəns] N ejemplo *m*; **for —** por ejemplo; **court of first —** tribunal de primera instancia *m*

instant [ínstənt] N instante *m*; **this —** ahora mismo; ADJ inmediato; **— coffee** café instantáneo *m*

instantaneous [ɪnstənténiəs] ADJ instantáneo

instead [ɪnstéd] ADV **she didn't want a sandwich, so she ordered a hamburger —** no quería un bocadillo, así que pidió una hamburguesa en su lugar; **— of** en lugar de, en vez de

instigate [ínstɪget] VT instigar

instill [ɪnstíł] VT inculcar

instinct [ínstɪŋkt] N instinto *m*

instinctive [ɪnstíŋktɪv] ADJ instintivo

institute [ínstɪtut] N instituto *m*; VT instituir

institution [ɪnstɪtúʃən] N institución *f*

instruct [ɪnstrʌ́kt] VT (teach) instruir; (command, advise) dar instrucciones; (command) mandar

instruction [ɪnstrʌ́kʃən] N instrucción *f* (also computer term); **—s** (orders) órdenes *f pl*; (information) instrucciones *f pl*, indicaciones *f pl*

instructive [ɪnstrʌ́ktɪv] ADJ instructivo

instructor [ɪnstrʌ́ktɚ] N (of skills) instructor -ra *mf*; (of knowledge) profesor -ra *mf*

instrument [ínstrəmənt] N instrumento *m*; **— panel** salpicadero *m*, tablero *m*

instrumental [ɪnstrəméntl] ADJ instrumental; **to be — in** ser fundamental para

insubordinate [ɪnsəbɔ́rdn̩ɪt] ADJ insubordinado

insufferable [ɪnsʌ́fəˑəbəł] ADJ insufrible

insufficiency [ɪnsəfíʃənsi] N insuficiencia *f*

insufficient [ɪnsəfíʃənt] ADJ insuficiente

insulate [ínsəlet] VT aislar

insulation [ɪnsəléʃən] N aislamiento *m*

insulator [ínsəleDɚ] N (material) aislante *m*; (device) aislador *m*

insulin [ínsəlɪn] N insulina *f*

insult [ínsʌłt] N insulto *m*, injuria *f*; [ɪnsʌ́łt] VT insultar, injuriar

insulting [ɪnsʌ́łtɪŋ] ADJ insultante, injurioso

insuperable [ɪnsúpəˑəbəł] ADJ insuperable

insurance [ɪnʃúrəns] N seguro *m*; **— agent** agente de seguros *mf*; **— company** compañía de seguros *f*; **— policy** póliza de seguro *f*

insure [ɪnʃúr] VI/VT asegurar(se)

insurmountable [ɪnsɚmáʊntəbəł] ADJ insuperable

insurrection [ɪnsərékʃən] N insurrección *f*

intact [ɪntǽkt] ADJ intacto

intangible [ɪntǽndʒəbəł] ADJ intangible

integer [íntɪdʒɚ] N (número) entero *m*

integral [íntɪgrəł] ADJ (complete) integral; (forming part of) integrante; N integral *f*; **— calculus** cálculo integral *m*

integrate [íntɪgret] VT integrar; VI integrarse a

integrity [ɪntégrɪDi] N integridad *f*

intellect [íntl̩ekt] N intelecto *m*

intellectual [ɪntl̩éktʃuəł] ADJ & N intelectual *mf*

intelligence [ɪntélɪdʒəns] N inteligencia *f* (also secret information); **— quotient** coeficiente intelectual / de inteligencia *m*

intelligent [ɪntélɪdʒənt] ADJ inteligente

intelligible [ɪntélɪdʒəbəł] ADJ inteligible

intend [ɪnténd] VT pensar; **to — to do something** pensar hacer algo; **a book —ed for children** un libro destinado / dirigido a los niños

intense [ɪnténs] ADJ intenso

intensify [ɪnténsɪfaɪ] VI/VT intensificar(se)

intensity [ɪnténsɪDi] N intensidad *f*

intensive [ɪnténsɪv] ADJ intensivo

intent [ɪntént] N intención *f*, propósito *m*; **to / for all —s and purposes** en la práctica; ADJ atento; **— on** resuelto a

intention [ɪnténʃən] N intención *f*

intentional [ɪnténʃənəł] ADJ intencional

intentionally [ɪnténʃənəli] ADV a propósito

inter [ɪntɚ́] VT sepultar

interact [ɪntɚǽkt] VI interactuar

interactive [ɪntɚǽktɪv] ADJ interactivo

intercede [ɪntɚsíd] VI interceder

intercept [ɪntɚsépt] VT interceptar

interception [ɪntɚsépʃən] N interceptación *f*

intercession [ɪntɚséʃən] N intercesión *f*

interchange [íntɚtʃendʒ] N cambio *m*; (on road) enlace *m*; *Sp* intercambiador *m*; [ɪntɚtʃéndʒ] VI/VT cambiar, intercambiar

intercourse [íntɚkɔrs] N (sexual) relación sexual *f*; (social) comunicación *f*, trato *m*

interest [íntrɪst] N interés *m*; (financial) interés *m*, rédito *m*; (share in a business)

participación *f;* **mining** —s los negocios
mineros; — **rate** tasa de interés *f;* VT
interesar; **may I — you in a cookie?** ¿te
puedo ofrecer una galleta?
interested [íntrɪstɪd] ADJ interesado; **to be /**
become — in interesarse en / por
interesting [íntrɪstɪŋ] ADJ interesante
interface [íntɚfes] N interface *mf,* interfaz *f*
interfere [ɪntɚfír] VI interferir; (meddle)
entrometerse; **to — with** interferir en
interference [ɪntɚfírəns] N interferencia *f*
interim [íntɚɪm] N ínterin *m;* ADJ (person)
interino; (decision) provisional
interior [ɪntíriɚ] ADJ & N interior *m;* —
decoration decoración de interiores *f;* —
design diseño de interiores *m*
interjection [ɪntɚdʒékʃən] N interjección *f,*
exclamación *f*
interlace [ɪntɚlés] VI/VT entrelazar(se)
interlinear [ɪntɚrlíniɚ] ADJ interlineal
interlock [ɪntɚlák] VI/VT (gears) engranar(se);
(branches, etc.) entrelazar(se); N interlock
m
interlocking [ɪntɚlákɪŋ] ADJ (gears)
engranado; (branches) entrelazado
interlude [íntɚlud] N (interval) intervalo *m;*
(musical) interludio *m;* (theatrical)
entremés *m*
intermediate [ɪntɚmídiɪt] ADJ intermedio
interment [ɪntɝmənt] N entierro *m*
interminable [ɪntɝmənəbəɫ] ADJ
interminable
intermingle [ɪntɚmíŋgəɫ] VI/VT
entremezclar(se)
intermission [ɪntɚmíʃən] N entreacto *m,*
intervalo *m*
intermittent [ɪntɚmítn̩t] ADJ intermitente
intern [íntɝn] VT internar, confinar; N
(prisoner, doctor) interno -na *mf*
internal [ɪntɝnəɫ] ADJ interno, interior;
—-**combustion engine** motor de
combustión interna *m;* — **revenue** rentas
internas *f pl;* — **Revenue Service**
Hacienda *f*
internalize [ɪntɝnəlaɪz] VT interiorizar,
internalizar
international [ɪntɚnǽʃənəɫ] ADJ
internacional; — **law** derecho
internacional *m*
Internet [íntɚnet] N internet *m*
internist [ɪntɝnɪst] N internista *mf*
internship [íntɝnʃɪp] N (medical) internado
m; (student) práctica *f*
interpersonal [ɪntɚpɝsənəɫ] ADJ
interpersonal
interpose [ɪntɚpóz] VI/VT interponer(se)
interpret [ɪntɝprɪt] VI/VT interpretar

interpretation [ɪntɝprɪtéʃən] N
interpretación *f*
interpreter [ɪntɝprɪdɚ] N intérprete *mf*
interracial [ɪntɚréʃəɫ] ADJ interracial
interrelated [ɪntɚrɪlédɪd] ADJ
interrelacionado
interrogate [ɪntérəget] VI/VT interrogar
interrogation [ɪntərəgéʃən] N interrogación
f, interrogatorio *m*
interrogative [ɪntərágəDɪv] ADJ
interrogativo; N palabra / oración
interrogativa *f*
interrupt [ɪntərÁpt] VI/VT interrumpir
interruption [ɪntərÁpʃən] N interrupción *f*
intersect [ɪntɚsékt] VI/VT (math)
intersecar(se); (road) cruzar(se)
intersection [íntɚsekʃən] N (math)
intersección *f;* (street) cruce *m,*
intersección *f*
intersperse [ɪntɚspɝs] VT (scatter) esparcir;
(intermingle) entremezclar, entreverar;
(spice up) salpicar
interstate [íntɚstet] ADJ interestatal; N —
highway autopista interestatal *f*
interstellar [ɪntɚstélɚ] ADJ interestelar
interstice [ɪntɝstɪs] N intersticio *m*
intertwine [ɪntɚtwáɪn] VI/VT entrelazar(se)
interval [íntɚvəɫ] N intervalo *m*
intervene [ɪntɚvín] VI intervenir; (mediate)
interponerse, mediar
intervention [ɪntɚvénʃən] N intervención *f;*
(mediation) mediación *f*
interview [íntɚvju] N entrevista *f;* (for
entertainment) Sp interviú *f;* VT
entrevistar; VI entrevistarse
intestine [ɪntéstɪn] ADJ & N intestino *m;*
small — intestino delgado *m;* **large** —
intestino grueso *m*
intimacy [íntəməsi] N intimidad *f*
intimate [íntəmɪt] ADJ íntimo; (knowledge)
profundo; [íntəmet] VT insinuar, dar a
entender
intimation [ɪntəméʃən] N insinuación *f*
intimidate [ɪntímɪdet] VT intimidar,
acobardar
into [íntu] PREP **she came — the room**
entró en la habitación; **he put it — the**
box lo metió en la caja; **he translated**
it — German lo tradujo al alemán; **he**
ran — a tree chocó contra un árbol; **it**
fell — oblivion cayó en el olvido; **he**
went — medicine entró a medicina;
I'm really — pop music me ha dado
por la música pop
intolerable [ɪntálɚəbəɫ] ADJ intolerable
intolerance [ɪntálɚəns] N intolerancia *f*
intolerant [ɪntálɚənt] ADJ intolerante

intonation [ɪntənéʃən] N entonación *f*

intoxicate [ɪntáksɪket] VI/VT embriagar (also exhilarate); (poison) intoxicar

intoxication [ɪntaksɪkéʃən] N (drunkenness) embriaguez *f*; (poisoning) intoxicación *f*

intransigent [ɪntrǽnzɪʤənt] ADJ intransigente

intransitive [ɪntrǽnzɪDɪv] ADJ intransitivo

intrauterine device [ɪntrəjúDərɪndɪváɪs] N dispositivo intrauterino *m*

intravenous [ɪntrəvínəs] ADJ intravenoso

intrepid [ɪntrépɪd] ADJ intrépido

intricate [íntrɪkɪt] ADJ intrincado

intrigue [ɪntríg] VI/VT intrigar; [íntrig] N intriga *f*

intrinsic [ɪntrínzɪk] ADJ intrínseco

introduce [ɪntrədús] VT (put in, bring) introducir; (to a person) presentar

introduction [ɪntrədákʃən] N (putting in, preface) introducción *f*; (to a person) presentación *f*

introspection [ɪntrəspékʃən] N introspección *f*

introvert [íntrəvɝt] N introvertido -da *mf*

introverted [íntrəvɝDɪd] ADJ introvertido

intrude [ɪntrúd] VI/VT interrumpir; (penetrate, of rock) penetrar

intruder [ɪntrúDɚ] N intruso -sa *mf*

intrusion [ɪntrúʒən] N (interruption) interrupción *f*; (penetration) intrusión *f*

intrusive [ɪntrúsɪv] ADJ (rock) intrusivo; (people) entrometido

intuition [ɪntuíʃən] N intuición *f*

intuitive [ɪntúɪDɪv] ADJ intuitivo

inundate [ínəndet] VT inundar

invade [ɪnvéd] VI/VT invadir

invader [ɪnvéDɚ] N invasor -ra *mf*

invalid [ínvəlɪd] ADJ & N (infirm) inválido -da *mf*; [ɪnvǽlɪd] ADJ (not valid) nulo

invaluable [ɪnvǽljuəbəl] ADJ invalorable, inestimable

invariable [ɪnvériəbəl] ADJ invariable

invariably [ɪnvériəbli] ADV siempre

invasion [ɪnvéʒən] N invasión *f*

invent [ɪnvént] VT inventar

invention [ɪnvénʃən] N (act of inventing, thing invented) invención *f*, invento *m*; (falsehood) invención *f*

inventive [ɪnvéntɪv] ADJ inventivo

inventor [ɪnvéntɚ] N inventor -ra *mf*

inventory [ínvəntɔri] N inventario *m*; VT inventariar

inverse [ɪnvɝ́s] ADJ & N inverso *m*

inversion [ɪnvɝ́ʒən] N inversión *f*

invert [ɪnvɝ́t] VT invertir

invest [ɪnvést] VI/VT (money) invertir; (a rank upon someone) investir

investigate [ɪnvéstɪget] VI/VT investigar, indagar

investigation [ɪnvestɪgéʃən] N investigación *f*

investigator [ɪnvéstɪgeDɚ] N investigador -ra *mf*

investment [ɪnvéstmənt] N (of money) inversión *f*; (of rank) investidura *f*; — **broker** corredor -ra de bolsa *mf*

investor [ɪnvéstɚ] N inversionista *mf*, inversor -ra *mf*

invigorate [ɪnvígəret] VT vigorizar

invincible [ɪnvínsəbəl] ADJ invencible

invisible [ɪnvízəbəl] ADJ invisible

invitation [ɪnvɪtéʃən] N invitación *f*

invite [ɪnváɪt] VI/VT invitar; **to — trouble** buscarse problemas; [ínvaɪt] N *fam* invitación *f*

inviting [ɪnváɪDɪŋ] ADJ atractivo, seductor

in vitro fertilization [ɪnvítrofɚd[ɪzéʃən] N fertilización in vitro *f*

invocation [ɪnvəkéʃən] N invocación *f*

invoice [ínvɔɪs] N factura *f*; VT facturar

invoke [ɪnvók] VT invocar

involuntary [ɪnválənteri] ADJ involuntario

involve [ɪnváɫv] VT (take, last) suponer; **how much time will this —?** ¿cuánto tiempo supone esto? (consist of, entail) consistir en, involucrar; **what does your work —?** ¿en qué consiste tu trabajo? (be in question) ser cuestión de; **national security is —d!** ¡es una cuestión de seguridad nacional! (implicate) implicar; **they tried to — her** trataron de implicarla; (wrapped up in) estar metido; **he's very —d in the family business** está muy metido en el negocio familiar; (have a liaison) enredarse; **she got —d with a married man** se enredó con un hombre casado

involved [ɪnváɫvd] ADJ complicado, enrevesado

inward [ínwɚd] ADV hacia dentro; ADJ interior

iodide [áɪədaɪd] N yoduro *m*

iodine [áɪədaɪn] N yodo *m*

ion [áɪɑn] N ión *m*

ionize [áɪənaɪz] VT ionizar

IQ (intelligence quotient) [aɪkjú] N coeficiente de inteligencia *m*

Iran [ɪrán] N Irán *m*

Iranian [ɪréniən] ADJ & N iraní *mf*

Iraq [ɪrǽk] N Irak *m*

Iraqi [ɪrǽki] ADJ & N iraquí *mf*

irascible [ɪrǽsəbəl] ADJ irascible

irate [aɪrét] ADJ airado

ire [aɪr] N ira *f*

Ireland [áɪrlənd] N Irlanda *f*

iridescent [ɪrɪdésənt] ADJ iridiscente, tornasolado

iridium [ɪrídiəm] N iridio *m*

iris [áɪrɪs] N (of eye) iris *m*; (plant, flower) lirio *m*; (rainbow) arco iris *m*

Irish [áɪrɪʃ] ADJ irlandés; N (language) irlandés *m*; **the —** los irlandeses

irk [ɜ·k] VT fastidiar; **—ed** fastidiado

irksome [ɜ·ksəm] ADJ engorroso, molesto

iron [áɪə·n] N (element, golf club) hierro *m*; (appliance) plancha *f*; **in —s** en grilletes; ADJ férreo, de hierro; **—work** herrajes *m pl*; **—works** fundición *f*; VI/VT planchar; **to — out a difficulty** allanar una dificultad

ironic [aɪránɪk] ADJ irónico

ironing [áɪə·nɪŋ] N planchado *m*

irony [áɪrəni] N ironía *f*; (mockery) ironía *f*, sorna *f*

irradiate [ɪréɒiet] VT irradiar

irrational [ɪrǽʃənəɫ] ADJ irracional

irrefutable [ɪrɪfjúɒəbəɫ] ADJ irrefutable

irregular [ɪrégjələ·] ADJ irregular

irrelevant [ɪréɫəvənt] ADJ no pertinente; **your age is —** tu edad no viene al caso

irreparable [ɪrépə·əbəɫ] ADJ irreparable

irreplaceable [ɪrɪplésəbəɫ] ADJ irreemplazable

irreproachable [ɪrɪprótʃəbəɫ] ADJ irreprochable

irresistible [ɪrɪzístəbəɫ] ADJ irresistible

irresponsible [ɪrɪspánsəbəɫ] ADJ irresponsable

irretrievable [ɪrɪtrívəbəɫ] ADJ irrecuperable

irreverent [ɪrévə·ənt] ADJ irreverente

irrevocable [ɪrévəkəbəɫ] ADJ irrevocable

irrigate [íɾɪget] VI/VT (a garden) irrigar, regar; (the eyes) irrigar

irrigation [ɪɾɪgéʃən] N riego *m*, irrigación *f*; **— ditch** acequia *f*

irritable [íɾɪɒəbəɫ] ADJ irritable, colérico

irritate [íɾɪtet] VT irritar

irritating [íɾɪteɒɪŋ] ADJ irritante

irritation [ɪɾɪtéʃən] N irritación *f*

IRS (Internal Revenue Service) [aɪɑrés] N Hacienda *f*

Islam [ízlɑm] N islamismo *m*, islam *m*

Islamic [ɪzlɑ́mɪk] ADJ islámico

island [áɪlənd] N isla *f*

islander [áɪləndə·] N isleño -ña *mf*

isle [aɪɫ] N isla *f*

isobar [áɪsəbɑr] N isobara *f*

isolate [áɪsəlet] VT aislar

isolation [aɪsəléʃən] N aislamiento *m*

isolationism [aɪsəléʃənɪzəm] N aislacionismo *m*

isometric [aɪsəmétrɪk] ADJ isométrico

isotope [áɪsətop] N isótopo *m*

Israel [ízriəɫ] N Israel *m*

Israeli [ɪzréli] ADJ & N israelí *mf*

issue [íʃu] N (of printed matter) tirada *f*; (of stock, bonds) emisión *f*; (copy of a magazine) número *m*, entrega *f*; (of a fluid) flujo *m*; (problem) problema *m*, tema *m*; (progeny) descendencia *f*; **he's got —s** es muy acomplejado; **to take — with** discrepar de; VT (written material) publicar; (a decree) promulgar; (a permit, document) expedir; (shares) emitir; (to flow) brotar; (to come out of) salir de; (to descend from) descender de

isthmus [ísməs] N istmo *m*

it [ɪt] PRON **— all started yesterday** todo empezó ayer; **— is necessary** es necesario; **— is raining** llueve, está lloviendo; **— is said that** se dice que; **— is two o'clock** son las dos; **— was broken** estaba roto; **who is —?** ¿quién es? **if — weren't five o'clock** si no fueran las cinco; **I saw —** lo/la vi; **he talked about —** habló de eso; **what time is — ?** ¿qué hora es? **how is — going?** ¿qué tal? **I don't get —** no entiendo; **you're —!** ¡tú te/la quedas!/¡tú la traes!

Italian [ɪtǽljən] ADJ & N italiano -na *mf*

italic [ɪtǽlɪk] ADJ itálico; N **—s** letra bastardilla/cursiva *f*

italicize [ɪtǽlɪsaɪz] VT poner en bastardilla/cursiva

Italy [ídli] N Italia *f*

itch [ɪtʃ] VI/VT picar; **to be —ing to** tener ganas de; N comezón *f*, picazón *f*; (longing) ansia *f*

itchy [ítʃi] ADJ que pica; **it feels — to me** me pica

item [áɪɒəm] N (piece of news) artículo *m*; (topic of gossip) tema de conversación *m*; (unit) ítem *m*; (couple) pareja *f*

itemize [áɪɒəmaɪz] VT (list) enumerar; (break down) desglosar

itinerant [aɪtínə·ənt] ADJ itinerante, ambulante

itinerary [aɪtínə·reri] N (schedule) itinerario *m*; (guidebook) guía de viajeros *f*

its [ɪts] POSS ADJ su/sus, de él, de ella, de ello

itself [ɪtséɫf] PRON **this story wrote —** esta historia se escribió sola; **the bike was standing by —** la bici estaba parada sola; **the dog bit —** el perro se mordió (a sí mismo); **the fox found — a hole** la zorra se encontró una guarida

Ivorian [aɪvóriən] ADJ & N marfileño -ña *mf*

ivory [áɪvri] N marfil *m*; **— tower** torre de marfil *f*

Ivory Coast [áɪvrɪkóst] N Costa de Marfil *f*
ivy [áɪvi] N hiedra *f*

Jj

jab [dʒæb] VI/VT (hit) golpear; (hit with elbow) codear; N (blow) golpe *m*; (blow with elbow) codazo *m*; (in boxing) jab *m*, puñetazo directo *m*
jabber [dʒǽbɚ] VI (unintelligibly) farfullar; (incessantly) charlotear; N (unintelligible) farfulla *f*; (incessant) charloteo *m*
jack [dʒæk] N (tool) gato *m*; (card) sota *f*; (plug-in) hembra *f*, toma *f*; (flag) bandera de proa *f*; **—ass** asno *m*, burro *m* (also person); **—hammer** martillo neumático *m*; **—knife** navaja *f*; **— of all trades** hombre orquesta *m*; **—pot** premio gordo *m*; **—rabbit** liebre americana *f*; **you don't know —** no sabes ni un comino; VI/VT **to — off** *vulg* hacer(se) una paja; VT **to — up** (a car) alzar con gato; (prices) subir
jackal [dʒǽkəl] N chacal *m*
jacket [dʒǽkɪt] N (clothing) chaqueta *f*; (of a book) forro *m*; (of a potato) piel *f*
jade [dʒed] N jade *m*
jaded [dʒédɪd] ADJ (disenchanted) de vuelta; (sated) hastiado
jagged [dʒǽgɪd] ADJ recortado, desigual
jaguar [dʒǽgwɑr] N jaguar *m*
jail [dʒeł] N cárcel *f*; **—break** fuga *f*; VT encarcelar
jailer [dʒélɚ] N carcelero -ra *mf*
jalopy [dʒəlápi] N cacharro *m*
jam [dʒæm] VT (stuff) embutir; (block) atestar; (immobilize) trabar; (make unworkable) obstruir, atascar, atorar; (stop radio signals) interferir; VI (become stuck or unworkable) atascarse; (crowd in) apiñarse; **to — on the brakes** frenar de golpe; **to — one's fingers** pillarse los dedos; N (jelly) mermelada *f*, dulce *m*; (difficult situation) aprieto *m*; (traffic) embotellamiento *m*; **— session** jam *m*
Jamaica [dʒəmékə] N Jamaica *f*
Jamaican [dʒəmékən] ADJ & N jamaicano -na *mf*, jamaiquino -na *mf*
janitor [dʒǽnɪdɚ] N conserje *m*
January [dʒǽnjuɛri] N enero *m*
Japan [dʒəpǽn] N Japón *m*
Japanese [dʒæpəníz] ADJ & N japonés -esa *mf*
jar [dʒɑr] VI/VT (shake) sacudir(se); (clash) chocar; **to — one's nerves** ponerle a uno los nervios de punta; N (container) tarro *m*, frasco *m*, pote *m*; (large earthen container) tinaja *f*; (collision) choque *m*; (shake) sacudida *f*
jargon [dʒárgən] N jerga *f*
jasmine [dʒǽzmɪn] N jazmín *m*
jasper [dʒǽspɚ] N jaspe *m*
jaundice [dʒɔ́ndɪs] N ictericia *f*
jaunt [dʒɔnt] N excursión *f*; VI pasear
javelin [dʒǽvlɪn] N jabalina *f*
jaw [dʒɔ] N (of animal) quijada *f*; (of human) mandíbula *f*; (of carnivores) fauces *f pl*; **—bone** mandíbula *f*, maxilar *m*
jay [dʒe] N arrendajo *m*
jazz [dʒæz] N jazz *m*; VI **to — up** animar
jealous [dʒéləs] ADJ (possessive) celoso; (envious) envidioso; (protective) protector
jealousy [dʒéləsi] N celos *m pl*
jeans [dʒinz] N jeans *m pl*, vaqueros *m pl*
jeer [dʒir] VI/VT (mock) mofarse (de), burlarse (de); (boo) abuchear, befar; N (act of mockery) mofa *f*, burla *f*; (boos) abucheo *m*, befa *f*
jelly [dʒéli] N jalea *f*; **—fish** medusa *f*
jeopardize [dʒépɚdaɪz] VT comprometer, poner en peligro
jeopardy [dʒépɚdi] ADV LOC **in —** en peligro
jerk [dʒɚk] N (quick pull) tirón *m*; (muscular contraction) espasmo *m*; (idiot) *pej* pelmazo *m*; VI/VT tironear; **to — around** manipular, *vulg* joder; **to — off** *vulg* hacerse una paja; **—water** de mala muerte
jerky [dʒɚki] ADJ espasmódico; N tasajo *m*
jersey [dʒɚzi] N jersey *m*
jest [dʒest] N broma *f*, chanza *f*; **in —** en broma; VI bromear
jester [dʒéstɚ] N bufón *m*
Jesuit [dʒézuɪt] N jesuita *m*
jet [dʒet] N (stream) chorro *m*; (spout) surtidor *m*; (stone) azabache *m*; **— (air)plane** avión a reacción *m*; **— engine** motor a reacción *m*; **— lag** jet lag *m*; **—liner** avión a reacción de pasajero *m*; **— propulsion** propulsión a chorro *f*; **— set** jet-set *m*; **— stream** (of air) corriente en chorro *f*; (of a jet) chorro *m*; ADJ **—-black** negro como el azabache; VI (stream out) salir a chorros; (travel) volar en avión a reacción; VT (spew out) lanzar a chorros; (transport) transportar en avión a reacción
jettison [dʒédɪsən] VT echar por la borda
Jew [dʒu] N judío -día *mf*
jewel [dʒúəl] N (ornament, prized person) joya *f*, alhaja *f*; (stone) gema *f*; (watch jewel) rubí *m*; **— box** joyero *m*

jeweler [ʤúələˈ] N joyero -ra *mf*; **—'s shop** joyería *f*

jewelry [ʤúəˈtri] N joyas *f pl*, alhajas *f pl*; **— box** alhajero *m*; **— store** joyería *f*

Jewish [ʤúɪʃ] ADJ judío

jiffy [ʤífi] ADV LOC **in a —** en un santiamén

jig [ʤɪg] N giga *f*; **—saw** sierra de vaivén *f*; **—saw puzzle** rompecabezas *m sg*; VI (dance) bailotear; **to — up and down** zangolotearse

jiggle [ʤígəˈt] VI/VT zangolotear(se), zarandear(se); N zangoloteo *m*, zarandeo *m*

jilt [ʤɪˈtt] VT dejar plantado

jingle [ʤíŋgəˈt] VI tintinear; VT agitar; N retintín *m*; (short song) jingle *m*

jinx [ʤɪŋks] N gafe *m*; VT gafar

job [ʤab] N (task) tarea *f*; (position) trabajo *m*, empleo *m*; (theft) golpe *m*; **to be out of a —** estar sin trabajo; *Sp* estar en (el) paro; **by the —** a destajo; **to do a good —** hacer buen trabajo; VI trabajar a destajo

jobber [ʤábəˈ] N (day-worker) trabajador -ra a destajo *mf*; (wholesaler) vendedor -ra mayorista *mf*

jobless [ʤáblɪs] ADJ sin trabajo; *Sp* en paro

jock [ʤak] N deportista *mf*; **— (strap)** suspensorio *m*

jockey [ʤáki] N jockey *m*; VI **to — for position** disputarse la posición

jocular [ʤákjələˈ] ADJ jocoso

jog [ʤag] VI (run) correr; VT (refresh) refrescar; N trote *m*; **to go for a —** salir a correr

john [ʤan] N (urinal) *fam* meadero *m*; (customer of a prostitute) *fam* putañero *m*

join [ʤɔɪn] VI/VT juntar(se); (pipes) acoplar(se), unir(se); (bones) articular(se); (a club) asociarse (a); (the navy, etc.) alistarse (en)

joint [ʤɔɪnt] N (point of contact) juntura *f*, junta *f*; (connection between bones) articulación *f*, coyuntura *f*; (nodule on a plant) nudo *m*; (marijuana cigarette) porro *m*; (public place) antro *m*; **out of —** descoyuntado; ADJ (shared) común; **— account** cuenta conjunta *f*; **— action** acción colectiva *f*; **— owner** copropietario -ria *mf*; **— session** sesión plena *f*; **— venture** joint venture *m*

joke [ʤok] N broma *f*, chiste *m*; VI bromear

joker [ʤókəˈ] N (person who jokes) bromista *mf*, guasón -ona *mf*; (card) comodín *m*

jokingly [ʤókɪŋli] ADV en broma

jolly [ʤáli] ADJ jovial

jolt [ʤoˈtt] N sacudida *f*; VT sacudir; **to — along** avanzar a los tumbos

Jordan [ʤórdn̩] N Jordania *f*

Jordanian [ʤɔrdénɪən] ADJ & N jordano -na *mf*

jostle [ʤásəˈt] VI/VT codear(se), dar empujones (a); N empujón *m*

jot [ʤat] VT **to — down** apuntar; N pizca *f*

journal [ʤэˈnəˈt] N (diary) diario *m*; (periodical) revista *f*; (logbook) cuaderno de bitácora *m*

journalism [ʤэˈnəlɪzəm] N periodismo *m*

journalist [ʤэˈnəlɪst] N periodista *mf*

journalistic [ʤэˈnəlístɪk] ADJ periodístico

journey [ʤэˈni] N viaje *m*; VI viajar

joust [ʤaust] N justa *f*

joy [ʤɔɪ] N (delight) alegría *f*, regocijo *m*, alborozo *m*; (source of delight) deleite *m*; **—ride** paseo en coche robado *m*; **—stick** joystick *m*, palanca de juegos *f*

joyful [ʤɔífəˈt] ADJ alborozado

joyous [ʤɔ́ɪəs] ADJ jubiloso, alegre

jubilant [ʤúbələnt] ADJ jubiloso

jubilee [ʤubəlí] N jubileo *m*

judge [ʤʌʤ] N juez -za *mf*; **to be a good — of character** saber juzgar a la gente; VI/VT juzgar; (estimate) calcular

judgment [ʤʌ́ʤmənt] N juicio *m*; (in court) fallo *m*; **— day** día del juicio final *m*

judicial [ʤudíʃəˈt] ADJ judicial

judicious [ʤudíʃəs] ADJ juicioso, sensato

judo [ʤúDo] N judo *m*

jug [ʤʌg] N (pitcher) jarro *m*, jarra *f*; (storage jar) pote *m*; **—s** *vulg* tetas *f pl*

juggle [ʤʌ́gəˈt] VI/VT hacer juegos malabares (con), hacer malabarismo (con); **to — the accounts** manipular las cuentas

juggler [ʤʌ́gləˈ] N malabarista *mf*

jugular [ʤʌ́gjələˈ] N yugular *f*

juice [ʤus] N jugo *m*; (fruit only) *Sp* zumo *m*

juicer [ʤúsəˈ] N exprimidor *m*

juicy [ʤúsi] ADJ jugoso; **a — story** un cuento sabroso

jukebox [ʤúkbaks] N juke-box *m*

July [ʤulái] N julio *m*

jumble [ʤʌ́mbəˈt] VI/VT revolver(se) *m*; N revoltijo *m*

jumbo [ʤʌ́mbo] ADJ jumbo, gigantesco; **— jet** jumbo *m*

jump [ʤʌmp] VI (spring) saltar; (increase, as temperature, prices) dar un salto; VT (capture in checkers) comer; (ride a horse over barrier) hacer saltar; (mug) asaltar; (cross a river, mountains, etc.) salvar; **to — at** abalanzarse sobre; **to — over** saltar; **to — the track** descarrilarse; **to — to conclusions** hacer deducciones precipitadas; N salto *m*; (in prices) subida repentina *f*; **— rope** cuerda de saltar *f*; **to —-start** hacer un puente; **—suit** mono *m*

jumper [dʒʌ́mpɚ] N (person who jumps) saltador -ra *mf*; (dress) jumper *m*; *Sp* pichi *m*; — **cable** puente *m*

jumpy [dʒʌ́mpi] ADJ nervioso, asustadizo

junction [dʒʌ́ŋkʃən] N (act or state of joining) unión *f*; (joining of two rivers) confluencia *f*; (of two railways) empalme *m*; (of roads) entronque *m*

juncture [dʒʌ́ŋktʃɚ] N (point where joined) juntura *f*; **at this** — en esta coyuntura

June [dʒun] N junio *m*

jungle [dʒʌ́ŋgəɫ] N selva *f*, jungla *f*; **the law of the** — la ley de la selva

junior [dʒúnjɚ] ADJ (younger) menor; (more recent) más nuevo, de menos antigüedad; — **college** institución para los dos primeros anõs de la licenciatura *f*; **John Smith,** — John Smith, hijo; N estudiante del tercer año *mf*

juniper [dʒúnəpɚ] N enebro *m*

junk [dʒʌŋk] N (useless articles) trastos viejos *m pl*; (metal) chatarra *f*; (Chinese boat) junco *m*; — **dealer** chatarrero -ra *mf*; — **food** comida basura *f*, porquerías *f pl*; — **mail** publicidad por correo *f*; —**yard** chatarrería *f*; VT desechar, echar a la basura

junkie [dʒʌ́ŋki] N *fam* drogata *mf*, drogota *mf*

jurisdiction [dʒʊrɪsdíkʃən] N jurisdicción *f*

jurisprudence [dʒʊrɪsprúdn̩s] N jurisprudencia *f*

juror [dʒúrɚ] N miembro de un jurado *m*, jurado -da *mf*

jury [dʒúri] N jurado *m*; — **box** banco de jurado *m*; **to —-rig** chapucear

just [dʒʌst] ADJ justo; ADV (exactly) exactamente; (only) sólo; **he** — **left** acaba de salir; **she is** — **a little girl** no es más que una niña; **you'll** — **have to wait** tendrás que esperar; — **barely** apenas; **the meeting is** — **starting** la reunión está empezando

justice [dʒʌ́stɪs] N (fairness) justicia *f*; (judge) juez -za *mf*; **to bring to** — enjuiciar; **the painting doesn't do him** — el retrato no le favorece

justification [dʒʌstəfɪkéʃən] N justificación *f*

justify [dʒʌ́stəfaɪ] VT justificar

jut [dʒʌt] VI sobresalir, proyectarse

juvenile [dʒúvənaɪɫ] ADJ juvenil; — **delinquent** delincuente juvenil *mf*

juxtapose [dʒʌ́kstəpoz] VT yuxtaponer

Kk

kangaroo [kæŋgərú] N canguro *m*

karat, carat [kǽrət] N quilate *m*

kayak [káɪæk] N kayak *m*

Kazak, Kazakh [kəzǽk] ADJ & N kazako -ka *mf*

Kazakhstan [kəzákstɑn] N Kazajstán *m*

keel [kiɫ] N quilla *f*; VI/VT volcar(se); **to** — **over** (ship) volcar(se); (person) caer de cabeza, desplomarse

keen [kin] ADJ (sharp) afilado; (ear) fino; (mind) agudo, penetrante

keenness [kínnɪs] N agudeza *f*

keep [kip] VI (continue) seguir; (not spoil) aguantar; VT (retain) guardar; (maintain) mantener; (employ) tener; (look after) cuidar; **to** — **a diary** llevar un diario; **to** — **a secret** guardar un secreto; **to** — **at it** persistir; **to** — **away** mantener(se) alejado; **to** — **back** (stay away) tener a raya; (restrain) contener; **to** — **bad company** andar en mala compañía; **to** — **from** (prevent) impedir; (protect) proteger; **to** — **(on) talking** seguir hablando; **to** — **the door open** mantener la puerta abierta; **to** — **off the grass** no pisar el cesped; **to** — **up** (perform as well) seguir el tren; (stay informed) mantenerse al tanto; **to** — **one's hands off** no tocar; **to** — **someone posted** mantener al corriente a alguien; **to** — **quiet** estarse callado; **to** — **to the right** mantenerse a la derecha; **to** — **track of** (do accounts) llevar la cuenta de; (consider) no perder de vista; **to** — **watch** vigilar; **he** —**s a maid** tiene una criada; **she kept me on the phone** me (re)tuvo en el teléfono; N **for** —**s** (forever) para siempre; (for real) en serio

keeper [kípɚ] N (of people) guardián *m*; (of things) custodio *m*

keeping [kípɪŋ] N custodia *f*; **in** — **with** en armonía con

keepsake [kípsek] N recuerdo *m*

keg [kɛg] N barril *m*

kennel [kénəɫ] N residencia de perros *f*

Kenya [kénjə] N Kenia *f*

Kenyan [kénjən] ADJ & N keniata *mf*

kernel [kɝ́nəɫ] N (seed) semilla *f*, grano *m*; (essence) meollo *m*

kerosene [kérəsin] N queroseno *m*

kestrel [késtrəɫ] N cernícalo *m*

ketchup [kétʃəp] N salsa de tomate *f*, cátsup *m*

kettle [kédl] N caldera *f*, hervidor *m*; (for tea) tetera *f*; — **drum** tímpano / timbal *m*; **that's another — of fish** es harina de otro costal

key [ki] N (for locks) llave *f*; (secret, book of answers) clave *f*; (for winding) clavija *f*; (for keyboard) tecla *f*; (island) cayo *m*; (music) clave *f*; —**board** teclado *m*; —**hole** ojo de la cerradura *m*; —**note** tónica *f*; —**note address** discurso de apertura *m*; —**pad** teclado numérico *m*; — **ring** llavero *m*; — **signature** armadura *f*; —**stone** piedra angular *f*; —**stroke** pulsación (de la tecla) *f*; — **word** palabra clave *f*; **to sing on** — cantar a tono; ADJ clave; VT (scratch) rayar; **to be —ed up** estar sobreexcitado

khaki [kǽki] N kaki *m*, caqui *m*

kick [kɪk] VI/VT (person) patear; (horse) dar coces (a), cocear; VI (gun) dar un culatazo, retroceder; **to — around** (discuss) discutir; (to mistreat) dar por la cabeza; **to — at** dar patadas; **to — out** echar a patadas; **to — the bucket** estirar la pata; **to — up a lot of dust** levantar una polvareda; **to — a habit** dejar un vicio; N patada *f*, puntapié *m*; (of a horse) coz *f*; *Am* patada *f*; (of a gun) culatazo *m*; (in the air) pataleo *m*; **this whisky has a —** este whisky es fuerte; **I get a — out of swimming** me encanta nadar; —**back** comisión ilegal *f*; *Mex* mordida *f*; —**stand** soporte *m*; **to —start** arrancar

kid [kɪd] N (young goat) cabrito *m*, chivo *m*; (leather) cabritilla *f*; (child) niño -ña *mf*, chico -ca *mf*; — **stuff** juego de niños *m*; VI bromear, embromar, tomar el pelo

kidnap [kídnæp] VT secuestrar, raptar

kidnapper [kídnæpɚ] N secuestrador -ra *mf*

kidnapping [kídnæpɪŋ] N secuestro *m*, rapto *m*

kidney [kídni] N riñón *m*; — **bean** judía *f*; — **stone** cálculo renal *m*

kill [kɪɫ] VI/VT matar; (drink completely) terminar; (turn off) apagar; **that comedian —s me** ese cómico me mata de risa; N (animal killed) caza *f*; (slaughter) matanza *f*; —**-joy** aguafiestas *mf sg*

killer [kílɚ] N asesino -na *mf*; **a — game** un partidazo; — **bee** abeja asesina *f*; — **whale** orca *f*

killing [kílɪŋ] N (slaughter) matanza *f*; (murder) asesinato *m*; (game killed) caza *f*; **to make a —** llenarse de oro

kilo [kílo] N kilo *m*

kilobyte [kíləbaɪt] N kilobyte *m*

kilometer [kɪlámɪdɚ] N kilómetro *m*

kilowatt [kíləwɑt] N kilovatio *m*; —**-hour** kilovatio-hora *f*

kin [kɪn] N parentela *f*, parientes *m pl*; —**sman** pariente *m*; —**swoman** parienta *f*; **to notify the next of —** avisar a los deudos

kind [kaɪnd] ADJ (benevolent) bondadoso, bueno; (words) amable; **to be — to animals** ser cariñoso con los animales; —**hearted** de buen corazón; — **of tired** algo cansado; N clase *f*, tipo *m*, género *m*; **to pay in —** (without money) pagar en especie; (retaliate) pagar con la misma moneda

kindergarten [kíndɚgɑrtn̩] N jardín de niños *m*; *Sp* parvulario *m*

kindle [kíndl] VT (fire) prender; (interest) despertar, provocar; VI encenderse

kindling [kíndlɪŋ] N leña ligera *f*, astillas *f pl*

kindly [káɪndli] ADJ bondadoso, bueno; ADV (with kindness) amablemente; (please) por favor; **we thank you —** le agradecemos mucho; **not to take — to criticism** no aceptar de buen grado las críticas

kindness [káɪndnɪs] N (state) bondad *f*, amabilidad *f*; (act) favor *m*

kindred [kíndrɪd] ADJ emparentado; — **spirits** espíritus afines *m pl*, almas gemelas *f pl*

king [kɪŋ] N rey *m* (also chess, cards); (in checkers) dama *f*; —**fisher** martín pescador *m*; —**pin** (in a mechanism) pivote central *m*; (in bowling) bolo central *m*; (person) figura central *f*; —**-sized** extra grande

kingdom [kíŋdəm] N reino *m*

kingly [kíŋli] ADJ real

kink [kɪŋk] N (bend) doblez *m*; (pain) tortícolis *f*

kinky [kɪŋki] ADJ crespo; (sex) pervertido, *Sp* morboso

kinship [kínʃɪp] N parentesco *m*; (likeness) afinidad *f*

kiosk [kíask] N quiosco *m*

Kiribati [kirəbádi] N Kiribati *m*

kiss [kɪs] VI/VT besar(se); N beso *m*

kit [kɪt] N (of tools) caja *f*; (of first aid) botiquín *m*; (sewing notions) costurero *m*

kitchen [kítʃɪn] N cocina *f*; —**ware** utensilios de cocina *m pl*

kite [kaɪt] N (toy) cometa *f*; (bird) milano *m*

kitten [kítn̩] N gatito *m*

kitty [kídi] N (young cat) gatito *m*, minino *m*; (petty cash) caja chica *f*, fondo *m*

knack [næk] N buena mano *f*, maña *f*; **once you get the —** una vez que le agarras la vuelta / onda

knapsack [nǽpsæk] N mochila *f*

knave [nev] N pícaro *m*; (in cards) sota *f*

knead [nid] VT amasar, sobar

knee [ni] N rodilla *f*; **—cap** rótula *f*; **—-deep** hasta las rodillas; **—-jerk liberal** liberal fanático *m*; **—-jerk reaction** reacción visceral *f*; VT dar un rodillazo

kneel [niɫ] VI arrodillarse

knell [nɛɫ] N doble *m*; VI doblar

knickknack [níknæk] N chuchería *f*, baratija *f*

knife [naɪf] N cuchillo *m*; (big) cuchilla *f*; (folding) navaja *f*; (for carving) trinchante *m*; VT acuchillar; **at —point** a punta de cuchillo

knight [naɪt] N caballero *m*; (in chess) caballo *m*; **— errant** caballero andante *m*; VT armar caballero

knighthood [náɪthʊd] N (all knights) caballería *f*; (title) orden de la caballería *f*

knit [nɪt] VI/VT tejer; **to — one's brow** fruncir el entrecejo / el ceño

knitting [nídɪŋ] N tejido *m*; **— needle** aguja de punto *f*

knob [nɑb] N (on a door) pomo *m*, perilla *f*, tirador *m*; (protuberance) protuberancia *f*

knock [nɑk] VI (pound) golpear; (of motors) golpetear; (call at the door) llamar; VT (criticize) criticar; **to — a hole in the wall** hacer un agujero en la pared a golpes; **to — down** derribar, echar abajo, tumbar; **to — off** (stop working) terminar; (reduce) rebajar; (make fall) tirar; (kill) liquidar; **— it off!** ¡basta! **to — into** golpearse contra; **to — out** noquear; **to — over** voltear, revolcar; **to — up** *vulg* preñar; N (pounding) golpe *m*, toque *m*; (criticism) crítica *f*; (in a motor) golpeteo *m*; **—-kneed** patizambo, zambo; **—out** (boxing) nócaut *m*; (attractive person) bomba *f*

knocker [nákɚ] N (handle on door) llamador *m*, aldaba *f*; (breast) *vulg* teta *f*

knoll [noɫ] N morro *m*, loma *f*

knot [nɑt] N nudo *m* (also in wood, unit of speed); (of people) grupo *m*; (swelling) chichón *m*; VI/VT anudar(se)

knotty [nádi] ADJ (full of knots) nudoso; (difficult) dificultoso, enredado

know [no] VI/VT (to have knowledge of; to know how to) saber; VT (to be acquainted with, have sexual intercourse with) conocer; (to recognize) reconocer; (distinguish) distinguir; **to — how to swim** saber nadar; **to — of** estar enterado de; N **to be in the —** estar al tanto; **—-how** conocimiento *m*; **—-it-all** sabelotodo *mf*

knowing [nóɪŋ] ADJ (complicitous) cómplice; (astute) astuto

knowingly [nóɪŋli] ADV a sabiendas

knowledge [nálɪdʒ] N (awareness) conocimiento *m*; (information known) saber *m*, conocimientos *m pl*; **not to my —** no que yo sepa

knuckle [nákəɫ] N nudillo *m*; **—head** tarambana *mf*; VI **to — down** arremangarse, aplicarse con empeño; **to — under** someterse

Korean [kɔríən] ADJ & N coreano -na *mf*

kosher [kóʃɚ] ADJ kosher

Kuwait [kuwét] N Kuwait *m*

Kuwaiti [kuwéɖi] ADJ & N kuwaití *mf*

Kyrgyzstan [kɝgistán] N Kirguistán *m*

Ll

label [lébəɫ] N etiqueta *f*, rótulo *m*; (brand) marca *f*; (of recording companies) sello *m*; VT etiquetar, rotular

labor [lébɚ] N trabajo *m*, labor *f*; (body of workers) mano de obra *f*; (working class) clase obrera *f*; (uterine contractions) trabajo de parto *m*; **—-intensive** que requiere mucha mano de obra; **— union** sindicato *m*; **to be in —** estar de parto; ADJ laboral; VI (work) trabajar; (dedicate oneself) afanarse; **to — under a disadvantage** sufrir una desventaja

laboratory [lǽbrətɔri] N laboratorio *m*

laborer [lébərɚ] N jornalero -ra *mf*; (unskilled) peón -ona *mf*

laborious [ləbóriəs] ADJ (industrious) laborioso; (difficult) trabajoso

labyrinth [lǽbərɪnθ] N laberinto *m*

lace [les] N (cloth) encaje *m*; (cord) cordón *m*; VT (to adorn with lace) bordar con encaje; (to insert laces into) poner cordones a; (to spike) echar alcohol; VI atarse

lack [læk] N falta *f*, carencia *f*; VI/VT carecer de, faltarle a uno; **he —s courage** le falta valentía; **—luster** mediocre

lackey [lǽki] N lacayo *m*

lacking [lǽkɪŋ] ADJ (deficient) deficiente; **good maids are — in this town** faltan buenas criadas en este pueblo; **— in** falto de, carente de

laconic [ləkánɪk] ADJ lacónico
lacquer [lǽkɚ] N laca f; VT lacar, laquear
lactic acid [lǽktɪkǽsɪd] N ácido láctico m
ladder [lǽDɚ] N escalera f
laden [lédn̩] ADJ cargado
ladle [lédl] N cucharón m, cazo m; VT servir con cucharón
lady [léDi] N señora f, dama f; **—bug** mariquita f; **—like** muy fina; **—love** amada f; **ladies' room** Sp aseo / servicio de damas m
lag [læg] VI (fall behind) quedarse atrás, rezagarse; (flag) disminuir; N retardo m, retraso m
lagoon [ləgún] N laguna f
lair [lɛr] N guarida f
lake [lek] N lago m
lamb [læm] N cordero m; (yearling) borrego m
lame [lem] ADJ cojo; Am rengo; **—brained** idiota; **— duck** funcionario -ria cesante mf; **— excuse** pretexto tonto m; VT dejar cojo
lament [ləmént] N lamento m; VI lamentar(se); VT llorar
lamentable [ləméntəbəł] ADJ lamentable
lamentation [læməntéʃən] N lamentación f, lamento m
laminate [lǽmənet] VT laminar
lamp [læmp] N lámpara f; (on a street) farol m; **—post** farol m; **—shade** pantalla f
lance [læns] N lanza f; (lancet) lanceta f; VT lancear; (a wound) abrir con una lanceta
lancet [lǽnsɪt] N lanceta f
land [lænd] N tierra f; (lot) terreno m; (country) país m, tierra f; **—fill** vertedero m; **— grant** con terrenos concedidos por el estado; **—lady** casera f, propietaria f; **—lord** casero m, propietario m; **—mark** hito m (also historical), mojón m; **— mine** mina f; **—owner** hacendado -da mf; **—scape** paisaje m; **—scape architecture** paisajismo m; **—slide** derrumbe m, desprendimiento m; (election) victoria aplastante f; VI/VT (a ship) atracar; (an airplane) aterrizaje; VT (a fish) Sp coger; Am pescar; (a job) conseguir; **you'll — in jail** terminarás en la cárcel
landing [lǽndɪŋ] N (of a ship) desembarco m; (of cargo) desembarque m; (of an airplane) aterrizaje m; (place) desembarcadero m; (on stairs) descanso m; **— field** campo de aterrizaje m; **— gear** tren de aterrizaje m; **— strip** pista de aterrizaje f
lane [len] N (country road) sendero m; (road

division) carril m; (for ships) ruta f
language [lǽŋgwɪdʒ] N lengua f, idioma m; (faculty, computer) lenguaje m
languid [lǽŋgwɪd] ADJ lánguido
languish [lǽŋgwɪʃ] VI languidecer
languor [lǽŋgɚ] N languidez f
lanky [lǽŋki] ADJ larguirucho, zancudo
lanolin [lǽnəlɪn] N lanolina f
lantern [lǽntɚn] N farol m; (of a lighthouse) faro m, linterna f
Laos [léɑs] N Laos m
Laotian [leóʃən] ADJ & N laosiano -na mf
lap [læp] N (part of body) regazo m; (part of a race) vuelta f; **—dog** perro faldero m; **—top** laptop m; **to live in the — of luxury** vivir en la abundancia; VI/VT lamer
lapel [ləpéł] N solapa f
lapidary [lǽpɪdɛri] ADJ & N lapidario -ria mf
lapse [læps] N (period of time) lapso m; (linguistic error) lapsus m; (defect in memory) fallo m; (fall) caída f; (termination) caducidad f; VI (fall) caer; (decline) decaer; (end) caducar, vencer
larceny [lársəni] N latrocinio m, hurto m
lard [lɑrd] N manteca f; VT enmantecar; (with bacon) mechar
large [lɑrdʒ] ADJ grande; **—-scale** de gran escala; **a — company** una gran compañía / una compañía grande; **at —** (not in jail) suelto, libre; (in general) en general; N tamaño grande m
lariat [lǽriət] N reata f
lark [lɑrk] N (bird) alondra f; (bit of fun) diversión f; **to go on a —** ir de jarana
larva [lárvə] N larva f
laryngitis [lærəndʒáɪDɪs] N laringitis f
larynx [lǽrɪŋks] N laringe f
lascivious [ləsíviəs] ADJ lascivo
laser [lézɚ] N laser m; **— printer** impresora laser f
lash [læʃ] N (blow with a whip, tail, etc.) azote m, latigazo m; (blow of waves) embate m; (part of eye) pestaña f; VT azotar; (tie) amarrar; **to — out at** fustigar
lasso [lǽso] N lazo m, reata f; VT lazar; Am enlazar
last [læst] ADJ (in a series) último; (definitive) final; **—-ditch** desesperado; **— minute** de último momento; **— name** apellido m; **— night** anoche; **— rites** extrema unción f, viático m; **— straw** colmo m; **— word** última palabra f; **— year** el año pasado; **next to the —** penúltimo; ADV último; **to arrive —** llegar al último; **when — seen** cuando se lo vio por última vez; **at —** finalmente; N el último;

(of a shoe) horma *f;* VI durar; (live on) perdurar

lasting [lǽstɪŋ] ADJ duradero, perdurable

lastly [lǽstli] ADV por último

latch [lætʃ] N pestillo *m,* picaporte *m,* cierre *m;* VI cerrar con el pestillo; **to — on** agarrarse de; **to — onto** pegarse a

late [let] ADJ (tardy) tardío; (hour) avanzada; (recent) reciente, último; (recently deceased) finado; **—comer** rezagado -da *mf;* **— afternoon** atardecer *m;* ADV tarde; **— in the night** a una hora avanzada de la noche; **— into the night** hasta cualquier hora de la noche; **— in the week** a finales de la semana; **it is —** ya es tarde; **of —** últimamente; **to be —** llegar tarde; **to work —** trabajar hasta tarde; **the train was ten minutes —** el tren llegó con diez minutos de retraso

lately [létli] ADV últimamente

lateness [létnɪs] N tardanza *f*

latent [létn̩t] ADJ latente

later [léɖɚ] ADJ posterior; **see you —** hasta luego; **— on** más tarde

lateral [léɖɚəɫ] ADJ lateral

latest [léɖɪst] ADJ último; **the — fashion** la última moda; **the — news** las últimas novedades; **at the —** a más tardar; N la última

latex [létɛks] N látex *m*

lathe [leð] N torno *m*

lather [lǽðɚ] N (foam) espuma *f;* (sweat) sudor *m;* **he got into a —** se puso histérico; VT enjabonar; VI hacer espuma

Latin [lǽtn̩] ADJ latino; N latín *m;* **— America** América Latina *f,* Latinoamérica *f;* **— American** latinoamericano -na *mf*

latitude [léɖɪtud] N latitud *f;* (freedom) flexibilidad *f*

latrine [lətrín] N letrina *f*

latter [léɖɚ] ADJ último; **in the — days of the Roman Republic** en los últimos días de la República Romana; **toward the — part of the week** a finales de la semana; **the —** este *m,* esta *f*

lattice [léɖɪs] N enrejado *m,* entramado *m;* (of a window) celosía *f*

Latvia [lǽtviə] N Letonia *f*

Latvian [lǽtviən] ADJ & N letón -ona *mf*

laud [lɔd] VT loar

laudable [lɔ́ɖəbəɫ] ADJ laudable, loable

laugh [læf] VI reír(se); **to — at** reírse de; **to — loudly** reírse a carcajadas; **to — up / in one's sleeve** reírse para sus adentros; **she —ed in his face** se rió en su cara; N risa *f;* **we did it for —s** lo hicimos por diversión

laughable [lǽfəbəɫ] ADJ risible

laughingstock [lǽfɪŋstak] N hazmerreír *m*

laughter [lǽftɚ] N risa *f*

launch [lɔntʃ] VT (put into water) botar; (a rocket, new product) lanzar; **to — forth / out** lanzarse; N lancha *f;* (act of launching a boat) botadura *f;* (act of launching a rocket) lanzamiento *m*

launder [lɔ́ndɚ] VI/VT (wash) lavar; (money) blanquear, lavar; (wash and iron) lavar y planchar

laundry [lɔ́ndri] N (business establishment) lavandería *f,* lavadero *m;* (room in house) cuarto de lavado *m,* lavadero *m;* (clothes to be washed) ropa sucia *f;* (washed clothes) ropa limpia *f*

laurel [lɔ́rəɫ] N laurel *m* (also honor); **to rest on one's —s** dormirse sobre los laureles

lava [lávə] N lava *f*

lavatory [lǽvətɔri] N (basin) lavabo *m;* (bathroom) baño *m,* retrete *m*

lavender [lǽvəndɚ] N espliego *m,* lavanda *f;* ADJ lavanda

lavish [lǽvɪʃ] ADJ INV (generous) pródigo, espléndido; (abundant) abundante, copioso; VT prodigar; **to — praise upon** colmar de alabanzas a

law [lɔ] N ley *f;* (discipline) derecho *m,* jurisprudencia *f;* (police) policía *f;* **— and order** orden público *m;* **—breaker** infractor -ora *mf,* transgresor -ora *mf;* **—maker** legislador -ra *mf;* **— student** estudiante de derecho *mf;* **—suit** pleito *m,* litigio *m;* **to practice —** ejercer la abogacía; **to take the — into one's hands** hacer justicia por mano propia; ADJ **—-abiding** respetuoso de las leyes

lawful [lɔ́fəɫ] ADJ (in accordance with the law) legal; (allowed by law) lícito; (recognized by law) legítimo

lawless [lɔ́lɪs] ADJ (anarchic) anárquico; (illegal) ilegal

lawn [lɔn] N césped *m,* grama *f;* **— mower** cortadora de césped *f*

lawyer [lɔ́jɚ] N abogado -da *mf*

lax [læks] ADJ laxo

laxative [lǽksəDɪv] ADJ & N laxante *m,* purgante *m*

laxity [lǽksɪDi] N flojedad *f,* laxitud *f*

lay [le] VT colocar; (eggs) poner; (a cable) tender; (to have sexual intercourse with) *fam* tirarse a; **to — aside** (abandon) dejar de lado; (save) guardar; **to — a wager** apostar; **to — bare** poner al descubierto; **to — bricks** poner ladrillos; **to — down arms** rendir las armas; **to — down the law** imponerse; **to — hold of** asir, agarrar; **to — into** atacar; **to — off a workman** despedir temporalmente a un obrero; **to — one's head on a pillow** recostar la cabeza sobre una almohada; **to — open** exponer; **to — out a plan** trazar un plan; **to — up** almacenar; **to be laid up** estar en cama; **to — waste** asolar; N situación *f*, orientación *f*; **she's an easy — fam** es una mujer fácil; **—man** (nonexpert) lego *m*; (clergy) laico *m*; **—out** trazado *m*; ADJ lego, laico

layer [léə‑] N capa *f*; (geological) estrato *m*; (hen) gallina ponedora *f*; **— cake** tarta de capas *f*

laziness [lézinɪs] N pereza *f*, holgazanería *f*, flojera *f*

lazy [lézi] ADJ perezoso, holgazán, flojo

lead [led] N (metal) plomo *m*; (graphite) mina *f*; **— poisoning** intoxicación con plomo *f*; [lid] VT (guide) guiar; (guide a horse) llevar de la rienda; (induce, take) llevar, inducir; (be in charge, be first) encabezar; (direct) dirigir; (be superior to) estar a la cabeza de; **to — a life of ease** llevar una vida fácil; **to — astray** llevar por mal camino; **to — the way** mostrar el camino; VI (afford passage to, result in) llevar a; (be first) estar a la cabeza; N (first position) delantera *f*, primer lugar *m*; (clue) indicio *m*; (most important role) papel principal *m*; **— story** noticia principal *f*

leaden [lédn̩] ADJ (of lead) de plomo; (color) plomizo; (oppressive, slow) pesado

leader [lídə‑] N (in politics) líder *mf*, caudillo *m*; (in a race) líder *mf*; (in music) director -ora *mf*; (as a guide) guía *mf*

leadership [lídə‑ʃɪp] N dirección *f*, liderazgo *m*

leading [lídɪŋ] ADJ (most important) principal; (arriving first) delantero; **— man** primer actor *m*

leadoff [lídɔf] ADJ comienzo

leaf [lif] N hoja *f*; VI echar hojas; **to — through a book** hojear un libro

leafless [líflɪs] ADJ sin hojas, deshojado

leaflet [líflɪt] N (small leaf) folíolo *m*; (printed matter) volante *m*; (folded printed matter) pliego *m*

leafy [lífi] ADJ (with foliage) frondoso; (in the form of leaves) de hoja

league [lig] N (alliance) liga *f*; (unit of distance) legua *f*; VI/VT aliar(se)

leak [lik] N (in a roof) gotera *f*; (in a boat, bucket, etc.) agujero *m*; (of information) filtración *f*; (of gas, steam, electricity) escape *m*, fuga *f*; VI (roof) gotear(se); (boat)

hacer agua; (gas) salirse, escaparse; (information) filtrarse; VT pasar información

leaky [líki] ADJ (roof) que tiene goteras; (boat) que hace agua; (gas, electricity) que pierde

lean [lin] VI/VT (incline) inclinar(se); (support) apoyar(se), reclinar(se), recostar(se); **to — on** presionar; ADJ magro; **— year** mal año *m*

leap [lip] VI/VT saltar; **to — at** aprovechar; **to — to mind** ocurrírsele a uno; N salto *m*; **—frog** pídola *f*; **— year** año bisiesto *m*

learn [lɜn] VI/VT aprender; (find out) enterarse de

learned [lɜ́nɪd] ADJ erudito, letrado

learner [lɜ́nə‑] N estudiante *mf*; (driver) aprendiz -za *mf*

learning [lɜ́nɪŋ] N (result) erudición *f*, saber *m*; (process) aprendizaje *m*; **— disability** problema de aprendizaje *m*

lease [lis] N (action) arrendamiento *m*; (contract) contrato de arrendamiento *m*; (period) período de arrendamiento *m*; **to have a new — on life** nacer de nuevo; VI/VT arrendar

leash [liʃ] N traílla *f*, correa *f*

least [list] ADJ **he doesn't have the — chance** no tiene la más mínima posibilidad; **the — amount of money** la menor cantidad de dinero; **— common denominator** mínimo común denominador *m*; ADV menos; **the — important** lo menos importante; **at — al** menos, por lo menos; N **I received the — of anyone** yo fui el que recibió menos de todos

leather [léðə‑] N cuero *m*; ADJ de cuero; **— strap** correa *f*

leave [liv] VT (a person, thing) dejar; (a place) salir de, irse de; VI salir, partir; **to — off** (stop) parar de; (omit) omitir; **to — out** omitir; **I have two books left** me quedan dos libros; N permiso *m*; **to be on —** estar de licencia; **to take — of** despedirse de

leaven [lévən] N levadura *f*; VT leudar

leavings [lívɪŋz] N (leftovers) sobras *f pl*; (refuse) desperdicios *m pl*; (act of leaving) partida *f*

Lebanese [lebəníz] ADJ & N libanés -esa *mf*

Lebanon [lébənɑn] N Líbano *m*

lecherous [létʃə‑əs] ADJ lujurioso

lecture [léktʃə‑] N (presentation) conferencia *f*, disertación *f*; (sermon) sermón *m*; (longwinded speech) perorata *f*; VI (present) dar una conferencia, disertar; VT (scold) sermonear

lecturer [lέktʃərɚ] N conferenciante *mf*; (academic rank) profesor -ra *mf*

LED (light-emitting diode) [ɛlidí] N LED *m*

ledge [lɛdʒ] N cornisa *f*

ledger [lέdʒɚ] N libro mayor *m*

leech [litʃ] N sanguijuela *f*

leer [lir] VT (sideways) mirar de soslayo; (lecherously) mirar con lujuria; N (sideways) mirada de soslayo *f*; (lecherous) mirada lujuriosa *f*

leeway [líwe] N margen de maniobra *m*; (of a ship) deriva *f*

left [lɛft] ADJ izquierdo; —-**handed** zurdo, con la mano izquierda; —-**handed compliment** alabanza irónica *f*; —-**handed tool** herramienta para zurdos *f*; —-**wing** de izquierdas; N izquierda *f*; **at / on / to / toward the** — a / hacia la izquierda; **make a** — dobla / gira a la izquierda

leftist [lέftɪst] N & ADJ izquierdista *mf*

leg [lɛg] N (human) pierna *f*; (animal, furniture) pata *f*; (wading bird) zanca *f*; (furniture) pie *m*; (of a trip) etapa *f*; **to be on one's last** —**s** estar en las últimas; **to pull someone's** — tomarle el pelo a alguien; **to stretch one's** —**s** estirar las piernas

legacy [lέgəsi] N legado *m*

legal [líɡəɫ] ADJ (in accordance with the law) legal; (permitted by law) lícito; (recognized by law) legítimo; — **age** mayoría de edad *f*; — **fees** honorarios del abogado *m pl*; — **holiday** día feriado *m*; — **procedure** procedimiento jurídico *m*; — **tender** moneda de curso legal *f*

legalize [líɡəlaɪz] VT legalizar

legation [lɪɡéʃən] N legación *f*

legend [lέdʒənd] N leyenda *f* (also inscription); (of a map) clave *f*

legendary [lέdʒəndɛri] ADJ legendario

leggings [léɡɪŋz] N (ankle to knee) polainas *f pl*; (trousers) leggings *m pl*

legible [lέdʒəbəɫ] ADJ legible

legion [lídʒən] N legión *f*

legislate [lέdʒɪslet] VI/VT legislar

legislation [lɛdʒɪsléʃən] N legislación *f*

legislative [lέdʒɪslɛDɪv] ADJ legislativo

legislator [lέdʒɪslɛDɚ] N legislador -ra *mf*

legislature [lέdʒɪsletʃɚ] N legislatura *f*

legitimate [lɪdʒídəmɪt] ADJ legítimo

legitimize [lədʒídəmaɪz] VT legitimar

legume [léɡjum] N legumbre *f*

leisure [líʒɚ] N ocio *m*, holgura *f*; — **hours** horas de ocio *f pl*, tiempo libre *m*; **to be at** — estar desocupado; **do it at your** —

hazlo cuando te convenga

leisurely [líʒɚli] ADJ lento, deliberado; ADV sin prisa

lemon [lémən] N limón *m*; ADJ de limón; — **tree** limonero *m*

lemonade [lɛmənéd] N limonada *f*

lend [lɛnd] VI/VT prestar; **to** — **a hand** dar una mano

lender [léndɚ] N (person who lends) prestador -ora *mf*; (professional) prestamista *mf*

length [lɛŋkθ] N largo *m*, largura *f*, longitud *f*; (of movie) duración *f*; (of a book) extensión *f*; **at** — (in detail) pormenorizadamente; (finally) finalmente; **by two** —**s** por dos cuerpos; **two meters in** — dos metros de largo; **to go to any** —**s** hacer lo imposible

lengthen [léŋkθən] VI/VT alargar(se)

lengthwise [léŋkθwaɪz] ADV & ADJ a lo largo

lengthy [léŋkθi] ADJ largo, prolongado

lenient [líniənt] ADJ indulgente

lens [lɛnz] N lente *m*; (of the eye) cristalino *m*

Lent [lɛnt] N Cuaresma *f*

lentil [léntɫ] N lenteja *f*

Leon [león] N León *m*

Leonese [liəníz] ADJ leonés

leopard [lépɚd] N leopardo *m*

leprosy [léprəsi] N lepra *f*

lesbian [lézbiən] ADJ lesbiano; N lesbiana *f*

lesion [líʒən] N lesión *f*

Lesotho [ləsóto] N Lesoto *m*

less [lɛs] ADJ, ADV & PREP menos; **I have** — **than you do** tengo menos que tú; — **and** — cada vez menos

lessen [lésən] VI/VT disminuir, aminorar

lesser [lésɚ] ADJ menor

lesson [lésən] N lección *f*

lest [lɛst] CONJ no sea que; — **you should think I'm teasing** para que no vayas a creer que estoy bromeando

let [lɛt] VT (permit) dejar, permitir; (rent) alquilar; — **him come** que venga; —'s **do it** hagámoslo; **to** — **be** dejar en paz; **to** — **down** (lower) bajar; (disappoint) decepcionar; **to** — **go** soltar; **to** — **in** dejar entrar; **to** — **know** hacer saber; **to** — **off** dejar ir; **to** — **through** dejar pasar; **to** — **up** (permit to stand) dejar incorporarse; (cease) disminuir; N —**down** desilusión *f*; —**up** tregua *f*

lethal [líθəɫ] ADJ letal

lethargy [léθɚdʒi] N letargo *m*, sopor *m*; **to fall into a** — aletargarse

letter [léDɚ] N (of alphabet) letra *f*; (missive) carta *f*; — **box** buzón *m*; — **carrier** cartero -ra *mf*; —**head** membrete *m*;

—head paper papel membretado *m*; **—s** letras *f pl*; **the — of the law** la letra de la ley; **to the —** al pie de la letra; VT escribir

lettuce [lédɪs] N lechuga *f*

leukemia [lukímiə] N leucemia *f*

levee [lévi] N dique *m*

level [lévəł] ADJ llano, plano; N nivel *m* (also tool); VT (make level) nivelar, igualar; (to demolish) arrasar, allanar; (to knock down a person) tumbar; (to aim criticism) dirigir; (to aim a gun) apuntar; **—-headed** sensato; **— with** a nivel de; **a — teaspoon** una cucharada al ras; **to be on the —** ser serio; **to — off** quedar paralelo al suelo; **to — with** hablar en serio con / a

lever [lévə-] N palanca *f*

leverage [lévə-ɪdʒ] N (influence) palanca *f*; (physical) apalancamiento *m*

levity [lévɪDi] N ligereza *f*

levy [lévi] N (of taxes) recaudación *f*; (of troops) leva *f*; VT (taxes) recaudar; (troops) reclutar, hacer una leva de

lewd [lud] ADJ lascivo

lewdness [lúdnɪs] N lascivia *f*

lexical [léksɪkəł] ADJ léxico

lexicography [lɛksɪkágrəfi] N lexicografía *f*

lexicon [léksɪkɑn] N léxico *m*

liability [laɪəbílɪDi] N (disadvantage) desventaja *f*; (debits) pasivo *m*; (debts) deudas *f pl*; (responsibility) responsabilidad legal *f*; **— insurance** seguro contra daños a terceros *m*; **liabilities** obligaciones *f pl*

liable [láɪəbəł] ADJ responsable; **— to** propenso a; **she's — to get angry** es probable que se enoje

liaison [liézɑn] N enlace *m*; (illicit love affair) aventura *f*

liar [láɪə-] N mentiroso -sa *mf*, embustero -ra *mf*

libel [láɪbəł] N libelo *m*, difamación *f*; VT difamar

liberal [líbə-əł] ADJ & N liberal *mf*

liberalism [líbə-əlɪzəm] N liberalismo *m*

liberality [lɪbərǽlɪDi] N (generosity) liberalidad *f*; (tolerance) tolerancia *f*

liberalize [líbə-əlaɪz] VI/VT liberalizar(se)

liberate [líbəret] VT (give freedom to) libertar, liberar; (release from obligation) librar; (give off) desprender

liberation [lɪbəréʃən] N liberación *f*

liberator [líbəreDə-] N libertador -ra *mf*

Liberia [laɪbíriə] N Liberia *f*

Liberian [laɪbíriən] ADJ & N liberiano -na *mf*

libertine [líbə-tin] ADJ & N libertino -na *mf*, calavera *m*

liberty [líbə-DI] N libertad *f*; **at —** autorizado

libido [lɪbíDo] N libido *f*

librarian [laɪbrériən] N bibliotecario -ria *mf*

library [láɪbreri] N biblioteca *f*

libretto [lɪbréDo] N libreto *m*

Libya [líbjə] N Libia *f*

Libyan [líbjən] ADJ & N libio -bia *mf*

license [láɪsəns] N permiso *m*; (driver's permit, poetic freedom) licencia *f*; **— plate** placa *f*, matrícula *f*; VT (issue license to) otorgar una licencia; (give permission) autorizar

licentious [laɪsénʃəs] ADJ licencioso

lick [lɪk] VT (touch with tongue) lamer (also waves); (thrash) dar una paliza; (defeat) derrotar; N lamida *f*, lengüetazo *m*; (blow) golpe *m*; **not to do a — of work** no mover un dedo

lickety-split [lɪkɪDisplít] ADV en un santiamén

licking [líkɪŋ] N paliza *f*

licorice [líkə-ɪʃ] N regaliz *m*

lid [lɪd] N tapadera *f*, tapa *f*; (of eye) párpado *m*; (on prices) tope *m*

lie [laɪ] N (falsehood) mentira *f*, embuste *m*; (orientation of an object) orientación *f*; **— detector** detector de mentiras *m*; **to give the — to** desmentir; VI mentir; **to — one's way out of a situation** salirse de una situación a mentiras; (be buried) yacer; (to be on a flat surface) estar; (to be situated) estar situado; (be horizontal) tumbarse, acostarse; **he's lying in bed** está acostado en la cama; **to — back** recostarse; **to — down** acostarse, tumbarse; **to — in wait** acechar

Liechtenstein [líktənstaɪn] N Liechtenstein *m*

Liechtensteiner [líktənstaɪnə-] N liechtensteiniano -na *mf*

lien [lin] N gravamen *m*, carga *f*

lieutenant [luténənt] N teniente *mf*; **— colonel** teniente coronel *mf*; **— governor** vicegobernador -ora *mf*

life [laɪf] N vida *f*; **—-and-death** de vida o muerte; **—boat** bote de salvamento *m*; **— cycle** ciclo vital *m*; **— expectancy** expectativa de vida *f*; **—guard** salvavidas *mf sg*; **— imprisonment** prisión perpetua *f*; **— insurance** seguro de vida *m*; **— jacket** salvavidas *m sg*; **—like** natural, que parece vivo; **—long** de toda la vida; **— of the party** alma de la fiesta *f*; **— preserver** salvavidas *m sg*; **— raft** balsa salvavidas *f*; **—-support system** (in space) equipo de vida *m*; (in a hospital) máquina corazón-pulmón *f*; **—style** estilo de vida *m*; **—time** vida *f*; ADJ (relative to life) vital; (for duration of life) vitalicio; **—-sized** de tamaño natural

lifeless [láɪflɪs] ADJ (without living things) sin vida; (dead) muerto, sin vida; (fainted) desfallecido; (without liveliness) sin animación

lifer [láɪfɚ] N (prisoner) condenado -da a cadena perpetua *mf*; (soldier) militar de carrera *m*

lift [lɪft] VT levantar; (steal) robar; (plagiarize) copiar; VI (disperse) disiparse; (go up) elevarse; N (upward force) empuje *m*; (feeling) mejoría de ánimo *f*; (device for lifting) montacargas *m sg*; **to give someone a —** llevar en coche; *Mex* dar un aventón; **—off** despegue *m*

ligament [lígəmənt] N ligamento *m*

ligature [lígətʃɚ] N ligadura *f*

light [laɪt] N luz *f*; (device) luz *f*, lámpara *f*; (for traffic) semáforo *m*; (perspective) perspectiva *f*; (for cigarettes) fuego *m*; **—house** faro *m*; ADJ (well-lighted) claro; (of little weight) ligero, leve; (of clothes) fresco; *Am* liviano; **— blue** azul claro *m*; **—-emitting diode** diodo electroiluminiscente *m*; **—-headed** mareado; **—hearted** alegre; **— rain** lluvia fina *f*; **—-skinned** de tez blanca; **— touch** mano delicada *f*; **—weight** de peso ligero; **—-year** año luz *m*; **to make — of** restar importancia a; VI/VT (turn on, ignite) encender(se), prender(se); (provide light, brighten) iluminar(se); (land on) posarse en; **to — up** prender, encender, alumbrar; **to — upon** caer sobre

lighten [láɪtn̩] VI/VT (make / become lighter) aligerar(se), alivianar(se); (brighten) iluminar(se); **— up!** ¡No tomes las cosas a la tremenda!

lighter [láɪDɚ] N encendedor *m*

lighting [láɪDɪŋ] N iluminación *f*; (in the street) alumbrado *m*

lightness [láɪtnɪs] N (little weight) ligereza *f*, levedad *f*; (brightness) claridad *f*

lightning [láɪtnɪŋ] N relámpago *m*; **— bug** luciérnaga *f*; **— rod** pararrayos *m sg*; **it happened at — speed** pasó como rayo; VI relampaguear

likable [láɪkəbəɫ] ADJ agradable, simpático

like [laɪk] ADV & PREP como; ADJ semejante, parecido; **in — manner** del mismo modo; **to feel — going** tener ganas de ir; **to look — someone** parecerse a alguien; **it looks — rain** parece que va a llover; **—-minded** del mismo parecer; N **—s** gustos *m pl*, preferencias *f pl*; VT gustarle a

uno; **he —s dogs** le gustan los perros; **do whatever you —** haz lo que quieras; CONJ **he talked — he was crazy** hablaba como si estuviera loco; **she came — you predicted she would** vino, tal como tú pronosticaste; **I'm —, "you're crazy"** yo pensé / dije, "estás loco"; INTERJ **he was, like, way too old** era como que demasiado viejo

likely [láɪkli] ADJ (probable) probable; (believable) creíble; (promising) prometedor; **John is — to win** es probable que gane Juan; ADV probablemente

liken [láɪkən] VT comparar, asimilar

likeness [láɪknɪs] N (similarity) parecido *m*; (portrait) retrato *m*

likewise [láɪkwaɪz] ADV (the same thing) lo mismo; **we did —** hicimos lo mismo; (similarly) asimismo; (also) también

liking [láɪkɪŋ] N preferencia *f*, gusto *m*

lilac [láɪlək] N lila *f*; ADJ lila *inv*

lily [líli] N lirio *m*, azucena *f*; ADJ **—-white** (very white) blanquísimo; (pure) puro; (for whites only) exclusivamente para blancos

limb [lɪm] N (branch) rama *f*; (appendage) miembro *m*

limber [límbɚ] ADJ flexible; VT hacer flexible; VI **to — up** estirarse

lime [laɪm] N (mineral) cal *f*; (fruit, color) lima *f*; **—light** candilejas *f pl*; **in the —light** en el candelero; **—stone** piedra caliza *f*; **— tree** limero *m*, lima *f*

limit [límɪt] N límite *m*; **to the —** al máximo; VT limitar

limitation [lɪmɪtéʃən] N limitación *f*

limitless [límɪtlɪs] ADJ ilimitado

limousine [líməzin] N limusina *f*

limp [lɪmp] N cojera *f*, renguera *f*; VI cojear, renguear, renquear; ADJ (body) flácido; (plants) mustio

limpid [límpɪd] ADJ límpido

line [laɪn] N (bus route, telephone connection) línea *f*; (of words) renglón *m*, línea *f*; (row) raya *f*, hilera *f*; (cord) cuerda *f*; (persons waiting) cola *f*, fila *f*; (business) ramo *m*; (wrinkle) arruga *f*; (boundary) límite *m*; **— of credit** línea de crédito *f*; **—s** (in a play) parte *f*; **—up** hilera de personas *f*; (sports) alineación *f*; **drop me a —** escríbeme unas líneas; **off-—** fuera de línea; **on-—** en línea; **out of —** irrespetuoso; **to get in —** hacer cola; VI/VT (border) alinear, bordear; (put in a lining) forrar; **to — up** alinear(se)

lineage [líniɪdʒ] N linaje *m*, estirpe *f*

linear [líniɚ] ADJ lineal

lined [laɪnd] ADJ (with lines) rayado; (with a lining) forrado

linen [línɪn] N (fabric) lino *m*; (bedclothes, etc.) ropa blanca *f*

liner [láɪnɚ] N (ocean) transatlántico *m*; (air) avión comercial *m*; (eye) delineador *m*

linger [líŋgɚ] VI (stay) quedarse, demorarse; (persist) persistir; (saunter) rezagarse; (contemplate) detenerse; (delay death) aguantar

lingerie [lɑnʒəré] N lencería *f*

linguist [líŋgwɪst] N lingüista *mf*

linguistics [lɪŋgwístɪks] N lingüística *f*

liniment [línəmənt] N linimento *m*

lining [láɪnɪŋ] N forro *m*; **every cloud has a silver —** no hay mal que por bien no venga

link [lɪŋk] N (of a chain) eslabón *m*; (bond, tie) vínculo *m*; (computer, rail, radio connection) enlace *m*; VI/VT enlazar(se), conectar(se), vincular(se)

linnet [línɪt] N pardillo *m*

linoleum [lɪnóliəm] N linóleo *m*

linseed [línsid] N linaza *f*; **— oil** aceite de linaza *m*

lint [lɪnt] N pelusa *f*

lion [láɪən] N león *m*; **—'s share** la parte del león

lioness [láɪənɪs] N leona *f*

lip [lɪp] N labio *m*; (of a pitcher) borde *m*; **—stick** lápiz de labios *m*; **to —read** leer los labios; **don't give me no —!** no me contestes

liposuction [láɪposʌkʃən] N liposucción *f*

liqueur [lɪkɝ] N licor *m*

liquid [líkwɪd] ADJ líquido; **— assets** activo líquido *m*; **— measure** medida para líquidos *f*; N líquido *m*

liquidate [líkwɪdet] VI/VT liquidar

liquidation [lɪkwɪdéʃən] N liquidación *f*

liquidity [lɪkwídɪDi] N liquidez *f*

liquor [líkɚ] N bebida espirituosa *f*

lira [lírə] N lira *f*

lisp [lɪsp] N ceceo *m*; VI cecear

list [lɪst] N lista *f*; (of a ship) escora *f*; **— price** precio de lista *m*; **— server** servidor de lista *m*; VT (make a list) hacer una lista de; VI (lean) escorar; **this chair —s for two hundred dollars** esta silla está a doscientos dólares

listen [lísən] VI/VT (hear) escuchar, oír; (heed) escuchar, prestar atención; **to — in** (on radio) sintonizar; (eavesdrop) escuchar a hurtadillas

listener [lísənɚ] N oyente *mf*; **radio —** radioescucha *mf*, oyente *mf*

listing [lístɪŋ] N listado *m*

listless [lístlɪs] ADJ lánguido

lit [lɪt] ADJ (provided with light) iluminado; (tipsy) alegre, alumbrado

literacy [líDɚəsi] N (action of making literate) alfabetización *f*; (rate) alfabetismo *m*

literal [líDɚəɫ] ADJ literal

literary [líDɚɛri] ADJ literario

literate [líDɚɪt] ADJ (who can read and write) alfabeto; (erudite) erudito, letrado; **he's barely —** apenas sabe leer y escribir

literature [líDɚətʃɚ] N literatura *f*; (handbills) impresos *m pl*, folletos *m pl*; **the scientific —** la literatura científica

lithium [líθiəm] N litio *m*

Lithuania [lɪθuéniə] N Lituania *f*

Lithuanian [lɪθuéniən] ADJ & N lituano -na *mf*

litigation [lɪDɪgéʃən] N litigio *m*, pleito *m*

litter [líDɚ] N (young animals) camada *f*, cría *f*; (stretcher) camilla *f*; (straw) cama de paja para animales *f*; (trash) basura *f*; (for cats) arena higiénica *f*; VI/VT (dirty) ensuciar; (strew) esparcir; VI (give birth) parir

little [líDɫ] ADJ (small) pequeño, chico; (not much) poco; **— brother** hermano menor *m*, hermanito *m*; **— finger** (dedo) meñique *m*; **— pig** puerquito *m*; **a — coffee** un poco de café; **a — while** un ratito, un poco; ADV & N poco; **— by —** poco a poco

live [lɪv] VI/VT vivir; **to — up to** cumplir; **to — it up** tirar la casa por la ventana; **all the —long day** todo el santo día; [laɪv] ADJ vivo; (ammunition) cargado; **— coal** ascua encendida *f*; **— oak** roble de Virginia *m*; **—stock** ganado *m*; **— wire** (electric) cable cargado *m*; (person) persona vivaz *f*; **before a — audience** en vivo; **—-in** con cama; ADV en vivo y en directo

livelihood [láɪvlihʊd] N sustento *m*

liveliness [láɪvlinɪs] N viveza *f*, animación *f*

lively [láɪvli] ADJ (party) animado; (person) vivaz, avispado; ADV con animación

liver [lívɚ] N hígado *m*

livid [lívɪd] ADJ (bluish) lívido; (angry) furibundo

living [lívɪŋ] N (life) vida *f*; **to earn / make a —** ganarse la vida; ADJ vivo, viviente; **— room** sala *f*, living *m*; **— wage** sueldo suficiente para vivir *m*; **the —** los vivos

lizard [lízɚd] N lagartija *f*

llama [lámə] N llama *f*

load [lod] N carga *f*; (weight) peso *m*; (of a ship) cargamento *m*; **—s of** montones de;

VI/VT cargar; **to — down** colmar; **to — oneself down** agobiarse

loaf [lof] N hogaza de pan *f*, pan *m*; VI holgar, holgazanear, haraganear

loafer [lófɚ] N (idler) holgazán -ana *mf*, haragán -na *mf*, gandul -la *mf*; (shoe) mocasín *m*

loan [lon] N préstamo *m*; (to a government) empréstito *m*; **— shark** usurero -ra *mf*; **—word** préstamo *m*; VI/VT prestar

loath [loθ] ADJ renuente; **to be — to** ser renuente a

loathe [loð] VT aborrecer

loathsome [lóðsəm] ADJ repugnante, abominable

lob [lab] VT tirar por lo alto; N (tennis) globo *m*

lobby [lábi] N (vestibule) vestíbulo *m*; (special interest) grupo de presión *m*, lobby *m*; VI/VT (influence) presionar

lobbyist [lábiɪst] N lobbista *mf*, lobista *mf*

lobe [lob] N lóbulo *m*

lobotomy [ləbádəmi] N lobotomía *f*

lobster [lábstɚ] N langosta *f*

local [lókəɫ] ADJ local; **— train** tren de cercanías *m*

localize [lókəlaɪz] VT localizar

locate [lóket] VI/VT (establish in a place) situar, ubicar; (find) localizar; VI (settle) radicarse, establecerse

location [lokéʃən] N (position) ubicación *f*; (finding) localización *f*; **on —** en exteriores

lock [lak] N (door) cerradura *f*; (canal) esclusa *f*; (firearms, wrestling) llave *f*; (of hair) mechón *m*; **to have a — on the award** tener asegurado el premio; **—-out** cierre patronal *m*; **—smith** cerrajero -ra *mf*; VI/VT cerrar con llave; (make immovable) trabar(se); **to — in** encerrar; **to — out** dejar afuera; **to — up** (door) cerrar con llave; (animal) encerrar; (prisoner) encarcelar; (valuables) poner bajo llave

locker [lákɚ] N (for athletic equipment) casillero *m*; (for frozen food) cámara frigorífica *f*; **— room** vestuario *m*

locket [lákɪt] N relicario *m*, guardapelo *m*

locomotive [lokəmóɾɪv] N locomotora *f*

locust [lókəst] N langosta *f*; **— tree** algarrobo *m*

lodge [ladʒ] N (of fraternal organization) logia *f*; (cabin) cabaña *f*; (hotel) posada *f*, mesón *m*; VI/VT alojar(se), hospedar(se); **to — a complaint** presentar una queja

lodger [láʤɚ] N inquilino -na *mf*

lodging [láʤɪŋ] N alojamiento *m*, hospedaje *m*

loft [lɔft] N (attic) desván *m*; (for choir) coro *m*; (for hay) pajar *m*; VT tirar por lo alto

lofty [lɔ́fti] ADJ elevado, encumbrado

log [lɔg] N leño *m*, madero *m*, rollizo *m*; (ship record) cuaderno de bitácora *m*; (record of activity) diario *m*; **— cabin** cabaña de troncos *f*; VI/VT (cut trees) cortar; VT (write down) anotar; **to — in** entrar (al sistema); **to — off / out** salir (del sistema)

logarithm [lágərɪðəm] N logaritmo *m*

logic [láʤɪk] N lógica *f*

logical [láʤɪkəɫ] ADJ lógico

logistics [ləʤístɪks] N logística *f*

loin [lɔɪn] N ijada *f*; (in animals) ijar *m*; (cut of meat) lomo *m*; **—s** entrañas *f pl*

loiter [lɔ́ɪɾɚ] VI (idly) holgazanear; (with intent) merodear; **to — behind** rezagarse

loll [laɫ] VI arrellanarse

lollipop [lálipap] N *Sp* pirulí *m*; *Mex* paleta *f*; *RP* chupetín *m*

lone [lon] ADJ (solitary) solitario; (only) único

loneliness [lónlɪnɪs] N soledad *f*

lonely [lónli] ADJ solo

lonesome [lónsəm] ADJ solo

long [lɔŋ] ADJ largo; **a — way home** lejos de casa; **to work — hours** trabajar muchas horas; **— distance** de larga distancia; **— division** división de más de una cifra *f*; **—hand** letra manuscrita *f*; **— johns** calzoncillos largos *m pl*; **— jump** salto largo *m*; **—-lasting** duradero, perdurable; **—-lived** (batteries) duradero; (people) longevo; **—-range** de largo alcance; **—shoreman** estibador *m*; **—-term** a largo plazo; **— underwear** calzoncillo largo *m*; **—-winded** verborrágico, palabrero; **it's a — shot** es muy improbable; ADV mucho, mucho tiempo; **— ago** hace mucho tiempo; **— before** mucho antes; **— live . . . !** ¡viva . . . ! **—-suffering** sufrido; **all winter —** todo el invierno; **how — did he stay?** ¿cuánto tiempo se quedó ? **not for —** no por mucho tiempo; **so — !** ¡hasta luego! **to be — in coming** tardar en venir; **three meters —** tres metros de largo; **will you be —?** ¿tardarás mucho? **the whole day —** todo el santo día; VI **to — for** anhelar

longer [lɔ́ŋgɚ] ADJ más largo; ADV más; **no — ya** no; **how much —?** ¿hasta cuándo?

longevity [lanʤévɪɾi] N longevidad *f*

longing [lɔ́ŋɪŋ] N anhelo *m*; ADJ anhelante

longitude [lánʤɪtud] N longitud *f*

look [lʊk] VI (see) mirar; (seem) parecer; **it —s good on you** te queda bien, te luce; **to — after** atender, cuidar; **to — alike**

parecerse; **to — down on someone** despreciar a alguien; **to — for** (search for) buscar; (anticipate) esperar; **I — forward to it** lo espero con ansia, me da mucha ilusión; **to — into** investigar; **she —s her age** aparenta la edad que tiene; **to — out on** dar a, tener vista a; **to — out of** asomarse a; **— out!** ¡cuidado! **to — over** dar un vistazo a; **to — up** (upwards) levantar la vista; (in a directory) buscar; **to — up to** admirar; N (gaze) mirada *f*; (examination) vistazo *m*; **—-alike** doble *mf*; **—out** (person) vigía *mf*; (place) mirador *m*, vigía *f*; **to be on the —out** estar alerta; **—s** aspecto *m*, pinta *f*; **good —s** belleza *f*

looking glass [lúkɪŋglæs] N espejo *m*

loom [lum] N telar *m*; VI (appear indistinctly) dibujarse; (threaten) cernerse

loony [lúni] ADJ chiflado

loop [lup] N (for fastening) presilla *f*; (in a rope) lazo *m*; (of a flight) rizo *m*; (electric) circuito cerrado *m*; (computer programming, ice-skating) bucle *m*; **—hole** resquicio *m*, agujero *m*; VI (make a loop) hacer un lazo; (curve around) serpentear; (loop the loop) rizar el rizo; VT enlazar

loose [lus] ADJ (free) suelto; (not tight) flojo; (approximate) libre; (unfettered) desatado; (immoral) disoluto; (promiscuous) fácil; **— cannon** mono con una metralleta *m*; **— change** suelto *m*, cambio *m*; **— end** cabo suelto *m*; **—-fitting** holgado; **—-jointed** de articulaciones flexibles; **—-leaf** (de) hojas sueltas; **to let —** soltar; VT desatar, soltar

loosen [lúsən] VI/VT (untie) soltar(se), desatar; (make / become less tight / dense / strict) aflojar(se)

looseness [lúsnɪs] N (of skin) flojedad *f*; (of morals) relajamiento *m*; (of clothing) holgura *f*; (of soil) friabilidad *f*; (of translation) lo libre

loot [lut] N botín *m*; VI/VT saquear

lop [lɑp] VT (cut) cortar; (eliminate) eliminar; VI caer(se); ADJ **—sided** (leaning to one side) ladeado; (unbalanced) desequilibrado; (listing) escorado

lope [lop] VI correr a pasos largos

loquacious [lokwéʃəs] ADJ locuaz

loquat [lókwɑt] N níspero *m*

lord [lɔrd] N señor *m*; (God) Señor *m*; (British title) lord *m*; **—'s Prayer** Padrenuestro *m*; **my —!** ¡Dios mío! VI **to — it over someone** tratarle a alguien con arrogancia

lordly [lɔ́rdli] ADJ (kingly) señorial; (haughty) altivo

lordship [lɔ́rdʃɪp] N (title) señoría *f*; (power) señorío *m*

lore [lɔr] N saber *m*

lose [luz] VI/VT perder; (a pursuer) dejar atrás; **to — sight of** perder de vista; **to — oneself in thought** ensimismarse

loser [lúzə] N perdedor -ra *mf*

loss [lɔs] N (destruction) pérdida *f*; (misplacement) pérdida *f*, extravío *m*; (sports) derrota *f*; **to be at a —** no saber qué hacer; **to sell at a —** vender con pérdida; **—es** bajas *f pl*

lost [lɔst] ADJ perdido; **— in thought** absorto; **to get —** perderse, extraviarse

lot [lɑt] N (parcel) lote *m*; (luck) suerte *f*, destino *m*; (piece of land) solar *m*, terreno *m*; **the —** todo; **a — of / —s of** mucho(s); **a — of money** mucho dinero; **by —** al azar; **to draw —s** echar suertes; **to fall to one's —** caerle en suerte a uno; ADV **a — better** mucho mejor

lotion [lóʃən] N loción *f*

lottery [lɑ́Dəri] N lotería *f*

loud [laʊd] ADJ (noisy) ruidoso; (strong) fuerte; (ostentatious) chillón; ADV fuerte, alto; **—speaker** altavoz *m*, altoparlante *m*; **—mouth** bocazas *mf sg*

lounge [laʊndʒ] VI repantigarse, arrellanarse; **to — away** pasar holgazaneando; N (waiting-room) sala de espera *f*; (room in bar) salón *m*; (divan) diván *m*; **— chair** diván *m*

louse [laʊs] N piojo *m*

lousy [láʊzi] ADJ (infested with lice) piojoso; (contemptible) despreciable; (poorly done) pésimo

lout [laʊt] N bruto *m*

lovable [lávəbəɫ] ADJ adorable

love [lʌv] N (affection) amor *m*; (fondness) afición *f*; (in tennis) nada *f*; **— affair** aventura *f*, amorío *m*; **— at first sight** amor a primera vista *m*, flechazo *m*; **— life** vida sentimental *f*; **— seat** confidente *m*; **books were her great —** los libros fueron su gran pasión; **to be in —** estar enamorado; **to fall in — with** enamorarse de; **to make — to** hacerle el amor a; VI/VT amar, querer; **I — to eat apples** me encanta comer manzanas

loveliness [lávlinɪs] N (beauty) hermosura *f*; (charm) encanto *m*

lovely [lávli] ADJ (beautiful) hermoso; (charming) encantador; (pleasant) ameno

lover [lávə] N (sexually involved) amante *mf*; (in love) enamorado -da *mf*, amante *mf*;

(interested in) aficionado -da *mf*
loving [lávɪŋ] ADJ cariñoso, afectuoso
low [lo] ADJ (not high) bajo; (base) vil; (humble) humilde; (downcast) abatido; (deep in pitch) grave; — **beam** luces cortas *f pl*; **—brow** poco culto; **—-cal** de bajas calorías; **—down** verdad *f*; **—-end** barato; — **gear** primera marcha *f*; **—-grade** (inferior) inferior; (low) bajo; **—-key** tranquilo; **—land** tierra baja *f*; **—-level** de bajo nivel; **—life** canalla *f*; **—-tech** sencillo; — **tide** bajamar *f*, marea baja *f*; **dress with a — neck** vestido escotado *m*; **to be — on something** estar escaso de algo; **to be in — spirits** estar abatido／desanimado; ADV bajo; **to buy —** comprar barato; N (sound of a cow) mugido *m*; VI mugir
lower [lóɚ] VI/VT bajar; (prices) rebajar; (flag, sail) arriar; ADJ más bajo, inferior; **—case** minúscula *f*; — **house** cámara de diputados *f*
lowliness [lólɪnɪs] N humildad *f*
lowly [lóli] ADJ humilde
loyal [lɔ́ɪəł] ADJ leal
loyalty [lɔ́ɪəłti] N lealtad *f*
LSD (lysergic acid diethylamide) [ɛlɛsdí] N LSD *m*
lubricant [lúbrɪkənt] ADJ & N lubricante *m*
lubricate [lúbrɪket] VI/VT lubricar
lucid [lúsɪd] ADJ lúcido
luck [lʌk] N suerte *f*; **in —** de suerte; **to be out of —** estar de mala suerte; **to — into** conseguir por un golpe de suerte; **to — out** tener suerte
lucky [lʌ́ki] ADJ afortunado; — **charm** amuleto de la suerte *m*; **to be —** tener suerte
lucrative [lúkrəDɪv] ADJ lucrativo
ludicrous [lúdɪkrəs] ADJ ridículo
lug [lʌg] VT acarrear
luggage [lʌ́gɪdʒ] N equipaje *m*; — **rack** rejilla *f*
lukewarm [lúkwɔ́rm] ADJ (not warm or cold) tibio; (indifferent) indiferente
lull [lʌł] VT (put to sleep) arrullar; VI/VT (soothe) calmar(se); N (calm) calma *f*, tregua *f*; (sound) arrullo *m*
lullaby [lʌ́ləbaɪ] N canción de cuna *f*, nana *f*
lumber [lʌ́mbɚ] N madera *f*; **—jack** leñador *m*; **—man** maderero *m*; — **mill** aserradero *m*; **—yard** almacén de maderas *m*; VI/VT (cut trees) talar; (move heavily) moverse pesadamente; (make a low noise) tronar
luminous [lúmənəs] ADJ luminoso
lump [lʌmp] N (in breast) bulto *m*; (in sauce) grumo *m*; (in throat) nudo *m*; (of coal)

trozo *m*; (of rice) plasta *f*; (on head) chichón *m*; (of sugar) terrón *m*; **to take one's —s** recibir palos; — **sum** pago global *m*; VT juntar; VI agrumarse
lumpy [lʌ́mpi] ADJ grumoso
lunar [lúnɚ] ADJ lunar; — **eclipse** eclipse lunar *m*
lunatic [lúnətɪk] ADJ & N lunático -ca *mf*, loco -ca *mf*; — **fringe** extremistas *mf pl*
lunch [lʌntʃ] N comida *f*, almuerzo *m*; **—time** hora de almorzar／comer *f*; **out to —** (crazy) en la luna; VI comer, almorzar
lung [lʌŋ] N pulmón *m*
lunge [lʌndʒ] N arremetida *f*; VI arremeter, abalanzarse; **to — at** arremeter contra, abalanzarse sobre
lurch [lɚtʃ] N tambaleo *m*; **to give a —** tambalearse; **to leave someone in the —** dejar a alguien en la estacada; VI tambalearse, dar barquinazos
lure [lur] N (thing that attracts) atractivo *m*, gancho *m*; (in hunting) señuelo *m*; (in fishing) cebo *m*; VT atraer, seducir
lurid [lúrɪd] ADJ (gruesome) sangriento; (shocking) escabroso
lurk [lɚk] VI (lie in wait) estar en acecho, acechar; (move furtively) moverse furtivamente
luscious [lʌ́ʃəs] ADJ (delicious) exquisito, delicioso; (sexy) voluptuoso
lust [lʌst] N (sexual desire) lujuria *f*, lascivia *f*; (craving) deseo *m*, ansia *f*; VI desear; **to — after** codiciar
luster [lʌ́stɚ] N lustre *m*, brillo *m*
lustful [lʌ́stfəł] ADJ lujurioso
lusty [lʌ́sti] ADJ (robust) robusto; (full of lust) lujurioso
Luxembourg [lʌ́ksəmbɚg] N Luxemburgo *m*
Luxembourger [lʌ́ksəmbɚgɚ] N luxemburgués -esa *mf*
Luxembourgian [lʌksəmbɚ́giən] ADJ luxemburgués
luxurious [lʌgʒúriəs] ADJ (characterized by luxury) lujoso; (luxuriant) exuberante
luxury [lʌ́gʒəri] N lujo *m*; — **tax** impuesto suntuario *m*; ADJ de lujo
lye [laɪ] N lejía *f*
lying [láɪɪŋ] ADJ mentiroso
lymph [lɪmf] N linfa *f*; — **node** nodo linfático *m*
lynch [lɪntʃ] VT linchar
lynx [lɪŋks] N lince *m*
lyric [lírɪk] N poema lírico *m*; **—s** letra *f*; ADJ lírico
lyrical [lírɪkəł] ADJ lírico
lyricism [lírɪsɪzəm] N lirismo *m*

Mm

ma'am [mæm] N señora *f*
Macao [məkáʊ] N Macao *m*
macaroni [mækəróni] N macarrones *m pl*
Macedonia [mæsɪdóniə] N Macedonia *f*
Macedonian [mæsɪdónɪən] ADJ & N
macedonio -nia *mf*
machine [məʃín] N máquina *f*; (of
government) maquinaria *f*, aparato *m*; —
gun (not portable) ametralladora *f*;
(portable) metralleta *f*; — **language**
lenguaje de máquina *m*; **—-made** hecho a
máquina; VT trabajar a máquina
machinery [məʃínəri] N maquinaria *f*
machinist [məʃínɪst] N maquinista *mf*,
operario -ria *mf*
mackerel [mǽkəəɫ] N caballa *f*
mad [mæd] ADJ (crazy) loco; (angry) rabioso,
enojado; (hydrophobic) rabioso; **to be —
about someone** estar loco por alguien;
to drive — enloquecer, volver loco; **to
get —** enojarse; **to go —** volverse loco,
enloquecerse; **like —** como loco; **—man**
loco *m*
Madagascan [mædəgǽskən] ADJ & N
malgache *mf*
Madagascar [mædəgǽskɑr] N Madagascar *m*
madam [mǽdəm] N señora *f*; (woman who
runs a brothel) madama *f*
maddening [mǽdn̩ɪŋ] ADJ enloquecedor
made [med] ADJ **—-to-measure** hecho a la
medida; **—-to-order** hecho por encargo;
—-up (invented) inventado, falso;
(wearing make-up) maquillado; **to be —
of** ser de; **to have something —**
mandar hacer algo; **I'm a — man** estoy
hecho; **to have it —** estar hecho
madness [mǽdnɪs] N (insanity) locura *f*;
(anger) rabia *f*
Mafia [máfiə] N mafia *f*
mafioso [mɑfióso] N mafioso *m*
magazine [mǽgəzin] N (publication) revista
f; (room for ammunition) polvorín *m*;
(part of gun) cargador *m*
magic [mǽdʒɪk] N magia *f*; ADJ mágico; —
bullet panacea *f*; — **wand** varita mágica
f
magical [mǽdʒɪkəɫ] ADJ mágico
magician [mədʒíʃən] N mago -ga *mf*
magistrate [mǽdʒɪstret] N magistrado -da *mf*
magma [mǽgmə] N magma *m*
magnanimous [mægnǽnəməs] ADJ

magnánimo
magnate [mǽgnet] N magnate *m*
magnesia [mægnízə] N magnesia *f*
magnesium [mægnízɪəm] N magnesio *m*
magnet [mǽgnɪt] N imán *m*
magnetic [mægnɛ́DɪK] ADJ magnético; —
pole polo magnético *m*; — **resonance
imaging** imagen por resonancia
magnética *f*; — **tape** cinta magnetofónica
f
magnetism [mǽgnɪtɪzəm] N magnetismo *m*
magnetize [mǽgnɪtaɪz] VT magnetizar,
imantar
magnificence [mægnífɪsəns] N magnificencia
f
magnificent [mægnífɪsənt] ADJ magnífico
magnify [mǽgnɪfaɪ] VT (to make larger)
aumentar; (to make louder) amplificar; (to
exaggerate) exagerar, magnificar
magnitude [mǽgnɪtud] N magnitud *f*
magnolia [mægnólʲə] N (flower) magnolia *f*;
(tree) magnolio *m*
magpie [mǽgpaɪ] N urraca *f* (also hoarder)
mahogany [məhágəni] N caoba *f*
maid [med] N criada *f*, sirvienta *f*; (in hotel)
camarera *f*; — **of honor** dama de honor *f*
maiden [médn̩] N *lit* doncella *f*, virgen *f*; —
voyage primer viaje *m*; — **name** nombre
de soltera *m*
mail [meɫ] N correo *m*; (electronic) mensaje
m; (of metal) malla *f*; **—bag** cartera *f*;
—box buzón *m*; **—man** cartero *m*; —
order pedido por correo *m*; VT echar al
correo
maim [mem] VT mutilar
main [men] ADJ principal; N (pipe) cañería principal *f*; (sea)
alta mar *f*; **—frame** *Sp* ordenador central
m, *Am* computadora central *f*; **—land**
continente *m*; **—spring** muelle real *m*;
—stream tendencia mayoritaria *f*; **—stay**
pilar *m*, puntal *m*; — **street** calle
principal *f*
maintain [mentén] VT mantener (also
support); (assert) afirmar
maintenance [méntnəns] N (repairs)
mantenimiento *m*; (monetary support)
manutención *f*
maize [mez] N maíz *m*
majestic [mədʒéstɪk] ADJ majestuoso
majesty [mǽdʒɪsti] N majestad *f*; **Your —** Su
Majestad
major [médʒɚ] ADJ (greater) mayor, más
grande; (large) grande; — **key** mayor *m*; N
(military rank) comandante *m*; (field of
study) especialidad *f*; — **league** liga
mayor *f*; VI especializarse

majority [mədʒɔ́rɪDi] N mayoría f; **the —** el grueso; (age) mayoría de edad f

make [mek] VT (do) hacer; (create) fabricar; (cause) causar; (earn) ganar; (a speech) pronunciar; **to — a clean breast of** sacarse del pecho; **to — a decision** tomar una decisión; **to — a living** ganarse la vida; **to — a train** llegar a tiempo para tomar un tren; **to — a turn** girar, doblar; **to — away with** fugarse con; **two plus two —s four** dos y dos son cuatro; **to — believe** hacer de cuenta que; **to — out** (see) vislumbrar, divisar; (read) descifrar; (kiss) *Sp* morrear; *Am* besuquearse; **to — too much of** exagerar; **what do you — of that?** ¿cómo interpretas eso? **to — up** (a story) inventar un cuento; (after a quarrel) hacer las paces; (for a loss) recuperar; (one's face) maquillarse; (one's mind) decidirse; **to — up for** suplir; **you'll — a good teacher** vas a ser un buen profesor; N marca f; **—-up** (composition) composición f; (character) carácter m; (cosmetics) maquillaje m; ADJ **—shift** provisional

maker [mékɚ] N (creator) creador mf, hacedor -ora mf; (manufacturer) fabricante m

makings [mékɪŋz] N (potential) potencial m; (ingredients) ingredientes m pl

maladjusted [mælədʒʌ́stɪd] ADJ inadaptado

malady [mǽləDi] N mal m

malaise [məléz] N malestar m

malaria [məlériə] N malaria f, paludismo m

Malawi [məláwi] N Malawi m

Malawian [məláwiən] ADJ & N malawiano -na mf

Malaysia [məléʒə] N Malasia f

Malaysian [məléʒən] ADJ & N malasio -sia mf

malcontent [mǽɫkəntent] ADJ & N descontento -ta mf

Maldives [mɔ́ɫdaɪvz] N Maldivas f pl

Maldivian [mɔɫdíviən] ADJ & N maldivo -va mf

male [meɫ] ADJ (animal, plant) macho; (person) varón; (trait) masculino; N (animal, plant) macho m; (person) varón m

malevolent [məlévələnt] ADJ malévolo

malfunction [mæɫfʌ́ŋkʃən] N funcionamiento defectuoso m; VI funcionar mal

Mali [máli] N Malí m

Malian [máliən] ADJ & N malí mf

malice [mǽlɪs] N malicia f; **with — aforethought** con premeditación y alevosía

malicious [məlíʃəs] ADJ malicioso

malign [məláɪn] VT calumniar, difamar

malignant [məlígnənt] ADJ maligno

mall [mɔɫ] N (closed street) paseo m; (enclosed shopping area) galería f, centro comercial m

mallet [mǽlɪt] N mazo m

malnourished [mæɫnɚ́rɪʃt] ADJ desnutrido

malnutrition [mæɫnutríʃən] N desnutrición f

malpractice [mæɫprǽktɪs] N negligencia f, mala práctica f

malt [mɔɫt] N malta f; **—ed milk** leche malteada f

Malta [mɔ́ɫtə] N Malta f

Maltese [mɔɫtíz] ADJ & N maltés -esa mf

mama, mamma [mámə] N mamá f; **—'s boy** nene de mamá m

mammal [mǽməɫ] N mamífero m

mammography [mæmágrəfi] N mamografía f

mammoth [mǽməθ] ADJ enorme; N mamut m

man [mæn] N hombre m; (servant) criado m; (in games) pieza f, ficha f; **— and wife** marido y mujer; **—hunt** persecución f; **—kind** humanidad f; **—-of-war** (ship) buque de guerra m; (jellyfish) medusa f; **—power** (for work) mano de obra f; (for war) soldados m pl; **every — for himself** cada cual para sí; **to a —** unánimemente; ADJ **—-eating** que come carne humana; **—-made** (fiber) sintético; (lake) artificial; INTERJ ¡hombre! VT (a fort) guarnecer; (a ship) tripular; **to —handle** violentar

manage [mǽnɪdʒ] VT (succeed in) conseguir, lograr; (direct) dirigir, administrar; (maneuver) manejar; VI **to — without help** arreglárselas sin ayuda; **—d care** asociación mutualista de salud f

manageable [mǽnɪdʒəbəɫ] ADJ manejable; (hair) dócil

management [mǽnɪdʒmənt] N (act of managing) manejo m, dirección f; (persons controlling a business) gerencia f, gestión f

manager [mǽnɪdʒɚ] N (of a store) gerente -ta mf; (of a company) director -ra mf

mandate [mǽndet] N mandato m; VT decretar

mandatory [mǽndətɔri] ADJ obligatorio

mandolin [mǽndəlɪn] N mandolina f

mane [men] N (of a lion) melena f; (of a horse) crin f

maneuver [mənúvɚ] N maniobra f; VI/VT maniobrar

manganese [mǽŋgəniz] N manganeso m

mange [mendʒ] N sarna *f*, roña *f*

manger [méndʒɚ] N pesebre *m*

mangle [mǽŋgəɫ] VT (mutilate) magullar, mutilar; (ruin) estropear

mango [mǽŋgo] N mango *m*

mangrove [mǽŋgrov] N mangle *m*

mangy [méndʒi] ADJ sarnoso

manhood [mǽnhʊd] N virilidad *f*; (male genitals) miembro viril *m*; (men collectively) hombres *m pl*; (adult age) edad adulta *f*

mania [méniə] N manía *f*

maniac [méniæk] N maníaco -ca *mf*, maniaco -ca *mf*

maniacal [mənáɪəkəɫ] ADJ maníaco

manic-depressive [mǽnɪkdɪprésɪv] ADJ maniaco-depresivo

manicure [mǽnɪkjʊr] N manicura *f*; VT manicurar

manifest [mǽnəfɛst] ADJ manifiesto; N (list of cargo) manifiesto *m*, hoja de ruta *f*; VT (show) manifestar, poner de manifiesto; (express) declarar

manifestation [mænəfɛstéʃən] N manifestación *f*

manifesto [mænɪfésto] N manifiesto *m*

manifold [mǽnəfoɫd] ADJ diverso; N colector *m*

manila [mənílə] N abacá *m*; — **envelope** sobre manila *m*

manioc [mǽniɑk] N mandioca *f*, yuca *f*

manipulate [mənípjəlet] VT manipular

manipulation [mənɪpjəléʃən] N manipulación *f*

manlike [mǽnlaɪk] ADJ (manly) varonil; (mannish) hombruna; (resembling a human) de hombre

manly [mǽnli] ADJ varonil, viril

manner [mǽnɚ] N (way) manera *f*, modo *m*, forma *f*; (type) tipo *m*; (air) aire *m*, ademán *m*; (outward bearing) porte *m*; —**s** modales *m pl*, crianza *f*; **in the — of** a la manera de

mannerism [mǽnərɪzəm] N peculiaridad *f*

mannish [mǽnɪʃ] ADJ hombruno, varonil

manor [mǽnɚ] N feudo *m*, solar *m*; — **house** casa solariega *f*

mansion [mǽnʃən] N mansión *f*

mantel [mǽntɫ] N repisa de chimenea *f*

mantle [mǽntɫ] N manto *m*

mantra [mǽntrə] N mantra *f*

manual [mǽnjuəɫ] ADJ & N manual *m*

manufacture [mænjəfǽktʃɚ] VT fabricar, manufacturar; (clothes, shoes) confeccionar; N fabricación *f*, manufactura *f*; (of clothes, shoes) confección *f*

manufacturer [mænjəfǽktʃərɚ] N fabricante *m*

manufacturing [mænjəfǽktʃɚɪŋ] N fabricación *f*, manufactura *f*; ADJ fabril, manufacturero

manure [mənúr] N estiércol *m*; VT estercolar, abonar

manuscript [mǽnjəskrɪpt] ADJ & N manuscrito *m*

many [méni] ADJ muchos; — **apples** muchas manzanas; — **came** vinieron muchos; — **a time** muchas veces; **a great** — muchísimos; **as — as** tantos como; **as — as five** hasta cinco; **how** — ¿cuántos? **three books too** — tres libros de más; **too** — demasiados

map [mæp] N (geographical) mapa *m*; (of streets) plano *m*; VT trazar un mapa de; **to — out** planear

maple [mépəɫ] N *Sp* arce *m*; *Am* maple *m*; — **syrup** miel de arce / maple *m*

mar [mɑr] VT estropear

marathon [mǽrəθɑn] N maratón *mf*

marble [mɑ́rbəɫ] N mármol *m*; (toy) canica *f*, bola *f*; **to play** —**s** jugar a las canicas; ADJ de mármol, marmóreo

march [mɑrtʃ] N marcha *f*; VI marchar; (leave) marcharse; **to — in** entrar; **to — out** marcharse; VT hacer marchar

March [mɑrtʃ] N marzo *m*

mare [mɛr] N yegua *f*

margarine [mɑ́rdʒɚɪn] N margarina *f*

margin [mɑ́rdʒɪn] N margen *m*

marginal [mɑ́rdʒənəɫ] ADJ marginal

marginalize [mɑ́rdʒənəlaɪz] VT marginar

marigold [mǽrɪgoɫd] N caléndula *f*, maravilla *f*

marijuana, marihuana [mærəwánə] N marihuana *f*

marinate [mǽrənet] VT marinar

marine [mərín] ADJ (of the sea) marino; (maritime) marítimo; — **corps** infantería de marina *f*; N soldado de infantería de marina *m*

marionette [mæriənét] N marioneta *f*

marital [mǽrɪdl] ADJ conyugal

maritime [mǽrɪtaɪm] ADJ marítimo

mark [mɑrk] N marca *f*, seña *f*; (token) señal *f*; (indication) seña *f*; (grade) nota *f*, calificación *f*; (former German currency) marco *m*; —**sman** tirador *m*; **he's a good** —**sman** tiene muy buena puntería / muy buen tino; **the halfway** — el punto medio, la mitad; **to hit the** — dar en el blanco; **on your** —, set, go! ¡en sus marcas, listos y ya! ¡en sus marcas, listos, fuera! **to make one's** — distinguirse; **to miss the** — errar el tiro; **easy** — blanco fácil *m*; VT marcar; (indicate) señalar; (observe) observar, notar; (grade) calificar; **—ed for greatness** destinado a la grandeza; **— my words!** ¡ya verás! **to — down prices** rebajar los precios; **to — off** acotar, deslindar; **to — up prices** subir los precios

markdown [márkdaʊn] N rebaja *f*

marker [márkɚ] N marcador *m*

market [márkɪt] N mercado *m*; **—place** mercado *m*; **— price** precio de mercado *m*; **— share** sector del mercado *m*; **I'm in the — for** estoy buscando; VT comercializar, mercadear

marketable [márkɪɾəbəł] ADJ vendible

marketing [márkɪɾɪŋ] N (field of study) mercadotecnia *f*, marketing *m*; (selling) comercialización *f*

marmalade [márməled] N mermelada de naranja *f*

maroon [mərún] ADJ & N bordó / bordeaux *m*; VT abandonar

marriage [mǽrɪʤ] N matrimonio *m*; (combination) combinación *f*; **— license** licencia de matrimonio *f*

marriageable [mǽrɪʤəbəł] ADJ casadero

married [mǽrid] ADJ (united in marriage) casado; (relation to marriage) conyugal; **— couple** matrimonio *m*; **to get —** casarse

marrow [mǽro] N (in the bones) médula *f*; (food) tuétano *m*; (essential part) meollo *m*

marry [mǽri] VT (to marry off) casar; (to get married) casarse con; VI casarse

marsh [marʃ] N pantano *m*, ciénaga *f*

marshal [márʃəł] N (military) mariscal *m*; (police chief) alguacil *m*; (of a parade) maestro de ceremonia *m*; VT (facts, forces) reunir; (troops) formar

Marshallese [marʃəlíz] ADJ & N marshalés -esa *mf*

Marshall Islands [márʃəláɪləndz] N Islas Marshall *f pl*

marshmallow [márʃmɛlo] N caramelo de azúcar y gelatina *m*

marshy [márʃi] ADJ pantanoso, cenagoso

martial [márʃəł] ADJ marcial; **— arts** artes marciales *f pl*; **— law** ley marcial *f*

martin [mártn̩] N avión *m*

martini [martíni] N martini *m*

martyr [márɾɚ] N mártir *m*; VT martirizar

martyrdom [márɾɚdəm] N martirio *m*

marvel [márvəł] N maravilla *f*; VI maravillarse

marvelous [márvələs] ADV maravilloso

Marxism [márksɪzəm] N marxismo *m*

mascara [mæskǽrə] N rímel *m*

mascot [mǽskɑt] N mascota *f*

masculine [mǽskjəlɪn] ADJ masculino

mash [mæʃ] VT aplastar, pisar; N (pulpy mass) puré *m*; (food for livestock) afrecho *m*; (malt) malta remojada *f*; **—ed potatoes** puré de papas / patatas *m*

mask [mæsk] N máscara *f*, careta *f*; VT enmascarar; **—ed ball** baile de máscaras *m*

masochism [mǽsəkɪzəm] N masoquismo *m*

mason [mésən] N (builder) albañil *m*; (freemason) masón *m*

masonry [mésənri] N (bricklaying) albañilería *f*; (fraternal order) masonería *f*

masquerade [mæskəréd] N mascarada *f*; VI **to — as** hacerse pasar por

mass [mæs] N masa *f*; (in church) misa *f*; **— communication** comunicación de masas *f*; **—-marketing** comercialización masiva *f*; **— media** medios de comunicación (de masas) *m pl*; **— production** fabricación en masa *f*; **— unemployment** desempleo / paro masivo *m*; **— transit** transporte público *m*; **the —es** las masas *pl*; VI/VT juntar(se) en masa; (troops) concentrar(se)

massacre [mǽsəkɚ] N masacre *m*; VT masacrar

massage [məsáʒ] N masaje *m*; **— parlor** salón de masajes *m*; VT (give a massage) masajear; (change data) manipular

masseur [məsɚ́] N masajista *m*

masseuse [məsús] N masajista *f*

massive [mǽsɪv] ADJ (severe) masivo; (solid) macizo; (large) enorme

mast [mæst] N mástil *m*, árbol *m*

mastectomy [mæstéktəmi] N mastectomía *f*

master [mǽstɚ] N (person in control) amo -a *mf*, señor -ora *mf*; (owner of slave or animal) amo -a *mf*; (best representative, skilled laborer) maestro *m*; (young boy) señorito *m*; (tape or disk) original *m*; **—'s degree** maestría *f*; ADJ (dominant) dominante; **— bedroom** dormitorio principal *m*; **— key** llave maestra *f*; **—piece** obra maestra *f*; VT dominar

masterful [mǽstɚfəł] ADJ magistral

masterly [mǽstɚli] ADJ magistral

mastery [mǽstɚi] N dominio *m*

mastiff [mǽstɪf] N mastín *m*, alano *m*

masturbate [mǽstɚbet] VI/VT masturbar

mat [mæt] N (floor covering) estera *f*; (for wiping feet) felpudo *m*; (in gymnastics) colchoneta *f*; (of hair) maraña *f*; VI enmarañarse

match [mætʃ] N (pair) pareja *f*; (chess game) partida *f*; (tennis game) partido *m*; (boxing encounter) combate *m*; (device for fire) fósforo *m*, cerilla *f*; **—box** cajita de fósforos *f*; **—maker** casamentero -ra *mf*; **he has no —** no tiene igual; **he is a good —** es un buen partido; **the hat and coat are a good —** el abrigo y el sombrero hacen juego; VI/VT hacer juego (con); VI (to correspond) estar de acuerdo; **the colors don't —** los colores no combinan; VT (equal) igualar; (come to correspond) poner de acuerdo; (form pairs) parear

matchless [mǽtʃlɪs] ADJ sin par

mate [met] N (one of a pair) pareja *f*; (friend) compañero -ra *mf*; (on a ship) oficial *m*; (in chess) mate *m*; VI/VT aparear(se)

material [mətíriəɫ] ADJ material; (pertinent) pertinente; N (substance) material *m*; (fabric) tejido *m*, género *m*

materialize [mətíriəlaɪz] VI/VT materializar(se)

maternal [mətɝ́nəɫ] ADJ (motherly) maternal; (on mother's side of family) materno

maternity [mətɝ́nɪDi] N maternidad *f*

math [mæθ] N matemática(s) *f (pl)*

mathematical [mæθəmǽDɪkəɫ] ADJ matemático

mathematician [mæθəmətíʃən] N matemático -ca *mf*

mathematics [mæθəmǽDɪks] N matemática(s) *f (pl)*

matinée [mætn̩é] N matiné *f*

matriarch [métriɑrk] N matriarca *f*

matriculate [mətríkjəlet] VI/VT matricular(se)

matriculation [mətrɪkjəléʃən] N matriculación *f*, matrícula *f*

matrimony [mǽtrəmoni] N matrimonio *m*

matrix [métrɪks] N matriz *f*

matron [métrən] N matrona *f*; (in a hospital) jefa de enfermeras *f*

matter [mǽDɚ] N (substance, pus) materia *f*; (affair) asunto *m*; (printed) impreso *m*; (reading) material de lectura *m*; **— for complaint** motivo de queja *m*; **a — of two minutes** cosa de dos minutos *f*; **as a — of fact** de hecho; **it is of no —** no tiene importancia; **no — what you say** no importa lo que digas; **to do something as a — of course** hacer algo por rutina; **what is the — ?** ¿qué pasa? VI importar; **it doesn't —** no importa

mattress [mǽtrɪs] N colchón *m*

mature [mətʃúr] ADJ maduro; **a — note** un pagaré vencido ∕ pagadero; **for — audiences** para adultos; VI/VT madurar(se); (a savings bond) vencer(se)

maturity [mətúrɪDi] N madurez *f*; (of a debt) vencimiento *m*

maul [mɔɫ] VT atacar, herir gravemente

Mauritania [mɔrɪténiə] N Mauritania *f*

Mauritanian [mɔrɪténiən] ADJ & N mauritano -na *mf*

Mauritian [mɔríʃən] ADJ & N mauriciano -na *mf*

Mauritius [mɔríʃəs] N Mauricio *m*

maverick [mǽvɚɪk] N cimarrón *m* (also person); (person) inconformista *mf*

maxim [mǽksɪm] N máxima *f*, sentencia *f*

maximum [mǽksəməm] ADJ & N máximo *m*

may [me] V AUX **— I sit down?** ¿puedo sentarme? **— you have a merry Christmas** que pases una feliz Navidad; **it — be that** puede ser que; **it — rain** puede (ser) que llueva, tal vez llueva; **she — have been late** puede (ser) que haya llegado tarde; **be that as it —** sea como fuere

May [me] N mayo *m*; **— Day** primero de mayo *m*; **—pole** mayo *m*

maybe [mébi] ADV quizá(s), tal vez

mayonnaise [méənez] N mayonesa *f*, mahonesa *f*

mayor [méɚ] N alcalde *m*

maze [mez] N laberinto *m*

me [mi] PRON **she sees —** me ve; **he talks to —** me habla; **he comes with —** viene conmigo; **he did it for —** lo hizo para mí

meadow [méDo] N pradera *f*, prado *m*; **—lark** alondra *f*

meager [mígɚ] ADJ escaso, exiguo

meal [miɫ] N comida *f*; (flour) harina *f*; **—time** hora de comer *f*

mean [min] ADJ (unkind) cruel; (petty) vil; (humble) humilde; (stingy) mezquino; (difficult) de mal genio; (middle) medio; **—-spirited** mezquino; **I make a — lasagna** me sale muy rica la lasagna; N (average) media *f*, promedio *m*; **—s** medios *m pl*; **the ends justify the —s** el fin justifica los medios; **a man of —s** un hombre adinerado; **by —s of** por medio de; **by all —s** (of course) por supuesto; (using all resources) por todos los medios; **by no —s** de ningún modo; VT (intend) querer, tener intenciones; (signify) querer decir, significar; **he —s well** tiene buenas intenciones; **winning —s everything to them** lo que más les importa es ganar; **they are meant for each other** son el uno para el otro

meander [miǽndɚ] VI (be winding) serpentear; (to wander) vagar

meaning [mínɪŋ] N (sense) significado *m*, sentido *m*; (purpose) sentido *m*; ADJ **well·—** bien intencionado

meaningless [mínɪŋlɪs] ADJ sin sentido

meanness [mínnɪs] N (cruelty) crueldad *f*; (pettiness) mezquindad *f*

meantime [míntaɪm] ADV LOC **in the —** mientras tanto

meanwhile [mínhwaɪɫ] ADV mientras tanto

measles [mízəɫz] N sarampión *m*

measurable [mɛ́ʒəˈəbəɫ] ADJ medible, mensurable

measure [mɛ́ʒə˞] N (dimension) medida *f*; (criterion) criterio *m*; (in musical bar) compás *m*; (bill) proyecto de ley *m*; **—s** medidas *f pl*; **beyond —** sobremanera; **dry —** medida de áridos *f*; **in large —** en gran parte; VI/VT medir; **to — up** compararse con; **measuring tape** cinta de medir *f*, metro *m*

measured [mɛ́ʒə˞d] ADJ (rhythmical) acompasado; (moderate) moderado, mesurado

measurement [mɛ́ʒə˞mənt] N (act of measuring) medición *f*; (dimension) medida *f*, dimensión *f*

meat [mit] N carne *f*; (essential point) meollo *m*; **—ball** albóndiga *f*; **— loaf** pan / pastel de carne *m*

meaty [míɾi] ADJ (with meat) con mucha carne; (substantial) sustancioso

mechanic [mɪkǽnɪk] ADJ & N mecánico *m*; N **—s** mecánica *f*

mechanical [mɪkǽnɪkəɫ] ADJ mecánico

mechanism [mɛ́kənɪzəm] N mecanismo *m*

medal [mɛ́dl̩] N medalla *f*; VI ganar una medalla

meddle [mɛ́dl̩] VI entrometerse, inmiscuirse

meddler [mɛ́dlə˞] N entrometido -da *mf*

meddlesome [mɛ́dl̩səm] ADJ entrometido

media [míɾiə] N media *m pl*, medios de comunicación (de masas) *m pl*

median [míɾiən] ADJ mediano; N (middle value, line) mediana *f*

mediate [míɾiet] VI/VT mediar

mediation [miɾiéʃən] N mediación *f*

mediator [míɾieɾə˞] N mediador -ra *mf*

medical [mɛ́dɪkəɫ] ADJ médico; **— school** facultad de medicina *f*

medication [mɛdɪkéʃən] N medicación *f*

medicine [mɛ́dɪsɪn] N medicina *f*, medicamento *m*; **— ball** balón medicinal *m*; **— cabinet** botiquín *m*; **— man** curandero *m*

medieval [mɪdívəɫ] ADJ medieval

mediocre [miɾióokə˞] ADJ mediocre

mediocrity [miɾiákrɪɾi] N mediocridad *f*

meditate [mɛ́dɪtet] VI meditar

meditation [mɛdɪtéʃən] N meditación *f*, recogimiento *m*

medium [míɾiəm] N medio *m*; (person who contacts spirits) médium *mf*; ADJ mediano; ADV término medio; **— of exchange** medio de cambio *m*

medley [mɛ́dli] N (music) popurrí *m*; (mixture) mezcla *f*

meek [mik] ADJ manso

meet [mit] VT (encounter) encontrarse con; (make acquaintance) conocer; (face in conflict) enfrentar; (satisfy) satisfacer; (pay) pagar; **to — a deadline** cumplir el plazo; **to — the expenses** sufragar los gastos; **to — halfway** partir la diferencia; **to — a train** esperar un tren; **I will — you at the station** nos encontramos / vemos en la estación; **have you met my brother?** ¿conoces a mi hermano? **we were met with disapproval** se nos recibió con desaprobación; VI (encounter) encontrarse; (make acquaintance) conocerse; (have a meeting) reunirse; (cross) cruzarse; **to — in battle** trabar batalla; **to — with** (intentional) reunirse con; (unintentional) tropezar con; N encuentro deportivo *m*, competición *f*

meeting [míɾɪŋ] N reunión *f*, junta *f*; (political) mitin *m*; (crossing of roads) cruce *m*

megabyte [mɛ́gəbaɪt] N megabyte *m*

megahertz [mɛ́gəhɚtz] N megahertz *m*, megahercio *m*

megaphone [mɛ́gəfon] N megáfono *m*, bocina *f*

melancholy [mɛ́lənkɑli] N melancolía *f*; ADJ melancólico

melanoma [mɛlənóomə] N melanoma *m*

meld [mɛɫd] VT fusionar

melee [méle] N reyerta *f*, tumulto *m*

mellow [mɛ́lo] ADJ (soft) dulce, suave; (gentle) tranquilo; VI/VT suavizar(se)

melodious [məlóɾiəs] ADJ melodioso

melodrama [mɛ́lodrɑmə] N melodrama *m*

melody [mɛ́ləɾi] N melodía *f*

melon [mɛ́lən] N melón *m*

melt [mɛɫt] VI/VT (liquefy) derretir(se); (dissolve) disolver(se); **—down** (fusion) catástrofe por fusión nuclear incontrolada *f*; (any developing disaster) catástrofe *f*

melting pot [mɛ́ɫtɪŋpɑt] M crisol *m*

member [mɛ́mbə˞] N miembro *m* (also body part)

membership [mɛ́mbə˞ʃɪp] N (number) número de miembros / socios *m*; (state) calidad de miembro / socio *f*

membrane [mémbren] N membrana *f*
memento [məménto] N recuerdo *m*
memoir [mémwɑr] N memoria *f*; **—s**
memorias *f pl*, autobiografía *f*
memorable [mémə-əbəɫ] ADJ memorable
memorandum [mɛmə-ǽndəm] N
memorándum *m*
memorial [məmɔ́riəɫ] N (monument)
monumento conmemorativo *m*; (petition)
memorial *m*; ADJ conmemorativo
memorize [méməraɪz] VI/VT memorizar
memory [mémə-i] N (faculty) memoria *f*;
(recollection) recuerdo *m*
menace [ménɪs] N amenaza *f*; VI/VT amenazar
mend [mɛnd] VT remendar; **to — matters**
enmendar la situación; **to — one's ways**
enmendarse, reformarse; VI (sick person)
mejorarse; (bones) soldarse; N remiendo *m*;
to be on the — ir mejorando
menial [mínɪəɫ] ADJ bajo; (job) servil; N
criado -da *mf*
meningitis [mɛnɪnʤaɪDIS] N meningitis *f*
menopause [ménəpɔz] N menopausia *f*
menstruation [mɛnstruéʃən] N
menstruación *f*
mental [méntl̩] ADJ mental; (insane) *fam*
chiflado; **— health** salud mental *f*; **—
illness** enfermedad mental *f*; **—
retardation** retraso mental *m*
mentality [mɛntǽlɪDi] N mentalidad *f*
mention [ménʃən] VT mencionar; **don't —
it** no hay de qué; N mención *f*
mentor [méntɔr] N mentor -ra *mf*
menu [ménju] N (list of dishes) carta *f*, menú
m; (computer) menú *m*
meow [mjaʊ] INTERJ miau
mercantile [mɝ́-kəntiɫ] ADJ mercantil
mercenary [mɝ́-sənɛri] ADJ mercenario
merchandise [mɝ́-tʃəndaɪs] N mercancía *f*,
mercadería *f*
merchandising [mɝ́-tʃəndaɪzɪŋ] N mercadeo
m, comercialización *f*
merchant [mɝ́-tʃənt] N (trader) comerciante
m, mercader *m*; ADJ mercante; **— marine**
marina mercante *f*
merciful [mɝ́-sɪfəɫ] ADJ misericordioso
merciless [mɝ́-sɪlɪs] ADJ despiadado
mercury [mɝ́-kjəri] N mercurio *m*; (on a
mirror) azogue *m*
mercy [mɝ́-si] N (compassion) misericordia *f*,
clemencia *f*, piedad *f*; **to be at the — of**
estar a merced de; **— killing** eutanasia *f*
mere [mir] ADJ mero, simple; **a — trifle** una
nonada
merge [mɝʤ] VI/VT (join) unir(se); (colors)
fundir(se); (companies) fusionar(se)
merger [mɝ́-ʤə-] N fusión *f*

meridian [məríDiən] ADJ & N meridiano *m*
merit [mérɪt] N mérito *m*; VT merecer
meritorious [mɛrɪtɔ́riəs] ADJ meritorio
mermaid [mɝ́-med] N sirena *f*
merriment [mérɪmənt] N alegría *f*, algazara *f*
merry [méri] ADJ alegre; **—-go-round**
tiovivo *m*; **—maker** fiestero *mf*, juerguista
mf; **—making** fiesta *f*, juerga *f*; **to make
—** divertirse; INTERJ **— Christmas** Feliz
Navidad *f*, Felices Pascuas
mesa [mésə] N mesa *f*
mesh [mɛʃ] N (of metal) malla *f*; (of fiber) red
f; (of gears) engranaje *m*; VI engranar
mesmerize [mézmə-aɪz] VI/VT hipnotizar
mess [mɛs] N (state of confusion) desorden *m*,
desarreglo *m*; (disorderly person)
desordenado -da *mf*, mugriento -ta *mf*;
(confused person) desastre *m*; (difficult
situation) lío *m*, jaleo *m*; (food for
soldiers) rancho *m*; (cafeteria) cantina *f*; **—
hall** cantina *f*; **— of fish** plato de
pescado *m*; **to make a — of** (a room)
ensuciar, desordenar; (a project) estropear;
VI/VT **to — around** (waste time) perder el
tiempo; (get involved with) meterse con;
(philander) correr detrás de las mujeres; **to
— up** (a room) alborotar, desordenar;
(clothes, hair) desarreglar; (a project)
estropear; (make a muddle of) *vulg* cagarla;
to — with meterse con
message [mésɪʤ] N mensaje *m*, recado *m*; **İ
get the —** ya caí en cuenta
messenger [mésəndʒə-] N mensajero -ra *mf*
messy [mési] ADJ (chaotic) desordenado;
(embarrassing) embarazoso
metabolism [mətǽbəlɪzəm] N metabolismo
m
metal [métl̩] N metal *m*; ADJ de metal,
metálico
metallic [mətǽlɪk] ADJ metálico
metallurgy [médl̩ɝ-ʤi] N metalurgia *f*
metamorphosis [mɛDəmɔ́rfəsɪs] N
metamorfosis *f*
metaphor [méDəfɔr] N metáfora *f*
metaphysics [mɛDəfízɪks] N metafísica *f*
metastasis [mətǽstəsɪs] N metástasis *f*
meteor [míDiɔr] N meteoro *m*; **— shower**
lluvia de meteoritos *f*
meteorite [míDiəraɪt] N meteorito *m*
meteorology [miDiərálə-ʤi] N meteorología *f*
meter [míDə-] N (unit of length) metro *m*;
(measuring device) contador *m*, medidor
m
methane [méθen] N metano *m*
method [méθəd] N método *m*
methodical [məθáDɪkəɫ] ADJ metódico
methodology [mɛθədálə-ʤi] N metodología *f*

meticulous [mətíkjələs] ADJ detallista
metric [métrɪk] ADJ métrico
metronome [métrənom] N metrónomo *m*
metropolis [mətrápəlɪs] N metrópoli *f*, urbe *f*
metropolitan [mɛtrəpálɪɒən] ADJ metropolitano
mettle [médl̩] N temple *m*, valor *m*
mew [mju] N maullido *m*; VI maullar
Mexican [méksɪkən] ADJ & N mexicano -na *mf*
Mexico [méksɪko] N México *m*
mezzanine [mézənin] N entrepiso *m*, entresuelo *m*
mickey mouse [míkimáʊs] ADJ poco serio, informal
microbe [máɪkrob] N microbio *m*
microcomputer [maɪkrokəmpjúɒɚ] N *Am* microcomputadora *f*; *Sp* microordenador *m*
microeconomics [maɪkroɛkənámɪks] N microeconomía *f*
microfiche [máɪkrofiʃ] N microficha *f*
microfilm [máɪkrofɪɫm] N microfilm *m*
micromanage [maɪkromǽnɪʤ] VI/VT administrar con excesivo control
micron [máɪkrɑn] N micrón *m*, micra *f*
Micronesia [maɪkroníʒə] N Micronesia *f*
Micronesian [maɪkrəníʒən] ADJ & N micronesio -sia *mf*
microorganism [maɪkroɔ́rgənɪzəm] N microorganismo *m*
microphone [máɪkrəfon] N micrófono *m*
microprocessor [maɪkroprásɛsɚ] N microprocesador *m*
microscope [máɪkrəskop] N microscopio *m*
microscopic [maɪkrəskápɪk] ADJ microscópico
microsurgery [maɪkrosɚ́ʤəri] N microcirujía *f*
microwave [máɪkrowev] N microonda *f*; — **oven** (horno) microondas *m sg*
mid [mɪd] ADJ medio; —**air** en el aire; —**day** (del) mediodía *m*; —**life** madurez *f*; —**night** (de) medianoche *f*; —**shipman** guardiamarina *m*; **in** —**stream** (of a river) en medio del río; (of a task) en plena actividad; —**summer** pleno verano *m*; —**term examination** examen a mitad del curso *m*; —**way** a medio camino, a mitad del camino; —**wife** partera *f*, comadre *f*
middle [mídl̩] ADJ (average) medio, mediano; (intermediate) intermedio; (central) central; —**aged** de mediana edad; — **Ages** Edad Media *f*; — **ear** oído medio *m*; — **finger** dedo mayor *m*, dedo del corazón *m*; —**man** intermediario *m*,

revendedor *m*; — **management** mandos medios *m pl*; — **name** segundo nombre *m*; —**sized** (de) tamaño mediano; N medio *m*; (waist) cintura *f*; **in the** — **of** en el medio de; **I'm in the** — **of something** estoy ocupado haciendo algo; —**-of-the-road** moderado; **toward the** — **of the month** a mediados del mes
midget [mídʒɪt] N enano -na *mf*
midst [mɪdst] N medio *m*, centro *m*; **in the** — **of** en medio de, entre; **in our** — entre nosotros
mien [min] N porte *m*
might [maɪt] V AUX **it** — **be that** podría ser que; **he said it** — **rain tomorrow** dijo que tal vez lloviera mañana; **she** — **have been late** puede ser que haya llegado tarde; N poder *m*, poderío *m*
mighty [máɪɒɪ] ADJ (strong) poderoso, potente; (large) imponente; ADV muy
migraine [máɪgren] N migraña *f*, jaqueca *f*
migrant [máɪgrənt] ADJ migratorio, migrante; N trabajador -ra itinerante *mf*, bracero -ra *mf*
migrate [máɪgret] VI emigrar
migration [maɪgréʃən] N migración *f*
mild [maɪɫd] ADJ (gentle) suave; (moderate) moderado; (not serious) leve
mildew [mízdu] N moho *m*
mildness [máɪɫdnɪs] N (gentleness) suavidad *f*; (lack of gravity) levedad *f*
mile [maɪɫ] N milla *f*; —**stone** hito *m*
mileage [máɪlɪʤ] N (distance, odometer reading) millaje *m*, kilometraje *m*; **this car gets good** — este coche es económico; **what kind of** — **are you getting?** ¿cuántos kilómetros por litro hace tu coche?
milieu [mɪljú] N ambiente *m*
militant [mílɪtənt] ADJ & N (fanatic) militante *mf*; (combatant) combatiente *mf*
military [mílɪteri] ADJ militar; N **the** — (armed forces) el ejército; (military personnel) los militares
militia [məlíʃə] N milicia *f*
milk [mɪɫk] N leche *f*; — **chocolate** chocolate con leche *m*; —**maid** lechera *f*; —**man** lechero *m*; — **shake** batido *m*; VT ordeñar; (exploit) exprimir; **he's** —**ing it for all it's worth** le está sacando todo el jugo
milky [mílki] ADJ (consistency) lechoso; (product) lácteo; — **Way** Vía Láctea *f*
mill [mɪɫ] N (building) molino *m*; (factory) fábrica *f*; (for sugar) trapiche *m*, ingenio *m*; (rotating tool) fresa *f*; (small grinder) molinillo *m*; —**stone** muela de molino *f*;

a —**stone around your neck** una piedra al cuello; VT (grind grain) moler; (cut wood) aserrar; (cut grooves on coins) acordonar; (machine) fresar; **to — around** dar vueltas

millennium [məlíniəm] N milenio *m*

miller [mílɚ] N (person who mills) molinero *m*; (machine for milling) fresadora *f*; (moth) mariposa nocturna *f*

milligram [mílɪɡræm] N miligramo *m*

milliliter [míləliɒɚ] N mililitro *m*

millimeter [mílэmiɒɚ] N milímetro *m*

milliner [mílənɚ] N sombrerero -ra *mf*

millinery [mílənɛri] N (shop) sombrerería *f*; (hats) sombreros de señora *m pl*

million [míljən] N millón *m*; **a — dollars** un millón de dólares

millionaire [mɪljənɛ́r] N millonario -ria *mf*

millionth [míljənθ] ADJ & N millonésimo *m*

mime [maim] N (actor) mimo *m*; (technique, performance) pantomima *f*; VI hacer la mímica

mimic [mímɪk] VT imitar, remedar; N mono -na *mf*, remedador -ra *mf*

mince [mɪns] VT picar, desmenuzar; **—meat** picadillo *m*; **not to — words** no tener pelos en la lengua; **I'm going to make —meat of you** te voy a hacer picadillo

mind [maind] N (thinking process) mente *f*; (person of intellect) inteligencia *f*; (opinion) parecer *m*, opinión *f*; **—-altering** alucinógeno; **— games** manipulación psicológica *f*; **— over matter** el espíritu sobre la materia; **—set** actitud *f*; **to be out of one's —** estar loco; **to change one's —** cambiar de parecer / opinión; **to give someone a piece of one's —** cantarle a alguien las cuarenta; **I have a — to** me dan ganas de; **to make up one's —** decidirse; **to my —** a mi modo de ver; **to speak one's — freely** hablar con toda franqueza; **what do you have in —?** ¿qué tienes en mente? **to call to —** recordar; **to keep one's — on one's work** concentrarse en el trabajo; VT (take care of) cuidar; (pay attention to) atender a; (obey) obedecer; **I don't —** no tengo inconveniente en ello; **— what you say** cuidado con lo que dices; **to — one's own business** no meterse en lo ajeno

mindful [máindfəł] ADJ atento (a)

mine [main] PRON **this book is —** este libro es mío; **these things are —** estas cosas son mías; **— is bigger** el mío / la mía es más grande; **a friend of —** un amigo mío / una amiga mía; N mina *f* (also

explosive device); **—field** campo minado *m*; **— sweeper** dragaminas *m sg*, barreminas *m sg*; VT (plant explosives) minar; (dig out minerals) extraer; (exploit an area for minerals) explotar; VI (lay mines) sembrar minas; (dig a mine) cavar una mina; **to — for** extraer

miner [máinɚ] N minero -ra *mf*

mineral [mínɚəł] ADJ & N mineral *m*; **— water** agua mineral *f*

mingle [míŋɡəł] VI mezclarse; (sounds) confundirse; VT mezclar

miniature [míniətʃɚ] N miniatura *f*; ADJ en miniatura

minicomputer [mɪnikəmpjúɒɚ] N *Am* minicomputadora *f*; *Sp* miniordenador *m*

minimal [mínəməł] ADJ mínimo

minimize [mínəmaiz] VT minimizar

minimum [mínəməm] ADJ & N mínimo *m*; **— wage** salario mínimo *m*

mining [máiniŋ] N (of minerals) minería *f*; (with explosives) minado *m*; ADJ minero; **— engineer** ingeniero -ra de minas *mf*

miniskirt [mínɪskɚt] N minifalda *f*

minister [mínɪstɚ] N (official) ministro -tra *mf*; (pastor) pastor -ora *mf*, clérigo *m*; VI **to — to** atender a

ministry [mínɪstri] N (government agency) ministerio *m*; (functions of pastor) clerecía *f*

minivan [mínivæn] N camioneta *f*

mink [mɪŋk] N visón *m*

minnow [míno] N pececillo *m*

minor [máinɚ] ADJ (smaller) menor, más pequeño; (of secondary importance) menor; **— key** tono menor *m*; **— league** liga menor *f*; N (young person) menor de edad *mf*; (musical interval) tono menor *m*; (subfield) asignatura secundaria *f*; VI tener como segunda especialización

minority [mənɔ́rɪdi] N (smaller part or group) minoría *f*; (state of being underage) minoridad *f*; (member of a minority) miembro de una minoría *m*; ADJ minoritario

mint [mɪnt] N (flavor) menta *f*, hierbabuena *f*; (candy) pastilla de menta *f*; (money) casa de la moneda *f*; VT acuñar

minus [máinəs] PREP **seven — four** siete menos cuatro; **we came — my brother** vinimos sin mi hermano; N signo de menos *m*; ADJ negativo

minuscule [mínəskjuł] ADJ minúsculo

minute [mínɪt] N minuto *m*; **— hand** minutero *m*; **—s** actas *f pl*; [mənjút] ADJ (small) diminuto; (detailed) detallado, minucioso

miracle [mírəkəɫ] N milagro *m*
miraculous [mɪrǽkjələs] ADJ milagroso
mirage [mɪráʒ] N espejismo *m*
mire [maɪr] N (mud) cieno *m*, fango *m*;
(muddy place) ciénaga *f*; VI/VT (bog down)
atascar(se) en el fango; (be or get covered
with mud) enlodar(se)
mirror [mírə‑] N espejo *m*; (large) luna *f*; —
image imagen especular *f*; VT reflejar
mirth [mɝθ] N risa *f*, hilaridad *f*
mirthful [mɝθfəɫ] ADJ risueño
miry [máɪri] ADJ cenagoso, fangoso
misappropriation [mɪsəpropriéʃən] N
malversación *f*
misbehave [mɪsbɪhév] VI portarse mal
miscarriage [mískæɾɪdʒ] N aborto
espontáneo *m*, malparto *m*; — **of justice**
injusticia *f*
miscarry [mɪskǽri] VI (abort) abortar
espontáneamente; (fail) malograrse,
frustrarse
miscellaneous [mɪsəléniəs] ADJ diverso; (of
texts) misceláneo; — **expenses** gastos
varios *mf*
mischief [místʃɪf] N travesura *f*, diablura *f*,
picardía *f*; (serious prank) barrabasada *f*,
bellaquería *f*; **this will come to** — va a
suceder una desgracia
mischievous [místʃəvəs] ADJ travieso, pícaro
misconception [mɪskənsépʃən] N concepto
erróneo *m*
misconduct [mɪskándʌkt] N (bad behavior)
mala conducta *f*; (malfeasance) mala
administración *f*; [mɪskəndákt] VT
administrar mal; **to** — **oneself** portarse
mal
miscue [mɪskjú] N pifia *f*; VI/VT pifiar
misdeed [mɪsdíd] N fechoría *f*
misdemeanor [mɪsdɪmínə‑] N delito menor
m
miser [máɪzə‑] N avaro -ra *mf*, tacaño -ña *mf*
miserable [mízə‑əbəɫ] ADJ infeliz,
desdichado, mísero; **a** — **day** un día
asqueroso; **a** — **failure** un fracaso
rotundo
miserly [máɪzə‑li] ADJ avariento, tacaño
misery [mízəri] N (wretchedness) desgracia *f*;
(poverty) miseria *f*; (unhappiness)
infelicidad *f*
misfit [mísfɪt] N inadaptado -da *mf*
misfortune [mɪsfɔ́rtʃən] N desgracia *f*,
desdicha *f*, desventura *f*
misgivings [mɪsgívɪŋz] N aprensión *f*, recelo
m
misguided [mɪsgáɪdɪd] ADJ mal aconsejado,
poco feliz
mishap [míshæp] N contratiempo *m*,
percance *m*
misinform [mɪsɪnfɔ́rm] VT desinformar, dar
información errónea
misjudge [mɪsdʒʌ́dʒ] VT juzgar mal
mislay [mɪslé] VT (lose keys, etc.) extraviar,
perder; (lose a document) traspapelar; (lay
wrong) colocar mal
mislead [mɪslíd] VT (lead in wrong direction)
guiar por mal camino; (lead into error)
engañar, confundir
mismanage [mɪsmǽnɪdʒ] VT administrar mal
misogyny [mɪsádʒəni] N misoginia *f*
misplace [mɪsplés] VT (lose keys, etc.)
extraviar; (lose a document) traspapelar;
(place wrong) colocar mal; **she** —**d her
trust** confió en la persona equivocada
misprint [mísprɪnt] N errata *f*, error de
imprenta *m*
misrepresent [mɪsreprɪzént] VT distorsionar,
tergiversar
misrepresentation [mɪsreprɪzentéʃən] N
distorsión *f*, tergiversación *f*
miss [mɪs] VI (fail to hit) errar; (misfire) fallar;
VT (fail to hit) errar, no acertar; (fail to be
on time for) perder; (fail to attend) faltar
a; (feel absence of) echar de menos; *Am*
extrañar; **he just** —**ed being killed** por
poco se mata; N (of a target) tiro errado *m*;
(in a motor) falla *f*; (from class) falta *f*;
(young woman) señorita *f*; — **Smith** la
señorita Smith
missile [mísəɫ] N (projectile) proyectil *m*;
(guided weapon) misil *m*
missing [mísɪŋ] ADJ (not present) ausente;
(lost) perdido; — **link** eslabón perdido *m*;
one book is — falta un libro
mission [míʃən] N misión *f*
missionary [míʃəneri] ADJ & N misionero -ra
mf; — **position** posición del misionero *f*
misspell [mɪsspéɫ] VT (written) escribir mal;
(oral) deletrear mal
misstep [místep] N paso en falso *m*
mist [mɪst] N (of water droplets) neblina *f*,
bruma *f*; (of perfume) rocío *m*; VI
lloviznar; VT rociar
mistake [mɪsték] N error *m*, equivocación *f*;
(orthographical) falta *f*; **to make a** —
equivocarse; VI/VT equivocar(se); **I
mistook my sister for my mother**
confundí a mi hermana con mi madre
mistaken [mɪstékən] ADJ equivocado; **to be**
— estar equivocado, equivocarse; **unless
I'm** — si no me equivoco
mister [místə‑] N señor *m*
mistletoe [mísəɫto] N muérdago *m*
mistreat [mɪstrít] VT maltratar
mistreatment [mɪstrítmənt] N maltrato *m*

mistress [místrɪs] N (of a household) señora f; (employing servants, animal owner) ama f; (lover) amante f
mistrial [místraɪł] N proceso viciado de nulidad m
mistrust [mɪstrʌ́st] N desconfianza f; VT desconfiar de
mistrustful [mɪstrʌ́stfəł] ADJ desconfiado, receloso
misty [místi] ADJ (foggy) neblinoso, brumoso; (in tears) nublado; (blurry) empañado
misunderstand [mɪsʌndɚstǽnd] VT comprender mal, malinterpretar
misunderstanding [mɪsʌndɚstǽndɪŋ] N (confusion) malentendido m; (failure to understand) equivocación f, mala inteligencia f; (argument) desavenencia f
misuse [mɪsjús] N (of drugs) abuso m; (of a word) mal uso m; (of funds) malversación f; [mɪsjúz] VT (drugs) abusar de; (a friend) maltratar; (a word) emplear mal; (funds) malversar
mite [maɪt] N ácaro m; **a — greedy** un poquito codicioso
mitigate [mídɪget] VT mitigar
mitten [mítn̩] N manopla f
mix [mɪks] VI/VT mezclar(se); **to — up** confundir; N mezcla f; (for baking) preparado m; **—-up** (confusion) confusión f; (fight) pelea f; **—ed bag** grupo heterogéneo m; **—ed drink** cóctel m; **—ed-up** confundido
mixed [mɪkst] ADJ mixto
mixer [míksɚ] N (appliance) batidora f; (party) fiesta f; (soda) refresco m; (sound technician) mezclador -ra mf; (sound device) mezcladora f
mixture [míkstʃɚ] N mezcla f
moan [mon] N quejido m, gemido m; VI gemir, quejarse; VI/VT lamentar
moat [mot] N foso m
mob [mab] N (disorderly crowd) tumulto m, turba f; (crowd) muchedumbre f, populacho m; (Mafia) mafia f; VT (attack) asaltar; (crowd) atestar
mobile [móbəł] ADJ móvil; (personnel) que tiene movilidad; **— home** casa prefabricada f; **— phone** (teléfono) móvil m, (teléfono) celular m
mobilize [móbəlaɪz] VI/VT movilizar(se)
moccasin [mákəsɪn] N mocasín m (also snake)
mock [mak] VI (ridicule) burlar(se); VT (imitate) remedar; **to — at** burlarse de; ADJ de práctica; **— battle** simulacro de batalla m; **—-up** maqueta f, modelo m
mockery [mákəri] N (ridicule) burla f;

(imitation) remedo m; (travesty) farsa f
mockingbird [mákɪŋbɚd] N sinsonte m
mode [mod] N modo m
model [mádl̩] N (guide) modelo m; (person) modelo mf, maniquí mf; ADJ modelo, ejemplar; **— school** escuela modelo f; VI/VT modelar; (display clothes) lucir
modem [módəm] N módem m
moderate [mádɚɪt] ADJ (not excessive) moderado, mesurado; (person) comedido; (weather) templado; (price) módico; N moderado -da mf; [mádɚet] VI/VT moderar(se) (also preside at meetings)
moderation [madɚéʃən] N moderación f, mesura f
modern [mádɚn] ADJ moderno
modernize [mádɚnaɪz] VI/VT modernizar(se)
modest [mádɪst] ADJ (humble) modesto; (chaste) recatado, honesto
modesty [mádɪsti] N (humility) modestia f; (chastity) recato m, pudor m
modification [madɚfɪkéʃən] N modificación f
modify [mádɚfaɪ] VT modificar
modulate [mádʒəlet] VI/VT modular(se)
mohair [móhɛr] N mohair m
moist [mɔɪst] ADJ húmedo
moisten [mɔ́ɪsən] VI/VT humedecer(se)
moisture [mɔ́ɪstʃɚ] N humedad f
moisturizer [mɔ́ɪstʃəraɪzɚ] N (crema) hidrante / humectante f
molar [mólɚ] ADJ molar; N muela f, molar m
molasses [məlǽsɪz] N melaza f
mold [mołd] N (form) molde m; (fungi) moho m; (mettle) temple m; VT (shape) moldear; (adapt) amoldar; (fuse) fundir; VI/VT (become moldy) enmohecer(se)
molder [mółdɚ] VI/VT descomponerse; (paper) enmohecerse
molding [mółdɪŋ] N (adornment) moldura f; (action of molding) moldeado m
Moldova [mɔłdóvə] N Moldavia f
Moldovan [mɔłdóvən] ADJ & N moldavo -va mf
moldy [mółdi] ADJ mohoso
mole [moł] N (blemish) lunar m; (animal, spy) topo m; (breakwater) rompeolas m sg
molecule [málɪkjuł] N molécula f
molest [məlést] VT abusar sexualmente de
mollify [málɪfaɪ] VT apaciguar, aplacar
mollusk [máləsk] N molusco m
molt [mołt] VI (birds) mudar la pluma; (snakes) mudar la piel; N muda f
molten [mółtn̩] ADJ fundido
molybdenum [məlíbdənəm] N molibdeno m
mom [mam] N mamá f; **— and pop store** tienda familiar f

moment [mómənt] N momento *m*; **being a parent has its —s** ser padre / madre tiene sus momentos de recompensa

momentary [mómənteri] ADJ momentáneo

momentous [moméntəs] ADJ importante, trascendental

momentum [moméntəm] N (in physics) momento *m*; (in politics, sports) empuje *m*

mommy [mámi] N mami *f*

Monaco [mánəko] N Mónaco *m*

monarch [mánɑrk] N monarca *mf*

monarchy [mánɚki] N monarquía *f*

monastery [mánəsteri] N monasterio *m*

Monday [mánde] N lunes *m*

Monegasque [mɑnɪgásk] ADJ & N monegasco -ca *mf*

monetary [mánɪteri] ADJ monetario

money [máni] N dinero *m*; **—** faltriquera en forma de cinturón *f*; **— changer** cambista *mf*; **— machine** cajero automático *m*; **—-making** lucrativo, rentable; **— market** mercado de valores *m*; **— order** giro postal *m*; **to get one's —'s worth** sacar jugo al dinero

Mongolia [mɑŋgóliə] N Mongolia *f*

Mongolian [mɑŋgóliən] ADJ & N mongol -la *mf*

mongoose [máŋgus] N mangosta *f*

mongrel [máŋgrəɫ] ADJ & N mestizo *m*

monitor [mánɪtɚ] N monitor *m*; (in a school) celador -ora *mf*; **— lizard** varano *m*

monk [mʌŋk] N monje *m*, religioso *m*

monkey [máŋki] N mono *m*, mico *m* (also child); **— bars** jaula de los monos *f*; **— business** (mischief) picardía *f*; (trickery) chanchullo *m*; **— wrench** llave inglesa *f*; **to have a — on one's back** estar adicto; VI **to — around** bobear, payasear; **to — with** bobear con

monogamy [mənágəmi] N monogamia *f*

monolog, monologue [mánələg] N monólogo *m*

mononucleosis [mɑnonukliósɪs] N mononucleosis *f*

monopolize [mənápəlaɪz] VT monopolizar

monopoly [mənápəli] N monopolio *m*

monotonous [mənátṇəs] ADJ monótono

monotony [mənátṇi] N monotonía *f*

monster [mánstɚ] N monstruo *m*; ADJ enorme, monstruo *inv*

monstrosity [mɑnstrásɪɒi] N monstruosidad *f*

monstrous [mánstrəs] ADJ monstruoso

month [mʌnθ] N mes *m*

monthly [mánθli] ADJ mensual; **— installment** mensualidad *f*; N

publicación mensual *f*, mensuario *m*; ADV mensualmente

monument [mánjəmənt] N monumento *m*

monumental [mɑnjəméntḷ] ADJ monumental

moo [mu] N mugido *m*; VI mugir

mooch [mutʃ] VI/VT gorronear

mood [mud] N (emotional state) humor *m*, vena *f*, ánimo *m*; (grammatical category) modo *m*; **to be in a good —** estar de buen humor; **to be in the — to** tener ganas de

moody [múɒi] ADJ (sullen) malhumorado; (changing) voluble

moon [mun] N luna *f*; **—beam** rayo de luna *m*; **—light** claro de la luna *m*, luz de la luna *f*; **—shine** bebida alcohólica destilada sin licencia *f*; **once in a blue —** de Pascuas a Ramos; VT *fam* mostrar el culo

moor [mur] VI/VT amarrar; N páramo *m*

Moor [mur] N moro -ra *mf*

Moorish [múrɪʃ] ADJ morisco, moro

moose [mus] N alce *m*

moot [mut] ADJ **it became a — point** dejó de tener importancia

mop [mɑp] N *Sp* fregona *f*, *Sp* mopa *f*; *Mex* trapeador *m*; (for dust) plumero *m*; (of hair) greña *f*; **—-up** (of an enemy) limpieza *f*; (of a task) remate *m*; VI/VT pasar la mopa (sobre); *Am* trapear; **to — one's brow** enjugarse la frente; **to — up** (a spill) limpiar; (an enemy) acabar con; (a task) rematar

mope [mop] VI andar abatido

moped [mópɛd] N ciclomotor *m*, scooter *m*

moral [mɔ́rəɫ] ADJ moral; N moraleja *f*; **—s** moral *f*

morale [məráɫ] N moral *f*

moralist [mɔ́rəlɪst] N moralista *mf*

morality [mɔráɛlɪɒi] N moralidad *f*

moralize [mɔ́rəlaɪz] VI/VT moralizar

morbid [mɔ́rbɪd] ADJ mórbido, morboso

more [mɔr] ADJ & ADV más; **— and —** cada vez más; **— or less** más o menos; **there is no —** no hay más; **—over** además

morgue [mɔrg] N depósito de cadáveres *m*, morgue *f*

moribund [mɔ́rəbʌnd] ADJ moribundo

morning [mɔ́rnɪŋ] N mañana *f*; **good —!** ¡buenos días! **tomorrow —** mañana por la mañana; ADJ de la mañana, matutino; **— glory** dondiego de día *m*; **— sickness** náuseas *f pl*; **— star** lucero del alba *m*

Moroccan [mərákən] ADJ & N marroquí *mf*

Morocco [məráko] N Marruecos *m*

moron [mɔ́rɑn] N imbécil *m*

morphine [mɔ́rfin] N morfina f
morsel [mɔ́rsəł] N bocado m
mortal [mɔ́rdl] ADJ & N mortal mf; — **sin** pecado mortal m
mortality [mɔrtǽlɪɾi] N (rate) mortalidad f; (toll) mortandad f
mortar [mɔ́rɾɚ] N (for pounding) mortero m (also ballistics); (for bricks) argamasa f, mezcla f; —**board** birrete m
mortgage [mɔ́rgɪʤ] N hipoteca f; VT hipotecar; ADJ hipotecario
mortgagor [mɔ́rgɪʤɚ] N deudor -ra hipotecario -ria mf
mortify [mɔ́rɾəfaɪ] VI/VT mortificar(se)
mosaic [mozéɪk] N mosaico m
Moslem [mázləm] ADJ & N musulmán -ana mf
mosque [mɔsk] N mezquita f
mosquito [məskíɾo] N mosquito m; — **net** mosquitero m
moss [mɔs] N musgo m
mossy [mɔ́si] ADJ musgoso
most [most] ADJ — **children are good** la mayoría de los niños son buenos; — **people** la mayoría de la gente; **the — money** más dinero m; **the — votes** el mayor número de votos; **for the — part** generalmente; PRON **the — that I can do** lo más que puedo hacer; **we ate the —** comimos más que nadie; — **of the guests are here** ha llegado la mayoría de los invitados; ADV **the — ambitious** el más ambicioso; **a — pleasant day** un día de lo más agradable
mostly [móstli] ADV generalmente
motel [motéł] N motel m
moth [mɔθ] N (pest) polilla f; (nocturnal insect) mariposa nocturna f; —**ball** bolita de naftalina f; —**-eaten** apolillado
mother [mʌ́ðɚ] N madre f; —**board** plaqueta madre f; — **country** madre patria f; —**fucker** offensive hijo de puta m; —**-in-law** suegra f; —**-of-pearl** madreperla f; — **tongue** lengua materna f; VT mimar a, cuidar de/a
motherhood [mʌ́ðɚhud] N maternidad f
motherly [mʌ́ðɚli] ADJ maternal
motif [motíf] N motivo m
motion [móʃən] N (movement) movimiento m; (signal) ademán m; (proposal) moción f; — **picture** película de cine f; —**-picture industry** industria cinematográfica f; — **sickness** mareo m; VI/VT hacer un ademán
motionless [móʃənlɪs] ADJ inmóvil
motivate [móɾəvet] VT motivar
motivation [moɾəvéʃən] N motivación f

motive [móɾɪv] N motivo m; ADJ motriz
motley [mátli] ADJ abigarrado
motor [móɾɚ] N motor m; —**bike** motocicleta pequeña f; —**boat** lancha a motor f; —**cycle** motocicleta f; —**cyclist** motociclista mf; — **home** casa rodante f, caravana f; — **scooter** scooter m; — **vehicle** vehículo motorizado m; VI pasear en coche
motorist [móɾɚɪst] N automovilista mf
motto [máɾo] N lema f
mound [maund] N montículo m; **burial —** túmulo m; — **of laundry** pila de ropa f
mount [maunt] VI/VT montar; VI (increase) subir; VT (assemble) armar; N (mountain) monte m; (getting on a horse) monta f; (animal for riding) montura f
mountain [maunṭn] N montaña f; ADJ (animal, person) montañés; (thing) de montaña; — **bike** bicicleta de montaña f; — **climber** alpinista mf; — **climbing** alpinismo m, montañismo m; — **goat** cabra montés f; — **lion** puma f, gato montés m; — **range** (large) cordillera f; (small) sierra f; —**side** ladera (de una montaña) f; —**top** cumbre (de una montaña) f
mountaineer [mauntṇír] N alpinista mf
mountainous [máunṭnəs] ADJ montañoso
mourn [mɔrn] VI estar de duelo/luto; VT llorar; **to — for** llorar a
mourner [mɔ́rnɚ] N doliente mf
mournful [mɔ́rnfəł] ADJ lúgubre, triste
mourning [mɔ́rnɪŋ] N luto m, duelo m; **to be in —** estar de luto/duelo; ADJ de luto
mouse [maus] N ratón m (also computer); — **pad** bandeja del ratón f; —**trap** ratonera f
mouth [mauθ] N boca f; (of a cave) abertura f; (of a river) desembocadura f; —**piece** (part of a trumpet) boquilla f; (spokesman) portavoz mf; —**-to-mouth resuscitation** respiración boca a boca f; —**wash** enjuague bucal m; —**-watering** delicioso; [mauð] VT articular silenciosamente una palabra; VI **to — off** contestar
mouthful [máuθfuł] N (of food) bocado m; (of liquid) bocanada f, buche m
movable [múvəbł] ADJ movible, móvil
move [muv] VI (change position) mover(se) (also board games); (change residence) mudar(se) de casa; (sell) venderse; **to — away** (distance oneself) apartarse; (change residence) irse; **to — forward** avanzar; **to — on** seguir adelante; **to — out** mudarse de casa; **to — up** anticipar; VT (propose) proponer; (affect

emotionally) conmover; N (act of moving) movimiento *m*; (change of residence) mudanza *f*; (action toward a goal) paso *m*; (play, in games) jugada *f*; **get a — on there!** ¡date prisa! **he made the first —** dio el primer paso

movement [múvmənt] N (motion, part of a watch) movimiento *m*; **to have a bowel —** mover el vientre

mover [múvɚ] N compañía de mudanzas *f*; **—s and shakers** la plana mayor

movie [múvi] N película *f*; **—s** cine *m*

moving [múvɪŋ] ADJ (target) móvil; (car) en movimiento; (company) de mudanzas; (story) conmovedor; **— picture** película *f*; **— van** camión de mudanzas *m*; N **I hate —** no me gusta mudarme de casa

mow [mo] VT cortar; (harvest) segar

mower [móɚ] N (for lawns) cortadora de céspedes *f*, cortacésped *m*; (farm implement) segadora *f*; (farm worker) segador -ra *mf*

Mozambican [mozæmbíkən] ADJ & N mozambiqueño -ña *mf*

Mozambique [mozæmbík] N Mozambique *m*

Mozarabic [mozǽrəbɪk] ADJ mozárabe

Mr. [místɚ] N Sr. *m*

Mrs. [mísɪz] N Sra. *f*

Ms. [mɪz] N Sra. *f*

much [mʌtʃ] ADJ & ADV mucho; **— the same** casi lo mismo; **— like the others** muy parecido a los demás; **as — as** tanto como; **how — ?** ¿cuánto? **too —** demasiado; **very —** muchísimo; **to make — of** dar mucha importancia a; **— as I'd like, I won't do it** aunque me gustaría, no lo voy a hacer; **that's not — of a book** ese libro no es gran cosa; **she cried so — that her eyes turned red** lloró tanto que se le enrojecieron los ojos; **they need water, — as they need sun** necesitan agua, del mismo modo que necesitan sol

muck [mʌk] N (manure) estiércol *m*; (mire) cieno *m*, lodo *m*; (filth) porquería *f*; **to — up** *vulg* cagarla

mucous [mjúkəs] ADJ mucoso

mucus [mjúkəs] N mucosidad *f*

mud [mʌd] N lodo *m*, barro *m*; **—slinging** difamación *f*

muddle [mʌdl] VT (confuse) confundir; (make turbid) enturbiar; VI **to — along** ir tirando; **to — through** salir del paso; N (confusion) confusión *f*; (confused situation) embrollo *m*

muddy [mʌdi] ADJ (path) lodoso, barroso; (shoes) embarrado; (vague) confuso; VT

(cover with mud) enlodar, embarrar; (make unclear) enturbiar

muff [mʌf] N manguito *m*; VT estropear

muffin [mʌfɪn] N mollete *m*

muffle [mʌfəl] VT amortiguar

muffler [mʌflɚ] N (scarf) bufanda *f*; (exhaust device) silenciador *m*

mug [mʌg] N (ceramic) tazón *m*; (glass) jarra *f*; (face) jeta *f*; VT atracar

mugger [mʌgɚ] N asaltante *mf*; atracador -ora *mf*

muggy [mʌgi] ADJ bochornoso

mulatto [mulÁDo] ADJ & N mulato -ta *mf*

mulberry [mʌlbɛri] N mora *f*; **— tree** moral *m*

mule [mjul] N mulo -la *mf* (also in drug trafficking)

mull [mʌl] VI/VT rumiar

multicultural [mʌltikʌltʃɚəl] ADJ multicultural

multiple [mʌltəpəl] N múltiplo *m*; ADJ múltiple; **—-choice** de opción múltiple; **— personality disorder** trastorno de personalidad múltiple *m*; **— sclerosis** esclerosis múltiple *f*

multiplication [mʌltəplɪkéʃən] N multiplicación *f*; **— sign** signo de multiplicación *m*; **— table** tabla de multiplicar *f*

multiplicity [mʌltəplísɪDi] N multiplicidad *f*

multiply [mʌltəplaɪ] VI/VT multiplicar(se)

multitasking [mʌltitǽskɪŋ] N multitarea *f*

multitude [mʌltɪtud] N multitud *f*

multi-user [mʌltijúzɚ] N multiusuario -ria *mf*

mum [mʌm] ADJ callado; **to keep —** callarse la boca

mumble [mʌmbəl] VI/VT mascullar; N refunfuño *m*

mumbo jumbo [mʌmboʤʌmbo] N jerigonza *f*

mummy [mʌmi] N momia *f*

mumps [mʌmps] N paperas *f pl*

munch [mʌntʃ] VT mascar

mundane [mʌndén] ADJ mundano

municipal [mjunísəpəl] ADJ municipal; **— council** concejo *m*

municipality [mjunɪsəpǽlɪDi] N municipio *m*, municipalidad *m*

munition [mjuníʃən] N munición *f*

mural [mjúrəl] ADJ & N mural *m*

murder [mɝ́Dɚ] N asesinato *m*, homicidio *m*; **to get away with —** salirse con la suya; **that exam was —** ese examen fue matador; VI/VT asesinar

murderer [mɝ́Dərɚ] N asesino *mf*, homicida *mf*

murderous [mɝ́-ɒ-əs] ADJ asesino, homicida
murky [mɝ́-ki] ADJ (of water, matter) turbio; (of sky) oscuro
murmur [mɝ́-mɚ] N (noise) murmullo *m*, susurro *m*; (complaint) queja *f*; VI/VT (make noise) murmurar, susurrar; (complain) quejarse
muscle [mʌ́səł] N músculo *m*
muscular [mʌ́skjələ·] ADJ (relative to muscles) muscular; (endowed with muscles) musculoso
muse [mjuz] VI meditar; VT cavilar; N musa *f*
museum [mjuzíəm] N museo *m*
mushroom [mʌ́ʃrum] N seta *f*, hongo *m*, champiñón *m*
mushy [mʌ́ʃi] ADJ (soft) fofo; (sentimental) sensiblero
music [mjúzɪk] N música *f*; — **stand** atril *m*; — **video** *Am* video musical *m*; *Sp* vídeo musical *m*
musical [mjúzɪkəł] ADJ (pertaining to music) musical; (fond of music) aficionado a la música, melómano; — **comedy** comedia musical *f*
musician [mjuzíʃən] N músico -ca *mf*
muskrat [mʌ́skræt] N ratón almizclero *m*
Muslim [mʌ́zləm] ADJ & N musulmán -ana *mf*
muslin [mʌ́zlɪn] N muselina *f*
muss [mʌs] VT revolver, alborotar; N revoltijo *m*
mussel [mʌ́səł] N mejillón *m*
must [mʌst] V AUX **you — arrive before nine** debes llegar antes de las nueve; **you really — eat at that restaurant** tienes que comer en ese restaurante; **you — be his son** debes (de) / has de ser su hijo; **they — have seen me** deben (de) haberme visto
mustache, moustache [mʌ́stæʃ] N bigote *m*; (large) mostacho *m*
mustard [mʌ́stɚd] N mostaza *f*; — **gas** gas mostaza *m*
muster [mʌ́stɚ] VT (troops) formar; (courage) juntar, reunir; VI (assemble for inspection) formar; (come together) reunirse; **to — out** dar de baja; **to — up one's courage** juntar valor; N revista *f*; **to pass —** ser aceptable
musty [mʌ́sti] ADJ (stale smelling) con olor a encierro / humedad; (antiquated) anticuado
mutant [mjútn̩t] ADJ & N mutante *mf*
mutation [mjutéʃən] N mutación *f*
mute [mjut] ADJ mudo; N (mute person) mudo -da *mf*; (for musical instruments) sordina *f*

mutilate [mjúdl̩et] VT mutilar
mutiny [mjútn̩i] N motín *m*; VI amotinarse
mutter [mʌ́dɚ] VI/VT refunfuñar, musitar; N refunfuño *m*
mutton [mʌ́tn̩] N carne de cordero *f*
mutual [mjútʃuəł] ADJ mutuo; — **fund** fondo mutuo / mutual *m*
muzzle [mʌ́zəł] N (snout) hocico *m*; (mouthguard) bozal *m*; (gun opening) boca *f*; VT (a dog) abozalar, poner bozal a; (critics) amordazar, silenciar
my [maɪ] POSS ADJ mi; **these are — friends** estos son mis amigos; **oh —!** ¡Dios mío! — **foot!** ¡ni lo pienses!
Myanmar [mjɑnmár] N Myanmar *m*
myopia [maɪópiə] N miopía *f*
myriad [míriəd] N miríada *f*, sinfín *m*; — **problems** un sinfín de problemas
myrtle [mɝ́-dl̩] N mirto *m*, arrayán *m*
myself [maɪsέłf] PRON **I — wrote the letters** yo mismo escribí las cartas; **I'm not — today** hoy no soy la misma de siempre; **I was sitting by —** estaba sentado solo; **I talk to —** hablo solo; **I looked at — in the mirror** me miré en el espejo; **I bought — a house** me compré una casa
mysterious [mɪstíriəs] ADJ misterioso
mystery [místəri] N misterio *m*
mystic [místɪk] ADJ & N místico -ca *mf*
mystical [místɪkəł] ADJ místico
myth [mɪθ] N mito *m*
mythology [mɪθálədʒi] N mitología *f*

Nn

nab [næb] VT pescar; *Sp* coger
nag [næg] N (horse) jaca *f*, rocín *m*, penco *m*; (complainer) quejica *mf*; VI/VT regañar, criticar
nail [neł] N (for nailing) clavo *m*; (of finger, toe) uña *f*; —**biter** situación angustiante *f*; — **file** lima *f*; — **polish** esmalte para uñas *m*; **to hit the — on the head** dar en el clavo; VT (fasten) clavar; (nab) pescar; *Sp* coger
naïve [nɑív] ADJ ingenuo, cándido, bonachón
naked [nékɪd] ADJ desnudo
nakedness [nékɪdnɪs] N desnudez *f*
name [nem] N nombre *m*; —**brand** marca *f*; —**plate** placa *f*; —**sake** tocayo *m*; —**tag** etiqueta de identificación *f*; — **of the game** lo esencial *m*; **to call someone**

—s motejar a alguien; **to make a — for oneself** hacerse un nombre; **what is your —?** ¿cómo te llamas? VT nombrar; **— your price** haz una oferta

namely [némli] ADV a saber, en concreto

Namibia [nəmíbiə] N Namibia *f*

Namibian [nəmíbiən] ADJ & N namibio -bia *mf*

nanny [nǽni] N niñera *f*

nanosecond [nǽnosɛkənd] N nanosegundo *m*

nap [næp] N (sleep) siesta *f*; (fibers) pelo *m*; **to take a —** echar / dormir una siesta; VI echar / dormir una siesta

napalm [népɑɫm] N napalm *m*

nape [nep] N nuca *f*

napkin [nǽpkɪn] N servilleta *f*

narcissism [nɑ́rsɪsɪzəm] N narcisismo *m*

narcissus [nɑrsísəs] N narciso *m*

narcolepsy [nɑ́rkəlɛpsi] N narcolepsia *f*

narcotic [nɑrkɑ́Dɪk] ADJ & N narcótico *m*, estupefaciente *m*

narco-trafficking [nɑrkotrǽfɪkɪŋ] N narcotráfico *m*

narrate [nǽret] VI/VT narrar

narration [næréʃən] N narración *f*

narrative [nǽrəDɪv] ADJ narrativo; N narrativa *f*

narrator [nǽreDɚ] N narrador -ora *mf*

narrow [nǽro] ADJ (of little width) estrecho, angosto; (exhaustive) exhaustivo; (limited in scope) limitado; (intolerant) intolerante; **to have a — escape** salvarse por poco; **— gauge** de vía angosta / estrecha; **—-minded** intolerante; N **—s** desfiladero *m*, estrecho *m*, angostura *f*; VI/VT angostar(se), estrechar(se); **to — down** reducir

narrowness [nǽronɪs] N (quality of being narrow) estrechez *f*, angostura *f*; (intolerance) estrechez *f*

nasal [nézəɫ] ADJ nasal

nastiness [nǽstɪnɪs] N (filth) suciedad *f*; (stinkiness) asquerosidad *f*; (rudeness, obscenity) grosería *f*

nasturtium [nəstɚ́ʃəm] N capuchina *f*

nasty [nǽsti] ADJ (mess) sucio; (smell) asqueroso; (comment) hiriente; (accident) feo; (word) grosero; (disposition) malo

natal [nédl] ADJ natal

nation [néʃən] N nación *f*; **—wide** a escala nacional

national [nǽʃənəɫ] ADJ nacional; **— park** parque nacional *m*; N ciudadano -na *mf*, nacional *mf*

nationalism [nǽʃənəlɪzəm] N nacionalismo *m*

nationality [næʃənǽlɪDi] N nacionalidad *f*; **adjective of —** gentilicio *m*

nationalize [nǽʃənəlaɪz] VT nacionalizar

native [néDɪv] ADJ nativo; **— language** lengua nativa *f*; **— plants** flora nativa *f*; **my — Italy** mi Italia natal *f*; (innate) innato; N (person born in a place) natural *m*; (member of a tribal group) indígena *mf*, nativo -va *mf*

nativity [nətívɪDi] N nacimiento *m*; **— scene** pesebre *m*; **the —** la Natividad

NATO (North Atlantic Treaty Organization) [néDo] N OTAN *f*

natural [nǽtʃɚəɫ] ADJ natural; (inborn) innato; **— childbirth** parto natural *m*; **— gas** gas natural *m*; **— resources** recursos naturales *m pl*; **— selection** selección natural *f*; N (musical sign) becuadro *m*; **he is a — for that job** tiene aptitud natural para ese puesto

naturalist [nǽtʃɚəlɪst] N naturalista *mf*

naturalization [nǽtʃɚəlɪzéʃən] N naturalización *f*

naturalize [nǽtʃɚəlaɪz] VI/VT naturalizar(se)

naturally [nǽtʃɚəli] ADV (of course) naturalmente; **I have — curly hair** tengo rizos naturales

naturalness [nǽtʃɚəɫnɪs] N naturalidad *f*

nature [nétʃɚ] N naturaleza *f*; (disposition) genio *m*, natural *m*

naught [nɔt] N (zero) cero *m*; (nothing) nada *f*

naughty [nɔ́Di] ADJ (child) travieso, pícaro, pillo; **— word** picardía *f*

Nauru [nɑúru] N Nauru *m*

Nauruan [nɑúruən] ADJ & N nauruano -na *mf*

nausea [nɔ́ziə] N náusea *f*, mareo *m*

nauseate [nɔ́ziet] VT dar náuseas; **to be —d** tener náuseas

nauseating [nɔ́zieDɪŋ] ADJ nauseabundo

nauseous [nɔ́ʃəs] ADJ (feeling nausea) mareado; (causing nausea) nauseabundo

nautical [nɔ́Dɪkəɫ] ADJ náutico

naval [névəɫ] ADJ naval; **— officer** oficial de marina *m*

nave [nev] N nave *f*

navel [névəɫ] N ombligo *m*; **— orange** naranja de ombligo *f*

navigable [nǽvɪgəbəɫ] ADJ navegable

navigate [nǽvɪget] VI/VT navegar

navigation [nævɪgéʃən] N navegación *f*; (science) náutica *f*

navigator [nǽvɪgeDɚ] N navegante *mf*

navy [névi] N marina (de guerra) *f*, armada *f*; **— bean** judía blanca *f*; **— blue** azul marino *m*

nay [ne] N (refusal) no *m*; (negative vote) voto negativo *m*

near [nɪr] ADV cerca; — **at hand** cerca, a la mano; **to come / go / draw** — acercarse; **—sighted** miope; PREP cerca de; — **the end of the month** hacia fines del mes; **to be** — **death** estar a punto de morir; ADJ cercano, próximo; — **East** Cercano Oriente *m*, Oriente Próximo *m*; **I had a** — **miss** por poco me sucede un accidente; VI/VT acercarse (a)

nearby [nírbái] ADV cerca; ADJ cercano, próximo

nearly [nírli] ADV casi, cerca de; **I** — **did it** casi lo hago

nearness [nírnɪs] N cercanía *f*, proximidad *f*

neat [nit] ADJ (clean) limpio, pulcro; (ordered) ordenado; (great) bueno

neatness [nítnɪs] N (cleanness) limpieza *f*, pulcritud *f*; (order) orden *m*

nebulous [nébjələs] ADJ nebuloso

necessary [nésɪseri] ADJ (needed) necesario; (involuntary) forzoso

necessitate [nəsésɪtet] VT requerir

necessity [nəsésɪdi] N necesidad *f*

neck [nɛk] N (of a human) cuello *m*; (of an animal) pescuezo *m*; (of clothes) escote *m*; (throat) garganta *f*; — **and** — parejos; **—lace** collar *m*; **—line** escote *m*; — **of land** istmo *m*; **—tie** corbata *f*

necrology [nəkrálədʒi] N necrología *f*

nectar [nɛ́ktɚ] N néctar *m*

nectarine [nɛktərín] N nectarina *f*

need [nid] N (lack) necesidad *f*; (poverty) carencia *f*; **in** — en aprietos; **if** — **be** en caso de necesidad; VT necesitar, precisar; **you** — **to come at four** tienes que venir a las cuatro

needle [nídl] N aguja *f*; **—point** bordado *m*; **—work** (embroidery) bordado *m*; (sewing) costura *f*; VT pinchar

needless [nídlɪs] ADJ innecesario; — **to say** huelga decir

needy [nídi] ADJ necesitado, menesteroso

ne'er-do-well [nérduwɛł] N inútil *mf*

negate [nɪgét] VT negar

negation [nɪgéʃən] N negación *f*

negative [négəDIV] ADJ negativo; **the search proved** — la búsqueda no dio resultado; N negativa *f*; (photographic) negativo *m*; **this plan has one** — este plan tiene una contra; INTERJ ¡negativo!

neglect [nɪglékt] VT postergar; (children) descuidar; (chores) desatender; **you're —ing your friends** tienes abandonados a tus amigos; **to** — **to** olvidarse de; N negligencia *f*, descuido *m*

neglectful [nɪgléktfəł] ADJ negligente, descuidado

negligence [néglɪdʒəns] N negligencia *f*

negligent [néglɪdʒənt] ADJ negligente, descuidado

negligible [néglɪdʒəbəł] ADJ despreciable

negotiate [nɪgóʃiet] VI/VT (a contract) negociar, gestionar; (an obstacle) salvar

negotiation [nɪgoʃiéʃən] N negociación *f*, gestión *f*

Negro [nígro] ADJ & N negro -gra *mf*

neigh [ne] N relincho *m*; VI relinchar

neighbor [nébɚ] N (person who lives near) vecino -na *mf*; (fellow human) prójimo -ma *mf*; ADJ vecino; VI **to** — **with** lindar con

neighborhood [nébɚhud] N vecindario *m*, barrio *m*; **in the** — **of a hundred dollars** alrededor de cien dólares

neighboring [nébərɪŋ] ADJ vecino, colindante

neither [níðɚ] PRON ninguno de los dos, ni (el) uno ni (el) otro; — **of the two** ninguno de los dos; ADJ ninguno de los dos; — **one of us** ninguno de nosotros dos; CONJ ni; — **hot nor cold** ni caliente ni frío; — **will I** yo tampoco

nemesis [némɪsɪs] N némesis *f*

neologism [niálədʒɪzəm] N neologismo *m*

neon [nían] N neón *m*

Nepal [nəpɔ́ł] N Nepal *m*

Nepalese [nepəlíz] ADJ & N nepalés -esa *mf*, nepalí *mf*

nephew [néfju] N sobrino *m*

nephritis [nəfráɪDɪs] N nefritis *f*

nepotism [népətɪzəm] N nepotismo *m*

nerd [nɝd] N (technological adept) persona aficionada a las computadoras / los ordenadores *f*; (socially inept person) persona socialmente inepta *f*

nerve [nɝv] N (anatomy) nervio *m*; (courage) presencia de ánimo *f*; (impertinence) descaro *m*, morro *m*; — **cell** neurona *f*; — **gas** gas nervioso *m*; **—-(w)racking** angustiante; **he gets on my —s** me saca de quicio

nervous [nɝ́vəs] ADJ nervioso; — **breakdown** ataque de nervios *m*

nervousness [nɝ́vəsnɪs] N nerviosismo *m*

nest [nɛst] N nido *m*; (brood) nidada *f*; — **egg** ahorros *m pl*; — **of thieves** guarida de ladrones *f*; VI/VT anidar; (fit together) encajarse

nestle [nésəł] VI acurrucarse; VT apoyar, recostar

net [nɛt] N red *f* (also network); (in hair) redecilla *f*; VT (catch a fish) pescar con red;

(cover with a net) cubrir con una red; (catch a criminal) atrapar; (hit the tennis net) dar en la red; (make money after expenses) producir/ganar neto; ADJ neto; — **price** precio neto *m*; — **profit** ganancia neta *f*; — **assets** activo neto *m*; — **income** ingreso neto *m*; —**work** red *f*; —**working** (social) relaciones profesionales *f pl*; (computer) diseño de redes y comunicaciones *m*

Netherlander [néðɚ-ləndɚ] N holandés -esa *mf*

Netherlands [néðɚ-ləndz] N Países Bajos *m pl*

nettle [nédl] N ortiga *f*

neural [núrəɫ] ADJ neural

neuron [núrɑn] N neurona *f*

neurosis [nurósɪs] N neurosis *f*

neurotic [nurɑ́dɪk] ADJ & N neurótico -ca *mf*

neuter [núpɚ] ADJ neutro; VT castrar

neutral [nútrəɫ] ADJ neutral; (of colors) neutro; N punto muerto *m*

neutrality [nutrǽlɪɒi] N neutralidad *f*

neutralize [nútrəlaɪz] VI/VT neutralizar(se)

neutron [nútrɑn] N neutrón *m*; — **bomb** bomba de neutrones *f*

never [névɚ] ADV nunca, jamás; — **mind** no te preocupes; **this will** — **do** esto no va a funcionar; —**ending** interminable

nevertheless [nɛvɚ-ðəlés] ADV & CONJ sin embargo, no obstante

new [nu] ADJ (not old) nuevo; (fresh) otro; **a** — **sheet of paper** otra hoja de papel; — **Age (music)** new age *f*; —**born baby** recién nacido -da *mf*; —**comer** recién llegado -da *mf*; —**fangled** moderno, recién inventado; —**found** nuevo; — **year** año nuevo *m*; — **Year's Eve** fin de año *m*; *Sp* nochevieja *f*

newly [núli] ADV recientemente; — **arrived** recién llegado; —**wed** recién casado

newness [núnɪs] N novedad *f*

news [nuz] N noticias *f pl*; (latest gossip) novedades *f pl*; (newspaper) periódico *m*; **it is** — **to me** recién me entero; **piece of** — noticia *f*; — **broadcast/bulletin** noticiero *m*, noticiario *m*; —**cast** noticiero *m*, noticiario *m*; — **clipping** recorte de diario *m*; —**letter** boletín informativo *m*; —**paper** periódico *m*, diario *m*; —**print** papel de periódico *m*; —**room** sala de redacción *f*; —**stand** quiosco *m*; —**worthy** de interés periodístico

newt [nut] N tritón *m*

New Zealand [nuzílənd] N Nueva Zelanda *f*

New Zealander [nuzíləndɚ] N neozelandés -esa *mf*

next [nɛkst] ADJ (future) próximo, entrante;

(following) siguiente; (contiguous) contiguo, de al lado; **who's** —? ¿quién sigue? ADV después, luego; — **best** segundo en calidad; **when** — **we meet** cuando nos volvamos a ver; PREP —-**door** de al lado; — **of kin** familiares *m pl*; — **to** junto a, al lado de

nibble [níbəɫ] VI/VT (bite) mordiscar, mordisquear; (eat) picotear; (of fish) picar; N (bite) mordisco *m*; (act of nibbling) mordisqueo *m*

Nicaragua [nɪkərágwə] N Nicaragua *f*

Nicaraguan [nɪkərágwən] ADJ & N nicaragüense *mf*

nice [naɪs] ADJ (kind) amable, simpático; (agreeable) *Am* lindo, *Sp* majo; **it's** — **and hot** está bien calentito

nicety [náɪsɪɒi] N (subtlety) sutileza *f*; (detail) exactitud *f*, precisión *f*

niche [nɪtʃ] N nicho *m* (also environmental); **I've found my** — he encontrado mi lugar

nick [nɪk] N (chip) muesca *f*; (cut) corte *m*; **in the** — **of time** justo a tiempo; VT (chip) hacer muescas; (cut) cortar

nickel [níkəɫ] N (metal) níquel *m*; (coin) moneda de cinco centavos *f*; —-**plated** niquelado

nickname [níknem] N apodo *m*, mote *m*, sobrenombre *m*; VT apodar

nicotine [níkətin] N nicotina *f*

niece [nis] N sobrina *f*

Niger [náɪʤɚ] N Níger *m*

Nigeria [naɪʤíriə] N Nigeria *f*

Nigerian [naɪʤírian] ADJ & N nigeriano -na *mf*

Nigerien [naɪʤírien] ADJ & N nigerino -na *mf*

niggardly [nígɚ-dli] ADJ mezquino

night [naɪt] N noche *f*; ADJ nocturno, de noche; —**club** club nocturno *m*; —**fall** anochecer *m*, atardecer *m*; —**gown** camisón *m*; —**life** vida nocturna *f*; *Sp* marcha *f*; —-**light** lamparilla *f*; —**mare** pesadilla *f*; — **owl** trasnochador -ora *mf*; — **shift** turno de la noche *m*; —**stand** veladora *f*, mesilla de noche *f*; —**time** noche *f*; — **watchman** sereno *m*

nightingale [náɪtŋgeɫ] N ruiseñor *m*

nightly [náɪtli] ADV todas las noches; ADJ nocturno

nihilism [náɪəlɪzəm] N nihilismo *m*

nil [nɪɫ] ADJ **your chances are** — tus probabilidades son nulas

nimble [nímbəɫ] ADJ ágil

nincompoop [nínŋkəmpup] N *fam* tarambana *mf*, bobalicón -ona *mf*

nine [naɪn] NUM nueve

nineteen [naɪntín] NUM diecinueve

ninety [náɪnti] NUM noventa

ninth [náɪnθ] ADJ & N noveno *m*

nip [nɪp] VT (pinch) pellizcar; (bite) mordiscar, mordisquear; (cause frostbite) helar; **to — in the bud** cortar de raíz; **to — off** despuntar; VI (drink in sips) dar sorbitos; N (pinch) pellizco *m*; (bite) mordisco *m*; (sip) traguito *m*, sorbito *m*; (cold) frío *m*; **it's going to be — and tuck** va a ser muy reñido

nipple [nípəł] N (on female breast) pezón *m*; (on male breast) tetilla *f*; (on bottle) tetina *f*

nitpick [nítpɪk] VI criticar detalles insignificantes

nitrate [náɪtret] N nitrato *m*

nitric acid [náɪtrɪkǽsɪd] N ácido nítrico *m*

nitrogen [náɪtrədʒən] N nitrógeno *m*

nitroglycerin [naɪtroglísə˞ɪn] N nitroglicerina *f*

nitty-gritty [nídɪgrídɪ] N **to get down to the —** ir al grano

no [no] ADV no; **— longer** ya no; **he was a —-show** no se presentó; **a —-win situation** una situación insoluble; **there is — more** no hay más; ADJ ningun(o); **— man's land** tierra de nadie *f*; **— matter how much** por mucho que; **— one** ninguno, nadie; **— smoking** se prohíbe fumar; **—where** (location) en ninguna parte / ningún lado; (direction) a ninguna parte / ningún lado; **I have — friends** no tengo amigos; **it's a —-brainer** la respuesta es obvia; **— friend of mine will go hungry** ningún amigo mío pasará hambre; **of — use** inútil; N (refusal) no *m*; (negative vote) voto negativo *m*

nobility [nobílɪɖi] N nobleza *f*, hidalguía *f*

noble [nóbəł] ADJ & N noble *mf*

nobody [nóbaɖi] PRON nadie, ninguno; N un don nadie, pelagatos *mf sg*

nocturnal [naktɝ́nəł] ADJ nocturno

nod [nad] VI/VT (signal affirmation) asentir con la cabeza; VI (doze) cabecear, dar cabezadas; **to — off** dormirse; N (as signal) inclinación de cabeza *f*, saludo con la cabeza *m*; (from sleepiness) cabezada *f*

node [nod] N (of cells) nódulo *m*; (in plants) nudo *m*; (in physics) nodo *m*

noise [nɔɪz] N ruido *m*; VI **it is being —d about that** corre el rumor que

noiseless [nɔ́ɪzlɪs] ADJ silencioso

noisy [nɔ́ɪzi] ADJ ruidoso

nomad [nómæd] N nómada *mf*

nomenclature [nómɪnkletʃɚ] N nomenclatura *f*

nominal [námənəł] ADJ nominal

nominate [námənet] VT nominar

nomination [namənéʃən] N nominación *f*

nominee [naməní] N candidato -ta *mf*

nonchalant [nanʃəlánt] ADJ despreocupado

nonconformist [nankənfɔ́rmɪst] ADJ & N incomformista *mf*

none [nʌn] PRON ninguno; **I want — of that** no me quiero meter en eso; **that is — of your business** no es asunto tuyo; ADV **— too soon** al último momento; **—theless** sin embargo

nonentity [nanéntɪɖi] N nulidad *f*

nonfiction [nanfíkʃən] N no ficción *f*

nonpartisan [nanpárɖɪzən] ADJ imparcial

nonproductive [nanprədáktɪv] ADJ improductivo

nonprofit [nanpráfɪt] ADJ sin fines de lucro

nonresident [nanrézɪdənt] ADJ & N no residente *mf*

nonsense [nánsɛns] N tonterías *f pl*, monsergas *f pl*, estupideces *f pl*; **to talk —** decir barbaridades / disparates

nonstop [nánstáp] ADJ sin escala, directo; ADV sin parar

noodle [núdl] N fideo *m*, tallarín *m*

nook [nʊk] N rincón *m*

noon [nun] N mediodía *m*; **—time** mediodía *m*

noose [nus] N soga *f*, lazo *m*; **with a — around his neck** con la soga al cuello; VT (catch with a rope) enlazar; (make a loop in) hacer un lazo corredizo en

nope [nop] ADV no

nor [nɔr] CONJ ni; **we have neither eggs — flour** no tenemos ni huevos ni harina

Nordic [nɔ́rdɪk] ADJ nórdico

norm [nɔrm] N norma *f*

normal [nɔ́rməł] ADJ normal; N (line) normal *f*; **to return to —** volver a la normalidad; (perpendicular line) línea perpendicular *f*

normalize [nɔ́rməlaɪz] VI/VT normalizar(se)

north [nɔrθ] N norte *m*; ADJ (in the north) norte, norteño; **the — entrance** la entrada norte; (from the north) del norte; **— America** América del Norte *f*; **— American** norteamericano -na *mf*; **—east** noreste, hacia el noreste; **—eastern** del noreste; **— Korea** Corea del Norte *f*; **— Korean** norcoreano -na; **— Pole** Polo Norte *m*; **—west** noroeste *m*, hacia el noroeste; **— wind** cierzo *m*, viento norte *m*; ADV al norte, hacia el norte

northern [nɔ́rðɚn] ADJ del norte; (from the north) norteño; (in the north) septentrional; **— lights** aurora boreal *f*

northerner [nɔ́rðɚnɚ] N norteño -ña *mf*
northward [nɔ́rθwəd] ADV hacia el norte
Norway [nɔ́rwe] N Noruega *f*
Norwegian [nɔrwíʤən] ADJ & N noruego -ga *mf*
nose [noz] N nariz *f*; (of an airplane) morro *m*; (of an animal) hocico *m*; (perspicacity) olfato *m*; **—bleed** hemorragia nasal *f*; **—dive** picado *m*; **— job** rinoplastia *f*; **keep your — clean** no te metas en líos; **on the —** exactamente; VI/VT (move forward) entrar de punta; (muzzle) hocicar; **to — around** husmear; **to pick one's —** hurgarse las narices
nostalgia [nɑstǽłʤə] N nostalgia *f*
nostalgic [nɑstǽłʤɪk] ADJ nostálgico
nostrils [nástrəłz] N narices *f pl*, ventanillas de la nariz *f pl*
nosy, nosey [nózi] ADJ entrometido
not [nɑt] ADV no; **I'm — your friend** no soy tu amigo; **— at all** (no way) de ningún modo; (you're welcome) de nada; **— at all sure** nada seguro; **— even a word** ni una palabra
notable [nódəbəł] ADJ notable, granado
notarize [nódəraɪz] VT notariar
notary [nódəri] N notario -ria *mf*; **— public** notario -ria público -ca *mf*
notation [notéʃən] N (system of signs) notación *f*; (act of writing) anotación *f*; (short note) anotación *f*, apunte *m*
notch [nɑtʃ] N (nick) muesca *f*, mella *f*; (degree) grado *m*; **a — above the rest** mejor que los demás; VT hacer una muesca; **he —ed another win** se anotó otra victoria
note [not] N nota *f*; (touch) toque *m*; **—book** cuaderno *m*; (small) libreta *f*; **—s** apuntes *m pl*; **—worthy** notable; **of —** de renombre / de nota; **to take — of** notar; VT (notice) notar; (write down) anotar, apuntar
noted [nódɪd] ADJ célebre
nothing [nʌ́θɪŋ] PRON nada; (score) cero, nada; N (insignificant person) don nadie *m*; (insignificant thing) nadería *f*; **— to it** no tiene ciencia; ADV **it was — like that** no fue así para nada; **we did it for —** (free) lo hicimos gratis; (fruitlessly) lo hicimos en balde
notice [nódɪs] N (information) aviso *m*; (warning) advertencia *f*; (attention) atención *f*; **a week's —** una semana de plazo; **to give —** renunciar; **to take —** hacer caso; VT (perceive) notar, advertir; (pay attention to) fijarse (en), reparar (en)
noticeable [nódɪsəbəł] ADJ perceptible, apreciable
notification [nodəfɪkéʃən] N notificación *f*
notify [nódəfaɪ] VT notificar
notion [nóʃən] N noción *f*, idea *f*; (whim) capricho *m*; **—s** mercería *f*
notorious [notóriəs] ADJ de mala fama; **he's a — liar** tiene fama de mentiroso
nougat [núgət] N turrón *m*
noun [naun] N sustantivo *m*
nourish [nɝ́ɪʃ] VT (a person) nutrir, alimentar; (a hope) abrigar
nourishing [nɝ́ɪʃɪŋ] ADJ nutritivo
nourishment [nɝ́ɪʃmənt] N (food) alimento *m*; (act of nourishing) alimentación *f*
novel [návəł] N novela *f*; ADJ novedoso
novelist [návəlɪst] N novelista *mf*
novelty [návəłti] N novedad *f*; **the — soon wore off** se pasó la novedad; **novelties** chucherías *f pl*
November [novémbɚ] N noviembre *m*
novice [návɪs] N novato -ta *mf*, pipiolo -la *mf*; (religious) novicio -cia *mf*
now [nau] ADV ahora; **— and then** de vez en cuando; **— that** ahora que; **he left just —** salió hace poco, recién salió; **—, —, calm down!** bueno, bueno, ¡cálmate!
nowadays [náuədez] ADV hoy (en) día
noxious [nákʃəs] ADJ nocivo
nuance [núɑns] N matiz *m*
nuclear [núkliɚ] ADJ nuclear; **— energy** energía nuclear *f*; **— family** familia nuclear *f*; **— fission** fisión nuclear *f*; **— fusion** fusión nuclear *f*; **— physics** física nuclear *f*; **— weapon** arma nuclear *f*
nucleus [núkliəs] N núcleo *m*
nude [nud] ADJ & N desnudo *m*
nudge [nʌʤ] VI/VT codear; N golpe suave con el codo *m*
nugget [nʌ́gɪt] N (gold) pepita *f*; (chicken) pedacito *m*; (wisdom) perla *f*
nuisance [núsəns] N molestia *f*; *Sp* pesadez *f*; (legal) perjuicio *m*; **you're such a —!** ¡qué pesado eres tú! **— tax** impuesto de consumo *m*
nuke [nuk] N arma nuclear *f*; VT (bomb) bombardear con armas nucleares; (cook) calentar en microondas
null [nʌł] ADJ nulo; **— and void** nulo
nullify [nʌ́ləfaɪ] VT anular
numb [nʌm] ADJ entumecido; **to get —** entumecerse; VT entumecer
number [nʌ́mbɚ] N número *m*; **— one** uno mismo *m*; **—-crunching** procesamiento de datos numéricos complejos *m*; VT numerar; VI (total) ascender a; **I — him among my friends** lo cuento entre mis amigos

numberless [nʌ́mbəlɪs] ADJ sin número
numbskull, numskull [nʌ́mskʌɫ] N
zopenco -ca *mf*
numeral [núməəɫ] N número *m*; ADJ
numeral
numerical [numérɪkəl] ADJ numérico
numerous [núməəs] ADJ numeroso
nun [nʌn] N monja *f*, religiosa *f*
nuptial [nʌ́pʃəɫ] ADJ nupcial; N —**s** nupcias *f*
pl
nurse [nɜ·s] N (for the sick) enfermero -a *mf*;
(for children) niñera *f*; VT (give milk)
amamantar, lactar; (tend to a sick person)
cuidar; **to — a grudge** guardar rencor; **to
— a cup of coffee** tomar una taza de
café a sorbitos; **to — a cold** cuidarse
durante un resfrío; VI (drink milk) mamar
nursery [nɜ́·sri] N (children's room) cuarto
para niños *m*; (day-care center) guardería
f; (place for growing plants) almáciga *f*,
vivero *m*, plantel *m*; — **school** pre-escolar
infantil *f*, ronda *f*; — **school** pre-escolar
m; *Sp* parvulario *m*; *Am* jardín infantil *m*
nursing [nɜ́·sɪŋ] N (profession) enfermería *f*;
(care) cuidado *m*; — **home** (for old
people) hogar de ancianos *m*; (for sick
people) casa de salud *f*
nurture [nɜ́·tʃə] VT (rear) criar; (feed) nutrir,
alimentar; (encourage) fomentar; N
(rearing) crianza *f*; (feeding) alimentación
f
nut [nʌt] N (fruit) fruto seco *m*; (device)
tuerca *f*; (person) excéntrico -ca *mf*;
—**cracker** cascanueces *m sg*; —**meg** nuez
moscada *f*; —**s** *vulg* cojones *m pl*; **he's** —**s**
está loco; —**s and bolts** los fundamentos;
—**shell** cáscara de fruto seco *f*; **in a**
—**shell** en pocas palabras
nutrient [nútriənt] N nutriente *m*
nutrition [nutríʃən] N nutrición *f*,
alimentación *f*
nutritious [nutríʃəs] ADJ nutritivo,
alimenticio
nylon [náɪlɑn] N nilón *m*, nailon *m*

Oo

oak [ok] N roble *m*, encina *f*; — **grove**
robledal *m*
oar [ɔr] N remo *m*; VI/VT remar, bogar; —**lock**
tolete *m*
OAS (Organization of American States)
[oeés] N OEA *f*

oasis [oésɪs] N oasis *m*
oat [ot] N avena *f*; —**meal** (flour) harina de
avena *f*; (breakfast food) gachas de avena *f*
pl; —**s** avena *f*
oath [oθ] N (pledge) juramento *m*; (curse)
maldición *f*; (swear word) palabrota *f*, taco
m; **to take an** — prestar juramento
obedience [obídiəns] N obediencia *f*
obedient [obídient] ADJ obediente
obese [obís] ADJ obeso
obesity [obísɪdi] N obesidad *f*
obey [obé] VI/VT obedecer
obituary [obítʃueri] N nota necrológica *f*,
obituario *m*
object [ábdʒɪkt] N objeto *m*; (of a verb)
complemento *m*; [əbdʒékt] VI/VT objetar
objection [əbdʒékʃən] N objeción *f*
objective [əbdʒéktɪv] ADJ objetivo; N objetivo
m
obligate [ábligeɪt] VT obligar
obligation [ablɪgéʃən] N obligación *f*; **under
no — to buy** sin compromiso de compra
obligatory [əblígətɔri] ADJ obligatorio
oblige [əbláɪdʒ] VT (make obliged) obligar; VI/
VT (do a favor for) complacer; VI (obey an
order) obedecer; **much —d!** ¡muchas
gracias! ¡muy agradecido!
obliging [əbláɪdʒɪŋ] ADJ complaciente; *Am*
comedido
oblique [oblík] ADJ oblicuo
obliterate [əblídəret] VT (blot out) tachar;
(destroy) arrasar, destruir
oblivion [əblíviən] N olvido *m*
oblivious [əblíviəs] ADJ inconsciente; — **to
the danger** ajeno al peligro
obnoxious [əbnákʃəs] ADJ (remark, behavior)
ofensivo; (person) molesto
oboe [óbo] N oboe *m*
obscene [əbsín] ADJ obsceno; **his salary is**
— lo que gana es escandaloso
obscenity [əbsénɪdi] N obscenidad *f*
obscure [əbskjúr] ADJ oscuro; VT oscurecer
obscurity [əbskjúrɪdi] N oscuridad *f*
obsequious [əbsíkwiəs] ADJ obsequioso
observance [əbzɔ́·vəns] N observancia *f*
observant [əbzɔ́·vənt] ADJ observador
observation [abzɔ·véʃən] N observación *f*
observatory [əbzɔ́·vətɔri] N observatorio *m*
observe [əbzɔ́·v] VT observar; (holidays,
rituals) guardar
observer [əbzɔ́·və] N observador -ra *mf*
obsess [əbsés] VI/VT obsesionar(se); **he's**
—**ing over it** está obsesionado
obsession [əbséʃən] N obsesión *f*
obsessive-compulsive [əbsésɪvkəmpʌ́ɫsɪv]
ADJ obsesivo-compulsivo
obsolescence [absəlésəns] N desuso *m*

obsolete [absəlít] ADJ anticuado, desusado

obstacle [ábstəkəɫ] N obstáculo *m*

obstetrics [abstétrɪks] N obstetricia *f*

obstinacy [ábstənəsi] N obstinación *f*, terquedad *f*, porfía *f*

obstinate [ábstənɪt] ADJ obstinado, terco, recalcitrante; **to be —** obstinarse

obstruct [əbstrʌ́kt] VI/VT obstruir; (traffic) atascar, obstruir

obstruction [əbstrʌ́kʃən] N obstrucción *f*

obtain [əbtén] VT obtener, procurar; VI prevalecer

obtainable [əbténəbəɫ] ADJ conseguible

obviate [ábviet] VT hacer innecesario

obvious [ábviəs] ADJ obvio, evidente

occasion [əkéʒən] N (moment) ocasión *f*; (chance) oportunidad *f*, ocasión *f*; (cause) motivo *m*; (event) acontecimiento *m*, ocasión *f*; VT ocasionar

occasional [əkéʒənəɫ] ADJ ocasional

occasionally [əkéʒənəli] ADV de vez en cuando, ocasionalmente

occidental [aksɪdéntɫ] ADJ & N occidental *mf*

occult [əkʌ́ɫt] ADJ oculto; N ocultismo *m*, ciencias ocultas *f pl*; VT ocultar

occupant [ákjəpənt] N ocupante *mf*

occupation [akjəpéʃən] N ocupación *f*

occupy [ákjəpaɪ] VI/VT ocupar

occur [əkɝ́] VI ocurrir, suceder; **it —red to me** se me ocurrió

occurrence [əkɝ́əns] N suceso *m*, acontecimiento *m*

ocean [óʃən] N océano *m*

oceanography [oʃənágrəfi] N oceanografía *f*

ocelot [ásəlat] N ocelote *m*

o'clock [əklák] ADV **it is one —** es la una; **it is two —** son las dos

octagon [áktəgan] N octágono *m*, octógono *m*

octane [ákten] N octano *m*

octave [áktɪv] N octava *f*

October [aktóbɚ] N octubre *m*

octopus [áktəpəs] N pulpo *m*

OD (overdose) [odí] N sobredosis *f*; VI tomar una sobredosis

odd [ad] ADJ (unusual) extraño; (not even) impar, non; **—ball** excéntrico -ca *mf*; **— change** suelto *m*, cambio *m*; **— job** trabajo ocasional *m*; **— shoe** zapato sin compañero *m*; **thirty-—** treinta y tantos

oddity [ádɪti] N rareza *f*; (person) excéntrico -ca *mf*

odds [adz] N (probabilities) probabilidades *f pl*; **— and ends** cachivaches *m pl*; **—-on favorite** favorito *m*; **the — are against me** llevo las de perder; **to be at —** estar en desacuerdo

ode [od] N oda *f*

odious [ódiəs] ADJ odioso

odor [ódɚ] N olor *m*; (bad) hedor *m*

odorless [ódɚlɪs] ADJ inodoro

odorous [ódɚəs] ADJ oloroso

of [ʌv] PREP de; **— course** por supuesto, desde luego; **a quarter — five** las cinco menos cuarto; **doctor — medicine** doctor -ra en medicina *mf*; **the smell — paint** el olor a pintura; **a friend — mine** un amigo mío

off [ɔf] ADV **— and on** de vez en cuando; **— the record** extraoficialmente; **ten cents —** rebaja de diez centavos *f*; **ten miles —** a diez millas de distancia; **to take a day —** tomarse un día libre; ADJ **— chance** posibilidad remota *f*; **—-color** verde; **— season** temporada baja *f*; **— year** de producción decreciente; **our deal is —** se canceló nuestro plan; **prices are —** los precios han caído; **you're — by a mile** estás equivocadísimo; **he's a little —** está tocadito; **with his hat —** sin el sombrero; **the electricity is —** está apagada la electricidad; **to be — to war** haberse ido a la guerra; **to be well —** tener mucho dinero; PREP **— course** fuera de curso; **he drove — the road** se salió de la carretera; **I bought it — a gypsy** se lo compré a un gitano; **he's — playing golf** se fue a jugar al golf; VT liquidar

off-duty [ɔfdúɖi] ADJ **to be —** no estar de turno

offend [əfénd] VI/VT (insult) ofender, afrentar; (affect disagreeably) desagradar

offender [əféndɚ] N delincuente *mf*

offense [əféns] N (sin, insult) ofensa *f*; (misdemeanor) delito *m*; **no — was meant** no te lo tomes a mal; [áfɛns] (in sports) ofensiva *f*

offensive [əfénsɪv] ADJ ofensivo; N ofensiva *f*

offer [ɔ́fɚ] VT ofrecer; **to — to** ofrecerse a; N oferta *f*

offering [ɔ́fɚɪŋ] N (thing given in worship) ofrenda *f*; (thing presented for sale) oferta *f*; (action of offering) ofrecimiento *m*

offhand [ɔ́fhǽnd] ADV **he remarked —** mencionó al descuido; ADJ **an — remark** un comentario descuidado

office [ɔ́fɪs] N (function) cargo *m*, función *f*; (place) oficina *f*, despacho *m*; (headquarters) oficinas *f pl*; **— boy** mandadero de oficina *m*; **— building** edificio para oficinas *m*; **through the —s of** por la intervención de

officer [ɔ́fɪsɚ] N (military) oficial *m*; (police) agente de policía *mf*; (of an organization)

directivo -va *mf*
official [əfíʃəł] ADJ oficial; N funcionario -ria *mf*
officiate [əfíʃiet] VI oficiar; (in sports) arbitrar
officious [əfíʃəs] ADJ oficioso
off-key [ɔfkí] ADJ desafinado
off-limits [ɔflímɪts] ADJ vedado
off-season [ɔfsízən] ADJ de temporada baja
offset [ɔfsét] N offset *m*; VT compensar
offshore [ɔfʃɔr] ADJ & ADV cerca de la costa; — **drilling** explotación petrolífera en el fondo del mar *f*
offspring [ɔ́fsprɪŋ] N prole *m*
offstage [ɔfstédʒ] ADV & ADJ entre bastidores, fuera de escena
often [ɔ́fən] ADV a menudo; **how** — ? ¿con qué frecuencia? ¿cada cuánto?
ogre [óɡɚ] N ogro *m*
ohm [om] N ohmio *m*
oil [ɔɪl] N (for cars, cooking) aceite *m*; (crude) petróleo *m*; —**can** alcuza *f*, aceitera *f*; —**cloth** hule *m*, tela de hule *f*; — **field** yacimiento petrolífero *m*; — **lamp** quinqué *m*; — **painting** pintura al óleo *f*, óleo *m*; — **pan** cárter *m*; — **rig** plataforma petrolífera *f*; — **slick** mancha de petróleo *f*; — **well** pozo de petróleo *m*; VT (apply oil) aceitar; (bribe) untar
oily [ɔ́ɪli] ADJ aceitoso, oleoso; (unctuous) untuoso
oink [ɔɪŋk] VI gruñir; N gruñido *m*
ointment [ɔ́ɪntmənt] N ungüento *m*
OK [oké] ADJ bueno; ADV bien; **he's an** — **guy** es un buen tipo; **it's** — (fine) está bien; (adequate) es regular; **to give one's** — dar el visto bueno; VT dar el visto bueno, aprobar
okra [ókrə] N quingombó *m*
old [old] ADJ viejo; (objects only) antiguo; (wine) añejo; — **age** vejez *f*, ancianidad *f*; —**-fashioned** (unfashionable) pasado de moda; (antiquated) anticuado; (morally prudish) chapado a la antigua; — **fogey** carcamal *m*, carca *m*; — **hat** pasado de moda; — **maid** solterona *f*; —**-time** antiguo, viejo; —**-timer** (long-time member) miembro de la vieja guardia *m*; (oldster) viejo *m*; — **wives' tale** superstición *f*; — **world** viejo mundo *m*; **days of** — antaño; **how** — **are you?** ¿cuántos años tienes? — **man** (husband) marido *m*; (father) *fam* viejo *m*; **I'm not** — **enough to drive** soy muy joven para conducir; **to be an** — **hand at** ser ducho en
olden [óldən] ADJ **in** — **days** antaño
oldie [óldi] N viejo éxito *m*

oleander [óliændɚ] N adelfa *f*
olfactory [ɔłfǽktəri] ADJ olfatorio
olive [áliv] N (tree) olivo *m*; (fruit) aceituna *f*, oliva *f*; — **branch** ramo de olivo *m*; — **grove** olivar *m*; — **oil** aceite de oliva *m*; — **wood** madera de olivo *m*; ADJ verde oliva
Olympiad [olímpiæd] N olimpiada *f*
Olympic [olímpɪk] ADJ olímpico; — **Games** Olimpiadas *f pl*, Juegos Olímpicos *m pl*
Oman [omán] N Omán *m*
Omani [ománi] ADJ & N omaní *mf*
omelet [ámlɪt] N tortilla francesa *f*
omen [ómən] N agüero *m*, presagio *m*
ominous [ámənəs] ADJ (threatening) amenazador; (like an omen) agorero
omission [omíʃən] N omisión *f*
omit [omít] VT omitir
omnipotence [ɑmnípətəns] N omnipotencia *f*
omnipotent [ɑmnípətənt] ADJ omnipotente
omniscience [ɑmníʃəns] N omnisciencia *f*
omniscient [ɑmníʃənt] ADJ omnisciente
omnivorous [ɑmnívɚəs] ADJ omnívoro
on [ɑn] PREP en, sobre, encima de; — **the table** en / sobre / encima de la mesa; — **all sides** por todos lados; — **arriving** al llegar; — **call** de guardia; — **credit** al fiado; — **drugs** drogado; — **horseback** a caballo; —**-line** en línea; — **Monday** el lunes; — **purpose** a propósito; —**-screen** en la pantalla; — **the house** la casa paga; — **time** a tiempo; **a book** — **stamps** un libro sobre sellos; **do you have any cigarettes** — **you?** ¿tienes cigarros? **drunk** — **beer** borracho de cerveza; **to talk** — **the phone** hablar por teléfono; ADV — **and** — dale que dale; ADJ **his hat is** — lleva puesto el sombrero; **the light is** — está encendida la luz; **there's a war** — estamos en guerra; **you're** — (broadcasting) estás en el aire
once [wʌns] ADV (in the past, a single time) una vez; (if ever) si alguna vez; — **and for all** una vez por todas; — **in a while** de vez en cuando; —**-over** vistazo *m*; — **upon a time** érase una vez; **at** — de inmediato; **just this** — sólo por esta vez; **cousin** — **removed** primo segundo *m*; CONJ una vez que, cuando; N una vez
oncology [ɑnkálədʒi] N oncología *f*
one [wʌn] ADJ uno; — **book** un libro; — **thousand** mil; —**-armed** manco; —**-armed bandit** tragaperras *mf sg*; —**-eyed** tuerto; — **John Smith** un tal John Smith; —**-man band** hombre orquesta *m*; — **on** — mano a mano;

—**-sided fight** pelea desigual *f*;
—**-upmanship** competitividad *f*; —**-way
street** calle de sentido único *f*; **his —
chance** su única oportunidad; **the —
and only** el único; **this is — smart dog**
es un perro muy listo; N & PRON uno *m*; —
at a time de a uno; — **by** — uno por
uno; **love — another** amaos los unos a
los otros; **the — who** el / la que; **the
green** — el verde; **this** — este / esta

oneself [wʌnsélf] PRON **to be** — ser uno
mismo; **to sit by** — estar sentado solo; **to
talk to** — hablar para sí; **to look at** —
in the mirror mirarse en el espejo; **to
buy — a house** comprarse una casa

ongoing [ángoɪŋ] ADJ continuo

onion [ánjən] N cebolla *f*; — **patch** cebollar
m

onlooker [ánlʊkɚ] N espectador -ra *mf*,
mirón -ona *mf*

only [ónli] ADJ único; ADV sólo, solamente; **I
— just caught the train** por poco
pierdo el tren; CONJ sólo que, pero

onomatopoeia [ɑnəmɑɒəpíə] N
onomatopeya *f*

onset [ánset] N comienzo *m*

onto [ɑntu] PREP en, sobre, encima de; **he
placed it — the top of the
refrigerator** lo colocó encima de la
nevera; **I'm — your plot** conozco tu
plan

onward [ánwɚd] ADV hacia adelante

onyx [ánɪks] N ónix *m*

oops [ʊps] INTERJ ¡huy!

ooze [uz] VI/VT rezumar(se); N cieno *m*

opal [ópəl] N ópalo *m*

opaque [opék] ADJ opaco

**OPEC (Organization of Petroleum
Exporting Countries)** [ópɛk] N OPEP *f*

open [ópən] VI/VT abrir(se); **to — into**
comunicarse con; **to — one's way** abrirse
paso; **to — onto** dar a; **to — up** abrirse;
ADJ abierto; — **and shut** claro, evidente;
— **door policy** política de acceso libre *f*;
—**-ended** abierto; —**-heart surgery**
cirujía de corazón abierto *f*; —**-minded**
de amplias miras; —**-mouthed**
boquiabierto; — **question** cuestión
discutible *f*; — **season** temporada de caza
f; — **to criticism** expuesto a la crítica; N
(outdoors) aire libre *m*; (tournament)
abierto *m*

opener [ópənɚ] N abridor *m*; (in sports)
primer partido *m*; **for —s** para empezar

opening [ópənɪŋ] N (open space) abertura *f*;
(act of making or becoming open,
ceremony) apertura *f*; (beginning)

comienzo *m*; (clearing) claro *m*; (vacancy)
vacante *m*; (pretext) oportunidad *f*; —
night estreno *m*

opera [ápərə] N ópera *f*; — **glasses** gemelos
m pl; — **house** ópera *f*

operable [ápɚəbəɫ] ADJ operable

operate [ápəret] VI (function) funcionar;
(intervene surgically) operar; **to — on a
person** operar a una persona; VT (run a
machine) manejar; (administrate) dirigir;
(make function) accionar

operating room [ápəreɒɪŋrum] N sala de
operaciones *f*, quirófano *m*

operation [ɑpəréʃən] N (surgical
intervention, mission, math function)
operación *f*; (function) funcionamiento *m*;
(use of a machine) manejo *m*; **to be in** —
(law) estar vigente; (machine) estar
funcionando

operative [ápɚəɒɪv] ADJ (law) vigente;
(contract provision) pertinente; (word)
clave; N (machine worker) operario -ria *mf*;
(spy) agente *mf*

operator [ápəreɒɚ] N (telephone, math)
operador -ra *mf*; (machine) operario -ria
mf; (stock) especulador -ra *mf*; **he's a
smooth** — es un astuto

opinion [əpínjən] N opinión *f*

opium [ópiəm] N opio *m*

opossum [əpásəm] N zarigüeya *f*

opponent [əpónənt] N oponente *mf*,
contrincante *mf*, adversario -ria *mf*

opportune [ɑpɚtún] ADJ oportuno

opportunistic [ɑpɚtunístɪk] ADJ oportunista,
aprovechado

opportunity [ɑpɚtúniɒi] N oportunidad *f*,
ocasión *f*

oppose [əpóz] VI/VT oponer(se)

opposing [əpózɪŋ] ADJ opuesto, contrario; —
thumb pulgar oponible *m*

opposite [ápəzɪt] ADJ (contrary) opuesto,
contrario; — **to** frente a; PREP frente a, en
frente de; N contrario *m*, opuesto *m*; ADV
en frente

opposition [ɑpəzíʃən] N oposición *f*; **they
met with little** — encontraron poca
resistencia

oppress [əprés] VT oprimir

oppression [əpréʃən] N opresión *f*

oppressive [əprésɪv] ADJ (harsh) opresivo;
(heat) bochornoso, sofocante

oppressor [əprésɚ] N opresor -ra *mf*

optic [áptɪk] ADJ óptico; N —**s** óptica *f*

optical [áptɪkəɫ] ADJ óptico; — **fiber** fibra
óptica *f*; — **illusion** ilusión óptica *f*

optician [aptíʃən] N óptico -ca *mf*

optimism [áptəmɪzəm] N optimismo *m*

optimist [áptəmɪst] N optimista *mf*

optimistic [aptəmístɪk] ADJ optimista

option [ápʃən] N opción *f* (also financial); (feature) extra *m*; **to leave one's —s open** no descartar posibilidades

optional [ápʃənəɫ] ADJ opcional, optativo

optometry [aptámɪtri] N optometría *f*

opulence [ápjələns] N opulencia *f*

opulent [ápjələnt] ADJ opulento

or [ɔr] CONJ o; **seven — eight** siete u ocho

oracle [ɔ́rəkəɫ] N oráculo *m*

oral [ɔ́rəɫ] ADJ oral; (hygiene) bucal

orange [ɔ́rɪndʒ] N naranja *f*; **— blossom** azahar *m*; **— grove** naranjal *m*; **— tree** naranjo *m*; ADJ anaranjado

orangutan [ərǽŋətæn] N orangután *m*

orator [ɔ́rəɾɚ] N orador -ra *mf*

oratory [ɔ́rətɔri] N (skill in speaking) oratoria *f*; (place for prayer) oratorio *m*

orbit [ɔ́rbɪt] N órbita *f*; VI/VT orbitar

orbital [ɔ́rbɪɾəɫ] ADJ orbital

orbiter [ɔ́rbɪɾɚ] N orbitador *m*

orchard [ɔ́rtʃɚd] N huerto *m*; (large) huerta *f*

orchestra [ɔ́rkɪstrə] N orquesta *f*

orchestrate [ɔ́rkɪstret] VT orquestar

orchid [ɔ́rkɪd] N orquídea *f*

ordain [ɔrdén] VT (as minister) ordenar; (with an edict) decretar

ordeal [ɔrdíɫ] N suplicio *m*, tortura *f*; **— by fire** ordalía de fuego *f*

order [ɔ́rɾɚ] N (command) orden *f*, mandato *m*; (request, commission) pedido *m*; (obedience to law, sequence, regime) orden *m*; **holy —s** órdenes sagradas *f pl*; **an apology is in —** corresponde una disculpa; **in — to** para; **in working —** en buen estado; **in — that** para que, a fin de que; **to the — of** a la orden de; **out of —** no funciona; **to put in —** ordenar; VI/VT (command, arrange) ordenar, mandar; (ask for) pedir

orderly [ɔ́rɾɚli] ADJ ordenado; N (military) ordenanza *m*; (hospital) camillero *m*

ordinal [ɔ́rdɪnəɫ] ADJ ordinal

ordinance [ɔ́rdnəns] N ordenanza *f*

ordinary [ɔ́rdnɛri] ADJ común, corriente, ordinario; **do it the — way** hazlo de la forma habitual

ore [ɔr] N mineral *m*

oregano [ərégəno] N orégano *m*

organ [ɔ́rgən] N órgano *m* (also musical instrument)

organic [ɔrgǽnɪk] ADJ orgánico; **— chemistry** química orgánica *f*

organism [ɔ́rgənɪzəm] N organismo *m*

organist [ɔ́rgənɪst] N organista *mf*

organization [ɔrgənɪzéʃən] N organización *f*

organize [ɔ́rgənaɪz] VI/VT organizar(se)

organizer [ɔ́rgənaɪzɚ] N organizador -ra *mf*

orgasm [ɔ́rgæzəm] N orgasmo *m*

orgy [ɔ́rdʒi] N orgía *f*

orient [ɔ́riənt] N oriente *m*; [ɔ́riɛnt] VT orientar

oriental [ɔriɛ́ntɫ] ADJ & N oriental *mf*

orientate [ɔ́riɛntet] VT orientar

orientation [ɔriɛntéʃən] N (guidance) orientación *f*; (tendency, leaning) tendencia *f*

orifice [ɔ́rəfɪs] N orificio *m*

origin [ɔ́rədʒɪn] N origen *m*; (of a river) naciente *f*, nacimiento *m*

original [ərídʒənəɫ] ADJ & N original *m*

originality [ərɪdʒənǽlɪɾi] N originalidad *f*

originate [ərídʒənet] VI/VT originar(se)

oriole [ɔ́rioɫ] N oropéndola *f*

Orlonᵗᵐ [ɔ́rlɑn] N orlón *m*

ornament [ɔ́rnəmənt] N adorno *m*, ornamento *m*; [ɔ́rnəmɛnt] VT adornar, ornamentar

ornamental [ɔrnəmɛ́ntɫ] ADJ ornamental

ornate [ɔrnét] ADJ adornado en exceso; **— style** estilo rebuscado *m*

ornithology [ɔrnəθálədʒi] N ornitología *f*

orphan [ɔ́rfən] ADJ & N huérfano -na *mf*; VT dejar huérfano a

orphanage [ɔ́rfənɪdʒ] N orfanato *m*, hospicio *m*

orthodontics [ɔrθədántɪks] N ortodoncia *f*

orthodox [ɔ́rθədɑks] ADJ ortodoxo

orthography [ɔrθágrəfi] N ortografía *f*

oscillate [ásəlet] VI oscilar; VT hacer oscilar

oscillation [asəléʃən] N oscilación *f*

osmosis [azmósɪs] N ósmosis *f*

osprey [áspre] N águila pescadora *f*

ostensible [asténsəbɫ] ADJ aparente

ostentation [astɛntéʃən] N ostentación *f*

ostentatious [astɛntéʃəs] ADJ ostentoso

osteoporosis [astiopərósɪs] N osteoporosis *f*

ostracize [ástrəsaɪz] VT aislar

ostrich [ástrɪtʃ] N avestruz *m*

other [ʌ́ðɚ] ADJ, PRON & N otro -tra *mf*; **— than Bob** salvo Bob; **every — day** cada dos días, un día sí y otro no; **—wise** de otro modo; **—worldly** fantástico

otter [ʌ́ɾɚ] N nutria *f*

ouch [autʃ] INTERJ ¡ay!

ought [ɔt] V AUX **you — to sit down** deberías sentarte; **we — to get up early** deberíamos levantarnos más temprano

ounce [auns] N onza *f*

our [aur] POSS ADJ nuestro

ours [aurz] ADJ nuestro; **this book is —** este libro es nuestro; **these things are —** estas cosas son nuestras; PRON el nuestro;

— is bigger el nuestro / la nuestra es más grande; **a friend of** — un amigo nuestro

ourselves [aʊrsélvz] PRON **we made the cake** — nosotros mismos hicimos la torta; **we were sitting by** — estábamos sentados solos; **we look at** — **in the mirror** nos miramos en el espejo; **we bought** — **a house** nos compramos una casa

oust [aʊst] VT echar, expulsar

out [aʊt] ADV (outside) fuera; ADJ (turned off, extinguished) apagado; INTERJ ¡fuera! N escape *m*; VT (expel) expulsar; (expose) descubrir; VI **the truth will** — se descubrirá la verdad; PREP **she ran** — **the door** salió corriendo por la puerta; **they locked me** — me dejaron fuera; — **and** — **criminal** criminal empedernido *f*; — **and** — **refusal** una negativa rotunda; — **of commission / order** fuera de servicio; —**-of-date** pasado de moda, anticuado; — **of fashion** pasado de moda; — **of fear** por miedo; — **of joint** dislocado; — **of money** sin dinero; — **of print / stock** agotado; — **of touch with** desconectado de; — **of tune** desentonado; — **of work** desempleado; **made** — **of** hecho de; **miniskirts are on the way** — las minifaldas se están dejando de usar; **I had it** — **with him** me peleé con él; **you were** — no estabas; **before the week is** — antes de que termine la semana; **the book is just** — acaba de publicarse el libro; **the secret is** — se ha divulgado el secreto; **we had some, but now we're** — teníamos, pero se nos acabó; **I'm** — **$10** perdí $10

outage [áʊdɪʤ] N apagón *m*

outbreak [áʊtbrek] N (of pimples) erupción *f*; (of war) comienzo *m*; (of disease) brote *m*

outburst [áʊtbɝst] N (emotional) arrebato *m*; (of tears) ataque *m*; (of violence) motín *m*, explosión *f*

outcast [áʊtkæst] ADJ & N marginado -da *mf*

outcome [áʊtkʌm] N resultado *m*

outcry [áʊtkraɪ] N clamor *m*, protesta *f*

outdated [aʊtdédɪd] ADJ anticuado

outdoor [áʊtdɔr] ADJ al aire libre; [aʊtdɔ́rz] ADV —**s** al aire libre, afuera

outer [áʊdɚ] ADJ exterior; — **ear** oído externo *m*; — **space** espacio exterior *m*

outfit [áʊtfɪt] N (gear) equipo *m*; (clothes) conjunto *m*; (soldiers) unidad *f*; VI/VT equipar, habilitar

outfox [aʊtfáks] VT ser más listo que

outgoing [áʊtgoɪŋ] ADJ (leaving) saliente; [aʊtgóɪŋ] (extrovert) extrovertido

outgrow [aʊtgró] VT **she will** — **her clothes** le quedará la ropa pequeña; **she will** — **her epilepsy** la epilepsia se le irá con la edad

outing [áʊdɪŋ] N excursión *f*, paseo *m*

outlandish [aʊtlǽndɪʃ] ADJ estrafalario

outlast [aʊtlǽst] VT (last longer than) durar más que; (live longer than) sobrevivir a

outlaw [áʊtlɔ] N bandido -da *mf*, forajido -da *mf*; VT prohibir

outlay [áʊtle] N gasto *m*, desembolso *m*; [aʊtlé] VT gastar, desembolsar

outlet [áʊtlɪt] N (exit) salida *f*; (stream) desagüe *m*, emisario *m*; (store) tienda *f*; (electric connection) toma de corriente *f*; **she needs an** — **for her talent** necesita canalizar su talento

outline [áʊtlaɪn] N (abstract) bosquejo *m*, esbozo *m*, trazado *m*; (boundary) contorno *m*; VT (summarize) bosquejar, esbozar; (draw) delinear; (plan) trazar

outlook [áʊtlʊk] N perspectiva *f*, panorama *m*

outlying [áʊtlaɪɪŋ] ADJ (marginal) periférico; (distant) remoto

output [áʊtpʊt] N (production) rendimiento *m*; (computer information) salida *f*

outrage [áʊtreʤ] N (offense) ultraje *m*, agravio *m*, atropello *m*; (indignation) indignación *f*; VT (offend) ultrajar, agraviar; (enrage) indignar

outrageous [aʊtréʤəs] ADJ (offensive) ultrajante; (exorbitant) exorbitante; (extravagant) extravagante

outreach [áʊtritʃ] N extensión *f*; [aʊtrítʃ] VT exceder

outright [aʊtráɪt] ADV completamente; **he bought it** — lo compró al contado; **he rejected it** — lo rechazó categóricamente; [áʊtraɪt] ADJ — **denial** negativa rotunda *f*; — **lie** mentira descarada *f*

outset [áʊtset] N comienzo *m*, principio *m*

outshine [aʊtʃáɪn] VT eclipsar

outside [aʊtsáɪd] ADV fuera, afuera; PREP fuera de; [áʊtsaɪd] ADJ (external) exterior; (foreign) foráneo; N exterior *m*; — **chance** posibilidad remota *f*; **in a week, at the** — en una semana, a lo sumo; **to close on the** — cerrar por fuera

outsider [aʊtsáɪdɚ] N forastero -ra *mf*

outskirts [áʊtskɝts] N alrededores *m pl*, afueras *f pl*

outspoken [aʊtspókən] ADJ franco

outstanding [aʊtstǽndɪŋ] ADJ (excellent) sobresaliente, destacado; (pending) pendiente

outstretched [aʊtstrɛ́tʃt] ADJ extendido

outward [áʊtwəɾd] ADJ exterior, externo; — **appearances** apariencias *f pl;* ADV hacia fuera; — **bound** que sale

outweigh [aʊtwé] VT (weigh more) pesar más que; (be more important) sobreponerse a, valer más que

outwit [aʊtwít] VT ser más listo que

oval [óvəł] ADJ oval, ovalado; N óvalo *m*

ovary [óvəri] N ovario *m*

ovation [ovéʃən] N ovación *f*

oven [ʌ́vən] N horno *m*

over [óvəɾ] PREP — **here** acá; — **in Japan** allá en Japón; — **many years** durante muchos años; — **the sea** al otro lado del mar; — **the hill** viejo; — **there** allá; **an umbrella** — **his head** un paraguas sobre la cabeza; **I heard it** — **the radio** lo oí por la radio; **he jumped** — **the fence** saltó por encima de la cerca; **he is** — **her in the hierarchy** él está por encima de ella en la jerarquía; **not** — **one year** no más de un año; **he hit him** — **the head with a rock** le golpeó en la cabeza con una piedra; **all** — **the city** por toda la ciudad; ADV — **again** de nuevo, otra vez; — **against** en contraste con; — **and** — una y otra vez; —**generous** demasiado generoso; **do it** — hazlo de nuevo, hazlo otra vez; **the world** — por todo el mundo; **it is** — **with** se acabó; INTERJ — **and out** cambio y fuera

overactive [ovəɾǽktɪv] ADJ hiperactivo, demasiado activo

overall [ovəɾɔ́ł] ADJ global, total; —**s** mono *m,* overol *m*

overbearing [ovəɾbérɪŋ] ADJ mandón -ona, dominante

overboard [óvəɾbɔrd] ADV (into the water) al agua; **she went** — **on her project** se le fue la mano con su proyecto

overcast [óvəɾkæst] ADJ nublado, encapotado; **to become** — nublarse, encapotarse

overcharge [ovəɾtʃárʤ] VI/VT cobrar demasiado

overcoat [óvəɾkot] N sobretodo *m,* gabán *m*

overcome [ovəɾkʌ́m] VI/VT (to get the better of) superar; (to overwhelm) embargar; **to be** — **by weariness** estar agobiado

overdose [óvəɾdos] N sobredosis *f;* VI tomar una sobredosis

overdraft [óvəɾdræft] N sobregiro *m,* descubierto *m*

overdraw [ovəɾdrɔ́] VI/VT sobregirar(se)

overdrawn [ovəɾdrón] ADJ en descubierto, sobregirado

overdrive [óvəɾdraɪv] N superdirecta *f*

overdue [ovəɾdú] ADJ (borrowed item) atrasado; (bill) vencido

overeat [ovəɾít] VI comer en exceso

overexcite [ovəɾɪksáɪt] VT sobreexcitar

overflow [ovəɾfló] VI desbordarse, rebosar; [óvəɾflo] N desborde *m*

overgrown [ovəɾgrón] ADJ cubierto, crecido; — **boy** muchacho demasiado crecido para su edad *m*

overhang [ovəɾhǽŋ] VI (jut) proyectarse; (hang over) estar suspendido; [óvəɾhæŋ] N saliente *m*

overhaul [ovəɾhɔ́ł] VT revisar; [óvəɾhɔł] N revisión *f*

overhead [óvəɾhɛd] N gastos generales *mf;* ADJ elevado; — **projector** retroproyector *m;* [ovəɾhéd] ADV en lo alto

overhear [ovəɾhír] VT oír por casualidad

overkill [óvəɾkɪł] N exageración *f*

overland [óvəɾlænd] ADV & ADJ por tierra

overlap [ovəɾlǽp] VI/VT solapar(se), superponer(se); [óvəɾlæp] N traslapo *m*

overlay [ovəɾlé] VT cubrir; (with gold, etc.) incrustar; [óvəɾle] N cubierta *f;* (with metal, wood) revestimiento *m,* chapa *f*

overload [ovəɾlód] VT sobrecargar, recargar, saturar; [óvəɾlod] N sobrecarga *f*

overlook [ovəɾlúk] VT (fail to mention) pasar por alto, omitir; (pardon) perdonar; (look from above) mirar desde arriba; (afford a view of) dar a, tener vista a; [óvəɾluk] N mirador *m*

overly [óvəɾli] ADV excesivamente

overnight [óvəɾnaɪt] ADJ — **delivery** entrega al otro día *f;* — **guest** invitado -da a dormir *mf;* [ovəɾnáɪt] ADV **he succeeded** — tuvo éxito de la noche a la mañana

overpass [óvəɾpæs] N paso elevado *m*

overpower [ovəɾpáʊəɾ] VT vencer

overqualified [ovəɾkwáləfaɪd] ADJ sobrecalificado

overreach [ovəɾrítʃ] VI **to** — **oneself** abarcar demasiado

overreact [ovəɾriǽkt] VI reaccionar exageradamente

override [ovəɾráɪd] VT anular

overrule [ovəɾrúł] VT anular

overrun [ovəɾrʌ́n] VT (overflow) desbordarse; (exceed) exceder; (invade) infestar; [óvəɾrʌn] N exceso *m*

overseas [ovəɾsíz] ADV (beyond the sea) en ultramar; (abroad) en el extranjero

oversee [ovəɾsí] VI dirigir, supervisar

overseer [óvəɾsir] N capataz -za *mf,* supervisor -ra *mf*

overshadow [ovəɾʃǽdo] VT eclipsar, opacar

overshoe [óvəʃu] N chanclo *m*
oversight [óvəsaɪt] N (mistake) descuido *m*; (act of overseeing) supervisión *f*
overstep [ovəstép] VT excederse en
overt [ovɝ́t] ADJ evidente
overtake [ovəték] VT (pass someone) pasar, rebasar; (befall) abatirse sobre
overtax [ovətǽks] VT (tax too much) gravar excesivamente; (demand too much) exigir demasiado
overthrow [ovəθró] VT derrocar, derribar; [óvəθro] N derrocamiento *m*
overtime [óvətaɪm] N (at work) horas extras *f pl*; (in a game) prórroga *f*; **to work —** hacer horas extras
overture [óvətʃɝ] N (musical composition) obertura *f*; (initial move) propuesta *f*
overturn [ovətɝ́n] VI/VT volcar(se); VT (a decision) anular; (a government) derrocar
overview [óvəvju] N vista global *f*, panorama *m*
overweight [ovəwét] ADJ **he's —** pesa demasiado; [óvəwet] N sobrepeso *m*
overwhelm [ovəhwéɫm] VT abrumar, agobiar
overwhelming [ovəhwéɫmɪŋ] ADJ (responsibility, task) abrumador, agobiante; (victory) arrollador
overwork [ovəwɝ́k] VI trabajar demasiado; VT hacer trabajar demasiado; [óvəwɝ́k] N exceso de trabajo *m*
ovulate [ávjəlet] VI ovular
owe [o] VI/VT deber; (a sum) adeudar, deber
owing [óɪŋ] ADJ debido; **— to** debido a
owl [auɫ] N lechuza *f*, búho *m*
own [on] ADJ & PRON propio; **a house of his —** una casa suya; **to be on one's —** ser independiente; **to come into one's —** conseguir lo que uno se merece; **to hold one's —** mantenerse firme; VT poseer; **to — up (to)** confesar
owner [ónə] N dueño -ña *mf*, propietario -ria *mf*
ownership [ónəʃɪp] N propiedad *f*
ox [aks] N buey *m*
oxidize [áksɪdaɪz] VI/VT oxidar(se)
oxygen [áksɪdʒən] N oxígeno *m*; **— tent** cámara de oxígeno *f*
oyster [ɔ́ɪstə] N ostra *f*; (large) ostión *m*
ozone [ózon] N ozono *m*; **— layer** capa de ozono *f*

Pp

pace [pes] N paso *m*; VT (traverse) ir y venir por; (set the pace) marcar al paso; (measure) medir a pasos; **—maker** marcapasos *m sg*
pacific [pəsífɪk] ADJ pacífico; **— Ocean** Océano Pacífico *m*
pacifier [pǽsəfaɪə] N chupete *m*
pacifism [pǽsəfɪzəm] N pacifismo *m*
pacify [pǽsəfaɪ] VT (a country) pacificar; (a person) apaciguar
pack [pæk] N (of wolves) manada *f*; (of dogs) jauría *f*; (of cigarettes) cajilla *f*, cajetilla *f*; (of cloth) compresa *f*; (of cards) baraja *f*; (of cyclists) pelotón *m*; **— animal** acémila *f*, bestia de carga *f*; **a — of lies** una sarta de mentiras; VT empacar, empaquetar; (carry a gun) portar; (crowd) atestar; (load) cargar; **to — off** despachar; **to — one's bags** hacer las maletas; **— rat** rata urraca *f*; (person who saves everything) urraca *f*
package [pǽkɪdʒ] N paquete *m* (also organized vacation); VT (gift) empaquetar; (food) envasar; (in advertising) presentar
packer [pǽkə] N empacador -ra *mf*, embalador -ra *mf*
packet [pǽkɪt] N paquete *m*; (of soup) sobre *m*
packing [pǽkɪŋ] N embalaje *m* (also cushioning material)
pact [pækt] N pacto *m*
pad [pæd] N (cushion) almohadilla *f* (also for ink); (block of paper) bloc *m*; (for aircraft) pista *f*; (for spacecraft) plataforma de lanzamiento *f*; VT (stuff with padding) acolchar; (add to dishonestly) rellenar
padding [pǽdɪŋ] N relleno *m*; (cotton) guata *f*; (of a speech) ripio *m*
paddle [pǽdl] N (for rowing) pala *f*, remo *m*; (for mixing, beating, ping-pong) paleta *f*; **— wheel** rueda de paleta *f*; VI remar; VT hacer avanzar remando; (hit) dar una paletada
paddock [pǽdək] N (field) prado *m*; (enclosure at racetrack) paddock *m*
padlock [pǽdlak] N candado *m*; VT cerrar con candado
pagan [pégən] ADJ & N pagano -na *mf*
paganism [pégənɪzəm] N paganismo *m*
page [pedʒ] N (sheet) hoja *f*, página *f*; (boy servant) paje *m*; (hotel employee) botones *m sg*; VT (number pages) paginar; (call)

llamar por altavoz; *Mex* vocear; **to —
through** hojear

pageant [pǽʤənt] N (parade) desfile *m*;
(show) espectáculo *m*

pail [peł] N balde *m*, cubeta *f*

pain [pen] N dolor *m*; (suffering) sufrimiento
m; **—killer** analgésico *m*; **—staking**
esmerado; **on — of** so pena de; **to take
—s** esmerarse; **he's a —** es un chinche; VT
(physical) doler; (mental) apenar

painful [pénfəł] ADJ (hurting) doloroso;
(distressing) penoso; (difficult) arduo

painless [pénlɪs] ADJ sin dolor, indoloro

paint [pent] N (substance) pintura *f*; (spotted
horse) pinto *m*; **—brush** (for art) pincel
m; (for a house) brocha *f*; VI/VT pintar; **to
— the town red** irse de juerga

painter [péntɚ] N pintor -ra *mf*

painting [péntɪŋ] N pintura *f*

pair [pɛr] N par *m*; (married couple) pareja *f*;
(span) yunta *f*; **a — of scissors** unas
tijeras, una tijera; VI/VT aparear(se),
emparejar(se); **to — off** aparearse

pajamas [pəʤáməz] N pijama / piyama *mf*

Pakistan [pǽkɪstæn] N Paquistán *m*

Pakistani [pækɪstǽni] ADJ & N paquistano
-na *mf*

pal [pæł] N compañero -ra *mf*, compadre *m*,
comadre *f*

palace [pǽlɪs] N palacio *m*

palate [pǽlɪt] N paladar *m*

palatial [pəléʃəł] ADJ suntuoso

Palau [pɑláu] N Paláu *m*

pale [peł] ADJ pálido, macilento; **beyond the
—** grosero; VI palidecer

paleness [péłnɪs] N palidez *f*

paleontology [peliəntáləʤi] N paleontología
f

palette [pǽlɪt] N paleta *f*

palisade [pælɪséd] N empalizada *f*; **—s**
acantilados *m pl*

pall [pɔł] VT (cover with a cloth) cubrir con
un paño mortuorio; (satiate) hartar; VI
cansar; N paño mortuorio *m*; **—bearer**
portador del féretro *m*; **to cast a — on**
empañar

pallid [pǽlɪd] ADJ pálido

pallor [pǽlɚ] N palidez *f*

palm [pɑm] N (part of hand) palma *f*; (tree)
palmera *f*, palma *f*; **— Sunday** Domingo
de Ramos *m*; VT (hide in palm)
escamotear; **to — something off on
someone** encajar algo a alguien

palpable [pǽłpəbəł] ADJ (perceptible)
palpable; (tangible) tangible

palpitate [pǽłpɪtet] VI palpitar

palpitation [pæłpɪtéʃən] N palpitación *f*

paltry [pɔ́łtri] ADJ miserable, despreciable

pamper [pǽmpɚ] VT mimar, consentir

pamphlet [pǽmflɪt] N (informative) folleto
m; (political) panfleto *m*

pan [pæn] N (for boiling) cazuela *f*, cacerola *f*,
cazo *m*; (for frying) sartén *f*; (for baking)
molde *m*; **—handle** mango de sartén *m*;
—handler pordiosero -ra *mf*; VT criticar
duramente; VI **to — for gold** extraer oro;
to — out dar buen resultado; **to
—handle** mendigar, pordiosear

panacea [pænəsíə] N panacea *f*

Panama [pǽnəmɑ] N Panamá *f*

Panamanian [pænəméniən] ADJ & N
panameño -ña *mf*

Pan-American [pænəmérɪkən] ADJ
panamericano

pancake [pǽnkek] N panqueque *m*; **flat as a
—** chato como una tabla

pancreas [pǽnkriəs] N páncreas *m*

panda [pǽndə] N panda *m*

pander [pǽndɚ] N proxeneta *mf*; VI consentir

pane [pen] N vidrio *m*, cristal *m*

panel [pǽnəł] N (wall, group of persons)
panel *m*; (of instruments) tablero *m*; VT
revestir con paneles

pang [pæŋ] N (sharp pain, hunger) punzada
f; (anguish) remordimientos *m pl*

panic [pǽnɪk] ADJ & N pánico *m*;
—-stricken sobrecogido de pánico

panorama [pænərǽmə] N panorama *m*

panoramic [pænərǽmɪk] ADJ panorámico

pansy [pǽnzi] N (flower) pensamiento *m*;
(sissy) *offensive* marica *m*

pant [pænt] VI jadear; **to — out** decir
jadeando

panther [pǽnθɚ] N pantera *f*

panties [pǽntiz] N *Sp* bragas *f pl*; *Mex*
pantaletas *f pl*; *RP* bombacha *f*

pantomime [pǽntəmaɪm] N pantomima *f*

pantry [pǽntri] N despensa *f*, alacena *f*

pants [pænts] N pantalones *m pl*, pantalón *m*

pantyhose [pǽntihoz] N panty *m*

papa [pápə] N papá *m*

papacy [pépəsi] N papado *m*

papaya [pəpáɪə] N papaya *f*; *Cuba* fruta
bomba *f*

paper [pépɚ] N (material) papel *m*;
(newspaper) periódico *m*; (assignment)
trabajo *m*; (oral learned contribution)
comunicación *f*; (written learned
contribution) artículo *m*; **—back** libro en
rústica *m*; **— clip** clip *m*, sujetapapeles *m
sg*; **— cutter** guillotina *f*; **— money** papel
moneda *m*; **—s** papeles *m pl*; **— shredder**
trituradora *f*; **—weight** pisapapeles *m sg*;
—work trámites *m pl*; **on —** por escrito;

VI/VT empapelar

paprika [pæpríka] N pimentón *m*, páprika *f*

Papua New Guinea [pǽpjuǝnugíni] N Papúa Nueva Guinea *f*

Papua New Guinean [pǽpjuǝnugíniǝn] ADJ & N papú *mf*

par [par] N (financial) paridad *f*; (in golf) par *m*; **at** — a la par; **below** —, bajo par; **to be on a** — **with** estar en pie de igualdad con; **to feel above** — sentirse mejor que lo normal; VT hacer el par

parachute [pǽrǝʃut] N paracaídas *m sg*

parachutist [pǽrǝʃutɪst] N paracaidista *mf*

parade [pǝréd] N (procession) desfile *m*; (military review) parada *f*; — **ground** campo de maniobras *m*; **to make a** — **of** ostentar, hacer ostentación de; VI desfilar; VT hacer ostentación de

paradigm [pǽrǝdaɪm] N paradigma *m*

paradise [pǽrǝdaɪs] N paraíso *m*

paradox [pǽrǝdaks] N paradoja *f*

paradoxical [pærǝdáksɪkǝł] ADJ paradójico

paraffin [pǽrǝfɪn] N parafina *f*

paragraph [pǽrǝgræf] N párrafo *m*; VT dividir en párrafos

Paraguay [pǽrǝgwaɪ] N Paraguay *m*

Paraguayan [pærǝgwáɪǝn] ADJ & N paraguayo -ya *mf*

parakeet [pǽrǝkit] N perico *m*, periquito *m*

parallel [pǽrǝlɛł] ADJ & N paralelo *m*; (geometry) paralela *f*; VT (run equidistant from) correr paralelo a; (compare) comparar

paralysis [pǝrǽlǝsɪs] N (of the body) parálisis *f*; (of a transportation system) paralización *f*

paralyze [pǽrǝlaɪz] VT paralizar

paramedic [pærǝmédɪk] ADJ & N paramédico -ca *mf*

parameter [pǝrǽmɪDɚ] N parámetro *m*

paramilitary [pærǝmílɪteri] ADJ & N paramilitar *mf*

paramount [pǽrǝmaʊnt] ADJ supremo, sumo

paranoia [pærǝnɔ́ɪǝ] N paranoia *f*

paranoid [pǽrǝnɔɪd] ADJ & N paranoico -ca *mf*; — **delusion** delirio paranoico *m*

paranormal [pærǝnɔ́rmǝł] ADJ paranormal

paraphernalia [pærǝfǝnéljǝ] N parafernalia *f*

paraphrase [pǽrǝfrez] N paráfrasis *f*; VI/VT parafrasear

parapsychology [pærǝsaɪkálǝʤi] N parapsicología *f*

parasite [pǽrǝsaɪt] N parásito *m*

parasol [pǽrǝsɔł] N parasol *m*, sombrilla *f*

paratroops [pǽrǝtrups] N tropas paracaidistas *f pl*

parcel [pársǝł] N (package) paquete *m*; (lot)

partida *f*; (land) parcela *f*; — **post** paquete postal *m*; VT (land) parcelar; **to** — **out** repartir

parch [parʧ] VT secar; **I'm —ed** estoy muerto de sed

parchment [párʧmǝnt] N pergamino *m*

pardon [párdn̩] N perdón *m*, gracia *f*; (legal) indulto *m*; **I beg your** — perdone; VT perdonar, disculpar; (legally) indultar

pare [pɛr] VT mondar, pelar; **to** — **down expenditures** reducir gastos

parent [pérǝnt] N padre *m*, madre *f*; —**s** padres *m pl*

parental [pǝréntl̩] ADJ parental

parenthesis [pǝrénθǝsɪs] N paréntesis *m*

pariah [pǝráɪǝ] N paria *mf*

parish [pǽrɪʃ] N parroquia *f*; — **priest** (cura) párroco *m*

parishioner [pǝríʃǝnɚ] N feligrés -esa *mf*, parroquiano -na *mf*

parity [pǽrɪDi] N paridad *f*

park [park] N parque *m*; (for baseball) estadio de béisbol *m*; VI/VT estacionar, aparcar

parking [párkɪŋ] N estacionamiento *m*, aparcamiento *m*; — **lot** estacionamiento *m*, aparcamiento *m*; — **place** lugar de estacionamiento / aparcamiento *m*

parlance [párlǝns] N habla *f*

parley [párli] N (peace negotiation) parlamento *m*; (discussion) discusión *f*; VI parlamentar

parliament [párlǝmǝnt] N parlamento *m*

parliamentary [parlǝméntri] ADJ parlamentario

parlor [párlɚ] N sala *f*, salón *m*; — **game** juego de salón *m*; **beauty** — salón de belleza *m*

parochial [pǝrókiǝł] ADJ (of a parish) parroquial; (provincial) pueblerino

parody [pǽrǝDi] N parodia *f*; VT parodiar

parole [pǝról] N libertad condicional *f*; VT poner en libertad condicional

parrot [pǽrǝt] N loro *m*, papagayo *m*; VT repetir como loro

parry [pǽri] VT (a blow) parar; (a remark) eludir; N parada *f*

parsley [pársli] N perejil *m*

parsnip [pársnɪp] N chirivía *f*

parson [pársǝn] N pastor *m*

part [part] N (component) parte *f*; (role) papel *m*; (in hair) raya *f*; — **and parcel** parte esencial *f*; —-**time** a tiempo parcial; **in foreign —s** en el extranjero; **spare —s** piezas de repuesto *f pl*, repuestos *m pl*; VI/VT (cut into parts) partir(se); (divide into parts) dividir(se); (separate, leave) separar(se); (apportion) repartir(se); **to** —

company separarse; **to — one's hair** hacerse la raya; **to — with** desprenderse de

partake [pɑrték] vi **to — in** participar; **to — of** (share) compartir; (eat) comer

partial [pɑ́rʃəł] ADJ parcial

participant [pɑrtísəpənt] ADJ & N participante *mf*, partícipe *mf*

participate [pɑrtísəpet] vi participar

participation [pɑrtɪsəpéʃən] N participación *f*

participle [pɑ́rDɪsɪpəł] N participio *m*

particle [pɑ́rDɪkəł] N partícula *f*; **— board** aglomerado *m*

particular [pə-tíkjəlɚ] ADJ particular; (fussy) quisquilloso; N **—s** particulares *m pl*; **in —** en particular

parting [pɑ́rDɪŋ] N (farewell) despedida *f*; (separation) separación *f*; **— of the ways** encrucijada *f*

partisan [pɑ́rDɪzən] N (supporter) partidario -ria *mf*; (guerrilla) partisano -na *mf*; ADJ (of supporters) partidario; (of guerrillas) de partisanos

partition [pɑrtíʃən] N (distribution) reparto *m*; (division) división *f*; (wall) tabique *m*, mampara *f*; vt (distribute) repartir; (divide) dividir; (divide with a wall) tabicar

partly [pɑ́rtli] ADV en parte

partner [pɑ́rtnɚ] N (in business) socio -cia *mf*; (in an activity) compañero -ra *mf*; (in dancing, sports, marriage) pareja *f*

partnership [pɑ́rtnɚʃɪp] N (business) sociedad *f*; (relationship) asociación *f*

partridge [pɑ́rtrɪʤ] N perdiz *f*

party [pɑ́rDi] N (get-together) fiesta *f*; (political group) partido *m*; (group of people) partida *f*; (litigant) parte *f*; **— of four** mesa para cuatro *f*; **— animal** fiestero -ra *mf*, parrandero -ra *mf*

pass [pæs] vi/vt pasar; (a law) aprobar; (an exam, test) aprobar, superar; **to — away** fallecer; **to — for** pasar por; **to — in review** pasar revista; **to — judgment** juzgar; **to — on** (die) fallecer; (approve) aceptar; (refuse) no querer; **to — oneself off as** hacerse pasar por; **to — out** desmayarse; **to — over** no tener en cuenta; **to — up an opportunity** perderse una oportunidad; **he —ed a kidney stone** expulsó un cálculo renal; **— me the salt** pásame la sal, alcánzame la sal; N (road through mountains) paso *m*; (motion, permission) pase *m*; (for transportation) abono *m*; (over a surface) pasada *f*; (on an exam) aprobación *f*;

(difficult event) trance *m*; **—key** llave maestra *f*; **—port** pasaporte *m*; **—word** contraseña *f*, clave de seguridad *f*; **he made a — at her** trató de ligar con ella

passable [pǽsəbəł] ADJ (penetrable) transitable; (mediocre) pasable

passage [pǽsɪʤ] N (fare, musical or textual phrase, alley) pasaje *m*; (passing of time) paso *m*, transcurso *m*; (hallway in a house) pasillo *m*; (secret pathway) pasadizo *m*; (crossing) travesía *f*; (approval of a bill) aprobación *f*; **—way** (corridor) corredor *m*, pasillo *m*; (alley) pasaje *m*

passenger [pǽsənʤɚ] N pasajero -ra *mf*

passerby [pǽsə-baɪ] N transeúnte *mf*, viandante *mf*

passing [pǽsɪŋ] ADJ **each — day** cada día que pasa; **a — grade** una nota de aprobado; **a — fancy** un capricho pasajero; **a — mention** una mención al pasar

passion [pǽʃən] N pasión *f*

passionate [pǽʃənɪt] ADJ apasionado

passive [pǽsɪv] ADJ pasivo; N pasiva *f*

past [pæst] ADJ pasado; **— participle** participio pasado *m*; **— perfect** pluscuamperfecto *m*; **— precedents** precedentes anteriores *m pl*; **— tense** tiempo pretérito *m*; **the — president** el expresidente; PREP **— hope** más allá de toda esperanza; **— noon** después de mediodía; **the house — the store** la casa pasando la tienda; **we went — the tower** pasamos al lado de la torre; **half — two** las dos y media; **a woman — forty** una mujer de más de cuarenta años; ADV **for some time —** desde hace algún tiempo; **they drove —** pasaron en coche; N (time) pasado *m*; (tense) pretérito *m*

pasta [pɑ́stə] N pasta *f*

paste [pest] N (soft material, purée) pasta *f*; (glue) engrudo *m*; **—board** cartón *m*; vt pegar

pastel [pæstéł] ADJ & N pastel *m*

pasteurize [pǽstʃəraɪz] vt pasterizar / pasteurizar

pastime [pǽstaɪm] N pasatiempo *m*

pastor [pǽstɚ] N pastor -ra *mf*

pastoral [pǽstə-əł] ADJ (literary) pastoril; (ecclesiastical) pastoral; N pastoral *f*; (literary work) égloga *f*

pastry [péstri] N (in general) pastelería *f*; (specific) pastel *m*; **— cook** pastelero -ra *mf*, repostero -ra *mf*; **— shop** pastelería *f*, repostería *f*

pasture [pǽstʃɚ] N (grassland) prado *m*;

(grass) pasto *m*; (for horses) potrero *m*; VI/VT pastar, pacer, apacentar

pasty [pésti] ADJ pastoso

pat [pæt] ADJ banal; **(down)** — al dedillo; **to stand** — mantenerse firme; VI/VT dar palmaditas (a); N palmadita *f*; — **of butter** porción de mantequilla *f*

patch [pætʃ] N (piece of cloth to repair clothes) remiendo *m*, parche *m* (also for eye); (spot or area, as of ice) tramo (con hielo) *m*; (plot) parcela *f*; VT (repair) remendar; **to — up a quarrel** hacer las paces

patent [pǽtn̩t] ADJ (evident) patente; (protected by patent) patentado; — **leather** charol *m*; N patente *f*; — **pending** patente en trámite; VT patentar

paternal [pətɝ́nəɫ] ADJ (fatherly) paternal; (of the father's lineage) paterno

paternity [pətɝ́nɪɖi] N paternidad *f*

path [pæθ] N senda *f*, sendero *m*; (of a projectile, storm) trayectoria *f*; **—way** senda *f*, sendero *m*

pathetic [pəθɛ́ɖɪk] ADJ (moving) patético; (contemptible) lamentable

pathogen [pǽθədʒən] N patógeno *m*

pathology [pæθáləʤi] N patología *f*

pathos [péθɑs] N patetismo *m*

patience [péʃəns] N paciencia *f*

patient [péʃənt] ADJ & N paciente *mf*

patriarch [pétriɑrk] N patriarca *m*

patriarchal [petriárkəɫ] ADJ patriarcal

patrimony [pǽtrəmoni] N patrimonio *m*

patriot [pétriət] N patriota *mf*

patriotic [petriáɖik] ADJ patriótico

patriotism [pétriətɪzəm] N patriotismo *m*

patrol [pətróɫ] VI/VT patrullar, rondar; N patrulla *f*, ronda *f*; — **car, — man** patrullero *m*

patron [pétrən] N (customer) cliente -ta *mf*; (benefactor) benefactor -ra *mf*, mecenas *mf*; (saint) patrono *m*

patronage [pétrənɪʤ] N (support of an artist) mecenazgo *m*; (clientele) clientela *f*; (political) clientelismo *m*; **we appreciate your —** agradecemos su preferencia

patronize [pétrənaɪz] VT (be condescending) tratar con condescendencia; (do business with) frecuentar

patter [pǽɖɚ] VI (strike lightly) golpetear; (chatter) parlotear; N (small blows) golpeteo *m*; (chatter) parloteo *m*

pattern [pǽɖɚn] N (for sewing) molde *m*; (for drawing) plantilla *f*; (of behavior) patrón *m*; VI/VT **to — something after** modelar algo a imitación de, basarse en el modelo de; **to — oneself after** seguir el ejemplo de

paucity [pɔ́sɪɖi] N escasez *f*

paunch [pɔntʃ] N panza *f*, barriga *f*

pause [pɔz] N pausa *f*; VI (while talking) hacer pausa; (while moving) detenerse

pave [pev] VT (with asphalt) pavimentar; (with bricks) enladrillar; (with flagstones) enlosar; **to — the way for** preparar el camino para

pavement [pévmənt] N calzada *f*; (of asphalt) pavimento *m*; (of bricks) enladrillado *m*; (of flagstones) enlosado *m*

pavilion [pəvíljən] N pabellón *m*

paw [pɔ] N pata *f*; (with claws) garra *f*; VT (touch with paw) tocar con la pata; (touch with claws) dar zarpazos; (grope) manosear

pawn [pɔn] N (object left in deposit) prenda *f*; (chess piece) peón *m*; (puppet) títere *m*; **—broker** prestamista *mf*; **—shop** casa de empeños *f*, monte de piedad *m*; **in —** en prenda; VT empeñar, dejar en prenda

pay [pe] VT (remit) pagar; VI (be profitable) ser provechoso, convenir; (be worthwhile) valer la pena; **to — attention** prestar atención, fijarse en; **to — back** (return) restituir; (retaliate) vengarse; **to — a compliment** hacer un cumplido; **to — homage** rendir homenaje; **to — one's respects** saludar; **to — off a debt** cancelar una deuda; **to — a visit** hacer una visita; **to — through the nose** pagar demasiado; **I will — for your meal** te pago la comida; N (payment) pago *m*; (wages) paga *f*, salario *m*; **—back** venganza *f*; **—check** cheque del sueldo *m*; **—day** día de pago *m*; **—load** carga útil *f*; **—off** (pay) pago *m*; (reward) recompensa *f*; (bribe) soborno *m*; **— phone** teléfono público *m*; **—roll** nómina *f*, planilla *f*; **to hit — dirt** encontrar una mina de oro

payable [péəbəɫ] ADJ pagadero

payee [peí] N tenedor -ra *mf*, beneficiario -ria *mf*

payment [pémənt] N pago *m*; **— in full** liquidación *f*

PC [pisí] N (personal computer) PC *m*; (political correctness) lo políticamente correcto; ADJ (politically correct) políticamente correcto

pea [pi] N guisante *m*; *Am* arveja *f*; **—nut** *Sp* cacahuete *m*; *Mex* cacahuate *m*; *Am* maní *m*; **—nut butter** *Sp* crema de cacahuete *f*; *Mex* crema de cacahuate *f*; *Am* manteca / mantequilla de maní *f*

peace [pis] N paz *f*; **— officer** oficial de policía *m*; **at —** en paz; **to keep the —**

mantener el orden público; **to hold one's** — callar

peaceful [písfəɫ] ADJ pacífico, tranquilo

peach [pitʃ] N durazno *m; Sp* melocotón *m;* (nice thing or person) delicia *f,* monada *f;* — **tree** durazno *m,* duraznero *m, Sp* melocotonero *m*

peacock [píkɑk] N pavo real *m,* pavón *m*

peak [pik] N pico *m,* cumbre *f;* (of production, of one's abilities) punto máximo *m;* — **load** carga máxima *f;* — **season** temporada alta *f;* — **time** hora punta *f*

peal [piɫ] N (of bells) repique *m;* (of laughter) carcajada *f;* VI/VT repicar

pear [pɛr] N pera *f;* — **tree** peral *m*

pearl [pɝɫ] N perla *f;* — **necklace** collar de perlas *m*

pearly [pɝli] ADJ (color) nacarado, perlado; (with pearls) perlado; **the** — **Gates** las puertas del cielo

peasant [pézənt] ADJ & N campesino -na *mf*

peat [pit] N turba *f*

pebble [pébəɫ] N guijarro *m,* piedrecilla *f;* (smooth) canto *m*

pecan [pɪkán] N pacana *f*

peccary [pékəri] N pecarí / pécari *m*

peck [pɛk] VI/VT (strike with beak) picar; (eat bit by bit) picotear; (kiss) dar un besito; **to** — **a hole** agujerear a picotazos; N (quick stroke) picotazo *m;* (kiss) besito *m;* (measure) medida de áridos (9 litros) *f;* **you're in a** — **of trouble** estás metido en un lío

pecking order [pékɪŋɔrdɚ] N jerarquía *f*

pectoral [péktɚəɫ] ADJ & N pectoral *m*

peculiar [pɪkjúljɚ] ADJ peculiar, particular

peculiarity [pɪkjuljǽrɪɖi] N peculiaridad *f*

pedagogue [pédəgɑg] N pedagogo -ga *mf*

pedagogy [pédəgɑʤi] N pedagogía *f*

pedal [pédl̩] N pedal *m;* VI/VT pedalear

pedant [pédn̩t] N pedante *mf*

pedantic [pədǽntɪk] ADJ pedante

peddle [pédɫ] VI/VT ir vendiendo de puerta en puerta; **to** — **gossip** repartir chismes

peddler [pédlɚ] N buhonero -ra *mf,* mercachifle *m*

pedestal [pédɪstəɫ] N pedestal *m*

pedestrian [pədéstriən] N peatón -ona *mf;* ADJ pedestre

pediatrician [piɖiətríʃən] N pediatra *mf*

pediatrics [piɖiǽtrɪks] N pediatría *f*

pedigree [pédəgri] N (of persons) linaje *m;* (of animals) pedigrí *m*

pee [pi] VI *fam* mear, hacer pipí; N *fam* pipí *m*

peek [pik] VI atisbar; N atisbo *m*

peel [piɫ] VI/VT (fruit, tree) pelar(se), descortezar(se); (paint) descascarar(se); **to keep one's eyes** —**ed** mantener los ojos abiertos; N cáscara *f*

peeler [pílɚ] N pelador *m*

peep [pip] VI/VT (begin to appear) asomar(se); VI (make sound of chicks) piar; **to** — **at** atisbar; N (look) atisbo *m;* (sound of chicks) pío *m;* —**hole** mirilla *f;* — **show** espectáculo de striptease *m*

peer [pir] N par *m* (also nobleman); — **group** grupo paritario *m;* VI (look attentively) escudriñar; (peep out) asomar

peerless [pírlɪs] ADJ incomparable, sin par

peeve [piv] VT irritar; **to get** —**d** ponerse de mal humor; N cosa que irrita *f*

peevish [pívɪʃ] ADJ malhumorado

peg [pɛg] N percha *f;* (on violin) clavija *f;* **to take a person down a** — bajarle los humos a alguien; VT clavar, clavetear; (price) estabilizar

pejorative [pɪʤɔrəɖɪv] ADJ peyorativo, despectivo

pelican [pélɪkən] N pelícano *m*

pellet [pélɪt] N (ball) bola *f,* bolita *f;* (shot) perdigón *m*

pell-mell [pélmɛɫ] ADJ confuso, tumultuoso; ADV a troche y moche

pelt [pɛɫt] N piel *f,* pellejo *m;* VI/VT acribillar; **to** — **with stones** apedrear

pelvis [péɫvɪs] N pelvis *f*

pen [pɛn] N (fountain) pluma *f;* (ballpoint) bolígrafo *m;* (for pigs) pocilga *f;* (for sheep) redil *m;* (for cows) corral *m;* — **holder** mango de pluma *m,* portaplumas *m sg;* — **name** seudónimo *m;* VT (write) escribir; (shut in) acorralar, encerrar

penal [pínəɫ] ADJ penal

penalize [pénəlaɪz] VT penar; (in sports) penalizar

penalty [pénəɫti] N (punishment) pena *f,* castigo *m;* (forfeiture) multa *f;* (in sports) penalidad *f;* — **kick** tiro de penalidad *f,* penalty *m*

penance [pénəns] N penitencia *f*

pencil [pénsəɫ] N (writing instrument) lápiz *m;* (beam of light) haz *m;* — **sharpener** sacapuntas *m sg*

pendant [péndənt] N colgante *m;* ADJ pendiente

pending [péndɪŋ] ADJ pendiente; PREP — **his arrival** hasta que llegue, mientras no llegue

pendulum [péndʒələm] N péndulo *m*

penetrate [pénɪtret] VT penetrar

penetrating [pénɪtreɖɪŋ] ADJ penetrante

penetration [penɪtréʃən] N penetración *f*

penguin [péŋgwɪn] N pingüino *m*

penicillin [pɛnɪsílɪn] N penicilina *f*
peninsula [pənínsələ] N península *f*
penis [pínɪs] N pene *m*
penitent [pénɪtənt] ADJ & N penitente *mf*
penitentiary [pɛnɪténʃəri] N penitenciaría *f*, penal *m*
penmanship [pénmənʃɪp] N escritura *f*, caligrafía *f*
pennant [pénənt] N banderín *m*, gallardete *m*
penniless [pénɪlɪs] ADJ pobre, sin dinero
penny [péni] N centavo *m*; —**-pincher** avaro -ra *mf*; **to cost a pretty** — costar un dineral
pension [pénʃən] N (paid to a worker) jubilación *f*; (paid to a worker's survivors) pensión *f*; — **fund** caja de jubilaciones *f*; VT jubilar, pensionar
pensioner [pénʃənɚ] N pensionista *mf*
pensive [pénsɪv] ADJ pensativo
pent [pɛnt] ADJ encerrado; —**-up** reprimido
pentagon [péntəgɑn] N pentágono *m*
penthouse [pénthaʊs] N penthouse *m*
penultimate [pɪnʌ́ɫtəmɪt] ADJ penúltimo
people [pípəɫ] N gente *f*; (national group) pueblo *m*; VT poblar
pep [pɛp] N energía *f*; VI **to — up** animar
pepper [pépɚ] N (black) pimienta *f*; (green) pimiento *m*; (plant, shaker) pimentero *m*; —**mint** menta *f*; VT pimentar; **to — with bullets** acribillar a balazos
peptic [péptɪk] ADJ — **ulcer** úlcera péptica *f*
per [pɚ] PREP (for each) por; (according to) según; — **capita** per capita; —**cent** por ciento; — **diem** viático *m*
percale [pɚkéɫ] N percal *m*
perceive [pɚsív] VT percibir
percentage [pɚséntɪdʒ] N porcentaje *m*
percentile [pɚséntaɪɫ] N percentil *m*
perceptible [pɚséptəbəɫ] ADJ perceptible
perception [pɚsépʃən] N percepción *f*
perceptive [pɚséptɪv] ADJ (pertaining to perception) perceptivo; (having keen perception) perspicaz
perch [pɚtʃ] N (rod for birds) percha *f*; (type of fish) perca *f*; VT (alight) posarse; VI/VT (set) encaramar(se)
percolate [pɚ́kəlet] VI/VT filtrar(se)
percussion [pɚkʌ́ʃən] N percusión *f*
perdition [pɚdíʃən] N perdición *f*
perennial [pərénɪəɫ] ADJ perenne; N — **plant** planta perenne *f*
perfect [pɚ́fɪkt] ADJ perfecto; **a — stranger** un completo desconocido; [pɚfékt] VT perfeccionar
perfection [pɚfékʃən] N perfección *f*
perforate [pɚ́fəret] VI/VT perforar(se); VT calar

perforation [pɚfəréʃən] N perforación *f*
perform [pɚfɔ́rm] VT (a task) ejecutar, realizar; (a rite, ceremony) celebrar; (a contract) cumplir; (a play) representar; VI (give a performance) actuar; (play music) interpretar; (function) funcionar; (do well) rendir
performance [pɚfɔ́rməns] N (of a task) ejecución *f*; (of a ceremony) celebración *f*; (of a contract) cumplimiento *m*; (of a motor) desempeño *m*, rendimiento *m*; (of a play) representación *f*; (of an actor) actuación *f*; (of music) interpretación *f*
perfume [pɚ́fjum] N perfume *m*; [pɚfjúm] VT perfumar
perfumery [pɚfjúməri] N (store) perfumería *f*; (collection) perfumes *m pl*
perhaps [pɚhǽps] ADV tal vez, quizá(s), acaso
peril [pérəɫ] N peligro *m*; VT poner en peligro
perilous [pérələs] ADJ peligroso
perimeter [pərímɪdɚ] N perímetro *m*
period [pírɪəd] N período *m*; (historical) época *f*; (punctuation) punto *m*; (menstruation) período *m*, regla *f*; **you can't go, —!** no puedes ir, y sanseacabó; **within a — of ten days** en el término de diez días
periodic [pɪriɑ́dɪk] ADJ periódico; — **table** tabla periódica *f*
periodical [pɪriɑ́dɪkəɫ] ADJ periódico; N revista *f*
peripheral [pərífɚəɫ] ADJ & N periférico *m*; — **vision** visión periférica *f*
periphery [pərífəri] N periferia *f*
periscope [périskop] N periscopio *m*
perish [pérɪʃ] VI perecer
perishable [pérɪʃəbəɫ] ADJ perecedero
peritonitis [pɛrɪtɑ́ɪdɪs] N peritonitis *f*
perjure [pɚ́dʒɚ] VI **to — oneself** perjurarse, jurar en falso
perjury [pɚ́dʒəri] N perjurio *m*
permanence [pɚ́mənəns] N permanencia *f*
permanent [pɚ́mənənt] ADJ permanente; (of a position) titular
permeable [pɚ́miəbəɫ] ADJ permeable
permeate [pɚ́miet] VI/VT permear
permissible [pɚmísəbəɫ] ADJ permisible, lícito
permission [pɚmíʃən] N permiso *m*
permissive [pɚmísɪv] ADJ permisivo
permit [pɚmít] VI/VT permitir; [pɚ́mɪt] N permiso *m*
permutation [pɚmjutéʃən] N permutación *f*
pernicious [pɚníʃəs] ADJ pernicioso
peroxide [pərɑ́ksaɪd] N peróxido *m*
perpendicular [pɚpɪndíkjələ] ADJ & N perpendicular *f*

perpetrate [pə́·pɪtret] VT perpetrar
perpetual [pə·pétʃuəł] ADJ perpetuo
perpetuate [pə·pétʃuet] VT perpetuar
perplex [pə·pléks] VT confundir, dejar perplejo; —**ed** perplejo
perplexity [pə·pléksɪɒi] N perplejidad f
persecute [pə́·sɪkjut] VT perseguir
persecution [pɜ·sɪkjúʃən] N persecución f
persecutor [pə́·sɪkjuɒə·] N perseguidor -ra mf
perseverance [pɜ·səvírəns] N perseverancia f
persevere [pɜ·səvír] VI perseverar, persistir
Persian [pə́·ʒən] ADJ & N persa mf
persist [pə·síst] VI (continue, endure) persistir; (to be insistent) insistir
persistence [pə·sístəns] N (endurance) persistencia f; (insistence) insistencia f
persistent [pə·sístənt] ADJ (lasting) persistente; (insisting) insistente, machacón
person [pə́·sən] N persona f
personable [pə́·sənəbəł] ADJ agradable
personage [pə́·sənɪdʒ] N personaje m
personal [pə́·sənəł] ADJ personal; — **computer** Sp ordenador personal m; Am computadora personal f; — **effects** efectos personales m pl; — **identification number** número de identificación personal m; — **pronoun** pronombre personal m; — **property** bienes muebles m pl; **to make a — appearance** presentarse en persona
personality [pɜ·sənǽlɪɒi] N personalidad f
personify [pə·sánəfaɪ] VT personificar
personnel [pɜ·sənéł] N personal m
perspective [pə·spéktɪv] N perspectiva f
perspicacious [pɜ·spɪkéʃəs] ADJ perspicaz
perspiration [pɜ·spəréʃən] N transpiración f
perspire [pə·spáɪr] VI transpirar
persuade [pə·swéd] VT persuadir, convencer
persuasion [pə·swéʒən] N persuasión f; (belief) convicción f
persuasive [pə·swésɪv] ADJ persuasivo, convincente
pert [pə́·t] ADJ (insolent) insolente; (lively) vivaz
pertain [pə·tén] VI atañer, corresponder
pertinent [pə́·tɲənt] ADJ pertinente
perturb [pə·tə́·b] VT perturbar
Peru [pərú] N Perú m
perusal [pərúzəł] N lectura f
peruse [pərúz] VT (read carefully) leer con cuidado; (read carelessly) hojear
Peruvian [pərúviən] ADJ & N peruano -na mf
pervade [pə·véd] VT difundirse por
perverse [pə·və́·s] ADJ perverso
perversion [pə·və́·ʒən] N perversión f
perversity [pə·və́·sɪɒi] N perversidad f

pervert [pə·və́·t] VT pervertir; (misconstrue) desvirtuar; [pə́·və·t] N pervertido -da mf
peso [péso] N peso m
pessimism [pésəmɪzəm] N pesimismo m
pessimist [pésəmɪst] N pesimista mf
pest [pest] N (insect, disease) peste f, plaga f; (person) pesado -da mf
pester [péstə·] VT molestar
pesticide [péstɪsaɪd] N pesticida m
pestilence [péstələns] N pestilencia f
pet [pet] N (animal) mascota f; (favorite) favorito -ta mf, preferido -da mf; ADJ predilecto; — **name** apodo cariñoso m; VT (caress) acariciar; (pat) dar palmaditas a
petal [pédł] N pétalo m
petition [pətíʃən] N petición f, solicitud f; VI/VT peticionar, solicitar
petrify [pétrəfaɪ] VI/VT petrificar(se)
petroleum [pətróliəm] N petróleo m; — **products** productos petrolíferos m pl; — **jelly** vaselina f
petticoat [pédɪkot] N enaguas f pl
petty [pédi] ADJ (trivial) trivial; (mean) mezquino; — **cash** caja chica f; — **larceny** ratería f; — **officer** suboficial de marina m
petunia [pɪtúnjə] N petunia f
pew [pju] N banco de iglesia m
pewter [pjúɒə·] N peltre m
peyote [peóɒi] N peyote m
phallus [fǽləs] N falo m
phantom [fǽntəm] N fantasma m
pharmaceutical [farməsúɒɪkəł] ADJ farmacéutico; N producto farmacéutico m
pharmacist [fárməsɪst] N farmacéutico -ca mf
pharmacology [farməkáləǰi] N farmacología f
pharmacy [fárməsi] N farmacia f
pharynx [fǽrɪŋks] N faringe f
phase [fez] N fase f; VI **to — out** retirar por etapas; **to — in** incorporar paulatinamente
pheasant [fézənt] N faisán m
phenomenon [fɪnámənən] N fenómeno m
philanthropy [fɪlǽnθrəpi] N filantropía f
philharmonic [fɪłharmánɪk] ADJ filarmónico; N filarmónica f
Philippine [fíləpin] ADJ & N filipino -na mf
Philippines [fíləpinz] N Filipinas f pl
philosopher [fɪlásəfə·] N filósofo -fa mf
philosophical [fɪləsáfɪkəł] ADJ filosófico
philosophy [fɪlásəfi] N filosofía f
phlegm [flem] N flema f
phobia [fóbiə] N fobia f
phone [fon] N teléfono m; VI/VT telefonear; — **card** tarjeta telefónica f

phonetics [fənέDɪks] N fonética *f*

phonograph [fónəgræf] N fonógrafo *m*

phonology [fənáləʤi] N fonología *f*

phony [fóni] ADJ falso

phosphate [fásfet] N fosfato *m*

phosphorus [fásfərəs] N fósforo *m*

photo [fóDo] N foto *f*; — **finish** final muy reñido *m*

photocopier [fóDəkɑpiɚ] N fotocopiadora *f*

photocopy [fóDəkɑpi] N fotocopia *f*; VI/VT fotocopiar

photoelectric [foDoɪléktrɪk] ADJ fotoeléctrico

photogenic [foDəʤénɪk] ADJ fotogénico

photograph [fóDəgræf] N fotografía *f*; VT fotografiar

photographer [fətágrəfɚ] N fotógrafo -fa *mf*

photography [fətágrəfi] N fotografía *f*

photon [fótɑn] N fotón *m*

photosynthesis [foDosínθəsɪs] N fotosíntesis *f*

phrase [frez] N frase *f*; VI/VT expresar; (musical) frasear

phylum [fáɪləm] N filo *m*

physical [fízɪkəł] ADJ físico; — **education** educación física *f*; — **geography** geografía física *f*; — **science** ciencia física *f*

physician [fɪzíʃən] N médico -ca *mf*; —'s **assistant** ayudante médico -ca sanitario -ria *mf*

physicist [fízɪsɪst] N físico -ca *mf*

physics [fízɪks] N física *f*

physiological [fɪzɪəláʤɪkəł] ADJ fisiológico

physiology [fɪziáləʤi] N fisiología *f*

physique [fɪzík] N físico *m*

piano [piǽno] N piano *m*; — **bench** banqueta de piano *f*; — **hammer** martinete *m*; — **stool** taburete de piano *m*

picaresque [pɪkərésk] ADJ picaresco

piccolo [píkələ] N flautín *m*, pícolo *m*

pick [pɪk] VT (choose) escoger, elegir; (gather flowers) juntar; (play a guitar) puntear; (clean teeth) mondarse; (eat with the bill) picotear; (provoke a fight) armar, entablar; VI picar; **to — at** picotear; **to — apart** criticar; **to — a lock** violar una cerradura con ganzúa; **to — on** meterse con; **to — out** (choose) escoger; (distinguish) distinguir; **to — pockets** ratear; **to — up** (gather) recoger; (lift) levantar; (learn) aprender; (order) ordenar; (improve) mejorar; (contact in hope of sex) ligar con; **to — up speed** acelerar la marcha; —**-proof** a prueba de ladrones; N (tool) pico *m*; (of a guitar) púa *f*; (act of selecting) selección *f*; (thing or person selected) elección *f*; (the best) lo selecto, lo

mejor; —**ax(e)** zapapico *m*; —**lock** ganzúa *f*; —**pocket** ratero -ra *mf*, carterista *mf*; —**up** (taking on freight) recolección *f*; (improvement in business) recuperación *f*; (casual sexual acquaintance) ligue *m*, plan *m*; (acceleration) aceleración *f*; —**up truck** camioneta *f*

picket [píkɪt] N piquete *m* (also union worker); — **fence** cerca de piquetes *f*; VT (fence) vallar; (block with workers) bloquear

pickle [píkəł] N pepinillo en vinagre *m*, curtido *m*; **to be in a —** hallarse en un aprieto; VT encurtir, escabechar; —**d fish** pescado al / en escabeche *m*, pescado adobado *m*

picnic [píknɪk] N picnic *m*; — **area** merendero *m*; VI hacer un picnic

picture [píktʃɚ] N (image) imagen *f*; (drawing) dibujo *m*; (photo) fotografía *f*; (situation) panorama *m*; (movie) película *f*; — **frame** marco *m*; — **gallery** galería de pinturas *f*; — **tube** tubo de imagen *m*; **she is the — of unhappiness** es la imagen de la infelicidad; VT (describe) describir; (imagine) imaginar

picturesque [pɪktʃərésk] ADJ pintoresco

pie [paɪ] N pastel *m*, tarta *f*; — **chart** gráfica circular *f*; — **in the sky** castillos en el aire *m pl*; **it's as easy as —** es pan comido

piece [pis] N (of music, in a board game, of furniture) pieza *f*; (of wood, rock, pie) pedazo *m*, trozo *m*; —**meal** por partes; — **of advice** consejo *m*; — **of cake** pan comido *m*; — **of land** parcela *f*, terreno *m*; — **of one's mind** regaño *m*; — **of news** noticia *f*; — **of shit** *vulg* mierda *f*; —**work** trabajo a destajo *m*; **to go to —s** descomponerse; VI remendar; **to — together** (assemble) armar; (make sense of) atar cabos

pier [pir] N muelle *m*, embarcadero *m*; (breakwater) rompeolas *m sg*

pierce [pirs] VI/VT (make a hole in) agujerear; (penetrate) penetrar; (cause a sharp pain) punzar; (make a sharp sound) quebrar

piercing [pírsɪŋ] ADJ (glance, sound) penetrante; (pain) punzante

piety [páɪDi] N piedad *f*

pig [pɪg] N puerco *m*, cerdo *m*, cochino *m*; *Sp* guarro *m*; —**-headed** testarudo, cabezón; —**-iron** hierro en lingotes *m*; — **Latin** jerigonza *f*; —**pen** pocilga *f*; —**tail** coleta *f*

pigeon [píʤən] N paloma *f*; (young) pichón

m; **—hole** casilla *f;* **to —hole** encasillar; **— loft** palomar *m*

piggy [pígi] N cerdito *m;* **—-bank** alcancía *f; Sp* hucha *f;* **—back** a hombros, a cuestas

pigment [pígmənt] N pigmento *m*

pike [paɪk] N (weapon) pica *f;* (fish) lucio *m*

pile [paɪɫ] N (ordered stack) pila *f;* (chaotic group) montón *m,* amontonamiento *m;* (surface of a carpet) pelo *m;* (post) pilote *m;* **— driver** martinete *m;* **—s** almorranas *f pl;* **—-up** accidente múltiple *m;* VI/VT apilar(se), amontonar(se)

pilfer [píɫfɚ] VI/VT ratear, sisar

pilgrim [píɫgrəm] N peregrino -na *mf,* romero -ra *mf*

pilgrimage [píɫgrəmɪdʒ] N peregrinación *f,* romería *f*

pill [pɪɫ] N píldora *f* (also birth control), pastilla *f;* (naughty child) pesado -da *mf*

pillage [pílɪdʒ] N pillaje *m,* saqueo *m,* rapiña *f;* VI/VT pillar, saquear

pillar [pílɚ] N pilar *m,* columna *f*

pillow [pílo] N almohada *f;* **—case** funda *f*

pilot [páɪlət] N piloto *mf* (also test, light); (of a boat) timonel *m,* piloto *mf;* VT pilotar, comandar

pimp [pɪmp] N proxeneta *mf,* rufián *m*

pimple [pímpəɫ] N grano *m,* barro *m*

pin [pɪn] N alfiler *m;* (ornament) prendedor *m;* (rod) pasador *m,* perno *m;* (bowling) bolo *m;* (electric) pata *f,* clavija *f;* **—cushion** alfiletero *m;* **—wheel** molinete *m,* remolino *m;* VT (affix with pins) prender; (in wrestling) inmovilizar; **to be on —s and needles** estar en ascuas; **to — someone down** (hold down) inmovilizar; (force to act) hacer que concrete detalles; **to — one's hopes on** poner sus esperanzas en; **to —point** localizar con precisión; **to — up** sujetar con alfileres

PIN (personal identification number) [pɪn] N PIN *m*

pincers [pínsɚz] N (of lobsters) pinzas *f pl;* (tool) tenazas *f pl*

pinch [pɪntʃ] VT (squeeze with fingers) pellizcar; (squeeze tightly, hamper) apretar; (steal) birlar; (arrest) prender; VI (be too tight) apretar; (economize) economizar; N (act of pinching) pellizco *m;* (small amount) pizca *f;* (trying circumstances) aprieto *m,* apuro *m*

pine [paɪn] N pino *m;* **—apple** piña *f,* ananá(s) *m;* **— cone** piña *f;* **— grove** pinar *m;* **— nut** piñón *m;* VI **to — away** languidecer; **to — for** anhelar, suspirar por

ping-pong [píŋpɑŋ] N ping-pong *m,* tenis de mesa *m*

pinion [pínjən] N piñón *m*

pink [pɪŋk] N rosado *m,* rosa *m;* **in the —** rebosante de salud; ADJ rosado, rosa *inv*

pinnacle [pínəkəɫ] N pináculo *m*

pint [paɪnt] N pinta *f;* **—-sized** diminuto

pinto bean [píntobin] N judía pinta *f*

pioneer [paɪənír] N pionero -ra *mf;* VI ser el primero en hacer algo; VT promover

pious [páɪəs] ADJ (religious) pío, piadoso; (hypocritical) beato

pipe [paɪp] N (for smoking) pipa *f;* (for water) tubo *m,* caño *m;* (of an organ) tubo *m;* (for playing music) caramillo *m,* flauta *f;* **— dream** ilusiones *f pl;* **—line** (for oil) oleoducto *m;* (for gas) gasoducto *m;* (for water) tubería *f;* **in the —line** en trámite; **— wrench** llave inglesa *f;* VT (convey water) conducir por cañerías; (make music) tocar la flauta; VI chillar; **to — down** callarse

piping [páɪpɪŋ] N (many pipes) cañería *f,* tubería *f;* (border on clothes) ribete *m;* (sound of pipes) sonido de la gaita / flauta *m;* **— hot** hirviendo

pipsqueak [pípskwik] N chisgarabís *m,* mequetrefe *m*

pirate [páɪrət] N pirata *mf;* VT piratear

piss [pɪs] VI/VT *fam* mear

pistol [pístəɫ] N pistola *f,* revólver *m;* **to —-whip** dar culatazos

piston [pístən] N pistón *m,* émbolo *m;* **— ring** segmento de compresión *m;* **— rod** eje del pistón *m*

pit [pɪt] N (hole) hoyo *m,* pozo *m;* (in a garage, theater) foso *m;* (trap) trampa *f;* (seed) hueso *m;* (part of a racetrack) box *m,* paddock *m;* (part of the stomach) boca *f;* **—fall** (trap) trampa *f;* (difficulty) dificultad *f;* **this is the —s** esto es lo peor; VI/VT (make holes) picarse; VT (set against) oponer, enfrentar

pitch [pɪtʃ] VT (throw) tirar, lanzar; (try to sell) pregonar; **to — a tent** armar una tienda de campaña; VI (plane, ship) cabecear; **to — in** colaborar; N (throw) tiro *m,* lanzamiento *m;* (in music) tono *m;* (in printing) espaciado *m;* (slope) grado de inclinación *m;* (tar) brea *f,* pez *f;* **— dark** oscuro como boca del lobo; **—fork** horca *f,* horquilla *f*

pitcher [pítʃɚ] N (vessel) cántaro *m,* jarro *m,* jarra *f;* (in baseball) lanzador *m*

pith [pɪθ] N (in plants, feathers) médula *f;* (essence) meollo *m*

pithy [píθi] ADJ sustancial

pitiful [pídɪfəł] ADJ (deserving pity) lastimoso; (deserving contempt) despreciable

pitiless [pídɪlɪs] ADJ despiadado

pituitary [pɪtúɪteri] ADJ pituitario; — **gland** glándula pituitaria f

pity [pídi] N compasión f, lástima f; **what a —! ¡**qué lástima! VT compadecerse (de)

pivot [pívət] N pivote m; VI pivotar

pixel [píksəł] N píxel m

pizza [pítsə] N pizza f

placard [plǽkə˞d] N cartel m

placate [pléket] VT apaciguar

place [ples] N (site) lugar m, sitio m; (position) puesto m; (passage in text) pasaje m; — **mat** mantel individual m; — **of business** oficina f; — **setting** cubierto para una persona m; — **of worship** templo m; **in — of** en lugar de; **it is not my — to do it** no me corresponde a mí hacerlo m; VT colocar; (identify) situar, ubicar; VI clasificarse; **to — an order** hacer un pedido; **to — an ad** poner un anuncio

placebo [pləsíbo] N placebo m

placement [plésmənt] N colocación f

placenta [pləséntə] N placenta f

placid [plǽsɪd] ADJ plácido

plagiarism [pléʤərɪzəm] N plagio m

plague [pleg] N plaga f, peste f; VT atormentar, apestar

plaid [plæd] N tela escocesa f

plain [plen] ADJ (without embellishment) sencillo, llano; (clear) claro; (downright, unadulterated) puro; (ordinary) común; (unattractive) poco atractivo; — **fool** tonto de capirote; **in — sight** en plena vista; —**-clothesman** policía en traje de civil m; —**-Jane** sencillo; ADV completamente; N llano m, llanura f

plaintiff [pléntɪf] N demandante mf, querellante mf

plan [plæn] N plan m; (drawing, sketch, map, outline) plano m; VI/VT planear, planificar; (diagram) hacer el plano de

plane [plen] N (airplane) avión m; (surface) plano m; (tool) cepillo m; ADJ plano; — **geometry** geometría plana f; — **tree** plátano m; VI (glide, hover) planear; VT (smooth) cepillar, planear

planet [plǽnɪt] N planeta m

planetarium [plænɪtériəm] N planetario m

plank [plæŋk] N (board) tabla f, tablón m; (tenet) principio m, base f; VT entarimar

plankton [plǽŋktən] N plancton m

plant [plænt] N (vegetation) planta f; (industrial installation) fábrica f, planta f;

(mole, spy) topo m; VT (plants) plantar; (ideas) sembrar; (a spy, evidence) colocar

plantation [plæntéʃən] N plantación f

plaque [plæk] N placa f; (on teeth) sarro m, placa f

plasma [plǽzmə] N plasma m

plaster [plǽstə˞] N (substance) yeso m; (preparation applied to body) emplasto m; — **of Paris** yeso m; VT (cover with plaster) revocar; (apply a preparation) emplastar; (cover with posters) cubrir, empapelar; (defeat) aplastar; **to — down one's hair** achatarse el pelo; **he got —ed** se emborrachó

plastic [plǽstɪk] ADJ plástico; — **surgery** cirugía plástica / estética f

plate [plet] N (for food) plato m; (for collections) bandeja f; (metal) plancha f, lámina f; (license) placa f; — **glass** vidrio cilindrado m; — **tectonics** tectónica de placas f; VT (apply metal covering) chapar, enchapar; (apply armor) blindar

plateau [plætó] N meseta f, macizo m

platform [plǽtfɔrm] N plataforma f (also political); (railway) andén m; (mobile) tarima f, tinglado m

platinum [plǽtn̩əm] N platino m

platitude [plǽdɪtud] N lugar común m, perogrullada f

platter [plǽɖə˞] N fuente f

plausible [plɔ́zəbəł] ADJ plausible

play [ple] VT (game) jugar; (an opponent) jugar contra; (an instrument) tocar; (a drama) representar; (a role) desempeñar; (bet on) apostar; VI (divert oneself, gamble) jugar; (kid) bromear; (make music) tocar; **to — a joke** gastar una broma; **to — along** seguir la corriente; **to — cards** jugar a los naipes; **to — down** minimizar; **to — havoc** hacer estragos; **to — tennis** jugar al tenis; **to — the fool** hacerse el tonto; **to be all —ed out** estar agotado; N (recreational activity, looseness) juego m; (instance of playing) jugada f; (theater work) obra de teatro f; — **on words** juego de palabras m; —**boy** playboy m; —**ground** recreo m, patio m; —**ing card** naipe m; —**mate** compañero -ra de juego mf; —**thing** juguete m

player [pléə˞] N (one who plays, gambler) jugador -ra mf; (musician) músico -ca mf; (actor) actor m, actriz f; (participant) participante mf; — **piano** pianola f

playful [pléfəł] ADJ juguetón

playwright [plérait] N dramaturgo -ga mf

plea [pli] N (entreaty) súplica f, ruego m; (allegation) alegato m; **to enter a — of**

guilty declararse culpable

plead [plid] VI/VT (entreat) suplicar, rogar; (defend) abogar, defender; **to — guilty** declararse culpable

pleasant [plézənt] ADJ agradable, grato, placentero

pleasantry [plézəntri] N cortesía *f*

please [pliz] ADV por favor; VI/VT agradar, complacer; **as you — como quieras; to be —d to** tener el gusto de, tener gusto en; **to be —d with** estar satisfecho con

pleasing [plízɪŋ] ADJ agradable

pleasure [pléʒɚ] N placer *m*, gusto *m*, agrado *m*; **— trip** viaje de placer *m*

pleat [plit] N pliegue *m*, tabla *f*; (wide) tabla *f*; VT plisar; (wide) tablear

pledge [pleʤ] N (promise) promesa *f*; (security deposit) prenda *f*; (in a fraternity) miembro provisorio *m*; **as a — of** en prenda de; VI/VT (promise) prometer; VT (give as a deposit) empeñar; **to — one's word** dar la palabra; **to — to secrecy** exigir promesa de discreción

plenary [plénəri] ADJ & N plenario *m*

plentiful [pléntɪfəł] ADJ abundante, copioso

plenty [plénti] N abundancia *f*; **— of time** suficiente tiempo *m*; **that's —** con eso basta

pliable [pláɪəbəł] ADJ (flexible) flexible; (docile) dócil

pliant [pláɪənt] ADJ (flexible) flexible; (docile) dócil

pliers [pláɪɚz] N alicates *m pl*, tenazas *f pl*

plight [plaɪt] N aprieto *m*

plod [plɑd] VI (walk) caminar trabajosamente; (work) trabajar laboriosamente

plop [plɑp] VI hacer plaf; VT dejar caer; N plaf *m*

plot [plɑt] N (storyline) trama *f*, argumento *m*; (conspiracy) complot *m*, conspiración *f*; (land) parcela *f*, era *f*; (floor plan) plano *m*; VI/VT (plan secretly) tramar, conspirar, maquinar; VT (make a graph) hacer un gráfico; **to — a course** trazar un curso

plotter [plɑDɚ] N (one who plots) conspirador -ora *mf*; (device) trazador de gráficos *m*

plover [plóvɚ] N chorlito *m*

plow [plaʊ] N arado *m*; **—share** reja de arado *f*; VI/VT arar; (fresh soil) roturar; **to — through** abrirse paso

plowing [pláʊɪŋ] N labranza *f*

pluck [plʌk] VT (a feather, flower) arrancar; (bird) desplumar; (guitar) puntear, pulsar; **to — at** tirar de; **to — out / off** desprender; **to — up courage** animarse, cobrar ánimo; N (act of plucking) tirón *m*;

(courage) valor *m*

plug [plʌg] N (stopper) tapón *m*; (horse) *pej* penco *m*; (electric) enchufe *m*; (advertisement) mención favorable *f*; (tobacco) rollo *m*; **—-in** enchufe *m*; VT tapar; (advertise) hacer una mención favorable de; VI **to — along** afanarse; **to — in** enchufar; **to — up** tapar

plum [plʌm] N (fruit) ciruela *f*; **— tree** ciruelo *m*; **that job is a real — ese** trabajo es estupendo

plumage [plúmɪʤ] N plumaje *m*

plumb [plʌm] N (lead weight) plomada *f*; **to be out of —** no estar a plomo; ADJ (perpendicular) a plomo; **— bob** plomada *f*; ADV (in a vertical direction) a plomo; (completely) completamente; VT (measure depth) sondear; (test for verticality) aplomar; (examine) examinar

plumber [plʌmɚ] N plomero -ra *mf*; *Sp* fontanero -ra *mf*

plumbing [plʌmɪŋ] N (work and trade) plomería *f*; *Sp* fontanería *f*; (system of pipes) cañerías *f pl*

plume [plum] N penacho *m*; VT adornar con plumas

plummet [plʌmɪt] VI precipitarse; N plomada *f*

plump [plʌmp] ADJ rechoncho, regordete, rollizo; ADV a plomo; VI/VT **to — down** dejar(se) caer

plunder [plʌndɚ] N (act of plundering) pillaje *m*, saqueo *m*; (loot) botín *m*; VI/VT pillar, saquear

plunge [plʌnʤ] VI/VT (into water) zambullir(se), sumergir(se); (into something solid) hundir(se); VI (fall) precipitarse; (slope downward) bajar repentinamente; **to — headlong** echarse de cabeza; N zambullida *f*; (rush) salto *m*

plunger [plʌnʤɚ] N (for a toilet) desatascador *m*; (of a pump) émbolo *m*

pluperfect [plupɚfɪkt] N pluscuamperfecto *m*

plural [plúrəł] ADJ & N plural *m*

plurality [plurǽlɪDi] N pluralidad *f*

plus [plʌs] PREP más; N signo más *m*; (advantage) ventaja *f*; **two — three** dos más tres *m*; **on the — side** en el lado positivo; **— sign** signo de más *m*

plush [plʌʃ] N felpa *f*; ADJ (fabric) afelpado; (hotel) lujoso

plutonium [plutóniəm] N plutonio *m*

ply [plaɪ] VT (use) manejar; (assail with questions) acosar; (navigate a body of water) surcar; VI (travel regularly) recorrer con regularidad; (work steadily) aplicarse; **to — a trade** ejercer un oficio; N (layer of cloth, rubber) capa *f*; (layer of plywood) chapa *f*; **—wood** madera compensada *f*, contrachapado *m*

pneumatic [numǽɒɪk] ADJ neumático

pneumonia [numónjə] N pulmonía *f*

poach [potʃ] VT (eggs) escalfar; VI/VT (game) cazar furtivamente

pocket [pákɪt] N bolsillo *m*; (vein of ore) filón *m*; (on a pool table) tronera *f*; (of air) bache *m*; (of poverty) bolsa *f*; **—book** cartera *f*, *Sp* bolso *m*; **— book** libro de bolsillo *m*; **—knife** navaja *f*; **— of resistance** foco de resistencia *m*; VT meterse en el bolsillo; (appropriate) embolsar; (knock in a billiard ball) meter en la tronera

pod [pɑd] N (seed vessel) vaina *f*; (herd of cetaceans) manada *f*

podium [pódiəm] N podio *m*

poem [póəm] N poema *m*, poesía *f*

poet [póɪt] N poeta *mf*

poetic [poéɒɪk] ADJ poético; **—s** poética *f*; **— justice** justicia divina *f*

poetry [póɪtri] N poesía *f*

poignant [pɔ́ɪnjənt] ADJ conmovedor

poinsettia [pɔɪnséɒə] N flor de Pascua *f*

point [pɔɪnt] N (place) punto *m*; (sharp end) punta *f*; **— of view** punto de vista *m*; **—-blank** a quemarropa; **it is not to the — no** viene al caso; **I don't see the —** no le veo el sentido; **on the — of** a punto de; VT (direct finger at) apuntar con, señalar con; (indicate) señalar; **to — out** señalar, indicar; **to — up** enfatizar

pointed [pɔ́ɪntɪd] ADJ (having a point) puntiagudo; (piercing) agudo; (aimed) a propósito; **— arch** arco ojival *m*

pointer [pɔ́ɪntɚ] N (stick) puntero *m*; (on a scale) indicador *m*; (dog) perro de muestra *m*; (advice) consejo *m*

pointless [pɔ́ɪntlɪs] ADJ inútil

poise [pɔɪz] N (balance, steadiness) equilibrio *m*; (dignified bearing) aplomo *m*; VI/VT equilibrar(se); VT (ready) preparar; VI (hover) cernerse

poison [pɔ́ɪzən] N veneno *m*, ponzoña *f*; **— ivy** hiedra venenosa *f*; VT envenenar, emponzoñar

poisoning [pɔ́ɪzənɪŋ] N intoxicación *f*

poisonous [pɔ́ɪzənəs] ADJ venenoso, ponzoñoso

poke [pok] VT (jab) clavar, pinchar; (stir a fire) atizar; (thrust out, as one's head) asomar; **to — out an eye** sacar un ojo; VI **to — along** andar perezosamente; **to — around** husmear; **to — fun at** burlarse de; **to — into** meterse en; **to — out**

(project) sobresalir; N pinchazo *m*

Poland [pólənd] N Polonia *f*

polar [pólɚ] ADJ polar; **— bear** oso polar *m*

polarity [pəlǽrɪɒi] N polaridad *f*

polarization [polɚɪzéʃən] N polarización *f*

polarize [pólɚaɪz] VI/VT polarizar(se)

pole [poł] N (long piece of wood, metal) poste *m*; (for a flag) asta *f*; (for vaulting) pértiga *f*, garrocha *f*; (earth's axis) polo *m*; (for skiing) bastón *m*; **— vault** salto con pértiga *m*

Pole [poł] N polaco -ca *mf*

polemic [pəlémɪk] ADJ polémico *m*; N polémica *f*

police [pəlís] N policía *f*; **— car** patrullero *m*; **— dog** perro policía *m*; **— force** cuerpo de policía *m*; **—man** policía *m*; **— officer** oficial de policía *mf*; **— state** estado policíaco *m*; **— station** comisaría de policía *f*; **—woman** policía *f*; VT patrullar

policy [pálɪsi] N (procedure) política *f*; (for insurance) póliza *f*

polio [pólio] N polio *f*

Polish [pólɪʃ] ADJ & N polaco -ca *mf*

polish [pálɪʃ] N (sheen) lustre *m*, refinamiento *m*; (refinement) urbanidad *f*, cultura *f*; (substance for furniture) cera *f*; (substance for shoes) betún *m*; VT (a speech) pulir; (a metal) sacar brillo; (a car) encerar; (shoes) lustrar, embetunar; VI lustrarse; **to — off** despachar; **to — up** (metal) sacar brillo; (speech) pulir

polite [pəláɪt] ADJ cortés

politeness [pəláɪtnɪs] N cortesía *f*

politic [pálɪtɪk] ADJ diplomático, político

political [pəlídɪkəł] ADJ político; **— prisoner** preso -sa político -ca *mf*; **— science** ciencias políticas *f pl*

politically correct [pəlídɪklikɔrékt] ADJ políticamente correcto

politician [pɑlɪtíʃən] N político -ca *mf*

politics [pálɪtɪks] N política *f*

polka [półkə] N polca *f*; **— dot** lunar *m*

poll [poł] N (survey) encuesta *f*; **—s** (elections) comicios *m pl*; (voting place) urna *f*; VT (survey) encuestar; (receive votes) obtener; (record vote of) registrar

pollen [pálən] N polen *m*

pollinate [pálənet] VT polinizar

pollute [pəlút] VI/VT contaminar

pollution [pəlúʃən] N contaminación *f*

polo [pólo] N polo *m*

polyester [pɑliéstɚ] N poliéster *m*

polygamy [pəlígəmi] N poligamia *f*

polyglot [páliglɑt] ADJ & N políglota *mf*

polygraph [páligræf] N polígrafo *m*

polymer [páləmɚ] N polímero *m*

polyp [pálɪp] N pólipo *m*
polyunsaturated [pɑliʌnsǽtʃəreɪDɪd] ADJ poliinsaturado
polyurethane [pɑlijúrəθen] N poliuretano *m*
pomegranate [pámɪgrænɪt] N granada *f*; — **tree** granado *m*
pomp [pɑmp] N pompa *f*, boato *m*, aparato *m*
pompous [pámpəs] ADJ pomposo, aparatoso
pond [pɑnd] N (natural) charca *f*; (artificial) estanque *m*; (for irrigation) balsa *f*
ponder [pándɚ] VI meditar; VT considerar
ponderous [pándɚəs] ADJ enorme
pontoon [pɑntún] N (on a bridge) pontón *m*; (on an airplane) flotador *m*
pony [póni] N póney *m*; —**tail** colita *f*, cola de caballo *f*; VI **to — up** soltar
poodle [púdl] N caniche *m*
pool [puł] N (puddle of water, blood, etc.) charco *m*; (swimming place) piscina *f*, *Mex* alberca *f*; (association of competitors) pool *m*; (game) pool *m*, billar *m*; (bets) pozo *m*; — **table** billar *m*; — **hall** billar *m*; VI acumularse; VT combinar fondos
poop [pup] N (part of ship) popa *f*; (excrement) *fam* caca *f*; VI *fam* hacer caca
poor [pur] ADJ (lacking money) pobre; (deficient) malo; **I'm a — cook** no sé cocinar; —**house** asilo para los pobres *m*; — **little thing** pobrecito -ta *mf*; **the —** los pobres
pop [pɑp] VI reventar, estallar; (eyes, cork) saltar; **to — in** entrar de paso; VT (make explode) hacer reventar; (take out cork) hacer saltar; (put) meter; (take, as pills) tomar (píldoras); **to — a question** espetar una pregunta; **to — corn** hacer palomitas; N estallido *m*, detonación *f*; —**corn** palomitas *f pl*; — **music** música popular *f*; — **quiz** prueba sorpresa *f*; — **of a cork** taponazo *m*
Pope [pop] N Papa *m*
poplar [páplɚ] N álamo *m*, chopo *m*; — **grove** alameda *f*
poppy [pápi] N amapola *f*
popular [pápjəlɚ] ADJ popular; **he's very — with the ladies** tiene mucho éxito con las mujeres
popularity [pɑpjəlǽrɪDi] N popularidad *f*
populate [pápjəlet] VT poblar
population [pɑpjəléʃən] N población *f*
populous [pápjələs] ADJ populoso
porcelain [pɔ́rsəlɪn] N porcelana *f*
porch [pɔ́rtʃ] N porche *m*
porcupine [pɔ́rkjəpaɪn] N puercoespín *m*
pore [pɔr] N poro *m*; VI **to — over a book** estudiar detenidamente un libro
pork [pɔrk] N carne de cerdo *f*; — **chop** chuleta de cerdo *f*
pornography [pɔrnágrəfi] N pornografía *f*
porous [pɔ́rəs] ADJ poroso
porpoise [pɔ́rpəs] N marsopa *f*
port [pɔrt] N (harbor, computer) puerto *m*; (wine) oporto *m*; (left side of ship) babor *m*; —**hole** ojo de buey *m*
portable [pɔ́rDəbəł] ADJ portátil
portal [pɔ́rdl] N portal *m* (also of Internet)
portent [pɔ́rtɛnt] N (omen) presagio *m*, agüero *m*; (marvel, prodigy) portento *m*
portentous [pɔrténtəs] ADJ (ominous) de mal agüero; (prodigious) portentoso
porter [pɔ́rDɚ] N mozo -za *mf*
portfolio [pɔrtfólio] N cartera *f*; (flat case for papers) carpeta *f*
portion [pɔ́rʃən] N porción *f*; VI **to — out** repartir
portly [pɔ́rtli] ADJ grueso
portrait [pɔ́rtrɪt] N retrato *m*
portray [pɔrtré] VT (draw, describe) retratar; (in a drama) representar
portrayal [pɔrtréəł] N (portrait) retrato *m*; (act of portraying) representación *f*
Portugal [pɔ́rtʃəgəł] N Portugal *m*
Portuguese [pɔ́rtʃəgiz] ADJ & N portugués -esa *mf*
pose [poz] N (posture) pose *f*, postura *f*; (affected attitude) afectación *f*; VI (sit as a model) posar; (act affectedly) afectar una actitud; VT (to make sit as model) hacer posar; (to present) plantear; **to — as** hacerse pasar por
position [pəzíʃən] N (place) posición *f*; (job) puesto *m*, colocación *f*
positive [pázɪDɪv] ADJ positivo; — **proof** prueba certera *f*; **I am —** estoy seguro
possess [pəzés] VT poseer
possession [pəzéʃən] N posesión *f*
possessive [pəzésɪv] ADJ & N posesivo *m*
possessor [pəzésɚ] N poseedor -ra *f*
possibility [pɑsəbílɪDi] N posibilidad *f*
possible [pásəbəł] ADJ posible
post [post] N (pole) poste *m*; (position) puesto *m*; (mail) correo *m*; —**card** tarjeta postal *f*; — **haste** a la brevedad; —**man** cartero *m*; —**mark** matasellos *m*; —**master** director de correos *m*; — **office** oficina de correos *f*, casa de correos *f*; —**-office box** apartado postal *m*; — **paid** porte pagado; VT (affix) fijar; (announce) anunciar; (list) poner en lista; (place) apostar, situar; (mail) echar al correo; **keep me —ed** mantenme al tanto
postage [póstɪdʒ] N franqueo *m*; — **meter** franqueadora *f*; — **stamp** *Sp* sello *m*; *Am* estampilla *f*; *Mex* timbre *m*

postal [póstəł] ADJ postal; **to go** — perpetrar un ataque homicida, volverse loco

poster [póstə-] N cartel *m*, póster *m*, afiche *m*; **— child** modelo *m*

posterior [pɑstíriə-] ADJ posterior; N trasero *m*

posterity [pɑstérɪDi] N posteridad *f*

postgraduate [postgrǽʤuɪt] ADJ de posgrado

posthumous [pástʃəməs] ADJ póstumo

postpone [postpón] VT posponer, aplazar

postponement [postpónmənt] N aplazamiento *m*

postscript [póstskrɪpt] N posdata *f*

postulate [pástʃəlet] VT postular; [pástʃələt] N postulado *m*

posture [pástʃə-] N (carriage, attitude) postura *f*; (affectation) afectación *f*; VI darse aires

posy [pózi] N ramillete *m*

pot [pɑt] N (vessel) olla *f*, marmita *f*; (marijuana) marihuana *f*; (hashish) *fam* chocolate *m*; **—-bellied** panzudo, barrigón; **—hole** bache *m*

potable [pópɐbəł] ADJ potable

potassium [pətǽsiəm] N potasio *m*

potato [pətéDo] N *Sp* patata *f*; *Am* papa *f*; **— chip** patata / papa frita a la inglesa *f*, chip *m*

potency [pótn̩si] N potencia *f*

potent [pótn̩t] ADJ potente

potentate [pótn̩tet] N potentado -da *mf*

potential [pəténʃəł] ADJ & N potencial *m*

potion [póʃən] N poción *f*

potter [pápə-] N alfarero -ra *mf*

pottery [pápəri] N (craft, shop) alfarería *f*; (objects) cerámica *f*, objetos de alfarería *m pl*

pouch [pautʃ] N bolsa *f*; (for mail) valija *f*; (for tobacco) petaca *f*

poultry [półtri] N aves de corral *f pl*

pounce [pauns] VI saltar; **to — upon / on** abalanzarse sobre; **to — on an opportunity** no dejar pasar una oportunidad; N salto *m*

pound [paund] N (unit of weight, British currency) libra *f*; (blow) golpazo *m*; (place for stray dogs) perrera *f*; VT (a door) golpear; (seeds) machacar; (a military target) bombardear; VI (beat) latir con fuerza

pour [pɔr] VT verter; VI (leave en masse) salir en tropel; (rain) llover a cántaros; **to — out one's feelings** desahogarse

pout [paut] VI hacer pucheros; N puchero *m*

poverty [pávə-Di] N pobreza *f*, penuria *f*; **—-stricken** indigente

powder [páuDə-] N polvo *m*; (for the face) polvos *m pl*; (for guns) pólvora *f*; **— compact** polvera *f*; **— puff** borla *f*; **to**

take a — poner pies en polvorosa; VI/VT (use powder) empolvar(se); (pulverize) pulverizar(se)

power [páuə-] N (control) poder *m*, poderío *m*; (might, in physics, in math) potencia *f*; (physical strength) fuerza *f*; (energy) energía *f*; **— of attorney** poder *m*; **— plant** central eléctrica *f*; **— steering** dirección asistida *f*; **legislative —s** atribuciones legislativas *f pl*

powerful [páuə-fəł] ADJ poderoso, potente

powerless [páuə-lɪs] ADJ impotente

practical [prǽktɪkəł] ADJ práctico; **— joke** broma pesada *f*; **— nurse** enfermero -ra sin título *mf*

practice [prǽktɪs] N práctica *f*; (habit) costumbre *f*; (doctor's office) consultorio *m*; (lawyer's office) bufete *m*; VI/VT practicar; VT (a profession) ejercer

practiced [prǽktɪst] ADJ experto, perito

practitioner [prǽktíʃənə-] N practicante *mf*; **general —** médico -ca general *mf*

pragmatic [prægmǽDɪk] ADJ pragmático

prairie [préri] N pradera *f*, llanura *f*

praise [prez] N alabanza *f*, elogio *m*; VT alabar, elogiar; **—worthy** loable, encomiable

prance [præns] VI cabriolar, hacer cabriolas; N cabriola *f*

prank [præŋk] N travesura *f*, chasco *m*; **to play —s** hacer travesuras

prawn [prɔn] N langostino *m*; *Sp* gamba pequeña *f*

pray [pre] VI/VT (religious) rezar, orar; (beg) rogar, suplicar

prayer [prɛr] N (devout petition to God) oración *f*, rezo *m*; (entreaty) ruego *m*, súplica *f*

praying mantis [préɪŋmǽntɪs] N mantis religiosa *f*

preach [pritʃ] VI/VT predicar; (moralize) sermonear

preacher [prítʃə-] N predicador -ra *mf*

preamble [príæmbəł] N preámbulo *m*

precarious [prɪkériəs] ADJ precario

precaution [prɪkɔ́ʃən] N precaución *f*

precede [prɪsíd] VI/VT preceder

precedence [présɪDəns] N precedencia *f*, prioridad *f*

preceding [prɪsíDɪŋ] ADJ precedente, anterior

precept [prísept] N precepto *m*

precinct [prísɪŋkt] N distrito *m*; (police station) comisaría *f*; **—s** límites *m pl*

precious [préʃəs] ADJ precioso; (overly refined) preciosista; **— little** muy poco; **— metal** metal precioso *m*; **— stone** piedra preciosa *f*

precipice [présəpɪs] N precipicio *m*, derrumbadero *m*

precipitate [prɪsípɪtet] VI/VT precipitar(se); [prɪsípɪtət] ADJ & N precipitado *m*

precipitation [prɪsɪpɪtéʃən] N precipitación *f*

precipitous [prɪsípɪɒəs] ADJ (steep) escarpado; (hasty) precipitado

precise [prɪsáɪs] ADJ preciso, exacto

precision [prɪsíʒən] N precisión *f*, exactitud *f*; (of expression) propiedad *f*

preclude [prɪklúd] VT excluir; **that doesn't — our considering your application** esto no obsta para que tengamos en cuenta su solicitud

precocious [prɪkóʃəs] ADJ precoz

precursor [prɪkɝ́sɚ] N precursor *m*

predator [prÉDətɚ] N depredador *m*

predatory [prÉDətɔri] ADJ (animal) depredador; (persona) rapaz

predecessor [prÉDɪsesɚ] N predecesor -ra *mf*, antecesor -ra *mf*

predestine [pridéstɪn] VT predestinar

predicament [prɪdíkəmənt] N aprieto *m*

predicate [prÉDɪkɪt] ADJ & N predicado *m*; [prÉDɪket] VT basar

predict [prɪdíkt] VT predecir

prediction [prɪdíkʃən] N predicción *f*, vaticinio *m*

predilection [predlékʃən] N predilección *f*

predispose [pridɪspóz] VI/VT predisponer

predominance [prɪdámənəns] N predominio *m*

predominant [prɪdámənənt] ADJ predominante

predominate [prɪdámənet] VI/VT predominar, preponderar

preface [préfɪs] N prefacio *m*, prólogo *m*; VT hacer una introducción; (a book) prologar

prefer [prɪfɝ́] VT preferir; **to — a claim** presentar una demanda

preferable [préfɚəbəl] ADJ preferible

preference [préfɚəns] N preferencia *f*

preferential [prefɚénʃəl] ADJ preferente

preferred [prɪfɝ́d] ADJ preferido; **— stocks** acciones preferentes *f pl*

prefix [prífɪks] N prefijo *m*; VT poner un prefijo

pregnancy [prégnənsi] N embarazo *m*; (of an animal) preñez *f*

pregnant [prégnənt] ADJ (person) embarazada, encinta; (animal) preñada; (full of meaning, rain) preñado, cargado

prehensile [prihénsəl] ADJ prensil

prehistoric [prihistórɪk] ADJ prehistórico

prejudge [priʤʌ́ʤ] VT prejuzgar

prejudice [préʤədɪs] N (bias) prejuicio *m*; (harm) perjuicio *m*; VT (cause bias against) predisponer en contra; (harm) perjudicar

preliminary [prɪlíməneri] ADJ & N preliminar *m*

prelude [prélud] N preludio *m*; VI/VT preludiar

premarital [primǽrɪDəl] ADJ prematrimonial

premature [primətʃúr] ADJ prematuro

premeditated [primÉDɪteDɪd] ADJ premeditado

premier [prɪmír] N primer ministro / primera ministra *mf*; ADJ principal

premiere [prɪmír] N estreno *m*, première *f*

premise [prémɪs] N premisa *f*; **—s** local *m*

premium [prímiəm] N (bonus) premio *m*; (insurance) prima *f*; (surcharge) recargo *m*; **at a —** muy escaso; ADJ superior

premonition [preməníʃən] N premonición *f*

prenatal [prinédl] ADJ prenatal

prenuptial [prinʌ́pʃəl] ADJ prenupcial

preoccupy [priákjəpaɪ] VT absorber

prepaid [pripéd] ADJ pagado de antemano; **to send —** enviar porte pagado

preparation [prepəréʃən] N (act of preparing) preparación *f*; (substance) preparado *m*; (for a trip) preparativos *m pl*

preparatory [prépɚətɔri] ADJ preparatorio, preparativo

prepare [prɪpér] VI/VT preparar(se)

preponderance [prɪpándɚəns] N preponderancia *f*

preponderant [prɪpándɚənt] ADJ preponderante

preposition [prepəzíʃən] N preposición *f*

preposterous [prɪpástɚəs] ADJ absurdo

prerequisite [prirékwəzɪt] N prerequisito *m*

prerogative [prɪrágəDɪv] N prerrogativa *f*

prescribe [prɪskráɪb] VT (order) prescribir; (medicine) recetar

prescription [prɪskrípʃən] N (order) prescripción *f*; (of medicine) receta *f*

presence [prézəns] N presencia *f*; **— of mind** aplomo *m*, presencia de ánimo *f*

present [prézənt] N (time) presente *m*; (gift) regalo *m*, presente *m*; **at —** ahora; **for the —** por ahora; ADJ (at a place) presente; (at this time) actual; **— company excepted** con perdón de los presentes; **—-day** actual; **— participle** gerundio *m*; **— perfect** pretérito perfecto *m*; [prɪzént] VT presentar, entregar

presentable [prɪzéntəbəl] ADJ presentable

presentation [prezəntéʃən] N presentación *f*, entrega *f*; (talk) ponencia *f*

presentiment [prɪzéntəmənt] N presentimiento *m*

presently [prézəntli] ADV (soon) pronto; (now) actualmente

preservation [prɛzɚvéʃən] N preservación *f*, conservación *f*

preservative [prɪzɚ́vəDɪv] N conservante *m*

preserve [prɪzɚ́v] VI/VT (protect) preservar; (keep food fresh) conservar; N (for game) coto *m*; (for animals) reserva *f*; **—s** mermelada *f*, dulce *m*

preside [prɪzáɪd] VI presidir; **to — over a meeting** presidir una reunión

presidency [prézɪDənsi] N presidencia *f*

president [prézɪDənt] N presidente -ta *mf*

presidential [prezɪdénʃəł] ADJ presidencial

press [prɛs] VI/VT (bear down, squeeze) apretar, oprimir; (iron) planchar; (force) presionar; (extract juice) prensar; (put under pressure) apremiar; **to — on** avanzar; **to — one's point** insistir en un argumento; **to — through** abrirse paso; N (newspapers) prensa *f*; (printing machine) imprenta *f*; (crowding) empuje *m*; **— conference** conferencia de prensa *f*; **— corps** cuerpo de prensa *m*; **— release** comunicado de prensa *m*

pressing [présɪŋ] ADJ apremiante, urgente

pressure [préʃɚ] N presión *f*; **— cooker** olla a presión *f*; **— gauge** manómetro *m*; **— group** grupo de presión *m*; VT apremiar, presionar

prestige [prɛstíʒ] N prestigio *m*

prestigious [prɛstíʤəs] ADJ prestigioso

presume [prɪzúm] VI (be presumptuous) presumir; VT (suppose) suponer; (dare) atreverse a

presumption [prɪzÁmpʃən] N presunción *f*

presumptuous [prɪzÁmptʃuəs] ADJ presuntuoso, presumido

presuppose [prisəpóz] VT presuponer

preteen [pritín] ADJ & N preadolescente *mf*

pretend [prɪténd] VI/VT (make believe) hacer de cuenta que; (feign) fingir; VT (claim) pretender; **to — to the throne** pretender el trono

pretense [prítɛns] N (faked action or belief) engaño *m*; (false show) apariencia *f*; **under — of** so pretexto de

pretension [prɪténʃən] N pretensión *f*; (pretext) pretexto *m*

pretentious [prɪténʃəs] ADJ (full of pretension) pretencioso; (showy) ostentoso

pretext [prítɛkst] N pretexto *m*

pretrial [pritráɪł] ADJ anterior al juicio

pretty [príDi] ADJ bonito; (human only) *Sp* guapo; ADV bastante; VI/VT **to — up** embellecer

prevail [prɪvéł] VI (win) prevalecer; (be widespread, dominant) preponderar, imperar; **to — on (upon)** persuadir

prevailing [prɪvélɪŋ] ADJ (dominant) predominante; (existing) reinante

prevalent [prévələnt] ADJ prevaleciente, preponderante

prevent [prɪvént] VT (keep from occurring) prevenir; VI/VT (impede) impedir

prevention [prɪvénʃən] N prevención *f*; (of a disease) prevención *f*, profilaxis *f*

preventive [prɪvéntɪv] ADJ preventivo

preview [prívju] N preestreno *m*

previous [príviəs] ADJ previo, anterior

prey [pre] N (animal) presa *f*; VI **to — on** alimentarse de cazar; **it —s upon my mind** me tiene preocupado

price [praɪs] N precio *m*; **at any — a** toda costa; **— control** control de precios *m*; **— fixing** fijación de precios *f*; **— index** índice de precios *m*; **— tag** etiqueta de precio *f*; VT (set price) poner precio a; (ask price) averiguar el precio de

priceless [práɪslɪs] ADJ (without price) invalorable; (amusing) divertidísimo

prick [prɪk] N (puncture) pinchazo *m*; (sharp point) púa *f*; (penis) *vulg* pija *f*; (creep) *offensive* hijo de puta *m*; VI/VT pinchar, punzar; **to — up one's ears** parar las orejas

prickly [príkli] ADJ espinoso; **— heat** sarpullido causado por el calor *m*; **— pear** tuna *f*, nopal *m*

pride [praɪd] N orgullo *m*; (excessive) soberbia *f*; VI **to — oneself on** enorgullecerse de

priest [prist] N sacerdote *m*; (Catholic only) cura *m*; **—hood** sacerdocio *m*

prim [prɪm] ADJ remilgado

primary [práɪmeri] ADJ primario; (main) fundamental, principal; **— colors** colores primarios *m pl*; **— election** elección primaria *f*; **— school** escuela primaria *f*

primate [práɪmet] N primate *m*

prime [praɪm] ADJ (principal) fundamental; (of a number) primo; (select) de primera; **— minister** primer ministro *m*, primera ministra *f*; N (stage) flor *f*; (number) número primo *m*; **to be in one's —** estar en la flor de la edad, estar en la plenitud de la vida; **— rate** tasa prima *f*; VT preparar; (a pump) cebar

primer [prímɚ] N (first book) manual elemental *m*; (pump part) cebador *m*

primitive [prímɪDɪv] ADJ & N primitivo -va *mf*

prince [prɪns] N príncipe *m*

princely [prínsli] ADJ noble, principesco; **a — sum** una suma muy grande

princess [prínsɛs] N princesa *f*

principal [prínsəpəł] ADJ principal; N

(money invested) capital *m*; (giver of power of attorney) poderdante *mf*, mandante *mf*; (head of a school) director -ora *mf*

principle [prínsəpəɬ] N principio *m*

print [prɪnt] VI/VT imprimir; (write in block letters) escribir en letra de molde; **to — out** imprimir; N (type) letra de imprenta *f*; (of art) lámina *f*; (of photographs) copia *f*; (of fingers) huella digital *f*; (on cloth) estampado *m*; **—out** listado *m*; **in —** publicado, en venta; **out of —** agotado

printer [príntɚ] N (person) impresor -ra *mf*, gráfico -ca *mf*; (machine) impresora *f*

printing [príntɪŋ] N (art, trade) imprenta *f*; (process) impresión *f*, tipografía *f*; (block letters) letra de molde *f*, letra de imprenta *f*; **— press** imprenta *f*; **this book is in its second —** este libro está en su segunda edición

prior [práɪɚ] ADJ previo; **— to** anterior a

priority [praɪɔ́rɪDi] N prioridad *f*

prism [prízəm] N prisma *m*

prison [prízən] N prisión *f*, cárcel *f*, presidio *m*

prisoner [prízənɚ] N (captive) prisionero -ra *mf*; (in jail) preso -sa *mf*, presidiario -ria *mf*; **— of war** prisionero -ra de guerra *mf*

pristine [prɪstín] ADJ (immaculate) puro; (perfect) perfecto

privacy [práɪvəsi] N privacidad *f*

private [práɪvɪt] ADJ (not public) privado; (individual) particular; **— enterprise** empresa privada *f*; **— eye** detective privado -da *mf*; **— parts** partes pudendas *f pl*; **— school** escuela privada *f*; **— sector** sector privado *m*; **a — citizen** un particular; **in —** en privado; N soldado raso *m*

privation [praɪvéʃən] N privación *f*

privilege [prívəlɪdʒ] N privilegio *m*

privileged [prívlɪdʒd] ADJ privilegiado

privy [prívi] ADJ **to be — to** estar enterado de; N retrete *m*

prize [praɪz] N (reward) premio *m*; (booty) botín *m*; **— fight** pelea de boxeo profesional *f*; **— fighter** boxeador -ora *mf*, pugilista *mf*; VT apreciar

pro [pro] N profesional *mf*

probability [prɑbəbílɪDi] N probabilidad *f*

probable [prɑ́bəbəɬ] ADJ probable

probation [probéʃən] N libertad condicional *f*

probe [prob] VI/VT (explore with a probe) sondear; (examine) examinar; N sonda *f* (also space); (investigation) indagación *f*

problem [prɑ́bləm] N problema *m*

procedure [prəsídʒɚ] N procedimiento *m*; (legal) trámite *m*

proceed [prəsíd] VI (originate) proceder; (continue) proseguir, continuar; **to — against** demandar a; **to — to** proceder a; N **—s** ganancia *f*, lo recaudado

proceedings [prəsídɪŋz] N (events) acontecimientos *m pl*; (record of a conference) actas *f pl*, memoria *f*; (legal action) procedimiento *m*

process [prɑ́sɛs] N proceso *m*; **in the — of** en vías de

procession [prəséʃən] N procesión *f*

pro-choice [protʃɔ́ɪs] ADJ proaborto

proclaim [prəklém] VT proclamar

proclamation [prɑkləméʃən] N proclamación *f*, proclama *f*

procrastinate [prəkrǽstənet] VI/VT dejar para último momento

procreate [prókriet] VI/VT procrear, engendrar

procure [prəkjúr] VT procurar, obtener; VI ser proxeneta

prod [prɑd] VT aguijonear; **they —ded me into going / to go** insistieron en que fuera

prodigal [prɑ́Dɪgəɬ] ADJ & N pródigo -ga *mf*

prodigious [prədíʤəs] ADJ prodigioso

prodigy [prɑ́DəʤI] N prodigio *m*

produce [pródus] N (vegetables) verduras *f pl*, hortalizas *f pl*; [prədús] VI/VT producir; VT (present) presentar

producer [prədúsɚ] N productor -ora *mf*

product [prɑ́Dəkt] N producto *m*

production [prədʌ́kʃən] N producción *f*; (TV, radio) producción *f*, realización *f*; (exaggerated situation) teatro *m*

productive [prədʌ́ktɪv] ADJ productivo

profane [profén] ADJ profano; (vulgar) grosero; VT profanar

profanity [prəfǽnɪDi] N groserías *f pl*, palabrotas *f pl*

profess [prəfés] VI/VT (publicly accept, take vows) profesar; VT (express) expresar

profession [prəféʃən] N profesión *f*

professional [prəféʃənəɬ] ADJ & N profesional *mf*

professor [prəfésɚ] N profesor -ra universitario -ria *mf*; (full) catedrático -ca *mf*

proffer [prɑ́fɚ] VT ofrecer; N oferta *f*

proficiency [prəfíʃənsi] N competencia *f*

proficient [prəfíʃənt] ADJ competente

profile [prófaɪl] N (contour) perfil *m*; **a high-— case** un caso muy sonado

profit [prɑ́fɪt] N (gain) ganancia *f*; **— and loss** ganancias y pérdidas *f pl*; **— sharing**

participación en las ganancias de una empresa *f*; **at a —** con ganancia; **to turn a —** dar ganancia; **not for —** sin fines de lucro; VI salir ganando; **to — from** (benefit) aprovechar, sacar provecho de; (use to get an advantage) aprovecharse de; VT servir

profitable [práfɪɒəbəɫ] ADJ (beneficial) provechoso; (lucrative) lucrativo, rentable

profound [prəfáund] ADJ profundo

profundity [prəfʌ́ndɪɒi] N profundidad *f*

profuse [prəfjús] ADJ profuso, pródigo

progesterone [proʤéstəron] N progesterona *f*

prognosis [prɑgnósɪs] N pronóstico *m*

program [prógræm] N programa *m*; VI/VT programar

programmer [prógræmə-] N programador -ora *mf*

programming [prógræmɪŋ] N programación *f*

progress [prágrɛs] N progreso *m*; [prəgrés] VI progresar

progressive [prəgrésɪv] ADJ (advancing) progresivo; ADJ & N (liberal) progresista *mf*, progresivo -va *mf*

prohibit [prohíbɪt] VT prohibir, vedar

prohibition [proəbíʃən] N prohibición *f*

project [práʤɛkt] N proyecto *m*; [prəʤékt] VI/VT proyectar(se); VI (jut out) sobresalir

projectile [prəʤéktaɪɫ] N proyectil *m*; ADJ arrojadizo

projection [prəʤékʃən] N proyección *f*; (jut) saliente *f*

projector [prəʤéktə-] N proyector *m*

proletariat [prolɪtériət] N proletariado *m*

pro-life [prolάɪf] ADJ antiaborto

prolific [prəlífɪk] ADJ prolífico

prologue [prólɔg] N prólogo *m*

prolong [prəlɔ́ŋ] VT prolongar

prolongation [prolɔŋgéʃən] N prolongación *f*

promenade [prɑmənéd] N paseo *m*; (prom) baile *m*; VI/VT pasear(se)

prominent [prámənənt] ADJ prominente

promiscuous [prəmískjuəs] ADJ promiscuo, liviano

promise [prámɪs] N promesa *f*; **he showed — prometía mucho; VI/VT prometer

promising [prámɪsɪŋ] ADJ prometedor, halagüeño

promissory [prámɪsɔri] ADJ promisorio; **— note** pagaré *m*

promontory [práməntɔri] N promontorio *m*

promote [prəmót] VT (foster) promover, fomentar; (advance in rank) ascender; (in school) pasar de año, promover; (advertise) promocionar

promoter [prəmóɒə-] N (fomenter) propulsor -ora *mf*; (organizer) promotor -ora *mf*

promotion [prəmóʃən] N (act of promoting) promoción *f*; (advance in rank) ascenso *m*

prompt [prɑmpt] ADJ (quick) rápido; (punctual) puntual; VT (cause) inducir; (in theater) apuntar; **to give someone a —** apuntarle a alguien

promptly [prámptli] ADV (soon) pronto; (punctually) puntualmente

promulgate [práməɫget] VT promulgar

prone [pron] ADJ (disposed) propenso, proclive; (face down) boca abajo; (prostrate) postrado

prong [prɔŋ] N púa *f*, diente *m*

pronoun [prónaun] N pronombre *m*

pronounce [prənáuns] VT (enunciate) pronunciar; (declare) declarar

pronounced [prənáunst] ADJ pronunciado

pronunciation [prənʌnsiéʃən] N pronunciación *f*

proof [pruf] N (evidence, test, trial printing) prueba *f*; (of alcohol) graduación *f*, grado *m*; **— of purchase** comprobante de compra *m*; **—reader** corrector -ra de pruebas *mf*; **fifty —** veinticinco por ciento de graduación alcohólica; ADJ **fire—** a prueba de incendios; **water—** impermeable; **bullet—** a prueba de balas

prop [prɑp] N (pole) puntal *m*; (in theater) accesorio *m*; (propeller) hélice *f*; (support) sostén *m*, apoyo *m*; (of a plant) tutor *m*; VT **to — against** apoyar en, sostener en; **to — up** apuntalar, sostener

propaganda [prɑpəgǽndə] N propaganda *f*

propagate [prápəget] VI/VT propagar(se)

propagation [prɑpəgéʃen] N propagación *f*

propane [própen] N propano *m*

propel [prəpéɫ] VT propulsar, impulsar

propeller [prəpélə-] N hélice *f*

propensity [prəpénsɪɒi] N propensión *f*

proper [prápə-] ADJ (appropriate) apropiado; (decorous) decoroso; (genuine) como Dios manda; (correct) correcto; (in math, grammar) propio; **to be — to** ser propio de

property [prápə-ɒi] N (characteristic) propiedad *f*; (real estate) propiedad *f*, finca *f*; (assets) bienes *m pl*

prophecy [práfɪsi] N profecía *f*

prophesy [práfɪsaɪ] VI/VT profetizar

prophet [práfɪt] N profeta -tisa *mf*

prophetic [prəféɒɪk] ADJ profético

propitious [prəpíʃəs] ADJ propicio

proponent [prəpónənt] N (person who proposes) proponente *mf*; (adherent) defensor -ra *mf*

proportion [prəpɔ́rʃən] N proporción *f*; **out of —** desproporcionado; VT proporcionar; **well —ed** bien proporcionado

proposal [prəpózəł] N (suggestion) propuesta *f*; (of marriage, dishonest) proposición *f*

propose [prəpóz] VI/VT (suggest) proponer; VI (ask in marriage) declararse, hacer una proposición de matrimonio; **to — to do something** proponerse hacer algo

proposition [prɑpəzíʃən] N proposición *f*; VT hacer proposiciones deshonestas

proprietor [prəpráɪɪɾɚ] N propietario -ria *mf*

propriety [prəpráɪɪɾi] N decoro *m*

propulsion [prəpʌ́łʃən] N propulsión *f*

prorate [prorét] VT prorratear

prosaic [prozéɪk] ADJ prosaico

prose [proz] N prosa *f*

prosecute [prásɪkjut] VI/VT (take to court) procesar, enjuiciar; VT (pursue) llevar adelante

prosecution [prɑsɪkjúʃən] N (act of prosecuting) procesamiento *m*; (officials who prosecute) ministerio público *m*, fiscalía *f*

prosecutor [prásɪkjuɾɚ] N fiscal *mf*

proselytize [prásəlɪtaɪz] VT convertir; VI ganar prosélitos

prospect [práspɛkt] N (outlook, possibility) perspectiva *f*, expectativa *f*; (candidate) candidato -ta *mf*; (possible client) posible cliente -ta *mf*; VT prospectar; VI **to — for** buscar

prospective [prəspéktɪv] ADJ posible, potencial

prospector [práspɛkɾɚ] N prospector -ora *mf*

prosper [práspɚ] VI prosperar

prosperity [prɑspɛ́rɪɾi] N prosperidad *f*, bonanza *f*

prosperous [práspərəs] ADJ próspero

prostate [prástet] N próstata *f*; **— gland** próstata *f*

prosthesis [prɑsθísɪs] N prótesis *f*

prostitute [prástɪtut] N prostituto -ta *mf*; VT prostituir

prostrate [prástret] VT postrar; ADJ (lying flat, overcome) postrado; (lying face down) boca abajo

protagonist [protǽɡənɪst] N protagonista *mf*

protect [prətɛ́kt] VI/VT proteger, amparar

protection [prətɛ́kʃen] N protección *f*

protectionist [prətɛ́kʃənɪst] ADJ & N proteccionista *mf*

protective [prətɛ́ktɪv] ADJ protector

protector [prətɛ́ktɚ] N protector -ra *mf*

protectorate [prətɛ́ktərɪt] N protectorado *m*

protégé, protégée [próɾəʒe] N protegido -da *mf*

protein [prótin] N proteína *f*

protest [prótɛst] N protesta *f*, reclamación *f*; [prətɛ́st] VI/VT protestar, reclamar

Protestant [práɪɪstənt] ADJ & N protestante *mf*

protestation [protɛstéʃən] N declaración *f*

protocol [próɾəkɔł] N protocolo *m*

proton [prótɑn] N protón *m*

protoplasm [próɾəplæzəm] N protoplasma *m*

prototype [próɾətaɪp] N prototipo *m*

protozoan [proɾəzóən] N protozoario *m*

protract [protrǽkt] VT prolongar

protrude [protrúd] VI sobresalir, proyectarse

protuberance [prətúbərəns] N protuberancia *f*

proud [praʊd] ADJ orgulloso; (haughty) soberbio; **to be — of** enorgullecerse de, ufanarse de

prove [pruv] VT (demonstrate) probar, demostrar; (verify) resultar; VI resultar; **events have —d me right** los hechos me han dado la razón

proverb [právɚb] N proverbio *m*, refrán *m*

provide [prəváɪd] VT (furnish) proveer, proporcionar; (supply) abastecer, aportar; (stipulate) estipular, prevenir; VI **to — for** (support) mantener; (stipulate) estipular; **to — with** proveer de, proporcionar

provided [prəváɪdɪd] CONJ **— (that)** con tal (de) que, siempre que

providence [právɪdəns] N providencia *f*

provider [prəváɪdɚ] N (supplier) proveedor -ra *mf*; (breadwinner) sostén *m*

province [právɪns] N (area) provincia *f*; (competence) competencia *f*

provincial [prəvínʃəł] ADJ (of a province) provincial; (rustic) provinciano, pueblerino; N provinciano -na *mf*

provision [prəvíʒən] N (act of providing, thing provided) provisión *f*, prestación *f*; (precaution) medida *f*, precaución *f*; (clause) estipulación *f*, prevención *f*; **—s** provisiones *f pl*, víveres *m pl*, bastimentos *m pl*

provisional [prəvíʒənəł] ADJ provisional

proviso [prəváɪzo] N condición *f*, estipulación *f*

provocation [prɑvəkéʃən] N provocación *f*

provoke [prəvók] VT provocar

provost [próvost] N vicerrector -ora *mf*

prow [praʊ] N proa *f*

prowess [práʊɪs] N valentía *f*

prowl [praʊł] VI/VT rondar en acecho

proximity [prɑksímɪɾi] N proximidad *f*

proxy [práksi] N (person) apoderado -da *mf*; (power of attorney) poder *m*; **by —** por poder

prude [prud] N mojigato -ta *mf*, gazmoño -ña *mf*

prudence [prúdn̩s] N prudencia *f*

prudent [prúdn̩t] ADJ prudente

prudery [prúDəri] N mojigatería *f*, gazmoñería *f*

prudish [prúDıʃ] ADJ mojigato, gazmoño

prune [prun] N ciruela pasa *f*; VI/VT podar

pry [praı] VT curiosear; **to — into** entrometerse; **to — open** abrir por la fuerza; **to — a secret out** extraer / arrancar un secreto

pseudonym [súdn̩ım] N seudónimo *m*

psoriasis [səráıəsıs] N psoriasis *f*

psychedelic [saıkıdélık] ADJ psicodélico

psychiatrist [saıkáıətrıst] N psiquiatra *mf*

psychiatry [saıkáıətri] N psiquiatría *f*

psychic [sáıkık] ADJ psíquico; N médium *mf*, psíquico -ca *mf*

psychological [saıkəládʒıkəł] ADJ psicológico

psychologist [saıkúlədʒıst] N psicólogo -ga *mf*

psychology [saıkúlədʒi] N psicología *f*

psychopath [sáıkəpæθ] N psicópata *mf*

psychosis [saıkósıs] N psicosis *f*

psychosomatic [saıkosəmǽDık] ADJ psicosomático

psychotherapy [saıkoθérəpi] N psicoterapia *f*

psychotic [saıkáDık] ADJ psicótico

puberty [pjúbə-Di] N pubertad *f*

public [páblık] ADJ público; **— domain** dominio público *m*; **— relations** relaciones públicas *f pl*; **— school** escuela pública *f*; **— service** servicio público *m*; N público *m*

publication [pʌblıkéʃən] N publicación *f*

publicity [pʌblísıDi] N publicidad *f*, propaganda *f*

publish [páblıʃ] VI/VT publicar, editar; **—ing house** editorial *f*

publisher [páblıʃə-] N editor -ra *mf*

puck [pʌk] N puck *m*

pucker [pákə-] VI/VT fruncir(se); N frunce *m*

pudding [púDıŋ] N budín *m*

puddle [pádl̩] N charco *m*

Puerto Rican [pɔrDəríkən] ADJ & N puertorriqueño -ña *mf*

Puerto Rico [pɔrDəríko] N Puerto Rico *m*

puff [pʌf] N (air) resoplido *m*, soplo *m*; (smoke) bocanada *f*; (on a cigarette) pitada *f*, chupada *f*; (of a sleeve) bullón *m*; **— pastry** masa de hojaldre *f*; VI (blow) resoplar; (breathe hard) jadear; (smoke a cigarette) echar bocanadas; **to — up** hincharse; **to — up with pride** henchirse de orgullo

pug [pʌg] N dogo *m*; **— nose** nariz chata *f*

puke [pjuk] VI/VT vomitar, lanzar; N vómito *m*

pull [pʊł] VI/VT (tug) tirar, jalar; (extract) arrancar, extraer; (stretch) estirar; (injure) desgarrarse; **to — apart** destrozar; **to — down** (demolish) demoler; (earn) sacar; **to — for** hinchar; **to — off** conseguir; **to — oneself together** calmarse; **to — over** parar; **to — up** parar; **to — through** salvarse; **to — strings** mover palancas; **to — out** (leave a place) salir; (back out) retirarse; **the train —ed into the station** el tren entró a la estación; N (act of pulling) tirón *m*; (force) fuerza *f*; (influence) influencia *f*; (injury) desgarro *m*

pullet [púlıt] N polla *f*

pulley [púli] N polea *f*, carrucha *f*

pulp [pʌłp] N (of paper, wood, fruit) pulpa *f*; (residue of grape, sugarcane, olive, etc.) bagazo *m*

pulpit [púłpıt] N púlpito *m*

pulsar [pálsɑr] N púlsar *m*

pulsate [pálset] VI latir

pulse [pałs] N pulso *m*; (single pulsation, act of pulsing) pulsación *f*

pulverize [páłvəraız] VT pulverizar(se)

pumice [pámıs] N piedra pómez *f*

pump [pʌmp] N bomba *f*; (shoe) zapatilla *f*, zapato escotado *m*; (for gasoline) surtidor *m*; VI/VT bombear; (inflate) inflar; **to — someone for information** sonsacar (información) a alguien

pumpkin [pámpkın] N calabaza *f*

pun [pʌn] N juego de palabras *m*, retruécano *m*; VI hacer juegos de palabras

punch [pʌntʃ] N (blow) puñetazo *m*; (drink) ponche *m*; (drill) sacabocados *m sg*; (force) fuerza *f*, empuje *m*; **— bowl** ponchera *f*; **— line** remate de un chiste *m*; VI/VT (hit) dar un puñetazo; VT (drive cattle) arriar; (make a hole) agujerear; **to — in / out** marcar tarjeta

punctual [páŋktʃuəł] ADJ puntual

punctuality [pʌŋktʃuǽlıDi] N puntualidad *f*

punctuate [páŋktʃuet] VI/VT puntuar; (interrupt) interrumpir; (accentuate) salpicar

punctuation [pʌŋktʃuéʃən] N puntuación *f*

puncture [páŋktʃə-] VI/VT pinchar(se); **—d tire** neumático pinchado *m*; N (action of perforating) perforación *f*; (hole) pinchazo *m*

pundit [pándıt] N experto -ta *mf*

pungent [pándʒənt] ADJ (acrid) acre; (sarcastic) mordaz

punish [pánıʃ] VT castigar, penar

punishment [pánıʃmənt] N castigo *m*

punitive [pjúnɪdɪv] ADJ punitivo; —
damages daños punitivos *m pl*
punk [pʌŋk] N (inexperienced boy) mocoso
m; (hoodlum) gamberro *m*; (rock) punk *m*;
(punker) punkero -ra *mf*
punt [pʌnt] N (kick) patada de despeje *f*;
(boat) balsa *f*; VI/VT despejar; VI andar en
balsa
puny [pjúni] ADJ endeble, ruin
pupil [pjúpəł] N escolar *mf*; — **of the eye**
pupila *f*, niña *f*
puppet [pápɪt] N títere *m*, monigote *m*; —
show teatro de títeres *m*
puppy [pápi] N cachorro *m*
purchase [pɝ́tʃəs] VI/VT comprar, adquirir; N
compra *f*; (hold) asidero *m*
purchaser [pɝ́tʃəsɚ] N comprador *mf*
pure [pjur] ADJ puro; ADJ & N **—bred**
purasangre *m*
puree [pjuré] N puré *m*
purgative [pɝ́gədɪv] ADJ & N purgante *m*
purgatory [pɝ́gətɔri] N purgatorio *m*
purge [pɝdʒ] VI/VT purgar(se); N purga *f*
purify [pjúrəfaɪ] VI/VT purificar(se),
depurar(se)
purist [pjúrɪst] N purista *mf*
puritanical [pjurɪtǽnɪkəł] ADJ puritano
purity [pjúrɪɖi] N pureza *f*
purple [pɝ́pəł] N morado *m*, púrpura *f*; ADJ
púrpura *inv*, morado
purport [pɝ́pɔrt] N (meaning) significado *m*;
(purpose) propósito *m*; [pɚpórt] VT
pretender
purpose [pɝ́pəs] N propósito *m*, objetivo *m*;
on — adrede, a propósito
purr [pɝ] N ronroneo *m* (also motors); VI
ronronear
purse [pɝs] N bolso *m*, cartera *f*; VT **to** —
one's lips fruncir los labios
pursuant [pɚsúənt] ADV LOC — **to** conforme
a, de acuerdo con
pursue [pɚsú] VT (follow) perseguir; (strive)
dedicarse a; (continue) continuar con;
(practice a profession) ejercer
pursuer [pɚsúɚ] N perseguidor -ora *mf*
pursuit [pɚsút] N (chase) persecución *f*,
seguimiento *m*; (striving for) búsqueda *f*;
(pastime) pasatiempo *m*; (practice)
ejercicio *m*; **in** — **of** (chasing) detrás de;
(striving for) en busca de
pus [pʌs] N pus *m*
push [puʃ] VI/VT (shove) empujar; VT
(pressure) presionar, promover; (sell drugs)
camellear; VI (in childbirth) pujar; **to** —
aside / away apartar; **to** — **forward**
abrirse paso, avanzar; **to** — **open** abrir de
un empujón; **to** — **through** hacer pasar;

to — **a button** apretar un botón; N
empujón *m*; (military) ofensiva *f*;
—-button de botones; **—-up** lagartija *f*
pusher [púʃɚ] N camello *mf*
pushy [púʃi] ADJ insistente
pussy [púsi] N (cat) minino *m*, gatito *m*;
(female genitalia) *vulg* coño *m*; *Am vulg*
concha *f*; **—-whipped man** *vulg*
calzonazos *m sg*; — **willow** sauce *m*
put [put] VT poner, colocar; **to** — **a**
question plantear una pregunta; **to** —
across expresar; **to** — **away** guardar; **to**
— **down** (write down) apuntar; (suppress)
sofocar; (attribute) atribuir; (humiliate)
humillar; (make a deposit) hacer un
depósito; **to** — **into** meter; **to** — **into**
words expresar, decir; **to** — **in writing**
poner por escrito; **to** — **off** (postpone)
aplazar, posponer; (perturb) desagradar; **to**
— **on** ponerse; **to** — **on airs** darse tono;
to — **on weight** engordar; **to** — **out**
(extinguish) apagar, extinguir; (annoy)
molestar; **to** — **the blame** echar la culpa;
to — **to sea** echar al mar; **to** — **up**
(construct) levantar; (lodge) alojar; **to** —
up for sale poner a la venta; **to** — **up**
with aguantar; **—-down** insulto *m*; **I**
felt —-upon sentí que se habían
aprovechado de mí
putrid [pjútrɪd] ADJ putrefacto
putter [pádɚ] VI entretenerse; N putter *m*
putty [pádi] N masilla *f*; VT rellenar con
masilla
puzzle [pázəł] N (jigsaw) rompecabezas *m sg*;
(riddle) acertijo *m*; (problem) enigma *m*;
(crossword) crucigrama *m*; VT dejar
perplejo, desconcertar; VI **to** — **out**
desentrañar; **to** — **over** meditar sobre; **to**
be —d estar perplejo
pygmy [pígmi] N pigmeo -a *mf*
pylon [páɪlɑn] N pilón *m*
pyramid [pírəmɪd] N pirámide *f*
pyromaniac [paɪroméniæk] N pirómano -na
mf
pyrotechnics [paɪrətéknɪks] N pirotecnia *f*
python [páɪθɑn] N pitón *mf*

Qq

Qatar [kətár] N Qatar *m*
Qatari [kətári] ADJ & N catarí *mf*
quack [kwæk] N (sound of duck) graznido *m*;
(charlatan) matasanos *mf*, charlatán -ana

mf; ADJ charlatán; VI graznar

quadrilateral [kwɑdrəlǽDɚəɫ] ADJ & N cuadrilátero *m*

quadriplegic [kwɑdrəplíʤɪk] ADJ & N tetraplégico -ca *mf*

quadruped [kwádrəpɛd] ADJ & N cuadrúpedo *m*

quadruplet [kwɑdrúplɪt] N cuatrillizo -za *mf*

quagmire [kwǽgmaɪr] N (bog) cenagal *m*, atascadero *m*; (crisis) atolladero *m*, atascadero *m*

quail [kweɫ] N codorniz *f*

quaint [kwent] ADJ pintoresco

quake [kwek] N (instance of quaking) temblor *m*; (earthquake) terremoto *m*; VI temblar

qualification [kwɑləfɪkéʃən] N (for a race) clasificación *f*; (requirement) requisito *m*; **without —** sin reservas

qualify [kwáləfaɪ] VT (characterize) calificar; (moderate) moderar; (provide with credentials) capacitar; VI (for a race) clasificarse; (for a position) estar capacitado

quality [kwálɪDi] N (characteristic) cualidad *f*; (excellence) calidad *f*

qualm [kwɔm] N escrúpulo *m*

quantify [kwántəfaɪ] VT cuantificar

quantity [kwántɪDi] N cantidad *f*

quantum mechanics [kwántəmmǝkǽnɪks] N mecánica cuántica *f*

quarantine [kwɔ́rəntin] N cuarentena *f*; VT poner en cuarentena

quarrel [kwɔ́rəɫ] N riña *f*, rencilla *f*; VI reñir, pelear

quarrelsome [kwɔ́rəɫsəm] ADJ pendenciero

quarry [kwɔ́ri] N (stone) cantera *f*; (game) presa *f*; VT explotar

quart [kwɔrt] N cuarto de galón (0.9463 litros) *m*

quarter [kwɔ́rɒɚ] N (one-fourth) cuarto *m*, cuarta parte *f*; (coin) moneda de 25 centavos *f*; (of a sporting match) tiempo *m*; (of a calendar or school year) trimestre *m*; (district) barrio *m*; **— note** negra *f*; **—s** alojamiento *m*; **from all —s** de todas partes; **to give no — to the enemy** no dar cuartel al enemigo; ADJ cuarto; VT (divide) cuartear, dividir en cuartos; (execute) descuartizar; (lodge troops) acuartelar, acantonar

quarterly [kwɔ́rɒɚli] ADV trimestralmente; ADJ trimestral; N publicación trimestral *f*

quartet [kwɔrtét] N cuarteto *m*

quartz [kwɔrts] N cuarzo *m*

quasar [kwézɑr] N cuásar *m*, quásar *m*

quash [kwɑʃ] VT (a rebellion) sofocar; (a decision) anular

quaver [kwévɚ] VI temblar; N temblor *m*; (in music) trémolo *m*

queasy [kwízi] ADJ nauseoso

queen [kwin] N reina *f*; (effeminate male homosexual) *offensive* loca *f*; *offensive* reinona *f*

queer [kwir] ADJ (strange) raro; (eccentric) excéntrico; (homosexual) *offensive* maricón; **to feel —** sentirse raro; N (homosexual) *offensive* marica *m*, maricón *m*; VT comprometer

quell [kwɛɫ] VT (suppress) reprimir, sofocar; (calm) calmar

quench [kwentʃ] VT (flames, thirst) apagar; (passions) aplacar, apagar

query [kwíri] N (question) pregunta *f*; (question mark) signo de interrogación *m*; (doubt) duda *f*; VT (ask) preguntar; (question) expresar dudas; (mark with a question mark) marcar con signo de interrogación

quest [kwɛst] N búsqueda *f*

question [kwéstʃən] N (thing asked) pregunta *f*; (issue) cuestión *f*; **— mark** signo de interrogación *m*; **beyond —** fuera de duda; **that is out of the —** ¡ni pensarlo! VT (ask) preguntar; (interrogate) interrogar; (call into doubt) dudar, cuestionar

questionable [kwéstʃənəbəɫ] ADJ (doubtful) cuestionable, discutible; (morally dubious) equívoco

questioner [kwéstʃənɚ] N interrogador -ra *mf*

questioning [kwéstʃənɪŋ] N interrogatorio *m*; ADJ (asking) interrogador; (doubting) cuestionador

questionnaire [kwɛstʃənér] N cuestionario *m*

quibble [kwíbəɫ] VI (split hairs) sutilizar; (evade) evadir; (argue) andar en dimes y diretes; N (hairsplitting) sutileza *f*; (evasion) evasiva *f*

quiche [kiʃ] N quiche *f*

quick [kwɪk] ADJ rápido, pronto; **—-tempered** irascible, geniudo; **—-witted** agudo; ADV rápido; N (flesh under nails) carne viva *f*; (the living) los vivos; **to cut to the —** herir en lo vivo; **—sand** arena movediza *f*; **—silver** mercurio *m*, azogue *m*

quicken [kwíkən] VI/VT (speed up) acelerar(se), aligerar(se); (liven) avivar(se)

quickly [kwíkli] ADV rápido, deprisa

quickness [kwíknɪs] N (speed) rapidez *f*; (of wit) agudeza *f*

quiet [kwáɪt] ADJ (not noisy) silencioso; (not talking) callado; (restrained) tranquilo; (peaceful, still) reposado; **be —!** ¡silencio!

¡cállate! N (freedom from noise) silencio *m*; (tranquility) tranquilidad *f*, sosiego *m*; VT (make quiet) acallar; (make tranquil) sosegar, tranquilizar, serenar; VI **to — down** calmarse

quill [kwɪł] N (feather) pluma *f*; (hollow base of feather) cañón *m*; (spine on a porcupine) púa *f*

quilt [kwɪłt] N edredón *m*; VI/VT acolchar

quip [kwɪp] N ocurrencia *f*; VI decir ocurrencias

quirk [kwɝk] N excentricidad *f*

quit [kwɪt] VT (a competition) abandonar; (a place) irse de, salir de; (a job) dejar; **to call it —s** abandonar; **to — smoking** dejar de fumar; VI (withdraw) abandonar; (stop) parar; (resign) renunciar

quite [kwaɪt] ADV (very) bastante; (entirely) del todo, enteramente; **— a person** una persona admirable *f*; **— a lot** bastante; **it's — the fashion** está muy de moda

quiver [kwívɚ] VI temblar; N (shake) temblor *m*; (sheath for arrows) carcaj *m*, aljaba *f*

quiz [kwɪz] N (test) prueba *f*; (show) concurso *m*; VI (give a quiz) examinar, poner una prueba; (interrogate) interrogar

quota [kwóᴅə] N cuota *f*

quotation [kwotéʃən] N cita *f*; (of a price) cotización *f*; **— marks** comillas *f pl*

quote [kwot] VI/VT citar; (prices) cotizar; **to — from** citar a; N cita *f*; (of a price) cotización *f*; **in —s** entre comillas

quotient [kwóʃənt] N cociente *m*

Rr

rabbi [rǽbaɪ] N rabino -na *mf*

rabbit [rǽbɪt] N conejo *m*

rabble [rǽbəł] N chusma *f*, plebe *f*, gentuza *f*

rabid [rǽbɪd] ADJ rabioso

rabies [rébiz] N rabia *f*

raccoon [rækún] N mapache *m*

race [res] N (lineage) raza *f*; (competition) carrera *f*; **—horse** caballo de carreras *m*; **—track** (for runners) pista *f*; (for horses) hipódromo *m*; VI (participate in competition) correr, competir en una carrera; (hurry) ir corriendo; (of heart) latir rápido; (of a motor) acelerar; VT (a horse) hacer correr; (an engine) acelerar; **I'll — you** te echo una carrera

racer [résɚ] N corredor -ra *mf*; (horse) caballo de carreras *m*

racial [réʃəł] ADJ racial

racism [résɪzəm] N racismo *m*

rack [ræk] N (for clothes) perchero *m*; (on a vehicle) baca *f*; (for spices) especiero *m*; (for towels) toallero *m*; (torture) potro de tormento *m*; **— and pinion** cremallera *f* y piñón *m*; VT **to be —ed with pain** estar transido de dolor; **to — one's brain** devanarse los sesos; **to — up** acumular

racket [rǽkɪt] N (sports) raqueta *f*; (noise of an impact) estrépito *m*, estruendo *m*; (noise of voices and movement) barahúnda *f*, batahola *f*; (swindle) estafa *f*; (extortion) extorsión *f*

racketeer [rækɪtír] N trapacero -ra *mf*; (swindler) estafador -ra *mf*; (extortionist) extorsionista *mf*; VI (swindle) estafar; (extort) extorsionar

radar [réᴅɑr] N radar *m*

radial [réᴅiəł] ADJ radial

radiance [réᴅiəns] N resplandor *m*, fulgor *m*

radiant [réᴅiənt] ADJ radiante, resplandeciente

radiate [réᴅiet] VI/VT irradiar, radiar; (health) derrochar

radiation [reᴅiéʃən] N radiación *f*

radiator [réᴅieᴅɚ] N radiador *m*

radical [rǽᴅɪkəł] ADJ & N radical *mf*

radicalism [rǽᴅɪkəlɪzəm] N radicalismo *m*

radio [réᴅio] ADJ **—active** radiactivo, radioactivo; N (device, system of communication) radio *f*; **— announcer** locutor -ra *mf*; **— listener** radioescucha *mf*; **— station** radiodifusora *f*; **— telescope** radiotelescopio *m*; **— transmitter** radiotransmisor *m*; **by —** por radio; VT (broadcast) transmitir por radio; VI/VT (call) llamar por radio

radiology [reᴅiálədʒi] N radiología *f*

radish [rǽᴅɪʃ] N rábano *m*

radium [réᴅiəm] N radio *m*

radius [réᴅiəs] N radio *m*

radon [réᴅɑn] N radón *m*

raffle [rǽfəł] N rifa *f*, sorteo *m*; VI rifar, sortear

raft [ræft] N balsa *f*

rafter [rǽftɚ] N viga *f*, cabrio *m*

rag [ræg] N (piece of cloth) trapo *m*, guiñapo *m*; (clothes) harapo *m*, andrajo *m*; **— doll** muñeca de trapo *f*

rage [redʒ] N ira *f*, rabia *f*, cólera *f*; **to be all the —** estar de moda; VI enfurecerse; **to — with anger** bramar de ira

ragged [rǽgɪd] ADJ (ill-clothed) andrajoso, harapiento, desharrapado; (voice) ronco, roto; (on an edge) irregular, desigual; **to be on the — edge** estar al borde

raid [red] N (military) incursión *f*; (by police) allanamiento *m*, redada *f*; (by air) bombardeo aéreo *m*; VI/VT hacer una incursión; VT (attack) atacar; (rob) asaltar; (by the police) allanar

rail [reł] N (of a railroad track) riel *m*, carril *m*; (railing) baranda *f*, barandilla *f*; — **fence** barrera *f*; —**road** ferrocarril *m*; —**road company** empresa ferroviaria *f*; —**road crossing** cruce de ferrocarril *m*; —**road employee** ferroviario -a *mf*; **to** —**road** (goods) transportar por ferrocarril; (laws) hacer aprobar apresuradamente; (a person) condenar injustamente; —**way** ferrocarril *m*; **by** — por ferrocarril

railing [réliŋ] N (barrier) baranda *f*; (on a bridge) pretil *m*; (on a stairway) pasamano *m*

rain [ren] N lluvia *f*; —**bow** arco iris *m*; —**coat** impermeable *m*; —**drop** gota de lluvia *f*; —**fall** precipitación *f*; — **forest** selva tropical *f*; — **gauge** pluviómetro *f*; —**storm** temporal de lluvia *f*; — **water** agua llovediza *f*; VI/VT llover; — **or shine** llueva o truene; **to** — **cats and dogs** llover a cántaros

rainy [réni] ADJ lluvioso

raise [rez] VI/VT (voice, hand, a house, spirits) levantar(se); VT (prices) subir; (an alarm) dar; (a flag) izar; (crops) cultivar; (animals, children) criar; (money) recabar, recaudar; **to** — **a question** plantear una pregunta; **to** — **a racket** armar un alboroto; N aumento *m*

raisin [rézin] N pasa (de uva) *f*

rake [rek] N rastrillo *m*; VI/VT rastrillar; **to** — **in money** amasar dinero

rally [ræli] VI/VT (reorganize troops) reunir(se), juntar(se); (inspire) reanimar; VI (demonstrate) concentrarse; (recuperate) recuperarse; (reinvigorate) recobrar ánimo; (rise in value) repuntar; **to** — **around someone** apoyar a alguien; N (demonstration) concentración *f*; (recovery) recuperación *f*; (rise in prices) subida *f*

RAM (random-access memory) [ræm] N RAM *m*

ram [ræm] N (male sheep) carnero *m*; (tool for battering) ariete *m*; (part of a ship) espolón *m*; VT chocar contra; **to** — **a boat** embestir un buque con el espolón

ramble [ræmbəł] VI vagar; **to** — **on** divagar; N paseo *m*

ramp [ræmp] N rampa *f*

rampage [ræmpeʤ] N **to go on a** — andar destrozando todo; VI andar destrozando todo

rampant [ræmpənt] ADJ desenfrenado

ranch [rænʧ] N hacienda *f*; *Mex* rancho *m*

rancid [rænsɪd] ADJ rancio

rancor [ræŋkɚ] N rencor *m*

random [rændəm] ADJ aleatorio, azaroso; **at** — al azar; — **access memory** memoria de acceso directo *f*

range [renʤ] N (gamut) gama *f*; (of a gun) alcance *m*; (amplitude of variation) fluctuación *f*; (of mountains) cadena *f*; (for shooting) campo de tiro *m*; (of an aircraft) autonomía *f*; (grazing place) campo abierto *m*; (stove) cocina *f*; *Mex* estufa *f*; — **finder** telémetro *m*; — **of vision** alcance visual *m*; VT (align) alinear; (of a gun) tener alcance; VI (vary) oscilar; (be found in an area) extenderse; **his children** — **in age between 2 and 10** sus hijos van en edad entre 2 y 10

ranger [rénʤɚ] N (in a park) guardabosques *mf*; (soldier) guardia de asalto *m*

rank [ræŋk] N (in a hierarchy) rango *m*, grado *m*; (line) fila *f*; — **and file** (of an army) tropa *f sg*; **the** —**s** (soldiers) la tropa; (union members) bases *f pl*; **a sculptor of the first** — un escultor de primer orden; VT (arrange) poner en orden de importancia; VI (rate) figurar; **to** — **high** tener alto rango; **to** — **second** estar clasificado en el segundo lugar; ADJ (smelly) hediondo; (growing vigorously) exuberante

ransack [rænsæk] VT saquear, desvalijar

ransom [rænsəm] N rescate *m*; VT rescatar

rant [rænt] VI/VT despotricar

rap [ræp] VI/VT (strike) golpear; (chat) charlar; VI rapear, cantar rap; N (blow) golpe *m*; (accusation) cargo *m*; **to take the** — ser el cabeza de turco; — **music** música rap *f*

rapacious [rəpéʃəs] ADJ rapaz

rape [rep] N (violation) violación *f*; (statutory) estupro *m*; (plant) colza *f*; (grape pulp) orujo *m*; VT violar

rapid [ræpɪd] ADJ rápido; N —**s** rápidos *m pl*

rapidity [rəpídɪti] N rapidez *f*

rapport [rəpór] N relación *f*

rapt [ræpt] ADJ extasiado

rapture [ræpʧɚ] N éxtasis *m*, embeleso *m*; **to go into a** — arrobarse

rare [rer] ADJ (infrequent) raro, poco frecuente, extraño; (of gas, earth) raro; (thin, of air) enrarecido; (excellent) excepcional; (not well-done) crudo; — **earths** tierras raras *f pl*

rarity [rériɾi] N rareza *f*; (of air) enrarecimiento *m*

rascal [ráeskəł] N bribón *m*, bellaco *m*, pícaro *m*; *Sp* golfo *m*; **you little —**! ¡bandido! ¡sinvergüenza!

rash [ræʃ] ADJ (thoughtless) precipitado, temerario; N sarpullido *m*

raspberry [ráezbɛri] N frambuesa *f*; **— bush** frambueso *m*

raspy [ráespi] ADJ ronco, áspero

rat [ræt] N rata *f*; **I smell a —** aquí hay gato encerrado; VI (one's hair) cardar; **to — on** chivar, delatar

ratchet [ráetʃit] N trinquete *m*

rate [ret] N (amount of interest) tasa *f*; (charge) tarifa *f*; (unit charge for insurance) prima *f*; (pace) paso *m*, ritmo *m*; **— of exchange** tipo de cambio *m*; **at any —** en todo caso; **at this —** a este ritmo; **at the — of** a razón de; VT (estimate) valorar, estimar; (esteem) considerar; **he —s as the best** se le considera como el mejor; **he —s high** se le tiene en alta estima

rather [ráeðɚ] ADV (somewhat) bastante; (more precisely) más bien; **— than** en vez de; **I would — die than** antes la muerte que; **I would — not go** prefiero no ir

ratify [ráɛɒəfaɪ] VT ratificar

rating [réɒɪŋ] N (act of adjudging) calificación *f*; (for credit) clasificación *f*; (TV quotient) rating televisivo *m*, índice de audiencia *m*

ratio [réʃio] N razón *f*, proporción *f*

ration [ráeʃən] N ración *f*; VT racionar

rational [ráeʃənəł] ADJ racional

rationale [ræʃənáeł] N motivo *m*

rationalize [ráeʃənəlaɪz] VI/VT racionalizar

rationing [ráeʃənɪŋ] N racionamiento *m*

rattle [ráedł] VI (bang) golpetear; (move noisily) traquetear; **to — on** parlotear; VT hacer sonar, sacudir; **to — off** recitar; N (banging) golpeteo *m*; (movement) traqueteo *m*; (toy) sonaja *f*, sonajero *m*; (of a rattlesnake) cascabel *m*; (of death) estertor *m*; **—snake** víbora de cascabel *f*

raucous [rɔ́kəs] ADJ (loud) estridente; (rowdy) escandaloso

ravage [ráevɪdʒ] VI/VT asolar, arruinar; N estrago *m*

rave [rev] VI (rant) desvariar, delirar; VI/VT (roar) bramar; **to — about** deshacerse en elogios; N crítica muy favorable *f*

raven [révən] N cuervo *m*; ADJ azabache

ravenous [ráevənəs] ADJ voraz, famélico; **to be —** tener un hambre canina

ravine [rəvín] N quebrada *f*, barranco *m*, cañada *f*

raving [révɪŋ] ADJ delirante; (extraordinary)

extraordinario; **— mad** loco de remate; N desvarío *m*

ravish [ráevɪʃ] VT (kidnap) raptar, secuestrar; (rape) violar

raw [rɔ] ADJ (uncooked, unprocessed, damp and cold) crudo; (of vegetables) fresco, crudo; (unadorned) descarnado; **— flesh** carne viva *f*; **— material** materia prima *f*; **— sugar** azúcar bruto *m*; N **—hide** cuero crudo *m*

ray [re] N (beam) rayo *m*; (stingray) raya *f*

rayon [réɑn] N rayón *m*

raze [rez] VT arrasar, asolar

razor [rézɚ] N (device with blade) maquinilla de afeitar *f*, rasuradora *f*; (barber's tool) navaja *f*; (electric) rasuradora electrica *f*; **— blade** hoja de afeitar *f*; **safety —** navaja de seguridad *f*

reach [ritʃ] VI/VT (extend) alcanzar; VT (arrive at) llegar a; (contact) ponerse en contacto con; **to — for** tratar de agarrar; *Sp* tratar de coger; **to — into** meter la mano en; **to — out one's hand** alargar la mano; N alcance *m*; **beyond his —** fuera de su alcance; **within his —** a su alcance; **far —es** zona remota *f*

react [riáekt] VI reaccionar

reaction [riáekʃən] N reacción *f*

reactionary [riáekʃənɛri] ADJ & N reaccionario -ria *mf*

reactor [riáektɚ] N reactor *m*

read [rid] VI/VT leer; VT (interpret) interpretar; (give as a reading) decir; (indicate) indicar, marcar; **it —s easily** es fácil de leer; N lectura *f*

reader [rídɚ] N (person who reads) lector -ra *mf*; (schoolbook) libro de lectura *m*, cartilla *f*; (anthology) antología *f*

readily [rédḷi] ADV fácilmente

readiness [rédɪnɪs] N estado de preparación *m*; (willingness) buena disposición *f*; **to be in —** estar preparado, estar listo

reading [rídɪŋ] N lectura *f*; (interpretation) interpretación *f*; **— room** sala de lectura *f*

readjust [riədʒʌ́st] VI/VT (improve fit) reajustar; (acclimate) readaptar

readjustment [riədʒʌ́stmənt] N (fitting) reajuste *m*; (acclimation) readaptación *f*

ready [rédi] ADJ (prepared) listo, preparado, pronto; (willing) dispuesto; (available) disponible; (quick) rápido; **—-made** de confección

reagent [riédʒənt] ADJ & N reactivo *m*

real [riɫ] ADJ real, verdadero; **— estate** bienes raíces *m pl*, bienes inmuebles *m pl*

realism [ríəlɪzəm] N realismo *m*

realist [ríəlɪst] N realista *mf*

realistic [riəlístɪk] ADJ realista

reality [riǽlɪɒi] N realidad *f*; **— check** ajuste de perspectiva *m*

realization [riəlɪzéʃən] N (making real) realización *f*; (understanding) comprensión *f*

realize [ríələaɪz] VT (achieve) realizar; (comprehend) darse cuenta de, comprobar

realm [rɛɫm] N (kingdom) reino *m*; (domain) terreno *m*, esfera *f*

realtortm [ríəɫtɚ] N agente inmobiliario -ria *mf*

reap [rip] VI/VT (cut with sickle) segar; (harvest) cosechar; **to — a benefit** obtener, sacar

reaper [rípɚ] N (person) segador -ora *mf*; (machine) segadora *f*; (death) la Parca, la Muerte

reappear [riəpír] VI reaparecer

rear [rir] ADJ trasero, posterior; **—guard** retaguardia *f*; N (space at the back) parte de atrás *f*, fondo *m*; (backside) trasero *m*, posaderas *f pl*; **— end** trasero *m*; **—view mirror** espejo retrovisor *m*; VT (raise) criar; VI (rise on back legs) encabritarse, empinarse

reason [rízən] N (faculty) razón *f*; (cause) motivo *m*, razón *f*; **by — of** por causa de; **it stands to —** es lógico; VT razonar; **to — out** resolver por medio de la razón; **to — with** hacer entrar en razón

reasonable [rízənəbəɫ] ADJ razonable; (in price) módico, moderado

reasoning [rízənɪŋ] N razonamiento *m*, raciocinio *m*; ADJ racional

reassure [riəʃúr] VT tranquilizar

rebate [ríbet] N reembolso *m*, reintegro *m*; VT reembolsar, reintegrar

rebel [rébəɫ] ADJ & N rebelde *mf*, insurrecto -ta *mf*; [ɪbéɫ] VI rebelarse

rebellion [ɪbéljən] N rebelión *f*

rebellious [ɪbéljəs] ADJ rebelde, insurrecto

rebelliousness [ɪbéljəsnɪs] N rebeldía *f*

rebound [ɪbáʊnd] VI (bounce) rebotar; (recover) recuperarse; [ríbaʊnd] N rebote *m*; **on the —** de rebote

rebuff [ɪbʌ́f] N desaire *m*, repulsa *f*; VT desairar, rechazar

rebuild [ribíɫd] VI/VT reconstruir, reedificar; (auto engine) reacondicionar

rebuke [ɪbjúk] VT reprender, reprochar; N reproche *m*, reprimenda *f*

recall [ɪkɔ́ɫ] VT (remember) recordar; (call back) retirar; (remove from office) destituir; [ríkɔɫ] N (memory) memoria *f*; (of a diplomat, product) retirada *f*; (from office) destitución *f*

recapitulate [rikəpítʃəlet] VI/VT recapitular

recast [rikǽst] VT refundir

recede [rɪsíd] VI retroceder; (of hairline) tener entradas

receipt [rɪsít] N recibo *m*; **upon — of** al recibo de; **—s** entradas *f pl*, ingresos *m pl*

receive [rɪsív] VI/VT recibir; (suggestions) acoger, recibir; (a broadcast) captar, recibir

receiver [rɪsívɚ] N recibidor -ora *mf*; (of a telephone) auricular *m*; (of a television or radio, in sports) receptor *m*; (of a business) síndico *m*

recent [rísənt] ADJ reciente

receptacle [rɪséptəkəɫ] N receptáculo *m*

reception [rɪsépʃən] N (hotel, social event, TV) recepción *f*; (act of receiving) recibimiento *m*, acogida *f*; **— room** recibidor *m*

recess [rísɛs] N (niche) nicho *m*, entrante *m*; (pause) descanso *m*; (playtime) recreo *m*; **in the —es of** en lo más recóndito de; VI/VT (a meeting) interrumpir; VT (a wall) hacer un nicho en

recession [rɪséʃən] N (act of receding) retroceso *m*; (economic) recesión *f*

recipe [résəpi] N receta *f*

recipient [rɪsípiənt] N destinatario -ria *mf*

reciprocal [rɪsíprəkəɫ] ADJ recíproco

reciprocate [rɪsíprəket] VI/VT corresponder (a)

recital [rɪsáɪdɫ] N recital *m*

recitation [rɛsɪtéʃən] N recitación *f*

recite [rɪsáɪt] VI/VT recitar

reckless [réklɪs] ADJ (driver) temerario, imprudente; (speed) desenfrenado

recklessness [réklɪsnɪs] N temeridad *f*, imprudencia *f*

reckon [rékən] VI/VT calcular; (consider) considerar; (think) suponer

reckoning [rékənɪŋ] N (computation) cálculo *m*; (settlement of accounts) ajuste de cuentas *m*; **the day of —** el día del juicio final

reclaim [rɪklém] VT (win back, recover) recuperar; (make land usable) ganar, sanear

recline [rɪkláɪn] VI/VT reclinar(se), recostar(se)

recluse [réklus] ADJ & N solitario -ria *mf*, ermitaño -ña *mf*

recognition [rɛkəgníʃən] N reconocimiento *m*

recognize [rékəgnaɪz] VT reconocer

recoil [ɪkɔ́ɪɫ] VI (firearm) dar un culatazo; (move back) retroceder; [ríkɔɪɫ] N (of a gun) culatazo *m*; (move back) retroceso *m*

recollect [rɛkəlékt] VI/VT recordar

recollection [rɛkəlékʃən] N recuerdo *m*

recommend [rɛkəmɛ́nd] VI/VT recomendar
recommendation [rɛkəmɛndéʃən] N recomendación *f*
recompense [rékəmpɛns] VI/VT recompensar; N recompensa *f*
reconcile [rékənsaɪł] VT (persons) reconciliar; (statements) conciliar; **to — oneself to** resignarse a, conformarse con
reconciliation [rɛkənsɪliéʃən] N reconciliación *f*
reconnoiter [rikənɔ́ɪDɚ] VT reconocer; VI hacer un reconocimiento
reconsider [rikənsíDɚ] VI/VT reconsiderar
reconstruct [rikənstrʌ́kt] VT reconstruir
reconstruction [rikənstrʌ́kʃən] N reconstrucción *f*
record [rékɚd] N (account) registro *m*, asiento *m*; (account of a meeting) acta *f*; (of criminal acts) antecedentes *m pl*; (of past activities) historial *m*, hoja de servicios *f*; (phonographic) disco *m*; (best performance) récord *m*, marca *f*; **— player** tocadiscos *m sg*; **off the —** extraoficialmente; [rɪkɔ́rd] VI/VT (write down) registrar, apuntar; (cut a recording) grabar
recorder [rɪkɔ́rDɚ] N (archivist) archivero -ra *mf*; (sound device) grabadora *f*; (musical instrument) flauta dulce *f*
recording [rɪkɔ́rDɪŋ] N grabación *f*; **— company** grabadora *f*
recount [rɪkáʊnt] VT (tell) narrar, relatar; [ríkaʊnt] (count again) recontar
recourse [ríkɔrs] N recurso *m*; **to have — to** recurrir a
recover [rɪkʌ́vɚ] VI/VT recobrar(se), recuperar(se); VI (lost health) restablecerse; VT (lost time, property) recuperar; (damages) obtener indemnización
recovery [rɪkʌ́vəri] N recuperación *f*, recobro *m*; (from a lawsuit) indemnización *f*
recreation [rɛkriéʃən] N recreación *f*, recreo *m*, esparcimiento *m*
recreational [rɛkriéʃənəł] ADJ de recreo; **— drug** droga de recreo *f*; **— vehicle** caravana *f*
recriminate [rɪkrímənet] VI/VT recriminar
recruit [rɪkrút] N recluta *mf*; VI/VT reclutar
recruitment [rɪkrútmənt] N reclutamiento *m*, recluta *f*
rectangle [réktæŋgəł] N rectángulo *m*
rectify [réktəfaɪ] VT rectificar
rector [réktɚ] N rector -ra *mf*
rectum [réktəm] N recto *m*
recuperate [rɪkúpəret] VI/VT recuperar(se), recobrar(se)
recur [rɪkɔ́] VI volver a ocurrir, repetirse

recycle [risáɪkəł] VI/VT reciclar
red [rɛd] ADJ & N rojo *m*, colorado *m*; **— blood cell** glóbulo rojo *m*; **—-handed** *fam* in fraganti; **—headed** pelirrojo; **—-hot** candente, al rojo vivo; **— light** luz roja *f*; **—neck** granjero -ra blanco -ca pobre *mf*; **— pepper** pimienta de cayena *f*; **— snapper** pargo *m*; **— tape** trámites *m pl*; **— wine** vino tinto *m*; **—wood** secoya / secuoya *f*; **in the —** en números rojos; **to see —** enfurecerse
redden [rédn̩] VI/VT enrojecer, ruborizar(se)
reddish [rédɪʃ] ADJ rojizo, bermejo
redeem [rɪdím] VT (deliver from sin) redimir; (pay off a mortgage) cancelar; (buy back) desempeñar; (exchange) canjear; (fulfill) cumplir
redemption [rɪdémpʃən] N redención *f*; (of something pawned) desempeño *m*
redness [rédnɪs] N rojez *f*; (inflammation) inflamación *f*
redress [rídrɛs] N reparación *f*, desagravio *m*; [rɪdrés] VT reparar, desagraviar
reduce [rɪdús] VI/VT reducir(se); **she was —d to tears** se echó a llorar
reduction [rɪdʌ́kʃən] N reducción *f*
redundant [rɪdʌ́ndənt] ADJ (repetitive) redundante; (superfluous) superfluo
reed [rid] N caña *f*, junco *m*, carrizo *m*; (of a musical instrument) lengüeta *f*
reef [rif] N (underwater ridge) escollo *m*; (of coral) arrecife *m*
reek [rik] VI heder, apestar; N hedor *m*
reel [rił] N carrete *m*, bobina *f*; VT (on a spool) bobinar; VI tambalearse; **to — off** recitar; **to — in a fish** sacar un pez del agua
reelect [riɪlékt] VT reelegir
reelection [riɪlékʃən] N reelección *f*
reestablish [riɪstǽblɪʃ] VT restablecer
refer [rɪfɚ́] VI referir; (direct to a source of information) remitir; (direct to a doctor) mandar; (mention) referirse a, aludir; (look up) consultar
referee [rɛfərí] N árbitro *m*; VT (a game) arbitrar; (a submission) hacer el referato
reference [réfərəns] N (mention) referencia *f*; **— book** libro de consulta *m*; **with — to** con respecto a, respecto de
referendum [rɛfəréndəm] N referéndum *m*
referral [rɪfɚ́əł] N **he gave me a — to a specialist** me mandó con un especialista
refill [rifíł] VI/VT rellenar; [rífɪł] N (for a pen) repuesto *m*; (for a lighter) carga *f*; **may I have a —?** ¿me sirve más?
refine [rɪfáɪn] VT (purify) refinar; (polish) refinar, pulir

refined [rɪfáɪnd] ADJ refinado

refinement [rɪfáɪnmənt] N (of manners) refinamiento *m*, pulimento *m*; (of oil) refinación *f*

refinery [rɪfáɪnəri] N refinería *f*; (of sugar) ingenio *m*

reflect [rɪflékt] VI/VT (mirror) reflejar; VI (ponder) reflexionar; **to — poorly on** desacreditar

reflection [rɪflékʃən] N (image) reflejo *m*; (consideration) reflexión *f*; (unfavorable observation) tacha *f*; **on —** pensándolo bien

reflector [rɪfléktɚ] N reflector *m*

reflex [rífleks] ADJ & N reflejo *m*

reflexive [rɪfléksɪv] ADJ reflexivo

reform [rɪfɔ́rm] VI/VT reformar(se); N reforma *f*

reformation [refɚméʃən] N reforma *f*

reformatory [rɪfɔ́rmətɔri] N reformatorio *m*

reformer [rɪfɔ́rmɚ] N reformador -ra *mf*, reformista *mf*

refraction [rɪfrǽkʃən] N refracción *f*

refractory [rɪfrǽktəri] ADJ (not malleable) refractario; (rebellious) rebelde

refrain [rɪfrén] VI abstenerse; N estribillo *m*

refresh [rɪfréʃ] VI/VT refrescar(se)

refreshing [rɪfréʃɪŋ] ADJ (drink) refrescante; (sleep) reparador; (honesty) agradable

refreshment [rɪfréʃmənt] N (drink) refresco *m*; (food) refrigerio *m*

refrigerate [rɪfrídʒəret] VT refrigerar

refrigeration [rɪfrɪdʒəréʃən] N refrigeración *f*

refrigerator [rɪfrídʒəreDɚ] N *Sp* frigorífico *m*, nevera *f*; *Am* refrigerador *m*; *RP* heladera *f*

refuge [réfjudʒ] N refugio *m*

refugee [refjudʒí] N refugiado -da *mf*

refund [rífʌnd] N reembolso *m*; [rɪfʌ́nd] VT reembolsar

refurbish [rɪfɚ́bɪʃ] VT restaurar

refusal [rɪfjúzəł] N negativa *f*, rechazo *m*; **first —** opción *f*

refuse [rɪfjúz] VI/VT (deny a request) rehusarse (a); (decline to accept) negarse (a); VT (reject) rechazar, desechar; **to — to** rehusarse a, negarse a; [réfjus] N desechos *m pl*, desperdicios *m pl*

refute [rɪfjút] VT refutar, rebatir

regain [rɪgén] VT (recover) recobrar; (get back to) volver a

regal [rígəł] ADJ regio, real

regard [rɪgárd] VT (consider) considerar; (esteem) estimar; **as —s** en cuanto a; N (consideration) consideración *f*; (esteem) respeto *m*, estima *f*; **—s** recuerdos *m pl*, saludos *m pl*; **with — to** con respecto a

regarding [rɪgárDɪŋ] PREP con respecto a

regardless [rɪgárdlɪs] ADV LOC **— of** independientemente de

regenerate [rɪdʒénəret] VI/VT regenerar(se)

regent [rídʒənt] N regente -ta *mf*

reggae [rége] N reggae *m*

regime [rɪʒím] N régimen *m*

regiment [rédʒəmənt] N regimiento *m*

region [rídʒən] N región *f*

register [rédʒɪstɚ] N (recording, range of voice) registro *m*; (entry) asiento *m*; VI/VT (enter into a list) registrar(se); (enroll) matricular(se), inscribir(se); VT (indicate) indicar, registrar; (a letter) certificar; VI (appear) aparecer; **that didn't —** no cayó en la cuenta

registered [rédʒɪstɚd] ADJ registrado; **— mail** correo certificado *m*; **— nurse** enfermero -ra titulado -da *mf*; **— trademark** marca registrada *f*

registrar [rédʒɪstrar] N secretario -ria de admisiones *mf*

registration [redʒɪstréʃən] N registro *m*; (of a car) matrícula *f*; (of a student) inscripción *f*

regret [rɪgrét] VT (feel sorry) lamentar; (feel rueful) arrepentirse de; N arrepentimiento *m*; **to send —s** enviar sus excusas

regretful [rɪgrétfəł] ADJ lleno de remordimientos

regrettable [rɪgréDəbəł] ADJ lamentable

regroup [rigrúp] VT reagrupar; VI reorganizarse

regular [régjəlɚ] ADJ (symmetrical, uniform) regular; (normal) normal; (habitual) habitual; **a — fool** un verdadero necio; **a — guy** un buen tipo; (habitual customer) parroquiano -na *mf*; (soldier) soldado de línea *m*

regularity [regjəlǽrɪDi] N regularidad *f*

regulate [régjəlet] VT (control) regular; (make regular) regularizar

regulation [regjəléʃən] N regulación *f*; **—s** reglamento *m*

regulator [régjəleDɚ] N regulador *m*

regurgitate [rigɚ́dʒɪtet] VI/VT regurgitar

rehabilitate [rihəbílɪtet] VI/VT rehabilitar(se)

rehearsal [rɪhɚ́səł] N ensayo *m*

rehearse [rɪhɚ́s] VI/VT ensayar

reign [ren] N reino *m*, reinado *m*; VI reinar

reimburse [riɪmbɚ́s] VI/VT reembolsar

reimbursement [riɪmbɚ́smənt] N reembolso *m*

rein [ren] N rienda *f* (also control); VI **to — in** dominar, refrenar

reincarnation [riɪnkɑrnéʃən] N reencarnación *f*

reindeer [réndɪr] N reno *m*

reinforce [riɪnfɔ́rs] VT reforzar
reinforcement [riɪnfɔ́rsmənt] N refuerzo *m*
reiterate [riíDəret] VT reiterar
reject [rɪʤékt] VT rechazar; [ríʤɛkt] N (thing) cosa rechazada *f*, desecho *m*; (person) rechazado -da *mf*
rejoice [rɪʤɔ́ɪs] VI regocijarse
rejoicing [rɪʤɔ́ɪsɪŋ] N regocijo *m*
rejoin [riʤɔ́ɪn] VT (come again into group) reincorporarse a; VI/VT (reunite) volver a unir(se); [riʤɔ́ɪn] VI/VT replicar
rejuvenate [rɪʤúvənet] VI/VT rejuvenecer
relapse [rɪlǽps] VI (into bad health) recaer; (into crime) reincidir; [rílæps] N (into bad health) recaída *f*; (into crime) reincidencia *f*
relate [rɪlét] VT (tell) relatar, narrar; (connect) relacionar; VI **to — to** relacionarse con
related [rɪléDɪd] ADJ (connected) relacionado; (kin) emparentado
relation [rɪléʃən] N (association) relación *f*; (act of narrating) narración *f*; (kinship) parentesco *m*; (relative) pariente -ta *mf*; **with — to** con respecto a
relationship [rɪléʃənʃɪp] N relación *f*
relative [réləDɪv] ADJ relativo; N pariente -ta *mf*, allegado -da *mf*; **— to** relativo a, referente a
relax [rɪlǽks] VI/VT relajar(se), distender(se); VT (grip) aflojar
relaxation [rilækséʃən] N (recreation) esparcimiento *m*, recreo *m*; (loosening) relajamiento *m*, relajación *f*
relay [ríle] N relevo *m*, posta *f*; (electrical) relé *m*; **— race** carrera de relevos / postas *f*; [rɪlé] VT transmitir; **to — a broadcast** transmitir un programa
release [rɪlís] VT (let go) soltar; (free prisoners) librar, poner en libertad; (energy) liberar; (news) divulgar; (discharge from hospital) dar de alta; N (liberation) liberación *f*; (permission) permiso *m*; (of film) estreno *m*; (of gas) escape *m*; (of energy) desprendimiento *m*
relegate [rélɪget] VT relegar
relent [rɪlént] VI aplacarse
relentless [rɪléntlɪs] ADJ implacable
relevant [rélɪvənt] ADJ pertinente
reliability [rɪlaɪəbílɪDi] N fiabilidad *f*, confiabilidad *f*
reliable [rɪláɪəbəł] ADJ fiable, confiable; (a person) formal
reliance [rɪláɪəns] N (dependency) dependencia *f*; (trust) confianza *f*
relic [rélɪk] N reliquia *f*
relief [rɪlíf] N (ease) alivio *m*; (aid) ayuda *f*; (projection) relieve *m*; (soldier) relevo *m*;

in — en relieve; **— map** mapa en relieve *m*
relieve [rɪlív] VT (alleviate) aliviar; (free) liberar; (replace) relevar; VI **to — oneself** orinar
religion [rɪlíʤən] N religión *f*
religious [rɪlíʤəs] ADJ religioso
relinquish [rɪlíŋkwɪʃ] VT (give up) renunciar; (let go) soltar
relish [rélɪʃ] VT (to like the taste) saborear, paladear; (enjoy) disfrutar; N (enjoyment) gusto *m*; (condiment) condimento de pepinillos en vinagre *m*
relocate [rilóket] VI/VT trasladar(se)
reluctance [rɪláktəns] N renuencia *f*
reluctant [rɪláktənt] ADJ renuente, reacio
rely [rɪláɪ] VI **to — on** (trust) confiar en; (depend on) depender de
REM (rapid eye movement) [ɑriém] N REM *m*
remain [rɪmén] VI (continue to be) seguir siendo; (stay) quedar(se), permanecer; (to be left) quedar, restar; (to be left over) sobrar; N **—s** restos *m pl*
remainder [rɪméndɚ] N resto *m*, remanente *m*
remake [rimék] VT rehacer; (film) hacer de nuevo; [rímek] N nueva versión *f*
remark [rɪmárk] VT (comment) comentar, observar; (notice) notar, observar; **to — on** comentar; N observación *f*, comentario *m*
remarkable [rɪmárkəbəł] ADJ notable
remedial [rɪmíDiəł] ADJ (rehabilitative) rehabilitador; (to improve skills) de recuperación
remedy [rémɪDi] N (solution) remedio *m*; (cure) cura *f*; VT (solve) remediar, subsanar; (heal) curar
remember [rɪmémbɚ] VI/VT recordar, acordarse (de); **— me to him** mándale saludos míos
remind [rɪmáɪnd] VT recordar
reminder [rɪmáɪndɚ] N (of a date, deadline) recordatorio *m*; (warning) advertencia *f*
reminiscence [remənísəns] N reminiscencia *f*, recuerdo *m*
remiss [rɪmís] ADJ negligente
remission [rɪmíʃən] N remisión *f*
remit [rɪmít] VI/VT remitir
remittance [rɪmítṇs] N remesa *f*, giro *m*
remnant [rémnənt] N (remainder) resto *m*; (of fabric) retazo *m*, retal *m*; (vestige) vestigio *m*
remodel [rimádł] VI/VT remodelar
remorse [rɪmɔ́rs] N remordimiento *m*
remote [rɪmót] ADJ (far away) remoto,

recóndito; (aloof) distante; (in kinship) lejano; N — **control** control remoto *m*, mando a distancia *m*

removal [rɪmúvəł] N (dismissal) deposición *f*; (elimination) eliminación *f*; (extirpation) extirpación *f*

remove [rɪmúv] VT (an obstacle) remover; (take away, take off) quitar; (dismiss) deponer; (eliminate) eliminar; (extirpate) extirpar; **to — from office** separar / apartar del cargo

renaissance [rénɪsɑns] N renacimiento *m*

rend [rɛnd] VI/VT desgarrar(se), rajar(se)

render [réndɚ] VT (give) dar; (cause to become) dejar; (depict) representar; (translate) traducir; (homage, account) rendir; (services, assistance) prestar; (fat) derretir; (a verdict) pronunciar; **to — useless** inutilizar

rendition [rɛndíʃən] N (translation) traducción *f*; (interpretation) interpretación *f*, versión *f*

renegade [rénɪged] N renegado -da *mf*

renew [rɪnú] VT (vows, contract) renovar; (furniture) restaurar; (friendship, effort) reanudar; (a loan) prorrogar

renewal [rɪnúəł] N (of vows, contract) renovación *f*; (of furniture) restauración *f*; (of friendship, effort) reanudación *f*; (of loan) prórroga *f*

renounce [rɪnáuns] VT (give up) renunciar a; (repudiate) repudiar, renegar de

renovate [rénəvet] VT renovar

renown [rɪnáun] N renombre *m*

renowned [rɪnáund] ADJ renombrado

rent [rɛnt] N (monthly payment) alquiler *m*, arrendamiento *m*; **for** — se alquila, se arrienda; (fissure) rajadura *f*, hendidura *f*; (tear) rasgadura *f*; (schism) escisión *f*; VI/VT (lease) alquilar, arrendar

rental [rɛntl] ADJ de alquiler; N alquiler *m*, arrendamiento *m*

renter [rɛntɚ] N inquilino -na *mf*

renunciation [rɪnʌnsiéʃən] N renuncia *f*

reopen [riópən] VI/VT (doors) reabrir(se); (negotiations) reanudar(se)

reorganize [riɔ́rgənaɪz] VI/VT reorganizar(se)

repair [rɪpér] VT (fix) reparar, arreglar, componer; (shoes) remendar; **to — to** acudir a; N (fixing) reparación *f*; (of shoes) remiendo *m*, compostura *f*; **in —** en buen estado; **—man** técnico -ca en reparaciones *mf*

reparation [rɛpəréʃən] N reparación *f*, indemnización *f*

repay [rɪpé] VT (return money, favor) devolver; (pay off) pagar

repayment [rɪpémənt] N (of an object) devolución *f*; (of a sum) reembolso *m*; (of a loan) pago *m*

repeal [rɪpíł] VT derogar, revocar, abrogar; N derogación *f*, revocación *f*, abrogación *f*

repeat [rɪpít] VI/VT repetir; N repetición *f*

repeated [rɪpíDɪd] ADJ repetido

repel [rɪpéł] VI/VT repeler; (an attack) rechazar

repellent [rɪpélənt] ADJ & N repelente *m*

repent [rɪpént] VI/VT arrepentirse (de)

repentance [rɪpéntəns] N arrepentimiento *m*

repentant [rɪpéntənt] ADJ arrepentido, pesaroso

repercussion [rɛpɚkáʃən] N repercusión *f*; **to have —s** repercutir

repertoire [répɚtwar] N repertorio *m*

repetition [rɛpɪtíʃən] N repetición *f*

replace [rɪplés] VT (place again) volver a colocar; (substitute for) reemplazar; (provide a substitute for) reponer

replaceable [rɪplésəbəł] ADJ reemplazable, sustituible

replacement [rɪplésmənt] N (substitute, substitution) reemplazo *m*; (making up for) reposición *f*

replenish [rɪplénɪʃ] VI/VT (supply) reabastecer; (fill again) rellenar

replete [rɪplít] ADJ repleto

replica [réplɪkə] N réplica *f*

replicate [réplɪket] VT reproducir

reply [rɪplái] VI replicar, contestar; N réplica *f*, contestación *f*

report [rɪpɔ́rt] VT (recount) relatar; (make a crime known, denounce) denunciar; (make an accident known) dar parte de; VI hacer un informe, informar; **to — for duty** presentarse; **to — on** hacer un informe sobre; **to — sick** dar parte de enfermo, reportarse enfermo; **it is —ed that** se dice que; N informe *m*; (rumor) rumor *m*; (loud noise) estallido *m*; **— card** boletín de calificaciones *m*

reporter [rɪpɔ́rDɚ] N reportero -ra *mf*

repose [rɪpóz] VI/VT reposar, descansar; N reposo *m*, descanso *m*

repository [rɪpázɪtɔri] N (object) depósito *m*; (person) depositario -ria *mf*

repossess [ripəzés] VT retomar posesión de

represent [rɛprɪzént] VT representar

representation [rɛprɪzɛntéʃən] N representación *f*

representative [rɛprɪzéntəDɪv] ADJ representativo; N representante *mf*

repress [rɪprés] VI/VT reprimir

repression [rɪpréʃən] N represión *f*

reprieve [rɪprív] VT (pardon) indultar;

(commute) conmutar; (delay) aplazar; N
(pardon) indulto *m*; (commutation)
conmutación *f*; (delay) aplazamiento *m*
reprimand [répɹəmænd] N reprimenda *f*,
regaño *m*; VT reprender, regañar
reprint [ríprɪnt] N reimpresión *f*; (offprint)
separata *f*
reprisal [rɪpráɪzəɫ] N represalia *f*
reproach [rɪprótʃ] VT reprochar; N reproche
m
reproduce [ripɹədús] VI/VT reproducir(se)
reproduction [ripɹədʌ́kʃən] N reproducción *f*
reproof [rɪprúf] N reprobación *f*
reprove [rɪprúv] VT reprobar
reptile [réptaɪɫ] N reptil *m*
republic [rɪpʌ́blɪk] N república *f*
republican [rɪpʌ́blɪkən] ADJ & N republicano
-na *mf*
repudiate [rɪpjúɒiet] VT repudiar
repugnance [rɪpʌ́gnəns] N repugnancia *f*
repugnant [rɪpʌ́gnənt] ADJ repugnante
repulse [rɪpʌ́ɫs] VT repeler, rechazar; N
repulsa *f*, rechazo *m*
repulsive [rɪpʌ́ɫsɪv] ADJ repulsivo
reputable [répjəɒəbəɫ] ADJ reputado
reputation [rɛpjətéʃən] N reputación *f*, fama
f
request [rɪkwést] N solicitud *f*, petición *f*,
requerimiento *m*; **at the — of** a solicitud
de, a instancias de; VT solicitar, pedir
require [rɪkwáɪr] VI/VT (need) requerir;
(demand) exigir
requirement [rɪkwáɪrmənt] N (demand)
requisito *m*; (need) necesidad *f*
requisite [rékwɪzɪt] ADJ requerido, necesario;
N requisito *m*
requisition [rɛkwɪzíʃən] N (taking over)
requisa *f*; (order) pedido *m*; VT (take over)
requisar; (order) pedir
rerun [rírʌn] N refrito *m*
rescind [rɪsínd] VT rescindir
rescue [réskju] VT rescatar, salvar; N rescate *m*,
salvamento *m*; **to go to the — of** acudir
al socorro de, salir al quite de
research [rísɚtʃ] N investigación *f*; [rɪsɚ́tʃ] VI/
VT investigar
researcher [rɪsɚ́tʃɚ] N investigador -ora *mf*
resell [riséɫ] VT revender
resemblance [rɪzémbləns] N semejanza *f*,
parecido *m*
resemble [rɪzémbəɫ] VT semejar, asemejarse a,
parecerse a
resent [rɪzént] VT resentirse de
resentful [rɪzéntfəɫ] ADJ resentido, rencoroso
resentment [rɪzéntmənt] N resentimiento *m*
reservation [rɛzɚ́véʃən] N reserva *f*; Am
reservación *f*; **to have one's —s** tener

reservas
reserve [rɪzɚ́v] VT reservar; N reserva *f*;
(shyness) pudor *m*
reserved [rɪzɚ́vd] ADJ reservado
reservoir [rézɚvwar] N (tank) depósito *m*,
alberca *f*; (artificial lake) embalse *m*,
represa *f*
reside [rɪzáɪd] VI residir
residence [rézɪɒəns] N residencia *f*
resident [rézɪɒənt] ADJ & N residente *mf*; (of
a neighborhood) vecino -na *mf*
residential [rɛzɪdéntʃəɫ] ADJ residencial
residue [rézɪdu] N residuo *m*
resign [rɪzáɪn] VI/VT renunciar (a), dimitir
(de); **to — oneself to** resignarse a
resignation [rɛzɪgnéʃən] N (act of resigning
an office) renuncia *f*, dimisión *f*;
(accepting attitude) resignación *f*
resilience [rɪzíljəns] N (elasticity) elasticidad
f; (adaptability) adaptabilidad *f*
resilient [rɪzíljənt] ADJ (elastic) elástico;
(adaptable) adaptable
resin [rézɪn] N resina *f*
resist [rɪzíst] VT (a temptation) resistir; VI/VT
(tyranny) resistirse (a)
resistance [rɪzístəns] N resistencia *f*
resistant [rɪzístənt] ADJ resistente
resolute [rézəlut] ADJ resuelto, decidido
resolution [rɛzəlúʃən] N resolución *f*
resolve [rɪzáɫv] VI/VT resolver(se); **to — into**
convertirse en; **to — to** decidir, resolver;
N resolución *f*
resonance [rézənəns] N resonancia *f*
resonate [rézənet] VI/VT resonar
resort [rɪzɔ́rt] VI **to — to** recurrir; N (seaside)
centro de veraneo *m*; (for skiing) estación
de esquí *f*; **as a last —** como último
recurso; **to have — to** recurrir a
resound [rɪzáund] VI/VT resonar
resource [rísɔrs] N recurso *m*
resourceful [rɪzɔ́rsfəɫ] ADJ ingenioso
respect [rɪspékt] N (esteem) respeto *m*; (detail)
aspecto *m*; **with — to** (con) respecto a,
respecto de; VT respetar; **as —s** por lo que
respecta a
respectable [rɪspéktəbəɫ] ADJ respetable
respectful [rɪspéktfəɫ] ADJ respetuoso
respective [rɪspéktɪv] ADJ respectivo
respiration [rɛspəréʃən] N respiración *f*
respite [réspɪt] N (pause) respiro *f*, tregua *m*;
(postponement) prórroga *f*
resplendent [rɪspléndənt] ADJ
resplandeciente, refulgente
respond [rɪspánd] VI/VT responder
response [rɪspáns] N respuesta *f*
responsibility [rɪspansəbílɪɒi] N
responsabilidad *f*

responsible [rɪspánsəbəɫ] ADJ responsable

rest [rɛst] N (repose) descanso *m*, reposo *m*; (musical) pausa *f*; (support) apoyo *m*; (remainder) resto *m*; **an object at** — un objeto en reposo; **he's at** — descansa en paz; — **home** (for convalescents) casa de reposo *f*; (for the aged) casa de ancianos *f*; — **room** servicio *m*; *Sp* aseo *m*; VI/VT descansar, reposar; VT (one's gaze) posar; (against a wall) reclinar; VI parar; **to** — **on** depender de; **let it** — déjalo en paz

restaurant [rɛ́stərɑnt] N restaurante *m*; *Am* restorán *m*

restitution [rɛstɪtúʃən] N restitución *f*

restless [rɛ́stlɪs] ADJ (worried) inquieto; (fidgety) movedizo, revuelto

restlessness [rɛ́stlɪsnɪs] N inquietud *f*, desasosiego *m*

restoration [rɛstəréʃən] N restauración *f*

restore [rɪstɔ́r] VT restaurar

restrain [rɪstrén] VT (hold back) refrenar, contener, moderar; (bring under control) reducir

restraint [rɪstrént] N (self-control) compostura *f*, moderación *f*; (device) seguro *m*; **under** — bajo control

restrict [rɪstríkt] VT restringir; (someone's liberty) coartar

restriction [rɪstríkʃən] N restricción *f*

result [rɪzʌ́ɫt] VI resultar; **to** — **from** resultar de; **to** — **in** dar por resultado; N resultado *m*; **as a** — de resultas, como resultado

resume [rɪzúm] VI/VT (take up again) reasumir, volver a asumir; (continue) reanudar

résumé [rézʊme] N currículum *m*, historial personal *m*

resurrection [rɛzərékʃən] N resurrección *f*

resuscitate [rɪsʌ́sɪtet] VI/VT resucitar

resuscitation [rɪsʌsɪtéʃən] N resucitación *f*

retail [rítɛɫ] N venta al por menor *f*; **at** — al por menor, al menudeo; — **trade** comercio minorista *m*; VI/VT vender al por menor

retailer [rítɛlɚ] N minorista *mf*, detallista *mf*

retain [rɪtén] VT (recall, confine, detain) retener; (keep) conservar, quedarse con; (hire) contratar

retainer [rɪténɚ] N (device that holds back) retén *m*; (payment) honorarios pagados por adelantado *m pl*

retaliate [rɪtǽliet] VI vengarse

retaliation [rɪtæliéʃən] N venganza *f*

retard [rɪtárd] VI/VT retardar

retarded [rɪtárdɪd] ADJ retrasado

retention [rɪténʃən] N retención *f*

reticence [rɛ́Dɪsəns] N reserva *f*

retina [rɛ́tṇə] N retina *f*

retinue [rɛ́tṇu] N séquito *m*, comitiva *f*

retire [rɪtáɪr] VI/VT (stop working) retirar(se), jubilar(se); (withdraw) retirar(se); (to bed) acostarse; (money, troops, machines) retirar

retirement [rɪtáɪrmənt] N retiro *m*, jubilación *f*

retort [rɪtɔ́rt] N (reply) réplica *f*; (vessel) retorta *f*

retouch [rɪtʌ́tʃ] VT retocar; N retoque *m*

retrace [ritrés] VT (mental steps) repasar; (one's route) volver sobre

retract [rɪtrǽkt] VT retractar; (claws) retraer(se); VI desdecirse, retractarse

retreat [rɪtrít] N (place of refuge, period of meditation) retiro *m*, refugio *m*; (military) retirada *f*, repliegue *m*; (bugle call) retreta *f*; VI batirse en retirada, retroceder, replegarse

retrench [rɪtréntʃ] VI economizar

retrieve [rɪtrív] VT (game) cobrar; (something lost) recuperar

retriever [rɪtrívɚ] N perro cobrador *m*

retroactive [rɛtroǽktɪv] ADJ retroactivo

retrospect [rɛ́trəspɛkt] ADV LOC **in** — mirando para atrás

retrovirus [rɛ́trovaɪrəs] N retrovirus *m*

return [rɪtɚ́n] VI (come back) volver, regresar; VT (put back) devolver, retornar; (a verdict) fallar; N (to a place) vuelta *f*, regreso *m*; (thing bought, of a thing) devolución *f*; (profit) ganancia *f*; (electoral) resultados *m pl*; — **address** señas del remitente *f pl*; — **game** revancha *f*; — **ticket** billete de vuelta *m*; **by** — **mail** a vuelta de correo; **election** —**s** resultados electorales *m pl*; **in** — a cambio; **in** — **for** a cambio de; **income tax** — *Sp* declaración de la renta *f*; *Am* declaración de impuestos *f*

reunion [rijúnjən] N reunión *f*

reunite [rijunáɪt] VI/VT reunir(se)

rev [rɛv] VI/VT acelerar en vacío

reveal [rɪvíɫ] VT revelar

revealing [rɪvílɪŋ] ADJ revelador; (neckline) atrevido

revel [rɛ́vəɫ] VI (enjoy) deleitarse, gozar; (party) parrandear; N parranda *f*

revelation [rɛvəléʃən] N revelación *f*; —**s** Apocalipsis *m sg*

revelry [rɛ́vəɫri] N parranda *f*, jarana *f*

revenge [rɪvɛ́ndʒ] N venganza *f*, revancha *f*

revengeful [rɪvɛ́ndʒfəɫ] ADJ vengativo

revenue [rɛ́vənu] N (of a government) rentas públicas *f pl*; (of a person) ingresos *m pl*; — **stamp** sello fiscal *m*

reverberate [rɪvɝ́bəret] vi reverberar; vt hacer reverberar

revere [rɪvír] vt reverenciar

reverence [révəəns] n reverencia f, veneración f; vt venerar

reverend [révəənd] adj & n reverendo -da mf

reverent [révəənt] adj reverente

reverie, revery [révəri] n ensueño m, ensoñación f

reverse [rɪvɝ́s] adj inverso, opuesto; **the — side** el revés; n (opposite) lo opuesto; (back of clothing, mishap) revés m; (back of a coin, medal) reverso m; (gear) marcha atrás f; (back of a piece of paper) dorso m; vi/vt invertir(se); vt (a policy, a vehicle) dar marcha atrás; (a verdict) revocar

revert [rɪvɝ́t] vi revertir

review [rɪvjú] n (inspection of a military unit, periodical publication) revista f; (repetition of studied material) repaso m; (critique of a book, drama) reseña f, crítica f; (examination of a judicial case) revisión f; vi/vt (examine) repasar, revisar; vt (reexamine) revisar, examinar; (inspect troops) pasar revista a; (write a critique of) reseñar

revile [rɪváɪɫ] vt vilipendiar, denostar

revise [rɪváɪz] vt corregir, enmendar

revision [rɪvíʒən] n (action of revising) corrección f; (revised version) versión corregida f

revival [rɪváɪvəɫ] n (of customs) retorno m; (of religious feeling) resurgimiento m, despertar m; (from unconsciousness) resucitación f; (of a play) reposición f, revisión f; (evangelical meeting) asamblea evangelista f

revive [rɪváɪv] vt (an unconscious person) reavivar, reanimar; (an apparently dead person) resucitar; (an old play) reponer; (a custom) restablecer; vi revivir, reanimarse; (be reestablished) restablecerse

revocation [rɛvəkéʃən] n revocación f

revoke [rɪvók] vt revocar

revolt [rɪvóɫt] n revuelta f, sublevación f; vi rebelarse, sublevarse; **it —s me** me da asco

revolting [rɪvóɫtɪŋ] adj repugnante, asqueroso

revolution [rɛvəlúʃən] n revolución f

revolutionary [rɛvəlúʃəneri] adj & n revolucionario -ria mf

revolve [rɪváɫv] vi/vt girar

revolver [rɪváɫvɚ] n revólver m

revue [rɪvjú] n revista f

revulsion [rɪváɫʃən] n repugnancia f, asco m

reward [rɪwɔ́rd] n recompensa f; vt recompensar

rewind [riwáɪnd] vi/vt rebobinar

rewrite [rɪráɪt] vi/vt reescribir; [ríraɪt] n corrección f

rhea [ríə] n ñandú m

rhetoric [rɛ́Dɚɪk] n retórica f

rheumatism [rúmətɪzəm] n reumatismo m, reuma m

Rh factor [ɑrétʃfæktɚ] n factor Rh m

rhinoceros [raɪnásərəs] n rinoceronte m

rhinovirus [ráɪnováɪrəs] n rinovirus m

rhododendron [roDədéndrən] n rododendro m

rhubarb [rúbɑrb] n (vegetable) ruibarbo m; (brawl) reyerta f

rhyme [raɪm] n rima f; **without — or reason** sin ton ni son; vi/vt rimar

rhythm [ríðəm] n ritmo m

rhythmical [ríðmɪkəɫ] adj rítmico; (breathing) acompasado

rib [rɪb] n (of person, animal) costilla f; (of umbrella) varilla f; (in garment) canalé m, cordoncillo m; **— cage** caja torácica f; vt burlarse de

ribbon [ríbən] n (of cloth) cinta f; (of land) franja f, faja f

rice [raɪs] n arroz m; **— field** arrozal m

rich [rɪtʃ] adj rico; (tasty) sabroso; (buttery) mantecoso; (colorful) vivo; n **—es** riquezas f pl

rickety [ríkɪDi] adj (shaky) desvencijado; (affected with rickets) raquítico

ricochet [ríkəʃe] n rebote m; vi rebotar

rid [rɪd] vt librar, desembarazar; **to get — of** librarse de, deshacerse de

riddle [rídɫ] n (puzzle) acertijo m, adivinanza f; (puzzling person) enigma m; vi hablar en enigmas; vt acribillar, perforar; **to be —d with graft** estar plagado de corrupción

ride [raɪd] vi (on a horse) cabalgar, jinetear; (on a bicycle) montar; (in a vehicle) andar, viajar / ir en; **this car —s well** este coche anda bien; **his hopes are riding on that** tiene las esperanzas puestas en eso; **just let it — ** déjalo tranquilo; vt (travel on horse, bicycle) montar; (travel on bus) andar en; (harass) hostigar; **to — away** irse; **to — by** pasar; **to — out** capear; **to — up** subirse; n paseo m, viaje m; **to give someone a —** acercar en coche; **to go on a —** dar un paseo

rider [ráɪdɚ] n (on a horse) jinete m; (on a bicycle) ciclista mf; (on an insurance policy) cláusula añadida f; (law) anexo m

ridge [rɪʤ] N (back of an animal) espinazo *m*, lomo *m*; (chain of hills) cadena *f*; (of a roof) caballete *m*; (of cloth) cordoncillo *m*

ridicule [rídɪkjuł] N burla *f*, mofa *f*; VT ridiculizar, poner en ridículo

ridiculous [rɪdíkjələs] ADJ ridículo

riffraff [rífræf] N *pej* gentuza *f*, chusma *f*

rifle [ráɪfəł] N rifle *m*, fusil *m*; VT robar; **to — through** revolver

rift [rɪft] N (opening) grieta *f*, hendidura *f*; (disagreement) desavenencia *f*

rig [rɪg] VT (sails) aparejar, equipar; (an election) amañar; **to — up** armar; N (on a ship) aparejo *m*, equipo *m*; (apparatus) aparato *m*; (truck) camión *m*

rigging [rígɪŋ] N jarcia *f*

right [raɪt] ADJ (not left) derecho; (not wrong) correcto, acertado; (suitable) adecuado; **— angle** ángulo recto *m*; **—-hand** derecho; **—-hand man** brazo derecho *m*; **—-handed** diestro; **—-to-life** antiaborto, pro vida; **— triangle** triángulo recto *m*; **—-wing** derechista, de derecha; **at the — moment** en el momento justo; **the — people** la gente indicada; **to be —** tener razón; **to be all — estar bien; he's not in his — mind** no está en sus cabales; **to turn out —** salir bien; ADV (straight) derecho, directamente; (correctly) correctamente; (to the right) a la derecha; **— after** justo después de; **—-face** media vuelta a la derecha; **— now** ahora mismo; **— there** allí mismo; **it is — where you left it** está exactamente donde lo dejaste; **to hit — in the eye** darle de lleno en el ojo; N (just claim) derecho *m*; (moral good) bien *m*; (direction, political persuasion) derecha *f*; **— of way** prioridad *f*, preferencia *f*; **make a — at the corner** gira / dobla a la derecha; **to the —** a la derecha; **to be in the —** tener razón; VI/VT (make upright) enderezar(se); VT (correct) corregir

righteous [ráɪtʃəs] ADJ recto, justo; **— rage** rabia justificada *f*

righteousness [ráɪtʃəsnɪs] N rectitud *f*, superioridad moral *f*

rightful [ráɪtfəł] ADJ legítimo

rightist [ráɪdɪst] N derechista *mf*

rightly [ráɪtli] ADV con razón

rigid [ríʤɪd] ADJ rígido

rigidity [rɪʤídɪti] N rigidez *f*

rigor [rígɚ] N rigor *m*

rigorous [rígɚəs] ADJ riguroso

rim [rɪm] N (edge) borde *m*; (on a car) llanta *f*; *Am* rin *m*; (on a bicycle) aro *m*; (on a plate) filete *m*; (of glasses) montura *f*

rind [raɪnd] N (cheese) corteza *f*; (fruit) cáscara *f*

ring [rɪŋ] N (on finger, of smoke) anillo *m*; (for women only) sortija *f*; (under the eyes) ojeras *f pl*; (in the nose) argolla *f*; (circle) círculo *m*, redondel *m*, ruedo *m*; (in a circus) pista *f*; (for bullfights) plaza de toros *f*; (for boxing) cuadrilátero *m*; (for gymnastics) anillas *f pl*; (of criminals) banda *f*; (undertone) tono *m*; (sound of telephone) timbrazo *m*, telefonazo *m*; (sound of bells) retintín *m*, repique *m*; **— finger** anular *m*; **—leader** cabecilla *mf*; **—worm** tiña *f*; VT (surround) cercar; (make doorbell sound) tocar; (make bell sound) tañer; VI (of ears) zumbar; (make sound, doorbell) sonar; (make sound, bell) repicar, repiquetear; **to — the nose of an animal** ponerle una argolla en la nariz a un animal; **to — the hour** dar la hora; **to — true** parecer verdad; **to — up the sale** marcar la venta

ringlet [ríŋlɪt] N (curl) rizo *m*, bucle *m*, sortija *f*; (small ring) pequeña sortija *f*

rink [rɪŋk] N pista de patinaje *f*

rinkydink [ríŋkidɪŋk] ADJ de pacotilla

rinse [rɪns] VI/VT enjuagar, aclarar; N enjuague *m*, aclarado *m*

riot [ráɪət] N (uprising) motín *m*, tumulto *m*; (excess) exceso *m*; **he's a —** es un cómico; VI amotinarse

riotous [ráɪədəs] ADJ (wanton) desenfrenado; (funny) graciosísimo

rip [rɪp] VI/VT rasgar(se), rajar(se); VT (something sewn) descoser; **to — away** desprender; **to — into** asaltar; **to — off** robar; **to — out a seam** descoser una costura; N rasgadura *f*, rajadura *f*; **— cord** cordón de apertura *m*; **—off** robo *m*

ripe [raɪp] ADJ maduro; **to be — for** estar preparado para, listo para; **— old age** edad avanzada *f*

ripen [ráɪpən] VI/VT madurar(se), sazonar(se)

ripeness [ráɪpnɪs] N madurez *f*

ripple [rípəł] VI/VT (water) rizar(se); (grass) agitar(se); N ondulación *f*, rizo *m*

rise [raɪz] VI (go up) subir; (increase) aumentar; (get up, stand up) levantarse; (slope up) elevarse; (arise) surgir; (of mist) levantarse; (of the sun, moon) salir; (of dough) crecer, leudar; **to — up in rebellion** sublevarse, alzarse; **to — above** superar; **to — to the challenge** aceptar el desafío; N (of prices, volume) subida *f*, aumento *m*; (of an empire, talent) surgimiento *m*; (slope upward) elevación *f*; **to get a — out of someone**

provocar a alguien; **to give — to** ocasionar

risk [rɪsk] N riesgo *m*; VT arriesgar, aventurar; **to — defeat** correr el riesgo de perder, exponerse a perder

risky [ríski] ADJ arriesgado, aventurado, azaroso

risqué [rɪské] ADJ subido de tono, atrevido, picante

rite [raɪt] N rito *m*

ritual [rítʃuəl] ADJ & N ritual *m*

ritzy [rítsi] ADJ elegante

rival [ráɪvəl] ADJ & N rival *mf*; VT rivalizar con, competir con

rivalry [ráɪvəlri] N rivalidad *f*

river [rívə-] N río *m*; —**bank** orilla *f*, ribera *f*

rivet [rívɪt] N remache *m*; VT (put rivets) remachar; (fix) fijar, clavar

RNA (ribonucleic acid) [arɪné] N ARN *m*

roach [rotʃ] N cucaracha *f*

road [rod] N (in the country) camino *m*; (highway) carretera *f*; **on the — to recovery** en vías de recuperación; — **map** mapa carretero *m*; — **rage** ira caminera *f*; —**side** borde del camino *m*; —**way** camino *m*

roam [rom] VI/VT vagar (por), errar (por), rodar (por); VI vagabundear

roar [rɔr] VI/VT rugir, bramar; **to — with laughter** reír a carcajadas; N rugido *m*, bramido *m*; — **of laughter** risotada *f*, carcajada *f*

roast [rost] VI/VT (meat, potatoes) asar(se); (coffee, nuts) tostar, torrar; (criticize) criticar; N (meat) asado *m*; (party) barbacoa *f*; — **beef** rosbif *m*

rob [rɑb] VI/VT robar; **to — someone of something** robarle algo a alguien

robber [rábə-] N ladrón -ona *mf*

robbery [rábəri] N robo *m*

robe [rob] N manto *m*, traje talar *m*, túnica *f*; (ceremonial dress) toga *f*; (bath wrap) bata *f*

robin [rábɪn] N petirrojo *m*

robot [róbɑt] N robot *m*

robotics [robáDɪks] N robótica *f*

robust [robást] ADJ (strong) robusto; (hearty) saludable; (solid) sólido

rock [rɑk] N roca *f*; (crag) peñasco *m*, peñón *m*; (diamond) diamante *m*; (music style) rock *m*; — **crystal** cristal de roca *m*; — **salt** sal de piedra *f*, sal gema / mineral *f*; **to go on the —s** tropezar en un escollo; *Am* escollar; **he hit —-bottom** tocó fondo; VI/VT (move to and fro) mecer(se); (stagger) sacudir, estremecer; **to — to sleep** arrullar

rocker [rákə-] N mecedora *f*

rocket [rákɪt] N cohete *m*

rocketry [rákɪtri] N cohetería *f*

rocking [rákɪŋ] N — **chair** mecedora *f*; — **horse** caballito de madera *m*, caballito mecedor *m*

rocky [ráki] ADJ (with rocks) rocoso; (difficult) difícil

rod [rɑd] N vara *f*, varilla *f*; (in engine) vástago *m*; medida de longitud *f* (aproximadamente 5 metros)

rodent [ródənt] N roedor *m*

rodeo [ródio] N rodeo *m*

rogue [rog] N pícaro -ra *mf*, bribón -ona *mf*; ADJ solitario y bravo

roguish [rógɪʃ] ADJ (rascally) pícaro, bribón; (mischievous) travieso

role [rol] N papel *m*, rol *m*; — **model** modelo ejemplar *m*; —-**playing** improvisación *f*

roll [rol] VI (move on wheels, rotate) rodar; (rotate one's eyes) revolear; (sway) balancearse, bambolearse; (reverberate) retumbar; (flow as waves) ondular; VT (steel) aplanar; (cigarettes) liar; (a drum) redoblar; (one's r's) pronunciar la erre; **to — over in the snow** revolcarse en la nieve; **to — up** arrollar, enrollar; **to — around** llegar; **to — back** reducir, rebajar; **to — by** pasar; **to — over** volcar, darse vuelta; **to get —ing** ponerse en marcha; N (of paper, fabric, etc.) rollo *m*; (of coins) cartucho *m*; (of a ship) balanceo *m*; (of thunder) retumbo *m*; (of a drum) redoble *m*; (catalog of members) lista *f*; (of waves) ondulación *f*; (of a typewriter) carro *m*; (piece of bread) bollo *m*, panecillo *m*; (of dice) tiro *m*; ADJ —-**on** de bolita

roller [rólə-] N (for painting, moving things) rodillo *m*; (hair) rulo *m*, rulero *m*; — **coaster** montaña rusa *f*; — **skate** patín de ruedas *m*

rolling pin [rólɪŋ pɪn] N rodillo *m*, palote *m*

roly-poly [rólipóli] ADJ rechoncho

ROM (read-only memory) [rɑm] N ROM *f*

Roman [rómən] ADJ & N romano -na *mf*; — **numeral** número romano *m*

romance [rómæns] N (love affair, story) romance *m*; (romantic atmosphere) romanticismo *m*; VT cortejar; ADJ romance, románico

romanesque [romənésk] ADJ románico

Romania [roméniə] N Rumania *f*

Romanian [roméniən] ADJ & N rumano -na *mf*

romantic [romǽntɪk] ADJ romántico

romanticism [romæntəsɪzəm] N
  romanticismo *m*

romp [rɑmp] VI retozar, brincar; (win easily)
  arrasar con; N (frolic) retozo *m*; (victory)
  victoria fácil *f*

roof [ruf] N (ceiling) techo *m*, tejado *m*; (flat
  roof) azotea *f*; — **of the mouth** paladar
  m; **to hit the** — poner el grito en el
  cielo; VT techar

rookie [rʊ́ki] N novato -ta *mf*

room [rum] N (in building) cuarto *m*; (large)
  sala *f*; (in a hotel) habitación *f*; (space)
  lugar *m*, sitio *m*; — **and board** pensión
  completa *f*; —**mate** compañero -ra de
  cuarto *mf*; — **service** servicio a la
  habitación *f*; **to take up** — ocupar
  espacio; **the whole** — **laughed** todos los
  presentes se rieron; VI hospedarse, alojarse

roomy [rʊ́mi] ADJ espacioso, amplio

roost [rust] N vara *f*; VI posarse (para dormir)

rooster [rʊ́stɚ] N gallo *m*

root [rut] N raíz *f*; **to take** — (a plant) echar
  raíces, prender; (an idea) arraigar(se); —
  canal tratamiento de conducto *m*; VI
  (grow roots) arraigar(se), echar raíces; (dig)
  hozar; **to** — **for** animar; **to** — **out / up**
  (uproot) arrancar de raíz; (eradicate)
  erradicar

rope [rop] N (cord) soga *f*, cuerda *f*; (lasso)
  reata *f*, lazo *m*; (on a ship) cabo *m*; (thick)
  maroma *f*; **to be at the end of one's** —
  no dar más; **to know the** —**s** conocer el
  paño, sabérselas todas; VT enlazar; **to** —
  off acordonar; **to** — **someone in** agarrar
  a alguien

rosary [rʊ́zəri] N rosario *m*

rose [roz] N rosa *f*; (color) rosa *m*; —**bud**
  capullo de rosa *m*, pimpollo de rosa *m*;
  —**bush** rosal *m*; —**-colored** de color rosa

rosemary [rʊ́zmɛri] N romero *m*

roster [rʊ́stɚ] N lista *f*

rostrum [rʊ́strəm] N tribuna *f*

rosy [rʊ́zi] ADJ (pink) rosado, color de rosa;
  (of cheeks) sonrosado; — **future** porvenir
  halagüeño *m*

rot [rɑt] VI/VT pudrir(se); N podredumbre *f*

rotary [rʊ́Dəri] ADJ rotatorio, rotativo

rotate [rʊ́tet] VI/VT rotar

rotation [rotéʃən] N rotación *f*, giro *m*

rotor [rʊ́Dɚ] N rotor *m*

rotten [rʊ́tn̩] ADJ (decomposing) podrido;
  (stinking) hediondo; (morally corrupt)
  corrupto; (despicable) odioso

rotund [rotʊ́nd] ADJ rollizo

rouge [ruʒ] N colorete *m*

rough [rʌf] ADJ (coarse) áspero, rugoso;
  (violent) violento; (rude) tosco;

(approximate) aproximado; (road)
desigual, irregular; (terrain) agreste,
bronco; (sea) picado, revuelto; —
diamond diamante en bruto *m*; — **draft**
borrador *m*; — **weather** mal tiempo *m*;
he had a — **time** le fue mal; ADV con
violencia; VI ponerse áspero; **to** — **it** vivir
sin lujos ni comodidades

roughly [rʌ́fli] ADV (not smoothly)
ásperamente; (rudely) groseramente,
rudamente; (approximately)
aproximadamente; **to estimate** — tantear

roughness [rʌ́fnɪs] N (lack of smoothness)
aspereza *f*; (rudeness) rudeza *f*;
(unevenness) desigualdad *f*; **the** — **of the
sea** lo picado del mar

roulette [rulét] N ruleta *f*

round [raʊnd] ADJ redondo; — **trip** viaje de
ida y vuelta *m*; N (of talks, drinks, dance)
ronda *f*; (of cheese) rodaja *f*; (in cards,
sports) vuelta *f*; (in boxing) round *m*,
asalto *m*; (of golf) partido *m*; (canon)
canon *m*; — **number** número redondo *m*;
— **of ammunition** carga de municiones
f; — **of applause** aplauso *m*; **to make
the** —**s** hacer la ronda; PREP & ADV
—**about** indirecto; —**-the-clock**
veinticuatro horas al día; —**up** (of cattle)
rodeo *m*; (of criminals) redada *f*; **all year**
— todo el año; **to come** — pasar; **to go**
— **a corner** doblar una esquina; VT (a
corner) doblar; (an edge, a number)
redondear; **to** — **off / out** redondear; **to**
— **up** juntar, reunir; **to** — **up cattle**
juntar el ganado

roundness [ráʊndnɪs] N redondez *f*

rouse [raʊz] VI/VT (wake) despertar(se); VT
(instigate) incitar

rout [raʊt] N (defeat) derrota aplastante *f*;
(flight) huida en desbandada *f*; VT (defeat)
derrotar, destrozar; (cause to flee) poner en
fuga

route [raʊt, rut] N ruta *f*, trayecto *m*; (of
newspaper delivery) reparto *m*; VT dirigir

routine [rutín] N rutina *f*

rove [rov] VI/VT vagar (por), errar (por)

rover [róvɚ] N vagabundo -da *mf*

row [raʊ] N (fight) riña *f*, pelea *f*, bronca *f*;
[ro] N (line) fila *f*, hilera *f*, ringlera *f*; **four
times in a** — cuatro veces seguidas; VI/VT
(propel with oars) remar, bogar; —**boat**
bote de remos *m*, barca *f*, chinchorro *m*

rowdy [ráʊDi] ADJ (person) alborotador;
(party) bullicioso; N camorrista *mf*

rower [róɚ] N remero -ra *mf*

royal [rɔ́ɪəɫ] ADJ real; — **blue** azul marino *m*;
— **flush** escalera real *f*

royalty [rɔ́ɪəɫti] N realeza f; (person) miembro de la realeza m; **royalties** derechos m pl, regalías f pl

RSVP (répondez s'il vous plaît) [ɑresvipí] LOC S.R.C.

rub [rʌb] VI/VT (apply friction) frotar(se); (massage) friccionar; (spread on) aplicar frotando; (make sore) rozar; **to — off** quitar(se) frotando; **to — out** borrar; **to — shoulders with** codearse con; **to — someone the wrong way** peinar a contrapelo; **don't — it in!** ¡no me lo refriegues por la cara! N (act of rubbing) fricción f; (difficulty) dificultad f; (abraded area) roce m, frote m

rubber [rʌ́bɚ] N caucho m, goma f; (condom) fam condón m; **— band** goma elástica f; **—s** chanclos m pl; **— stamp** sello de goma m; **— tree** gomero m

rubbish [rʌ́bɪʃ] N (trash) basura f; (nonsense) pamplinas f pl

rubble [rʌ́bəɫ] N (debris) escombros m pl; (stone fragments) ripios m pl, cascote m

rubric [rúbrɪk] N rúbrica f

ruby [rúbi] N rubí m

ruckus [rʌ́kəs] N barahúnda f, jaleo m

rudder [rʌ́Dɚ] N timón m

ruddy [rʌ́Di] ADJ rubicundo

rude [rud] ADJ (impolite) grosero; (uncouth, crude, simple) tosco; (harsh) rudo

rudeness [rúdnɪs] N (impoliteness) grosería f; (harshness) rudeza f; (crudeness) tosquedad f

rueful [rúfəɫ] ADJ (sad) triste; (repentant) arrepentido

ruffian [rʌ́fiən] N rufián m

ruffle [rʌ́fəɫ] VI/VT (gather cloth) fruncir(se); (raise feathers) erizar(se); (water) agitar(se), rizar(se); (hair) desgreñar(se); (bother) molestar(se), fastidiar(se); N (frill on clothes) volante m; (gathering in cloth) frunce m, pliegue m; (ripples in water) ondulación f, rizo m

rug [rʌg] N alfombra f; (hairpiece) peluquín m

rugby [rʌ́gbi] N rugby m

rugged [rʌ́gɪd] ADJ (terrain) escarpado, áspero, fragoso; (face) recio; (manners) tosco; (way of life) duro; (man) robusto

ruin [rúɪn] N ruina f; **to go to —** arruinarse, venirse abajo; VI/VT arruinar(se), estropear(se); (spoil) echar(se) a perder

ruinous [rúɪnəs] ADJ ruinoso

rule [ruɫ] N (principle) regla f; (line separating newspaper columns) filete m; (government) mando m, gobierno m; **the — of law** el imperio de la ley; **as a — of thumb** por regla general, a ojo de buen cubero; VI/VT (govern) reinar, gobernar; (decree) fallar, dictaminar, sentenciar; (put lines on paper) rayar, poner renglones; **to — out** excluir; **to — over** reinar, gobernar

ruler [rúlɚ] N (governor) gobernante mf; (instrument) regla f

ruling [rúlɪŋ] N (decision) fallo m, sentencia f, dictamen m; (line on paper) renglón m; ADJ (governing) gobernante

rum [rʌm] N ron m

rumble [rʌ́mbəɫ] VI (roar) retumbar; (of stomach) hacer ruido; (fight) pelear; N (roar) retumbo m; (of stomach) ruido m; (fight) pelea f

ruminate [rúmənet] VI rumiar

rummage [rʌ́mɪdʒ] VI/VT rebuscar, hurgar; N cachivaches m pl; **— sale** venta de beneficencia f

rumor [rúmɚ] N rumor m; VT murmurar; **it is —ed that** se rumorea que, corre la voz que

rump [rʌmp] N (of quadruped) anca f, grupa f; (of bird) rabadilla f; (of person) trasero m

run [rʌn] VI (person, tears, water) correr; (stockings, dyes) correrse; (function) funcionar; (travel briefly) hacer una escapadita; (circulate) circular, hacer el recorrido; (drip) chorrear; (be a candidate) presentarse como candidato; (suppurate) supurar; VT (a mile, a risk) correr; (one object through another) pasar; (a business) manejar, dirigir; (a red light) comerse; (a news story) publicar; (a sum of money) costar; (a computer program) ejecutar; (a fever) tener; **— along now!** ¡vete! **to — across someone** encontrarse con alguien; **to — after** perseguir; **to — around with** andar con; **to — away** fugarse, escaparse; **to — down** (stop working) dejar de funcionar; (capture) aprehender; (criticize) hablar mal de; (run over) atropellar; (tire) cansar; **to — dry** secarse; **to — into** (encounter) tropezar con, encontrarse con; (collide) chocar con; **to — out** salir corriendo; **to — out of money** quedarse sin dinero; **to — over** (spill) derramarse; (run down) atropellar, arrollar; (move along a surface) deslizar por; **to — through** (stab) atravesar; (squander) despilfarrar; (repeat) repetir; **the play ran for three months** la obra estuvo en cartel durante tres meses; **it —s in the family** es un rasgo de familia; N (act of running) carrera f, corrida f; (defect in stockings) carrera f, corrida f; (routine

trip) recorrido *m*; (of newspapers) tirada *f*;
(of a play) temporada en cartel *f*; (on a
bank) pánico *m*, corrida *f*; **—away**
fugitivo -va *mf*; **—away horse** caballo
desbocado *m*; **—-down** desvencijado; **—
of good luck** racha de buena suerte *f*; **—
of performances** temporada en cartel *f*;
— of the mill del montón; **—way** (for
planes) pista *f*; (for models) pasarela *f*; **to
be on the —** estar huyendo; **in the long
—** a la larga; **the —s** *vulg* cagalera *f*; **he
gave me the —around** contestó con
evasivas
rung [rʌŋ] N (of a chair) barrote *m*; (of a
ladder) peldaño *m*
runner [rʌnɚ] N (one who runs) corredor
-ora *mf*; (on a table) tapete *m*; (on a sled)
patín *m*; (on a skate) cuchilla *f*; (on a
plant) estolón *m*; (of drugs, contraband)
contrabandista *mf*; **—-up** segundo -da *mf*
running [rʌnɪŋ] N (race) corrida *f*, carrera *f*;
(direction) manejo *m*, dirección *f*; (flow)
flujo *m*; (of machines) funcionamiento *m*;
(of a car) rodaje *m*; **to be out of the —**
estar fuera de combate; **— board** estribo
m; ADJ (of horses) de carrera; (of plants)
trepador; (of sores) supurante; **— water**
agua corriente *f*; **in — condition** en
buen estado; **for ten days —** durante
diez días seguidos
runt [rʌnt] N (animal) animal más pequeño
de la camada *m*; (person) *pej* mequetrefe *m*
rupture [rʌptʃɚ] N (of relations, internal
organ) ruptura *f*; (of a tire) rotura *f*;
(hernia) hernia *f*; VI/VT romper(se),
reventar(se)
rural [rúrəɫ] ADJ rural
rush [rʌʃ] VI/VT (hurry) apresurar(se); *Am*
apurar(se); VT (to dispatch) llevar con
prisa, llevar rápido; (to attack) precipitarse,
abalanzarse sobre; **to — by / past** pasar
corriendo; **to — out** salir corriendo; N
(haste) prisa *f*; *Am* apuro *m*; (attack)
acometida *f*; (hurried activity) bullicio *m*;
(plant) junco *m*; **— of air** ráfaga *f*; **— of
people** tumulto *m*; **— of water** torrente
m; **— order** pedido urgente *m*
Russia [rʌʃə] N Rusia *f*
Russian [rʌʃən] ADJ & N ruso -sa *mf*
rust [rʌst] N (oxidation) herrumbre *f*, orín *m*;
(disease) tizón *m*; **—-colored** color
herrumbre; **—-proof** inoxidable; VI/VT
herrumbrar(se)
rustic [rʌstɪk] ADJ rústico; N campesino -na
mf, paleto -ta *mf*
rustle [rʌsəɫ] VI susurrar, crujir; VT hacer
susurrar, hacer crujir; **to — cattle** robar

ganado; N susurro *m*, crujido *m*
rusty [rʌsti] ADJ (oxidized) herrumbrado,
oxidado; (rust-colored) color herrumbre;
(out of practice) falto de práctica; **my
German is —** se me ha olvidado el
alemán
rut [rʌt] N (furrow) surco *m*; (of a wheel)
rodada *f*; (routine) rutina *f*; (heat) celo *m*;
to be in a — ser esclavo de la rutina; VI
estar en celo
ruthless [rúθlɪs] ADJ despiadado
ruthlessness [rúθlɪsnɪs] N crueldad *f*
Rwanda [ruándə] N Ruanda *f*
Rwandan [ruándən] ADJ & N ruandés -esa *mf*
rye [raɪ] N centeno *m*; **— bread** pan de
centeno *m*

Ss

saber [sébɚ] N sable *m*
sabotage [sǽbətɑʒ] N sabotaje *m*; VT sabotear
saccharine [sǽkərɪn] ADJ empalagoso; N
sacarina *f*
sack [sæk] N (bag) saco *m*, bolso *m*; (looting)
saqueo *m*; **in the —** en la cama; VT (bag)
embolsar, ensacar; (loot) saquear; (fire)
despedir
sacrament [sǽkrəmənt] N sacramento *m*
sacred [sékrɪd] ADJ sagrado
sacrifice [sǽkrəfaɪs] N sacrificio *m*; **at a —**
con pérdida; VT sacrificar
sacrilege [sǽkrəlɪdʒ] N sacrilegio *m*
sacrilegious [sækrəlídʒəs] ADJ sacrílego
sad [sæd] ADJ triste
sadden [sǽdn̩] VI/VT entristecer(se); VT pesar
saddle [sǽdl̩] N (for horse) silla de montar *f*,
montura *f*; (for bicycle) sillín *m*; **—bag**
alforja *f*; **— horse** caballo de silla *m*; **—
pad** carona *f*; **— tree** arzón *m*; VT ensillar;
to — up ensillar; **to — someone with
responsibilities** cargar a alguien de
responsabilidades
sadism [sédɪzəm] N sadismo *m*
sadistic [sədístɪk] ADJ sádico
sadness [sǽdnɪs] N tristeza *f*
sadomasochism [seɪdoʊmǽsəkɪzəm] N
sadomasoquismo *m*
safari [səfári] N safari *m*
safe [sef] ADJ (secure) seguro, salvo;
(trustworthy) digno de confianza; (careful)
precavido, prudente; **— and sound** sano
y salvo; **—-conduct** salvoconducto *m*;
—guard salvaguarda *f*; **to —guard**

salvaguardar; — **in jail** confinado;
—**keeping** custodia *f*; — **sex** sexo seguro
m; N caja fuerte *f*
safety [séfti] N seguridad *f*; — **belt** cinturón
de seguridad *m*; — **device** mecanismo de
seguridad *m*, seguro *m*; — **glass** vidrio
inastillable *m*; — **net** red *f*; — **pin**
imperdible *m*
saffron [sǽfrən] N (spice) azafrán *m*; (color)
color azafrán *m*
sag [sæg] VI/VT (wall) combar(se), pandear(se);
VI (stock market, breast) caer; (spirits)
decaer; (rope) aflojarse; (pants) abolsarse;
his shoulders — tiene las espaldas
caídas; N (of a wall) pandeo *m*, comba *f*;
(in prices) caída *f*
sage [seʤ] ADJ sabio; N (wise person) sabio
-bia *mf*; (plant) salvia *f*
sail [seɫ] N (part of a boat) vela *f*; (trip) viaje
en barco *m*; —**boat** velero *m*; —**fish** pez
vela *m*; **under full** — a toda vela; **to set**
— zarpar; VI/VT (travel by boat) navegar;
(set sail) zarpar; **to — along** deslizarse,
navegar; **to — along the coast** costear;
to — through an exam aprobar un
examen con facilidad
sailor [sélɚ] N marinero -ra *mf*
saint [sent] N santo -ta *mf*; — **John** San Juan
saintly [séntli] ADJ santo, piadoso
sake [sek] N **for the — of** por; **for my** —
por mí; **for pity's** — por el amor de Dios;
for brevity's — para ser breve; **for the
— of argument** por vía de argumento;
art for art's — el arte por el arte
salad [sǽləd] N ensalada *f*; — **dressing**
aderezo *m*
salamander [sǽləmændɚ] N salamandra *f*
salary [sǽləri] N sueldo *m*; — **bracket**
categoría salarial *f*
sale [seɫ] N (act of selling) venta *f*; (special
sales event) liquidación *f*, saldo *m*; —**s
force** personal de ventas *m*; —**sperson**
vendedor -ora *mf*; (in a store) dependiente
-ta *mf*; —**s tax** impuesto sobre las ventas
m; **for** — en venta
salient [séliənt] ADJ & N saliente *m*
saline [sélin] ADJ salino
saliva [səláɪvə] N saliva *f*
sally [sǽli] N (sortie) salida *f*; (excursion)
excursión *f*; VI salir, hacer una salida; **to
— forth** salir
salmon [sǽmən] N salmón *m*
salmonella [sæɫmənélə] N salmonela *f*
salon [səlún] N salón *m*; (beauty parlor) salón
de belleza *m*, peluquería *f*
saloon [səlún] N salón *m*, taberna *f*, bar *m*
salt [sɔɫt] N sal *f*; (for smelling) sales *f pl*; **the**

— **of the earth** la sal de la tierra; **old** —
lobo de mar *m*; —**cellar** salero *m*; — **lick**
salegar *m*; — **mine** salina *f*; —**shaker**
salero *m*; —**water** agua salada *f*; VT salar;
to — away ahorrar
salty [sɔ́ɫti] ADJ salado; (land) salobre
salutation [sæljətéʃən] N saludo *m*
salute [səlút] N saludo *m*; (of guns) salva *f*;
VI/VT (greet) saludar; (acknowledge)
reconocer
Salvadoran, Salvadorian [sæɫvədór(i)ən]
ADJ & N salvadoreño -ña *mf*
salvage [sǽlvɪʤ] N (recovery) salvamento *m*;
(objects recovered) objetos salvados *m pl*;
VT salvar
salvation [sæɫvéʃən] N salvación *f*
salve [sæv] N ungüento *m*, pomada *f*
salvo [sǽɫvo] N salva *f*
same [sem] ADJ (identical) mismo; (similar)
igual; **it is all the — to me** me da igual,
me da lo mismo; **all the** — de todos
modos; —-**sex marriage** matrimonio
homosexual *m*
Samoa [səmóə] N Samoa *f*
Samoan [səmóən] ADJ & N samoano -na *mf*
sample [sǽmpɫ] N muestra *f*; VT (try) probar;
(take samples) muestrear
sampling [sǽmplɪŋ] N muestreo *m*
sanctify [sǽŋktəfaɪ] VT santificar
sanction [sǽŋkʃən] N sanción *f*; VT sancionar
sanctity [sǽŋktɪɾi] N santidad *f*
sanctuary [sǽŋktʃuɛri] N (church
auditorium, place of refuge) santuario *m*;
(game preserve) reserva *f*
sand [sænd] N arena *f*; —**box** arenero *m*; —
dollar erizo de mar plano *m*; —**paper**
papel de lija *m*; **to —paper** lijar; —**stone**
arenisca *f*; —**storm** tormenta de arena *f*;
VT lijar, pulir
sandal [sǽndl] N sandalia *f*
sandwich [sǽndwɪtʃ] N bocadillo *m*,
emparedado *m*; VT intercalar; **to be —ed
between** quedar apretado entre
sandy [sǽndi] ADJ (full of sand) arenoso,
arenisco; (yellowish red) rubio
sane [sen] ADJ cuerdo
sanitarium [sænɪtériəm] N sanatorio *m*
sanitary [sǽnɪteri] ADJ sanitario; — **napkin**
paño higiénico *m*
sanitation [sænɪtéʃən] N (sewers)
saneamiento *m*; (hygiene) salubridad *f*
sanity [sǽnɪɾi] N cordura *f*
San Marinese [sænmærəníz] ADJ & N
sanmarinense *mf*, sanmarinés -esa *mf*
San Marino [sænməríno] N San Marino *m*
Sanskrit [sǽnskrɪt] N sánscrito *f*
Santa Claus [sǽntəklɔz] N Papá Noel *m*,

Santa Claus *m*

São Tomean [saʊtoméən] ADJ & N santotomense *mf*

São Tome and Principe [saʊtoméændprínsipe] N Santo Tomé y Príncipe *m*

sap [sæp] N (juice) savia *f*; (fool) tonto -ta *mf*; VT (exhaust) agotar

sapling [sǽplɪŋ] N (tree) árbol joven *m*; (person) jovenzuelo -la *mf*

sapphire [sǽfaɪr] N zafiro *m*

sarcasm [sárkæzəm] N sarcasmo *m*, socarronería *f*

sarcastic [sɑrkǽstɪk] ADJ sarcástico, socarrón

sarcoma [sɑrkómə] N sarcoma *m*

sarcophagus [sɑrkáfəgəs] N sarcófago *m*

sardine [sɑrdín] N sardina *f*

sardonic [sɑrdánɪk] ADJ sardónico

sash [sæʃ] N (around waist) faja *f*; (around shoulder) banda *f*; (on window) marco *m*, bastidor *m*

sassy [sǽsi] ADJ insolente

satanic [sətǽnɪk] ADJ satánico

satchel [sǽtʃəɫ] N cartera *f*

satellite [sǽdlaɪt] N satélite *m*; — **dish** (antenna) parabólica *f*

satiate [séʃiet] VT saciar, hartar

satin [sǽtn̩] N raso *m*, satén *m*

satire [sǽtaɪr] N sátira *f*

satirical [sətírɪkəɫ] ADJ satírico

satirize [sǽdəraɪz] VT satirizar

satisfaction [sæDɪsfǽkʃən] N satisfacción *f*

satisfactory [sæDɪsfǽktəri] ADJ satisfactorio

satisfied [sǽDɪsfaɪd] ADJ satisfecho

satisfy [sǽDɪsfaɪ] VI/VT satisfacer

saturate [sǽtʃəret] VI/VT (impregnate) saturar(se); (soak) empapar(se); —**d fat** grasa saturada *f*

Saturday [sǽDə·De] N sábado *m*

sauce [sɔs] N salsa *f*; —**pan** cacerola *f*; VT aderezar con salsa

saucer [sɔ́sə·] N platillo *m*

saucy [sɔ́si] ADJ descarado, insolente; (who talks back) respondón

Saudi Arabia [sɔ́Diərébiə] N Arabia Saudí *f*, Arabia Saudita *f*

Saudi Arabian [sɔ́Diərébiən] ADJ & N saudí *mf*, saudita *mf*

saunter [sɔ́ntə·] VI pasearse, deambular

sausage [sɔ́sɪdʒ] N (thick) chorizo *m*; (thin) salchicha *f*; (cured) longaniza *f*; —**-making** charcutería *f*

savage [sǽvɪdʒ] ADJ salvaje; (furious) rabioso; (rugged) agreste; N salvaje *m*; VT hacer trizas

savagery [sǽvɪdʒri] N salvajismo *m*, barbarie *f*

save [sev] VT (a sinner, a person in danger)

salvar; (furniture) salvaguardar, proteger; (money, time, energy) ahorrar, economizar; (data) guardar; VI (lay up money, be economical) ahorrar; (protect) salvaguardar; **to — from** librar de; **to — one's eyes** cuidarse la vista; PREP salvo, menos

savings [sévɪŋz] N ahorros *m pl*; — **account** cuenta de ahorros *f*; — **bank** caja de ahorros *f*

savior [sévjə·] N salvador -ora *mf*

savor [sévə·] N (taste) sabor *m*; (trace) dejo *m*; VT saborear

savory [sévəri] ADJ sabroso

savvy [sǽvi] N astucia *f*; ADJ astuto

saw [sɔ] N sierra *f*; —**horse** caballete *m*; VI/VT aserrar(se); —**dust** aserrín *m*, serrín *m*; —**mill** aserradero *m*

saxophone [sǽksəfon] N saxofón *m*

say [se] VI/VT decir; VT (a clock) marcar; (a sign) rezar, decir; (a prayer) rezar; —**!** ¡oye! **that is to** — es decir; — **I bought it** supongamos que yo lo comprara; **it goes without** —**ing** huelga decirlo; **there's a lot to be said for** es muy recomendable; **when all is said and done** al fin y al cabo; **you can** — **that again** tú lo has dicho; **the final** — la última palabra; **to have one's** — dar su opinión; ADV **you could earn,** —**, 1 million dollars** podrías ganar pongamos un millón de dólares

saying [séɪŋ] N dicho *m*, refrán *m*

scab [skæb] N (of a wound) costra *f*; (on plants) roña *f*; (strikebreaker) esquirol *m*, amarillo -lla *mf*; VI (wound) encostrarse; (break a strike) ser esquirol

scabby [skǽbi] ADJ (of wounds) costroso; (of plants) roñoso; (of scalp) tiñoso

scaffold [skǽfəɫd] N (in construction) andamio *m*; (of a gallows) patíbulo *m*

scald [skɔɫd] VI/VT escaldar(se); N escaldadura *f*

scale [skeɫ] N (progression) escala *f*; (for weighing) balanza *f*; (for heavy weights) báscula *f*; (on fish, reptiles, human skin) escama *f*; **pair of** —**s** balanza *f*; VT (climb) escalar; (remove scales) escamar; VI/VT (adjust proportionately) graduar; **to** — **down** rebajar proporcionalmente

scallion [skǽljən] N cebollino *m*

scallop [skǽləp] N (mollusk) vieira *f*; (of beef) escalope *m*; (of fabric) festón *m*; VT festonear

scalp [skæɫp] N cuero cabelludo *m*; VT (to skin) arrancar la cabellera; (to resell) revender

scalpel [skǽɫpəɫ] N bisturí *m*
scalper [skǽɫpɚ] N revendedor -ra *mf*
scam [skæm] N timo *m*, estafa *f*
scamp [skæmp] N pícaro -ra *mf*, tunante -ta *mf*, pillo -lla *mf*
scamper [skǽmpɚ] VI (run) escabullirse, escaparse; (caper) cabriolar
scan [skæn] VT (horizon) escudriñar, escrutar; (with radar) explorar; (brain) hacer una tomografía; (page) echar un vistazo a; (verse) escandir; (digitalize for computer) escanear; N tomografía *f*
scandal [skǽndl̩] N escándalo *m*
scandalize [skǽndl̩aɪz] VT escandalizar
scandalous [skǽndl̩əs] ADJ escandaloso
scanner [skǽnɚ] N escáner *m*
scant [skænt] ADJ escaso
scanty [skǽnti] ADJ (scant) escaso; (of a skirt) muy corto; (of a bikini) breve
scapegoat [sképgot] N chivo expiatorio *m*, cabeza de turco *m*
scar [skɑr] N cicatriz *f*, lacra *f*; VT dejar una cicatriz
scarce [skɛrs] ADJ escaso; **to be —** escasear
scarcely [skérsli] ADV (barely) apenas; **he's — a genius** no es un genio ni mucho menos
scarcity [skérsɪDi] N escasez *f*, pobreza *f*, carestía *f*
scare [skɛr] VI/VT espantar(se), asustar(se); **to — away** ahuyentar; **to — up** reunir; N susto *m*, sobresalto *m*; (of war) amago *m*; **—crow** espantapájaros *m sg*
scarf [skɑrf] N (woolen) bufanda *f*; (silk, cotton) pañuelo *m*; VI **to — up** engullir
scarlet [skárlɪt] N escarlata *m*, grana *f*; **— fever** escarlatina *f*
scary [skéri] ADJ (causing fright) de miedo; (easily frightened) asustadizo
scat [skæt] INTERJ ¡fuera!
scatter [skǽDɚ] VI/VT (seeds) esparcir(se), desparramar(se), desperdigar(se); (crowd) dispersar(se); **—brain** cabeza de chorlito *mf*; **—brained** atolondrado
scavenge [skǽvɪndʒ] VT recoger, rescatar; VI hurgar
scenario [sɪnério] N guión *m*; **worst-case —** el peor de los casos
scene [sin] N escena *f*; (sphere) ambiente *m*, ámbito *m*; **to make a —** montar una escena; **behind the —s** entre bastidores
scenery [sínəri] N paisaje *m*; (on a stage) decorado *m*
scenic [sínɪk] ADJ panorámico
scent [sɛnt] N (smell) olor *m*; (fragrance) perfume *m*; (trace) pista *f*, rastro *m*; (sense of smell) olfato *m*; VI/VT (perceive through

smell) olfatear; (intuit) presentir; (give fragrance to) perfumar
schedule [skédʒuɫ] N (plan) calendario *m*; (timetable) horario *m*; (appendix) apéndice *m*; (list) lista *f*; **on —** en fecha; **ahead of —** adelantado; VT programar, fijar
scheme [skim] N (plan) plan *m*, proyecto *m*; (plot) ardid *m*, trama *f*; (of colors) combinación *f*; VI/VT maquinar, intrigar, tramar
schemer [skímɚ] N maquinador -ra *mf*, intrigante *mf*
scheming [skímɪŋ] ADJ intrigante; N maquinación *f*
schizophrenia [skɪtsəfréniə] N esquizofrenia *f*
schmuck [ʃmʌk] N *pej* pendejo -ja *mf*, gilipollas *mf sg*
scholar [skálɚ] N (student) alumno -na *mf*; (fellow) becario -ria *mf*; (erudite person) erudito -ta *mf*, estudioso -sa *mf*
scholarly [skálɚli] ADJ erudito
scholarship [skálɚʃɪp] N (erudition) erudición *f*; (award) beca *f*
school [skuɫ] N (primary) escuela *f*, colegio *m*; (secondary) secundaria *f*; *Sp* instituto *m*; (university) universidad *f*; (of law, etc.) facultad *f*; (of language, driving) academia *f*; (of thought) escuela *f*; (of fish) banco *m*, cardumen *m*; **—boy** escolar *m*; **—girl** escolar *f*; **—house** escuela *f*; **—master** maestro -tra *mf*; **—mate** compañero -ra de escuela *mf*; **—room** aula *f*, sala de clase *f*; **—teacher** maestro -tra *mf*; **— year** año lectivo *m*; VT instruir, entrenar
schooling [skúlɪŋ] N instrucción *f*
schooner [skúnɚ] N goleta *f*
sciatic nerve [saɪǽDɪknɝv] N nervio ciático *m*
science [sáɪəns] N ciencia *f*; **— fiction** ciencia ficción *f*
scientific [saɪəntífɪk] ADJ científico; **— method** método científico *m*
scientist [sáɪəntɪst] N científico -ca *mf*
scintillate [síntl̩et] VI (diamonds) centellear, destellar; (stars) titilar
scissors [sízɚz] N tijeras *f pl*
sclerosis [sklərósɪs] N esclerosis *f*
scoff [skɑf] N mofa *f*, burla *f*; VI mofarse; **to — at** mofarse de, burlarse de
scold [skoɫd] VI/VT reprender, regañar, reñir; N regañón -ona *mf*
scolding [skóɫdɪŋ] N regaño *m*, reprimenda *f*
scoliosis [skoliósɪs] N escoliosis *f*
scoop [skup] N (ladle) cucharón *m*; (spoon for ice-cream) cuchara *f*; (shovel) pala *f*; (news

item) primicia *f*; VT sacar con cuchara; (report first) adelantarse a; **to — in a good profit** sacar buena ganancia; **to — out** (water) achicar; (a hole) cavar; **to — up** recoger

scoot [skut] VI (go fast) correr; (go away) largarse

scooter [skúDɚ] N (with motor) scooter *m*; (toy) monopatín *m*, patinete *m*

scope [skop] N (range) alcance *m*, ámbito *m*; (sphere) esfera *f*; VT observar

scorch [skɔrtʃ] VI/VT chamuscar(se), quemar(se); N chamuscadura *f*; *Am* quemadura *f*

score [skor] N (partial result) tanteo *m*; (total result) resultado *m*; (in a test) calificación *f*; (scratch) arañazo *m*; (twenty) veintena *f*; (of music) partitura *f*; **on that** — a ese respecto; **to keep** — llevar la cuenta; **to settle old —s** ajustar cuentas; VT (a test) calificar; (to orchestrate) orquestar; (to scratch) arañar; VI/VT (points) marcar, tantear; (sexually) ligar

scorn [skɔrn] N desdén *m*, menosprecio *m*; VI/VT desdeñar, menospreciar

scornful [skɔ́rnfəɫ] ADJ desdeñoso

scorpion [skɔ́rpiən] N escorpión *m*, alacrán *m*

Scotch [skɑtʃ] ADJ escocés; — **whisky** whisky escocés *m*

Scotland [skɑ́tlənd] N Escocia *f*

Scotsman [skɑ́tsmən] N escocés *m*

Scotswoman [skɑ́tswumən] N escocesa *f*

Scottish [skɑ́DIʃ] ADJ escocés

scoundrel [skáʊndrəɫ] N bellaco *m*, infame *m*, truhán *m*

scour [skaʊr] VT (clean) fregar, restregar; (search) recorrer

scourge [skɝʤ] N azote *m*; VT azotar

scout [skaʊt] N (military) explorador -ra *mf*; (child explorer) explorador -ra *mf*, scout *mf*; (for talent) cazatalentos *mf sg*; **a good** — una buena persona; VI/VT explorar; VI **to — for** buscar

scowl [skaʊɫ] N ceño fruncido *m*; VI fruncir el ceño

scram [skræm] VI largarse

scramble [skrǽmbəɫ] VI (climb) subir a gatas; VT (eggs) revolver; (numbers) mezclar; **to — for** pelearse por; **to — up** subir a gatas; **—d eggs** huevos revueltos *m pl*; N (difficult climb) subida difícil *f*; (struggle for possession) arrebatiña *f*

scrap [skræp] N (fragment) fragmento *m*, pedacito *m*; (of truth) ápice *m*; (fight) riña *f*, reyerta *f*; **—book** álbum de recortes *m*; — **iron** chatarra *f*; **—s** sobras *f pl*, desperdicios *m pl*; VT (break apart)

desguazar; (discard) desechar; VI pelearse, reñir

scrape [skrep] VI/VT (rub) raspar; (damage) arañar; **to — along** ir tirando, ir pasándola; **to — by** arreglárselas; **to — together** reunir; **to bow and** — ser muy servil; N (act of scraping) raspado *m*; (injury) raspón *m*, raspadura *f*; (sound) chirrido *m*; (fight) pelea *f*; (difficult situation) aprieto *m*

scraper [skrépɚ] N raspador *m*

scratch [skrætʃ] VI/VT (mark) arañar, rasguñar; (relieve itching) rascar(se); (cancel from a race) retirar(se); (cause itching) picar; VI (to dig, as a hen) escarbar; **to — out** (words) tachar; (eyes) sacar; N (injury) arañazo *m*, rasguño *m*; (sound) chirrido *m*; **to start from —** empezar de cero

scrawny [skrɔ́ni] ADJ esmirriado

scream [skrim] N grito *m*, alarido *m*; **he's a** — es un payaso; VI/VT gritar

screech [skritʃ] N (of brakes) chirrido *m*; (of voice) chillido *m*; — **owl** lechuza *f*; VI (of brakes) chirriar; (of voice) chillar

screen [skrin] N (movie, computer) pantalla *f*; (divider) biombo *m*; (on window) mosquitero *m*; (sifter) tamiz *m*; — **door** puerta con mosquitero *f*; **—play** guión *m*; **—writer** guionista *mf*; VT (conceal) tapar; (sift) tamizar; (project) proyectar; (select) seleccionar

screw [skru] N tornillo *m*; (one turn) vuelta *f*; (propeller) hélice *f*; (sexual intercourse) *fam* polvo *m*; **—driver** destornillador *m* (also cocktail); VT (turn) atornillar; (have intercourse) *Sp vulg* follar; *Am vulg* coger, culear; **to — on** enroscar; **to — up one's courage** cobrar ánimo; **to — around** (waste time) perder tiempo; (be promiscuous) ser promiscuo; **to — something up** *vulg* chingar algo, joder algo; **I —ed up** *vulg* la cagué; **to — with** *vulg* chingar

scribble [skríbəɫ] VI/VT garabatear, garrapatear; N garabato *m*

script [skrɪpt] N (writing) escritura *f*; (screenplay) guión *m*

scripture [skríptʃɚ] N escritura sagrada *f*

scroll [skroɫ] N (roll) rollo *m*; (adornment) voluta *f*; VI **to — down** bajar el cursor

scrotum [skróDəm] N escroto *m*

scrub [skrʌb] VI/VT (rub) fregar, restregar; VT (cancel) cancelar; **to — up** lavarse las manos; N (cleaning) friega *f*, fregada *f*; (bushes) maleza *f*; (rough terrain) breña *f*; — **pine** pino achaparrado *m*; — **team**

equipo suplente *m*; —**woman** fregona *f*
scruple [skrúpəł] N escrúpulo *m*
scrupulous [skrúpjələs] ADJ escrupuloso
scrutinize [skrútn̩aɪz] VI/VT escrutar
scrutiny [skrútn̩i] N escrutinio *m*, examen minucioso *m*
scuba [skúbə] N escafandra *f*; VI **to** —-**dive** bucear
scuff [skʌf] VT (shoes) rayar; (floor) marcar; N (on shoes) raya *f*; (on floor) marca *f*
scuffle [skʌ́fəł] N refriega *f*, riña *f*; VI pelear, reñir; (shuffle) arrastrar los pies
sculptor [skʌ́łptɚ] N escultor -ra *mf*
sculpture [skʌ́łptʃɚ] N escultura *f*; VI/VT esculpir
scum [skʌm] N (in a glass) capa de suciedad *f*; (in a pond) verdín *m*; (people) escoria *f*; (vile person) *pej* canalla *mf*; —**bag** *pej* canalla *mf*; VI cubrirse de espuma; VT espumar
scurrilous [skɝ́ələs] ADJ (coarse) grosero; (injurious) injurioso
scurry [skɝ́i] VI correr; **to** — **away** / **off** escabullirse; N carrera *f*
scuttle [skʌ́dl̩] VI (run) correr; **to** — **away** / **off** escabullirse; VT (sink a ship) hundir; (abandon a plane) abandonar
scythe [saɪð] N guadaña *f*
sea [si] N mar *mf*; **at** — en el mar; **by** — por barco; **to put to** — hacerse a la mar; **on the high** —**s** en alta mar; ADJ marino; — **battle** batalla naval *f*; —**board** costa *f*, litoral *m*; —**coast** costa *f*, litoral *m*; — **cow** vaca marina *f*; — **current** corriente marina *f*; —**faring** marinero; —**food** frutos del mar *m pl*; — **green** verdemar *m*; —**gull** gaviota *f*; — **horse** caballito de mar *m*; — **level** nivel del mar *m*; — **lion** léon marino *m*; —**man** marino *m*, marinero *m*; —**plane** hidroavión *m*; —**port** puerto de mar *m*; — **power** potencia naval *f*; —**shore** costa *f*; —**sick** mareado; **to get** —**sick** marearse; —**sickness** mareo *m*; —**side** costa *f*, litoral *m*; — **turtle** tortuga marina *f*; — **urchin** erizo de mar *m*; —**weed** alga (marina) *f*; —**worthy** marinero
seal [sił] N (stamp) sello *m*; (on a jar) precinto *m*; (animal) foca *f*; **to set one's** — **to** sellar; —**ing wax** lacre *m*; VT (put a seal on) sellar; (close with a seal) precintar; **to** — **one's fate** determinar el destino de uno; **to** — **off** acordonar; **to** — **in** cerrar herméticamente; **to** — **with sealing wax** lacrar
seam [sim] N (sewing) costura *f*; (in rock) grieta *f*; (in ore deposits) veta *f*; VT coser

seamstress [símstrɪs] N costurera *f*
seamy [sími] ADJ sórdido
sear [sir] VT chamuscar
search [sɝtʃ] VI/VT (an area) rastrear, requisar; (a suitcase) registrar; (a person) cachear; — **me!** ¡a mí que me registren! ¡yo que sé! **to** — **for** buscar; N (for something) búsqueda *f*; (of baggage, ships) registro *m*; (of an area) rastreo *m*; — **engine** motor de búsqueda *m*, máquina de búsqueda *f*; —**light** reflector *m*; — **warrant** orden de registro *m*; **in** — **of** en busca de
season [sízən] N (of the year) estación *f*; (period of time) temporada *f*, época *f*; **in** — en temporada / época; — **ticket** billete de abono *m*; **open** — temporada de caza / pesca *f*; **out of** — fuera de temporada / época; VT (to spice) sazonar, aderezar; VI (wood) secarse; **a** —**ed pilot** un piloto experimentado
seasoning [sízənɪŋ] N condimento *m*, aliño *m*
seat [sit] N (furniture) asiento *m*; (of bicycle) sillín *m*; (in parliament) escaño *m*; (of government) sede *f*; (in the theater) localidad *f*; (buttocks) asentaderas *f pl*; (of clothes) fondillos *m pl*; **to take a** — sentarse, tomar asiento; — **belt** cinturón de seguridad *m*; VT (cause to sit) sentar; (accommodate with seats) tener capacidad para; (place) colocar; **to** — **oneself** sentarse
seclude [sɪklúd] VT aislar; **to** — **oneself from** recluirse de, aislarse de
secluded [sɪklúdɪd] ADJ apartado, aislado
seclusion [sɪklúʒən] N recogimiento *m*, aislamiento *m*
second [sékənd] ADJ & N segundo -da *mf*; — **fiddle** segundón -ona *mf*; — **floor** primer piso *m*; —**hand** de segunda mano; — **lieutenant** subteniente *mf*; **on** — **thought** pensándolo bien; —-**rate** mediocre, de segunda; N (part of a minute) segundo *m*; (helper in a duel) padrino *m*; — **child** segundón -ona *mf*; — **cousin** primo -ma segundo -da *mf*; — **nature** automático; —**s** artículos de segunda *m pl*; **may I have** —**s?** ¿puedo repetir? **to** —-**guess** cuestionar; VT (support) secundar, apoyar; (assist in duels) apadrinar; (support a motion) apoyar
secondary [sékəndɛri] ADJ secundario; — **school** escuela secundaria *f*
secondly [sékəndli] ADV en segundo lugar
secrecy [síkrɪsi] N secreto *m*
secret [síkrɪt] ADJ & N secreto *m*

secretariat [sɛkrɪtǽriət] N secretaría *f*
secretary [sékrɪteri] N (assistant) secretario
-ria *mf*; (government) ministro -tra *mf*;
(furniture) escritorio *m*
secrete [sɪkrít] VT (discharge) secretar,
segregar; (hide) ocultar
secretion [sɪkríʃən] N secreción *f*
secretive [síkrɪDɪv] ADJ hermético
sect [sɛkt] N secta *f*
section [sékʃən] N sección *f*; (of a chapter)
apartado *m*; (passage) trozo *m*; (of a city)
sector *m*; (incision) corte *m*; (of orange)
gajo *m*; VT seccionar
sector [séktɚ] N sector *m*
secular [sékjələ˞] ADJ secular; N seglar *mf*, lego
-ga *mf*
secure [sɪkjúr] ADJ (certain, safe) seguro;
(firm) firme; VT (make certain, guarantee)
asegurar, afianzar; (make firm) afirmar,
cimentar; (obtain) obtener; (protect)
proteger; (lock) cerrar con llave; (capture)
capturar; (tie) amarrar
security [sɪkjúrɪDi] N (safety, freedom from
worry) seguridad *f*; (guarantee) fianza *f*,
garantía *f*; (guarantor) fiador -ora *mf*;
securities valores *m pl*
sedan [sɪdǽn] N sedán *m*
sedate [sɪdét] ADJ sosegado, tranquilo; VT
sedar
sedation [sɪdéʃən] N sedación *f*
sedative [séDətɪv] ADJ & N calmante *m*,
sedante *m*
sedentary [sédn̩teri] ADJ sedentario
sediment [séDəmənt] N sedimento *m*; (dregs)
heces *f pl*
sedition [sɪdíʃən] N sedición *f*
seduce [sɪdús] VI/VT seducir (a)
seduction [sɪdÁkʃən] N seducción *f*
see [si] VI/VT (perceive, find out, meet, visit)
ver; (understand) entender; (make sure)
fijarse, asegurarse; (date) salir con; (help)
ayudar; (accompany) acompañar; **to — to**
encargarse de, atender; **let me —** a ver;
to — off despedir; **to — through**
someone calar a alguien; **to — about**
ocuparse de; **to — out** acompañar a la
puerta; N sede *f*
seed [sid] N (grains) semilla *f*; (semen)
simiente *f*; **to go to —** echarse a perder;
— bed semillero *m*; VI/VT (sow) sembrar;
VT despepitar, quitar las semillas; (player)
clasificar; VI producir semillas
seedy [sídi] ADJ sórdido
seek [sik] VT (search for) buscar; (ask for)
pedir; **to — after** buscar; **to — to** tratar
de, esforzarse por
seem [sim] VI parecer; **they — to be here**

parece que están aquí; **it —s to me** me
parece
seemingly [símɪŋli] ADV aparentemente
seep [sip] VI/VT rezumar(se)
seer [sir] N vidente *mf*
seesaw [sísɔ] N balancín *m*, subibaja *m*; VI
oscilar
seethe [sið] VI bullir, hervir; **he was
seething** hervía de rabia
segment [ségmənt] N segmento *m*
segregate [ségrɪget] VI/VT segregar
seismic [sáɪzmɪk] ADJ sísmico
seize [siz] VT (grab) asir, agarrar; (take
possession) apoderarse de; (take advantage
of) aprovecharse de; (confiscate) embargar,
incautarse de, secuestrar; **to — upon** asir;
VI **to — (up)** agarrotarse; **to — upon**
valerse de
seizure [síʒɚ] N (of power) toma *f*; (of
property) confiscación *f*; (of drugs, guns)
incautación *f*, secuestro *m*; (epileptic)
ataque *m*
seldom [séɫdəm] ADV rara vez, raramente
select [sɪlékt] ADJ selecto; VI/VT elegir,
seleccionar
selection [sɪlékʃən] N selección *f*, elección *f*
selective [sɪléktɪv] ADJ selectivo
self [sɛɫf] N (ego) yo *m*; **—-assurance**
desenvoltura *f*; **—-control** autocontrol *m*;
—-defense defensa propia *f*; (juridical
term) legítima defensa *f*; **—-denial**
abnegación *f*; **—-discipline**
autodisciplina *f*; **—-esteem** autoestima *f*;
—-government autogobierno *m*;
—-help autoayuda *f*; **—-image**
autoimagen *f*; **—-improvement** mejora
personal *f*; **—-interest** interés personal *m*;
—-made man hombre que debe su éxito
a sus propios esfuerzos *m*; **—-pity**
autocompasión *f*; **—-reliance**
independencia *f*; **—-respect** amor propio
m; **—-sacrifice** sacrificio *m*;
—-satisfaction autosatisfacción *f*; **his
better —** su lado bueno *m*; **his former
—** lo que era antes *m*; ADJ **—-assured**
desenvuelto; **—-centered** egocéntrico;
—-composed tranquilo; **—-confident**
con confianza de sí mismo; **—-conscious**
(shy) cohibido; (with complexes)
acomplejado; **—-destructive**
autodestructivo; **—-employed** que trabaja
por cuenta propia; **—-evident** evidente;
—-explanatory claro, fácil de entender;
—-propelled autopropulsado;
—-righteous que afecta superioridad
moral; **—-satisfied** pagado de sí,
satisfecho de sí; **—-service** autoservicio;

—**-serving** interesado; —**-sufficient** autosuficiente

selfish [sɛ́łfɪʃ] ADJ egoísta

selfishness [sɛ́łfɪʃnɪs] N egoísmo *m*

selfless [sɛ́łflɪs] ADJ desinteresado, generoso

sell [sɛł] VI/VT vender(se); **this book sold a thousand copies** se vendieron mil ejemplares de este libro; **to be sold on** estar entusiasmado con; **to — out** (dispose of) liquidar; (betray) traicionar, vender; (run out) agotarse; N —**-off** (liquidation) liquidación *f*; (decline) baja *f*; —**out** traición *f*

seller [sɛlə-] N vendedor -ora *mf*

semantics [sɪmǽntɪks] N semántica *f*

semblance [sémbləns] N apariencia *f*

semen [símɪn] N semen *m*

semester [səméstə-] N semestre *m*

semicircle [sémɪsɜ-kəł] N semicírculo *m*

semicolon [sémɪkolən] N punto y coma *m*

semiconductor [sɛmɪkəndʌ́ktə-] N semiconductor *m*

semifinal [sémɪfaɪnəł] ADJ & N semifinal *f*

seminar [sémənɑr] N seminario *m*

seminary [séməneri] N seminario *m*

Semitic [səmídɪk] ADJ semítico

senate [sénɪt] N senado *m*

senator [sénətə-] N senador -ora *mf*

send [send] VT enviar, mandar; **that sent chills down my spine** me dio escalofríos; **to — away** hacer salir; **to — for** mandar buscar a; **to — in** remitir; **to — out for** encargar; **to — word** mandar decir

sender [séndə-] N remitente *m*

Senegal [sénɪgɔ̀ł] N Senegal *m*

Senegalese [sɛnɪgəlíz] ADJ & N senegalés -esa *mf*

senile [sínaɪł] ADJ senil, chocho

senility [sɪnílɪDi] N senilidad *f*, chochera *f*, chochez *f*

senior [sínjə-] ADJ (with more seniority) más antiguo; (in school) de cuarto año; (for the elderly) para ancianos; **John Smith —** John Smith padre; N (person of higher rank) superior *mf*; (fourth year student) estudiante de cuarto año *mf*; (elderly person) persona de la tercera edad *f*; **to be somebody's —** ser mayor que alguien; **— citizen** persona de la tercera edad *f*

seniority [sinjɔ́rɪDi] N antigüedad *f*

sensation [sɛnséʃən] N sensación *f*

sensational [sɛnséʃənəł] ADJ sensacional

sense [sens] N (of humor, honor, direction) sentido *m*; (of pain, insecurity) sensación *f*; (meaning) significado *m*, sentido *m*; **to make —** tener sentido; **to make — of**

something entender algo; **in a —** en cierto sentido; **to take leave of one's —s** volverse loco; **to come to one's —s** (wake up) volver en sí; (be reasonable) recobrar el juicio; VT (perceive) percibir, sentir; (intuit) intuir

senseless [sénslɪs] ADJ (meaningless) sin sentido; (unconscious) inconsciente

sensibility [sɛnsəbílɪDi] N sensibilidad *f*

sensible [sénsəbəł] ADJ sensato, razonable

sensitive [sénsɪDɪv] ADJ (to emotions) sensible; (to stimuli) sensitivo

sensitivity [sénsɪtɪvɪDi] N sensibilidad *f*

sensitize [sénsɪtaɪz] VT sensibilizar

sensor [sénsɔr] N sensor *m*

sensory [sénsəri] ADJ sensorial

sensual [sénʃuəł] ADJ sensual

sensuality [sɛnʃuǽlɪDi] N sensualidad *f*

sensuous [sénʃuəs] ADJ sensual

sentence [séntəns] N (to prison) sentencia *f*, condena *f*; (phrase) oración *f*; VT condenar, sentenciar

sentiment [séntəmənt] N sentimiento *m*

sentimental [sɛntəméntḷ] ADJ sentimental; (excessively) sensiblero

sentimentality [sɛntəmɛntǽlɪDi] N sentimentalismo *m*; (excessive) sensiblería *f*

sentinel [séntənəł] N centinela *m*

sentry [séntri] N centinela *m*; **— box** garita *f*

separate [séprɪt] ADJ (apart) separado; [sépəret] VI/VT separar(se)

separation [sɛpəréʃən] N separación *f*

Sephardi [səfárdi] N sefardí *mf*, sefardita *mf*

September [sɛptémbə-] N septiembre *m*

sequel [síkwəł] N continuación *f*

sequence [síkwəns] N secuencia *f*; (of events) serie *f*; **in —** en orden; VT secuenciar

serenade [sərənéd] N serenata *f*, ronda *f*; VI/VT dar (una) serenata (a), rondar (a)

serene [sərín] ADJ sereno

serenity [sərénɪDi] N serenidad *f*

sergeant [sárdʒənt] N sargento *m*

serial [síriəł] N novela por entregas *f*; ADJ (published in installments) por entregas; (murder) en serie

series [síriz] N serie *f*

serious [síriəs] ADJ serio; (illness) grave

seriousness [síriəsnɪs] N seriedad *f*; (of an illness) gravedad *f*

sermon [sɜ́-mən] N sermón *m*

serpent [sɜ́-pənt] N sierpe *f*

serrated [sɛ́rɛDɪd] ADJ serrado

serum [sírəm] N suero *m*

servant [sɜ́-vənt] N sirviente -ta *mf*, criado -da *mf*

serve [sɜ-v] VI/VT (in a restaurant, in a store)

servir, atender; (in tennis) sacar; **to — a term in prison** cumplir una condena; **to — a warrant** entregar una orden judicial; **to — as** servir de; **to — notice** advertir; **to — one's purpose** resultarle útil a alguien; **it —s me right** me lo merezco; N saque *m*

server [sɚ́vɚ] N (one who serves) servidor -ra *mf*; (in a restaurant) camarero -ra *mf*; (for pie) utensilio para servir *m*; (computer) servidor *m*

service [sɚ́vɪs] N servicio *m*; (in tennis) saque *m*; (of a warrant) entrega *f*; **at your — a** su servicio; **— entrance** entrada de servicio *f*; **—man** (soldier) militar *m*; (for repairs) reparador *m*; **— station** estación de servicio *f*; VT (a car) revisar; (an industry) atender, servir; (a debt) pagar

serviceable [sɚ́vɪsəbəɫ] ADJ (practical) práctico; (durable) duradero

servile [sɚ́vaɪɫ] ADJ servil

servitude [sɚ́vɪtud] N servidumbre *f*

sesame [sésəmi] N sésamo *m*

session [séʃən] N sesión *f*; (semester) semestre *m*; (of Congress) período de sesiones *m*

set [sɛt] VT (place) colocar; (fix) fijar, establecer; (sic) azuzar; (print) componer; VI (cement) fraguar; (jelly) cuajar; (sun) ponerse; (glue) endurecerse; **to — a bone** reducir un hueso dislocado; **to — a diamond** engastar un diamante; **to — an example** dar ejemplo; **to — a poem to music** ponerle música a un poema; **to — a precedent** establecer un precedente; **to — a trap** tender una trampa; **to — a watch** poner el reloj en hora; **to — about** disponerse a; **to — aside** apartar; (money) ahorrar; (a claim) rechazar; (a verdict) anular; **to — back** (hinder, make earlier) atrasar; (cost) costar; (a clock) retrasar; **to — forth** exponer; **to — forth on a journey** ponerse en camino; **to — free** librar; **to — off** (make explode) hacer estallar; (start on a journey) ponerse en camino; (intensify) resaltar; **to — one's heart on** tener la esperanza puesta en; **to — one's mind on** resolverse a; **to — out for** partir para; **to — out to** proponerse; **to — right** rectificar; **to — the table** poner la mesa; **to — up** (assemble) armar; (set a trap for) tender; (establish) establecer; **to — upon someone** acometer a alguien; ADJ (fixed) fijo; (ready) listo; (hard) duro; N (ensemble) juego *m*; (group) conjunto *m*; (TV) aparato *m*; (scenery) escenario *m*; (of tennis) set *m*; **—back** revés *m*; **— of**

teeth dentadura *f*; **—up** (arrangement) arreglo *m*; (assembly) montaje *m*; (trap) tongo *m*, timo *m*

setter [sɛ́Dɚ] N sétter *m*

setting [sɛ́Dɪŋ] N (act of putting down) colocación *f*; (jewel) engaste *m*; (in theater) escenario *m*; (of sun, moon) puesta *f*; **— sun** sol poniente *m*

settle [sɛ́dɫ] VT (a territory) colonizar, poblar; (affairs) arreglar; (argument) zanjar; (lawsuit) arreglar; (an estate) liquidar; (a bill) saldar, solventar; (one's nerves) calmar; VI (end a dispute) llegar a un arreglo; (take up residence) establecerse; (alight) posarse; (sink to bottom) depositarse; **to — down** (get married) casarse; (mend one's ways) sentar cabeza; (take up residence) instalarse; (become calm) calmarse; **to — on a date** fijar / señalar una fecha; **to — for** conformarse con; **to — up** pagar

settlement [sɛ́dɫmənt] N (community) colonia *f*, población *f*; (agreement) acuerdo *m*; (of a lawsuit) arreglo *m*; (of a bill) pago *m*, finiquito *m*; (final disposition) liquidación *f*

settler [sɛ́tlɚ] N colono -na *mf*, poblador -ra *mf*

seven [sévən] NUM siete

seventeen [sevəntín] NUM diecisiete

seventh [sévənθ] ADJ séptimo

seventy [sévənti] NUM setenta

sever [sévɚ] VT (an arm) cortar; (relations) romper

several [sévɚəɫ] ADJ varios

severe [səvír] ADJ (criticism, standards) severo; (winter, test) duro; (storm, heat) intenso; (illness) grave

severity [səvérɪDi] N (of criticism, standards) severidad *f*; (of water, test) dureza *f*; (of storm, heat) intensidad *f*; (of illness) gravedad *f*

sew [so] VI/VT coser

sewage [súɪdʒ] N aguas negras *f pl*; **— system** alcantarillado *m*

sewer [súɚ] N alcantarilla *f*, cloaca *f*, colector *m*

sewing [sóɪŋ] N costura *f*; **— machine** máquina de coser *f*

sex [sɛks] N sexo *m*; **to have —** tener relaciones (sexuales); **— appeal** atractivo sexual *m*; **— symbol** símbolo sexual *m*; VT sexar

sexism [séksɪzəm] N sexismo *m*

sexton [sékstən] N sacristán *m*

sexual [sékʃuəɫ] ADJ sexual; **— assault** violación *f*; **— harassment** acoso sexual

m; — **intercourse / relations** relaciones sexuales *f pl*; **—ly transmitted disease** enfermedad de transmisión sexual *f*
sexuality [sɛkʃuǽlɪɒi] N sexualidad *f*
sexy [séksi] ADJ sexy, morboso
Seychelles [seʃéɫ] N Seychelles *f pl*
shabby [ʃǽbi] ADJ (worn) gastado; (slovenly) andrajoso; (tawdry) sórdido; (mean) mezquino; **not too** — no está mal
shack [ʃæk] N casucha *f*, choza *f*
shackle [ʃǽkəɫ] N grillete *m*; **—s** cadenas *f pl*, grillos *m pl*; VT (put in chains) engrillar; (impede) estorbar
shad [ʃæd] N sábalo *m*
shade [ʃed] N (shadow) sombra *f*; (nuance) matiz *m*; (for windows) persiana *f*; (phantom) espectro *m*; (of a lamp) pantalla *f*; **a — longer** un poco más largo; **in the** — a la sombra; **—s** lentes negros / oscuros *m pl*; *Sp* gafas de sol *f pl*; VT (protect from sun) sombrear, dar sombra; (darken a picture) sombrear
shadow [ʃǽdo] N (dark image, shade) sombra *f*; (phantom) espectro *m*; **in the** — **of** a la sombra de; **without a** — **of doubt** sin sombra de duda; VT (darken) sombrear; (make gloomy) ensombrecer; **to** — **someone** seguirle la pista a alguien
shady [ʃéɒi] ADJ sombreado, umbrío; — **character** sospechoso *m*; — **dealings** negocios turbios *m pl*
shaft [ʃæft] N (of a mine) pozo *m*; (of a feather) cañón *m*; (of an elevator) hueco *m*; (of an arrow) asta *f*
shaggy [ʃǽgi] ADJ peludo, lanudo
shake [ʃek] VI (tremble) temblar; VI/VT (move back and forth) sacudir(se); (in order to mix) agitar(se); (elude) deshacerse de; **to** — **hands** darse la mano; **to** — **one's head** menear la cabeza; **to** — **with cold** tiritar; **to** — **with fear** temblar de miedo; **to** — **off** (a cold, disappointment, etc.) deshacerse de; (depression) librarse de; **to** — **up** (a liquid) agitar; (a person) trastornar; N (violent) sacudida *f*; (of milk) batido *m*; **hand—** apretón de manos *m*; **the —s** escalofríos *m pl*; **—-up** reorganización *f*
shaky [ʃéki] ADJ (hand) tembloroso; (start) vacilante
shall [ʃæɫ] V AUX **I** — **come** vendré; — **I help you?** ¿te ayudo? **thou shalt not steal** no robarás
shallow [ʃǽlo] ADJ (plate) llano; (water) poco profundo; (breathing) superficial; (explanation) superficial, somero
shallowness [ʃǽlonɪs] N (of plate) lo llano;

(of water) poca profundidad *f*; (of person) superficialidad *f*
sham [ʃæm] N (hoax) farsa *f*; (trickster) farsante *mf*; — **battle** simulacro de batalla *m*
shambles [ʃǽmbəɫz] N desorden *m*, caos *m*
shame [ʃem] N (embarrassment) vergüenza *f*; (dishonor) deshonra *f*; (pity) lástima *f*; — **on you!** ¡qué vergüenza! **to bring** — **upon** deshonrar; VT avergonzar
shameful [ʃémfəɫ] ADJ vergonzoso
shameless [ʃémlɪs] ADJ desvergonzado, descarado
shamelessness [ʃémlɪsnɪs] N desvergüenza *f*
shampoo [ʃæmpú] N (product) champú *m*; (wash) lavado del cabello *m*; VI/VT lavar con champú
shamrock [ʃǽmrɑk] N trébol *m*
shank [ʃæŋk] N (part of leg) canilla *f*, espinilla *f*; (cut of meat) pierna *f*, pata *f*
shanty [ʃǽnti] N casucha *f*; *Sp* chabola *f*; **—town** suburbio *m*
shape [ʃep] N (form) forma *f*; (condition) condición *f*; (silhouette) bulto *m*; **to be in bad** — andar mal; **to get in** — ponerse en forma; VT dar forma a; **to** — **up** reformarse
shapeless [ʃéplɪs] ADJ informe
share [ʃɛr] N (portion) parte *f*, porción *f*; (stock) acción *f*; **—cropper** aparcero *m*; **—holder** accionista *mf*; VI/VT compartir; **to** — **in** participar en
shark [ʃɑrk] N (fish) tiburón *m*; (swindler) estafador -ra *mf*
sharp [ʃɑrp] ADJ (blade) afilado, filoso; (needle) puntiagudo; (curve) cerrado; (contrast) marcado, nítido; (smell) acre; (wind) cortante; (pain) punzante; (remark) mordaz, agudo; (mind) perspicaz; (musical note) sostenido; (dresser) elegante; (cheese) picante; (ear) fino; — **eye** vista aguzada *f*; **—-tongued** mordaz; **—-witted** agudo; **—shooter** tirador -ra de primera *mf*; N sostenido *m*
sharpen [ʃɑ́rpən] VI/VT (knife) afilar(se); VT (pencil) sacar punta a; (skill) afinar
sharpness [ʃɑ́rpnɪs] N (of a blade) lo afilado; (of a needle) lo puntiagudo; (of a curve) lo cerrado; (of a contrast) nitidez *f*; (of a smell) acritud *f*; (of pain) intensidad *f*; (of a remark) mordacidad *f*; (of a mind) perspicacia *f*, agudeza *f*; (of cheese) lo picante
shatter [ʃǽɒɚ] VI/VT (glass) astillar(se), hacer(se) añicos; (nerves) destrozar(se); (health) quebrantar(se); (hopes) frustrar
shave [ʃev] VI/VT (beard, legs) afeitar(se),

rasurar(se); VT (wood) cepillar; (graze) rozar; **to — off** rapar; N afeitado *m*, rasurado *m*; **he had a close —** se salvó por poco

shaver [ʃévə⋅] N afeitadora *f*

shavings [ʃévɪŋz] N virutas *f pl*

shawl [ʃɔɫ] N mantón *m*, chal *m*

she [ʃi] PRON ella; **— who** la que, quien; N **—-bear** osa *f*

sheaf [ʃif] N (of corn) gavilla *f*; (of arrows) haz *m*; (of paper) fajo *m*

shear [ʃir] VT esquilar, trasquilar; N **—s** (for sheep) tijeras para esquilar *f pl*; (for plants) tijeras para podar *f pl*; (for metal) cizallas *f pl*; (for hair) tijeras de peluquero *f pl*

shearing [ʃírɪŋ] N esquila *f*, esquileo *m*

sheath [ʃiθ] N (of sword, peas) vaina *f*; (of knife, umbrella) funda *f*

sheathe [ʃið] VT (a sword) envainar; (a knife) enfundar

shed [ʃɛd] N cobertizo *m*, galpón *m*, tinglado *m*; VT (tears) derramar; (light) arrojar; (leaves) perder; (skin, hair) mudar, perder; VI (be waterproof) ser impermeable; (lose hair) pelechar; (lose leaves) deshojarse; (lose skin) mudar la piel

sheen [ʃin] N brillo *m*

sheep [ʃip] N oveja *f*; **—dog** perro pastor *m*, ovejero *m*; **—skin** (hide) piel de oveja *f*; (leather) badana *f*; (parchment) pergamino *m*; (diploma) diploma *m*

sheepish [ʃípɪʃ] ADJ vergonzoso, tímido

sheer [ʃir] ADJ (absolute) puro, total; (fine) fino; (vertical) vertical, acantilado

sheet [ʃit] N (bedding) sábana *f*; (of ice) capa *f*; (of paper) hoja *f*; (of glass) lámina *f*; (of rain) cortina *f*; **— metal** chapa de metal *f*; **— music** música en hojas de partitura *f*

shelf [ʃɛɫf] N estante *m*, repisa *f*, anaquel *m*; (of rock) saliente *f*

shell [ʃɛɫ] N (turtles, snail) caparazón *f*; (of mollusk) concha *f*; (of egg, nut) cáscara *f*; (of peas) vaina *f*; (of a ship) casco *m*; (of a building) armazón *m*; (of artillery) proyectil *m*; (of a rifle) cartucho *m*; **—fish** mariscos *m pl*; VT (nuts, eggs) pelar; (peas) desgranar; (military target) bombardear

shelter [ʃɛ́ɫtə⋅] N (refuge) refugio *m*, resguardo *m*, abrigo *m*; **to take —** refugiarse, guarecerse; VI/VT (take or give refuge) refugiar(se), resguardar(se), abrigar(se)

shelve [ʃɛɫv] VT (place on a shelf) colocar en un estante; (defer) archivar

shepherd [ʃɛ́pə⋅d] N pastor *m*; (dog) perro pastor *m*

sherbet [ʃɚ́bɪt] N sorbete *m*

sheriff [ʃɛ́rɪf] N alguacil *m*

sherry [ʃɛ́ri] N jerez *m*

shield [ʃiɫd] N escudo *m*; VI/VT (protect) escudar(se); VT (conceal) ocultar

shift [ʃɪft] VI/VT (gears) cambiar; **to — for oneself** arreglárselas solo; **to — the blame** echar la culpa a otro; N (of gears, of wind) cambio *m*; (dress) vestido suelto *m*; (of workers) turno *m*; **— key** tecla (de) mayúscula *f*

shiftless [ʃɪ́ftlɪs] ADJ holgazán

shimmer [ʃímə⋅] VI titilar; N titileo *m*

shin [ʃɪn] N espinilla *f*, canilla *f*; VI **to — up** trepar

shine [ʃaɪn] VI brillar, relucir; VT (shoes) limpiar, lustrar; (furniture) lustrar; N brillo *m*, resplandor *m*; (of shoes) lustre *m*

shingle [ʃíŋɡəɫ] N (on roof) teja *f*; (sign) chapa *f*; **—s** culebrilla *f*, zona *f*; **to hang out one's —** abrir un consultorio; VT cubrir con tejas

shiny [ʃáɪni] ADJ (bright) brillante; (worn) brilloso

ship [ʃɪp] N (on water) buque *m*, navío *m*; (in air) avión *m*; **—builder** constructor -ra naval *mf*; **—mate** camarada de a bordo *mf*; **—wreck** naufragio *m*; **—yard** astillero *m*; ADJ **—shape** ordenado; VT transportar; **to —wreck** hacer naufragar; **to — off** sacarse de encima; VI **to —wreck** naufragar

shipment [ʃípmənt] N cargamento *m*, remesa *f*

shipper [ʃípə⋅] N (sender) expedidor -ra *mf*; (carrier) transportista *mf*

shipping [ʃípɪŋ] N envío *m*; **— charges** gastos de envío *m pl*; **— and handling** gastos de envío *m pl*

shirk [ʃɚk] VT evadir, esquivar, rehuir

shirt [ʃɚt] N camisa *f*; **in — sleeves** en mangas de camisa; **—tail** faldón *m*

shit [ʃɪt] N (excrement) *vulg* mierda *f*; (stuff) porquerías *f pl*; **the —s** *fam* cagalera; **that's a crock of —** y una polla (como una olla); **he doesn't know —** *vulg* no sabe un carajo; VI/VT (defecate) *vulg* cagar; (lie to) *vulg* joder; **to — bricks** *vulg* cagarse de miedo; **he's on my —list** estoy enojado con él; INTERJ *vulg* carajo; *Sp vulg* joder

shitty [ʃídi] ADJ *vulg* de mierda

shiver [ʃívə⋅] VI (from cold) tiritar; (from cold, fear, etc.) temblar; N temblor *m*; **—s** escalofríos *m pl*

shoal [ʃoɫ] N (sandbank) bajío *m*, banco de arena *m*; (school of fish) banco *m*, bandada *f*

shock [ʃɑk] N (impact, disturbance) choque

m; (of electricity) sacudida *f*; (of wheat) hacina *f*; (physical convulsion) shock *m*, choque *m*; — **absorber** amortiguador *m*; — **of hair** guedeja *f*; — **troops** tropas de choque *f pl*; — **wave** onda expansiva *f*; VT (bewilder) chocar, horrorizar, azorar; (discharge electricity) dar una descarga eléctrica; (make bundles of grain) hacinar, hacer gavillas de

shocking [ʃákɪŋ] ADJ chocante, escandaloso

shoddy [ʃádi] ADJ chapucero

shoe [ʃu] N zapato *m*; (for brakes) zapata *f*; (for horses) herradura *f*; —**horn** calzador *m*; —**lace** cordón *m*; —**maker** zapatero -ra *mf*; — **polish** betún *m*; — **repairman** zapatero -ra remendón -ona *mf*; — **store** zapatería *f*; —**string** cordón *m*; **to live on a** —**string** vivir con poco dinero; **to tie one's** —**s** atarse los zapatos; VT (a person) calzar; (a horse) herrar

shoo-in [ʃúɪn] N favorito -ta *mf*

shoot [ʃut] VT (wound with a bullet) pegar un tiro, abatir; (discharge a firearm) disparar; (film a movie) rodar; VI (discharge bullet, arrow) disparar, tirar; (be discharged) dispararse; (hunt with a gun) cazar; (germinate) brotar; (throw) lanzar; (take a photo) fotografiar; (film) filmar; (kick a ball) chutar; **to** — **at** disparar a, tirar a; **to** — **by** pasar rápidamente; **to** — **down** (plane) derribar; (argument) refutar; **to** — **forth** brotar; **to** — **up** (grow) crecer rápidamente; (damage by shooting) tirotear; (inject drugs) chutar; N (new growth) yema *f*, retoño *m*, vástago *m*; (filming) rodaje *m*

shooter [ʃúðɚ] N (of guns) tirador -ra *mf*; (of balls, soccer) goleador -ra *mf*

shooting [ʃúðɪŋ] N (discharge of a gun) tiro *m*, disparo *m*; (exchange of shots) tiroteo *m*; — **match** concurso de tiro *m*; — **pain** punzada *f*; — **star** estrella fugaz *f*

shop [ʃɑp] N (store) tienda *f*; (artisan's place of business, carpentry course) taller *m*; (business) planta *f*; —**keeper** tendero -ra *mf*; —**lifter** mechero -ra *mf*; **to** —**lift** mechar; — **window** escaparate *m*, vitrina *f*; **to talk** — hablar de negocios; VI ir de compras; **to** — **for** ir a comprar

shopper [ʃápɚ] N cliente -ta *mf*, comprador -ra *mf*

shopping [ʃápɪŋ] N **to go** — ir de compras; — **center** centro comercial *m*

shore [ʃɔr] N costa *f*, ribera *f*; (of a lake) orilla *f*; VT **to** — **up** apuntalar

short [ʃɔrt] ADJ (not long in duration) corto, breve; (not long in length) corto; (not tall)

bajo; (scanty) escaso; (curt) brusco; — **circuit** cortocircuito *m*; —**comings** limitaciones *f pl*; —**cut** atajo *m*, cortada *f*; —**fall** agujero *m*; —**hand** taquigrafía *f*; —-**handed** escaso de personal; —-**legged** pernicorto; —**sighted** miope, corto de vista; — **story** cuento *m*; —**wave** onda corta *f*; **in the** — **run (haul, term)** a corto plazo; **for** — para abreviar; **in** — en resumen, en suma; **in** — **order** rápidamente; **to be** — **on** estar escaso de, estar alcanzado de; **to be** — **on something** faltarle a uno algo; **to cut** — interrumpir; **I'm running** — **on sugar** se me está acabando el azúcar; ADV **to stop** — parar de repente, parar en seco; **to come up** — quedarse corto; N (circuit) cortocircuito *m*; —**s** short *m*, pantalón corto *m*; VI/VT (a circuit) cortocircuitar(se); (change) dar de menos; **to** —**change** dar de menos; **to** — **out** fundir

shortage [ʃɔrdɪdʒ] N escasez *f*, penuria *f*

shorten [ʃɔrtn̩] VI/VT acortar(se); VT recortar

shortening [ʃɔrtnɪŋ] N (lard) manteca *f*; (abbreviation) acortamiento *m*

shortly [ʃɔrtli] ADJ (soon) en breve, pronto; (curtly) bruscamente, secamente

shortness [ʃɔrtnɪs] N (of length, height) cortedad *f*; (of time) brevedad *f*; (of breath) falta *f*; (of a reply) brusquedad *f*

shot [ʃɑt] N (discharge) tiro *m*, disparo *m*; (photograph) foto *f*; (pellet) perdigón *m*, plomo *m*; (ball in shot-putting) bala *f*; (injection) inyección *f*; (swallow) trago *m*; (throw) tirada *f*; —**gun** escopeta *f*; — **put** lanzamiento de bala *m*; **not by a long** — ni con mucho; **he is a good** — tiene buena puntería; **to take a** — disparar; **to take a** — **at** intentar

should [ʃud] V AUX **I** — **think so** ya lo creo; **you** — **arrive before nine** deberías llegar antes de las nueve; **you** — **eat less** tendrías que comer menos; **you** — **have seen her** tendrías que haberla visto; **were he to come, I** — **be pleased** si viniera, me alegraría

shoulder [ʃóɫdɚ] N (of a person, coat) hombro *m*; (cut of meat) paletilla *f*; (of a road) arcén *m*; — **blade** (person) homóplato *m*; (animal) paletilla *f*; **to turn a cold** — **to** hacerle el vacío a; **the responsibility is on your** —**s** tú tienes la responsabilidad; VT (a load) cargar al hombro; (an expense) cargar con, asumir; (a door) empujar con el hombro

shout [ʃaut] VI/VT gritar; N grito *m*

shove [ʃʌv] VI/VT empujar; **to** — **aside** echar

a un lado; **to — off** (go away) largarse; (push off) desatracar; N empujón *m*, empellón *m*

shovel [ʃʌvəł] N pala *f*; VT echar con la pala

show [ʃo] VT (exhibit) mostrar, manifestar; (prove) demostrar; (indicate) indicar, marcar; (a film, a TV program) dar; VI (be visible) verse, asomar; (make an appearance) aparecerse; — **him in** hazle entrar; **to — a film** dar una película; **to — mercy** tener piedad; **to — off** hacer alarde, aparentar; **to — up** aparecer; **to — someone up** poner en evidencia; **to — the way** señalar el camino; N (exhibition) exposición *f*; (display) demostración *f*; (ostentation) ostentación *f*, alarde *m*; (performance) espectáculo *m*; (showing) función *f*; (on TV) programa *m*; (movie theater) cine *m*; — **business** farándula *f*; —**case** vitrina *f*; **to** —**case** presentar; —**down** confrontación *f*; —**-off** fanfarrón -ona *mf*; **to go to the** — ir al cine

shower [ʃáuɚ] N (rain) aguacero *m*, chubasco *m*; (bath) ducha *f*; (for brides) fiesta para novias *f*; (of sparks, blows) lluvia *f*; VI (bathe) ducharse; (rain) llover; VT (with gifts) inundar; (with praise) colmar

showy [ʃói] ADJ ostentoso; (attractive) vistoso

shred [ʃred] N (of paper) tira *f*; (of evidence) pizca *f*; **to be in —s** estar hecho jirones; **to tear to —s** hacer trizas; VI/VT (documents) triturar; (vegetables) rallar

shrew [ʃru] N (animal) musaraña *f*; (woman) arpía *f*

shrewd [ʃrud] ADJ astuto, sagaz

shriek [ʃrik] VI/VT chillar; N chillido *m*

shrill [ʃrɪł] ADJ chillón

shrimp [ʃrɪmp] N (animal) camarón *m*; (small person) renacuajo *m*; VI pescar camarones

shrine [ʃraɪn] N (chapel) capilla *f*; (altar) altar *m*

shrink [ʃrɪŋk] VI/VT encoger; VI (value) reducirse; **to — from** retroceder; N *fam* loquero -ra *mf*

shrinkage [ʃríŋkɪʤ] N (of clothes) encogimiento *m*; (of value) reducción *f*

shrivel [ʃrívəł] VI/VT secar(se), marchitar(se)

shroud [ʃraud] N mortaja *f*; VT (to wrap for burial) amortajar; (to hide) cubrir

shrub [ʃrʌb] N arbusto *m*

shrug [ʃrʌg] VI encogerse de hombros; VT encogerse de; **to — off** minimizar, ignorar; N encogimiento de hombros *m*

shudder [ʃʌdɚ] VI (from cold) tiritar; (from fear) temblar, estremecerse; N temblor *m*, estremecimiento *m*

shuffle [ʃʌfəł] VT (mix) mezclar; VI (walk)

arrastrar los pies; (dance) bailar arrastrando los pies; VI/VT (cards) barajar; **to — along** ir arrastrando los pies; N (of cards) barajadura *f*; (of feet) arrastrapiés *m sg*

shun [ʃʌn] VT rehuir, evitar

shut [ʃʌt] VI/VT cerrar(se); **to — down** cerrar; **to — off** cortar; **to — out** impedir la entrada de; **to — up** (close) cerrar bien; (lock up) encerrar; (be quiet) callarse; —**-down** cese de actividades *m*; —**-eye** sueño *m*; —**-in** enfermo -ma confinado -da a la casa *mf*

shutter [ʃʌdɚ] N (of a window) postigo *m*, contraventana *f*; (of a camera) obturador *m*

shuttle [ʃʌdł] N (in loom) lanzadera *f*; (spaceship) transbordador espacial *m*; (airplane) puente aéreo *m*; (bus, train) servicio regular *m*; VI ir y venir; VT llevar y traer

shy [ʃaɪ] ADJ tímido, retraído; (wary) esquivo; (lacking) escaso; VI asustarse, respingar; **to — away** (start) asustarse, respingar; (avoid) esquivar

shyness [ʃáɪnɪs] N timidez *f*, retraimiento *m*

shyster [ʃáɪstɚ] N *fam* picapleitos *m sg*

sic [sɪk] VT azuzar

sick [sɪk] ADJ (ill) enfermo; (deranged) enfermizo, morboso; (at heart) angustiado; — **and tired** harto; **to be — of** estar harto de; **to be — to one's stomach** tener náuseas; **to make —** (disgust) dar asco; (anger) dar rabia, enfermar; — **leave** licencia por enfermedad *f*

sicken [síkən] VI/VT (with illness) enfermar(se), poner(se) enfermo; (to disgust) dar asco; (to anger) dar rabia, enfermar

sickening [síkənɪŋ] ADJ repugnante

sickle [síkəł] N hoz *f*; — **cell anemia** anemia falciforme *f*

sickly [síkli] ADJ enfermizo, enclenque

sickness [síknɪs] N enfermedad *f*

side [saɪd] N lado *m*; (of coin, piece of paper) cara *f*; (of a person) costado *m*; (of hill) ladera *f*; (of beef) media res *f*; (of boat) banda *f*; (team) equipo *m*; (garnish) acompañamiento *m*; — **by** — uno al lado del otro; **by his** — a su lado; **by the — of** al lado de; **on all —s** por todos lados; ADJ (on the side) lateral; (secondary) secundario; —**arm** arma de mano *f*; —**board** aparador *m*; —**burns** patillas *f pl*; —**-glance** mirada de soslayo / reojo *f*; —**light** (illumination) luz lateral *f*; (detail) detalle incidental *m*; —**line** (in sports) línea de banda *f*; **to sit on the —lines** no intervenir; **to —step** evitar, esquivar; (in business) negocio suplementario *m*; **to —track** (a train) desviar; (attention) distraer; **—walk** acera *f*; *Mex* banqueta *f*; **—wall** flanco *m*; VI **to — with** ponerse del lado de

sideways [sáɪdwez] ADV (walk) de costado; (glance) de soslayo

siege [siʤ] N sitio *m*, asedio *m*, cerco *m*; **to lay — to** sitiar

Sierra Leone [siérəlión] N Sierra Leona *f*

sieve [sɪv] N tamiz *m*, cedazo *m*

sift [sɪft] VT cerner, tamizar; **to — through** revisar

sigh [saɪ] VI suspirar; N suspiro *m*

sight [saɪt] N (sense) vista *f*; (attraction) punto de interés *m*; (ridiculous thing or person) adefesio *m*, mamarracho *m*; (on a gun) mira *f*; **—seeing** turismo *m*; **in —** a la vista; **on —** en el acto; **he is out of —** ya no se ve; **at first —** a primera vista; **to catch — of** divisar; **to lose — of** perder de vista; **you're a — for sore eyes** dichosos los ojos que te ven; VT (a ship) avistar, divisar; (a gun) apuntar

sign [saɪn] N (gesture) seña *f*, señal *f*; (indication) muestra *f*, señal *f*, indicio *m*; (placard) letrero *m*; (omen) agüero *m*, presagio *m*; (astrological, mathematical) signo *m*; (on road) cartel *m*, letrero *m*; VI/VT (write name) firmar; (signal) hacer señas (de); VT (hire) contratar; (use sign language) hablar por señas; **— language** lenguaje de signos *m*; **to — over property** ceder una propiedad; **to — up** (in a club) anotarse; (in the army) alistarse

signal [sígnəɫ] N señal *f*; VI/VT señalar, hacer señas (a); ADJ notable

signature [sígnətʃəˣ] N firma *f*

signer [sáɪnəˣ] N firmante *mf*, signatario -ria *mf*

significance [sɪgnífɪkəns] N significación *f*

significant [sɪgnífɪkənt] ADJ significativo; **my — other** mi media naranja *f*

signify [sígnəfaɪ] VT significar

silence [sáɪləns] N silencio *m*; VT (child, fears) acallar; (criticism) silenciar, enmudecer

silencer [sáɪlənsəˣ] N silenciador *m*

silent [sáɪlənt] ADJ (machine) silencioso; (person) callado, silencioso; **— agreement** acuerdo tácito *m*; **— film** película muda *f*

silhouette [sɪluét] N silueta *f*; VT **to be —d against** perfilarse contra

silicon [sílɪkɑn] N silicio *m*

silk [sɪɫk] N seda *f*; **— industry** industria

sedera *f*; **—worm** gusano de seda *m*

silken [síɫkən] ADJ (of silk) de seda; (like silk) sedoso

silky [síɫki] ADJ sedoso

sill [sɪɫ] N alféizar *m*, antepecho *m*

silly [síli] ADJ necio, bobo, lelo

silo [sáɪlo] N silo *m*

silt [sɪɫt] N cieno *m*, limo *m*

silver [síɫvəˣ] N (metal, color) plata *f*; (tableware) cubiertos de plata *m pl*; ADJ (of silver) de plata; (silver-colored) plateado; **— anniversary** las bodas de plata *f pl*; **—-plated** bañado en plata; **—-plating** plateado *m*; **—smith** platero -ra *mf*; **—ware** cubiertos de plata *m pl*; VT platear; (a mirror) azogar

similar [símələˣ] ADJ semejante, similar

similarity [sɪmələ́rɪDi] N semejanza *f*, parecido *m*

simile [síməli] N símil *m*

simmer [síməˣ] VI/VT hervir a fuego lento; **to — down** calmarse

simple [símpəɫ] ADJ (uncomplicated) simple, sencillo; (naive) simple; **—minded** simple, simplón

simpleton [símpəɫtən] N simplón -ona *mf*, mentecato -ta *mf*

simplicity [sɪmplísɪDi] N (lack of complication) sencillez *f*, simplicidad *f*; (naiveté) simpleza *f*

simplify [símpləfaɪ] VI/VT simplificar

simplistic [sɪmplístɪk] ADJ simplista

simulate [símjəlet] VI/VT simular

simultaneous [saɪməɫténiəs] ADJ simultáneo

sin [sɪn] N pecado *m*; VI pecar

since [sɪns] CONJ (continuously) desde que; (inasmuch as) puesto que, ya que; PREP (continuously) desde; (from a past time) a partir de; ADV desde entonces; **ever —** desde entonces; **he died long —** murió hace mucho tiempo; **she has — agreed** después de eso consintió; **we have been here — five** estamos aquí desde las cinco

sincere [sɪnsír] ADJ sincero

sincerity [sɪnsérɪDi] N sinceridad *f*

sinew [sínju] N tendón *m*

sinewy [sínjuwi] ADJ (full of tendons) nervudo; (vigorous) membrudo; (chewy) estropajoso

sinful [sínfəɫ] ADJ (act) pecaminoso; (person) pecador

sing [sɪŋ] VI/VT cantar; **—song** sonsonete *m*

Singapore [síŋəpɔr] N Singapur *m*

Singaporean [sɪŋəpóriən] ADJ & N singapurense *mf*

singe [sɪnʤ] VT chamuscar, socarrar; N chamusquina *f*, socarrina *f*

singer [síŋɚ] N cantante *mf*

single [síŋgəł] ADJ (only one) solo, único; (for one person) individual; (unmarried) soltero; — **bed** cama de una plaza *f;* — **entry bookkeeping** teneduría por partida simple *f;* — **file** fila india *f;* —**-handed** solo, sin ayuda; —**-minded** resuelto; —**-spacing** sencillo *m;* **every** — **one** cada uno; **not a** — **word** ni una sola palabra; N (bill) billete de uno *m;* (unmarried person) soltero -ra *mf;* (record) disco sencillo *m;* (in tennis) —**s** single *m;* VT **to** — **out** elegir

singular [síŋgjəlɚ] ADJ & N singular *m*

sinister [sínɪstɚ] ADJ siniestro

sink [sɪŋk] VI/VT hundir(se); VT (invest) invertir; (dig) cavar; (put in ground) enterrar; **it finally sank in** finalmente nos dimos cuenta de eso; **to** — **one's teeth into** clavar los dientes en; **to** — **to one's knees** caer de rodillas; **sunk in thought** absorto; **my heart sank** se me fue el alma al piso; **the sun was** —**ing** se iba poniendo el sol; N (in the kitchen) fregadero *m;* (in bathroom) lavabo *m;* (pond for sewage) pozo negro *m;* —**hole** socavón *m,* sumidero *m*

sinner [sínɚ] N pecador -ora *mf*

sinuous [sínjuəs] ADJ sinuoso

sinus [sáɪnəs] N seno *m*

sip [sɪp] VI/VT sorber; N sorbo *m*

siphon [sáɪfən] N sifón *m;* VI/VT (liquid) sacar con sifón; (money) desviar

sir [sɚ] N señor *m*

siren [sáɪrən] N sirena *f*

sirloin [sɚ́lɔɪn] N solomillo *m*

sissy [sísi] ADJ & N afeminado *m; offensive* marica *m,* maricón *m*

sister [sístɚ] N hermana *f;* —**-in-law** cuñada *f;* — **Mary** Sor María *f*

sit [sɪt] VI sentar(se); (pose) posar; (be seated) estar sentado; (be located) estar situado; **to** — **down** sentarse; **to** — **in on a class** ir de oyente a una clase; **to** — **on** posponer; **to** — **out a dance** saltearse una pieza; **to** — **still** estarse quieto; **to** — **tight** mantenerse firme en su puesto; **to** — **up** incorporarse; **to** — **up all night** quedarse en vela; **to** — **well** caer bien; —**-in** sentada *f;* —**-up** abdominal *m*

sitcom [sítkɑm] N comedia de situación *f*

site [saɪt] N (for construction) terreno *m,* solar *m;* (on the Internet) sitio *m*

sitter [síDɚ] N niñera *f*

sitting [síDɪŋ] N sesión *f;* **in one** — de una sentada, de un tirón; ADJ — **duck** blanco fácil *m;* — **room** cuarto de estar *m*

situated [sítʃueDɪd] ADJ situado, ubicado

situation [sɪtʃuéʃən] N situación *f*

six [sɪks] NUM seis; —**-pack** paquete de seis *m;* —**-shooter** revólver de seis tiros *m*

sixteen [sɪkstín] NUM dieciséis

sixth [sɪksθ] ADV & N sexto *m*

sixty [síksti] NUM sesenta

size [saɪz] N tamaño *m;* (clothing) talla *f;* VT clasificar según el tamaño; **to** — **up** juzgar

sizeable, sizable [sáɪzəbəł] ADJ de tamaño considerable

sizzle [sízəł] VI chisporrotear; N chisporroteo *m*

skate [sket] N patín *m;* VI/VT patinar; —**board** monopatín *m*

skein [sken] N madeja *f*

skeleton [skélɪtən] N esqueleto *m,* osamenta *f;* (of a building) armazón *m;* — **key** llave maestra *f*

skeptic, sceptic [sképtɪk] N escéptico -ca *mf*

skeptical [sképtɪkəł] ADJ escéptico

skepticism [sképtɪsɪzəm] N escepticismo *m*

sketch [skɛtʃ] N (of a drawing) boceto *m,* croquis *m;* (outline) esbozo *m,* bosquejo *m;* (skit) sketch *m;* VI/VT (outline) bosquejar; (draw) dibujar

skew [skju] VT (cloth) sesgar; (data) tergiversar

skewer [skjúɚ] N brocheta *f*

ski [ski] N esquí *m;* VI/VT esquiar (en); — **jump** (sport) salto con esquís *m;* (course) pista de saltos *f;* — **lift** telesquí *m*

skid [skɪd] N patinazo *m;* VI patinar

skill [skɪł] N destreza *f,* habilidad *f,* maña *f*

skilled [skɪłd] ADJ diestro, habilidoso; — **worker** obrero -ra calificado -da *mf*

skillet [skílɪt] N sartén *f*

skillful, skilful [skíłfəł] ADJ diestro, habilidoso

skim [skɪm] VT (milk) desnatar; (a broth) espumar; (move near surface) rozar; VI/VT (read) leer por encima, repasar; **to** — **over** rozar; — **milk** *Sp* leche desnatada *f; Am* leche descremada *f*

skimp [skɪmp] VI escatimar; **to** — **on** escatimar

skimpy [skímpi] ADJ (funds) escaso; (dress) corto; (bikini) pequeño

skin [skɪn] N piel *f* (also of animal, sausage, potato); (of the face) cutis *m,* tez *f;* (for carrying wine) pellejo *m;* (of boiled milk) nata *f;* (of grapes) hollejo *m;* —**-deep** superficial; —**-diving** natación submarina *f;* — **flick** película pornográfica *f;* — **flint** roña *mf;* —**head** cabeza rapada *mf;* **to save one's** — salvar el pellejo; **to be saved by the** — **of one's teeth** salvarse por un pelo; VT (animal) despellejar, desollar; (fruit) pelar; (a person) quitarle a uno el dinero

skinny [skíni] ADJ flaco; **to —-dip** nadar desnudo

skip [skɪp] VI (jump) brincar, ir dando saltos en un pie; (omit) saltarse; (bounce) rebotar; VT (a page) saltar(se); (class) faltar a; (a stone) hacer rebotar; **to — out** escaparse; N salto *m*, brinco *m*

skipper [skípɚ] N (captain) patrón -ona *mf*, capitán -ana *mf*; (jumper) saltador -ora *mf*

skirmish [skɚ́mɪʃ] N escaramuza *f*; VI escaramuzar

skirt [skɚt] N falda *f*; VT bordear; **to — an issue** evitar un tema

skit [skɪt] N sketch *m*

skull [skʌɫ] N cráneo *m*, calavera *f*; **— and crossbones** calavera *f*

skunk [skʌŋk] N mofeta *f*; *Am* zorrillo *m*

sky [skaɪ] N cielo *m*; **— blue** azul celeste *m*; **—diving** paracaidismo *m*; **—-high** muy alto; **—lark** alondra *f*; **—light** claraboya *f*; **—line** horizonte *m*; **—scraper** rascacielos *m sg*; **to —rocket** subir vertiginosamente

slab [slæb] N (of wood) trozo *m*; (of stone) losa *f*, laja *f*; (of meat) tajada *f*

slack [slæk] ADJ (not taut) flojo; (careless) descuidado; (sluggish) lento; **— season** temporada baja *f*; **to take up the —** llenar el vacío; **—s** pantalones *m pl*; VI holgazanear; **to — off** aflojar

slag [slæg] N escoria *f*

slalom [sláləm] N slalom *m*

slam [slæm] VI/VT cerrar(se) de un golpe; VI (hit) chocar; VT (throw down) hacer golpear; (criticize) criticar; **to — on the brakes** dar un frenazo; **to — the door** dar un portazo; N (blow) golpazo *m*; (criticism) crítica *f*; (of a door) portazo *m*

slander [slǽndɚ] N calumnia *f*, difamación *f*; VT calumniar, difamar

slanderous [slǽndərəs] ADJ calumnioso, difamatorio

slang [slæŋ] N (jargon) jerga *f*; (argot) argot *m*

slant [slænt] N (orientation, bias) sesgo *m*; (of a roof) inclinación *f*; VI/VT (bias) sesgar; (slope) inclinar(se), ladear(se)

slap [slæp] N (to the body) palmada *f*; (to the face) bofetada *f*, torta *f*, cachetada *f*; (with a glove) guantada *f*; **—happy** aturdido; **—stick** de golpe y porrazo; **a — in the face** un desaire; **a — on the wrist** un tirón de orejas; **a — on the back** una palmadita en la espalda; VT abofetear; **to — down** reprimir

slash [slæʃ] VI/VT (cut) acuchillar; *Am* tajear; VT (whip) azotar; (reduce) reducir, rebajar; N (sweeping stroke, wound) cuchillada *f*, tajo *m*; (typographical sign) barra *f*

slat [slæt] N tablilla *f*

slate [slet] N (rock, roofing) pizarra *f*; (color) color pizarra *m*; (list of candidates) lista de candidatos *f*; VT empizarrar; **this building is —d for destruction** se ha programado la demolición de este edificio

slaughter [slɔ́ɾɚ] N matanza *f*; **—house** matadero *m*; VT (animals) matar; (people, opponents) masacrar

slave [slev] N esclavo -va *mf*; **— driver** capataz de esclavos *m*; **— labor** (workers) mano de obra esclava *f*; (work) trabajo de esclavos *m*; VI trabajar como esclavo -va

slavery [slévəri] N esclavitud *f*

Slavic [slávɪk] ADJ eslavo

sleazy [slízi] ADJ (squalid) sórdido; (contemptible) despreciable

sled [slɛd] N trineo *m*

sledgehammer [slɛ́ʤhæmɚ] N almádena *f*

sleek [slik] ADJ (hair) lustroso; (sports car) elegante

sleep [slip] VI/VT dormir; **it —s three** tiene espacio para que duerman tres personas; **to — around** ser promiscuo; **to — in** dormir hasta tarde; **to — it off** dormir la mona; **to — something off** dormir para que desaparezca algo; **to — over** dormir en casa ajena; **to — together** acostarse juntos; **to — with** acostarse con; **to — on it** consultarlo con la almohada; N sueño *m*; **—walker** sonámbulo -la *mf*; **to go to —** dormirse; **to put to —** (put to bed) dormir a; (euthanize) sacrificar

sleeper [slípɚ] N (one who sleeps) persona que duerme *f*; (beam) durmiente *m*; (on a train) coche cama *m*; (unexpected success) éxito inesperado *m*; (sofa bed) sofá-cama *m*

sleepily [slípɪli] ADV con somnolencia

sleepiness [slípɪnɪs] N sueño *m*, somnolencia *f*

sleeping [slípɪŋ] N sueño *m*; ADJ dormido; **— bag** saco de dormir *m*; **— pill** píldora para dormir *f*, somnífero *m*; **— sickness** enfermedad del sueño *f*

sleepless [slíplɪs] ADJ (person) desvelado; (night) en blanco

sleepy [slípi] ADJ somnoliento, adormilado; **to be —** tener sueño

sleet [slit] N cellisca *f*; VI caer cellisca

sleeve [sliv] N manga *f*; **to have something up one's —s** tener algo en la manga

sleigh [sle] N trineo *m*; **— bell** cascabel *m*; VI

pasear en trineo

sleight [slaɪt] N — **of hand** prestidigitación *f*

slender [sléndɚ] ADJ delgado, esbelto

sleuth [sluθ] N sabueso *m*

slice [slaɪs] N (of bread, cheese) rebanada *f*; (of fruit) tajada *f*, raja *f*; (of meat) lonja *f*; VT cortar, rebanar, tajar

slick [slɪk] ADJ (unctuous) untuoso; (sly) astuto; (slippery) resbaladizo

slicker [slíkɚ] N impermeable *m*

slide [slaɪd] VI/VT deslizar(se); **to — in** cerrar(se) deslizando; **to — out** abrirse deslizando; **to let something —** dejar pasar algo; N deslizamiento *m*; (playground equipment) tobogán *m*; (of a trombone) vara corredora *f*; (photographic) diapositiva *f*; (for microscopes) portaobjeto *m*

slight [slaɪt] N desaire *m*; VT (snub) desairar; (neglect) descuidar; ADJ (slim) delgado; (delicate) delicado, tenue; (small in degree) leve, ligero

slim [slɪm] ADJ delgado, esbelto; **a — chance** una posibilidad remota

slime [slaɪm] N (in rivers) limo *m*, fango *m*; (of snails) baba *f*; (despicable person) asqueroso -sa *mf*

slimy [sláɪmi] ADJ (muddy) fangoso; (slobbery) baboso, gomoso; (despicable) asqueroso

sling [slɪŋ] N honda *f*; (for arm) cabestrillo *m*; **—shot** (toy) tirachinas *m sg*, tirador *m*; (weapon) honda *f*; VT lanzar; **to — a rifle over one's shoulder** ponerse el rifle en bandolera

slink [slɪŋk] VI (move furtively) andar furtivamente; (move provocatively) caminar provocativamente; **to — away** escurrirse

slip [slɪp] VI (slide) deslizarse; (slide accidentally) resbalar(se); (fail to engage) patinar; (deteriorate) empeorar; VT (make slip) hacer resbalar; (put) meter; **to — away** escaparse, escabullirse; **to — by** correr; **to — in** meter(se); **to — one's dress on** ponerse el vestido; **to — out** (leave) salir inadvertido; (say inadvertently) escapársele a uno algo; **to — up** meter la pata; **to let an opportunity — by** dejar pasar una oportunidad; **it —ped my mind** se me olvidó; **it —ped off** se zafó; N (act of slipping) resbalón *m*, traspié *m*; (mistake) equivocación *f*; (pillow cover) funda *f*; (underskirt) viso *m*; (piece of paper) papeleta *f*, tira de papel *f*; (space for boats) embarcadero *m*; **— of the tongue** lapsus

(linguae) *m*; **—knot** nudo corredizo *m*; **Freudian —** acto fallido *m*

slipper [slípɚ] N zapatilla *f*, pantufla *f*

slippery [slípəri] ADJ resbaloso, resbaladizo; (evasive) evasivo, escurridizo

slipshod [slípʃad] ADJ chapucero

slit [slɪt] VT cortar a lo largo; **to — someone's throat** degollar a alguien; **to — into strips** cortar en tiras; N raja *f*

slither [slíðɚ] VI serpentear, culebrear; N serpenteo *m*, culebreo *m*

sliver [slívɚ] N astilla *f*; VI/VT astillar(se)

slob [slab] N (unkempt) dejado -da *mf*; (uncouth) bruto -ta *mf*

slobber [slábɚ] N baba *f*; VI/VT babosear, babear(se)

slogan [slógən] N eslogan *m*, lema *m*

slop [slap] VT (splash) salpicar; (feed) dar de comer; N (pigswill) bazofia *f*; (mud) fango *m*

slope [slop] VI/VT inclinar(se); N vertiente *f*, declive *m*, cuesta *f*; (in math) pendiente *f*

sloppiness [slápɪnɪs] N chapucería *f*

sloppy [slápi] ADJ (ground) fangoso; (splashed) salpicado; (slovenly) cochino; (poorly done) chapucero

slot [slat] N (for coins, letters) ranura *f*; (place in a series) casilla *f*; (job) puesto *m*; **— machine** tragamonedas *mf sg*, tragaperras *mf sg*; VT hacer una ranura

sloth [slɔθ] N (vice) pereza *f*; (animal) perezoso *m*

slouch [slaʊtʃ] N (posture) encorvamiento *m*; (inept person) torpe *mf*; (lazy person) holgazán -ana *mf*; VI/VT (crouch) andar agachado, encorvar(se); (shuffle) andar caído de hombros

Slovakia [slovákiə] N Eslovaquia *f*

Slovakian [slovákiən] ADJ & N eslovaco -ca *mf*

Slovene [slóvin] ADJ & N esloveno -na *mf*

Slovenia [slovíniə] N Eslovenia *f*

slovenliness [slávənlinɪs] N (of a person) desaseo *m*, desaliño *m*; (of work) descuido *m*

slovenly [slávənli] ADJ (unclean) desaseado; (unkempt) desaliñado

slow [slo] ADJ (not fast) lento, tardo; (running behind) atrasado; (sluggish) lerdo, torpe, pesado; ADV lentamente, despacio; VI/VT **to — down / up** andar más despacio, frenar; **—down** (in business) disminución de actividades *f*; (in labor disputes) huelga de celo *f*; **in — motion** en cámara lenta

slowness [slónɪs] N (of speed) lentitud *f*; (of intelligence) torpeza *f*

slug [slʌg] N (bullet) bala *f*; (coin) moneda

falsa *f*; (animal) babosa *f*; (swallow) trago *m*; (blow with fist) puñetazo *m*; VT aporrear; **to — it out** agarrarse a puñetazos

sluggard [slÁgɚd] N holgazán -ana *mf*

sluggish [slÁgɪʃ] ADJ (slow) lento; (torpid) aletargado, torpe

sluggishness [slÁgɪʃnɪs] N torpeza *f*

sluice [slus] N (channel with a gate) esclusa *f*; (channel) canal *m*; **— gate** compuerta *f*

slum [slʌm] N barrio bajo *m*; **—s** tugurios *m pl*; **—lord** propietario de tugurio *m*; VI visitar los barrios bajos; **to — it** divertirse en lugares de poca categoría

slumber [slÁmbɚ] VI dormitar; N sueño ligero *m*; **— party** fiesta de niñas que se quedan a dormir *f*

slump [slʌmp] VI (a person) desplomarse; (prices, markets) bajar repentinamente; N (in prices) baja repentina *f*; (in the economy) ralentización *f*; (in sports) mala racha *f*

slur [slɚ] VT (pronounce indistinctly) pronunciar mal; (connect notes) ligar; N (connection of notes) ligado *m*; (insult) insulto *m*

slush [slʌʃ] N (melted snow) nieve a medio derretir *f*; (sludge) nieve fangosa *f*; (mud) fango *m*; (refuse) desperdicios *m pl*; **— fund** (illicit fund) cuenta para fines ilícitos *f*; (petty cash) caja chica *f*

slut [slʌt] N (slovenly woman) *pej* puerca *f*; (loose woman) *offensive* mujerzuela *f*, puta *f*

sly [slaɪ] ADJ astuto, taimado; **on the —** a escondidas

smack [smæk] N (taste) dejo *m*; *Sp* deje *m*; (kiss) beso ruidoso *m*; (loud eating) chasquido *m*; (slap) palmada *f*, sopapo *m*; (heroin) *fam* caballo *m*; VT (kiss) dar un beso ruidoso; (eat loudly) chascar, chasquear; (slap) dar una palmada; **to — of** tener un dejo de

small [smɔł] ADJ (not large) pequeño, chico; (of build) menudo; (narrow) estrecho; (lower case) minúsculo; (petty) mezquino; N (size) pequeño *m*; **— change** cambio suelto *m*; **— fry** gente menuda *f*; **— intestine** intestino delgado *m*; **— of the back** baja espalda *f*; **—pox** viruela *f*; **— talk** cháchara *f*; **to feel —** avergonzarse

smallness [smɔłnɪs] N pequeñez *f*

smart [smɑrt] ADJ (intelligent) listo, inteligente; (astute) astuto; (stylish) elegante; **— alec, aleck** sabihondo -da *mf*; **— ass** *fam* sabihondo -da *mf*; **— bomb** bomba inteligente *f*; **— money**

inversión inteligente *f*; **— remark** insolencia *f*; N escozor *m*; VI picar; **I'm —ing from his rude remarks** todavía me duelen sus groserías

smash [smæʃ] VT estrellar, destrozar; (a rebellion) aplastar; **to — into** estrellarse contra; N (sound) estrépito *m*; (blow) choque violento *m*; **a — hit** un exitazo

smear [smir] VT (daub) untar; (spot, vilify) manchar; (blur) correrse; (defeat) reventar; **to — with paint** pintorrear, pintarrajear; N (stain) mancha *f*; (culture) frotis *m*; **— campaign** campaña de difamación *f*

smell [smeł] VI/VT oler; **to — of** oler a; **that —s** huele mal, apesta; **to — up** apestar; N (odor) olor *m*; (sense) olfato *m*; **— of** olor a

smelly [sméli] ADJ hediondo, apestoso

smile [smaɪł] VI sonreír(se); **to — approval** sonreír en aprobación; N sonrisa *f*

smiling [smáɪlɪŋ] ADJ risueño, sonriente

smirk [smɚk] N sonrisa suficiente *f*; VI sonreír con suficiencia

smith [smɪθ] N herrero -ra *mf*

smog [smɑg] N smog *m*

smoke [smok] N humo *m*; (cigarette) cigarro *m*, cigarrillo *m*; **— detector** detector de humo *m*, detector de incendios *m*; **— screen** cortina de humo *f*; **— stack** chimenea *f*; **to have a —** fumar; VI (put off smoke) echar humo; (go fast) volar; VT (tobacco) fumar; (ham, fish, glass) ahumar; **to — out** (drive out) ahuyentar con humo; (expose) poner al descubierto

smoker [smókɚ] N fumador -ora *mf*; (train car) vagón de fumar *m*

smoking [smókɪŋ] ADJ humeante; **— car** vagón de fumar *m*; **— gun** prueba irrefutable *f*; **— room** cuarto de fumar *m*; N (use of tobacco) tabaquismo *m*

smoky [smóki] ADJ humoso

smolder, smoulder [smółdɚ] VI arder

smooth [smuð] ADJ (surface) liso; (skin) suave, terso; (tire) gastado; (sea) sereno, tranquilo; (polished) agradable, fino; (ingratiating) zalamero; VT (make surface even) alisar; (make easy) allanar; **to — away** hacer desaparecer; **to — one's hair** atusarse el cabello; **to — over** limar asperezas

smoothness [smúðnɪs] N (evenness) lisura *f*; (of skin) tersura *f*, suavidad *f*; (of sea) tranquilidad *f*; (polish) fineza *f*; (suaveness) zalamería *f*

smother [smÁðɚ] VT (stifle) ahogar(se), sofocar(se), asfixiar(se); (envelop) cubrir; (overprotect) sobreproteger

smudge [smʌʤ] N borrón *m*, mancha *f*; VI/VT borronear(se), manchar(se)

smug [smʌg] ADJ suficiente, petulante

smuggle [smʌ́gəɫ] VI/VT contrabandear, hacer contrabando; **to — in** entrar de contrabando; **to — out** sacar de contrabando

smuggler [smʌ́glɚ] N contrabandista *mf*

smut [smʌt] N (soot) hollín *m*; (obscenity) obscenidad *f*

snack [snæk] N tentempié *m*, bocadillo *m*; — **bar** cafetería *f*

snafu [snæfú] N relajo *m*

snag [snæg] N (a branch) gancho *m*; (in fabric) enganchón *m*; (any obstacle) pega *f*, obstáculo *m*, contrariedad *f*; **to hit a —** tropezar con un obstáculo; VI/VT enganchar(se); VT agarrar

snail [sneɫ] N caracol *m*; — **mail** correo regular *m*; —**'s pace** paso de tortuga *m*

snake [snek] N serpiente *f*; —**bite** mordedura de serpiente *f*; — **in the grass** víbora *f*; —**skin** piel de serpiente *f*; VI serpentear

snap [snæp] VI (make sound) chasquear, dar un chasquido; (lose control) estallar, perder los estribos; VT (a photograph) sacar; VI/VT (break) quebrar(se); **to — at** (try to bite) tirar un mordiscón; (speak harshly) ladrar; **to — one's fingers** chasquear los dedos, castañetear con los dedos; **to — out of** recuperarse de; **to — shut** cerrar(se) de golpe; **to — together** abrochar; **to — up** llevarse; N (sound) chasquido *m*; (fastener) broche *m*; (bite) tarascada *f*; **it's a —** es pan comido; — **judgment** decisión atolondrada *f*; —**dragon** dragón *m*; —**shot** instantánea, foto *f*

snappy [snǽpi] ADJ (that bites) mordedor; (elegant) elegante; **make it —!** ¡en seguida!

snare [snɛr] N (trap) trampa *f*; — **drum** tambor con bordón *m*; VT atrapar

snarl [snɑrɫ] VI/VT (growl) regañar; (tangle) enmarañar(se), enredar(se); N (growl) gruñido *m*; (tangle) maraña *f*, enredo *m*

snatch [snætʃ] VT (seize) arrebatar; (kidnap) secuestrar; VI **to — at** dar manotazos; N (act of snatching) arrebato *m*; (fragment) fragmento *m*

snazzy [snǽzi] ADJ llamativo

sneak [snik] VI andar furtivamente; VT (put away) meter a escondidas; **to — in** entrar a escondidas; **to — something in** meter a escondidas; **to — out** salir a hurtadillas; **to — something out** sacar a escondidas; **to — a cigarette** fumar a escondidas; N

persona solapada *f*

sneakers [sníkɚz] N zapatillas (deportivas) *f pl*, tenis *m pl*

sneer [snir] VI (smile) sonreír con sorna; **to — at** mofarse de; N expresión de sorna *f*

sneeze [sniz] VI estornudar; **that's nothing to — at** no es nada desdeñable; N estornudo *m*

snicker [sníkɚ] VI reírse burlonamente; N risita burlona *f*

snide [snaɪd] ADJ malévolo

sniff [snɪf] VI/VT husmear, olfatear; **to — at** husmear; (ridicule) menospreciar; N (act of sniffing) husmeo *m*, olfateo *m*; (smell) bocanada *f*

sniffle [snífəɫ] VI (with a cold) sorberse los mocos; (when crying) gimotear; N (when crying) gimoteo *m*; **the —s** un resfrío

snip [snɪp] VT tijeretear; **to — off** cortar de un tijeretazo; N (act of snipping) tijeretada *f*, tijeretazo *m*; (piece cut off) pedacito *m*, recorte *m*; — **of conversation** retazo de conversación *m*

sniper [snáɪpɚ] N francotirador -ora *mf*

snitch [snɪtʃ] VI (tell on) chivar, chivatar; VT (rob) ratear; N soplón -ona *mf*, chivato -ta *mf*

snob [snɑb] N esnob *mf*

snoop [snup] VI fisgar, fisgonear; N fisgón -ona *mf*

snooze [snuz] VI dormitar; N siesta *f*; **to take a —** echar un sueñecito / sueñito

snore [snɔr] VI roncar; N ronquido *m*

snorkel [snɔ́rkəɫ] N esnórquel *m*

snort [snɔrt] VI resoplar, bufar; VI/VT (drugs) esnifar; N resoplido *m*, bufido *m*; (drink) trago *m*

snot [snɑt] N (mucus) *fam, vulg* moco *m*; (person) *pej* mocoso -sa *mf*

snout [snaʊt] N hocico *m*, jeta *f*, morro *m*; (nose) napias *f pl*

snow [sno] N nieve *f* (also cocaine, heroin); —**ball** bola de nieve *f*; **to —ball** aumentar rápidamente; —**board** monopatín de nieve *m*; —**drift** ventisquero *m*; —**fall** nevada *f*; —**flake** copo de nieve *m*; —**man** muñeco de nieve *m*; —**mobile** motonieve *f*; —**plow** quitanieves *m sg*; —**shoe** raqueta *f*; —**storm** ventisca *f*; VI nevar; **the airport was —ed in** cerraron el aeropuerto por nieve; **to — under** (cover in snow) cubrir de nieve; (overwhelm) abrumar

snowy [snói] ADJ nevado; (white) níveo

snub [snʌb] VT volverle la cara a, desairar; (reject) despreciar; N desprecio *m*, desaire *m*; —**-nosed** chato; *Am* ñato

snuff [snʌf] VI **to — out** apagar, extinguir; N rapé *m*; **to be up to —** dar la talla

snug [snʌg] ADJ (tight-fitting) ajustado; (comfortable) cómodo

so [so] ADV (in this way) así; (to this degree) tan; (so much) tanto; **— am I** yo también; **—-and-—** fulano (de tal); **—-called** llamado; **— as to** para; **— far as I know** que yo sepa; **— many** tantos; **— much** tanto; **—-— regular; — much the better** tanto mejor; **— that** de modo que; **I was — a beauty queen!** ¡sí que fui reina de belleza! **— long!** ¡hasta luego! **and — forth** etcetera, y así sucesivamente; **I believe —** creo que sí; **is that — ?** ¿en serio? ¡no me digas! **ten minutes or —** unos diez minutos; INTERJ ajajá; CONJ (in order that) de modo que; (consequently) así que, entonces

soak [sok] VI/VT (immerse) remojar(se); (drench) empapar(se); **it finally —ed in on him that** por fin se dio cuenta de que; **to — through** colarse por; **to — up** absorber, embeber; **to be —ed through** estar empapado, estar calado hasta los huesos; N remojón *m*

soap [sop] N jabón *m*; (soap opera) telenovela *f*; **— bubble** pompa de jabón *f*; **— dish** jabonera *f*; VT enjabonar

soapy [sópi] ADJ jabonoso

soar [sɔr] VI/VT (airplane) elevar(se); (kite) remontar(se); (hopes) aumentar(se); (prices) disparar(se); (glider) planear(se); VI (bird) volar

sob [sab] VI sollozar, hipar; N sollozo *m*, hipo *m*

SOB (son of a bitch) [esobí] N *offensive* hijo de puta *m*, *offensive* hijo de perra *m*

sober [sóbɚ] ADJ (not drunk) sobrio; (temperate) moderado; (serious, subdued) serio, sobrio; VI **to — up** (get over drunkenness) despejarse; (become more serious) sentar cabeza

sobriety [səbráɪɪDi] N (not being drunk) sobriedad *f*; (moderation) moderación *f*; (seriousness) seriedad *f*

soccer [sákɚ] N fútbol *m*, balompié *m*

sociable [sóʃəbəɫ] ADJ sociable

social [sóʃəɫ] ADJ (of society) social; (friendly) sociable; N reunión social *f*; **— climber** arribista *mf*; **— science** ciencias sociales *f pl*; **— security** seguridad social *f*; **— welfare** asistencia social *f*; **— work** asistencia social *f*

socialism [sóʃəlɪzəm] N socialismo *m*

socialist [sóʃəlɪst] ADJ & N socialista *mf*

socialize [sóʃəlaɪz] VT socializar; VI salir, tener trato social

society [səsáɪɪDi] N sociedad *f*; (companionship) compañía *f*

socioeconomic [sosioɛkənámɪk] ADJ socioeconómico

sociology [sosiáləʤi] N sociología *f*

sociopath [sósiəpæθ] N sociópata *mf*

sock [sak] N (garment) calcetín *m*; (blow) puñetazo *m*, zumbido *m*; VT pegar, zumbar; **to — away** ahorrar

socket [sákɪt] N (of eye) cuenca *f*; (electrical outlet) enchufe *m*; (for bulb) portalámparas *m sg*, casquillo *m*

sod [sad] N (lawn) césped *m*; (piece) tepe *m*; VT cubrir de césped

soda [sóDə] N (drink) gaseosa *f*; (sodium hydroxide) soda *f*, sosa *f*; **— fountain** bar de bebidas sin alcohol *m*; **— pop** gaseosa *f*; **— water** agua con gas *f*

sodium [sóDiəm] N sodio *m*

sodomy [sáDəmi] N sodomía *f*

sofa [sófə] N sofá *m*; **— bed** sofá-cama *m*

soft [sɔft] ADJ (butter, bed, water, penalty) blando; (life) fácil, cómodo; (hair, skin) suave; (light) tenue; **—ball** softball *m*; **—-boiled eggs** huevos pasados por agua *m pl*; **— coal** carbón bituminoso *m*; **— drink** gaseosa *f*; **— palate** velo del paladar *m*; **—ware** software *m*

soften [sɔfən] VI/VT (butter) ablandar(se); (skin) suavizar(se); VT (a blow) amortiguar; (voice) bajar

softness [sɔftnɪs] N (of butter) blandura *f*; (of hair, skin) suavidad *f*; (of light) tenuidad *f*

soggy [sági] ADJ (clothes) empapado; (day) húmedo

soil [sɔɪɫ] N suelo *m*, tierra *f*; VI/VT ensuciar(se), manchar(se)

solace [sálɪs] N consuelo *m*; VT consolar

solar [sólɚ] ADJ solar; **— eclipse** eclipse de sol *m*; **— energy** energía solar *f*; **— plexus** plexo solar *m*; **— system** sistema solar *m*

solder [sáDɚ] VI/VT soldar(se); N soldadura *f*

soldering iron [sáDə-ɪŋaɪrn] N soldador *m*

soldier [sóɫʤɚ] N (of low rank) soldado *m*; (of any rank) militar *m*

sole [soɫ] ADJ solo, único; N (of a foot) planta *f*; (of a shoe) suela *f*; (fish) lenguado *m*

solemn [sáləm] ADJ solemne

solemnity [səlémnɪDi] N solemnidad *f*

solenoid [sólənɔɪd] N solenoide *m*

solicit [səlísɪt] VT (aid) pedir; (a prostitute) ofrecerse; VI (sell) vender, ofrecer productos

solicitor [səlísɪDɚ] N abogado *m*; **— General** Subsecretario -ria de Justicia *mf*

solicitous [səlísɪtəs] ADJ solícito
solid [sálɪd] ADJ (firm) sólido; (dense) denso; — **blue** azul liso *m*; — **geometry** geometría del espacio *f*; — **gold** oro puro *m*; — **line** línea continua *f*; —-**state** de estado sólido; **for one — hour** por una hora entera; N sólido *m*
solidarity [salɪdǽrɪɒi] N solidaridad *f*
solidify [səlídəfaɪ] VI/VT solidificar(se)
solidity [səlídɪti] N solidez *f*
solitary [sálɪteri] ADJ solitario; **to be in — confinement** estar incomunicado
solitude [sálɪtud] N soledad *f*
solo [sólo] N solo *m*
soloist [sóloɪst] N solista *mf*
Solomon Islander [sáləmənáɪləndɚ] N salomonense *mf*
Solomon Islands [sáləmənáɪləndz] N Islas Salomón *f pl*
solstice [sóɫstɪs] N solsticio *m*
soluble [sáljəbəɫ] ADJ soluble
solution [səlúʃən] N solución *f*
solve [saɫv] VT resolver, solucionar
solvent [sáɫvənt] N solvente *m*, disolvente *m*
Somalia [somáljə] N Somalia *f*
Somalian [somáljən] ADJ & N somalí *mf*
somber [sámbɚ] ADJ sombrío
some [sʌm] ADJ alguno; **I worked for — time** trabajé por un rato; **that is — dog!** ¡menudo perro! PRON algunos; **and then — y más todavía**; ADV — **twenty people** unas veinte personas; **I like it —** me gusta un poco
somebody [sámbɑɒi] PRON alguien
someday [sámde] ADV algún día
somehow [sámhaʊ] ADV de alguna manera; — **or other** de alguna manera u otra
someone [sámwʌn] PRON alguien
somersault [sámɚsɔɫt] N (on ground) voltereta *f*; (in air) salto mortal *m*; VI (on ground) dar una voltereta; (in air) dar un salto mortal
something [sámθɪŋ] N algo *m*; — **else** otra cosa; **thirty—** treinta y tantos
sometime [sámtaɪm] ADV algún día, en algún momento; —**s** a veces, de vez en cuando
somewhat [sámhwɑt] ADV algo
somewhere [sámhwɛr] ADV en alguna parte; — **else** en alguna otra parte
son [sʌn] N hijo *m*; —-**in-law** yerno *m*; — **of a bitch** *offensive* hijo de puta *m*; — **of a gun** *fam* hijo de su madre *m*
sonar [sónɑr] N sonar *m*
song [sɔŋ] N canción *f*; (of a bird) canto *m*; — **and dance** cuento chino *m*; —**writer** compositor -ora *mf*; —**bird** ave canora *f*, pájaro cantor *m*; **to buy something for**

a — comprar algo muy barato
sonic barrier [sánɪkbǽriɚ] N barrera del sonido *f*
sonnet [sánɪt] N soneto *m*
sonorous [sánɚəs] ADJ sonoro
soon [sun] ADV pronto; — **after nine** poco después de las nueve; **as — as** tan pronto como, en cuanto; **see you —** hasta pronto; **how — do you want it?** ¿para cuándo lo necesitas? —**er or later** tarde o temprano; **I'd —er stay here** prefiero quedarme aquí
soot [sʊt] N hollín *m*, tizne *m*
soothe [suð] VT calmar, aliviar
soothsayer [súθseɚ] N agorero -ra *mf*
sooty [súɒi] ADJ tiznado
sop [sɑp] VT empapar; **to — up** absorber; **to be —ping wet** estar empapado; N sopa *f*
sophisticated [səfístɪkeɒɪd] ADJ sofisticado
sophomore [sáfəmɔr] N estudiante de segundo año *mf*
soprano [səprǽno] N soprano *m*
sorcerer [sórsərɚ] N brujo *m*, hechicero *m*
sorceress [sórsɚɪs] N hechicera *f*
sordid [sórdɪd] ADJ sórdido, escabroso
sore [sɔr] ADJ (painful) dolorido, doloroso; (grieved) dolorido; (angry) enojado; —**head** cascarrabias *mf*; **my arm is —** me duele el brazo; **to have a — throat** tener dolor de garganta; N llaga *f*, úlcera *f*
soreness [sórnɪs] N dolor *m*
sorority [sərórɪɒi] N asociación femenina de estudiantes *f*
sorrow [sáro] N (sadness) pena *f*, pesar *m*, pesadumbre *f*; (cause of sadness) fuente de disgustos *f*
sorrowful [sárəfəɫ] ADJ triste, pesaroso
sorry [sári] ADJ **I am —** lo siento; **I am — about that** lo lamento; **I am — for her** la compadezco; —**?** ¿Cómo? **a — SOB** *pej* un desgraciado; **you'll be —** te arrepentirás; **he was in — shape** estaba en un estado lamentable
sort [sɔrt] N clase *f*, tipo *m*; — **of tired** algo cansado; **all —s of** toda clase de; **out of —s** (depressed) de mal humor; (ill) indispuesto; VT (classify) clasificar; **to — out** separar, apartar; **to — out a problem** resolver un problema
SOS [ésoés] N SOS *m*
soul [soɫ] N alma *f*; — **music** música soul *f*; **not a —** nadie, ni un alma; **the — of tact** la imagen del tacto
sound [saʊnd] N sonido *m*; (inlet) brazo de mar *m*; — **wave** onda sonora *f*; ADJ (healthy) sano; (sane) cuerdo; (well founded) bien fundado, lógico; — **advice**

buen consejo *m*; — **barrier** barrera del sonido *f*; —**proof** a prueba de sonido; —**sleep** sueño profundo *m*; —**track** banda sonora *f*; **a** — **beating** una buena paliza; **of** — **mind** en su sano juicio; **safe and** — sano y salvo; VI sonar; VT (an alarm) tocar; (a channel) sondar; (opinion) sondear; **to** — **out** tantear, sondear

soup [sup] N sopa *f*; — **dish** plato sopero *m*; —**spoon** cuchara sopera *f*; — **tureen** sopera *f*

sour [saUr] ADJ (acidic) agrio, ácido; (peevish) agrio, avinagrado; **to go** — cortarse, agriarse; — **cream** *Sp* nata agria *f*; *Am* crema agria *f*; — **milk** leche cortada *f*; —**puss** cascarrabias *mf*, avinagrado -da *mf*; VI/VT agriar(se), avinagrar(se); (milk) cortar(se)

source [sɔrs] N fuente *f*, origen *m*

sourness [sáUrnɪs] N acidez *f*

souse [saUs] VI/VT (plunge) zambullir(se); (soak) empapar(se); N borracho -cha *mf*, esponja *f*

south [saUθ] N sur *m*; ADJ meridional; — **Africa** Sudáfrica *f*; — **African** sudafricano -na *mf*; — **America** América del Sur *f*, Sudamérica *f*; — **American** sudamericano -na *mf*; —**bound** con rumbo al sur; —**east** sureste, sudeste; —**eastern** sureste, sudeste; — **Korea** Corea del Sur *f*; — **Korean** surcoreano -na *mf*; —**paw** zurdo -da *mf*; — **pole** polo sur *m*; —**west** sudoeste, suroeste; —**western** sudoeste, suroeste; ADV hacia el sur

southern [sáðɚn] ADJ meridional, sureño

southerner [sáðɚnɚ] N sureño -ña *mf*, meridional *mf*, habitante del sur *mf*

southward [sáUθwɚd] ADV hacia el sur, rumbo al sur

souvenir [suvənír] N recuerdo *m*

sovereign [sávɚɪn] ADJ & N soberano -na *mf*

sovereignty [sávɚɪnti] N soberanía *f*

sow [saU] N puerca *f*; [so] VI/VT sembrar

soy [sɔi] N *Sp* soja *f*; *Am* soya *f*; —**bean** *Sp* semilla de soja *f*; *Am* semilla de soya *f*; — **sauce** *Sp* salsa de soja *f*; *Am* salsa de soya *f*

spa [spɑ] N balneario *m*

space [spes] N espacio *m*; —**-age** de la era espacial; —**bar** barra espaciadora *f*; —**craft** nave espacial *f*; —**ship** nave espacial *f*; — **shuttle** transbordador espacial *m*; — **station** estación espacial *f*; — **suit** traje espacial *m*; VT espaciar

spacious [spéʃəs] ADJ espacioso, amplio

spade [sped] N pala *f*; (in cards) pica *f*; **to call a** — **a** — al pan, pan y al vino, vino

Spain [spen] N España *f*

span [spæn] N (of hand) palmo *m*; (of time) espacio *m*; (of attention) lapso *m*, período *m*; (of bridge) tramo *m*; (of wing) envergadura *f*; (of life) duración *f*; VT (time) abarcar; (a river) atravesar, salvar

Spaniard [spǽnjɚd] N español -ola *mf*

Spanish [spǽnɪʃ] ADJ (of Spain) español; (Spanish-speaking) hispano; N (language) español *m*

Spanish America [spǽnɪʃəmérɪkə] N Hispanoamérica *f*

spank [spæŋk] VT dar nalgadas; N palmada *f*, nalgada *f*

spanking [spǽŋkɪŋ] N zurra en las nalgas *f*; ADJ — **new** flamante

spare [sper] VT (embarrassment) ahorrar, evitar; (money) prestar; (an enemy) perdonar la vida a; (a worker) prescindir de; — **me!** ¡ten piedad de mí! **to** — **no expense** no escatimar gastos; **to have time to** — tener tiempo de sobra; ADJ (austere) austero; (extra) de sobra, de más; — **cash** dinero disponible *m*; — **parts** repuestos *m pl*; — **time** tiempo libre *m*; N (part) repuesto *m*; (tire) neumático de repuesto *m*

spark [spɑrk] N chispa *f*; — **plug** bujía *f*; VI chispear, echar chispas; VT (a riot) desencadenar; (interest, criticism) provocar

sparkle [spárkəl] VI (diamond) centellear; (sparkler) chispear; (eyes) brillar; N (flashing) brillo *m*, centelleo *m*; (spirit) viveza *f*, animación *f*

sparkling [spárklɪŋ] ADJ (diamond) centelleante; (eyes) brillante; — **water** agua con gas *f*; — **wine** vino espumoso *m*

sparrow [spǽro] N gorrión *m*

sparse [spɑrs] ADJ escaso; (hair) ralo

spasm [spǽzəm] N espasmo *m*

spastic [spǽstɪk] ADJ espástico

spat [spæt] N riña *f*

spatial [spéʃəl] ADJ espacial

spatter [spǽDɚ] VI/VT salpicar; N salpicadura *f*

spatula [spǽtʃələ] N espátula *f*

spawn [spɔn] VI desovar; VT engendrar; N (of fish) huevas *f pl*; (of frogs) huevos *m pl*

spay [spe] VT esterilizar, castrar

speak [spik] VI hablar; VT (language) hablar; (truth, amusement) decir; (lines) recitar, decir; **so to** — por decirlo así, valga la expresión; **to** — **for** hablar en nombre de / a favor de; **to** — **one's mind** hablar sin rodeos; **to** — **out against** denunciar; **to** — **out for** defender; **to** — **up** hablar fuerte

speaker [spíkɚ] N orador -ra *mf*; (at a conference) conferenciante *mf*; **— of the House** presidente -ta de la cámara de representantes *mf*; **—phone** teléfono con parlante *m*

spear [spir] N lanza *f*; (for fishing) arpón *m*; (sprout) brote *m*; VT (wound with lance) alancear, herir con lanza; (fish with lance) arponear

spearmint [spírmɪnt] N mentaverde *f*

special [spéʃəɫ] ADJ especial; **— delivery** entrega inmediata *f*; **— education** educación especial *f*; **— effects** efectos especiales *m pl*; **— interest (group)** grupo de presión *m*; N (sale item) especialidad *f*; (TV program) especial *m*

specialist [spéʃəlɪst] N especialista *mf*

specialization [spɛʃəlɪzéʃən] N especialización *f*, especialidad *f*

specialize [spéʃəlaɪz] VI/VT especializar(se)

specialty [spéʃəɫti] N especialidad *f*

species [spíʃiz] N especie *f*

specific [spɪsífɪk] ADJ específico; **— gravity** peso específico *m*; N **—s** detalles *m pl*

specify [spésəfaɪ] VI/VT especificar

specimen [spésəmən] N (representative) espécimen *m*, ejemplar *m*; (sample) muestra *f*

speck [spɛk] N (small dot) mota *f*, manchita *f*; (small amount) pizca *f*

speckle [spékəɫ] N manchita *f*, mota *f*; VT salpicar, motear; **—d** moteado

spectacle [spéktəkəɫ] N espectáculo *m*; **—s** gafas *f pl*, anteojos *m pl*; **to make a — of oneself** dar un espectáculo, ponerse en ridículo

spectacular [spɛktǽkjəlɚ] ADJ espectacular

spectator [spéktedɚ] N espectador -ra *mf*

spectrum [spéktrəm] N espectro *m*

speculate [spékjəlet] VI/VT especular

speculation [spɛkjəléʃən] N especulación *f*

speculator [spékjəledɚ] N especulador -ora *mf*

speech [spitʃ] N (faculty of speaking) habla *f*; (formal) discurso *m*; (in a play) parlamento *m*; **to make a —** pronunciar un discurso; **— defect** defecto de pronunciación *m*

speechless [spítʃlɪs] ADJ (dumb) mudo; (astonished) estupefacto

speed [spid] N velocidad *f* (also gear), rapidez *f*; (amphetamine) anfeta *f*; **— limit** límite de velocidad *m*; **at full —** a toda velocidad; VI (break speed limit) ir con exceso de velocidad; **to — by** pasar a toda velocidad; **to — off / away** irse a toda velocidad; **to — up** acelerar; VT (supplies) hacer llegar a toda velocidad; (work) acelerar

speedometer [spɪdámɪdɚ] N velocímetro *m*

speedy [spíDi] ADJ veloz, rápido

spell [spɛɫ] N (charm) hechizo *m*, sortilegio *m*, conjuro *m*; (period) temporada *f*; (sickness) ataque *m*; **—bound** hechizado; **to put under a —** hechizar; VT (spoken) deletrear; (written) escribir; (represent) significar, representar; **to —-check** comprobar el deletreo; **I —ed it out for him** se lo dije con todas las letras

spelling [spélɪŋ] N ortografía *f*; **— bee** concurso de ortografía *m*

spend [spɛnd] VT (money) gastar; (time) pasar; **—thrift** derrochador -ra *mf*, gastador -ra *mf*, pródigo -ga *mf*

sperm [spɝm] N esperma *mf*, semen *m*; **— bank** banco de semen / esperma *m*; **— whale** cachalote *m*

sphere [sfir] N esfera *f*

spherical [sférɪkəɫ] ADJ esférico

spice [spaɪs] N especia *f*; VT condimentar; **to — up** dar sal

spiciness [spáɪsɪnɪs] N lo picante

spick and span [spíkənspǽn] ADJ impecable

spicy [spáɪsi] ADJ picante

spider [spáɪDɚ] N araña *f*; **— monkey** mono araña *m*; **—'s web** telaraña *f*

spigot [spígət] N grifo *m*, espita *f*

spike [spaɪk] N (sprout) espiga *f*; (sharp object) púa *f*, pincho *m*; (on shoes) clavo *m*; **—s** zapatillas con clavos *f pl*; VT (impale) clavar; (add alcohol to) echar alcohol a; (hit a volleyball) picar

spill [spɪɫ] VI/VT volcar(se), derramar(se), verter(se); VT (a rider) hacer caer; **to — the beans** descubrir el pastel; VI **to — over** (a liquid) desbordarse; (a conflict) extenderse; N (of water) derrame *m*; (of blood) derramamiento *m*; (fall) caída *f*

spin [spɪn] VT (wool) hilar; (a top, one's partner) hacer girar; VI dar vueltas, girar; **to — yarns** contar cuentos; N (turning) giro *m*, vuelta *f*; (of an airplane) barrena *f*; (political) sesgo *m*; **to take a —** dar una vuelta

spinach [spínɪtʃ] N espinaca *f*

spinal [spáɪnəɫ] ADJ espinal, vertebral; **— column** columna vertebral *f*, espina dorsal *f*; **— cord** médula espinal *f*

spindle [spíndɫ] N (for weaving) huso *m*; (on machines) eje *m*

spine [spaɪn] N espina *f*, espinazo *m*

spinning [spínɪŋ] N (action) hilado *m*; (art) hilandería *f*; **— machine** máquina de hilar *f*; **— mill** hilandería *f*; **— top**

trompo *m*, peonza *f*; — **wheel** rueca *f*

spinster [spínstɚ] N solterona *f*

spiral [spáɪrəł] ADJ & N espiral *m*; — **notebook** cuaderno de espiral *m*; — **staircase** escalera de caracol *f*

spire [spaɪr] N aguja *f*, chapitel *m*

spirit [spírɪt] N (ghost) espíritu *m*; (animation) ánimo *m*, brío *m*; (alcohol) alcohol *m*; **low —s** abatimiento *m*; **to be in good —s** estar de buen humor; VT **to — away** llevar como por arte de magia

spirited [spírɪDɪd] ADJ fogoso, brioso

spiritual [spírɪtʃuəł] ADJ & N espiritual *m*

spit [spɪt] VI/VT escupir; N (saliva) escupitajo *m*; (for roasting) asador *m*; (of sand) banco *m*

spite [spaɪt] N despecho *m*, inquina *f*; **in — of** a pesar de; **out of —** por despecho; VT contrariar

spiteful [spáɪtfəł] ADJ malicioso

splash [splæʃ] VI/VT salpicar; VI chapotear, chapalear; N salpicadura *f*, chapoteo *m*; **to make a —** hacer olas

splatter [splǽDɚ] VI/VT salpicar; N salpicadura *f*

spleen [splin] N bazo *m*; (ill humor) mal humor *m*

splendid [spléndɪd] ADJ espléndido

splendor [spléndɚ] N esplendor *m*

splice [splaɪs] VT (tape, genes) empalmar, unir; N empalme *m*, unión *f*

splint [splɪnt] N tablilla *f*; VT entablillar

splinter [splíntɚ] N astilla *f*; VI/VT astillar(se)

split [splɪt] VI/VT (stone, wood) hender(se), rajar(se); (candy bar) partir(se), dividir(se); **to — hairs** hilar fino; **to — one's sides with laughter** desternillarse de risa; **to — the difference** partir la diferencia; ADJ (wood) partido, hendido; (a group) dividido; **—-level** en desnivel; **— personality** doble personalidad *f*; **— screen** pantalla dividida *f*; **— second** fracción de segundo *f*; N hendidura *f*, grieta *f*; (in a group) escisión *f*, división *f*

spoil [spɔɪł] VI (milk) cortar(se); (food) echarse a perder, averiarse; VT (vacation, performance) estropear, arruinar; (plans) desbaratar; (enjoyment) aguar; (child) malcriar, mimar demasiado; N **—s** botín *m*

spoiler [spɔ́ɪlɚ] N alerón *m*

spoke [spok] N rayo *m*

spokesperson [spókspɚsən] N portavoz *mf*, vocero -ra *mf*

sponge [spʌndʒ] N (animal, utensil) esponja *f*; (parasite) gorrón -ona *mf*; **— cake** *Am* bizcochuelo *m*; *Sp* bizcocho *m*; VI **to — off** quitar con esponja; **to — off of**

gorronear; **to — up** absorber con una esponja

sponger [spʌ́ndʒɚ] N gorrón -ona *mf*, parásito *m*

spongy [spʌ́ndʒi] ADJ esponjoso, esponjado

sponsor [spánsɚ] N (of the arts) mecenas *mf*; (of sports, TV program) patrocinador -ora *mf*; (of a bill) proponente *mf*; VT (a child) apadrinar; (arts, sports, TV show) patrocinar; (bill) proponer

sponsorship [spánsɚʃɪp] N patrocinio *m*

spontaneity [spantənéɪDi] N espontaneidad *f*

spontaneous [spantén iəs] ADJ espontáneo

spook [spuk] N (ghost) espectro *m*; (spy) espía *mf*

spool [spuł] N carrete *m*, carretel *m*; VT (wool) devanar; (tape) enrollar

spoon [spun] N cuchara *f*; VT cucharear, poner con una cuchara; **to —-feed** dar de comer en la boca

spoonful [spúnfuł] N cucharada *f*

spore [spɔr] N espora *f*

sport [spɔrt] N deporte *m*; **to be a good —** tener espíritu deportivo; VT lucir; ADJ deportivo; **— utility vehicle** vehículo utilitario deportivo *m*; **—s car** coche deportivo *m*; **—s jacket** saco de sport *m*, americana *f*; **—sman** (hunter) cazador *m*; (in sports) hombre de espíritu deportivo *m*; **—smanship** espíritu deportivo *m*, deportividad *f*; **—swriter** cronista deportivo -va *mf*

sporty [spɔ́rDi] ADJ deportivo

spot [spat] N (stain) mancha *f*, mota *f*; (blemish) espinilla *f*; (insect bite) roncha *f*; (place) lugar *m*, paraje *m*; (scrape) aprieto *m*; **on the —** en el acto; **—-check** inspección al azar *f*; **—light** (in theater) foco *m*; (outdoors) reflector *m*; **to be in the —light** ser el centro de atención; **— remover** quitamanchas *m sg*; VI/VT (stain) manchar, ensuciar; VT (see in the distance) divisar; (notice) notar; (give advantage) dar como ventaja

spotless [spátlɪs] ADJ inmaculado

spotted [spáDɪd] ADJ manchado, moteado

spouse [spaʊs] N cónyuge *mf*

spout [spaʊt] VT (throw) arrojar chorros de; (talk) soltar tonterías; VI (flow out) salir a chorros; (talk) perorar; N (of a fountain) caño *m*; (of a gutter) canalón *m*; (of a teapot) pico *m*

sprain [spren] VT torcerse; N torcedura *f*

sprawl [sprɔł] VI (spread limbs) despatarrarse; (extend) extenderse; (fall) tumbarse; N postura despatarrada *f*

spray [spre] N (of liquid) rociada *f*; (foam)

espuma *f*; (of flowers) ramillete *m*; VI/VT
rociar(se); — **can** aerosol *m*; — **paint**
pintura en aerosol *f*
spread [sprɛd] VI/VT (arms, newspaper)
extender(se); (butter) untar(se); (map)
desdoblar(se); (legs) abrir(se); (seeds)
esparcir(se); (news) difundir(se),
diseminar(se); (rumor) propalar; (panic)
sembrar; VT (panic, news) sembrar; N (of
ideas) difusión *f*; (of opinion)
diseminación *f*; (of disease) propagación *f*;
(of nuclear weapons) proliferación *f*; (for a
bed) cubrecama *m*; (for bread) pasta *f*; (of
food) festín *m*; (ranch) hacienda *f*;
—**sheet** (paper) planilla de cálculo *f*;
(program) planilla electrónica *f*
spree [spri] N parranda *f*, farra *f*; **to go on a**
— ir de parranda/farra; **to go on a**
shopping — gastar dinero
desenfrenadamente
spring [sprɪŋ] VI saltar; **to** — **at** abalanzarse
sobre; **to** — **from** nacer de; **to** — **to**
mind venir a la mente; **to** — **up** surgir;
VT **to** — **a leak** (boat) hacer agua; (pipe)
comenzar a gotear; **to** — **news** dar una
noticia de sopetón; **to** — **open** abrir(se)
de golpe; N (season) primavera *f*; (coil)
muelle *m*, resorte *m*; (elasticity) elasticidad
f; (jump) salto *m*; (water) manantial *m*,
fuente *f*; —**board** trampolín *m*; — **fever**
fiebre de primavera *f*; — **mattress**
colchón de muelles *m*; —**time** primavera
f; — **water** agua de manantial *f*; **he's no**
— **chicken** no se cuece en el primer
hervor
sprinkle [spríŋkəł] VT (with sugar)
espolvorear; (with droplets) salpicar,
rociar; (rain) gotear, chispear
sprint [sprɪnt] VI (run) echarse una carrera;
(run a competitive race) (e)sprintar; N
(run) corrida corta *f*; (race) (e)sprint *m*
sprocket [sprákɪt] N piñón *m*, rueda dentada
f
sprout [spraʊt] VI (leaf) brotar, salir; (plants)
retoñar; (seeds) germinar; (houses) surgir;
VT echar; **he** —**ed horns** le salieron
cuernos; N retoño *m*, brote *m*, renuevo *m*
spruce [sprus] N picea *f*; VI **to** — **up**
arreglarse
spunk [spʌŋk] N agallas *f pl*, *vulg* cojones *m*
pl
spur [spɝ] N espuela *f*; (stimulus) aguijón *m*;
(of a rooster) espolón *m*; (of a mountain)
estribación *f*; (of a railroad track) ramal *m*;
on the — **of the moment**
espontáneamente; VT espolear; **to** — **on**
animar

spurious [spjúriəs] ADJ espurio
spurn [spɝn] VT rechazar, desdeñar
spurt [spɝt] VI salir a chorros; N (of water)
chorro *m*; (of a runner) esfuerzo repentino
m; **in** —**s** por rachas
sputter [spʌ́Dɚ] VI (fire) chisporrotear;
(person) refunfuñar; N (fire) chisporroteo
m
sputum [spjútəm] N esputo *m*
spy [spaɪ] N espía *mf*; VI espiar; **to** — **on**
espiar, avizorar; —**glass** catalejo *m*
squabble [skwábəł] VI reñir; N reyerta *f*
squad [skwɑd] N (of police) patrulla *f*; (for
execution) pelotón *m*; (of athletes) equipo
m; (for guarding) retén *m*; — **car** (coche)
patrullero *m*
squadron [skwádrən] N (in navy) escuadra *f*;
(in army) escuadrón *m*
squalid [skwálɪd] ADJ escuálido
squall [skwɔł] N (rain) chubasco *m*, borrasca
f; (sound) berrido *m*; VI berrear
squalor [skwálɚ] N miseria *f*, escualidez *f*
squander [skwándɚ] VT despilfarrar,
derrochar, disipar
squanderer [skwándərɚ] N derrochador -ora
mf
square [skwɛr] N (shape) cuadrado *m*; (on a
pattern) cuadro *m*; (plaza) plaza *f*; (tool in
carpentry) escuadra *f*; (on chessboard)
casilla *f*; **he is a** — es muy conservador;
VT (make square) cuadrar; (draw squares
on) cuadricular; (multiply by itself) elevar
al cuadrado; **to** — **one's shoulders**
erguirse; ADJ (in shape) cuadrado; (at
ninety degrees) en ángulo recto; (tied)
empatado; (frank) franco; — **dance**
cuadrilla *f*; — **knot** nudo de rizo *m*; —
meal comida completa *f*; — **root** raíz
cuadrada *f*; **to be** — **with someone** estar
a mano con alguien; ADV **right** —
between the eyes justo entre los ojos
squash [skwɑʃ] N (gourd) calabaza *f*; (sport)
squash *m*; VT aplastar, despachurrar
squat [skwɑt] VI (sit low) acuclillarse;
(occupy) ocupar sin autorización; ADJ
(sitting low) acuclillado; (thick set)
rechoncho, achaparrado; N **in a** — en
cuclillas
squawk [skwɔk] VI (of chickens) cacarear;
(complain) quejarse; N (of chickens)
cacareo *m*; (complaint) quejido *m*
squeak [skwik] VI (door) rechinar, chirriar;
(shoe) rechinar; (mouse) chillar; N (of
door) rechinamiento *m*, chirrido *m*; (of
shoe) rechinamiento *m*; (of mouse)
chillido *m*
squeaky [skwíki] ADJ (door) chirriante;

(shoes) rechinante

squeal [skwił] VI chillar; (complain) protestar; (snitch) chivatar, delatar; N chillido *m*

squeamish [skwímɪʃ] ADJ delicado

squeegee [skwíʤi] N escurridor de goma *m*, limpiavidrios *m sg*

squeeze [skwiz] VT apretar; (press very hard) estrujar; (an orange) exprimir; (hug) abrazar; **to — into** meter(se) con dificultad en, encajar(se) en; **to — out** (an orange) exprimir; (a towel) escurrir; **to — through a crowd** abrirse paso entre la multitud; N (of hands) apretón *m*; (excessive squeeze) estrujón *m*; (hug) abrazo *m*; (lack) restricción *f*

squelch [skwɛłtʃ] VT (revolt) aplastar, sofocar; (criticism) acallar

squid [skwɪd] N calamar *m*

squint [skwɪnt] VI (partially close eyes) entrecerrar los ojos; (look askance) mirar de soslayo; N (look with partially closed eyes) mirada con los ojos entrecerrados *f*; (side-glance) mirada de soslayo *f*

squirm [skwɜˑm] VI retorcerse; **to — out of a difficulty** zafarse de un aprieto

squirrel [skwə́ˑəł] N ardilla *f*

squirt [skwɜˑt] VT echar un chisguete en; VI salir a chorritos; N chisguete *m*, chorrito *m*; **— gun** pistola lanzaagua *f*, pistola de agua *f*

Sri Lanka [sriláŋkə] N Sri Lanka *f*

Sri Lankan [sriláŋkən] ADJ & N cingalés -esa *mf*

stab [stæb] VI/VT apuñalar, acuchillar; **to — at** tirar puñaladas a; N (with a dagger) puñalada *f*; (with a knife) cuchillada *f*; (with a pocketknife) navajazo *m*; (of pain) punzada *f*, pinchazo *m*; **— wound** cuchillada *f*

stability [stəbílɪɾi] N estabilidad *f*

stable [stébəł] ADJ estable; N establo *m*, cuadra *f*; (for horses) caballeriza *f*; VT poner en el establo

stack [stæk] N pila *f*, montón *m*; (of a chimney) chimenea *f*; (in a library) estantería *f*; VT amontonar, apilar

stadium [stédiəm] N estadio *m*

staff [stæf] N (stick) cayado *m*; (of a flag) asta *f*; (personnel) personal *m*, plantel *m*; (of music) pentagrama *m*; **— of life** pan de cada día *m*; **— officer** oficial de estado mayor *m*; **editorial —** redacción *f*; **teaching —** cuerpo docente *m*; VT contratar personal

stag [stæg] N (of deer) venado *m*, ciervo *m*; (of other animals) macho *m*; **— beetle**

ciervo volante *m*; **— party** fiesta para hombres *f*

stage [steʤ] N (showplace) escenario *m*; (for popular entertainment) tablado *m*; (theater) teatro *m*, las tablas *f pl*; (period) etapa *f*, estadio *m*; (distance) etapa *f*; **—coach** diligencia *f*; **— fright** miedo al escenario *m*, fiebre de candilejas *f*; **—hand** tramoyista *mf*; **by —s** por etapas; VT (a play) poner en escena; (an attack) organizar

stagger [stǽgɚ] VI (totter) tambalearse, dar tumbos; VT (hit hard) hacer tambalear; (overwhelm) dejar azorado; (alternate) escalonar; N tambaleo *m*

stagnant [stǽgnənt] ADJ estancado

stagnate [stǽgnet] VI estancarse

staid [sted] ADJ serio

stain [sten] VI/VT (spot) manchar(se); (color) teñir(se); **—ed-glass window** vitral *m*; N (spot) mancha *f*; (color) tinte *m*, tintura *f*

stainless [sténlɪs] ADJ sin mancha; **— steel** acero inoxidable *m*

stair [stɛr] N peldaño *m*, escalón *m*; **—case** escalera *f*; **—s** escalera *f*; **—way** escalera *f*

stake [stek] N (pole) estaca *f*; (investment) interés *m*; (bet) apuesta *f*; **at —** en juego; **to die at the —** morir en la hoguera; VT estacar; **to — out** vigilar

stalactite [stəlǽktaɪt] N estalactita *f*

stalagmite [stəlǽgmaɪt] N estalagmita *f*

stale [stel] ADJ (bread) duro; (air) viciado; (joke) viejo; **—mate** punto muerto *m*

stalk [stɔk] N tallo *m*; VT acechar

stall [stɔł] N (at a market) puesto *m*; (at a fair) caseta *f*, barraca *f*; (in a stable) compartimiento *m*; VI (airplane) entrar en pérdida; (talks) llegar a un punto muerto; (motor) pararse; **he is —ing** está arrastrando los pies; VT (airplane) hacer entrar en pérdida; (talks) paralizar; (motor) parar

stallion [stǽljən] N semental *m*

stamina [stǽmənə] N resistencia *f*, aguante *m*

stammer [stǽmɚ] VI balbucear; N balbuceo *m*

stamp [stæmp] VT (a letter) sellar; *Mex* timbrar; *Am* estampillar; (an official document) sellar, timbrar; (a coin) acuñar; VI (with foot) pisotear, patalear; (horse) piafar; **to — out** eliminar; N (on a letter) *Sp* sello *m*; *Mex* timbre *m*; *Am* estampilla *f*; (on an official document) sello *m*, timbre *m*; (instrument, character) sello *m*; (on the ground) pisotón *m*; (sound) paso *m*

stampede [stæmpíd] N estampida *f*; VI huir en estampida; VT hacer huir en estampida

stance [stæns] N posición *f*, postura *f*

stanch, staunch [stɔntʃ] VT restañar; ADJ (strong) firme; (loyal) fiel

stand [stænd] VI (take a standing position) ponerse de pie, levantarse; *Am* parar(se); (to be in a standing position) estar de pie; *Am* estar parado; (stop) detenerse; (withstand, tolerate) aguantar, tolerar, soportar; (remain valid) mantenerse; —**by** recurso viejo *m*; —**by passenger** pasajero -ra en la lista de espera *mf*; **to — aside** apartarse; **to — back** retroceder; **to — behind** respaldar; **to — by** (be uninvolved) mantenerse al margen; (be alert) estar alerta; (support) respaldar; **to — for** (mean) significar; (tolerate) tolerar; **to — one's ground** mantenerse firme; **to — out** destacarse, sobresalir; **to — up for** defender; **it —s to reason** es razonable; **it —s one meter tall** mide un metro de alto; **to — a chance of** tener posibilidad de; **where do you — on this issue?** ¿qué opinas al respecto? N (at a market) puesto *m*; (at a fair) caseta *f*; (of trees) bosque *m*; (opinion) posición *f*; (for music) atril *m*; (for taxis) parada *f*; —**off** empate *m*; —**point** punto de vista *m*; **to come to a —still** pararse; **to be at a —still** estar parado

standard [stændɚd] N (of behavior) norma *f*; (of living, performance) nivel *m*; (of weights) patrón *m*; (banner) estandarte *m*; **gold —** patrón oro *m*; **to be up to —** satisfacer los requisitos; —-**bearer** portaestandarte *mf*; **— of living** nivel de vida *m*; ADJ (normal) normal; (standardized) estándar; **— deviation** desviación estándar *f*; **— time** hora oficial *f*

standardization [stændɚdɪzéʃən] N estandarización *f*

standardize [stændɚdaɪz] VT estandarizar, uniformar

standing [stændɪŋ] N (position) posición *f*; (rank) rango *m*; (reputation) reputación *f*; ADJ (not seated) derecho, en pie; (permanent) permanente; (stagnant) estancado; **— order** pedido fijo *m*; **— ovation** ovación de pie *f*

stanza [stænzə] N estrofa *f*

staple [stépəł] N (for paper) grapa *f*; (main product) producto principal *m*; (food) alimento básico *m*; ADJ (principal) principal; (basic) básico; VT engrapar

stapler [stéplɚ] N grapadora *f*

star [stɑr] N estrella *f* (also actor); (asterisk) asterisco *m*; **— attraction** atracción principal *f*; —**fish** estrella de mar *f*; —**light** luz de las estrellas *f*; —-**spangled** salpicado de estrellas; **a — student** un(a) estudiante sobresaliente; VT (act in) protagonizar; (put asterisk on) marcar con asterisco; (cover with stars) estrellar

starboard [stɑ́rbərd] N estribor *m*; ADV a estribor

starch [stɑrtʃ] N almidón *m* (also food); VT almidonar

stardom [stɑ́rDəm] N estrellato *m*

stare [stɛr] VI/VT mirar fijamente; N mirada fija *f*

stark [stɑrk] ADJ (landscape) yermo; (truth) descarnado, desnudo; (contrast) marcado; **— naked** en cueros; **— raving mad** loco de remate

starling [stɑ́rlɪŋ] N estornino *m*

starry [stɑ́rɪ] ADJ estrellado

start [stɑrt] VI/VT (begin) comenzar, empezar; (a car) poner(se) en marcha, arrancar; VT (a fire) provocar; VI (jump) sobresaltarse; **to — off / out / up** empezar; N (beginning) comienzo *m*, principio *m*; (of a race) salida *f*; (nervous jump) sobresalto *m*; (nervous jump of a horse) respingo *m*

starter [stɑ́rDɚ] N (on an automobile) arranque *m*; (for a race) juez de salida *m*; **for —s** para empezar

startle [stɑ́rdl] VI/VT asustar(se), sobresaltar(se)

startling [stɑ́rdlɪŋ] ADJ asombroso, sorprendente

starvation [stɑrvéʃən] N inanición *f*

starve [stɑrv] VI/VT hambrear; VI morirse de hambre; VT matar de hambre; (for affection) privar de cariño

starving [stɑ́rvɪŋ] ADJ hambriento, muerto de hambre

stash [stæʃ] VI **to — away** ir ahorrando; N alijo *m*

state [stet] N estado *m*; **— of the art** con los últimos avances; —**room** (on a ship) camarote *m*; (on a train) compartimiento *m*; —**sman** estadista *m*; —**swoman** estadista *f*; VT (declare) declarar, aseverar, manifestar; (describe) exponer

stately [stétli] ADJ majestuoso, imponente

statement [stétmənt] N (declaration) declaración *f*, aseveración *f*; (bill) estado de cuentas *m*

static [stæDɪk] ADJ estático; N interferencia *f*; **— electricity** electricidad estática *f*; **don't give me any —** no me compliques la vida

station [stéʃən] N estación *f*; (of radio) emisora *f*; (of television) canal *m*; (social

rank) condición *f*; — **wagon** camioneta *f*;
VT (a sentry) apostar; (troops) estacionar
stationary [stéʃənɛri] ADJ (not moving)
estacionario; (stopped) detenido; (fixed)
fijo
stationery [stéʃənɛri] N (material) artículos
de papelería *m pl*; (paper) papel de carta *m*
statistics [stətístɪks] N (science) estadística *f*;
(data) estadísticas *f pl*
statue [stǽtʃu] N estatua *f*
stature [stǽtʃɚ] N estatura *f*; (moral) talla *f*
status [stǽɾəs] N (prestige, rank) status *m*;
(legal, financial) situación *f*; (marital)
estado *m*; — **symbol** símbolo de status *m*
statute [stǽtʃut] N (by-law) estatuto *m*; (law)
ley *f*; — **of limitations** ley de
prescripción *f*
statutory rape [stǽtʃətɔrirép] N estupro *m*
stave [stev] N (of a barrel) duela *f*; VI **to —
off** evitar
stay [ste] VI (remain) quedarse, permanecer;
to — away mantenerse alejado; **to — in**
quedarse en casa; **to — out of trouble**
no meterse en líos; **to — up** quedarse
levantado; VT **to — an execution** aplazar
una ejecución; N (time spent) estancia *f*,
estadía *f*, permanencia *f*; (support) sostén
m, soporte *m*
STD (sexually transmitted disease) [ɛstidí]
N ETS *f*
stead [stɛd] N **in her —** en su lugar; **to
stand one in good —** ser de provecho
para uno
steadfast [stédfæst] ADJ fijo, firme
steadiness [stédɪnɪs] N (firmness) firmeza *f*;
(of the hand) pulso *m*; (constancy)
constancia *f*; (continuity) continuidad *f*
steady [stédi] ADJ (not shaky) firme;
(constant) constante; (continuous)
continuo; — **boyfriend** novio formal *m*;
— **customer** cliente -ta asiduo -dua *mf*;
— **income** ingreso fijo *m*; VI/VT (an
object) asegurar; (nerves) calmar
steak [stek] N bistec *m*, churrasco *m*
steal [stil] VI/VT (a thing) robar, hurtar; (a
girlfriend) soplar; VI **to — away / out**
escabullirse, escaparse; N ganga *f*
stealth [stɛlθ] M sigilo *m*; **by —** furtivamente
stealthy [stélθi] ADJ furtivo
steam [stim] N (evaporated water) vapor *m*;
(arising from an object) vaho *m*; —
engine máquina de vapor *f*; — **roller**
apisonadora *f*, aplanadora *f*; — **ship**
(buque de) vapor *m*; — **shovel** excavadora
f; VT (cook) cocer al vapor; VI (give off
steam) echar vapor; **to get —ed up**
(angry) indignarse; (covered with vapor)

empañarse
steamer [stímɚ] N buque de vapor *m*
steed [stid] N corcel *m*
steel [stil] N acero *m*; — **blue** azul acero *m*;
— **industry** siderurgia *f*; — **mill** acería *f*;
— **wool** lana de acero *f*; VT acerar; **to —
oneself** prepararse
steep [stip] ADJ (hill) empinado, escarpado,
acantilado; (decline) marcado; (price)
excesivo; VT infusionar; VI estar en
infusión, infusionarse
steeple [stípəl] N (spire) aguja *f*, chapitel *m*;
(bell tower) campanario *m*
steer [stir] N (young) novillo *m*; (grown) buey
m; VI/VT (a car) conducir, manejar; (a ship)
gobernar, timonear; VI (turn) girar, doblar;
to — clear of evitar; **to — a
conversation** desviar una conversación;
the car —s easily el coche es fácil de
conducir; **—ing** dirección *f*; **—ing wheel**
volante *m*
stellar [stélɚ] ADJ estelar
stem [stɛm] N (of a plant) tallo *m*; (of a leaf)
pedúnculo *m*, rabo *m*; (of a glass) pie *m*;
(of a pipe) cañón *m*; — **cell** célula
estaminal / embrional *f*; VT detener,
contener, estancar; **to — from** provenir
de
stench [stɛntʃ] N hedor *m*, hediondez *f*, tufo
m
stencil [sténsəl] N plantilla *f*, matriz *f*
stenographer [stənágrəfɚ] N taquígrafo -fa
mf
step [stɛp] N (in walking, dancing) paso *m*;
(on stairs) peldaño *m*, escalón *m*; (in
music) tono *m*; **to take —s to** tramitar;
— **by** — paso a paso; **—ladder** escalera *f*;
in — with the music al compás de la
música; **to take —s** (walk) dar pasos; (act)
tomar medidas; VI dar un paso; — **this
way** pase por aquí; **to — aside** hacerse a
un lado; **to — back** retroceder; **to —
down** (descend) bajar; (resign) renunciar;
to — off bajar; **to — off a distance**
medir a pasos una distancia; **to — on**
pisar, pisotear; **to — on the gas** pisar el
acelerador; **to — out** salir; **to — up** subir
stepbrother [stépbrʌðɚ] N hermanastro *m*
stepdaughter [stépdɔːɾɚ] N hijastra *f*
stepfather [stépfaðɚ] N padrastro *m*
stepmother [stépmʌðɚ] N madrastra *f*
steppe [stɛp] N estepa *f*
stepsister [stépsɪstɚ] N hermanastra *f*
stepson [stépsʌn] N hijastro *m*
stereo [stério] ADJ & N estéreo *m*
stereotype [stériətaɪp] N estereotipo *m*
sterile [stérəl] ADJ estéril

sterility [stərílɪDi] N esterilidad *f*
sterilize [stérəlaɪz] VT esterilizar
stern [stɜ˞n] ADJ austero, severo, adusto; N popa *f*
sternum [stɜ˞nəm] N esternón *m*
steroid [stérɔɪd] N esteroide *m*
stethoscope [stéθəskop] N estetoscopio *m*
stew [stu] VI/VT (cook) estofar(se), guisar(se); VI (worry) preocuparse; N estofado *m*, guiso *m*; **to be in a** — estar preocupado
steward [stúwə˞d] N (manager) administrador *m*; (on a ship) camarero *m*; (on an airplane) auxiliar de vuelo *m*
stewardess [stúwə˞dɪs] N (on a ship) camarera *f*; (on an airplane) azafata *f*
stick [stɪk] N (of wood) palo *m*, vara *f*; (of firewood) raja *f*; (of dynamite) cartucho *m*; — **shift** palanca de cambios *f*; —**-up** atraco *m*, asalto *m*; VI/VT (adhere) pegar(se), adherir(se); VT (place) poner, meter; (stab) clavar, pinchar; VI (become jammed) atascarse; — '**em up!** ¡arriba las manos! **to** — **out** salir, sobresalir; **to** — **out one's head** asomar la cabeza; **to** — **out one's tongue** sacar la lengua; **to** — **to a job** persistir en una tarea; **to** — **up** estar parado de punta; **to** — **up for** defender; **to** — **someone up** asaltar / atracar a alguien
sticker [stíkə˞] N (thistle) abrojo *m*; (adhesive) etiqueta adhesiva *f*
sticky [stíki] ADJ pegajoso
stiff [stɪf] ADJ (leather, cardboard) tieso, duro; (drink) fuerte, cargado; (shirt) almidonado; (back) entumecido; (test) difícil; (breeze) fuerte; (personality) envarado; (climb) arduo; (price) alto; **to get** — entumecerse; N (cadaver) *fam* fiambre *m*
stiffen [stífən] VI/VT (leather) atiesar(se); (back) entumecer(se); (shirt) almidonar(se); **to** — **up** agarrotar(se)
stiffness [stífnɪs] N (of leather) dureza *f*, tiesura *f*; (of one's back) entumecimiento *m*; (of one's personality) envaramiento *m*; (of resistance) firmeza *f*
stifle [stáɪfəɫ] VI/VT ahogar(se), sofocar(se); **to** — **a yawn** contener un bostezo
stigma [stígmə] N estigma *m*
stigmatize [stígmətaɪz] VI/VT estigmatizar
still [stɪɫ] ADJ (not moving) quieto; (quiet) silencioso; —**born** nacido muerto; — **life** naturaleza muerta *f*; VT acallar; ADV todavía, aún; CONJ de todos modos; N (for distilling) alambique *m*; (quiet) silencio *m*
stillness [stíɫnɪs] N quietud *f*, silencio *m*
stilt [stɪɫt] N (for walking) zanco *m*; (support) pilote *m*

stilted [stíɫtɪd] ADJ (personality) envarado; (style) afectado
stimulant [stímjələnt] ADJ & N estimulante *m*
stimulate [stímjəlet] VT estimular
stimulation [stɪmjəléʃən] N estimulación *f*
stimulus [stímjələs] N estímulo *m*
sting [stɪŋ] VI/VT (insects, thorns) picar; (insects) aguijonear; VT (shampoo) hacer picar; (rain) azotar; (cheat) timar; N (pain) picadura *f*; (stinger) aguijón *m*; (confidence game) golpe *m*; — **of remorse** punzada de remordimiento *f*; —**ray** manta raya *f*
stinger [stíŋə˞] N aguijón *m*
stinginess [stíndʒinɪs] N tacañería *f*, mezquindad *f*
stingy [stíndʒi] ADJ mezquino, tacaño
stink [stɪŋk] VI (smell bad) heder, apestar; **to** — **of** heder a; **to** — **up** dar mal olor a; **your performance stank** tu actuación fue un desastre; N hedor *m*
stipend [stáɪpɪnd] N (fellowship) beca *f*; (salary) estipendio *m*
stipulate [stípjəlet] VT estipular
stipulation [stɪpjəléʃən] N estipulación *f*
stir [stɜ˞] VI/VT (move) bullir, rebullir; VT (mix) revolver; (move emotionally) conmover; (awake) despertar; (stoke) atizar; **to** — **up** (trouble) provocar, suscitar; (an old grudge) remover; N **to give something a** — revolver algo; **to cause a** — causar revuelo; —**crazy** claustrofóbico; **to** —**-fry** saltear
stirring [stɜ˞ɪŋ] ADJ conmovedor
stirrup [stɜ˞rəp] N estribo *m*
stitch [stɪtʃ] N puntada *f*; (on a wound) punto *m*; **to be in** —**es** desternillarse de risa; VI/VT coser
St. Kitts and Nevis [sentkítsənnívis] N San Cristóbal y Nieves *m*
St. Lucia [sentlúʃə] N Santa Lucía *f*
St. Lucian [sentlúʃən] ADJ & N santalucense *mf*
stock [stɑk] N (selection) surtido *m*; (reserves) existencias *f pl*; (livestock) ganado *m*; (lineage) estirpe *f*; (shares) acciones *f pl*, valores *m pl*; (in grafting) patrón *m*; (broth) caldo *m*; **out of** — agotado; **in** — en existencia; ADJ (common) trillado; —**broker** corredor -ra de bolsa *mf*, bolsista *mf*; — **company** sociedad anónima *f*; — **exchange** bolsa de valores *f*; —**holder** accionista *mf*; — **market** mercado de valores *m*, bolsa de valores *f*; — **options** opciones *f pl*; —**pile** acopio *m*; —**room** depósito *m*; — **size** tamaño

ordinario *m*; **—yard** corral *m*; VT (sell) vender; (fill shelves) abastecer; **to — up on** surtirse de, acumular; **to —pile** acopiar

stockade [stɑkéd] N (fence) estacada *f*, empalizada *f*; (prison) prisión militar *f*

stocking [stɑ́kɪŋ] N (hose) media *f*; (sock) calcetín *m*

stocky [stɑ́ki] ADJ robusto

stoic [stóɪk] ADJ & N estoico -ca *mf*

stoke [stok] VT (fire) atizar; (engine) alimentar

stomach [stʌ́mək] N (organ) estómago *m*; (belly) panza *f*, barriga *f*; **he has a big —** es barrigón; **to lie on one's —** estar panza abajo; VT aguantar

stomp [stɑmp] VI pisar fuerte; VT (crush) pisotear; (defeat) aplastar

stone [ston] N (rock, gem) piedra *f*; (in fruit) hueso *m*; (in kidneys) cálculo *m*; **within a —'s throw** a tiro de piedra; **— Age** Edad de Piedra *f*; **—-deaf** sordo como una tapia; VT (a person) lapidar; (a fruit) deshuesar; **to get —d** *fam* volarse; *Sp fam* colocarse

stony [stóni] ADJ (made of stone) pétreo; (driveway) pedregoso; (silence) sepulcral

stool [stuɫ] N (furniture) taburete *m*, banqueta *f*; (excrement) materia fecal *f*; **— pigeon** soplón -ona *mf*, chivato -ta *mf*

stoop [stup] VI (bend over) agacharse; (have bad posture) encorvarse; **to — to** rebajarse a; N (posture) encorvamiento *m*; (porch) entrada *f*, porche *m*; **to walk with a —** andar encorvado; **—-shouldered** encorvado, cargado de espaldas

stop [stɑp] VI (halt) parar, detenerse; (malfunction) parar(se); VT (halt) parar, detener; (cancel) cancelar; (suspend) suspender; (plug) tapar; **to — at nothing** no tener escrúpulos; **to — by / in** visitar; **to — from** impedir; **to — over at** hacer escala en; **to — short** parar en seco; **to — up** tapar, atascar; **it —ped raining** paró / dejó de llover; N parada *f*, detención *f*; (on organ) registro *m*; **—gap** arreglo provisorio *m*; **—light** semáforo *m*; **—over** escala *f*; **— sign** *Sp* stop *m*; *Am* señal de pare *f*; *Mex* alto *m*; **—watch** cronómetro *m*; **to bring to a —** parar; **to make a —** parar

stoppage [stɑ́pɪʤ] N interrupción *f*; (strike) huelga *f*

stopper [stɑ́pɚ] N tapón *m*

storage [stɔ́rɪʤ] N almacenaje *m*, almacenamiento *m*; **— battery** acumulador *m*; **to keep in —** almacenar

store [stɔr] N (shop) tienda *f*, almacén *m*; (supply) reserva *f*, provisión *f*; **—house** (warehouse) almacén *m*, depósito *m*; (source) mina *f*, fuente *f*; **—keeper** tendero -ra *mf*, almacenista *mf*; **—room** almacén *m*, depósito *m*; **what is in — for us?** ¿Qué nos espera? VT (commercial goods) almacenar; (personal effects) guardar; **to — up** acumular

stork [stɔrk] N cigüeña *f*

storm [stɔrm] N tormenta *f*; (at sea) tempestad *f*, temporal *m*; (of protest) ola *f*; **— troops** tropas de asalto *f pl*; VT tomar por asalto; VI **to — in / out** entrar / salir en tromba

stormy [stɔ́rmi] ADJ tormentoso, tempestuoso

story [stɔ́ri] N (tale) cuento *m*, historia *f*; (newspaper article) artículo *m*; (lie) mentira *f*; (information) información *f*; (plot) argumento *m*, trama *f*; (floor) piso *m*

stout [staut] ADJ (fat) corpulento; (robust) robusto, fornido; (strong) fuerte; (courageous) valiente

stove [stov] N (for heating) estufa *f*; (for cooking) cocina *f*; *Mex* estufa *f*

stow [sto] VT (keep) guardar; (hide) esconder; (put in cargo hold) estibar; **to — away on a ship** viajar de polizón

stowaway [stóəwe] N polizón -ona *mf*

straddle [strǽdl] VI/VT estar a horcajadas; VT (a fence) ponerse a horcajadas; (one's legs) abrir; (not take sides) no comprometerse

strafe [stref] VT ametrallar

straggle [strǽgəl] VI **to — along / behind** rezagarse; **to — in** entrar de a pocos

straight [stret] ADJ (not curved) recto; (not tilted) derecho; (in succession) seguido; (hair) lacio, liso; (teeth) parejo; (frank) franco; (heterosexual) heterosexual; **— A's** sobresaliente en todo; **— face** cara seria *f*; **— flush** escalera de color *f*; **—forward** campechano; **—edge** regla *f*; ADV **— ahead** todo derecho, todo recto; **for two hours** dos horas seguidas; **to come — home** volver derecho a casa; **to leave — after lunch** irse justo después de comer; **to set a person —** aclararle algo a alguien; **tell me —** dímelo francamente; **he can't think —** no puede pensar con claridad; **—forward** (honest) honesto; (simple) sencillo; (clear) claro

straighten [strétn̩] VI/VT enderezar(se); (situation) arreglar(se); VT (hair) alisar, *RP* laciar; **to — out a child** enderezar a un niño

straightness [strétnɪs] N derechura *f*

strain [stren] VI (pull) tironear; (try hard)

esforzarse; VT (exhaust) agotar; (hurt voice) forzar; (injure a joint) torcer; (injure a muscle) sufrir un tirón en; (hurt a relationship) crear una tirantez en; VI/VT (filter) colar(se); N (effort) esfuerzo *m*; (injury) torcedura *f*; (pressure) presión *f*; (trouble in a relationship) tirantez *f*; (lineage) cepa *f*; (style) veta *f*

strainer [strénɚ] N colador *m*

strait [stret] N estrecho *m*; **in dire —s** en aprietos; ADJ **—jacket** camisa de fuerza *f*, chaleco de fuerza *m*; **—laced** puritano

strand [strænd] VI/VT (a ship) encallar, varar; VT (a person) dejar plantado; **to be —ed** (boat) estar encallado; (person) quedar plantado; N (beach) costa *f*, playa *f*; (of rope) ramal *m*; (of thread) hebra *f*; (of hair) mechón *m*

strange [strendʒ] ADJ (bizarre) extraño, raro; (unknown) desconocido

strangeness [stréndʒnɪs] N (unusualness) lo extraño, rareza *f*; (unexpectedness) lo inesperado

stranger [stréndʒɚ] N (unknown person) extraño -ña *mf*, desconocido -da *mf*; (outsider) forastero -ra *mf*; **to be no — to something** saber bien lo que es algo

strangle [stréŋgəł] VI/VT estrangular(se); **—hold** (in wrestling) llave al cuello *f*; (in markets) monopolio *m*; VT (creativity) coartar

strap [stræp] N (leather band) correa *f*, tira *f*; (on a dress) tirante *m*; VT atar con correa; **to — in** amarrar(se)

stratagem [strǽtədʒəm] N estratagema *f*

strategic [strətídʒɪk] ADJ estratégico

strategy [strǽɖədʒi] N estrategia *f*

stratosphere [strǽɖəsfir] N estratosfera *f*

stratum [strǽɖəm] N estrato *m*

straw [strɔ] N paja *f* (also for drinking); **—berry** fresa *f*; **-colored** pajizo; **— man** testaferro *m*; **— vote** votación de prueba *f*

stray [stre] VI (deviate, digress) desviarse; (get lost) perderse; (wander) vagar; (morally) descarriarse, perderse; ADJ extraviado, perdido; N perro / gato mostrenco *m*

streak [strik] N (line) raya *f*; (vein) vena *f*; (of luck) racha *f*; (of light) rayo *m*; VI (run naked) correr desnudo; (get discolored) aclararse

stream [strim] N (jet) chorro *m*; (river) río *m*; (brook) arroyo *m*; VI (water) correr, fluir; (blood) derramar; **—lined** aerodinámico; **to — out** brotar, manar; **to — in** entrar a raudales

street [strit] N calle *f*; **—car** tranvía *f*;

—lamp / lamp farol *m*, poste de alumbrado *m*; **— sweeper** barrendero -ra *mf*; **—walker** prostituta *f*

strength [streŋθ] N fuerza *f*; (spiritual) firmeza *f*; **on the — of** en base a

strengthen [stréŋθən] VI/VT fortalecer(se), reforzar(se)

strenuous [strénjuəs] ADJ arduo

strep throat [strépθrót] N infección por estreptococo *f*

stress [stres] N (tension) tensión *f*; (strain) estrés *m*; (pressure) esfuerzo *m*; (emphasis) énfasis *m*; (accent) acento *m*; VT (emphasize) enfatizar; (accentuate) acentuar; (exert force) someter a un esfuerzo; (put under pressure) estresar; **to — out** estresar

stretch [stretʃ] VI/VT (make or become longer) estirar(se), alargar(se); (extend) extender(se); (exaggerate) exagerar; **to — oneself** estirarse, desperezarse; **to — out** (lengthen) extender(se); (lie) tumbarse, tenderse; N (act of stretching) desperezo *m*; (length) trecho *m*, tramo *m*, tirada *f*; (period) período *m*; (exaggeration) exageración *f*; **— mark** estría *f*

stretcher [strétʃɚ] N camilla *f*

strew [stru] VT esparcir

stricken [stríkən] ADJ (with disease) aquejado; (by a flood) afectado; (with fear) aterrado

strict [strɪkt] ADJ estricto; **in — confidence** en absoluta confianza

stride [straɪd] VI caminar a paso largo, dar zancadas; N (gait) paso *m*; (long step) zancada *f*, tranco *m*

strident [stráɪdənt] ADJ estridente

strife [straɪf] N conflictos *m pl*

strike [straɪk] VI/VT (hit) golpear, pegar; (stop work) hacer huelga (contra); VT (find) dar con, encontrar; (occur to) ocurrírsele a uno; (cross out) tachar; (mark by chimes) dar; (light) encender; (coin) acuñar; **to — a compromise** llegar a un acuerdo; **to — one's fancy** antojársele a uno; **to — out** (cross out) tachar; (set forth) encaminarse; (fail) fracasar; **to — up a conversation** entablar conversación; **to — up a friendship** trabar amistad; **how does she — you?** ¿qué tal te parece? N (work stoppage) huelga *f*; (attack) ataque *m*; (finding of oil) descubrimiento *m*; **—breaker** esquirol *m*, rompehuelgas *m sg*

striker [stráɪkɚ] N (person on strike) huelguista *mf*; (of a bell) badajo *m*

striking [stráɪkɪŋ] ADJ (unusual, conspicuous) notable; (attractive) llamativo; (on strike) en huelga

string [strɪŋ] N (cord) cuerda *f*, cordel *m*; (of pearls, lies) sarta *f*; (of questions) serie *f*; (of beans) fibra *f*; (of garlic) ristra *f*; — **bean** habichuela *f*, judía verde *f*; **—s** cuerdas *f pl*; VT (beads) ensartar; (a musical instrument) encordar; **to — along** tener en ascuas; **to — out** extender(se), prolongar(se); **to — up** colgar, ahorcar; **to be strung out** estar muy tenso

stringent [stríndʒənt] ADJ (law, need) riguroso; (time limit) estrecho, ajustado

strip [strɪp] VI/VT (make / get naked) desnudar(se); VT (remove bark) descortezar; (remove leaves) deshojar; (remove sheets) deshacer; (remove varnish) quitar el barniz; (damage gears) estropear el engranaje; **to —-mine** explotar a cielo abierto; N tira *f*; (of land) faja *f*; — **mall** centro comercial *m*; **—tease** strip-tease *m*

stripe [straɪp] N (band) raya *f*, lista *f*, banda *f*; (military insignia) galón *m*; (type) tipo *m*

striped [straɪpt, stráɪpɪd] ADJ listado, rayado

stripper [strɪpɚ] N striptisero -ra *mf*

strive [straɪv] VI esforzarse por, luchar por

stroke [strok] N (in golf, tennis, of luck, of genius) golpe *m*; (cerebral hemorrhage) derrame cerebral *m*; (movement in swimming) brazada *f*; (style in swimming) estilo *m*; (of a piston) carrera *f*; (of a painter's brush) pincelada *f*; (of lightning) rayo *m*; **at the — of ten** al dar las diez; VT (pet) acariciar; (praise) halagar

stroll [stroł] VI dar un paseo, pasearse; N paseo *m*, caminata *f*

stroller [strólɚ] N cochecito de bebé *m*

strong [strɔŋ] ADJ fuerte; (husky) recio; (eyesight, probability) bueno; (protest) enérgico; (views, faith, support) firme; (features, resemblance) marcado; (argument) sólido; **—hold** (fortress) fortaleza *f*; (center of activity) baluarte *m*; **—-willed** (resolute) resuelto, decidido; (stubborn) terco; **to —-arm** intimidar; ADV **to be going —** seguir activo

structural [stráktʃərəł] ADJ estructural

structure [stráktʃɚ] N (manner of construction) estructura *f*; (thing constructed) construcción *f*

struggle [strágəł] VI (with difficulties) luchar, bregar; (with an assailant) forcejear; **she —s in math** la pasa mal en matemáticas; N lucha *f*; (of ideas) pugna *f*, lucha *f*; (fight) contienda *f*, forcejeo *m*; **it's a —** da mucho trabajo

strut [strʌt] VI pavonearse; N pavoneo *m*;

(support) tirante *m*, puntal *m*; (on a car) amortiguador *m*

strychnine [stríknaɪn] N estricnina *f*

stub [stʌb] N talón *m*; VT **to — one's toe** dar(se) un tropezón, reventarse el dedo

stubble [stábəł] N (of a crop) rastrojo *m*; (of a beard) barba de unos días *f*

stubborn [stábə·n] ADJ terco, testarudo

stubbornness [stábə·nnɪs] N terquedad *f*, testarudez *f*

stucco [stáko] N estuco *m*; VT estucar

stuck [stʌk] ADJ atascado; **to be — on someone** estar loco por alguien; **—-up** estirado, presumido

stud [stʌd] N (knob) tachuela *f*; (earring) arete *m*; (cufflink) gemelo *m*; (on shirtfront) botón *m*; (horse, man) semental *m*, garañón *m*; VT tachonar

student [stúdn̩t] N alumno -na *mf*; (secondary, university) estudiante *mf*; — **body** alumnado *m*; ADJ estudiantil *m*

studio [stúdio] N estudio *m*, taller *m*; — **apartment** estudio *m*

studious [stúdiəs] ADJ estudioso

study [stádi] N estudio *m*; VT estudiar

stuff [stʌf] N (material) materia *f*, material *m*; (things) trastos *m pl*, bártulos *m pl*; (cloth) paño *m*, tela *f*; (affair) cosa *f*; (junk) cachivaches *m pl*; VT (mattress) rellenar; (dead animal) embalsamar, disecar; **to — into** meter en; **I'm —ed** estoy lleno

stuffing [stáfɪŋ] N relleno *m*

stuffy [stáfi] ADJ (person) envarado; (air) viciado

stumble [stámbəł] VI (trip) tropezar, trastabillar, dar un traspié; (stutter) balbucear; **to — out** salir a tropezones; **to — upon** tropezar con; N tropezón *m*, tropiezo *m*, traspié *m*; **stumbling block** obstáculo *m*

stump [stʌmp] N (of a tree) tocón *m*, cepa *f*; (of a tooth) raigón *m*; (of a limb) muñón *m*; **to be on the —** hacer una campaña electoral; VT (baffle) dejar perplejo; (remove stumps) arrancar los tocones de; **to — the country** recorrer el país haciendo campaña

stun [stʌn] VT (shock, surprise) dejar atónito, pasmar; (render unconscious) dejar sin sentido; — **gun** pistola tranquilizante *f*

stunning [stánɪŋ] ADJ (shocking) pasmoso; (beautiful) elegante, bellísimo

stunt [stʌnt] VT (stop growth) atrofiar; (do acrobatic tricks) hacer acrobacia; N (feat) acrobacia *f*; (for publicity) maniobra *f*; **—man** doble *m*; **—woman** doble *f*; **to pull a —** hacerse el listo

stupefy [stúpəfaɪ] VT (make lethargic) atontar, embrutecer; (astonish) dejar estupefacto, alelar

stupendous [stupéndəs] ADJ estupendo

stupid [stúpɪd] ADJ tonto, estúpido, majadero

stupidity [stupíDɪti] N tontería f, estupidez f, majadería f

stupor [stúpə] N estupor m

sturdy [stɜ́Di] ADJ (person) fornido, fuerte; (construction) sólido, robusto

stutter [stʌ́Də] VI tartamudear, tartajear; VT decir tartamudeando; N (act of stuttering) tartamudeo m; (speech defect) tartamudez f

stutterer [stʌ́Dərə] N tartamudo -da mf

stuttering [stʌ́Dərɪŋ] ADJ tartamudo; N (act of stuttering) tartamudeo m; (speech defect) tartamudez f

St. Vincent and the Grenadines [sentvínsəntənðəgrénədinz] N San Vicente y las Granadinas m

sty [staɪ] N (for pigs) pocilga f; (in eye) orzuelo m

style [staɪɫ] N estilo m; (type) modelo m; **out of —** fuera de moda; **like it's going out of —** como loco; VT (a book) intitular; (hair) peinar; **he —s himself Professor Smith** se hace llamar Profesor Smith

stylish [stáɪlɪʃ] ADJ elegante, de moda

stymie, stymy [stáɪmi] VT obstaculizar

Styrofoamᵗᵐ [stáɪrəfom] N poliestireno m

suave [swɑv] ADJ urbano, educado

subconscious [sʌbkánʃəs] ADJ subconsciente

subcontract [sʌbkántrækt] VT subcontratar

subdivision [sʌ́bdɪvɪʒən] N subdivisión f; (of land) parcelación f

subdue [səbdú] VT (overcome, vanquish) sojuzgar, someter, rendir; (repress) reprimir; (attenuate) atenuar

subdued [səbdúd] ADJ (atmosphere) tranquilo; (mood) deprimido; (lighting, color) tenue

subject [sʌ́bdʒɪkt] N (of a king) súbdito -ta mf; (of a sentence, in an experiment) sujeto m; (in school) asignatura f, materia f; **— matter** tema m; ADJ **— to** (changes, laws, conditions) sujeto a; (depression, earthquakes) propenso a; [səbdʒékt] VT someter

subjection [səbdʒékʃən] N sometimiento m

subjective [səbdʒéktɪv] ADJ subjetivo

subjugate [sʌ́bdʒəget] VT sojuzgar, avasallar

subjunctive [səbdʒʌ́ŋktɪv] ADJ & N subjuntivo m

sublet [sʌblét] VI/VT subarrendar

sublime [səbláɪm] ADJ sublime

submarine [sʌbmərín] ADJ submarino;
[sʌ́bmərin] N submarino m

submerge [səbmɜ́dʒ] VI/VT sumergir(se)

submission [səbmíʃən] N (humility) sumisión f; (subjugation) sometimiento m, sumisión f; (sending) entrega f, envío m

submissive [səbmísɪv] ADJ sumiso

submit [səbmít] VI/VT someter(se); (to a judge) elevar(se); **to — a report** presentar un informe

subordinate [səbɔ́rdŋɪt] ADJ & N subordinado -da mf, subalterno -na mf; [səbɔ́rdŋet] VT subordinar

subpoena [səpínə] N citación f, orden de comparecencia f

subroutine [sʌ́brutin] N subrutina f

subscribe [səbskráɪb] VI (underwrite, sign) suscribir; (receive a magazine) abonarse, suscribirse; (agree with) adherirse a

subscriber [səbskráɪbə] N (to shares) suscriptor -ora mf; (to services) abonado -da mf; (to a magazine) suscriptor -ora mf, abonado -da mf; (to an idea) partidario -ria mf

subscription [səbskrípʃən] N suscripción f, abono m

subsequent [sʌ́bsɪkwənt] ADJ subsiguiente

subservient [səbsɜ́-viənt] ADJ servil

subside [səbsáɪd] VI (sediment) hundirse; (water level) bajar; (volcano, storm, anger) calmarse, aquietarse

subsidiary [səbsíDiƐri] ADJ subsidiario; N sucursal f

subsidize [sʌ́bsɪdaɪz] VT subvencionar

subsidy [sʌ́bsɪdi] N subvención f

substance [sʌ́bstəns] N sustancia f; **— abuse** abuso de sustancias m

substantial [səbstǽnʃəɫ] ADJ (changes) sustancial; (food, lecture) sustancioso; (furniture) sólido; (amount) considerable, importante; **to be in — agreement** estar básicamente de acuerdo

substantiate [səbstǽnʃiet] VT (verify) verificar; (prove) probar

substantive [sʌ́bstəntɪv] ADJ & N sustantivo m

substitute [sʌ́bstɪtut] VT **I —d water for milk** usé agua en vez de leche, sustituí / reemplacé la leche por agua; VI **John —d for Mary** Juan sustituyó / reemplazó a María; N (one who substitutes) sustituto m, reemplazo m; (teacher, athlete) suplente -ta mf; (thing) sucedáneo m

substitution [sʌbstɪtúʃən] N sustitución f; **the — of water for milk** la sustitución de leche por agua

subterfuge [sʌ́btəfjudʒ] N subterfugio m

subterranean [sʌbtəréniən] ADJ subterráneo

subtitle [sʌ́btaɪdl̩] N subtítulo *m*
subtle [sʌ́dl̩] ADJ sutil
subtlety [sʌ́dl̩ti] N sutileza *f*
subtract [səbtrǽkt] VT (deduct) restar; (take away) sustraer
subtraction [səbtrǽkʃən] N sustracción *f*, resta *f*
suburb [sʌ́bɝb] N barrio residencial periférico *m*
suburban [səbɝ́bən] ADJ (residential) residencial; (on the outskirts) periférico
subversive [səbvɝ́sɪv] ADJ subversivo
subway [sʌ́bwe] N metropolitano *m*, metro *m*, subterráneo *m*
succeed [səksíd] VI (be successful) tener éxito; (manage) lograr; **to — to** heredar; VT (follow) suceder a
success [səksés] N éxito *m*
successful [səksésfəl] ADJ exitoso; **to be —** tener éxito
succession [səkséʃən] N sucesión *f*
successive [səksésɪv] ADJ sucesivo
successor [səksésɚ] N sucesor -ora *mf*
succinct [səksíŋkt] ADJ sucinto, escueto
succor [sʌ́kɚ] N socorro *m*; VT socorrer
succumb [səkʌ́m] VI sucumbir
such [sʌtʃ] ADJ tal; **he's — an idiot!** ¡es tan idiota! **in — a case** en tal caso/en semejante caso; **— as** tal como; **at — and — a place** en tal o cual lugar; **there's no — thing** eso no existe; PRON **hobbies, pastimes, and —** hobbies, pasatiempos y cosas por el estilo; **a car — as yours** un coche como el tuyo; ADV **— nice neighbors** vecinos tan simpáticos
suck [sʌk] VI/VT chupar; (suckle) mamar; (vacuum, pump) aspirar; (perform fellatio) *vulg* mamarla; **to be —ed into** ser arrastrado a; VI **this book —s!** *vulg* ¡este libro es una cagada! **to — in** (air) aspirar; (stomach) meter; (fools) timar; **to — up to someone** *vulg* lamerle el culo a alguien; N chupada *f*; (sexual) *vulg* mamada *f*
sucker [sʌ́kɚ] N (gullible person) primo -ma *mf*; (lollipop) *Sp* pirulí *m*; *Mex* paleta *f*; *RP* chupetín *m*
suction [sʌ́kʃən] N succión *f*, aspiración *f*
Sudan [sudǽn] N Sudán *m*
Sudanese [sudn̩íz] ADJ & N sudanés -esa *mf*
sudden [sʌ́dn̩] ADJ súbito, repentino, brusco; **all of a —** de repente, de improviso
suddenness [sʌ́dn̩nɪs] N brusquedad *f*, lo repentino
suds [sʌdz] N espuma *f*
sue [su] VI/VT demandar, poner pleito; **to — for** pedir, suplicar; **to — for damages** demandar por daños y perjuicios
suede [swed] N gamuza *f*, ante *m*
suffer [sʌ́fɚ] VI/VT (feel pain) sufrir, padecer; VT (tolerate) tolerar
sufferer [sʌ́fərɚ] N paciente *mf*
suffering [sʌ́fə-ɪŋ] N sufrimiento *m*, padecimiento *m*
suffice [səfáɪs] VI/VT bastar, ser suficiente
sufficient [səfíʃənt] ADJ suficiente, bastante
suffix [sʌ́fɪks] N sufijo *m*
suffocate [sʌ́fəket] VI/VT ahogar(se), sofocar(se); (to die, kill) asfixiar(se)
suffocation [sʌfəkéʃən] N ahogo *m*, sofoco *m*
suffrage [sʌ́frɪdʒ] N sufragio *m*
sugar [ʃúgɚ] N azúcar *mf*; (endearment) cariño *m*; **— cane** caña de azúcar *f*; VT azucarar; **to — the pill** dorar la píldora
suggest [səgdʒést] VT (propose) sugerir; (hint) insinuar
suggestion [səgdʒéstʃən] N (proposal) sugerencia *f*; (in hypnosis) sugestión *f*
suggestive [səgdʒéstɪv] ADJ insinuante; **to be — of** evocar
suicide [súɪsaɪd] N (act) suicidio *m*; (person) suicida *mf*; **to commit —** suicidarse
suit [sut] N traje *m*; (in cards) palo *m*, color *m*; (lawsuit) demanda *f*, pleito *m*, querella *f*; **—case** maleta *f*, valija *f*; VT (adapt) adaptar, ajustar; (satisfy) satisfacer; (look good) quedarle bien a, sentarle bien a; (be convenient, appropriate) convenir, venir bien; **— yourself** haz lo te parezca
suitable [súɾəbəl] ADJ (appropriate) apropiado; (apt) apto
suitably [súɾəbli] ADV como corresponde
suite [swit] N (series) serie *f*; (series of rooms, musical composition) suite *f*; (furniture) juego *m*
suitor [súɾɚ] N pretendiente *m*, galán *m*
sulk [sʌlk] VI enfurruñarse; N **to be in a —** estar enfurruñado
sulky [sʌ́lki] ADJ malhumorado, enfurruñado
sullen [sʌ́lən] ADJ hosco, huraño
sully [sʌ́li] VT mancillar, ensuciar
sulphate, sulfate [sʌ́lfet] N sulfato *m*
sulphide, sulfide [sʌ́lfaɪd] N sulfuro *m*
sulphur, sulfur [sʌ́lfɚ] N azufre *m*
sulphuric, sulfuric [sʌlfjúrɪk] ADJ sulfúrico
sultry [sʌ́ltri] ADJ (hot) bochornoso, sofocante; (sensual) sensual
sum [sʌm] N suma *f*, adición *f*; **in —** en resumen; VI **to — up** resumir, recapitular
summarize [sʌ́mɚaɪz] VI/VT resumir
summary [sʌ́mɚi] N resumen *m*; ADJ sumario
summer [sʌ́mɚ] N verano *m*, estío *m*; **— resort** balneario *m*, lugar de veraneo *m*;

— **school** cursos de verano *m pl*; **—time** verano *m*; VI veranear

summit [sÁmɪt] N cumbre *f*, cima *f*

summon [sÁmən] VT (witness) citar; (employee, police) llamar; N **—s** citación judicial *f*

sumptuous [sÁmptʃuəs] ADJ suntuoso

sun [sʌn] N sol *m*; **to —bathe** tomar el sol; **—beam** rayo de sol *m*; **—block** protector solar *m*; **—burn** quemadura de sol *f*; **to —burn** quemar(se) al sol; **—dial** reloj de sol *m*; **—down** puesta de(l) sol *f*; **—flower** girasol *m*; **—glasses** gafas de sol *f pl*, anteojos de sol *m pl*; — **lamp** lámpara solar *f*; **—light** luz del sol *f*; **—rise** salida de(l) sol *f*, amanecer *m*; **—screen** protector solar *m*; **—set** puesta de(l) sol *f*; **—shine** luz (del sol) *f*; **—spot** mancha solar *f*; **—stroke** insolación *f*; **—tan** bronceado *m*; **—up** salida del sol *f*; VI **to — oneself** tomar el sol

Sunday [sÁnde] N domingo *m*; — **school** escuela dominical *f*

sundry [sÁndri] ADJ diversos

sunny [sÁni] ADJ (day, patio) soleado; (disposition) alegre

super [súpɚ] N conserje *m*; ADJ súper, bárbaro

superb [supɝ́b] ADJ excelente

supercharger [súpɚtʃɑrdʒɚ] N sobrealimentador *m*

supercomputer [súpɚkəmpjuDɚ] N *Am* supercomputadora *f*; *Sp* superordenador *m*

superego [supɚígo] N superego *m*, superyó *m*

superficial [supɚfíʃəɫ] ADJ superficial

superfluous [supɝ́fluəs] ADJ superfluo

superhuman [supɚhjúmən] ADJ sobrehumano

superimpose [supɚɪmpóz] VT superponer, sobreponer

superintendent [supɚɪnténdənt] N (of work) superintendente *mf*, supervisor -ora *mf*; (of building) portero -ra *mf*, conserje *mf*

superior [supíriɚ] ADJ & N superior *m*

superiority [supiriɔ́rɪDi] N superioridad *f*

superlative [supɝ́ləDɪv] ADJ & N superlativo *m*

supermarket [súpɚmɑrkɪt] N supermercado *m*

supernatural [supɚnǽtʃɚəɫ] ADJ sobrenatural

superpower [súpɚpaʊɚ] N superpotencia *f*

superscript [súpɚskrɪpt] N número volado *m*

supersede [supɚsíd] VT reemplazar

supersonic [supɚsánɪk] ADJ supersónico

superstar [súpɚstɑr] N superestrella *f*

superstition [supɚstíʃən] N superstición *f*

superstitious [supɚstíʃəs] ADJ supersticioso

supervise [súpɚvaɪz] VI/VT supervisar

supervision [supɚvíʒən] N supervisión *f*

supervisor [súpɚvaɪzɚ] N supervisor -ra *mf*

supper [sÁpɚ] N cena *f*

supplant [səplǽnt] VT suplantar

supple [sÁpəɫ] ADJ (flexible) flexible, elástico; (agile) ágil, grácil

supplement [sÁpləmənt] N (of a newspaper) suplemento *m*; (of a book) apéndice *m*; (of one's diet) complemento *m*; [sÁpləmɛnt] VT complementar, suplementar

supply [səplái] VT abastecer, suministrar; N (act of supplying) abastecimiento *m*; — **and demand** oferta y demanda *f*; **supplies** suministros *m pl*, provisiones *f pl*; **office supplies** artículos de oficina *m pl*; **military supplies** pertrechos *m pl*; **in short —** escaso

support [səpɔ́rt] VT (keep from falling) sostener, soportar; (encourage) mantener, apoyar; (corroborate) corroborar; N (of a structure) sostén *m*, soporte *m*; (of a family) sustento *m*; (of a candidate, idea) apoyo *m*; (of a theory) respaldo *m*; — **group** grupo de apoyo *m*

supporter [səpɔ́rDɚ] N partidario -ria *mf*; (in sports) hincha *mf*

suppose [səpóz] VT suponer; **we are —d to go** tenemos que ir

supposition [sʌpəzíʃən] N suposición *f*, supuesto *m*

suppository [səpázɪtɔri] N supositorio *m*

suppress [səprés] VT (repress) reprimir; (eliminate) suprimir; (a revolt) sofocar

suppression [səpréʃən] N (repression) represión *f*; (elimination) supresión *f*

supremacy [suprémɪsi] N supremacía *f*

supreme [suprím] ADJ supremo

surcharge [sɝ́tʃɑrdʒ] N recargo *m*, prima *f*

sure [ʃur] ADJ seguro; (judgment) certero; (hand) firme; **to make — of** asegurarse de; ADV **he — drinks a lot** es una esponja; **may I sit here? —!** ¿me puedo sentar? ¡cómo no!

surely [ʃúrli] ADV seguramente, ciertamente; **— you jest** no hablarás en serio; **he will — come** seguramente vendrá

surf [sɝf] N (breaking waves) rompientes *mf pl*; (foam) espuma *f*; (undertow) resaca *f*; **—board** tabla de surf *f*; VI/VT (on water) hacer surfing (en), surfear; (on Internet) navegar, surfear

surface [sɝ́fɪs] N superficie *f*; (of a solid) cara *f*; VI (come to top) emerger; (turn up) salir a la luz; VT (a submarine) sacar a la superficie; (a road) revestir

surfeit [sɝ́fɪt] N (excess) exceso *m*; (feeling of

fullness) hartazgo *m*; VI/VT hartar(se)
surfing [sɚ́-fɪŋ] N surfing *m*
surge [sɚ-ʤ] N (of people, disgust) oleada *f*; (of waves) oleaje *m*; (of electricity) tensión *f*; VI (people) precipitarse; (current) subir; — **protector** protector de tensión *m*
surgeon [sɚ́-ʤən] N cirujano -na *mf*
surgery [sɚ́-ʤəri] N cirujía *f*; (room) quirófano *m*
surgical [sɚ́-ʤɪkəł] ADJ quirúrgico
Surinam, Suriname [súrɪnam(ə)] N Surinam *m*
Surinamese [sʊrɪnamíz] ADJ & N surinamés -esa *mf*
surly [sɚ́-li] ADJ malhumorado, hosco, arisco
surmise [sɚ-máɪz] VT conjeturar, suponer; N conjetura *f*, suposición *f*
surmount [sɚ-máʊnt] VT superar
surname [sɚ́-nem] N apellido *m*
surpass [sɚ-pǽs] VT superar, sobrepujar
surplus [sɚ́-plʌs] N excedente *m*, sobrante *m*, sobra *f*; (of funds) superávit *m*
surprise [sɚ-práɪz] N sorpresa *f*; VT sorprender
surprising [sɚ-práɪzɪŋ] ADJ sorprendente
surrealism [səríəlɪzəm] N surrealismo *m*
surrender [səréndɚ] VI (accept defeat) rendir(se), darse por vencido; (give oneself up) entregarse; VT entregar; N rendición *f*
surreptitious [sɚ-əptíʃəs] ADJ subrepticio
surrogate [sɚ́-əgɪt] ADJ sustituto; — **mother** madre de alquiler *f*
surround [səráʊnd] VT rodear, circundar; (a city) sitiar
surrounding [səráʊndɪŋ] ADJ circundante; **—s** alrededores *m pl*, inmediaciones *f pl*
surveillance [sɚ-véləns] N vigilancia *f*
survey [sɚ-vé] VT (evaluate) evaluar; (measure) medir; (contemplate) contemplar; (poll) encuestar; [sɚ́-ve] N (inspection) reconocimiento *m*, inspección *f*; (measure) medición *f*; (overview) panorama *m*; (poll) encuesta *f*, sondeo *m*; — **course** curso general *m*
surveyor [sɚ-véɚ] N agrimensor -ra *mf*
survival [sɚ-váɪvəł] N supervivencia *f*, sobrevivencia *f*; (subsistence) subsistencia *f*; **the — of the fittest** la supervivencia del más apto
survive [sɚ-váɪv] VI/VT sobrevivir (also live longer than); (subsist) subsistir
survivor [sɚ-váɪvɚ] N sobreviviente *mf*
susceptible [səséptəbəł] ADJ susceptible; **to be — of proof** poderse demostrar; **to be — to pneumonia** ser propenso a la pulmonía
suspect [sʌ́spɛkt] N sospechoso -sa *mf*; [səspɛ́kt] VT sospechar, barruntar, recelar

suspend [səspénd] VT suspender
suspenders [səspéndɚz] N tirantes *m pl*
suspense [səspéns] N (uncertainty) incertidumbre *f*; (in movie) suspenso *m*; *Sp* suspense *m*; **to keep in —** mantener en suspenso, tener en vilo
suspension [səspénʃən] N suspensión *f*; (of a ban) levantamiento *m*; — **bridge** puente colgante *m*
suspicion [səspíʃən] N sospecha *f*, barrunto *m*
suspicious [səspíʃəs] ADJ (causing suspicion) sospechoso; (experiencing suspicion) suspicaz, desconfiado
sustain [səstén] VT (weight) sostener, sustentar; (pretense, effort) mantener; (an injury) sufrir; (an objection) admitir; (a musical note) sostener
sustenance [sʌ́stənəns] N sustento *m*, alimento *m*
suture [sútʃɚ] N sutura *f*
swab [swɑb] N hisopo *m*, bola de algodón *f*; VT pasar un hisopo sobre
swagger [swǽgɚ] VI (walk) pavonearse, contonearse; (boast) fanfarronear; N (walk) pavoneo *m*, contoneo *m*; (bluster) fanfarronería *f*
swallow [swɑ́lo] N (drink) trago *m*; (bird) golondrina *f*; VI/VT tragar; **to — up** consumir
swamp [swɑmp] N pantano *m*, ciénaga *f*; **—land** cenagal *m*; VI/VT (flood) inundar(se); (overwhelm) abrumar(se), agobiar(se)
swampy [swɑ́mpi] ADJ pantanoso, cenagoso
swan [swɑn] N cisne *m*; — **dive** salto del ángel *m*; — **song** canto de cisne *m*
swap [swɑp] VT cambiar, canjear; N cambio *m*, canje *m*
swarm [swɔrm] N enjambre *m*; VI (of bees) salir en enjambre; (of people, tourists) pulular, hormiguear; **to be —ing with** ser un hervidero de, abundar en
swarthy [swɔ́rði] ADJ trigueño, moreno
swat [swɑt] VT (a person) pegar; (flies) aplastar; **to — at** manotear; N manotazo *m*
sway [swe] VI/VT (move to and fro) balancear(se), bambolear(se); (move hips) menear(se); (influence) influir (en); N (movement) balanceo *m*, vaivén *m*, bamboleo *m*; (influence) influencia *f*; **to hold — over** dominar
Swazi [swázi] N suazi *mf*
Swaziland [swázilænd] N Suazilandia *f*
swear [swer] VI/VT (vow) jurar; (use profanity) decir palabrotas; *Sp* soltar tacos; **to — in** (give oath) juramentar; (take oath) prestar

juramento; **she —s by canned peaches** para ella no hay nada como los duraznos enlatados; **to — off** renunciar a; **to — to** jurar por

sweat [swɛt] VI (perspire) sudar; (ooze) exudar, sudar; (worry) preocuparse; N sudor *m*; **—shirt** sudadera *f*; **—suit** equipo deportivo *m*; *Sp* chándal *m*; **no —** no hay problema

sweater [swéDɚ] N suéter *m*, jersey *m*

sweaty [swéDi] ADJ sudoroso, sudado

Swede [swid] N sueco -ca *mf*

Sweden [swídn̩] N Suecia *f*

Swedish [swídɪʃ] ADJ sueco

sweep [swip] VI/VT (clean with broom, scan) barrer; (dredge) dragar; VT (touch) rozar; (search) rastrear; VI (spread) extenderse; **to — away** llevar, arrastrar; **to — down upon** caer sobre, asolar; **to — off** limpiar; **to — into** (majestically) entrar majestuoso; (quickly) entrar rápidamente; **to — up** recoger; N (cleaning) barrida *f*; (extension) extensión *f*; (movement) barrido *m*; (search) rastreo *m*

sweeping [swípɪŋ] ADJ (statement) (demasiado) general; (victory) aplastante

sweet [swit] ADJ (in flavor, personality) dulce; (in smell) bueno, fragante; **—and-sour** agridulce; **—heart** querido -da *mf*; **— pea** *Sp* guisante de olor *m*; **— potato** batata *f*, boniato *m*; *Mex* camote *m*; **to have a — tooth** ser goloso; N dulce *m*, golosina *f*; **my —** mi vida, mi alma; **to —-talk** halagar

sweeten [switn̩] VI/VT (a food) endulzar(se); (an experience) dulcificar(se)

sweetener [swítn̩ɚ] N endulzante *m*, edulcorante *m*

sweetness [swítnɪs] N (of personality) dulzura *f*; (of taste) dulzor *m*

swell [swɛɫ] VI/VT (limbs, with pride) hinchar(se), henchir(se); VI (river) crecer; (population) crecer, engrosar(se); VT (make grow) hacer crecer, hacer aumentar, engrosar; N (of ocean) oleaje *m*; ADJ estupendo, bárbaro

swelling [swélɪŋ] N hinchazón *f*

swelter [swéɫtɚ] VI sofocarse de calor

swerve [swɝv] VI/VT (in a car) virar; (from a goal) desviar(se); N viraje *m*

swift [swɪft] ADJ ligero, veloz, raudo; N vencejo *m*

swiftness [swíftnɪs] N velocidad *f*, rapidez *f*

swim [swɪm] VI/VT nadar; (float) flotar; **to — across** atravesar nadando; **my head is —ming** me da vueltas la cabeza; N **—ming pool** piscina *f*; *Mex* alberca *f*;

—suit traje de baño *m*; **to take a —** ir a nadar, dar una nadada

swimmer [swímɚ] N nadador -ra *mf*

swindle [swíndl̩] VT estafar; N estafa *f*, trapacería *f*

swine [swaɪn] N puerco *m*, cerdo *m*; (person) *offensive* puerco -ca *mf*, sinvergüenza *mf*

swing [swɪŋ] VI/VT (on a swing) columpiar(se); (move to and fro) balancear(se), bambolear(se); VI (change) virar; VT (make turn) hacer girar; (influence) influir sobre; (baseball, golf) dar un swing con; **to — a deal** concretar un negocio; **to — around** dar vueltas; **to — open** abrirse; **I can't — a new car** no me puedo dar el lujo de comprar un auto nuevo; N (playground toy) columpio *m*; (oscillation) balanceo *m*, vaivén *m*, bamboleo *m*; (in golf, baseball, music) swing *m*; (change) cambio *m*; **in full —** en su apogeo; **to get into the — of things** agarrarle la onda a algo, cogerle el tranquillo a algo

swipe [swaɪp] VT (steal) afanar, sisar; (slide) deslizar; N (insult) insulto *m*; **to take a — at someone** (physical) tirarle un manotazo a alguien; (verbal) insultar

swirl [swɝɫ] VI/VT arremolinar(se); (dancers) girar; N remolino *m*; (smoke) espiral *f*

Swiss [swɪs] ADJ & N suizo -za *mf*; **— cheese** queso suizo *m*

switch [swɪtʃ] N (change) cambio *m*; (electrical) interruptor *m*, llave *f*; (stick for whipping) varilla *f*; (on railways) agujas *f pl*; **—blade** navaja automática *f*; **—board** centralita *f*; **—man** guardagujas *m sg*; VI/VT cambiar (de); (traincars) desviar; **to — off** (current) cortar; (light, TV) apagar; **to — on** encender, prender

Switzerland [swítsɚlənd] N Suiza *f*

swivel [swívəɫ] N pivote *m*; **— chair** silla giratoria *f*

swollen [swólən] ADJ hinchado

swoon [swun] VI desvanecerse, desmayarse; **to — over someone** morirse por alguien; N vahído *m*

swoop [swup] VI **to — down upon** abalanzarse sobre; N descenso súbito *m*; **at one fell —** de un tirón

sword [sɔrd] N espada *f*; **—fish** pez espada *m*

sycamore [síkəmɔr] N sicomoro *m*

syllable [síləbəɫ] N sílaba *f*

syllabus [síləbəs] N programa (de estudios) *m*

syllogism [síləʤɪzəm] N silogismo *m*

symbiosis [sɪmbiósɪs] N simbiosis *f*

symbol [símbəɫ] N símbolo *m*

symbolic [sɪmbálɪk] ADJ simbólico

symbolism [símbəlızəm] N simbolismo *m*
symmetrical [sɪmétrɪkəł] ADJ simétrico
symmetry [símɪtri] N simetría *f*
sympathetic [sɪmpəθéɗɪk] ADJ
(compassionate) compasivo;
(understanding) comprensivo; (favoring)
favorable; (nervous system) simpático
sympathize [símpəθaɪz] VI (be
compassionate) compadecer(se); (be
understanding) comprender; **to — with**
estar a favor de
sympathy [símpəθi] N compasión *f*,
comprensión *f*; (condolence) condolencia
f, pésame *m*; **to extend one's —** dar el
pésame
symphony [símfəni] N sinfonía *f*; **—
orchestra** orquesta sinfónica *f*
symposium [sɪmpóziəm] N simposio *m*
symptom [símptəm] N síntoma *m*
synagogue [sínəgɑg] N sinagoga *f*
synchronize [síŋkrənaɪz] VI/VT
sincronizar(se)
syndicate [síndɪkɪt] N sindicato *m*; [síndɪket]
VI/VT (form a syndicate) sindicar(se); VT
(sell rights) vender los derechos de
syndrome [síndrom] N síndrome *m*
synonym [sínənɪm] N sinónimo *m*
synonymous [sɪnánəməs] ADJ sinónimo
synopsis [sɪnápsɪs] N sinopsis *f*
syntax [síntæks] N sintaxis *f*
synthesis [sínθəsɪs] N síntesis *f*
synthesize [sínθəsaɪz] VI/VT sintetizar
synthetic [sɪnθéɗɪk] ADJ sintético
syphilis [sífəlɪs] N sífilis *f*
Syria [síriə] N Siria *f*
Syrian [síriən] ADJ & N sirio -ria *mf*
syringe [sərínʤ] N jeringa *f*
syrup [sírəp] N (food) almíbar *m*, jarabe *m*;
(medicine) jarabe *m*
system [sístəm] N sistema *m*
systematic [sɪstəmǽɗɪk] ADJ sistemático
systematize [sístəmətaɪz] VI/VT sistematizar
systemic [sɪstémɪk] ADJ sistémico

Tt

tab [tæb] N (on typewriter) tabulador *m*; (on
index cards) pestaña *f*, ceja *f*; (bill) cuenta
f; **— key** tecla de tabulación *f*
table [tébəł] N (furniture) mesa *f*; (list) tabla
f; **— lamp** lámpara de mesa *f*; **— of
contents** tabla de contenido *f*, índice *m*;
at — a la mesa; VT posponer

indefinidamente, dar carpetazo a; **—cloth**
mantel *m*; **—spoon** (spoon) cuchara
grande *f*; (measurement) cucharada *f*;
—spoonful cucharada *f*; **— tennis** tenis
de mesa *m*; **—ware** vajilla *f*, servicio de
mesa *m*
tablet [tǽblɪt] N (pill) pastilla *f*, tableta *f*;
(paper) bloc *m*; (stone) tabla *f*, lápida *f*;
(portable writing surface) tablilla *f*
tabloid [tǽblɔɪd] N (paper size) tabloide *m*;
(type of press) prensa amarilla ∕
sensacionalista *f*
taboo [tæbú] N tabú *m*
tabulate [tǽbjəlet] VT tabular
tachometer [tækámɪɗɚ] N tacómetro *m*
tacit [tǽsɪt] ADJ tácito
taciturn [tǽsɪtɚn] ADJ taciturno
tack [tæk] N (nail) tachuela *f*; (stitch) hilván
m; (heading of a boat) rumbo *m*; (course
of action) táctica *f*; (equipment for a
horse) arreos *m pl*; VT (to nail) clavar con
tachuelas; (to stitch) hilvanar; **to — on**
agregar; VI virar, cambiar de rumbo
tackle [tǽkəł] N (for fishing, hoisting)
aparejo *m*; (in rugby, football) placaje *m*;
(person) atajador *m*; VT (a problem)
enfrentar, abordar; (a task) emprender; (a
horse) poner arreos; VI/VT (rugby,
American football) placar, atajar; **the
cowboy —d the calf** el vaquero tiró al
suelo al becerro
tacky [tǽki] ADJ (in bad taste) de mal gusto,
chabacano; *Sp* hortera *inv*; (sticky)
pegajoso
tact [tækt] N tacto *m*
tactful [tǽktfəł] ADJ que tiene tacto
tactics [tǽktɪks] N táctica *f*
tactile [tǽktəł] ADJ táctil
tactless [tǽktlɪs] ADJ falto de tacto
tag [tæg] N (label) etiqueta *f*; (question)
coletilla *f*; (nickname) apodo *m*; **to play
—** jugar al pillapilla; VT etiquetar; (in the
game of tag) pillar; **to — along**
acompañar; **to — on** agregar
tail [teł] N cola *f*, rabo *m*; (of a shirt) faldón
m; (pursuer) perseguidor -ra *mf*; (buttocks)
vulg culo *m*; **—bone** rabadilla *f*; **— end**
(of a concert) final *m*; (of a procession)
cola *f*; **to —gate** seguir demasiado de
cerca (a otro coche); **—light** luz trasera *f*;
—pipe tubo de escape *m*; **—s** (of a coin)
cruz *f*; (tuxedo) frac *m*; **—spin** barrena *f*
tailor [télɚ] N sastre *m*; **— shop** sastrería *f*;
VT hacer a medida; (adapt) adaptar
taint [tent] N (stain) mancha *f*;
(contamination) contaminación *f*; VI/VT
(stain) manchar(se); (contaminate)

contaminar(se)

Taiwan [taɪwán] N Taiwán *m*

Taiwanese [taɪwɑníz] ADJ & N taiwanés -esa *mf*

Tajik [tɑdʒík] ADJ & N tayiko -ka *mf*

Tajikistan [tɑdʒíkɪstæn] N Tayikistán *m*

take [tek] VT (carry) llevar; (conduct) conducir; (steal) robar, llevarse; (subtract) restar; (prisoner, medicine, measures, a course) tomar; (one of a set) elegir, coger; (a bribe) aceptar; (a prize) recibir; (advice) seguir; (a walk) dar; (a vacation) irse; (a trip) hacer; (a piece of news) recibir; (remove from) sacar; (a photo) sacar; **to — a bath** bañarse; **to — a chance** arriesgarse, correr un riesgo; **to — after** salir a, parecerse a; **to — a fancy to** entusiasmarse con; **to — a look at** echar un vistazo a; **to — a nap** dormir la siesta; **to — a notion to** ocurrírsele a uno; **to — an oath** prestar juramento; **to — apart** desarmar, desmontar; **to — aside** apartar; **to — away** (carry away) llevarse; (steal) sustraer; **to — back** devolver; **to — back one's words** retractarse; **to — by surprise** tomar desprevenido; **to — care of** (a person) cuidar de; (a matter) atender a; **to — charge of** encargarse de; **to — down in writing** anotar, apuntar; **to — effect** entrar en vigencia; **to — exercise** hacer ejercicio; **to — in** (include) incluir; (comprehend) absorber; (deceive) embaucar; (orphans) albergar; (a dress) tomar, achicar; **to — leave** despedirse; **to — off** (a coat) quitar(se); (to jail) llevar; (discount) rebajar; (an airplane) despegar; **to — offense** ofenderse; **to — office** asumir un cargo; **to — on** (accept) asumir; (hire) tomar, contratar; (acquire) adquirir; **to — out** (withdraw) sacar; (carry out [food], take on a date) llevar; **to — place** tener lugar; **to — revenge** vengarse; **to — stock** hacer un balance; **to — stock in** tener confianza en; **to — the floor** tomar la palabra; **to — to heart** tomar a pecho; **to — to one's heels** poner pies en polvorosa; **to — to task** reprender, regañar; **to — up a matter** tratar un asunto; **to — up space** ocupar espacio; **I — it that** supongo que; **it —s ten minutes** lleva diez minutos; **the vaccination didn't —** la vacuna no prendió; N (profits) ingresos *m pl*; (of fish) pesca *f*, captura *f*; (of a film production) toma *f*; (opinion) opinión *f*; (approach) enfoque *m*; **—off** (of an airplane) despegue *m*; (parody) parodia *f*; **—over** (of

a government) toma de poder *f*; (of a company) adquisición *f*

talcum [tǽlkəm] N talco *m*; **— powder** polvo de talco *m*

tale [teɫ] N (story) cuento *m*, relato *m*; (lie) mentira *f*

talent [tǽlənt] N talento *m*

talented [tǽləntɪd] ADJ talentoso

talk [tɔk] VI/VT hablar; (chat) charlar; VT (nonsense) decir; (French) hablar; (politics) hablar de; **to — back** contestar con impertinencia; **to — down to** hablar con arrogancia a; **to — someone into something** convencer a alguien para que haga algo; **to — out of** disuadir de; **to — over** discutir; **to — up** alabar, hacer propaganda; N (formal speech) charla *f*; (gossip) habladurías *f pl*; (lingo) habla *f*; **— of the town** la comidilla del pueblo *f*; **— show** programa de entrevistas *m*

talkative [tɔ́kəDIV] ADJ hablador, parlanchín, charlatán

tall [tɔɫ] ADJ alto; **— order** misión imposible *f*; **— tale** cuento chino *m*, patraña *f*; **six feet —** de seis pies de altura; **how — are you?** ¿cuánto mides?

tallow [tǽlo] N sebo *m*

tally [tǽli] N (account) cuenta *f*; VT llevar la cuenta; **to — up** sumar; **to — with** concordar con

tambourine [tæmbərín] N pandereta *f*

tame [tem] ADJ (docile) manso, dócil; (domesticated) domesticado; (dull) aburrido; VT (make docile) amansar, domar; (domesticate) domesticar

tamper [tǽmpɚ] VI **to — with** (a jury) sobornar; (a lock) intentar forzar; (a document) alterar, amañar

tampon [tǽmpɑn] N tampón *m*

tan [tæn] VI/VT (cure) curtir(se); (sunburn) broncear(se), tostar(se); VT (cure) adobar; (spank) zurrar; N color tostado *m*; (of skin) bronceado *m*; ADJ (car) color tostado; (skin) bronceado, tostado

tandem [tǽndəm] N tándem *m*; **in — with** en colaboración con

tangent [tǽndʒənt] ADJ & N tangente *f*; **to go off on a —** salirse por la tangente

tangerine [tændʒərín] N mandarina *f*; *Am* tangerina *f*

tangible [tǽndʒəbɫ] ADJ tangible

tangle [tǽŋgəɫ] VI/VT enredar(se), enmarañar(se); N enredo *m*, maraña *f*; (in hair) nudo *m*, enredijo *m*

tank [tæŋk] N tanque *m* (also military), depósito *m*; VT guardar en un tanque; **to — up** (with gasoline) llenar el tanque;

(with alcohol) emborracharse

tannery [tǽnəri] N curtiduría *f*, tenería *f*; *Am* curtiembre *f*

tantalize [tǽntʃaɪz] VT atormentar con tentaciones

tantamount [tǽntəmaʊnt] ADJ **to be — to** equivaler a

tantrum [tǽntrəm] N berrinche *m*, perrera *f*, rabieta *f*

Tanzania [tænzənía] N Tanzania *f*

Tanzanian [tænzénien] ADJ & N tanzano -na *mf*

tap [tæp] N golpecito *m*; (repeated) golpeteo *m*; (with the hand) palmadita *f*; (faucet) llave *f*; *Sp* grifo *m*; **— dance** claqué *m*; **— water** agua de llave *f*; VI/VT (once) tocar; (repeatedly) golpetear; (with fingers) tamborilear; (utilize) explotar; (draw off liquid) extraer; **to — a tree** sangrar un árbol; **to — a telephone** intervenir un teléfono

tape [tep] N cinta *f* (also adhesive); **— measure** cinta métrica *f*; **— recorder** grabadora *f*, grabador *m*; **— recording** grabación *f*; **to —-record** grabar; **—worm** lombriz *f*, solitaria *f*; VT (tie up) atar con cinta; VI/VT (record) grabar

taper [tépɚ] N (diminished size) estrechamiento *m*; (candle) vela *f*, candela *f*; VI/VT afinar(se); **to — off** (become smaller) afinar(se); (diminish) ir disminuyendo

tapestry [tǽpɪstri] N (wall hanging) tapiz *m*; (art, industry) tapicería *f*

tapioca [tæpiókə] N tapioca *f*

tapir [tépər] N tapir *m*

tar [tɑr] N alquitrán *m*, brea *f*; VT alquitranar; **to — and feather** emplumar

tarantula [tərǽntʃələ] N tarántula *f*

tardy [tárɒi] ADJ **to be —** llegar tarde

target [tárɡɪt] N blanco *m*; **— practice** tiro al blanco *m*

tariff [tǽrɪf] N tarifa *f*, arancel *m*

tarnish [tárnɪʃ] VI/VT (metal) deslustrar(se), empañar; (reputation) manchar(se)

tart [tɑrt] ADJ (fruit) agrio, ácido; (remark) mordaz; N (pie) tarta *f*; (woman) *pej* fulana *f*

tartar [tárɒɚ] N (in wine) tártaro *m*; (on teeth) sarro *m*; **— sauce** salsa tártara *f*

task [tæsk] N tarea *f*, labor *f*, quehacer *m*; **to take to —** reprender, regañar; **— force** fuerza de tarea *f*; **—master** tirano -na *mf*

tassel [tǽsəł] N borla *f*

taste [test] N (test) VT (perceive) sentir el gusto / sabor de; (try) probar; (try wine) catar; VI **to — of onion** saber a cebolla; **it —s sour**

tiene un sabor agrio; N (sense, esthetic judgment) gusto *m*; (flavor) sabor *m*; (small amount of food) bocadito *m*; (small amount of drink) sorbo *m*; **— bud** papila gustativa *f*

tasteless [téstlɪs] ADJ (with no taste) soso, desabrido; (in bad taste) de mal gusto

tasty [tésti] ADJ sabroso

tatter [tǽɒɚ] N andrajo *m*, harapo *m*, pingajo *m*

tattered [tǽɒɚd] ADJ harapiento, andrajoso

tattle [tǽdl] VI acusar; **to — on** acusar a; N **—tale** alcahuete -ta *mf*, acusetas *mf sg*

tattoo [tætú] N tatuaje *m*; VI/VT tatuar(se)

taunt [tɔnt] VT provocar, burlarse de; N provocación *f*, pulla *f*

taut [tɔt] ADJ tenso, tirante

tavern [tǽvə-n] N taberna *f*, cantina *f*

tawdry [tɔ́dri] ADJ (affair) sórdido; (outfit) charro

tax [tæks] N impuesto *m*, contribución *f*, gravamen *m*; (burden) carga *f*; VT (a product) gravar; (a person) cobrarle impuestos a; (patience, resources) poner a prueba; **—-deductible** desgravable; **—-exempt** no gravable, exento de impuestos; **—payer** contribuyente *mf*; **— return** declaración de impuestos *f*; **— shelter** refugio fiscal *m*

taxation [tæksé ʃən] N (result of taxing) impuestos *m pl*; (act of taxing) imposición de contribuciones *f*

taxi [tǽksi] N taxi *m*; VI ir en taxi; (an airplane) rodar por la pista; **—cab** taxi *m*

taxidermy [tǽksɪdɚmi] N taxidermia *f*

taxonomy [tæksánəmi] N taxonomía *f*

tea [ti] N té *m*; **— bag** bolsita de té *f*; **—cup** taza de té *f*; **—kettle** tetera *f*; **— party** té *m*; **—pot** tetera *f*; **—spoon** (spoon) cucharita *f*, cucharilla *f*; (measurement) cucharadita *f*; **—spoonful** cucharadita *f*; **—time** hora del té *f*

teach [titʃ] VI/VT enseñar; **to — a class** dar clase

teacher [títʃɚ] N (primary school) maestro -tra *mf*; (secondary school) profesor -ora *mf*; **—'s college** (escuela) normal *f*

teaching [títʃɪŋ] N enseñanza *f*; **—s** enseñanzas *f pl*

team [tim] N equipo *m*; (of yoked animals) yunta de bueyes *f*; (of horses) tiro *m*, enganche *m*; VI **to — up** unirse, formar un equipo

teamster [tímstɚ] N transportista *mf*, camionero -ra *mf*

tear [tir] N lágrima *f*; **—drop** lágrima *f*; **— gas** gas lacrimógeno *m*; **to burst into**

—s romper a llorar; [tɛr] VI/VT rasgar(se); (rip a hole) hacer(se) un siete; VT (snatch) arrancar; (disrupt) desgarrar; **to — along** ir a toda velocidad; **to — apart** (rip up) romper, destrozar; (separate) separar; **to — away** apartar(se); **to — down** (a building) demoler, derribar; (a machine) desarmar, desmontar; (a person) denigrar; **to — one's hair** arrancarse los cabellos; N desgarrón *m*, desgarradura *f*, rasgón *m*

tearful [tírfəɫ] ADJ (look) lloroso; (farewell) triste

tease [tiz] VT (make fun of a person) molestar, fastidiar; (tantalize sexually) provocar; (comb wool, hair) cardar; **to — out** sacar; N provocadora *f*

teat [tit] N teta *f*

technical [téknɪkəɫ] ADJ técnico

technician [tɛkníʃən] N técnico -ca *mf*, perito -ta *mf*

technique [tɛkník] N técnica *f*

technology [tɛknáləʤi] N tecnología *f*, técnica *f*

tectonics [tɛktánɪks] N tectónica *f*

tedious [tíɖiəs] ADJ tedioso, aburrido

tedium [tíɖiəm] N hastío *m*

tee [ti] N (T-shirt) camiseta *f*; (golf ball support) tee *m*; (start of hole in golf) punto de salida *m*

teem [tim] VI **to — with** abundar en, estar lleno de

teenager [tínɛʤɚ] N adolescente *mf*

teens [tinz] N (teenage years) adolescencia *f*; (numbers 13–19) números de trece a diecinueve *m pl*

teethe [tið] VI **the baby is teething** al bebé le están saliendo los dientes

teetotaler [títódlɚ] N abstemio -mia *mf*

telecast [téləkæst] N teledifusión *f*

telecommunications [tɛlɪkəmjunɪkéʃənz] N telecomunicaciones *f pl*

teleconference [télɪkɑnfɚəns] N teleconferencia *f*

telegram [téləgræm] N telegrama *m*

telegraph [téləgræf] N telégrafo *m*; VI/VT telegrafiar

telegraphic [tɛləgræfɪk] ADJ telegráfico

telemarketing [tɛləmárkɪɖɪŋ] N telemercadeo *m*, telemarketing *m*

telepathy [təlépəθi] N telepatía *f*

telephone [téləfon] N teléfono *m*; **— book** guía telefónica *f*; **— booth** cabina telefónica *f*; **— number** número telefónico *m*; **— operator** telefonista *mf*; **— receiver** auricular *m*, tubo de teléfono *m*; VI/VT telefonear, llamar por teléfono

telescope [télɪskop] N telescopio *m*; VI

plegarse

television [téləvɪʒən] N (medium) televisión *f*; (device) televisor *m*; **— viewer** televidente *mf*

tell [tɛɫ] VI/VT (the truth) decir; (a story) contar; **to — apart** distinguir; **to — on someone** acusar a alguien; **to — someone off** regañar a alguien; **to — time** decir la hora; **I can't — if he's old or young** no sé si es viejo o joven; **his age is beginning to —** se le comienza a notar la edad; **a —tale sign** una señal reveladora; **he is a —tale** es un acusica

teller [télɚ] N (narrator) narrador -ora *mf*; (in a bank) cajero -ra *mf*

temerity [təmérɪɖi] N temeridad *f*

temper [témpɚ] N (hardness) temple *m*; (bad humor) mal genio *m*; VT templar; **to keep one's —** mantener la calma; **to lose one's —** perder los estribos, encolerizarse

temperament [témpɚəmənt] N temperamento *m*, genio *m*, talante *m*

temperance [témpɚəns] N (moderation) templanza *f*, temperancia *f*; (abstinence from alcohol) abstinencia de bebidas alcohólicas *f*

temperate [témpɚɪt] ADJ (weather) templado; (opinions, habits) moderado

temperature [témpɚətʃur] N temperatura *f*; **to have a —** tener fiebre

tempest [témpɪst] N tempestad *f*

tempestuous [tempéstʃuəs] ADJ tempestuoso

temple [témpəɫ] N (church) templo *m*; (side of the forehead) sien *f*

temporal [témpɚəɫ] ADJ temporal

temporary [témpəreri] ADJ temporal, provisional

tempt [tɛmpt] VT tentar

temptation [temptéʃən] N tentación *f*

tempting [témptɪŋ] ADJ tentador

ten [tɛn] NUM diez

tenacious [tənéʃəs] ADJ tenaz

tenacity [tənǽsɪɖi] N tenacidad *f*

tenant [ténənt] N inquilino -na *mf*, arrendatario -ria *mf*

tend [tɛnd] VT (care for) cuidar; **to — to** ocuparse de; VI (lean toward) tender, inclinarse

tendency [téndənsi] N tendencia *f*

tender [téndɚ] ADJ tierno; (painful) sensible; N (offer) oferta *f*; (legal currency) curso legal *m*; (person who tends) cuidador -ra *mf*, vigilante *mf*; VT presentar, ofrecer

tenderness [téndɚnɪs] N (of feeling) ternura *f*; (of meat) terneza *f*, ternura *f*; (sensitivity to pain) sensibilidad *f*

tendon [téndən] N tendón *m*

tendonitis [tɛndənáɪdɪs] N tendinitis *f*
tendril [téndrəł] N zarcillo *m*
tenement [ténəmənt] N casa de vecindad *f*
tenet [ténɪt] N principio *m*
tennis [ténɪs] N tenis *m*; — **court** cancha de tenis *f*, pista de tenis *f*; — **player** tenista *mf*; — **shoes** tenis *m pl*
tenor [ténɚ] N tenor *m*
tense [tɛns] ADJ tenso; N tiempo *m*
tension [ténʃən] N tensión *f*; (tautness) tirantez *f*
tent [tɛnt] N tienda de campaña *f*; (circus) carpa *f*; VI acampar
tentacle [téntəkəł] N tentáculo *m*
tentative [téntəDIV] ADJ tentativo
tenth [tɛnθ] ADJ & N décimo *m*
tenuous [ténjuəs] ADJ (light, color, cloth) tenue; (peace) frágil; (rarefied) enrarecido
tenure [ténjɚ] N (of professorship) titularidad *f*; (of an office) ocupación *f*
tepid [tépɪd] ADJ tibio
terabyte [térəbaɪt] N terabyte *m*
term [tɝm] N (word, mathematical expression) término *m*; (period) período *m*; (time in office) mandato *m*; (semester) semestre *m*; (trimester) trimestre *m*; (set date for payment) plazo *m*; — **paper** trabajo final *m*; —**s** condiciones *f pl*; **at** — a término; **to be on good** —**s** estar en buenas relaciones; **not to be on speaking** —**s** no hablarse; **to come to** —**s** aceptar; VT denominar
terminal [tɝmənəł] ADJ terminal; N (of airport, computer) terminal *mf*; (electric) terminal *m*
terminate [tɝmənet] VI/VT terminar(se)
termination [tɝmənéʃən] N terminación *f*; (of an employee) despido *m*
terminology [tɝmənáləʤi] N terminología *f*
termite [tɝmaɪt] N termita *f*
terrace [térɪs] N terraza *f*, escalón *m*; VT poner terrazas en, escalonar
terrain [tərén] N terreno *m*
terrestrial [təréstriəł] ADJ terrestre
terrible [térəbəł] ADJ terrible, tremendo
terrier [tériɚ] N terrier *m*
terrific [tərífɪk] ADJ estupendo
terrify [térəfaɪ] VT aterrar, aterrorizar, espeluznar
territory [térɪtɔri] N territorio *m*
terror [térɚ] N terror *m*
terrorism [térəɪzəm] N terrorismo *m*
terrorist [térəɪst] N terrorista *mf*
terse [tɝs] ADJ lacónico
test [tɛst] N (trial, experiment) prueba *f*; (of intelligence, multiple choice) test *m*;

(examination) examen *m*, prueba *f*; **to** —**-drive** probar; — **pilot** piloto de pruebas *m*; — **tube** tubo de ensayo *m*, probeta *f*; —**-tube baby** bebé de probeta *mf*; **to undergo a** — someterse a una prueba; **to take a** — dar un examen; **to give a** — poner un examen; **to put to the** — poner a prueba; VT (try) probar, poner a prueba; (give an exam) poner una prueba, examinar; VI **girls** — **better than boys** en los exámenes salen mejor las niñas que los niños
testament [téstəmənt] N testamento *m*; (testimony) testimonio *m*
testicle [téstɪkəł] N testículo *m*
testify [téstəfaɪ] VI testificar; (confirm) dar fe
testimony [téstəmoni] N testimonio *m*
testosterone [tɛstástəron] N testosterona *f*
tetanus [tétɲəs] N tétano(s) *m*
Teutonic [tutánɪk] ADJ teutónico
text [tɛkst] N texto *m*; —**book** libro de texto *m*; — **editor** editor de texto(s) *m*
textile [tékstaɪł] ADJ textil; N textil *m*, tejido *m*; — **mill** fábrica de tejidos *f*
texture [tékstfɚ] N textura *f*
Thai [taɪ] ADJ & N tailandés -esa *mf*
Thailand [táɪlænd] N Tailandia *f*
Thailander [táɪlændɚ] ADJ & N tailandés -esa *mf*
than [ðæn] CONJ que; **I have more** — **you** tengo más que tú; **more** — **once** más de una vez
thank [θæŋk] VT dar las gracias, agradecer; **to have oneself to** — **for** tener la culpa de; INTERJ — **heaven!** ¡gracias a Dios! — **you** gracias; —**s** gracias *f pl*
thankful [θǽŋkfəł] ADJ agradecido
thankfulness [θǽŋkfəłnɪs] N gratitud *f*, agradecimiento *m*
thankless [θǽŋklɪs] ADJ ingrato
thanksgiving [θæŋksgívɪŋ] N acción de gracias *f*; — **Day** día de acción de gracias *m*
that [ðæt] ADJ (something nearer the speaker) ese, esa; (something more remote from speaker) aquel, aquella; — **dog** ese / aquel perro *m*; — **one** (nearer) ese, esa; DEMON PRON (nearer to speaker) ese, esa; (more remote from speaker) aquel, aquella; (neuter) eso, aquello; — **is my daughter** esa / aquella es mi hija; — **was a nightmare** eso / aquello fue una pesadilla; REL PRON que; **the bike** — **disappeared** la bici que desapareció; **the pen** — **I was writing with** la lapicera con la que / cual escribía; — **is** es decir; CONJ que; **she said** — **she would come**

dijo que vendría; ADV tan; **it's not — far**
no queda tan lejos; **— much** tanto; **she
was — tall** era así de alta

thatch [θætʃ] N paja *f*; *Am* quincha *f*; VT
techar con paja; *Am* quinchar; **—ed roof**
techo de paja *m*; *Am* quincha *f*

thaw [θɔ] VI/VT (food) descongelar(se); (ice
and snow) derretir(se); (relations,
refrigerator) deshelar(se); N deshielo *m*

the [ðə, ði] DEF ART (singular) el *m*, la *f*; —
boy el chico *m*; (plural) los *m*, las *f*; —
girls las chicas *f pl*; — **good thing** lo
bueno; ADV — **more I work, — less I
accomplish** cuanto más trabajo, menos
consigo

theater [θíəDɚ] N teatro *m*

theatrical [θiǽtrɪkəɫ] ADJ teatral

theft [θɛft] N hurto *m*, robo *m*

their [ðɛr] POSS ADJ **this is — dog** este es su
perro, este es el perro de ellos

theirs [ðɛrz] PRON **this book is —** este libro
es suyo, este libro es de ellos/ellas; **these
things are —** estas cosas son suyas/de
ellos/de ellas; **— is bigger** el suyo/la
suya/el de ellos/la de ellos es más
grande; **a friend of —** un amigo suyo,
un amigo de ellos

them [ðɛm] PRON los *m pl*, las *f pl*; **I see —**
los/las veo; **I talk to —** les hablo a ellos;
I went with — fui con ellos/ellas

thematic [θɪmǽDɪk] ADJ temático

theme [θim] N tema *m*; (essay) ensayo *m*,
redacción *f*; **— park** parque temático *m*;
— song tema *m*

themselves [ðɛmsélvz] PRON **they — built
their house** ellos mismos se
construyeron la casa; **they are not —
today** hoy no son los mismos de siempre;
they were sitting by — estaban
sentados solos; **they looked at — in the
mirror** se miraron en el espejo; **they
talk to —** hablan solos; **they bought —
a yacht** se compraron un yate

then [ðɛn] ADV (at that time) entonces, en
aquel tiempo; **it was cheaper —** era más
barato en aquel tiempo; (after) luego,
después; **from — on** a partir de entonces;
now and — de vez en cuando; **until —**
hasta entonces; **I ate, — I paid** comí,
luego pagué; ADJ entonces; **the —
president** el entonces presidente; CONJ
entonces; **if not, — you should stay** si
no, entonces deberías quedarte; **now —**
ahora bien; **are you sorry —?** ¿estás
arrepentido pues?

theology [θiáləʤi] N teología *f*

theoretical [θiərέDɪkəɫ] ADJ teórico

theory [θíəri] N teoría *f*

therapeutic [θɛrəpjúDɪk] ADJ terapéutico

therapist [θɛ́rəpɪst] N terapeuta *mf*;
(psychologist) psicólogo -ga *mf*

therapy [θɛ́rəpi] N terapia *f*

there [ðɛr] ADV ahí; *Am* allí; (more remote)
allá; *Sp* allí; **—abouts** por ahí, más o
menos; **—after** (after) después;
(subsequently) de allí en adelante; **—by**
así, de ese modo; **— ensued a war** a
continuación hubo una guerra; **—fore** por
consiguiente, por lo tanto; **—in** en eso,
allí; **— is, — are** hay; **— goes the bus**
ahí va el autobús; **— — bueno, bueno;
—of de eso; **—on** (on that) encima; (after)
luego, después; **—upon** (after) luego,
después; (for this reason) por consiguiente;
(upon that) encima; **—with** (with that)
con eso; (after that) luego, en seguida;
who's —? ¿quién es? **is Mary —?** ¿está
María? **we got — at 5** llegamos a las 5

thermal [θɝ́məɫ] ADJ termal; **— energy**
energía térmica *f*

thermodynamic [θɝmodaɪnǽmɪk] ADJ
termodinámico

thermometer [θɚmámɪDɚ] N termómetro *m*

thermonuclear [θɝmonúkliɚ] ADJ
termonuclear

thermos [θɝ́məs] N termo *m*

thermostat [θɝ́məstæt] N termostato *m*

thesaurus [θɪsɔ́rəs] N (synonym dictionary)
diccionario de sinónimos *m*; (large
dictionary) diccionario *m*

these [ðiz] ADJ & PRON estos, estas

thesis [θísɪs] N tesis *f*

they [ðe] PRON ellos, ellas

thick [θɪk] ADJ (slice) grueso; (fog, soup)
espeso; (accent) marcado; (wit) torpe; **one
inch —** una pulgada de espesor; **— as
thieves** como carne y uña; ADV
—-headed estúpido; **—-set** grueso;
—-skinned insensible; N **the — of the
fight** lo más reñido de la pelea; **through
— and thin** pase lo que pase

thicken [θíkən] VI/VT espesar(se), trabar(se);
the plot —s la trama se complica

thicket [θíkɪt] N soto *m*, matorral *m*, boscaje
m

thickness [θíknɪs] N (of paper, wood) espesor
m, grosor *m*; (of soup) lo espeso; (of lips)
lo grueso; (of a beard) lo tupido; (of hair)
lo abundante

thief [θif] N ladrón -ona *mf*

thieve [θiv] VI/VT hurtar, robar

thigh [θaɪ] N muslo *m*

thimble [θímbəɫ] N dedal *m*

thin [θɪn] ADJ (ice, wire) delgado, fino;

(person) flaco; (vegetation, beard, hair) ralo; (voice) tenue, fino; (air) enrarecido; (excuse) débil; (soup) aguado; VI/VT (paint, soup, sauce) diluir; (hair) entresacar; **to — out** (hair) ralear; (crowd) dispersarse

thing [θɪŋ] N cosa *f*; **there's no such —** eso no existe; **that is the — to do** eso es lo que hay que hacer; **the — about Mary** lo que pasa con María

thingamajig [θíŋəmədʒɪg] N chisme *m*, coso *m*

think [θɪŋk] VI/VT (reason) pensar, razonar; (believe) creer, opinar; **to — about** pensar en; **to — back** recordar; **to — it over / through** pensarlo bien, reflexionar sobre; **I'm —ing of you** pienso en ti; **what do you — of Mary?** ¿qué piensas de María? **I thought of a plan** se me ocurrió un plan; **to — up an excuse** inventar / elucubrar una excusa; **I don't — so** no creo; **who does he — he is?** ¿quién se cree que es? **to — well of** tener buena opinión de; **she —s nothing of spending $1000** no le importa nada gastar $1000; **to my way of —ing** a mi parecer

thinner [θínɚ] N disolvente *m*

thinness [θínnɪs] N (of ice, person) delgadez *f*, flacura *f*; (of hair) escasez *f*; (of air) enrarecimiento *m*; (of soup) fluidez *f*

third [θɝd] ADJ tercer(o); **— chapter** capítulo tercero *m*, tercer capítulo *m*; ADV tercero; N tercio *m*; (gear, musical interval) tercera *f*; **— person** tercera persona *f*; **—-rate** de poca categoría; **— World** Tercer Mundo *m*; **the — of March** el tres de marzo

thirst [θɝst] N sed *f*; VI tener sed; **to — for** tener sed de, estar sediento de

thirsty [θɝ́sti] ADJ sediento; **to be —** tener sed

thirteen [θɝtín] NUM trece

thirty [θɝ́Di] NUM treinta

this [ðɪs] ADJ & PRON este *m*, esta *f*, esto (neuter); **— dog** este perro; **— is a disaster** esto es un desastre

thistle [θísəł] N cardo *m*

thong [θɔŋ] N (strip of leather) correa *f*; (garment) tanga *mf*; (shoe) chancleta *f*

thorax [θɔ́ræks] N tórax *m*

thorn [θɔrn] N (sharp growth) espina *f*; (plant) espino *m*

thorny [θɔ́rni] ADJ espinoso, escabroso

thorough [θɝ́o] ADJ (exhaustive) exhaustivo, minucioso, detenido; (conscientious) concienzudo

thoroughbred [θɝ́əbrɛd] ADJ de pura sangre;

N purasangre *m*

those [ðoz] ADJ & PRON (nearer) esos *m*, esas *f*; PRON (more remote) aquellos *m*, aquellas *f*; **— of you** los de vosotros / ustedes; **— that / who** los / las que

though [ðo] CONJ aunque; **as —** como si; ADV sin embargo

thought [θɔt] N (act, product of thinking) pensamiento *m*; (idea) idea *f*; (opinion) opinión *f*; (concern) consideración *f*; **to be lost in —** estar abstraído; **to give it no —** no darle importancia; **the very —** la mera idea; **at the — of** ante la idea de; **on second —** pensándolo bien; **my —s are with you** te acompaño en el sentimiento

thoughtful [θɔ́tfəł] ADJ (considerate) considerado, atento; (well thought out) bien pensado; (reflective) pensativo, reflexivo

thoughtfulness [θɔ́tfəłnɪs] N consideración *f*

thoughtless [θɔ́tlɪs] ADJ (inconsiderate) desconsiderado; (careless) descuidado; (not reflective) irreflexivo

thoughtlessness [θɔ́tlɪsnɪs] N (lack of consideration) desconsideración *f*; (carelessness) descuido *m*; (lack of reflection) falta de reflexión *f*

thousand [θáuzənd] NUM mil

thrash [θræʃ] VI/VT (whip, defeat) zurrar, vapulear, apalear; (thresh) trillar, desgranar; **to — around** revolverse, agitarse; **to — out a matter** ventilar un asunto

thread [θrɛd] N hilo *m*; (on a screw) rosca *f*; **—bare** raído; VT (a needle) enhebrar; (beads) ensartar; (a screw) enroscar; **to — one's way** abrirse paso

threat [θrɛt] N amenaza *f*

threaten [θrɛ́tn̩] VI/VT amenazar

threatening [θrɛ́tn̩ɪŋ] ADJ amenazador

three [θri] NUM tres; **—-dimensional** tridimensional

thresh [θrɛʃ] VT trillar

threshold [θrɛ́ʃhołd] N umbral *m*

thrift [θrɪft] N economía *f*

thrifty [θrífti] ADJ económico, ahorrativo

thrill [θrɪł] VI/VT emocionar(se), ilusionar(se); N emoción *f*, ilusión *f*

thrive [θraɪv] VI prosperar; (plants) florecer

throat [θrot] N garganta *f*

throb [θrɑb] VI latir, palpitar; N latido *m*, palpitación *f*

throes [θroz] ADV LOC **in the — of war** en plena guerra; **in the — of death** agonizando

throne [θron] N trono *m*

throng [θrɔŋ] N muchedumbre f, turbamulta f; VI apiñarse, llegar en tropel

throttle [θrádl̩] N (of a motor) válvula reguladora / de aceleración f, regulador m; (of a motorcycle) puño giratorio del gas m; **— lever** palanca del regulador f; VT ahogar, estrangular

through [θru] PREP por, a través de; (as intermediary) por medio de; **Monday — Friday** de lunes a viernes; **all — the night** toda la noche; ADV (completely) de un lado a otro; (from beginning to end) de principio a fin, de cabo a rabo; **loyal — and —** leal a toda prueba; **an aristocrat — and —** un aristócrata de pura cepa; **to carry —** llevar a cabo; ADJ (ticket, train) directo; **to be —** (with a task) haber terminado; (in a profession) estar acabado; **we're —!** (with a boyfriend) ¡se acabó entre nosotros!

throughout [θruáut] PREP (all through) por todo; (during) a lo largo de, durante; ADV (duration) de principio a fin; (space) por todas partes

throw [θro] VI/VT (a ball) tirar, lanzar; (a light, voice) arrojar; (a switch) conectar; (a pot on a wheel) modelar en un torno; (a punch) lanzar; (a wrestler) tumbar; (a game for a bribe) dejarse perder; (a rider) desmontar; (a party) dar, organizar; **that really threw me** eso me confundió; **to — away** (dispose of) tirar, arrojar; (squander) malgastar; **to — down** tirar al suelo; **to — in** añadir; **to — into gear** engranar; **to — in the clutch** embragar; **to — out** (garbage) tirar, arrojar; (unruly guest) echar; **to — up** vomitar, devolver; N (act or instance of throwing) tiro m; (of dice) tirada f; (shawl) chal m; (blanket) manta f

thrush [θrʌʃ] N tordo m, zorzal m

thrust [θrʌst] VT (stab) clavar; (shove) empujar; **to — oneself upon** meterse en; **to — a task upon someone** imponerle una tarea a alguien; **to — aside** echar a un lado; **to — someone through** atravesar a alguien; VI (push) dar un empujón; (stab at) lanzar una estocada; (push through) empujar para pasar; N (stab) estocada f; (force of a jet engine) empuje m; (shove) empujón m; (military assault) arremetida f, acometida f

thud [θʌd] N golpe sordo m; VI caer con un golpe sordo

thug [θʌg] N matón m

thumb [θʌm] N pulgar m; **under the — of** bajo la bota de; VT hojear; **to give the —s up** aprobar; **—tack** chinche f, tachuela f

thump [θʌmp] N golpe sordo m; VI hacer un ruido sordo

thunder [θʌndɚ] N trueno m; VI tronar; **—bolt** rayo m; **—head** nubarrón m; **—storm** tormenta eléctrica f, tronada f

thunderous [θʌndɚəs] ADJ atronador, estruendoso

Thursday [θɚ́zde] N jueves m

thus [ðʌs] ADV así; **— far** (space) hasta aquí; (time) hasta ahora

thwart [θwɔrt] VT frustrar

thyme [taɪm] N tomillo m

thyroid [θáɪrɔɪd] N tiroides m sg

Tibet [tɪbét] N Tíbet m

Tibetan [tɪbétn̩] ADJ & N tibetano -na mf

tic [tɪk] N tic m, manía f

tick [tɪk] N (sound of a clock) tic tac m; (cover of a pillow) funda f; (check mark) marca f; (insect) garrapata f; VI hacer tic tac; **to — off** (check off) marcar; (anger) enojar

ticket [tíkɪt] N billete m; Am boleto m; (slate of candidates) candidatura f; (summons) multa f; (tag) etiqueta f; **— office** taquilla f; VT (give passage) vender billetes; (give summons) multar

tickle [tíkl̩] VT (poke) cosquillear, hacer cosquillas; (amuse) dar ilusión; VI picar; N picazón f, cosquilleo m

ticklish [tíklɪʃ] ADJ (prone to tickles) cosquilloso; (delicate) delicado

tidal [táɪdl̩] ADJ **— wave** (tsunami) maremoto m; (large wave) marejada f

tidbit [tídbɪt] N (snack) golosina f; (gossip) chisme jugoso m

tide [taɪd] N marea f; (of opinion) corriente f; **—water** (water) agua de marea f; (land) marisma f; VT **to — over** cubrir

tidy [táɪdi] ADJ (orderly) ordenado; (large) considerable; VI/VT arreglar; **to — oneself up** arreglarse

tie [taɪ] VI (fasten) atarse; (make same score) empatar; VT (fasten) atar; (make a knot) hacer un nudo; (make same score as) empatar con; **to — down** atar; **to — in** cuadrar; **to — one on** emborracharse; **to — tight** atar fuerte; **to — up** (bind) atar; (hinder) bloquear; (occupy) ocupar; (moor a ship) amarrar; N (cord) cuerda f; (relations) lazo m, vínculo m; (cravat) corbata f; (score) empate m; (railway) durmiente m, traviesa f

tier [tir] N nivel m

tiger [táɪgɚ] N tigre m

tight [taɪt] ADJ (knot, nut) apretado, ajustado;

(clothes) ceñido, ajustado; (control) firme, estricto; (race) reñido; (stingy) tacaño, mezquino; (drunk) borracho; **—-fisted** agarrado; **—rope** cuerda floja *f*; **—wad** tacaño -ña *mf*; **to be in a — spot** estar en un aprieto; ADV bien, herméticamente; **to hold on —** agarrarse bien

tighten [táɪtn̩] VI/VT (knot, nut, belt) apretar(se); (control) estrechar(se)

tightness [táɪtnɪs] N estrechez *f*; (stinginess) tacañería *f*

tile [taɪl] N (on a roof) teja *f*; (on a floor) baldosa *f*; (on a wall) azulejo *m*; **— roof** tejado *m*; VT (roof) tejar; (floor) embaldosar; (wall) azulejar

till [tɪl] PREP hasta; CONJ hasta que; VI/VT labrar, arar; N caja *f*

tilt [tɪlt] VI/VT ladear(se), inclinar(se); N (act or instance of tilting) ladeo *m*, inclinación *f*; (incline) declive *m*; (joust) justa *f*; **at full —** a toda velocidad

timber [tímbɚ] N (cut wood) madera (de construcción) *f*; (trees) árboles para madera *m pl*; (beam) viga *f*; **—line** límite de la vegetación arbórea *m*; **— wolf** lobo gris *m*

timbre [tímbɚ] N timbre *m*

time [taɪm] N (past, present, future) tiempo *m*; (hour) hora *f*; (occasion) vez *f*; (period) período *m*, momento *m*, época *f*; **— bomb** bomba de tiempo *f*; **—keeper** cronometrador -ra *mf*; **— out** descanso *m*; **—piece** reloj *m*; **— signature** compás *m*; **—table** horario *m*; **— zone** huso horario *m*; **at —s** a veces; **at the same —** a la vez, al mismo tiempo; **at this —** en este momento; **behind —** atrasado; **lunch—** hora del almuerzo *f*; **from — to —** de vez en cuando; **for the — being** por el momento; **in — a** tiempo; **in no —** en seguida; **it's about —** ya era hora; **on —** puntual; **to buy on —** comprar a plazo; **— after —** una vez tras otra; **to do —** cumplir una condena; **to have a good —** divertirse; **what — is it?** ¿qué hora es? VT (a race) cronometrar; (a test) fijar la duración de; (one's arrival) fijar la hora de; **to — an attack well** atacar en el momento oportuno

timeless [táɪmlɪs] ADJ eterno

timely [táɪmli] ADJ oportuno

timer [táɪmɚ] N (person) cronometrador -ra *mf*; (device) reloj *m*

timid [tímɪd] ADJ tímido, apocado

timidity [tɪmídɪdi] N timidez *f*, apocamiento *m*

timing [táɪmɪŋ] N (measurement)

cronometraje *m*; (synchronization) sincronización *f*; **that was good —** lo hiciste en el momento oportuno

timorous [tímɚəs] ADJ timorato

tin [tɪn] N (metal) estaño *m*; (tin plate) hojalata *f*; **— can** lata *f*; **— foil** papel de estaño *m*, papel de aluminio *m*; VT estañar

tincture [tíŋktʃɚ] N tintura *f*

tinder [tíndɚ] N yesca *f*

tinge [tɪndʒ] VT (tint) teñir; (hint) matizar; N (of color) tinte *m*, matiz *m*; (of taste) dejo *m*; (of irony) matiz *m*

tingle [tíŋgəl] VI sentir hormigueo, hormiguear; **to — with excitement** estremecerse de entusiasmo; N hormigueo *m*

tinker [tíŋkɚ] VI ocuparse, entretenerse; **to — with** toquetear, hacer ajustes

tinkle [tíŋkəl] VT (ring lightly) tintinear; (urinate) hacer pipí; N tintineo *m*

tinsel [tínsəl] N (Christmas trim) espumillón *m*, guirnalda *f*; (tawdry decoration) oropel *m*

tint [tɪnt] N (hue) matiz *m*; (for hair) tinte *m*, tintura *f*; (for glass) coloreado *m*; VT (hair) teñir; (glasses) colorear

tiny [táɪni] ADJ diminuto, chiquito

tip [tɪp] N (point) punta *f*; (gratuity) propina *f*; (piece of advice) consejo *m*; VI/VT (tilt) inclinar(se), ladear(se); (give a gratuity) dar propina (a); **to — a person off** advertir a alguien; **to — one's hat** sacarse / quitarse el sombrero; **to — over** volcar(se)

tipsy [típsi] ADJ alegre

tiptoe [típto] N punta del pie *f*; **on —s** de puntillas; VI andar de puntillas

tirade [táɪred] N diatriba *f*

tire [taɪr] N neumático *m*, cubierta *f*; *Mex* llanta *f*; *Am* goma *f*; VI/VT cansar(se), fatigar(se); **to — out** cansar, fatigar; ADJ **—d** cansado, fatigado; **—d out** cansado, fatigado

tireless [táɪrlɪs] ADJ incansable

tiresome [táɪrsəm] ADJ aburrido, pesado, plasta *inv*

tissue [tíʃu] N (cell aggregate) tejido *m*; (handkerchief) pañuelo de papel *m*; **— paper** papel tisú *m*

tit [tɪt] N (bird) paro *m*; (breast) *vulg* teta *f*

titanic [taɪtǽnɪk] ADJ titánico

titanium [taɪténiəm] N titanio *m*

tithe [taɪð] N diezmo *m*; VI pagar el diezmo

titillate [tídlet] VT excitar; (interest) despertar interés

title [táɪdl̩] N título *m*; (of a picture) rótulo *m*; **— deed** título de propiedad *m*; **— page** portada *f*

TNT [tiɛntí] N TNT *m*

to [tu] PREP **I gave it — you** te lo di a ti; **to count — ten** contar hasta diez; **I called — find out** llamé para averiguar; **— my surprise** para mi sorpresa; **a quarter — five** las cinco menos cuarto; **bills — be paid** cuentas por pagar; **things — do** cosas que hacer; **frightened — death** muerto de susto; **from house — house** de casa en casa; ADV **— and fro** de acá para allá; **to come —** volver en sí

toad [tod] N sapo *m*; **—stool** seta *f*, hongo no comestible *m*

toast [tost] VI/VT (brown) tostar(se); VT (congratulate) brindar por; N tostada *f*; (congratulation) brindis *m*

toaster [tóstɚ] N tostadora *f*; **— oven** horno tostador *m*

tobacco [təbǽko] N tabaco *m*

today [tədé] ADV hoy; (nowadays) hoy día

toddler [tádlɚ] N niño -ña pequeño -ña *mf*

toe [to] N dedo del pie *m*; (of shoe, sock) punta *f*; **—nail** uña del dedo del pie *f*; VT (touch with toe) tocar con el dedo del pie; **to — the line** hacer buena letra, entrar en vereda

together [təgéðɚ] ADV (in union) juntos; (at the same time) al mismo tiempo; **— with** junto con; **all —** todos juntos

Togo [tógo] N Togo *m*

Togolese [togəlíz] ADJ & N togolés -esa *mf*

toil [tɔɪł] N esfuerzo *m*, trabajo *m*; VI trabajar, esforzarse, bregar

toilet [tɔ́ɪlɪt] N (bowl) inodoro *m*; (lavatory) aseo *m*, lavabo *m*; **— paper** papel higiénico *m*; **—-trained** que ya no usa pañales

token [tókən] N (symbol) señal *f*; (keepsake) recuerdo *m*; (coinlike metal piece) ficha *f*; **— payment** pago nominal *m*; **as a — of friendship** en prenda de amistad

tolerance [tálərəns] N tolerancia *f*

tolerant [tálərənt] ADJ tolerante

tolerate [táləret] VT tolerar

toll [toł] N (of bells) tañido *m*; (payment) peaje *m*; (charges) tarifa *f*; (of victims) balance *m*; **— bridge** puente de peaje *m*; **— road** carretera de peaje *f*; VI/VT tañer (a muerto)

tomato [təmédo] N tomate *m*

tomb [tum] N tumba *f*, sepulcro *m*, sepultura *f*; **—stone** lápida *f*

tomboy [támbɔɪ] N marimacho *m*

tomcat [támkæt] N gato macho *m*

tomorrow [təmɔ́ro] ADV & N mañana *f*; **— morning** mañana por la mañana *f*

ton [tʌn] N tonelada *f*

tone [ton] N (pitch) tono *m*; (of a speech) tono *m*, tónica *f*; VI **to — down** moderar, matizar

toner [tónɚ] N tóner *m*

Tonga [táŋgə] N Tonga *m*

Tongan [táŋgən] ADJ & N tongano -na *mf*

tongs [tɔŋz] N tenazas *f pl*

tongue [tʌŋ] N (body part, language, of a flame) lengua *f*; (of a shoe) lengüeta *f*; **to —-lash** reprender; **to be —-tied** tener trabada la lengua; **on the tip of my —** en la punta de la lengua; **to hold one's —** callarse la boca; **— in cheek** irónicamente; **— twister** trabalenguas *m sg*; VI tocar con la lengua

tonic [tánɪk] ADJ tónico; N (medicine) tónico *m*; (water, key note) tónica *f*; **— water** agua tónica *f*

tonight [tənáɪt] ADV esta noche

tonsil [tánsəł] N amígdala *f*

tonsillitis [tɑnsəláɪdɪs] N amigdalitis *f*, anginas *f pl*

too [tu] ADV (in addition) también; (excessively) demasiado; **— bad!** ¡qué lástima! **— many** demasiados; **— much** demasiado

tool [tuł] N herramienta *f*; **—box** caja de herramientas *f*; **—shed** cobertizo para herramientas *m*

toot [tut] VI/VT (horn) sonar; (whistle) pitar; (trumpet) tocar; **to — one's own horn** darse autobombo; N (of horn, trumpet) toque *m*; (of horn) bocinazo *m*; (of whistle) pitido *m*

tooth [tuθ] N (front) diente *m*; (back) muela *f*; **—ache** dolor de muelas *m*; **—brush** cepillo de dientes *m*; **— decay** caries (dental) *f sg*; **— fairy** ratoncito Pérez *m*; **— mark** dentellada *f*; **—paste** pasta dental *f*, pasta dentífrica *f*; **—pick** mondadientes *m sg*, palillo de dientes *m*; **to fight — and nail** luchar a brazo partido; **to have a sweet —** ser goloso

toothed [tuθt] ADJ dentado

toothless [túθlɪs] ADJ desdentado

top [tɑp] N (of a mountain) cumbre *f*, cima *f*; (of a page) parte superior *f*; (of a jar) tapa *f*; (of a convertible) capota *f*; (of a table) superficie *f*; (of a tree) copa *f*; (toy) trompo *m*, peonza *f*; (blouse) blusa *f*; **he's at the — of his class** es el mejor de su clase; **at the — of one's voice** a voz en cuello; **filled up to the —** lleno hasta el tope; **from — to bottom** de arriba abajo; **on — of** encima de; ADJ (officer, floor) superior; (shelf, step) más alto; **—coat** abrigo *m*; **to be — dog** ir a la cabeza; **—**

dollar precio exorbitante *m*; — **hat** sombrero de copa *m*; —-**flight** de primera; —-**heavy** desbalanceado; —**most** superior; —-**notch** de primera; **at** — **speed** a velocidad máxima; VT (a tree) desmochar; (a list) encabezar; (a performance) superar; (a level) exceder; **to** — **off** (an action) rematar; (a tank) llenar hasta el tope; **that —s everything!** ¡eso es el colmo!

topaz [tópæz] N topacio *m*

topic [tápɪk] N tema *m*, materia *f*

topical [tápɪkəɫ] ADJ (of medicine) tópico; (current) de actualidad

topless [táplɪs] ADJ topless; — **swimsuit** monokini *m*

topple [tápəɫ] VT (knock over) derribar; (overthrow) derrocar; VI (fall) volcarse; (lose power) caer; **to — over** volcarse

topsy-turvy [tápsitɝvi] ADJ & ADV patas arriba

torch [tɔrtʃ] N antorcha *f*

torment [tɔ́rment] N tormento *m*; [tɔrmént] VT atormentar, martirizar

tornado [tɔrnéDo] N tornado *m*

torpedo [tɔrpíDo] N torpedo *m*; — **boat** torpedero *m*; VT torpedear

torpor [tɔ́rpɚ] N letargo *m*, torpor *m*

torque [tɔrk] N par de torsión *m*

torrent [tɔ́rənt] N torrente *m*

torrential [tɔréɲʃəɫ] ADJ torrencial

torrid [tɔ́rɪd] ADJ tórrido

torsion [tɔ́rʃən] N torsión *f*

torso [tɔ́rso] N torso *m*, tronco *m*

tortoise [tɔ́rDɪs] N tortuga *f*

tortuous [tɔ́rtʃuəs] ADJ tortuoso

torture [tɔ́rtʃɚ] N tortura *f*; VT torturar

torturous [tɔ́rtʃɚəs] ADJ torturante, torturador

toss [tɔs] VT (a ball, coin) tirar; (one's head) echar; (a salad) revolver; **to — aside** echar a un lado; VI (waves) cabecear; (in bed) dar vueltas; N (of coin, ball) tiro *m*; (of head) sacudida *f*

total [tódl̩] ADJ & N total *m*; — **amount** importe total *m*, montante *m*

totalitarian [totælɪtériən] ADJ totalitario

totter [táDɚ] VI tambalear(se), titubear

touch [tʌtʃ] VI/VT tocar; (move deeply) conmover, enternecer; (compare with) compararse con, igualar; (affect) afectar; **to — down** aterrizar; **to — off** provocar; **to — up** retocar; **to — upon** mencionar; N (contact) contacto *m*, roce *m*, toque *m*; (sense) tacto *m*; (knack) mano *f*; (slight amount) poquito *m*; —-**and-go** precario; **a woman's** — un toque femenino;

—**screen** pantalla táctil *f*; —**stone** piedra de toque *f*; —-**tone** de botones; **finishing** — toque final *m*; **to keep in** — **with** mantener(se) en contacto con

touching [tʌ́tʃɪŋ] ADJ conmovedor

touchy [tʌ́tʃi] ADJ hipersensible

tough [tʌf] ADJ (leather) fuerte, resistente; (fighter) duro, fuerte; (steak) duro, correoso; (situation) difícil; (neighborhood) bravo

toughen [tʌ́fən] VI/VT (leather) curtir(se); (meat) endurecer(se); (person) endurecerse

toughness [tʌ́fnɪs] N (of leather) resistencia *f*; (of a fighter, steak) dureza *f*; (of a situation) dificultad *f*; (of a neighborhood) lo bravo

toupee [tupé] N peluquín *m*

tour [tur] N (professional, artistic) gira *f*; (touristic) tour *m*, excursión *f*; (of a building) visita *f*; VI/VT (artistic, political) hacer una gira (por); (touristic) hacer un tour

tourism [túrɪzəm] N turismo *m*

tourist [túrɪst] N turista *mf*; — **class** clase turista / turística *f*

tournament [tɝnəmənt] N torneo *m*

tourniquet [tɝnɪkɪt] N torniquete *m*

tow [to] VT remolcar; N (pull) remolque *m*; (fiber) estopa *f*; —**rope** cuerda de remolque *f*; — **truck** remolque *m*, grúa *f*; **in** — a cuestas

toward, towards [təwɔ́rd(z)] PREP (in the direction of) hacia; (for) para; — **four o'clock** a eso de las cuatro; **to feel angry** — estar enojado con

towel [táuəɫ] N toalla *f*

tower [táuɚ] N torre *f*; VI elevarse; **to — over** dominar, descollar

towering [táuɚɪŋ] ADJ (tall) elevado, muy alto; (excessive) desmedido

town [taun] N (large) ciudad *f*; (small) pueblo *m*, localidad *f*; (downtown) centro *m*; — **hall** ayuntamiento *m*, municipio *m*; **out of** — de viaje

toxic [táksɪk] ADJ tóxico

toxin [táksɪn] N toxina *f*

toy [tɔɪ] N juguete *m*; — **poodle** caniche enano *m*; VI **to — with** (fiddle with) juguetear con; (consider) considerar

trace [tres] N (path, mark, footprint) huella *f*; (mark) rastro *m*, traza *f*; (vestige) vestigio *m*; (strap) tirante *m*; VT (a plan) trazar; (history) examinar; (an image) calcar; (a criminal) rastrear

trachea [trékiə] N tráquea *f*

track [træk] N (of a heel, animal) huella *f*; (of a wheel) rodada *f*; (for racing) pista *f*;

(path) senda *f*, sendero *m*; (of a railroad) vía *f*; (on a record) surco *m*; (of study) orientación *f*; — **and field** atletismo *m*; — **meet** encuentro de atletismo *m*; **to be off the** — estar descarrilado; **to keep — of** seguir el hilo de; VI/VT (a criminal) rastrear, seguir la pista de; (an aircraft, a student, progress) seguir; VI (wheels) estar alineado; (stylus) seguir los surcos; **to — down** perseguir; **to — in mud** traer lodo en los pies

tract [trækt] N (of land) terreno *m*; (political) octavilla *f*; (digestive) tubo *m*

traction [trǽkʃən] N tracción *f*

tractor [trǽktɚ] N tractor *m*; —-**trailer** tractocamión *m*

trade [tred] N (buying and selling) comercio *m*, trato *m*; (industry) industria *f*; (swap) canje *m*, cambio *m*; (manual labor) oficio *m*; (profession) profesión *f*; (people in a business) gremio *m*; —-**in** entrega como parte de pago *f*; —-**off** compensación *f*; —**mark** marca registrada *f*, marca de fábrica *f*; — **name** (of product) nombre comercial *m*; (of company) razón social *f*; — **school** escuela industrial *f*; — **union** sindicato *m*; VI/VT (buy and sell) comerciar, negociar; (exchange) canjear; (traffic) traficar; **to — in** entregar

trader [trédɚ] N comerciante *mf*; (at fairs) feriante *mf*; (of slaves) tratante *mf*

tradition [trədíʃən] N tradición *f*

traditional [trədíʃənəl] ADJ tradicional

traffic [trǽfɪk] N (of drugs) tráfico *m*; (of vehicles) tránsito *m*, tráfico *m*; — **light** semáforo *m*; VI traficar

tragedy [trǽdʒɪdi] N tragedia *f*

tragic [trǽdʒɪk] ADJ trágico

trail [treɫ] VI/VT (drag) arrastrar(se); (follow in a race) ir detrás (de); (track) seguir la pista (de), rastrear; VT (leave a trace) dejar una estela / un reguero de; **to — off** desvanecerse, apagarse; N (trace) rastro *m*, huella *f*; (path) trocha *f*, sendero *m*, senda *f*; (of smoke) estela *f*; (of blood) reguero *m*; — **bike** motocicleta de trail *f*

trailer [trélɚ] N (of a truck) remolque *m*; (house) caravana *f*; (of a film) sinopsis *f*, trailer *m*, avance *m*

train [tren] N (railroad) tren *m*; (of a dress) cola *f*; — **of thought** hilo de pensamiento *m*; VI/VT (worker) capacitar(se); (troops, athlete) adiestrar(se); *Am* entrenar(se); VT (an animal) amaestrar; (a child) educar, formar; (a cannon) apuntar; **to — on** (a camera, eye) enfocar

trainee [trení] N aprendiz -iza *mf*,

practicante *mf*

trainer [trénɚ] N (of animals) amaestrador -ora *mf*; (of workers, troops, athletes) entrenador -ora *mf*

training [trénɪŋ] N (of animals) amaestramiento *m*; (of workers, troops, athletes) adiestramiento *m*, entrenamiento *m*; (of children) educación *f*

trait [tret] N rasgo *m*, seña *f*

traitor [trédɚ] N traidor -ora *mf*

trajectory [trədʒéktəri] N trayectoria *f*

tramp [træmp] VT (trample) pisar; VI andar con pasos pesados; (roam, as a hobo) vagabundear; N (hobo) vagabundo -da *mf*; (promiscuous woman) *fam* fulana *f*; *Sp fam* golfa *f*

trample [trǽmpəɫ] VT pisotear; **to — on / over** pisotear, atropellar; **to — out** apagar de un pisotón

trampoline [trǽmpəlín] N trampolín *m*, cama elástica *f*

trance [træns] N trance *m*

tranquil [trǽŋkwɪɫ] ADJ tranquilo

tranquility [trænkwílɪDi] N tranquilidad *f*

tranquilizer [trǽŋkwɪlaɪzɚ] N tranquilizante *m*

transact [trænzǽkt] VT hacer, llevar a cabo

transaction [trænzǽkʃən] N transacción *f*, negocio *m*; —**s** actas *f pl*

transatlantic [trænzɪtlǽntɪk] ADJ transatlántico

transcend [trænsénd] VI/VT trascender

transcendence [trænséndəns] N trascendencia *f*

transcendental [trænsɛndéntɫ] ADJ trascendental, trascendente

transcribe [trænskráɪb] VT transcribir

transcript [trǽnskrɪpt] N transcripción *f*

transfer [trǽnsfɚ] VI/VT (bus, train) trasbordar; (a prisoner, worker) trasladar(se); VT (loyalty, rights, money) transferir; (property) traspasar; N (of loyalty, rights, money) transferencia *f*; (of a prisoner, worker) traslado *m*; (of property) traspaso *m*; (on a bus, train) trasbordo *m*; — **of ownership** traspaso de propiedad *m*

transferable [trænsfɚəbəɫ] ADJ transferible

transfix [trænsfíks] VT (paralyze) paralizar; (impale) traspasar, atravesar

transform [trænsfórm] VI/VT transformar(se)

transformation [trænsfɚméʃən] N transformación *f*

transformer [trænsfórmɚ] N transformador *m*

transfusion [trænsfjúʒən] N transfusión *f*

transgress [trænzgrés] VT transgredir; **to —**

against pecar contra; **to — the bounds of** traspasar los límites de

transgression [trænzgréʃən] N transgresión *f*, pecado *m*

transient [trǽnziənt] ADJ transeúnte, pasajero; N transeúnte *mf*, vagabundo -da *mf*

transistor [trænzístɚ] N transistor *m*

transit [trǽnzɪt] N tránsito *m*; **in —** en tránsito, de paso

transition [trænzíʃən] N transición *f*

transitive [trǽnzɪDɪv] ADJ transitivo

transitory [trǽnzɪtɔri] ADJ transitorio, pasajero

translate [trænzlét] VI/VT traducir

translation [trænzléʃən] N (rendering in different language) traducción *f*; (movement) translación *f*

translator [trǽnzleDɚ] N traductor -ora *mf*

transmission [trænzmíʃən] N transmisión *f*

transmit [trænzmít] VI/VT transmitir

transmitter [trænzmíDɚ] N transmisor *m*

transom [trǽnsəm] N travesaño *m*, montante *m*

transparency [trænzpérənsi] N transparencia *f*

transparent [trænspérənt] ADJ transparente; **to be —** traslucirse

transpire [trænspáɪr] VI (happen) ocurrir; (become known) descubrirse; VI/VT (perspire) transpirar

transplant [trænsplǽnt] VI/VT trasplantar; [trǽnsplænt] N trasplante *m*

transport [trænspórt] VT transportar, acarrear; [trǽnspɔrt] N (moving) transporte *m*, acarreo *m*; (airplane) avión de transporte *m*; (rapture) éxtasis *m*; (of freight) flete *m*

transportation [trænspɚtéʃən] N transporte *m*

transpose [trænspóz] VI/VT (letters) transponer; (a song) transportar

transsexual [trænsékʃuəł] ADJ & N transexual *mf*

transverse [trænsvɝ́s] ADJ transversal; (flute) transverso

transvestite [trænzvéstaɪt] N travestí *mf*, travesti *mf*, travestido -da *mf*

trap [træp] N trampa *f*; (for hunting) trampa *f*, cepo *m*; (under a sink) sifón *m*; **— door** trampilla *f*; VI/VT (to capture animals) cazar con trampa, atrapar; VT (to pinch) atrapar; (to pin) aprisionar

trapeze [træpíz] N trapecio *m*

trapezoid [trǽpəzɔɪd] N & ADJ trapezoide *m*

trash [træʃ] N basura *f*, desechos *m pl*; (people) *pej* gentuza *f*; **— can** cubo de basura *m*

trashy [trǽʃi] ADJ ordinario

trauma [trɔ́mə] N (physical) traumatismo *m*; (psychological) trauma *m*

traumatic [trəmǽDɪk] ADJ traumático

travel [trǽvəł] VI/VT viajar (por); VI (sound waves) propagarse; N (traveling) viajar *m*; **— agency** agencia de viajes *f*; **—s** viajes *m pl*

traveler [trǽvəlɚ] N viajero -ra *mf*; **—'s check** cheque de viajero *m*

traverse [trəvɝ́s] VI/VT atravesar, cruzar; (skiing) bajar en diagonal; N (crossbar) travesaño *m*; (crossing) travesía *f*

travesty [trǽvɪsti] N farsa *f*

tray [tre] N bandeja *f*

treacherous [trétʃɚəs] ADJ traicionero, alevoso

treachery [trétʃɚi] N traición *f*, alevosía *f*

tread [trɛd] VI/VT (trample) pisar, pisotear; VI (walk) andar, caminar; N (step) paso *m*; (on tire) banda de rodadura / rodaje *f*; (on shoe) dibujo *m*; **—mill** cinta rodante *f*

treason [trízən] N traición *f*

treasure [tréʒɚ] N tesoro *m*; **— hunt** búsqueda del tesoro *f*; VT atesorar

treasurer [tréʒərɚ] N tesorero -ra *mf*

treasury [tréʒəri] N tesorería *f*, tesoro *m*; **Secretary of the —** Ministro -tra de Hacienda *mf*

treat [trit] VI/VT tratar (de); **I —ed myself to ice cream** me di un festín de helado; N (pleasure) placer *m*; (gift) regalo *m*; **my —** yo invito

treatable [tríDəbəł] ADJ tratable

treatise [tríDɪs] N tratado *m*

treatment [trítmənt] N trato *m*, tratamiento *m*; (artistic handling) interpretación *f*

treaty [tríDi] N tratado *m*

treble [trébəł] ADJ (triple) triple; (of higher clef) de tiple; **— clef** clave de sol *f*; N tiple *m*; VI/VT triplicar

tree [tri] N árbol *m*; **— hugger** ecologista *mf*; **—top** copa de árbol *f*; **up a —** en aprietos

treeless [trílɪs] ADJ pelado, sin árboles

trek [trɛk] N expedición *f*; VI viajar con dificultad

tremble [trémbəł] VI temblar; N temblor *m*

tremendous [trɪméndəs] ADJ tremendo

tremor [trémɚ] N temblor *m*, sacudida *f*

tremulous [trémjələs] ADJ trémulo

trench [trɛntʃ] N (military) trinchera *f*; (for pipes) zanja *f*; (on sea floor) fosa *f*; **— coat** trinchera *f*, gabardina *f*

trend [trɛnd] N tendencia *f*

trendy [tréndi] ADJ de moda

trespass [tréspæs] N (illegal entry) entrada

ilegal *f;* (religious) deuda *f;* VI (enter illegally) entrar ilegalmente; **to — against** violar; (sin) pecar; **no —ing** prohibida la entrada

triage [triáʒ] N triaje *m,* clasificación *f*

trial [tráɪəɬ] N (testing) ensayo *m,* prueba *f;* (attempt) tentativa *f;* (affliction) aflicción *f;* (in a court of law) juicio *m,* proceso *m;* **— balloon** globo sonda *m;* **— by fire** prueba de fuego *f;* **— flight** vuelo de prueba *m;* **— run** ensayo *m,* prueba *f;* **by — and error** por ensayo y error

triangle [tráɪæŋgəɬ] N triángulo *m*

triangular [traɪǽŋgjələ˞] ADJ triangular

tribe [traɪb] N tribu *f*

tribulation [trɪbjəléʃən] N tribulación *f*

tribunal [traɪbjúnəɬ] N tribunal *m*

tributary [tríbjətɛri] ADJ & N tributario *m,* afluente *m*

tribute [tríbjut] N (tax) tributo *m;* (testimonial) homenaje *m*

triceps [tráɪsɛps] N triceps *m sg*

trick [trɪk] N (ruse) treta *f,* trampa *f,* trapisonda *f;* (magician's) truco *m;* (prank) broma *f;* (in cards) baza *f;* (of a prostitute) *fam* chapa *f;* **to be up to one's old —s** hacer de las suyas; **to play a — on someone** gastarle una broma a alguien; **to turn —s** prostituirse; *slang* hacer chapas; VT hacer trampa, engañar; **to — someone into something** hacer que alguien haga algo por medio de artilugios

trickery [tríkəri] N engaños *m pl,* argucias *f pl*

trickle [tríkəɬ] VI gotear; **to — in (out)** llegar (irse) de a poco; N goteo *m*

trickster [tríkstə˞] N embustero -ra *mf*

tricky [tríki] ADJ (artful) mañoso; (difficult) complicado

tricycle [tráɪsɪkəɬ] N triciclo *m*

trifle [tráɪfəɬ] N (worthless thing) fruslería *f,* nadería *f,* bobada *f;* (cheap purchase) bagatela *f;* (small sum) miseria *f;* VI **to — with** jugar con; **to — away** perder

trigger [trígə˞] N gatillo *m;* VT desencadenar; (suddenly) disparar

trill [trɪɬ] VI/VT (birds) trinar; (musical instrument) tremolar; (the r sound) pronunciar con vibración; N (of birds, etc.) trino *m;* (of the r sound) vibración *f*

trillion [tríljən] N billón *m*

trilogy [tríləʤi] N trilogía *f*

trim [trɪm] VT (adorn) adornar, guarnecer; (an edge) bordear; (fingernails, hair, threads) recortar; (hedge) podar; (airplane) equilibrar; (a wick) despabilar; ADJ (neat) cuidado; (slim) delgado; (fit) en buen

estado físico; N (embellishment) adorno *m;* (of sails) orientación *f;* (cutting of hair) recorte *m;* (cutting of hedge) poda *f;* (of an airplane) equilibrio *m*

trimming [trímɪŋ] N (act of cutting) recorte *m;* (on a uniform) orla *f,* ribete *m;* **—s** (embellishments) adornos *m pl;* (food) guarniciones *f pl;* (parts cut off) recortes *m pl*

Trinidad and Tobago [trínɪdædəntəbégo] N Trinidad y Tobago *f*

Trinidadian [trɪnɪdǽɒɪən] ADJ & N trinitense *mf*

trinket [tríŋkɪt] N chuchería *f,* baratija *f*

trio [trío] N trío *m*

trip [trɪp] N (journey, drug-induced condition) viaje *m;* (experience) experiencia *f;* (light step) paso ligero *m;* (accidental stumble) tropezón *m;* (throwing down) zancadilla *f;* VT (cause to stumble) hacer una zancadilla a; (cause to make error) confundir; (release a catch) soltar; (blow a fuse) hacer saltar; VI (stumble) tropezar; (skip) andar con paso ligero; (make a mistake) equivocarse; (hallucinate) viajar; (blow a fuse) saltar

triphthong [trípθɔŋ] N triptongo *m*

triple [trípəɬ] ADJ & N triple *m;* VI/VT triplicar

triplet [tríplɪt] N trillizo *m*

tripod [tráɪpɑd] N trípode *m*

trite [traɪt] ADJ trivial, trillado

triumph [tráɪəmf] N triunfo *m;* VI triunfar

triumphant [traɪʌ́mfənt] ADJ triunfante

trivial [tríviəɬ] ADJ trivial, baladí, fútil

trolley [tráli] N (electric bus) trole *m,* trolebús *m;* (on tracks) tranvía *m*

trombone [trámbon] N trombón *m*

troop [trup] N (of scouts) tropa *f;* (of soldiers) escuadrón *m;* (of tourists) horda *f;* **—s** tropas *f pl*

trophy [trófi] N trofeo *m*

tropic [trápɪk] N trópico *m*

tropical [trápɪkəɬ] ADJ tropical

trot [trɑt] VI trotar; VT hacer trotar; **to — out** sacar a relucir; N trote *m;* **the —s** *fam* cagalera *f*

trouble [trábəɬ] VT (make turbid) enturbiar; (afflict) aquejar; VI/VT (bother) molestar(se); (disturb) preocupar(se); N (problem) problema *m;* (difficulty) dificultad *f,* sinsabor *m;* (disturbance) disturbio *m;* (effort) molestia *f;* (ailment) enfermedad *f,* trastorno *m;* (mechanical breakdown) avería *f,* desperfecto *m;* **to be in —** estar en un aprieto; **it is not worth the —** no vale la pena; **—maker** agitador -ra *mf,* revoltoso -sa *mf;* **—shoot**

solucionar problemas; **—shooter** solucionador -ra *mf*, localizador -ra de averías *mf*; **to make** — causar problemas

trough [trɔf] N (for food) pesebre *m*, comedero *m*; (for water) abrevadero *m*, bebedero *m*; (of weather, on ocean floor) depresión *f*

trousers [tráuzɚz] N pantalones *m pl*

trousseau [trúso] N ajuar *m*

trout [traut] N trucha *f*

trowel [tráuəɫ] N (for mortar) llana *f*, paleta *f*; (for digging) desplantador *m*

truant [trúənt] N alumno -na que falta a clase sin permiso *mf*

truce [trus] N tregua *f*

truck [trʌk] N (vehicle) camión *m*; *Mex* troca *f*; (dealings) trato *m*; (vegetables) hortalizas *f pl*; **— driver** camionero -ra *mf*; *Mex* troquero -ra *mf*; VI/VT transportar en camión; *Mex* transportar en troca

trudge [trʌdʒ] VI andar con dificultad; N caminata difícil *f*

true [tru] ADJ verdadero; (story) verídico; (copy, translation) fiel; (well) a plomo; (wheel) alineado, centrado; **—-blue** leal; **—-false test** prueba de verdadero o falso *f*; **his dream came** — su sueño se hizo realidad

truly [trúli] ADV (surprisingly) verdaderamente; (sincerely) sinceramente; (actually) en realidad, realmente; (accurately) fielmente; **very — yours** su seguro servidor, atentamente

trumpet [trʌ́mpɪt] N trompeta *f*; VI/VT trompetear; (an elephant) barritar

trunk [trʌŋk] N (of tree, body) tronco *m*; (receptacle) baúl *m*; (of elephant) trompa *f*; (of a car) maletero *m*, *Mex* cajuela *f*; **—s** traje de baño *m*

trust [trʌst] N (responsibility) confianza *f*; (hope) esperanza *f*; (credit) crédito *m*; (charge) cargo *m*; (firm) trust *m*; (fund) fondo fideicomiso *m*; VI/VT (rely on) confiar en, fiarse de; VT (believe) creer; (hope) esperar

trustee [trʌstí] N (person holding property of another) fideicomisario -ria *mf*; (administrator) administrador -ra *mf*

trusteeship [trʌstíʃɪp] N (position of holding property) fideicomiso *m*; (administrative position) cargo de administrador *m*

trustful [trʌ́stfəɫ] ADJ confiado

trusting [trʌ́stɪŋ] ADJ confiado

trustworthy [trʌ́stwɚði] ADJ fidedigno, digno de confianza

trusty [trʌ́sti] ADJ leal

truth [truθ] N verdad *f*

truthful [trúθfəɫ] ADJ (account) verídico; (person) veraz

truthfulness [trúθfəɫnɪs] N veracidad *f*

try [traɪ] VT (attempt) tratar de, intentar; (test, taste) probar; (strain) poner a prueba; (put on trial) procesar, enjuiciar; **to — on** probarse; **to — one's luck** probar fortuna; **to — and** tratar de; **to — out** (test) probar; (for a team) presentarse para; **—out** prueba *f*; N intento *m*, tentativa *f*

trying [tráɪɪŋ] ADJ penoso

tryst [trɪst] N cita romántica *f*

T-shirt [tíʃɚt] N camiseta *f*

tub [tʌb] N (for bathing) bañera *f*; (for butter) envase *m*; (for washing) tina *f*

tuba [túbə] N tuba *f*

tube [tub] N tubo *m* (also electronic); (television) televisor *m*

tuberculosis [tubɚkjəlósɪs] N tuberculosis *f*

tubular [túbjəlɚ] ADJ tubular

tuck [tʌk] VT (stick in) meter; (make fold) alforzar; **to — in one's shirt** meter la camisa dentro del pantalón; **to — into bed** arropar; **to — something under one's arm** meterse algo bajo el brazo; N alforza *f*

Tuesday [túzde] N martes *m*

tuft [tʌft] N (of feathers) penacho *m*, copete *m*; (of hair) mechón *m*; (of plants) mata *f*

tug [tʌg] VI/VT (pull) tirar, jalar; (drag) arrastrar; **to — at** tironear; N tirón *m*; (boat) remolcador *m*

tuition [tuíʃən] N matrícula *f*

tulip [túlɪp] N tulipán *m*

tumble [tʌ́mbəɫ] VI (fall) caer; (collapse) venirse abajo; (do handsprings, etc.) dar volteretas; **to — down** rodar; **to — dry** secar en la secadora; **to — over** tropezarse; N (fall) caída *f*; (gymnastic trick) voltereta *f*

tumbler [tʌ́mblɚ] N (glass) vaso *m*; (person) acróbata *mf*

tummy [tʌ́mi] N barriguita *f*

tumor [túmɚ] N tumor *m*

tumult [túmʌɫt] N tumulto *m*

tumultuous [tumʌ́ɫtʃuəs] ADJ tumultuoso

tuna [túnə] N (fish) atún *m*, bonito *m*; (prickly pear) tuna *f*

tune [tun] N (melody) tonada *f*, aire *m*; (electronic adjustment) sintonía *f*; **to be in** — (in pitch) estar afinado; (adjusted) sintonizado; **to be out of** — estar desafinado; VT (engine) afinar; (musical instrument) afinar, templar; (radio) sintonizar; **to — in** sintonizar; **to — out** ignorar; **—-up** afinación *f*

tuner [túnɚ] N afinador -ra *mf*; (electronics)

sintonizador *m*
tungsten [tʌ́ŋstən] N tungsteno *m*
tunic [túnɪk] N túnica *f*
Tunisia [tuníʒə] N Túnez *m*
Tunisian [tuníʒən] ADJ & N tunesino -na *mf*
tunnel [tʌ́nəɫ] N túnel *m*; (for traffic) viaducto *m*; VI cavar; VT hacer un túnel
turban [tɝ́bən] N turbante *m*
turbine [tɝ́baɪn] N turbina *f*
turbocharger [tɝ́botʃɑrdʒɚ] N turbocompresor *m*
turbojet [tɝ́bodʒet] N turborreactor *m*
turbulent [tɝ́bjələnt] ADJ turbulento
turd [tɝd] N *vulg* zurullo *m*, mojón *m*
turf [tɝf] N (lawn) césped *m*; (peat) turba *f*; (track for horseraces) pista *f*; (territory) territorio *m*; VT cubrir con césped
Turk [tɝk] N turco -ca *mf*
turkey [tɝ́ki] N pavo *m*; — **vulture** buitre pavo *m*
Turkey [tɝ́ki] N Turquía *f*
Turkish [tɝ́kɪʃ] ADJ turco; — **bath** baño turco *m*
Turkmen [tɝ́kmən] ADJ & N turcomano -na *mf*
Turkmenistan [tɝkmɛnɪstǽn] N Turkmenistán *m*
turmoil [tɝ́mɔɪɫ] N confusión *f*, agitación *f*
turn [tɝn] VT (corner) doblar, dar vuelta; (wheel, key) girar, dar vuelta; (page) dar vuelta; (soil) labrar; (stomach) revolver; (ankle) torcerse; (a river) desviar; VI (change color) cambiar de color; (become) ponerse; (rotate) girar; (change direction) girar, dar la vuelta; (be nauseated) revolvérsele a uno; **to — against** volverse en contra de; **to — around** dar la vuelta, girar; **to — away** (face) volver; (eyes) apartar; (person) rechazar; **to — back** (return) volver; (a clock) atrasar; **to — down** (offer) rechazar; (radio) bajar; (request) rechazar; **to — in** (hand in / over) entregar; (go to bed) acostarse; **to — inside out** dar vuelta al revés; **to — into** convertir(se) en; **to — off** (light) apagar; (faucet) cerrar; (a road) salir de; (person in general sense) disgustar; (person in sexual sense) quitarle las ganas a alguien; **to — on** (light) encender, prender; (faucet) abrir; (person) excitar; **to — out** (light) apagar; (people) expulsar; (product) producir; **—out** concurrencia *f*; **to — out well** salir bien; **to — over** (car) volcar(se); (engine) arrancar; (thought, idea, etc.) dar vueltas a; (criminal, weapon, etc.) entregar; **—over** (of employees) renovación *f*; (of merchandise)

volumen *m*; (pastry) empanada *f*, pastelito *m*; (of a ball) pérdida *f*; **—pike** autopista *f*; **—stile** torniquete *m*, molinete *m*; **—table** plato giratorio *m*; **to — to** (have recourse to) acudir a, recurrir a; (become) volver(se); **to — up** aparecer; **to — up one's nose** desdeñar; **to — up one's sleeves** arremangarse; **to — upside down** dar vuelta; N (rotation) vuelta *f*, revolución *f*; (change of direction) giro *m*, vuelta *f*; (change in condition) cambio *m*; (curve) recodo *m*, curva *f*; (opportunity) turno *m*; **— of mind** actitud *f*; **— of phrase** giro *m*; **— signal** intermitente *m*; **at every —** a cada paso; **bad —** mala pasada *f*; **good —** favor *m*; **it's my —** me toca a mí; **to take —s** turnarse
turnip [tɝ́nɪp] N nabo *m*
turpentine [tɝ́pəntaɪn] N trementina *f*, aguarrás *m*
turquoise [tɝ́kɔɪz] N turquesa *f*
turret [tɝ́ɪt] N (small tower, gun tower) torreta *f*; (on a ship) torre *f*
turtle [tɝ́dḷ] N tortuga *f*; **—dove** tórtola *f*; **—neck** cuello vuelto *m*
tusk [tʌsk] N colmillo *m*
tutor [túdɚ] N profesor -ora particular *mf*; VI/VT dar clases particulares
Tuvalu [túvəlu] N Tuvalu *m*
Tuvaluan [tuvəlúən] ADJ & N tuvaluano -na *mf*
tuxedo [tʌksído] N esmoquin *m*
TV (television) [tíví] N tele *f*
twang [twæŋ] N (in music) tañido *m*; (of speech) nasalidad *f*; VI (vibrate) vibrar; VT hacer vibrar; VI/VT (speak nasally) ganguear
twangy [twǽŋi] ADJ gangoso
tweak [twik] VT (pinch) pellizcar; (adjust) ajustar; N (pinch) pellizco *m*; (adjustment) ajuste *m*
tweed [twid] N tweed *m*
tweezers [twízɚz] N pinzas *f pl*
twelve [twɛlv] NUM doce
twenty [twɛ́nti] NUM veinte
twerp [twɝp] N idiota *mf*, papanatas *mf sg*
twice [twaɪs] ADV dos veces
twig [twɪg] N ramita *f*
twilight [twáɪlaɪt] N crepúsculo *m*, ocaso *m*; **— zone** zona gris *f*
twin [twɪn] ADJ & N mellizo -za *mf*, gemelo -la *mf*; **— bed** cama individual *f*
twine [twaɪn] N cuerda *f*; VI/VT (twist) enroscar(se); (interlace) entrelazar(se)
twinge [twɪndʒ] N punzada *f*
twinkle [twíŋkəɫ] VI (star) titilar, parpadear; (eyes) brillar; N (of stars) titileo *m*,

parpadeo *m*; (of eyes) brillo *m*

twirl [twɝɫ] VI/VT girar, dar vueltas (a); N giro *m*, vuelta *f*; (of ice cream) espiral *m*

twist [twɪst] VI/VT torcer(se); (distort) tergiversar(se); (writhe) retorcer(se); (coil) enroscar(se); N (of an ankle) torcedura *f*; (in a road, coil) vuelta *f*; (unforeseen event) vuelta de tuerca *f*; (distortion) tergiversación *f*

twister [twístɚ] N tornado *m*

twitch [twɪtʃ] VI/VT crispar(se), mover(se); N (tic) tic *m*; (pang) punzada *f*; (tug) tirón *m*

twitter [twíDɚ] VI gorjear; N gorjeo *m*

two [tu] NUM dos; **—-bit** de chicha y nabo; **my — cents' worth** mi opinión *f*; **—-edged** de doble filo; **—-faced** (with two faces) de dos caras; (hypocritical) hipócrita, falso; **—-fisted** pendenciero; **—-way** de dos sentidos

tycoon [taɪkún] N magnate *mf*

type [taɪp] N tipo *m*, índole *f*; VI/VT (a letter) escribir a máquina, mecanografiar; VT (blood) determinar el grupo sanguíneo; **—script** texto escrito a máquina *m*; **to —set** componer; **to —write** escribir a máquina; **—writer** máquina de escribir *f*; **—writing** mecanografía *f*; **—written** escrito a máquina

typhoid [táɪfɔɪd] N tifoidea *f*; **— fever** fiebre tifoidea *f*, tifus *m*

typhoon [taɪfún] N tifón *m*

typical [típɪkəɫ] ADJ típico

typist [táɪpɪst] N mecanógrafo -fa *mf*

typographical [taɪpəgrǽfɪkəɫ] ADJ tipográfico; **— error** error de imprenta *m*, errata *f*

typology [taɪpúlədʒi] N tipología *f*

tyrannical [tɪrǽnɪkəɫ] ADJ tiránico

tyranny [tírəni] N tiranía *f*

tyrant [táɪrənt] N tirano -na *mf*

Uu

ubiquitous [jubíkwɪDəs] ADJ ubicuo

U-boat [júbot] N submarino *m*

udder [ʌ́Dɚ] N ubre *f*

UFO (**unidentified flying object**) [juɛfó] N OVNI *m*

Uganda [jugǽndə] N Uganda *f*

Ugandan [jugǽndən] ADJ & N ugandés -esa *mf*

ugliness [ʌ́glɪnɪs] N fealdad *f*

ugly [ʌ́gli] ADJ feo; (incident) deplorable;

(mood) de perros

uh-huh [ʌhʌ́] INTERJ sí

Ukraine [jukrén] N Ucrania *f*

Ukrainian [jukréniən] ADJ & N ucraniano -na *mf*

ulcer [ʌ́ɫsɚ] N úlcera *f*

ulterior [ʌɫtíriɚ] ADJ ulterior; **— motive** segunda intención *f*

ultimate [ʌ́ɫtəmɪt] ADJ (destination) último, final; (authority) final, máximo; (principle) fundamental; (vacation) perfecto; N súmmum *m*

ultimatum [ʌɫtəméDəm] N ultimátum *m*

ultralight [ʌ́ɫtrəlaɪt] ADJ & N ultraligero *m*

ultramodern [ʌɫtrəmáDɚn] ADJ ultramoderno

ultraviolet [ʌɫtrəváɪələt] ADJ & N ultravioleta *m*

umbilical cord [ʌmbíɫɪkəɫkɔrd] N cordón umbilical *m*

umbrella [ʌmbrélə] N paraguas *m sg*

umpire [ʌ́mpaɪr] N árbitro *m*; VI/VT arbitrar

unable [ʌnébəɫ] ADJ **to be — to** no poder

unaccented [ʌnǽksɛntɪd] ADJ sin acento

unacceptable [ʌnɪkséptəbəɫ] ADJ inaceptable

unaccustomed [ʌnəkʌ́stəmd] ADJ (not used to) no acostumbrado; (uncommon) insólito

unadulterated [ʌnədʌ́ɫtəreDɪd] ADJ puro

unaffected [ʌnəféktɪd] ADJ (sincere) natural, sincero; (unpretentious) sin afectación

unanimity [junənímɪDi] N unanimidad *f*

unanimous [junǽnəməs] ADJ unánime

unarmed [ʌnármd] ADJ desarmado

unassuming [ʌnəsúmɪŋ] ADJ modesto, sin pretensiones

unattached [ʌnətǽtʃt] ADJ (piece of paper) suelto; (person) soltero

unavoidable [ʌnəvɔ́ɪDəbəɫ] ADJ inevitable

unaware [ʌnəwér] ADJ inconsciente; ADV **to be — of** ignorar; **—s** sin darse cuenta

unbalanced [ʌnbǽlənst] ADJ desequilibrado

unbearable [ʌnbérəbəɫ] ADJ inaguantable, insoportable

unbeatable [ʌnbíDəbəɫ] ADJ imbatible

unbeaten [ʌnbítn̩] ADJ invicto

unbecoming [ʌnbɪkʌ́mɪŋ] ADJ (inappropriate) impropio; (unflattering) que no queda bien

unbelief [ʌnbɪlíf] N incredulidad *f*, descreimiento *m*

unbelievable [ʌnbɪlívəbəɫ] ADJ increíble

unbeliever [ʌnbɪlívɚ] N descreído -da *mf*

unbending [ʌnbéndɪŋ] ADJ inflexible

unbiased [ʌnbáɪəst] ADJ imparcial

unbounded [ʌnbáʊndɪd] ADJ ilimitado

unbridled [ʌnbráɪdld̩] ADJ desenfrenado

unbroken [ʌnbrókən] ADJ (intact) intacto; (not tamed) indomado; (uninterrupted) ininterrumpido

unbuckle [ʌnbákəɫ] VT desabrochar

unbutton [ʌnbátn̩] VI/VT desabotonar, desabrochar

uncalled-for [ʌnkɔ́ɫdfɔr] ADJ injustificado

uncanny [ʌnkǽni] ADJ inexplicable, misterioso

uncertain [ʌnsɝ́tn̩] ADJ incierto

uncertainty [ʌnsɝ́tn̩ti] N incertidumbre *f*

unchanged [ʌntʃénʤd] ADJ inalterado

uncharitable [ʌntʃǽrɪɒəbəɫ] ADJ duro, poco caritativo

uncivilized [ʌnsívəlaɪzd] ADJ incivilizado

uncle [ʌ́ŋkəɫ] N tío *m*; **to say —** darse por vencido

unclean [ʌnklín] ADJ (dirty) sucio; (impure) impuro

uncomfortable [ʌnkámfɚɒəbəɫ] ADJ incómodo

uncommon [ʌnkámən] ADJ (unusual) poco común; (extraordinary) extraordinario

uncompromising [ʌnkámprəmaɪzɪŋ] ADJ (intransigent) intransigente; (unfailing) incondicional

unconcerned [ʌnkənsɝ́nd] ADJ indiferente

unconditional [ʌnkəndíʃənəɫ] ADJ incondicional

unconscious [ʌnkánʃəs] ADJ inconsciente

unconstitutional [ʌnkɑnstɪtúʃənəɫ] ADJ inconstitucional

uncontrollable [ʌnkəntrólǝbəɫ] ADJ (movement) incontrolable; (urge, laughter) incontenible

unconventional [ʌnkənvénʃənəɫ] ADJ poco convencional

uncouth [ʌnkúθ] ADJ tosco

uncover [ʌnkávɚ] VI/VT descubrir(se); VI (remove bedcovers) destaparse

unctuous [ʌ́ŋktʃuəs] ADJ untuoso, zalamero

uncultivated [ʌnkʌ́ɫtəveɒɪd] ADJ (talent) inculto, no cultivado; (land) no cultivado

uncultured [ʌnkʌ́ɫtʃɚd] ADJ inculto

undaunted [ʌndɔ́ntɪd] ADJ impávido, intrépido

undecided [ʌndɪsáɪDɪd] ADJ indeciso

undeniable [ʌndɪnáɪəbəɫ] ADJ innegable

under [ʌ́ndɚ] PREP (below) bajo, debajo de, abajo de; (in a ranking) por debajo de; (less) menos de; **— the democrats** durante el mandato de los demócratas; **— a pseudonym** bajo un seudónimo; **— cost** a menos del costo/coste, por debajo del costo/coste; ADV (below) debajo, abajo; (less than) menos; **to be —** estar inconsciente

underage [ʌndɚéʤ] ADJ menor de edad; **— drinking** consumo de alcohol por menores de edad *m*

underarm [ʌ́ndɚɑrm] N axila *f*

underbrush [ʌ́ndɚbrʌʃ] N maleza *f*

underclass [ʌ́ndɚklæs] N subproletariado *m*

undercover [ʌndɚkávɚ] ADJ clandestino, secreto

undercut [ʌndɚkʌ́t] VT (undermine) socavar; (sell for less) vender por menos que

underdeveloped [ʌndɚdɪvéləpt] ADJ subdesarrollado

underdog [ʌ́ndɚdɔg] N el/la de abajo

underemployed [ʌndɚɛmplɔ́ɪd] ADJ subempleado

underestimate [ʌndɚéstəmet] VT (person) subestimar; (price) subvaluar

underfed [ʌndɚféd] ADJ desnutrido

underfoot [ʌndɚfút] ADJ (beneath the feet) bajo los pies; (in the way) estorbando

undergird [ʌndɚgɝ́d] VT reforzar

undergo [ʌndɚgó] VT (an operation) someterse a; (a change) experimentar, sufrir

undergraduate [ʌndɚgrǽʤuɪt] N estudiante de pregrado *mf*; **— course** programa de pregrado *m*

underground [ʌ́ndɚgraʊnd] ADJ (under the earth) subterráneo; (secret) clandestino; N resistencia *f*, grupo clandestino *m*; ADV (under the earth) bajo tierra; (secretly) en secreto

underhanded [ʌndɚhǽndɪd] ADJ (secret) secreto, solapado; (illicit) ilícito

underlie [ʌndɚláɪ] VI/VT subyacer (a)

underline [ʌ́ndɚlaɪn] VT subrayar

undermine [ʌndɚmáɪn] VT minar, menoscabar

underneath [ʌndɚníθ] PREP bajo, debajo de, abajo de; ADV debajo, abajo; N la parte inferior

underpants [ʌ́ndɚpænts] N (for men) calzoncillos *m pl*; (for women) *Sp* bragas *f pl*; *Mex* pantaletas *f pl*; *RP* bombacha *f*

undersecretary [ʌndɚsékrətɛri] N subsecretario -ria *mf*

undersell [ʌndɚséɫ] VT (to sell at a low price) malbaratar; (to sell cheaper than) vender a menos precio que

undershirt [ʌ́ndɚshɝt] N camiseta *f*

underside [ʌ́ndɚsaɪd] N parte inferior *f*

undersigned [ʌndɚsáɪnd] N abajofirmante *mf*, infrascrito -ta *mf*

underskirt [ʌ́ndɚskɝt] N enaguas *f pl*

understaffed [ʌndɚstǽft] ADJ falto de personal

understand [ʌndɚstǽnd] VI/VT comprender,

entender; **I — you're leaving** tengo entendido que te vas; **to — about** saber de∕entender de

understandable [ʌndɚstǽndəbəł] ADJ comprensible

understanding [ʌndɚstǽndɪŋ] N (comprehension) comprensión *f*, entendimiento *m*; (tolerance) comprensión mutua *f*; (agreement) acuerdo *m*; ADJ comprensivo

understate [ʌndɚstét] VT minimizar

understood [ʌndɚstúd] ADJ entendido; (implicit) sobreentendido

understudy [ándɚstʌDi] N suplente *mf*, sobresaliente *mf*; VI/VT servir de sobresaliente (para), suplir (a)

undertake [ʌndɚték] VT emprender, acometer; **to — to** comprometerse a

undertaker [ándɚtekɚ] N director -ra de funeraria∕pompas fúnebres *mf*, funerario -ria *mf*

undertaking [ʌndɚtékɪŋ] N empresa *f*

under-the-table [ándɚðətébəł] ADJ ilícito, bajo cuerda

undertone [ándɚton] N (low voice) voz baja *f*; (undercurrent) tónica *f*

undertow [ándɚto] N resaca *f*

underwater [ándɚwɔtɚ] ADJ submarino; [ándɚwɔ́tɚ] ADV por debajo del agua

underwear [ándɚwɛr] N ropa interior *f*

underweight [ándɚwet] ADJ de peso insuficiente

underworld [ándɚwɝłd] N (of criminals) hampa *f*; (netherworld) el más allá

underwrite [ándɚraɪt] VI/VT (finance) financiar; (sign) suscribir; (insure) asegurar

undesirable [ʌndɪzáɪrəbəł] ADJ indeseable

undisturbed [ʌndɪstɝ́bd] ADJ (unworried, uninterrupted) tranquilo; (unspoiled) virgen

undo [ʌndú] VT (reverse an action) deshacer; (unfasten) desabrochar, desabotonar; (destroy) destruir; (loosen hair) soltar

undoing [ʌndúɪŋ] N (reversal) deshacer *m*; (destruction) destrucción *f*, perdición *f*; (of buttons) desabrochar *m*

undone [ʌndʌ́n] ADJ (unfinished) sin terminar; (ruined) perdido; (unfastened) desabrochado; **to come —** (clothing) desabrocharse; (person) desquiciarse

undoubtedly [ʌndáʊDɪdli] ADV indudablemente, sin duda

undress [ʌndrés] VI/VT desnudar(se), desvestir(se)

undue [ʌndú] ADJ (inappropriate) indebido; (excessive) excesivo

undulate [ándʒəlet] VI/VT ondular

undying [ʌndáɪɪŋ] ADJ imperecedero, eterno

unearth [ʌnɝ́-θ] VT desenterrar

uneasiness [ʌnízinɪs] N (feeling) inquietud *f*, desasosiego *m*, desazón *f*; *Sp* grima *f*; (of peace) precariedad *f*; (of silence, situation) incomodidad *f*

uneasy [ʌnízi] ADJ (feeling) inquieto; (peace) precario; (silence) incómodo; (situation) molesto; (sleep) agitado

uneducated [ʌnédʒəkeDɪd] ADJ inculto, ignorante

unemployed [ʌnemplɔ́ɪd] ADJ (jobless) desocupado, desempleado, parado; (unused) ocioso

unemployment [ʌnemplɔ́ɪmənt] N desocupación *f*, desempleo *m*, paro *m*; **— compensation** seguro de paro *m*; *Sp* paro *m*

unending [ʌnéndɪŋ] ADJ interminable

unequal [ʌníkwəł] ADJ desigual; **to be — to a task** no ser capaz de cumplir una tarea

unequivocal [ʌnɪkwívəkəł] ADJ inequívoco, tajante

uneven [ʌnívən] ADJ (rough) irregular, accidentado; (inequitable) desigual; (not uniform) desparejo; (odd, of numbers) impar

uneventful [ʌnɪvéntfəł] ADJ sin incidente

unexpected [ʌnɪkspéktɪd] ADJ inesperado

unexpressive [ʌnɪksprésɪv] ADJ inexpresivo

unfailing [ʌnfélɪŋ] ADJ (inexhaustible) inagotable; (dependable) infalible

unfair [ʌnfér] ADJ (measure, price) injusto; (competition) injusto, desleal

unfaithful [ʌnféθfəł] ADJ infiel

unfamiliar [ʌnfəmíljɚ] ADJ (unknown) poco familiar, desconocido; (unacquainted) poco familiarizado

unfasten [ʌnfǽsən] VI/VT desabrochar(se), desprender(se)

unfavorable [ʌnfévɚəbəł] ADJ desfavorable

unfeeling [ʌnfílɪŋ] ADJ insensible

unfettered [ʌnféDɚd] ADJ desatado

unfinished [ʌnfínɪʃt] ADJ (matter) inacabado, inconcluso; (business) pendiente; (wood) sin terminar, sin barnizar; (task) inconcluso, sin terminar

unfit [ʌnfít] ADJ (unsuitable) no apto; (incapable) incapaz

unfold [ʌnfółd] VT (open out) desdoblar, desplegar; VI (happen) desarrollarse; (appear) extenderse; (reveal) revelarse

unforeseen [ʌnfɔrsín] ADJ imprevisto

unforgettable [ʌnfɚgéDəbəł] ADJ inolvidable

unfortunate [ʌnfɔ́rtʃənɪt] ADJ desgraciado, desafortunado, desventurado

unfounded [ʌnfáʊndɪd] ADJ infundado

unfriendly [ʌnfréndli] ADJ (forces) hostil; (person) antipático

unfurl [ʌnfɔ́ː+] VI/VT desplegar(se)

unfurnished [ʌnfɔ́ːnɪʃt] ADJ sin amueblar, desamueblado

ungainly [ʌngénli] ADJ (ungraceful) desgarbado, desmadejado; (clumsy) torpe

ungrateful [ʌngrétfə+] ADJ ingrato, desagradecido

unguarded [ʌngárdɪd] ADJ (incautious) descuidado, desprevenido; (unattended) sin vigilancia; (defenseless) indefenso; **an — moment** un momento de descuido

unhappiness [ʌnhǽpɪnɪs] N infelicidad f

unhappy [ʌnhǽpi] ADJ (sad) infeliz, desdichado, desgraciado; (dissatisfied) insatisfecho; (infelicitous) poco afortunado

unharmed [ʌnhármd] ADJ ileso

unhealthy [ʌnhélθi] ADJ (climate, food, lifestyle) malsano, insalubre; (complexion, obsession) enfermizo

unheard-of [ʌnhɔ́ː ɑv] ADJ inaudito, desconocido

unhinge [ʌnhíndʒ] VT desquiciar

unholy [ʌnhóli] ADJ (noise) infernal; (alliance) nefasto

unhook [ʌnhúk] VT (disentangle) desenganchar; (undo) desabrochar

unhurt [ʌnhɔ́ːt] ADJ ileso

uniform [júnəfɔrm] ADJ & N uniforme m

uniformity [junəfɔ́rmɪdi] N uniformidad f

unify [júnəfaɪ] VI/VT unificar(se)

unilateral [junəlǽɒəə+] ADJ unilateral

unimportant [ʌnɪmpɔ́rtṇt] ADJ insignificante, sin importancia

uninhabited [ʌnɪnhǽbɪdɪd] ADJ deshabitado

uninhibited [ʌnɪnhíbɪdɪd] ADJ desinhibido, desenfadado

uninspired [ʌnɪnspáɪrd] ADJ poco inspirado

unintelligible [ʌnɪntélɪdʒəbə+] ADJ ininteligible

union [júnjən] N unión f; (labor) sindicato m, gremio m; **— labor** mano de obra sindicalizada / agremiada f; **— leader** dirigente sindical mf

unionize [júnjənaɪz] VI/VT sindicar(se), agremiar(se)

unique [juník] ADJ único, singular; **that feature is — to the South** ese rasgo es peculiar del sur

unisex [júnəseks] ADJ unisex

unison [júnəsən] ADV LOC **in —** al unísono

unit [júnɪt] N unidad f

unite [junáɪt] VI/VT unir(se)

United Arab Emirates [junáɪdɪdǽɾəbémə‑ɪts] N Emiratos Árabes Unidos m pl

United Kingdom [junáɪdɪdkíŋdəm] N Reino Unido m

United States [junáɪdɪdstéts] N Estados Unidos m pl

unity [júnɪdi] N unidad f; (concord) unión f

universal [junəvɔ́ː‑sə+] ADJ universal; **— joint** acoplamiento universal de cardán m

universe [júnəvɔ‑s] N universo m

university [junəvɔ́ː‑sɪdi] N universidad f; **— degree** título universitario m

unjust [ʌndʒʌ́st] ADJ injusto

unjustifiable [ʌndʒʌstəfáɪəbə+] ADJ injustificable

unkempt [ʌnkémpt] ADJ (uncombed) desgreñado, despeinado; (messy) desaliñado

unkind [ʌnkáɪnd] ADJ antipático, poco amable

unknown [ʌnnón] ADJ desconocido; **— quantity** incógnita f; **it is —** se ignora

unlawful [ʌnlɔ́fə+] ADJ ilegal

unleaded [ʌnlédɪd] ADJ sin plomo

unleash [ʌnlíʃ] VT desatar

unless [ənlés] CONJ a menos que, a no ser que

unlicensed [ʌnláɪsənst] ADJ sin permiso, ilícito

unlike [ʌnláɪk] ADJ distinto, diferente; **he is — me** es diferente de mí; PREP a diferencia de; **how — you to forget!** ¡me extraña que te hayas olvidado!

unlikely [ʌnláɪkli] ADJ (improbable) improbable; (not realistic) inverosímil; (exotic) exótico; **I am — to come** es improbable que venga

unlimited [ʌnlímɪdɪd] ADJ ilimitado

unload [ʌnlód] VI/VT (take cargo from) descargar; VI (pour out one's feelings) desahogarse; (sell) liquidar

unlock [ʌnlák] VI/VT abrir con llave

unlucky [ʌnláki] ADJ (unfortunate) desafortunado; (ominous) aciago, funesto; **an — number** un número de mala suerte

unmanageable [ʌnmǽnɪdʒəbə+] ADJ (crisis, situation) inmanejable; (person) poco dócil

unmanned [ʌnmǽnd] ADJ (deprived of courage) achicado; (with no crew) no tripulado

unmarried [ʌnmǽrid] ADJ soltero

unmask [ʌnmǽsk] VI/VT desenmascarar(se)

unmistakable [ʌnmɪstékəbə+] ADJ inconfundible

unmitigated [ʌnmídɪgedɪd] ADJ absoluto

unmoved [ʌnmúvd] ADJ (unflinching) impasible; (indifferent) indiferente

unnatural [ʌnnǽtʃə‑ə+] ADJ (contrary to nature) no natural; (unloving) desnaturalizado; (monstrous) monstruoso; (affected) afectado

unnecessary [ʌnnésəseri] ADJ innecesario

unnoticed [ʌnnóDIst] ADJ inadvertido, desapercibido

unobserved [ʌnəbzɔ́-vd] ADJ inadvertido

unobtrusive [ʌnəbtrúsɪv] ADJ discreto

unoccupied [ʌnákjəpaɪd] ADJ (house) desocupado; (territory) no ocupado

unofficial [ʌnəfíʃəł] ADJ extraoficial, no oficial

unoriginal [ʌnəríʤənəł] ADJ poco original

unorthodox [ʌnɔ́rθədɑks] ADJ heterodoxo

unpack [ʌnpǽk] VT (a suitcase) deshacer, desempacar; (a carton) desembalar

unpaid [ʌnpéd] ADJ (debt) impagado, por pagar; (work) no remunerado

unpleasant [ʌnplézənt] ADJ desagradable

unpleasantness [ʌnplézəntnɪs] N (quality or state of being unpleasant) lo desagradable; (unpleasant episode) desavenencia *f*, disgusto *m*

unplug [ʌnplʌ́g] VI/VT desenchufar

unpopular [ʌnpápjələ-] ADJ (decision) impopular; **she was — in school** tenía pocos amigos en la escuela

unprecedented [ʌnprésɪdentɪd] ADJ sin precedente, inaudito

unpredictable [ʌnprɪdíktəbəł] ADJ impredecible, imprevisible

unpremeditated [ʌnpriméDɪteDɪd] ADJ impremeditado; (murder) sin premeditación

unprepared [ʌnprɪpérd] ADJ (surprised) desprevenido; (not ready) no preparado

unpretentious [ʌnprɪténʃəs] ADJ modesto, sin pretenciones

unprincipled [ʌnprínsəpəłd] ADJ sin escrúpulos, falto de principios

unprintable [ʌnpríntəbəł] ADJ impublicable

unproductive [ʌnprədʌ́ktɪv] ADJ improductivo

unprofessional [ʌnprəféʃənət] ADJ poco profesional

unprofitable [ʌnpráfiDəbəł] ADJ no rentable

unpublished [ʌnpʌ́blɪʃt] ADJ inédito, sin publicar

unqualified [ʌnkwáləfaɪd] ADJ (worker) *Sp* no cualificado; *Am* no calificado; (support) incondicional; (disaster) absoluto

unquestionable [ʌnkwéstʃənəbəł] ADJ incuestionable, indiscutible

unravel [ʌnrǽvəł] VI/VT (a rope) desenredar(se); (a sweater) destejer(se); (cloth) deshilachar(se); (a plan) deshacer(se); VT (a mystery) desentrañar

unreal [ʌnríəł] ADJ (not real) irreal;

(unbelievable) increíble

unreasonable [ʌnrízənəbəł] ADJ (excessive) exagerado; (irrational) irracional, poco razonable

unrecognizable [ʌnrɛkəgnáɪzəbəł] ADJ irreconocible

unrefined [ʌnrɪfáɪnd] ADJ (oil, sugar) no refinado; (behavior) inculto, grosero

unreliable [ʌnrɪláɪəbəł] ADJ (person) informal; (machine, information) *Sp* poco fiable; *Am* poco confiable

unrest [ʌnrést] N malestar *m*, agitación *f*

unroll [ʌnrół] VI/VT desenrollar(se)

unruly [ʌnrúli] ADJ (students) indisciplinado, revoltoso, díscolo; (country) ingobernable; (hair) rebelde

unsafe [ʌnséf] ADJ (uncertain) inseguro; (dangerous) peligroso

unsatisfactory [ʌnsæDɪsfǽktəri] ADJ no satisfactorio, insatisfactorio

unscrew [ʌnskrú] VT desatornillar, destornillar

unscrupulous [ʌnskrúpjələs] ADJ sin escrúpulos

unseasonable [ʌnsízənəbəł] ADJ impropio de la estación

unseat [ʌnsít] VT derribar

unseen [ʌnsín] ADJ invisible, oculto

unselfish [ʌnséłfɪʃ] ADJ desinteresado

unselfishness [ʌnséłfɪʃnɪs] N desinterés *m*

unsettled [ʌnsédł̣d] ADJ (situation) desordenado; (life) sin domicilio fijo; (wilderness) sin colonizar; (case) pendiente; (weather) variable

unsightly [ʌnsáɪtli] ADJ feo, antiestético

unskilled [ʌnskíłd] ADJ (not trained) inexperto; (not qualified) *Sp* no cualificado; *Am* no calificado

unsophisticated [ʌnsəfístɪkeDɪd] ADJ sencillo, no sofisticado

unsound [ʌnsáund] ADJ (argument) erróneo, falso; (body) enfermizo; (mind) demente; (foundation) poco sólido; (investment) poco seguro

unspeakable [ʌnspíkəbəł] ADJ indecible

unstable [ʌnstébəł] ADJ inestable

unsteady [ʌnstéDi] ADJ (walk) inseguro, inestable; (flame) tembloroso; (pulse) irregular

unsuccessful [ʌnsəksésfəł] ADJ sin éxito, infructuoso

unsuitable [ʌnsúDəbəł] ADJ (person) no apto; (place) inadecuado, inapropiado

unsuspected [ʌnsəspéktɪd] ADJ insospechado

untenable [ʌnténəbəł] ADJ insostenible

unthinkable [ʌnθíŋkəbəł] ADJ impensable

untidy [ʌntáɪDi] ADJ (dress) desaliñado,

desastrado; (room) desordenado

untie [ʌntái] VI/VT desatar(se), destrabar(se)

until [əntíɫ] PREP hasta; CONJ hasta que

untimely [ʌntáimli] ADJ (ill-timed) inoportuno; (premature) prematuro

untiring [ʌntáiriŋ] ADJ incansable, denodado

untold [ʌntóɫd] ADJ (riches) incalculable; (suffering) inaudito

untouched [ʌntʌ́tʃt] ADJ (not injured) ileso; (not affected) no afectado; **he left his dessert** — no tocó el postre

untrained [ʌntrénd] ADJ (worker) *Sp* no cualificado; *Am* no calificado; (animal) no amaestrado; (eye) inexperto

untried [ʌntráid] ADJ (untested) no probado, no ensayado; (not taken to trial) no juzgado

untrue [ʌntrú] ADJ (incorrect) falso; (unfaithful) infiel; (disloyal) desleal

untutored [ʌntútəɾd] ADJ (unschooled) sin instrucción; (unsophisticated) inculto

untwist [ʌntwíst] VT desenroscar

unused [ʌnjúzd] ADJ sin usar; (unaccustomed) no habituado

unusual [ʌnjúʒuəɫ] ADJ (infrequent) desacostumbrado, raro; (highly abnormal) inusitado, insólito

unvarnished [ʌnvárnɪʃt] ADJ (without varnish) sin barnizar; (straightforward) puro

unveil [ʌnvéɫ] VT (remove a veil) quitar el velo a; (reveal) descubrir

unwarranted [ʌnwɔ́rəntɪd] ADJ injustificado

unwelcome [ʌnwéɫkəm] ADJ (untimely) inoportuno; (unpleasant) desagradable; (poorly received) mal recibido

unwholesome [ʌnhóɫsəm] ADJ malsano

unwieldy [ʌnwíɫdi] ADJ poco manejable, difícil de manejar

unwilling [ʌnwílɪŋ] ADJ **to be — to** no estar dispuesto a

unwise [ʌnwáiz] ADJ imprudente

unwonted [ʌnwɔ́ntɪd] ADJ inusitado, inacostumbrado

unworthy [ʌnwɔ́ɾ-ði] ADJ indigno

unwrap [ʌnrǽp] VT desenvolver

unwritten [ʌnrítn̩] ADJ no escrito; (agreement) de palabra

unzip [ʌnzíp] VT abrir la cremallera

up [ʌp] ADV (position) arriba; (direction) hacia arriba; ADJ levantado, derecho, erecto; (assembled) armado; (finished) terminado, concluido; **—-and-coming** prometedor; **—-to-date** actualizado; **—-front** (paid in advance) inicial; (frank) franco; **he's — for reelection** se presenta para la reelección; **I'm feeling —** me siento

optimista; **I'm — for golf** tengo ganas de jugar al golf; **prices are —** los precios han subido; **that is — to you** queda en tus manos, es cosa tuya; **the children are already —** ya se levantaron los niños; **the moon is —** salió la luna; **the wheat is —** germinó el trigo; **time is —** se terminó el tiempo; **to be — on the news** estar al corriente de las noticias; **to be — to one's old tricks** hacer de las suyas; **— and down** de arriba para abajo; **— against** enfrentado con; **what's —?** ¿qué pasa? PREP **— the current** contra la corriente; **— the river** rio arriba; **— the street** calle arriba; **— to now** hasta ahora; N **—s and downs** altibajos *m pl*; VI **he — and went** agarró y se fue

upbeat [ʌ́pbit] ADJ optimista

upbringing [ʌ́pbrɪŋɪŋ] N crianza *f*

update [ʌpdét] VT actualizar

upend [ʌpénd] VI/VT (stand on end) poner(se) de punta; (defeat) derrotar

upgrade [ʌ́pgred] VT (facilities) mejorar; (computer) actualizar; N (facilities) mejora *f*; (computer) actualización *f*

upheaval [ʌphívəɫ] N trastorno *m*

uphill [ʌ́phíɫ] ADV cuesta arriba; [ʌ́phiɫ] ADJ penoso, arduo

uphold [ʌphóɫd] VT sostener, apoyar; (legal decision) refrendar

upholster [ʌphóɫstɚ] VT tapizar

upholstery [ʌphóɫstəri] N tapicería *f*

upkeep [ʌ́pkip] N mantenimiento *m*

uplift [ʌplíft] VT (physically) elevar; (spiritually) edificar

upload [ʌ́plod] VT cargar

upon [əpán] PREP sobre, encima de; **— arriving** al llegar; **once — a time** érase una vez

upper [ʌ́pɚ] ADJ (higher) superior; (high) alto; **to have the — hand** dominar, llevar la ventaja; N (of shoe) pala *f*; (of berth) litera superior *f*; **— class** clase alta *f*; **— crust** flor y nata *f*; **—case** mayúsculo; **—cut** gancho al mentón *m*; **—most** (highest) de más arriba; (most important) mayor; **—s** dentadura postiza superior *f*

uppity [ʌ́pɪdi] ADJ presumido

upright [ʌ́prait] ADJ (posture) erecto, erguido; (position) vertical; (just) íntegro, recto, cabal; **— piano** piano vertical *m*; N (column) montante *m*; (piano) piano vertical *m*; (post) poste *m*

uprightness [ʌ́praitnɪs] N rectitud *f*

uprising [ʌ́praizɪŋ] N alzamiento *m*, levantamiento *m*

uproar [ʌ́prɔr] N tumulto *m*, alboroto *m*, bulla *f*

uproarious [ʌpróriəs] ADJ (tumultuous) tumultuoso; (funny) graciosísimo

uproot [ʌprút] VT arrancar de raíz, desarraigar

upscale [ʌ́pskeɫ] ADJ de lujo

upset [ʌpsét] VI/VT (overturn) volcar(se), tumbar; (distress) trastornar(se), perturbar(se), alterar(se); VT (in sports) derrotar al favorito; ADJ (overturned) volcado; (ill) indispuesto; (distressed) disgustado, enojado; [ʌ́psɛt] N (overturning) vuelco *m*; (unexpected defeat) derrota inesperada *f*; (emotional state) trastorno *m*, disgusto *m*; (illness) malestar *m*

upshot [ʌ́pʃɑt] N consecuencia *f*

upside [ʌ́psaɪd] N (upper part) parte superior *f*; (positive prospect) lo bueno; **— down** al revés, patas arriba

upstage [ʌpstéʤ] VT eclipsar

upstairs [ʌpstérz] ADV (location) arriba, en el piso de arriba; (movement) (para) arriba; [ʌ́pstɛrz] ADJ de arriba; N piso de arriba *m*

upstart [ʌ́pstɑrt] N advenedizo -za *mf*

uptake [ʌ́ptek] N **quick on the —** listo; **slow on the —** duro de entendederas

uptight [ʌptáɪt] ADJ (nervous) nervioso; (conventional) estreñido

upturn [ʌ́ptɚn] N (prices) aumento *m*, subida *f*; (markets) tendencia alcista *f*

upward [ʌ́pwəd] ADV (toward a higher place) hacia arriba; **— of** más de; ADJ ascendente; N **— mobility** ascenso social *m*

uranium [jʊréniəm] N uranio *m*

urban [ɚ́bən] ADJ urbano; **— blight** tuguarización *f*; **— legend** leyenda urbana *f*; **— renewal** renovación urbana *f*; **— sprawl** expansión urbana *f*

urchin [ɚ́tʃɪn] N pilluelo -la *mf*, guaje -ja *mf*

urethra [jʊríθrə] N uretra *f*

urge [ɚʤ] VT (exhort) exhortar, urgir; (beg) rogar; (propose) propugnar; **to — on** animar; N impulso *m*, gana *f*

urgency [ɚ́ʤənsi] N urgencia *f*

urgent [ɚ́ʤənt] ADJ urgente

urinal [jʊ́rɪnəɫ] N urinario *m*, mingitorio *m*

urinary [jʊ́rənɛri] ADJ urinario

urinate [jʊ́rɪnet] VI/VT orinar

urine [jʊ́rɪn] N orina *f*

URL (Uniform Resource Locator) [jʊɑréɫ] N URL *m*

urn [ɚn] N urna *f*

urologist [jʊrálədʒɪst] N urólogo -ga *mf*

Uruguay [jʊ́rəgwaɪ] N Uruguay *m*

Uruguayan [jʊrəgwáɪən] ADJ & N uruguayo

-ya *mf*

us [ʌs] PRON nos; **she saw —** nos vio; **he came with —** vino con nosotros; **he gave it to —** nos lo dio (a nosotros)

USA (United States of America) [juɛsé] N EEUU *m sg/pl*

usable [júzəbəɫ] ADJ utilizable, aprovechable

usage [júsɪʤ] N uso *m*, costumbre *f*

use [juz] VT usar, utilizar (also exploit); (consume) gastar; (take advantage of) aprovecharse de; VI **I —d to smoke** antes fumaba, solía fumar; **to — up** gastar, agotar; [jus] N (application) uso *m*; (utilization) empleo *m*, utilización *f*, aprovechamiento *m*; (usefulness) utilidad *f*; **it is of no —** es inútil; **out of —** en desuso; **to have no — for** no soportar; **to make — of** usar, utilizar; **to put to — utilizar; what is the — of it?** ¿para qué sirve?

used [juzd] ADJ usado; [just] **to be — to** estar acostumbrado a

useful [júsfəɫ] ADJ útil

usefulness [júsfəɫnɪs] N utilidad *f*

useless [júslɪs] ADJ inútil, inservible

uselessness [júslɪsnɪs] N inutilidad *f*

user [júzɚ] N usuario -ria *mf*; **—-friendly** fácil de utilizar

usher [ʌ́ʃɚ] N acomodador -ra *mf*; VT conducir, acompañar; **to — in** (a person) acompañar; (an era) anunciar, marcar el comienzo

usual [júʒuəɫ] ADJ usual, habitual; (of clothes) de todos los días; **as —** como siempre; **she wasn't her — self** no era la de siempre; **the — thing** lo normal; **more than — más** que de costumbre

usurp [jusɚ́p] VI/VT usurpar

usury [júʒəri] N usura *f*

utensil [juténsəɫ] N utensilio *m*, útil *m*

uterus [júɒ꜔əs] N útero *m*

utilitarian [jutɪlɪtériən] ADJ utilitario

utility [jutílɪɒi] N utilidad *f*; (public service) empresa de servicio público *f*; **— furniture** muebles prácticos *m pl*; **— program** programa utilitario *m*; **— room** lavadero *m*

utilization [judlɪzéʃən] N utilización *f*

utilize [júdlaɪz] VT utilizar

utmost [ʌ́tmost] ADJ (extreme) sumo, extremo; (farthest) más distante; N máximo *m*; **he did his —** hizo cuanto pudo; **to the —** al máximo

utopia [jutópiə] N utopía *f*

utter [ʌ́dɚ] VT (emit) dar, proferir; (say) decir, pronunciar; (make circulate) poner en circulación; ADJ absoluto, completo

utterance [ÁDə-əns] N (of words) enunciado *m*; (of money) emisión *f*
uvula [júvjələ] N campanilla *f*, úvula *f*
Uzbek [úzbɛk] ADJ & N uzbeko -ka *mf*
Uzbekistan [ʊzbékɪstæn] N Uzbekistán *m*

Vv

vacancy [vékənsi] N (job) vacante *f*; (room in hotel) habitación libre *f*; **no —** completo
vacant [vékənt] ADJ (position) vacante; (expression) vacío; (seat, room) libre
vacate [véket] VI/VT (a room) desalojar, desocupar; (a contract) anular; (a position) dejar vacante
vacation [vekéʃən] N vacaciones *f pl*
vaccinate [vǽksənet] VI/VT vacunar
vaccination [væksənéʃən] N vacunación *f*
vaccine [væksín] N vacuna *f*
vacillate [vǽsəlet] VI vacilar
vacuum [vǽkjum] N vacío *m*; **— cleaner** aspiradora *f*; **—-packed** envasado al vacío; **— tube** tubo de vacío *m*; VI/VT aspirar, pasar la aspiradora
vagabond [vǽgəband] ADJ & N vagabundo -da *mf*
vagina [vədʒáɪnə] N vagina *f*
vagrancy [végrənsi] N vagancia *f*
vagrant [végrənt] ADJ & N vagabundo -da *mf*
vague [veg] ADJ vago, indistinto
vain [ven] ADJ (futile) vano, hueco; (proud of appearance) vanidoso; **in —** en vano
valentine [vǽləntaɪn] N (card) tarjeta del día de San Valentín *f*; (person) querido -da *mf*; **—'s Day** día de San Valentín *m*, día de los enamorados *m*
valet [vælé] N (manservant) criado *m*; (in a hotel) mozo de habitación *m*; (car parker) aparcacoches *m sg*
valiant [vǽljənt] ADJ valiente
valid [vǽlɪd] ADJ válido, valedero
validity [vəlídɪti] N validez *f*
valise [vəlíz] N maleta *f*, valija *f*
valley [vǽli] N valle *m*
valor [vǽlə-] N valor *m*, valentía *f*
valorous [vǽlə-əs] ADJ valeroso, valiente
valuable [vǽljəbəł] ADJ valioso, preciado; N **—s** objetos de valor *m pl*
valuation [væljuéʃən] N (value) valoración *f*; (appraisal) tasación *f*, valuación *f*
value [vǽlju] N valor *m*; VT valorar
valve [vǽłv] N (on mollusks) valva *f*

vamp [væmp] N vampiresa *f*; VT seducir
vampire [vǽmpaɪr] N vampiro *m*
van [væn] N camioneta *f*
vandal [vǽndḷ] N vándalo *m*
vane [ven] N (for weather) veleta *f*; (of a fan, windmill) aspa *f*; (of propeller) paleta *f*
vanilla [vənílə] N vainilla *f*
vanish [vǽnɪʃ] VI desaparecer, esfumarse
vanity [vǽnɪDi] N vanidad *f*; **— table** tocador *m*
vanquish [vǽnkwɪʃ] VT vencer
vantage [vǽntɪdʒ] N **— point** mirador *m*
Vanuatu [vɑnuátu] N Vanuatu *m*
Vanuatuan [vɑnuátuən] ADJ & N vanuatuense *mf*
vapor [vépə-] N vapor *m*, humo *m*
vaporize [vépə-aɪz] VI/VT vaporizar(se)
variable [vériəbəł] ADJ & N variable *f*
variance [vériəns] N discrepancia *f*, desacuerdo *m*; **to be at —** no concordar
variant [vériənt] N variante *f*
variation [veriéʃən] N variación *f*
varicose [vǽrɪkos] ADJ varicoso; **— veins** *Sp* varices *f pl*; *Am* várices *f pl*
varied [vérid] ADJ variado, vario
variegated [vériɪɡeDɪd] ADJ variopinto
variety [vəráɪɪDi] N variedad *f*
various [vériəs] ADJ vario
varnish [várnɪʃ] N barniz *m*, charol *m*; VT barnizar, charolar
varsity [vársɪDi] N equipo universitario *m*
vary [véri] VI/VT variar
vascular [vǽskjələ-] ADJ vascular
vase [ves] N jarrón *m*; (for flowers) florero *m*
vasectomy [vəséktəmi] N vasectomía *f*
Vaselineᵗᵐ [væsəlín] N vaselina *f*
vast [væst] ADJ vasto, inmenso
vastly [vǽstli] ADV radicalmente
vastness [vǽstnɪs] N inmensidad *f*
vat [væt] N tina *f*, barrica *f*
Vatican City [vǽDɪkənsíDi] N Ciudad del Vaticano *f*
vaudeville [vɔ́dvɪł] N vodevil *m*
vault [vɔ́łt] N (arched structure) bóveda *f*; (burial chamber) panteón *m*; (place for valuables) cámara acorazada *f*; (jump) salto *m*; VT (cover with a vault) abovedar; VI/VT saltar
VCR (videocassette recorder) [visiár] N video *m*; *Sp* vídeo *m*
VD (venereal disease) [vidí] N enfermedad venérea *f*
veal [vił] N ternera *f*; **— cutlet** chuleta de ternera *f*
veer [vir] VI/VT virar; N virada *f*
vegan [vígən] ADJ & N vegan *mf*
vegetable [védʒtəbəł] N (food) verdura *f*,

hortaliza *f*; (plant, paralyzed person)
vegetal *m*; — **garden** huerto *m*; (large)
huerta *f*; — **kingdom** reino vegetal *m*; —
oil aceite vegetal *m*
vegetarian [vɛdʒətériən] ADJ & N vegetariano
-na *mf*
vegetate [védʒətet] VI vegetar
vegetation [vɛdʒətéʃən] N vegetación *f*
vehemence [víəməns] N vehemencia *f*
vehement [víəmənt] ADJ vehemente
vehicle [víɪkəł] N vehículo *m*
veil [veł] N velo *m*; VT velar
vein [ven] N (blood vessel, style) vena *f*;
(small deposit of ore) veta *f*; (large deposit
of ore) filón *m*
veined [vend] ADJ veteado; (leaf) nervado
velocity [vəlásɪDi] N velocidad *f*
velvet [véłvɪt] N terciopelo *m*; ADJ (of velvet)
de terciopelo; (like velvet) aterciopelado
velvety [véłvɪDi] ADJ aterciopelado
vendetta [vɛndéDə] N vendetta *f*
vending machine [véndɪŋməʃin] N máquina
expendedora *f*
vendor [véndɚ] N vendedor -ora *mf*; (in a
stall) puestero -ra *mf*
veneer [vənír] N (layer of wood) chapa *f*;
(outward appearance) barniz *m*; VT chapar,
enchapar
venerable [vénɚəbəł] ADJ venerable
venerate [vénəret] VT venerar
veneration [vɛnəréʃən] N veneración *f*
venereal [vəníriəł] ADJ venéreo; — **disease**
enfermedad venérea *f*
venetian blind [vəníʃənbláɪnd] N veneciana
f
Venezuela [vɛnɪzwélə] N Venezuela *f*
Venezuelan [vɛnɪzwélən] ADJ & N
venezolano -na *mf*
vengeance [véndʒəns] N venganza *f*; **with a**
— (violently) con furia; (energetically) con
ganas
vengeful [véndʒfəł] ADJ vengativo
venison [vénəsən] N carne de venado *f*
venom [vénəm] N veneno *m*
venomous [vénəməs] ADJ venenoso
vent [vɛnt] N (outlet for air) ventilación *f*;
(opening of a volcano) chimenea *f*; **to**
give — **to anger** desahogar la ira; VI/VT
desahogar(se), descargar(se)
ventilate [véntłet] VI/VT ventilar(se)
ventilation [vɛntłéʃən] N ventilación *f*
ventilator [véntłeDɚ] N ventilador *m*
ventricle [véntrɪkəł] N ventrículo *m*
venture [véntʃɚ] N (adventure) aventura *f*;
(business enterprise) empresa *f*; — **capital**
capital de riesgo *m*; VI/VT aventurar(se),
arriesgar(se)

venue [vénju] N lugar *m*
veranda [vərǽndə] N porche *m*, terraza *f*
verb [vɝb] N verbo *m*
verbal [vɝ́bəł] ADJ (linguistic, related to
verbs) verbal; (not written) oral
verbatim [vɚbéDəm] ADJ textual; ADV
textualmente
verbiage [vɝ́biɪdʒ] N palabrerío *m*
verbose [vɚbós] ADJ verboso
verdict [vɝ́dɪkt] N veredicto *m*
verge [vɝdʒ] ADV LOC **on the** — **of** al borde
de, a punto de; VI **to** — **on** rayar en,
lindar con
verification [vɛrəfɪkéʃən] N verificación *f*,
comprobación *f*
verify [vérəfaɪ] VT verificar, constatar
veritable [vérɪDəbəł] ADJ verdadero
vermillion [vɚmíljən] ADJ & N bermellón *m*
vermin [vɝ́mɪn] N bichos *m pl*
vermouth [vɚmúθ] N vermú *m*
vernacular [vɚnǽkjəlɚ] ADJ vernáculo; N
(plain language) lengua vernácula *f*
versatile [vɝ́səDəł] ADJ versátil
verse [vɝs] N verso *m*; (stanza) estrofa *f*; (line
of poem) verso *m*; (in Bible) versículo *m*
versed [vɝst] ADJ versado
version [vɝ́ʒən] N versión *f*
versus [vɝ́səs] PREP contra; (in sports) versus
vertebra [vɝ́Dəbrə] N vértebra *f*
vertebrate [vɝ́Dəbrɪt] ADJ vertebrado
vertical [vɝ́Dɪkəł] ADJ vertical
vertigo [vɝ́Dɪgo] N vértigo *m*
very [véri] ADV muy; — **many** muchísimos;
— **much** muchísimo; **it is** — **cold today**
hace mucho frío hoy; ADJ (same) mismo;
(mere) mero
vessel [vésəł] N (container) vasija *f*; (duct)
vaso *m*; (ship) nave *f*
vest [vɛst] N chaleco *m*; VT conferir; —**ed**
interests intereses creados *m pl*
vestibule [véstəbjuł] N vestíbulo *m*, zaguán
m
vestige [véstɪdʒ] N vestigio *m*
vet [vɛt] N (veterinarian) veterinario -ria *mf*;
(veteran) veterano -na militar *mf*
veteran [véDɚən] ADJ & N veterano -na *mf*
veterinarian [vɛDɚənériən] N veterinario -ria
mf
veterinary [véDɚəneri] ADJ veterinario; —
medicine veterinaria *f*
veto [víto] N veto *m*; VT vetar
vex [vɛks] VT molestar, irritar
via [váɪə, víə] PREP (by way of) vía; (by means
of) por
viable [váɪəbəł] ADJ viable
vial [váɪəł] N ampolla *f*, frasco *m*
vibrate [váɪbret] VI/VT vibrar

vibration [vaɪbréʃən] N vibración *f*
vibrator [váɪbreɒɚ] N vibrador *m*
vicarious [vaɪkériəs] ADJ indirecto
vice [vaɪs] N vicio *m*
vice-president [váɪspréziɒənt] N vicepresidente -ta *mf*
viceroy [váɪsrɔɪ] N virrey *m*
viceroyalty [vaɪsrɔ́ɪəɫti] ADJ virreinato
vice versa [váɪsəvɚ́·sə] ADV viceversa
vicinity [vɪsínɪɒi] N vecindad *f,* cercanías *f pl,* aledaños *m pl*
vicious [víʃəs] ADJ (having vices) vicioso; (violent) violento, sanguinario; (evil) maligno, perverso; (malicious) malicioso; — **circle** círculo vicioso *m;* — **dog** perro fiero *m,* perro bravo *m*
vicissitude [vɪsísɪtud] N vicisitud *f,* peripecia *f*
victim [víktəm] N víctima *f*
victimize [víktəmaɪz] VT (make victim) victimizar; (dupe) estafar
victor [víktɚ] N vencedor -ora *mf*
victorious [vɪktóriəs] ADJ victorioso
victory [víktəri] N victoria *f*
video [víɒio] N *Am* video *m; Sp* vídeo *m;* —**cassette** *Am* video *m; Sp* vídeo *m;* —**cassette recorder** videocasete *m;* —**conference** videoconferencia *f;* — **game** videojuego *m;* —**tape** *Am* cinta de video *f; Sp* cinta de vídeo *f*
vie [vaɪ] VI competir; **to — for power** disputarse el poder
Vietnam [viɛtnám] N Vietnam *m*
Vietnamese [viɪtnəmíz] ADJ & N vietnamita *mf*
view [vju] N (field of vision) vista *f;* (opinion) opinión *f;* (panorama) visión panorámica *f;* —**point** punto de vista *m;* **in — of** en vista de; **to be within — of** estar a la vista; **with a — to** con el propósito de; VT (see) ver; (consider) enfocar
viewpoint [vjúpɔɪnt] N punto de vista *m*
vigil [víʤəɫ] N vigilia *f,* vela *f;* **to keep —** velar
vigilance [víʤələns] N vigilancia *f*
vigilant [víʤələnt] ADJ vigilante
vigor [vígɚ] N vigor *m,* pujanza *f,* dinamismo *m*
vigorous [vígɚəs] ADJ vigoroso
vile [vaɪɫ] ADJ (evil) vil, ruin; (foul, bad) pésimo
villa [vílə] N quinta *f,* casa de campo *f*
village [vílɪʤ] N aldea *f,* villa *f*
villager [vílɪʤɚ] N aldeano -na *mf*
villain [vílən] N villano -na *mf*
villainous [vílənəs] ADJ vil, villano
villainy [víləni] N villanía *f,* vileza *f*

vindicate [víndɪket] VT reivindicar, vindicar
vindictive [vɪndíktɪv] ADJ vengativo
vine [vaɪn] N (grapevine) vid *f;* (decorative) parra *f;* (stem) sarmiento *m;* (climbing plant) enredadera *f*
vinegar [vínɪgɚ] N vinagre *m*
vineyard [vínjɚd] N viña *f,* viñedo *m*
vintage [víntɪʤ] N (act or season of gathering grapes) vendimia *f;* (harvest of grapes) cosecha *f;* (year) año *m;* ADJ (wine) añejo; (classic) excelente; (old) antiguo, de colección; (typical) típico
vinyl [váɪnəɫ] N vinilo *m*
viola [vióɫə] N viola *f*
violate [váɪəlet] VT violar; (a law) violar, quebrantar
violation [vaɪəléʃən] N violación *f;* (traffic) infracción *f*
violence [váɪələns] N violencia *f*
violent [váɪələnt] ADJ violento
violet [váɪəlɪt] N (flower) violeta *f;* (color) violeta *m;* ADJ violeta *inv*
violin [vaɪəlín] N violín *m*
violinist [vaɪəlínɪst] N violinista *mf*
viper [váɪpɚ] N víbora *f*
virgin [vɚ́ʤɪn] ADJ & N virgen *f;* (uninitiated) no iniciado -da *mf;* — **Islands** Islas Vírgenes *f pl*
virginal [vɚ́ʤɪnəɫ] ADJ virginal
virile [vírəɫ] ADJ viril
virility [vərílɪɒi] N virilidad *f*
virtual [vɚ́tʃuəɫ] ADJ virtual; — **reality** realidad virtual *f*
virtue [vɚ́tʃu] N virtud *f*
virtuoso [vɚtʃuóso] ADJ & N virtuoso -sa *mf*
virtuous [vɚ́tʃuəs] ADJ virtuoso
virulent [vírələnt] ADJ virulento
virus [váɪrəs] N virus *m*
visa [vízə] N *Am* visa *f; Sp* visado *m*
vis-à-vis [vizavíʃ] PREP con respecto a
visceral [vísɚəɫ] ADJ visceral
viscous [vískəs] ADJ viscoso
vise [vaɪs] N tornillo de banco *m*
visible [vízəbəɫ] ADJ visible
Visigoth [vízɪgɒθ] N visigodo -da *mf*
vision [víʒən] N (sense, apparition) visión *f;* (eyesight) vista *f*
visionary [víʒəneri] ADJ & N visionario -ria *mf*
visit [vízɪt] VT visitar; (afflict) infligir; VI estar de visita; **to — with** charlar con; N (stay) visita *f;* (chat) charla *f*
visitation [vɪzɪtéʃən] N (apparition) visitación *f;* (punishment) castigo *m;* (parental right) régimen de visita *m*
visitor [vízɪɒɚ] N visita *f,* visitante *mf*
visor [váɪzɚ] N visera *f*

vista [vístə] N (visual) vista *f*; (mental) perspectiva *f*

visual [víʒuəɬ] ADJ visual

visualize [víʒuəlaɪz] VT visualizar, imaginar

vital [váɪdl] ADJ vital; — **signs** signos vitales *m pl*

vitality [vaɪtǽlɪDi] N vitalidad *f*

vitamin [váɪDəmɪn] N vitamina *f*

vituperation [vaɪtupəréʃən] N vituperación *f*, vituperio *m*

vivacious [vaɪvéʃəs] ADJ vivaz, vivaracho

vivacity [vaɪvǽsɪDi] N vivacidad *f*

vivid [vívɪd] ADJ vívido, vivo

vivisection [vívɪsɛkʃən] N vivisección *f*

vocabulary [vokǽbjəlɛri] N vocabulario *m*

vocal [vókəɬ] ADJ (musical) vocal; (outspoken) vociferante; — **cords** cuerdas vocales *f pl*

vocalic [vokǽlɪk] ADJ vocálico

vocation [vokéʃən] N vocación *f*

vociferous [vosífəəs] ADJ vociferante

vodka [vádkə] N vodka *m*

vogue [vog] N boga *f*, moda *f*; **in —** en boga, de moda

voice [vɔɪs] N voz *f*; — **mail** contestador automático *m*; VT expresar

void [vɔɪd] ADJ (devoid, empty) vacío; (not binding) nulo, inválido; **—ed check** cheque anulado *m*; — **of** desprovisto de; N vacío *m*; VT (intestines) evacuar; (a check) anular

volatile [váləd̶l] ADJ (liquid) volátil; (political situation) explosivo; (stock market) voluble; (temperament) cambiante

volcanic [vɑɬkǽnɪk] ADJ volcánico

volcano [vɑɬkéno] N volcán *m*

volition [vəlíʃən] N volición *f*; **of one's own —** por su propia voluntad

volley [váli] N (of firearms) descarga *f*; (of protests, arrows, stones) lluvia *f*; (of balls) volea *f*; VI/VT (bullets) descargar; (balls) volear; **—ball** voleibol *m*, balonvolea *m*

volt [voɬt] N voltio *m*

voltage [vóɬtɪʤ] N voltaje *m*

volume [váljəm] N volumen *m*, tomo *m*

voluminous [vəlúmɪnəs] ADJ voluminoso

voluntary [válənteri] ADJ voluntario

volunteer [vɑləntír] ADJ & N voluntario -ria *mf*; VI/VT (offer) ofrecer(se), brindar(se); *RP* comedir(se); VI (do volunteer work) trabajar de voluntario -ria

voluptuous [vəláptʃuəs] ADJ voluptuoso

vomit [vámɪt] N vómito *m*; VI/VT vomitar

voodoo [vúDu] N vudú *m*

voracious [vɔréʃəs] ADJ voraz

vortex [vɔ́rtɛks] N vórtice *m*

vote [vot] N (right, ballot) voto *m*; (act of voting) votación *f*; VI votar; VT (a bill)

aprobar; (a party) votar a / por; **to — do something** votar por hacer algo

voter [vóDə] N votante *mf*

vouch [vautʃ] VI **to — for** dar fe de, salir de fiador a, fiar a; VT **to — that** dar fe de que

voucher [váutʃə] N (receipt) comprobante *m*; (coupon) vale *m*; (person) fiador -ra *mf*, garante *mf*

vow [vau] N voto *m*; **to take a —** prometer; VT jurar

vowel [váuəɬ] N vocal *f*

voyage [vɔɪɪʤ] N viaje *m*; (by sea) travesía *f*; VI viajar

voyeur [vɔɪɚ] N mirón -ona *mf*

vulgar [váɬgə] ADJ (rude) ordinario, grosero, soez; (popular, vernacular) vulgar

vulgarity [vʌɬgǽrɪDi] N ordinariez *f*

vulnerable [váɬnəəbəɬ] ADJ vulnerable

vulture [váɬtʃə] N buitre *m*

vulva [váɬvə] N vulva *f*

Ww

wacky [wǽki] ADJ (person) chiflado; (idea) descabellado

wad [wɑd] N (for artillery, for filling) taco *m*; (ball) pelota *f*, pelotón *m*; (of money) rollo *m*, fajo *m*; VI/VT (a firearm) atacar; (a piece of paper) hacer una pelota (con)

waddle [wádl] VT anadear, andar como un pato; N anadeo *m*

wade [wed] VI andar por el agua; **to — through a book** leer con dificultad un libro

wafer [wéfə] N (cookie) oblea *f*; (in Catholic ritual) hostia *f*; (computer) lámina / oblea de silicio *f*

waffle [wáfəɬ] N *Sp* gofre *m*; *Am* wafle *m*; — **iron** *Sp* plancha para hacer gofres *f*; *Am* waflera *f*

waft [wæft] VI flotar; VT llevar por el aire; N (of air) ráfaga *f*; (of odor) ola *f*

wag [wæg] VI/VT menear(se), mover(se); **to — the tail** colear; N (movement) meneo *m*, movimiento *m*; (joker) bromista *mf*

wage [weʤ] N — **earner** asalariado -da *mf*; (paid daily) jornalero -ra *mf*; **—s** salario *m*; (daily) jornal *m*; — **scale** escala salarial *f*; VT (war) hacer; (battle) librar

wager [wéʤə] N apuesta *f*; VI/VT apostar

wagon [wǽgən] N (horsedrawn) carro *m*; (covered) carreta *f*; (toy) carrito *m*; **to fix**

someone's — vengarse de alguien; **to be on the** — abstenerse de las bebidas alcohólicas

wail [weɫ] VI lamentar; N lamento *m*

waist [west] N cintura *f*; (of garment) talle *m*; **—band** pretina *f*; **—coat** chaleco *m*; **—line** talle *m*, cintura *f*

wait [wet] VI/VT esperar; **to — for** esperar; **to — on** servir; **to — tables** trabajar de camarero -ra; N espera *f*; **to lie in — for** estar en / al acecho de

waiter [wéɖɚ] N camarero *m*, mozo *m*, mesero *m*

waiting [wéɖɪŋ] N espera *f*; **— list** lista de espera *f*; **— room** sala de espera *f*

waitress [wétrɪs] N camarera *f*, moza *f*, mesera *f*

waive [wev] VT (rights) renunciar a; (rule) hacer una excepción

waiver [wévɚ] N (of rights) renuncia *f*; (of rules) excepción *f*

wake [wek] VI/VT despertar(se); **to — up** despertar(se); N (at death) velatorio *m*; (of a ship) estela *f*, surco *m*; **in the — of** después de, detrás de; **—-up call** (in a hotel) llamada del servicio despertador *f*; (to action) llamada de atención *f*

wakeful [wékfəɫ] ADJ (awake) despierto; (insomniac) insomne

waken [wékən] VI/VT despertar(se)

Wales [weɫz] N Gales *m sg*

walk [wɔk] VI andar, caminar; (to a place) ir a pie; (go away) marcharse; **to — back** volver a pie; **to — down** bajar a pie; **to — in** entrar caminando; **to — out** (to go out) salir caminando; (to abandon) dejar; (to strike) declararse en huelga; **—out** huelga *f*; **to — up** subir a pie; VT (to cause to walk) hacer caminar; (to trace on foot) recorrer; **to — the streets** callejear; N (period of walking) paseo *m*, caminata *f*; (pace) paso *m*; (gait) andar *m*; **— of life** condición *f*; **to take a —** pasear, dar un paseo

walker [wɔ́kɚ] N (to aid walking) andador *m*; (one who walks) caminante *mf*; (in sports) marchista *mf*

walking [wɔ́kɪŋ] ADJ andante; **— papers** despido *m*; **— stick** bastón *m*

wall [wɔɫ] N (interior) pared *f*; (garden) muro *m*, tapia *f*; (fort) muralla *f*; (of silence) barrera *f*; **to have one's back to the —** estar entre la espada y la pared; **to drive someone up the —** sacar a alguien de quicio; **I was climbing the —s** me moría de aburrimiento; **—-to-—** de pared a pared; **—flower** alhelí *m*; **she was a**

—flower no la sacaban a bailar; **—paper** papel de empapelar *m*; **to —paper** empapelar

wallet [wáɫɪt] N cartera *f*

wallow [wáɫo] VI (roll) revolcarse; (indulge oneself) regodearse

walnut [wɔ́ɫnʌt] N nuez *f*; **— tree** nogal *m*

walrus [wɔ́ɫrəs] N morsa *f*

waltz [wɔɫts] N vals *m*; VI valsar

wand [wɑnd] N (rod) vara *f*; (magic) varita *f*

wander [wándɚ] VI/VT vagar (por), errar (por); **to — away** perderse; **my mind —s easily** me distraigo fácilmente

wanderer [wándərɚ] N vagabundo -da *mf*

wane [wen] VI menguar, flaquear; N mengua *f*; **to be on the —** ir menguando

wannabe [wánəbi] N imitador -ora *mf*

want [wɑnt] VI/VT (desire) querer; **he —s judgment** le falta juicio; **he's —ed in Texas** se lo busca en Texas; N (desire) deseo *m*; (lack) falta *f*; (scarcity) escasez *f*; **to be in —** estar necesitado; **— ad** (aviso) clasificado *m*

wanting [wántɪŋ] ADJ (lacking) falto; (deficient) deficiente

wanton [wántən] ADJ (immoderate) desenfrenado; (immoral) lascivo; (senseless, unprovoked) gratuito

war [wɔr] N guerra *f*; **— crime** crimen de guerra *m*; **— games** juegos de guerra *m pl*, simulacro de batalla *m*; **—head** ojiva *f*; **—ship** acorazado *m*; VI guerrear, hacer la guerra

warble [wɔ́rbəɫ] VI gorjear; N gorjeo *m*

warbler [wɔ́rblɚ] N (European) curruca *f*; (American) arañero *m*

ward [wɔrd] N (district) distrito *m*; (of a building) pabellón *m*; (of a tutor) pupilo -la *mf*; VI **to — off** resguardarse de, conjurar

warden [wɔ́rdn̩] N guardián -na *mf*; (of prison) alcaide *m*

wardrobe [wɔ́rdrob] N (room) guardarropa *m*; (furniture) ropero *m*, armario *m*; (garments) vestuario *m*, guardarropa *m*

warehouse [wérhaʊs] N almacén *m*, depósito *m*

wares [wɛrz] N mercancías *f pl*

warfare [wɔ́rfɛr] N guerra *f*

warlike [wɔ́rlaɪk] ADJ bélico

warm [wɔrm] ADJ (bath) caliente; (clothes) abrigado; (weather) caluroso; (colors, reception) cálido; **—-blooded** de sangre caliente; **—hearted** de buen corazón; **it is — today** hace calor hoy; VI/VT calentar(se); **to — over** recalentar; **to — up** calentar(se), templar(se); **—up**

precalentamiento *m*; **it —s my heart** me alegra el corazón; **she —ed to the idea** se entusiasmó con la idea

warmth [wɔrmθ] N calor *m*, tibieza *f*

warn [wɔrn] VI/VT (advise of danger) advertir; (urge to behave) amonestar

warning [wɔ́rnɪŋ] N (of danger) advertencia *f*; (of punishment) amonestación *f*

warp [wɔrp] N (yarn) urdimbre *f*; (curve) comba *f*, alabeo *m*; VI/VT (wood) combar(se), alabear(se); (character) deformar(se); **he has a —ed personality** tiene una personalidad retorcida

warrant [wɔ́rənt] N orden *f*; **a — for his arrest** una orden de arresto contra él; VT garantizar

warranty [wɔ́rənti] N garantía *f*; VT garantizar

warrior [wɔ́riɚ] N guerrero -ra *mf*

wart [wɔrt] N verruga *f*

wary [wéri] ADJ cauteloso, cauto; **to be — of** desconfiar de

wash [waʃ] VI/VT lavar(se); **to — down** bajar; **to — out** (clean) quitar; (demolish) destruir; **to — up** lavarse; **he was —ed away by the waves** fue arrastrado por las olas; **his excuse won't —** su excusa no va a colar; **the bottle was —ed up on the shore** la botella fue traída por el mar; **—-and-wear** de lava y pon, de no planchar; **—ed-up** fracasado; **—ed-out** desteñido; **—out** (erosion) derrubio *m*; (failure) fracaso *m*; N (act of washing) lavado *m*; (clothes to be washed) ropa para lavar *f*; (washed clothes) ropa lavada *f*; **—cloth** toallita para lavarse *f*; **—room** lavabo *m*, lavatorio *m*

washable [wáʃəbəł] ADJ lavable

washer [wáʃɚ] N (washing machine) máquina de lavar *f*; (ring) arandela *f*; **— woman** lavandera *f*

washing [wáʃɪŋ] N lavado *m*; **— machine** lavadora *f*, máquina de lavar *f*

wasp [wasp] N avispa *f*

WASP (white Anglo-Saxon Protestant) [wasp] N persona blanca, anglosajona y protestante *f*

waste [west] VI/VT (squander resources) malgastar, desperdiciar; **to — away** consumirse; VT (squander time) perder; (murder) liquidar; N (of resources) desperdicio *m*, malgasto *m*, derroche *m*; (of time) pérdida *f*; (refuse) desperdicios *m pl*, desechos *m pl*; **to go to —** desperdiciarse; **—paper basket** papelera *f*; **— products** productos de desecho *m pl*; **—land** tierra yerma *f*, páramo *m*; **to**

lay — to asolar

wasted [wéstɪd] ADJ (squandered) desperdiciado; (debilitated) consumido; (drunk) borracho

wasteful [wéstfəł] ADJ despilfarrador, gastador; (method) antieconómico

watch [watʃ] VI (look) mirar; (be careful) cuidarse; (be vigilant) vigilar; VT (view) mirar, ver; (observe) observar; (tend) cuidar; **— out for the cars!** ¡cuidado con los coches! **to — for** estar a la espera de; **to — over** proteger; N (timepiece) reloj *m*; (period of wakefulness) vela *f*, vigilia *f*; (vigilant guard) guardia *mf*; (duty shift) guardia *f*; (lookout) centinela *m*; **—band** pulsera *f*; **—dog** (type of dog) perro guardián *m*; (organization) organismo de control *m*; **—maker** relojero -ra *mf*; **—making** relojería *f*; **—man** vigilante *m*, sereno *m*; **—tower** atalaya *f*, torre de vigilancia *f*; **—word** (password) contraseña *f*; (motto) consigna *f*, lema *m*; **to be on the —** estar alerta; **to keep — on / over** vigilar a

watchful [wátʃfəł] ADJ alerta, atento

water [wɔ́Dɚ] N agua *f*; **—bed** cama de agua *f*; **—bird** ave acuática *f*; **— buffalo** búfalo de agua *m*; **—color** acuarela *f*; **—cress** berro *m*; **—fall** (small) cascada *f*; (large) catarata *f*; **—front** muelles *m pl*; **— heater** calentador de agua *m*; **— lily** nenúfar *m*; **—logged** empapado; **—melon** sandía *f*; **— pistol** pistola de agua *f*; **— power** energía hidráulica *f*; **— proof** (fabric) impermeable; (watch) sumergible; **to —proof** impermeabilizar; **—shed** vertiente *f*; **— ski** esquí acuático *m*; **to —-ski** hacer esquí acuático; **— softener** ablandador de agua *m*; **— sports** deportes acuáticos *m pl*; **—spout** (pipe) tubo de desagüe *m*; (tornado) tromba *f*; **— supply** abastecimiento de agua *m*; **— table** capa freática *f*; **—tight** hermético; **— vapor** vapor de agua *m*; **—way** vía navegable *f*; **my — broke** se me rompieron las aguas, se me rompió la fuente; VT (irrigate) regar; (dilute) aguar; VI/VT (animals) abrevar; **—ed-down** (with water) aguado; (simplified) simplificado; (softened) suavizado; **my eyes are —ing** me lloran los ojos; **it makes my mouth —** se me hace agua la boca

watery [wɔ́Dəri] ADJ (watered-down) aguado; (like water) acuoso; (boggy) húmedo

watt [wat] N vatio *m*

wattage [wáDɪdʒ] N vataje *m*

wave [wev] N (of radio) onda *f*; (of water,

heat, fashion) ola *f*; (of disgust, of people) oleada *f*; (with the hand) saludo *m*; **—length** longitud de onda *f*; VI/VT (flag) ondear; (hair) ondular(se); VI (greeting) saludar con la mano; **to — good-bye** decir adiós con la mano

waver [wévəʳ] VI (hesitate) vacilar, titubear; (falter) flaquear

wavy [wévi] ADJ ondeado, ondulado

wax [wæks] N cera *f*; (for seals) lacre *m*; **— paper** papel encerado *m*; VT encerar; (defeat) derrotar; VI crecer; **to — poetic** ponerse poético

way [we] N (road) camino *m*; (manner) modo *m*, manera *f*; **— in** entrada *f*; **— out** salida *f*; **to —lay** (wait in ambush) estar al acecho de; (attack) asaltar; (stop) detener; **—farer** caminante *mf*; **—-out** estrafalario; **—s** costumbres *f pl*; **—side** borde del camino *m*; **— through** paso *m*, pasaje *m*; **a long — off** muy lejos; **by — of London** por Londres; **by — of comparison** a modo de comparación; **by the —** a propósito; **in no — de** ningún modo; **on the — to** rumbo a; **to get out of the —** apartarse; **to go out of one's —** desvivirse por; **to look the other —** hacer la vista gorda; **to lead the — ir** a la cabeza; **to be in a bad —** hallarse mal de salud; **to give —** (yield) ceder; (break) quebrarse; **to get one's —** salirse con la suya; **to make — for** abrir paso para

wayward [wéwəd] ADJ (disobedient) desobediente; (willful) porfiado

we [wi] PRON nosotros -as *mf*

weak [wik] ADJ débil; (deficient) flojo; **— force** fuerza débil *f*; **—-kneed** achicado; **— sister** (coward) cobarde *mf*; **— link** parte más delgada del hilo *f*

weaken [wíkən] VI/VT debilitar(se), quebrantar(se)

weakling [wíklɪŋ] N alfeñique *m*

weakness [wíknɪs] N debilidad *f*, flaqueza *f*; (deficiency) flojedad *f*

wealth [wɛlθ] N riqueza *f*

wealthy [wélθi] ADJ rico, adinerado, pudiente

wean [win] VT destetar; **to — oneself of** quitarse el vicio de

weapon [wépən] N arma *f*

wear [wɛr] VT (have on) llevar, tener puesto; (dress in habitually) usar; VI/VT (waste away) desgastar(se); **to — away** gastar(se), desgastar(se); **to — down** (a person) agotar; (a pencil) desgastar; **to — off** perder efecto; **to — on** prolongarse; **to — out** (make unfit) gastar(se), degastar(se),

sobar(se); (expend) agotar; **it —s well** es duradero; N (use) gasto *m*; (clothes) ropa *f*; (durability) durabilidad *f*; (deterioration) desgaste *m*; **— and tear** desgaste *m*

weariness [wírinɪs] N cansancio *m*, fatiga *f*

wearing [wérɪŋ] ADJ (causing wear) desgastante; (causing fatigue) cansado

wearisome [wírisəm] ADJ fastidioso

weary [wíri] ADJ cansado, fatigado; VI/VT cansar(se), fatigar(se)

weasel [wízəɫ] N comadreja *f*

weather [wéðəʳ] N tiempo *m*; (storm) tempestad *f*; **—-beaten** desgastado/ curtido por la intemperie; **— bureau** oficina meteorológica *f*; **— conditions** condiciones atmosféricas *f pl*; **—man** meteorólogo *m*; **—proof** resistente a la intemperie; **—vane** veleta *f*; **it is fine —** hace buen tiempo; **to be under the —** estar enfermo; VI/VT gastar(se); (skin) curtir; **to — a storm** capear un temporal

weave [wiv] VT (cloth, basket) tejer, entretejer; (to put together) urdir, tramar; **to — together / into** entretejer, entrelazar; **to — one's way** zigzaguear; N tejido *m*

weaver [wívəʳ] N tejedor -ra *mf*

web [wɛb] N (of a spider) telaraña *f*; (of lies) sarta *f*; (membrane) membrana *f*; **—foot** (foot) pata palmada *f*; (animal) palmípedo *m*; **— page** página web *f*; **—site** sitio web *m*

wed [wɛd] VI/VT casarse (con); VT casar a

wedding [wédɪŋ] N boda *f*, casamiento *m*; **— day** día de boda *m*; **— dress** traje de novia *m*; **— ring** anillo de boda *m*

wedge [wɛdʒ] N cuña *f*; **to drive a — between** separar; VT acuñar, meter cuñas; **to be —d between** estar apretado entre

Wednesday [wénzde] N miércoles *m*

wee [wi] ADJ chiquito, pequeñito

weed [wid] N mala hierba *f*; (marijuana) hierba *f*; **—killer** herbicida *m*; VT deshierbar, escardar; **to — out** eliminar

week [wik] N semana *f*; **—day** día de semana *m*; **—end** fin de semana *m*; **a — from today** de aquí en una semana

weekly [wíkli] ADJ semanal; ADV semanalmente; N semanario *m*

weep [wip] VI llorar, lagrimear

weeping [wípɪŋ] ADJ lloroso; **— willow** sauce llorón *m*; N llanto *m*

weevil [wívəɫ] N gorgojo *m*

weigh [we] VI/VT pesar; (consider) ponderar, sopesar, barajar; **to — anchor** levar anclas; **to — down** agobiar, abrumar; **to — on one's conscience** pesar en la conciencia de uno

weight [wet] N (heaviness, importance) peso *m*; (for clocks, scales, barbells) pesa *f*; **—lifting** levantamiento de pesas *m*, halterofilia *f*; **— training** levantamiento de pesas *m*, halterofilia *f*; **—-watcher** persona a dieta *f*; **to put on —** engordar; **to lose —** adelgazar; VT (add weight) añadir peso; (in statistics) ponderar; **to — someone down** agobiarle a uno

weightless [wétlɪs] ADJ ingrávido

weighty [wéɖi] ADJ importante

weird [wírd] ADJ (strange) extraño; (supernatural) misterioso

weirdo [wírɖo] N bicho raro *m*, ente *m*

welcome [wɛ́łkəm] N bienvenida *f*; ADJ bienvenido; **—!** ¡bienvenido! **— mat** alfombrilla *f*, felpudo *m*; **— rest** descanso agradable *m*; **you are —** no hay de qué, de nada; **you are — here** estás en tu casa; **you are — to use it** a tus órdenes; VT (friendly) dar la bienvenida, acoger; (unfriendly) recibir

weld [wɛłd] VI/VT soldar(se); N soldadura *f*

welfare [wɛ́łfɛr] N (good fortune) bienestar *m*; (public assistance) asistencia social *f*; **— state** estado de bienestar *m*

well [wɛł] ADV bien; **— then** pues bien; **—-being** bienestar *m*; **—-bred** bien educado; **—-defined** bien definido; **—-done** (steak) bien cocido; (a task) bien hecho; **—-fed** bien alimentado; **—-fixed** adinerado; **—-founded** bien fundamentado; **—-groomed** bien arreglado, aseado; **—-heeled** adinerado; **—-informed** bien informado; **—-known** (of a fact) bien sabido; (of a person) bien conocido, notorio; **—-made** bien hecho; **—-meaning** bien intencionado; **—-nigh** casi, muy cerca de; **he is — over fifty** tiene mucho más de cincuenta años; **—-off** adinerado, acomodado; **—-read** leído, educado; **—-rounded** completo; **—-spoken** bien hablado; **—-to-do** adinerado; **all is —** todo está bien; INTERJ ¡bueno! ADJ (healthy) bien de salud, sano; N (of water, oil) pozo *m*; (of staircase) caja *f*; **—spring** fuente *f*, manantial *m*; VI **tears —ed up in her eyes** se le llenaron los ojos de lágrimas

wellness [wɛ́łnɪs] N (health) salud *f*; (health care) medicina preventiva *f*

welsh [wɛłʃ] VI **to — on** (a debt) no pagar; (a promise) no cumplir

Welsh [wɛłʃ] ADJ & N galés -esa *mf*

welt [wɛłt] N verdugón *m*

west [wɛst] N (cardinal point) oeste *m*; (hemisphere) occidente *m*; **— Berlin** Berlín occidental *m*; **— Indies** Antillas *f pl*; **— wind** viento del oeste *m*; ADV (direction) hacia el oeste; (location) al oeste

western [wɛ́stə⋅n] ADJ occidental, del oeste; N película del oeste *f*

westerner [wɛ́stə⋅nə⋅] N occidental *mf*

westward [wɛ́stwə⋅d] ADV hacia el oeste; ADJ occidental

wet [wɛt] ADJ (drenched) mojado; (damp, rainy) húmedo; **—back** *offensive* espalda mojada *mf*, mojado -da *mf*; **— blanket** aguafiestas *mf sg*; **— dream** sueño húmedo *m*; **—land** humedal *m*; **— nurse** nodriza *f*; **— paint** pintura fresca *f*; **— suit** traje de buzo *m*; VI/VT mojar(se); (dampen) humedecer(se)

wetness [wɛ́tnɪs] N humedad *f*

whack [hwæk] VI/VT golpear, pegar; **to — off** (cut) cortar; (masturbate) *vulg* hacer(se) una paja; N golpazo *m*; *Sp* hostia *f*; **to take a — at** hacer un intento de; **out of —** descompuesto, averiado

whale [hwel] N ballena *f*; VI pescar ballenas

wharf [hwɔrf] N muelle *m*, embarcadero *m*

what [hwɑt] INTERR PRON, N & ADJ qué; **— did you say?** ¿qué dijiste? **— books did you want?** ¿qué libros querías? **—'s the matter?** ¿qué pasa? **— for?** ¿para qué? **and —not** y demás; REL PRON lo que; **come — may** venga lo que venga; **take — books you need** toma los libros que necesites; **any place —soever** en cualquier lugar; ADJ qué; **— happy children!** ¡qué niños más felices! **— luck!** ¡qué buena suerte! INTERJ cómo, qué; **so —?** ¡y qué?

whatever [hwɑtévə⋅] PRON lo que; **— do you mean?** ¿qué demonios quieres decir? **do it, — happens** hazlo, pase lo que pase; **— you may think** pienses lo que pienses; ADJ **any person —** una persona cualquiera / cualquier persona; **no money —** nada de dinero; INTERJ ¡lo que sea!

wheat [hwit] N trigo *m*; **— germ** germen de trigo *m*

wheel [hwił] N (disc) rueda *f*; (of cheese) horma *f*; (for pottery) torno *m*; (for steering a car) volante *m*; (on a ship) timón *m*; **—barrow** carretilla *f*; **—base** batalla *f*, paso *m*; **—chair** silla de ruedas *f*; **—s** coche *m*; VT (a round object) hacer rodar; (a person, bicycle, wheelchair) empujar; VI **to — out** sacar rodando; **to — in** entrar rodando; **to — around** girar sobre los talones

wheeze [hwiz] N resuello ruidoso *m*; VI resollar

when [hwɛn] ADV & CONJ cuando; INTERJ, ADV & N cuándo

whenever [hwɛnévə·] CONJ — **I see him** cada vez que lo veo; ADV — **you arrive tomorrow** cuando llegues

where [hwɛr] ADV, N & INTERR PRON dónde *m*; (direction) adónde; CONJ donde; (direction) adonde

whereabouts [hwérəbaʊts] N paradero *m*; INTERR ADV dónde

whereas [hwɛrǽz] CONJ mientras que; (in preambles) visto que, considerando que

whereby [hwɛrbái] ADV por lo cual

wherefore [hwérfɔr] ADV por lo cual

wherein [hwɛrín] ADV en donde

whereof [hwɛráv] REL PRON de que; INTERR PRON de qué

whereupon [hwɛrəpán] ADV después de lo cual

wherever [hwɛrévə·] ADV dondequiera que

wherewithal [hwérwɪðɔł] N medios *m pl*, fondos *m pl*

whet [hwɛt] VT (sharpen) afilar; (stimulate) estimular; —**stone** piedra de afilar *f*

whether [hwéðə·] CONJ — **we like it or not** nos guste o no nos guste; **I doubt — we can do it** dudo (de) que lo podamos hacer; **he asked — I was coming** me preguntó si venía

which [hwɪtʃ] INTERR PRON cuál(es); — **do you want?** ¿cuál(es) quieres? REL PRON que; **the apple — I just bought** la manzana que acabo de comprar; **the book — I was talking about** el libro del que / cual estaba hablando; **that — you don't know can hurt you** lo que no sabes puede hacerte daño; INTERR ADJ qué, cuál(es) de; — **house is it?** ¿qué casa es? ¿cuál de las casas es?

whichever [hwɪtʃévə·] PRON & ADJ (no matter which) cualquiera (que); — **you choose, you'll regret it later** elijas el que elijas, te arrepentirás después; (anyone that) el que / la que; **choose — you like** elije el que quieras

whiff [hwɪf] N (waft) soplo *m*; (odors, scandal) bocanada *f*, tufillo *m*; **to take a** — oler

while [hwaɪł] N rato *m*; **a short** — un ratito; **a short — ago** hace poco; CONJ (during) mientras; (whereas) mientras que; (even though) aunque; VT **to — away** pasar

whim [hwɪm] N capricho *m*, antojo *m*

whimper [hwímpə·] VI/VT lloriquear, gimotear; N lloriqueo *m*, gimoteo *m*

whimsical [hwímzɪkəł] ADJ caprichoso, antojadizo

whine [hwaɪn] VI (whimper) gemir; (complain) quejarse; N (whimper) gemido *m*; (complaint) quejido *m*

whiner [hwáɪnə·] N llorón -ona *mf*, quejica *mf*

whiny [hwáɪni] ADJ quejoso, quejica, ñoño

whip [hwɪp] N azote *m*, látigo *m*, rebenque *m*; VT (hit with a whip) azotar, fustigar; (spank) zurrar, dar una paliza; (beat to a froth) batir; (defeat) vencer; **to** — **out** sacar; **to** — **up** (prepare) preparar rápidamente; (incite) incitar

whipping [hwípɪŋ] N zurra *f*, paliza *f*; — **cream** crema para batir *f*

whir [hwɝ] VI zumbar; N zumbido *m*

whirl [hwɝ̃ł] VI girar; **to** — **around** arremolinarse; **my head** —**s** me da vueltas la cabeza; N (rotation) giro *m*; (of water) remolino *m*; —**pool** remolino *m*; —**wind** torbellino *m*, remolino de viento *m*; —**wind tour** gira relámpago *f*; **my head is in a** — me da vueltas la cabeza; **to give it a** — probarlo

whisk [hwɪsk] VT (sweep) barrer; (beat) batir; **to** — **away** llevarse de prisa; VI **to** — **by** pasar rápidamente; N (broom) escobilla *f*; (beater) batidor *m*

whisker [hwískə·] N (hair of beard) pelo de la barba *m*; (sideburn) patilla *f*; (of animals) bigote *m*

whiskey, whisky [hwíski] N whisky *m*

whisper [hwíspə·] VI/VT (voices) cuchichear, secretear; (leaves, water) susurrar; N (voices) cuchicheo *m*; (leaves, water) susurro *m*; **to talk in a** — cuchichear en voz baja

whistle [hwísəł] VI/VT silbar; (loud) chiflar; (in protest) rechiflar; VI (referee, train) pitar; **to** — **for someone** llamar a uno con un silbido; N (sound) silbido *m*; (loud sound) chiflido *m*; (of a referee) pitido *m*; (instrument) silbato *m*, pito *m*; — **blower** acusador -ora *mf*

white [hwaɪt] ADJ (of color, ethnicity) blanco; — **blood cell** glóbulo blanco *m*; — **bread** pan blanco *m*; —-**bread** soso; —**caps** cabrillas *f pl*; —-**collar** administrativo, de cuello blanco; — **gold** oro blanco *m*; — **hair** cana *f*; — **lie** mentirilla *f*; — **noise** ruido blanco *m*; — **trash** *offensive* sureño -ña blanco -ca pobre *mf*; **to** —**wash** (paint) blanquear, enjalbegar; (cover up) encubrir; —**wash** (paint) lechada *f*; (cover-up) encubrimiento *m*; N blanco *m* (also ethnicity); (of egg) clara *f*

whiten [hwaɪtn̩] VI/VT blanquear(se), emblanquecer

whiteness [hwáitnɪs] N blancura *f*

whitish [hwáɪdɪʃ] ADJ blancuzco, blanquecino

whittle [hwídl]] VI/VT tallar; **to — away** ir gastando; **to — down expenses** reducir los gastos

whiz [hwɪz] VI zumbar; **to — by** pasar zumbando; N (sound) zumbido *m*; (ace) as *m*; VT hacer zumbar; **— kid** niño -ña prodigio *mf*

who [hu] REL PRON quien(es); INTERR PRON quién(es); **he —** el que

whoa [hwo] INTERJ (to express amazement) ¡jo! (to stop a horse) ¡so!

whoever [huévə˞] REL PRON (whatever person) quienquiera que, el que; INTERR PRON (who) quién

whole [hoɫ] ADJ (complete) completo, íntegro; (unbroken) entero; (uninjured) ileso; **—-grain** integral; **—hearted** sincero; **—heartedly** de todo corazón; **— milk** leche entera *f*; **— note** redonda *f*; **—sale** (in bulk) al por mayor; (massive) masivo; **—saler** comerciante al por mayor *mf*, mayorista *mf*, almacenista *mf*; **—sale slaughter** matanza *f*; **—-wheat** integral; **the — day** todo el día; **to go — hog** tirar la casa por la ventana; N todo *m*; (for amounts) totalidad *f*; **—sale** venta al por mayor *f*, mayoreo *m*; **as a —** en su totalidad; **on the —** en general; ADV **—sale** al por mayor; VI/VT **to —sale** vender al por mayor

wholesome [hóɫsəm] ADJ sano

whom [hum] REL PRON a quien(es); INTERR PRON a quién(es); **for / with —** para / con quien

whoop [hwup] N (shout) grito *m*; (gasp) respiración convulsiva *f*; VI (person) gritar; (owl) ulular; **to — it up** armar jaleo

whopper [hwápə˞] N (large thing) cosa enorme *f*; (lie) mentira *f*, trola *f*

whopping [hwápɪŋ] ADJ enorme

whore [hor] N *offensive* puta *f*; **—house** *vulg* casa de putas *f*

whose [huz] REL PRON cuyo; **the man — son is here** el hombre cuyo hijo está aquí; INTERR PRON de quién; **— book is this?** ¿de quién es este libro?

why [hwaɪ] ADV & CONJ por qué; **that's the reason — he left** es por eso que se fue; N porqué *m*; INTERJ **—, of course!** ¡pero, claro!

wick [wɪk] N mecha *f*, pabilo *m*

wicked [wíkɪd] ADJ malvado, perverso

wickedness [wíkɪdnɪs] N maldad *f*, perversidad *f*

wicker [wíkə˞] N mimbre *m*; **— chair** silla de mimbre *f*

wide [waɪd] ADJ (broad) ancho; (of great range) amplio; (spacious) vasto, extenso; **— apart** muy apartados; **—-awake** muy despierto, despabilado; **— body** avión de fuselaje ancho *m*; **—-eyed** ojiabierto, con los ojos bien abiertos; **— of the mark** lejos del blanco; **—-open** abierto de par en par; **—spread** (over a wide area) extendido; (among many people) generalizado; **to open —** (a door) abrir de par en par; (one's mouth) abrir bien; **two feet —** dos pies de ancho

widely [wáɪdli] ADV **it is — known that** es bien sabido que; **he is a — known artist** es un artista muy conocido; **he is — read** es muy leído; **— different versions** versiones muy diferentes

widen [wáɪdn̩] VI/VT ensanchar(se), ampliar(se)

widow [wído] N viuda *f*

widower [wídoə˞] N viudo *m*

width [wɪdθ] N ancho *m*, anchura *f*

wield [wiɫd] VT (power) ejercer; (tool) manejar; (weapon) blandir, esgrimir

wife [waɪf] N esposa *f*, mujer *f*, señora *f*

wig [wɪg] N peluca *f*

wiggle [wígəɫ] VI/VT (hips) menear(se); (toes) mover(se); N (of hips) meneo *m*; (of toes) movimiento *m*; **— room** flexibilidad *f*

wigwam [wígwɑm] N tienda indígena *f*

wild [waɪɫd] ADJ (animals, savages) salvaje, bravío, bronco; (plant) silvestre; (party) desenfrenado; (conduct) alocado; (storm, temperament) violento; (hair) desordenado; (look) extraviado, desencajado; (enthusiasm) delirante; **— boar** jabalí *m*; **— card** comodín *m*; **—cat** gato montés *m*; **—-eyed** de mirada extraviada, con los ojos desencajados; **—fire** fuego arrasador *m*; **—flower** flor silvestre *f*; **— goose chase** búsqueda inútil *f*; **—life** fauna *f*; **I'm just — about Mary** estoy loco por María; **not in your —est dreams** ni lo pienses; **to drive someone —** volver loco a alguien; **to talk —** decir disparates; N **—s** regiones salvajes *f pl*

wilderness [wíɫdə˞nɪs] N (near mountains) monte *m*; (desert) desierto *m*; (jungle) jungla *f*

wile [waɪɫ] N artimaña *f*, treta *f*

will [wɪɫ] VT (use will power) conseguir a

fuerza de voluntad; (bequeath) legar, dejar; V AUX **if you —** si quieres; **she — come** va a venir, vendrá; **this motorcycle — go 100 mph** esta motocicleta puede hacer 100 millas por hora; **in spite of everything, he — not stop complaining** a pesar de todo, no deja de quejarse; **she — just sit for hours doing nothing** se pasa horas sentada sin hacer nada; **that — do** basta; N (wish) voluntad *f*; (testament) testamento *m*; **—power** fuerza de voluntad *f*; **at —** a discreción, a voluntad

willful, wilful [wílfəł] ADJ testarudo, porfiado

willies [wíliz] N escalofríos *m pl*

willing [wílɪŋ] ADJ dispuesto, voluntarioso

willingly [wílɪŋli] ADV de buena gana, gustoso

willingness [wílɪŋnɪs] N buena voluntad *f*, buena gana *f*

willow [wílo] N sauce *m*

wilt [wɪłt] VI/VT (plant) marchitar(se); VI (person) languidecer

wily [wáɪli] ADJ astuto, artero

wimp [wɪmp] N pelele *m*

win [wɪn] VI/VT ganar; VT (support, fame, affection) ganarse; (victory) alcanzar, conseguir; **to — out** ganar, triunfar; **to — over** conquistar; **a —-— situation** una situación beneficiosa para ambas partes

wince [wɪns] VI hacer una mueca; N mueca *f*

winch [wɪntʃ] N cabrestante *m*, torno *m*

wind [wɪnd] N (air) viento *m*; (gas) gases *m pl*; **—bag** charlatán -ana *mf*; **—breaker**ᵗᵐ cazadora *f*; **—fall** ganancia inesperada *f*; **— instrument** instrumento de viento *m*; **—mill** molino de viento *m*; **—pipe** tráquea *f*; **—shield** parabrisas *m sg*; **—shield wiper** limpiaparabrisas *m sg*; **—sock** manga de viento *f*; **—surfing** windsurf *m*; **— tunnel** túnel aerodinámico *m*; **to get — of** enterarse de; **to break —** ventosear; **to catch one's —** recobrar el aliento; ADJ **—ward** de barlovento; ADV **—ward** hacia / a barlovento; [waɪnd] VT enrollar; (watch) dar cuerda a; VI (take a bending course) serpentear; **to — around** enrollarse; **to — down** (relax) tranquilizarse; (come to a conclusion) irse terminando; **to — up** (string) enrollar; (a clock) dar cuerda; (a project) completar; (in jail) acabar; N (turn) vuelta *f*; (bend) recodo *m*; **—up** conclusión *f*

winding [wáɪndɪŋ] ADJ sinuoso; **— staircase** escalera de caracol *f*

window [wíndo] N (in building) ventana *f*; (in car, plane) ventanilla *f*; (in a shop) escaparate *m*; *Am* vidriera *f*; **—pane** cristal *m*, vidrio *m*; **— shade** visillo *m*; **—sill** alféizar *m*

windy [wíndi] ADJ ventoso; **it is —** hace / hay viento

wine [waɪn] N vino *m*; **— cellar** bodega *f*; **—glass** copa *f*; **—grower** viticultor -ora *mf*, viñatero -ra *mf*; **— industry** industria vinícola *f*; **—skin** odre *m*; **— tasting** cata de vinos *f*

winery [wáɪnəri] N bodega *f*

wing [wɪŋ] N ala *f* (also of building, table, army); **— nut** tuerca (de) mariposa / palomilla *f*; **—span / spread** envergadura *f*; **—tip** extremo del ala *m*; **in the —s** en los bastidores; **under one's —** al amparo de alguien; **to take —** levantar vuelo; VI volar; VT (transport) transportar por aire; (wound slightly) herir en el ala / brazo; **to — it** improvisar

wink [wɪŋk] VI/VT guiñar; **to — approval** guiñar en aprobación; **to — at** hacer la vista gorda; N guiño *m*, guiñada *f*; **I didn't sleep a —** no pegué un ojo

winner [wínɚ] N ganador -ora *mf*

winning [wínɪŋ] ADJ (successful) ganador, vencedor; (charming) atractivo; **—s** ganancias *f pl*

wino [wáɪno] N borracho -cha *mf*

winter [wíntɚ] N invierno *m*; **— weather** clima invernal *m*; VI invernar

wintry [wíntri] ADJ invernal

wipe [waɪp] VT (sweat, tears) enjugar; (wet surfaces) secar; (dry surface) limpiar; **to — away** enjugar; **to — off** limpiar; **to — out** aniquilar; **to — up** limpiar

wiper [wáɪpɚ] N limpiaparabrisas *m sg*

wire [waɪr] N (filament) alambre *m*; (telegram) telegrama *m*; **by —** por telégrafo; **— fence** alambrado *m*; **—tap** intervención del teléfono *f*, pinchazo *m*; **to —tap** intervenir un teléfono, pinchar un teléfono; VT (an appliance) alambrar; (a house) electrificar; VI/VT (a message) telegrafiar; (money) girar; **to — together** atar con alambre

wired [waɪrd] ADJ (installed) alambrado; (tied) atado con alambre; (electrified) electrificado; (enthusiastic) sobreexcitado

wireless [wáɪrlɪs] ADJ inalámbrico

wiring [wáɪrɪŋ] N cableado *m*

wiry [wáɪri] ADJ (skinny) nervudo; (like wire) crespo

wisdom [wízdəm] N (moral) sabiduría *f*; (scholarly) saber *m*; **— tooth** muela del juicio *f*

wise [waɪz] ADJ (discerning) sabio; (prudent) sensato, prudente; (erudite) erudito; **—ass** sabihondo -da *mf*; **—crack** broma *f*, chiste *m*; **— guy** sabihondo *m*; **the Three — Men** los Tres Reyes Magos; N **in no —** de ningún modo; VI **to — up** avisparse

wish [wɪʃ] VT desear; **I — you were here** ojalá estuvieras aquí; **I — you the best** te deseo lo mejor; **to — for** pedir; **to — upon a star** pedir un deseo; N deseo *m*; **to make a —** pedir un deseo; **best —es** saludos

wishy-washy [wíʃiwaʃi] ADJ indeciso

wistful [wístfəł] ADJ (pensive) pensativo; (nostalgic) nostálgico

wit [wɪt] N (intelligence) agudeza *f*, ingenio *m*; (verbal humor) gracejo *m*, sal *f*, chispa *f*; (person) persona aguda *f*, persona ingeniosa *f*; **to be at one's —s' end** no saber qué más hacer; **to live by one's —s** vivir de su ingenio; **to lose one's —s** perder el juicio; **to use one's —s** valerse de su ingenio

witch [wɪtʃ] N bruja *f*; **—craft** brujería *f*; **—hunt** cacería de brujas *f*

with [wɪθ, wɪð] PREP con; **rice — chicken** arroz con pollo *m*; **the man — glasses** el hombre de gafas; **I left my son — Mary** dejé a mi hijo al cuidado de María; **to be — it** está al día; **— me** conmigo; **— you** contigo, con usted

withdraw [wɪðdrɔ́ł] VI/VT retirar(se)

withdrawal [wɪðdrɔ́əł] N (of troops) retirada *f*; (from public office) alejamiento *m*; (from a bank) *Am* retiro *m*; *Sp* retirada *f*; **— (symptoms)** síndrome de abstinencia *m*

wither [wíðɚ] VI/VT (of a plant) marchitar(se); (of a person) consumir(se); **she —ed him with a look** lo fulminó con la mirada

withhold [wɪθhóɫd] VT (approval) negar; (funds) retener; (truth) ocultar

withholding tax [wɪθhóɫdɪŋtæks] N impuesto deducido del salario *m*

within [wɪðín] PREP dentro de; **— five miles** a menos de cinco millas; ADV dentro, adentro

without [wɪðáʊt] PREP sin; **— my seeing him** sin que yo lo vea; ADV fuera, afuera

withstand [wɪθstǽnd] VI/VT resistir

witness [wítnɪs] N (person) testigo *mf*; (testimony) testimonio *m*; **to bear —** atestiguar; VT (see) presenciar; (sign) firmar como testigo

witticism [wídɪsɪzem] N ocurrencia *f*

witty [wídi] ADJ ocurrente, dicharachero

wizard [wízɚd] N (sorcerer) mago *m*, brujo *m*, hechicero *m*; (genius) genio *m*

wobble [wábəł] N bamboleo *m*, tambaleo *m*; VI/VT tambalear(se), bombolear(se)

woe [wo] N aflicción *f*; **— is me!** ¡pobre de mí!

woeful [wófəł] ADJ lamentable

wok [wɑk] N wok *m*

wolf [wʊłf] N lobo *m*; **— spider** araña lobo *f*

woman [wúmən] N mujer *f*; **a —'s touch** un toque femenino; **women's lib(eration)** movimiento de liberación femenina *m*; **women's rights** derechos de la mujer *m pl*

womanhood [wúmənhʊd] N (condition) condición de mujer *f*; (group of women) las mujeres *f pl*

womanizer [wúmənaɪzɚ] N mujeriego *m*

womankind [wúmənkaɪnd] N las mujeres *f pl*

womanly [wúmənli] ADJ femenino

womb [wum] N (uterus) útero *m*, matriz *f*; (insides) vientre *m*; (center) seno *m*

wonder [wándɚ] VI/VT preguntarse; **to — at** admirarse de, maravillarse de; **I — what time it is** ¿qué hora será? N (marvel) maravilla *f*; (surprise) asombro *m*; (miracle) milagro *m*; **it's a — that** es asombroso que; **it's no — that** no es de extrañar que

wonderful [wándɚfəł] ADJ maravilloso, estupendo

woo [wu] VI/VT cortejar

wood [wʊd] N (material) madera *f*; (firewood) leña *f*; **—cutter** leñador -ora *mf*; **—louse** cochinilla *f*; **—pecker** pájaro carpintero *m*; **—s** bosque *m*; **— shaving** viruta *f*; **—shed** leñera *f*; **—sman** leñador *m*; **—winds** maderas *f pl*; **—work** carpintería *f*, maderaje *m*; **to come out of the —work** salir de la nada

wooded [wʊdɪd] ADJ arbolado

wooden [wʊdn̩] ADJ (of wood) de madera; (lifeless) inexpresivo

woody [wʊdi] ADJ (with trees) arbolado; (like wood) leñoso

woof [wʊf] N trama *f*; INTERJ ¡guau!

wool [wʊł] N lana *f*; **— sweater** suéter de lana *m*

woolen [wʊlən] ADJ de lana; N **—s** (fabric) tejido de lana *m*; (clothes) ropa de lana *f*

woolly [wʊli] ADJ lanudo

word [wɝd] N (lexical unit) vocablo *m*; palabra *f* (also promise); (news) noticia *f*, aviso *m*; (order) mandato *m*, orden *m*;

may I have a — with you? ¿podemos hablar? — **processing** procesamiento de textos *m*; *Sp* tratamiento de texto(s) *m*; **by — of mouth** de palabra; **—s (of a song)** letra (de una canción) *f*; **to eat one's —s** tragarse / comerse las palabras; **— for —** palabra por palabra; VT (oral) expresar; (written) formular

wordy [wɜ́ɾ·ɒi] ADJ verboso, prolijo

work [wɜ·k] N (effort) trabajo *m*; (employment) empleo *m*, trabajo *m*; (artistic product, fortification) obra *f*; **—book** cuaderno / libro de trabajo *m*; **—day** día laborable *m*; **—force** mano de obra *f*; **—load** cantidad / carga de trabajo *f*; **—man** obrero *m*; **— of art** obra de arte *f*; **—place** lugar de trabajo *m*; **—shop** taller *m*; **— station** terminal de trabajo *m*; **—s** fábrica *f*; **the —s** todo; **—week** semana de trabajo *f*; **he's hard at —** está trabajando duro; VI (labor) trabajar; (function) funcionar; VT (change) efectuar; (metal, land) trabajar; (a crowd) manipular; (a mine) explotar; (employees) hacer trabajar; **to — in(to)** introducir; **to — loose** soltarse, aflojarse; **to — on** (repair) arreglar; (improve) tratar de mejorar; **to — one's way through college** pagarse los estudios trabajando; **to — one's way up** ascender a fuerza de trabajo; **to — out** (a plan) urdir; (a problem) resolver; **he —s out every day** hace ejercicio todos los días; **it all —ed out** al final todo salió bien; **to be all —ed up** estar sobreexcitado; **to get —ed up** agitarse

worker [wɜ́·kɚ] N trabajador -ora *mf*; (in a factory) obrero -ra *mf*; (in an office) oficinista *mf*

working [wɜ́·kɪŋ] N (act of someone who works, shaping of metals) trabajo *m*; (operation) funcionamiento *m*, operación *f*; (of a problem) cálculo *m*; (of a mine) explotación *f*; ADJ (class) obrero, trabajador; (majority) suficiente; **— class** clase obrera / trabajadora *f*; **— lunch** comida de trabajo *f*; **—man** obrero *m*

workmanship [wɜ́·kmənʃɪp] N (skill) habilidad *f*, destreza *f*; (quality) confección *f*

world [wɜ·ɫd] N mundo *m*; **—view** cosmovisión *f*; **— war** guerra mundial *f*; **—wide web** web *f*, red (mundial electrónica) *f*; ADJ **—-class** de categoría mundial; **—-shaking** trascendental; **—wide** mundial

worldly [wɜ́·ɫdli] ADJ (mundane) mundano,

temporal; (sophisticated) de mundo, corrido; (material) material

worm [wɜ·m] N gusano *m*; ADJ **—-eaten** comido por los gusanos, carcomido; VT desparasitar, quitar las lombrices; **to — a secret out of someone** extraerle / sonsacarle un secreto a alguien; **to — oneself into** insinuarse en

worn [wɔrn] ADJ desgastado, usado

worrisome [wɜ́·risəm] ADJ preocupante

worry [wɜ́·i] VI/VT preocupar(se), inquietar(se); VT (harass) atacar; VI **to — with** juguetear con; N preocupación *f*, inquietud *f*, zozobra *f*; **—wart** preocupón -ona *mf*

worse [wɜ·s] ADJ & ADV peor; **— and —** cada vez peor; **— than ever** peor que nunca; **from bad to —** de mal en peor; **so much the —** tanto peor; **to be — off** estar peor que antes; **to change for the —** empeorar(se); **to get —** empeorar(se)

worship [wɜ́·ʃɪp] N (act of worshiping) adoración *f*; (ceremony) culto *m*; VT (revere) adorar, venerar; VI (attend services) asistir al culto

worshiper [wɜ́·ʃɪpɚ] N (one who worships) adorador -ora *mf*; **—s** fieles *mf pl*

worst [wɜ·st] ADJ & ADV peor; **the — one** el / la peor; **the — thing** lo peor; **—-case scenario** el peor de los casos; VT derrotar

worth [wɜ·θ] ADJ **to be — a dollar** valer un dólar; **to be — hearing** ser digno de oírse; **to be —while** valer la pena; **it's — doing** vale la pena hacerlo; N valor *m*, valía *f*; **ten cents — of** diez centavos de; **to get one's money's — out of** aprovechar al máximo

worthless [wɜ́·θlɪs] ADJ (useless) inútil; (despicable) despreciable

worthy [wɜ́·ði] ADJ digno, meritorio; (esteemed) benemérito; **— cause** causa noble *f*; **— of praise** digno de elogio; N notable *mf*

would [wʊd] V AUX **I — do it if I could** lo haría si pudiera; **— you please open the door?** ¿podrías abrir la puerta por favor? **he said he — do it** dijo que lo haría; **as a child, I — play all the time** de niño, jugaba todo el tiempo; **— that she were alive!** ¡ojalá estuviera viva!

wound [wund] N herida *f*; VI/VT herir; (with an arrow) flechar

wow [waʊ] VT impresionar; INTERJ ¡huy!

wrangle [ɾǽŋgəɫ] VI/VT (quarrel) discutir; (obtain) agenciarse de; VT (herd) juntar; *Am* rodear; N riña *f*, pendencia *f*

wrangler [ɾǽŋglɚ] N vaquero -ra *mf*

wrap [ræp] VT envolver; **to — up** (a present) envolver; (a baby) arropar; (a task) terminar; (against the cold) abrigar(se); **to be wrapped in** estar envuelto en; **to be wrapped up in** estar absorto en; N (coat) abrigo *m*; (shawl) chal *m*; **—-up** (summary) resumen *m*; (end) final *m*

wrapper [ræpɚ] N envoltura *f*, envoltorio *m*

wrapping [ræpɪŋ] N envoltura *f*; **— paper** papel para envolver *m*

wrath [ræθ] N ira *f*, cólera *f*

wreak [rik] VT **to — havoc** hacer estragos

wreath [riθ] N corona *f*; **— of smoke** espiral de humo *f*

wreck [rɛk] N (building) ruina *f*; (car, plane) restos *m pl*; (a ship) pecio *m*; (shipwreck) naufragio *m*; (person) desastre *m*, ruina *f*; (accident) accidente *m*; VI tener un accidente; VT (a ship) naufragar; (a car, totally) destrozar; (a car, with minor damage) chocar; (a building) demoler

wreckage [rékɪʤ] N (of a car, plane) restos de un accidente *m pl*; (of a ship) pecio *m*; (of a building) escombros *m pl*

wrecker [rékɚ] N (tow truck) grúa *f*, camión de remolque *m*; (worker) obrero -ra de demolición *mf*

wrench [rɛntʃ] VT torcer, retorcer; **to — off / out** arrancar de un tirón, arrebatar; N (twist) torcedura *f*; (pull) tirón *m*; (tool) llave de tuercas *f*

wrest [rɛst] VT (pull) arrancar; (take away) arrebatar

wrestle [résəɫ] VI/VT luchar (con / contra); N lucha *f*

wrestler [réslɚ] N luchador -ra *mf*

wrestling [réslɪŋ] N lucha libre *f*

wretch [rɛtʃ] N miserable *mf*, infeliz *mf*

wretched [rétʃɪd] ADJ (unfortunate) desdichado, infeliz; (despicable) vil, miserable, arrastrado; (inferior) pésimo

wriggle [rígəɫ] VI culebrear, serpentear; VT menear, retorcer; **to — out of** escabullirse de

wring [rɪŋ] VT (twist) torcer, retorcer; (extract) arrancar; **to — one's hands** retorcerse las manos; **to — out** escurrir

wrinkle [ríŋkəɫ] N arruga *f*, surco *m*; (problem) problema *m*; VI/VT arrugar(se)

wrist [rɪst] N muñeca *f*; **—watch** reloj (de) pulsera *m*

writ [rɪt] N auto *m*, mandato *m*

write [raɪt] VI/VT escribir; **to — back** contestar; **to — down** apuntar; **to — off** cancelar; **to — out** escribir en forma completa; **to — up** hacer un reportaje sobre; **it's written all over his face** se

le ve en la cara; **she —s for a living** es escritora; N **—-up** reportaje *m*

writer [ráɪDɚ] N escritor -ora *mf*, literato -ta *mf*

writhe [raɪð] VI retorcerse

writing [ráɪDɪŋ] N (act of writing) escritura *f*; (handwriting) letra *f*, escritura *f*; (style) estilo *m*; **— desk** escritorio *m*; **— paper** papel de escribir *m*; **—s** obra *f*; **to put in —** poner por escrito

wrong [rɔŋ] ADJ (incorrect) incorrecto, equivocado; (improper) inapropiado; **what's — with you?** ¿qué te pasa? **you are —** estás equivocado; **the — side of a fabric** el revés de una tela; **— side out** con lo de adentro para afuera; **to be on the — side of the road** ir a contramano / en sentido contrario; **that is the — book** ese no es el libro; **it is in the — place** está fuera de lugar; ADV mal; **to go —** salir mal; N (evil) mal *m*; (injustice) injusticia *f*; **to be in the —** (not be right) estar equivocado; (be to blame) tener la culpa; **to do —** hacer mal; VT perjudicar

wrought [rɔt] ADJ forjado; **— iron** hierro forjado *m*

wry [raɪ] ADJ (smile) torcido; (remark, humor) irónico; **to make a — face** hacer una mala cara

Xx

xenophobia [zɛnəfóbiə] N xenofobia *f*

Xeroxᵗᵐ [zírɑks] N fotocopia *f*; VI/VT fotocopiar

x-rated [éksreDɪd] ADJ pornográfico

x-ray [éksre] N rayos X *m pl*, radiografía *f*; VI/VT radiografiar

xylophone [záɪləfon] N xilofón *m*, xilófono *m*

Yy

yacht [jɑt] N yate *m*; VI navegar en yate

y'all [jɔɫ] PRON ustedes *mf*; *Sp* vosotros -as *mf*

Yankee [jǽŋki] ADJ & N estadounidense del norte del país *mf*

yard [jɑrd] N (measure) yarda (0.9144m) *f*;

(spar) verga *f*; (courtyard) patio *m*; (grassy area) jardín *m*; —**stick** (stick) vara de medida (de una yarda) *f*; (criterion) patrón *m*, norma *f*

yarn [jɑrn] N (material) hilo *m*; (story) cuento *m*

yawn [jɔn] VI bostezar; N bostezo *m*

year [jɪr] N año *m*; —**book** anuario *m*; —-**round** de todo el año

yearling [jírlɪŋ] N animal de un año *m*; (of cows) añojo -ja *mf*

yearly [jírli] ADJ anual; ADV anualmente

yearn [jɜn] VI anhelar, suspirar por

yearning [jɜ́nɪŋ] N anhelo *m*

yeast [jist] N levadura *f*

yell [jɛɫ] VI/VT gritar; N grito *m*

yellow [jélo] ADJ (color) amarillo; (coward) cobarde; — **fever** fiebre amarilla *f*; — **jacket** avispa *f*; — **pages** páginas amarillas *f pl*; N amarillo *m*; VI/VT poner(se) amarillo, amarillear

yellowish [jéloɪʃ] ADJ amarillento

yelp [jɛɫp] VI gañir, aullar; N gañido *m*, aullido *m*

Yemen [jémən] N Yemen *m*

Yemeni [jéməni] ADJ & N yemení *mf*

yen [jɛn] N (currency of Japan) yen *m*; (desire) anhelo *m*; VI anhelar

yes [jɛs] ADV sí; —-**no question** pregunta de sí o no *f*

yesterday [jéstɚde] ADV & N ayer *m*; **the day before** — anteayer

yet [jɛt] ADV & CONJ **are they here** —? ¿ya llegaron? **they aren't here** — todavía no llegan, aún no han llegado; — **another** otro más; **ugly** — **charming** feo pero encantador; **as** — todavía, aún

yield [jiɫd] VI/VT (surrender, give in) ceder, plegar(se); (produce) rendir, redituar; **to** — **five percent** dar un cinco por ciento de interés; N (production) rendimiento *m*, producción *f*; (of stocks) rédito *m*

yodel [jódl̩] VI cantar a la tirolesa; N canto tirolés *m*

yoga [jógə] N yoga *m*

yogurt [jógɚt] N yogur *m*

yoke [jok] N (crossbar) yugo *m*; (pair of animals) yunta *f*; (on a shirt) canesú *m*; VT uncir

yolk [jok] N yema *f*

yonder [jándɚ] ADJ aquel; ADV (location) allá; (direction) hacia allá

yore [jɔr] N **in days of** — antaño

you [ju] PRON — **came** (sg informal) tú viniste; (sg formal) usted vino; (pl informal) *Sp* vosotros vinisteis; *Am* ustedes vinieron; (formal) ustedes vinieron; **I see**

— (sg informal) te veo; (sg formal) lo veo; (pl informal) *Sp* os veo; *Am* los veo; (pl formal) los veo; **I talk to** — (sg informal) te hablo; (sg formal) le hablo; (pl informal) *Sp* os hablo; *Am* les hablo; (pl formal) les hablo; **I went with** — (sg informal) fui contigo; (sg formal) fui con usted; (pl informal) *Sp* fui con vosotros; *Am* fui con ustedes; (pl formal) fui con ustedes; **it's for** — (sg informal) es para ti; (sg formal) es para usted; (pl informal) *Sp* es para vosotros; *Am* es para ustedes; (pl formal) es para ustedes; **this is how** — **make bread** así se hace el pan

young [jʌŋ] ADJ joven; — **man** joven *m*; — **people** gente joven *f*; — **woman** joven *f*; N (offspring) cría *f*

youngster [jʌ́ŋstɚ] N muchacho -cha *mf*, jovencito -ta *mf*

your [jɔr] POSS ADJ **this is** — **dog** (sg informal) este es tu perro; (sg formal) este es su perro; (pl informal) *Sp* este es vuestro perro; *Am* este es su perro; (pl formal) este es su perro

yours [jɔrz] PRON **this book is** — (sg informal) este libro es tuyo; (sg formal) este libro es suyo/de usted; (pl informal) *Sp* este libro es vuestro; *Am* este libro es suyo/de ustedes; (pl formal) este libro es suyo/de ustedes; — **is bigger** (sg informal) el tuyo/la tuya es más grande; (sg formal) el suyo/el de usted/la suya/ la de usted es más grande; (pl informal) *Sp* el vuestro/la vuestra es más grande; *Am* el suyo/el de ustedes es más grande; (pl formal) el suyo/el de ustedes es más grande; **a friend of** — (sg informal) un amigo tuyo; (sg formal) un amigo suyo/ de usted; (pl informal) *Sp* un amigo vuestro; *Am* un amigo suyo/de ustedes; — **truly** atentamente

yourself [jɔrsɛ́ɫf] PRON **you** — **wrote the letter** (sg informal) tú mismo escribiste la carta; (sg formal) usted mismo escribió la carta; **you yourselves wrote the letter** (pl informal) *Sp* vosotros mismos escribisteis la carta; *Am* ustedes mismos escribieron la carta; (pl formal) ustedes mismos escribieron la carta; **you are not** — **today** (sg informal) hoy no eres el mismo de siempre; (sg formal) hoy no es el mismo de siempre; **you are not yourselves today** *Sp* hoy no sois los mismos de siempre; *Am* hoy no son los mismos de siempre; (pl formal) hoy no son los mismos de siempre; **you were sitting by** — (sg informal) tú estabas sentado solo; (sg formal) usted estaba sentado solo; **you were sitting by yourselves** (informal) *Sp* vosotros estabais sentados solos; *Am* ustedes estaban sentados solos; (pl formal) ustedes estaban sentados solos; **you look at — at the mirror** (sg informal) tú te miras en el espejo; (sg formal) usted se mira en el espejo; **you look at yourselves at the mirror** (pl informal) *Sp* vosotros os mirais en el espejo; *Am* ustedes se miran en el espejo; (pl formal) ustedes se miran en el espejo; **you bought — a house** (sg informal) te compraste una casa; (sg formal) usted se compró una casa; **you bought yourselves a house** (pl informal) *Sp* os comprasteis una casa; *Am* se compraron una casa; (pl formal) se compraron una casa

youth [juθ] N (person) joven *m*; (young age) juventud *m*

youthful [júθfəł] ADJ juvenil

yo-yo [jójo] N yo-yo *m*

yucca [jʌ́kə] N yuca *f*

yuck [jʌk] INTERJ puaj, puaf

Yugoslavia [jugosláviə] N Yugoslavia *f*

Yugoslavian [jugoslávian] ADJ & N yugoslavo -va *mf*

Yuletide [júłtaɪd] N Navidad *f*

yummy [jámi] ADJ delicioso; INTERJ ¡qué rico!

yuppie [jápi] N yuppie *mf*

Zimbabwe [zɪmbábwe] N Zimbabue *m*

Zimbabwean [zɪmbábweən] ADJ & N zimbabuo -a *mf*

zinc [zɪŋk] N cinc *m*, zinc *m*

zip [zɪp] VI/VT cerrar / abrir con cremallera; **to — by** pasar volando; **to — over** ir corriendo; N cero *m*; — **code** código postal *m*

zipper [zípɚ] N cremallera *f*, cierre (relámpago) *m*

zirconium [zɚkóniəm] N circonio *m*

zodiac [zóɒɪæk] N zodíaco *m*

zombie [zámbi] N zombi *mf*

zone [zon] N zona *f*; VT dividir en zonas

zoo [zu] N zoológico *m*; *Sp* zoo *m*; —**keeper** guardián -ana del zoológico *mf*

zoological [zoəláʤɪkəł] ADJ zoológico

zoology [zoáləʤi] N zoología *f*

zoom [zum] VI zumbar; **to — off** salir zumbando; N zumbido *m*; — **lens** teleobjetivo *m*, zoom *m*

zucchini [zukíni] N calabacín *m*

zygote [záɪgot] N cigoto *m*, zigoto *m*

Zz

Zambia [zǽmbiə] N Zambia *f*

Zambian [zǽmbiən] ADJ & N zambiano -na *mf*

zany [zéni] ADJ absurdo

zap [zæp] VT liquidar

zeal [ził] N celo *m*, fervor *m*

zealot [zélət] N fanático -ca *mf*

zealous [zéləs] ADJ celoso, fervoroso

zebra [zíbrə] N cebra *f*

zenith [zínɪθ] N cenit *m*

zephyr [zéfɚ] N céfiro *m*

zeppelin [zépəlɪn] N zepelín *m*, dirigible *m*

zero [ziro] N cero *m*; **there's — possibility that he'll come** las posibilidades de que venga son nulas

zest [zɛst] N entusiasmo *m*

zigzag [zígzæg] N zigzag *m*; ADJ & ADV en zigzag; VI zigzaguear, andar en zigzag; VT hacer zigzaguear